East Hall #307

The Junior Classic Series

Junior Classic
French Dictionary

FRENCH-ENGLISH and ENGLISH-FRENCH

By
J. E. WESSELY

REVISED EDITION

FOLLETT PUBLISHING COMPANY
CHICAGO   ILLINOIS

1947

PREFACE

In the compilation of the first edition of the Junior Classic Series of Foreign Language Dictionaries the endeavor of the authors was to produce efficient texts in the smallest possible compass.

That they were successful is testified to by the fact that thousands upon thousands of copies of these volumes are now used daily by students, travelers, and business men all over the civilized world.

Since the publishing of the first edition, however, there has come into current use many words of a somewhat special nature that were not included in the original texts.

Many of these new words or new meanings of old words and phrases have been inserted in their proper place in the body of the dictionary. Some, because of certain typographical difficulties, have been set off to themselves in A List of Popular Words to be found just before the dictionary proper.

It is hoped that these new words will add considerably to the value of these dictionaries and make them even more useful than they have been.

Inasmuch as the aim of the work is to include the largest number of words in the smallest possible space, the translations are necessarily brief and to the point.

Supplementing the general vocabularies themselves are valuable appendixes on pronunciation, proper names, and verb forms.

It is hoped that the many changes, additions, and revisions will add considerably to the everyday usefulness of these volumes and that the new edition will be given an even better reception than that so generously accorded the first.

THE PUBLISHERS.

List of abbreviations used in both parts
of this dictionary.

Abréviations employées dans les deux parties du dictionnaire.

a. = adjective, *adjectif.*
ad. = adverb, *adverbe.*
(agr.) = agriculture, *agriculture.*
(alg.) = algebra, *algèbre.*
(an.) = anatomy, *anatomie.*
(ar.) = arithmetic, *arithmétique.*
(arch.) = architecture, *architecture.*
art. = article, *article.*
(astr.) = astronomy, *astronomie.*
(bot.) = botany, *botanique, plantes.*
(chim.) = chemistry, *chimie.*
(chir.) = surgery, *chirurgie.*
(com.) = commerce, trade, *commerce.*
c. = conjunction, *conjonction.*
(culin.) = culinary, *culinaire.*
f. = feminine, *féminin.*
fam. = familiarly, *familièrement.*
fig. = figuratively, *figurément.*
(géom.) = geometry, *géométrie.*
(gr.) = grammar, *grammaire.*
(hort.) = horticulture, *horticulture.*
ir. = irregular, *irrégulier.*
(jur.) = jurisprudence, law, *jurisprudence.*
(log.) = logics, *logique.*

m. = masculine, *masculin.*
(mach.) = machinery, *machines.*
(mar.) = marine, navy, *marine.*
(math.) = mathematics, *mathématiques.*
(méd.) = medicine, *médecine, pathologie.*
(mil.) = military art, *art militaire.*
(min.) = mines, mineralogy, *mines, minéralogie.*
(mus.) = music, *musique.*
(parl.) = parliamentary, *parlement.*
(peint.) = painting, *peintre.*
(phys.) = physics, *physique.*
pl. = plural, *pluriel.*
(poét.) = poetically, *poétiquement.*
pr. = pronoun, *pronom.*
prp. = preposition, *préposition.*
qc. = *quelque chose.*
qn. = *quelqu'un.*
(rail.) = railway, *chemin de fer.*
s. = substantive, *substantif.*
sing. = singular, *singulier.*
(tech.) = technical, *technique.*
(typ.) = typography, *typographie.*
v. a. = verb active, *verbe actif.*
v. n. = verb neuter, *verbe neutre.*

Throughout the dictionary the *tilde* (~) stands for the main word unaltered, as given at the beginning of each separate article; *e. g.* abandon, m.... || à l'~, at random.

Before flexional endings and suffixes and in compounds a "dash" replaces the main word; *e. g.* ablution, f.; faire ses –s, to perform one's ablutions.

The various equivalents in one language for the corresponding different meanings of a given word in the other are separated by the sign ||.

The endings of the feminine forms of French nouns and adjectives are given after the masculine word, thus: abandonné, e, m. & f., abortif, ve, a.

Le signe ~ sert à éviter la répétition du mot qui fait l'objet de l'article, p. exemple: abandon, m ... || à l'~, at random.

Les flexions et les affixes sont représentés par un tiret –, comme: ablution ... || faire ses –s, to perform one's ablutions.

Le mot initial a-t-il plusieurs significations, le signe || sert à séparer ces diverses acceptions d'entre elles; ainsi: pension, f. pension || annuity || boarding-house, boarding-school || board and lodging || livery (of horses).

Le genre féminin des mots qui n'ont pas la parité du genre, est indiqué de la manière suivante: abandonné, e, m. & f., abortif, ve, a.

UNE LISTE DES MOTS POPULAIRES
FRENCH–ENGLISH

aérodrome, m. airdrome
aéroplane, m. (see avion)
aileron, m. aileron   [biles]
allumage, m. ignition (of automo-
altimètre, m. altimeter
amortisseur, m. shock absorber
ampèremètre, m. ammeter (see galvanomètre)
amplificateur, m. amplifier
ampoule amplificatrice (or génératrice), f. power tube
ampoule (f.) de détection, f. detecting tube
ampoule de radio, f. radio tube
antenne, f. antenna
arbre à cames, f. cam shaft
arbre (m.) de distribution, f. cam
shaft (see arbre à cames)
arbre principal, m. crank shaft
association, f. merger
atterrissage, m. landing (of planes)
autobus, m. bus
avertisseur, m. horn (see trompe)
aviateur, m. airman
aviatrice, f. airwoman
avion, m. airplane

ballon d'observation, m. blimp (see
"saucisse")
bielle, f. connecting rod
biplan, m. biplane
bougie, f. sparkplug
                                      [taurant]
"cafétéria", f. cafeteria (see res-
carburateur, m. carburetor
char de combat, m. tank (war)
chariot (m.) d'atterrissage, m. land-
châssis, m. chassis   [ing gear
clé anglaise, f. monkey wrench
cohéreur, m. radio receiver
condensateur, m. condenser
crevaison, f. puncture (of tires)

déraper, v. a. skid (of automobiles)
diffuser, v. a. broadcast
diffusion, f. broadcast
drogue, f. dope (see renseignement)

embrayage, m. clutch (of motors)
engrenage, m. gear (of motors)
essence, f. gasoline

feu (signal), m. stop light
film, m. film
film parlant, m. talkie
four à air chaud, m. air furnace
frein à air, m. air brake

galvanomètre, m. ammeter (see am
pèremètre)
générateur, m. generator
glissoirs, m. runners (of planes)

hangar, m. hangar
haut-parleur, m. loudspeaker
haut-parleur électrodynamique, m
dynamic speaker
hydravion, m. hydroplane, seaplane
hydroaéroplane, m. hydroplane, seaplane (see hydravion)

ignition, f. ignition (see allumage)

lettre (f.) de change, m. trade acceptance

magnéto, f. magneto
malthusianisme, m. birth control
mécanicien, m. mechanic
monoplan, m. monoplane
montage, m. hook-up
moratoire, m. moratorium

pare-choc, m. bumper (of automobiles)
pneu, m. tire (of automobiles)
poste (m.) de radio, f. radio set
prise de terre, f. ground wire

radiateur, m. radiator
"radio", f. radio
radiotélégraphie, f. radio
radiotéléphonie, f. radio
récepteur, m. receiver (telephone)
renseignement(s), m. dope (see
drogue)
réservoir, m. tank (for gasoline)
restaurant, m. cafeteria (see "café-
rhéostat, m. rheostat   [téria")

"saucisse", f. blimp   [light
signaux (lumineux), m. pl. traffic

tank, m. tank (war)
télévision, f. television
tracteur, m. tractor
tramway, m. street-car
triplan, m. triplane
trompe, f. horn (see avertisseur)
tuyau d'échappement, m. exhaust
pipe

ventilateur, m. fan
vol, m. flight (of aeroplanes)
volant, m. steering wheel

See page 232 for ENGLISH-FRENCH *of* A List of Popular Words

Remarques sur la prononciation anglaise.

ā se prononce comme é dans *fée, épée*.

ă se prononce comme a dans *matin*.

â se prononce comme a dans *fable*.

aw se prononce comme le dernier élément de la diphthongue française *oï*.

ē se prononce comme î dans *épître*.

ĕ se prononce comme e dans *mettre*.

ė se prononce à peu près comme eu dans *fleur*.

ī se prononce comme aï dans *ail, aïeul*, mais d'une seule émission de voix, en évitant d'en faire deux syllabes comme dans *caïc, laïque, mosaïque*.

ĭ se prononce comme i dans *illustre*.

ō se prononce comme o dans *globe*.

ŏ se prononce comme o dans *motte*.

ô se prononce comme ou dans *mouvoir*.

ow se prononce comme aou d'une seule émission de voix.

oy se prononce comme oie, mais d'une seule émission de voix, en y ajoutant un *ï*.

oo se prononce comme ou dans *foule*.

ū se prononce comme iou dans *chtourme*, mais d'une seule émission de voix.

ŭ se prononce comme eu dans *neuf*.

ch se prononce comme tch dans *tcherkesse*.

j se prononce comme dj dans *adjutant*.

g se prononce comme g dans *gamme*.

y se prononce comme y dans *yeux*.

s se prononce comme s dans *sœur*.

z se prononce comme z dans *zouave*.

th se prononce en avançant le bout de la langue entre les dents en sifflant un peu fortement, comme si l'on voulait prononcer s.

th se prononce de même, seulement d'un son plus doux, comme si l'on voulait faire entendre le *z*.

FRENCH AND ENGLISH.

A.

a (à), pr. to, at, in ‖ into ‖ by, for, on, from, after, about ‖ as a, as ‖ under ‖ against ‖ according to ‖ between ‖ enough ‖ or ‖ and ‖ good-bye till ‖ ne savoir ni A ni B, not to know a B from a bull's foot.

abaisse, f. dough ‖ thinly rolled paste.

abaissement, m. lowering, abatement ‖ humiliation, meanness ‖ disgrace ‖ depression.

abaisser, v. a. to lower, to diminish, to reduce ‖ to humble, to mortify ‖ s'~, to fall, to sink, to decrease ‖ to humble oneself.

abajoue, f. cheek-pouch. [self.

abalourdir, v. a. (fam.) to stultify ‖ to put out, to nonplus.

abandon, m. relinquishment ‖ dereliction ‖ destitution ‖ à l'~, at random.

abandonné, e, m. & f. profligate ‖ unfortunate ‖ abandoned character.

abandonné, e, a. deserted ‖ abandoned, shameless. [bauchery.

abandonnement, m. dissoluteness, de-

abandonner, v. a. to abandon, to forsake, to give over ‖ s'~, to give oneself up, to give way, to trust to ‖ to indulge in ‖ to throw off all constraint.

abaque, m. abacus.

abasourdir, v. a. to stun.

abat, m.; ~-jour, m. skylight ‖ shade of a lamp ‖ ~-vent, m. pent-house ‖ ~-voix, m. sounding-board.

abatage, m. cutting, felling ‖ slaughter, killing ‖ (mar.) heeling. [counter.

abatant, m. raisable flap of a table or

abâtardir, v. a. to deteriorate ‖ s'~, to degenerate.

abâtardissement, m. degeneracy.

abatis, m. demolition, felling, cutting down ‖ ~ de volaille, giblets.

abats, m. pl. offal, cats' and dogs' meat.

abattement, m. weakness, faintness, dejection. [(fam.) braggart.

abatteur, m. feller (of wood) ‖ caster down ‖

abattoir, m. slaughter-house.

abattre, v. a. ir. to beat down, to fell ‖ to cut down, to cut off, to demolish ‖ to weaken ‖ to dishearten, to humble, to damp (one's spirits) ‖ s'~, to abate, to relent ‖ to despond ‖ to alight ‖ to pounce (of birds).

abattu, e, a. cast down, low-spirited.

abbatial, e, a. abbatial.

abbaye, f. abbey.

abbé, m. abbot ‖ Abbé.

abbesse, f. abbess.

abcéder, v. a. to form into an abscess.

abcès, m. abscess.

abdication, f. abdication, resignation.

abdiquer, v. a. to abdicate, to resign.

abdomen, m. abdomen.

abdominal, e, a. abdominal.

abécédaire, m. abecedary, primer.

abée, f. sluice ‖ mill-dam.

abeille, f. bee ‖ ~-mère, f. queen-bee.

aberration, f. aberration ‖ (méd.) disturbance.

abêtir, v. a. to stupify ‖ to stultify.

abhorrer, v. a. to abhor, to detest.

abime, m. abyss, hell, chasm.

abimer, v. a. to throw into an abyss ‖ to destroy ‖ s'~, to fall into an abyss, to ruin oneself.

abject, e, a. abject, base, low, mean.

abjection, f. abjectness ‖ vileness, meanness. [to abjure.

abjuration, f. abjuration ‖ faire ~ de,

abjurer, v. a. to abjure.

ablatif, m. (gr.) ablative (case).

ablation, f. (chir.) ablation.

ablette, f. bleak, ablet (fish) ‖ ~ de mer, whitebait. [one's ablutions.

ablution, f.; faire ses ~s, to perform

abnégation, f. abnegation ‖ self-denial ‖ faire ~ de, to renounce, to sacrifice.

aboiement, m. barking, baying.

abois, m. pl. agony of death ‖ desperate situation.

abolir, v. a. to abolish. [situation.

abolissement, m., **abolition,** f. abolition ‖ indemnity.

abominable, a. abominable, detestable ‖ ~-ment, ad. abominably.

abomination, f. abomination ‖ avoir en ~, to abominate.

abondamment, ad. abundantly.

abondance, f. abundance, plenty ‖ common wine greatly diluted with water ‖ parler d'~, to extemporise.

abondant, e, a. abundant, plentiful.

abonder, v. n. to abound in ou with.

abonné, m. subscriber.

abonnement, m. subscription.

abonner, (s'~), to subscribe to.

abonnir, v. a. & n. to improve.

abord, m. approach, access, arrival ‖ du premier ~, at first sight.

abordable, a. accessible. [fouling.
abordage, m. boarding || landing || (mar.)
aborder, v. a. to approach, to accost || to
board || ~, v. n. to land, to disembark, to
arrive at || (mar.) to run foul of, to foul.
aborigènes, m. pl. aborigines.
abortif, ve, a. abortive.
aboucher, v. a. to bring together || s'~, to
have an interview.
aboutir, v. n. to confine, to border upon ||
to terminate in || to have a result.
aboutissants, m. pl. bounds, limits, pl.
aboyer, v. a. to bark.
aboyeur, m. barker || dun.
abrégé, m. abstract, compendium, sum-
mary || en ~, compendiously.
abréger, v. a. to abridge, to abbreviate.
abreuver, v. a. to water || to soak || s'~,
to drink plentifully.
abreuvoir, m. horse-pond, watering-place.
abréviation, f. contraction, abbreviation.
abri, m. shelter || à l'~ de, under cover,
under the protection of.
abricot, m. apricot.
abricotier, m. apricot-tree.
abriter, v. a. to shelter, to shade.
abrivent, m. wind-screen.
abrogation, f. abrogation, repeal.
abroger, v. a. to abrogate, to repeal.
abrupt, e, a. abrupt || rugged. [stupid.
abrutir, v. a. to stupify || s'~, to grow
abrutissement, m. brutishness.
absence, f. absence || absence of mind.
absent, e, m. & f. absentee.
absent, e, a. absent, not present.
absentéisme, m. absenteeism. [sent.
s'absenter, to absent oneself || to be ab-
absinthe, f. wormwood || bitters || (fig.)
grief.
absolu, e, a. absolute, arbitrary || im-
perious, despotic ||-ment, ad. absolutely,
positively.
absolution, f. absolution || (jur.) acquittal.
absolutisme, m. absolute government,
absolutisme, m. absolutist. [absolutism.
absolutoire, a. absolutory.
absorbant, a. absorbent.
absorber, v. a. to absorb, to swallow up,
to imbibe || (fig.) to waste || s'~, to be ab-
sorbed ou swallowed up.
absorption, f. absorption.
absoudre, v. a. ir. to absolve.
absoute, f. general absolution.
s'abstenir, v. ir. to abstain. [drawal.
abstention, f. abstention || (jur.) with-
abstraction, f. abstraction ||-s, pl. ab-
sence of mind || ~ faite de, setting aside.
abstractivement, ad. abstractedly.
abstraire, v. a. ir. to abstract.
abstrait, e, a. abstracted || abstruse ||
absent in mind.
abstrus, e, a. abstruse, obscure, intricate.
absurde, m. absurdity.
absurde, a. absurd ||-ment, ad. absurdly.
absurdité, f. absurdity.
abus, m. abuse, ill use || error.
abuser, v. a. to abuse || to seduce || to
violate || s'~, to be mistaken.
abusif, ve, a. abusive || abuseful.

abusivement, ad. abusively.
acabit, m. quality of a thing.
acacia, m. (bot.) acacia.
académicien, m. academician.
académie, f. academy || academy for young
noblemen. [(ly).
académique(ment), a. (& ad.) academical
acagnarder, v. a. to make lazy || s'~, to
acajou, m. mahogany. [get lazy.
acanthe, f. acanthus.
acariâtre, a. peevish.
accablant, e, a. heavy, troublesome.
accablement, m. heaviness, extreme dejection, low spirits.
accabler, v. a. to overwhelm, to oppress ||
to fatigue, to plague || to depress.
accaparement, m. forestalling(the market).
accaparer, v. a. to forestall.
accapareur, m. forestaller.
accéder, v. n. to accede (à, to).
accélérateur, trice, a. accelerating.
accéléré, f. mail-coach. [accelerative.
accélérer, v. a. to accelerate, to hasten.
accent, m. accent || tone.
accentuation, f. accentuation.
accentuer, v. a. to accent.
acceptation, f. acceptance.
accepter, v. a. to accept.
accepteur, m. (com.) accepter.
acception, f. regard, respect || acceptation,
sense, meaning (of a word).
accès, m. access, approach || fit || attack.
accession, f. accession || consent.
accessit, m. accessit, second prize.
accessoire, a. accessory ||-ment, ad.
accessorily.
accident, m. accident, chance, mischance
accidentel, le, a. (-lement, ad.) ac-
accise, f. excise. [cidental(ly).
acclamer, v. a. to acclaim || to cheer.
acclamation, f. cheer, acclamation || shout.
acclimatation, f. acclimatisation.
acclimater, v. a. to accustom, to acclimatise. [timacy.
accointance, f. (fam.) acquaintance, in-
accolade, f. embracing, hug || brace, pair
(of game) || (typ.) brace.
accoler, v. a. to embrace, to hug, to prop.
accommodage, m. cooking, dressing.
accommodement, m. accommodation,
agreement, arrangement.
accommoder, v. a. to fit up, to adapt, to
dress || to cook || to settle, to appease, to
make up || to furnish || s'~, to accom-
modate oneself, to take one's ease || to
agree || to suit. [accompanist.
accompagnateur, trice, m. & f. (mus.)
accompagnement, m. accompanying ||
(mus.) accompaniment.
accompagner, v. a. to accompany || to
suit with.
accompli, e, a. accomplished, perfect.
accomplir, v. a. to accomplish || to per-
form || s'~, to be fulfilled.
accomplissement, m. accomplishment,
performance || execution.
accord, m. accord, agreement, concord,
harmony, consent || d'~, granted, agreed ||
in tune.

accordéon, m. (mus.) accordion.
accorder, v. a. to allow, to grant || to adjust, to reconcile || (mus.) to tune || s'~, to agree.
accordeur, m. (mus.) tuner.
accordoir, m. (mus.) tuning-key.
accort, e, a. civil, complaisant.
accoster, v. a. to accost || s'~, to frequent.
accoter, v. a. to prop up, to lean (sideways).
accotoir, m. prop, stay.
accouchée, f. woman confined.
accouchement, m. delivery, childbed, lying-in, confinement.
accoucher, v. a. to deliver (a woman) || ~, v. n. to be brought to bed, to be confined.
accoucheur, m. accoucheur, man-midwife.
accoucheuse, f. midwife.
s'accouder, to lean on one's elbow.
accoudoir, m. elbow-rest.
accouplement, m. coupling, pairing.
accoupler, v. a. to couple, to yoke || to match, to pair.
accourcir, v. a. to shorten.
accourcissement, m. shortening.
accourir, v. n. ir. to run to ou up.
accoutrement, m. (fam.) get-up, dress-up.
accoutrer, v. a. to dress, to rig out.
accoutumé, e, a. customary, accustomed, usual.
accoutumer, v. a. to accustom, to use, to inure || s'~, to get used [into credit.
accréditer, v. a. to accredit || s'~, to get
accroc, m. rent || (fig.) impediment.
accroche-cœur, m. (curl) heart-breaker || en ~, curled up.
accrocher, v. a. to hang upon, to hasp || (fam.) to delay, to put off || s'~, (mar.) to grapple || to stick to.
accroire, v. a. ir. faire ~, to make one believe || en faire ~, to impose upon.
accroissement, m. increase.
accroître, v. a. & n. ir. to increase.
s'accroupir, to squat || to roll oneself up || to sink. [ing.
accroupissement, m. squatting || cower-
accueil, m. reception, welcome.
accueillir, v. a. ir. to receive, to welcome || (com.) to honour. [to back (against).
acculer, v. a. to drive into a corner || s'~,
accumulateur, m. (mach.) accumulator.
accumulation, f. accumulation.
accumuler, v. a. to accumulate.
accusateur, trice, m. & f. accuser || (jur.) plaintiff, complainant.
accusatif, m. (gr.) accusative (case).
accusation, f. accusation, impeachment, charge || (jur.) indictment.
accusé, e, m. & f. (jur.) accused || culprit || ~ de réception, m. acknowledgment of receipt. [to acknowledge || (jur.) to indict.
accuser, v. a. to accuse, to impeach || (com.)
acerbe, a. acerb, sharp, rough.
acéré, e, a. sharp-edged, steely.
acérer, v. a. to steel, to sharpen.
acescence, f. accescency.
acétate, m. (chim.) acetate.
acétique, a. (chim.) acetic. [tomers.
achalandage, m. custom, goodwill, cus-
achalandé, e, a. having custom.

achalander, v. a. to procure custom, to bring custom to || s'~, to get custom.
acharné, e, a. maddened, infuriated || furious || desperate || inveterate.
acharnement, m. animosity, fury.
acharner, v. a. to madden, to set on, to enrage || s'~, to fall furiously upon.
achat, m. purchase || bargain.
acheminement, m. step, means, set on.
acheminer, v. a. to forward || s'~, to set out, to go on.
acheter, v. a. to buy, to purchase.
acheteur, m. buyer, purchaser.
achèvement, m. finish, completion.
achever, v. a. to finish, to accomplish, to perfect || to close. [lock, rub.
achoppement, m.; pierre d'~, stumbling-
achromatique, a. achromatic.
acide, a. acid, sour.
acidité, f. acidity, sourness.
aciduler, v. a. to acidulate.
acier, m. steel.
aciérie, f. steel-works.
acolyte, m. acolyte || confederate.
acompte, m. instalment.
aconit, m. (bot.) aconite, wolf's bane.
acoquiner, v. a. (fam.) to allure || to captivate || s'~, to get fond of.
à-coup, m. jerk || par ~, by fits and starts.
acoustique, f. acoustics (pl.).
acoustique, a. acoustic.
acquéreur, m. purchaser.
acquérir, v. a. ir. to acquire, to purchase.
acquiescement, m. acquiescence.
acquiescer, v. n. to acquiesce, to comply.
acquis, m. acquirement. [chase.
acquisition, f. acquisition, getting, pur-
acquit, m. acquittance, discharge || par manière d'~, for form's sake || pour ~, paid. [(jur.) acquittal.
acquittement, m. discharge, payment ||
acquitter, v. a. to acquit, to discharge, to pay || s'~, to pay off, to clear.
âcre, a. acrid, tart, sour.
âcreté, f. acrity, acrimony, tartness.
acrimonie, f. acrimony.
acrimonieux, se, a. acrimonious.
acrobate, m. rope-dancer || acrobat.
acrostiche, m. acrostic.
acte, m. act, action, deed || certificate || -s, pl. registers, pl. || faire ~ de, to show proof of. [actress.
acteur, m., actrice, f. actor, stage-player ||
actif, m. assets, funds || (gr.) active (voice).
actif, ve, a. (-vement, ad.) active(ly).
action, f. action, deed, operation || suit at law || battle || share || -s, pl. stock || par -s, by shares || joint-stock.
actionnaire, m. actionary, share-holder.
actionner, v. a. to sue at law, to bring an action.
activer, v. a. to put in motion, to forward.
activité, f. activity || despatch || active service. [of the hour.
actualité, f. present state || -s, pl. questions
actuel, le, a. (-lement, ad.) actual(ly) || real, present || now.
adage, m. adage, proverb.
adaptation, f. adaptation.

adapter, v. a. to adapt, to apply, to fit.
addition, f. addition, additament.
additionnel, le, a. additional.
additionner, v. a. to cast *ou* add up.
adepte, m. adept.
adéquat, e, a. adequate.
adhérent, e, a. adherent, sticking.
adhérer, v. n. to adhere, to side with.
adhésion, f. adhesion, compliance.
adieu, m. adieu, farewell ‖ **dire ~,** to bid farewell ‖ **sans ~,** I won't say good-bye, I shall see you again.
adjacent, e, a. adjacent, contiguous.
adjectif, m. (gr.) adjective.
adjectivement, ad. adjectively.
adjoindre, v. a. ir. to adjoin ‖ **to associate** ‖ **s'~,** to take as an assistant ‖ to be joined.
adjoint, m. assistant, adjunct.
adjonction, f. association.
adjudant, m. (mil.) adjutant.
adjudicataire, m. highest bidder ‖ contractor. [ing.
adjudicataire, a. purchasing ‖ contract-
adjudication, f. adjudication ‖ bargain knocked down to the highest bidder.
adjuger, v. a. to adjudge, to award ‖ **adjugé!** gone! sold!
adjurer, v. n. to adjure.
admettre, v. a. ir. to admit.
administrateur, trice, m. & f. administrator, manager ‖ director of a company ‖ trustee ‖ steward ‖ administratrix.
administratif, ve, a. (**-vement,** ad.) administrative(ly).
administration, f. administration, management, government.
administrer, v. a. to administer, to govern ‖ to dispense ‖ to officiate.
admirable, a. admirable, wonderful ‖ **-ment,** ad. admirably.
admirateur, trice, m. & f. admirer.
admiration, f. admiration, wonderment.
admirer, v. a. to admire, to wonder at.
admissibilité, f. admissibility.
admissible, a. admissible.
admission, f. admission, admittance.
admonestation, f. admonition, admonishment. [mand.
admonester, v. a. to admonish ‖ to repri-
admonition, f. admonition ‖ (jur.) reprimand.
adolescence, f. adolescence.
adolescent, e, m. & f. young man, youth ‖ maid, lass.
adolescent, e, a. young.
adoniser, v. a. to dress out, to adorn.
s'adonner, to apply oneself ‖ to become attached ‖ to be addicted.
adopter, v. a. to adopt.
adoptif, ve, a. adoptive, adopted.
adoption, f. adoption. [shipper.
adorateur, trice, m. & f. adorer, worshipper.
adoration, f. adoration, worship.
adorer, v. a. to adore, to worship.
ados, m. shelving-bed.
adosser, v. a. to set back to back ‖ to lean (against) ‖ **s'~,** to lean one's back (against).
adouber, v. a. (at chess) to set a piece right ‖ (mar.) to repair, to mend.

adoucir, v. a. to sweeten, to soften, to calm, to moderate, to alleviate, to mend ‖ **s'~,** to become sweet ‖ to soften.
adoucissant, m. emollient.
adoucissant, e, a. emollient.
adoucissement, m. softening, sweetening ‖ mitigation ‖ alleviation ‖ relief.
adresse, f. address, direction ‖ petition ‖ dexterity, ability ‖ **à l'~ de,** addressed to ‖ intended for ‖ **bureau d'~,** directory.
adresser, v. a. & n. to address, to direct ‖ to dedicate ‖ to hit the mark ‖ **s'~,** to address oneself, to apply, to speak to one ‖ to be addressed *ou* directed ‖ **s'~ ici!** Enquire within! [ning.
adroit, e, a. dexterous, skilful, sly, cunningly.
adroitement, ad. dexterously, skilfully, cunningly.
adulateur, trice, m. & f. flatterer.
adulateur, trice, a. adulatory.
aduler, v. a. to fawn upon.
adulte, m. adult.
adultération, f. adulteration.
adultère, m. adultery ‖ adulterer ‖ ~, f.
adultère, a. adulterous. [adulteress.
adultérer, v. a. to adulterate.
adultérin, e, a. adulterine.
advenir, v. imp. to occur, to happen.
adverbe, m. (gr.) adverb. [(ly).
adverbial, e, a. (**-ement,** ad.) adverbial
adversaire, m. adversary.
adverse, a. adverse, contrary.
adversité, f. adversity, misfortune.
aérage, s. airing, ventilation.
aéré, e, a. airy, well-aired.
aérer, v. a. to air, to ventilate.
aérien, ne, a. aerial, ethereal ‖ high.
aérolithe, m. aerolite, meteoric stone.
aéromètre, m. aerometer.
aéronaute, m. aeronaut.
aéronautique, f. aeronautics, pl.
aéroplane, m. aeroplane, flying-machine.
aérostatique, a. aerostatic ‖ **art ~,** aero-
aérostation, f. aerostation. [statics (pl.).
affabilité, f. affability.
affable, a. affable, courteous. [sicken.
affadir, v. a. to make insipid ‖ to cloy ‖ to
affadissement, m. cloying ‖ insipidity, nausea. [to grow weak.
affaiblir, v. a. to enfeeble, to weaken ‖ **s'~,**
affaiblissement, m. weakening ‖ allaying.
affaire, f. affair, business, matter ‖ quarrel, trouble ‖ law-suit ‖ action, fight ‖ **~ d'honneur,** affair of honour ‖ duel ‖ **~ d'intérêt,** money-concern ‖ **homme d'~s,** man of business, agent ‖ **avoir ~ à,** to have to deal with ‖ **être en ~,** to be engaged ‖ **être dans les ~s,** to be in business ‖ **faire l'~ de,** to suit, to do for ‖ **pour ~,** on business ‖ **j'en fais mon ~,** I will manage it ‖ **voilà mon ~!** that is
affairé, e, a. busy. [what I want!
affaissement, m. giving way, sinking ‖ weakness ‖ collapse.
affaisser, v. a. & n. to press down, to cause to sink ‖ **s'~,** to sink.
affaler, v. a. to overhaul ‖ **s'~,** (mar.) to be embayed upon a lee-shore.
affamé, e, a. starved, famished ‖ greedy.

affamer, v. a. to famish, to starve.
affectation, f. affectation, pretension.
affecter, v. a. to affect, to appropriate, to
affection, f. affection. [attach.
affectionné, e, a. affectionate || loving.
affectionner, v. a. to love, to be fond of ||
s'~, to become attached.
affectueux, se, a. (-sement, ad.) affec-
tionate(ly) || kind(ly).
affermer, v. a. to farm, to lease.
affermir, v. a. to strengthen, to secure || to
harden || to fix firmly. [ing.
affermissement, m. firmness, strengthen-
afféterie, f. affectation.
affichage, m. bill-sticking.
affiche, f. bill, placard.
afficher, v. a. to post up, to publish, to
advertise || défense d'~, Stick no bills ||
s'~, to make oneself the talk of the town.
afficheur, m. bill-sticker.
affidé, m. secret agent || trusty person.
affiler, v. a. to set, to sharpen.
affilier, v. a. to affiliate, to adopt.
affiloir, m. whetstone, hone.
affinage, m. refining.
affiner, v. a. to refine.
affineur, m. refiner.
affinité, f. affinity.
affiquets, m. pl. trinkets, gewgaws.
affirmatif, ve, a. (-vement, ad.) affir-
mative(ly) || positive(ly) || in the affirmative.
affirmation, f. affirmation || (jur.) oath.
affirmer, v. a. to affirm, to assert.
affleurer, v. a. to level.
afflictif, ve, a. penal || corporal.
affliction, f. affliction || trouble, **distress** ||
trial || heart-ache.
affliger, v. a. to afflict, to grieve.
affluence, f. affluence, abundance, plenty ||
affluent, m. affluent, tributary. [crowd.
affluent, e, a. tributary.
affluer, v. n. to flow into || to abound.
affolé, e, a. defective. [dote upon.
affoler, v. a. (fam.) to infatuate || s'~, to
affouage, m. (mach.) coaling || right to
gather fuel in forests.
affourché, e, a. astride. [woman.
affranchi, e, m. & f. freedman || freed-
affranchir, v. a. to set free || to pay the
p stage, to stamp.
affranchissement, m. enfranchisement,
discharge, privilege || postage.
affres, f. pl. pangs, terrors.
affrètement, m. freighting of a ship.
affréter, v. a. to fright a ship, to charter.
affréteur, m. freighter, charterer.
affreux, se, a. (-sement, ad.) fright-
ful(ly) || horrible || atrocious(ly) || terribly.
affriander, v. a. to make dainty || to allure,
to entice.
affrioler, v. a. to allure || to make dainty.
affront, m. insult, outrage || disgrace ||
avaler un ~, to pocket an affront.
affronter, v. a. to affront, to face || to
brave, to defy.
affablement, m. odd dress.
affubler, v. a. to dress oddly || s'~, to put
on an odd costume.
affût, m. (mil.) gun-carriage.

affûtage, m. sharpening || set of tools.
affûter, v. a. to sharpen tools.
affûtiau, m. knicknack || gewgaw.
afin, c. to, in order to, in order that.
agacement, m. setting on edge || irritation.
agacer, v. a. to set one's teeth on edge || to
provoke, to excite || to allure.
agacerie, f. encitement || pretty ways ||
advances || ogling, raillery.
agape, f. love-feast.
agate, f. agate.
âge, m. age, time || old age || bas ~, in-
fancy || entre deux —s, middle-aged.
âgé, e, a. aged, old.
agence, f. agency.
agencement, m. arrangement.
agencer, v. a. (fam.) to dress, to fit up ||
s'~, to trim oneself.
agenda, m. memorandum-book.
s'agenouiller, v. a. to kneel down.
agenouilloir, m. hassock.
agent, m. agent || accountant || ~ de
change, exchange-broker.
agglomérer, v. a. to agglomerate.
agglutiner, v. a. to agglutinate || s'~, to
aggraver, v. a. to aggravate. [adhere.
agile, a. agile, nimble ||, -ment, ad. nimbly.
agilité, f. agility, nimbleness.
agio, m. exchange || stock-jobbing.
agiotage, m. stock-jobbing.
agioter, v. n. to stock-job.
agioteur, m. stock-jobber.
agir, v. a. & n. to act, to do, to operate ||
to be in action, to move || de quoi s'agit-
il ? what's the matter ? what is it ?
agissant, e, a. active, busy.
agitateur, m. agitator.
agitation, f. agitation, stir, bustle.
agiter, v. a. to agitate, to move, to shake ||
to disturb, to confound, to torment || to
debate, to discuss || s'~, to be in move-
ment, to stir || to be debated.
agneau, m. lamb.
agneler, v. a. to ewe, to yean, to lamb.
agnelet, m. lambkin.
Agnès, f. raw young girl.
agonie, f. agony || à l'~, dying, in the
throes of death.
agonir, v. a. (fam.) to insult grossly.
agonisant, e, a. dying.
agoniser, v. a. to be at the point of death.
agrafe, f. clasp, locket.
agrafer, v. a. to clasp, to hook.
agraire, a. agrarian.
agrandir, v. a. to enlarge, to aggrandise,
to raise || s'~, to get larger, to increase.
agrandissement, m. increase, enlarge-
ment || promotion.
agréable, a. agreeable, pleasant || -ment,
agréé, m. attorney. [ad. agreeably.
agréer, v. a. & n. to accept || to allow || to
approve || to please, to be liked.
agrégation, f. admission || aggregate ||
fellowship.
agrégé, m. fellow (of a university).
agréger, v. a. to admit (into a society).
agrément, m. comeliness || consent ||
pleasure || -s, pl. ornaments of dress ||
arts or talents d'~, accomplishments.

agrès, m. pl. rigging (of a ship).
agresseur, m. aggressor.
agressif, ve, a. aggressive.
agression, f. aggression.
agreste, a. wild, rustic.
agricole, a. agricultural.
agriculteur, m. agriculturist.
agriculture, f. agriculture, husbandry.
s'agriffer, to cling fast.
agripper, v. a. to clutch.
agronome, m. agronomist.
agronomie, f. theory of agriculture.
agronomique, a. agronomical.
aguerrir, v. a. to inure to war.
aguets, m. pl. watch || aux ~, on the lookout, on the watch.
ah ! oh ! hah ! || ~ ça ! now then !
aheurtement, m. obstinacy.
s'aheurter, to be obstinate, to persist in.
ahurir, v. a. to astound, to startle, to dumbfound.
aide, m. & f. assistant, helper, mate || aid, help, assistance || ~ de camp, (mil.) aide-de-camp.
aider, v. a. to aid, to help.
aïe ! oh dear !
aïeul, –e, m. & f. grandfather || ancestor || grandmother.
aïeux, m. pl. forefathers, ancestors.
aigle, m. eagle || (fig.) star || reading-desk || ~, f. eagle (standard).
aiglon, m. eaglet.
aigre, m. sourness, sharpness.
aigre, a. (–ment, a.) sour, tart || churlish(ly) || sharp(ly) || harsh(ly) || ~-doux, ce, a. half sweet, half sour, bitter-sweet.
aigrefin, m. cunning fellow, sharper.
aigrelet, te, a. somewhat sour.
aigremoine, f. (bot.) agrimony.
aigremore, m. coal-dust, pulverised charcoal.
aigret, te, a. sourish.   [coal.
aigrette, f. tuft of feathers, crest.
aigretté, e, a. tufted.
aigreur, f. sourness, sharpness, spite || –s, pl. heart-burn.
aigrir, v. a. to sour || to exasperate || s'~, to turn sour || to be exasperated.
aigu, ë, a. acute, sharp-pointed || piercing, sharp, violent || accent ~, (gr.) acute accent.
aiguade, s. watering-place || water.
aiguayer, v. a. to water || to rinse.
aigue-marine, f. aqua marina, beryllus.
aiguière, f. ewer.
aiguillade, f. goad.
aiguille, f. needle || hand (of a clock) || (rail.) points, switch || ~ à tricoter, knitting needle || ~ à emballer, packing-needle || ~ à passer, bodkin.
aiguillée, f. needleful.
aiguillette, f. shoulder-knot || slice || tag, trimming.
aiguilleur, m. (rail.) switchman.
aiguillier, m. needle-case || needle-maker.
aiguillon, m. sting || goad, spur || incitement.   [to incite.
aiguillonner, v. a. to goad || to stimulate.
aiguiser, v. a. to whet, to sharpen.
ail, m. (bot.) garlic.

aile, f. wing || (poét.) pinion || bout d'~, the first quill || tirer de l'~, to make   [wing.
ailé, e, a. winged.
aileron, m. pinion || fin (of a fish).
aillade, f. garlic sauce.
ailleurs, ad. elsewhere || d'~, otherwise, besides, moreover.
aimable, a. amiable, lovely, pleasant.
aimant, m. loadstone, magnet.
aimant, e, a. loving, fond.
aimanté, e, a. magnetic.
aimanter, v. a. to magnetise.
aimer, v. a. to love, to like, to be fond of ||
aine, f. groin.   [to choose.
aîné, –e, a. elder, eldest.   [birthright.
aînesse, f. primogeniture || droit d'~,
ainsi, ad. & c. so, thus, after this manner || ~ que, even as, so as || ~ soit-il, be it so, amen.
air, m. air || tune, song || look, appearance || manner || avoir l'~ bien portant, to
airage, m. ventilation.   [look well.
airain, m. brass.
aire, f. area || threshing-floor || aerie || ~ de vent, (mar.) point of the compass.
airelle, f. (bot.) whortle-berry, bilberry.
airer, v. n. to nest.
ais, m. pl. board, plank, shelf.
aisance, f. ease, convenience || comfort || dans l'~, well off || cabinet d'~, water-closet.
aise, f. ease || –s, pl. comfort || à l'~, with ease, comfortably || à son ~, comfortably, free || en prendre à son ~, to take it
aise, a. glad, joyful, happy.   [easy.
aisé, e, a. easy || well off || –ment, ad.   [easily.
aisselle, f. armhole.
ajonc, m. (bot.) furze, broom, thorn-broom.
ajournement, m. adjournment, summons.
ajourner, v. a. to adjourn, to summon || to put off, to delay, to prorogue.
ajouter, v. a. to add, to subjoin.
ajustage, f. adjustment of coins to legal weight.   [agreement || attire.
ajustement, m. adjustment, arrangement.
ajuster, v. a. to adjust, to fit up || to trim || to reconcile || to aim (at).
ajusteur, m. adjuster.
alambic, m. alembic, still.   [refine.
alambiquer, v. a. to distil || to strain || to
alanguir, v. a. to cause to languish, to render languid || s'~, to become languid, to languish.
alarme, f. alarm, fright, trouble.
alarmer, v. a. to alarm.
alarmiste, m. alarmist.
albâtre, m. alabaster.
albatros, m. albatros.
albinos, m. albino.
album, m. album || sketch-book.
albumine, f. white of egg, albumen.
albumineux, euse, a. albuminous.
alcali, m. (chim.) alkali.
alcalin, e, a. (chim.) alkaline.
alchimie, f. alchemy.
alchimiste, m. alchemist.
alcool, m. alcohol.
alcooliser, v. a. to alcoholise.
alcoolomètre, m. alcoholometer.

alcôve, f. recess, alcove.
aléatoire, a. (jur.) eventual.
alène, f. awl.
alentour, ad. about, around || d'~, neighbouring || -s, pl. environs || company,
alépine, f. bombazine. [circle.
alerte, f. (mil.) alarm. [briskly.
alerte, a. alert, brisk || -ment, ad. quickly,
alésage, m. (mach.) boring, drilling.
aléser, v. a. (mach.) to bore, to drill.
alevin, m. fry. [horse.
alezan, e, m. sorrel, chestnut || chestnut
alezan, e, a. sorrel, chestnut.
algarade, f. (fam.) insult, blowing up,
tirade.
algèbre, f. algebra.
algue, f. seaweed. [to prove an alibi.
alibi, m. (jur.) alibi || prouver son ~,
aliboron, m. ass, blockhead.
aliéné, e, m. & f. lunatic, madman.
aliéné, e, a. alienated || insane || lunatic.
aliéner, v. a. to alienate || to estrange.
aligné, e, a. in line || straight.
alignement, m. line || row.
aligner, v. a. to lay out in line || to square ||
to string together.
aliment, m. food || fuel || maintenance.
alimentaire, a. alimentary.
alimenter, v. a. to maintain, to feed.
alinéa, m. paragraph, break.
alise, f. (bot.) beam-berry.
aliser, m. beam-tree, service-tree, lote-tree.
alité, e, a. bedridden.
aliter, v. a. to confine to one's bed.
alizé, a., vents -s, s. pl. trade-winds.
allaitement, m. lactation, suckling.
allaiter, v. a. to suckle, to nurse.
allant, e, m. & f. goer.
allant, e, a. active || going.
allécher, v. a. to allure, to entice.
allée, f. walk, alley || -s et venues,
goings and comings.
allégation, f. allegation || quotation.
allége, m. (mar.) lighter.
allégement, m. alleviation, relief.
alléger, v. a. to lighten || to ease, to relieve.
allégorie, f. allegory.
allégorique, a. (-ment, ad.) allegorical(ly).
allégoriser, v. n. to allegorise.
allègre, a. gay, lively, brisk.
allégresse, f. cheerfulness, mirth.
alléguer, v. a. to allege.
alléluia, m. Hallelujah.
aller, v. n. ir. to go, to walk || to lead to ||
to gather || to hunt || to ask || to reach, to
fit || to amount || to chance, to happen ||
~ à cheval, to ride on horseback || ~ en
voiture, to go ou ride in a carriage || se
laisser ~, to give way, to yield || le pis
~, the worst that may happen || make-
shift || au pis ~, let the worst come to
the worst || ~ et retour, there and back.
alliage, m. alloy.
alliacé, e, a. alliaceous.
alliance, f. alliance, league || relationship ||
wedding-ring.
allié, m. & f. ally || female relation || kins-
man || kinswoman.

allier, v. a. to alloy || to combine || to match.
allobroge, m. clown. [lowance.
allocation, f. allocation || grant || al-
allocution, f. address.
allonge, f. piece joined to another.
allongement, m. lengthening. [to hit.
allonger, v. a. to lengthen, to stretch out,
allopathe, s. allopathist.
allouer, v. a. to allow, to grant.
allumer, v. a. to light, to kindle || to
excite || s'~, to catch fire. [vesta.
allumette, f. match || fusee || ~ bougie, f.
allumeur, m. lamp-lighter.
allure, f. pace, gait.
allusion, f. allusion || hint.
alluvion, f. alluvium, alluvion.
almanach, m. almanac.
aloès, m. (bot.) aloes.
aloi, m. standard || quality || condition.
alors, ad. then, at that time.
alose, f. shad. [spur.
alouette, f. lark || pied d'~, (bot.) lark-
alourdir, v. a. (fam.) to dull, to make
aloyau, m. sirloin. [dull ou heavy.
alpaga, m. alpaca.
alpage, m. alpine meadow.
alpestre, a. alpine.
alphabet, m. alphabet. [betical(ly).
alphabétique, a. (-ment, ad.) alpha-
alpin, e, a. of the Alps, alpine.
altérant, e, a. causing thirst, thirst-
compelling.
altérateur, trice, a. altering || de-
teriorating || counterbalancing || weaken-
ing.
altération, f. alteration, adulteration ||
debasement (of coin) || excessive thirst.
altercation, f. altercation, dispute.
altéré, e, a. altered, changed || thirsty.
altérer, v. a. to alter, to change || to adul-
terate, to counterfeit, to deprave, to cor-
rupt || to disorder || to make thirsty || s'~,
(of the voice) to falter, to tremble.
alternatif, ve, a. (-vement, ad.) alter-
native(ly) || alternate(ly).
alternative, f. alternative.
alterne, a. alternate.
alterner, v. a. to alternate, to change.
Altesse, f. Highness.
altier, ère, a. (-èrement, ad.) haughty ||
proud(ly) || haughtily.
altitude, f. altitude, height.
alto, m. (mus.) alto, tenor-violon.
alun, m. alum. [tooth).
alvéole, m. honey-comb cell || socket (of a
amabilité, f. amiability || -s, pl. civilities.
amadou, m. tinder.
amadouer, v. a. to flatter, to cajole.
s'amaigrir, to grow thin, to fall away.
amaigrissement, m. emaciation.
amalgame, m. amalgam.
amalgamer, v. a. to amalgamate.
amande, f. almond || kernel.
amandé, m. almond-milk.
amandier, m. almond-tree.
amant, m. lover, paramour || suitor.
amante, f. mistress, sweetheart.
amarante, f. (bot.) amaranth.
amarante, a. amaranth-coloured.

amariner, v. a. (mar.) to man (a prize) ‖ to accustom to the sea.
amarrage, m. (mar.) mooring.
amarre, f. (mar.) mooring ‖ cable.
amarrer, v. a. (mar.) to moor, to tie fast.
amas, m. heap, pile ‖ store.
amasser, v. a. to heap *ou* hoard up ‖ to gather, to collect, to stock ‖ ~ de l'argent, to hoard up money ‖ s'~, to gather, to assemble, to accumulate.
amateur, m. amateur, lover, virtuoso.
amazone, f. amazon ‖ riding-habit ‖ rider.
ambassade, f. embassy.
ambassadeur, drice, m. & f. ambassador, ambassadress.
ambiant, e, a. circumambient.
ambigu, m. ambigu (medley of dishes).
ambigu, ë, a. ambiguous.
ambiguïté, f. ambiguity.
ambitieux, se, a. (-sement, ad.) ambitious(ly) ‖ desirous of ‖ high-minded(ly).
ambition, f. ambition.
ambitionner, v. a. to covet ambitiously, to aspire to, to be ambitious of.
amble, m. ambling, amble.
ambre, m. amber ‖ ~ gris, ambergris.
ambré, e, a. amber-scented ‖ amber-coloured.
ambrer, v. a. to amber.
ambroisie, f. ambrosia.
ambulance, f. (mil.) field-hospital.
ambulant, e, a. moveable, itinerant ‖ strolling, walking.
âme, f. soul, spirit, mind ‖ heart, life ‖ conscience ‖ bore (of a gun) ‖ sounding-post ‖ small wood (in faggots).
amélioration, f. improvement, amelioration.
améliorer, v. a. to improve, to better, to mend, to ameliorate.
aménager, v. a. to superintend the keeping of a forest ‖ to cut up (a tree).
amende, f. fine, penalty.   [ment.
amendement, m. amendment, improvement.
amender, v. a. to mend, to improve.
amener, v. a. to bring, to introduce ‖ to cause ‖ (mar.) to lower.
aménité, f. amenity.
amenuiser, v. a. to thin.
amer, m. bitterness ‖ gall ‖ land-mark.
amer, ère, a. (-èrement, ad.) bitter(ly) ‖ grievous(ly).   [way.
américain, m. American phaeton ‖ tramamertume, f. bitterness.
améthyste, f. amethyst.
ameublement, m. furniture.
ameublir, v. a. to mellow.
ameublissement, m. mellowing.
ameulonner, v. a. to stack.
ameuter, v. a. to train hounds to hunt together ‖ s'~, to gather in a mob.
ami, e, m. & f. friend ‖ sweetheart ‖ ~ de cœur, bosom friend ‖ ~ de cour, false ami, a. a. friendly.   [friend.
amiable, a. amicable ‖ à l'~, amicably ‖ privately ‖ -ment, ad. amicably.
amical, e, a. amicable, friendly ‖ -ement, ad. amicably, kindly.
amidon, m. starch.
amidonnerie, f. starch-manufactory.

amidonnier, m. starch-maker.
amincir, v. a. to make thinner, to thin ‖ s'~, to become thinner.
amincissement, m. thinness.
amiral, m. admiral ‖ flagship ‖ grand-~, high-admiral ‖ contre-~, rear-admiral.
amirauté, f. admiralty.
amitié, f. amity, friendship, favour, kindness ‖ -s, pl. caresses, compliments.
ammoniac, que, a. ammoniac.
ammoniaque, f. ammonia.
amnistie, f. amnesty.
amnistier, v. a. to grant an amnesty.
amoindrir, v. a. to lessen.
amoindrissement, m. lessening, decrease.
amollir, v. a. to mollify ‖ to enervate, to effeminate ‖ s'~, to grow tender, to grow effeminate.
amollissement, m. softening ‖ effeminacy.
amonceler, v. a. to heap up ‖ to gather.
amoncellement, m. heap.
d'amont, ad. up stream ‖ upwards.
amorce, f. priming ‖ bait, allurement.
amorcer, v. a. to prime a gun ‖ to put on a percussion-cap ‖ to bait, to allure.
amortir, v. a. to deaden, to weaken ‖ to calm ‖ to pay off ‖ to redeem (a rent).
amortissable, a. redeemable.
amortissement, m. amortisation ‖ decrease, abatement, extinction ‖ caisse d'~, sinking-fund.
amour, m. love, passion, affection ‖ ~ propre, self-love.
s'amouracher, to fall in love with.
amourette, f. slight love-affair.
amoureux, m. lover.
amoureux, se, a. (-sement, ad.) amorous(ly) ‖ enamoured.
amovibilité, f. removability.
amovible, a. removable.
ampère, m. ampère, unit of intensity of an electric current.
amphibie, m. amphibian, amphibium.
amphibie, a. amphibious, amphibian.
amphibologie, f. amphibology.
amphigouri, m. nonsense, rigmarole.
amphigourique, a. nonsensical.
amphithéâtre, m. amphitheatre ‖ first gallery ‖ lecture-room ‖ dissecting-room.
amphitryon, m. (fig.) host, entertainer.
ample, a. ample, large, full ‖ -ment, ad. amply, largely.
ampleur, f. amplitude, fulness.
ampliation, f. duplicate ‖ office copy ‖ true copy.
amplificateur, m. amplifier.   [on.
amplifier, v. a. to amplify, to expatiate
ampoule, f. blister.
ampoulé, e, a. bombastic, high-flown.
amputer, v. a. to amputate.
amulette, m. amulet.
amure, f. (mar.) tack of a sail.
amusement, m. amusement, pastime.
amuser, v. a. to amuse, to entertain ‖ to feed with vain hopes, to play with ‖ s'~, to amuse oneself, to tarry, to trifle one's time away.
amusette, f. trifle, toy ‖ pastime.
amygdale, f. tonsil.

an, m. year || par ~, yearly || **premier jour de l'~**, New Year's day.
anabaptiste, m. anabaptist.
anachorète, m. anchorite.
anachronisme, m. anachronism || pro-
anagramme, m. anagram. [lepsis.
analogie, f. analogy.
analogique, a. analogical.
analogue, a. analogous.
analyse, f. analysis || (gr.) parsing.
analyser, v. a. to analyse.
analytique, a. (-ment,ad.) analytical(ly).
ananas, m. pine-apple.
anarchie, f. anarchy.
anarchique, a. anarchical.
anarchiste, m. anarchist.
anathématiser, v. a. to anathematise.
anathème, m. anathema.
anathème, a. anathematised.
anatomie, f. anatomy.
anatomique, a. anatomical.
anatomiser, v. a. to anatomise.
ancêtres, m. pl. ancestors, forerunners.
anche, f. (mus.) reed || miller's scuttle.
anchois, m. anchovy.
ancien, m. senior, elder || old codger.
ancien, ne, a. ancient, old || late || **–ne-ment**, ad. anciently || formerly.
ancienneté, f. antiquity || seniority.
ancrage, m. (mar.) bracing || anchorage.
ancre, f. anchor || (fig.) refuge || **~ de miséricorde,~de salut,~maîtresse,** (mar.) sheet-anchor.
ancrer, v. n. to anchor || **s'~**, to get a
andain, m. swath. [footing.
andalou(s), m. Andalusian horse.
andouille, f. haggis || roll of tobacco.
andouiller, m. antler.
andouillette, f. small sausage.
âne, m. ass || donkey || fool.
anéantir, v. a. to destroy, to bring to no-thing || **s'~**, to come to nothing, to humble oneself || to vanish.
anéantissement, m. annihilation, de-struction || self-humiliation.
anecdote, f. anecdote.
ânerie, f. gross ignorance || gross blunder.
ânesse, f. she-ass.
anémie, f. (méd.) anæmia.
anévrisme, m. (méd.) aneurism.
anfractueux, se, a. anfractuous || intri-cate. [to be in extasies.
ange, m. angel || angel-fish || **être aux –s,**
angélique, f. (bot.) angelica.
angélique, a. angelic.
angine, f. sore-throat || **~ couenneuse,**
anglaiser, v. a. to nick. [diphtheria.
angle, m. angle || corner.
anglican, e, a. Anglican || (of the) Church of England.
anglicisme, m. Anglicism.
anglomane, m. & f. Anglomaniac.
anglomanie, f. Anglomania.
angoisse, f. anguish, pang.
angora, m. Angora-cat.
anguillade, f. lashing.
anguille, f. eel || **~ de haie,** hedge, grass-ou water-snake || **~ tremblante,** electric
anguillère, f. eel-pond. [eel.

angulaire, a. angular.
anguleux, se, a. many-cornered.
anicroche, m. obstacle, difficulty.
ânier, ère, m. & f. ass-driver.
animal, m. animal, beast || blockhead.
animal, e, a. animal, bestial.
animé, a. animated || gay, sprightly.
animer, v. a. to animate, to enliven || to encourage, to excite || to provoke || **s'~,** to encourage one another, to cheer up, to
animosité, f. animosity. [take fire.
anis, m. anise || **(graine d'~)** anise-seed.
ankylose, f. (méd.) stiff joint, anchylosis.
annales, f. pl. annals.
anneau, m. ring || link.
année, f. year, twelve-month || **à l'~,** by the year || **~ commune (moyenne),** (agr.) taking one year with another.
annelé, e, a. annulated.
annelet, m. annulet, small ring.
annexe, f. annex || schedule || chapel of
annexer, v. a. to annex. [ease.
annexion, f. annexation.
annihiler, v. a. to annihilate.
anniversaire, m. anniversary.
anniversaire, a. anniversary.
annonce, f. advertisement || banns (among
protestants).
annoncer, v. a. to announce, to make known, to inform, to warn || to foretell || **s'~,** to present oneself || to announce its coming || to be preceded || **s'~ bien,** to promise well.
Annonciation, f. Lady-day, Annuncia-
annotateur, m. annotator. [tion.
annoter, v. a. to note down || to annotate.
annuaire, m. annuary || year-book.
annuel, le, a. (-lement, ad.) annual(ly) ||
yearly.
annuité, f. annuity. [finger.
annulaire, a. annular || **doigt ~,** m. ring-
annuler, v. a. to annul, to cancel || to
anoblir, v. a. to ennoble. [quash.
anoblissement, m. ennoblement || no-
anodin, e, a. anodyne. [bility.
anodin, e, a. gentl- || unmeaning.
anomal, e, a. anomalous.
anomalie, f. anomaly.
ânon, m. ass's colt, young ass.
ânonner, v. n. to falter || to foal.
anonyme, m. anonymity || anonymous person || **garder l'~,** not to give one's name, to preserve one's incognito.
anonyme, a. anonymous || joint-stock.
anormal, e, a. abnormal || anomalous.
anse, f. handle || (mar.) small bay || **~ du panier,** servants' perquisites.
antagonisme, m. antagonism.
antagoniste,m.& f. antagonist, adversary.
antagoniste, a. antagonistic.
antan, m. last year.
antarctique, a. antarctic.
antécédent, m. precedent || antecedent.
antécédent, e, a. antecedent, preceding.
Antéchrist, m. Antichrist.
antédiluvien, ne, a. antediluvian.
antenne, f. feeler, antenna.
antépénultième, f. antepenultimate.
antépénultième, a. antepenultimate.

antérieur, e, a. (-ement, ad.) anterior ‖ former(ly) ‖ previous(ly) ‖ before.
antériorité, f. priority.
anthère, f. (bot.) anther.
anthologie, f. anthology.
anthropophage, m. & f. cannibal.
antichambre, f. antechamber, hall ‖ **faire ~**, to dance attendance.
antichrétien, ne, a. antichristian.
anticipation, f. anticipation ‖ par ~, beforehand.   [to preclude.
anticiper, v. a. to anticipate, to forestall,
antidater, v. a. to antedate.
antidote, m. antidote.
antienne, f. anthem.
antilope, f. antelope.
antimoine, m. antimony.
antinational, e, a. antinational.
antipape, m. antipope.
antipathie, f. antipathy, aversion.
antipathique, a. antipathetic.
antiphrase, f. antiphrasis, irony.
antipode, m. antipode.
antiputride, a. antiseptic.
antiquaille, f. antiquity ‖ old rubbish.
antiquaire, m. antiquary.
antique, a. antique, old, ancient ‖ à l'~, old-fashioned.
antiquité, f. antiquity.
antiseptique, m. antiseptic.
antiseptique, a. antiseptic.
antisocial, e, a. antisocial.
antithèse, f. antithesis.
antre, m. cave ‖ den (of beasts).
anus, m. (anat., bot.) anus.
anxiété, f. anxiety.
aorte, f. (anat.) aorta.
août, m. August ‖ harvest-time.
aoûté, e, a. ripened.
apaiser, v. a. to appease ‖ to calm, to quiet ‖ to quench ‖ to quell ‖ s'~, to abate ‖ to get calm, to calm down.
apanage, m. appanage ‖ appendage.
aparté, m. aside, words spoken aside.
apathie, f. spathy.
apathique, a. apathetic.
apercevoir, v. a. ir. to perceive, to descry, to remark ‖ s'~, to perceive, to discover.
aperçu, m. sketch, glimpse, glance ‖ slight notion ‖ general idea ‖ brief account ‖ en ~, summarily ‖ par ~, at a rough guess.
apéritif, m. (méd.) aperient.
apéritif, ve, a. (méd.) aperient.
aphonie, f. (méd.) loss of voice, aphony.
aphorisme, m. aphorism.   [-s, thrush.
aphthe, m. slight ulcer (in the mouth) ‖
apitoyer, v. a. to move to pity ‖ s'~, to be moved to pity.
aplaner, v. a. to nap, to raise the nap.
aplanir, v. a. to plane, to level, to smoothe.
aplanissement, m. levelling ‖ levelness, smoothness.
aplatir, v. a. to flatten.
aplatissement, m. flattening ‖ flatness.
aplomb, m. level ‖ perpendicular line ‖ steadiness ‖ self-possession ‖ d'~, perpendicularly ‖ in equilibrium.
apocryphe, a. apocryphal.
apode, a. footless.

apogée, f. apogee ‖ acme.
apologétique, a. apologetic.
apologie, f. apology ‖ praise.
apologiste, m. apologist.
apophthegme, m. apophthegm, **maxim**.
apoplectique, a. apoplectic.
apoplexie, f. apoplexy.
apostasie, f. apostasy.
apostasier, v. n. to apostatise.
apostat, m. apostate.
apostat, e, a. apostate. [station, to secrete.
aposter, v. a. to lay in ambuscade, to
apostille, f. marginal note ‖ postscript ‖ recommendation.   [write.
apostiller, v. a. to write notes, to under-
apostolat, m. apostleship.
apostolique, a. apostolic.
apostropher, v. a. apostrophise.
apothéose, f. apotheosis.
apothicaire, m. apothecary ‖ **mémoire d'~**, exorbitant bill.
apôtre, m. apostle ‖ saint.
apparaître, v. n. ir. to appear.
apparat, m. pomp, state, show.
appareil, m. preparation ‖ equipage, attendance ‖ machinery ‖ dressing of a wound ‖ (mar.) purchase.
appareillage, m. getting under sail.
appareiller, v. a. & n. to match ‖ (mar.) to set sail ‖ to get under sail.
apparemment, ad. apparently.
apparence, f. appearance.
apparent, e, a. apparent, evident, conspicuous.   [spicuous.
apparenté, e, a. related to.
apparenter, v. a. to connect by marriage ‖ s'~, to become related to ‖ to marry.
appariement, m. matching ‖ pairing.
apparier, v. a. to match ‖ to pair.
appariteur, m. beadle.   [ghost.
apparition, f. apparition ‖ appearance ‖
appartement, m. apartment, lodging.
appartenance, f. appartenance.
appartenir, v. a. ir. to appertain, to belong ‖ s'~, to be one's own master.
appas, m. pl. charms, allurement.
appât, m. bait, decoy, allurement.
appâter, v. a. to allure, to bait ‖ to feed.
appauvrir, v. a. to empoverish, to pauperise ‖ s'~, to grow poor.
appeau, m. bird-call.
appel, m. appeal, challenge ‖ call ‖ calling over ‖ (mil.) muster.
appeler, v. a. to call, to name ‖ (faire ~) to send for, to invite ‖ s'~, to be called.
appendice, m. appendix.
appendre, v. a. to hang up.
appentis, m. shed, penthouse.
appesantir, v. a. to dull, to make heavy or dull ‖ to lie heavy upon ‖ s'~, to grow dull ‖ to descant or expatiate.   [ness.
appesantissement, m. heaviness ‖ dul-
appétissant, e, a. relishing ‖ desirable, delicious, inviting, appetising.
appétit, m. appetite ‖ relish.
applaudir, v. a. & n. to applaud ‖ s'~, to applaud oneself, to admire.
applaudissement, m. applause.
applaudisseur, m. applauder, clapper.
application, f. application.

applique, f. inlaying || bracket.
appliqué, e, a. diligent, studious.
appliquer, v. a. to apply, to put, to lay on *ou* upon || **s'~,** to apply oneself.
appoint, m. balance || odd money.
appointé, e, a. agreed || paid.
appointements, m. pl. wages, salary.
appointer, v. a. to salary, to give a salary.
apport, m. share of capital || personal estate. [to use.
apporter, v. a. to bring, to cause, to apply,
apposer, v. a. to affix, to put.
apposition, f. setting || apposition.
appréciateur, m. appraiser.
appréciatif, ve, a. appreciating || **état ~,** estimate.
appréciation, f. valuation, appraising.
apprécier, v. a. to appreciate || to value.
appréhender, v. a. to apprehend, to dread || to lay hold of || **~ au corps,** to arrest.
apprendre, v. a. ir. to learn, to teach || to understand || to advise || **~ par cœur,** to learn by heart.
apprenti, e, f. apprentice || (fig.) novice.
apprentissage, m. apprenticeship || trial.
apprêt, m. preparation || cooking || painting on glass || dressing || (fig.) stiffness, affectation. [to dress.
apprêter, v. a. to prepare, to get ready ||
apprivoisement, m. taming.
apprivoiser, v. a. to tame || to make sociable || **s'~,** to grow tame *ou* sociable.
approbateur, trice, m. & f. approver.
approbateur, trice, a. approving, approbatory. [tory.
approbatif, ve, a. approving, approba-
approchant, e, a. somewhat like || **~,** ad. & pr. near, about.
approche, m. approach || (typ.) space.
approcher, v. a. & n. to approach, to bring near || to draw near || to border (upon) || to be like.
approfondir, v. a. to deepen || to dive into || to search into, to explore.
approprier, v. a. to appropriate, to adapt || to clean || to tidy (a room).
approuver, v. a. to approve (of).
approvisionnement, m. supply of provisions || stores || victualling.
approvisionner, v. a. to supply with provisions.
approvisionneur, m. victualler.
approximatif, ve, a. (**-vement,** ad.) approximate(ly). [guess.
approximation, f. approximation || rough
appui, m. prop, stay, support || protection || **à l'~,** in support of || **point d'~,** m. fulcrum, basis || **à hauteur d'~,** breast-high || **~-main,** m. (peint.) maulstick || hand-rest.
appuyer, v. a. & n. to prop up, to stay, to support || to favour, to defend || to press upon, to lean, to rest || **s'~,** to lean upon *ou* against || to rely upon || to dwell.
âpre, a. rough, harsh, sour, bitter || greedy, eager || **-ment,** ad. roughly, harshly, sharply, eagerly.
après, ad. & pr. after, next to || upon || about || **~ tout,** after all || **d'~,** to, from || according to || **et ~?** what next? what

then? || **~-demain,** m. & ad. the day after to-morrow || **~-midi,** m. & f. afternoon.
âpreté, f. asperity, sourness || roughness, harshness, severity || greediness.
apte, a. fit (to) || qualified.
aptitude, f. aptitude, aptness.
apurement, m. closing of an account.
apurer, v. a. to audit.
aquarelle, f. water-colour || painting in water-colours || **peindre à l'~,** to paint in water-colours.
aquatique, a. aquatic.
aqueduc, m. aqueduct || inlet.
aqueux, se, a. watery.
aquilin, a. aquiline, hooked, Roman (nose).
aquilon, m. north wind || **-s,** pl. cold stormy winds.
arabe, m. usurer || dun, screw.
arabesque, m. arabesque.
araignée, f. spider.
aratoire, a. agricultural.
arbalète, f. cross-bow.
arbalétrier, m. cross-bowman.
arbitrage, m. arbitration.
arbitraire, a. arbitrary || voluntary || **-ment,** ad. arbitrarily.
arbitralement, ad. by arbitration.
arbitre, m. arbiter, umpire || ruler || disposer.
arbitrer, v. a. to arbitrate. [poser.
arborer, v. a. to set up || to hoist || to proclaim.
arborisé, e, a. arborised. [claim.
arbouse, f. arbute-berry.
arbousier, m. arbute.
arbre, m. tree || beam || **~ en espalier,** wall-tree || **~ fruitier,** fruit-tree || **~ vert,** evergreen.
arbrisseau, arbuste, m. shrub.
arc, m. bow || arch || arc || **~-boutant,** m. buttress || prop, stay || **~-en-ciel,** m. rainbow.
arcade, m. arcade || arch. [rainbow.
arceau, m. arch of a vault.
archaïsme, m. archaism.
archal, m. fil d'~, wire.
archange, m. archangel.
arche, m. arch || ark.
archéologie, f. archæology.
archéologique, a. archæological.
archéologue, m. archæologist.
archer, m. archer, bowman.
archet, m. violin-bow, fiddlestick.
archevêché, m. archbishopric || archiepiscopal palace.
archevêque, m. archbishop. [deaconry.
archidiaconat, archidiaconé, m. arch-
archidiacre, m. archdeacon.
archiduc, m. archduke.
archiduché, m. archdukedom.
archiduchesse, f. archduchess.
archipel, m. archipelago.
archiépiscopal, e, a. archiepiscopal.
archiprêtre, m. archpriest.
architecte, m. architect || **~ de jardins, ~ paysagiste,** landscape-gardener.
architectural, e, a. architectural.
archives, f. pl. archives || record-office.
archiviste, m. archivist || keeper of the archives.
arçon, m. saddle-bow. [archives.
arctique, a. arctic, northern.
ardemment, ad. ardently.

ardent, m. ignis fatuus, Will o' the Whisp, Jack o' Lantern.
ardent, e, a. ardent ‖ vehement, eager ‖ burning ‖ red-hot. [eagerness, passion.
ardeur, f. ardour, fervency ‖ vehemence,
ardillon, m. tongue (of a buckle).
ardoise, f. slate.
ardoisé, e, a. slated.
ardoisière, f. slate-quarry.
ardu, e, a. arduous.
are, m. are (100 square metres).
arène, f. sand ‖ arena.
aréopage, m. areopagus.
arête, f. fish-bone ‖ beard ‖ edge.
argent, m. silver ‖ money, cash ‖ coin ‖ change, small change ‖ **~ comptant,** ready money ‖ **prendre pour ~ comptant,** to be too credulous, to take literally.
argenter, v. a. to silver, to silver-plate.
argenterie, f. plate, silver-plate.
argenteur, m. silverer.
argentifère, a. argentiferous.
argentin, e, a. silvery, silver-coloured ‖ bright ‖ sonorous.
argenture, f. silver-plating.
argile, f. potter's clay.
argileux, se, a. clayey.
argilière, f. clay-pit.
argot, m. slang. [wood.
argoter, v. a. (hort.) to prune away dead
argousin, m. convict-keeper.
arguer, v. n. to argue, to infer.
argumentateur, m. arguer.
argument, v. n. to argue.
argutie, f. quibble.
aride, a. arid, dry, barren.
aridité, f. dryness ‖ barrenness.
ariette, f. (mus.) arietta.
aristocrate, m. aristocrat.
aristocratie, f. aristocracy. [cratic(ally).
aristocratique, a. (-ment, ad.) aristo-
arithméticien, m. arithmetician.
arithmétique, f. arithmetic.
arithmétique, a. (-ment, ad.) arith-
arlequin, m. harlequin. [metical(ly).
armateur, m. fitter-out ‖ privateer ‖ ship-owner.
arme, f. arm, weapon ‖ **~ à feu,** fire-arm ‖ **~ de trait,** cross-bow ‖ **-s,** pl. arms, coat of arms ‖ troops ‖ place **d'-s,** drill-ground ‖ **aux -s!** to arms! **faire des -s,** to learn fencing ‖ **faire passer par les -s,** (mil.) to shoot. [navale, fleet.
armée, f. army, troops ‖ **~ de mer,**
armeline, f. ermine. [parations.
armement, m. armament ‖ warlike pre-
armer, v. a. to arm ‖ to prepare ‖ (mar.) to fit out ‖ to cock (a gun) ‖ **s'~,** to arm oneself, to take up arms ‖ (fig.) to provide oneself ‖ (fig.) to provide against ‖ to sum-
armillaire, a. armillary. [mon up.
armistice, m. armistice.
armoire, f. clothes-press ‖ cupboard ‖ **~ à glace,** wardrobe with glass doors.
armoiries, f. pl. arms, armorial bearings.
armorial, m. book of heraldry.
armorier, v. a. to put one's arms upon.
armure, f. armour. [armourer.
armurier, m. gunsmith ‖ sword-cutler ‖

aromate, m. aromatic.
aromatique, a. aromatic, spicy.
aromatiser, v. a. to perfume.
arome, m. aroma, flavour.
arpège, m. (mus.) arpeggio.
arpent, m. acre.
arpentage, m. land-surveying.
arpenter, v. a. to survey, to measure land ‖ (fam.) to walk fast (over) ‖ to devour the ground, to cover miles of.
arpenteur, m. surveyor.
arqué, e, a. arched ‖ bent ‖ crooked.
arquebuse, f. arquebuse, hand-gun.
arquebuserie, f. gun-smithery.
arquebusier, m. gunsmith.
arquer, v. a. to arch, to bend.
arrachage, m. pulling up of plants.
arrachement, m. plucking ‖ pulling ‖ wringing ‖ digging up.
(d')arrache-pied, ad. without interruption.
arracher, v. a. to tear out, to pluck up, to wrest out, to root up ‖ to pull away, to snatch away ‖ to force ‖ to draw (a tooth) ‖ **s'~,** to tear oneself away ‖ to detach one-
arracheur, m. tooth-drawer. [self from.
arrangement, m. arrangement ‖ order ‖ management ‖ measures (pl.).
arranger, v. a. to arrange, to place in order ‖ to dispose, to settle, to class ‖ **s'~,** to take proper measures, to agree amicably ‖ to compound ‖ **arrangez-vous!** I manage
arrenter, v. a. to rent. [as you can!
arrérager, v. n. to be in arrears.
arrérages, m. pl. arrears.
arrestation, f. arrest ‖ apprehension.
arrêt, m. decree, sentence, judgment ‖ arrest of one's person ‖ **à l'~, en ~,** (of dogs) setting ‖ **maison d'~,** prison ‖ **chien d'~,** setter ‖ **temps d'~,** stopping-time.
arrêté, m. decree, resolution, settlement.
arrête-porte, m. door-porter ‖ gate-stop.
arrêter, v. a. & n. to arrest, to stop ‖ to detain, to withhold ‖ to strike a bargain ‖ to settle ‖ to come to a resolution, to deter-mine upon ‖ to give over ‖ **s'~,** to stop, to halt, to stay ‖ to forbear ‖ to suspend.
arrhes, f. pl. earnest-money ‖ deposit.
arrière, m. back part ‖ (mar.) stern ‖ **~-main,** f. back of the hand ‖ backstroke ‖ **~-neveu,** m. grand-nephew ‖ **~-pensée,** f. after-thought ‖ mental reservation ‖ **~-petite-fille,** f. great-granddaughter ‖ **~-petit-fils,** m. great-grandson ‖ **~-plan,** m. background ‖ **~-saison,** f. autumn, end of the season ‖ **~-train,** m. after-carriage.
arriéré, m. arrears (pl.).
arriéré, e, a. in arrears.
arriérer, v. a. to put in arrears, to delay ‖ to defer ‖ **s'~,** to stay behind ‖ to be in
arrimer, v. a. (mar.) to stow. [arrears.
arrivage, m. (mar.) arrival.
arrivée, f. arrival, coming.
arriver, v. n. to arrive, to come to, to land, to approach ‖ to happen, to befall.
arrogamment, ad. arrogantly.
arrogant, e, a. arrogant.
s'arroger, to arrogate to oneself.

arrondir, v. a. to round, to enlarge || s'~, to grow round || (fam.) to increase one's estate.

arrondissement, m. rounding || district.

arrosage, m. irrigation, watering.

arrosement, m. watering, sprinkling || basting. [to bathe (of a river).

arroser, v. a. to water || to sprinkle || (fig.)

arrosoir, m. watering-pot.

arsenal, m. arsenal || ~ de marine, dockyard || (Am.) navy-yard.

arsenic, m. (chim.) arsenic.

arsenical, a. (chim.) arsenical.

arsénieux, se, a. (chim.) arsenious.

art, m. art || profession || ability || maître-artère, f. artery. [ès--s, master of arts.

artériel, le, a. arterial.

artésien, ne, a. artesian (of wells).

artichaut, m. (bot.) artichoke || spiked fence.

article, m. article, point || matter, clause || ~ de fond, ~ principal, leading article.

articulaire, a. articular.

articulation, f. articulation || joint.

articuler, v. a. to articulate.

artifice, m. artifice, art, skill || craft, trick, deceit || feu d'~, fireworks || sans ~, roundly, plainly. [(ly).

artificiel, le, a. (-lement, ad.) artificial

artificier, m. firework-maker || (mil.) filler of explosive shells. [ful(ly), cunning(ly).

artificieux, se, a. (-sement, ad.) art-

artillerie, f. artillery.

artilleur, m. gunner, artilleryman.

artimon, m. (mar.) mizzen.

artisan, m. artisan, mechanic || architect.

artiste, m. artist. [author.

artistement, ad. skilfully || artistically.

artistique, a. relating to the arts || artistic.

as, m. ace. [influence.

ascendant, m. ascendant || ascendency ||

ascendant, e, a. ascending || upward.

ascenseur, m. passenger-lift.

Ascension, ascension, f. Ascension-day || ascent, ascension.

ascensionnel, le, a. ascensional || mouvement ~, up-stroke.

ascétique, a. ascetic.

ascétisme, m. asceticism.

asile, m. asylum, refuge || ~ des pauvres, poorhouse, workhouse || salle d'~, infant-school.

asine, a. assinine || bête ~, ass, dunce.

aspect, m. aspect, view, appearance ||

asperge, f. asparagus. [sketch.

asperger, v. a. to sprinkle.

aspergerie, f. asparagus-bed.

aspergès, m. holy-water sprinkler.

aspérité, f. asperity, roughness.

aspersion, f. sprinkling.

aspersoir, m. holy-water sprinkler.

asphalte, m. asphalt.

asphaltite, a. asphaltic.

asphyxie, f. asphyxia.

asphyxier, v. a. to suffocate, to asphyxiate.

aspic, m. aspic, asp.

aspirant, e, m. candidate || midshipman.

aspiration, f. aspiration.

aspirer, v. a. & n. to aspirate || to inhale ||

assaillant, m. assailant, aggressor.

assaillir, v. a. to assail, to assault, to attack. [drain.

assainir, v. a. to render wholesome || to

assainissement, m. rendering wholesome || draining.

assaisonnement, m. seasoning.

assaisonner, v. a. to season || to heighten || to temper.

assassin, m. assassin, murderer.

assassin, e, a. murderous, murdering || killing.

assassinat, m. assassination, murder.

assassiner, v. a. to assassinate, to murder || to plague.

assaut, m. assault, attack || ~ d'armes, fencing-match || faire ~ de, to vie in.

assemblage, m. assemblage, joining, union || mixture.

assemblée, f. assembly, meeting, society.

assembler, v. a. to assemble, to collect || to join || to gather || s'~, to assemble, to meet together. [blow.

asséner, v. a. to strike hard, to deal a

assentiment, m. assent.

assertion, f. assertion, statement.

asseoir, v. a. ir. to set, to lay, to fix || to establish || s'~, to sit, to sit down.

assermenter, v. a. to swear in.

asservir, v. a. to enslave, to subdue.

asservissant, e, a. slavish.

asservissement, m. subjection || bondage.

assesseur, m. assessor.

assez, ad. enough, sufficiently || ~ bien, pretty well || c'est ~, that will do.

assidu, e, a. assiduous.

assiduité, f. assiduity || regular attendance.

assidûment, ad. assiduously.

assiégeant, e, m. besieger. [to dun.

assiéger, v. a. (mil.) to besiege || to beset ||

assiette, f. seat, state, situation || assessment || plate || plateful || fund || trim.

assiettée, f. plateful.

assignation, f. assignation || (jur.) assignment, summons || subpœna.

assigner, v. a. to assign, to summon.

assimiler, v. a. to assimilate, to compare.

assise, f. course || layer || -s, pl. assizes.

assistance, f. assistance, attendance || assembly. [auditor.

assistant, m. assistant, helper || bystander.

assister, v. a. & n. to assist, to stand by, to help, to succour, to relieve || to be present at, to attend.

association, f. association, partnership.

associé, m. associate, partner || accomplice || fellow.

associer, v. a. to associate, to join in company, to take into partnership || s'~, to enter into partnership || to keep company with.

assolement, m. (agr.) rotation of crops.

assoler, v. a. (agr.) to distribute crops.

assombrir, v. a. to darken || s'~, to get gloomy. [some.

assommant, a. killing, oppressive, tire-

assommer, v. a. to knock down, to kill || to beat soundly || to overpower, to beat down || to tease, to torment.

assommeur, m. killer.

assommoir, m. bludgeon || life-preserver || trap || gin-palace.   [tion || assumption.
Assomption, assomption, f. Assump-
assortiment, m. assortment, set.
assortir, v. a. & n. to sort, to match, to
assortissant, e, a. matching.   [suit.
assoter, v. a. to infatuate.
assoupir, v. a. to make drowsy ou sleepy || to calm, to assuage || to deaden || s'~, to fall asleep.
assoupissant, e, a. soporiferous.
assoupissement, m. sleepiness, drowsiness || carelessness, slovenliness.
assouplir, v. a. to make supple, to bend, to break.   [muffle || to deaden.
assourdir, v. a. to deafen, to stun || to
assouvir, v. a. to satiate, to glut.
assouvissement, m. satiating || glutting.
assujettir, v. a. to subdue, to master, to overcome || to fix, to fasten.
assujettisant, e, a. slavish.
assujettissement, m. subjection || con-
assumer, v. a. to assume.   [straint.
assurance, f. assurance, confidence || security || firmness || insurance.
assuré, e, a. sure, certain, bold, confident || —ment, ad. assuredly.
assurer, v. a. to assure || to affirm || to encourage || to insure || to fix || s'~, to be certain, to make sure of || to rely (upon).
assureur, m. insurer.
astérisque, m. (typ.) asterisk.
asthmatique, a. (méd.) asthmatic.
asthme, m. (méd.) asthma.
asticot, m. maggot.
asticoter, v. a. (fam.) to tease.
astiquer, v. a. to polish.
astre, m. star, fixed star.
astreindre, v. a. n. ir. to bind || to compel.
astreinte, f. fine, penalty, forfeit.
astringent, e, a. astringent.
astrologie, f. astrology.
astrologue, m. astrologer.
astronome, m. astronomer.
astronomie, f. astronomy.
astronomique, a. astronomical.
astuce, f. cunning, craft.
astucieux, se, a. (—sement, ad.) cunning(ly) || crafty.
ataxie, f. (méd.) ataxy.   [dio.
atelier, m. work-shop, manufactory || stu-
atermoiement, m. (com.) delay.
atermoyer, v. a. to delay (a payment).
athée, m. & f. atheist.
athée, a. atheistic(al).
athéisme, m. atheism.
athénée, m. athenæum.
athlète, m. athlete.
athlétique, a. athletic.
atmosphère, f. atmosphere.
atmosphérique, a. atmospheric.
atome, m. atom.   [tone.
atonie, f. (méd.) atonia, atony, want of
atours, m. pl. attire.
atout, m. trump (at cards).
atrabilaire, a. splenetic.
âtre, m. hearth, fire-place.
atroce, a. (—ment, ad.) atrocious(ly).
atrocité, f. atrocity.

atrophié, e, a. withered, wasted || stunted.
s'attabler, to sit down to table (for long).
attachant, e, a. attractive, engaging, interesting || confining.
attache, f. tether || tie || string, bond, leash || attachment || à l'~, tied up.
attaché, m. attaché (to an embassy).
attachement, m. attachment, affection || tie, bond || constant application.
attacher, v. a. to attach, to fasten, to join, to tie, to apply || to entice || to hold, to fix (one's eye) || s'~, to stick to || to take hold, to conceive an affection for || to endeavour.
attaquant, m. assailant.
attaque, f. attack, assault || (méd.) fit.
attaquer, v. a. to attack, to assault || to begin to sue || s'~, to challenge || to meddle with.
attarder, v. a. to make late, to delay || s'~, to stay ou start late || to be out late.
atteindre, v. a. n. ir. to touch, to reach, to attain, to overtake || to strike.
atteinte, f. blow, hit, touch, reach || reproach, injury.   [oxen).
attelage, m. team (of horses) || yoke (of
atteler, v. a. to harness, to put to (of horses, etc.).
attenant, e, a. close to, contiguous.
attendant, e, a. expecting || en ~, in the mean time.
attendre, v. a. & n. to expect, to wait, to stay for, to tarry || s'~, to rely, to depend (upon) || to trust (to).
attendrir, v. a. to make tender, to move || to affect || s'~, to be moved to pity.
attendrissement, m. tenderness, emotion.
attendu, pr. considering, on account of || ~ que, considering that.
attentat, m. attempt, outrage, violation.
attentatoire, a. attempting, hostile.
attente, f. waiting || expectation, hope.
attenter, v. n. to attempt.   [tive(ly).
attentif, ve, a. (—vement, ad.) atten-
attention, f. attention, carefulness || faire ~, to pay attention.   [polite.
attentionné, e, a. considerate, attentive,
atténuation, f. attenuation, weakness || extenuation.   [to extenuate.
atténuer, v. a. to attenuate || to weaken ||
atterrage, m. (mar.) making land.
atterrer, v. a. to throw down || to destroy.
atterrir, v. n. (mar.) to land.
atterrissage, m. (mar.) landing.
atterrissement, m. alluvion.
attester, v. a. to attest, to witness, to attic(ism), to atticism.   [testify.
atticisme, m. atticism.
attiédir, v. a. to cool.
attiédissement, m. lukewarmness.
attifer, v. a. to dress, to trick up, to rig out.
attique, m. (arch.) attic.
attique, a. attic || elegant.
attirail, m. implements (pl.) || equipage.
attirant, e, a. attractive.
attirer, v. a. to attract, to allure, to entice || to gain, to bring over || s'~, to bring upon oneself, to gain, to win.
attiser, v. a. to stir, to poke.
attitré, e, a. regular || appointed || recognised.
attitude, f. attitude, posture.

attouchement, m. touch, contact.
attractif, ve, a. attractive.
attrait, m. enticement, charm || taste.
attrape, f. trick, take-in || ~-mouche, m. (bot.) fly-trap || ~-nigaud, m. (fam.) fool's-trap.
attraper, v. a. to catch, to ensnare || to cheat, to take in || to obtain, to gain, to arrive at || to bring upon oneself.
attrapeur, m. deceiver || catcher.
attrayant, e, a. attractive.
attribuer, v. a. to attribute, to attach || s'~, to take upon oneself, to claim.
attribut, m. attribute.
attribution, f. conferring || privilege || -s, pl. functions, pl.
attristant, e, a. afflicting, sad.
attrister, v. a. to afflict, to grieve.
attroupement, m. mob.
attrouper, v.a. to assemble || to gather in crowds.
au = à le.
aubade, f. serenade.
aubaine, f. escheat || windfall.
aube, f. dawn || alb || paddle-board || à -s, paddle ...
aubépine, f. haw-thorn.
auberge, f. inn, tavern.
aubergine, f. mad-apple.
aubergiste, m. inn-keeper, landlord.
aubette, f. newspaper stall, bookstall.
aubier, m. sapwood.
aucun, e, pn. no one, none, not any.
aucunement, ad. not at all.
audace, f. audacity, boldness.
audacieux, se, a. (-sement, ad.) audacious(ly) || bold(ly).
au-delà, pr. on the other side, beyond.
audience, f. audience || auditory, assembly.
audiencier, m. usher, crier.
auditeur, m. auditor, hearer.
auditif, ve, a. auditory.
audition, f. hearing || audit.
auditoire, m. audience, auditory.
auge, f. trough, tray.
augée, f. troughful || hodful.
auget, m. trough || spout.
augmentation, f. augmentation, increase || rise.
augmenter, v. a. & n. to augment, to increase || to better, to enhance || to aggravate.
augure, m. augury.
augurer, v. a. to augur.
auguste, a. august, sacred.
augustin, m. Austin friar.
aujourd'hui, ad. to-day, nowadays.
aulique, a. aulic.
aumône, f. alms (pl.), charity.
aumônerie, f. almonry.
aumônier, m. almoner || chaplain.
aumônière, f. alms-bag.
aunage, m. ell-measure, alnage.
aunaie, f. alder-plot.
aune, m. (bot.) alder-tree.
aune, f. ell.
auner, v. a. to measure.
auparavant, ad. before, first.
auprès, pr. & ad. hard by, near, close to, next to, nigh || with.
auréole, f. glory, halo.
auriculaire, a. auricular || témoin ~, ear-witness.
aurifère, a. auriferous.

aurore, f. dawn, break of day.
ausculter, v. a. (méd.) to auscultate.
auspice, m. auspice, omen || sous les -s de, under the auspices of.
aussi, c. also, too, likewise, therefore, so, equally || ~ bien que, as well as.
aussitôt, ad. immediately, directly, presently || ~ que, as soon as.
austère, a. (-ment, ad.) austere(ly).
austérité, f. austerity.
austral, e, a. austral.
autan, m. south-wind, stormy wind.
autant, ad. as much, as many, so much, so many || tout ~, as much || ~ que, as much as, as far as || d'~ plus, d'~ mieux, the better, the rather, the more || d'~ moins, so much the less, the less so.
autel, m. altar || maître ~, great altar.
auteur, m. author, authoress || inventor.
authenticité, f. authenticity.
authentique, a. (-ment, ad.) authentic(ally).
autocrate, m. autocrat.
autocratie, f. autocracy.
autographe, m. autograph || autographer.
autographe, a. autographic.
automate, m. automaton || automatic machine.
automate, a. automatic.
automnal, e, a. autumnal.
automne, m. & f. autumn.
autonomie, f. autonomy.
autopsie, f. self-contemplation || autopsy, post-mortem examination.
autorisation, f. authorisation || authority.
autoriser, v. a. to authorise, to empower || to establish by authority || s'~, to get authority ou power || to justify oneself on the authority of || to think oneself warranted (by).
autorité, f. authority || power.
autour, m. goshawk.
autour, ad. & pr. about, round, around, round about || ici ~, hereabouts || tout ~ round about, all round.
autre, a. other, another || different || else || à d'~s ! ad. tell that to the marines !
autrefois, a. formerly || d'~, bygone.
autrement, ad. otherwise, else.
autruche, f. ostrich.
autrui, pn. others, other people.
auvent, m. penthouse, shed.
aux = à les || (cookery) with, done in.
auxiliaire, m. auxiliary.
auxiliaire, a. auxiliary.
s'avachir, to get flabby ou loose ou out of shape.
aval, ad. downwards, down the river.
avaler, v. a. to swallow || to drink up || to endure || to go down the river || s'~, to hang down.
avaleur, m. glutton || swallower.
avaloire, f. gullet || crupper (of horses).
avançage, m. cab-stand.
avance, f. projection || distance before one || improvement, gain, ground gained || advance || anticipation || d'~, par ~, beforehand, in advance.
avancé, e, p. & a. advanced, forward.
avancement, m. advancement, promotion || progress, improvement.

avancer, v. a. & n. to advance, to forward, to hasten || to raise, to promote || to propose || to pay in advance || to go on || to make progress || to jut, to project || s'~, to come ou go forward || to be preferred, to improve || to jut out.

avanie, f. affront, extortion.

avano, m. shrimp-net.

avant, m. (mar.) prow, bows (pl.).

avant, pr. & ad. before, forward, far || ~ de, ~ que de, before || ~-coureur, m. forerunner, harbinger || ~-dernier, ère, a. the last but one || ~-garde, f. (mil.) vanguard, van || ~-hier, ad. the day before yesterday || ~-midi, m. forenoon || ~-port, m. outer-port || ~-poste, m. outpost || ~-propos, m. preamble || preface || ~-quart, m. warning (of a clock) || ~-scène, f. proscenium || ~-train, m. fore-carriage || limbers || ~-veille, f. two days before.

avantage, m. advantage, gain, profit || odds (at play).

avantager, v. a. to advantage, to give over and above || to favour || to settle upon.

avantageux, se, a. (-sement ad.) advantageous(ly).

avare, m. niggard, miser.

avare, a. avaricious, covetous.

avarice, f. avarice, covetousness.

avaricieux, se, a. avaricious, covetous, stingy.

avarie, f. (mar.) average.

avarié, e, a. damaged at sea.

à vau-l'eau, ad. with the current || aller ~, to come to naught, to fall to the ground.

avec, pr. with, for, against.

aveline, f. filbert.

avelinier, m. (bot.) filbert-tree.

avenant, e, a. well-looking, handsome, suitable || à l'~ de, proportionately, in proportion to.

avènement, m. accession, coming.

avenir, m. future, posterity || à l'~, for the future. [fall out, to come to pass.

avenir, v. n. ir. to happen, to chance, to

Avent, m. Advent.

aventure, f. adventure || hazard, risk, chance || amorous intrigue || par ~, perchance || à l'~, at random.

aventurer, v. a. to venture, to hazard.

aventureux, se, a. adventurous.

aventurier, ère, m. & f. adventurer, intriguer || adventuress. [void.

avenu, e, a. done || non ~, null and

avenue, f. avenue, alley.

avérer, v. a. to affirm, to prove.

averse, f. sudden heavy shower.

aversion, f. aversion, antipathy || dislike, disinclination.

avertir, v. a. to warn, to advise, to inform.

avertissement, m. advertisement, warning || advice || notice.

aveu, m. confession, avowal, consent || homme sans ~, vagabond.

aveugle, a. blind.

aveuglement, m. blindness.

aveuglément, ad. blindly.

aveugler, v. a. to blind, to dazzle || s'~, to be blinded.

à l'aveuglette, ad. gropingly, in the dark.

avide, a. greedy || eager || -ment, ad. greedily || eagerly.

avidité, f. avidity, greediness. [grace.

avilir, v. a. to vilify, to abase, to disavilissement, m. degradation, debasement || disparagement, contempt.

aviné, a. drunken.

aviner, v. a. to season with wine.

aviron, m. (mar.) oar || ~ à couple, scull.

avis, m. advice, counsel || account, advertisement || motion || à mon ~, in my opinion || (il) m'est ~, I rather think.

avisé, e, a. prudent, circumspect.

aviser, v. a. & n. to advise, to warn, to caution || to think advisable, to resolve, to consider || s'~, to advise, to bethink [oneself.

aviso, m. advice-boat.

avitaillement, m. provisions (pl.).

avitailler, v. a. to victual.

aviver, v. a. to polish, to heighten.

avocasser, v. a. to pettifog.

avocasserie, f. pettifogging, pettifoggery.

avocassier, ière, a. of those wretched lawyers, pettifogging.

avocat, m. barrister, pleader, lawyer || ~ consultant, chamber-counsel.

avoine, f. oats.

avoir, m. property, credit || creditor.

avoir, v. a. ir. to have, to hold || to get || ~ raison, to be right || ~ chaud, froid, to be hot, cold || qu'avez-vous? what ails you? what's the matter? || ~, v. imp. il y a, there is, there are, it is.

avoisiner, v. a. to be near, to border [upon.

avorté, e, a. abortive.

avortement, m. abortion, miscarriage.

avorter, v. n. to miscarry || not to succeed, to fail.

avorton, m. abortive child || dwarf.

avoué, m. attorney, solicitor.

avouer, v. a. to avow, to confess || to own.

avril, m. April || poisson d'~, April-fool.

avunculaire, a. avuncular.

axe, m. axis || axle-tree.

axiome, m. axiom.

axonge, f. hog's lard.

ayant; ~-cause, m. representative, trustee || ~-droit, m. party, assign.

azalée, f. (bot.) azalia.

azur, m. azure.

azurer, v. a. (peint.) to azure, to blue.

azyme, a. unleavened, azymous.

B.

baba, m. bun || plum-cake.

Babel, f. (fig.) Babel, confusion.

babeurre, m. butter-milk.

babil, m. c atter, chitchat, prattle.

babillage, m. tittle-tattle.

babillard, e, m. & f. chatterer, prattler.

babiller, v. n. to prattle, to chatter.

babine, f. lip (of animals) || chops (pl.).

babiole, f. bauble, trifle || toy.

bâbord, m. (mar.) larboard.
babouche, f. Turkish slipper.
babouin, m. baboon || monkey.
bao, m. ferry-boat.   [bachelorship.
baccalauréat, m. bachelor's degree ||
bacchanal, m. great noise || (fam.) row,
rumpus.
bacchanale, a. bacchanal(ian).
bacchante, f. Bacchante || bachanalian.
bâche, f. cistern || car-tilt.
bachelier, m. bachelor of a university.
bâcher, v. a. to tilt (a cart).
bachique, a. bacchic, drunken || convivial.
bachot, m. wherry || cockle-shell || bachelor
bachoteur, m. ferryman.   [(of arts).
bâcler, v. a. to hurry over || to patch up ||
to settle.
badaud, e, m. & f. booby, cockney.
baderne, f. (mar.) platting, paunch,
paunch-mat || (fig.) good-for-nothing.
badigeon, m. plaster of Paris.
badigeonner, v. a. to whitewash.
badigeonneur, m. whitewasher.
badin, e, a. facetious, playful.
badinage, m. sport, joke, play || trifle.
badine, f. switch.
badiner, v. n. to jest, to joke, to play.
bafouer, v. a. to scoff at.
bâfre, f. spread, blow-out.   [oneself.
bâfrer, v. a. (fam.) to guzzle, to gorge
bâfreur, m. guzzler.
bagage, m. baggage, luggage || plier ~,
to pack off || to march off.
bagarre, f. scuffle, fray, squabble || crowd.
bagatelle, f. trifle, toy, nonsense || ~ I
pshaw! stuff |
bagne, m. bagnio || convict prison.
bagout, m. gabble.   [gain, sinecure.
bague, f. ring || ~ au doigt, (fig.) clear
baguenaude, f. bladder-nut.
baguenauder, v. n. to dally.
baguenaudier, m. (bot.) bladder-nut tree.
baguette, f. wand, switch || ramrod ||
drum-stick || ~s, pl. gauntlet || ~s à
gants, glove-stretchers.
baguier, m. ring-box.
bah ! pooh ! pshaw ! never mind !
bahut, m. trunk, chest.
bai, e, a. (of horses) bay.
baie, f. berry || bay, gulf.
baigner, v. a. & n. to bathe, to wash || to
soak || to welter.
baigneur, m., baigneuse, f. bather ||
bath-keeper || bathing-woman.
baignoire, f. bathing-tub || pit-box.
bail, m. lease.
bâillement, m. yawning.
bâiller, v. n. to yawn, to gape.
bailleur, m. lessor || ~ de fond, money-
lender || sleeping partner.
bâilleur, m. yawner.
bailli, m. bailiff.
bâillon, m. gag.
bâillonner, v. a. to gag.
bain, m. bath, bathing || ~ de siège, hip-
bath || ~marie, m. (chim.) sand-bath.
baïonnette, f. bayonet.
baisemain, m. kissing of hands || compli-
baisement, m. kissing.   [ments (pl.).

baiser, m. kiss, buss.
baiser, v. a. to kiss.
baisotter, v. a. to be always kissing.
baisse, f. fall, decline.
baisser, v. a. & n. to let down, to lower
(the voice, sails) || to lessen || to fall (in
value) || to hang (one's head) || se ~, to
stoop, to bend down.   ["bear."
Baissier, m. speculator for the fall.
baissière, f. tiltings of wine || sediment.
baisure, f. kissing-crust.
bajoue, f. hog's cheek.
bal, m. ball || ~ masqué, masked ball ||
~costumé or travesti, fancy ball || ~
paré, dress ball.
baladin, e, m. & f. juggler, buffoon.
balafre, f. gash, scar, slash.
balafrer, v. a. to gash, to slash.
balai, m. broom, besom || ~ de crin, hair-
broom || ~ de plume, duster || ~ de jonc,
carpet-broom || faire ~ neuf, to do one's
work well at first || rôtir le ~, to drudge
in obscurity || to lead a wild life.
balais, m. balass, balass-ruby.
Balance, f. (astr.) Libra.
balance, f. scale, pair of scales || balance
(of an account) || equality.
balancement, m. balancing || swing, wa-
ving, rocking.
balancer, v. a. & n. to balance, to weigh ||
to hesitate, to fluctuate, to waver.
balancier, m. pendulum, beam of the
scales || pole || flier || gimbal || coining-
engine || balance-maker.
balançoire, f. see-saw || swing.
balayage, m. sweeping.
balayer, v. a. to sweep.
balayeur, se, m. & f. sweeper.
balayures, f. pl. sweepings (pl.).
balbutiement, m. stuttering, stammering.
balbutier, v. n. to stammer, to stutter ||
balcon, m. balcony.   [to lisp.
baldaquin, m. baldachin || canopy.
baleine, f. whale || whalebone.
baleiné, e, a. with whalebone, whale-
baleineau, m. young whale.   [bone . . .
baleinier, m. whaler, whaling-vessel.
baleinière, f. whaler's boat.
balisage, m. (mar.) buoying.
balise, f. (mar.) buoy, beacon.
baliser, v. a. (mar.) to buoy.
balivage, m. staddling.
baliveau, m. staddle.
baliverner, v. n. to trifle.
ballade, f. ballad.
ballant, e, a. swinging.
balle, f. ball || bullet || bale of goods || husk ||
bob || renvoyer la ~, to give tit for tat ||
prendre la ~ au bond, to improve one's
opportunity, to take time by the forelock ||
charger à ~, to load with ball.
ballerine, f. ballet-dancer.
ballet, m. ballet.   [captive balloon.
ballon, m. balloon || foot-ball || ~captif,
ballonnement, m. swelling.
ballonner, v. a. & n. to swell.
ballot, m. bale (of goods).
ballotin, m. small bale (of goods).
ballottage, m. balloting.

ballottement, m. shuffling.
ballotter, v. a. & n. to toss || to ballot || to debate || to shake.
balnéaire, m. sea bathing-place.
balourd, e, m. & f. dunce, blockhead.
balourdise, f. stupidity || stupid thing.
balsamier, m. (bot.) balsam-tree.
balsamine, f. balsamine.
balsamique, a. balsamic || balmy.
balustre, m. baluster || railing.
balzan, e, m. white-footed horse.
balzane, f. white spot, blaze.
bambin, m. babe, brat.   [cature.
bambochade, f. grotesque picture || carl-
bamboche, f. large puppet || shrimp || prank, spree || stuff.
bambocheur, m. pot-companion, tippler.
bambou, m. bamboo.   [(marriage).
ban, m. ban || exile || ~s, pl. banns (of
banal, e, a. commonplace || vulgar || trite || -ement, ad. trivially.
banalité, f. vulgarity || banality.
banane, f. banana.
bananier, m. banana-tree.
banc, m. bench, form || pew, seat || (mar.) reef, shoal, bank || ~ de sable, sand-bank || -s, pl. school-forms, college.
bancal, e, bancroche, a. bandy-legged.
bandage, m. bandage, truss.
bandagiste, m. truss-maker.
bande, f. band || fillet || strip || wrapper || shoal || gang || cushion.
bandeau, m. head-band || diadem || bandage || fillet || frontlet || en -x, plain.
bandelette, f. little band.
bander, v. a. & n. to bind, to bend, to stretch || to be tight.
banderole, f. streamer || shoulder-belt.
bandière, f. ensign, colours || front line.
bandit, m. bandit, robber.
bandoulière, f. shoulder-belt || en ~, slung over the shoulder.
banlieue, f. precincts of a city.
banne, f. tilt, awning || hamper.
banner, v. a. to cover with a tilt.
bannière, f. banner, flag.
bannir, v. a. to banish.
bannissement, m. banishment, exile.
banque, f. bank || banking.
banqueroute, f. bankruptcy || faire ~, to go ou become bankrupt.
banqueroutier, ère, m. & f. bankrupt.
banquet, m. banquet, feast.
banquette, f. stuffed bench || window-seat || outside (of a coach).
banquier, m. banker.
banquise, f. ice-berg.
baptême, m. baptism || christening.
baptiser, v. a. to baptise, to christen.
baptismal, e, a. baptismal.
baptistaire, a. of baptism || extrait ~, certificate of baptism.
baptistère, m. (arch.) baptistery.
baquet, m. bucket, tub || trough.
baragouin, baragouinage, m. gib-berish, jargon.   [berish.
baragouiner, v. n. to jabber || to talk gib-
baragouineur, m. jabberer.
baraque, f. barrack, booth.

baratte, f. churn.
baratter, v. a. to churn.
baratterie, f. (mar.) barratry.
barbacane, f. barbican.
barbare, m. barbarian.
barbare, a. barbarous, inhuman || uncivil.
barbarie, f. barbarity, barbarous act.
barbarisme, m. barbarism.
barbe, f. beard, whiskers || van || feather || Barbary horse || ~ d'une plume, down of a quill || à sa ~, to one's face || faire la ~, to shave || faire la ~ à, to beard || to
barbelé, e, a. bearded.   [cut out.
barbet, m. water-spaniel.
barbiche, f. beard, Imperial || (bot.) devil
barbichon, m. lap-dog.   [in a bush.
barbier, m. barber.
barbifier, v. a. to shave.   [barbles.
barbillon, m. little barbel || wattle || -s, pl.
barbon, m. graybeard || dotard.
barbote, f. eel-pout.
barboter, v. a. to muddle, to dabble.
barboteur, m. tame duck.
barbouillage, m. daub || scrawl || non-sensical speech.   [to scribble || to bungle.
barbouiller, v. a. to daub, to besmear ||
barbouilleur, m. dauber, scribbler || bab-
barbu, e, a. bearded.   [bler.
barbue, f. (fish) brill || quickset vine.
barcelonnette, f. cot, bassinet.
bard, m. hand-barrow.
bardane, f. bardock, burr.
barde, m. -bard.
barder, v. a. to cover with a slice of bacon || to load a hod || (fig.) to bedizen.
bardeur, m. hodman.   [to remove.
bardot, m. small mule || drudge || butt.
barège, m. barege.
barème, m. ready-reckoner.
barguignage, m. haggling.
barguigner, v. n. to haggle.
barguigneur, m. haggler.   [rooms.
barigoule, à la ~, (Culin.) with mush-
baril, m. barrel, small cask.
barillet, m. small barrel, rundlet, keg.
bariolage, m. medley of colours.
barioler, v. a. to speckle.
baromètre, m. barometer.
baron, m. baron.
baronnage, m. baronage.
baronne, f. baroness.
baronnet, m. baronet.
baronnie, f. barony.
baroque, a. odd, irregular.
barque, f. bark, large boat.
barquée, f. boat-load.
barquerolle, f. ferry-boat.
barrage, m. stoppage || dam || turnpike-money, toll.
barre, f. bar || cross-bar || helm || stroke || -s, pl. prison-bars.   [wire.
barreau, m. wooden or iron bar || splat ||
barrer, v. a. to bar, to stop || to strike out
barrette, f. cap.
barricade, f. barricade.
barricader, v. a. to barricade.
barrière, f. barrier || rail, enclosure || ob-stacle || turnpike || boundary || guardhouse for bailiffs || starting-post.

barriquaut, m. little cask, keg.

barrique, f. cask || hogshead.

bartavelle, f. red partridge.

baryton, m. (mus.) baritone.

bas, m. stocking, hose || lower part, bottom, foot || ~ blen, blue-stocking.

bas, se, a. low, shallow || mean, cheap, short || small || vile || ~, ad. low || softly || in a whisper || être au ~, to be getting low (of a cask, a bottle) || à ~ le roi! down with the king!

basalte, m. basalt.

basane, f. sheepskin.

basané, e, a. tawny, sun-burnt.

bascule, f. see-saw || weigh-bridge || path-way.

base, f. base, basis. [way.

baser, v. a. to base, to ground (on). [flat.

bas-fond, m. shoal, shallow || valley ||

basilic, m. basilisk || (bot.) sweet basil.

basilique, f. (arch.) basilica.

basin, m. dimity.

basoche, f. jurisdiction of clerks of Paris parliamentary solicitors.

basque, m. skirt (of a coat).

bas-relief, m. bas-relief.

basse, f. (mus.) bass || shoal, sandbank || ~-contre, f. (mus.) counter-bass || ~-cour, f. poultry-yard || stable-yard || ~-fosse, f. dungeon || ~-taille, f. (mus.) counter-tenor.

bassement, ad. meanly, vulgarly.

bassesse, f. base action || vulgarity.

bassin, m. basin || scale || plate || dock ||

bassine, f. pan. [haven.

bassiner, v. a. to warm (a bed, etc.) || to foment || to bathe.

bassinoire, f. warming-pan.

basson, m. (mus.) bassoon.

bast(e)! pooh! nonsense! [netting.

bastingage, m., bastingue, f. (mar.)

bastinguer, v. a. (mar.) to barricade.

bastionné, e, a. fortified with bastions.

bastonnade, f. cudgelling. [bastioned.

bastringue, m. low-class public ball.

bât, m. pack-saddle.

bataclan, m. rattle, confusion || crowd.

bataille, f. battle, fight || battle-array || beggar-my-neighbour (card-game).

batailler, v. n. to battle, to fight.

batailleur, se, a. pugnacious, disputatious. [major.

bataillon, m. battalion || chef de ~, bâtard, m. bastard || mongrel.

bâtard, e, a. a bastard, spurious || porte ~e, private door.

batardeau, m. coffer-dam.

bâtardise, f. bastardy.

bateau, m. boat.

batelée, f. boat-load.

batelet, m. small boat.

bateleur, se, m. & f. juggler, mounte-batelier, ère, m. & f. waterman, boat-man || boatwoman.

bâter, v. a. to load with a pack-saddle.

bâti, e, a. & part. built || made, shaped || comme vous voilà ~! a pretty figure you are!

batifoler, v. n. to toy. [ship.

bâtiment, m. building, edifice || vessel,

bâtir, v. a. to build, to baste || to tack.

bâtisse, f. building.

bâtisseur, m. sorry builder || person with a mania for building.

batiste, f. cambric.

bâton, m. stick, cudgel || staff || à ~s rompus, by fits and starts.

bâtonner, v. a. to cudgel || to cancel || papier bâtonné, water-lined paper.

bâtonnet, m. small stick || cat, tip-cat.

bâtonnier, m. staff-bearer || president.

bâtonniste, m. cudgel-player.

battage, m. (agr.) thrashing.

battant, m. clapper || fold of a door || à deux ~s, folding . . . [folding.

battant, e, a. pelting, driving || swing.

batte, f. beater || wooden sword || ~ à beurré, churn-staff.

battement, m. beating || clapping (of hands) || stamping || throbbing.

batterie, f. fighting, scuffle || (mil., phys.) battery || (mar.) broadside || ~ de cuisine, kitchen utensils.

batteur, m. beater || thrasher || ~ d'estrade, spy || ~ de pavé, lounger, loafer || (Am.) bummer.

battoir, m. battledoor || beetle.

battre, v. a. & n. ir. to beat, to strike || to mint || to defeat || to convince || to loose || ~ aux champs, to beat a salute || ~ froid à, to give the cold shoulder to || ~ en brèche or en ruine, to batter down || se ~, to fight. [worn.

battu, e, a.; avoir les yeux ~s, to look

battue, f. battue (of game).

bau, m. (mar.) beam.

baudet, m. donkey.

baudrier, m. shoulder-belt.

baudruche, f. goldbeater's skin.

bauge, f. lair || filth || mud || pugging mor-

baume, m. balsam, balm. [tar.

baumier, m. (bot.) balsam-tree.

bavard, e, m. & f. babbler, gossip.

bavardage, m. prattling.

bavarder, v. n. to blab, to babble, to

bavarderie, f. prattle. [gossip.

bave, f. dribbel, slaver || slime, foam.

baver, v. n. to dribbel, to slobber, to

bavette, f. bib. [slaver || to foam.

baveux, se, m. & f. slobberer.

baveux, se, a. slobbering.

bavoir, m. bib.

bavolet, m. head-gear || curtain.

bayer, v. n. to gape || ~ aux corneilles, to stand gaping, to star-gaze.

béant, e, a. gaping, wide open.

béat, e, m. & f. devout, pious person || sanctimonious person.

béat, e, a. saintly, sanctimonious.

béatifier, v. a. beatify.

béatilles, f. pl. dainties. [beau.

beau, m. beauty, fairness || perfection || fop,

beau, (bel), belle, a. fine, fair, beautiful || charming, graceful || excellent, glorious || happy || ~ temps, fine weather || ~ monde, people of fashion || ~ sexe, the fair sex || ~-fils, m. son-in-law || stepson || ~-frère, m. brother-in-law || stepbrother || ~-père, m. father-in-law || stepfather.

2*

beaucoup, ad. much, many || de ~, by
beaupré, m. (mar.) bowsprit.   [far.
beauté, f. beauty || beautiful woman.
bébé, m. baby.
bec, m. beak, bill || snout || nib (of a pen) ||
   spout || burner (of a lamp) || ~-de-corbin,
   m. bill-head || ripping-iron || ~-de-grue,
   m. crane's bill || ~-de-lièvre, m. hare-
bécarre, m. (mus.) natural.   [lip.
bécasse, f. woodcock || idiot.
bécasseau, m. young woodcock.
bécassine, f. snipe.
becfigue, m. fig-pecker (bird).
béchamel, f. cream-sauce.
bêche, f. spade.
bêcher, v. a. to dig.
becquée, f. billful.
becqueter, v. a. to peck || to pick || to kiss.
bedaine, f. paunch.
bedeau, m. beadle.
bedon, m. (fig.) obese person, fatsides.
beffroi, m. belfry || alarm-bell.
bégaiement, m. stammering.
bégayer, v. a. to stammer.
bègue, m. & f. stammerer.
bégueule, f. prude || prudish woman.
bégueule, a. squeamish, strait-laced ||
   finical, nimini-pimini.
bégueulerie, f. squeamishness, prudery.
béguin, m. child's cap.
béguinage, m. convent for beguins.
béguine, f. nun || bigot.
beige, a. (of wool) natural.
beignet, m. fritter.
béjaune, m. ninny.
bel, le vide beau.
bélandre, m. (mar.) bilander.
bêlement, m. bleating of sheep.
bêler, v. n. to bleat.
bel-esprit, m. witty writer.
belette, f. weasel.
bélier, m. ram.
Bélier, m. (astr.) Aries.
belle, f. beauty, belle || rubber, winning
   game (at cards) || ~-de-jour, f. (bot.)
   day-lily || convolvulus || ~-de-nuit, f.
   (bot.) marvel of Peru || ~-fille, f. daughter-
   in-law || stepdaughter || ~-mère, f. mother-
   in-law || stepmother || ~-sœur, f. sister-
bellement, ad. softly.   [in-law || stepsister.
belligérant, e, a. belligerent.
belliqueux, se, a. warlike, bellicose.
bellot, te, a. pretty.
belvédère, m. belvedere, turret, terrace.
bémol, m. (mus.) flat.
bénédicité, m. grace (before a meal).
bénédiction, f. benediction, blessing.
bénéfice, m. benefice || profit || living ||
   représentation à ~, benefit-night.
bénéficiaire, a. beneficiary.   [cumbent.
bénéficier, m. beneficed clergyman || in-
benêt, m. booby, ninny, simpleton.
bénévole, a. (-ment, ad.) kind(ly).
béni, e, a. blessed.   benign(ly).
bénigne, a. (-ment, ad.) kind(ly) ||
bénin, a. benign, kind and easy.
bénir, v. a. to bless, to consecrate.
bénit, e, a. consecrated || holy.
bénitier, m. holy-water vessel.

benjoin, m. benzoin.
benzine, f. (chim.) benzine, benzole.
béquillard, m. old cripple.
béquille, f. crutch.
béquiller, v. n. to walk on crutches.
bercail, m. sheep-fold.
berceau, m. cradle || bower || vault.
bercer, v. a. to rock, to lull asleep.
berceuse, f. rocker.
béret, m. Tam o' Shanter (cap).
bergamote, f. bergamot-pear.
berge, f. bank || bluff.
berger, m. shepherd, swain.
bergère, f. shepherdess || lass || easy chair.
bergerie, f. sheep-fold.
bergeronnette, f. wagtail.
berline, f. berlin (coach).   [ness.
berlue, f. dimness of sight || (fig.) blind-
berne, f., bernement, m. tossing in a
   blanket || (fam.) raillery.   [to chaff.
berner, v. a. to toss in a blanket || (fam.)
bernique, ad. (fam.) not at all!
berthe, f. cape || fur-collarette.
besace, f. wallet || beggary.
besaigre, a. sourish.
besicles, m. pl. spectacles.
besogne, f. work, task.
besoigneux, se, a. needy.
besoin, m. need, want || necessity || misery ||
   avoir ~ (de), to want || au ~, if neces-
   sary || on the occasion || as the case may
bestiaire, m. beast-fighter.   [be.
bestial, e, a. beastly, brutish || -ement,
   ad. bestially.
bestiasse, f. (fam.) simpleton.
bestiaux, m. pl. cattle.
bestiole, f. small beast || (fig.) young fool.
bêta(s), m. blockhead, fool.
bétail, m. cattle.
bête, f. beast, animal || fool || ~ à cornes,
   horned cattle || ~ à laine, lanigerous
   animal, sheep || ~ noire, aversion || ~ à
   bon Dieu, ~ de la Vierge, lady-bird.
bête, a. stupid, foolish || c'est ~! it is a
   nuisance! || pas si ~! (fam.) not such a
   fool! || -ment, ad. foolishly.
bêtise, f. folly, stupidity, nonsense || trifle.
bette, f. (bot.) beet.
betterave, f. beet-root || mangel-wurzel.
beuglement, m. bellowing.
beugler, v. n. to bellow, to roar.
beurre, m. butter || au ~ noir, with
   browned butter sauce || faire son ~, to
   make nice pickings.
beurrée, f. slice of bread and butter.
beurrer, v. a. to butter.
beurrier, m. butter-dish || butter-cooler.
bévue, f. blunder, mistake.
bézy or bésigue, m. bezique (a card-game).
biais, m. slope, slant || bias, method, man-
   ner || de ~, en ~, sloping(ly).
biaiser, v. n. to slope || to shuffle.
biaiseur, m. shuffler.
bibelot, m. knicknack, gewgaw.
biberon, ne, m. & f. wine-bibber || suck-
   ing-bottle.
bibliographe, m. bibliographer.
bibliographie, f. bibliography.
bibliographique, a. bibliographic.

bibliomane, m. bibliomaniac.
bibliomanie, f. bibliomania.
bibliophile, m. bibliophile, book-lover.
bibliothécaire, m. librarian.
bibliothèque, f. library || book-shelves (pl.) || book-case.
biblique, a. biblical.
biceps, m. (anat.) biceps.
biche, f. hind || (person)dear, love, darling.
bichette, f. little dear.
bichon, ne, m. & f. lapdog || dear.
bichonner, v. a. to curl || to trim up.
bicoque, f. mean hamlet || hut, hovel || shabby household.
bicycle, m. bicycle.
bicycliste, m. bicyclist.
bidet, m. nag, bidet.
bidon, m. can || bidon.
bief, m. mill-course, mill-race.
bielle, f. (mach.) connecting-rod.
bien, m. good || fortune, wealth, estate || favour, kindness || probity || ~ public, public weal || homme de ~, honest man.
bien, ad. well || ~-aimé, e, a. well-beloved || ~-dire, m. fine speaking || ~-être, m. well-being, welfare || ~-faire, s. well-doing || ~-fonds, m. landed property || ~-vivre, m. comfort.
bienfaisance, f. beneficence || kindness.
bienfaisant, e, a. beneficent || kind.
bienfait, m. benefit, favour || good office.
bienfaiteur, trice, m. & f. benefactor || benefactress.   [blissful.
bienheureux, se, a. blessed, happy,
biennal, e, a. biennial.
bienséance, f. decency, decorum.
bienséant, e, a. decent, becoming.
bientôt, ad. soon, ere long, immediately.
bienveillance, f. kindness, goodwill.
bienveillant, e, a. kind.
bienvenu, e, a. welcome.
bienvenue, f. welcome || footing.
bière, f. bier, coffin.
biez, m. mill-course, mill-race.
biffer, v. a. to cancel, to erase.
bifteck, m. beefsteak || ~ chateau-briand, rumpsteak.
se bifurquer, v. to be forked, bifurcated.
bigame, m. & f. bigamist.
bigame, a. guilty of bigamy.
bigamie, f. bigamy.   [streaked.
bigarré, e, a. motley, mottled, freckled ||
bigarreau, m. white-heart cherry.
bigarrer, v. a. to variegate, to dapple.
bigarrure, f. variegation, medley.
bigle, m. beagle   [periwinkle (shell).
bigorneau, m. bickern, horned anvil ||
bigot, e, m. & f. bigot || hypocrite.
bigot, e, a. bigoted.
bigoterie, f., bigotisme, m. bigotry.
bigre! hang it! bother!
bijou, m. jewel, trinket.
bijouterie, f. jewelry.
bijoutier, ère, m. & f. jeweller.
bilan, m. balance-sheet || balance || schedule.
bilboquet, m. cup and ball.
bile, m. bile, gall || anger.
bilieux, se, a. bilious || choleric.
billard, m. billiards, billiard-table.

bille, f. billiard-ball || marble || log.
billebaude, f. confusion.
billet, m. note, billet || hand-bill, bill || ~ d'aller et retour, return-ticket || ~ de banque, bank-note || ~ doux, love-letter || ~ de complaisance, (com.) accommodation bill || ~ de faire part, circular letter to announce a marriage, &c. || ~ de faveur, free pass || ticket at reduced price || ~ de santé, bill of health.
billevesée, f. silly trash || crotchet.
billion, m. thousand millions.
billon, m. copper-money || base coin.
billot, m. block, log || dog-yoke, clog.
bimane, m. two-handed.
bimbeloterie, f. toy-trade.
bimbelotier, m. toy-man.
binard, f. truck, four-wheeled waggon.
binet, m. save-all.
binette, f. hoe || face || (fam.) phiz.
binocle, m. double eyeglass || binocle.
biographe, m. biographer.
biographie, f. biography.
biographique, a. biographical.
bipède, m. biped.
bipède, a. biped.
bique, f. she-goat.
biquet, m. kid || balance.
bis, e, a. brown.
bis, ad. twice || encore, again (at theatres).
bisaïeul, e, m. & f. great-grandfather || great-grandmother.
bisannuel, le, a. biennial.
bisbille, f. bickering.
biscaïen, m. small cannon-ball.
biscornu, e, a. odd, irregular, queer.
biscotte, f. rusk.
biscuit, m. (sea-)biscuit || sponge-cake.
bise, f. north-east wind, cold wind.
biseau, m. bevel || foot-stick || kissing-crust.
biset, m. stockdove || National Guard on duty in plain clothes.
bisque, f. bisk || broth, soup || odds, bisque.
bisquer, v. n. to be vexed, to fret.
bissac, m. wallet.
bisser, v. a. & n. to encore || to cry encore.
bissextil, e, a. bissextile || année –e, leap-year.
bistouri, m. bistoury (surgery).
bistourner, v. a. to twist.
bistreux, se, a. of bistre.
bitume, m. bitumen.
bitum(in)er, v. a. to bituminate.
bitumineux, se, a. bituminous.
bivac, bivouac, m. (mil.) bivouac.
bivaquer, bivouaquer, v. n. (mil.) to bivouac, to watch.
bizarre, a. (-ment, ad.) odd(ly) || strange-
bizarrerie, f. oddness, whim.   [(ly).
blafard, e, a. pale, dull, wan.
blague, f. tobacco-pouch || fudge, humbug || random chit-chat || (fam.) gift of the gab || blarney.
blaguer, v. n. to humbug, to hoax.
blagueur, m. humbug, hoaxer.
blaireau, m. badger.
blâmer, v. a. to blame.
blanc, m. white colour || white mark, target || blank cartridge || white man || linen || melted

butter||breast|| ~ de baleine, spermaceti ||
~ d'Espagne, whiting.

blanc, che, a. white, clean || clear, blank ||
dead || sleepless || vin ~, white wine || ~-
bec, m. novice, greenhorn || ~-manger,
blanchaille, f. fry.   [m. blanc-mange.
blanchâtre, a. whitish.
blanche, f. (mus.) minim.
blancheur, f. whiteness.
blanchiment, m. whitening, bleaching.
blanchir, v. a. & n. to whiten, to bleach,
   to wash, to clear || to grow white ou gray.
blanchissage, m. washing, bleaching ||
   ~ de fin, clear-starching.   [works.
blanchisserie, f. bleaching-field || bleach-
blanchisseur, m. bleacher, washer.
blanchisseuse, f. laundress.
blanquette, f. stew with melted butter ||
   blanket.
blaser, v. a. to weaken, to blunt, to pall ||
   être blasé, to be sick of everything ||
   se ~, to become palled, surfeited ou used
blason, m. heraldry || coat of arms. [up.
blasonner, v. a. to blazon.
blasphémateur,trice,m.&f. blasphemer.
blasphémateur, trice, a. blasphemous.
blasphématoire, a. blasphemous.
blasphème, m. blasphemy.
blasphémer, v. a. to blaspheme.
blatte, f. moth, black-beetle.
blé, m. wheat, corn || corn-field || ~ noir,
   buck-wheat || ~ de Turquie, Indian corn.
blême, a. pale, pallid, wan.
blêmir, v. n. to grow pale, to pale.
blennorrhagie, f. (méd.) blennorrhœa.
blessant, e, a. offensive.
blesser, v. a. to wound, to hurt || to offend,
   to shock, to injure || se ~, to hurt oneself ||
   to take offence.
blessure, f. wound || injury.
blet, te, a. mellow.
bleu, m. blue || blue colour.
bleu, e, a. blue.
bleuâtre, a. bluish.
bleuet, m. vide bluet.   [blue.
bleuir, v. a. to make blue || ~, v. n. to turn
blindage, m. blinding || plating || sheeting.
blinde, f. blind.
blindé, e, a. iron-plated.
blinder, v. a. to cover with blinds || to plate.
bloc, m. block, lump || en ~, in a lump.
blocage, m., blocaille, f. rubbish, pebble-
blockhaus, m. (mil.) block-house. [stone.
blocus, m. blockade.
blond, e, a. light, fair.
blonde, f. fair woman, blonde || blond-lace.
blondin, m. fair young man || fop.
blondine, f. fair young woman.
bloquer, v. a. to block up, to blockade.
se blottir, to squat, to cower down.
blouse, f. smock-frock || pocket || pinafore.
blouser, v. a. to pocket || to deceive || se ~,
   to pocket one's own ball (at billiards) || to
   make a mess of it.
bluet, m. corn-flower.
bluette, f. spark || flash (of wit).
blutage, m. bolting.
bluter, v. a. to bolt, to sift.
bluterie, f. bolting-room.

blutoir, m. bolter.
bobèche, f. socket of a candle-stick.
bobine, f. bobbin, quill for silk.
bobo, m. (child's language) slight hurt.
bocage, m. grove, copse.
bocal, m. bottle || jar || glass bowl || globe.
bocard, m. stamp || crushing-mill.
bocarder, v. a. to stamp, to crush.
bœuf, m. ox || du ~, beef.
bohémien, ne, m. & f. gipsy || Bohemian.
boire, m. drink, drinking.
boire, v. a. & n. ir. to drink || to soak, to
   blot || to be puckered || se ~, to be drunk.
bois, m. wood || forest || horns of a deer ||
   ~ de charpente, timber || ~ de lit, bed-
   stead || ~ de rose, tulip-wood || de or en
   ~, wooden.
boisage, m. timber, wainscot.
boisé, e, a. wainscoted || woody.
boiser, v. a. to wainscot.
boiserie, f. wainscot, wainscoting || floor-
boisseau, m. bushel.   [boards.
boisselier, m. white-cooper.
boisson, f. drink, drinking.
boite, f. box || watch-case || caddy || ~ aux
   lettres, letter-box || (Am.) post-box.
boite, f. maturity, ripeness || en ~, fit to
   drink.
boiter, v. n. to limp, to halt, to go lame.
boiteux, se, a. lame, limping.
boitier, m. surgeon's case.
bol, m. bolus || bowl, basin.
bolide, m. (astr.) bolis.
bombance, f. feasting.
bombarde, f. bomb-ketch.
bombardement, f. bombardment.
bombarder, v. a. to bombard.
bombe, f. bomb, shell.
bombé, e, a. arched || convex || barrelled.
bombement, m. convexity || bulging.
bomber, v. a. & n. to make convex || to
   barrel || to be convex.
bon, m. good quality || bond, order || faire
   un ~, to give a voucher.
bon, ne, a. good, useful || able, fit, proper ||
   en ~ état, sound || à quoi ~ ? to what
   purpose? || à la ~e heure ! be it so! ||
   ~! well! pshaw! || ~-mot, m. witticism.
bonasse, a. simple, silly.
bonbon, m. sweetmeat.
bonbonne, f. carboy || demijohn.
bonbonnière, f. sugar-plum box || neat
   little house.   [to fail || to disappoint.
bond, m. rebound, gambol || faire faux ~,
bonde, f. floodgate || bung || bung-hole.
bondir, v. n. to rebound || to skip.
bondissement, m. bound || skipping (of
   animals).   [cheese.
bondon, m. bung || bung-hole || round
bondonner, v. a. to bung.
bonheur, m. happiness, good luck || bless-
   ing || par ~, luckily.
bonhomie, f. good-nature || simplicity.
bonhomme, m. good-natured man.
boni, m. bonus || I.O.U.
bonification, f. improvement.
bonifier, v. a. to improve.
boniment, m. (fam.) cheating || mounte-
   bank's trick.

bonjour, m. good day, good morning.
bonne, f. nursery-maid, nurse.
bonnement, ad. simply ‖ plainly ‖ foolishly.
bonnet, m. cap ‖ ~ à poil, bear-skin cap ‖ ~ de coton, man's nightcap ‖ ~ de police, forage-cap.
bonneterie, f. hosiery.
bonneteur, m. sharper, ring-dropper.
bonnetier, m. hosier.
bonnette, f. bonnet ‖ (mar.) studding-sail.
bonsoir, m. good evening, good-night ‖ ~! not a bit of it ‖ ‖ that's enough! ‖ ‖ gone! go to!
bonté, f. goodness ‖ kindness.   [bowels.
borborygme, m. (méd.) rumbling in the
bord, m. border, edge, brim ‖ skirt ‖ shore, sea-shore, bank ‖ shipboard ‖ tack, limit ‖ lace ‖ rim (of a hat) ‖ ~ à ~, (mar.) along-
bordage, m. (mar.) side-planking.   [side.
bordeaux, m. (wine) claret.
bordé, m. hem, edging.
bordée, f. broadside ‖ volley ‖ tack.
border, v. a. to border, to edge, to trim ‖ to plank ‖ (mar.) to lay a deck.
bordereau, m. memorandum.
bordure, f. border, edge, edging, frame.
boréal, e, a. northern.
borée, m. north-wind.
borgne, a. blind of one eye ‖ dingy.
borgnesse, f. one-eyed woman.
bornage, m. setting bounds.
borne, f. bound, boundary, limit ‖ post ‖ mile-stone ‖ ~-boîte, f. pillar-box ‖ ~-fontaine, f. water-plug, hydrant.
borné, e, a. limited, shallow, small, narrow, mean.   [fine.
borner, v. a. to bound, to limit ‖ to con-
bornoyer, v. a. to look with one eye closed, to squint along ‖ to set marks in.
bosquet, m. grove, thicket.   [bruise.
bosse, f. hump, bump, protuberance ‖
bosser, v. a. (mar.) to stopper.
bosselage, m. embossing.   [relievo.
bosseler, v. a. to emboss, to work in
bosselure, f. embossment.
bossetier, m. glass-blower.
bossette, f. boss, bridle-stud.
bossoir, m. (mar.) cat-head.
bossu, e, m. & f. hunchback, humpback.
bossué, e, a. hunch-backed, humpbacked.
bossuer, v. a. to bruise, to indent.
bot, a. club-footed ‖ pied ~, m. club-foot.
botanique, f. botany.
botanique, a. botanic(al).
botaniste, m. botanist.
botte, f. boot ‖ bunch, thrust ‖ bundle ‖ truss ‖ ~s fines, dress boots ‖ ~s à revers, top-boots.
botté, e, a. booted ‖ in boots.
bottelage, m. putting up in bundles.
botteler, v. a. to put up in bundles.
botter, v. a. to help one on with one's boots ‖ to fit ‖ se ~, to put one's boots on.
bottier, m. boot-maker.
bottine, f. half-boot ‖ ~ à élastique, boot with elastic sides.   [scapegoat.
bouc, m. goat ‖ goat-skin ‖ ~ émissaire,
boucan, m. smoking-place ‖ gridiron ‖ row ‖ dust.   [hunt wild oxen.
boucaner, v. a. & n. to smoke dry ‖ to

boucanier, m. buccaneer.
boucaut, m. bogshead.
bouche, f. mouth ‖ living ‖ food ‖ table ‖ kitchen ‖ ~ à feu, piece of ordnance ‖ ~ de chaleur, hot air-hole ‖ bonne ~, tit-bit ‖ de ~, by word of mouth ‖ ~-trou.
bouché, e, a. dull, stupid.   [m. stop-gap.
bouchée, f. mouthful.
boucher, ère, m. & f. butcher ‖ butcher's wife ‖ ~ en gros, carcass-butcher.
boucher, v. a. to stop, to cork, to bung.
boucherie, f. butchery, shambles ‖ slaughter.   [tavern-bush ‖ tavern.
bouchon, m. stopple, cork ‖ wisp of straw ‖
bouchonner, v. a. to rumple, to rub down.
boucle, f. buckle ‖ curl.
boucler, v. a. to buckle ‖ to curl (hair).
bouclier, m. buckler, shield.
bouder, v. n. to pout, to sulk.
bouderie, f. pouting, sulking.
boudeur, se, m. & f. pouter, sulker.
boudeur, se, a. sullen, sulky.
boudin, m. black-pudding ‖ ~ blanc, poultry sausage.
boudoir, m. lady's room, boudoir.
boue, f. mud, dirt, mire.
bouée, f. (mar.) buoy ‖ ~ de sauvetage, **boueur**, m. dustman.   [life-buoy.
boueux, se, a. miry, muddy, dirty.
bouffant, e, à. puffing.
bouffarde, f. tobacco-pipe.   [(in Paris)
bouffe, m. buffoon ‖ ~s, pl. Italian opera
bouffée, f. puff ‖ whiff ‖ fit.
bouffer, v. n. to puff, to swell ‖ to feed.
bouffette, f. ear-knot ‖ sail.
bouffir, v. a & n. to swell, to puff up.
bouffissure, f. swelling, tumour, bombast.
bouffon, m. buffoon.
bouffon, ne, a. droll, comical.
bouffonner, v. n. to play the buffoon.
bouffonnerie, f. buffoonery.
bouge, m. closet ‖ hole ‖ den.
bougeoir, m. chamber-candlestick.
bouger, v. n. to budge, to stir.
bougie, f. wax-candle ‖ taper.
bougon, ne, m. & f. grumbler.
bougonner, v. n. to grumble.
bougran, m. buckram.
bouillant, e, a. boiling ‖ hot ‖ fiery ‖ hasty.
bouille, f. fishing-pole.   [water.
bouiller, v. a. to stir up mud, to trouble
bouilleur, m. boiler-tube.
bouilli, m. boiled beef.
bouillie, f. pap ‖ hasty-pudding ‖ pulp.
bouillir, v. n. ir. to boil ‖ ~ à gros bouillons, to boil fast ‖ ~ à petits bouillons, to simmer.
bouilloire, f. boiler, kettle.
bouillon, m. broth ‖ bubble ‖ puff (in a garment) ‖ burst ‖ boire un ~, to make a bad speculation.   [ebullition.
bouillonnement, m. boiling, bubbling.
bouillonner, v. n. to bubble, to gush out ‖ to boil up ‖ ~, v. a. to put puffs to (a gar-
bouillotte, f. boiler ‖ kettle.   [ment).
boulanger, m. baker.
boulangère, f. baker's wife.
boulangerie, f. bakehouse.
boule, f. bowl ‖ ball ‖ sconce ‖ ~ d'eau

chaude, hot-water bottle || de ~, Buhl ... || jeu de ~, bowls || ~-dogue, m. bull-dog.

bouleau, m. birch-tree.

boulet, m. bullet, cannon-ball || ~ ramé, bar-shot, chain-shot.

boulette, f. little ball || forced-meat ball.

bouleux, m. short thickset horse || drudge.

boulevard, m. bulwark, rampart.

bouleversement, m. overthrow, confusion, disorder.

bouleverser, v. a. to overthrow, to upset.

boulevue; à la ~, ad. hastily.

boulin, m. pigeon-hole.

bouline, f. (mar.) bowline || gauntlet.

bouliner, v. n. (mar.) to haul the wind || to sail close to the wind.

boulingrin, m. bowling-green || grass-plot.

boulon, m. bolt || pin.

boulonner, v. a. to bolt || to pin.

bouquet, m. nosegay, tuft, bunch || flavour (of wine) || birthday-ode || crowning-piece.

bouquetier, m. flower-seller || flower-pot.

bouquetière, f. flower-girl.

bouquetin, m. wild goat.   [book.

bouquin, m. old he-goat || buck-hare || old

bouquiner, v. n. to hunt after old books.

bouquineur, m. bookworm.

bouquiniste, m. dealer in old books.

bouracan, m. barracan, camlet.

bourbe, f. (mar.) mud, mire, dirt.

bourbeux, se, a. muddy, miry.

bourbier, m. slough, plash || scrape.

bourdaine, f. (bot.) black alder.

bourdalou, m. hat-band.

bourde, f. fib, sham, humbug.

bourdon, m. drone || pilgrim's staff || great bell || humble-bee || bass.   [tingling.

bourdonnement, m. buzzing, humming ||

bourdonner, v. n. to buzz, to hum || to

bourg, m. borough.   [murmur.

bourgade, f. small borough.

bourgeois, e, m. & f. burgess, burgher, citizen, commoner.

bourgeois, e, a. citizen-like || civil || private, homely || common || vulgar || -ement, ad. plainly, commonly.

bourgeoisie, f. citizenship || middle class.

bourgeon, m. bud || pustule.

bourgeonné, e, a. pimply.

bourgeonnement, m. budding.

bourgeonner, v. n. to bud || to break out in pimples.

bourgmestre, m. burgomaster.

Bourgogne, m. Burgundy (wine).

bourrache, f. (bot.) borage.   [hit.

bourrade, f. snapping || cuff || (fig.) hard

bourrasque, f. squall || fit of anger || tiff || caprice, whim.

bourre, f. cow's hair || wadding || trash.

bourreau, m. executioner, hangman || tormentor || ~ d'argent, spendthrift.

bourrée, f. brush-wood.   [sting.

bourreler, v. a. to torment, to goad || to

bourrelet, m. pad || cushion || tumbling-

bourrelier, m. harness-maker.   [cap.

bourrer, v. a. to ram (a gun) || to stuff with hair || (fam.) to thrash.

bourriche, f. hamper for fowls.

bourrique, f. she-ass || blockhead.

bourriquet, m. ass's colt || hand-barrow.

bourru, e, a. peevish.

bourse, f. purse, bag || bursery || scholarship || stock-exchange || money-market.

boursicaut, m. small purse || savings (pl.).

boursier, m. bursar || speculator on 'Change.

boursouflage, m. bombast.

boursouflé, e, a. swollen || puffed up || bombastic || turgid.

boursoufler, v. n. to puff up, to bloat.

boursouflure, f. swelling || bombast || fustian || turgidness.

bousculer, v. a. to put in confusion, to turn upside down || to bully.

bouse, f. cow's-dung.

bousillage, m. mud-wall || very bad work.

bousiller, v. a. & n. to bungle || to build with mud.

bousilleur, m. (fam.) mud-waller || botcher.

bousin, m. row, dust.

boussole, f. sea-compass || (fig.) guide.

boustifaille, f. grub, stuffing.

bout, m. top, end, tip || nipple || extremity.

boutade, f. whim, fit, freak, frolic.

boute; ~-en-train, m. merry companion || life and soul || ~-feu, m. firebrand || ~-selle, m. (mil.) signal to saddle.

bouteille, f. bottle || flask || jar.

bouterolle, m. iron way for wheels.

boutique, f. shop || stall || stock || set of

boutiquier, m. shop-keeper.   [tools.

boutoir, m. snout || buttress, parer.

bouton, m. button || stud || knob || handle || bud || pimple || ~ d'or, (bot.) buttercup.

boutonné, e, a. buttoned || close.

boutonner, v. a. & n. to button || to bud.

boutonnerie, f. button-ware.

boutonnier, m. button-maker.

boutonnière, f. button-hole.

bouts-rimés, m. pl. poetry made to rhyme with given words || dumb-crambo (game).

bouture, f. cutting from a tree || sucker.

bouverie, f. ox-stall.

bouvier, m. ox-driver.

bouvreuil, m. bullfinch.

bovine, a. bovine.

boxe, f. boxing.

boxer, v. n. to box.   [hose.

boxeur, m. boxer.

boyau, m. gut || narrow place || passage ||

boyaudier, m. fiddle-string maker.

boycottage, m. boycotting || Irish terrorism.

boycotter, v. a. to boycott.   [rorism.

bracelet, m. bracelet, armlet.

braconnage, m. poaching.

braconner, v. n. to poach.

braconnier, m. poacher.

braguette, f. flap || (bot.) cowslip.

brahmane, m. Brahmin.

brai, m. pitch, tar.

braillard, e, m. & f. bawler.

braillard, e, a. bawling.

brailler, v. n. to brawl, to be noisy.

brailleur, m. brawler, squaller.

braiment, m. braying.

braire, v. n. to bray.

braise, f. embers (pl.) || live coal.

braiser, v. a. to stew, to broil.

bûcher, v. a. & n. to fell wood, to rough-hew || to work hard.

bûcheron, m. wood-cutter || seller of wood.

bûchette, f. fallen-wood, sticks.

bucolique, m. bucolic.

bucolique, a. bucolic (poet or poem).

budget, m. budget.

buée, f. lye.

buffet, m. buffet, sideboard || refreshment-room.

buffle, m. buffalo.

buffleterie, f. buff-belts of a soldier.

buffletin, m. young buffalo.

bugle, m. bugle || (mus.) key-bugle.

buis, m. box, box-wood.

buisson, m. bush, thicket || ~ creux, nothing || nobody.

buissonneux, se, a. bushy, woody.

buissonnier, ère, a. bush || faire l'école -ère, to play truant.

bulbe, f. bulb.

bulbeux, se, a. bulbous.

bulle, f. bubble || (papal) bull.

bulletin, m. bulletin || summary of news || little ticket, ballot.

buraliste, m. office-keeper.

bure, f. drugget || shaft (of a mine).

bureau, m. office || writing-desk || davenport || ~ d'adresses, intelligence-office.

bureaucrate, m. bureaucrat.

bureaucratie, f. bureaucracy || red-tapism.

bureaucratique, a. bureaucratic.

burette, f. cruet || flagon.

burin, m. burin, graver.

buriner, v. a. to engrave.

burlesque, a. (–ment, ad.) comical(ly) || jocular(ly).

burnous, m. burnous, Arabian cloak.

busard, m. (moor-)buzzard.

busc, m. busk (of stays).

buse, f. buzzard || (fig.) simpleton.

busqué, e, a. curved.

busquer, v. a. to put a busk in ou on.

buste, m. bust.

but, m. mark, aim, design || ~ à ~, even, on a par || de ~ en blanc, point blank || bluntly || without any preamble.

buter, v. n. to set (against) || se ~, to stick || to be bent || to oppose.

butin, m. booty || prize.

butiner, v. n. to pilfer || to get booty.

butor, m. bittern || pig-headed churl.

butte, f. mound || butt || hill, rise || en ~, exposed to. [to stumble.

butter, v. a. & n. to earth ou bank up ||

buvable, a. drinkable.

buvard, m. blotter || blotting-pad || ~ de voyage, despatch-box.

buvette, f. refreshment-booth || tap-room.

buveur, se, m. & f. toper, drunkard.

buvotter, v. n. to sip || to tipple.

C.

çà, ad. here || ~ et là, here and there || to and fro || ~ ! come on ! || ~, pn. (fam.) this, that || c'est ~, that's it.

cabale, f. cabal || (jewish) cabala.

cabaler, v. n. to cabal.

cabaleur, m. caballer.

cabalistique, a. cabalistic.

caban, m. cloak with a cape ou hood.

cabane, f. cottage, cabin || hut || kennel.

cabanon, m. small cabin, cell.

cabaret, m. public-house || set of tea-things.

cabaretier, ière, m. & f. tavern-keeper || publican's wife.

cabas, m. basket || work-bag.

cabestan, m. (mar.) capstan.

cabillaud, m. codfish

cabinet, m. closet, study, cabinet || Cabinet-council || ~ d'affaires, agency office || ~ d'aisance, water-closet || ~ de lecture, reading-room || circulating library.

câble, m. (mar.) cable || hawse.

câbleau, m. boat-rope.

caboche, f. noddle || head-piece.

cabotage, m. coasting-trade.

caboter, v. n. to coast.

caboteur, cabotier, m. coaster.

cabotin, e, m. & f. strolling comedian.

se cabrer, to rear, to prance || to get into a passion. [a passion.

cabri, m. kid.

cabriole, f. capriole || caper.

cabrioler, v. n. to caper.

cabriolet, m. gig || hansom cab.

cabrioleur, m. caperer.

cacade, f. (fam.) evacuation || (fig.) failure.

cacao, m. cocoa-nut. [mess.

cacaoyer, cacaotier, m. cocoa-tree.

cacatoès, m. cockatoo.

cachalot, m. sperm-whale.

cache, f. hiding-place || fly-leaf || ~-cache, m. hide-and-seek (game).

cachemire, m. cashmere.

cache-nez, m. comforter.

cacher, v. a. to hide, to conceal || se ~, to hide oneself, to live retired || to make a mystery of. [mystery of.

cachet, m. seal || signet.

cacheter, v. a. to seal.

cachette, f. hiding-place || en ~, secretly.

cachot, m. dungeon || cell.

cachotterie, f. (air of) mystery.

cachottier, ère, a. mysterious, sly.

cachou, m. cachou.

cacolet, m. mule-litter. [ance.

cacophonie, f. cacophony || (mus.) dissonance.

cadastre, m. land survey and valuation, cadastre || doomsday-book.

cadavéreux, se, a. cadaverous.

cadavre, m. corpse, dead body.

cadeau, m. gift, present.

cadenas, m. padlock.

cadenasser, v. a. to padlock. [shake.

cadence, f. cadency || (mus.) cadence, trill,

cadencer, v. a. to cadence || to shake.

cadène, f. chain for galley-slaves || chain-gang. [junior || cadet.

cadet, m. younger brother, youngest,

cadet, te, a. younger, junior.

cadette, f. youngest sister || small paving-stone. [dial.

cadran, m. dial-plate || ~ solaire, sun-

cadre, m. frame || list of officers || rolls (pl.).

cadrer, v. n. to square, to agree with.

caduc, que, a. frail, decrepit, decayed, perishable || mal ~, epilepsy.

caducée, m. caduceus.
caducité, f. caducity, decay.			[son.
cafard, e, m. & f. hypocrite, canting per-
cafard, e, a. hypocritical, canting || air~,
	mask of hypocrisy.
cafarderie, f. hypocrisy.
café, m. coffee || coffee-house || moulin à
	~, coffee-mill || garçon de ~, waiter.
caféière, f. coffee-plantation.
cafetier, m. coffee-house keeper.
cafetière, f. coffee-pot.
cafier, m. coffee-plant.
cage, m. cage, bird-cage.
cagnard, m. lazy-bones, sluggard || (mar.)
	weather-cloth.
cagnard, e, a. idle, lazy, skulking.
cagnarder, v. n. to waste one's time.
cagnardise, f. laziness.
cagneux, se, a. bandy-legged.
cagnotte, f. money-box.
cagot, e, a. bigoted, hypocritical.
cagoterie, f. bigotry.
cagotisme, m. bigotry.
cahier, m. small paper volume || copy-
	book, manuscript-book || sheet (in print-
cahin-caha, ad. (fam.) so-so.		[ing).
cahot, m. jolt.
cahotage, m. jolting.
cahoter, v. a. & n. to jolt.
cahute, f. hut, hovel.
caïeu, m. (hort.) sucker, off-set || clove.
caille, f. quail.
caillé, m. curd.
caillebotte, f. curds (of milk).
caille-lait, m. cheese-rennet.
cailler, v. a. to curdle || to clot.
cailletage, m. gossiping.
cailleteau, m. young quail.
caillette, f. rennet-bag || gossip.
caillot, m. clot of blood.
caillou, m. flint-stone, pebble.
cailloutage, m. stoning || heap of stones ||
	pebble-work || rock-work.
caillouter, v. a. to stone.
caillouteux, se, a. stony, pebbly.
caïman, m. alligator.
caïque, m. Turkish boat.
caisse, f. chest, box, trunk || till || case ||
	drum || body of a coach || cashier's desk ||
	counting-house || cash-account || frame,
	body || en ~, in hand || livre de ~, cash-
caissier, m. cashier.			[book.
caisson, m. ammunition-waggon, tumbril.
cajoler, v. a. to wheedle.
cajolerie, f. wheedling.
cajoleur, m. wheedler.
cal, m. callosity.
calaison, m. (mar.) draft, load water-line.
calamité, f. calamity.
calamiteux, se, a. calamitous.
calandrage, m. calendering.
calandre, f. weevil || lark || calender, hot-
	press.
calandrer, v. a. to calender.
calandreur, se, m. & f. calenderer.
calangue, f. (mar.) cove, creek.
calcaire, a. calcarious, chalky.
calcédoine, f. chalcedony.
calciner, v. a. to calcine.

calcul, m. calculation || ciphering || (méd.)
	calculus || de ~ fait, all things con-
	sidered, after mature deliberation.
calculateur, m. calculator.		[cipher.
calculer, v. a. to calculate, to reckon || to
cale, f. wedge || (mar.) hold || stocks, slips ||
	slope || à fond de ~, (mar.) down in the
calebasse, f. calabash.			[hold.
calèche, f. calache, open carriage.
caleçon, m. drawers, pair of drawers.
caléfacteur, m. economic cooking-appara-
calembour, m. pun.			[tus.
calembouriste, m. punster.
calembredaine, f. fib, subterfuge, cock-
	and-bull story.
calendes, f. pl. calends.
calendrier, m. calendar.
calepin, m. note-book.			[to sink.
caler, v. a. to wedge || to lower || ~, v. n.
calfat, m. (mar.) caulker.
calfatage, m. (mar.) caulking.
calfater, v. a. (mar.) to caulk.
calfeutrage, m. stopping up of chinks.
calfeutrer, v. a. to stop up chinks || se ~,
	to make oneself snug.
calibre, m. size, bore, stamp.
calice, m. chalice || flower-cup.
calicot, m. calico || counter-jumper.
calife, m. caliph.
à califourchon, ad. astraddle.
câlin, e, m. & f. do-nothing || wheedler.
câlin, e, a. coaxing, wheedling.
câliner, v. a. to wheedle, to coax || se ~,
	to take one's ease || to coddle oneself.
câlinerie, f. wheedling.
calleux, se, a. callous, hard, horny.
calligraphe, m. calligrapher, copyist.
calligraphie, f. calligraphy.
calligraphique, a. calligraphic.
callosité, f. callosity.		[draught, anodyne.
calmant, m. (méd.) sedative, composing-
calme, m. calmness || calm.
calme, a. calm, tranquil, quiet || (com.) dull.
calmer, v. a. to calm, to appease, to quiet.
calomniateur, m. slanderer.
calomnie, f. calumny, slander.
calomnier, v. a. to calumniate, to slander.
calomnieux, se, a. (-sement, ad.) ca-
	lumnious(ly) || slanderous(ly).
calorifère, m. hot-air stove.
calorique, m. caloric, heat.
calotte, f. skull-cap || coif || box on the
	ear || priesthood || canopy.
calotter, v. a. to box (anyone's) ears.
calottin, m. priest || white choker.
calque, m. tracing || copy.
calquer, v. a. to trace, to copy.
calus, m. callosity || callousness || obduracy.
Calvaire, m. Calvary.
calvitie, f. baldness.
camaïeu, m. cameo.
camarade, m. & f. comrade, mate, com-
	panion, partner.
camaraderie, f. association, companion-
	ship, close fraternity.
camard, e, a. flat-nosed || la -e, Death.
cambouis, m. coom, cart-grease.
cambrer, v. a. to camber, to crook, to
	bend || se ~, to warp || to arch one's back.

cambrioleur, m. pick-lock (thief).
cambrure, f. bending.
cambuse, f. (mar.) steward's room.
cambusier, m. (mar.) steward's mate.
camée, m. cameo.
camélia, camellia, m. (bot.) camelia.
camelot, m. camlet.
camelotte, f. shoddy || trash, rubbish.
caměriste, f. waiting-woman.
camion, m. truck, dray.
camionnage, m. cartage in a dray.
camionneur, m. drayman.
camisole, f. under-waistcoat || ~ de force,
strait-waistcoat || ~ de nuit, short night-
dress.
camomille, f. (bot.) camomile.
camouflet, m. whiff of smoke (in the face) ||
(fig.) affront || rap over the knuckles.
campagnard, e, m. & f. countryman ||
countrywoman.
campagnard, e, a. churlish.
campagne, f. country || (mil.) campaign,
expedition || battre la ~, to scour the
country || to speak at random || to beat
about the bush || to be delirious.
campanile, m. (arch.) campanile.
campanule, f. bell-flower.
campêche, m. logwood.
camper, v. n. & n. (mil.) to encamp || se
~, to plant ou place oneself.
camphre, m. camphor.
camphré, e, a. camphorated.
camphrer, v. a. to camphorate.
camphrier, m. camphor-tree.
campos, m. holiday (at school).
camus, e, a. snub-nosed, flat-nosed || cut-
ting a poor figure, fooled, disappointed.
canaille, f. rabble, mob || scoundrel.
canal, m. canal, channel, water-conduit.
canaliser, v. a. to cut canals, to canalise.
canapé, m. sofa.   [paper report.
canard, m. duck || water-dog || false news-
canarder, v. a. to shoot from ambush.
canardière, f. decoy for wild ducks ||
duck-gun || loop-hole.
canari, m. canary-bird.
cancan, m. tittle-tattle || cancan (indecent
dance).   [cancan.
cancaner, v. n. to tattle || to dance the
cancanier, ière, m. & f. gossip.
cancéreux, se, a. (méd.) cancerous.
cancre, m. crab-fish || miser.
cancrelat, m. American cockroach.
candélabre, m. candelabrum || candle-
candeur, f. candour.   [stick || lamp-post.
candi, m. sugar-candy.
candidat, m. candidate.
candidature, f. candidateship.
candide, a. (-ment, ad.) candid(ly) ||
se candir, to candy.   [frank.
cane, f. duck.
caneton, m. duckling.
canette, f. duckling || pint || tap.
canevas, m. canvass || sketch.
caniche, f. poodle.   [days.
caniculaire, a. canicular || jours -s, dog-
canicule, f. dog-star || dog-days (pl.).
canif, m. penknife.
canine, a. canine.

canne, f. cane, walking-stick || reed || ~
plombée, loaded stick || ~ à sucre,
sugar-cane.   [reed.
canneler, v. a. to channel, to flute || to
cannelle, f. cinnamon || tap.
cannelure, f. fluting.
canon, m. cannon || barrel of a gun || nose ||
(mus.) canon || quarter-pint || ~ rayé,
rifled gun || à ~ rayé, rifle-barrelled.
canonicat, m. canonry.
canonique, a. canonical.
canoniser, v. a. to canonise.
canonnade, f. cannonade.
canonner, v. a. to cannonade.
canonnier, m. gunner.
canonnière, f. pop-gun || gun-boat.
canot, m. barge || canoe.   [keeper.
canotier, m. rower || bargeman || boat-
cantate, f. (mus.) cantata.
cantaloup, m. (bort.) cantaloup, cantélope.
cantatrice, f. songstress.
cantharide, f. Spanish-fly.
cantine, f. canteen, bottle-case.
cantinier, ière, m. & f. sutler || canteen-
cantique, m. canticle, song.   [woman.
canton, m. canton, district.
cantonnement, m. cantonment.
cantonner, v. a. & n. (mil.) to canton || to
be in cantonments.   [keeper.
cantonnier, m. road-mender || (rail.) line-
canule, f. injection-pipe || tube.
canuler, v. a. to bore, to plague.
caoutchouc, m. Indian-rubber.
cap, m. (mar.) cape, headland || où est
le ~ ? (mar.) how is her head? || ~ -de-
mouton, m. (mar.) dead-eye.
capable, a. capable, fit, skilful || assum-
ing || c'est un homme très—, he is
the right man in the right place.
capacité, f. capacity, ability || capacious-
caparaçon, m. caparison.   [ness.
caparaçonner, v. a. to caparison.
cape, f. cloak with a hood || riding-hood.
capeline, f. woman's hat.
capillaire, m. (bot.) maiden-hair.
capillaire, a. capillary.
capilotade, f. hash.
capitaine, m. captain || ~ de cavalerie,
horse-captain || ~ d'infanterie, foot-
captain.
capitainerie, f. captaincy.
capital, m. capital, stock || main point.
capital, e, a. capital, chief, main.
capitale, f. chief city, capital || capital
capitaliser, v. a. to capitalise. [letter.
capitaliste, m. capitalist.
capitan, m. boaster, hector.
capitation, f. poll-tax.
capiteux, se, a. heady, strong.
Capitole, m. Capitol of Rome || capitol.
capiton, m. silk-flock, cappadine.
capitonner, v. a. to pad (arm-chairs, &c).
capitulaire, a. capitulary.
capituler, v. n. to capitulate.   [crite.
capon, m. coward || sneak || skulker || hypo-
caponner, v. n. to be cowardly || to sneak ||
to skulk away.
caporal, m. corporal || shag (tobacco).
capot, a.: être ~, to have lost every trick.

capote, f. hooded cloak || (mil.) great-coat || hood, mantle, capuchin.

câpre, f. caper.

caprice, m. caprice, whim, fancy.

capricieux, se, a. (-sement, ad.) capricious(ly).

Capricorne, m. (astr.) Capricorn.

câprier, m. (bot.) caper-bush.

capsule, f. capsule || percussion-cap.

captation, f. inveigling || (jur.) undue influence.

capter, v. a. to gain insidiously || (jur.) to exercise undue influence.   (ly).

captieux, se, a. (-sement, ad.) captious.

captif, ve, m. & f. captive, prisoner || ballon ~, m. captive balloon.

captiver, v. a. to captivate.

captivité, f. captivity.

capturer, v. a. to capture || to arrest.

capuce, capuchon, m. cowl || riding-cloak.

capucin, m. Capuchin friar.

capucinade, f. dull, prosy sermon.

capucine, f. Capuchin nun || (bot.) nasturtium.

caquage, m. barrelling || curing.

caque, f. keg, barrel.

caquer, v. a. to barrel (herrings) || to cure.

caquet, m. prattling || cackle of geese.

caquetage, m. babbling, prattling.

caqueter, v. n. to prattle || to cackle.

caqueteur, se, m. & f. prattler.

caqueur, m. fish-curer.

car, c. for, because, forasmuch as.

carabe, m. beetle.

carabin, m. saw-bones (medical student).

carabine, f. carbine, rifle.

carabiner, v. a. to rifle a gun-barrel || carabiné, rifled || (mar.) stiff.

carabinier, m. carabineer, rifleman.

caraco, m. bodice.

caracoler, v. n. to caracole, to prance.

caractère, m. character, mark || stamp || letter, type || handwriting, temper, humour, genius || dignity, quality.

caractériser, v. a. to characterise.

caractéristique, f. characteristic || (math.) characteristic, index.

caractéristique, a. characteristic.

carafe, f. decanter, bottle.   [wine-cooler.

carafon, m. liquor-bottle || half-pint bottle ||

carambolage, m. (at billiards) cannon.

caramboler, v. n. to cannon (at billiards).

caramel, m. burnt sugar.

carapace, f. carapace, calapash.

caraque, f. best cocoa.

caravane, f. caravan.

caravansérail, m. caravansary.

carbone, m. (chim.) carbon.

carboné, a. carbonated.

carboniser, v. a. to carbonise.

carbonnade, f. carbonado.

carcan, m. pillory, carcan.

carcasse, f. carcass || skeleton.

carcinome, m. (méd.) carcinoma.

carde, f. card.

carder, v. a. to card, to comb wool.

cardeur, se, m. & f. carder.

cardiaque, a. (méd. & anat.) cardiac.

cardinal, m. Cardinal || cardinal (bird).

cardinal, e, a. cardinal.

cardinalat, m. cardinalship.

cardon, m. (bot.) cardoon || shrimp. [tide.

carême, m. Lent || ~-prenant, m. Shrove-

carénage, m. (mar.) careening || careenage.

carence, f. (jur.) absence of assets.

carène, f. (mar.) keel || careening.

caréner, v. a. (mar.) to careen.

caresse, f. caress.   [fawn upon, to pat.

caresser, v. a. to caress, to fondle || to

cargaison, f. cargo, ship-load.

carguer, v. a. (mar.) to brail the sails.

carie, f. caries || decay || brown rust.

carier, v. a. to make carious, to rot, to putrify || se ~, to grow carious.

carillon, m. chime of bells, peal || row.

carillonnement, m. chiming.

carillonner, v. n. to chime, to ring away.

carillonneur, m. chimer.

carlin, m. pug-dog.

carme, m. carmelite.

carmin, m. carmine.

carnage, m. slaughter, massacre.

carnassier, ère, a. carnivorous.

carnassière, f. game-bag.

carnaval, m. carnival.

carné, e, a. flesh-coloured.

carnet, m. note-book || ~ d'échéances, carnier, m. game-bag.   [bill-book.

carnivore, a. carnivorous.

carotte, f. carrot || roll || tirer une ~ à . . ., to get something out of.

carotter, v. a. & n. to chouse || to play low.

caroube, m. (bot.) carob.

caroubier, m. carob-tree.

carpe, f. carp (fish).

carpeau, m. young carp.

carpillon, m. small ou young carp.

carquois, m. quiver.   [shoulders.

carre, f. crown (of a hat) || toes || back and

carré, m. square, garden-bed || landing.

carré, e, a. (-ment, ad.) square(ly) || bold(ly) || plainly.

carreau, m. square paving-tile, cushion || floor || diamond (at cards) || tailor's goose || pane of glass || à -x, checked.

carrefour, m. crossways || crowded thoroughfare.   [ment.

carrelage, m. brick-paving || brick-pave-

carreler, v. a. to pave with tiles ou bricks || to mend shoes.

carrelet, m. square fishing-net || awl.

carreleur, m. brick-paver || itinerant cobbler.

carrelure, f. re-soling (of shoes).

carrer, v. a. to square || se ~, to strut.

carrick, m. box-coat || gig.

carrier, m. quarryman.

carrière, f. career, course || race || quarry.

carriole, f. light van, jaunting car.

carrosse, m. coach.

carrossier, m. coach-builder.

carrousel, m. tournament, tilt.

carrure, f. breadth of shoulders.

carte, f. card || map || pasteboard || ticket || bill of fare || chart || à la ~, from the bill of fare || jeu de -s, pack of cards || ~ blanche, full power || perdre la ~, to be put out.   [ing-clock.

cartel, m. cartel, challenge || antique hang-

cartésien, m. cartesian.
cartilage, m. cartilage.
cartilagineux, se, a. cartilaginous.
cartomancie, f. fortune-telling by cards.
carton, m. pasteboard || cartoon || band-box ||
book of charts || cancel, leaf || ~-pâte, f.
mill-board || ~-pierre, f. statuary paste-
board.
cartonnage, m. boarding of books.
cartonner, v. a. to put in boards.
cartonnerie, f. pasteboard-manufactory.
cartonneur, m. boarder of books.
cartonnier, m. pasteboard-maker || paste-
board chest of drawers.
cartouche, f. cartridge.
cartouchier, m., cartouchière, f. car-
tridge-box.
cas, m. case, accident || matter, fact ||
value || en ~ de, in case of, in point of ||
en tout ~, at all events, in any case ||
en-tout-~, m. light mackintosh.
casanier, ère, m. & f. stay-at-home.
casanier, ère, a. home-keeping, seden-
tary || stay-at-home.
casaque, f. cassock || cloak || jacket ||
tourner ~, to change sides.
casaquin, m. jacket, short gown.
cascade, f. cascade, waterfall.
cascatelle, f. small cascade.
case, f. cabin || compartment || pigeon-hole ||
box || square || (mar.) berth.
caséine, f. (chim.) caseine.
casemate, e, a. with casemates.
caser, v. a. to place || se ~, to get settled ||
to find a place.
caserne, f. (mil.) barrack.
casernement, m. barracking of troops.
caserner, v. a. & n. to barrack || to be in
barracks.
casier, m. set of pigeon-holes || cabinet of
small drawers || ~ à musique, canter-
casimir, m. kerseymere.   [bury.
casque, m. helmet || ~ à mèche, man's
night-cap.   [eyes.
casquette, f. cap with a shade for the
cassant, e, a. brittle || bluff || unsociable.
cassation, f. annulment || reversal || repeal.
casse, f. (bot.) cassia || case || breakage ||
~-cou, m. breakneck || dare-devil || ~-
noisette, m. nut-cracker || ~-sucre, s.
sugar-nippers || ~-tête, m. tomahawk ||
life-preserver || deafening noise || bewilder-
ing work || anxiety || puzzle.
casser, v. a. to break, to crack || to annul ||
to split || to wear out || to puzzle || to re-
verse || to dissolve || (mil.) to reduce to the
ranks.   [table-dish.
casserolle, f. saucepan, stewpan || vege-
cassette, f. casket || cash-box || privy purse.
casseur, m. breaker || ~ d'assiettes,
blusterer.   [wine.
cassis, m. black-currant || black-currant-
cassolette, f. incense-pan || scent-box.
cassonade, f. moist sugar.
cassure, f. fracture, crack.
castagnette, f. castanet.
caste, f. caste.
castor, m. beaver || beaver(hat).
casuel, m. emolument, fees, perquisites.

casuel, le, a. (-lement, ad.) casual(ly) ||
fortuitous, precarious.
casuiste, m. casuist.
catacombes, f. pl. catacombs (pl.).
cataclysme, m. cataclysm || overthrow.
catafalque, m. bed of state, catafalque ||
catalepsie, f. catalepsy.   [canopy.
cataleptique, a. cataleptic.
catalogue, m. catalogue, list, roll.
cataloguer, v. a. to catalogue.
cataplasme, m. poultice, cataplasm.
cataracte, f. cataract, waterfall.
catarrhe, m. catarrh.
catastrophe, f. catastrophe, tragical end.
catéchiser, v. a. to catechise.
catéchisme, m. catechism.
catéchiste, m. catechist.
catéchumène, m. & f. catechumen.
catégorie, f. category.
catégorique, a. (-ment, ad.) categorical
cathédrale, f. cathedral church.   [(ly).
catholicisme, m. catholicism.
catholicité, f. catholicism || catholic coun-
catholique, m. & f. catholic.   [tries.
catholique, a. (-ment, ad.) catholic ||
catholically, like a catholic.
cati, m. gloss || lustre.
(en) catimini, ad. secretly, stealthily.
catin, f. harlot.
catir, v. a. to press cloth, to gloss.
catissage, m. glossing.
cauchemar, m. nightmare || bore || nuisance
caudataire, m. train-bearer.
cause, f. cause || source, occasion || motive,
reason || side, party || suit at law, trial ||
à ~ que, because || à ~ de, on account of,
for the sake of.
causer, v. a. & n. to cause, to occasion ||
to chat, to talk || to prate.
causerie, f. chat || prattling, gossiping.
causeur, se, m. & f. babbler, prattler.
causeuse, f. small sofa.
causticité, f. causticity.
caustique, m. caustic.
caustique, a. caustic.   [craftily.
cauteleux, se, a. (-sement, ad.) crafty ||
cautère, m. (chir.) cautery, issue.
cautériser, v. a. to cauterise.
caution, f. bail, security || il est sujet à
~, he is not to be trusted, he is "a perfect caution".
cautionnement, m. bail, security.
cautionner, v. a. to bail, to warrant.
cavalcade, f. cavalcade.
cavale, f. mare.
cavalerie, f. cavalry, horse.
cavalier, m. horseman, rider || cavalier,
gentleman || partner || dancer.
cavalier, ère, a. (-èrement, ad.) cava-
lier(ly) || free || unceremonious(ly).
cave, f. cellar || liquor-case || sarcophagus ||
pool.
cave, a. hollow (of cheeks, eyes).
caveau, m. cellar || little vault.
caver, v. a. to hollow out || to stake at play.
caverne, f. cavern || cave, den.
caverneux, se, a. cavernous.
caviar, m. caviare, caviar.
cavité, f. cavity, hollowness.

ce, (cet), cette, pn. this, that, it.

ceci, pn. this.

cécité, f. blindness.

céder, v. a. & n. to cede, to give up, to yield || to transfer || to dispose of || le ~ à,

cédille, f. (gr.) cedilla.   [to be second to.

cèdre, m. (bot.) cedar.

cédule, f. (jur.) note of hand || cedule.

ceindre, v. a. ir. to gird, to enclose, to en-circle, to encompass, to surround.

ceinture, f. girdle, sash, waistband, belt || enclosure, circle.

ceinturier, m. belt-maker.

ceinturon, m. belt.

cela, pn. that || ce n'est pas ~, it is not   [so.

céladon, m. sea-green || sentimental lover.

célèbre, a. celebrated, famous.

célébrer, v. a. to celebrate.

célébrité, f. celebrity || fame.

céler, v. a. to conceal, to hide.

céleri, m. (bot.) celery.

célérité, f. celerity, swiftness.

céleste, a. celestial, heavenly.

célibat, m. celibacy, single life.

célibataire, m. bachelor.

celle, pn. she, that.

cellérier, m. cellarer.

cellier, m. cellar, store-room.

cellulaire, a. cellular.

cellule, f. cell, cellule.

celui, pn. he, him, her, that || who || ~-ci, the latter, this one || ~-là, the former || that one || the other.

cendre, f. ashes || cinder || jour, mercredi des Cendres, Ash-Wednesday.

cendré, e, a. ash-coloured.

cendrée, f. dust-shot.

cendreux, se, a. ashy, full of ashes.

cendrier, m. ash-pan, ash-hole.

Cendrillon, f. Cinderella.

cène, f. the Lord's supper.

cénelle, f. (bot.) haw.

cénotaphe, m. cenotaph.

cens, m. electoral qualification || quit-rent.

censé, e, a. reputed, accounted for || ~-ment, ad. virtually || as it is supposed.

censeur, m. censor, censurer, critic || press-censitaire, a. qualified.   [censor.

censure, f. censorship || censure.

censurer, v. a. to censure.

cent, m. cent, hundred.

centaine, f. hundred.

centaure, m. centaur.

centaurée, f. (bot.) centaury.

centenaire, m. & f. centenary || centenarian.

centenaire, a. centenary.

centenier, m. centurion.

centième, a. hundredth.

centigrade, m. centigrade thermometer.

centigramme, m. the hundredth part of a gramme.

centilitre, m. the hundredth part of a litre.

centime, m. centime, the hundredth part of a franc.

centimètre, m. the hundredth part of a central, e, a. central.   [metre.

centraliser, v. a. to centralise.

centre, m. centre.

centrifuge, a. centrifugal.

centripète, a. centripetal.

centupler, v. a. to centuplicate.

cep, m. vine || vine-stock.

cèpe, m. (bot.) esculent boletus.

cépée, f. tuft of shoots.

cependant, ad. & c. in the mean time, in the meanwhile, however, yet.

céramique, f. ceramic, fictile art.

cérat, m. ointment, cold cream.

Cerbère, m. Cerberus (also fig.).

cerceau, m. hoop.

cercle, m. circle, hoop, ring, assembly, company || vin en -s, wine in the cask.

cercler, v. a. to hoop.   [death.

cercueil, m. coffin, bier || grave, tomb ||

céréal, e, a. a cereal.   [brain-fever.

cérébral, e, a. cerebral || fièvre -e,

cérémonie, f. ceremony, formality || en (grande) ~, in state.

cérémonieux, se, a. ceremonious.

cerf, m. stag, hart || ~-volant, m. paper-) kite || stag-beetle.

cerfeuil, m. (bot.) chervil.

cerisaie, f. cherry-orchard.

cerise, f. cherry.

cerisier, m. cherry-tree

cerné, e, a. surrounded || with dark circles round the eyes.

cerneau, m. (half of the) kernel of a green walnut || unripe walnut.

cerner, v. a. to cut round || to encircle, to surround || (mil.) to invest (a fortress).

certain, e, a. (-ement, ad.) certain(ly) ||

certes, ad. truly, indeed.   [sure || some.

certificat, m. certificate, testimonial.

certifier, v. a. to certify, to assure.

certitude, f. certainty.

céruse, f. ceruse, white-lead.

cervaison, f. season for stag-hunting.

cerveau, m. brain || ~ brûlé, m. crazy fel-cervelas, m. cervelas.   [low.

cervelet, m. (anat.) cerebellum.

cervelle, f. brains.

ces, pn. pl. these, those.

césarienne, a. (chir.) Cesarean.

cessation, f. cessation || stop.

cesse, f. cessation, rest || respite.

cesser, v. a. to cease, to discontinue.

cessible, a. transferable.

cession, f. cession, giving up.

cessionnaire, m. grantee.

ceste, m. cestus, gauntlet (of the ancients).

césure, f. (poés.) cæsura.

cet, pn. this, that.

cétacé, m. cetacean.

cétacé, e, a. cetaceous.

ceux, pn. pl. these, those.

chabot, m. gull || bull-head (fish).

chabraque, f. caparison.

chacal, m. jackal.

chacun, e, pn. each || everyone.   [fellow.

chafouin, m. deep fellow, mean-looking

chafouin, e, a. ill-shaped, shabby.

chagrin, m. grief, sorrow, vexation, afflic-tion, displeasure || shagreen.

chagrin, e, a. sad || peevish, sullen, cross.

chagrinant, e, a. grievous, vexatious.

chagriner, v. a. to grieve, to vex || to shagreen || se ~, to fret, to grieve.

chaîne, f. chain ‖ weaver's warp ‖ gang of galley-slaves.
chaînetier, m. chain-maker.
chaînette, f. little chain.
chaînon, m. link (of a chain).
chair, f. flesh, meat ‖ pulp ‖ flesh-side ‖ ~ **vive,** quick.
chaire, f. pulpit ‖ see ‖ professorship.
chaise, f. chair, seat ‖ ~ **longue,** lounging chair ‖ ~ **à porteur,** sedan-chair ‖ ~ **percée,** close-stool.
chaisier, m. chair-maker.
chaland, m. customer ‖ barge.
chalande, f. female customer.
châle, m. shawl.
chalet, m. Swiss-cottage.
chaleur, f. heat, warmth ‖ ardour of temper, vivacity, eagerness.   [sanguine.
chaleureux, se, a. naturally warm ‖
chaloupe, f. sloop ‖ ~ **canonnière,** gunboat.   [(mus.) pipe.
chalumeau, m. stalk of a straw, reed ‖
chamade, f. (mil.) parley.
se chamailler, to squabble.
chamaillis, m. squabble.
chamarrer, v. a. to bedizen.
chamarrure, f. gaudy ornaments ‖ medley.
chambellan, m. chamberlain.
chambranle, m. door-case, window-case ‖ mantelpiece.
chambre, f. chamber, room, apartment ‖ court of justice ‖ ~ **à coucher,** bedroom ‖ ~ **garnie,** furnished room ‖ ~ **obscure,** camera obscura.
chambrée, f. sleeping-room ‖ roomful ‖ number in a room ‖ number of spectators.
chambrette, f. little room.   ["the house."
chameau, m. camel ‖ (mar.) camel, caisson.
chamelier, m. camel-driver.
chamelle, f. she-camel.
chamois, m. chamois.
chamoiserie, f. chamois-leather-factory.
chamoiseur, m. chamois-leather-dresser.
champ, m. field ‖ career ‖ matter, subject, theme.   [iced champagne.
champagne, m. champagne ‖ ~ **frappé,**
champêtre, a. rural.
champignon, m. mushroom ‖ toadstool ‖ thief in a candle ‖ bonnet-stand.
champignonnière, f. mushroom-bed.
champion, m. champion.
chance, f. chance, hazard ‖ good luck.
chanceler, v. n. to stagger, to totter, to reel ‖ to waver.
chancelier, m. chancellor.
chancelière, f. foot-bag, boot of a carriage.
chancellerie, f. chancery.
chanceux, se, a. lucky ‖ uncertain.
chancre, m. canker (on a tree) ‖ (méd.)
Chandeleur, f. Candlemas.   [chancre.
chandelier, m. candlestick.
chandelle, f. candle, candle-light ‖ **le jeu n'en vaut pas la ~,** the game is not worth the candle, it is not worth powder and shot.   [rabbet.
chanfrein, m. chanfrin ‖ (arch.) chamfer,
change, m. change ‖ exchange ‖ **lettre de ~,** bill of exchange ‖ **agent de ~,** stockbroker.

changeant, e, a. changeable, fickle ‖ variable (of colours) ‖ unsettled (of weather).
changement, m. change, alteration.
changer, v. a. & n. to change ‖ to exchange, to alter ‖ to turn ‖ to shift.
changeur, m. money-changer.
chanoine, m. canon.
chanoinesse, f. canoness.   [rub, hitch.
chanson, f. song, ballad ‖ ditty ‖ nonsense ‖
chansonner, v. a. to lampoon.
chansonnette, f. light *ou* comic song.
chansonnier, ère, m. & f. ballad-maker ‖ song-book.
chant, m. singing, song, tune, air.
chantage, m. extortion of hush-money.
chantant, e, a. singing ‖ tunable, fit to be
chanteau, m. hunch of bread.   [sung.
chanter, v. a. & n. to sing, to praise ‖ to warble, to crow ‖ **c'est comme si vous chantiez,** you might as well talk to the wind.
chanterelle, f. treble-string ‖ call-bird.
chanteur, se, m. & f. (female) singer, vocalist.
chantier, m. workshop ‖ timber-yard, wood-yard ‖ dock-yard, stocks ‖ cask-stand
chantonner, v. a. to hum (a song).
chantre, m. chanter, chorister.
chantrerie, f. precentorship.
chanvre, m. hemp.
chaos, m. chaos ‖ **de ~,** chaotic.
chapardage, m. (mil.) marauding.
chape, f. cope.
chapeau, m. hat ‖ bonnet ‖ cap ‖ ~ **chinois,** (mus.) Chinese bells ‖ ~ **bas !** hats off !
chapelain, m. chaplain.
chapeler, v. n. to rasp bread.
chapelet, m. beads ‖ string.   [wife.
chapelier, ère, m. & f. hatter ‖ hatter's
chapelle, f. chapel ‖ church-plate ‖ ~ **ardente,** catafalque lighted up ‖ with
chapellenie, f. chaplainship.   [candles.
chapellerie, f. hat-trade.
chapelure, f. raspings of bread.
chaperon, m. hood ‖ riding-hood ‖ shoulderknot ‖ coping.   [to hood.
chaperonner, v. a. to chaperon ‖ to cope ‖
chapiteau, m. capital of a column ‖ top.
chapitre, m. chapter ‖ chapter-house ‖
chapitrer, v. a. to reprimand.   [matter.
chapon, m. capon.
chaponneau, m. young capon.
chaponner, v. a. to caponise.
chaque, pn. each, every.   [jaunting-car.
char, m. car, chariot ‖ hearse ‖ ~ **à bancs,**
charabia, m. broken French, gibberish.
charade, f. charade.
charançon, m. weevil.
charbon, m. coal, ember ‖ carbuncle ‖ mildew ‖ ~ **de bois,** charcoal ‖ ~ **de terre,** pit-coal.
charbonné, e, a. mildewed.
charbonner, v. a. to daub with charcoal ‖ ~, v. n. to carbonise.
charbonneux, se, a. carbuncled.
charbonnier, ère, m. & f. charcoalburner ‖ coalheaver, coalman ‖ coal-cellar, coal-hole ‖ (mar.) collier ‖ coal-woman ‖ charcoal-kiln.

French and English.

charbouiller, v. a. to blight.
charcuter, v. a. to hack meat.
charcuterie, f. pork-butcher's trade || hog's flesh || pork-dressing.
charcutier, ère, m. & f. pork-butcher.
chardon, m. thistle || ~ à foulon, fuller's thistle.
chardonneret, m. goldfinch.
charge, f. charge, load, burden, weight || commission || condition || duty, tax, cost || place, employment || accusation, imputation || attack, onset || à la ~ de, upon condition that || à la ~ d'autant, upon condition of a return.
chargé-d'affaires, m. chargé d'affaires, ambassador's substitute.
chargement, m. cargo, load || bill of lading.
charger, v. a. to charge, to load, to burden || to entrust, to give the care of || to load with powder and ball || to attack || to accuse, to exaggerate || to write down || to crowd || to overload || (jur.) to charge, to accuse || (mil.) to charge || (chim.) to impregnate, to saturate || se ~, to take charge of, to be answerable for.
chargeur, m. loader || porter.
chariot, m. waggon, cart.
charitable, a. (-ment, ad.) merciful(ly) || charitable || charitably.
charité, f. charity || alms || alms-house.
charivaresque, a. noisy.
charivari, m. discordant music || rattle, hubbub || Punch (a French satirical journal) || faire or donner un ~, to make a disturbance, a scene.
charivariser, v. n. to make a great noise.
charlatan, m. quack. [quackery.
charlatanerie, f., charlatanisme, m.
charlotte, f. apple-charlotte || ~ russe, charlotte-russe (whipped cream with biscuits).
charmant, e, a. charming, delightful.
charme, m. charm, spell || yoke-elm.
charmer, v. a. to charm, to delight, to bewitch. [yoke-elm.
charmille, f. yoke-elm || row ou hedge of
charmoie, f. yoke-elm grove.
charnel, le, a. (-ment, ad.) carnal(ly) || sensual(ly).
charnier, m. charnel-house || larder.
charnière, f. hinge.
charnu, e, a. fleshy.
charnure, f. flesh, skin.
charogne, f. carrion.
charpente, f. timber-work || skeleton.
charpenter, v. a. to work timber, to hack.
charpenterie, f. carpentry.
charpentier, m. carpenter.
charpie, f. lint.
charretée, f. cart-load.
charretier, m. carman, carter, waggoner.
charrette, f. cart.
charriage, m. cartage.
charrier, v. a. & n. to cart || to carry by waggon.
charroi, m. cartage. [waggon.
charron, m. wheelwright.
charronnage, m. wheelwright's work.
charroyer, v. a. & n. vide charrier.
charrue, f. plough. [charter-party.
charte, f. charter || ~~partie, f. (mar.)

chartre, f. charter || ~ privée, arbitrary ou illegal confinement. [convent.
chartreuse, f. Carthusian nun || Carthusian
chartreux, m. Carthusian friar.
Charybde, m. Charybdis || tomber de ~ en Scylla, out of the frying-pan into the fire.
chas, m. eye of a needle || starch.
chasse, f. hunting, coursing || game || chase || pursuit || chien de ~, hound || ~ au tir, shooting || ~ aux oiseaux, fowling || à courre, coursing || ~-infernale, Arthur's chase || ~-marée, m. fish-cart || lugger || ~-mouches, m. fly-flap || ~-pierres, m. (rail.) cow-catcher, guard-irons || ~-roues, m. spur-post.
châsse, f. shrine || frame.
chasser, v. a. & n. to put to flight, to drive out, to discharge || to dislodge, to dispel || to hunt || to shoot || to pursue || to drag || ~ de race, to take after one's parent.
chasseresse, f. (poét.) huntress.
chasseur, m. huntsman, sportsman || -s, pl. light infantry ou cavalry.
chasseuse, f. huntress.
chassie, f. blearedness.
chassieux, se, a. blear-eyed.
châssis, m. sash, frame.
chassoir, m. cooper's driver.
chaste, a. (-ment, ad.) chaste(ly) || decent(ly) || innocent(ly).
chasteté, f. chastity.
chat, m. cat || darling || acheter ~ en poche, to buy a pig in a poke || ~-huant, m. screech-owl.
châtaigne, f. chestnut.
châtaigneraie, f. grove of chestnut-trees.
châtaignier, m. chestnut-tree.
châtain, e, a. chestnut colour, nut-brown.
château, m. castle, fort || mansion || -x en Espagne, castles in the air.
chateaubriand, m. rumpsteak.
châtelain, m. lord of a manor || castellan.
châtelaine, f. lady of a manor || chain || scarf.
châtelet, m. little castle.
châtier, v. a. to chastise, to punish, to scourge.
chatière, f. cat's hole.
châtiment, m. chastisement, punishment.
chatoiement, s. play of colours, glistening.
chaton, m. kit || bezil || catkin. [ling.
chatouillement, m. tickling.
chatouiller, v. a. to tickle.
chatouilleux, se, a. ticklish || touchy.
chatoyant, e, a. changing colour || glistening || shot-coloured.
châtrer, v. a. to castrate, to geld.
chattée, f. cat's litter.
chattemit(t)e, f. bland hypocrite || faire la ~, to put on a demure look. [sweets.
chatterie, f. petting, coquetry, flattery ||
chaud, m. heat, warmth.
chaud, e, a. hot, warm || ardent || passionate || vivid || fresh || avoir ~, faire ~, to be warm.
chaudement, ad. warmly, eagerly.
chaudière, f. large kettle, boiler.
chaudron, m. caldron, boiler.
chaudronnerie, f. coppersmith's trade ou wares.

chaudronnier, m. brazier || coppersmith ||
chauffage, m. fuel || warming.   [tinker.
chauffe, m. warmer || ~-assiettes, m.
plate-warmer.
chauffer, v. a. & n. to heat, to warm, to
get up steam || to get hot *ou* warm || to give
heat.   [dish.
chaufferette, f. foot-warmer || chafing-
chauffeur, m. stoker || chauffeur.
chauffeuse, f. low-seated chair.
chauffoir, m. warming-place || warm cloth.
chaufour, m. lime-kiln.
chaufournier, m. lime-burner.
chaulage, m. liming seed-corn.
chauler, v. a. to lime seed-corn.
chaume, m. stubble || stubble-field || thatch.
chaumière, f. thatched house, cottage.
chaussée, f. causeway || road || bank.
chausse, ~-pied, f. shoe-horn || ~-trape,
f. (mil.) caltrop || trap, snare.
chausser, v. a. & n. to put on shoes *ou*
boots || to make shoes *ou* boots || to suit,
to fit || to have a foot of a certain length ||
se ~, to put on one's shoes, etc. || to be-
come possessed of (an idea).
chaussette, f. half-stocking, sock.
chausson, m. sock || list-shoe || pump ||
chaussure, f. shoes, boots, etc. || dumpling.
chauve, a. bald || ~-souris, f. bat.
chauvinisme, m. party fanaticism || jin-
chaux, f. lime || lime-stone.   [goism.
chavirer, v. a. to upset || (mar.) to capsize.
chébec, m. xebec.
chef, m. chief, head, leader, commander ||
foreman || principal || fag-end || degree ||
count || own right || ~-d'œuvre, m.
master-piece, trial-piece || ~-lieu, m.
chief-town, county-town.
chemin, m. way, path, road || means || ~
de fer, railway || ~ de traverse, cross-
road || en ~, ~ faisant, by the way.
cheminée, f. chimney, fire-place || chimney-
piece || mantelpiece || nipple.
cheminer, v. a. to walk, to go on.
chemise, f. shirt, shift || cover.
chemisette, f. front || under-waistcoat.
chemisier, ère, m. & f. shirt-maker.
chênaie, f. grove of oaks.
chenal, m. channel || track.
chenapan, m. vagabond, scamp.
chêne, m. oak.
chenet, m. andiron || fire-dog.
chènevière, f. hemp-field.
chènevis, m. hemp-seed.
chenil, m. dog-kennel.
chenille, f. caterpillar || silk-velvet twist.
chenu, e, a. hoary, gray-headed || bald.
cheptel, m. lease of cattle.
chéquard, m. check-bearer.
chèque, m. check (in banking) || (rail.)
luggage-bill.
cher, ère, a. & ad. dear(ly) || fond(ly).
chercher, v. a. to search, to look for || to try
chercheur, se, m. & f. seeker, searcher.
chère, f. cheer, fare, living || faire bonne
~, to live high *ou* well.
chèrement, ad. dearly || at a high price.
chérir, v. a. to cherish, to love dearly.
cherté, f. dearness.

chérubin, m. cherub.
chérubinique, a. chubby, cherry-cheeked.
chervis, m. skirret.
chester, s. Chester cheese.
chétif, ve, a. (-vement, ad.) mean(ly) ||
vile(ly) || pitiful(ly) || poor(ly).
cheval, m. horse || ~ entier, stallion || ~
de bât, pack-horse || ~ de trait, draught-
horse || ~ de relais, fresh horse || ~ de
course, race-horse || ~ de bataille,
charger || ~ de main, led-horse || ~ de
race, blood-horse, thoroughbred || ~ de
selle, saddle-horse.
chevaleresque, a. chivalrous.
chevalerie, f. chivalry || knighthood.
chevalet, m. wooden horse || (violin's)
bridge || easel || buttress.
chevalier, m. knight || defender || suitor ||
~ d'industrie, card-sharper, swindler.
chevalière, f. knight's lady || ring.
chevaline, a. equine.
chevaucher, v. n. to ride || to overlap.
chevau-léger, m. (mil.) light horseman ||
light horse.
chevaux-de-frise, m. pl. (mil.) chevaux-
de-frise, defensive iron spikes.
chevelu, e, a. hairy || long-haired.
chevelure, f. hair of the head || crest,
beard || head of hair.
chevet, m. bolster || bed-side || bedhead.
cheveu, m. hair.
cheville, f. peg, bolt || plug || ankle || ~
ouvrière, pole-bolt || main spring.
cheviller, v. a. to peg, to pin || to bolt.
chevillette, f. small peg.
chèvre, f. she-goat || gin || crane.
chevreau, m. kid.
chèvre-feuille, m. (bot.) honey-suckle.
chevrette, f. roe, doe || shrimp.
chevreuil, m. roe-buck.
chevrier, m. goat-herd.
chevrillard, m. young roe-buck.
chevron, m. rafter || coping || stripe.
chevrotant, e, a. tremulous.
chevrotement, m. singing with a quiver-
ing voice.   [tremulous voice || to shake.
chevroter, v. n. to kid || to sing in a
chevrotine, f. deer-shot.
chez, pr. at, to, in (one's house) || among,
amongst || ~ soi, at home || avoir un ~
soi, to have a home of one's own.
chiasse, f. dirt || scum.
chic, m. knack || style.
chicane, f. chicanery, pettifogging || cavil ||
chercher ~ à, to pick a quarrel with one.
chicaner, v. a. & n. to cavil, to wrangle
(with) || to shuffle || to quibble || (mar.) to
hug (the wind).
chicanerie, f. chicanery, cavilling.
chicaneur, m. chicaner, quibbler, caviller,
wrangler.
chicanier, ère, m. & f. chicaner, wrangler.
chiche, a. stingy, niggard || -ment, ad.
chicorée, f. chicory || endive.   [stingily.
chicot, m. stump.   [nibble.
chicoter, v. n. (fam.) to split hairs || to
chicotin, m. juice of bitter apples.
chien, m. dog || cur || cock (of a gun) || ~
courant, beagle || ~ couchant, ~ d'ar-

rêt, pointer || ~ basset, terrier || entre ~ et loup, in the dusk of the evening || faire le ~ couchant, to cringe.

chien, ne, a. dogged || hard || close || ~ de, de ~, wretched.   [grass.

chiendent, m. (bot.) couch-grass, dog's-

chienne, f. bitch.

chier, v. a. & n. (fam.) to shite.

chiffe, f. poor cloth, rag.

chiffon, m. rag || ~s, pl. dress, finery.

chiffonné, e, a. rumpled || delicate and irregular.

chiffonner, v. a. to rumple, to tease.

chiffonnier, ère, m. & f. rag-picker || tell-tale || chiffonnier (furniture).

chiffre, m. cipher || figure, number.

chiffrer, v. a. & n. to cipher || to write in cipher.

chiffreur, m. calculator.   [ciphers.

chignon, m. nape || chignon, hair twisted in a knot behind.

chimère, f. chimera.

chimérique, a. chimerical.

chimie, f. chemistry.

chimique, a. chemical.

chimiste, m. chemist.

chiné, e, a. variegated.

chinoiserie, f. chinese ornaments || folly || oddity.

chiourme, f. convicts (on a galley).

chiper, v. a. (fam.) to crib, to prig, to bag.

chipie, f. pert woman ou girl.

chipoter, v. n. to trifle || to haggle || to chipotier, m. trifler.   [nibble.

chique, f. quid of tobacco.

chiquenaude, f. fillip.

chiquer, v. n. to chew tobacco || to grub.

chiquet, m. dribblet.

chiqueur, m. tobacco-chewer.

chiragre, f. (méd.) chiragra.

chiromancien, m. chiromancer.

chirurgical, e, a. surgical.

chirurgie, f. surgery.

chirurgien, m. surgeon.

chiste, m. cyst (tumor).

chiure, f. dirt || fly-blow.

chlore, m. chlorine.   [drochloric.

chlorhydrique, a. (chim.) muriatic, hy-

chloroforme(is)er, v. a. to chloroform.

chlorose, f. green-sickness.

chlorure, m. (chim.) chloride.

choc, m. shock, collision, attack, onset.

chocolat, m. chocolate.

chocolatier, m. chocolate-seller.

chocolatière, f. chocolate-pot.

chœur, m. choir || chorus.

choir, v. n. ir. to fall, to tumble.

choisi, e, a. choice, select.

choisir, v. n. to choose, to elect || to select.

choix, m. choice, election, option || best

cholérine, f. cholerine.   [part.

cholérique, m. & f. person affected with cholera, cholera patient.

cholérique, a. choleric.   [rest.

chômage, m. want of work || stoppage ||

chômer, v. a. & n. to keep holiday || to want work || to strike || (agr.) to lie fallow || ~ de besogne, to be out of work.

chope, f. pint.

chopine, f. half pint.

choquant, e, a. shocking, offensive.

choquer, v. a. & n. to shock, to strike against, to clash || to offend || se ~, to strike against one another, to clash together || to take offence || to engage.

chorégraphie, f. choregraphy.

choriste, m. chorister.

chose, f. thing, matter || quelque ~, something || ~ publique, common weal || sur toutes ~s, above all, above all things || ce n'est pas grand' ~, 'tis no great matter.

chou, m. cabbage || puff-cake || faire ~ blanc, to draw a blank || ~ cabus, ~ pommé, cabbage || ~ frisé, Savoy cabbage || ~ gras, (fig.) delight || profit || ~ marin, sea-kale || ~ navet, turnip-cabbage || ~ vert, bore-cole, kale || ~-fleur, cauliflower.

choucas, m. jackdaw.   [m. cauliflower.

choucroute, f. sourcrout.

chouette, f. owl, owlet.

choyer, v. a. to fondle, to pamper || to take great care of.

chrême, m. chrism.

chrestomathie, f. selection of extracts.

chrétien, ne, m. & f. Christian.

chrétien, ne, a. (~nement, ad.) christian(ly) || christianlike.

chrétienté, f. Christianity || Christendom.

christianisme, m. Christianity.

chromatique, a. (mus.) chromatic.

chromolithographie, f. chromo-litho-chronique, f. chronicle.   [graphy.

chronique, a. chronic.

chroniqueur, m. chronicler.

chronologie, f. chronology.

chronologique, a. chronological.

chronomètre, m. chronometer.

chrysalide, f. chrysalis.

chrysanthème, m. (bot.) chrysanthemum.

chuchotement, m. whispering in the ear.

chuchoter, v. n. to whisper in the ear.

chuchoterie, f. whispering.

chuchoteur, m. whisperer.

chut! hush!

chute, f. fall, falling, downfall || ruin, failure, miscarriage || cadence.

chuter, v. n. to fail, to be damned (of theatre pieces).

ci, ad. here || ~-après, hereafter || ~-devant, former(ly) || (of) late || ~-dessous, hereafter, underneath || ~-dessus, above-said || ~-joint, hereto annexed || par ~, par là, here and there || ~-gît, here lies.

cible, f. target.

ciboire, m. pyx.

ciboule, f. scallion, eschalot.

ciboulette, f. chives.

cicatrice, f. scar.

cicatriser, v. a. to heal || to scar.

cidre, m. cider.

ciel, m. sky, heaven || air, climate, country.

cierge, m. wax-taper.

cieux, m. pl. de ciel, heavens (pl.).

cigale, f. grass-hopper.

cigare, m. cigar.

cigarette, f. cigarette.

cigogne, f. stork.

ciguë, f. (bot.) water-hemlock.

cil, m. eye-lash.

cilice, m. hair-cloth.   [winking.
cillement, m. twinkling of the eye-lids ‖
ciller, v. a. to twinkle, to wink.
cime, f. top, summit.
ciment, m. cement ‖ tie, bond.
cimenter, v. a. to cement.
cimeterre, f. scimitar, falchion.
cimetière, f. cemetery, churchyard.
cimier, m. crest ‖ buttock.
cinabre, m. cinnabar.
cinéma(tographe), m. cinema(tograph).
cinéraire, a. cinerary, full of ashes.
cingler, v. a. & n. to lash, to switch.
cinq, m. a five (at cards) ‖ cinque (at
cinq, a. five.   [dice).
cinquantaine, f. fifty ‖ age of fifty.
cinquante, a. fifty.
cinquantième, m. fiftieth, fiftieth part.
cinquantième, a. fiftieth.
cinquième, m. fifth, fifth part ‖ fifth floor.
cinquième, a. (-ment, ad.) fifth(ly).
cintre, m. arch, semicircle.
cintré, e, a. (of windows) bow
cintrer, v. a. to arch.
cipaye, m. Sepoy.
cirage, m. waxing, blacking.
circoncire, v. a. to circumcise.
circonflexe, a. (gr.) circumflex.
circonscrire, v. a. ir to circumscribe.
circonspect, e, a. circumspect, cautious.
circonstance, f. circumstance ‖ occasion ‖
  de ~, made for ou necessitated by the occasion ‖ accidental ‖ transient.
circonstancié, e, a. circumstantial.
circonstancier, v. a. to detail.
circonvenir, v. a. ir. to circumvent, to
deceive.   [rounding.
circonvoisin, e, a. neighbouring, sur-
circuit, m. (fig.) circumlocution.
circulaire, f. circular ‖ circular letter.
circulaire, a. (-ment, ad.) circular(ly).
circulant, e, a. circulating ‖ in circulation.   [traffic.
circulation, f. circulation, currency ‖
circulatoire, a. circulatory.
circuler, v. n. to circulate, to move round.
cire, f. wax.   [black.
cirer, v. a. to wax ‖ to clean, to polish ‖ to
cireux, se, a. waxy.
cirier, m. wax-chandler ‖ wax-shrub.
ciron, m. flesh-worm.
cirque, m. circus.
cisaille, f. shears ‖ clippings.   [shears.
ciseau, m. chisel ‖ -x, m. pl. scissors ‖
ciseler, v. a. to carve ‖ to chisel.
ciselet, m. graver ‖ small chisel.
ciseleur, m. chaser ‖ carver.
ciselure, f. chasing ‖ carving.
citadelle, f. citadel.
citadin, m. townsman, citizen.
citadine, f. townswoman ‖ cab.
citateur, m. quoter.   [tion.
citation, f. citation, summons ‖ quota-
cité, f. city ‖ the citizens.
citer, v. a. to cite, to summon ‖ to quote.
citérieur, e, a. hither.
citerne, f. cistern ‖ pit.
citoyen, m. citizen.
citoyenne, f. free-woman of a city.

citron, m. lemon ‖ lemon-colour.
citronnat, m. candied lemon-peel.
citronné, e, a. lemon-flavoured.   [wood.
citronnelle, f. citron-water ‖ southern-
citronnier, m. lemon-tree ‖ satin-wood.
citrouille, f. pumpkin.   [hare.
civet, m. stew ‖ ~ de lièvre, jugged
civette, f. chives ‖ civet-cat ‖ civet.
civière, f. hand-barrow ‖ stretcher.
civil, e, a. (-ement, ad.) civil(ly).
civilisateur, trice, a. civilising.
civilisation, f. civilisation.
civiliser, v. a. to civilise ‖ se ~, to become civilised.
civilité, f. civility ‖ -s, pl. compliments.
civique, a. civic.   [noise.
clabaudage, m. barking ‖ troublesome
clabauder, v. n. to bark without cause ‖
to bawl.
clabauderie, f. clamour, bawling.
clabaudeur, se, m. & f. bawler.
claie, f. hurdle ‖ screen.
clair, m. light ‖ light part ‖ sure part ‖ ~
de lune, moonlight.
clair, e, a. clear, bright, light, transparent ‖
clean ‖ limpid, pure ‖ perspicuous, intelligible ‖ ~ et net, (com.) all expenses
deducted ‖ ~, ad. clearly, plainly ‖ evidently.
clairement, ad. clearly, evidently.
clairet, te, a. light red, pale.
claire-voie, f. opening of a garden-wall ‖
à ~, in open-work ‖ open.
clairière, f. glade.   [light and shade.
clair-obscur, m. (peint.) clare-obscure.
clairon, m. clarion.
clair-semé, e, a. thinly sown ‖ scarce.
clairvoyance, f. perspicacity ‖ self-con-
templation.
clairvoyant, e, a. clear-sighted.
clameur, f. clamour, outcry.   [lazy dog.
clampin, clanpin, m. slowcoach, laggard ‖
clampiner, v. n. to lag ‖ to linger.
clandestin, e, a. (-ement, ad.) clandes-
tine(ly) ‖ secret(ly).
clapet, m. clapper, clack.
clapier, m. rabbit-burrow, hutch.
clapir, v. n. to squeak (like a rabbit) ‖ se
~, to squat.
clapotage, m. (mar.) chopping.
clapoter, v. n. to chop.
clapoteux, se, a. rolling, swelling.
claque, f. slap ‖ clog ‖ (in theatres) clap-
claque, m. opera hat.   [pers.
claquement, m. clapping ‖ snapping ‖
chattering ‖ smacking ‖ cracking.
claquemurer, v. a. to shut up.
claquer, v. a. & n. to clap, to flap ‖ to
smack, to clack ‖ to smack (a whip) ‖ to
snap (one's fingers).   [box.
claquet, m. mill-clapper, rattle ‖ chatter-
claqueur, m. clapper.
clarifier, v. a. to clarify ‖ se ~, to' get
clarine, f. little bell.   [clear.
clarinette, f. clarinet.
clarté, f. clearness, brightness ‖ light.
classe, f. class, order, rank ‖ set ‖ form,
school, school-room ‖ scholars of a class ‖
school-time ‖ en ~, at school.

classement, m. classing.
classer, v. a. to class.
classification, f. classification.
classifier, v. a. to classify.
classique, a. classic(al) || correct || standard||
claude, m. simpleton.   [school . . .
claudication, f. lameness, limping.
clause, f. clause.
claveau, m. rot || key-stone.
clavecin, m. harpsichord.
clavelé, e, a. infected with the rot.
clavelée, f. rot || scab (of sheep).
clavette, f. (mus.) key || peg || collar.
clavicule, f. collar-bone.
clavier, m. (mus.) key-ring || key-board.
clayon, m. small hurdle || stand.
clayonnage, f. wattle-fence || wicker.
clé, clef, f. key || plug || crown || wrench ||
  (mus.) tuning-hammer || leader || (mus.)
  clef || ~ de voûte, key-stone || sous ~,
  under lock and key.
clématite, f. (bot.) clematis.
clémence, f. clemency.
clément, e, a. clement.
clerc, m. clerk || clergyman || scholar.
clergé, m. clergy.
clérical, e, a. (–ement, ad.) clerical(ly).
clichage, m. stereotyping.
cliché, m. stereotype plate.
clicher, v. a. to stereotype.
clicheur, m. stereotyper.
client, e, m. & f. client || customer || patient.
clientèle, f. clientship || clients || practice ||
  custom || good-will.
clignement, m. winking.
cligner, v. a. to wink || to twinkle.
clignotement, m. twinkling || winking.
clignoter, v. n. to twinkle || to wink.
climat, m. climate, clime.
climatérique, a. climacteric.
clin (d'œil), m. twinkling (of an eye) ||
  trice.   [ou hospital.
clinique, f. clinical medicine ou surgery
clinquant, m. tinsel || foil.
clique, f. set, gang, party, clique.
cliquet, m. mill-clapper || hitch, stop.
cliqueter, v. n. to clack.
cliquetis, m. clashing.
cliquettes, f. pl. snappers, clappers.
clisse, f. wicker || splint.
clisser, v. a. to case in wicker-work.
cloaque, m. sink, sewer.
cloche, f. bell || glass-bell || diving-bell ||
  dish-cover || blister.
clochement, m. limping || limp.
(à)cloche-pied, ad. hopping || sauter à
  ~, to hop.   [hobble, to go lame.
clocher, m. steeple || parish || ~, v. n. to
clocheton, m. bell-turret.
clochette, f. hand-bell || bell-flower.
cloison, f. partition || of masonry).
cloisonnage, m. partition-work || wain-
cloître, m. cloister.   [scoting.
cloîtrer, v. a. to cloister || to immure.
clopin-clopant, ad. hobbling along.
clopiner, v. a. to hobble.
cloporte, m. wood-louse.
clore, v. a. ir. to close || to enclose || to
  end || to seal up.

clos, m. close (of a cathedral) || enclosure.
clos, e, a. closed, shut up.
closeau, m., closerie, f. small close ||
  little orchard.   [seclusion || closure.
clôture, f. enclosure, fence || closing ||
clôturer, v. a. to close (an account).
clou, m. nail, stud || boil || chief attraction
  of an exhibition || ~ de girofle, clove ||
  ~ à crochet, tenter-hook || mettre au
  ~, to pawn.
clouer, v. a. to nail, to tack || to spike.
clouter, v. a. to stud.
clouterie, f. nail-trade || nail-forge || nails.
cloutier, m. nail-maker.
cloyère, f. oyster-basket.
clubiste, m. member of a club.
clysoir, m. injection-tube, enema.
clysopompe, m. injecting-apparatus,
  clyster-pump.
clystère, m. enema || injection.
coaccusé, e, m. & f. (jur.) accomplice ||
  fellow-prisoner.
coadjuteur, trice, m. & f. coadjutor ||
  coadjutrix.
coaguler, v. a. to coagulate.
se coaliser, v. to league.
coalition, f. coalition || combination.
coassement, m. croaking.
coasser, v. n. to croak.
coassocié, m. co-partner.
cocagne, f.; pays de ~, land of milk and
  honey || mât de ~, greasy pole.
cocarde, f. cockade.   [rum.
cocasse, a. odd, comical, funny, (fam.)
coccinelle, f. lady-bird.
coccyx, m. (anat.) coccyx.
coche, m. stage-coach || barge || ~, f. notch
  || la mouche du ~, a busybody.
cochenille, f. cochineal.
cocher, m. coachman, driver.
cochère, a.; porte–~, f. carriage-entrance.
cochon, m. hog, pig || pork || ~ d'Inde,
  Guinea-pig || ~ de lait, sucking-pig.
cochonnée, f. farrow.   [bungle.
cochonner, v. a. & n. to farrow || to
cochonnerie, f. filthiness, nastiness ||
  blackguard trick.
cochonnet, m. (jeu) the "jack" at bowls.
coco, m. cocoa || liquorice-water || chap.
cocon, m. cocoon.   [saucepan.
cocotte, f. chickabiddy || pet || egg-boiler ||
cocotier, m. cocoa-tree.
cocotte, f. fast woman, street-walker.
cocu, m. cuckold.
codébiteur, m. joint-debtor.
codétenteur, m. joint-holder.
codex, m. code || (méd.) pharmacopœia.
codicille, m. codicil.
codifier, v. a. to codify.
cœur, m. heart || courage || vigour || mind,
  desire || inner part, centre || soul || à
  contre–~, against one's will || de tout
  mon ~, with all my heart || par ~, by
  heart || mal de ~, qualmishness, sickness
  || avoir mal au ~, to be sick at the
  stomach.
coexister, v. n. to coexist.   [stomach.
coffre, m. chest, trunk, coffer || box || bin ||
  seat.
coffrer, v. a. to put in a box || to lock up.

coffret, f. little chest *ou* trunk.

coffretier, m. trunk-maker.

cognac, m. Cognac brandy.

cognasse, f. wild quince.

cognassier, m. quince-tree.

cognée, f. hatchet, axe.

cogner, v. a. to drive *ou* knock in || to beat.

cohabiter, v. n. to cohabit.

cohérent, e, a. coherent.

cohéritier, ère, m. & f. joint-heir || joint-heiress.

cohorte, f. cohort, band.

cohue, f. rout, tumultuous crowd.

coi, te, a. quiet, still || snug.

coiffe, f. head-dress || lining || child's caul.

coiffer, v. a. & n. to coif, to dress (another's) head, to curl (another's) hair || to fit well, to become || se ~, to dress one's head || to grow fond of (an opinion) || to get tipsy.

coiffeur, m. hair-dresser.   [ing the hair.

coiffure, f. head-dress || manner of dress-

coin, m. corner, angle || marking-iron || stamp || wedge || clock (of a stocking) || les quatre ~s, puss in the corner (game).

coïncider, v. n. to coincide.

coing, m. quince.

col, m. neck || stock, collar.

colback, m. busby.

coléoptère, m. coleoptera || beetle.

colère, f. anger, wrath, passion || en ~, angry.

colère, colérique, a. choleric, irascible.

colibri, m. humming-bird.   [cake.

colifichet, m. trifle, gew gaw, toy || bird-

colimaçon, m. snail.

colin-maillard, m. blindman's-buff

colique, f. colic, gripes.   [(game).

colis, m. bale of goods, package.

Colisée, m. coliseum.

collaborateur, m. fellow-labourer || assistant || associate || contributor.

collaboration, f. co-operation || aid || contribution.   [fining || size.

collage, m. sizing, pasting || hanging ||

collant, e, a. tight.

collation, f. luncheon.

collationner, v. a. & n. to collate || to make a light repast.

colle, f. glue, paste, size || ~ à bouche, lip-glue || ~ de poisson, isinglass.

collecte, f. collect || collection.

collecteur, m. collector.   [(ly).

collectif, ve, a. (-vement, ad.) collective

collectionner, v. a. to make a collection

collectionneur, m. collector.   [(of).

collège, m. college, school || academy.

collégial, e, a. collegial, collegiate || église ~e, collegiate church.

collégien, m. collegian || school-boy.

collègue, m. colleague.

coller, v. a. & n. to paste, to glue together || (at billiards) to get the ball against the cushion || to stick || to fit tight.

collerette, f. tucker || collar.

collet, m. collar || snare || cape || neck || ~ monté, stiff, formal, strait-laced.

colleter, v. a. tc collar, to seize by the collar.   [pasteboard-maker.

colleur, m. paper-hanger || bill-sticker,

collier, m. necklet || necklace || collar || ~ de force, training-collar || ~ de misère,

colline, f. hill, hillock.   [drudgery.

collision, f. collision || conflict.

collocation, f. (jur.) classing.   [logue.

colloque, m. colloquy || conference || dia-

colloquer, v. a. to place || to give || to rank.

collusoire, a. collusive.

collyre, m. eye-salve.

colombaire, m. mortuary chapel with niches for funeral urns.

colombe, f. dove.

colombier, m. pigeon-house.

colombine, f. pigeon's dung.

colon, m. colonist || planter.

colonel, m. colonel.

colonial, e, a. colonial.

colonie, f. colony, settlement.

colonisation, f. colonisation.

coloniser, v. a. to colonise.

colonne, f. column, pillar || defender.

colophane, f. colophony, rosin.

coloquinte, f. colocynth.   [etc.).

colorer, colorier, v. a. to colour (prints

coloris, m. colouring (of a picture) || tint.

coloriste, m. colourist.

colossal, e, a. colossal.

colosse, m. colossus.   [bookstall trade.

colportage, m. hawking || news-vending ||

colporter, v. a. to hawk about.

colporteur, m. pedlar || news-vender.

combat, m. battle, fight || conflict || opposition || ~ singulier, duel || ~ naval, sea-fight || hors de ~, disabled.

combativité, f. combativeness.

combattant, m. combatant.

combattre, v. a. & n. to engage, to fight || to withstand, to struggle against.

combien, ad. how much, how many.

combinaison, f. combination, contrivance || management.

combiner, v. a. to combine || to contrive.

comble, m. top, summit || roof || overmeasure || au ~, complete, to the full || pour ~ de, to crown . . .   [full.

comble, a. full to the top || (fam.) choke-

combler, v. a. to heap, to heap up, to fill, to fill up || to overwhelm (with).

combustible, m. fuel, firing.

comédie, f. comedy, play || play-house || sport, diversion.

comédien, m. player, actor || hypocrite.

comédienne, f. female-player || actress.

comestible, a. eatable || ~s, pl. provisions.

comète, f. comet.

comice, m. meeting || society.

comique, m. comic art || comic || comic author.   [cal(ly).

comique, a. (-ment, ad.) droll(y) || comi-

comité, m. committee || en petit ~, snug little party || among ourselves (themselves).

commandant, m. commander || governor.

commande, f. order || de ~, to order || ordered || feigned || at command || sur ~, to order.   [mand || word of command.

commandement, m. commandment, com-

commander, v. a. & n. to command, to govern, to order || to rule || to overlook ||

se ~, to command oneself || to come at one's call.

commandeur, m. commander.

commanditaire, m. sleeping partner.

commandite, f. limited joint-stock company.

commanditer, v. a. to advance funds to || to take an interest in (as a sleeping partner).

comme, ad. as, as if || like || almost || whereas || how || ~ si, as if, as though.

commémoratif, ve, a. commemorative.

commençant, m. beginner, novice.

commencement, m. beginning.

commencer, v. a. & n. to begin.

commensal, m. messmate.

comment, ad. how, in what manner ? || why ? || ~ donc ! oh dear yes ! || oh dear no ! || to be sure! || ~ donc ? what do you mean ?

commentaire, m. commentary, comment.

commentateur, m. commentator.

commenter, v. a. to comment on.

commérage, m. idle gossiping.

commerçant, m. dealer, trader, merchant.

commerçant, e, a. commercial.

commerce, m. commerce, trade, traffic || intercourse, correspondence.

commercer, v. n. to trade.

commercial, e, a. commercial.

commère, f. godmother || gossip.

commettant, m. (com.) constituent || employer.

commettre, v. a. ir. to commit || to assign, to constitute || to entrust with || to compromise || to set at variance || se ~, to expose oneself.   [m. commercial traveller.

commis, m. clerk || shopman || ~ voyageur,

commissaire, m. commissary, commissioner || ~ de police, commissary of police || ~ priseur, m. appraiser, auctioneer.

commissariat, m. trusteeship || ~ de police, police-station || police-commissaryship.   [errand || committee.

commission, f. commission || message ||

commissionnaire, m. factor || commission-agent || agent || errand-boy.

commissionner, v. a. to commission.

commode, f. chest of drawers.

commode, a. convenient, comfortable || fit || easy || easy to deal with.   [veniently.

commodément, ad. commodiously, con-

commode-toilette, f. toilet-table.

commodité, f. comfort, convenience || accommodation || ~s, pl. water-closet.

commodore, m. (mar.) commodore.

commotion, f. concussion || shock.

commuable, a. commutable.

commuer, v. a. to commute.

commun, m. common || bulk, generality || lower class || ~s, pl. outbuildings || le ~ des martyrs, the common herd.

commun, e, a. common, vulgar || public || ordinary, usual.

communal, e, a. parish, communal.

communard, e, m. & f. follower of the "Commune" of Paris (1871).   [mune."

communard, e, a. belonging to the "Com-

communautaire, a. communistic(al).

communauté, f. commonalty, community, company, corporation || common property.

communaux, m. pl. commons.

commune, f. parish || inhabitants, townhall || ~s, pl. commons.

communément, ad. commonly, generally.

communiant, e, m. & f. communicant.

communicatif, ve, a. communicative.

communication, f. communication, connexion || intercourse.

communier, v. a. & n. to administer the sacrament || to communicate.

communion, f. communion || fellowship.

communiquer, v. a. & n. to communicate, to impart || to inform || to be contiguous to || to have intercourse with.

communisme, m. communism.

commutation, f. commutation.

compacité, f. compactness.

compacte, a. compact, solid, dense.

compagne, f. female companion || spouse.

compagnie, f. company, society || fellowship, partnership || covey.

compagnon, m. companion, associate, colleague, partner, fellow || journeyman || trades-unionist.

compagnonnage, m. trades-union.

comparable, a. comparable.

comparaison, f. comparison || par ~, comparatively.

comparaître, v. a. ir. to appear.

comparatif, m. (gr.) comparative degree, comparative.   [comparative(ly).

comparatif, ve, a. (-vement, ad.)

comparer, v. a. to compare.

comparse, m. figurant, supernumerary.

compartiment, m. compartment.

comparution, f. appearance.

compas, m. compass || pair of compasses || ~ de proportion, sector.   [stiff,

compassé, e, a. very exact || formal,

compassement, m. measurement with compasses || studied regularity.

compasser, v. a. to measure, to arrange || to regulate.   [tion.

compassion, f. compassion, commisera-

compatibilité, f. compatibility.

compatir, v. n. to sympathise with, to compassionate.

compatissant, e, a. compassionate.

compatriote, m. & f. fellow-countryman ou woman.

compenser, v. a. to compensate.

compérage, m. compaternity || godfathership || confederacy || complicity || (fig.) trickery.

compère, m. godfather || pal, accomplice || irony || merry companion || cunning fellow || ~-loriot, m. stye (on the eye).

compétence, f. (jur.) competency || sphere, province, department.

compétent, e, a. competent || suitable.

compétiteur, m. competitor.

compilateur, m. compiler.

compiler, v. a. to compile.   [lament.

complainte, f. complaint || lamentation,

complaire, v. n. ir. to please || se ~, to delight in.

complaisamment, ad. obligingly, with kindness.   [complaisance.
complaisance, f. kindness, compliance.
complaisant, e, m. & f. fawner ‖ panderer.
complaisant, e, a. obliging ‖ compliant, complaisant.
complément, m. complement ‖ object.
complémentaire, a. completing, complementary.
complet, m. full number.
complet, ète, a. complete, perfect ‖ utter.
complétement, m. completion.
complètement, ad. completely, fully.
compléter, v. a. to complete.
complexe, a. complex ‖ compound.
complexion, f. constitution, disposition.
complication, f. complication ‖ intricacy.
complice, m. (jur.) accomplice, accessory ‖ co-respondent (in divorce cases).
complice, a. accessory, privy (to).
complicité, f. complicity.
complies, f. pl. compline.
compliment, m. compliment ‖ congratulation ‖ -s empressés, best compliments ‖ présenter ses -s à, to pay one's compliments, one's respects to.
complimenter, v. a. to compliment, to congratulate.
complimenteur, se, m. & f. complimenter, payer of compliments.
complimenteur, se, a. complimentary.
compliquer, v. a. to complicate.
complot, m. plot, conspiracy, complot.
comploter, v. a. to plot, to conspire.
componction, f. compunction.
comporter, v. a. to allow, to permit ‖ to require ‖ se ~, to behave.
composé, m. compound.   [affected.
composé, e, a. compound, complex ‖ stiff,
composer, v. a. & n. to compose ‖ to write, to invent ‖ to set up type ‖ to compound, to make up, to agree ‖ se ~, to be composed, to consist of.
compositeur, m. composer ‖ compositor.
composition, f. composition, construction ‖ written work, written examination ‖ agreement, accommodation ‖ (peint.) composition.
composteur, m. composing-stick.
compote, f. stewed fruit.
compotier, m. dish for stewed fruit.
comprendre, v. a. ir. to comprehend, to include ‖ to understand, to conceive.
compresse, f. compress.
comprimer, v. a. to compress.
compris, e, a. understood, included ‖ y ~, including, inclusive of, together with.
compromettre, v. a. & n. ir. to compromise ‖ to implicate ‖ to pledge ‖ to put to arbitration ‖ to agree ‖ se ~, to expose
compromis, m. compromise.   [oneself.
comptabilité, f. book-keeping.
comptable, m. accountant.
comptable, a. accountable.
comptant, e, a. ready ‖ argent ~, ready money, cash ‖ au ~, for cash ‖ for delivery.
compte, m. account, reckoning, calculation, computation ‖ a certain number ‖

value ‖ profit ‖ à ~, on account ‖ à bon ~, cheap ‖ ~ rond, even money ‖ ~pas, m. perambulator ‖ ~-rendu, m. report ‖ return.
compter, v. a. & n. to count, to reckon, to pay ‖ to calculate ‖ to value, to estimate ‖ to purpose, to think ‖ to settle accounts ‖ to rely upon ‖ to comprise.
compteur, m. reckoner ‖ teller ‖ meter ‖ gas-meter ‖ trigger.   [bar (of a public house).
comptoir, m. counter, counting-house ‖
compulser, v. a. to examine.
comte, m. count, earl.
comté, m. county, earldom.
comtesse, f. countess.
concasser, v. a. to pound, to bruise.
concasseur, m. crushing-mill.
concave, a. hollow, concave.
concavité, f. concavity.
concéder, v. a. to concede, to grant, to
concentration, f. concentration.   [yield.
concentrer, v. a. to centre, to concentrate.
conception, f. conception ‖ apprehension.
concernant, pr. concerning, relating to.
concerner, v. a. to concern.
concert, m. concert ‖ concert-room ‖ good understanding ‖ de ~, in concert, jointly.
concertant, e, m. & f. performer in a concert.
concerter, v. a. to concert, to contrive ‖ to adjust ‖ se ~, to consult together.
concession, f. concession, grant.
concessionnaire, m. grantee ‖ ~ d'un privilège, patentee.
concevoir, v. a. ir. to conceive, to understand ‖ to entertain ‖ to express, to word.
conchyliologie, f. (hist. nat.) conchology, conchiliology.
concierge, m. door-keeper.
conciergerie, f. porter's lodge ‖ door-keeper's place ‖ a prison in Paris.
concile, m. council.
conciliable, a. reconcilable.
conciliabule, m. conventicle.
conciliateur, m. conciliator.
concilier, v. a. to conciliate ‖ to reconcile.
concis, e, a. concise, short.
concision, f. conciseness, brevity.
concitoyen, m. fellow-citizen.
concluant, e, a. conclusive.
conclure, v. a. & n. ir. to conclude, to finish, to close, to decide ‖ to infer (from).
conclusion, f. conclusion, end ‖ final inference ‖ motion.
concombre, m. cucumber.
concordat, m. concordat, composition ‖ (d'un failli) bankrupt's certificate.
concorde, f. concord, harmony.
concorder, v. n. to agree.
concourir, v. n. ir. to concur, to compete.
concours, m. concourse (of people) ‖ concurrence, co-operation ‖ meeting ‖ competitive examination.
concret, ète, a. concrete.
concubinage, m. (jur.) concubinage.
concupiscence, f. concupiscence.
concurremment, ad. concurrently, in competition with.
concurrence, f. competition.

concurrent, m. competitor.
concussion, f. extortion || peculation.
concussionnaire, m. exactor || peculator.
condamnation, f. condemnation, judgment || passer ~, to pass sentence || to own oneself in fault || not to wish to press the point || ~ en masse, sweeping condemnation.
condamner, v. a. to condemn, to sentence to punishment || to blame, to censure.
condensateur, m. (phys.) condenser.
condenseur, m. (phys.) condenser.
condescendance, f. condescension.
condescendre, v. n. to condescend, to condisciple, m. school-fellow. [comply.
condition, f. condition, quality, property || state, rank, character || place, service || stipulation || –s, pl. terms.
conditionné, e, a. (com.) marketable, in good condition. [ditional(ly).
conditionnel, le, a. (–lement, ad.) conconditionner, v. a. to make conditions.
condoléance, f. condolence.
conducteur, m. conductor, guide, director || (rail.) guard, conductor.
conductrice, f. conductress.
conduire, v. a. ir. to conduct, to lead, to guide, to direct, to rule, to superintend || to accompany, to escort || se ~, to behave || to take care of oneself.
conduit, m. conduit, canal, pipe.
conduite, f. conduct, behaviour || management || leading || driving.
confection, f. making || completion || ready-made clothes department || ready-made clothes || outfitting. [plish.
confectionner, v. a. to make, to accomconfectionneur, m. maker || ready-made clothier || slop-seller || outfitter.
confédération, f. confederation, confederacy.
confédéré, e, m. & f. confederate.
se confédérer, to confederate.
conférence, f. conference || comparison || lecture. [to confer.
conférer, v. a. &n. to compare || to collate ||
confesse, f. confession.
confesser, v. a. to confess || to hear confession || se ~, to confess one's sins || aller se ~, to go to confession.
confesseur, m. confessor.
confiance, f. confidence || reliance || trust.
confiant, e, a. confiding || confident || sanguine.
confidemment, ad. in confidence.
confidence, f. confidence, trust || secrecy || faire une ~, to tell a secret.
confident, m. confident || confidant.
confidentiel, le, a. (–lement, ad.) confidential(ly). [trust.
confier, v. a. to confide || to entrust || to
configuration, f. configuration.
confiner, v. a. &n. to confine (to) || to border (on).
confins, m. pl. confines, limits.
confire, v. a. ir. to preserve || to pickle.
confirmer, v. a. to confirm.
confiserie, f. confectionery.
confiseur, m. confectioner.

confisquer, v. a. to confiscate, to seize confiture, f. jam || sweetmeats. [upon.
conflagration, f. conflagration.
conflit, m. conflict || clashing.
confluent, m. confluent.
confluent, e, a. (méd.) confluent.
confluer, v. n. to meet (with).
confondre, v. a. to confound, to blend, to mingle || to puzzle, to put out of countenance, to stupify || se ~, to mix || to be perplexed || to be lost in || to make no end of. [able.
conforme, a. conformable, agreeable, suitconformément, ad. conformably, suitably.
conformer, v. a. to conform.
conformité, f. conformity.
confort, m. comfort. [comfortably.]
confortable, a. comfortable || –ment, ad.
conforter, v. a. to comfort, to strengthen.
confraternité, f. brotherhood.
confrère, m. brother, fellow-member || contemporary.
confrérie, f. brotherhood.
confrontation, f. confrontation || collation (of writings).
confronter, v. a. to confront || to compare.
confus, e, a. confused || overpowered || jumbled.
confusément, ad. confusedly, dimly.
confusion, f. confusion, confusedness || medley || tumult || shame.
congé, m. leave, furlough || dismissal || warning to quit || jour de ~, holiday.
congédier, v. a. to discharge, to dismiss, to disband.
congélateur, m. refrigerator.
congeler, v. a. to congeal.
congénère, a. congeneric, congenerous.
congénital, e, a. congenital, congenite.
congestion, f. (méd.) congestion, determination of blood.
congre, m. conger, sea-eel.
congrégation, f. congregation.
congrès, m. congress.
conifère, m. coniferous tree.
conique, a. conical, conic.
conjecturalement, ad. by conjecture.
conjecturer, v. a. to conjecture, to guess.
conjoindre, v. a. ir. to unite.
conjoints, m. pl. man and wife.
conjonctive, f. (anat.) conjunctive.
conjoncture, f. conjuncture.
conjonction, f. union (of man and wife) || (gr.) conjunction || (astr.) conjunction, synod.
conjugaison, f. (gr.) conjugation.
conjugal, e, a. (–ement, ad.) conjugal(ly).
conjuguer, v. a. (gr.) to conjugate.
conjurateur, m. plotter, conjuror.
conjuration, f. conspiracy || entreaty || incantation || exorcism.
conjuré, m. conspirator, plotter.
conjuré, e, a. conspiring || leagued.
conjurer, v. a. to conjure || to implore, to conspire.
connaissance, f. knowledge, skill, notion, acquaintance, familiarity || –s, pl. learning, acquirements || âge de ~, years of discretion || de ~, of one's acquaintance ||

familiar || en ~ de cause, knowingly || sans ~, senseless || perdre ~, to faint, to swoon.

connaissement, m. bill of lading.

connaisseur, m. connoisseur, judge || acquaintance-maker.

connaître, v. a. & n. ir. to know || to be acquainted with || to distinguish, to experience || to take cognizance of || se ~, to know oneself || to be a judge of.

connétable, m. constable || Grand Connétable, High Constable.

connexion, f. connection.

connivence, f. connivance.

conniver, v. n. to connive.

connu ! that is an old story !

conque, f. conch || sea-shell.

conquérant, m. conqueror.

conquérir, v. a. ir. to conquer, to subdue || to gain.

conquête, f. conquest.

consacrer, v. a. to consecrate, to dedicate.

consanguin, e, a. consanguineous.

consanguinité, f. consanguinity.

conscience, f. conscience, consciousness || scruple, difficulty || en ~, indeed || avoir de la ~, to be a man of integrity.

consciencieux, se, a. (-sement, ad.) conscientious(ly).

conscription, f. enrolling || recruiting || conscription.

conscrit, m. recruit || greenhorn.

consécutif, ve, a. (-vement, ad.) consecutive(ly).

conseil, m. counsel, advice || counsellor, advocate || council, council-board || ~ d'administration, managing committee || ~ de famille, family council || commission of lunacy || ~ de guerre, court-martial.

conseiller, m. counsellor, adviser || councillor || ~ municipal, alderman.

conseiller, v. a. to counsel, to give advice.

conseillère, f. female adviser || councillor's wife.

consentement, m. consent.

consentir, v. n. ir. to consent, to assent, to agree.   [sistently.

conséquemment, ad. consequently, consequence, f. consequence, conclusion || importance || en ~, consequently || tirer à ~, to be of importance || to be drawn into a precedent.   [sequently.

conséquent, e, a. consistent || par ~, consequently.

conservateur, m. conservator, preserver, defender || commissioner || keeper.

conservation, f. conservation, preservation.   [servatory.

conservatoire, m. school for music || conserve, f. pickle || sweetmeats || (mar.) convoy || -s, pl. preserves.

conserver, v. a. to conserve, to preserve || to maintain || to defend, to protect || se ~, to keep || to take care of one's health.

considérablement, ad. considerably, a great deal.

considérant, m. (jur.) preamble.

considération, f. consideration, regard, esteem.

considérément, ad. considerately.

considérer, v. a. to consider, to examine, to sift || to value, to esteem.

consignataire, m. trustee, consignee.

consignateur, m. consigner.

consignation, f. consignation, deposit.

consigne, f. (mil.) watchword || cloak-room.

consigner, v. a. to consign, to entrust, to deposit || to confine (to a place) || to record.

consistance, f. consistency || thickness || firmness || extent of an estate || credit.

consister, v. n. to consist.

consistoire, m. consistory.

consolateur, trice, m. & f. consoler, comforter || triste ~, Job ou sorry comforter.

consoler, v. a. to console, to comfort.

consolider, v. a. to consolidate.

consolidés, m. pl. consols.

consommateur, m. consumer.

consommation, f. consummation || expense || consumption || refreshments.

consommé, m. jelly-broth, gravy-soup.

consommer, v. a. to consummate || to consume.

consomption, f. consumption || (méd.) atrophy, consumption, decline.

consonne, f. (gr.) consonant.

consorts, m. pl. associates.

consoude, f. comfrey.

conspirateur, m. conspirator.

conspiration, f. conspiracy.

conspirer, v. a. & n. to conspire, to plot.

conspuer, v. a. to scorn.

constamment, ad. constantly.

constance, f. constancy.

constant, e, a. constant, steady, certain || faithful.

constatation, f. proof || statement || authentication.   [establish.

constater, v. a. to aver, to prove || to constellation, f. (astr.) constellation.

consternation, f. consternation, amazement.   [ment.

consterner, v. n. to dismay.

constipation, f. costiveness.

constipé, e, a. costive.

constiper, v. a. to constipate || to bind.

constituant, e, a. constituent.

constituer, v. a. to constitute, to erect || to set, to settle, to establish, to place || to assign, to appoint, to empower || ~ prisonnier, to commit to prison || se ~ prisonnier, to give oneself up.

constitution, f. constitution || settlement.

constitutionnel, le, a. (-lement, ad.) constitutional(ly).

constricteur, m. constrictor.

constructeur, m. builder.

construction, f. construction, building || erection.   [(gr.) to construe.

construire, v. a. ir. to construct, to build ||

consulaire, a. consular.

consulat, m. consulate || consulship.

consultatif, ve, a. consultative.

consulter, v. a. to consult.

consumer, v. a. to consume, to waste, to destroy, to consume.

contact, m. contact || connection.

contagieux, se, a. contagious.

contaminer, v. a. to contaminate.

conte, m. tale, story || ~ **à dormir debout,** stupid stuff || ~ **en l'air,** idle story.

contemplateur, trice, m. & f. contemplator.

contemplatif, ve, a. contemplative.

contempler, v. a. & n. to contemplate || to behold.

contemporain, e, m. & f. contemporary.

contemporain, e, a. contemporary, contemporaneous.

contempteur, m. contemner.

contenance, f. capaciousness || contents || look, deportment.

contenant, m. holder, container.

contenir, v. a. ir. to contain, to hold, to comprise || to restrain from.

content, m. fill, bellyful || **tout son ~,** all one wants.

content, e, a. content, satisfied, pleased.

contentement, m. content, satisfaction, joy.   [satisfied.

contenter, v. a. to content || **se ~,** to be

contentieux, m. law business.

contentieux, se, a. disputable, quarrelsome.

contention, f. contention || contest, debate || intensity.

contenu, m. contents.

conter, v. a. to relate, to tell || **en ~,** to impose upon one || to talk soft nonsense to a woman.

contestable, a. disputable.

contestation, f. contest || debate || strife.

conteste, f. (jur.) dispute.

contester, v. a. to contest.

conteur, se, m. & f. story-teller.

conteur, se, m. & f. fond of relating stories.

contigu, ë, a. contiguous to.

contiguïté, f. contiguity.

continent, m. continent, mainland.

continent, e, a. abstemious || moderate.

continental, e, a. continental.

contingent, m. contingent || share, quota.

contingent, e, a. contingent.

continu, e, a. continual.

continuateur, m. continuer.   [(ly).

continuel, le, a. (-lement, ad.) continual

continuer, v. a. & n. to continue, to go on with, to prolong || to last.

continuité, f. continuance || continuity.

contondant, e, a. blunt.

contorsion, f. contortion.

contour, m. outline || circumference.

contourner, v. a. to outline a figure || to go round, to distort.

contractant, m. contractor.

contractant, e, a. contracting.

contracter, v. a. & n. to contract || to get, to acquire.

contractuel, le, a. stipulated.

contradicteur, m. contradictor, contradictory person.

contradictoire, a. contradictory, inconsistent || **-ment,** ad. contradictorily || inconsistently.   [compel, to restrain.

contraindre, v. a. ir. to constrain, to

contrainte, f. constraint, compulsion, restraint || force || **~ par corps,** arrest (for debt).

contraire, m. contrary.

contraire, a. contrary, adverse, opposite ||

au ~, on the contrary || **au ~ de,** contrary to.   [to incommode.

contrarier, v. a. to contradict, to oppose ||

contrariété, f. contrariety, opposition.

contraste, m. contrast.   [annoyance.

contraster, v. a. & n. to contrast.

contrat, m. contract, compact, covenant.

contravention, f. contravention || offence.

contre, pr. against || contrary to || near by || **par ~,** by way of compensation || **tout ~,** close by || **~-allée,** f. side-alley || **~-amiral,** m. rear-admiral || **~-appel,** m. second call || **~-coup,** m. rebound || result || **~-cœur, (à ~-cœur)** ad. reluctantly, against the grain || **~-danse,** f. countrydance || **~-fort,** m. counterfort || **~-interrogatoire,** m. cross-examination || **~-jour,** m. counterlight, false light || **~-maître,** m. boatswain's mate || foreman || **~-marche,** f. counter-march || **~-mur,** m. counter-mure || **~-murer, v. a.** to countermure || **~-partie,** f. counterpart || reverse || **~-pied,** m. reverse, contrary || **~-poil,** m. wrong way of the hair ou of the nap || **à ~-poil,** against the grain || the wrong way || **~-pointer, v. a.** to quilt on both sides || to thwart || **~-porte,** f. double-door || **~-rail,** m. guard-rail || **~-vérité,** f. irony.

contrebande, f. contraband || smuggling || **faire la ~,** to smuggle.

contrebandier, m. smuggler.

contrecarrer, v. a. to thwart, to oppose.

contredire, v. a. ir. to contradict, to refute.

contredit, m. contradiction || **sans ~,** unquestionably.

contrée, f. country, region.

contrefaçon, f. counterfeiting || literary piracy || plagiarism || spurious edition.

contrefacteur, m. counterfeiter, pirate || imitator || plagiarist.

contrefaire, v. a. ir. to counterfeit, to forge || to copy, to imitate || to disguise, to disfigure || to pirate || **se ~,** to dissemble.

contremandement, m. counter-order.

contremander, v. a. to countermand.

contremarque, f. counter-mark || check

contrescarpe, f. counter-scarp.   [(ticket).

contresens, m. opposite || misconstruction || contrary sense || wrong side.

contresignataire, m. countersigner.

contresigner, v. a. to countersign.

contretemps, m. contrary accident, disappointment, mischance || **à ~,** unseasonably.

contrevallation, f. countervallation.

contrevenant, m. transgressor, offender.

contrevenant, e, a. transgressing, offending.   [to offend (against).

contrevenir, v. n. ir. to act contrary (to) ||

contrevent, m. outside shutter.

contribuable, m. tax-payer || rate-payer.

contribuant, m. contributor.

contribuer, v. n. to contribute.

contribution, f. contribution || tax.

contrister, v. a. to grieve.

contrit, e, a. contrite.

contrôle, m. control, control-book || rolls (pl.) || file || controller's office.

contrôler, v. a. to control, to register || to stamp || to try.

contrôleur, m. controller || ticket-collector || censurer. [falsely.

controuver, v. a. to forge, to contrive

controverse, f. controversy.

controverser, v. a. to controvert.

controversiste, m. controversialist.

contumace, f. contumacy, non-appearance, default.

contusion, f. contusion, bruise.

contusionner, v. a. to bruise.

convaincant, e, a. convincing. [vict.

convaincre, v. a. ir. to convince || to convalescent, e, a. convalescent.

convenable, a. becoming, suitable, proper, seasonable || —ment, ad. duly || suitably, becomingly, conformably || expediently.

convenance, f. convenience, congruity, suitableness, fitness, propriety, decency || harmony, agreement, proportion || —s, pl. good manners.

convenir, v. n. ir. to agree, to become || to own, to grant, to confess || to fit, to be [suitable.

conventicule, f. conventicle.

convention, f. convention, treaty, meeting.

conventionnel, m. member of the French national assembly.

conventionnel, le, a. (—lement, ad.) conventional || by agreement.

conventuel, le, a. (—lement, ad.) conventual(ly).

convergent, e, a. converging.

converger, v. n. to converge.

convers, e, a. lay.

conversation, f. conversation, discourse.

converser, v. n. to converse, to talk.

converti, e, m. & f. convert.

convertir, v. a. to convert, to turn, to change || se ~, to be converted, to turn.

convertissement, m. conversion.

convertisseur, m. converter.

convexe, a. convex.

convexité, f. convexity

convié, m. guest.

convier, v. a. to invite || to incite, to allure.

convive, m. convive, guest || table-companion. [summons.

convocation, f. convocation, requisition ||

convoi, m. burial, funeral procession || convoy (of provisions) || railway-train.

convoiter, v. a. to covet.

convoitise, f. (fam.) covetousness.

convoler, v. n. to marry, to marry again.

convoquer, v. a. to convoke, to summon.

convoyer, v. a. (mar., mil.) to convoy.

convoyeur, m. (mar.) convoy-ship.

convulsif, ve, a. (—vement, ad.) convulsive(ly).

conyze, f. (bot.) flea-bane.

coopérateur, m. co-operator.

coopérer, v. a. to co-operate.

coordination, f. co-ordination.

coordonner, v. a. to render co-ordinate.

copahu, m. (bot.) copaiva.

copain, m. joint-share holder, partner || school-friend || être le ~ de, (fam.) to go halves with. [(in).

copartageant, m. co-partner, joint-sharer

copeau, m. chip || —x, pl. shavings.

copie, f. copy, duplicate || manuscript.

copier, v. a. to copy, to imitate.

copieux, se, a. (—sement, ad.) copious (ly) || hearty || heartily.

copiste, m. copyist, copier.

copropriétaire, m. joint-proprietor.

coq, m. cock || male (of birds) || weather-cock || ~ de bruyère, heath-cock, grouse || ~ d'Inde, turkey-cock || ~-à-l'âne, m. nonsense.

coque, f. shell || cocoon || cockle || hull.

coquecigrue, f. fiddle-faddle.

coquelicot, m. (bot.) wild poppy.

coqueluche, f. whooping-cough || être la ~ de, to be a great favourite with.

coquemar, m. boiler.

coquet, m. beau, dandy || cock-boat.

coquet, te, a. coquettish || fond of dress || stylish, elegant.

coqueter, v. n. to flirt || to coquette.

coquetier, m. egg-cup.

coquette, f. coquette, flirt, jilt.

coquetterie, f. flirtation, coquetry || love of dress || spruceness, quaintness.

coquillage, m. shell-fish || shell-work.

coquille, f. shell || pat.

coquillier, m. collection of shells.

coquin, m. rogue, rascal, knave.

coquine, f. slut, wretch, jade.

coquinerie, f. roguish trick, knavery.

cor, m. horn || corn || ~ de chasse, French horn || à ~ et à cri, loudly || vehemently.

corail, m. coral.

corailleur, m. coral-fisher.

corbeau, m. raven.

corbeille, f. little osier-basket || wedding-presents || flower-bed.

corbillard, m. hearse.

corbillat, m. young raven.

corbillon, m. small basket.

cordage, m. cordage, rigging, ropes.

corde, f. cord, rope, line || string || thread of cloth || cat-gut || chord || ~ de violon, [violin-string.

cordeau, m. line, string.

cordeler, v. a. to twist.

cordelette, f. small cord.

cordelier, m. Franciscan friar.

cordelière, f. Franciscan nun || Franciscan's [girdle.

cordelle, f. tow-line.

corder, v. a. to twist, to cord.

corderie, f. rope-walk, rope-yard, ropery.

cordial, m. cordial, stimulant.

cordial, e, a. (—ement, ad.) cordial(ly).

cordialité, f. cordiality.

cordier, m. rope-maker.

cordon, m. lace, string, band || edge (of a coin) || twist || le ~, s'il vous plaît! open the door, please! || ~ bleu, first-rate cook || knight of the Holy Ghost.

cordonner, v. a. to twist, to entwine || to line || to edge.

cordonnerie, f. shoe-maker's trade.

cordonnet, m. twist, netting-silk.

cordonnier, m. shoe-maker.

cordouan, m. cordwain.

coreligionnaire, m. & f. co-religionist.

coriace, a. tough as leather.

coriandre, f. coriander.

corinthien, m. Corinthian order.
corme, m. sorb-apple.
cormier, m. service-tree.
cormoran, m. cormorant || (fig.) glutton.
cornac, m. elephant-driver.
cornage, m. blowing, roaring (of horses).
cornaline, m. cornelian stone.
cornard, a. cuckold.
corne, f. horn || hoof || shoe-horn || corner || dog's ear (in books).
corné, e, a. horny.
cornée, f. (anat.) cornea.
corneille, f. rook, crow.
cornement, m. tingling of the ears.
cornemuse, f. bag-pipe.
corner, v. a. & n. to blare out, to blurt out || to speak through a speaking-trumpet || (of the ears) to tingle.
cornet, m. horn || speaking-trumpet || dice-box || inkhorn || paper-cornet || rolled wafer || ~ acoustique, ear-trumpet || ~ à pistons, key-horn. [pendant.
cornette, f. lady's night-cap || (mar.) broad
corneur, m. French-horn blower.
corniche, f. cornice.
cornichon, m. little horn || gherkin || ninny.
cornier, ère, a. corner.
cornière, f. (tech.) corner channel || corner-iron || angle-iron.
cornouille, f. dog-berry.
cornouiller, m. cornel-tree, dog-wood.
cornu, e, a. horned || angular || absurd.
cornue, f. (chim.) retort. [extravagant.
corollaire, m. corollary.
corolle, f. corolla, petal.
corporation, f. corporation, body corporate.
corporel, le, a. (-lement, ad.) corporeal (ly) || material(ly).
corps, m. body || corporation, company || ~ à ~, hand to hand || à ~ perdu, head-long || with might and main || ~ mort, dead body, corpse || ~ d'un vaisseau, hull of a ship || ~ de logis, shell of a house || suit of rooms || ~ de bataille, the main army || ~ de garde, guard-house || garde-du-~, (mil.) life-guard.
corpulent, e, a. corpulent.
corpusculaire, a. corpuscular.
corpuscule, m. corpuscle.
correct, e, a. (-ement, ad.) correct(ly).
correcteur, m. corrector, reformer || reader.
correctrice, se, a. corrective, correcting.
correctif, m. corrective.
correctif, ve, a. corrective.
correction, f. correction || correctness || reading || punishment. [ninal.
correctionnel, le, a. correctional || cri-
corrélatif, ve, a. correlative.
correspondance, f. correspondence, inter-course || omnibus-ticket. [dian.
correspondant, m. correspondent || guar-
correspondant, e, a. corresponding.
correspondre, v. n. to correspond || to communicate.
corridor, m. corridor, gallery.
corrigé, m. corrected copy || key.
corriger, v. a. to correct, to mend, to re-claim || to rid || to temper || se ~, to correct oneself, to amend, to get rid of.

corroborer, v. a. to corroborate, to
corroder, v. a. to corrode. [strengthen.
corroi, m. currying || claying.
corrompre, v. a. to corrupt || to taint, to spoil, to bribe || se ~, to putrify || to fester || to be tainted.
corrosif, m. corrosive.
corrosif, ve, a. corrosive.
corroyer, v. a. to curry || to beat up || to
corroyeur, m. currier. [puddle.
corrupteur, trice, m. &f. corrupter || cor-ruptress || briber. [tiona.
corrupteur, trice, a. corrupting || infec-
corruptibilité, f. corruptibility.
corruption, f. corruption, bribery.
cors, m. pl. horns || cerf de dix ~, full-grown stag.
corsage, m. shape || bust || body.
corsaire, m. corsair, privateer || shark.
corsé, e, a. rich, full-bodied.
corselet, m. corselet, corcelet.
corser, v. a. to fit || se ~, to put on one's
corset, m. corset, stays. [corset.
corsetier, m. corset-maker.
cortège, m. cortege, train, retinue.
corvée, f. statute-labour || (mil.) fatigue duty || drudgery || unpleasant task || bore.
corvette, f. sloop of war, corvette.
coryphée, m. corypheus || leading man.
coryza, m. (méd.) coryza.
Cosaque, m. Cossack.
cosmétique, m. cosmetic || ~, f. art of using cosmetics.
cosmétique, a. cosmetic.
cosmopolite, m. cosmopolitan.
cosmopolite, a. cosmopolitan, cosmopolite.
cosse, f. pod, husk, shell.
cosser, v. n. to butt (of rams).
cosson, m. weevil || vine-shoot.
cossu, e, a. husky, shelly || rich || sub-stantial || warm || smart.
costume, m. costume, dress.
costumer, v. a. to dress. [robe-keeper.
costumier, m. dealer in costumes || ward-
cote, f. number || quota, share || faire une ~ mal taillée, to settle in the lump.
côte, f. rib || sea-coast || hill || slice.
côté, m. side || way || quarter || party || à ~, near, by, on one side || de ~, sideways || to oneself, aside.
coteau, m. hillock, little hill.
côtelette, f. chop, cutlet.
coter, v. a. to quote, to number.
coterie, f. set, society, club.
cothurne, m. buskin || (fig.) tragedy.
côtier, m. coaster, coasting pilot.
côtier, e, a. coasting.
cotignac, m. quince marmalade.
cotillon, m. under-petticoat || cotillon (dance). [contribution.
cotisation, f. clubbing (together) || share ||
cotiser, v. a. to rate || se ~, to club to-gether || to get up a subscription.
coton, m. cotton || down || ~ plat, darn-ing cotton || ~-poudre, gun-cotton.
cotonnade, m. cotton-cloth.
cotonner (se ~), to get downy ou mealy.
cotonnerie, f. cotton-plantation.
cotonneux, se, a. cottony, downy.

cotonnier, m. (bot.) cotton-plant.
cotonnine, f. cotton canvass.
côtoyer, v. a. to coast along, to go by the
cotre, m. (mar.) cutter. [side.
cotret, m. little faggot || stick || huile de
~, stirrup-oil, cudgelling.
cotte, f. petticoat || coat.
cotuteur, m. joint-guardian.
cotylédon, m. (anat.) cotyledon || (bot.)
navel-wort.
cou, m. neck || ~-de-pied, instep.
couardise, f. cowardice.
couchant, m. west, decline.
couchant, e, a. setting.
couche, f. bed || bedstead || lying-in, con-
finement, child-bed || child's linen || hot-
bed || layer, stratum || fausse ~, mis-
carriage.
couchée, f. night's lodging || resting-place.
coucher, m. retirement for the night, going
to bed || bed-time || bedding || place of re-
pose || sunset.
coucher, v. a. & n. to put to bed, to lay,
to lay down || to slope, to incline || to
stake (money) || to knock down || to sleep ||
~ en joue, to aim at || se ~, to go to bed,
to lie down || to set.
couchette, f. bedstead || berth || crib.
coucheur, m. bed-fellow || mauvais ~,
disagreeable fellow.
couci-couci, ad. (fam.) so-so.
coucou, m. cuckoo || cowslip || wooden
clock || coach.
coude, m. elbow || turning || bend, knee.
coudée, f. cubit || arm's length || ~s
franches, elbow-room.
couder, v. a. to bend. [huddle.
coudoyer, v. a. to elbow, to jostle || to
coudraie, f. hazel-copse. [to tack.
coudre, v. a. & n. ir. to sew, to stitch ||
coudrier, m. hazel-tree.
couenne, f. pork-rind, crackling.
coulage, m. leakage.
coulamment, ad. fluently.
coulant, m. slide. [slip (of knots).
coulant, e, a. flowing, smooth || easy ||
coulé, m. slur || slide.
coulée, f. running hand || path.
couler, v. a. & n. to strain, to melt || to
flow, to run, to drop, to trickle down, to
gutter || (mar.) to leak || to glide away, to
slip || se ~, to slide away || to slip, to
creep, to steal. [colour, pretext.
couleur, f. colour || paint || (fig.) pretence,
couleuvre, f. adder. [of air.
coulis, m. cullis || jelly || vent ~, draught
coulisse, f. groove || running-string || side-
scene || behind the scenes.
coulissier, m. outsider.
couloir, m. strainer || filter || passage, lobby.
couloire, f. strainer.
coulure, f. dropping.
coup, m. blow, throw, stroke, wound ||
action, deed, event || effect, time || move
(at chess) || ~ d'aile, flap || ~ d'air, cold ||
~ de balai, sweep || ~ de bec, peck || by-
stroke || fling || ~ de bonheur, lucky hit ||
piece of good fortune || lucky event || ~ de
grâce, finishing blow || ~ de poignard,

stab || ~ de poing, cuff || ~ d'épée,
sword-thrust || ~ de canon, cannon-shot ||
~ de fusil, gun-shot || ~ de pied, kick ||
~ d'œil, glance || d'un ~ d'œil, at a
glance || au premier ~ d'œil, at first
sight || ~ de plume, dash with a pen ||
flourish || ~ de sifflet, hissing || ~ de
fouet, lash || ~ de foudre, thunderbolt ||
~ de tonnerre, thunderclap || ~ de mer,
billow || ~ de vent, gust of wind || ~
d'essai, trial, attempt || ~ de maître,
master-stroke || ~ de théâtre, clap-trap,
striking event || ~ d'état, politic stroke,
unexpected state-measure || ~ de ha-
sard, mere chance || ~ d'éclat, xploit ||
~ de sang, apoplectic fit || ~ de tête,
start || freak, fit, crotchet, whim.
coupable, m. culprit.
coupable, a. culpable, guilty of.
coupage, m. mixing.
coupant, m. edge.
coupant, e, a. cutting.
coupe, f. cut, cutting, section || cut (as
cards) || cup || ~ des cheveux, hair-
cutting.
coupé, m. brougham || front part of a stage-
coach, coupé || ~-lit, invalid carriage.
coupe-gorge, m. cut-throat place, den
of thieves.
coupe-jarret, m. cut-throat.
coupelle, f. cupel, test.
coupeller, v. a. to test.
couper, v. a. & n. to cut, to cut out, to
cut off, to fell || to divide || to carve || to
mix || to intercept, to hinder || se ~, to cut
oneself || to contradict oneself || to cross,
to intersect.
coupe-racines, m. root-cutter.
couperet, m. chopper, cleaver.
couperose, f. copperas || (méd.) acne.
couperosé, e, a. pimply, red.
coupeur, m. cutter || ~ d'eau, cut-water.
couple, m. & f. couple || pair || brace.
coupler, v. a. to couple.
couplet, m. stanza, verse.
coupoir, m. cutter, knife.
coupole, f. cupola. [railway-ticket.
coupon, m. remnant || dividend-warrant ||
coupure, f. cut, slit || (mil.) intrenchment ||
(fig.) suppression.
cour, f. court, court-yard || courtship || juris-
diction || faire la ~ à, to court.
courage, m. courage, bravery, valour.
courageux, se, a. (-sement, ad.) coura-
geous(ly) || spirited(ly).
couramment, ad. fluently.
courant, e, a. current, running || present ||
fair, middling.
courante, f. running hand || (méd.) diarrhœa.
courbatu, e, a. foundered (of horses).
courbature, f. foundering (of a horse) ||
extreme weariness.
courbaturé, e, a. stiff all over, cramped.
courbe, f. curve || knee.
courbe, a. crooked, bent.
courber, v. a. to bend, to bow, to inflect ||
se ~, to bend || to stoop, to humble one-
courbette, f. curvet || cringing. [self.
courbetter, v. n. to curvet (of horses).

courbure, f. curvity, crookedness.
coureur, m. runner, racer || stroller || scout || gay man || running footman, groom.
coureuse, f. gad-about || street-walker.
courge, f. gourd, pumpkin.
courir, v. a. & n. ir. to run, to hunt after, to frequent, to pursue || to drive fast, to walk fast, to ramble || to circulate || to travel over.
courlis, courlieu, m. curlew.
couronne, f. crown || coronet || wreath.
couronnement, m. coronation || top-piece || crowning || (mar.) taffrail || perfection.
couronner, v. a. to crown.
courre, v. a. ir. to hunt.
courrier, m. courier, post-boy, **express**, messenger || mail.
courroie, f. strap || belt.
courroucer, v. a. to irritate.
courroux, m. anger, wrath.
cours, m. course || current, stream || way || public walk || price-current || (méd.) flux.
course, f. running, race || hunting, chase || walk, journey, voyage || invasion || career || (mar.) cruise.
coursier, m. courser, steed.
coursière, f. errand-girl.
court, e, a. short || concise || ~, ad. short.
courtage, m. brokerage, brokership.
courtaud, m. short thick-set man || cropped horse.
courtaud, e, a. short and thick || cropped.
courtauder, v. a. to curtail.
courte-pointe, f. quilt.
courtier, m. broker, agent || ~ **marron**, [outside-broker.
courtine, f. curtain.
courtisan, m. courtier.
courtisane, f. courtesan.
courtiser, v. a. to court.
courtois, e, a. (-ement, ad.) courteous(ly).
courtoisie, f. courtesy. [frequented.
couru, e, a. sought after || in fashion ||
couseuse, f. seamstress || sewing-machine.
cousin, m. cousin || gnat.
cousinage, m. cousinship, relations.
cousine, f. female cousin.
cousiner, v. a. & n. to call cousin || to spunge upon one's friends || **se ~**, to call each other cousin.
cousinière, f. mosquito-net.
coussin, m. cushion.
coussinet, m. small **cushion** || pad.
coût, m. cost, price.
couteau, m. knife || hunting-knife || dagger || ~ **pliant**, folding-knife || ~ **à découper**, ~ **de cuisine**, carving-knife || ~ **de coutelas**, m. cutlass. [chasse, hanger.
coutelier, m. cutler.
coutellerie, f. cutlery || cutlery works.
coûter, v. a. & n. to cost || to be expensive || to be painful || to be an effort.
coûteux, se, a. costly, expensive.
coutier, m. tick-weaver.
coutil, m. ticking.
coutre, m. coulter.
coutume, f. custom, habit || practice.
coutumier, ère, a. customary, usual, wonted, habitual || ~ **du fait**, an old offender.

couture, f. sewing || seam, suture || scar || à plate ~, hollow.
couturer, v. a. to seam.
couturière, f. mantua-maker, **seamstress**.
couvain, m. nest of eggs.
couvaison, f. breeding-time.
couvée, f. brood, covey, set.
couvent, m. convent.
couver, v. a. & n. to brood *ou* sit on, **to** breed || to hatch, to incubate || to lurk.
couvercle, m. cover, lid.
couvert, m. table-cloth || cover (plate with knife, fork and spoon) || shelter, cover || roof of a building.
couvert, e, a. covered, loaded || clad || ambiguous || hidden || cloudy || shady || woody.
couverte, f. glazing || (mar.) deck.
couverture, f. cover || wrapper || blanket, roof || (com.) guaranty, security || -s, pl.
couveuse, f. brood-hen. [bed-clothes.
couvi, a.; **œuf ~** m. addled egg.
couvre; ~-chef, m. head-covering || ~-**feu**, m. curfew || ~-**lit**, m. coverlet || ~-**pieds**, m. covering for the feet || quilt coverlet || ~-**plat**, m. dish-cover || meat-cover.
couvreur, m. tiler, slater || thatcher.
couvrir, v. a. ir. to cover, to wrap, to envelop || to clothe || to disguise, to conceal || to protect || to copulate || to leap || **se ~**, to put one's hat on || to be overcast || to defend oneself.
crabe, m. crab.
crac, m. crack, cracking noise || ~! crack! [suddenly.
crachat, m. spittle || star. [of.
craché, e, a.; **tout(e) ~**, the very image
crachement, m. spitting.
cracher, v. a. & n. to spit (out) || to sputter || to disburse || (fam.) to fork out (money).
cracheur, m. spitter.
crachoir, m. spitting-box.
crachotement, m. frequent spitting.
crachoter, v. n. to spit often.
craie, f. chalk.
craindre, v. a. ir. to fear, to dread, to be afraid of || to dislike || to be injured by || to be unable to stand. [for fear of.
crainte, f. fear, dread, awe || de ~ **de**,
craintif, ve, a. (-vement, ad.) fearful(ly) || [timid(ly).
cramoisi, m. crimson.
cramoisi, e, a. crimson.
crampe, f. cramp. [nail.
crampon, m. cramp-iron || calkin || frost-
cramponner, v. n. to cramp || **to rough-**shoe || **se ~**, to cling (to).
cran, m. notch, cog, peg.
crâne, m. skull || swaggerer.
crâne, a. (-ment, ad.) swaggering(ly).
crânerie, f. swaggering.
crapaud, m. toad.
crapaudière, f. toad-hole.
crapaudine, f. toad-stone || (bot.) iron-wort, siderite || valve || water-plug || **à la** ~, broiled.
crapoussin, m. shrimp, dwarf.
crapule, f. low habits || low people || dissolute life. [drunken.
crapuleux, se, a. crapulous, intemperate,

craque, f. lie, humbug.
craquelin, m. cracknel.   [crepitation.
craquement, m. crack, cracking noise,
craquer, v. n. to crack, to crackle, to
  creak || to fib, to brag.
craquerie, f. bragging.
craqueter, v. n. to crackle, to crepitate.
craqueur, se, m. & f. bragger, boaster.
crasse, f. dandriff || filth, dirt || rudeness ||
  stinginess || dross.
crasse, a. thick, gross, coarse.
crasseux, se, m. & f. slovenly fellow ||
  miser || slut.   [stingy, sordid.
crasseux, se, a. dirty, filthy, nasty ||
cratère, m. crater.
cravache, f. horse- ou riding-whip.
cravate, f. neck-cloth || ~ longue, scarf.
crayeux, se, a. chalky.
crayon, m. crayon, pencil || sketch.
crayonner, v. a. to draw with a pencil,
  to sketch, to chalk.
crayonneux, se, a. chalky.
créance, f. trust, credit || power, authority,
  influence || lettres de ~, credentials.
créancier, m. creditor.
créateur, m. creator || maker, author.
créateur, trice, a. creative.
créature, f. creature.
crécelle, f. rattle.
crécerelle, f. kestrel.
crèche, f. crib, manger || infant-asylum.
crédence, f. credence || buttery.
crédibilité, f. credibility.
crédit, m. credit || trust, honour, estima-
  tion || power, influence, sway || à ~, upon
créditer, v. a. to credit.   [trust.
créditeur, m. creditor.
credo, m. creed, belief.
crédule, a. credulous.
crédulité, f. credulity.
créer, v. a. to create, to settle.
crémaillère, f. pot-hanger, pot-hook ||
  rack || pendre la ~, to give a house-
  warming.
crémaillon, m. small pot-hook.
crémation, f. cremation.
crématoire, a. crematory || four ~, cre-
  matory furnace.
crématorium, m. crematorium.
crème, f. cream || custard || (fig.) the best.
crémer, v. n. to cream.
crèmerie, f. milk-shop || coffee-house.
crémier, ère, m. & f. dairy-man || coffee-
  house keeper || milk-woman.
crémone, f. kind of window-fastener.
créneau, m. battlement.   [dented.
crénelé, a. embattled, crenelated, in-
crénelure, f. indenting.
crêpe, m. crape || ~, f. pancake.
crêper, v. a. to crisp, to frizzle.
crépi, m. rough-cast.
Crépin (Saint), m. (fam.) one's all.
crépine, f. fringe.   [crisp.
crépir, v. a. to roughcast, to grain || to
crépitation, f. crepitation, crackling ||
  (méd.) crepitatus.
crépu, a. a. crisped || frizzled, crisp.
crépusculaire, a. crepuscular.
crépuscule, m. twilight.

créquier, m. wild plum-tree.
cresson, m. cress || water-cresses (pl.).
cressonnière, f. cress-bed.
crête, f. comb of a cock ou hen || crest,
crêté, e, a. crested, tufted.   [top, tuft.
crételer, v. n. to cackle.
crétin, m. (méd.) cretin || idiot. [an idiot.
crétiniser, v. a. to stupefy || se ~, to become
crétinisme, m. (méd.) cretinism.
cretonne, f. cotton-cloth || chintz.
cretons, m. pl. greaves || cracklings.
creuser, v. a. to dig, to excavate, to
  deepen || se ~, to become hollow.
creuset, m. crucible || test.
creux, m. pit, hole, hollow, cavity || hol-
  low ou bass voice.   [ish, vain.
creux, se, a. hollow, deep || empty, fool-
crevasse, f. crevice, crevasse, chink, cleft ||
  chap.   [chink || to chap.
crevasser, v. a. to crevice, to crack, to
crève-cœur, m. heart-break.
crever, v. a. & n. to break, to rend || to
  kill || to burst || to die || ~ de rire, to
  split one's sides with laughing.
crevette, f. shrimp || prawn.
cri, m. cry, shriek, scream || lamentation.
criailler, v. n. to bawl, to scold.
criaillerie, f. bawling || scolding.
criailleur, se, m. & f. bawler || scold.
criailleur, se, a. scolding.   [bawler.
criard, e, m. & f. noisy fellow || clamourer,
criard, e, a. clamorous, noisy, squalling.
criblage, m. sifting.
crible, m. sieve, riddle.
cribler, v. a. to sift, to riddle || to pierce with
  holes || (fig.) criblé de dettes, over head
cribleur, m. sifter.   [and ears in debt.
criblure, f. siftings.
crio, m. jack, hand-screw.
cri-cri, m. cricket || small rattle imitating
  the chirping of a cricket.
criée, f. proclamation of sale, auction.
crier, v. a. & n. to proclaim, to promul-
  gate || to scold || to sell by auction || to ex-
  claim || to scream, to complain || to shout.
crierie, f. cry, outcry || scolding.
crieur, m. crier || auctioneer.
crime, m. crime || offense, sin.
criminalité, f. criminality.
criminel, le, m. & f. criminal, culprit.
criminel, le, a. (-lement, ad.) criminal
  (ly) || guilty.
crin, m. horse-hair || hair-cloth.
crin-crin, m. squeaking-fiddle || scraper.
crinier, m. horse-hair worker.
crinière, f. mane || horse-hair || mop.
crique, f. (mar.) creek, cove.
criquet, m. cricket || (of horses) tit || (fig.)
  tom-tit, whippersnapper.
crise, f. crisis || fit.   [irritation || fidgets.
crispation, f. shrivelling, contraction ||
crisper, v. a. to shrivel, to contract, to
  irritate, to fidget.
crisser, v. a. to gnash one's teeth.
cristal, m. crystal || glass.   [glass-works.
cristallerie, f. crystal manufactory ||
cristallin, m. (an.) crystalline || lens ||
  (astr.) crystalline heaven.
cristallin, e, a. crystalline.

French and English.

cristalliser, v. a. to crystallise.
critérium, m. criterion.
critiquable, a. censurable.
critique, f. criticism, critique || censure, stricture || ~, m. critic || fault-finder.
critique, a. critic(al).
critiquer, v. a. to criticise.
croassement, m. croaking.
croasser, v. n. to croak.
croc, m. hook || boat-hook || fang, tusk || canine tooth || curling moustache || ~-en-jambe, m. tripping up, Cornish hug.
croche, f. (mus.) quaver || double ~, semiquaver.
crochet, m. hook || pick-lock || steel-yard || clasp || sudden turn || shoulder-strap || fang || curl || bracket.
crocheter, v. a. to pick (a lock).
crocheteur, m. street-porter || pick-lock.
crochu, e, a. hooked, crooked.
crocodile, m. crocodile.
croire, v. a. & n. ir. to believe, to think, to suppose || se ~, to believe oneself, to [be believed.
croisade, f. crusade.
croisé, m. Crusader || twill.
croisé, e, a. cross, crossed || folded || twilled || double-milled || double-breasted.
croisée, f. window, sash, casement.
croisement, m. crossing.
croiser, v. a. & n. to cross, to set across || to cancel || to obstruct, to hinder || (mar.) to cruise || se ~, to cross each other || to meet || to take up the Cross.
croiseur, m. (mar.) cruiser.
croisière, f. (mar.) cruise || cruising-party || (rail.) intersection of two lines.
croisillon, m. crossbar (of a window).
croissance, f. growth. [pruning-hook.
croissant, e, m. crescent (of the moon) ||
croître, v. n. ir. to increase || to grow || to thrive, to swell. [row, trouble.
croix, f. cross || mark || dagger || (fig.) sor-
croquant, m. gristle.
croquant, e, a. crisp.
croquemitaine, m. black bogey.
croque; ~-mort(s), m. death-hunter, undertaker's man || ~-notes, m. wretched musician. [sketch.
croquer, v. a. to crunch || to eat up || to
croquet, m. crisp biscuit. [potato, etc.).
croquette, f. (culin.) croquette (of rice,
croqueur, m. glutton.
croquignole, f. fillip || cracknel.
croquis, m. rough sketch.
crosse, f. crosier || butt-end || hockey-stick.
crosser, v. n. to rate soundly || to bully || to spurn, to kick.
crotte, f. mud, dirt || dung.
crotter, v. a. to dirty || se ~, to get dirty
crottin, m. dry manure. [(in walking).
croulement, m. falling down, fall.
crouler, v. n. to tumble down, to sink.
croupe, f. crupper, croup, rump || top,
croupi, e, a. stagnant, putrid. [ridge.
croupier, m. partner.
croupière, f. crupper (of a horse) || tailler des (les) ~s à, to cut out work for.
croupion, m. rump.
croupir, v. n. to stand, to stagnate.

croupissant, e, a. standing, stagnant.
croustade, f. pie, pasty.
croustillant, e, a. crisp, crusty.
croustille, f. little crust.
croustiller, v. n. to gnaw a crust.
croustilleux, se, a. humorous || (fam.) smutty. [picture.
croûte, f. crust || shell || scab, scurf || paltry
croûtelette, f. little crust.
croûton, m. crust-end || bit of toast ||
croyable, a. credible. [dauber || fogey.
croyance, f. belief, creed || credit.
croyant, m. believer || one of the Faithful.
crû, m. growth || vine-estate || (fig.) invention, fabrication.
cru, e, a. crude, raw || uncooked || undigested || rough || unripe || unmannerly || [stiff.
cruauté, f. cruelty.
cruche, f. pitcher || dunce.
cruchée, f. pitcherful.
cruchon, m. small pitcher, jug.
crucifère, f. (bot.) cruciferous plant.
crucifère, a. (bot.) cruciferous || (arch.) surmounted by a cross.
crucifiement, m. crucifixion.
crucifier, v. a. to crucify.
crucifix, m. crucifix, cross.
crudité, f. crudity, rawness || crude thing.
crue, f. growth, increase || swelling, rise.
cruel, le, a. (~lement, ad.) cruel(ly) ||
crûment, ad. bluntly. [sore(ly).
crustacé, m. crustacean.
crustacé, e, a. crustaceous.
crypte, f. crypt. [dite.
cryptogame, f. (bot.) cryptogam, aphro-
cubage, m. cubature.
cube, m. (géom.) cube.
cube, a. (géom.) cubic.
cubèbe, f. cubeb.
cuber, v. a. to cube.
cubique, a. cubic.
cueillette, f. gathering || nutting.
cueillir, v. a. ir. to gather, to crop, to pluck.
cueilloir, m. fruit-basket || fruit- (grape-, flower-)gatherer.
cuiller, cuillère, f. spoon || ladle || ~ à café, tea-spoon || ~ à bouche, table-spoon || ~ à soupe, soup-ladle.
cuillerée, f. spoonful, ladleful.
cuir, m. leather, hide, skin || ~ à semelle, sole-leather.
cuirasse, f. cuirass, breast-plate.
cuirassé, m. (mar.) ironclad. [iron-plated.
cuirassé, e, a. breast-plated || hardened,
cuire, v. a. & n. ir. to cook, to dress, to do || to stew || to digest || to burn || to ripen || to smart.
cuisant, e, a. smarting, sharp || severe.
cuisine, f. kitchen, cookery || living || garçon de ~, m. under-cook.
cuisiner, v. n. to cook.
cuisinier, m. cook. [meat-screen.
cuisinière, f. cook-maid || Dutch oven ||
cuisse, f. thigh || leg || quarter.
cuisson, f. cooking || baking || smart.
cuissot, m. haunch (of a stag ou deer).
cuistre, m. college-fag || clownish pedant.
cuite, f. burning, baking.
cuivre, m. copper || ~ jaune, brass.

cuivré, e, a. copper-coloured.
cuivrer, v. a. to copper.
cuivreux, se, a. coppery.
cul, m. breech, tail ǀǀ posterior, bottom ǀǀ ~-de-basse-fosse, m. dungeon ǀǀ ~-de-jatte, m. cripple ǀǀ ~-de-lampe, m. tail-piece ǀǀ ~-de-sac, m. blind alley.
culasse, f. breech (of a cannon).
culbute, f. somersault ǀǀ tumble, fall.
culbuter, v. a. & n. to overturn ǀǀ to overthrow ǀǀ to destroy, to ruin ǀǀ to tumble down, to be ruined.
culée, f. abutment of a bridge.
culinaire, a. culinary.
culminant, e, a. culminating ǀǀ highest.
culminer, v. n. to culminate.
culot, m. youngest ǀǀ bottom.
culotte, f. breeches ǀǀ rump of beef ǀǀ spree ǀǀ blow-out.
culotter, v. a. to put on breeches ǀǀ to colour (a pipe) ǀǀ (fig.) to inure.
culottier, m. breeches-maker.
culpabilité, f. culpability.
culte, m. worship, adoration ǀǀ honour.
cultivateur, trice, m. husbandman, agriculturist, tiller.
cultiver, v. a. to cultivate.
cultuel, le, a. belonging to divine office.
culture, f. culture, cultivation.
cumul, m. holding of several offices.
cumulard, m. pluralist.
cumuler, v. n. to hold several offices.
cunéiforme, a. cuneiform, wedge-shaped.
cupide, a. cov tous, greedy.
cupidité, f. cupidity.
Cupidon, m. Cupid.
cupule, f. cup.
curage, m. cleansing.
curatelle, f. trusteeship.
curateur, m. guardian, trustee.
curatif, m. curative agent.
curatif, ve, a. curative.
cure, f. cure ǀǀ living ǀǀ parsonage ǀǀ rectory ǀǀ vicarage ǀǀ ~-dents, m. toothpick ǀǀ ~-langue, m. tongue-scraper ǀǀ ~-oreilles, m. ear-pick.
curé, m. parson ǀǀ vicar ǀǀ rector.
curée, f. quarry (hunting) ǀǀ prey ǀǀ booty ǀǀ
curement, m. cleansing.   [gain.
curer, v. a. to cleanse, to pick.
curette, f. scoop ǀǀ scraper.
cureur, m. cleanser.
curial, e, a. curial, parochial.
curieux, m. curious part ǀǀ inquisitive person ǀǀ looker-on ǀǀ antiquary ǀǀ amateur.
curieux, se, a. (-sement, ad.) curious(ly) ǀǀ inquisitive ǀǀ fond ǀǀ singular(ly) ǀǀ careful(ly).
curiosité, f. curiosity.
cursif, ve, a. cursive, running.
curures, f. pl. cleansings ǀǀ sewage.
curviligne, a. curvilinear.
custode, m. warden, keeper ǀǀ ~, f. curtain, veil ǀǀ covering of the pyx.
cutané, e, a. cutaneous.
cuve, f. large tub.
cuveau, m. bucket.
cuvée, f. tubful.
cuvelage, m. lining ǀǀ tubbing.
cuveler, v. a. to line ǀǀ to case ǀǀ to tub.

cuver, v. a. & n. to work, to ferment ǀǀ to settle.   [hand-basin ǀǀ cap.
cuvette, f. cistern (of barometers) ǀǀ wash-
cuvier, m. lie-tub ǀǀ wash-tub.
cyclamen, m. (bot.) cyclamen ǀǀ sow-bread.
cycle, m. cycle (time).
cycliste, m. cyclist.
cyclone, m. cyclone.
cygne, m. swan ǀǀ jeune ~, cygnet.
cylindrage, m. mangling.
cylindre, m. cylinder ǀǀ mangle ǀǀ glass
cylindrer, v. a. to mangle.   [shade.
cylindrique, a. cylindrical.
cymaise, f. (arch.) ogee.
cymbale, f. (mus.) cymbal.
cynique, m. cynic.
cynique, a. cynic, cynical.
cynisme, m. cynicalness, cynicism.
cyprès, m. cypress.
cyste, m. (anat.) cyst.
cytise, m. (bot.) cytisus.

D.

dada, m. hobby-horse, cock-horse.
dadais, m. booby, ninny.
dague, f. dagger.
daigner, v. n. to deign, to vouchsafe.
daim, m. deer, buck.
daine, f. doe, deer.
dais, m. canopy.
dallage, m. flagging.
dalle, f. flag-stone, slab of marble.
daller, v. a. to pave with flag-stones.
dalmatique, f. dalmatic, tunic.
damas, m. damask (stuff) ǀǀ Damascus blade ǀǀ damson (plum).
damasquiner, v. a. to damaskeen.
damasquinerie, damasquinure, f. de- maskeening.
damassé, m. damasked linen.
damasser, v. a. to damask.
damasseur, m. damask-worker.
damassure, f. damasking.
dame, f. lady ǀǀ queen (at cards) ǀǀ dam ǀǀ sluice ǀǀ ~s, pl. draughts (game) ǀǀ ~-jeanne, f. demi-john, large bottle, jar.
dame ! nay ǀ indeed ! forsooth !
damer, v. a. to crown (at draughts) ǀǀ ~ le pion à, to out-do.
dameret, m. ladies' man ǀǀ beau.
damier, m. draught-board, chess-board.
damnation, f. damnation.
damné, e, m. damned soul, soul in Hell.
damner, v. a. to damn ǀǀ faire ~, to drive
damoiseau, m. fop, spark.   [mad.
damoiselle, f. damsel.
dandin, m. noddy, ninny.
dandinement, m. waddling ǀǀ swinging.
dandiner, v. n. (se ~), to waddle ǀǀ to swing.
dangeau, m. leader of fashion.
danger, m. danger ǀǀ risk.
dangereux, se, a. (-sement, ad.) dan- gerous(ly).
dans, pr. in, into, at, with, within.
dansant, e, a. dancing, lively ǀǀ dance-inviting.

danse, f. dance || dancing.

danser, v. a. & n. to dance.

danseur, se, m. & f. dancer || partner.

da; oui-~, yes certainly.

dard, m. dart || sting.

darder, v. a. to dart || to throw || to beam.

dariole, f. cream-cake.

darne, f. slice.

darse, f. (mar.) wet-dock.

dartre, f. tetter, ring-worm.

dartreux, se, a. scurvy.

date, f. date (time).

dater, v. a. to date.

datte, f. date (fruit).

dattier, m. (bot.) date-tree.

daube, f. stew, stewed meat.

dauber, v. a. to stew || to cuff || to banter.

daubière, f. stew-pan.

dauphin, m. dolphin || Dauphin, eldest son of the kings of France.

dauphine, f. Dauphiness.

davantage, ad. more, any more.

de, pr. of || from || in || with || by || about || after || at || upon || ~ par, in the name of.

dé, m. die || thimble || dado || block.

débâcher, v. a. to untilt (waggons, etc.).

débâclage, m. clearing (of a harbour).

débâcle, f. breaking up of ice || cleansing (of a harbour) || break-down, overthrow, fatal collapse.   [to break up (of ice).

débâcler, v. a. & n. to clear || to unbar ||

déballage, m. unpacking.

déballer, v. a. to unpack.

débandade, f. disbanding || à la ~, helter-skelter, in confusion.

débandement, m. disbanding.

débander, v. a. to unbend, to unloosen || se ~, to disband, to grow loose, to grow slack.   [to call by a wrong name.

débaptiser, v. a. to change the name of ||

débarbouiller, v. a. to wash another's face || to extricate.

débarcadère, m. landing-place || wharf || railway-station, terminus.

débardage, m. unlading.

débarder, v. a. to unlade.

débardeur, m. lighterman || lumper.

débarquement, m. landing, disembarking.   [embark.

débarquer, v. a. & n. to land || to dis-

débarras, m. riddance.

débarrasser, v. a. to clear, to disencumber || se ~, to get rid of, to get clear of, to extricate oneself from.

débarrer, v. n. to unbar.

débat, m. debate, contest, strife.

débâter, v. a. to unsaddle.

débattre, v. a. to debate, to discuss || se ~, to struggle, to strive.

débauché, m. debauchee, profligate, rake.

débauchée, f. lewd woman.

débaucher, v. a. to debauch || to corrupt, to seduce || to entice away || se ~, to become debauched, to follow ill courses, to go astray.

débaucheur, m. debaucher.

débet, m. (com.) balance due.

débile, a. feeble, weak.

débilité, f. debility, weakness.

débiliter, v. a. to debilitate, to weaken.

débine, f. destitution, distress, need || (fam.) mess, hole, difficulty.

débit, m. sale by retail || quick and easy sale || utterance, delivery || (com.) debtor

débitant, m. retailer, dealer.   [side.

débiter, v. a. to sell by retail || to spread about, to tell || to declaim || (com.) to carry to the debtor's account.

débiteur, trice, m. & f. debtor || tittle-tattler.

déblai, m. clearing || digging || -s, pl. rubbish.   [to rant.

déblatérer, v. n. to break out into abuse,

déblayer, v. a. to clear away, to free from.

débloquer, v. a. (mil.) to raise the blockade.

déboire, m. after-taste || trouble, grief.

déboîtement, m. dislocation.

déboîter, v. a. to dislocate, to disjoint.

débonder, v. a. & n. to open the sluice of a pond, to unbung || to gush out || to burst forth.

débondonner, v. a. to unbung.

débonnaire, a. easy-tempered, kind || -- ment, ad. gently, meekly.

débordé, e, a. overflowed || dissolute.

débordement, m. overflowing || (fig.) flood || invasion || debauchery.

déborder, v. a. & n. to unborder || to outflank || to overflow, to jut out.

débosseler, v. a. to remove, smoothe away bruises, dents, &c.

débotter, v. a. to pull off one's boots || au ~, immediately after arriving.

débouché, m. vent || sale, market || expedient.

débouchement, m. opening, unstopping.

déboucher, v. a. & n. to uncork, to unstop, to open || to pass || to debouch.

déboucler, v. a. to unbuckle, to uncurl.

débouquer, v. n. to disembogue.

débourber, v. a. to cleanse, to remove mud.   [polish.

débourrer, v. a. to worm || to empty || to

déboursé, m. disbursement.

déboursement, m. disbursement.

débourser, v. a. to disburse, to lay out.

debout, ad. up, standing, upright.

débouter, v. a. to reject in law.

déboutonner, v. a. to unbutton || se ~, to unbosom oneself.

se débrailler, v. to expose one's breast.

débrider, v. a. to unbridle || to halt || to stop || sans ~, at a stretch.   [(of a ship).

débris, m. remains (pl.) || ruins (pl.) || wreck

débrouiller, v. a. to disentangle.

débrutir, v. a. to polish.

débrutissement, m. polishing.

débucher, v. a. & n. to dislodge, to start (game).

débusquement, m. driving out.

débusquer, v. a. to dislodge, to oust || (fig.) to supplant.

début, m. first step, first cast, first throw || beginning || first appearance (of an actor ou actress).

débutant, e, m. & f. actor ou actress appearing for the first time || beginner || new performer.

débuter, v. n. to begin || to play first, to

have the lead ‖ to make a first appearance. [on this side.

deçà, pr. & ad. on this side ‖ au ~, par ~,

décacheter, v. a. to unseal.

décade, f. decade.

décadence, f. decay, decline.

décagone, m. decagon.

décagramme, m. decagramme = 5.64 drams avoirdupois. [box.

décaisser, v. a. to take out of a chest ou décalitre, f. decalitre = 2.9 gallons.

décalquer, v. a. to counterdraw.

décamper, v. n. to decamp, to march off ‖

décanat, m. deanery. [to bolt.

décanter, v. a. to decant.

décaper, v. a. (mar.) to double a cape.

décapitation, f. beheading.

décapiter, v. a. to behead.

décarreler, v. a. to unpave.

décatir, v. a. to spunge woollen cloth.

décatissage, m. spunging of woollen cloth.

décéder, v. n. to decease, to die.

décèlement, m. disclosure.

déceler, v. a. to disclose, to betray.

Décembre, m. December.

décemment, ad. decently.

décence, f. decency.

décennal, e, a. decennial.

décent, e, a. decent.

décentraliser, v. a. to decentralise.

déception, f. deception ‖ deceit, fraud.

décerner, v. a. to decree, to bestow, to award ‖ to issue.

décès, m. decease, death.

décevant, e, a. deceitful.

décevoir, v. a. ir. to deceive.

déchaînement, m. unchaining, letting loose ‖ fury.

déchaîner, v. a. to unchain ‖ to exasperate, to irritate ‖ se ~, to break loose ‖ to rail at.

déchanter, v. n. to change one's tone, to lower one's key

décharge, f. discharge, release, receipt, acquittal ‖ running, water-course, outlet ‖ lumber-room.

déchargement, m. discharging, unloading.

décharger, v. a. to discharge, to unload, to release, to ease ‖ to clear, to open ‖ se ~, to unload, to ease oneself.

déchargeur, m. unlader.

décharner, v. a. to strip off the flesh ‖ décharné, emaciated, meagre, poor.

déchaussé, a. bare-footed.

déchaussement, m. baring of the roots, hoeing up.

déchausser, v. a. to pull off one's shoes ou stockings ‖ to bare (the roots).

déchaussoir, m. gum-lancet.

dèche, f. pinching need.

déchéance, f. forfeiture ‖ deposition ‖

déchet, m. loss, waste. [downfall.

décheveler, v. a. to dishevel.

déchevêtrer, v. a. to take the halter off ‖

déchiffrable, a. legible. [to disentangle.

déchiffrement, m. deciphering.

déchiffrer, v. a. to decipher ‖ to spell out ‖ (mus.) to play at sight ‖ to clear up.

déchiffreur, m. decipherer. [slash.

déchiqueter, v. a. to mangle, to cut, to

déchirage, m. ripping up of a ship's

déchirant, e, a. heartrending. [planks.

déchirement, m. tearing, rending ‖ anguish.

déchirer, v. a. to tear ‖ to rend ‖ to destroy ‖ to defame ‖ to be all in rags.

déchireur, m. boat-ripper.

déchirure, f. rent, slit, tear. [feit.

déchoir, v. n. ir. to fall ‖ to sink ‖ to for-

décidément, ad. decidedly, positively.

décider, v. a. to decide ‖ to determine ‖ to put an end to ‖ se ~, to resolve, to come to a resolution.

décimal, e, a. decimal.

décime, m. penny (1/10 franc) ‖ tenth ‖ tithe.

décimer, v. a. to decimate ‖ to thin.

décimètre, m. tenth part of a metre.

décisif, ve, a. (-vement, ad.) decisive(ly) ‖ positive(ly). [nation.

décision, f. decision ‖ resolution ‖ determi-

déclamateur, m. stump-orator, declaimer.

déclamateur, a. declamatory ‖ declaiming.

déclamation, f. declamation ‖ elocution ‖ rant ‖ public speech.

déclamatoire, a. declamatory.

déclamer, v. a. & n. to declaim ‖ to recite ‖ to inveigh. [affidavit ‖ verdict.

déclaration, f. declaration ‖ disclosure ‖

déclarer, v. a. to declare, to proclaim ‖ to denounce ‖ se ~, to declare for ‖ to declare oneself ‖ to break out.

déclassé, e, a. one who has socially lost caste, or has become degraded from a former ou pretended position in society.

déclasser, v. a. to change the class of ‖ to cause one to lose one's social position.

déclin, m. decline, decay ‖ wane ‖ ebb.

déclinaison, f. (gr.) declension ‖ declina-

déclinatoire, m. declinatory plea. [tion.

décliner, v. a. & n. (gr.) to decline ‖ to shun, to refuse, to fall off ‖ to decay ‖ ~ ses qualités, to give an account of oneself.

déclivité, f. declivity.

déclore, v. a. ir. to unclose, to open.

déclouer, v. a. to unnail.

décocher, v. a. to shoot ‖ to discharge.

décoction, f. decoction.

décoiffer, v. a. to take off one's head-dress, to uncoif ‖ to uncork.

décollement, m. unglueing, unpasting.

décoller, v. n. to behead ‖ to unglue, to unpaste ‖ se ~, to come off.

décolleté, e, a. in a low dress ‖ (fig. of conversation) free, broad.

(se) décolleter, v. a. & r. to uncover one's neck and shoulders ‖ to wear a low dress.

décolorer, v. a. to discolour ‖ se ~, to lose colour.

décombrer, v. a. to clear from rubbish.

décombres, m. pl. rubbish (of a building).

décommander, v. a. (com.) to counter-mand.

décompléter, v. a. to make incomplete.

décomposer, v. a. to discompose ‖ to disorder, to undo ‖ se ~, to become discom-posed. [composure.

décomposition, f. decomposition ‖ dis-

décompte, m. discount, deficiency ‖ disappointment.

décompter, v. a. & n. to discount, to deduct || to abate, to diminish.

déconcerter, v. a. to disconcert || to baffle || se ~, to be disconcerted.

déconfire, v. a. ir. to discomfit, to rout.

déconfiture, f. havoc || break-down, ruin || insolvency.

déconseiller, v. a. to dissuade.

déconsidération, f. disfavour, discredit.

déconsidérer, v. a. to discredit.

décontenancer, v. a. to discountenance.

déconvenue, f. disaster, discomfiture.

décor, m. decoration || scenery.

décorateur, m. decorator || scene-painter.

décoration, f. decoration, scenery || star of the order of the Legion of Honour.

décorder, v. a. to untwist.

décorer, v. a. to decorate, to adorn || to paint || to dignify || to confer the cross of the Legion of Honour.

décortiquer, v. a. (hort.) to decorticate || to bark || to pulp.

décorum, m. decorum || propriety, decency.

découcher, v. a. ir. to sleep out.

découdre, v. a. to unsew, to unstitch.

découler, v. n. to flow, to trickle, to drop || to proceed.

découper, v. a. to carve || to cut up, to pink || se ~, to come out, to show off.

découpeur, m. pinker.

découplé, e, a.; **bien ~,** well-shaped.

découpler, v. a. to uncouple.

découpure, f. cutting into figures || figure cut out.　　　　[spondency.

découragement, m. discouragement, de-

décourager, v. a. to discourage || se ~, to be discouraged, to despond.

découronner, v. a. to uncrown.

décours, m. decrease, decline || wane (of the moon).

décousu, m. looseness.

décousu, e, a. unsewed || loose || desultory, unconnected || unsteady.

décousure, f. ripped place || seam-rent.

découvert, m. deficit.

découvert, e, a. uncovered, open, plain.

découverte, f. discovery || reconnoitring || (mar.) looking out.

découvrir, v. a. ir. to uncover || to unmask || to discover, to reveal || se ~, to uncover oneself || to pull one's hat off || to make oneself known || to be found out || to expose oneself.　　　　[to polish.

décrasser, v. a. to remove dirt, to clean,

décréditement, m. discrediting.

décréditer, v. a. to discredit || se ~, to fall into discredit.

décrépit, e, a. decrepit.

décrépiter, v. a. (chim.) to decrepitate ||

décrépitude, f. decrepitude.　　[to crackle.

décret, m. decree.

décréter, v. a. to decree.

décri, m. crying down || disrepute.

décrier, v. a. to decry, to cry down.

décrire, v. a. ir. to describe.

décrochement, m. unhooking.

décrocher, v. a. to unhook, to take down.

décroissance, f., décroissement, m. decrease.　　　　[to wane (of the moon).

décroître, v. n. ir. to decrease, to shorten ||

décrotter, v. a. to rub off dirt, to clean || to brush clothes.

décrotteur, m. shoe-black || (à l'hôtel)

décrottoir, m. door-scraper.　　　[boots.

décrottoire, f. hard shoe-brush.

décrue, f. decrease.

décruer, v. a. to scour.

décupler, v. a. to increase tenfold.

dédaigner, v. a. to disdain, to scorn.

dédaigneux, se, a. (-sement, ad.) disdainful(ly).

dédain, m. disdain, scorn.

dédale, m. labyrinth, maze, confusion.

dédaller, v. a. to unpave, to take up pave-

dedans, m. (the) inside.　　　　[ment.

dedans, ad. in, within || au ~, inwardly.

dédicace, f. dedication.

dédicatoire, a. dedicatory.

dédier, v. a. to dedicate || to inscribe.

dédire, v. a. ir. to disown, to deny, to unsay, to gainsay || se ~, to retract, to recant.

dédit, m. forfeit, forfeiture || retractation.

dédommagement, m. indemnification, indemnity, amends.　　　[amends for.

dédommager, v. a. to indemnify, to make

dédorer, v. a. to ungild || se ~, to get ungilt.　　　　[two || to halve.

dédoubler, v. a. to unline || to divide into

déduction, f. deduction || inference || par ~, deductively.

déduire, v. a. ir. to deduct || to deduce, to

déesse, f. goddess.　　　　[infer.

défaillance, f. fainting fit, swoon.

défaillant, m. defaulter.

défaillant, e, a. fainting, decaying.

défaillir, v. n. ir. to fail, to decay, to faint away.

défaire, v. a. ir. to unmake, to undo || to defeat || to rid of || to untie, to break || to outshine || se ~, to rid oneself || to make away || to despatch || to leave off || to part with || to get thin ou flat || to get out of shape.

défait, e, a. undone || meagre || wasted.

défaite, f. defeat, overthrow || pretence, evasion || sale || riddance.

défalcation, f. defalcation, deduction.

défalquer, v. a. to defalcate, to deduct.

défaut, m. defect, imperfection, want || non-appearance (in a court of justice) || à ~ de, au ~ de, for want of.

défaveur, f. disfavour, disgrace.

défavorablement, ad. unfavourably.

défectif, ve, a. (gr.) defective.

défection, f. defection || falling off ou away.

défectueux, se, a. (-sement, ad.) defectuous || defective(ly).

défectuosité, f. defect.

défençable, a. defensible || tenable.

défendeur, eresse, m. & f. (jur.) defendant || respondent.

défendre, v. a. to defend, to protect || to uphold || to prohibit, to forbid || se ~, to defend ou shelter oneself || to excuse oneself || to forbear, to help || to haggle.

défense, f. defence || guard, security || justification, apology || prohibition || -s, pl. tusks of a wild boar || (mil.) outworks.

défenseur, m. defender || counsel for the
défensif, ve, a. defensive. |defence.
déférence, f. deference || consideration.
déféquer, v. a. to defecate.
déférant, a. complying, yielding.
déférer, v. a. & n. to confer || to accuse,
   to impeach || to comply (with) || to submit.
déferler, v. a. (mar.) to unfurl || ~, v. n.
   to break into foam (of waves).
déferrer, v. a. to unshoe (a horse) || to take
   off the irons from || to perplex || se ~, to
   be unshod || to be confounded.
défet, m. waste || sheets (in printing).
défeuillaison, f. defoliation.
défeuiller, v. a. to strip off the leaves.
défi, m. defiance, challenge.
défiance, f. diffidence, distrust, mistrust.
défiant, e, a. distrustful, suspicious.
déficit, m. deficit, deficiency.
défier, v. a. & n. to defy, to brave, to chal-
   lenge || (mar.) to bear off || se ~, to
   suspect, to apprehend || to distrust.
défigurer, v. a. to disfigure, to deform.
défilé, m. defile, narrow passage || diffi-
défilement, m. (mil.) filing off. |culty.
défiler, v. a. & n. to unthread, to unstring ||
   (mil.) to file off.
défini, e, a. definite.   [describe.
définir, v. n. to define || to determine || to
définissable, a. definable.
définitif, ve, a. (–vement, ad.) defini-
   tive(ly) || on ~, definitely || positively.
définition, f. definition, description || de-
   cision, determination.
défloraison, f. falling of a blossom.
défloration, f. deflowering, defloration.
défleurir, v. a. & n. to nip the blossoms ||
   to lose the blossoms.
déflorer, v. a. to deflower.
défoncement, m. staving || digging up.
défoncer, v. a. to stave || to dig up || to
   break up.   [~, to become deformed.
déformer, v. a. to deform, to distort || se
défraîchi, e, a. no longer fresh.
défraîchir, v. a. to take the freshness off.
défrayer, v. a. to defray.   [grubbing up.
défrichement, m. (agr.) clearing (of land) ||
défricher, v. a. (agr.) to clear ground.
défricheur, m. (agr.) clearer.
défriper, v. a. to unrumple.
défriser, v. a. to uncurl.
défroncer, v. a. to unplait || to smoothe
   (one's brow).
défroque, f. old clothes, left-off clothes.
défroquer, v. a. to unfrock.
défunt, e, a. deceased, late.
dégagé, e, a. disengaged, free.
dégagement, m. disengagement || re-
   demption || extrication || release || escape ||
   discharge || back-door || back-room.
dégager, v. a. to disengage, to release, to
   redeem, to free from || to pay off || se ~,
   to free ou extricate oneself.
dégaîne, f. odd manner ou figure.
dégaîner, v. a. to unsheath, to draw (a
   sword) || to fork out.
déganter, v. a. to pull off one's gloves.
dégarnir, v. a. to unfurnish || to strip ||
   (mar.) to unrig || (mil.) to ungarrison || se

~, to leave off some of one's clothes || to
   part with || to lose the leaves, to grow thin.
dégât, m. damage || havoc || waste.
dégauchir, v. a. to smoothe || to polish ||
dégel, m. thaw.   [to straighten.
dégeler, v. a. & n. to thaw.
dégénération, f. degeneracy.
dégénérer, v. n. to degenerate.
dégingandé, e, a. awkward || loose || dis-
dégluer, v. a. to unglue.   [jointed.
dégobiller, v. a. (fam.) to spew || to bring
   ou throw up, to vomit.
dégoiser, v. a. & n. to blab, to chatter.
dégommer, v. a. to ungum || to oust.
dégonder, v. a. to unhinge.
dégonflement, m. reduction || falling,
   collapse.   [se ~, to decrease.
dégonfler, v. a. to remove a swelling ||
dégorgement, m. clearing, cleansing ||
   overflowing.
dégorger, v. a. & n. to clear, to open, to
   cleanse || to scour, to soak || se ~, to over-
   flow, to discharge itself.
dégourdi, e, a. lively || sharp.
dégourdir, v. a. to revive, to quicken || to
   form, to polish.   [tion || reviving.
dégourdissement, m. return of circula-
dégoût, m. disgust, dislike || nausea.
dégoûté, e, a. squeamish || weary of || out
   of conceit.
dégoûter, v. a. to disgust || se ~, to take
   a dislike to || to get disgusted.
dégoutter, v. n. to drop, to trickle down.
dégradation, f. degradation ||dilapidation||
   damage || waste.   [to damage || to waste.
dégrader, v. a. to degrade || to dilapidate ||
dégrafer, v. a. to unclasp, to unpin.
dégraissage, m. scouring.
dégraisser, v. a. to scour, to clean || to
   skim off || to impoverish, to fleece.
dégraisseur, m. scourer.
degré, m. degree, step, stage || stair || extent.
dégrèvement, m. reduction || relief.
dégréver, v. a. to reduce || to relieve.
dégringolade, f. going down, tumble ||
   (fig.) decline, fall.
dégringoler, v. n. to roll, to tumble down.
dégrisement, m. returning to one's senses.
dégriser, v. a. to sober.
dégrossir, v. a. to clear up || to hew || to
   take off the rough.
déguenillé, e, a. ragged, all in rags.
déguerpir, v. n. to pack off, to be off.
dégueuler, v. n. to vomit, to spew.
déguisement, m. disguise.
déguiser, v. a. to disguise.
dégustateur, m. taster.
dégustation, f. tasting.
déguster, v. a. to taste.
déhâler, v. a. to take off the sun-burning.
déhanché, e, a. hipshot || ungainly.
déharnacher, v. a. to unharness || to un-
déhonté, e, a. shameless.   [rig.
dehors, m. outside, appearance || outworks.
dehors, ad. out, out of doors, without,
   abroad || independent of || au ~, out-
   wardly || de ~, from without, outward ||
   en ~, par ~, without, out of.

déifier, v. a. to deify.

déisme, m. deism.

déiste, m. & f. deist.

déiste, a. deistical.

déjà, ad. already, before.

déjection, f. (méd.) dejection, ejection.

se déjeter, v. to warp.

déjeuner, m. breakfast || lunch.

déjeuner, v. n. to breakfast.

déjoindre, v. a. ir. to disjoin.

déjouer, v. a. to baffle.

déjucher, v. a. to unroost || to drive away.

delà, pr. thence, from that time, from that place || beyond, on the other side || au ~, beyond, further on, upwards.

délabré, e, a. broken, dilapidated, cracked.

délabrement, m. broken state, disorderly state, dilapidation.

délabrer, v. a. to tear to pieces || to pull down, to ruin || to lessen.

délacer, v. a. to unlace.

délai, m. delay, interval, term.　[ment.

délaissement, m. destitution, abandon-

délaisser, v. a. to abandon, to forsake.

délassement, m. rest || relaxation.

délasser, v. a. to rest || to refresh.

délateur, trice, m. & f. informer || accuser.

délation, f. information.

délayant, m. (méd.) diluent, diluter.

délayement, m. diluting.

délayer, v. a. to dilute.

délecter, v. a. to delight.

délégué, m. delegate.

déléguer, v. a. to delegate.

délestage, m. (mar.) unballasting.

délester, v. a. (mar.) to unballast.

délétère, a. (méd.) deleterious.

délibérant, e, a. deliberative.

délibératif, ve, a. deliberative.

délibération, f. deliberation, resolution.

délibéré, m. (jur.) final resolution.

délibéré, e, a. (–ment, ad.) deliberate(ly) || resolved || bold(ly) || resolute(ly) || courageous || easy || with ease || free.　[resolve.

délibérer, v. a. & n. to deliberate || to

délicat, e, a. (–ment, ad.) delicate(ly) || dainty || nice(ly) || tender || daintily.

délicatesse, f. delicacy, daintiness, nicety.

délices, f. pl. delight, pleasure.

délicieux, se, a. (–sement, ad.) delicious(ly) || delightful(ly).

délié, m. thin stroke.　[sharp, glib.

délié, e, a. loose, slender, thin || subtle,

délier, v. a. to untie, to release.

délimitation, f. delimitation, fixing of

délimiter, v. a. to fix limits.　[limits.

délinéation, f. delineation.

délinquant, m. delinquent, offender.

déliquescence, f. (chim.) deliquescence.

délirant, e, a. delirious, frenzied.

délire, m. delirium, frenzy.

délirer, v. n. to delirate.　[very act.

délit, m. offence || en flagrant, ~, in the

délivrance, f. deliverance, delivery, release || rescue.　[to issue.

délivrer, v. a. to deliver, to free, to rid,

délogement, m. removal.

déloger, v. a. & n. to dislodge, to turn out || to remove || to run away.

déloyal, e, a. (–ement, ad.) disloyal(ly) || perfidious || treacherously.

déloyauté, f. disloyalty.　[torrent.

déluge, m. deluge, flood, inundation ||

déluré, e, a. wide-awake, sharp.

délustrer, v. a. to take the gloss from.

déluter, v. a. to unlute.

démagogie, f. demagogy.

démagogique, a. demagogic.

démailloter, v. a. to unswathe.

demain, m. morrow, next day.

demain, ad. to-morrow.　[jointed.

démanché, e, a. awkward, loose, dis-

démancher, v. a. to take off the handle, to dislocate || se ~, to lose its handle.

demande, f. demand, question, request, claim, petition || suit.

demander, v. a. to ask, to call for || to inquire after || to beg, to crave, to sue for, to request || to claim || to require, to desire, to wish || se ~, to ask oneself ou each other || to be asked.

demanderesse, f. female plaintiff.

demandeur, m. demander, dun || plaintiff.

demandeuse, f. female dun.

démangeaison, f. itch, itching.

démanger, v. n. to itch.

démanteler, v. a. (mil.) to dismantle.

démantibuler, v. a. to put out of order, to break.　[ceeding, attempt.

démarche, f. step, pace, walk || gait, pro-

démarier, v. a. to unmarry.

démarquer, v. a. to take off the mark.

démarrage, m. (mar.) unmooring.

démarrer, v. n. (mar.) to unmoor, to put to sea || to move.

démasquer, v. a. to unmask.

démâter, v. a. to dismast.

démêlé, m. dispute, strife.

démêler, v. a. to disentangle, to separate, to part || to discover, to unravel, to distinguish || to contest, to dispute.

démêloir, m. large-toothed comb.

démembrer, v. a. to dismember.

déménagement, m. removal.

déménager, v. n. to move, to change one's lodgings || (fig.) to become childish.

démence, f. insanity, madness.

se démener, to struggle, to stir, to strive, to make a great bustle.

démenti, m. lie || flat contradiction ou denial || disappointment || en avoir le ~, to be balked || to find oneself wrong.

démentir, v. a. to give the lie, to belie, to contradict || se ~, to contradict oneself, to belie oneself || to change || to relax.

démérite, m. demerit.

démériter, v. n. to deserve blame.

démesuré, e, a. (–ment, ad.) huge(ly) || excessive(ly) || immoderate, boundless.

démettre, v. a. ir. to put out of joint || to dismiss || se ~, to be put out of joint || to abdicate || to resign.

démeublement, m. unfurnishing.

démeubler, v. a. to unfurnish.

demeurant; au ~, ad. as for the rest || after all || notwithstanding.

demeure, f. dwelling, abode, habitation || delay.

demeurer, v. n. to live in *ou* at, to dwell, to stay, to remain || to delay || to last.

demi, e, a. half || à ~, half, by half, by halves, almost || à ~-voix, in an under-tone.

demie, f. half an hour. [tone.

demi-monde, m. the questionable portion of society.

démission, f. resignation.

démissionnaire, m. resigner.

démissionnaire, a. resigned.

démocrate, m. democrat.

démocratie, f. democracy. [(ally).

démocratique, a. (-ment, ad.) democratic

demoiselle, f. miss, young lady, unmarried gentlewoman || rammer || dragon-fly.

démolir, v. a. to demolish, to pull down.

démolisseur, m. demolisher.

démolition, f. demolition || -s, pl. rubbish of a building.

démon, m. demon, devil || wild child.

démonétisation, f. calling in (of money *ou* coin).

démonétiser, v. a. to call in (money).

démoniaque, a. demoniac.

démonstrateur, m. demonstrator.

démonstratif, ve, a. (-vement, ad.) demonstrative(ly) || making a show of earnestness.

démonstration, f. demonstration, show.

démontage, m. taking to pieces.

démonter, v. a. to dismount || to take to pieces || to confound || to disappoint.

démontrer, v. n. to demonstrate, to show || to prove.

démoralisateur, trice, a. demoralising.

démoraliser, v. a. to demoralise.

démordre, v. n. ir. to let go one's hold || to desist || to depart.

démoucheter, v. a. to uncap.

démunir, v. a. to deprive of ammunition || se ~, to part with.

démurer, v. a. to unwall.

démuseler, v. a. to unmuzzle.

(se) dénantir, to give up (securities).

dénationaliser, v. a. to denationalise.

dénatter, v. a. to unmat || to unplait.

dénaturé, e, a. unnatural.

dénaturer, v. a. to disfigure || to misrepresent || to alter || to sophisticate.

dénégation, f. denegation || denial.

déni, m. denial, refusal.

déniaisé, m. cunning man, sharp man.

déniaiser, v. a. to sharpen one's wits || to cheat, to take in || se ~, to grow sharp.

dénicher, v. a. & n. to take out of the nest *ou* niche || to hunt out || (fam.) to dislodge || to brush off. [hunter.

dénicheur, m. bird's-nester || (fig.) fortune-

denier, m. money, funds || hard cash || mite || farthing || pence (pl.) || ~ à Dieu, earnest-money. [traverse.

dénier, v. a. to deny || to refuse || (jur.) to

dénigrement, m. disparagement.

dénigrer, v. a. to disparage.

dénigreur, m. disparager.

dénombrement, m. enumeration || census.

dénominateur, m. (ar.) denominator.

dénommer, v. a. to name.

dénoncer, v. a. to denounce, to inform against.

dénonciateur, trice, m. & f. denouncer, informer.

dénonciation, f. denunciation, information.

dénoter, v. a. to denote. [tion.

dénouer, v. a. to untie, to loose, to undo, to unravel || to resolve || se ~, to grow loose, to loosen || to grow more supple.

dénoûment, m. event, issue, end || catastrophe (of a play). [produce.

denrée, f. commodity, provisions || food ||

densité, f. density. [lion, f. (bot.) dandelion.

dent, f. tooth || notch || cog || prong || ~-de-dentaire, a. dental.

dental, e, a. (gr.) dental.

denté, e, a. dented, notched || cogged.

dentée, f. bite.

dentelé, e, a. denticulated, notched, jagged.

denteler, v. a. to indent, to jag, to notch.

dentelle, f. lace, lace-work.

dentelure, f. indentation || denticulation ||

dentier, m. set of teeth. [embrasure.

dentifrice, m. dentifrice.

dentiste, m. dentist.

dentition, f. teething.

denture, f. set of teeth.

dénuder, v. a. to denude.

dénué, e, a. destitute, void.

dénuer, v. a. to deprive, to strip.

dénûment, m. deprivation, destitution.

dépaqueter, v. a. to unpack.

de par, pr. by order of.

dépareillé, e, a. incomplete, odd.

dépareiller, v. a. to spoil a set *ou* a pair.

déparer, v. a. to undress || to disparage.

déparler, v. a. to unmatch.

déparler, v. a. to cease talking.

déparquer, v. a. to unpen.

départ, m. departure.

départager, v. a. to give the casting vote.

département, m. department, province || -s, pl. country.

départemental, e, a. departmental.

départeur, m. (chim.) separator.

départir, v. a. to divide, to distribute || se ~, to desist, to abandon, to give over.

dépasser, v. a. to draw out || to go beyond, to outrun || to overreach.

dépaver, v. a. to unpave.

dépayser, v. a. to take out of one's native country || to get one out of a habit || to remove || to put on a wrong scent.

dépècement, m. cutting in pieces.

dépecer, v. a. to carve, to cut in pieces, to cut up.

dépêche, f. despatch || message || mail || -s, pl. correspondence || post-bags.

dépêcher, v. a. to despatch || se ~, to hasten, to make haste.

dépeindre, v. a. ir. to paint, to portray || to describe. [dressed.

dépenaillé, e, a. ragged, tattered, loosely

dépenaillement, m. raggedness || disorder.

dépendance, f. dependence, dependency || appendage || outbuilding.

dépendant, m. dependent.

dépendant, e, a. dependent.

dépendre, v. a. & n. to take down || to depend on, to be in a state of dependence.

dépens, m. pl. expense, cost.

dépense, f. expense || expenditure || outlay || larder, pantry.
dépenser, v. a. to spend.
dépensier, m. spendthrift.
dépensier, **ère**, a. prodigal || extravagant.
déperdition, f. loss, waste || (méd.) discharges (pl.). [away.
dépérir, v. n. to decay, to fall off, to pine
dépérissement, m. decay, decline, withering. [contrary.
dépersuader, v. a. to persuade to the
dépêtrer, v. a. to disengage, to disentangle || to extricate || to rid.
dépeuplement, m. depopulation.
dépeupler, v. a. to depopulate || to unstock.
dépilatif, **ve**, a. depilatory.
dépilatoire, m. depilatory.
dépiler, v. a. to depilate || **se ~**, to lose one's *ou* its hair.
dépiquer, v. a. to unquilt || to cheer up.
dépister, v. a. to track, to hunt out.
dépit, m. spite || vexation.
dépiter, v. a. to vex || **se ~**, to be vexed || to get out of humour.
déplacement, m. displacing, removal.
déplacer, v. a. to displace, to transpose || to misplace || **se ~**, to leave one's seat.
déplaire, v. n. ir. to displease || to vex, to trouble, to offend || **se ~**, to dislike, to be displeased with || not to thrive.
déplaisant, **e**, a. unpleasant.
déplaisir, m. displeasure, grief, sorrow.
déplanter, v. a. to displant.
déplantoir, m. trowel.
déplier, v. a. to unfold.
déplisser, v. a. to unplait. [ploying.
déploiement, m. unfolding || display, de-
déplomber, v. a. to unseal || to unstop.
déplorablement, ad. deplorably, miser-
déplorer, v. a. to deplore. [ably.
déployer, v. a. to unfold || to display || to spread || to unfurl || to deploy.
déplumer, v. a. to unplume || **se ~**, to lose one's feathers, to moult.
dépolir, v. a. to take off the polish.
dépolissage, m. roughing.
dépopulariser, v. a. to render unpopular.
déportation, f. transportation.
déporté, m. transported convict.
déportements, m. pl. misconduct.
déporter, v. a. to transport || **se ~**, to desist from. [witness.
déposant, m. (jur.) depositor || deponent ||
déposer, v. a. & n. to depose, to degrade || to give up || to deposit || to settle, to bear witness.
dépositaire, m. depositary, trustee.
déposition, f. deposition, evidence, testimony.
déposséder, v. a. to dispossess.
déposter, v. a. (mil.) to dislodge.
dépôt, m. deposit || store-house, warehouse || trust, charge || sediment, settling || **~ de mendicité**, work-house. [cant.
dépoter, v. a. to unpot (a plant) || to de-
dépouille, f. skins || spoil || remains || wardrobe || **~s**, pl. booty.
dépouillement, m. stripping || renouncing || close examining of an account.

dépouiller, v. a. to strip, to take off (the clothes, skin etc.) || to uncase || to gather the crop of, to rob, to plunder || to examine, to make extracts from || to cast off.
dépourvoir, v. a. ir. to deprive, to divest.
dépourvu, a. unprovided, destitute || **au ~**, unawares, unprovided.
dépravation, f. depravation, depravity.
dépraver, v. a. to deprave.
dépréciation, f. depreciation. [value.
déprécier, v. a. to depreciate || to under-
déprédateur, **trice**, m. & f. depredator.
déprédateur, **trice**, a. predatory.
déprier, v. a. to disinvite.
déprimer, v. a. to depress.
dépriser, v. a. to undervalue.
depuis, pr. since || **~ longtemps**, long ago.
dépuratif, **ve**, v. a. cleansing. [tion.
député, m. deputy.
députer, v. a. to depute, to send a deputa-
déracinement, m. rooting out, eradication. [eradicate.
déraciner, v. a. to root out, to root up, to
dérader, v. n. (mar.) to be driven out to sea.
déraidir, v. a. to remove stiffness || **se ~**, to lose one's stiffness.
déraillement, m. running off the rails.
dérailler, v. a. to run off the rails, to derail. [tion.
déraison, f. unreasonableness || infatua-
déraisonnablement, ad. unreasonably.
déraisonner, v. n. to speak nonsense.
dérangé, **e**, a. out of order || deranged || relaxed. [disturbance, perplexity.
dérangement, m. disorder, confusion,
déranger, v. a. to derange, to disorder || to displace || to incommode, to disturb || **se ~**, to take to bad courses, to live a disorderly life || to inconvenience oneself.
dératé, **e**, a. lively, sharp.
dérater, v. a. to extract the spleen.
derechef, adv. over again, again.
déréglé, **e**, a. (-ment, ad.) out of order || disorderly || irregular(ly) || dissolute, licentious. [debauchery.
dérèglement, m. disorder, irregularity.
dérégler, v. a. to disturb the order || to unsettle. [to cheer up.
dérider, v. a. to unwrinkle, to smoothe ||
dérision, f. derision || **tourner en ~**, to turn into ridicule, to deride || to trifle.
dérisoire, a. derisory. [la ~, adrift.
dérive, f. (mar.) drift || lee-way || **en ~**, à
dérivé, m. (gr.) derivative.
dérivé, **e**, a. derivative.
dériver, v. n. to derive || (mar.) to get clear of the shore, to drive.
dernier, m. the last || last reply.
dernier, **ère**, a. (-èrement, ad.) last(ly) || highest, utmost || lately.
dérobé, **e**, a. stolen || private || spare || à la -e, by stealth.
dérober, v. a. to rob, to steal, to plunder, to pilfer || to deprive of || to hide, to conceal || **se ~**, to steal away || to put out || to disappear || to shun.
dérogatoire, a. dérogeant, **e**, a. derogatory.
déroger, v. n. to derogate.
dérouillement, m. rubbing away of rust.

dérougir, v. a. to remove redness || ~, v. n. to lose one's redness.

dérouiller, v. a. to rub off rust, to polish.

déroulement, m. unrolling.

dérouler, v. a. to unroll, to spread out.

déroute, f. rout, disorder, ruin.

dérouter, v. a. to lead astray || to confuse || to put out || to baffle. [(mil.) rear.

derrière, m. backside || posterior || -s, pl.

derrière, ad. & pr. behind, back, after.

derviche, m. dervish.

dès, pr. from, since || ~ que, as soon as, since || ~ lors, from then || thence, therefore. [subscription.

se désabonner, to discontinue one's

désabuser, v. a. to disabuse, to undeceive.

désaccord, m. disunion, disagreement.

désaccorder, v. a. to untune, to put out of tune.

désaccoupler, v. a. to uncouple.

désaccoutumer, v. a. to disaccustom.

désachalander, v. a. to make one lose one's customers.

désaffection, f. disaffection.

désagréable, a. disagreeable, unpleasant || -ment, ad. disagreeably.

désagrément, m. disagreeableness, unpleasantness || disgust || imperfection.

désajuster, v. a. to disarrange, to put out of order. [to refresh.

désaltérer, v. a. to quench one's thirst,

désapparier, v. a. to unmatch (of birds).

désappointement, m. disappointment || éprouver, essuyer un ~, to meet with a disappointment.

désappointer, v. a. to disappoint.

désapprendre, v. n. ir. to unlearn, to forget. [approver] censurer.

désapprobateur, trice, m. & f. disapprover || censurer.

désapprobateur, trice, a. disapproving || censuring. [approval.

désapprobation, f. disapprobation, disapproval.

désapprouver, v. a. to disapprove, to blame.

désarçonner, v. a. to unhorse || to throw down || to silence || to shut up.

désargenter, v. a. to unsilver || to drain of cash || se ~, to lose its plating.

désarmement, m. disarming || (mar.) unrigging of ships.

désarmer, v. a. to disarm || to appease, to quiet || (mar.) to unrig || to uncock (a gun) || to disband (an army).

désarroi, m. disorder, confusion.

désarticuler, v. a. (chir.) to disjoint || to amputate.

désassembler, v. a. to take to pieces.

désassortir, v. a. to unmatch.

désastre, m. disaster. [astrous(ly).

désastreux, se, a. (-sement, ad.) disastrous(ly).

désavantage, m. disadvantage.

désavantager, v. a. to disadvantage, to wrong. [disadvantageous(ly).

désavantageux, se, a. (-sement, ad.)

désaveu, m. disavowal, denial.

désaveugler, v. a. to open the eyes of, to undeceive. [to retract.

désavouer, v. a. to disavow || to disown.

desceller, v. a. to unseal, to unfasten.

descendance, f. descent.

descendant, m. descendant, offspring.

descendant, e, a. descending.

descendre, v. a. & n. to descend, to bring down || to go down, to walk down || to fall (as a river) || to make a descent, to invade || to condescend || to fall down.

descente, f. descent, going down || alighting || declivity || landing || irruption, invasion || defluxion (of humours) || gutter || rupture || ~ de lit, bedside carpet.

descriptif, ve, a. descriptive.

déséchouer, v. a. to set afloat.

désemballage, m. unpacking.

désemballer, v. a. to unpack.

désembarquement, m. disembarking, landing. [land.

désembarquer, v. a. to disembark, to

désembourber, v. a. to take out of the mire. [(mar.) to disable (a ship).

désemparer, v. a. & n. to quit a place ||

désempeser, v. a. to unstarch.

désemplir, v. a. & n. to empty a little to grow empty || se ~, to grow empty || ne pas ~, to be always full.

désenchanter, v. a. to disenchant.

désenclouer, v. a. (mil.) to unspike.

désencroûter, v. a. to polish.

désenfiler, v. a. to unthread (a needle) || to unstring.

désenfler, v. a. to remove ou reduce a swelling || se ~, to get less swollen.

désenflure, f. cessation ou diminution of swelling. [sober again.

désenivrer, v. a. to sober || se ~, to get

désenlaidir, v. a. & n. to render less ugly || to grow less ugly.

désennuyer, v. a. to drive away melancholy, to divert, to cheer.

désenrayer, v. a. to unskid (a wheel).

désenrhumer, v. a. to cure a cold.

désenrouer, v. a. to remove hoarseness.

désensevelir, v. a. to unwrap (a body) || to exhume, to disinter.

désensorceler, v. a. to unbewitch.

désensorcellement, m. unbewitching.

désentêter, v. a. to cure of obstinacy.

désentortiller, v. a. to untwist.

désert, m. desert, wilderness.

désert, e, a. desert, solitary, abandoned, wild, waste, uncultivated. [to abandon.

déserter, v. a. & n. to desert, to forsake,

déserteur, m. (mil.) deserter.

désertion, f. desertion.

désespérance, f. despair.

désespéré, m. desperate fellow, madman.

désespéré, e, a. desperate, hopeless || past recovery || very sorry.

désespérer, v. a. & n. to bereave of all hopes, to grieve to excess || to despair, to give up all hope || se ~, to fall into despair.

désespoir, m. despair.

déshabillé, m. undress, morning-wrapper.

déshabiller, v. a. to undress.

déshabituer, v. a. to disaccustom.

déshérence, f. (jur.) escheat.

déshériter, v. a. to disinherit.

déshonnête, a. (-ment, ad.) indecent(ly).

déshonnêteté, f. indecency.

déshonneur, m. dishonour, disgrace.

déshonorant, e, a. dishonourable, shameful.   [grace ‖ to ruin.

déshonorer, v. a. to dishonour, to disgrace ‖ to ruin.

désignation, f. designation ‖ indication ‖ election, choice.

désigner, v. a. to designate, to describe, to denote, to point out ‖ to assign, to appoint.   [reality.

désillusion, f. loss of illusions, return to

désillusionner, v. a. to free from illusion.

désincorporer, v. a. to disincorporate.

désinence, f. (gr.) desinence, ending.

désinfatuer, v.a. to undeceive, to disabuse.

désinfectant, m. disinfecting agent ‖ deodorising powder.   [odorise.

désinfecter, v. a. to disinfect ‖ to de-

désinfection, f. disinfection ‖ fumigation.

désintéressé, e, a. disinterested ‖ uninterested ‖ indemnified ‖ impartial.

désintéressement, m. disinterestedness.

désintéresser, v. a. to indemnify.

désinvestir, v. a. (jur.) to divest.

désinviter, v. a. to recall an invitation.

désinvolture, f. easy and graceful manner.

désir, m. desire, wish.

désirer, v. a. to desire, to wish for.

désireux, se, a. desirous ‖ anxious.

désistement, m. desistance ‖ (jur.) nonsuit.

se désister, to desist, to give over ‖ to waive.   [obedient.

désobéir, v. n. to disobey ‖ to be dis-

désobéissance, f. disobedience.

désobéissant, e, a. disobedient.

désobligeamment, ad. unkindly.

désobligeance, f. unkindness.

désobliger, v. a. to disoblige.

désobstruer, v. a. to clear.

désoccupé, e, a. unoccupied, disengaged.

désœuvré, m. idler.

désœuvré, e, a. idle, unoccupied.

désœuvrement, m. idleness.

désolant, e, a. grievous, distressing.

désolateur, m. destroyer.

désolation, f. desolation ‖ grief, affliction.

désoler, v. a. to desolate, to ruin, to destroy ‖ to grieve, to afflict, to vex, to harass ‖ **se ~,** to be grieved, to lament.

désopiler, v. a. (méd.) to clear ‖ **~ la rate,** to excite to laughter, to dispel one's spleen.

désordonner, v. a. to disorder.

désordre, m. disorder, irregularity, confusion ‖ tumult, bustle, riot.

désorganisateur, m. disorganiser.

désorganiser, v. a. to disorganise.

désorganisation, f. disorganisation.

désorienter, v. a. to make one lose his way ‖ to disconcert.

désormais, ad. henceforth.

désossement, m. taking out of bones,

désosser, v. a. to bone.   [boning.

désoxyder, v. a. (chim.) to deoxydise.

despote, m. despot.

despotique, a. (—ment, ad.) despotic(ally).

despotisme, m. despotism.

se dessaisir, to part with, to give up.

dessaisissement, m. parting with ‖ divesting oneself (of).

dessaisonner, v. a. to change the rotation of crops.

dessalaison, f. freshening, becoming less salt (of water) ‖ soaking of cod-fish.

dessaler, v. a. to unsalt, to soak in water.

dessangler, v. a. to ungird.

desséchement, m. drying up ‖ draining ‖ withering.

dessécher, v. a. to dry up, to parch ‖ to drain ‖ to wither ‖ to waste.

dessein, m. design, intention, purpose ‖ scheme, aim, plan ‖ **à ~,** on purpose.

desseller, v. a. to unsaddle.

desserrer, v. a. to loosen ‖ **~ les dents,** dessert, m. dessert.   [to open one's lips.

desserte, f. leavings ‖ officiating.

desservant, m. officiating clergyman ‖ curate.

desservir, v. a. & n. to remove the cloth ‖ to do an ill office (to) ‖ to do duty ‖ to ply on ‖ to wait on ‖ to connect.

dessiccatif, ve, a. (méd.) dessicative, drying.

dessiller, v. a. to open (one's eyes).

dessin, m. drawing ‖ plan ‖ pattern.

dessinateur, m. draughtsman, patterndrawer ‖ **~ de jardins,** landscape-gardener.

dessiner, v. a. to draw, to design, to sketch ‖ to set off ‖ **se ~,** to assume a form ‖ to appear.

dessoler, v. a. *vide* **dessaisonner.**

dessouder, v. a. to unsolder.

dessoûler, v. a. & n. to sober ‖ to get sober.

dessous, m. under part, undermost part ‖ wrong side ‖ **(de lampe)** lamp-mat ‖ **avoir le ~,** to have the worst of it.

dessous, pr. & ad. under, below ‖ underneath, undermost.

dessus, m. upper part *ou* side, top, right side ‖ advantage, superiority ‖ the best of it ‖ **prendre le ~,** to get the best of it.

dessus, pr. & ad. on, upon, uppermost ‖ **au ~,** above, beyond.

destin, m. destiny, fate.

destinataire, m. receiver (of a letter).

destinée, f. destiny, doom, fate.

destiner, v. a. to destine ‖ to doom ‖ to intend.

destitué, e, a. destitute, devoid.

destituer, v. a. to dismiss.

destitution, f. dismissal.

destructeur, m. destroyer.

destructeur, a. destructive ‖ destroying.

destructif, ve, a. destructive.

désuétude, f. disuse.   [cord.

désunion, f. disunion ‖ separation ‖ dis-

désunir, v. a. to disunite, to disjoin, to divide, to separate ‖ **se ~,** to fall out.

détaché, e, a. loose ‖ indifferent.

détachement, m. (mil.) detachment ‖ total disengagement ‖ indifference.

détacher, v. a. to detach, to loosen ‖ to separate ‖ to disengage (from) ‖ to take out (spots from) ‖ to send after ‖ **se ~,** to come off, to grow loose ‖ to quit ‖ to stand out in relief.   [**~,** by retail.

détail, m. detail, particulars ‖ retail ‖ **en**

détaillant, m. retailer.

détailler, v. a. to cut up ‖ to detail ‖ to retail. [gnat-strainer.

détailliste, m. minute describer ‖ (fig.)

détalage, m. packing up ‖ taking in of goods from a shop-window.

détaler, v. a. & n. to pack up (goods) ‖ to shut up shop ‖ to scamper away.

déteindre, v. a. & n. ir. to discolour, to take out the colour ‖ to fade.

dételer, v. a. to unyoke, to unharness.

détendre, v. a. to unbend, to slacken ‖ to take down. [to confine.

détenir, v. a. ir. to detain, to withhold ‖

détente, f. trigger ‖ detention ‖ stop ‖ stop-

détenteur, **trice**, m. & f. holder. [page.

détenu, **e**, m. & f. prisoner. [to spoil.

détériorer, v. a. to damage ‖ to impair.

déterminé, **e**, a. (**-ment**, ad.) determined ‖ determinate(ly) ‖ resolute(ly).

déterminer, v. a. to determine, to settle ‖ to decide ‖ to excite ‖ **se ~**, to be resolved **ou** decided.

déterrer, v. a. to disinter ‖ to discover.

détestablement, ad. detestably.

détester, v. a. to detest, to abhor.

détirer, v. a. to draw out, to stretch.

détiser, v. a. to rake out (the fire).

détisser, v. a. to unweave.

détoner, v. n. (chim.) to detonate.

détonner, v. n. (mus.) to be out of tune.

détordre, v. a. to untwist.

détors, **e**, a. untwisted.

détortiller, v. a. to untwist.

détour, m. turning, by-way, way about ‖ evasion, excuse, subterfuge ‖ **prendre des ~s**, to beat about the bush ‖ **sans ~**, straightforward. [cation.

détournement, m. turning aside ‖ defal-

détourner, v. a. to turn aside, to put out of the way, to avert ‖ to take away, to divert ‖ to pervert ‖ to embezzle ‖ to dissuade ‖ **se ~**, to turn aside ‖ to go out of one's way, to swerve. [slander.

détracter, v. a. to detract ‖ to traduce, to

détracteur, **trice**, m. & f. detractor.

détraction, f. detraction.

détraquer, v. a. to spoil a horse's pace ‖ to lead astray, to distract, to divert.

détrempe, f. water-colours.

détremper, v. a. to dilute ‖ to soften steel ‖ to weaken.

détresse, f. distress.

détresser, v. a. to untwist, to unweave.

détriment, m. detriment, prejudice ‖ **-s**, pl. (géol.) remains (pl.).

détritus, m. (géol.) detritus.

détroit, m. straits ‖ (British) Channel.

détromper, v. a. to undeceive.

détrôner, v. a. to dethrone. [to rob.

détrousser, v. a. to untuck ‖ to let down ‖

détruire, v. a. ir. to destroy, to ruin ‖ **se ~**, to fall to ruin ‖ to make away with oneself.

dette, f. debt ‖ **~ active**, debt due to us ‖ **~ passive**, debt due to others.

deuil, m. mourning ‖ mourning-dress ‖ time of mourning ‖ grief, sorrow ‖ mourners.

deux, m. deuce, two.

deux, a. two ‖ **~ à ~**, two and two.

deuxième, m. second ‖ second floor ‖ second class ‖ fore-cabin.

deuxième, a. (**-ment**, ad.) second(ly).

dévaler, v. n. to slope.

dévaliser, v. a. to rifle, to strip.

devancer, v. a. to go before, to precede, to outrun ‖ to surpass ‖ to anticipate.

devancier, **ère**, m. & f. predecessor.

devant, m. front, forepart.

devant, pr. d. ad. before ‖ **in front of** ‖ ahead of ‖ before it **ou** them.

devanture, f. shop-front.

dévastateur, **trice**, m. & f. destroyer.

dévastateur, **trice**, a. destructive.

dévaster, v. a. to devastate. [to bad.

déveine, f. change of a run of good luck

développement, m. development, unfolding. [to display, to explain.

développer, v. a. to develope ‖ to unfold,

devenir, v. n. ir. to become, to grow.

dévergondage, m. shamelessness ‖ dissoluteness. [irregular.

dévergondé, **e**, a. impudent ‖ dissolute ‖

déverrouiller, v. a. to unbolt.

devers, pr.; **par ~ soi**, in one's possession.

dévers, **e**, a. leaning, not upright, on an incline. [to lean ‖ to throw ‖ to reflect.

déverser, v. a. to bend, to incline,

déversoir, m. (tech.) weir ‖ sluice.

dévêtir, v. a. to undress, to divest, **to unclothe**, to strip.

déviation, f. deviation, deflection.

dévidage, m. winding into a skein.

dévider, v. a. to reel.

dévideur, **se**, m. & f. winder.

dévidoir, m. reel, spindle.

dévier, v. n. to deviate.

devin, m. diviner, soothsayer.

deviner, v. a. to divine, to guess.

devineresse, f. divineress.

devineur, m. guesser.

devis, m. estimate.

dévisager, v. a. to disfigure ‖ **to scratch** one's face ‖ to stare one in the face.

devise, f. device, motto.

deviser, v. n. to chat, to talk costly.

dévisser, v. a. to unscrew. [the belly).

dévoiement, m. (méd.) looseness, flux (of

dévoiler, v. a. to unveil, to discover.

devoir, m. duty, obligation, task ‖ **-s**, pl. respects.

devoir, v. a. & n. ir. to owe, to be indebted to, to be obliged for ‖ to be bound, to be obliged ‖ must, ought ‖ to be necessary.

dévolu, m. lapse of right ‖ (fig.) choice.

dévolu, **e**, a. devolved.

dévorant, m. glutton.

dévorant, **e**, a. devouring, consuming ‖ ravenous.

dévorer, v. a. to devour, to eat greedily ‖ to gorge oneself ‖ to suppress ‖ to brook ‖ **~ des yeux**, to gaze at ‖ to pore over.

dévoreur, m. devourer ‖ **~ de livres**, book-worm.

dévot, **e**, m. & f. devotee ‖ devout woman.

dévot, **e**, a. (**-ement**, ad.) devout(ly) ‖ pious(ly) ‖ bigot.

dévotion, f. devotion, devoutness, piety.

dévouement, devoûment, m. devotion, devotedness || self-denial.

dévouer, v. a. to devote, to dedicate.

dévoyer, v. a. to take *ou* place the wrong way || to put out of order.

dextérité, f. dexterity, skill.

diabète, m. (méd.) diabetes.

diabétique, a. (méd.) diabetic.

diable, m. devil, deuce || wild child || truck || drag || rub || rap.

diablement, ad. devilishly.

diablerie, f. devilish trick, witchcraft.

diablesse, f. wicked woman, shrew.

diablotin, m. little devil || chocolate-cracker.   [(ly) || devilish(ly).

diabolique, a. (**-ment,** ad.) diabolical

diaconat, m. deaconry.

diacre, m. deacon.

diaconesse, f. deaconess.

diadème, m. diadem.

diagnose, f. (méd.) diagnosis.

diagonalement, ad. diagonally.

dialecte, m. dialect.

dialectique, f. dialectics.

dialogique, a. dialogistic.

dialogue, m. dialogue.

dialoguer, v. a. to put in dialogue || ~, v. n. to converse.   [(fig.) gem.

diamant, m. diamond, adamant || jewel ||

diamantaire, m. diamond-cutter.

diamétralement, ad. diametrically.

diamètre, m. diameter.   [gun.

diane, f. (mil.) reveille || (mar.) morning-

diantre ! the deuce ! || **-ment,** ad. deucedly.

diapason, m. (mus.) pitch || tuning-fork.

diaphane, a. transparent.

diaphragme, m. (an.) diaphragm.

diaprer, v. a. to diaper.

diarrhée, f. diarrhœa.

diatribe, f. diatribe.

dictame, m. dittany.

dictateur, m. dictator.

dictatorial, e, a. dictatorial.

dictature, f. dictatorship.

dictée, f. dictation.

dicter, v. a. to dictate || to suggest.

diction, f. diction, style || delivery.

dictionnaire, m. dictionary.

diction, m. saying.

dièse, m. (mus.) sharp.

dièse, a. (mus.) sharp.

diète, f. diet || low diet.

Dieu, m. God || ~ merci ! thank God ! || plût à ~ ! God grant it ! || à ~ ne plaise ! God forbid ! || ~ veuille ! God grant !

diffamant, e, a. defamatory.

diffamateur, m. defamer, libeller, slan-derer.   [slandering.

diffamation, f. defamation, libel(ling).

diffamatoire, a. defamatory, slanderous, libellous.   [libel.

diffamer, v. a. to defame, to slander || to

différemment, ad. differently.

différencier, v. a. to distinguish.

différend, m. difference.

différent, e, a. different, various.

différer, v. a. & n. to defer, to put off || to differ.

difficile, a. (**-ment,** ad.) difficult || hard-

(ly) || unaccommodating || peevish || ticklish || not compliant, rigid, austere || particular || with difficulty.

difficulté, f. difficulty, impediment || embarrassment || tiff || fuss.

difficultueux, se, a. squeamish, peevish.

difforme, a. deformed.

difformité, f. deformity.

diffus, e, a. diffuse || wordy.

diffusément, ad. diffusely.

digérer, v. a. & n. to digest || to brook || to stomach || to put up with || to swallow.

digeste, m. digest.

digestif, m. (méd.) digestive.

digestif, ve, a. (méd.) digestive.

digitale, f. (bot.) fox-glove.

digne, a. (**-ment,** ad.) worthy of, deserving || dignified || worthily, deservedly.

dignitaire, m. dignitary.

dignité, f. dignity, title.

digression, f. digression.

digue, f. dike, dam, mole || bank || obstacle.

diguer, v. a. to dike.

dilapidateur, m. dilapidator.

dilapider, v. a. to dilapidate || to waste.

dilater, v. a. to dilate, to expand, to widen.

dilemme, m. dilemma.

diligemment, ad. diligently.

diligence, f. diligence || speed, dispatch ||

diligent, e, a. diligent.   [stage-coach.

diligenter, v. a. & n. to forward || to push on || se ~, to hasten, to make haste.

diluer, v. a. to dilute (liquids).

diluvien, ne, a. diluvial.

dimanche, m. Sunday.

dîme, f. tithe.

dimension, f. dimension.

diminuer, v. a. & n. to diminish, to decrease || to shorten || to sink, to fall.

diminutif, ve, m. & f. (gr.) diminutive.

diminutif, ve, a. diminutive.

diminution, f. diminution, abatement, decrease.

dinanderie, f. brass-wares.

dinandier, m. brazier.

dînatoire, a. ; **déjeûner~,** hearty luncheon || late lunch.

dinde, f. turkey-hen.

dindon, m. turkey-cock || ninny.

dindonneau, m. young turkey.

dîné, dîner, m. dinner || dinner-time || dinner-party.   [without one's dinner.

dîner, v. n. to dine || ~ par cœur, to go

dînette, f. little dinner.

dîneur, m. dinner-guest || great eater.

diocèse, m. diocese.

diocésain, a. diocesan.

diphthérite, f. (méd.) diphtheritis.

diphthongue, f. diphthong.

diplomate, m. diplomatist.

diplomatie, f. diplomacy.

diplomatique, a. (**-ment,** ad.), diplomatic(ally).

diplôme, m. diploma, patent.

diplômé, e, a. with a diploma, certificated.

dire, m. saying, opinion || words.

dire, v. a. ir. to tell, to say, to relate || to mean, to signify || to bid || c'est-à-~, that is to say || pour ainsi ~, as it were.

direct, e, a. (**-ement,** ad.) direct(ly) || straight(ly) || in a straight line.
directeur, m. director, manager, confessor.
direction, f. direction, management || directoire, m. directory.   [rectorship.
directorial, e a. directorial.
directrice, f. directress.   [dirigible.
dirigeable, m. dirigible balloon || ~, a.
diriger, v. a. to direct, to manage, to guide.
discernement, m. discernment, distinction.
discerner, v. a. to discern.   [tion.
disciplinaire, a. disciplinarian.
discipliner, v. a. to discipline.
discontinuer, v. a. & n. to discontinue.
disconvenance, f. unsuitableness || dissimilarity || disproportion.
disconvenir, v. n. ir. to deny.
discordant, e, out of tune.
discorde, f. discord.
discoureur, se, m. & f. talker.
discourir, v. n. ir. to discourse.
discours, m. discourse || speech || talk || discourtois, e, a. discourteous.   [lecture.
discréditer, v. a. to discredit.
discret, ète, a. (**-ètement,** ad.) discreet(ly) || prudent || reserved(ly).
discrétion, f. discretion, discreetness, prudence || mercy || à ~, at one's discretion *ou* will || freely || as much as one likes.
discrétionnaire, a. discretionary.
disculper, v. a. to exculpate, to clear.
discussion, f. discussion, dispute, debate.
discuter, v. a. to discuss, to debate.
disert, e, a. eloquent, fluent.
disette, f. dearth, scarcity, penury || want.
diseur, m. teller || talker.
disgrâce, f. disgrace, disfavour || ill-fortune.
disgracié, e, a. out of favour || deformed.
disgracier, v. a. to disgrace.
disgracieux, se, a. (**-sement,** ad.) ungraceful(ly) || disagreeable, unsightly || awkward(ly).
disjoindre, v. a. ir. to disjoin.
dislocation, f. (chir.) dislocation || (mil.) dismemberment, breaking up.
disloquer, v. a. to dislocate.
disparaître, v. n. ir. to disappear || to go.
disparate, f. incongruity.
disparate, a. incongruous || ill-matched || unsymmetrical.
disparité, f. disparity.
disparition, f. disappearance.
dispendieux, se, a. expensive.
dispensaire, m. dispensary.
dispensateur, m. dispenser || ruler.
dispense, f. dispensation || exemption || license.   [empt from || to bestow.
dispenser, v. a. to dispense with, to exdisperser, v. a. to disperse, to scatter.
dispersion, f. dispersion || (mil.) breaking up.
disponibilité, f. quality of that which can be disposed of || en ~, unattached.
disponible, a. disposable || disengaged.
dispos, a. active, nimble.   [willing.
disposé, e, a. disposed, ready, inclined,
disposer, v. a. & n. to dispose, to adjust, to prepare || to have at command || se ~, to get ready || to be about.

disposition, f. disposition, arrangement, order || aptitude || inclination || disposal, command || tendency, taste || humour || resolution || provision.
disproportionné, e, a. disproportionate.
disputailler, v. n. to cavil.
disputaillerie, f. wrangling.
disputailleur, se, m. & f. wrangler, caviller.   [cussion.
dispute, f. dispute, quarrel, wrangle || discuter, v. a. & n. to dispute, to contend for || to vie || se ~, to contend for || to be disputed || le ~ à, to struggle for the mastery with.
disputeur, m. wrangler, disputant.
disputeur, a. disputatious, quarrelsome.
disque, m. disk, quoit.
dissemblable, a. dissimilar.
dissemblance, f. dissimilarity.
disséminer, v. a. to disseminate.
dissension, f. dissension || disagreement.
dissentiment, m. dissenting.
disséquer, v. a. to dissect.
disséqueur, m. dissector.
dissertateur, m. dissertator.
disserter, v. n. to discourse.
dissidence, f. dissent.
dissident, m. dissenter.
dissident, e, a. dissenting.
dissimulateur, m. dissembler.
dissimulé, e, m. & f. dissembler.
dissimulé, e, a. dissembling.
dissimuler, v. a. & n. to dissemble, to conceal, to feign not to notice.
dissipateur, m. spendthrift.
dissipation, f. dissipation, waste || relaxation.
dissiper, v. a. to dissipate || to disperse, to waste, to dispel.
dissolu, e, a. dissolute.
dissoluble, a. dissoluble.
dissolution, f. dissolution || looseness of manners, dissoluteness.
dissolvant, m. dissolvent.
dissonance, f. (mus.) dissonance.
dissonant, e, a. dissonant.
dissonner, v. n. to be dissonant || to jar.
dissoudre, v. a. ir. to dissolve.
dissuader, v. a. to dissuade.
dissyllabe, a. dissyllabic.
distance, f. distance, interval.
distancer, v. a. to lay out at equal distances || to distance.
distant, e, a. distant.
distendre, v. a. to distend.
distillateur, m. distiller.
distiller, v. a. & n. to distil || to discharge, to vent || to drop.
distillerie, f. distillery.
distinct, e, a. (**-ement,** ad.) distinct(ly).
distinctif, ve, a. distinctive.
distinction, f. distinction, difference || superiority || homme de ~, man of note.
distingué, e, a. distinguished || eminent || gentlemanly || ladylike.
distinguer, v. a. to distinguish || to single out || to treat with regard || se ~, to distinguish oneself || to be distinguished.
distique, m. distich.

distors, e, a. distorted.

distraction, f. distraction, separation || want of attention, absence of mind || diversion, recreation.

distraire, v. a. & n. ir. to distract, to separate, to part || to subdue, to take away || to divert from, to disturb.

distrait, e, a. inattentive, absent.

distribuer, v. a. to distribute, to deal out || to dispense || to dispose.

distributeur, m. distributor, dispenser.

distributif, ve, a. distributive.

distribution, f. distribution, division || (typ.) distributing || cast (of a play).

district, m. district.

dit, m. saying, maxim.

dit, e, a. said, spoken || concluded, decided || surnamed.

dito, ad. do., ditto.

diurétique, a. (méd.) diuretic.

diurne, e, a. daily.

divagant, e, a. wandering.

divagation, f. rambling, wandering.

divaguer, v. n. to go astray, to wander, to ramble.

divan, m. Divan (sultan's council) || divan, [sofa-bed.

dive, a. divine.

divergence, f. divergence || difference.

divergent, e, divergent.

diverger, v. n. to diverge.

divers, e, a. (-ement, ad.) diverse(ly) || different(ly) || various || several(ly) || in various ways.

diversifier, v. a. to diversify, to vary.

diversité, f. diversity, variety.

divertir, v. a. to divert || to amuse || to embezzle || se ~, to amuse oneself.

divertissement, m. recreation, pastime || sport. [unclaimed dividend.

dividende, m. dividend || ~ arriéré, m.

divin, e, a. (-ement, ad.) divine(ly) || godlike, heavenly || admirable.

divinatoire, a. divinatory || divining.

diviniser, v. a. to deify.

divinité, f. divinity, godhead. [part.

diviser, v. a. to divide || to separate, to

divisibilité, f. divisibility. [divorced.

divorcer, v. a. & n. to divorce, to be

divulgation, f. divulgation || matter divulger, v. a. to divulge. [vulged.

dix, m. ten || tenth.

dix, a. ten || tenth || ~-huit, a. eighteen || ~-huitième, ad. eighteenth || ~-neuf, a. nineteen || ~-neuvième, a. nineteenth || ~-sept, a. seventeen.

dixième, m. tenth.

dixième, a. (-ment, ad.) tenth(ly).

dizain, m. stanza of ten verses.

dizaine, f. ten || decennary.

docart, m. dog-cart.

docile, a. (-ment, ad.) docile(ly) || tractable || with docility.

docilité, f. docility.

dock, m. (mar.) dock.

docte, a. (-ment, ad.) learned(ly).

docteur, m. doctor.

doctoral, e, a. (-ement, ad.) doctoral(ly).

doctorat, m. doctorship.

doctrinaire, m. doctrinary.

doctrine, f. doctrine.

document, m. document || instrument || (jur.) title-deed.

dodeliner, v. a. & n. to rock || to nod.

dodo, m. sleep || bed || **faire** ~, to sleep || **aller faire** ~, to go to bye-bye.

dodu, e, a. plump.

dogaresse, f. the wife of a doge.

doge, m. doge. [(ally).

dogmatique, a. (-ment, ad.) dogmatic

dogmatiser, v. n. to dogmatise.

dogme, m. dogma, tenet.

dogre, m. (mar.) dogger-boat.

dogue, m. bulldog, mastiff.

doguin, m. young house-dog.

doigt, m. finger || (du pied) toe || knuckle || little bit || digit.

doigté, **doigter**, m. (mus.) fingering.

doigter, v. a. (mus.) to finger.

doigtier, m. finger-stall.

doit, m. (com.) debit || debtor.

dol, m. (jur.) fraud, deceit.

doléance, f. complaint || grievance.

dolemment, ad. dolefully.

dolent, e, a. doleful, mournful.

doler, v. a. to adze, to chip with the adze.

domaine, m. domain || estate || property || department.

domanial, e, a. belonging to a domain.

dôme, m. dome, cathedral || cupola.

domesticité, f. domesticity || domestics || tameness.

domestique, m. & f. domestic, servant || home. [menial || tame.

domestique, a. domestic || internal ||

domestiquer, v. a. to tame.

domicile, m. domicile, dwelling, abode || à ~, at home.

domiciliaire, a. domiciliary.

domicilié, a resident || settled || domiciled.

dominant, e, a. leading || predominant, prevalent.

dominateur, trice, m. & f. ruler.

dominateur, trice, a. ruling.

domination, f. domination, dominion, government.

dominer, v. a. & n. to predominate, to domineer, to rule, to prevail || to rise above || to command a view of.

dominicain, m. Dominican friar.

dominicaine, f. Dominican nun.

dominical, e, a. dominical || **oraison -e**, Lord's prayer. [(game).

domino, m. masquerade-dress || dominoes

dominoterie, f. stained paper.

dominotier, m. paper-stainer.

dommage, m. damage, hurt, injury, detriment, loss || c'est ~, it is a pity.

dommageable, a. injurious || prejudicial.

domptable, a. tameable.

dompter, v. a. to tame || to subdue, to vanquish, to conquer.

dompteur, m. tamer || subduer.

don, m. gift, present || knack.

donataire, m. donee.

donateur, trice, m. & f. donor, giver.

donation, f. donation || deed of gift.

donc, c. then, therefore, accordingly.

dondon, f. stout, red-faced woman.

donjon, m. dungeon ‖ turret.

donjonné, e, a. turreted.

donnant, e, a. liberal, generous‖~~, give and take.

donne, f. deal (at cards).

donnée, f. notion, idea ‖ **-s**, pl. information ‖ data (pl.).

donner, v. a. & n. to give, to bestow, to confer ‖ to deliver ‖ to impart, to communicate ‖ to grant, to allow ‖ to deal (at cards) ‖ to engage, to fight, to conflict ‖ (mar.) to heel, to incline to one side ‖ **se ~**, to give oneself up ‖ to be addicted ‖ to assume ‖ to take place ‖ to be fought ‖ to strike ‖ to knock ‖ to hit ‖ **s'en ~**, to enjoy oneself.

donneur, euse, m. & f. giver.

dont, pn. whose, whereof, of which, of whom ‖ for whom ‖ from **ou** by whom **ou** which.

donzelle, f. damsel ‖ wench.

dorade, f. gold-fish.

dorénavant, ad. henceforth.

dorer, v. a. to gild ‖ (**pâtisserie**) to glaze.

doreur, se, m. & f. gilder.

dorloter, v. a. to fondle.

dormant, e, a. sleeping ‖ stagnant ‖ dull.

dormeur, se, m. & f. sleeper ‖ sluggard.

dormeuse, f. lounging-chair ‖ easy travelling carriage ‖ ear-ring.

dormir, m. sleeping, rest.

dormir, v. n. ir. to sleep, **to be sleeping** ‖ to be stagnant **ou** still.

dormitif, ve, m. & f. soporific.

dormitif, ve, a. soporific.

dortoir, m. dormitory.

dcrure, f. gilding ‖ glazing.

dos, m. back ‖ **(du nez)** bridge ‖ **saddleback** ‖ shelving-ridge.

dose, f. dose ‖ portion.

doser, v. a. to dose.

dossier, m. back (of a seat) ‖ head-board ‖ bundle of papers ‖ bag.

dot, f. portion, dowry. [property.

dotal, e, a. of one's dowry **ou** separate

dotation, f. endowment.

doter, v. a. to portion, to endow.

douaire, m. jointer, dower.

douairière, f. dowager.

douane, f. custom-house‖duty upon goods.

douaner, v.a. to clear at the custom-house.

douanier, m. custom-house officer ‖ tidewaiter.

douar, m. (Arabian) village. [waiter.

doublage, m. (mar.) sheathing.

double, a. double ‖ deceitful ‖ strong ‖ downright ‖ **-ment**, ad. doubly.

doubler, v. a. to double ‖ to line ‖ (mar.)

doublon, m. doubloon. [to sheath.

doublure, f. lining ‖ substitute (of a player).

douceâtre, a. sweetish.

doucement, ad. softly, gently, slowly, patiently, kindly, tenderly ‖ indifferently, so-so, pretty well.

doucereux, se, a. sweetish ‖ soft, tender.

doucet, te, a. demure, affectedly modest.

doucette, f. corn-salad.

douceur, f. sweetness, softness, mildness, gentleness ‖ good-nature, pleasure ‖ advantage, profit ‖ gratification ‖ **-s**, pl. flattering words.

douche, f. shower-bath.

douer, v. a. to bestow, to endow.

douillet, te, a. (**-tement**, ad.) downy ‖ soft(ly) ‖ tender(ly) ‖ nice ‖ at ease.

douillette, f. wadded silk-gown.

douilletter v. a. to coddle.

douleur, f. pain, sorrow, grief, affliction, anguish, dolor, woe.

douloureux, se, a. (**-sement**, ad.) painful(ly) ‖ smarting ‖ grievous(ly) ‖ afflicting.

doute, f. doubt ‖ **révoquer en ~**, to question.

douter, v. n. to doubt, to question, to scruple, to suspect ‖ **se ~**, to suspect, to mistrust. [certain.

douteux, se, a. doubtful, dubious, uneasy.

douvain, m. stave-wood.

douve, f. stave. [easy.

doux, ce, a. sweet ‖ mild, soft, smooth,

douzaine, f. dozen ‖ **à la ~**, by **ou** to the dozen ‖ of little value.

douze, m. twelve ‖ twelfth.

douze, a. twelve ‖ twelfth.

douzième, m. twelfth.

douzième, a. (**-ment**, ad.) twelfth(ly).

doyen, m. dean, senior.

doyenné, m. deanery.

dragage, m. dredging.

dragée, f. sugar-plum ‖ small shot ‖ bull's

drageoir, m. confit-box. [eye.

drageon, m. shoot, sucker.

drageonner, v. n. to put forth suckers.

dragon, m. dragon ‖ dragoon ‖ termagant.

dragonnade, f. dragonnade ‖ **livrer aux ~s**, to dragoon.

dragonne, f. sword-knot.

drague, f. dredge.

draguer, v. a. to dredge.

draille, f. (mar.) stay ‖ stay-sail.

drainage, m. (agr.) drainage.

drainer, v. a. to drain.

dramatique, m. drama.

dramatique, a. (**-ment**, ad.) dramatic (ally).

dramatiser, v. a. to dramatise.

dramaturge, m. dramatist.

drame, m. drama.

drap, m. cloth ‖ sheet (for a bed).

drapé, e, a. cloth-like.

drapeau, m. colours, banner ‖ **sous les -x**, in the service.

draper, v. a. & n. to cover **ou** hang with cloth ‖ to cover with mourning ‖ to jeer, to banter ‖ **se ~**, to dress ‖ to make a show ‖ to boast. [making.

draperie, f. drapery, cloth-trade ‖ cloth-

drapier, m. draper, woollen-draper.

drêche, f. malt, grains.

drelin, m. tinkling.

dresser, v. a. & n. to raise, to set up, to make straight ‖ to erect, to build ‖ to bring up, to instruct ‖ to rise on end, to stand ‖ **se ~**, to stand, to stand upright ‖ to rise on end.

dressoir, m. sideboard.

drille, m. fellow ‖ **bon ~**, jolly fellow ‖ **-s**, f. pl. rags for making paper.

drisse, f. (mar.) gear ‖ halliard.

drogman, m. dragoman.

French and English.

drogue, f. drug || rubbish; stuff.
droguer, v. a. to physic || to adulterate || to dance attendance || to drudge.
droguerie, f. drugs || drug-trade.
droguet, m. drugget.
droguier, m. drug-box || travelling medi-
droguiste, m. druggist.   [cine-chest.
droit, m. right, justice, equity || power, title, claim, prerogative, privilege || law || jurisprudence || tax, duty || de ~, by rights, rightfully.
droit, e, a. (& ad.) right || straight(ly) || just || honest(ly) || upright || direct(ly) || judicious || stand-up, stick-up || single-breasted || sound.
droite, f. right hand || à ~, on the right hand, to ou on the right.   [sincerely.
droitement, ad. righteously, uprightly,
droiture, f. uprightness, honesty, integrity.
drolatique, a. amusing, laughable.
drôle, a. (-ment, ad.) droll, funny || co-mical(ly) || ~ de corps, m. queer fellow.
drôlerie, f. drollery.
drôlesse, f. wench, hussy.
dromadaire, m. dromedary.
dru, e, a. fledged || pert, lively, healthy || thick (of corn) || ~, ad. in great quantity,
druide, m. Druid.   [thick.
druidique, a. druidic(al).
druidisme, f. druidism.
dû, m. due.
dû, due, a due, owing.
dualisme, m. dualism.
dualité, f. duality.   [doubt.
dubitatif, ve, a. dubious, expressive of
duc, m. duke || born-owl.
duché, m. dukedom, duchy.
duchesse, f. duchess || couch.
ductilité, f. ductility.
duègne, f. duenna || old governess.
duel, f. duel || appeler en ~, to challenge.
duelliste, m. dueller.
dulcifier, v. a. (chim.) to dulcify.
dûment, ad. duly.
dune, f. sand-hill || down.
dunette, f. (mar.) poop royal.
duo, m. (mus.) duet.
dupe, f. dupe, fool, gull.
duper, v. a. to dupe || to gull.
duperie, f. cheat, trickery, take-in.
dupeur, se, m. & f. cheat, trickster.
duplicata, m. duplicate.   [deceit.
duplicité, f. duplicity || double-dealing,
duquel = de lequel.
dur, e, a. & ad. (-ement, ad.) hard(ly) || close, firm || painful || austere, severe || harsh(ly) || rough(ly) || merciless, inhuman, cruel || tough, stale || disagreeable.
durable, a. durable, lasting.
durant, pr. during.
durcir, v. a. & n. to harden, to indurate || se ~, to grow hard.
durcissement, m. hardening, induration.
dure, f. ground, floor || hard bed.
durée, f. duration.
durement, ad. hard, harshly, roughly.
durer, v. n. to last, to continue, to endure.
duret, te, a. somewhat hard, rather tough.

dureté, f. hardness, firmness, toughness, callosity || obduracy || savageness, rough-ness || cruelty || dulness (of hearing).
durillon, m. callosity || hard skin || corn.
duriuscule, a. rather hard || somewhat
duvet, m. down.   [tough.
duveteux, se, a. downry.
dynamite, f. dynamite.
dynamique, f. dynamics (pl.).
dynamique, a. dynamic.
dynastie, f. dynasty.
dynastique, a. dynastic.
dyspepsie, f. (méd.) dyspepsía.
dyssenterie, f. (méd.) dysentery.

E.

eau, f. water || rain || lake, sea || sweat || urine || juice (of some fruits) || gloss, lustre || ~ de mer, salt water || ~x, fresh water || ~ de mer, salt water || ~x, pl. watering place || mineral waters || fountains |, tide || ~ de source, ~ de fontaine, spring-water || ~ bénite, holy-water || ~ forte, aqua fortis || ~ de savon, soap-suds || ~-de-vie, brandy || ~ de Cologne, Cologna-water || ~x mortes, pl. (mar.) neap tide || ~x vives, pl. (mar.) spring tide || ~ panée, toast-water || ~ rougie, wine and water |; ~ de vaisselle, dish-water || faire ~, to leak || faire de l'~, to take in water.
s'ébahir, to be amazed.
ébahissement, m. amazement.
ébarber, v. a. to clip the rough edges (of paper) || to strip quills || to scrape.
ébat, m. pleasure, pastime, diversion || prendre ses -s, vide **s'ébattre** || mener à l'~, to exercise (hunting dogs).
s'ébattre, to frolic, to gambol.
ébaubi, e, a. astonished, amazed.
ébauche, f. rough draught, sketch.
ébaucher, v. a. to sketch || to rough-model || to half-finish.
ébauchoir, m. roughing-chisel.
ébène, f. ebony.
ébéner, v. a. to ebonise.   [burnum.
ébénier, m. (bot.) ebony-tree || faux ~, la-
ébéniste, m. cabinet-maker.
ébénisterie, f. cabinet-work.
éblouir, v. a. to dazzle.
éblouissement, m. dazzling, dimness.
éborgner, v. a. to blind in one eye || to put out one eye.
éboueur, m. road-scraper.
ébouillir, v. n. to boil away.
éboulement, m. falling down || earth-slip.
s'ébouler, to fall down.   [land-slip.
éboulis, m. rubbish.
ébouriffé, e, a. put out of order, dis-ordered (of hair).
ébouriffer, v. a. to disorder || to ruffle || to dumbfound || to scandalise.
ébranchement, m. lopping.
ébrancher, v. a. to lop.
ébranlement, m. shaking, tottering || shock, concussion || decay || fear, trouble.

ébranler, v. a. to shake, to move, to shock || to disturb, to affright || s'~, to move, to waver || to be frightened || to give way, to fall back. [in.

ébrécher, v. a. to notch, to make a gap

ébriété, f. intoxication || drunkenness.

ébrouement, m. snorting (of a horse).

s'ébrouer, to snort.

ébruiter, v. a. to divulge || s'~, to be talked of, to spread about || to get wind.

ébullition, f. ebullition || boiling.

écacher, v. a. to crush, to squash.

écaille, f. scale, shell || tortoise-shell.

écailler, ère, m. & f. oyster-man, oyster-woman. [scale ou peel off.

écailler, v. a. to scale, to open || s'~, to

écailleux, se, a. scaly.

écale, f. shell (of nuts, eggs, etc.).

écaler, v. a. to shell.

écarbouiller, v. a. to crush.

écarlate, f. scarlet. [one's legs).

écarquillement, m. spreading wide (of

écarquiller, v. a. to open wide.

écart, m. stepping aside, going out of the way || excursion || digression, swerving.

écarté, m. écarté (game at cards).

écarté, e, a. lonely.

écartèlement, m. quartering.

écarteler, v. a. to quarter.

écartement, m. removal || scattering || separation.

écarter, v. a. to disperse, to drive away, to remove, to turn off, to mislead, to lead from || to discard || s'~, to go out of the way, to lose one's way || to recede || s'~ du but, to be wide of the mark.

ecchymose, f. (méd.) ecchymosis.

ecclésiastique, m. clergyman || ecclesias-

ecclésiastique, a. ecclesiastical. [tic.

écervelé, m. mad-cap.

écervelé, e, a. hare-brained.

échafaud, m. scaffold || stage.

échafaudage, m. scaffolding || preparations, fuss || display. [scaffolding.

échafauder, v. a. to scaffold, to erect

échalas, m. pole || stick || lath.

échalassement, m. propping of vines.

échalasser, v. a. to prop vines.

échalier, m. fence.

échalote, f. (bot.) shallot.

échancrer, v. a. to slope || to hollow out.

échancrure, f. slope, cut.

change, m. exchange, barter || interchange.

échanger, v. a. to exchange, to barter || to reciprocate.

échanson, m. cup-bearer. [specimen.

échantillon, m. pattern, sample || (fig.)

échantillonner, v. a. to sample.

échappade, f. mistake, slip.

échappatoire, f. shuffle, creep-hole.

échappée, f. prank || snatch || short interval || ~ de lumière, accidental light || ~ de vue, vista.

échapper, v. n. to escape || to avoid, to shun, to slip, to drop || s'~, to make one's escape || (fig.) to forget oneself.

écharde, f. splinter || thorn.

échardonner, v. a. to clear of thistles.

écharner, v. a. to excarnate || to flesh.

écharpe, f. scarf || sash || sling || en ~, over the shoulder || in a sling || oblique.

écharper, v. a. to slash, to cut to pieces.

échasse, f. stilt.

échassier, m. wading bird || grallic.

échaudé, m. cracknel. [one's fingers.

échauder, v. a. to scald || s'~, to burn

échaudoir, m. scalding-house || scalding-vessel. [ment.

échauffement, m. heating || over-excite-

échauffer, v. a. to warm, to heat || to excite || s'~, to overheat oneself || to get warm || to grow angry, to fly into a passion || to fume.

échauffourée, f. skirmish || affray.

échauguette, f. watch-tower.

échéance, f. expiration, falling due || term of payment || à longue ~, long-dated.

échéant, p. occurring.

échec, m. check || misfortune || ~ et mat, check-mate || ~s, pl. chess || chessmen.

échelle, f. ladder, scale || sea-port || ~ double, trestles || pair of steps.

échelon, m. step of a ladder || stepping-stone || degree || (mil.) echelon.

échelonner, v. a. to arrange in ranks || (fig.) to marshal.

écheniller, v. a. to clear of caterpillars.

écheveau, m. skein.

échevelé, e, a. dishevelled.

échevin, m. sheriff, alderman.

échine, f. chine || spine || back.

échinée, f. chine of pork.

échiner, v. a. to break the backbone, to chine || to beat to death.

échiqueté, e, a. checkered.

échiquier, m. chess-board || exchequer || échó, m. echo. [square-net.

échoir, v. n. ir. to fall || to expire || to fall

échoppe, f. stall. [due.

échouage, m. stranding. [ing.

échouement, m. running aground, strand-

échouer, v. a. & n. (mar.) to run aground, to strand || to be stranded || (fig.) to mis-

écimer, v. a. to top. [carry.

éclaboussement, m. splashing.

éclabousser, v. a. to splash.

éclaboussure, f. splash, dirt.

éclair, m. lightning, flash.

éclairage, m. lighting (of streets, etc.).

éclaircie, f. glade || vista || opening || clear spot in a cloudy sky.

éclaircir, v. a. to clear, to brighten || to clarify || to thin || to explain || to instruct.

éclaircissement, m. clearing up || explanation.

éclaire, f. (bot.) pilewort. [planation.

éclairer, v. a. & n. to light, to enlighten, to illuminate || to give light || to shine, to sparkle || to observe, to watch || s'~, to enlighten oneself, to get information.

éclaireur, m. (mil.) scout.

éclat, m. shiver, splinter || brightness || splendour, magnificence || explosion || bounce, crash || burst || noise || scandal.

éclatant, e, a. bright, sparkling, glittering, brilliant, eminent, glorious.

éclater, v. n. to split, to shiver || to make a great noise || to sparkle, to glitter || to break out, to appear || to fly into a passion.

éclectique a. eclectic.

éclectisme, m. eclectic philosophy.

éclipser, v. a. to eclipse ‖ s'~, to be eclipsed, to vanish, to disappear.

éclisse, f. splint ‖ cheese-hurdle.

éclisser, v. a. to splint.

écloppé, e, a. lame, limping.

éclore, v. n. ir. to be hatched ‖ to open, to come to light ‖ to dawn.

éclosion, f. hatching ‖ blowing.

écluse, f. sluice, dam, wear, floodgate.

éclusée, f. lock of water.

écluser, v. a. to lock.

éclusier, m. sluice-keeper.

écœurer, v. a. to sicken, to dishearten.

école, f. school ‖ academy ‖ school-time ‖ apprenticeship ‖ ~ d'application, practical school ‖ ~ maternelle, infant-school ‖ petite ~, day-school.

écolier, m. school-boy, pupil.

écolière, f. female scholar.

éconduire, v. a. ir. to deny, to refuse, to shift off, to put off.

économat, m. stewardship.

économe, m. economist, housekeeper ‖ steward, manager.

économe, a. economical, saving, sparing.

économie, f. economy, frugality ‖ saving ‖ system ‖ faire des ~s de bouts de chandelles, to be penny-wise and pound-foolish.   [(ly).

économique, a. (-ment, ad.) economical

économiser, v. a. to economise, to manage with economy, to save, to husband.

économiste, m. economist.

écope, f. scoop.

écoper, v. a. to scoop, to bale.

écorce, f. bark, rind, peel ‖ outside.

écorcer, v. a. to rind, to peel, to bark.

écorché, m. object deprived of its skin.

écorchée, f.; à l'~, in small lots.

écorcher, v. a. to flay, to skin ‖ to gall ‖ (fig.) to fleece ‖ s'~, to tear one's skin off.

écorcherie, f. knacker's yard ‖ fleecing.

écorcheur, m. flayer ‖ knacker ‖ fleecer.

écorchure, f. rubbing off of the skin ‖ sore.

écorner, v. a. to break the horns ou corners off ‖ to curtail ‖ to round off.

écornifler, v. a. to sponge.

écornure, f. corner broken off.

écosser, v. a. to shell.

écot, m. bill, reckoning (of one's expenses) ‖ share ‖ club, company.

écoulement, m. running, flowing ‖ draining ‖ emanation, issue ‖ sale.

écouler, v. n. to sell ‖ s'~, to run ou flow out ‖ to slide, to slip away, to go by, to steal away.

écourter, v. a. to crop, to cut short.

écoute, f. corner ou place for listening ‖ sheet of a sail.

écouter, v. a. to hear, to hearken, to listen, to attend ‖ to follow ‖ s'~, to like to hear oneself ‖ to indulge.

écouteur, m. listener.

écouteux, se, a. shy, skittish.

écoutille, f. (mar.) hatchway.

écouvillon, m. mop ‖ (mil.) sponge ‖ rammer.

écouvillonner, v. a. to mop ‖ to sponge (a cannon).   [minée, cheval-screen.

écran, m. screen, fire-screen ‖ ~ de che-

écrasant, e, a. humiliating ‖ excessive.

écrasement, m. crushing, destruction.

écraser, v. a. to crush in pieces, to destroy, to ruin.   [skim (milk).

écrémer, v. a. to take off the cream, to

écrêter, v. a. to take off the top.

écrevisse, f. crawfish, crab, lobster ‖ s'écrier, to cry out, to exclaim. [Cancer.

écrille, f. grate.

écrin, m. jewel-box, casket.

écrire, v. a. ir. to write ‖ to spell ‖ s'~, to write to each other ‖ to be written ou spelt.

écrit, m. writing, written agreement ‖ pamphlet ‖ par ~, in writing.

écriteau, m. bill ‖ board.

écritoire, f. ink-horn.

écriture, f. hand, handwriting ‖ Scripture ‖ -s, pl. books.

écrivailler, v. a. to scribble.

écrivaillerie, f. scribbling.

écrivailleur, m. scribbler.

écrivain, m. writer ‖ ~ public, petition-

écrivassier, m. scribbler.   [writer.

écrou, m. screw-nut ‖ (entry in the) jail-

écrouelles, f. pl. scrofula.   [book.

écrouer, v. a. to enter in the jail-book.

écrouir, v. a. (tech.) to hard-hammer (metals).

écroulement, m. falling, tumbling down.

écrouler, (s'~), v. a. to fall ou tumble down.

écroûter, v. a. to cut off the crust.

écru, e, a. raw, unbleached.

écu, m. shield ‖ crown ‖ petit ~, half a crown ‖ -s, pl. money, cash.

écubier, m. (mar.) hawse-hole ‖ plomb d'~, (mar.) hawse-pipe.

écueil, m. rock ‖ sandbank ‖ (fig.) stumbling-block ‖ danger.

écuelle, f. basin ‖ bowl.

écuellée, f. bowlful.

éculer, v. a. to tread down at the heels ‖ s'~, to wear down at the heels.

écume, f. froth, foam, scum, dross, yeast.

écumer, v. a. & n. to skim, to scum, to foam, to spume, to froth, to sponge.

écumeur, m. skimmer ‖ sponger ‖ ~ de marmites, parasite ‖ ~ de mer, pirate.

écumeux, se, a. foaming, frothy, foamy,

écumoire, f. skimmer ‖ slice.   [yeasty.

écurage, m. scouring.

écurer, v. a. to scour, to cleanse.

écureuil, m. squirrel.   [maid.

écureur, se, m. & f. scourer ‖ scullery-

écurie, f. stable ‖ equipage ‖ (rail.) horse-box ‖ -s, pl. stabling ‖ mews ‖ repository.

écusson, m. escutcheon ‖ leaf-bud.

écussonner, v. a. to ingraft.

écussonnoir, m. grafting-knife.

écuyer, m. squire, esquire ‖ equerry ‖ riding-master, horse-breaker ‖ attendant ‖ ~ tranchant, carver.   [Hessian boots.

écuyère, f. horsewoman ‖ bottes à l'~,

édenté, e, a. toothless.

édenter, v. a. to break the teeth (of a saw).

édifice, m. edifice, building ‖ construction, fabric.

édifier, v. a. to edify.
édilité, f. edileship ‖ town-council ‖ corporation.
édit, m. edict, decree.
éditer, v. a. to edit ‖ to publish (a book).
éditeur, m. editor, publisher.
édredon, m. eider-down ‖ eider-down quilt.
éducation, f. education. rearing.
édulcorer, v. a. (chim.) to edulcorate, to sweeten.
éduquer, v. a. to rear, to bring up.
éfaufiler, v. a. to reeve out.
effaçable, a. effaceable.
effacer, v. a. to efface, to deface, to strike ou blot out, to erase. to expunge ‖ to destroy ‖ to surpass, to eclipse ‖ s'~, to come out ‖ to wear away ou off ‖ to keep in the background ‖ to stand sideways.
effarement, m. fright, terror.
effarer, v. a. to scare.
effaroucher, v. a. to scare, to terrify ‖ to frighten away, to disgust ‖ s'~, to be scared, to be frightened, to take fright.
effectif, m. (mil.) effective force.
effectif, ve, a. (-vement, ad.) effective (ly) ‖ really, actually, indeed.
effectuer, v. a. to effect, to perform, to accomplish, to bring about.
efféminé, e, a. effeminate.
efféminer, v. a. to render effeminate.
effervescence, f. effervescence.
effet, m. effect, result, consequence, performance, deed ‖ sight, appearance, illusion ‖ note ‖ bill ‖ en ~, indeed, in fact.
effeuillaison, f. fall of the leaves.
effeuiller, v. a. to pull ou strip off leaves ‖ s'~, to lose the leaves.   [effectual(ly).
efficace, a. (-ment, ad.) efficient(ly) ‖
efficacité, f. efficiency.
effigie, f. effigy.
effilé, m. ravelled-out fringe.
effilé, e, a. slender ‖ tapering.
effiler, v. a. to ravel, to unweave.
effilochage, m. tearing-up ‖ shoddy ‖
effiloché, m. shoddy.   [shoddy-trade.
effilocher, v. a. to undo cotton.
effilocheur, m. shoddy-manufacturer.
effilocheuse, f. shoddy-mill.
effiloquer, v. a. to ravel out.
efflanqué, m. bag-o'-bones, spindle-shanks.
efflanquer, v. a. to emaciate.
effleurer, v. a. to graze, to touch lightly ‖ to skim ‖ to glance at ‖ to strip of flowers.
effluves, m. pl. (méd.) effluvia.
effondrement, m. (agr.) deep digging.
effondrer, v. a. to dig deep ‖ to break open ‖ s'~, to sink down.
effondrilles, f. pl. dregs.
s'efforcer, to endeavour, to labour, to strain, to attempt, to strive.   [strength.
effort, m. effort, endeavour, exertion of
effraction, f. breaking open ‖ vol avec ~, robbery with house-breaking ‖ (de nuit) burglary.
effrai, f. barn-owl.
effrayable, a. dreadful, surprising.
effrayant, e, a. frightful, dreadful.
effrayer, v. a. to fright, to frighten, to terrify ‖ s'~, to be frightened, to startle.
effréné, e, a. unbridled ‖ unruly ‖ immoderate,

effriter, v. a. (agr.) to exhaust.
effroi, m. fright, terror.
effronté, e, a. (-ment, ad.) brazen-faced, bold, shameless ‖ impudent(ly).
effronterie, f. impudence.
effroyable, a. (-ment, ad.) frightful(ly).
effusion, f. effusion, shedding ‖ overflowing ‖ flow of tenderness.
égal, m. equal, match, fellow, peer.
égal, e, a. (-ement, ad.) equal(ly) ‖ alike ‖ like ‖ even, level, uniform ‖ indifferent ‖ c'est ~, never mind.   [pare.
égaler, v. a. to equal, to match ‖ to com-
égaliser, v. a. to equalise ‖ to level ‖ to
égalitaire, m. leveller.   [square.
égalitaire, a. levelling.
égalité, f. equality, evenness ‖ uniformity ‖ ~ d'âme, equanimity.
égard, m. regard, respect, consideration, account ‖ attention, observance, relation ‖ à l'~ de, in comparison to, with respect.
égaré, e, a. strayed, misled, misguided ‖ raving.
égarement, m. straying ou going out of the way ‖ wandering, deviation ‖ disorder, ill behaviour ‖ mistake.
égarer, v. a. to mislead ‖ to mislay ‖ to disorder ‖ to bewilder ‖ s'~, to go astray, to deviate, to wander ‖ to rave.
égayer, v. a. to cheer up, to exhilarate ‖ to thin ‖ s'~, to make oneself merry, to
égide, f. ægis, shield.   [divert oneself.
églantier, m. (bot.) dog-rose bush ‖ ~ odorant, sweet-briar.
églantine, f. (bot.) wild rose ‖ sweet-briar.
église, f. church.
églogue, f. eclogue.
égoïsme, m. selfishness.
égoïste, m. & f. egotist.
égoïste, a. selfish.   [slaughter, to kill.
égorger, v. a. to cut the throat, to
s'égosiller, to talk oneself hoarse.
égotisme, f. egotism.
égotiste, m. egotist, egoist.
égout, m. sink, drain, common sewer.
égoutier, m. night-man.
égouttage, m. draining.
égoutter, v. a. & n. to drain, to drop ‖ to
égouttoir, m. drainer.   [drip
égoutture, f. droppings.
égrainer, v. a. vide égrener.
égrapper, v. a. to pick the grapes from the bunch ‖, to dress.
égratigner, v. a. to scratch.
égratignure, f. scratch.
égrener, v. a. to shell, to pick ‖ s'~, to fall from the stalk.
égrillard, m. grig.
égrillard, e, a. sprightly.
égrugeoir, m. wooden mortar.
égruger, v. a. to pound.
égueulement, m. break at the mouth ot a cannon.   [of a pot ou glass vessel.
égueuler, v. a. to break the gullet ou neck
éhanché, e, a. hip-shot.
éhonté, e, a. shameless.
éjaculer, v. a. to ejaculate.
élaborer, v. a. to elaborate.
élagage, m. lopping.

élaguer, v. a. to prune, to lop.
élagueur, m. pruner.
élan, m. elk || jerk, sudden motion || impulse || life || warmth, transport.
élancé, e, a. slender || thin.   [yearning.
élancement, m. shooting || transport ||
élancer, v. n. to shoot || s'~, to rush upon, to dash, to shoot, to give a jerk.
élargir, v. a. to widen, to make wide, to stretch, to enlarge || to release.
élargissement, m. widening, enlargement || release, discharge from prison.
élargissure, f. eking-piece, inlay.
élasticité, f. elasticity.
élastique, a. elastic, springy.
élastiques, f. pl. springs.
électeur, m. elector || Elector (in Germany).
électif, ve, a. elective.
électoral, e, a. electoral.
électorat, m. Electorate.
électrice, f. Elector's consort.
électricien, m. electrician.
électricité, f. electricity.
électrique, a. electric || machine ~, f. electric machine.
électriser, v. a. to electrify.
élégamment, ad. elegantly.   [politeness.
élégance, f. elegance, nicety, delicacy ||
élégant, e, m. & f. fashionable man ou woman.
élégant, e, a. elegant, nice || polite.   [man.
élégiaque, a. elegiac.
élégie, f. elegy.
élémentaire, a. elementary.
élevage, m. breeding (of cattle, etc.).
élévation, f. lifting up || preferment || hill || eminence || raising of the host.
élève, m. & f. pupil, scholar || (mar.) midshipman|| en chambre, parlour-boarder.
élevé, e, a. raised, elevated, sublime || high, lofty || educated, brought up.
élever, v. a. to raise, to lift up || to erect, to promote, to exalt || to educate, to cultivate || s'~, to rise, to arise, to go up || to grow proud ou elated.
éleveur, m. cattle-breeder || lift, elevator.
élevure, f. blister, pimple, blotch.
élider, v. a. to cut off.
éligibilité, f. eligibility.
éliminer, v. a. to eliminate, to strike out.
élire, v. a. ir. to elect, to choose.
élision, f. (gr.) elision.
élite, f. choice || flower, prime, best || d'~, select || picked || superior.
elle, pn. she, her, it.
ellébore, m. (bot.) hellebore.
ellipse, f. ellipsis.
elliptiquement, ad. elliptically.
éloge, m. eulogy, praise.
éloignement, m. remove, removal || absence, separation || distance || indifference, aversion, estrangement.
éloigner, v. a. to remove || to put away, to drive away, to banish || to estrange || to delay || s'~, to go away || to swerve || to deviate, to ramble from.
éloquemment, ad. eloquently.
éloquent, e, a. eloquent.
élu, m. elect.
élu, e, a. & p. elected.

élucider, v. a. to elucidate.
élucubration, f. lucubration.
éluder, v. a. to elude.
émacié, a. emaciated.
émail, m. enamel.
émailler, v. a. to enamel.
émailleur, m. enameller.
émaillure, f. enamelling.
émanation, f. emanation.
émanciper, v. a. to emancipate || s'~, to take too much liberty.
émaner, v. n. to emanate.
émargement, m. marginal note.
émarger, v. a. to write on the margin.
embabouiner, v. a. to wheedle, to coax.
emballage, m. packing up.
emballer, v. a. to pack up.
emballeur, m. packer.
embarcadère, m. wharf || (rail.) terminus.
embarcation, f. small vessel.
embargo, m. embargo.
embariller, v. a. to barrel up.
s'embarlificoter, to get muddled, to get into a mess.   [ping.
embarquement, m. embarcation, shipembarquer, v. a. to embark, to engage || to involve.
embarras, m. embarrassment, clog, incumbrance, hinderance, impediment, inconvenience, intricacy.   [fling.
embarrassant, e, a. embarrassing || puzzembarrasser, v. a. to embarrass, to entangle, to clog, to encumber, to disconcert, to puzzle, to perplex || s'~, to entangle oneself, to be encumbered.
embâter, v. a. to saddle.
embauchage, m. hiring || kidnapping.
embaucher, v. a. to hire a journeyman || to entice away || to enlist.   [enticer.
embaucheur, m. recruiter || (nav.) crimp ||
embauchoir, m. boot-tree, boot-crimp.
embaumement, m. embalming.
embaumer, v. a. to embalm, to perfume || ~, v. n. to smell very sweet.
embéguiner, v. a. to muffle up || (fig.) to wrap up || to infatuate || s'~, to become infatuated.   [handsome.
embellir, v. a. & n. to embellish || to grow
embellissement, m. embellishment.
s'emberlucoquer, to be prepossessed ombesogné, e, a. busy.   [with.
embêtement, m. bother, botheration.
embêter, v. a. to bother || to worry || s'~, to bother oneself || to find it dreadfully dull ou slow.
emblaver, v. a. to sow with wheat.
d'emblée, ad. at the first onset.
emblématique, a. emblematic.
emblème, m. emblem.
emboîtement, m. jointing, setting in.
emboîter, v. a. to joint, to set in || to put in a box || ~ le pas, (mil.) to lock up.
emboîture, f. joint, juncture || socket (of a joint).
embonpoint, m. stoutness, corpulence.
embosser, v. a. (mar.) to bring a broadside to bear upon.
emboucher, v. a. to put to the mouth || to prepare || to coach up || s'~, to fall in.

embouchure, f. mouth (of a river) ‖ mouth-piece ‖ bridle-bit.
embouquer, v. n. (mar.) to enter a strait.
embourber, v. a. to put in a mire, to be-mire, to sink in the mud.
embourser, v. a. to pocket.
embranchement, m. branching off ‖ (rail.) branch-line.
s'embrancher, to branch off.
embrasement, m. conflagration, burning.
embraser, v. a. to set on fire ‖ to in-flame ‖ s'~, to take fire ‖ to glow.
embrassade, f. embrace.
embrassement, m. embrace.
embrasser, v. a. to embrace ‖ to hug ‖ to kiss ‖ to comprehend, to comprise ‖ to encompass ‖ to avail oneself of.
embrasure, f. embrasure.
embrocher, v. a. to spit.
embrouillamini, embrouillement, m. confusion, intricacy, perplexity.
embrouiller, v. a. to embroil, to confuse, to perplex, to entangle ‖ s'~, to get con-fused ‖ to become intricate.
embrumé, e, a. foggy, cloudy.
embrun, m. (mar.) spray. [dwarf.
embryon, m. embryo, foetus ‖ germ ‖
embûche, f. ambush ‖ snares.
embuscade, f. ambuscade, ambush ‖ être en ~, to lie in wait.
embusquer, v. a. to place in ambuscade.
émeraude, f. emerald.
émerger, v. n. to emerge.
émeri, m. emery.
émérite, a. retired, pensioned.
émerveiller, v. a. to astonish, to amaze, to surprise ‖ s'~, to wonder at.
émétique, m. (méd.) emetic.
émétique, a. (méd.) emetic. [utter.
émettre, v. a. ir. to emit, to issue ‖ to
émeute, f. riot, mutiny.
émeutier, m. rioter.
émietter, v. a. to crumble.
émigré, e, m. & f. emigrant.
émigrer, v. n. to emigrate.
émincé, m. mince-meat.
émincer, v. a. to mince.
éminemment, ad. eminently.
éminent, e, a. eminent, high, lofty.
éminentissime, a. most eminent.
émissaire, m. emissary ‖ overflow-pipe ‖ bouc ~, scape-goat.
émission, f. emission, issue, uttering.
emmagasinage, m. warehousing.
emmagasiner, v. a. to warehouse.
emmailloter, v. a. to swathe, to swaddle.
emmanchement, m. hafting, fitting with a handle, helving.
emmancher, v. a. & n. to haft, to helve ‖ to make a beginning of.
emmancheur, m. handle-setter.
emmanchure, f. arm-hole.
emmannequiner, v. a. to put in hampers.
emmariner, v. a. (mar.) to man (a ship).
emmêler, v. a. to entangle. [tion.
emménagement, m. removal, installa-
emménager, v. a. to move in, to settle.
emmener, v. a. to lead ou take away.
emmenotter, v. a. to handcuff.

emmieller, v. a. to sweeten with honey ‖ to coax.
emmitoufler, v. a. to muffle up with furs.
émoi, m. care, trouble, anxiety. [cent.
émollient, m. (méd.) emollient ‖ demul-
émolument, m. emolument ‖ fee ‖ (jur.)
émondage, m. pruning. [share.
émonder, v. a. to prune.
émondes, f. pl. prunings.
émotion, f. emotion, commotion, trouble.
émotter, v. a. to break clods of earth.
émoucher, v. a. to drive flies away.
émouchet, m. sparrow-hawk.
émouchette, f. fly-net (for horses).
émouchoir, m. fly-flap.
émoudre, v. a. ir. to grind.
émouleur, m. grinder.
émousser, v. a. to take the moss off ‖ to blunt, to dull the edge ou point ‖ to weaken ‖ s'~, to grow blunt ou dull.
émoustiller, v. a. to brisk up.
émouvoir, v. a. ir. to move ‖ to agitate ‖ to stir up ‖ to excite, to affect ‖ s'~, to be moved, etc.
empaillage, m. stuffing with straw.
empailler, v. a. to cover ou stuff with straw ‖ to pack up with straw.
empailleur, m. chair-bottomer ‖ bird-
empaler, v. a. to impale. [stuffer.
empan, m. span (of the hand).
empanacher, v. a. to plume.
empanner, v. a. (mar.) to back the sails.
empaqueter, v. a. to pack, to pack up, to make up into a bundle.
s'emparer, to take possession of, to mas-ter, to seize upon.
empâtement, m. stickiness, clamminess.
empâter, v. a. to make sticky ‖ to cram ‖ to fatten ‖ to impaste.
empaumer, v. a. to strike with the palm of the hand or with a racket (at tennis) ‖ to grasp ‖ to allure, to decoy, to trap.
empêchement, m. obstacle, impediment.
empêcher, v. a. to hinder, to prevent ‖ to stop ‖ s'~, to forbear, to abstain from.
empeigne, f. upper-leather (of a shoe).
empellement, m. sluice, dam.
empenner, v. a. to feather.
empereur, m. emperor.
empesage, m. starching.
empeser, v. a. to starch. [horribly.
empester, v. a. & n. to infect ‖ to stink
empêtrer, v. a. to entangle, to hamper, to encumber ‖ to saddle.
emphase, f. emphasis ‖ bombast.
emphatique, a. (~ment, ad.) emphatic (ally) ‖ bombastic(ally).
empierrement, m. stoning, ballasting ‖ broken stones, ballast.
empierrer, v. a. to stone a road.
empiéter, v. a. to encroach (upon).
empiffrer, v. a. to cram.
empilement, m. piling up.
empiler, v. a. to pile up. [ment.
empire, m. empire, power, reign, govern-
empirer, v. a. & n. to make worse ‖ to
empirique, m. empiric. [grow worse.
empirique, a. empiric.
empirisme, m. empiricism.

emplacement, m. site || building-lot.
emplâtre, m. plaster || sickly person.
emplette, f. purchase.
emplir, v. a. to fill (up).
emploi, m. employ, application, use || office || employment, occupation, trade || **double ~,** useless repetition. [ployed.
employé, m. clerk || official || person employer, **v. a.** to employ || to use || to occupy, to bestow, to spend || **s'~,** to apply oneself to || to amuse oneself in || to be used.
emplumé, e, a. feathered || (mus.) quilled.
emplumer, v. a. (mus.) to quill.
empocher, v. a. to pocket.
empoigner, v. a. to grasp, to lay hold of, **empois,** m. starch. [to seize.
empoisonnement, m. poisoning.
empoisonner, v. a. & n. to poison || to stink horribly. [very bad cook.
empoisonneur, m. poisoner || corruptor ||
empoisser, v. a. to pitch over.
empoissonnement, m. stocking with fish.
empoissonner, v. a. to stock with fish.
emporté, e, a. carried away || passionate, hot-headed. [rage.
emportement, m. transport, passion,
emporte-pièce, m. punch.
emporter, v. a. to take *ou* carry away || to cut off, to kill || to take by assault || to prevail, to surpass, to have the advantage, to excel || to obtain || **s'~,** to fly into a passion, to rail against.
empoter, v. a. to pot.
empourprer, v. a. to purple.
empreindre, v. a. ir. to imprint, to stamp, to impress.
empreinte, f. impression, stamp.
empressé, e, a. bustling, eager, anxious, hasty, forward.
empressement, m. eagerness, earnestness, zeal || keenness, ardour, haste.
s'empresser, to be eager, to be earnest or forward. [finement.
emprisonnement, m. imprisonment, confine.
emprisonner, v. a. to imprison, to confine.
emprunt, m. loan, borrowing || **d'~,** borrowed || assumed || supposed || affected.
emprunter, v. a. to borrow, to take upon credit || to assume.
emprunteur, se, m. & f. borrower.
empuantir, v. a. to infect.
empuantissement, m. stench.
empyrée, m. empyrean.
ému, e, a. moved || affected || agitated.
émule, m. & f. competitor, rival.
en, pn. of him, of her, of it, of them || with him, with her, with it, with them || for him, for her, for it, for them || about him, about her, about it, about them || thence || some, any, none || **~,** pr. in, into, to, from, by, as, like.
encâblure, f. (mar.) cable's-length.
encadrement, m. framing.
encadrer, v. a. to frame || to insert.
encager, v. a. to cage.
encaisse, f. cash in hand || **~ métal- lique,** metallic reserve.

encaissé, e, a. with high and steep banks || embanked.
encaissement, m. packing up || (com.) payment of a bill *ou* note.
encaisser, v. a. to pack up, to put in cases || (com.) to deposit a bill *ou* note with a banker || to lay up (money).
encan, m. auction.
s'encanailler, to keep low company.
encapuchonner, v. a. to put on a cowl || to muffle up.
encaquer, v. a. to barrel up.
en-cas, m. sun-shade.
encastelé, e, a. hoof-bound.
encastrer, v. a. to fit in.
encaustique, f. encaustic.
encaustique, a. encaustic.
encavement, m. laying in a cellar.
encaver, v. a. to put in a cellar.
enceindre, v. a. ir. to enclose.
enceinte, f. enclosure || precincts.
enceinte, a. pregnant, big with child.
encens, m. incense || (fig.) flattery.
encensement, m. incensing.
encenser, v. a. to incense || to worship ||
encenseur, m. flatterer. [to flatter.
encensoir, m. censer || **coups d'~,** fulsome flattery. [series || concatenation.
enchaînement, m. chain || links (pl.) ||
enchaîner, v. a. to chain || to fetter || to connect || to charm || **s'~,** to be connected with, to be linked with.
enchantement, m. enchantment || delight.
enchanter, v. a. to enchant || to delight.
enchanteur, teresse, m. & f. enchanter, sorcerer || enchantress.
enchaperonner, v. a. to hood (a hawk).
enchâsser, v. a. to enchase || to set || to enchâssure,** f. setting. [introduce.
enchère, f. outbidding, higher bid, enhancing of the price.
enchérir, v. a. & n. to outbid || to enhance the price || to grow dearer || (sur) to outdo, to surpass.
enchérissement, m. rising in price.
enchérisseur, m. bidder.
enchevêtrer, v. a. to entangle || **s'~,** to get entangled.
enchevêtrure, f. binding || halter-cast.
enchifrènement, m. stopping up (of the nose) || cold in the head.
enchifrener, v. a. to give one a cold in the head.
enclave, f. land shut in by foreign territory.
enclaver, v. a. to enclose, to shut in.
enclin, e, a. inclined, prone || apt (to).
enclore, v. a. ir. to enclose.
enclos, m. enclosure. [to spike a gun.
enclouer, v. a. to prick a horse in shoeing ||
enclouure, f. prick (of a nail) || hitch.
enclume, f. anvil.
encoche, f. notch.
encocher, v. a. to notch, to fit (an arrow) to
encoffrer, v. a. to lay up. [the bow.
encognure, f. corner, angle || corner-piece
encollage, m. sizing. [(of furniture).
encoller, v. a. to size.
encolure, f. neck and shoulders of a horse || (fig.) look, appearance.

encombre, m. hindrance.
encombrement, m. encumbering, encumbrance.
encombrer, v. a. to encumber, to clog, to stop, to embarrass.
encontre, ad. (à l'~) against.
encore, ad. yet, as yet || still, more, once more, again, too, also, besides, over and above, at least, only || however.
encorné, e, a. horned.
encourager, v. a. to encourage.
encourir, v. a. ir. to incur.
encrasser, v. a. to soil, to make greasy ou nasty || s'~, to grow greasy ou nasty || to debase oneself.
encre, f. ink || ~ de Chine, Indian ink.
encrer, v. a. to ink.
encrier, m. ink-stand || ink-trough.
encroûté, e, a. full of prejudices.
encroûter, v. a. to crust || s'~, to gather a crust || to get stupid.
encuver, v. a. to put into a tub.
encyclique, a. encyclical, circular.
encyclopédie, f. encyclopædia.
endémique, a. endemic.
endenter, v. a. to indent, to notch.
endetter, v. a. to get into debt.
endêver, v. n. to be mad || faire ~, to tease, to bait.
endiablé, e, a. possessed, mad, furious.
s'endimancher, to put on Sunday clothes.
endoctriner, v. a. to teach, to instruct || to gain over.
endolori, e, a. aching.
endolorir, v. a. to make sore.
endommagement, m. (fam.) damage.
endommager, v. a. to damage.
endormeur, m. (fig.) wheedler.
endormi, e, a. asleep, sleepy || sluggish || drowsy || benumbed.
endormir, v. a. ir. to lull to sleep || to amuse || to benumb || s'~, to fall asleep, to be sleepy, to slumber || to be lulled asleep || to neglect. [ment.
endos, endossement, m. (com.) indorse-
endosser, v.a. (com.) to endorse || to put on.
endosseur, m. indorser.
endroit, m. place || part, passage || right side (of a stuff etc.). [to coat.
enduire, v.a. ir. to do over with, to plaster ||
enduit, m. layer, coat.
endurant, e, a. enduring, patient.
endurcir, v. a. to harden, to inure.
endurcissement, m. obduracy, hardness.
endurer, v. a. to endure, to bear, to suffer.
énergie, f. energy.
énergique, a. (-ment, ad.) energetic(ally) || forcible || vigorous(ly) || forcibly.
énergumène, m. demoniac || frantic ou wild person || fanatic. [enervated.
énerver, v. a. to enervate || s'~, to become
enfaitement, m. ridge-lead.
enfaîter, v. a. to cover the ridge of.
enfance, f. infancy, childhood || puerility, childishness || young people.
enfant, m. child, infant || ~ de chœur, singing-boy || ~ naturel, natural child || ~ de troupe, soldier's boy || ~ trouvé, foundling.

enfantement, m. childbirth. [livered of.
enfanter, v. a. to bring forth, to be de-
enfantillage, m. childishness || triviality.
enfantin, e, a. childish.
enfariner, v. a. to sprinkle with flour.
enfer, m. hell || -s, pl. infernal regions.
enfermer, v. a. to shut up, to lock up || to enclose || to comprehend, to comprise.
enferrer, v. a. to run through (with a sword), to transfix || s'~, to run oneself through || to entangle oneself || to make a mess of it.
enfilade, f. suit || long string || d'~, raking.
enfiler, v. a. to thread, to file || to run through || to enter into || (mil.) to rake || to engage in.
enfin, ad. in fine, finally, after all, at last || in short, to conclude || in a word.
enflammer, v. a. to inflame, to kindle || to incense, to irritate, to exasperate || s'~, to catch fire || to grow hot.
enflé, e, a. swelled, inflated, puffed up, proud, flatulent.
enfler, v. a. to swell, to puff up || to blow, to bloat || to elate. [vanity.
enflure, f. swelling, tumour || pride ||
enfoncement, m. breaking open || bottom, hollow place || depths (pl.) || background.
enfoncer, v. a. to thrust, to drive into || to break open, to break through || to pull down || to sink, to ruin || s'~, to go deep in, to dive, to sink. [boarding.
enfonçure, f. cavity || bottom pieces (pl.) ||
enforcir, v. a. to strengthen.
enfouir, v. a. to bury.
enfouissement, m. hiding in the ground.
enfourcher, v. a. to bestride.
enfourchure, f. forked head of a stag.
enfourner, v. a. to put in the oven || s'~, to get into a scrape.
enfreindre, v. a. ir. to infringe.
s'enfuir, to run away, to escape, to make one's escape || to be leaky.
enfumé, e, a. smoked || smoky. [dung.
enfumer, v. a. to smoke, to besmoke || to
engageant, e, a. engaging, prepossessing.
engagement, m. engagement || pawning || mortgage || enlistment.
engager, v. a. to engage || to pawn, to pledge || to induce, to persuade || to enlist || s'~, to engage oneself, to pass one's word, to be bound || to hire oneself out || to enlist || to bail || to run into debt || to entangle oneself.
engainer, v. a. to sheath. [oneself.
engeance, f. race, set, breed, brood || lot ||
engelure, f. chilblain. [gender.
engendrer, v. a. to engender, to beget, to produce, to breed || to cause. [into sheaves.
engerber, v. a. (agr.) to sheave, to bind up
engin, m. engine || machinery || tackle.
englober, v. a. to clap together, to unite, to mix. [sipate.
engloutir, v. a. to swallow up || to dis-
engluer, v. a. to daub with bird-lime || s'~, to be caught (as in bird-lime).
engoncer, v. a. to smother, to cover up.
engorgement, m. stoppage.
engorger, v. a. to obstruct || to stop up || s'~, to become obstructed.

engouement, m. infatuation.

engouer, v. a. to choke up ‖ to infatuate.

engouffrer, v. a. to ingulf, to swallow up ‖ s'~, to be ingulfed, to rush.

engouler, v. a. to gobble.

engourdi, e, a. dull, benumbed, torpid.

engourdir, v. a. to benumb ‖ to enervate ‖ s'~, to grow numb ‖ to grow stupid.

engourdissement, m. numbness, torpor ‖ dulness.

engrainer, v. a. to feed with grain ou corn.

engrais, m. pasture ‖ manure ‖ à l'~, fattening.

engraissement, m. fattening.   [ting.

engraisser, v. a. & n. to fat, to fatten, to feed ‖ to manure, to enrich ‖ to grow fat ‖ s'~, to grow fat ‖ to grow rich.

engranger, v. a. to house corn.

engravement, m. (mar.) stranding.

engraver, v. a. & n.; s'~, (mar.) to run aground, to strand.   [wheel.

engrenage, m. gear ‖ roue d'~, brake-

engrener, v. a. & n. to put the corn into the mill-hopper ‖ to tooth ‖ ~, v. n. to begin ‖ to catch ‖ s'~, to work into each

engrenure, f. catching.   [other.

engrosser, v. a. to get with child.

s'engrumeler, v. a. to clot, to coagulate.

engueuler, v. a. to shout ‖ to humbug, to chaff.

enhardir, v. a. to embolden ‖ s'~, to grow bold, to take courage.   [pings.

enharnachement, m. harnessing, trap-

enharnacher, v. a. to harness ‖ to rig out.

énigmatique, a. (-ment, ad.) enigmatic (ally).

énigme, f. riddle ‖ enigma.

enivrement, m. intoxication.

enivrer, v. a. to intoxicate ‖ s'~, to get drunk ‖ to be infatuated with.

enjambée, f. stride, wide step.

enjambement, m. running of a verse into the next line to complete the sense.

enjamber, v. a. & n. to stride, to stride over, to step wide ‖ to jut out ‖ to encroach upon ‖ to run into another line.

enjaveler, v. a. (agr.) to bind corn into sheaves.   [sheaves.

enjeu, m. stake (at play).

enjoindre, v. a. ir. to enjoin.

enjôler, v. a. to wheedle, to coax.

enjôleur, se, m. & f. wheedler, coaxer.

enjolivement, m. embellishment, ornament.   [set,off.

enjoliver, v. a. to embellish, to adorn, to

enjoliveur, m. setter-off.

enjolivure, f. ornament, set-off.

enjoué, e, a. cheerful, lively, sprightly, merry, mirthful, playful, sportive.

enjouement, m. cheerfulness, sprightliness, playfulness, sportiveness.

enlacement, m. twisting, entangling.

enlacer, v. a. to lace, to twist ‖ to string ‖ to interweave.   [ugly.

enlaidir, v. a. & n. to disfigure ‖ to grow

enlaidissement, m. growing ugly.

enlèvement, m. carrying off, removal, abduction.

enlever, v. a. to lift up, to raise, to heave up ‖ to blow up ‖ to carry off, to take away, to abduct ‖ to buy up ‖ to delight,

to charm ‖ s'~, to rise ‖ to come off, to peel off.

enligner, v. a. to place ou range in line.

enluminer, v. a. to colour, to illuminate.

enlumineur, m. colourer.   [redness.

enluminure, f. colouring ‖ coloured print ‖

ennemi, e, m. & f. enemy, foe.

ennemi, e, a. hostile ‖ adverse ‖ opposing.

ennoblir, v. a. to ennoble.

ennui, m. tediousness, weariness, dulness, lassitude, idleness ‖ spleen ‖ sorrow.

ennuyant, e, a. tedious, tiresome.

ennuyer, v. a. to tire, to weary ‖ s'~, to be tired ou weary ‖ to bother oneself.

ennuyeux, se, a. (-sement, ad.) tedious (ly) ‖ tiresome(ly) ‖ wearisome(ly) ‖ dull(y).

énoncé, m. assertion, declaration.

énoncer, v. a. to state ‖ to give out ‖ to express ‖ to word.

énonciation, f. enunciation, expression, utterance ‖ statement.

enorgueillir, v. a. to make proud ‖ s'~, to grow ou be proud.

énorme, a. enormous, huge.

énormément, ad. enormously.

énormité, f. enormity, hugeness.

s'enquérir, to inquire.

enquête, f. inquest, inquiry.

enraciner, v. a. to root ‖ s'~, to take root.

enragé, m. madman.

enragé, e, a. mad, enraged, furious ‖ (of music) rough and noisy.

enrageant, e, a. enraging, provoking.

enrager, v. n. to enrage, to be mad, to run mad ‖ to be provoked ‖ faire ~, to madden.   [skid (a wheel).

enrayer, v. a. to put spokes to ‖ to lock ou

enrayure, f. drag, skid.

enrégimenter, v. a. to enroll, to embody ‖ to form into regiments.

enregistrement, m. registering, enrolment, entry.   [to enroll.

enregistrer, v. a. to register, to record,

enrhumé, e, a. with a cold.   [to catch cold.

enrhumer, v. a. to give one a cold ‖ s'~,

enrichi, e, m. & f. upstart.

enrichir, v. a. to enrich ‖ to adorn ‖ to store ‖ s'~, to grow rich.

enrichissement, m. enriching ‖ ornament.

enrôler, v. a. to enroll, to enlist.

enroué, e, a. hoarse.

enrouement, m. hoarseness.

enrouer, v. a. to make hoarse ‖ s'~, to become hoarse.

enroulement, m. rolling.

enrouler, v. a. to roll up.

ensablement, m. sand-bank.

ensabler, v. a. (s'~) (mar.) to run on a sand-bank.

ensacher, v. a. to bag.   [sand-bank.

ensanglanter, v. a. to stain with blood.

enseigne, m. (mil.) ensign ‖ (mar.) midshipman ‖ ~, f. sign, signal, colours ‖ sign-post ‖ à bonnes -s, justly ‖ deservedly ‖ on good security ‖ à telles -s que, so much so that, as proof.

enseignement, m. instruction, precept ‖ information ‖ (jur.) title, proof, document.

enseigner, v. a. to teach, to instruct, to direct to ‖ to show.

ensellé, e, a. saddle-backed.
ensemble, m. whole || whole appearance || harmony || (mus.) part-music.
ensemble, ad. together.
ensemencement, m. sowing.
ensemencer, v. a. to sow.
enserrer, v. a. to encompass.   [engulf.
ensevelir, v. a. to lay out || to bury || to
ensevelissement, m. burying.
ensoleillé, e, a. sunny.
ensorceler, v. a. to bewitch.
ensorceleur, se, m. & f. bewitcher || enchantress, sorceress.
ensorcellement, m. bewitching.
ensuite, ad. afterwards, then, after || ~ **de cela,** after which, after that.
s'ensuivre, to follow || to ensue.
entablement, m. entablature.
entacher, v. a. to taint.
entaille, f. notch, slash, gash.
entailler, v. a. to notch.
entame, f. first cut.
entamer, v. a. to cut, to make the first cut, to break, to open || to begin, to enter upon.   [cision.
entamure, f. cut, the first cut || small in-
entassé, e, a. thick-set.
entassement, m. heap.
entasser, v. a. to heap up || to cram.
ente, f. graft, scion.
entendement, m. understanding.
entendeur, m. intelligent.
entendre, v. a. to hear, to hearken || to listen || to understand, to apprehend, to know || to expect || à ~, according to || s'~, to be heard || to understand. each other || to be understood || to be skilful in.
entendu, e, a. heard, understood || intelligent.   [skill.
entente, f. understanding || meaning ||
enter, v. a. to graft, to ingraft.
entérinement, m. ratification.
entériner, v. a. to ratify.
enterrement, m. funeral, burial.
enterrer, v. a. to bury || to outlive || to
en-tête, m. heading.   [terminate.
entêté, e, a. obstinate || infatuated.
entêtement, m. obstinacy || infatuation.
entêter, v. a. & n. to make giddy || to make vain || to infatuate || s'~, to take into one's head, to be prepossessed || to get obstinate.
enthousiasme, m. enthusiasm, rapture.
enthousiasmer, v. a. to transport || to enrapture || s'~, to become enthusiastic.
enthousiaste, m. enthusiast || fanatic.
enticher, v. a. to taint || s'~, to be taken with.
entier, ière, a. (-èrement, ad.) entire (ly) || whole || wholly || complete, perfect || obstinate, self-willed || **en ~,** totally, wholly.
entité, f. entity.   [vass.
entoilage, m. lining || mounting on can-
entoiler, v. a. to line || to mount on canvass.
entomologie, f. entomology.   [vass.
entonner, v. a. to tun || to intonate || to strike up || to begin || to sing || to quaff || s'~, to rush.

entonnoir, m. funnel.
entorse, f. sprain || shock.   [tanglement.
entortillage, m. equivocal language || en-
entortillement, m. winding about, twisting || entanglement.
entortiller, v. a. to wrap, to wind about, to twist || to entangle || (fig.) to bring round.
entourage, m. setting || associates || company || circle || attendants.
entourer, v. a. to surround, to enclose, to environ, to shut in.
entournure, f. sloping.
entours, m. pl. environs, adjacent country.
en-tout-cas, m. sun-shade.
entr'acte, m. interval between the acts.
s'entr'aider, to help one another.
entrailles, f. pl. entrails, bowels || feeling, tender affection.
s'entr'aimer, to love one another.
entrain, m. spirits || animation || life || sans ~, listless(ly).
entraînement, m. force || sway, rapture.
entraîner, v. a. to carry away, to lead away, to draw along || to entice || to hurry away.
entrant, e, m. ingoer.   [hinder.
entraver, v. a. to shackle, to fetter || to
entraves, f. pl. shackles || obstacle.
entre, pr. between, among, in || into || ~ **bâillé, e,** a. ajar, half-open || ~ **bâiller,** v. a. to open half-way || s'~ **choquer,** to knock ou to dash one against another || to contradict each other || ~ **côte,** f. piece off the ribs || s'~ **croiser,** to cross each other || s'~ **déchirer,** to tear each other || s'~ **détruire,** ir. to destroy one another || ~ **deux,** m. intermediate space || pier-piece (of furniture) || s'~ **dévorer,** to devour each other. || ~ **ligne,** f. interlineation || ~ **luire,** v. n. ir. to glimmer || s'~ **nuire,** ir. to injure each other || s'~ **quereller,** to quarrel with each other || s'~ **secourir,** ir. to assist each other || ~ **temps,** m. interval || meantime || s'~ **tuer,** to kill each other || ~ **voie,** f. space between the lines.
entrechat, m. caper.
entrecouper, v. a. to break off, to interrupt, to intersect || to intersperse.
entrée, f. entry, entrance, passage || access, admittance, introduction || beginning || duty || course of dishes.
entrefaites, f. pl.; **sur ces ~,** meanwhile.
s'entr'égorger, to cut each other's throat.
entrefilet, m. short newspaper article.
entregent, m. tact, shrewdness.
entrelacement, m. interweaving.
entrelacer, v. a. to interweave || s'~, to
entrelacs, m. pl. twine.   [entwine.
entrelarder, v. a. to interlard.
(s')entremêler, v. a. & n. to intermingle, to intersperse.
entremets, m. side-dish, relish.
entremetteur, se, m. & f. go-between.
s'entremettre, ir. to intermeddle, to interpose.   [intervention.
entremise, f. interposition, mediation,
entrepas, m. ambling pace.
entrepont, m. (mar.) 'tween-decks (pl.).

entreposer, v. a. to store, to lay up.
entrepôt, m. mart, staple || storehouse, bonding-warehouse.
s'entrepousser, to push each other.
entreprenant, e, a. enterprising, venturous || daring.
entreprendre, v. a. ir. to undertake, to attempt || to attack || to contract for.
entrepreneur, m. contractor || masterbuilder || ~ des pompes funèbres, undertaker.   [awkward || impotent.
entrepris, e, a. undertaken || disconcerted ||
entreprise, f. enterprise, undertaking, attempt || encroachment, usurpation.
entrer, v. n. to enter, to come in, to get in, to step in, to march into, to drop in || to penetrate || to share, to participate.
entresol, m. suite of rooms between the ground floor and the first floor.
entretenir, v. a. ir. to hold fast together, to keep up || to keep, to maintain || to preserve || to keep in good order || to converse with || to amuse, to divert || s'~, to keep up || to maintain ou supply oneself || to feed || to converse, to talk.
entretien, m. maintenance, livelihood, keeping || conversation, discourse || supply.
entretoise, f. tie-piece.   [port, defence.
entrevoir, v. a. to have a glimpse of || to foresee || s'~, to have an interview with ||
entrevue, f. interview.   [to meet.
entr'ouvert, e, a. half open, ajar.
entr'ouvrir, v. a. ir. to open a little || s'~, to open ou to unclose itself || to gape.
enture, f. cut, incision.
énumérer, v. a. to enumerate.
envahir, v. a. to invade, to usurp || to encroach on.   [ment.
envahissement, m. invasion || encroach-
envahisseur, m. invader.
enveloppe, f. envelope, wrapper, cover.
envelopper, v. a. to envelop, to wrap up, to fold up || to involve || to invest.
envenimer, v. a. to envenom || to irritate, to exasperate || to inflame || s'~, to fester || to rankle.
enverger, v. a. to deck with small willow-branches.   [at the yard.
enverguer, v. a. (mar.) to tie the sails
envergure, f. span (of the wings) || (mar.) width (of sails).
envers, m. wrong side (of stuff).
envers, pr. towards, to || ~ et contre tous, against each and all, through thick and à l'envi, ad. in emulation.   [thin.
envie, f. envy || mind, desire, longing, fancy || mark || flaw || hang-nail.
envier, v. a. to envy, to grudge.
envieux, se, a. envious.
enviné, e, a. smelling of wine.
environ, ad. about || thereabouts.
environner, v. a. to surround.
environs, m. pl. country round || neighbourhood.   [consider.
envisager, v. a. to look in the face, to
envoi, m. sending, conveyance, invoice, message || address, consignment || lettre d'~, letter of advice.   [bours.
envoisiner, v. a. to surround with neigh-

s'envoler, to fly away.
envoûtement, m. magic charm.
envoûter, v. a. to cast one under a spell by transfixing one's image in wax.
envoyé, m. envoy, messenger.
envoyer, v. a. to send, to dispatch.
envoyeur, m. (com.) sender.
épagneul, m. spaniel.
épais, se, a. thick || heavy.   [depth.
épaisseur, f. thickness, thick part || breadth ||
épaissir, v. a. & n. to thicken.
épaississement, m. thickening || thickness.   [leaves of a vine.
épamprer, v. a. to lop off the superfluous
épanchement, m. pouring out, shedding || effusion.
épancher, v. a. to pour out || to open || to vent || s'~, to overflow || to discloso one's
épandre, v. a. to spread.   [heart.
épanouir, v. n. to blow, to bloom || to grow cheerful.
épanouissement, m. blossoming of flowers || cheerfulness.
épargne, f. parsimony, saving.
épargner, v. a. to spare, to save.
éparpillement, m. scattering.
éparpiller, v. a. to scatter.
épars, e, a. scattered, thin, dishevelled.
éparvin, m. spavin.
épaté, e, a. flattened || (of glasses) with the foot broken off || (of the nose) flat || (fam.) amazed.
s'épater, to sprawl || to fall plump.
épaule, f. shoulder.   [starts.
épaulée, f. shouldering || –s, pl. fits and
épaulement, m. earthwork, rampart.
épauler, v. a. to splay || to bring to the shoulder || to press (the butt-end) against the shoulder || to support, to help.
épaulette, f. epaulet, shoulder-piece.
épave, f. strayed || waif || wreck.
épave, a. strayed.
épeautre, f. spelt.
épée, f. sword || ~-de-mer, sword-fish.
épeler, v. a. to spell.
épellation, f. spelling.
éperdu, e, a. (–ment, ad.) dismayed || distracted(ly) || desperate(ly).
éperlan, m. smelt.
éperon, m. spur || buttress || wrinkles (in the corner of the eye) || beak-head.
éperonner, v. a. to spur.
épervier, m. sparrow-hawk || sweep-net.
éphémère, m. day-fly.
éphémère, a. ephemeral.
épi, m. ear, spike || tuft || feather || cluster.
épice, f. spice || pain d'~, ginger-bread.
épicer, v. a. to spice.
épicerie, f. grocery.
épicier, ère, m. & f. spicer, grocer.
épicurien, m. epicure.
épicurien, ne, a. epicurean.
épicurisme, m. epicurism.
épidémie, f. epidemic (disease).
épidémique, a. epidemic.
épiderme, m. epidermis.
épier, v. a. & n. to espy, to watch || to ear.
épierrer, v. a. to clear of stones.
épieu, m. boar-spear.

épigastre, m. epigastrium.
épigrammatique, a. epigrammatic.
épigramme, f. epigram.
épigraphe, f. epigraph.
épilatoire, a. depilatory.
épilepsie, f. epilepsy.
épileptique, m. epileptic.
épileptique, a. epileptic.
épiler, v. a. to depilate.
épilogue, m. epilogue.
épiloguer, v. a. & n. to find fault with.
épilogueur, m. fault-finder || hair-splitter.
épinards, m. pl. spinage.
épine, f. thorn, prickle || ~-vinette, f. (bot.) barberry-bush.
épineux, se, a. spiny || thorny, prickly || intricate, difficult, ticklish.
épingle, f. pin || peg || scarf-pin || -s, pl. pin-money.
épinglette, f. pricker.
épinglier, m. pin-maker.
épinière, a. (an.) spinal.
épinoche, m. stickle-back.
Épiphanie, f. Epiphany.
épique, a. epic.
épiscopal, e, a. episcopal || episcopalian.
épiscopat, m. episcopacy, bishopric.
épisode, m. episode.
épispastique, m. epispastic.
épispastique, a. epispastic.
épisser, v. a. (mar.) to splice.
épistolaire, m. epistolary || letter-writer.
épistolaire, a. epistolary.
épitaphe, f. epitaph.
épithalame, m. nuptial song.
épithète, f. epithet.
épître, f. epistle, letter.
épizootie, f. epizooty, murrain.
épizootique, a. epizootic.
éploré, e, a. all in tears.
éployé, e, a. displayed, spread.
épluchage, **épluchement**, m. picking.
éplucher, v. a. to pick (out), to clean || to sift.
éplucheur, se, m. & f. picker || fault-finder.
épluchoir, m. paring-knife.
épluchure, f. picking.
épointer, v. a. to blunt, to dull the point.
éponge, f. sponge.
éponger, v. a. to sponge, to mop.
épontille, f. (mar.) stanchion, pillar.
épopée, f. epopee, epic poem.
époque, f. epoch, epocha, period.
époumonner, v. a. to tire the lungs.
épousailles, f. pl. wedding.
épouse, f. spouse, wife.
épousée, f. newly married woman.
épouser, v. a. to espouse, to marry.
épouseur, m. marrying man.
épousseter, v. a. to dust.
époussette, f. duster.
épouvantable, a. (-ment, ad.) frightful (ly) || dreadful(ly).
épouvantail, m. scarecrow, bugbear.
épouvante, f. fright, terror.
épouvanter, v. a. to frighten, to terrify || s'~, to be frightened ou terrified.
époux, m. husband, bridegroom || ~, pl. husband and wife, married couple.

épreindre, v. a. ir. to squeeze out.
s'éprendre, to be smitten, to fall in love.
épreuve, f. trial, proof, test || à l'~, on trial.
épris, e, a. enamoured, charmed, inflamed.
éprouver, v. a. to try || to experience || to be sensible of.
éprouvette, f. probe, gauge.
épucer, v. a. to free from fleas.
épuisable, a. exhaustible.
épuisement, m. exhaustion || drainage.
épuiser, v. a. to exhaust, to drain || to waste || to use up.
épuisette, f. hand-net (to take birds).
épuration, f. purifying, clarifying.
épure, f. draught.
épurer, v. a. to purify, to refine.
équarrir, v. a. to square || to kill and skin.
équarrissage, m. squareness || squaring || killing and skinning.
équarrissement, m. squaring.
équarrisseur, m. knacker.
équateur, m. equator.
équation, f. (math. & astr.) equation.
équatorial, a. (astr.) equatorial.
équerre, f. square, square rule || d'~, square.
équestre, a. equestrian.
équiangle, a. equi-angular.
équilibre, m. equilibrium || balance.
équilibrer, v. a. to poise.
équilibriste, m. equilibrist.
équinoxe, m. equinox.
équinoxial, e, a. equinoctial.
équipage, m. equipage || equipment || carriage || crew || plight || rouler ~, to ride in one's carriage.
équipée, f. foolish enterprise, prank.
équipement, m. equipment, fitting-out.
équiper, v. a. to equip, to fit out, to man.
équitablement, ad. equitably.
équitation, f. riding || horsemanship.
équité, f. equity, justice.
équivalent, m. equivalent.
équivalent, e, a. equivalent.
équivaloir, v. n. ir. to be equivalent to.
équivoque, f. equivocation, ambiguity.
équivoque, a. equivocal, ambiguous || doubtful || suspicious.
équivoquer, v. n. to equivocate || s'~, to make a mistake.
érable, m. maple-tree. [make a mistake.
éradication, f. eradication.
érafler, v. a. to scratch slightly, to graze.
éraflure, f. light scratch.
éraillement, m. (méd.) eversion of the eyelids.
éraillé, e, a. bloodshot || frayed.
érailler, v. a. to fray.
éraillure, f. fraying.
ératé, e, a. a brisk, sprightly, cunning.
érater, v. a. to pull out the milt ou spleen || to cheer up.
ère, f. era, epoch. [to cheer up.
érection, f. erection || raising.
éreinter, v. a. to break the back || to knock up.
érémitique, a. eremitical. [knock up.
érésipèle, m. (méd.) erysipelas.
ergot, m. spur (of a cock) || smut, blight.
ergoté, a. spurred || horned.
ergoter, v. n. to cavil.
ergoterie, f. cavilling.

ergoteur, se, m. & f. caviller.
ériger, v. a. to erect, to raise || s'~, to set
ermitage, m. hermitage.   [up for.
ermite, m. hermit.
érosion, f. (méd.) erosion.
érotique, a. erotic.
errant, e, a. errant, wandering, rambling.
erratique, a. erratic || intermittent.
errements, m. pl. footsteps.
errer, v. n. to rove, to ramble, to wander ||
erres, f. pl. track.   [to err, to mistake.
erreur, f. error, mistake || ~ I nay !
erroné, e, a. erroneous.
érudit, m. scholar.
érudit, e, a. learned.
éruption, f. eruption || teething || (méd.)
    eruption, rash.
érysipèle, m. (méd.) erysipelas.
ès, pr. (contr. of en les) maître-ès-
    arts, Master of arts.
esbrouffe, f. fuss, show.
escabeau, m. stool || steps.
escadre, f. squadron (of ships).
escadrille, f. little squadron.
escadron, m. squadron (of horse) || chef
    d'~, lieutenant-colonel.
escalade, f. climbing over, scaling.
escalader, v. a. to scale.
escale, f. putting in || stay.
escalier, m. staircase || flight of stairs ||
    de service, ~ de dégagement, back-
    staircase || ~ à vis, ~ en limaçon, wind-
escamotage, m. juggling.   [ing staircase.
escamoter, v. a. to juggle, to pick, to
    pilfer away.   [gentleman.
escamoteur, m. juggler || light-fingered
escampette, f.; prendre de la poudre
    d'~, to scamper away.
escapade, f. prank || spree.
escarbilles, f. pl. coal-cinders.
escarbot, m. black-beetle.
escarboucle, f. carbuncle.
escargot, m. edible snail || spiral staircase.
escarmouche, f. skirmish.
escarmoucher, v. n. to skirmish.
escarole, f. (bot.) endive.
escarpe, f. (mil.) scarp.
escarpé, e, a. steep.
escarpement, m. escarpment || steepness.
escarper, v. a. to cut down steep.
escarpin, m. pump.
escarpolette, f. swing.   [ingly.
escient, m. knowledge || à bon ~, know-
esclandre, f. noise, scandal, exposure.
esclavage, m. slavery.
esclave, m. & f. slave, drudge.
esclave, a. slavish.
escobard, m. shuffler.
escobarder, v. n. to shuffle.
escobarder', f. shuffling.
escoffier, v. a. to do for || to settle || to kill.
escogriffe, m. sharper || lanky lout.
escompte, m. (com.) discount.
escompter, v. a. (com.) to discount, to cash.
escompteur, m. (com.) discounter.
escopette, f. carbine, hand-gun.
escorte, f. escort, convoy.
escorter, v. a. to escort.
escouade, f. squad || scout.

escrime, f. fencing || salle d'~, fencing-
    school.
escrimer, v. n. to fence || s'~, to dabble
    in || to endeavour.
escroc, m. sharper, swindler.
escroquer, v. a. to trick, to cheat.
escroquerie, f. swindler's trick.
escroqueur, m. swindler.
espace, m. space, room.
espacement, m. interval || spacing.
espacer, v. a. to place apart || to space.
espadon, m. two-handed sword || sword-fish.
espagnolette, f. sash-fastening.
espalier, m. fruit-wall.
espars, m. pl. (mar.) spars (pl.).
espèce, f. species, sort, kind, race, tribe ||
    ~s, pl. specie, cash || ~s sonnantes,
    hard cash, ready money.
espérance, f. hope, expectation || trust.
espérer, v. a. & n. to hope, to expect, to
espiègle, m. wag.   [trust.
espiègle, a. waggish, frolicsome.
espièglerie, f. frolic || roguish trick.
espingole, f. blunderbuss.
espion, m. spy.
espionnage, m. spying || spy-system.
espionner, v. a. to spy.
esplanade, f. esplanade.
espoir, m. hope, expectation.
esprit, m. spirit, soul, ghost, apparition ||
    genius, ingenuity, wit, witty thought,
    understanding, mind || temper, disposi-
    tion, sense, meaning || principle, motive ||
    homme d'~, man of genius, man of wit ||
    ~ de corps, fellow-feeling || ~ fort, free-
    thinker || bel ~, wit, genius || ~ de parti,
    party-spirit || ~ de suite, consistency ||
    notions ou habits of regularity.
esquif, m. skiff.
esquille, f. splinter.
esquinancie, f. quinsy.
esquinter, v. a. to knock up.
esquipot, m. money-box.
esquisse, f. sketch || outline.
esquisser, v. a. to sketch.
esquiver, v. a. to avoid || s'~, to steal
    away.
essai, m. essay || trial, proof, experiment ||
    sample || effort || à l'~, on trial.
essaim, m. swarm || multitude.
essaimer, v. n. to swarm.
essanger, v. a. to soak.
essartage, essartement, m. grubbing.
essarter, v. a. to grub up.
essayer, v. a. to try, to attempt || to assay ||
    s'~, to try one's hand ou skill.
essayeur, m. assayer (of metals).
essence, f. essence || attar
essentiel, m. main point.
essentiel, le, a. (—lement, ad.) essen-
    tial(ly) || material(ly).
essieu, m. axle, axle-tree.
essor, m. flight || soaring || strain || play ||
    scope || prendre l'~, to soar.
essoriller, v. a. to cut the ears off || to crop.
essouffler, v. a. to put out of breath.
essui, m. drying-place.
essuie; ~-main, m. towel || ~-pieds, m.
    mat || ~-plume, m. pen-wiper.

essuyer, v. a. to wipe (off, away), to rub off, to dust, to dry up || to bear, to suffer.

est, m. east.

estacade, f. stockade.

estafette, f. express messenger.   [bully.

estafier, m. footman || livery servant ||

estafilade, f. slash || rent, cut (in cloth).

estafilader, v. a. to slash.

estaminet, m. smoking-room || tavern || tap-room.

estampe, f. stamp, print, engraving.

estamper, v. a. to stamp.

estampille, f. stamp.

estampiller, v. a. to stamp.

esthétique, a. æsthetic.

estimateur, m. appraiser.

estimation, f. estimate, valuation.

estime, f. esteem, estimation.

estimer, v. a. to esteem, to estimate, to value || to prize || to deem.

estival, a. æstival || summer.

estoc, m. long rapier || stock || point of a sword || tuck.

estocade, f. thrust.   [sword || tuck.

estocader, v. a. to thrust.

estomac, m. stomach || breast.

s'estomaquer, to take offence || to exhaust oneself.

estompe, f. stump.   [haust oneself.

estomper, v. a. to stump.

estrade, f. platform, stage || battre l'~, to scout.

estragon, m. tarragon.   [to scout.

estrapade, f. strappado.

estropié, m. lame, cripple.

estropié, e, a. crippled, maimed.

estropier, v. a. to maim, to cripple, to lame || to mutilate.

estuaire, m. estuary.

esturgeon, m. sturgeon.

et, c. and || ~ . . ~, both . . . and.

établage, m. stabling.

étable, m. stable || cattle-shed || sty.

établer, v. a. to stable.

établi, m. work-bench || counter.

établir, v. a. to establish, to settle, to erect, to found, to ground, to appoint, to create || to state, to aver, to assert.

établissement, m. establishment, establishing, settling || settlement, foundation, institution || state, condition.

étage, m. story, floor || degree, quality, rank.

étager, v. a. to cut slanting || to taper (the hair) || to place in tiers.

étagère, f. set of shelves, whatnot.

étai, m. stay || shore || prop, support.

étaim, m. carded wool.

étain, m. tin, pewter.

étal, m. butcher's stall.

étalage, m. stallage || show || goods exposed for sale || show-window.

étalagiste, m. stall-keeper.

étaler, v. a. to stall, to expose for sale || to show, to make a show of, to make a parade of || s'~, to lie along, to stretch oneself out, to fall all along.

étalier, m. stall-butcher.

étalon, m. stallion || standard.   [ing.

étalonnage, étalonnement, m. stamp-

étalonner, v. a. to stamp (measures ou weights).

étamage, m. tinning || plating.

étambot, m. (mar.) stern-post.

étamer, v. a. to tin || to plate.

étameur, m. tinker.

étamine, f. bolting-cloth || stamen || passer par l'~, to sift || to be sifted.

étamure, f. tinning.

étanchement, m. stanching, stopping (of a fluid) || quenching.   [quench.

étancher, v. a. to stanch, to stop || to

étançon, m. stay, prop.

étançonner, v. a. to stay, to prop.

étang, m. (fish-)pond, pool.

étape, f. rations || halting-place.

étapier, m. sutler.

état, m. state, condition || place, rank, quality || commonwealth, government || -s, pl. dominions || Parliament || ~-major, m. staff || staff-office.

étau, m. vice, screw-vice.   [to support.

étayer, v. a. to prop, to stay, to hold up,

été, m. summer.

éteignoir, m. extinguisher.

éteindre, v. a. ir. to extinguish, to put out, to quench, to suffocate || to strike out, to destroy || s'~, to go out || to abate, to decrease.

éteint, e, a. extinguished, out, extinct.

étendage, m. drying-lines.

étendard, m. standard, colours, banner.

étendoir, m. drying-place || clothes-lines (pl.) || peel.

étendre, v. a. to extend, to spread, to stretch, to expand || to lengthen || s'~, to stretch oneself || to extend, to spread, to reach, to enlarge, to expatiate (upon).

étendu, e, a. stretched, spread out || large || tedious || extensive || sprawling.

étendue, f. extent, compass, length.

éternel, le, a. (-lement, ad.) eternal(ly) || everlasting(ly).   [s'~, to last for ever.

éterniser, v. a. to eternise, to make eternal ||

éternité, f. eternity.

éternuement, m. sneezing.

éternuer, v. n. to sneeze.

étêter, v. a. to lop off the top of a tree.

éteule, f. stubble.

éthéré, e, a. ethereal.

éthique, f. ethics.

ethnographie, f. ethnography.

étiage, m. low-water mark.

étinceler, v. n. to sparkle, to glitter, to

étincelle, f. sparkle, flash.   [flash.

étincellement, m. sparkling, glittering, flashing.

étiolement, m. etiolation || emaciation.

étioler, v. a. to etiolate || to emaciate.

étique, a. consumptive, hectic.

étiqueter, v. a. to label, to ticket.

étiquette, f. label || ceremonies || ceremonial.

étirer, v. a. to stretch.   [monial.

étisie, f. consumption.

étoffe, f. stuff, cloth || matter.

étoffé, e, a. stuffed || furnished || full, rich || comfortably off.

étoffer, v. a. to put stuff in.

étoile, f. star || blaze || à la belle ~, in the star-light.   [light.

étoilé, e, a. starry, full of stars || star-

étoiler, v. a. to star || to stud || s'~, to crack.

étonnamment, ad. wonderfully.

étonnement, m. astonishment ‖ wonder.

étonner, v. a. to astonish, to amaze ‖ to startle ‖ **s'~,** to be astonished ‖ to wonder

étouffade, f. stew.   [at.

étouffant, e, a. sultry.

étouffement, m. stifling, suffocation.

étouffer, v. a. & n. to stifle, to suffocate, to choke, to smother ‖ to conceal, to extinguish ‖ to be stifled, to be choked.

étouffoir, m. damper ‖ cinder-pail.

étoupe, tow, oakum.

étouper, v. a. to stop (with tow).

étoupille, f. quick-match ‖ **~ fulminante,** friction-tube.   [blunder.

étourderie, f. giddiness, thoughtlessness.

étourdi, m. giddy-head.

étourdi, e, a. giddy, light-headed ‖ heedless ‖ **—ment,** ad. giddily ‖ à l'—e, giddily, thoughtlessly.

étourdir, v. a. to stun (with noise *ou* by a blow), to deafen, to make giddy ‖ to benumb, to daunt, to discourage ‖ to surprise, to astound ‖ to assuage ‖ **s'~,** to shake off the thoughts of, to divert one's mind from.   [dizziness, shock.

étourdissement, m. stunning, giddiness,

étourneau, m. starling ‖ silly coxcomb.

étrange, a. (—ment, ad.) strange(ly) ‖ odd.

étranger, ère, m. foreigner, stranger ‖ à l'~, abroad.

étranger, ère, a. strange, foreign, outlandish, exotic ‖ extraneous.

étrangeté, f. strangeness.   [tion.

étranglement, m. strangling ‖ strangula

étrangler, v. a. & n. to strangle, to garrote ‖ to make too scanty ‖ to be choked ‖ **étranglé,** scanty ‖ too narrow *ou* tight.

étrangleur, m. garotter.

étrave, f. (mar.) stem.   [outs of a house.

être, m. being, existence ‖ **—s,** pl. ins and

être, v. n. ir. to be, to exist ‖ to consist of ‖ to dwell ‖ to side with ‖ to be concerned in ‖ to come ‖ **y ~,** to have hit it ‖ to be up to the mark ‖ to be at home.

étrécir, v. a. to straiten ‖ **s'~,** to shrink, to get narrower.   [narrowness.

étrécissement, m. shrinking, straitness,

étreindre, v. a. ir. to bind, to press close, to twist.

étreinte, f. binding, tying close, grasp ‖ embrace ‖ clasping, pressing.

étrenne, f. handsel ‖ **—s,** pl. New-Year's gift, Christmas-box.

étrenner, v. a, & n. to give a New-Year's gift *ou* Christmas-box ‖ to give handsel ‖ to take handsel.

étrier, m. stirrup ‖ strap.

étrille, f. curry-comb.

étriller, v. a. to curry ‖ to drub ‖ (fig.) to

étriper, v. a. to gut.   [fleece.

étriqué, e, a. narrow, scanty ‖ paltry.

étrivière, f. stirrup-leather.

étroit, e, a. (—ement, ad.) strait ‖ narrow(ly) ‖ close(ly) ‖ scanty ‖ strict(ly) ‖ limited ‖ intimate.

étron, m. filth ‖ excrement.

étronçonner, v. a. to lop off (the top of a tree).

étude, f. study, learning ‖ study (room) ‖ usher's room ‖ office, chambers.

étudiant, m. student.

étudié, e, a. studied, affected.

étudier, v. a. & n. to study ‖ **s'~,** to endeavour.

étui, m. case, box, sheath ‖ pin-case.

étuve, f. stove, hot-house ‖ drying-place.

étuvée, f. stewing ‖ stewed meat.

étuvement, m. fomentation.

étuver, v. a. to stew ‖ to bathe, to foment.

étymologie, f. etymology.

étymologique, a. etymological.

eucharistie, f. Eucharist.

eunuque, m. eunuch.

euphémisme, m. euphemism.

euphonie, f. euphony ‖ **par ~,** for the sake of sound.

euphonique, a. euphonic.

euphorbe, m. (bot.) euphorbia ‖ milkwort ‖ (méd.) euphorbium.

eux, pn. m. pl. them, they.

évacuer, v. a. to evacuate.

s'évader, to make one's escape, to elope.

évaluation, f. valuation, estimate.

évaluer, v. a. to value, to appraise, to estimate.   [(ally).

évangélique, a. (—ment, ad.) evangelic

évangéliser, v. n. to evangelise.

évangéliste, m. evangelist.

évangile, m. Gospel.

s'évanouir, to faint, to swoon, to vanish.

évanouissement, m. swoon, fainting fit.

évaporation, f. evaporation ‖ thoughtlessness.

évaporé, e, a. evaporated, giddy-brained.

évaporer, v. a. to evaporate, to vent ‖ **s'~,** to pass off in vapour ‖ to get giddy.

évasé, e, a. wide, bell-mouthed.

évasement, m. width.

évaser, v. a. to widen.

évasif, ve, a. (—vement, ad.) evasive(ly).

évasion, f. escape.

évêché, m. bishopric ‖ episcopal palace.

éveil, m. warning, hint ‖ alarm.

éveillé, e, a. awake, awaked ‖ lively, brisk, sprightly, alert ‖ attentive, vigilant.

éveiller, v. a. to wake, to awake, to brisk up, to quicken, to animate.

événement, m. event ‖ emergency ‖ incident.   [hole.

évent, m. smack, twang ‖ open air ‖ vent

éventail, m. fan.

éventailliste, m. fan-maker ‖ fan-painter.

éventaire, m. flat basket.

éventé, e, a. fanned ‖ giddy.

éventer, v. a. to fan, to ventilate, to air ‖ to winnow ‖ to spread abroad ‖ **s'~,** to fan oneself ‖ to evaporate, to flatten, to die.

éventoir, m. fire-fan.

éventrer, v. a. to rip up ‖ to cut open.

éventualité, f. eventuality.

éventuel, m. contingency ‖ course-fees.

éventuel, le, a. (—lement, ad.) eventual (ly).

évêque, m. bishop.

s'évertuer, to strive, to exert oneself.

évidemment, ad. evidently.

évidence, f. evidence.

évident, e, a. evident ‖ undeniable.

évider, v. a. to unstarch || to hollow || to scoop out.

évier, m. sink (in a kitchen) || sink-stone.

évincer, v. a. to evict || to oust.

évitage, m. swinging.

évitée, f. (mar.) berth.

évitement; gare d'~, shunt, siding.

éviter, v. a. & n. to avoid, to shun, to save || to swing.

évocation, f. evocation, raising up.

évoluer, v. n. (mil.) to perform evolutions || to revolve.

évolution, f. (mil. & mar.) evolution.

évoquer, v. a. to evoke, to call forth.

exact, e, a. (-ement, ad.) exact(ly) || accurate(ly) || precise(ly) || strict, correct, punctual.

exacteur, m. exactor.

exactitude, f. exactness, punctuality, accuracy.

exagérer, v. a. to exaggerate.

exalté, e, a. exalted, excited.

exalter, v. a. to exalt || to extol.

examen, m. examination.

examinateur, m. examiner.

examiner, v. a. to examine, to inquire into || to inspect, to scrutinise.

exaspérer, v. a. to exasperate.

exaucement, m. granting, hearing.

exaucer, v. a. to grant, to hear.

excédant, e, m. & f. overplus, surplus.

excéder, v. a. to exceed, to weary || to wear out.

excellence, f. excellence || Excellency || par ~, in an eminent degree.

excellent, e, a. excellent.

excellentissime, a. most excellent.

exceller, v. n. to excel, to surpass.

excentricité, f. eccentricity.

excentrique, m. eccentric wheel.

excentrique, a. eccentric.

excepté, e, pr. except, save.

excepter, v. a. to except.

exceptionnel, le, a. (-lement, ad.) exceptional(ly).

excès, m. excess || abuse.

excessif, ve, a. (-vement, ad.) excessive(ly) || unreasonable || superfluous(ly) || immoderate(ly).

exciper, v. n. to plead an exception || to allege.

excitabilité, f. excitability.

excitant, e, m. & f. stimulant.

excitateur, m. exciter.

excitation, f. excitement || stimulation.

exciter, v. a. to excite, to provoke, to animate, to stimulate, to urge, to stir up.

s'exclamer, v. a. to exclaim, to clamour || to protest.

exclure, v. a. ir. to exclude.

exclusif, ve, a. (-vement, ad.) exclusive(ly).

excommunier, v. a. to excommunicate.

excorier, v. a. (chir.) to excoriate.

excrément, m. excrement.

excroissance, f. excrescence.

excursion, f. excursion, ramble.

excuse, f. excuse || apology.

excuser, v. a. to excuse || to apologise for || s'~, to excuse oneself || to decline.

exeat, m. permission to go, pass, exeat.

exécrablement, ad. execrably.

exécrer, v. a. to execrate.

exécutable, a. practicable.

exécutant, m. performer.

exécuter, v. a. to execute, to perform, to effect, to complete || to put to death || s'~, to do for oneself || to be one's own executor || to act against one's own interests.

exécuteur, trice, m. & f. executor || executioner, hangman || executrix.

exécution, f. execution, performance || capital punishment || homme d'~, bold and enterprising man || practical man.

exécutoire, a. executory.

exemplaire, m. copy (of a book).

exemplaire, a. exemplary.

exemple, m. example, copy || slip || par ~, for example, for instance.

exempt, e, a. exempt, free from.

exempter, v. a. to exempt, to free from, to dispense with.

exemption, f. exemption, dispensation.

exéquatur, m. exequatur, full power.

exercer, v. a. to exercise || to train up to || to practise || to exert || to follow || to drill.

exercice, m. exercise, use, practice || performance || action || fatigue, trouble.

exergue, m. exergue (of a coin).

s'exfolier, v. to exfoliate.

exhalaison, f. exhalation.

exhalation, f. exhalation.

exhaler, v. a. to exhale, to evaporate || to breathe out, to vent || s'~, to evaporate, to transpire || to break out.

exhaussement, m. raising, height.

exhausser, v. a. to raise.

exhiber, v. a. to exhibit.

exhorter, v. a. to exhort.

exhumer, v. a. to disinter, to exhume.

exigeant, e, a. exacting, unreasonable, particular || ableness, claim.

exigence, f. exigence, exigency, unreasonableness, claim.

exiger, v. a. to exact, to require, to demand || to want.

exigible, a. demandable.

exigu, ë, a. exiguous, small || slender, minute.

exiguïté, f. smallness || scantiness.

exil, m. exile (place).

exilé, e, m. & f. exile (person).

exiler, v. a. to exile, to banish.

existence, f. existence, being, subsistence || life || standing.

exister, v. n. to exist, to be || to live.

exode, m. exodus.

exonérer, v. a. to exonerate || to discharge.

exorbitamment, ad. excessively.

exorbitant, e, a. excessive.

exorciser, v. a. to exorcise.

exorcisme, m. exorcism.

exorde, m. exordium.

exotique, a. exotic.

expansif, ve, a. expansive.

expatrier, v. a. to expatriate || s'~, to leave one's country.

expectative, f. expectation || expectancy.

expectorer, v. a. to expectorate.

expédient, m. expedient, shift.

expédient, a. proper, fit || advisable.

expédier, v. a. to expedite, to forward, to send off || to hasten || to send from || (fam.) to send quickly.

expéditeur, m. sender || commission-agent || shipper.

expéditif, ve, a. expeditious, quick.

expédition, f. expedition, dispatch || dis-patching, sending off || shipment || march || copy.   [copyist, copier, clerk.

expéditionnaire, m. commissioner.

expéditionnaire, a. expeditionary.

expérience, f. experience || experiment.

expérimental, a. experimental.

expérimentateur, m. experimentalist.

expérimenter, v. a. to experience, to try.

expert, e, m. appraiser || valuer || surveyor ||

expertement, ad. expertly.   [expert.

expertise, f. examination, estimate, valua-tion || report || survey.

expertiser, v. a. to examine technically, to examine and report upon.

expiation, f. expiation, atonement.

expiatoire, a. expiatory.

expier, v. a. to expiate, to atone for.

expirer, v. n. to expire || to die.

explétif, m. (gr.) expletive.

explétif, ve, a. expletive || emphatic.

explicateur, m. explainer.

explicatif, ve, a. explanatory.

explication, f. explanation, interpretation, illustration || reading.

explicitement, ad. explicitly.

expliquer, v. a. to explain, to declare, to expound, to illustrate, to interpret, to translate || s'~, to explain oneself, to speak plainly, to give one's candid opinion.

exploit, m. exploit, achievement || feat || (jur.) writ.

exploitable, a. that may be worked ou cultivated || (jur.) distrainable.

exploitant, m. worker || cultivator, farmer.

exploitation, f. improving of lands, fell-ing of woods, working of mines.

exploiter, v. a. & n. to work, to employ || to farm, to cultivate || to make use of || to manage || (jur.) to serve warrants || to distrain.   [tivator || speculator.

exploiteur, m. manager, worker, cul-

explorateur, m. explorer.

explorer, v. a. to explore.

explosion, f. explosion.

exportateur, m. exporter.

exportation, f. exportation || exported

exporter, v. a. to export.   [goods.

exposant, m. petitioner || exhibitor || (ar.) exponent.   [count || allegation.

exposé, m. (jur.) statement || recital, ac-

exposer, v. a. to expose, to lay out, to display, to discover || to venture || to allege || to explain, to expound.

exposition, f. exposition, exhibition || ex-posure || situation || explanation, inter-pretation || recital, statement.

exprès, m. express (messenger).

exprès, esse, a. express || expressed || plain, in express terms, positive || ~, ad. purposely, on purpose.

expressément, ad. expressly.

expressif, ve, a. expressive.

expression, f. expression || expressive-ness || wording.

exprimable, a. expressible.

exprimer, v. a. to express || to squeeze out.

expropriation, f. expropriation || dis-possession || appropriation.

exproprier, v. a. to expropriate, to dis-possess.

expulser, v. a. to expel.   [possess.

exquis, e, a. exquisite.

exsangue, a. (méd.) bloodless, anæmic.

exsudation or **exudation,** f. exudation.

extase, f. ecstasy.

extasier, v. a. to ecstasy, to ravish.

extatique, a. ecstatic.

extension, f. extension, extent, strain.

exténuer, v. a. to extenuate || to exhaust.

extérieur, m. exterior, outside, outward surface, appearance.

extérieur, e, a. (-ment, ad.) exterior || external(ly) || outward(ly) || foreign || pu-blic || à l'~, exteriorly, abroad.   [stroyer.

exterminateur, m. exterminator, de-

exterminateur, a. exterminating.

exterminer, v. a. to exterminate, to de-

externat, m. day-school.   [stroy.

externe, m. day-scholar.

externe, a. external, exterior, outward.

exterritorialité, f. ex-territoriality, in-violability of a foreign ambassador's dwelling and belongings.

extinction, f. extinction, extinguishment || suppression, putting an end (to) || redemp-tion of annuities.   [pator.

extirpateur, m. destroyer || weed-extir-

extirpation, f. extirpation, total destruc-

extirper, v. a. to extirpate.   [tion.

extorquer, v. a. to extort.

extorsion, f. extortion.

extra, m. extra || ~-muros, ad. extra-muros || (London) off the stones.

extraction, f. extraction, descent, birth, extradition || extradition.   [origin.

extraire, v. a. ir. to extract, to select.

extrait, m. extract || abstract.

extrajudiciaire, a. (-ment, ad.) extra-judicial(ly).   [unusual expense.

extraordinaire, m. extraordinary thing ||

extraordinaire, a. extraordinary, out of the common course || -ment, ad. extra-ordinarily || uncommonly.

extravagance, f. extravagance || extra-vagant thing.   [wild, mad.

extravagant, e, a. extravagant, excessive ||

extravaguer, v. n. to extravagate || to rave, to talk idly.

s'extravaser, to be extravasated.

extrême, m. extremity.   [utmost.

extrême, a. (-ment, ad.) extreme(ly) ||

extrémité, f. extremity, extreme, utmost parts || utmost distress || last moments || à l'~, dying || to the last moment.

extrinsèque, a. extrinsic.

exubérance, f. exuberance || luxuriance.

ex-voto, m. votive offering.

F.

fable, f. fable || mythology || story.

fabliau, m. (poés.) metrical tale.

fabricant, m. manufacturer.

fabricateur, m. maker || forger.

fabrication, f. fabrication, manufacturing, manufacture || coining || forgery (of a deed).

fabrique, f. fabric, frame, building, construction || manufacture, factory || revenue of a church || vestry-board.

fabriquer, v. a. to fabricate, to manufacture || to coin || (fig.) to invent, to forge.

fabuleux, se, a. (-sement, ad.) fabulous

fabuliste, m. fabulist.   [(ly).

façade, f. front || frontage || face.

face, f. face, visage || surface, superficies || front, forepart (of a building) || appearance, state, turn (of affairs), condition || en ~ de, in the sight of, in presence of, before, over-against.

facétie, f. facetiousness, joke, jest.

facétieux, se, a. (-sement, ad.) facetious(ly) || jocular.

facette, f. facet, small surface.

facetter, v. a. to cut with facets.

fâché, e, a. angry, displeased || sorry, vexed.

fâcher, v. a. to anger, to make angry, to grieve, to afflict || to offend || se ~, to be grieved, to be displeased || to be sorry, to be angry, to grumble, to quarrel.

fâcherie, f. disagreement, trouble.

fâcheux, m. intruder, bore.

fâcheux, se, a. grievous, sad, troublesome, vexatious || difficult || peevish.

facial, a. (anat.) facial.

facies, m. (méd.) facies.

facile, a. easy || ready || yielding || offhand || fluent || -ment, ad. easily.

facilité, f. facility, easiness, ease, readiness, dexterity || fluency.

faciliter, v. a. to facilitate.

façon, f. fashion, shape, form || workmanship, making || composition, make || ornament || manner, way, mode, custom || look, presence || ceremony, affectation || (agr.)

faconde, f. eloquence, loquacity.   [dressing.

façonner, v. a. to fashion, to make, to form, to shape || to figure || to accustom to || (agr.) to till, to dress.

façonnier, ère, a. ceremonious, formal.

factage, m. carriage || goods-delivery || porterage.   [letter-carrier, postman.

facteur, m. maker || porter || factor, agent ||

factice, a. factitious.

factieux, m. factionist.

factieux, se, a. factious.   [duty.

faction, f. faction || (mil.) sentry, watch ||

factionnaire, m. (mil.) sentinel, sentry.

factorerie, f. factory.

facture, f. (com.) invoice, bill.

facturer, v. a. (com.) to invoice.

facultatif, ve, a. optional.

faculté, f. faculty.

fadaise, f. trifle, fiddle-faddle || silliness.

fadasse, a. most insipid.

fade, a. insipid, tasteless, mawkish || dull, heavy.   [insipid compliment.

fadeur, f. insipidity || silliness, empty talk ||

fagot, m. fagot, bundle || idle story.

fagotage, f. fagot-making.   [bundle up.

fagoter, v. a. to fagot, to tie in fagots || to

fagoteur, m. fagot-maker || bungler || scribbler.   [clothes || Pug || clown.

fagotin, m. monkey dressed in man's

faible, m. foible, weak side.

faible, a. (-ment, ad.) feeble || weak(ly) || poor || languishing || light, fragile || slight (ly) || faintly.

faiblesse, f. feebleness, weakness, faintness, languor || swoon, fainting fit || failing.

faiblir, v. n. to get weak || to slacken || to flag || to yield.

faïence, f. earthenware, delf.

faïencerie, f. manufacture of earthenware || crockery-ware.

faïencier, m. crockery-ware man.

failli, m. bankrupt.

faillibilité, f. fallibility.

faillir, v. n. ir. to fail, to err, to be mistaken, to be deficient || to go bankrupt || to be on the point of.

faillite, f. failure, bankruptcy || insolvency || faire ~, to go bankrupt.

faim, f. hunger || avoir ~, to be hungry.

faîne, f. beech-nut.

fainéant, m. idler || drone.

fainéant, e, a. idle, lazy.

fainéanter, v. n. to idle.

fainéantise, f. idleness, laziness, sloth.

faire, m. doing, execution || manner, style.

faire, v. a. ir. to make, to do, to perform, to execute, to accomplish || to create, to get, to beget || to cause || to compose, to constitute || to counterfeit || to commit, to practise || to think, to esteem || to fit, to suit || to deal || se ~, to be made, to be done || to turn, to become, to use, to inure || to grow, to happen.   [practicable.

faisable, a. feasible, that may be done,

faisan, e or **de**, m. & f. pheasant || henpheasant.

faisandeau, m. young pheasant.

faisander, v. a. to keep meat till it gets high || se ~, to get high (of meat).

faisanderie, f. pheasantry.

faisandier, m. pheasant-breeder.

faisceau, m. bundle, truss, sheaf.

faiseur, m. maker, doer, performer, monger || swindler || jobber.

fait, m. fact, matter of fact || act, action, deed || case, affair, business || share || en ~ de, in point of || de ~, in reality, truly || ~ d'armes, exploit || -s et gestes, pl. sayings and doings (pl.).

fait, e, a. made, done || over, out.

faîte, m. top, summit.

faix, m. burden, weight.

falaise, f. cliff.   [coast.

falaiser, v. n. (mar.) to break upon the

falbala, m. furbelow, flounce.   [(ly).

fallacieux, se, a. (-sement, ad.) fallacious

falloir, v. imp. ir. to be necessary, to be needful, to be requisite || to be in need, to want.

falot, m. large lantern.   [want.

falot, e, a. ludicrous || funny.

falourde, f. bundle of logs.

falsificateur, m. falsifier.

falsification, f. falsification, counterfeit, forgery || adulteration.

falsifier, v. a. to falsify, to adulterate.

6*

falun, m. shell-marl.

faluner, v. a. to manure with shell-marl.

famé, e, a. famed ‖ **mal ~,** of bad repute.

famélique, a. starved, hungry.

fameux, se, a. (**-sement,** ad.) famous (ly) ‖ famed, distinguished.

familiariser, v. a. to familiarise ‖ to tame, to habituate ‖ **se ~,** to familiarise oneself, to accustom oneself to.

familiarité, f. familiarity.

familier, ère, a. (**-èrement,** ad.) familiar(ly) ‖ intimate(ly) ‖ free(ly).

famille, f. family ‖ race, kindred, relations ‖ house, household ‖ **affaire de ~,** f. domestic concern ‖ **en ~,** with one's family ‖ without ceremony.

famine, f. famine.

fanage, m. hay-making ‖ hay-maker's wages (pl.) ‖ leaves (pl.).

fanal, m. light-house ‖ watch-light, beacon ‖ (fig.) guide.

fanatique, a. fanatic.

fanatique, m. fanatic.

fanatiser, v. a. to fanaticise.

fanatisme, m. fanaticism.

fane, f. fallen leaf ‖ tops.

faner, v. a. to make hay, to spread hay ‖ to dry up, to cause to fade ‖ **se ~,** to fade away.

faneur, se, m. & f. hay-maker.

fanfan, m. darling, duck.

fanfare, f. flourish (of trumpets).

fanfaron, m. bully, boaster, hector.

fanfaron, ne, a. boasting, bragging.

fanfaronnade, fanfaronnerie, f. bragging, boasting, ostentation.

fanfinot, m. baby ‖ (fam.) ducky.

fanfreluche, f. gewgaw.

fange, f. mire, mud, dirt.

fangeux, se, a. miry, dirty.

fanion, m. small flag (before baggage-waggons).

fanon, m. dewlap ‖ fetlock ‖ pendants (of a bishop's mitre).

fantaisie, f. fantasy ‖ fancy ‖ whim.

fantaisiste, m. & f. fanciful artist ‖ imaginative author ‖ fantasist, humourist.

fantasmagorie, f. phantasmagoria ‖ dissolving views.

fantasmagorique, a. phantasmagoric.

fantasque, a. fantastic ‖ fanciful ‖ whimsical.

fantassin, m. foot-soldier.

fantastique, a. (**-ment,** ad.) fantastical(ly).

fantôme, m. phantom, apparition, spectre ‖ fancy.

faon, m. fawn, doe.

faonner, v. n. to fawn.

faquin, m. coxcomb, fob, jackanapes.

faraud, m. vulgar coxcomb.

farce, f. farce ‖ stuffing, force-meat ‖ after-piece, interlude, laughable scene.

farceur, m. farce-player, buffoon ‖ droll person.

farcin, m. farcy, glanders.

farcir, v. a. to stuff, to cram.

fard, m. paint, varnish ‖ disguise.

fardeau, m. burden, load.

farder, v. a. & n. to fard ‖ to paint ‖ to gloss, to varnish, to disguise ‖ to sink.

fardier, m. stone-and-timber dray.

farfadet, m. hobgoblin.

farfouiller, v. a. & n. to rummage, to fumble, to poke.

faribole, f. idle story, trifle.

farine, f. meal, flour ‖ pollen, grist.

fariner, v. a. to flour.

farineux, m. pl. mealy substances (pl.), [farinaceous food.

farineux, se, a. farinaceous, mealy.

farinier, m. meal-man.

farinière, f. meal-tub, flour-bin.

farouche, a. wild, savage ‖ unsociable, shy.

fascicule, m. bundle ‖ nosegay ‖ (of publications) number, part ‖ (bot.) fascicle.

fascine, f. fascine, fagot, bavin.

fasciner, v. a. to fascinate.

faséole, f. kidney-bean.

faste, m. pomp, stateliness ‖ ostentation ‖ **-s,** pl. annals (pl.) ‖ archives (pl.).

fastidieux, se, a. (**-sement,** ad.) tedious(ly).

fastueux, se, a. (**-sement,** ad.) ostentatious(ly) ‖ pompous(ly).

fat, m. fop, coxcomb.

fat, a. foppish.

fatal, e, a. (**-ement,** ad.) fatal(ly).

fatalisme, m. fatalism.

fataliste, m. fatalist.

fatalité, f. fatality.

fatidique, a. (poés.) prophetic.

fatigant, e, a. fatiguing, tiresome.

fatigue, f. fatigue, lassitude, weariness ‖ toil, pain, hardship.

fatiguer, v. a. & n. to fatigue, to tire, to wear out ‖ to worry ‖ **se ~,** to fatigue oneself ‖ to get tired. [medley.

fatras, m. rubbish, stuff, trash ‖ confusion.

fatuité, f. conceitedness ‖ foppishness.

faubourg, m. suburb ‖ outskirt.

faubourien, ne, m. & f. suburban.

faubourien, ne, a. a suburban.

fauchage, m. mowing.

fauchaison, f. mowing-season.

fauche, m. mowing ‖ mowing-time.

fauchée, f. day's mowing.

faucher, v. a. & n. to mow.

faucheur, m. mower.

faucheuse, f. mowing-machine.

faucheux, m. field-spider, daddy long-legs.

faucille, f. sickle.

faucon, m. falcon, hawk.

fauconnerie, f. falconry, hawking.

fauconnier, m. falconer.

faufiler, v. a. to baste, to sew badly ‖ **se ~,** to intrude ‖ to curry favour ‖ to creep in.

faune, m. faun ‖ **~,** f. fauna (pl.).

faussaire, m. forger (of writings).

fausse-couche, f. miscarriage.

faussement, ad. falsely.

fausser, v. a. to bend ‖ to violate ‖ to falsify ‖ to put out of tune ‖ **se ~,** to be warped. [spigot, peg.

fausset, m. (mus.) falsetto, faint treble ‖

fausseté, f. falsity, falseness, falsehood, imposture, fib, lie.

faute, f. fault, failing ‖ error, mistake, defect, want ‖ sin, crime ‖ failure.

fauteuil, m. elbow-chair, arm-chair ‖ seat in the French Academy ‖ **~ à la Voltaire,** reclining-chair.

fauteur, trice, m. & f. favourer || abettor.
fautif, ve, a. faulty.
fauve, m. fallow-deer.
fauve, a. fallow || reddish || dismal.
fauvette, f. warbler.
faux, f. scythe.
faux, m. falsehood, forgery.
faux, fausse, a. false, untrue, counterfeit, forged, perfidious, deceitful, fictitious, pretended, feigned, erroneous || ~, ad. falsely, erroneously, wrongfully || **~-fuyant,** m. by-place || (fig.) evasion, shift.
faveur, f. favour || interest || vogue || grace || ribbon || **à la ~ de,** by favour of || **en ~ de,** in behalf of.
favorable, a. (—ment, ad.) favourable || propitious(ly) || favourably.
favori, m. favourite || whisker.
favori, te, a. favourite, agreeable.
favoriser, v. a. to favour, to befriend, to patronise.
favoritisme, m. favouritism.
fébrifuge, m. (méd.) febrifuge.
fébrifuge, a. (méd.) antifebrile.
fébrile, a. (méd.) febrile.
fécond, e, a. fecund, prolific || fruitful, fertile, productive.
féconder, v. a. to fecundate, to fertilise.
fécondité, f. fecundity, fertility.
fécule, f. fecula || lees (pl.), sediment.
fédéraliser, v. a. to federalise.
fédéraliste, m. federalist.
fédératif, ve, a. federative.
fédération, f. confederation.
fédéré, e, a. federate.
fée, f. fairy.
féerie, f. enchantment || fairy-land || fairy-scene || pantomime.
féerique, a. fairy-like.
feindre, v. a. & n. ir. to feign, to sham, to pretend, to dissemble.
feinte, f. feint, pretence, sham.
fêler, v. a. to crack.
félicitation, f. congratulation.
félicité, f. happiness.
féliciter, v. a. to congratulate, to wish joy || **se ~,** to congratulate oneself || **(de)** to be pleased with.
félin, e, a. feline.
félon, m. traitor.
félon, ne, a. felonious, traitorous.
félonie, f. felony, disloyalty || treason.
félouque, f. (mar.) felucca.
fêlure, f. crack, chink.
femelle, f. female.
femelle, a. female.
féminin, e, a. feminine.
femme, f. woman, wife, female || **~ sage,** wise woman, prudent woman || **sage-~,** midwife || **~ de charge,** house-keeper || **~ de chambre,** waiting-maid || **~-peintre,** female painter, lady-painter.
femmelette, f. silly woman || milksop.
fémur, m. thigh-bone.
fenaison, f. hay-making season.
fendant, m. (fam.) bully, hector.
fenderie, f. slitting-mill.
fendeur, m. slitter, cleaver.
se fendiller, to crack, to split.

fendre, v. a. & n. to cleave, to split || to crack, to cut, to rend, to rift || to be ready to split || to break. [long-legged.
fendu, e, a. cleft, split || cloven || **bien ~,**
fenêtrage, m. windows.
fenêtre, f. window || **~ cintrée,** bow-window || **~ à coulisse,** **~ à guillotine.**
fenil, m. hay-loft. [sash-window.
fenouil, m. fennel.
féodal, e, a. feudal.
féodalité, f. feodalism.
fer, m. iron || (fig.) sword || **~ forgé,** wrought iron || **~ à (de) cheval,** horse-shoe || **~s,** pl. fetters, chains || **~ à repasser,** smoothing-iron || **~ à friser,** curling-iron || **~ à gratiner,** salamander || **~ à glace,** frost-shoe || **cela ne vaut pas les quatre —s d'un chien,** that's not worth a straw, a rap || **~-blanc,** m. tin, latten || **~-chaud,** m. heart-burn.
ferblanterie, f. tin-ware.
ferblantier, m. tinman.
férié, e, a. ; **jour ~,** holiday.
férir, v. a. to strike || **sans coup ~,** without striking a blow.
ferler, v. a. to furl the sails.
fermage, m. rent of a farm.
fermant, e, a. closing || with lock and key.
ferme, f. farm, farmer's house || truss || rib || **à ~,** on lease || **bail à ~,** lease of ground.
ferme, a. firm, fast, strong, steady, stable, compact, hard, solid || resolute || **~,** ad. firmly, steadily, steadfastly || stoutly, resolutely || **faire ~,** to keep one's ground || **~-porte,** m. door-spring.
fermement, ad. firmly, steadily, stoutly, resolutely.
ferment, m. ferment || yeast.
fermentation, f. fermentation, fermenting.
fermenter, v. n. to ferment. [ing.
fermer, v. a. & n. to shut, to shut up || to fasten, to close, to obstruct || to be shut || **(au loquet)** to latch || to hasp || **(au verrou)** to bolt. [resolution.
fermeté, f. firmness, steadiness, strength ||
fermeture, f. closing, shutting || fastening.
fermier, ère, m. & f. farmer || tenant || farmer's wife.
fermoir, m. clasp.
féroce, a. ferocious, savage.
férocité, f. ferocity.
ferrage, m. shoeing (of horses).
ferraille, f. old iron. [wrangle.
ferrailler, v. a. to fence, to tilt || (fam.) to
ferrailleur, m. dealer in old iron || (fam.) fighter || wrangler.
ferré, e, a. shod **ou** mounted with iron || versed, skilled, strong || chalybeate stoned || **chemin ~,** m. stoned road || **voie —e,** f. railroad. [iron-work.
ferrement, m. iron-tool || ironing || **—s,** pl.
ferrer, v. a. to bind **ou** to hoop with iron-work || to shoe (a horse) || to tag || **~ à glace,** to rough-shoe.
ferret, m. tag || tin-pipe.
ferronnerie, f. iron-foundry || iron-store.
ferronnier, m. ironmonger.
ferrugineux, se, a. ferruginous.

ferrure, f. iron-work ‖ shoeing.
fertile, a. (–ment, ad.) fertile‖fruitful(ly).
fertiliser, v. a. to fertilise.
fertilité, f. fertility, fruitfulness.
férule, f. ferule, rod.
fervent, e, a. fervent.
ferveur, f. fervour.
fesse, f. buttock, breech ‖ **~-mathieu,** m. niggard, skinflint.
fessée, f. (fam.) whipping, flogging.
fesser, v. a. to flog.
fessier, m. buttocks (pl.).
festin, m. feast, banquet.
festival, m. (mus.) festival.
feston, m. festoon.
festonner, v. a. to festoon.
festoyer, v. a. to feast.
fête, f. feast, festival, festivity ‖ Saint's day ‖ birthday ‖ diversion ‖ **jour de ~,** holiday.
Fête-Dieu, f. Corpus-Christi-day.
fêter, v. a. to keep as a holiday, to feast ‖
fétiche, m. fetich. [to welcome.
fétichisme, m. fetichism.
fétide, a. fetid, stinking.
fétidité, f. fetidness.
fétoyer, v. a. to feast.
fétu, m. straw ‖ (fig.) straw, rush, fig.
feu, m. fire, burning ‖ light ‖ flame ‖ hearth, chimney ‖ combustion, conflagration ‖ brightness, briskness, fervour ‖ passion, love ‖ spirit ‖ **~ de joie,** bonfire ‖ **~ d'artifice,** firework ‖ **~ du ciel,** lightning ‖ **~ grégeois,** Greek fire ‖ **~ follet,** Jack-o'-lantern ‖ **~ de paille,** sudden blaze, more flash ‖ **au ~ ! fire !** ‖ **à petit ~,** on a slow fire ‖ by inches ‖ **ni ~ ni lieu,** neither house nor home ‖ **faire ~,** to fire ‖ **faire du ~,** to make a fire ‖ **faire long ~,** to hang fire.
feu, e, a. late, deceased.
feudataire, m. feudatory.
feuillage, m. foliage.
feuillaison, f. foliation.
feuille, f. leaf ‖ sheet ‖ paper, newspaper ‖ **'pass,** furlough ‖ **~ blanche,** blank page ‖ **vin de trois –s,** wine three years old ‖ **~-morte,** m. dead leaf ‖ **~-morte,** a. faded-leaf coloured.
feuillé, m. foliage.
feuillé, e, a. leafy.
feuillée, f. bower. [to get leaves.
feuiller, v. n. to draw ou paint leaves ‖
feuillet, m. leaf (of a book) ‖ edge (of a
feuilletage, m. puff-paste. [pannel).
feuilleter, v. a. to turn over, to peruse, to read cursorily, to skim through.
feuilleton, m. fly-sheet ‖ feuilleton (bottom part of a newspaper, reserved for light literature or fiction).
feuilletoniste, m. writer of "feuilletons."
feuillette, f. quarter-cask.
feuillu, e, a. leafy.
feutre, m. felt ‖ felt-hat.
feutrer, v. a. to felt, to stuff with felt.
feutrier, m. felt-maker.
fève, f. bean ‖ berry ‖ chrysalis (of silk-
féverole, f. horse-bean. [worms).

février, m. February.
fi ! fie ! fie upon ! ‖ **~ donc ! for shame!**
fiacre, m. hackney-coach.
fiançailles, f. pl. betrothal.
fiancé, m. bridegroom.
fiancée, f. bride.
fiancer, v. a. to betroth.
fiasco, m. dismal failure, fiasco.
fibre, f. fibre, string ‖ feeling ‖ constitution.
fibreux, se, a. fibrous.
fibrine, f. (chim.) fibrine.
ficeler, v. a. to tie with packthread.
ficelle, f. packthread ‖ dodge, trick.
fichant, e, a. darting ‖ bothering.
fiche, f. pin ‖ fish.
ficher, v. a. to drive, to thrust in, to fasten in, to fix upon ‖ **se ~ (de),** to laugh at, to make game of, to trifle ‖ not to care for ‖ to snap one's fingers at.
fichet, m. peg (for marking at games).
fichtre ! hang it! ‖ bless me! indeed!
fichu, m. neckerchief ‖ **corps de ~,** habit-shirt. [for.
fichu, e, a. sorry, pitiful, silly ‖ lost ‖ done
fictif, ve, a. (–vement, ad.) fictitious(ly).
fiction, f. fiction ‖ figment. [sum.
fidéicommis, m. (jur.) trust, fideicommis-
fidéicommissaire, m. (jur.) trustee.
fidèle, a. faithful, true, loyal, trusty, constant, persevering ‖ upright ‖ –ment, ad. faithfully, truly, honestly, exactly.
fidélité, f. fidelity, faithfulness, loyalty, allegiance, exactness.
fief, m. fief, fee.
fieffé, e, a. enfeoffed ‖ downright ‖ regular.
fiel, m. gall, bile ‖ (fig.) rancour.
fiente, f. dung, muck.
fienter, v. n. to dung.
fier, v. a. to intrust ‖ **se ~,** to rely upon.
fier, ère, a. (–èrement, ad.) haughty ‖ haughtily ‖ proud(ly) ‖ high-minded, high-spirited ‖ bold(ly) ‖ arrogant(ly) ‖ sound(ly).
fier-à-bras, m. bully, hector.
fierté, f. haughtiness, pride, arrogance.
fièvre, f. fever, ague ‖ uneasiness ‖ **accès de ~,** cold fit ‖ **~ chaude,** burning fever ‖ **~ intermittente,** intermittent fever ‖ **~ lente,** hectic fever ‖ **~ tierce,** tertian
fiévreux, se, a. feverish. [ague.
fifre, m. fife ‖ fifer.
figement, m. congealment, coagulation.
figer, v. a. to congeal, to curdle.
figue, f. fig.
figuerie, f. orchard of fig-trees.
figuier, m. fig-tree. [tive(ly).
figuratif, ve, a. (–vement, ad.) figura-
figure, f. figure, form, shape ‖ person, physiognomy, human face, outside, appearance ‖ statue, image ‖ type, letter, character, number.
figuré, m. figurative sense.
figuré, e, a. (–ment, ad.) figurative(ly).
figurer, v. a. & n. to figure, to represent ‖ to match ‖ to appear ‖ to make a figure ‖ **se ~,** to imagine, to suppose, to fancy.
figurine, f. little figure ‖ postage-stamp.
figuriste, m. figurist.
fil, m. thread ‖ **~ retors,** twine ‖ **~ de la Vierge,** gossamer ‖ **sans ~,** wireless,

filage, m. spinning.
filagramme, m. watermark (in paper).
filamenteux, se, a. filamentous, filaceous.
filandière, f. (fam.) spinster || **les sœurs** **-s,** the three Fates. [weeds.
filandres, f. pl. gossamer || strings || sea-
filandreux, se, a. stringy || diffuse.
filant, e, a. ropy || shooting.
filasse, f. tow || harl || bast.
filateur, m. spinner.
filature, f. spinning || **spinning-mill.**
file, f. file, row || line.
filé, m. gold *ou* silver wire.
filer, v. a. & n. to spin || to file, to march in a file || to purr (of cats) || to rope || (mar.) to veer || **~ doux,** to give way, to lower one's tone. [wire-mill.
filerie, f. spinning-house || rope-walk ||
filet, m. fibre, string, lace || net || fillet, chine of meat || ligament of the tongue || **~ d'eau,** small stream of water.
fileur, se, m. & f. spinner, spinster || wire-drawer.
filial, e, a. (**-ement,** ad.) filial(ly).
filière, f. draw-plate || screw-plate || string.
filiforme, a. filiform.
filigrane, m. filigree || watermark.
filigrané, e, a. filigreed.
fille, f. daughter || girl, lass, maid.
fillette, f. young girl.
filleul, e, m. & f. godson || goddaughter.
filoche, f. large rope, network.
filon, m. lead *ou* vein of metal.
filoselle, f. floss-silk.
filou, m. pickpocket, sharper, cheat.
filouter, v. a. to pickpocket, to swindle.
filouterie, f. picking of pockets, filching.
fils, m. son, male child.
filtrage, m. filtering.
filtration, f. straining.
filtre, m. filter, strainer.
filtrer, v. a. to filter, to strain.
filure, f. spinning.
fin, f. end, extremity, conclusion, termination, expiration, issue, death || end, aim, design, intention.
fin, m. chief point, essential part, quintessence.
fin, e, a. fine, small, thin || clear, pure || ingenious, delicate, refined || subtile, cunning, sharp, sly.
fin-de-siècle, m. the nervousness and extravagance of mind which marks the close of the 19th century.
fin-de-sièclard, m. contemporary of the close of the 19th century.
final, e, a. (**-ement,** ad.) final(ly) || last(ly).
finance, f. ready money || cash || finance || financiers.
financer, v. n. to pay *ou* disburse money || (fam.) to come down, to fork out.
financiel, le, a. financial.
financier, ère, m. & f. financier.
financier, ère, a. financial.
finasser, v. n. to finesse.
finasserie, f. finesse, artifice.
finasseur, m. one who finesses.
finaud, m. sly-boots.
finaud, e, a. (fam.) artful, sly.

finement, ad. artfully, skilfully, slily, cunningly || ingeniously.
finesse, f. fineness, thinness, smallness || finesse || artifice, stratagem || clearness, purity || elegance, beauty || artfulness || ingenuity.
finette, f. swansdown calico. [plete.
fini, m. finish || finite.
fini, e, a. finished, done, completed || com-
finir, v. a. & n. to finish, to end, to complete || to have an end, to have done.
finisseur, se, m. & f. finisher.
fiole, f. phial. [embellishments (pl.).
fioritures, f. pl. (mus.) flourishes (pl.) ||
firmament, m. firmament, sky.
fisc, m. fisc, exchequer.
fiscal, e, a. fiscal.
fiscalité, f. fiscal zeal.
fissure, f. fissure, cleft.
fiston, fistot, m. son, lad.
fistule, f. (méd.) fistula.
fixation, f. fixation || fixing || assessment.
fixe, a. fixed, settled, firm, fast, steady, set || **-ment,** ad. fixedly || steadfastly || earnestly || in the face || **prix ~,** set price.
fixer, v. a. to fix, to settle, to appoint || to
fixité, f. fixity, fixedness. [stare at.
flacon, m., flagon, decanter || scent-bottle.
flagellation, f. flagellation, scourging, flogging.
flageller, v. a. to flagellate, to scourge.
flageoler, v. n. to tremble, to shake.
flageolet, m. (mus.) flageolet.
flagorner, v. a. to flatter servilely, to toady, to fawn upon.
flagornerie, f. mean flattery, toadyism.
flagorneur, se, m. & f. sycophant || toad-eater. [the very act.
flagrant, e, a. flagrant || **en ~ délit,** in
flair, m. scent.
flairer, v. a. to scent, to smell.
flaireur, m. smeller || **~ de cuisine,** parasite.
flamant, m. red ibis, flamingo. [parasite.
flambart, m. will-o'-the-wisp || (mar.) two-masted coaster || pirate || charcoal partly
flambé, e, a. lost || done for. [burned.
flambeau, m. flambeau, taper, torch, link || candlestick || firebrand || luminary.
flambée, f. blaze. [blaze.
flamber, v. a. & n. to singe || to flame, to
flamberge, f. heavy sword || **mettre ~** **au vent,** (fig.) to draw one's sword.
flamboyer, v. n. to glisten, to flame.
flamme, f. flame || (fig.) passion || fleam.
flammèche, f. spark, flake of fire.
flan, m. custard || flan || blank.
flanc, m. flank, side || womb.
flandrin, m. lanky fellow.
flanelle, f. flannel. [stroll || to idle.
flâner, v. n. to lounge, to saunter || to
flânerie, f. lounging || idling || strolling.
flâneur, se, m. & f. lou·ger || stroller.
flanquer, v. a. (mil.) to flank || to fortify || to give || to throw || to thrust || to put, to
flaque, f. plash || puddle. [clap.
flaquée, f. dash of water, dab.
flaquer, v. a. to dash.
flasque, a. lax, slack, languid, loose, flabby, weak.

flatter, v. a. to flatter, to caress, to coax, to wheedle ‖ to please, to delight ‖ **se ~,** to flatter oneself, to be in hopes of.

flatterie, f. flattery.

flatteur, se, m. & f. flatterer.

flatteur, se, a. flattering.

flatuosité, f. flatulency, windiness, wind.

fléau, m. flail ‖ bar ‖ beam ‖ (fig.) plague.

flèche, f. arrow, bolt ‖ flitch of bacon ‖ beam (of a coach) ‖ spire ‖ tandem.

fléchir, v. a. & n. to bend, to bow ‖ to submit ‖ to move to pity, to appease ‖ to give way.   ‖ing ‖ giving way.

fléchissement, m. act of bending ‖ kneel-

flegmatique, a. phlegmatic.

flegme, m. phlegm ‖ indifference.

flétrir, v. a. & n. to fade, to tarnish ‖ to wither, to wear, to destroy ‖ to stain, to disgrace ‖ to burn (with a hot iron) ‖ **se ~,** to fade, to lose colour, to wither.

flétrissure, f. fading, decaying, withering ‖ blemish ‖ spot, stain ‖ mark with a hot iron, branding.

fleur, f. flower ‖ blossom ‖ (fig.) choice, quintessence ‖ **à ~ de,** even with, level with.

fleuraison, f. blooming ‖ blooming-time.

fleurdeliser, v. a. to brand malefactors with a fleur-de-lis.

fleuret, m. ferret ‖ foil (for fencing).

fleurette, f. little flower ‖ **conter ~,** to make love.

fleuri, e, a. florid, flowery, prime, fresh.

fleurir, v. a. & n. to deck with flowers ‖ to flower, to blossom, to bloom.

fleuriste, m. florist ‖ flower-maker.

fleuron, m. flower-work ‖ gem ‖ tail-piece.

fleuve, m. river, great stream.

flexibilité, f. flexibility.

flexible, a. flexible, pliant.

flibot, m. fly-boat.

flibuster, v. a. to rob, to steal, to swindle.

flibustier, m. buccaneer, freebooter, pirate.

flocon, m. flock, flake.

floconneux, se, a. flaky.

floraison, f. blossom-time.

flore, f. flora, anthology.

florence, m. sarcenet.

florès; faire ~, to cut a dash ‖ to make a show.

florin, m. florin.

flot, m. wave, surge ‖ flood, tide ‖ float of wood ‖ crowd ‖ **à ~,** afloat.

flottable, a. navigable for rafts.

flottage, m. floating of timber ou wood.

flottaison, f. water-line.

flotte, f. fleet ‖ float.

flottement, m. undulation.

flotter, v. a. & n. to float ‖ to waft ‖ to swim ‖ to hesitate, to waver.

flotteur, m. raftsman ‖ buoy.

flottille, f. little fleet.

flou, e, a. light and soft (of painting).

flouer, v. a. to cheat, to diddle.

flouerie, f. cheating.

floueur, m. cheat, sharper, gull-catcher.

flou-flou, m. rustling.

fluet, te, a. slender, thin.

fluide, m. fluid ‖ liquid, liquor.

fluide, a. fluid.

fluidité, f. fluidity.

flûte, f. flute ‖ flutist ‖ long roll ‖ thin shank.

flûté, e, a. fluted ‖ soft, sweet.

flûter, v. n. to pipe ‖ to tipple.

flûteur, m. piper ‖ tippler.

flûtiste, m. flutist, flute-player.

fluvial, e, a. fluvial, river.

flux, m. flux ‖ flood, tide ‖ flush.

fluxion, f. inflammation ‖ cold ‖ swelling.

foe, m. (mar.) jib.

foi, f. faith ‖ faithfulness, fidelity ‖ promise ‖ proof ‖ trust ‖ **ma ~,** upon my faith.

foie, m. liver.

foin, m. hay ‖ choke.

foire, m. fair, market ‖ diarrhœa.

fois, f. time ‖ une ~, once ‖ **deux ~,** twice ‖ **trois ~,** thrice ‖ **quatre ~,** four times ‖ **plusieurs ~,** several times.

foison, f. plenty, abundance ‖ **à ~,** in abundance.

foisonner, v. n. to abound.

fol, vide **fou.**

folâtre, a. frolicsome, playful, merry.

folâtrer, v. n. to dally, to sport, to play ‖ to gambol.

folichon, ne, a. waggish, frolicsome.

folichonner, v. n. to sport.

folie, f. folly, imbecility of mind, insanity, madness, frenzy.

follement, ad. foolishly, madly.

follet, te, a. foolish, frolicsome, playful, wanton ‖ **poil ~,** downy beard ‖ **esprit ~,** hobgoblin, puck.

fomenter, v. a. to foment.

foncé, e, a. moneyed, rich, (fam.) warm ‖ of a deep colour ‖ versed in.

foncement, m. sinking.

foncer, v. a. & n. to put a bottom to ‖ to sink ‖ to deepen ‖ to pitch, to dash.

fonceur, m. sinker (of wells).

foncier, a. landed ‖ on land ‖ **rente foncière,** f. ground-rent.

foncièrement, ad. at the bottom ‖ thoroughly.

fonction, f. function, office, duty.

fonctionnaire, m. functionary.

fonctionnement, m. working, activity.

fonctionner, v. a. to work, to operate.

fond, m. bottom, ground, groundwork ‖ depth, inside, extremity ‖ the main point ‖ **sans ~,** bottomless ‖ **à ~,** thoroughly, to the bottom ‖ exactly.

fondamental, e, a. (**-ement,** ad.) fundamental(ly) ‖ principal.

fondant, e, a. melting.

fondateur, trice, m. & f. founder ‖ foundress.

fondation, f. foundation ‖ endowment.

fondé de pouvoirs, m. attorney ‖ proxy.

fondement, m. foundation ‖ ground, groundwork ‖ (fig.) reliance, trust.

fonder, v. a. to found, to lay the foundation of, to ground ‖ to establish, to give birth, to originate ‖ **se ~,** to be grounded upon, to rely upon.

fonderie, f. foundry, melting-house.

fondeur, m. founder.

fondre, v. a. & n. to melt, to cast, to liquefy, to dissolve ‖ to blend ‖ to become liquid ‖ to sink, to fall away ‖ to rush

fondrière, f. quagmire, slough. [upon.

fondrilles, f. pl. dregs (pl.).

fonds, m. soil, land, ground ‖ estate, landed property ‖ fund, stock, capital ‖ ~ **publics,** pl. public funds (pl.), stocks (pl.).

fongueux, se, a. fungous.

fontaine, f. fountain, spring, well ‖ cistern, waterspout ‖ jet ‖ ~ **de jouvence,** fountain of youth.

fontainier, m. fountain-maker ‖ turncock.

fontanelle, f. fontanel.

fonte, f. melting, casting ‖ mixture of metals, brass ‖ mixture of colours ‖ (printing) cast, fcount, set of letters ‖ holster.

fonts, m. pl. font.

for, m. tribunal ‖ ~ **intérieur,** conscience.

forage, m. boring, drilling.

forain, e, a. foreign, outlandish ‖ **marchand ~,** m. hawker.

forban, m. pirate, corsair.

forçat, m. galley-slave.

force, f. force, strength, power, vigour, violence ‖ necessity, compulsion, virtue, efficacy ‖ fortitude, boldness ‖ energy ‖ great number, great deal, plenty ‖ à ~, much, extremely ‖ à ~ **de,** by strength of, by dint of ‖ à toute ~, by all means ‖ absolutely ‖ **maison de ~,** house of correction ‖ ~**s,** pl. troops, forces.

forcé, e, a. forced, cramped ‖ unnatural ‖ ~**ment,** ad. forcibly, by violence, compulsorily.

forcené, m. madman. [pulsorily.

forcené, e, a. furious, mad.

forcer, v. a. to force, to compel, to press ‖ to urge ‖ to assault ‖ to violate ‖ to take by force ‖ to break open, to wrest.

forer, v. a. to bore, to drill.

forestier, m. ranger, forester.

forestier, ère, a. forest.

foret, m. borer, drill.

forêt, f. forest, woodland.

forfaire, v. n. ir. to forfeit, to fail.

forfait, m. great crime, great fault ‖ à ~, in the lump.

forfaiture, f. forfeiture ‖ (jur.) prevarication.

forfanterie, f. boasting. [tion.

forge, f. forge ‖ farrier's shop ‖ ~**s,** pl. iron-works (pl.).

forger, v. a. & n. to forge ‖ to fabricate ‖ to coin ‖ to contrive ‖ to trump up ‖ **se ~,** to imagine, to fancy.

forgeron, m. blacksmith.

forgeur, m. forger ‖ contriver.

se formaliser, to take offence at.

formalisme, m. formalism.

formaliste, m. formalist.

formaliste, a. formal.

formalité, f. formality.

format, m. size (of a book).

forme, f. form, shape, figure, fashion ‖ manner, system, method, practice ‖ ceremony, formality ‖ mould ‖ bench, stall, last ‖ en ~, formally.

formé, e, a. full-grown.

formel, le, a. (~**lement,** ad.) formal(ly) ‖ express(ly).

former, v. a. to form, to fashion, to model ‖ to contrive ‖ to frame, to arrange ‖ to bring up, to instruct ‖ to train, to produce.

formidable, a. formidable ‖ tremendous.

formier, m. last-maker.

formulaire, m. formulary.

formule, f. formula, form ‖ (méd.) prescription. [tion ‖ to express.

formuler, v. n. (méd.) to write a prescription.

fors, pr. save, except, but.

fort, m. fort, stronghold ‖ strongest part ‖ vigour, strength ‖ le ~ **portant le faible,** on an average.

fort, e, a. strong, stout, robust, vigorous ‖ powerful ‖ violent, impetuous ‖ thick, close ‖ copious, plentiful ‖ offensive, displeasing, hard, painful, difficult ‖ skilled ‖ emphatic ‖ c'est ~, that is strange, that is hard to swallow.

fort, ad. strongly, resolutely ‖ much, very, excessively, extremely.

fortement, ad. strongly, forcibly, stoutly, vehemently, vigorously.

forteresse, f. fortress, stronghold.

fortifiant, m. (méd.) tonic.

fortifier, v. a. to fortify, to strengthen, to invigorate.

fortin, m. small fort.

à fortiori, a fortiori, much more.

fortrait, e, a. overspent (of horses).

fortuit, e, a. (~**ement,** ad.) fortuitous(ly) ‖ casual(ly).

fortune, f. fortune, destiny, chance, hazard ‖ prosperity ‖ estate, possessions ‖ de ~, by chance ‖ self-made ‖ risen from the ranks.

fortuné, e, a. fortunate, happy.

forure, f. bore, hole.

fosse, f. pit, hole ‖ grave.

fossé, m. ditch ‖ moat.

fossette, f. chuck-hole ‖ dimple (in the cheek) ‖ chuck-farthing.

fossile, m. fossil.

fossile, a. fossil.

fossoyage, m. ditching ‖ grave-making.

fossoyer, v. a. to ditch about.

fossoyeur, m. sexton ‖ grave-digger.

fou, m., **folle,** f. fool ‖ madman, madwoman ‖ jester ‖ bishop (at chess).

fou, (fol) **folle,** a. mad, foolish, imprudent, senseless ‖ wanton, frolicsome.

fouailler, v. a. to whip.

foudre, m. large tun ‖ great warrior ‖ ~, f. thunderbolt ‖ thunder ‖ lightning.

foudroiement, m. striking with a thunderbolt.

foudroyant, e, a. thundering, fulminatory, flashing ‖ terrible, tremendous.

foudroyer, v. a. & n. to thunderstrike ‖ to batter down ‖ to crush ‖ to confound.

fouet, m. whip, scourge ‖ **donner le ~ à,** to whip.

fouetter, v. a. & n. to whip ‖ to flog, to lash, to scourge ‖ to blow hard ‖ to sweep (as a cannon).

fouetteur, m. flogger, whipper.

fougasse, f. (mil.) fougade.

fougeraie, f. fern-plot.

fougère, f. (bot.) fern ‖ brake.

fougue, f. mettle, fieriness, sprightliness ‖ rage, passion ‖ (mar.) mizzen-mast.

fougueux, se, a. mettlesome, fiery, fierce, impetuous, passionate, full of spirit.

fouille, f. trenching, digging.

fouiller, v. a. & n. to dig, to excavate ‖ to investigate ‖ to fumble ‖ to retouch ‖ to rummage.

fouillis, f. medley, confusion.

fouine, f. marten.

fouir, v. a. to dig, to delve.

foulage, m. fulling.

foulant, e, a.; **pompe —e,** forcing-pump.

foulard, m. silk handkerchief ‖ scarf.

foule, f. crowd, throng, common herd.

fouler, v. a. to tread, to stamp upon, to rack, to press, to squeeze, to crush, to bruise, to full, to mill ‖ to oppress, to [hurt, to sprain.

foulerie, f. fullery.

fouleur, m. fuller ‖ wine-presser.

fouloir, m. beater ‖ rammer.

foulon, foulonnier, m. fuller.

foulque, f. coot.   [of a stag.

foulure, f. sprain ‖ fulling [‖—s, pl. foiling

four, m. oven ‖ kiln, stove, hot room ‖ bake-house.

fourbe, m. deceiver, cheat ‖ knave.

fourbe, f. cheat, knavery.

fourbe, a. deceitful.

fourber, v. a. to cheat.

fourberie, f. cheat.

fourbir, v. a. to furbish.

fourbisseur, m. furbisher, sword-cutler.

fourbissure, f. furbishing.

fourbu, e, a. foundered.

fourbure, f. foundering of a horse.

fourche, f. fork, pitch-fork.

fourcher, v. n. to grow forked ‖ to divide into two ‖ to branch off ‖ to trip.

fourchette, f. fork ‖ breast-bone ‖ frog.

fourchon, m. prong.

fourchu, e, a. forked ‖ **pied —,** m. cloven-

fourchure, f. splitting, fork.   [foot.

fourgon, m. waggon, carriage for luggage ‖ poker, fire-poker, coal-rake.

fourgonner, v. a. to poke *ou* stir the fire ‖ (fam.) to rummage, to poke, to fumble.

fourmi, f. ant, emmet.

fourmilier, m. ant-bear, ant-eater.

fourmilière, f. ant-hill ‖ swarm.

fourmi-lion, m. ant-eater.

fourmillement, m. tinging, itching ‖ (méd.) formication.

fourmiller, v. n. to swarm *ou* abound with, to be full of ‖ to tingle.

fournage, m. baking.

fournaise, f. furnace.

fourneau, m. cooking-stove, kitchen-range ‖ furnace ‖ bowl ‖ (mil.) chamber.

fournée, f. ovenful, batch, baking.

fourni, e, a. furnished, thick.

fournier, m. oven-keeper, baker.

fournil, m. bake-house.   [(pl.).

fourniment, m. powder-flask ‖ cross-belts

fournir, v. a. & n. to furnish, to provide, to supply, to procure ‖ to produce ‖ to complete, to fit up ‖ to support, to pay for, to bear the charge of ‖ to suffice ‖ se **~,** to deal with.

fournissement, m. share of capital.

fournisseur, m. contractor, purveyor.

fourniture, f. furnishing, providing, supplying, provision ‖ remittance.

fourrage, m. forage, fodder ‖ foraging.

fourrager, v. a. & n. to forrage ‖ to plunder ‖ to rummage.

fourrageur, m. forager.

fourré, m. thicket, jungle.   [haste.

fourré, e, a. thickly covered ‖ done in

fourreau, m. case, cover, scabbard ‖ sheath ‖ holster.

fourrer, v. a. to put in, to thrust in ‖ to stuff with, to cram ‖ to force ‖ to fur ‖ se **~,** to introduce oneself into ‖ to intrude.

fourreur, m. furrier.

fourrier, m. quarter-master.

fourrière, f. pound ‖ pinfold ‖ **mettre en ~,** to impound.

fourrure, f. fur ‖ fell ‖ (mar.) service.

fourvoyer, v. a. (fam.) to mislead, to lead astray ‖ se **~,** to go astray, to stray, to

fouteau, m. (bot.) beech-tree.   [err.

foutelaie, f. plantation of beech-trees.

foyer, m. hearth, fireside ‖ focus ‖ home, house ‖ saloon of a theatre, green-room.

frac, m. dress-coat.

fracas, m. heavy crash, great crack, bustle, noise, disturbance, tumult, uproar.

fracasser, v. a. to break in pieces, to crash.

fraction, f. fraction, breaking ‖ (ar.) **~ décimale,** decimal fraction.

fractionnaire, a. fractional.

fracture, f. fracture, rupture, break.

fracturer, v. a. to fracture.

fragile, a. fragile, brittle ‖ weak, feeble ‖ frail ‖ **~ !** with care!

fragilité, f. fragility, frailty.

fragment, m. fragment ‖ piece.

frai, m. spawn (of fish) ‖ spawning season ‖ fry, young fish.

fraîche, a.; **à la ~,** out in the cool air.

fraîchement, ad. freshly, coolly, newly, recently.   [vigour ‖ bloom.

fraîcheur, f. freshness, coolness ‖ chill ‖

fraîchir, v. n. (mar.) to freshen.

frais, m. freshness, coolness, cool air ‖ stiff breeze.

frais, m. pl. expenses (pl.) ‖ cost ‖ charges (pl.) ‖ efforts (pl.) ‖ **faux ~,** incidental expenses (pl.) ‖ **faire ses ~,** to cover one's expenses.

frais, fraîche, a. fresh, cool ‖ sweet ‖ new, recent ‖ fresh-coloured ‖ brisk, strong.

fraise, f. strawberry ‖ ruff, frill.

fraiser, v. a. to plait ‖ to ruffle.

fraisier, m. (bot.) strawberry-plant.

fraisière, f. strawberry-plantation.

fraisil, m. cinders, charcoal-dust.

framboise, f. raspberry.   [berry.

framboiser, v. a. to give a flavour of rasp-

framboisier, m. (bot.) raspberry-bush.

franc, m. franc (silver coin worth about 10 pence).

franc, che, a. (—chement, ad.) free(ly) ‖ exempted ‖ frank(ly) ‖ open(ly) ‖ sincere (ly) ‖ upright, candid ‖ honest(ly) ‖ true ‖ whole, entire, mere, very ‖ ingenuous(ly) ‖ plain(ly) ‖ clean, quite ‖ **~-alleu,** m. free-

hold || ~-maçon, m. freemason || ~-
maçonnerie, f. freemasonry || ~-tireur,
m. a French guerilla soldier on French
territory during the Franco-German war
(1870—71) || sharpshooter.
français, m. the French language.
français, e, a. French || à la -e, in the
French fashion.
franchir, v. a. to leap over, to pass over
by leaping, to outleap, to overpass, to
overcome.
franchise, f. frankness, openness, sin-
cerity, plainness, honesty || exemption,
privilege, immunity.
franciscain, m. franciscan ou grey friar.
franciser, v. a. to frenchify.
francisque, f. battle-axe.
franco, ad. free of expense, post-paid.
frange, f. fringe.
franger, frangier, m. fringe-maker.
franger, v. a. to fringe.
frangipane, f. cream and almond cake.
franquette, f.; à la bonne ~, ad.
frankly || without ceremony.   [ing.
frappant, e, a. striking, surprising, affect-
frappement, m. striking, clapping of
hands.
frapper, v. a. & n. to strike || to beat, to
tap, to hit || to stamp, to coin || to knock ||
~ juste, to strike home.
frappeur, se, m. & f. beater.
frappeur, a. rapping.
frasque, f. prank, trick || freak.
fraternel, le, a. (-lement, ad.) fraternal
(ly) || brotherly.
fraterniser, v. n. to fraternise.
fraternité, f. fraternity, brotherhood.
fratricide, m. fratricide (crime) || ~, m. &
f. fratricide (person).
fraude, f. deceit, imposture, cheat, trick ||
smuggling || en ~, fraudulently.
frauder, v. a. to defraud || to smuggle.
fraudeur, m. defrauder, smuggler.
frauduleux, se, a. (-sement, ad.) frau-
dulent(ly).
frayer, v. a. & n. to open || to trace || to
chalk out || to clear ou point out the way ||
to set the example || to graze, to touch ou
rub lightly in passing || to agree || to milt.
frayeur, f. fright, terror.
fredaine, f. frolic, prank.   [ming.
fredonnement, m. quaver, trilling, hum-
fredonner, v. n. to trill, to warble, to
hum.
frégate, f. (mar.) frigate || sea-swallow.
frégaté, e, a. frigate-built.
frein, m. bit || bridle, curb, check || (rail.)
frelatage, m. adulteration.   [brake.
frelater, v. a. to adulterate.
frelaterie, f. adulteration.
frêle, a. frail, weak.
frelon, m. hornet || (fig.) drone.
freluche, f. silk tuft.
freluquet, m. dandy, prig, puppy.
frémir, v. n. to shudder, to quake, to
tremble, to shake, to shiver, to vibrate.
frémissement, m. shivering, shuddering,
trembling, vibration || din (of a bell) || agi-
frêne, m. (bot.) ash-tree.   [tation.

frénésie, f. frenzy.
frénétique, m. & f. frantic, raving person.
frénétique, a. frantic.
fréquemment, ad. frequently.
fréquence, f. frequency || quickness.
fréquent, e, a. frequent || quick.
fréquentation, f. frequenting || company.
fréquenter, v. a. to frequent, to haunt ||
to keep company with.
frère, m. brother || fellow-christian || friar ||
monk || école de -s, f. ragged school.
fresaie, f. screech-owl.
fresque, f. fresco.
fressure, f. pluck.
fret, m. (mar.) freight.
fréter, v. a. (mar.) to freight, to charter.
fréteur, m. charterer, freighter.
frétillant, e, a. brisk, lively || frisky.
frétillement, m. frisking.
frétiller, v. n. to frisk.
frétillon, m. frisky, lively person.
fretin, m. fry, young fish || trash || rubbish.
freux, m. rook.
friable, a. friable || arenaceous.
friand, e, m. & f. dainty person || epicure.
friand, e, a. dainty, nice || fond.
friandise, f. daintiness || -s, pl. dainties,
delicacies (pl.).
fricandeau, m. slice of veal larded.
fricassée, f. fried hash || medley.
fricasser, v. a. to cut up and fry || to
squander away.
fricasseur, m. paltry cook.
friche, f. untilled land || en ~, uncultivated.
fricot, m. stew || grub, stuffing.
fricoter, v. n. to mess, to grub, to feast.
friction, f. friction, rub.
frictionner, v. a. to rub.
frigidité, f. frigidity.
frigorifique, a. frigorific.
frileux, se, a. chilly.   [snow || winter.
frimas, m. hoar-frost || ~, m. pl. frost and
frime, f. sham, pretence.
frimousse, f. face || (fam.) phiz.
fringale, f. sudden hunger.
fringant, e, a. frisky, lively, brisk,
fringuer, v. n. to frisk.   [mettlesome.
fripé, e, a. tumbled, rumpled || no longer
fresh.
friper, v. a. to rumple, to wrinkle, to ruf-
fle || to spoil, to waste, to gobble down.
friperie, f. frippery, old clothes || trade in
old clothes || place where old clothes are
sold.   [furniture-broker.
fripier, ière, m. & f. second-hand clothier ||
fripon, m. rogue, knave, sharper, thief.
fripon, ne, a. roguish, wicked, wanton.
friponne, f. knavish woman.
friponner, v. a. & n. to cheat || to pilfer.
friponnerie, f. knavish trick, roguery.
frire, v. a. ir. to fry.
frise, f. frieze || dreadnought.
friser, v. a. to curl, to crisp, to frizzle, to
twist || to graze, to border upon || to fall in
curls, to curl of itself.
frisotter, v. a. to frizzle, to curl.
frisson, m. shivering, shaking with cold
ou fear || chilliness.   [shudder.
frissonnement, m. slight shiver ||

frissonner, v. n. to shiver, to shudder.
frisure, f. curling || curls (pl.).
frit, e, a. fried || done for.
friture, f. frying || fried fish || dripping.
frivole, a. frivolous, trifling.
frivolité, f. frivolity, futility.
froc, m. frock || jeter le ~ aux orties,
to forsake one's monkish order, to apostatise.
froid, m. coldness, chilliness || coolness,
indifference, gravity || il fait ~, it is cold
|| avoir ~, to be cold.
froid, e, a. (–ement, ad.) cold(ly) || cool
(ly) || indifferent || dull || à ~, without fire.
froideur, f. coldness, indifference || coolness.
froidure, f. cold, coldness, cold weather.
froissement, m. bruising || clashing,
friction.
froisser, v. a. to bruise || to rumple || to
wound, to hurt || to clash, to ruffle || se
~, to take offence.
froissure, f. bruise || rumple.
frôlement, m. grazing, touching slightly,
rustling.
frôler, v. a. to graze.
fromage, m. cheese || ~ de cochon, brawn.
fromager, m., fromagère, f. cheese-
maker || cheesemonger || cheese-mould.
fromagerie, f. cheese-dairy || cheese-trade.
fromageux, se, a. cheesy.
froment, m. wheat.
fromental, m. rye-grass.
froncement, m. frowning, knitting of the
brows.   [to knit the brow.
froncer, v. a. to pucker || ~ le sourcil,
froncis, m. pucker (of clothes).
fronde, f. sling, band || opposition.
fronder, v. a. to sling, to fling, to throw,
to cast || to jeer, to criticise, to blame.
frondeur, m. slinger || fault-finder || railer.
front, m. forehead, face, head || front,
forepart || impudence, boldness, assurance,
confidence || de ~, in the front, abreast ||
~ à ~, face to face || ~ d'airain, brazen-
face || ~ de bandière, (mil.) front line ||
~ d'un bâtiment, front of a building ||
avoir le ~ de, (mil.) to have the impudence
to || faire ~, (mil.) to front.
fronteau, m. frontlet, frontal (among the
Jews) || (mar.) breastwork.
frontière, f. frontier, border.
frontispice, m. frontispiece || title-page.
fronton, m. frontal, pediment.
frottage, m. rubbing, polishing, scrubbing.
frottement, m. friction, rubbing.
frotter, v. a. & n. to rub, to bang, to
beat || to lash, to anoint || to graze || se ~,
to rub oneself || to meddle, to have to do
(with).
frotteur, m. rubber, floor-scrubber.
frottoir, m. rubbing-cloth || rubber, scrub-
bing-brush || cushion.
frottoire, f. scouring-barrel.
frouer, v. n. to whistle || to peep.
frou-frou, m. rustling of silk || faire ~,
to cut a dash || to make a fuss.
fructidor, m. fruit-month (18. Aug. —
16. Sept.).

fructification, f. fructification || fecunda-
tion.   [ful.
fructifier, v. n. to bear fruit || to be fruit-
fructueux, se, a. (–sement, ad.) fruit-
ful, profitable || profitably.
frugal, e, a. (–ement, ad.) frugal(ly) ||
sparing(ly) || sober, temperate.
frugalité, f. frugality.
frugivore, a. frugivorous.
fruit, m. fruit, product, production || ad-
vantage, profit, consequence, result || last
course, dessert || être ~ sec, to be plucked
(at an examination).   [trade.
fruiterie, f. fruitery, fruit-loft || fruit-
fruitier, m. fruiterer || greengrocer || fruit-
loft.   [fruit-tree.
fruitier, ère, a. fruit-bearing || arbre ~,
frusquin, m.; son saint ~, one's all.
fruste, a. defaced (of medals).
frustrer, v. a. to frustrate, to disappoint,
to defraud.
fugitif, ve, m. & f. fugitive || runaway.
fugitif, ve, a. transitory.
fugue, f. (mus.) fugue.
fuie, f. coop || small pigeon-house.
fuir, v. a. & n. ir. to shun, to avoid, to
flee, to run away, to escape, to evade || to
leak.   [evasion, subterfuge || leakage.
fuite, f. flight, running away || avoiding,
fulmi-coton, m. gun-cotton.
fulminant, e, a. fulminant, fulminatory ||
thundering, storming.   [to thunder.
fulminer, v. a. & n. to fulminate, to storm,
fumable, a. smokable.
fumée, f. smoke, vapour, steam || (fig.)
vain hope || phantom || dung (of deer).
fumer, v. a. & n. to smoke || to smoke-dry ||
to dung, to manure || to steam || to smoke
(tobacco) || to be in a rage, to fume.
fumeron, m. smoking coal.
fumet, m. flavour.
fumeterre, f. fumitory.
fumeur, m. smoker (of tobacco).
fumeuse, f. smoking-chair.   [wine).
fumeux, se, a. smoky, fumy || heady (of
fumier, m. dung, manure || dunghill.
fumiger, v. a. to fumigate.
fumiste, m. bricklayer for fire-places ||
(fam.) chimney-doctor.
fumisterie, f. swagger, brag.
fumivore, m. smoke-consumer.
fumivore, a. fumivorous.
fumoir, m. smoking-room || smoking-divan.
fumure, f. manure.
funambule, m. rope-dancer.
funèbre, a. funeral || mournful || dismal.
funérailles, f. pl. funeral.
funéraire, a. funeral.
funéral, e, a. funereal.
funeste, a. fatal.
funiculaire, a. funicular.   [to.
fur, m.; au ~ et à mesure, in proportion
furet, m. ferret || ferreter, Paul Pry.
fureter, v. a. to ferret, to hunt with a
ferret || to search.
fureteur, m. ferreter || prier || hunter.
fureur, f. fury, frenzy, madness || violent
desire, passion || avec ~, furiously.
furibond, e, a. furious.

furie, f. fury ‖ rage.

furieux, se, m. & f. mad man (*ou* woman).

furieux, se, a. (-sement, ad.) furious (ly) ‖ violent(ly) ‖ raging ‖ impetuous ‖ prodigious(ly) ‖ excessively.

furoncle, m. furuncle, boil.

furtif, ve, a. (-vement, ad.) furtive(ly) ‖ stealthy.

fusain, m. prick-wood ‖ crayon.

fuseau, m. spindle.

fusée, f. rocket ‖ (mil.) fusee ‖ barrel.

fuselé, e, a. spindle-shaped, slender.

fusiforme, a. (bot.) fusiform, spindle-shaped.

fusil, m. steel (used to strike fire), tinder-box ‖ butcher's steel ‖ gun, musket, fire-lock ‖ pierre à ~, flint ‖ ~ à aiguille, needle-gun ‖ ~ de chasse, fowling-piece ‖ ~ de munition, musket ‖ ~ rayé, rifled gun ‖ ~ à deux coups, double-barrelled gun ‖ ~ à vent, air-gun ‖ ~ à piston, percussion-gun ‖ coup de ~, musket-shot ‖ report of a musket ‖ portée de ~, gun-shot ‖ battre le ~, to strike fire.

fusilier, m. fusileer.

fusillade, f. discharge of musketry ‖ firing.

fusiller, v. a. to shoot (to death).

fusion, f. fusion, melting ‖ blending ‖ coalition.

fustigation, f. whipping.

fustiger, v. a. to whip, to flog.

fût, m. stock (of a gun) ‖ cask ‖ fust, shaft ‖ barrel (of a drum).

futaie, f. trees of long standing (pl.) ‖ forest of old trees ‖ arbre de haute ~, full-grown forest tree.

futaille, f. (wine-)cask.

futaine, f. fustian.

futé, e, a. sly, crafty, cunning.

futile, a. futile, trifling, worthless, frivolous, paltry.

futilité, f. futility, triflingness.

futur, m. (gr.) future (tense) ‖ ~, e, m. & f. intended (future) husband or wife.

futur, e, a. future, to come.

fuyard, m. runaway.

fuyard, e, a. fugitive.

G.

gabare, f. (mar.) schuyt ‖ lighter ‖ drag-net.

gabari, m. (mar.) model ‖ maître ~, mid-ship mould ‖ faux ~, slab timber.

gabarier, m. (mar.) lighterman.

gabelou, m. custom-house officer ‖ toll-gabier, m. (mar.) topman. [collector.

gabionner, v. a. to cover with gabions.

gâche, f. staple (of a lock).

gâcher, v. a. to mix mortar ‖ to rinse ‖ to bungle. [locks) follower.

gâchette, f. tumbler (of a musket) ‖ (of gâcheur, m. mason's labourer ‖ bungler.

gâcheux, se, a. splashy, miry.

gâchis, m. slop ‖ mess.

gadoue, f. nightsoil, sewage, drainage.

gaffe, f. gaff, boat-hook ‖ faire une ~, to do a foolish thing.

gaffer, v. a. to hook with the gaff.

gaffeur, se, m. & f. dunce ‖ goose.

gage, m. pawn, pledge, deposit, plight, mark, testimony ‖ ~s, pl. wages (pl.) ‖ à ~s, hired.

gager, v. a. to hire, to give wages to ‖ to lay a wager, to bet, to wager.

gageur, se, m. & f. bettor, wagerer.

gageure, f. bet, wager.

gagiste, m. hireling ‖ under-clerk.

gagnage, m. grazing-land.

gagnant, e, m. & f. winner.

gagne ; ~-pain, m. livelihood ‖ ~-petit, m. knife-grinder.

gagner, v. a. & n. to gain, to obtain, to get, to receive ‖ to acquire, to win, to earn ‖ to reach, to arrive at, to persuade, to prevail upon ‖ to entice, to allure, to attract ‖ to bribe, to corrupt ‖ se ~, to be catching ‖ to be caught.

gai, e, a. (-ement, ad.) gay ‖ gaily ‖ cheerful(ly) ‖ lively, pleasant ‖ merrily.

gaïac, m. guaiacum.

gaieté, f. merriment, mirth, cheerfulness.

gaillard, m. jovial fellow *ou* companion ‖ ~ d'avant, (mar.) forecastle ‖ ~ d'ar-rière, (mar.) quarter-deck.

gaillard, e, a. (-ement, ad.) gay, merry, jovial, cheerful ‖ fresh, healthy ‖ gallant, sprightly, courageous ‖ merrily ‖ boldly ‖ bluntly.

gaillarde, f. gay *ou* bold woman.

gaillardette, f. flag at the foretop.

gaillardise, f. cheerfulness ‖ rather free talk, broad, wanton language.

gain, m. gain, profit, lucre ‖ winnings (pl.).

gaine, f. sheath, case.

gainier, m. sheath-maker, case-maker.

gala, m. gala. [lantly.

galamment, ad. genteelly, elegantly, gal-galant, m. wooer, suitor, lover ‖ vert ~, dashing ladies' man.

galant, e, a. genteel, well-bred, elegant, refined ‖ upright, honest ‖ courtly, civil, courteous ‖ ~ homme, honest man, up-right man, gentleman ‖ homme ~, gal-lant man, beau ‖ billet ~, love-letter, billet-doux.

galanterie, f. politeness ‖ compliment ‖ love-affair, love-making ‖ love-intrigue.

galantin, m. ladies' man, dangler, beau.

galantine, f. galantine, poultry flavoured with herbs ‖ (bot.) snow-drop.

galaxie, f. milky-way.

galbe, m. graceful outline.

gale, f. itch, scab, mange.

galère, f. (mar.) galley ‖ drudgery ‖ vogue la ~ ! come what may !

galerie, f. gallery ‖ cornice ‖ spectators.

galérien, m. galley-slave.

galet, m. pebble ‖ shingle.

galetas, m. garret ‖ hole. [bannock.

galette, f. flat, thin cake ‖ buttered roll ‖ galeux, se, a. itchy, scabby, mangy.

galimatias, m. balderdash, bosh.

galiote, f. (mar.) galiot ‖ ~ à bombes, bomb-vessel.

galle, f. gall ‖ noix de ~, gall-nut.

gallicisme, m. gallicism.

gallinacés, m. pl. gallinaceans (pl.).

galoche, f. golosh, clog ‖ (mar.) clamp ‖ **menton de ~,** m. turned-up chin.

galon, m. galloon, lace.

galonner, v. a. to lace.

galonnier, m. lace-maker.

galop, m. gallop ‖ blowing up ‖ **grand ~,** full gallop ‖ **petit ~,** hand gallop.

galopade, f. galloping.

galoper, v. a. & n. to gallop ‖ to hunt after.

galopin, m. errand-boy ‖ dirty fellow ‖ blackguard.

galvanique, a. galvanic.

galvaniser, v. a. to galvanise.

galvanisme, m. galvanism.

galvanoplastie, f. electro-typing.

galvauder, v. a. to abuse ‖ to disturb ‖ to throw into disorder.

gambade, f. gambol.

gambader, v. n. to gambol.

gamelle, f. bowl ‖ mess.

gamin, m. street-urchin, blackguard-boy, cad ‖ urchin ‖ little boy ‖ mere boy.

gamme, f. (mus.) gamut ‖ scale ‖ lecture ‖ tone ‖ **être hors de ~,** to be at one's wits' end.   [head ‖ fogey.

ganache, f. nether-jaw of a horse ‖ block-

gandin, m. swell, fop.

gangrène, f. (méd.) gangrene, mortification ‖ canker.   [canker.

se gangrener, (méd.) to mortify ‖ to

ganse, f. loop, string.

gant, m. glove ‖ gauntlet.

gantelet, m. gauntlet ‖ bandage for the hand.

ganter, v. a. & n. to put on gloves ‖ to fit well ‖ **se ~,** to put on one's gloves.

ganterie, f. glove-making, glove-trade.

gantier, m. glover.

garage, m. garage ‖ (rail.) shunt ‖ **voie de ~,** shunt-line.

garance, f. (bot.) madder.

garance, a. madder-coloured.

garancer, v. a. to dye with madder.

garancière, f. madder-field.

garant, e, m. & f. guarantee ‖ (jur.) surety.

garantie, f. guaranty, warranty.

garantir, v. a. to guarantee, to warrant, to answer for ‖ to indemnify ‖ to affirm ‖ to secure (from) ‖ to protect.

garce, f. wretch ‖ wench ‖ lass.

garçon, m. boy, lad ‖ bachelor ‖ journeyman, fellow, groom ‖ manservant, waiter.

garçonnière, f. romp, tom-boy.

garde, m. guard, keeper, warden ‖ (rail.) line-keeper ‖ **~ du commerce,** bailiff ‖ **~,** f. keeping, watching ‖ guard, custody, care, heed, attention ‖ defence, protection, charge, security ‖ posture of defence ‖ sick-nurse ‖ fly-leaf ‖ **à la ~!** police! **prendre ~,** to take care, to mind ‖ **n'avoir ~ de,** to take care not to ‖ **se donner de ~,** to beware ‖ **~-bois,** m. forest-keeper ‖ **~-boutique,** m. unsalable goods ‖ **~-cendres,** m. fender ‖ **~-chasse,** m. game-keeper ‖ **~-côte,** m. (mar.) guard-ship, cruiser ‖ **~-corps,** m. (rail.) hand-rail ‖ **~-crotte,** m. splash-board ‖ **~-feu,** m. fender ‖ **~-fou,** m. rails along bridges, etc. (pl.) ‖ **~-frein,** m. (rail.)

brakesman ‖ **~-magasin,** m. storekeeper, warehouseman ‖ unsalable goods ‖ **~-malade,** m. & f. sick-nurse ‖ **~-manche,** m. false sleeves ‖ **~-manger,** m. safe, larder, pantry ‖ **~-ménagerie,** m. ship's poulterer ‖ **~-meubles,** m. lumber-room ‖ furniture repository ‖ pantechnicon ‖ **~-nappe,** m. table-mat ‖ **~-national,** m. National Guard ‖ **~-pêche,** m. water-bailiff ‖ **~-robe,** f. wardrobe ‖ water-closet ‖ **~-vue,** m. screen.

garder, v. a. to preserve, to keep, to save, to reserve ‖ to guard, to protect, to defend ‖ to watch, to look after, to have an eye upon ‖ to attend to, to observe ‖ to perform ‖ **se ~,** to keep, to last ‖ to preserve oneself from, to beware of.

gardeur, se, m. & f. keeper, herd.

gardien, m. guardian, warden ‖ protector.

gardon, m. roach (fish).

gare! I have a care, out of the way!

gare, f. railway station, terminus ‖ basin ‖ **chef de ~,** station-master.

garenne, f. warren.

garennier, m. warrener.

garer, v. a. to put into dock ‖ to shunt ‖ **se ~,** to get out of the way.

se gargariser, to gargle.

gargarisme, m. gargle.   [mess.

gargotage, m. wretched cooking, dirty

gargote, f. cheap eating-house, pot-house.

gargoter, v. n. to frequent cheap eating-houses and low ale-houses.

gargotier, m. low publican, bad cook.

gargouille, f. spout of a gutter.

gargouillement, m. rumbling in the gargouiller, v. n. to dabble.   [bowels.

gargouillis, m. splashing.

gargousse, f. (cannon-)cartridge.

garnement, m. rake-hell, bad fellow.

garni, e, a. garnished ‖ **hôtel ~,** lodging house.

garnir, v. a. to furnish, to provide with ‖ to strengthen ‖ to adorn, to decorate, to

garnisaire, m. bailiff's man.   [trim.

garnison, f. garrison.

garnissage, m. trimming.

garniture, f. garniture, garnishment, furniture, ornaments, trimming ‖ (mar.) rigging ‖ **~ de cheminée,** set of chimney-ornaments ‖ **~ de foyer,** fire-irons.

garrot, m. withers ‖ packing-stick.

garrotte, f. strangulation, garroting.

garrotter, v. a. to tie down ‖ to garrote,

gars, m. young fellow, lad.

gascon, m. bragger, boaster.

gasconnade, f. brag, boasting.

gasconner, v. n. to boast.

gaspillage, m. wasting.

gaspiller, v. a. to waste, to squander.

gaspilleur, m. spendthrift.

gastralgie, f. (méd.) gastralgia.

gastrique, a. gastric.

gastrite, f. (méd.) gastritis.

gastronome, m. glutton.

gastronomie, f. gastronomy.

gastronomique, a. gastronomic.

gâteau, m. cake ‖ honeycomb ‖ (fig.) profit ‖ **~ des rois,** twelfth-cake.

gâte; **~-enfant**, m. spoiler of children ‖ **~-métier**, m. spoil-trade ‖ underworker ‖ **~-papier**, m. scribbler ‖ **~-sauce**, m. bad cook.

gâter, v. a. to spoil, to corrupt, to hurt, to impair ‖ to foul, to dirty ‖ to injure ‖ to squander ‖ se ~, to be spoiled ‖ to get damaged, to decay, to rot.

gâtour, se, m. & f. spoiler.

gâteux, m. (méd.) insane paralytic.

gâteux, a. (méd.) paralytic and insane.

gauche, f. left hand *ou* side.

gauche, a. left ‖ crooked ‖ awkward ‖ à ~, on the left hand, to the left.

gauchement, ad. awkwardly.

gaucher, ère, a. left-handed.

gaucherie, f. awkwardness ‖ blunder.

gauchir, v. n. to turn aside, to shuffle ‖ to warp.

gauchissement, m. shrinkage, warping.

gaude, f. maize hasty-pudding ‖ dyer's

gaudisserie, f. broad humour.   [weed.

gaudriole, f. broad joking ‖ broad joke.

gaufre, f. honeycomb ‖ wafer.

gaufrer, v. a. to figure (stuffs) ‖ to emboss ‖ to gauffer.

gaufreur, m. gaufferer.

gaufrier, m. wafer-iron.

gaufrure, f. figuring stuffs, gauffering.

gaule, f. long pole ‖ switch.   [long pole.

gauler, v. a. to beat down (fruit) with a

se gausser, to jeer, to banter, to chaff.

gausserie, f. jeering, banter.

gausseur, m. jeerer, story-teller.

gaver, v. a. to cram with food.

gavotte, f. gavot.

gaz, m. gas ‖ gas-light ‖ **bec de ~**, gas-burner ‖ **éclairage au ~**, gas-lighting.

gaze, f. gauze.   [veil.

gazer, v. a. to cover with gauze ‖ (fig.) to

gazetier, m. gazetteer, news-writer.

gazette, f. newspaper.

gazeux, se, a. gaseous ‖ effervescing.

gazier, m. gauze-maker ‖ gas-fitter.

gazomètre, m. gasometer.

gazon, m. turf ‖ (fam.) wig.

gazonnement, m. covering with turf.

gazonner, v. a. to turf.

gazouillement, m. warbling ‖ purling (of a stream) ‖ prattle.   [purl ‖ to prattle.

gazouiller, v. n. to warble, to chirp ‖ to

geai, m. jay ‖ jackdaw.

géant, e, m. & f. giant ‖ giantess.

geindre, v. n. ir. to whine, to whimper.

gélatine, f. gelatine.

gélatineux, se, a. gelatinous.

gelée, f. frost ‖ jelly ‖ **~ blanche**, hoar-

geler, v. a. & n. to freeze.   [frost.

gélinotte, f. hazel-hen.   [(pl.)

gémeaux, m. pl. (astr.) Gemini, Twins

gémir, v. n. to groan, to sigh ‖ to moan, to mourn, to bewail ‖ to coo.   [tion.

gémissement, m. groan, moan, lamenta-

gemme, f. (bot.) gem ‖ leafy bud ‖ (min.) gem ‖ (of animals) bud.

gemme, a.; **sel ~**, m. mineral salt.

gênant, e, a. troublesome, embarrassing, wearisome, tedious, irksome, teasing, difficult.

gencive, f. gum.

gendarme, m. armed policeman ‖ virago, termagant ‖ (of diamonds) flaw ‖ (of fire) spark.   [bluster.

se gendarmer, to fall into a passion, to bluster.

gendarmerie, f. armed police, constabulary.   [lary.

gendre, m. son-in-law.

gêne, f. rack, torture ‖ pain, torment ‖ constraint, inconvenience ‖ **sans ~**, without ceremony, at one's ease.

généalogie, f. genealogy, lineage.

généalogique, a. genealogical.

gêner, v. a. to constrain, to pinch, to cramp, to straiten ‖ to impede, to hinder, to be troublesome to, to incommode ‖ **se ~**, to restrain oneself, to put oneself about, to incommode oneself.

général, m. general, chief commander, chief ‖ generality ‖ **en ~**, in general.

général, e, a. (-ement, ad.) general(ly) ‖ universal, common ‖ usually).

généralat, m. generalship.

générale, f. (mil.) general ‖ fire-drum.

généraliser, v. a. to generalise.

généralissime, m. commander-in-chief

généralité, f. generality.

générateur, trice, a. generating.

génération, f. generation ‖ posterity, descent.   [handsomely.

généreusement, ad. generously, nobly,

généreux, se, a. generous.

générique, a. generic.   [bounty.

générosité, f. generosity, liberality,

genêt, m. (bot.) broom ‖ furze.

genet, m. Spanish horse ‖ jennet.

genévrier, m. (bot.) juniper-tree.

génie, m. genius, spirit ‖ engineering ‖ body of engineers ‖ **officier du ~**, engineer ‖ **soldat du ~**, sapper and miner.

genièvre, m. (bot.) juniper ‖ gin.

génisse, f. heifer.   (-es, pl. genitals (pl.).

génital, e, a. genital, generative ‖ **parties**

génitif, m. (gr.) genitive (case).

genou, m. knee ‖ **à -x**, kneeling.

genouillère, f. knee-piece (of a boot) ‖ knee-pan ‖ top.

genre, m. genus ‖ (gr.) gender ‖ kind, sort, species, manner, style.

gens, m. pl. people, men (pl.) ‖ servants, attendants, hands, persons (pl.) ‖ **droit des ~**, right of nations ‖ **~ de lettres**, literary people (pl.) ‖ **~ d'église**, churchmen (pl.) ‖ **~ de guerre**, **~ d'épée**, military men (pl.) ‖ **~ de condition, gentilfolk** (pl.) ‖ **~ de mer**, naval *ou* seafaring people (pl.) ‖ **~ de bien**, honest men (pl.) ‖ **les vieilles ~**, old people (pl.).

gent, f. nation, tribe, race ‖ gentry (pl.).

gentiane, f. (bot.) gentian.

gentil, m. gentile.

gentil, le, a. genteel, well-bred ‖ elegant, pretty, pleasing, agreeable, graceful.

gentilhomme, m. gentleman, nobleman.

gentilhommerie, f. gentility, gentry.

gentilhommière, f. small country-seat.

gentilité, f. paganism ‖ gentile nations.

gentillâtre, m. lordling.

gentillesse, f. prettiness ‖ pretty thing ‖ pretty saying ‖ pretty trick.

gentiment, ad. genteelly, prettily.
génuflexion, f. genuflexion, kneeling.
géodésie, f. geodesy.
géographe, m. geographer.
géographie, f. geography.
géographique, a. geographical.
geôlage, m. jailor's fees (pl.).
geôle, f. jail.
geôlier, m. jailor.
géologie, f. geology.
géologue, m. geologist.
géométral, e, a. geometrical.
géomètre, m. geometrician || surveyor.
géométrie, f. geometry.   [cal(ly).
géométrique, a. (-ment, ad.) geometri-
gérance, f. management.
gérant, m. manager || principal || respon-
sible editor of a newspaper.
gerbe, f. sheaf || ~ d'eau, spout of water.
gerber, v. n. to make up in sheaves || to
pile casks upon each other.
gerboise, f. jerboa, jumping mouse.
gercer, v. a. & n. to chap, to crack.
gerçure, f. chap, crack, chink.
gérer, v. a. to manage.
gerfaut, m. gerfalcon.
germain, e, a. first, german || **cousin** ~,
first cousin || **cousin issu de** ~, second
germanisme, m. germanism.   [cousin.
germe, m. germ, sprout, shoot || sperme,
treadle.   [shoot, to spring up.
germer, v. n. to germinate, to sprout, to
germoir, m. malt-house.
gérondif, m. (gr.) gerund.
gésier, m. gizzard.
gésir, v. n. def. ir. to lie || **ci-gît**, here lies.
gesse, f. chickling-vetch.
gestation, f. gestation, gravidity.
geste, m. gesture || manner || sign || **beck** ||
nod || **-s**, pl. doings.
gesticuler, v. n. to gesticulate.
gestion, f. management.
gibbeux, se, a. gibbous.
gibbosité, f. gibbosity.
gibecière, f. game-bag || courier-bag ||
juggler's pouch.
gibelotte, f. rabbit-stew.
giberne, f. cartridge-pouch.
gibet, m. gibbet || gallows (pl.).
gibier, m. game || ~ **de potence, jail-bird.**
giboulée, f. April-shower.
giboyeux, se, a. abounding in game.
gifle, f. slap in the face, smacker, stinger.
gifler, v. a. to box (one's) ears.
gigantesque, a. gigantic.
gigot, m. leg of mutton.
gigotter, v. n. to kick about.
gigue, f. jig (dance) || shank, leg.
gilet, m. waistcoat, underwaistcoat, vest ||
~ **à châle**, roll-collar waistcoat.
gille, m. clown, ninny.
gimblette, f. crisp biscuit.
gingembre, m. ginger.
girafe, f. giraffe, camelopard.
girandole, f. chandelier.
giratoire, a. gyratory.
girofle, m. clove.
giroflée, f. gilliflower || wall-flower.
giroflier, m. (bot.) clove-tree.

giron, m. lap || pale.
girouette, f. weathercock || (mar.) vane of
gisant, e, a. lying (ill ou dead).   [a ship.
gisement, m. (mar.) bearing (of a sea-
coast) || (min.) layer, bed. [**gisent**, here lie.
gît, (de **gésir**); **ci-gît**, here lies || **ci-**
gîte, m. home, lodging, dwelling-house,
resting-place || form (of a hare) || layer.
gîter, v. n. to lodge, to stay || to sleep.
givre, m. hoar-frost, rime.
glabre, a. (bot.) glabrous, smooth.
glace, f. ice || coach-window || looking-
glass || plate-glass || plate-glass door ||
coldness || flaw (in a diamond) || ice-cream
|| **à la** ~, iced || **chandelle de** ~, f. icicle.
glacé, e, a. frozen, iced || freezing, chilling
|| **gants –s**, glazed gloves.
glacer, v. a. & n. to ice, to cover with ice ||
to freeze, to chill || to candy || to glaze ||
to overpower, to paralyse.
glacial, e, a. glacial, icy, frozen || (fig.)
biting || sharp.
glacier, m. glacier || plate-glass maker,
glass-maker || dealer in ice.
glacière, f. ice-house || freezing-machine,
refrigerator, ice-box.   [glazing.
glacis, m. (mil.) glacis || sloping-bank ||
glaçon, m. icicle, piece of ice || floe.
gladiateur, m. gladiator.
glaïeul, m. gladiole.
glaire, f. white of egg || glair.
glairer, v. a. to glair || ~, v. n. to ex-
pectorate.
glaise, f. clay || **terre** ~, potter's earth.
glaiser, v. a. to clay over.
glaiseux, se, a. clayey.
glaisière, f. clay-pit.
glaive, m. sword || steel.
glanage, m. gleaning.
gland, m. acorn || tassel.
glande, f. gland.
glandé, e, a. glandered || acorned.
glandée, f. crop of acorns.
glane, f. gleanings (pl.) || rope.
glaner, v. n. to glean.
glaneur, se, m. & f. gleaner.
glanure, f. gleanings (pl.).
glapir, v. n. to yelp, to squeak.
glapissement, m. yelping, squeaking.
glas, m. knell, passing-bell.
glauque, a. glaucous.
glèbe, f. glebe || soil, earth.
glissade, f. slip, slide.
glissant, e, a. slippery.
glisser, v. a. & n. to slip, to slide, to
glide || to touch lightly || **se** ~, to creep in
ou into || to insinuate.
glisseur, m. slider.
glissoire, f. slide.
globe, m. globe, ball, sphere, orb || ter-
restrial globe || glass shade.
globuleux, se, a. globular.
gloire, f. glory.
gloria, m. coffee with brandy.
gloriette, f. countryhouse, pavilion.
glorieux, m. vain man, braggart.
glorieux, se, a. (-sement, ad.) glorious
(ly) || illustrious || renowned || self-con-
ceited || ostentatious(ly).

glorifier, v. a. to glorify || se ~, to pride in, to take glory in, to boast of.

gloriole, f. vainglory.

glose, f. gloss || carping.

gloser, v. n. to gloss, to comment || to carp

gloseur, m. carper. [af.

glossaire, m. glossary.

glossateur, m. glossarist.

glotte, f. (an.) glottis.

glouglou, m. gurgling. [etc.).

glouglouter, v. n. to gobble (of turkeys,

gloussement, m. clucking.

glousser, v. n. to cluck.

glouteron, m. burdock.

glouton, m. glutton. [ous(ly).

glouton, ne, a. (-nement, ad.) glutton-

gloutonnerie, f. gluttony.

glu, f. birdlime.

gluant, e, a. limy || sticky.

gluau, m. lime-twig.

gluer, v. a. to lime, to cover with bird-

glui, m. coarse straw. [lime.

gluten, m. (chim.) gluten.

glutineux, se, a. glutinous, clammy.

glycerine, f. (chim.) glycerine.

gniaf, m. (fam.) bungler. [beer.

gnognotte, f. trash, rubbish || (fam.) small

gnomique, a. gnomical, sententious.

gnomonique, f. dialling.

go; tout de ~, ad. freely, directly.

gobe, f. poison-ball || ~-mouches, m. fly-catcher || gull || trifler.

gobelet, m. goblet, drinking-cup, juggler's box || joueur de -s, juggler || tours de ~, thimble-rigging.

gobelin, m. hobgoblin.

gobeloter, v. n. to tipple.

gober, v. a. to swallow greedily, to gulp down || to catch.

goberge, m. cross-bar || handle || veneering-cramp.

se goberger, to take one's ease, to indulge oneself.

gobeur, m. (fam.) swallower || gull.

godailler, v. n. to tipple.

godailleur, m. drunkard, toper.

godelureau, m. fop.

godenot, m. (juggler's) puppet.

goder, v. n. to pucker, to crease.

godet, m. small cup, mug.

godiche, godichon, m. simpleton.

godiveau, m. veal pie.

goëland, m. sea-gull.

goëlette, f. schooner. [blow-out.

gogaille, f. (fam.) a high time || a good à gogo, ad. luxuriously, in clover.

goguenard, m. jeerer.

goguenard, e, a. jovial.

goguenarder, v. n. to jeer.

goguenarderie, f. jeer.

goguettes, f. pl. merry stories || en ~, in a merry humour.

goinfre, m. gormandiser, guzzler.

goinfrer, v. n. to gormandise.

goinfrerie, f. gluttony.

goitre, m. (méd.) wen, goître.

goitreux, se, a. (méd.) goitrous.

golfe, m. gulf.

gommage, m. gumming.

gomme, f. gum || ~ élastique, India-rubber || ~ gutte, gamboge.

gommer, v. a. to gum.

gommeux, m. dandy, fop.

gommeux, se, a. gummy.

gommier, m. (bot.) gum-tree.

gonagre, m. (méd.) gout in the knee.

gond, m. hinge.

gondole, f. gondola.

gondolier, m. gondolier.

gonflement, m. swelling || inflation of a balloon. [inflate.

gonfler, v. a. & n. to swell, to puff up || to

gord, m. fishery. [knot.

gordien, a. Gordian || nœud ~, m. Gordian

goret, m. little pig, young hog.

gorge, f. forepart of the neck and breast, throat, gullet || tucker || defile || rendre ~, to disgorge, to refund || ~-chaude, f. hawk's fee || faire des -s-s, to laugh at the expense of another || ~-de-pigeon, m shot || shot-colour || ~-de-pigeon, a. shot || shot-colour.

gorgée, f. draught || mouthful.

gorger, v. a. to cram, to glut, to cloy.

gosier, m. throat || gullet || voice.

gosse, f. bad joke || fib, hoax.

gothique, f. old English, black letter || Elizabethan type.

gothique, a. gothic || (fam.) antiquated.

gouache, f. water-colours || painting in water-colours.

gouailler, v. a. to rally, to joke.

goudron, m. pitch and tar.

goudronnage, m. tarring.

goudronner, v. a. to tar.

gouffre, m. gulf, abyss || whirlpool.

gouger, v. a. to gouge.

goujat, m. vulgar fellow, snob || blackguard.

goujon, m. gudgeon. [guard.

goulée, f. gulp, mouthful.

goulet, m. narrow entrance (of a harbour).

goulîafre, m. greedy-gut.

goulot, m. neck of a bottle.

goulu, m. glutton.

goulu, e, a. gluttonous.

goulûment, ad. gluttonously.

goupille, f. pin, peg. [brush.

goupillon, m. holy-water sprinkler || bottle-

goupillonner, v. a. to cleanse with a gourd, e, a. benumbed. [bottle-brush.

gourde, f. gourd || pilgrim's bottle.

gourdin, m. club, cudgel.

gourdiner, v. a. to cudgel.

goure, f. adulterated drug.

gourgandine, f. woman of the town.

gourmade, f. cuff, punch.

gourmand, m. greedy fellow || epicure, gastronomist, good liver.

gourmand, e, a. greedy, gluttonous || fond of good living.

gourmander, v. a. to chide, to snub, to scold || to blame || to check.

gourmandise, f. greediness, daintiness.

gourme, f. strangles || teething eruptions || ill humours || jeter sa ~, to sow one's wild oats.

gourmer, v. a. to curb (a horse) || to box.

gourmet, m. judge of wine || epicure.

French and English.

gourmette, f. curb.

gousse, f. cog, husk || ~ **d'ail,** clove of garlic.

gousset, m. gusset || arm-pit, fob || bracket.

goût, m. taste, savour || smell, relish || fancy, liking || style || manner.

goûter, m. late lunch.

goûter, v. a. & n. to taste, to smell, to like, to relish || to enjoy, to delight in || to try || to eat something.

goutte, f. drop || dram || (disease) gout || ~ **sereine,** (méd.) gutta serena.

goutte, ad. not at all.

gouttelette, f. small drop, driplet.

goutteux, se, a. gouty.

gouttière, f. gutter || spout || roof.

gouvernail, m. rudder, helm.

gouvernante, f. governess || housekeeper (of a single man).

gouverne, f. guidance.

gouvernement, m. government || management.

gouverner, v. a. to govern, to rule, to manage, to command || to take care of || (mar.) to steer || **se** ~, to govern oneself || to behave || to be governed.

gouverneur, m. governor || ruler || tutor.

goyave, s. guava.

goyavier, s. (bot.) guava-tree.

grabat, m. pallet, stump-bed || **sick-bed.**

grabataire, a. bed-ridden.

grabuge, m. squabble, brawl, row.

grâce, f. grace, goodness, virtue || favour, kindness || good office || gracefulness || genteel deportment || beauty, charm || pardon, forgiveness || **-s,** pl. Graces || de ~, pray, for mercy's sake || **par** ~, by favour || **avec** ~, graceful(ly) || **sans** ~, graceless(ly) || **de bonne** ~, genteelly || **an de** ~, year of our Lord || **actions de** ~, f. pl. thanksgiving || ~ **à Dieu,** God be thanked || **dire (ses) -s,** to say grace || **faire** ~, to pardon.

gracier, v. a. to pardon.

gracieuseté, f. kindness, civility.

gracieux, se, a. (-ement, ad.) gracious (ly) || pleasant, elegant || favourable, benevolent || kindly || gracefully.

gracilité, f. slenderness.

gradation, f. gradation || climax.

grade, m. grade, rank, degree, quality.

gradin, m. (foot-)step || bench ou seat in tiers.   (ou university).

gradué, e, m. & f. graduate (in a college

graduel, le, a. (-lement, ad.) gradual(ly).

graduer, v. a. to graduate.

graillement, m. hoarse sound.

graillon, m. burnt fat, broken victuals.

grain, m. corn, grain, berry || seed || bead || squall || shower || ~ **de beauté,** mole || ~ **de raisin,** berry of a grape.

graine, f. seed || set, lot || berry || ~ **de niais,** fool's trap.

grainer, v. a. to granulate || to corn || to grain || to stipple.

graineterie, f. seed-trade.

grainetier, m. seedsman || corn-chandler.

grainier, m. seedsman.

graissage, m. greasing.

graisse, f. grease, fat || dripping || **-s,** pl. kitchen-stuff.

graisser, v. a. to grease || to make greasy || (fig.) ~ **la patte,** to bribe.

graisseux, se, a. greasy.

graminée, f. pl. (bot.) grasses || grass tribe.

grammaire, f. grammar.

grammairien, m. grammarian.

grammatical, e, a. (-ement, ad.) grammatical(ly).

gramme, m. gram (1000 gr. = one kilogram).

grand, m. greatness, nobleness, great, grandee, nobleman || **-s,** pl. high people || big boys || **trancher du** ~, to carry it high.

grand, e, a. grand, great || large, tall, high || broad || wide || open || deep || full || hard || loud || important, weighty || chief, principal || illustrious || ~-**merci,** ad. many thanks || ~-**oncle,** m. great-uncle || ~-**père,** m. grandfather.

grandelet, te, a. biggish, tallish.

grandement, ad. greatly, very much, highly || nobly.

grandesse, f. grandeeship.

grandeur, f. greatness, tallness, largeness, bulkiness, magnitude, hugeness || enormity, heinousness || grandeur, nobleness, magnificence, magnanimity || dignity, importance || **de** ~ **naturelle,** life-size.

grandiose, m. grandeur.

grandiose, a. grand.

grandir, v. n. to grow || to **increase** || **to rise.**

grandissime, a. very great.

grange, f. barn.

granit, m. granite.

granitique, a. granitic.

grand'mère, f. grandmother.

grand'tante, f. great-aunt.

granuler, v. a. to granulate.

granuleux, se, a. granulous.

graphique, a. graphic.

grappe, f. bunch, cluster || grape-shot.

grappillage, m. gleaning (in a vineyard) || small picking.

grappiller, v. a. & n. to glean (after the vintage) || to scrape up || to pilfer.

grappilleur, m. grape-gleaner || pilferer.

grappillon, m. little cluster.

grappin, m. grapnel.

gras, m. fat, fatness || fat bit || calf || **au** ~, dressed in meat-gravy || **faire** ou **manger** ~, to eat flesh.

gras, se, a. fat, fleshy, plump || bulky || oily, unctuous || fertile, rich || muddy (of wine) || **jour** ~, flesh-day || **les jours** ~, shrove-tide || ~-**double,** m. tripe || ~ **fondu,** m. mucous irritation.

grassement, ad. plentifully.

grasset, te, a. rather fat.

grasseyement, m. thickness of pronunciation.

grasseyer, v. a. to speak thickly.

grassouillet, te, a. plump.

grat, m. scratching-place (of fowls).

gratification, f. gratuity || gift.

gratifier, v. a. to favour, to confer, to bestow || to attribute.

gratin, m. burnt part || scraping || crackling || **au** ~, dressed with bread raspings.

gratiné, e, a. burnt, browned.

gratiner, v. n. to begin to burn, to stick at the bottom of the pan ‖ ~, v. a. to brown.

gratis, ad. gratis, free, for nothing.

gratitude, f. gratefulness.

gratte; ~cul, m. hip, hop ‖ ~langue, m. tongue-scraper ‖ ~papier, m. scribbler.

gratteleux, se, a. itchy. [bler.

gratter, v. a. to scratch, to scrape ‖ to rub.

grattoir, m. scratching-knife, scraper.

gratuit, e, a. (~ement, ad.) gratuitous (ly) ‖ groundless.

gratuité, f. gratuity ‖ free gift.

gravas, m. rubbish.

grave, a. heavy, grave, solemn, serious, important, of importance, weighty ‖ sedate ‖ (mus.) low, deep.

gravé, e, a. engraved ‖ pock-marked.

gravelée, f. dried dregs ‖ cendres ~s, f. pl. pearl-ashes.

graveleux, se, a. gravelly ‖ gritty ‖ obscene, smutty. [scene, smutty.

gravelle, f. gravel.

gravelure, f. broadness, smut.

gravement, ad. gravely, seriously ‖ grievously ‖ (mus.) slowly.

graver, v. a. to engrave, to impress ‖ ~ à l'eau forte, to etch ‖ ~ en creux, to sink. [sink.

graveur, m. engraver.

gravier, m. gravel ‖ grit.

gravir, v. a. & n. to climb.

gravité, f. gravity, heaviness ‖ graveness.

graviter, v. n. to gravitate.

gravois, m. rubbish out (of buildings).

gravure, f. engraving ‖ carving ‖ cut ‖ ~ à l'eau forte, etching ‖ ~ en creux, diesinking.

gré, m. will, inclination, liking ‖ consent, thankfulness, gratitude ‖ de bon ~, willingly ‖ contre son ~, against one's will, grudgingly ‖ de ~ à ~, amicably ‖ de ~ ou de force, willingly or unwillingly, willy nilly ‖ bon ~, mal ~, whether one will or not.

greo, m. card-sharper, blackleg ‖ miser ‖ Greek fashion ‖ Greek language.

gréciser, v. n. to Grecianise.

grécisme, m. Grecism.

grecque, f. fretwork.

gredin, e, m. scurvy fellow, scoundrel.

gredinerie, f. villany.

gréement, m. (mar.) rigging.

gréer, v. a. (mar.) to rig. [ing.

greffe, m. record-office ‖ ~, f. graft, grafting.

greffer, v. a. to graft.

greffeur, m. grafter.

greffier, m. registrar, recorder.

greffoir, m. grafting-knife.

grège, a. raw (of silk). [fire.

grégeois, e, a.; feu ~, m. Greek-fire, wildgrêle, f. hail ‖ hailstorm ‖ grain de ~, hail-stone.

grêle, a. lank, slender, shrill.

grêlé, e, a. ravaged by hail ‖ pock-marked.

grêler, v. a. & n. to destroy by hail ‖ to hail. [hail.

grelin, m. stream-cable.

grêlon, m. hail-stone. [bell the cat.

grelot, m. little bell ‖ attacher le ~, to

grelotter, v. n. to shiver.

greluchon, m. (fam.) favourite admirer.

grenade, f. pomegranate ‖ (mil.) grenade.

grenadier, m. pomegranate-tree ‖ grenadille, f. passion-flower. [dier.

grenaille, f. minute grains ‖ small-shot.

grenat, m. garnet.

grené, m. stippling.

greneler, v. a. to grain leather.

grener, v. a. & n. to granulate, to pound, to grind ‖ to seed, to produce seed.

grenier, m. granary, loft, garret, cornhouse ‖ lumber-room.

grenouille, f. frog. [place ‖ fen.

grenouillère, f. place full of frogs ‖ damp

grenu, e, a. grainy, full of corn, seedy ‖ grained ‖ clotted.

grès, m. grit-stone, sand-stone ‖ stonegrésil, m. sleet. [ware.

grésillement, m. shrivelling ‖ pattering.

grésiller, v. a. & n. to shrivel ‖ to sleet ‖ to patter. [ware.

gressorie, f. sand-stone quarry ‖ earthengrève, f. sandy shore ‖ strike (of workmen) ‖ faire ~, to strike work.

grever, v. a. to aggrieve ‖ to overburden.

gréviste, m. striker.

gribouillage, m. scrawl.

gribouiller, v. a. to scrawl.

gribouillette, f. scramble. [plaint.

grief, m. grievance, wrong, injury, comgrièvement, ad. grievously, seriously.

griffade, f. clawing, scratch. [grasp.

griffe, f. claw, paw, talon, fang, clutch,

griffer, v. a. to scratch with the claws.

griffonnage, m. scrawl, scribble.

griffonner, v. a. to scrawl, to scribble.

griffonneur, m. scrawler, scribbler.

grignon, m. hard, crust.

grignoter, v. n. to nibble.

grigou, m. sordid miser.

gril, m. gridiron ‖ toaster.

grillade, f. broiling ‖ broiled meat.

grillage, m. grate, wire-lattice ‖ frame of timber.

grillageur, m. wire-worker.

grille, f. grate ‖ iron-barred gate ‖ grating ‖ ~pain, m. gridiron, toaster.

griller, v. a. & n. to grate ‖ to broil, to scorch ‖ to toast ‖ to parch.

grillon, m. cricket. [sham.

grimace, f. grimace, wry face ‖ grin ‖ ~s, pl.

grimacer, v. n. to grin ‖ to pucker.

grimacier, ière, m. & f. grinner ‖ simperer ‖ canter.

grimacier, ière, a. grimacing ‖ affected ‖

grimaud, m. scribbler. [canting.

grime, m. dotard.

se grimer, to wrinkle one's face.

grimoire, m. conjuring-book ‖ (fig.) anything incomprehensible ‖ savoir le ~, to know the ins and outs of. [creep.

grimper, v. n. to clamber, to climb up, to

grimpereau, m. creeper.

grimpeur, m. climber.

grincement, m. gnashing ‖ grating.

grincer, v. a. & n. to gnash ‖ to grind ‖ to grate ‖ faire ~, to set on edge.

gringalet, m. slender man ‖ bit of a man.

griotte, f. egriot, black-heart cherry.

griottier, m. (bot.) black-cherry tree.

grippe, f. influenza ‖ dislike ‖ ~-sou, m. penny-scraper.

grippeminaud, m. Grimalkin.

gripper, v. a. to gripe ‖ to clutch ‖ to snatch ‖ to crib ‖ se ~, to shrivel.

gris, m. grey ‖ ~ de lin, gridelin ‖ en voir de -es, to have hot work.

gris, e, a. grey ‖ tipsy ‖ dull.

grisaille, f. grey painting ‖ hair partly grey.

grisailler, v. a. to daub with grey.

grisâtre, a. greyish.　　　　[tipsy.

griser, v. a. to make tipsy ‖ se ~, to get

griset, m. young goldfinch.

grisette, f. gay work-girl, grisette.

grisoller, v. n. to warble (of larks).

grison, m. greybeard ‖ donkey.

grison, ne, a. grey-haired.

grisonner, v. n. to grow grey.

grisou, m. fire-damp.

grive, f. thrush.

grivelé, e, a. speckled.

grivois, m. jolly companion.

grivois, e, a. jovial, brisk, merry.

grog, m. grog.

grognard, m. grumbler, grumbling fellow.

grognard, e, a. grumbling.

grognement, m. grunting, grumbling.

grogner, v. n. to grunt, to grumble, to growl, to snarl.

grogneur, m. grumbler.

grognon, m. grumbler.

grognon, a. grumbling.

groin, m. snout (of a hog).

grolle, f. rook.　　　　[to mutter.

grommeler, v. n. to grumble ‖ to growl ‖

grommeleur, m. grumbler.

grondement, m. rumbling, roaring, booming.

gronder, v. a. & n. to chide, to scold at, to grumble, to growl ‖ to rumble, to boom.

gronderie, f. scolding.

grondeur, se, m. & f. grumbler ‖ grumbling woman, shrew.

grondeur, se, a. grumbling.

grondin, m. red gurnet ‖ grey gurnet.

gros, m. the greater part, gross, main, bulk, lump ‖ main point ‖ dram.

gros, se, a. big, bulky, great, large, coarse, thick, huge, corpulent, stout ‖ considerable, numerous ‖ ~, ad. much, a great deal ‖ en ~, wholesale, by the lump ‖ ~-bec, m. gross-beak.

groseille, f. currant ‖ gooseberry ‖ ~ à maquereau, gooseberry.

groseillier, m. (bot.) currant-tree, gooseberry-bush.

grosse, f. gross, twelve dozen ‖ large hand ou text ‖ (com. & mar.) bottomry ‖ copy (of a deed) ‖ à la ~, slowly ‖ at a jog-trot.

grossesse, f. pregnancy.

grosseur, f. bigness, size ‖ bulk ‖ swelling.

grossier, ère, a. (-èrement, ad.) coarse (ly) ‖ grossly ‖ thick, plain ‖ rude(ly) ‖ uncivil, unpolished, clownish, rustic ‖ vulgar, mean ‖ palpable.

grossièreté, f. grossness, coarseness, rudeness, roughness, bluntness, vulgarity, obscenity ‖ unmannerliness.

grossir, v. a. & n. to make bigger, to enlarge, to increase, to augment, to swell ‖ to exaggerate ‖ se ~, to grow big, to grow, to augment, to increase, to swell, to rise.

grossissement, m. magnifying ‖ exaggeration.　　　　[deed.

grossoyer, v. a. to engross the copy of a

grotesque, a. (-ment, ad.) grotesque(ly).

grotte, f. grot, grotto.

grouillement, m. rumbling, grumbling.

grouiller, v. n. to stir, to rumble, to rattle ‖ to swarm.

group, m. (com.) sealed bag of money.

groupe, m. group ‖ flock.

groupement, m. grouping.

grouper, v. a. to group.

gruau, m. groats, oatmeal ‖ small crane.

grue, f. crane ‖ ninny ‖ faire le pied de ~, to dance attendance.　　　　[out.

gruger, v. a. to crunch, to devour ‖ to eat

grume, f. bark ‖ en ~, in the rough ‖ with the bark on.

grumeau, m. clot, lump.

se grumeler, to clot.

grumeleux, se, a. clotty ‖ rugged.

gruyère, m. Swiss cheese, gruyere.

guano, m. guano.

gué, m. ford.

guéable, a. fordable.

guède, f. woad.　　　　[wash (linen).

guéer, v. a. to ford ‖ to water (a horse) ‖ to

guenille, f. rag, tatter.　　　　[harridan.

guenon, f. she-monkey ‖ (fig.) fright ‖

guenuche, f. young she-monkey.

guêpe, f. wasp.

guêpier, m. wasp's nest ‖ bee-eater.

guère, guères, ad. little; but little, but few, not many, not much, not very ‖ hardly, scarcely.

guéret, m. headland ‖ field.

guéridon, m. stand for candlesticks ‖ loo-table ‖ centre-table.

guérir, v. a. & n. to cure, to heal, to remedy ‖ to be ou get cured.

guérison, f. cure, recovery.

guérisseur, m. curer.

guérite, f. sentry-box, watch-tower ‖ belvidere ‖ ~-urinoir, urinal with a pillar to post up advertisements.

guerre, f. war, warfare ‖ petite ~, shamfight ‖ skirmishing ‖ desultory war ‖ homme de ~, warrior ‖ gens de ~, soldiers.

guerrier, m. warrior, martial man.

guerrier, ère, a. warlike, military, valiant.

guerroyer, v. n. to war, to wage war.

guerroyeur, m. warrior.

guet, m. watch ‖ ~-apens, m. ambush ‖ lying in wait ‖ wilful injury.

guêtre, f. gaiter ‖ legging.

guêtrier, m. gaiter-maker.

guetter, v. a. to watch, to lie in wait for.

gueulard, m. mouth of a furnace ‖ bawler.

gueule, f. mouth, jaw.

gueulée, f. mouthful.

gueuler, v. n. to bawl.　　　　[mump.

gueusaille, f. rabble.

gueusailler, v. n. to be a lazy beggar, to

gueusard, m. blackguard, scoundrel.

gueuse, f. bad woman || pig of iron.
gueuser, v. a. & n. to beg.
gueuserie, f. beggary. [muffin.
gueux, m. scoundrel, scurvy fellow, raga-
gueux, se, a. beggarly, poor.
gui, m. mistletoe.
guichet, m. wicket || window.
guichetier, m. jailor.
guide, m. & f. guide || rein || stage-fee || **à
grandes —s**, four-in-hand || **~-âne**, m.
directory || drill || **~-main**, m. hand-guide.
guider, v. a. to guide, to lead, to manage.
guidon, m. flag || standard-bearer || broad
pennant || sight || direction || reference,
guigne, f. black-heart cherry. [mark.
guigner, v. a. to leer, to peep at || to look
after.
guignier, m. (bot.) black-heart cherry-tree.
guignon, m. ill luck (at play).
guillaume, m. rabbet-plane.
guilledou, m.: **courir le ~**, to frequent
low resorts.
guillemet, m. (gr.) inverted comma.
guillemeter, v. a. to mark with inverted
commas.
guilleret, te, a. merry, gay, sprightly.
guilleri, m. chirping.
guillocher, v. a. to engine-turn.
guillochis, m. engine-turning, engine-
guillotine, f. guillotine. [turned work.
guillotiner, v. a. to behead.
guimauve, f. (bot.) marsh-mallow.
guimbarde, f. waggon, van || Jew's-harp.
guimpe, f. inside chemisette || veil, stom-
acher (for nuns).
guindage, m. (mar.) hoisting.
guindé, e, a. bombastic, stiff.
guinder, v. a. (mar.) to hoist up || (fig.)
guinée, f. guinea. [to strain.
guingois, m. crookedness || **de ~**, ath-
wartly, crookedly.
guinguette, f. tea-garden, public-house.
guipure, f. vellum-lace, silk-lace.
guirlande, f. garland, wreath.
guise, f. manner, mode, humour, fancy ||
en ~ de, by way of, instead of || like.
guitare, f. guitar || **pincer de la ~**, to
gustation, f. taste. [play on the guitar.
guttural, e, a. guttural.
gymnase, m. gymnasium.
gymnastique, f. gymnastics.
gymnastique, a. gymnastic.
gynécée, m. women's work-shop.
gynécologiste, m. specialist in diseases
of women.
gypse, m. plaster-stone || gypsum.
gypseux, se, a. gypseous.

H.

habile, m. sharp practitioner.
habile, a. able, fit, proper, clever, skilful ||
quick || cunning. [cunningly.
habilement, ad. ably || skilfully || quickly ||
habileté, f. ability, cleverness, skill.
habilité, f. (jur.) competency.

habiliter, v. a. (jur.) to qualify.
habillage, m. dressing.
habillement, m. clothing, habit, dress ||
~ complet, suit of clothes.
habiller, v. a. to dress || to clothe, to
attire, to equip || to make clothes || to
abuse, to ridicule || **s'~**, to dress oneself,
to put one's clothes on || to abuse each
other.
habit, m. habit, dress, coat || suit of clothes ||
~ habillé, dress-coat || **prendre l'~**, to
become a nun *ou* a monk.
habitable, a. habitable, tenantable.
habitacle, m. dwelling || (mar.) binacle.
habitant, m. inhabitant, dweller || planter,
colonist.
habitation, f. habitation, dwelling, resi-
dence, domicile || plantation, colony.
habiter, v. a. & n. to inhabit, to dwell in,
to live in.
habitude, f. habit, custom, use, usage,
wont || practice || **d'~**, usual(ly). [quenter,
habitué, e, m. & f. regular customer, fre-
habituel, le, a. (**-lement**, ad.) habitual
(ly) || usual(ly). [to inure.
habituer, v. a. to habituate, to accustom,
hâbler, v. n. to brag, to boast.
hâblerie, f. bragging, boasting.
hâbleur, m. bragger, boaster.
hache, f. axe, hatchet || **~ d'armes**, battle-
axe || **~-paille**, m. chaff-cutter.
hacher, v. a. to hew with an axe, to hash,
to mince, to hack || to hatch.
hachereau, f. little axe, hatchet.
hachette, f. hatchet.
hachis, m. hash, minced meat.
hachoir, m. chopping-board || chopping-
hachure, f. hatching. [knife.
hagard, e, a. haggard, wild.
haie, f. hedge, fence, row.
haillon, m. rag, tatter.
haine, f. hate, hatred || spite.
haineux, se, a. hateful, spiteful.
haïr, v. a. to hate.
haire, f. hair-shirt.
haïssable, a. hateful, odious.
halage, m. towage || towing.
halali, m. whoop, holloa (in hunting).
halbran, m. young wild-duck.
hâle, m. sun-burning || sultry air.
hâlé, e, a. sunburnt.
haleine, f. breath, wind || **ouvrage de
longue ~**, work of time || **à perte d'~**,
out of breath || long-winded || **tenir en ~**,
to keep in exercise || to keep at bay.
halenée, f. breathing || whiff.
haler, v. a. to haul || to set on, to excite.
hâler, v. a. to tan || to burn.
haleter, v. n. to pant || to be out of breath.
haleur, m. (mar.) hauler.
hallage, m. market-duty.
halle, f. market-place || **dames de la ~**,
market-women || **fort de la ~**, market-
porter || **langage des —s**, Billingsgate
language.
hallebarde, f. halberd || **pleuvoir (tom-
ber) des —s**, to rain cats and dogs.
hallier, m. thicket. [delusion.
hallucination, f. hallucination || (méd.)

halot, m. rabbit-hole.
halte, f. halt, stop || faire ~, to halt, to make a halt || ~ I (mil.) halt! stop!
haltère, m. dumb-bell.
hamac, m. (mar.) hammock.
hameau, m. hamlet.
hameçon, m. hook, fish-hook.
hampe, f. staff (of a halberd) || handle.
hanche, f. hip, haunch.
hangar, m. shed, cart-house.
hanneton, m. cockchafer || giddy goose.
hanter, v. a. to haunt, to frequent.
hantise, f. intercourse.
happe, f. cramp-iron || axle-tree bed.
happer, v. a. to snap up, to snatch.
haquenée, f. back || (fam.) gawky.
haquet, m. dray.
haquetier, m. drayman.
harangue, f. speech, public address.
haranguer, v. a. to harangue, to address || ~, v. n. to speechify.
harangueur, m. speech-maker || speechifier.
haras, m. stud || breed of horses.
harasser, v. a. to harass, to tire || to tease.
harceler, v. a. to harass || to torment.
harde, f. herd || leash.
harder, v. a. to leash (dogs).
hardes, f. pl. clothes (pl.), attire.
hardi, e, a. hardy, bold, daring, fearless || forward, impudent, audacious.
hardiesse, f. boldness, liberty || impudence.
hardiment, ad. boldly || impudently.
hareng, m. herring || ~ saur, red herring, bloater.   (fishery.)
harengaison, f. herring-season || herring-
harengère, f. fish-woman.
hargneux, se, a. peevish || surly, snappish.
haricot, m. kidney-bean || ~ vert, French bean || ~ d'Espagne, scarlet runner || ~ de mouton, Irish stew.
haridelle, f. jade, harridan.
harmonie, f. harmony || choral singing.
harmonier, v. n. to harmonise.
harmonieux, se, a. (-sement, ad.) harmonious(ly).   (ally).
harmonique, a. (-ment, ad.) harmonic
harmoniste, m. harmonist.
harnachement, m. harnessing, harness.
harnacher, v. a. to harness, to rig out.
harnacheur, m. harness-maker.
harnais, m. harness, armour || horse-trappings (pl.).
haro, m. hue and cry.
harpagon, m. niggard.
harpe, f. harp || toothing.
harpie, f. harpy || shrew.
harpiste, m. harpist, harper.
harpon, m. harpoon.
harponner, v. a. to harpoon.
harponneur, m. harpooner.
hart, f. withe || halter || hanging.
hasard, m. hazard, chance, accident, fortuitous event, casualty, hap || danger, risk || au ~, at random || par ~, by chance, accidentally.   (tainted.)
hasardé, e, a. ventured || bold || stale,
hasarder, v. a. to hazard, to venture, to risk, to stake, to expose, to run the risk of.

hasardeux, se, a. (-sement, ad.) hazardous(ly) || venturous, perilous.
hase, f. doe-hare.
hâte, f. haste, speed, hurry || à la ~, hastily, quickly.
hâter, v. a. to hasten, to forward, to hurry, to urge, to push on, to accelerate || se ~, to haste, to hasten, to make haste.
hâtier, m. spit-rack.
hâtif, ve, a. hasty, forward, premature.
hâtiveau, m. early pear, early fruit.
hâtivement, ad. hastily, speedily || before the season, early.
hâtiveté, f. forwardness.
hauban, m. (mar.) shroud.
haubert, m. coat of mail.
hausse, f. block || piece || bridge || rise in stocks || ~-col, m. (mil.) neck-piece, gorget.
haussement, m. raising || shrug.
hausser, v. a. & n. to raise || to lift up || to increase || to shrug || to rise.
haussier, m. speculator for the rise in the public funds, "bull".
haut, m. height, ridge, top, upper end || au ~ de, at the top of || du ~ en bas, from top to bottom.
haut, e, a. (-ement, ad.) high(ly) || elevated|| great, exalted, eminent(ly) || sublime, excellent, magnanimous, illustrious || proud (ly) || haughty || aloft || loud(ly) || bold(ly) || en ~, above, upstairs || ~-fond, m. (mar.) shoal-water || ~-fourneau, m. blast-furnace || ~-goût, m. high-flavour || ~-le-corps, m. start || retching.
hautain, e, a. haughty, proud, arrogant || -ement, ad. haughtily.
hautbois, m. hautboy.
haute-contre, f. (mus.) counter-tenor || ~-école, f. high horsemanship.
Hautesse, f. Highness (title).
hauteur, f. height, hill || depth || eminence, sublimity, greatness, excellence, perfection || haughtiness, scorn || à la ~ de, equal to || off.
Havane, f. Havannah cigar.
hâve, a. pale, wan || emaciated.
havir, v. a. & n. to scorch.
havre, m. haven, harbour.
havre-sac, m. knapsack.
he! ha! ho! hoy! halloo! I say!
hebdomadaire, a. weekly.
héberger, v. a. to lodge, to entertain.
hébété, e, m. & f. dolt, dunce.
hébéter, v. a. to stupify || to dull, to blunt || to besot.
hébraïsant, m. Hebraist.
hébreu, m. Hebrew language.
hécatombe, f. hecatomb.   (lish.)
hectare, m. hectare (about 2½ acres Eng-
hectolitre, m. hectolitre (100 litres, ou somewhat more than 22 gallons English).
hégémonie, f. hegemony.
hein! eh!
hélas! alas!
héler, v. a. (mar.) to hail.
hélianthe, m. (bot.) sun-flower.
hélice, f. spiral line || screw || en ~, spiral, winding.

héliotrope, m. (bot.) heliotrope ‖ (min.) blood-stone.

hémérocalle, f. (bot.) day-lily.

hémisphère, f. hemisphere.

hémistiche, m. hemistich.

hémorragie, f. hemorrhage.

hémorroïdes, f. pl. (méd.) piles.

hennir, v. n. to neigh.

hennissement, m. neighing.

hépatique, a. (an. et méd.) hepatic.

héraldique, a. heraldic.

héraut, m. herald.

herbacé, e, a. herbaceous.

herbage, m. herbage ‖ grass ‖ pasture, meadow.

herbager, m. grazier.

herbe, f. herb, grass ‖ **–s potagères,** pl. pot-herbs (pl.), vegetables (pl.) ‖ **mauvaises ~,** pl. weeds (pl.).

herbette, f. herblet, tender grass.

herbeux, se, a. herbous, grassy.

herbier, m. herbal.

herbière, f. herb-woman.

herbivore, a. herbivorous.

herboriser, v. a. to herborise.

herboriste, m. herbalist.

herbu, e, a. grassy.

herculéen, ne, a. herculean.

hère, m. sorry fellow, poor wretch.

héréditaire, a. (–ment, ad.) hereditary ‖ hereditarily.

hérédité, f. heirship, inheritance, hereditary right.

hérésiarque, m. heresiarch.

hérésie, f. heresy.

hérétique, m. heretic.

hérétique, a. heretical.   [rough.

hérissé, e, a. bristling, brushy, shaggy,

hérisser, v. a. (of animals) to erect, to bristle ‖ **se ~,** to stand erect ‖ to be armed ou covered.

hérisson, m. hedgehog ‖ spikes ‖ spur-wheel.

hérisson, ne, a. cross, capricious.

héritage, m. heritage, inheritance, succession ‖ legacy.

hériter, v. a. & n. to inherit.

héritier, tière, m. & f. heir ‖ heiress.

hermaphrodite, m. hermaphrodite.

hermétique, a. (–ment, ad.) hermetic (ally).

hermine, f. ermine.

hernie, f. (méd.) hernia, rupture.

héroïne, f. heroine.

héroïque, a. (–ment, ad.) heroic(ally).

héroïsme, m. heroism.

héron, m. heron.

héronnière, f. heronry.

héros, m. hero.

hersage, m. harrowing of a field.

herse, f. harrowing ‖ (min.) portcullis.

herser, v. a. to harrow.

herseur, m. harrower.

hésiter, v. n. to hesitate.

hétéroclite, a. (gr.) heteroclitic ‖ irregular, whimsical, odd.

hétérodoxe, a. heterodox, heretical.

hétérodoxie, f. heterodoxy.

hétérogène, a. heterogeneous.

hêtre, m. beech-tree, beech.

heure, f. hour ‖ time, epoch ‖ moment ‖ **de bonne ~,** early ‖ **à la bonne ~ !** well! be it so! that is all right! ‖ **à cette ~,** now ‖ **tout à l'~,** immediately ‖ **–s,** pl. prayer-book.

heureux, se, a. (–sement, ad.) happy, fortunate(ly), lucky, successful, propitious, favourable ‖ happily ‖ safely.

heurter, v. a. & n. to strike against, to hit against, to clash, to knock ‖ to run against, to shock, to offend ‖ to hurt, to disoblige.

heurtoir, m. door-knocker.   [disoblige.

hexamètre, m. (poét.) hexameter.

hiatus, m. (gr.) hiatus.

hibernal, e, a. hibernal, winter.

hibou, m. owl.

hic, m. rub, difficulty.

hideux, se, a. (–sement, ad.) hideous(ly).

hie, f. paver's beetle ‖ rammer.

hièble, f. (bot.) wall-wort, dwarf-elder.

hier, ad. yesterday.

hiérarchie, f. hierarchy.   [chical(ly).

hiérarchique, a. (–ment, ad.) hierarchical(ly).

hiéroglyphe, m. hieroglyph.

hiéroglyphique, a. hieroglyphic.

hilarité, f. hilarity.

hippique, a. of horses, hippic.

hippocampe, m. hippocampus, sea-horse.

hippodrome, m. hippodrome ‖ circus ‖ race-course.   [tamus.

hippopotame, m. river-horse, hippopotamus.

hirondelle, f. swallow.

hisser, v. a. (mar.) to hoist.

histoire, f. history, narration, record ‖ **–s,** pl. fuss ‖ quarrel ‖ lot of things ‖ **peintre d'~,** m. historical painter.

historien, m. historian.

historier, v. a. to embellish.

historiette, f. story ‖ love-tale.

historiographe, m. historiographer.

historique, m. history ‖ genealogy.

historique, a. (–ment, ad.) historical(ly).

histrion, m. stage-player.

hiver, m. winter.

hivernage, m. wintering, winter-time.

hiverner, v. n. to winter.

hobereau, m. poor country squire.

hoche, f. notch.

hochement, m. head-shaking.

hochequeue, m. wag-tail (bird).

hocher, v. a. to toss.   [bauble.

hochet, m. coral ‖ rattle ‖ toy, plaything.

holà, m. hindrance, end, stop.

holà ! holloa!

hollander, v. a. to dress (a quill).

holocauste, m. holocaust, burnt-offering.

hom ! hum! humph!

homard, m. lobster.

hombre, f. ombre (game at cards).

homélie, f. homily.

homéopathe, m. homœopathist.

homéopathie, f. homœopathy.

homéopathique, a. homœopathic.

homicide, m. homicide (person or act) ‖ **~ involontaire,** manslaughter.

homicide, a. homicidal ‖ murderous.

hommage, m. homage ‖ present ‖ testimony ‖ **–s,** pl. respects, duty ‖ **~ de l'auteur,** presented by the Author.

hommasse, a. mannish.
homme, m. man || gentleman || husband || old man || good man || mankind.
homogène, a. homogeneous.
homologation, f. confirmation.
homologue, a. homologous.
homologuer, v. a. to confirm.
homonyme, m. namesake.
homonyme, a. homonymous.
homonymie, f. homonymy.
honchets, m. pl. spellicans (game).
hongre, m. gelding.
hongre, a. gelded.
hongrer, v. a. to geld.
honnête, a. honest, just, equitable, fair, sincere, unreserved || proper, fit, decent, suitable, becoming, civil, mannerly, moderate, reasonable, judicious || —ment, ad. honestly, in a becoming manner, fairly, civilly, courteously || decently || chastely, sufficiently.
honnêteté, f. honesty, fairness, genteelness, probity, integrity || courtesy, politeness, civility, kindness || decency, chastity, virtue.
honneur, m. honour || respect || credit || chastity || good name || decoration || **homme d'~**, man of probity || **parole d'~**, word of honour || **dame d'~**, lady-in-waiting || **demoiselle** ou **fille d'~**, bridesmaid || **garçon d'~**, bridesman || **affaire d'~**, affair of honour || **point d'~**, point of honour || **en l'~ de**, in honour of.
honnir, v. a. to disgrace || **honni soit qui mal y pense**, evil be to him who evil thinks.
honorable, a. honourable, respectable || creditable || —ment, ad. honourably, nobly, creditably, respectably.
honoraire, m. fee, salary || (of barristers) retainer.
honoraire, a. honorary.
honorer, v. a. to honour || to do credit to || **s'~**, to honour oneself || to esteem it an honour || to pride oneself.
honorifique, a. honorary.
honte, f. shame, dishonour, disgrace, discredit || bashfulness, ignominy, infamy || **fausse ~**, **mauvaise ~**, bashfulness, false shame.
honteux, se, a. (—sement, ad.) shameful(ly) || scandalous, disgraceful, ignominious, infamous || ashamed || shamedly.
hôpital, m. hospital || wreck and ruin, dogs, misery || work-house.
hoquet, m. hiccough, hiccup.
horaire, a. horary, horal.
horion, m. thump.
horizon, m. horizon.
horizontal, e, a. (—ement, ad.) horizontal (ly).
horloge, f. clock.
horloger, m. watch-maker, clock-maker.
horlogerie, f. clock-making, watch-making || clockwork.
hormis, pr. except, save, but.
horoscope, m. horoscope.
horreur, f. horror, terror, dread, abomination, detestation || destruction, desolation.

horrible, a. (—ment, ad.) horrible || horribly || frightful(ly) || shocking(ly).
horripilation, f. (méd.) horripilation.
hors, pr. except, out of || **~ ligne**, unsurpassed.
hors-d'œuvre, m. outwork || digression || **~**, pl. side-dishes (pl.), by-dishes (pl.), dainties (pl.).
horticulteur, m. horticulturist.
horticultural, e, a. horticultural.
hospice, m. hospital, alms-house (for monks).
hospitalier, ère, a. hospitable. [monks].
hospitalité, f. hospitality.
hostie, f. host, victim.
hostile, a. (—ment, ad.) hostile, inimical || hostilely || adversely.
hostilité, f. hostility.
hôte, m. host, innkeeper, landlord, publican || guest || **table d'~**, m. ordinary, table-d'hôte.
hôtel, m. hotel, inn, lodging-house || mansion || **~ de ville**, town-house, guildhall || **~ Dieu**, hospital || **~ garni** ou **meublé**, lodging-house.
hôtelier, ère, m. & f. innkeeper || landlord. [lady.
hôtellerie, f. hostelry, inn.
hôtesse, f. hostess, landlady || guest, visitor. [tor.
hotte, f. dosser, basket.
hottée, f. basketful.
hotteur, m. basket-carrier.
houblon, m. (bot.) hop.
houblonner, v. a. to pick hops.
houblonnière, f. hop-plantation.
houe, f. hoe.
houer, v. a. to hoe.
houille, f. pit-coal.
houiller, ère, a. coaly.
houillère, f. coal-mine, coal-pit.
houilleur, m. collier.
houilleux, se, a. coaly.
houka, m. hookah.
houle, f. surge || swell.
houlette, f. crook || sheep-hook || trowel.
houleux, se, a. rough.
houppe, f. tuft || puff.
houppelande, f. overcoat.
houpper, v. a. to tuft || to comb (wool).
hourder, v. a. to rough-wall, to pug.
hourque, f. (mar.) hooker.
hourra, m. hurrah || **~!** hurrah!
hourvari, m. hubbub.
houspiller, v. a. to pull, to touse, to tug, to worry || to abuse.
houssage, m. dusting.
houssaie, f. holly-grove.
housse, f. horse-cloth || body-cloth || saddle-cloth || hammer-cloth || cover (for a chair, etc.).
housser, v. a. to dust with a feather-broom.
houssine, f. switch. [broom.
houssiner, v. a. to switch.
houssoir, m. feather-broom.
houx, m. (bot.) holly.
hoyau, m. mattock.
hublot, m. (mar.) light-port || air-hole ||
huche, f. kneading-trough || bin. [scuttle.
hue! gee! gee ho! go on!
huée, f. hooting, shouting.
huer, v. a. to hoot after, to shout.

huette, f. owlet.
Huguenot, m. Huguenot.
huguenot, a. Huguenot.
huile, f. oil.
huiler, v. a. to oil.
huilerie, f. oil-works (pl.).
huileux, se, a. oily || greasy.
huilier, m. oil-cruet, cruet-stand.
huis, m. door || à ~ clos, with closed doors, privately.   [officer.
huissier, m. usher || bailiff || summoning
huit, a. eight.
huitain, m. stanza of eight verses.
huitaine, f. eight days.   [f. eighth class.
huitième, m. eighth || the eighth part || ~,
huitième, a. (—ment, ad.) eighth(ly).
huître, f. oyster || booby.
hulotte, f. large owl.
humain, m. human being || man.
humain, e, a. (—ement, ad.) human(ly) || humane(ly).
humaniser, v. a. to humanise.
humaniste, m. humanist.
humanitaire, m. humanitarian.
humanitaire, a. humanitarian.
humanité, f. humanity || mankind.
humble, a. humble, lowly, meek, submissive || —ment, ad. humbly, submissively || meanly.
humecter, v. a. to moisten, to water.
humer, v. a. to suck in || to inhale.
humeur, f. humour, moisture || temper, disposition || —s froides, f. pl. (méd.) scrofula.
humide, m. moisture, humidity, dampness.
humide, a. humid, moist, wet, damp || watery || —ment, ad. in a damp place.
humidité, f. humidity, moisture, dampness.
humilier, v. a. to humiliate, to humble.
humilité, f. humility, humbleness.
humoriste, m. humourist || cross, peevish person.
humoriste, a. humourist || cross, peevish.
humoristique, a. humouristic.
humus, m. soil.
hune, f. (mar.) top.
hunier, m. (mar.) top-sail || top-mast.
huppe, f. tuft, crest || hoopoo, peewit (bird).
huppé, e, a. tufted, crested.   [salmon].
hure, f. head (of a wild boar) || jole (of a
hurlement, m. howl, howling, roar, roaring, yelling.
hurler, v. n. to howl, to roar, to yell.
hurluberlu, m. giddy fellow.
hurluberlu, ad. bluntly, inconsiderately.
hussard, m. hussar.
hutte, f. hut, cottage.
hyacinthe, f. (bot.) hyacinth.
hybride, a. hybrid, mongrel.
hydraulique, f. hydraulics (pl.).
hydraulique, a. hydraulic.
hydre, f. hydra.
hydrogène, m. (chim.) hydrogen.
hydrographe, m. hydrographer.
hydrographie, f. hydrography.
hydropathe, m. (méd.) water-cure doctor || hydropathist.
hydropathie, f. (méd.) hydropathy.
hydropathique, a. (méd.) hydropathic.

hydrophobe, m. (méd.) hydrophobe.
hydrophobe, a. (méd.) hydrophobe.
hydrophobie, f. (méd.) hydrophobia.
hydropique, a. (méd.) dropsical.
hydropisie, f. (méd.) dropsy.
hydrothérapie, f. vide hydropathie.
hyène, f. hyena.
hygiène, f. preservation of health, hygiene.
hygiénique, a. for the preservation of health || of health || hygienic.
hymen, hyménée, m. (poét.) marriage || nuptials (pl.).
hymne, m. hymn.   [bolic(ally).
hyperbolique, a. (—ment, ad.) hyper-
hyperborée, a. hyperborean, northern.
hypnotiser, v. a. (méd.) to hypnotise.
hypnotisme, m. (méd.) hypnotism.
hypocondre, m. hypochondre || hypochondriac.
hypocondriaque, a. hypochondriacal.
hypocondrie, f. (méd.) hypochondria.
hypocrisie, f. hypocrisy.
hypocrite, m. hypocrite.
hypocrite, a. hypocritical.
hypothécaire, a. belonging to a mortgage || créancier ~, m. mortgagee.
hypothèque, f. mortgage.
hypothéquer, v. a. to mortgage, to pledge.
hypothèse, f. hypothesis.
hypothétique, a. (—ment, ad.) hypo-
hysope, f. (bot.) hyssop.   [thetical(ly).
hystérie, f. (méd.) hysterics (pl.), hysteria.
hystérique, a. hysteric.

I.

iambe, m. iambic || iambic verse.
ibis, m. ibis.   [ichnography.
ichnographie, f. (arch.) ground-plot ||
ichthyolithe, m. ichthyolite.
ici, ad. here, hither, in this place || d'~, from hence, hence || par ~, this way || d'~ là, between now and then || jusqu'~, hitherto.
iconographie, f. iconography.   [hitherto.
iconostase, f. (litur.) large three-doored screen between the altar and nave in Greek
idéal, m. ideal.   [churches.
idéal, e, a. ideal.
idéalisme, m. idealism.
idée, f. idea, thought, opinion, notion, mind, fancy || hint, outline || en ~, ideally || a-t-on ~! what an idea!
idem, ad. ditto (do.).
identifier, v. a. to identify.
identique, a. (—ment, ad.) identical(ly).
identité, f. identity.
idéologue, m. ideologist.
idiome, m. idiom, dialect.
idiopathie, f. inclination, propensity || (méd.) idiopathy.
idiot, m. idiot, simpleton.
idiot, e, a. simple, silly.
idiotie, f. idiotcy.
idiotisme, m. (méd.) idiotism || (gr.) idiom.
idolâtre, m. idolater.
idolâtre, a. idolatrous, extremely fond of.
idolâtrer, v. a. to idolise.

idolâtrie, f. idolatry.
idolâtrique, a. idolatrous.
idole, f. idol.
idylle, f. idyl.   [minations).
if, m. (bot.) yew(-tree) || lamp-stand (for illuminare, m. ignoramus.
iguare, m. ignoramus.
ignare, a. illiterate, ignorant.
igné, e, a. igneous.   [Ignobly.
ignoble, a. ignoble, base || —ment, ad.
ignominie, f. ignominy.
ignominieux, se, a. (—sement, ad.) ignominious(ly).
ignoramus, m. ignoramus.
ignorant, e, a. ignorant || unlettered.
ignorantin, m. lay-brother devoted to the elementary instruction of the poor.
ignorer, v. a. to be ignorant of, not to know.
il, pn. he, it || ~ y a, there is, there are.
île, f. island.
iléon, m. (an.) ileum.
iliaque, a. (an.) iliac.   [unlawful(ly).
illégal, e, a. (—ement, ad.) illegal(ly) ||
illégalité, f. illegality, unlawfulness.
illégitime, a. (—ment, ad.) illegitimate (ly) || unlawful(ly).   [ness || spuriousness.
illégitimité, f. illegitimacy; unlawful-
illettré, e, a. illiterate.   [mechanical.
illibéral, e, a. (—ement, ad.) illiberal(ly) ||
illibéralité, . illiberality.   [(ly).
illicite, a. (—ment, ad.) illicit || unlawful
illimité, e, a. unlimited.
illisible, a. (—ment, ad.) illegible, unreadable || illegibly.
illogique, a. (—ment, ad.) illogical(ly).
illuminé, e, m. & f. visionary || les –s, m. pl. illuminati.   [to light up.
illuminer, v. a. to illuminate, to enlighten,
illusion, f. illusion, delusion || se faire ~, to delude oneself.
illusionner, v. a. to delude, to deceive.
illusoire, a. (—ment, ad.) illusive(ly) || fallacious(ly).   [glory.
illustration, f. illustration, celebrity ||
illustre, a. illustrious.   [illustrate.
illustrer, v. a. to make illustrious, to
illustrissime, a. most illustrious.
îlot, m. small island, islet || block of houses.
ilote, m. helot.
ilotisme, m. helotism.
image, f. image, representation, picture.
imaginaire, a. imaginary.
imaginatif, ve, a. imaginative.
imagination, f. imagination, fancy.
imaginative, f. faculty of inventing.
imaginer, v. a. to imagine, to conceive.
imbécile, a. imbecile, silly || —ment, ad. in a silly manner.
imbécillité, f. imbecility, silliness, folly.
imberbe, a. beardless.
imbiber, v. a. to imbibe || to soak, to imbue.
imbriqué, e, a. imbricated.
imbroglio, m. complicated plot || confusion.
imbu, e, a. imbued.
imitateur, trice, a. imitative.
imitatif, ve, a. imitative.
imiter, v. a. to imitate || to mimic.
immaculé, e, a. immaculate.
immangeable, a. uneatable.

immanquable, a. (—ment, ad.) infallible, infallibly.
immatérialité, f. immateriality.
immatériel, le, a. (—lement, ad.) immaterial(ly).
immatriculation, f. matriculation.
immatriculer, v. a. to matriculate.
immédiat, e, a. (—ement, ad.) immediate
immémorial, e, a. immemorial.   [(ly).
immense, ad. immense.
immensément, ad. immensely.
immensité, f. immensity.
immensurable, a. immeasurable.
immerger, v. a. to immerse.
immeuble, m. immoveable possession || real estate.
immigration, f. immigration.
imminent, e, a. imminent, impending.
s'immiscer, to intermeddle.
immobile, a. immoveable, motionless.
immobilier, ère, a. immoveable, real.
immobiliser, v. a. to render immoveable, to fix.
immobilité, f. immobility.   [(ly).
immodéré, a. (—ment, ad.) immoderate
immodeste, a. (—ment, ad.) immodest(ly).
immodestie, f. immodesty.
immolation, f. immolation, sacrifice.
immoler, v. a. to immolate, to sacrifice || [to slay.
immonde, a. unclean, foul.
immondices, f. pl. filth, dirt.
immondicité, f. dirtiness.
immoral, e, a. (—ment, ad.) immoral(ly).
immoralité, f. immorality.
immortaliser, v. a. to immortalise.
immortalité, f. immortality.
immortel, a. immortal, everlasting.
immortelle, f. (bot.) everlasting flower.
immuable, a. immutable, unchangeable || —ment, ad. immutably, unchangeably.
immunité, f. immunity.
immutabilité, f. immutability.   [(ly).
impair, e, a. (—ement, ad.) odd || uneven
impalpabilité, f. unpalpableness.
impalpable, a. unpalpable.
impardonnable, a. unpardonable.
imparfait, m. imperfect tense.   [(ly).
imparfait, e, a. (—ement, ad.) imperfect
imparité, f. inequality.   [(ly).
impartial, e, a. (—ment, ad.) impartial
impartialité, f. impartiality.   [lock.
impasse, f. blind alley || hobble, fix, dead-
impassibilité, f. impassibility.
impassible, a. impassible, insensible || —ment, ad. impassively.
impatiemment, ad. impatiently, eagerly.
impatience, f. impatience || eagerness ||
impatient, e, a. impatient.   [longing.
impatienter, v. a. to tire out one's patience || s'~, to fret, to grow impatient, to grow
impatriotique, a. unpatriotic.   [angry.
s'impatroniser, to become master.
impayable, a. invaluable, inestimable || admirable.
impeccable, a. sinless, impeccable.
impénétrabilité, f. impenetrability.
impénétrable, a. impenetrable, impervious || —ment, ad. impenetrably.
impénitence, f. impenitence, obduracy.

impénitent, e, a. impenitent, obdurate.
impenses, f. pl. (jur.) expenses (pl.).
impératif, m. (gr.) imperative (mood).
impératif, ve, a. (-vement, ad.) im-
impératrice, f. empress.   [perative(ly).
imperceptible, a. imperceptible, insensible ‖ -ment, ad. imperceptibly.
imperdable, a. that cannot be lost.
imperfection, f. imperfection.
impérial, m. imperialist.
impérial, e, a. (-ement, ad.) imperial(ly).
impériale, f. imperial ‖ top of a coach.
impérialiste, m. imperialist.
impériaux, m. pl. (the) imperialists.
impérieux, se, a. (-sement, ad.) im-
perious(ly)
impérissable, a imperishable.   [fulness.
impéritie, f. want of experience, unskil-
imperméable, a. impervious, waterproof.
impersonnel, le, a. (-lement, ad.) (gr.)
impersonnel(ly).
impertinemment, ad. impertinently.
impertinence, f. impertinence, impropriety.
impertinent, m. saucy fellow, intruder.
impertinent, e, a. impertinent, extravagant.
imperturbabilité, f. imperturbability.
imperturbable, a. (-ment, ad.) firm(ly) ‖
unshaken ‖ steadily.   [duate ‖ recipient.
impétrant, m. patentee, grantee ‖ gra-
impétueux, se, a. (-sement, ad.) im-
petuous(ly).   [petus.
impétuosité, f. impetuosity, force, im-
impie, a. impious, irreligious.
impiété, f. impiety.
impitoyable, a. (-ment, ad.) unmerciful,
merciless(ly) ‖ pitiless(ly) ‖ unsparing.
implacabilité, f. implacability.
implacable, a. implacable ‖ -ment, ad.
implacably.
implanter, v. a. to implant, to insert.
implicite, a. (-ment, ad.) implicit(ly).
impliquer, v. a. to implicate, to involve,
implorer, v. a. to implore.   [to imply.
impoli, e, a. (-ment, ad.) uncivil(ly).
impolitesse, f. incivility, rudeness.
impolitique, a. impolitic.
impondérabilité, f. imponderability.
impondérable, a. imponderable.
impopulaire, a. unpopular.
impopularité, f. unpopularity.
importance, f. importance, consequence,
moment ‖ d'~, very much ‖ famously.
important, m. important ou main point ‖
consequential man.
important, e, a. important.
importateur, m. importer.
importation, f. importation ‖ import.
importer, v. a. to import goods ‖ ~, v. imp.
to be of consequence, to be of moment, to
concern ‖ n'importe, it does not matter ‖
qu'importe ? what does it matter?
importun, m. hanger-on, intruder.
importun, e, a. importunate, troublesome.
importunément, ad. importunately.
importuner, v. a. to importunate, to
trouble, to tease.
importunité, f. importunity.

imposable, a. taxable.
imposer, v. a. & n. to impose, to prescribe,
to lay duties on ‖ to impute, to charge ‖
to awe, to overawe ‖ en ~, to impose on,
to deceive.   [ment.
imposition, f. imposition, tax ‖ assess-
impossibilité, f. impossibility.
impossible, m. impossibility ‖ a great
deal ‖ par ~, supposing an impossibility.
impossible, a. impossible.
imposteur, m. impostor.
imposture, a. deceitful.
impôt, m. impost, tax, duty, toll.
impotent, e, a. impotent, infirm.
impraticable, a. impracticable, unmanageable ‖ impassable.
imprécation, f. imprecation.
imprégner, v. a. to impregnate.
imprenable, a. impregnable.
imprescriptibilité, f. imprescriptibility
impression, f. impression, stamping,
print ‖ edition.   [sensitive.
impressionable, a. impressive, excitable,
impressionner, v. a. to impress ‖ to make
an impression upon, to move ‖ s'~, to be
impressed ou moved.
imprévoyance, f. improvidence.
imprévoyant, e, a. improvident.
imprévu, m. adventure, surprise.
imprévu, e, a. unforeseen, unexpected.
imprimé, m. printed paper ou book.
imprimer, v. a. to impress, to imprint, to
print, to stamp ‖ to prime (cloth).
imprimerie, f. printing ‖ printing-house,
printing-office ‖ typography.
imprimeur, m. printer.
improbabilité, f. improbability.
improbateur, m. reprover.
improbateur, trice, a. disapproving.
improbation, f. disapprobation.
improbe, a. dishonest.
improbité, f. dishonesty.
improductif, ve, a. unproductive.
impromptu, m. impromptu.   [rary.
impromptu, e, a. impromptu, extempo-
impropre, a. (-ment, ad.) improper(ly) ‖
unbecoming, incongruous.
impropriété, f. impropriety.
improuver, v. a. to disapprove.
improvisateur, trice, m. & f. extem-
poriser.   [poraneous speaking.
improvisation, f. improvisation ‖ extem-
improviser, v. a. to extemporise, to improvise.   [den.
à l'improviste, ad. unawares, on a sud-
imprudemment, ad. imprudently.
imprudence, f. imprudence, indiscretion.
imprudent, e, a. imprudent.
impudemment, ad. impudently.
impudent, e, a. impudent, shameless,
brazen-faced.
impudeur, f. immodesty.   [lewd act.
impudicité, f. unchasteness ‖ lewdness ‖
impudique, a. (-ment, ad.) unchaste ‖
lewd(ly).   [powerlessness.
impuissance, f. impotence, inability,
impuissant, e, a. impotent, powerless, in-
impulsif, ve, a. impulsive.   [efficacious.
impulsion, f. impulsion, impulse.

impunément, ad. with impunity.
impuni, e, a. unpunished.
impunité, f. impunity.
impur, e, a. (—ement, ad.) impure(ly).
impureté, f. impurity.
imputer, v. a. to impute, to ascribe, to lay to one's charge.
inabordable, a. inaccessible.
inabrité, e, a. unsheltered.
inacceptable, a. unacceptable.
inaccessibilité, f. inaccessibleness.
inaccordable, a. ungrantable, irreconcilable ‖ untunable.   [usual.
inaccoutumé, e, a. unaccustomed, unusual.
inachevé, e, a. unfinished.
inactif, ve, a. inactive.
inactivité, f. inactivity.
inadmissibilité, f. inadmissibility.
inadvertance, f. inadvertency, oversight.
inaliénabilité, f. inalienableness.
inaltérable, a. unchangeable ‖ incorruptible.
inaltérabilité, f. unchangeableness.
inamovibilité, f. unremovableness, permanency.
inamovible, a. unremovable.   [manency.
inanimé, e, a. inanimate.
inanité, f. emptiness.
inanition, f. inanition, starvation.
inaperçu, e, a. unperceived.
inappétence, f. (méd.) inappetence, want of appetite.
inapplicabilité, f. inapplicability.
inappliqué, e, a. inattentive, heedless.
inappréciable, a. invaluable.
inarticulé, e, a. inarticulate.
inattaquable, a. unassailable, unimpeachable.
inattendu, e, a. unexpected.   [able.
inattentif, ve, a. inattentive.
inattention, f. inattention, heedlessness.
inaugurer, v. a. to inaugurate.
incandescence, f. incandescence ‖ lumière par ~, f. incandescent light.
incandescent, -e, a. white-hot, incandescent.
incapable, a. incapable, unable, unfit.
incapacité, f. incapacity, inability ‖ incompetence.
incarcérer, v. a. to incarcerate.
incarnat, m. flesh-colour.
s'incarner, to become incarnate.
incartade, f. insult ‖ prank.
incendiaire, m. & f. incendiary.
incendiaire, a. incendiary.
incendie, m. fire, conflagration.
incendié, e, m. & f. sufferer from fire.
incendier, v. a. to burn, to set fire to.
incertain, e, a. uncertain.
incertitude, f. uncertainty.
incessamment, ad. incessantly, immediately, continually.
incessible, a. inalienable.
inceste, m. incestuous person ‖ incest.
inceste, a. incestuous.   [cestuous(ly).
incestueux, se, a. (—sement, ad.) incidemment, ad. incidently.
incidence, f. (géom.) incidence.
incident, m. incident, occurrence ‖ difficulty.   [subordinate.
incident, e, a. incidental ‖ casual ‖ (gr.)

incidenter, v. n. to raise incidents ou difficulties.
incinération, f. (chim.) incineration.
inciser, v. a. to cut, to make an incision.
incisif, ve, a. incisive, incisory.
incisive, f. incisor (tooth).
incitateur, m. inciter.
incitation, f. incitement, instigation.
inciter, v. a. to incite.
incivil, e, a. (—ement, ad.) uncivil(ly).
incivilité, f. incivility.
inclémence, f. inclemency.
inclément, e, a. inclement.
inclinaison, f. inclination.
inclination, f. inclination ‖ proneness, stooping ‖ love ‖ mariage d'~, lovematch.
incliner, v. a. & n. to incline, to bend, to bow, to lean, to tend towards, to be disposed to.
inclus, e, a. inclosed.   [posed to.
incluse, f. enclosure, enclosed (of letters, etc.).   [sive(ly).
inclusif, ve, a. (—vement, ad.) inclusivo.
incognito, m. incognito ‖ garder l'~, to preserve one's incognito.
incognito, ad. incognito, incog.
incohérent, e, a. incoherent, unconnected.
incolore, a. colourless.   [to lie upon.
incomber, v. n. to be incumbent ‖ to fall
incombustible, a. incombustible.
incommode, a. incommodious, inconvenient, troublesome, pestering.
incommode, e, a. indisposed.
incommodément, ad. inconveniently, uncomfortably.
incommoder, v. a. to incommode, to annoy, to trouble, to embarrass.   [tion.
incommodité, f. inconvenience, indisposition.
incommutable, a. indefeasible ‖ (jur.) that cannot be dispossessed.
incomparable, a. (—ment, ad.) peerless, matchless ‖ incomparably.
incompatibilité, f. incompatibility.
incompatible, a. (—ment, ad.) incompatible, inconsistent ‖ incompatibly.
incompétemment, ad. incompetently.
incompétence, f. incompetency.
incompétent, e, a. incompetent.
incomplet, ète, a. (—ètement, ad.) unfinished ‖ incomplete(ly).
incompréhensible, a. incomprehensible, unintelligible ‖ inscrutable.
incompris, e, a. not understood ‖ unappreciated.
inconcevable, a. (—ment, ad.) inconceivable, strange ‖ inconceivably.
inconciliable, a. irreconcilable.
inconduite, f. misconduct.
incongru, e, a. incongruous ‖ indecent.
incongruité, f. incongruity ‖ impropriety.
incongrûment, ad. incongruously ‖ improperly.
inconnu, m. unknown ‖ stranger.
inconnu, e, a. unknown ‖ strange.
inconséquemment, ad. inconsequently.
inconséquence, f. inconsistency.
inconséquent, e, a. inconsistent ‖ inconsiderate, thoughtless.   [rashness.
inconsidération, f. inconsiderateness,

inconsidéré, e, a. (-ment, ad.) inconsiderate(ly) || rash(ly).

inconsolable, a. (-ment, ad.) inconsolable, inconsolably.

inconstance, f. inconstancy, fickleness, unsteadiness, uncertainty.

inconstant, e, a. inconstant, unsteady, variable, fickle.

inconstitutionnel, le, a. unconstitutional.

incontestable, a. (-ment, ad.) incontestable, indisputable || incontestably, indisputably.

incontesté, e, a. undisputed.

incontinent, e, a. incontinent, unchaste || ~, ad. immediately, forthwith.

inconvenance, f. impropriety.

inconvenant, e, a. unbecoming, improper.

inconvénient, m. inconvenience, disadvantage.

incorporel, le, a. incorporeal.

incorporer, v. a. to incorporate, to embody.

incorrect, e, a. (-ement, ad.) incorrect(ly).

incorrection, f. incorrectness, inaccuracy.

incorrigible, a. incorrigible.

incorruptibilité, f. incorruptibility

incorruptible, a. incorruptible.

incrédibilité, f. incredibility.

incrédule, m. unbeliever.

incrédule, a. incredulous.

incrédulité, f. incredulity, unbelief.

incréé, e, a. uncreated.

incriminer, v. a. to incriminate.

incroyable, a. (-ment, ad.) incredible || incredibly.

incrustation, f. incrustation || inlaid work.

incruster, v. a. to incrust || to inlay || to lay over

incuit, m. underdone part.

incuit, e, a. underdone.

inculpation, f. crimination, charge.

inculper, v. a. to accuse, to charge, to criminate.

inculquer, v. a. to inculcate.

inculte, a. uncultivated, uncivilised || unploughed, untilled, waste.

incultivable, a. uncultivable.

incunable, a. relating to incunabula.

incurable, a. incurable, past curing

incurie, f. carelessness.   [sion.

incursion, f. incursion || inroad || excursion

indébrouillable, a. inextricable || inexplicable.

indécemment, ad. indecently.

indécence, f. indecency.

indécent, e, a. indecent, unbecoming.

indéchiffrable, a. undecipherable || illegible || unintelligible, unaccountable

indécis, e, a. undecided, undetermined, doubtful || vague, wavering.

indéclinable, a. (gr.) undeclinable.

indécrottable, a. unpolished, unpolite || (fig.) uncivilised, untractable.

indéfendable, a. indefensible.

indéfini, e, a. (-ment, ad.) unlimited || indefinite(ly) || indeterminate(ly).

indéfinissable, a. undefinable || unaccountable, nondescript.

indélébile, a. indelible.   [(ly).

indélicat, e, a. (-ement, ad.) indelicate

indélicatesse, f. indelicacy.

indemnisation, f. indemnification.

indemniser, v. a. to indemnify

indemnité, f. indemnity.

indépendamment, ad. independently.

indépendance, f. independence.

indépendant, e, a. independent.

indescriptible, a. indescribable.

indestructibilité, f. indestructibility.

indéterminé, e, a. indeterminate, undecided, unsettled || -ment, ad. indeterminately, in general.

indevinable, a. not to be guessed.

indévot, e, a. (-ement, ad.) undevout(ly).

index, m. table of contents, index || forefinger || mettre à l'~, to forbid.

indicateur, m. indicator || denouncer || forefinger || index-book || time-bill.

indicateur, a. indicating.

indicatif, m. (gr.) indicative (mood).

indicatif, ve, a. indicative, indicating.

indication, f. indication, information, sign, symptom.

indice, m. sign, mark || clue, trace.

indicible, a. unspeakable, inexpressible, indescribable.

indienne, f. printed calico.

indifféremment, ad. indifferently, indiscriminately.   [ness.

indifférence, f. indifference, unconcernedindifférent, m. impartial person.

indifférent, e, a. indifferent, unconcerned.

indigène, a. indigenous, native.

indigent, e, a. indigent, penurious, poor, needy.   [crude, raw.

indigeste, a. indigestible || undigested

indigestion, f. indigestion.

indigne, a. indign, unworthy, undeserving, ignoble, mean.

indigné, e, a. indignant.

indignement, ad. unworthily, infamously

indigner, v. a. to excite indignation, shock || s'~, to be indignant.

indignité, f. indignity, worthlessness.

indigoterie, f. indigo-manufactory.

indigotier, m. indigo-plant.

indiquer, v. a. to indicate, to point out, to show || to acquaint with || to direct to || to recommend || to appoint || to mention.

indirect, e, a. (-ement, ad.) indirect(ly).

indisciplinable, a. unruly.

indiscipline, f. insubordination.

indiscipliné, e, a. undisciplined.

indiscret, ète, a. (-ètement, ad.) indiscreet(ly) || inconsiderate(ly) || inquisitive.

indiscrétion, f. indiscretion, imprudence || piece of indiscretion.   [vertible.

indiscutable, a. indisputable, uncontroindispensabilité, f. indispensableness.

indispensable, a. (-ment, ad.) indispensable || indispensably.   [posed of.

indisponible, a. (jur.) that cannot be disindisposé, e, a. indisposed, unwell.

indisposer, v. a. to indispose, to disincline, to disaffect.

indisposition, f. indisposition, dislike, distemper.

indisputable, a. indisputable, incontrovertible.

indissolubilité, f. indissolubility.

indissoluble, a. (-ment, ad.) indissoluble || indissolubly.

indistinct, e, a. (-ement, ad.) indistinct(ly) || indiscriminately.

individu, m. individual || self, inside.

individualité, f. individuality || entity.

individuel, le, a. (-lement, ad.) individual(ly).

indivis, e, a. undivided || par ~, jointly.

indivisé, e, a. undivided.

indivisibilité, f. indivisibility.

indivisible, a. (-ment, ad.) indivisible || indivisibly.

in-dix-huit, m. decimo-octavo.

indocile, a. indocile, ungovernable, unmanageable.

indocilité, f. indocility.   [tractable.

indolemment, ad. indolently, lazily.

indolence, f. indolence, laziness.

indolent, e, a. indolent, lazy, careless.

indomptable, a. untameable, unmanageable.   [invincible, undaunted.

indompté, e, a. untamed, unconquered.

in-douze, m. duodecimo.   [proper.

indu, e, a. undue || unseasonable || im-

indubitable, a. (-ment, ad.) indubitable || beyond doubt || indubitably, undoubtedly.

induction, f. induction, inference.

induire, v. a. ir. to induce, to infer || to lead.   [forgiveness of sins.

indulgence, f. indulgence, forbearance ||

indulgent, e, a. indulgent.

indûment, ad. unduly.   [ing.

induration, f. (méd.) induration, harden-

industrie, f. industry, ingenuity, dexterity, skill, address, art || manufactures (pl.) || chevalier d'~, sharper || vivre d'~, to live by one's wits.

industriel, m. manufacturer.   [ing.

industriel, le, a. industrial || manufactur-

industrieux, se, a. (-sement, ad.) industrious(ly) || ingenious(ly).

inébranlable, a. (-ment, ad.) immovable || firm(ly) || unshakable || immovably, steadily, unshakably.

inédit, e, a. unpublished.

ineffable, a. unspeakable.

ineffaçable, a. indelible.

inefficace, a. inefficient.

inefficacité, f. inefficiency.

inégal, e, a. (-ement, ad.) unequal(ly) || uneven(ly) || irregular(ly).

inégalité, f. inequality, unequalness, unevenness, irregularity, unsteadiness.

inélégant, e, a. inelegant.

inéligible, a. ineligible.

inénarrable, a. inexpressible, unspeak-

inepte, a. inept, silly, unfit.   [able.

ineptie, f. silliness, absurdity.

inépuisable, a. inexhaustible.

inerte, a. inert, sluggish.

inertie, f. inertia, indolence, sluggishness || force d'~, f. passive resistance.

inespéré, e, a. unhoped for, unexpected.

inévitable, a. (-ment, ad.) inevitable, unavoidable || inevitably.

inexact, e, a. inexact, inaccurate, careless.

inexactement, ad. inaccurately, incorrectly.

inexactitude, f. inaccuracy, inaccurateness, incorrectness, carelessness.

inexcusable, a. inexcusable || unjustifiable.

inexécutable, a. impracticable.

inexécution, f. non-performance.

inexercé, e, a. unpractised || untrained.

inexigible, a. not demandable.

inexorable, a. (-ment, ad.) inexorable || inexorably.

inexpérimenté, e, a. inexperienced.

inexprimable, a. inexpressible.

inexpugnable, a. inexpugnable, impregnable.

in-extenso, ad. in extenso, in full.

inextinguible, a. unextinguishable || irrepressible.

infaillibilité, f. infallibility.

infaillible, a. (-ment, ad.) unerring(ly) || infallible.

infaisable, a. impracticable.   [infallibly.

infamant, e, a. infamous, ignominious.

infâme, a. infamous || filthy.

infamie, f. infamy || infamous thing.

infant, m. infante, f. Infante, Infanta.

infanterie, f. infantry, foot-soldiers.

infatigable, a. (-ment, ad.) indefatigable || indefatigably.

infatuer, v. a. to infatuate.

infécond, e, a. unfruitful, barren.

infécondité, f. barrenness, unfruitfulness.

infect, e, a. infectious.   [sterility.

infecter, v. a. to infect, to taint || ~, v. n. to stink horribly.

inféoder, v. a. to infeoff.

inférer, v. a. to infer.

inférieur, e, a. inferior, lower || -ement, ad. in an inferior manner, below.

infériorité, f. inferiority.

infernal, e, a. infernal, hellish.

infertile, a. unfruitful, barren.

infester, v. a. to infest.

infidèle, m. infidel || unbeliever.

infidèle, a. (-ment, ad.) unfaithful(ly) || disloyal(ly) || false, unbelieving, perfidious.

infidélité, f. infidelity, unfaithfulness, disloyalty, unbelief, deceit.

s'infiltrer, to infiltrate || to creep.

infime, a. lowest.

infini, e, a. (-ment, ad.) infinite(ly) || numberless, endless || à l'~, without end, infinitely || exceedingly, extremely.

infinité, f. infinity, infiniteness.

infinitif, m. (gr.) infinitive (mood).

infirme, a. infirm, sickly.

infirmer, v. a. to invalidate.   [ward.

infirmerie, f. infirmary || sick-room || sick-

infirmier, m. hospital-attendant.

infirmière, f. sick-nurse.

infirmité, f. infirmity.

inflammatoire, a. inflammatory.

inflation, f. inflation.

inflexibilité, f. inflexibility, inexorability.

inflexible, a. (-ment, ad.) inflexible || inflexibly.

inflexion, f. inflection.

infliger, v. a. to inflict.

influence, f. influence, sway.

influencer, v. a. to influence.

influent, e, a. influential.

influer, v. n. to have influence over ‖ to
influenza, f. (méd.) influenza. [influence.
in-folio, m. folio-book.
information, f. information, inquiry ‖
aller aux —s, prendre des —s, to
make inquiries.
informe, a. shapeless.
informé, m. investigation.
informer, v. a. & n. to inform ‖ to advise ‖
(jur.) to institute an enquiry ‖ s'~, to
inquire, to ask after.
infortune, f. misfortune.
infortuné, e, a. unfortunate, unhappy.
infracteur, m. infringer.
infraction, f. infraction, breach, infringe-
ment. [able.
infranchissable, a. impassable, insuper-
infructueusement, ad. unprofitably, to
no purpose.
infructueux, se, a. unfruitful, unprofit-
infus, e, a. intuitive. [able.
infuser, v. a. to infuse, to steep.
infusion, f. infusion, instilling ‖ intuition.
ingambe, a. nimble, alert.
s'ingénier, v. r. to set one's wits to work.
ingénieur, m. engineer.
ingénieux, se, a. (–sement, ad.) in-
genious(ly). [open.
ingénu, e, a. ingenuous, sincere, frank,
ingénuité, f. ingenuity, frankness.
ingénûment, ad. ingenuously, frankly.
s'ingérer, v. r. to meddle, to intermeddle
ingouvernable, a. ungovernable. [with.
ingrat, e, a. ungrateful.
inhabile, a. incapable, unqualified, unfit,
inept, unskilful.
inhabileté, f. unskilfulness.
inhabilité, f. (jur.) incapacity.
inhabitable, a. uninhabitable.
inhabité, e, a. uninhabited.
inhalation, f. (phys.) inhalation.
inhérent, e, a. inherent.
inhospitalier, ère, a. inhospitable.
inhospitalité, f. inhospitality.
inhumain, e, a. (–ement, ad.) inhuman-
(ly) ‖ cruel(ly).
inhumanité, f. inhumanity, cruelty.
inhumation, f. interment.
inhumer, v. a. to inter.
inimaginable, a. unimaginable.
inimitable, a. (–ment, ad.) inimitable ‖
inimitably.
inimitié, f. enmity, hatred.
inintelligibilité, f. unintelligibility.
inintelligible, a. (–ment, ad.) unintelligible ‖ unintelligibly.
inique, a. (–ment, ad.) iniquitous(ly).
iniquité, f. iniquity, unrighteousness.
initiale, f. initial.
initiation, f. initiation. [power.
initiative, f. initiative ‖ originating
initier, v. a. to initiate, to admit.
injecter, v. a. to inject.
injonction, f. injunction. [abuse.
injure, f. injury, insult ‖ dire des —s, to
injurier, v. a. to abuse, to insult.
injurieux, se, a. (–sement, ad.) in-
jurious(ly) ‖ outrageous, offensive ‖ abu-
sive(ly) ‖ adverse.

injuste, a. (–ment, ad.) unjust(ly).
injustice, f. injustice ‖ act of injustice.
inlisible, a. illegible.
inné, e, a. innate, inborn.
innocemment, ad. innocently, foolishly.
innocence, f. innocence ‖ simplicity.
innocent, m. simpleton.
innocent, e, a. innocent, simple.
innocuité, f. harmlessness. [less.
innombrable, a. innumerable, number-
innovateur, trice, m. & f. innovator.
innover, v. a. to innovate.
inobservation, f. non-observance.
inoccupé, e, a. unoccupied.
in-octavo, m. in-octavo, octavo.
inoculateur, m. (méd.) inoculator.
inoculation, f. (méd.) inoculation.
inoculer, v. a. (méd.) to inoculate.
inodore, a. inodorous, scentless.
inoffensif, ve, a. inoffensive.
inondation, f. inundation, flood.
inonder, v. a. to inundate, to overflow,
to deluge.
inopiné, e, a. (–ment, ad.) unthought-
of ‖ unexpected(ly) ‖ unawares. [able.
inopportun, e, a. inopportune, unseason-
inopportunément, ad. inopportunely.
inopportunité, f. unseasonableness.
inouï, e, a. unheard-of, surprising, strange.
inoxydable, a. (chim.) inoxydisable.
in-quarto, m. quarto.
inquiet, ète, a. unquiet, uneasy, restless,
anxious.
inquiéter, v. a. to disquiet, to alarm, to
vex, to disturb ‖ s'~, to fret at, to be
anxious. [quietude, uneasiness.
inquiétude, f. disquiet, disquietude, in-
inquisiteur, m. inquisitor.
insaisissable, a. indiscernible ‖ not distrainable.
insalubre, a. unhealthy, unwholesome.
insalubrité, f. insalubrity, unwholesome-
insanité, f. insanity. [ness.
insatiabilité, f. insatiableness.
insatiable, a. (–ment, ad.) insatiable ‖
insatiably.
inscription, f. inscription, title.
inscrire, v. a. ir. to inscribe ‖ s'~, to get
one's name inscribed.
insecte, m. insect.
insecticide, m. vermin–ou insect-destroyer.
insecticide, a. insect-destroying.
insectivore, a. insectivorous.
insécurité, f. insecurity.
in-seize, m. book in sixteens.
in-seize, a. 16mo.
insensé, m. madman.
insensé, e, a. insane, senseless, mad.
insensibilité, f. insensibility.
insensible, a. (–ment, ad.) insensible,
unconscious, unfeeling ‖ insensibly.
inséparabilité, f. inseparability.
inséparable, a. (–ment, ad.) inseparable ‖
inseparably.
insérer, v. a. to insert. [(ly).
insidieux, se, a. (–ment, ad.) insidious
insigne, a. egregious, notorious.
insignes, m. pl. insignia (pl.).
insignifiant, e, a. insignificant. [hint.
insinuation, f. insinuation, suggestion,

insinuer, v. a. to insinuate, to suggest, to hint ‖ s'~, to insinuate oneself, to steal into ‖ to introduce oneself into.
insipide, a. (-ment, ad.) insipid(ly) ‖ unsavoury, tasteless ‖ heavy, dull.
insipidité, f. insipidity.
insistance, f. insistance.
insister, v. n. to insist upon.
insociabilité, f. unsociability.
insociable, a. unsociable.
insolation, f. exposure to the sun ‖ (méd.) insolation, sun-stroke.
insolemment, ad. insolently.
insolence, f. insolence, impudence, sauciness.
insolent, e, a. insolent. [ness.
insolite, a. unusual.
insoluble, a. insoluble ‖ unsolvable.
insolvabilité, f. insolvency.
insolvable, a. insolvent.
insomnie, f. (méd.) sleeplessness, insomnia.
insondable, a. fathomless.
insouciance, f. carelessness.
insouciant, e, a. careless.
insoumis, e, a. unsubdued.
insoutenable, a. insupportable ‖ indefensible.
inspecter, v. a. to inspect. [sible.
inspecteur, m. inspector, overseer, superintendent.
inspection, f. inspection, superintendence.
inspirateur, trice, a. inspiring.
inspiration, f. inspiration ‖ suggestion.
inspirer, v. a. to inspire.
instabilité, f. instability.
installation, f. instalment.
installer, v. a. to instal, to inaugurate ‖ to establish. [urgently.
instamment, ad. instantly, earnestly.
instance, f. entreaty, solicitation, importunity ‖ earnestness ‖ degree of jurisdiction ‖ suit ‖ avec ~, earnestly.
instant, m. instant, moment ‖ à l'~, immediately ‖ un ~! hold hard! not so fast! one moment!
instant, e, a. instant, urgent.
instantané, e, a. (-ment, ad.) instantaneous(ly).
instantanéité, f. instantaneousness.
à l'instar, pr. like, similar to.
instigateur, m. instigator, inciter.
instinct, m. instinct ‖ par ~, instinctively.
instinctif, ve, a. (-ment, ad.) instinctive(ly). [to appoint.
instituer, v. a. to institute, to establish.
institut, m. institute ‖ institute.
instituteur, m. founder ‖ schoolmaster ‖ private tutor.
institution, f. institution, establishment, school. [schoolmistress.
institutrice, f. governess ‖ foundress ‖
instructeur, m. instructor ‖ drill-instructor.
instructif, ve, a. instructive. [tor.
instruction, f. instruction, mandate, information, education ‖ order, direction ‖ proc edings (pl.).
instruire, v. a. to instruct, to educate, to teach, to inform, to acquaint, to take information on ‖ ~ mal, to misteach.
instruit, e, a. learned ‖ informed.

instrument, m. instrument, tool ‖ deed.
instrumental, e, a. instrumental.
instrumenter, v. a. (jur.) to draw up (a deed).
instrumentiste, m. instrumentalist.
insu, m. ignorance ‖ à l'~ de, unknown to ‖ à son ~, unwittingly, unknowingly.
insubordonné, e, a. insubordinate.
insuccès, m. bad success.
insuffisamment, ad. insufficiently.
insuffisance, f. insufficiency.
insuffisant, e, a. insufficient, inadequate.
insufflation, f. insufflation ‖ (méd.) inspiration.
insulaire, m. islander. [spiration.
insulaire, a. insular.
insulte, f. insult, affront.
insulter, v. a. to insult, to affront.
insupportable, a. (-ment, ad.) insufferable ‖ insupportably.
insurgé, e, m. & f. insurgent.
insurgé, e, a. insurgent.
insurger, v. a. to excite to insurrection ‖ s'~, to rebel.
insurmontable, a. insurmountable.
insurrectionnel, e, a. insurrectionary.
intact, e, a. intact, untouched ‖ pure.
intaille, f. intaglio.
intangible, a. intangible.
intarissable, a. inexhaustible.
intégral, e, a. integral, whole ‖ -ement, ad. entirely, wholly.
intégralité, f. integrality, the whole.
intégrant, e, a. integral.
intègre, a. upright, honest.
intégrité, f. integrity, honesty, entireness.
intellect, m. intellect, understanding.
intellectuel, le, a. intellectual.
intelligemment, ad. intelligently ‖ knowingly.
intelligence, f. understanding, intellect, comprehension ‖ concord ‖ être d'~, to have an understanding together.
intelligent, e, a. intelligent.
intelligibilité, f. intelligibility.
intelligible, a. (-ment, ad.) intelligible, audible ‖ intelligibly, audibly.
intempérant, e, a. intemperate.
intempérie, f. inclemency (of the weather).
intempestif, ve, a. (-vement, ad.) unseasonable ‖ unseasonably.
intendance, f. direction, superintendance, management ‖ commissariat.
intendant, m. intendant, surveyor, steward ‖ Lord-Lieutenant ‖ ~ militaire, commissary of stores.
intense, a. intense, violent.
intensité, f. intensity.
intenter, v. a. to begin, to enter ‖ to bring.
intention, f. intention, intent, purpose, design ‖ avec l'~, intentionally.
intentionné, e, a. intentioned, meaning.
intentionnel, le, a. intended ‖ of intention.
intercalaire, a. intercalar.
intercaler, v. a. to intercalate, to insert.
intercéder, v. a. to intercede (for).
intercepter, v. a. to intercept.
intercesseur, m. intercessor.
interdiction, f. interdict, prohibition.

interdire, v. a. ir. to interdict, to forbid, to suspend || (jur.) to declare incapable of managing his affairs.
interdit, m. interdict. [speechless.
interdit, e, a. interdicted || confused ||
intéressé, e, m. & f. interested party.
intéressé, e, a. interested || selfish.
intéresser, v. a. & n. to interest || to have a share in || to excite interest, to move || **s'~,** to be concerned, to take an interest in.
intérêt, m. interest, concern, self-interest, advantage || **mettre hors d'~,** to consider one harmless.
interfolier, v. a. to interleave.
intérieur, m. interior, inside || home || thoughts (pl.) || private life.
intérieur, m. interior, inner, inward || **—ement,** ad. internally || inwards.
intérim, m. interim || **par ~,** ad interim.
intérimaire, a. ad interim.
interjection, f. (gr.) interjection || (jur.) lodging (of appeals etc.). [etc.).
interjeter, v. a. (jur.) to lodge (appeals.
interligne, f. space between two lines || (typ.) lead.
interligner, v. a. (typ.) to lead.
interlinéaire, a. interlineary.
interlinéer, v. a. to interline.
interlocuteur, m. interlocutor.
interlope, m. interloper.
interlope, a. interloping.
interloquer, v. a. to puzzle, to shut up.
intermède, m. interlude.
intermédiaire, m. medium.
intermédiaire, a. intermediate.
interminable, a. interminable, long-
intermittence, f. intermission. [winded.
internat, m. boarding-school.
international, a. a. international.
interne, m. boarder || house-surgeon.
interne, a. internal, interior, inward.
interner, v. a. & n. to confine within the country || to introduce into the country || to reside within the country.
internonce, m. papal internuncio.
interpellation, f. interpellation, summons || question in parliament.
interpeller, v. a. to require peremptory answers, to summon, to challenge.
interpolateur, m. interpolator.
interpoler, v. a. to interpolate, to insert.
interposer, v. a. to interpose.
interprétation, f. interpretation || con-
interprète, m. interpreter. [struction.
interpréter, v. a. to interpret || to construe.
interrègne, m. interregnum.
interrogateur, trice, m. & f. interrogator, questioner.
interrogatif, ve, a. interrogative.
interrogation, f. interrogation, question.
interrogatoire, m. examination.
interroger, v. a. to interrogate, to examine, to question. [off || to cut short.
interrompre, v. a. to interrupt || to break
interrupteur, m. interrupter.
intersection, f. (géom.) intersection.
intervalle, m. interval.
intervenir, v. n. ir. to intervene, to interfere || to happen.

French and English.

interversion, f. inversion.
intervertir, v. a. to invert, to overturn || [to change.
intestat, m. intestate.
intestat, e, a. intestate.
intestin, e, a. intestine.
intestins, m. pl. bowels (pl.).
intimation, f. notification, summons.
intime, m. intimate friend, intimate.
intime, a. (—ment, ad.) intimate(ly).
intimé, e, m. (jur.) defendant.
intimer, v. a. to give notice, to notify.
intimité, f. intimacy.
intitulé, m. (jur.) title.
intituler, v. a. to entitle.
intolérable, a. (—ment, ad.) insufferable || insufferably.
intolérance, f. intolerance.
intolérant, e, a. intolerant.
intonation, f. intonation.
intoxication, f. poisoning || (méd.) morbid absorption || infection.
intraduisible, a. untranslatable.
intraitable, a. untractable, unmanageable.
intransitif, ve, a. (gr.) intransitive.
intrépide, a. (—ment, ad.) intrepid(ly).
intrépidité, f. intrepidity.
intrigant, m. intriguer.
intrigant, e, a. intriguing.
intrigue, f. intrigue, plot.
intriguer, v. a. & n. to puzzle, to perplex || to intrigue. [(ally).
intrinsèque, a. (—ment, ad.) intrinsic
introducteur, trice, m. & f. introducer.
introduire, v. a. ir. to introduce || **s'~,** to introduce oneself, to gain admittance.
intronisation, f. enthroning.
introniser, v. a. to enthrone.
introuvable, a. not to be found.
intrus, e, m. & f. intruder.
intrusion, f. intrusion, obtrusion.
intuitif, ve, a. (—vement, ad.) intuitive
intuition, f. intuition. [(ly).
inusable, a. that will never wear out.
inusité, e, a. unused, not in use, unusual.
inutile, a. (—ment, ad.) useless(ly) || fruitless(ly) || unserviceable || needless(ly).
inutilité, f. uselessness || **—s,** pl. useless things (pl.). [person.
invalide, m. invalid, disabled soldier || sick
invalide, a. invalid, disabled.
invalider, v. a. to invalidate.
invalidité, f. invalidity.
invariabilité, f. invariability.
invariable, a. (—ment, ad.) invariable || invariably.
invasion, f. invasion || (méd.) accession.
invective, f. invective.
invectiver, v. a. to inveigh.
invendable, a. unsaleable.
invendu, e, a. unsold.
inventaire, m. inventory || **faire l'~,** to take stock || **sous bénéfice d'~,** with liability for the debts of the succession only up to the amount of the goods in the inventory.
inventer, v. a. to invent, to contrive.
inventeur, trice, m. & f. inventor, contriver || inventress.
inventif, ve, a. inventive.

invention, f. invention, contrivance.
inventorier, v. a. to make an inventory.
inversable, a. that cannot be overturned.
inverse, m. reverse.
inverse, a. inverse, inverted.
investigateur, trice, m. & f. investigator.
investigateur, trice, a. investigating.
investigation, f. investigation, inquiry.
investir, v. a. to invest.
investissement, m. investment.
investiture, f. investiture || donner l'~ à, (jur.) to invest || to feoff.
invétéré, e, a. inveterate, rooted.
s'invétérer, to become inveterate.
invincible, a. (-ment, ad.) invincible, unconquerable || invincibly, unconquerably, insuperably.
inviolabilité, f. inviolability.
inviolable, a. (-ment, ad.) inviolable || inviolably.
invisibilité, f. invisibility.　　　[invisibly.
invisible, a. (-ment, ad.) invisible ||
invité, e, m. & f. guest.　　　　[advise.
inviter, v. a. to invite || to engage || to
involontaire, a. (-ment, ad.) involuntary || involuntarily.　　　　　[appeal.
invoquer, v. a. to invoke, to implore, to
invraisemblable, a. (-ment, ad.) improbable, unlikely || improbably.
invraisemblance, f. unlikeliness, unlikelihood, improbability.
invulnérable, a. invulnerable.
iode, m. (chim.) iodine.
irascibilité, f. irascibility.
iris, f. iris, rainbow.
irisé, e, a. rainbow-coloured, irisate.
ironie, f. irony.
ironique, a. (-ment, ad.) ironical(ly).
Iroquois, m. eccentric fellow || (fam.) rum chap.
irrachetable, a. irredeemable.
irradiation, f. (phys.) irradiation || (méd.) radiation.
irraisonnable, a. irrational.
irrationnel, le, a. (-lement, ad.) irrational(ly).
irréalisable, a. unrealisable.
irréconciliable, a. (-ment, ad.) irreconcilable || irreconcilably.
irrécusablement, ad. unexceptionably.
irréductible, a. irreducible.
irréfléchi, e, a. thoughtless.
irréflexion, f. thoughtlessness.
irréfragable, a. irrefragable, undeniable.
irréfutable, a. irrefutable.
irrégularité, f. irregularity.
irrégulier, ère, a. (-èrement, ad.) irregular(ly).　　　　　　[ligious(ly).
irréligieux, se, a. (-sement, ad.) irreremédiable, a. (-ment, ad.) irremediable, irretrievable || irremediably.
irrémissible, a. (-ment, ad.) irremissible || irremissibly.
irréparable, a. (-ment, ad.) irreparable, irretrievable || irreparably, irretrievably.
irrépréhensible, a. (-ment, ad.) blameless, faultless || irreprehensibly.
irréprochable, a. (-ment, ad.) irreproachable, unexceptionable || irreproachably.

irrésistibilité, f. irresistibility.
irrésistible, a. (-ment, ad.) irresistible || irresistibly.
irrésolu, e, a. (-ement, ad.) irresolute(ly).
irrespectueux, se, a. (-sement, ad.) disrespectful(ly).
irresponsable, a. irresponsible.
irrévérencieux, se, a. disrespectful.
irrévocabilité, f. irrevocableness.
irrévocable, a. (-ment, ad.) irrevocable || irrevocably.
irrigateur, m. watering-engine, gardenengine || injecting apparatus || enema.
irritabilité, f. irritability.
irriter, v. a. to irritate, to exasperate, to anger, to excite || s'~, to fly into a passion.
irruption, f. irruption || (com.) run.
isabelle, a. light bay, dun.
ischiatique, a. (an.) ischiatic.
isolé, e, a. (-ment, ad.) isolated, lonely || solitarily.　　　　　　　　　[tude.
isolement, m. retirement, loneliness, solitude.
isoler, v. a. to insulate || to isolate, to detach, to separate || s'~, to live lonely, to shun society.
issu, e, a. sprung, descended, born,
issue, f. issue, egress, outlet.
isthme, m. isthmus.
italique, m. italic letter.
italique, a. italic.
item, m. item.
item, ad. item, also.
itinéraire, m. itinerary.
itinéraire, a. itinerary.
ivoire, f. ivory.
ivraie, f. tare || (bot.) darnel.
ivre, a. inebriated, intoxicated, fuddled.
ivre-mort, a. dead drunk.
ivresse, f. intoxication, drunkenness || frenzy.
ivrogne, esse, m. & f. drunkard.
ivrogne, a. drunken.
ivrognerie, f. drunkenness.

J.

jabot, m. crop || (de chemise) frill.
jaboter, v. a. to jabber, to prattle.
jacasse, f. chatter-box.
jacasse, a. chattering.
jacasser, v. n. to chatter like a mag-pie.
jacent, a. a. (jur.) in abeyance.
jachère, f. fallow || fallow-ground.
jacinthe, f. (bot.) hyacinth.
Jacobin, m. Jacobin.
jaconas, m. jaconet.
Jacques, m.; Maître ~, Jack-of-all-trades.
jactance, f. boasting, bragging.
jaculatoire, a. ejaculatory.
jadis, ad. of old, formerly.
jaillir, v. n. to spout out, to spurt out || to burst out.　　　　　　　　　[out.
jaillissement, m. spouting out, gushing
jais, m. jet.
jalon, m. pole, stake || landmark.

jalonner, v. a. to stick poles in the ground, to mark || to plant landmarks.

jalouser, v. a. to envy, to be jealous.

jalousie, f. jealousy, envy, enviousness || uneasiness || Venetian blind.

jaloux, se, a. jealous, envious.

jamais, ad. ever || ne ~, never || à ~, à tout ~, for ever and ever || au grand ~, never || pour ~, for ever.

jambage, m. jamb, side-post || stroke.

jambe, f. leg, shank || os de la ~, shin-bone || à toutes —s, at full speed.

jambette, f. small pocket-knife || (mar.) stem-timber || (mar.) bracket || (arch.) jamb.

jambé, e, a. ankled || legged.

jambière, f. armour for the leg.

jambon, m. ham, gammon.

jambonneau, m. small ham.

janissaire, m. janissary.

jansénisme, m. Jansenism.

jante, f. felly (of a wheel).

janvier, m. January.

jappement, m. yelping.

japper, v. n. to yelp.

jaquemart, m. Jack (of the clock).

jaquette, f. jacket, short coat || child's coat.

jardin, m. garden || ~ potager, kitchen-garden || ~ des plantes, botanical garden.

jardinage, m. gardening.

jardiner, v. n. to garden.

jardinet, m. small garden.

jardinier, m. gardener.

jardinière, f. female gardener, gardener's wife || flower-stand || mixed carrots and turnips || à la ~, dressed with various vegetables.

jargonner, v. a. & n. to talk jargon ou gibberish.

jarnac, m. small poniard || coup de Jarnac, m. treacherous blow ou stroke.

jarre, f. (water-)jar.

jarret, m. ham, knuckle || shin || elasticity ou strength in the legs.

jarretière, f. garter.

jars, m. gander.   [to chatter, to blab.

jaser, v. n. to prattle, to prate, to tattle,

jaserie, f. chattering, prattling.   [terer.

jaseur, se, m. & f. blab, prattler, chat-

jasmin, m. jasmine, jessamine.

jaspe, m. jasper.

jaspé, e, a. streaked, veined, marbled.

jasper, v. a. to marble.

jaspure, f. marbling.

jatte, f. wooden bowl, platter.

jattée, f. bowlful.

jauge, f. gauge || (mar.) tonnage.

jaugeage, m. gauging.

jauger, v. a. to gauge.

jaugeur, m. gauger.

jaunâtre, a. yellowish.

jaune, m. yellow colour || yolk (of an egg).

jaune, a. yellow.

jaunet, m. (bot.) buttercup || (coin) yellow-boy.

jaunir, v. a. & n. to make yellow, to grow yellow, to dye yellow || to ripen || to wither.

jaunissant, e, a. turning yellow, ripening.

jaunisse, f. (méd.) jaundice.   [dry.

javeler, v. a. to lay corn in small heaps to

javeline, f. javelin, spear.

javelle, f. small heap of corn laid to dry || faggot of vine-branches.

javelot, m. short javelin.

je, j', pn. I.

jectisses, a. f. pl. earth that has been re-moved from another place || stones laid [by hand.

Jéhovah, f. Jehovah.

Jérémiade, f. jeremiad || faiseur de —s,   [croaker.

jésuite, m. Jesuit.

jésuitique, a. jesuitical.

Jésus, m. long royal || grand ~, imperial.

jet, m. throw, cast, fling || shoot, sprig || ray || ~ d'eau, waterspout || fountain.

jetée, f. mole, pier, jetty.

jeter, v. a. & n. to throw (away, out, down) || to cast, to hurl, to fling, to shoot || to toss || to strike || to shed || to utter || to suppurate, to run || to swarm || to fetch || to lay || se ~, to throw oneself, to fling oneself, to fall ou rush upon || to be thrown away.

jeton, m. counter || (fig.) brass shilling.

jeu, m. play, game, gaming, sport, per-formance of an actor ou musician || de bon ~, fairly || bon ~ bon argent, in right earnest || ~ de cartes, game at cards || pack of cards || ~ de boule, bowling-green || ~ d'esprit, witticism || ~ de hasard, game of chance || ~ de mots, pun, quibble || ~ de paume, ten-nis-court || ~ de bourse, stock-jobbing || jouer gros ~, to play high || mettre en ~, to stake.

jeudi, m. Thursday || ~ Saint, Maundy-Thursday || ~ gras, Shrove-Thursday.

à jeun, ad. fasting || having not yet break-fasted.

jeune, a. young, youthful || green, not ripe.

jeûne, m. fast, fasting.

jeûner, v. n. to fast.   [people.

jeunesse, f. youth, youthfulness, young

jeunet, te, a. very young.

jeûneur, se, m. & f. faster.

joaillerie, f. jewelry || jeweller's trade.

joaillier, ère, m. & f. jeweller.

jobard, m. ninny.

jobarderie, f. silliness.

jocrisse, m. simpleton.

joie, f. joy, joyfulness, gladness, mirth.

joignant, e, a. next to, joining, bordering upon.

joindre, v. a. ir. to join, to put together, to unite, to connect, to meet, to overtake || to close, to adhere.

joint, m. joint, seam.

joint, e, a. joined, united || ci-~, herewith, annexed.

jointé, e, a. legged.

jointée, f. double handful.

jointure, f. joint || juncture.

joli, e, a. pretty, neat, pleasing, genteel || -ment, ad. prettily, nicely || famously.

joliet, te, a. rather pretty.   [keeper.

jonc, m. rush || Malacca cane || plain ring ||

jonchaie, f. rush-bed.

jonchée, f. branches, flowers, herbs ou reeds strewed on the ground (pl.).

joncher, v. a. to strew, to spread over.

jonchets, m. pl. spellicans (game).

jonction, f. junction.

jongler, v. n. to juggle.

jonglerie, f. juggle, juggling.

jongleur, m. juggler.

jonque, m. junk (Chinese vessel).

jonquille, f. jonquil.

jouable, a. fit to be acted.

jouailler, v. n. to play for a trifle.

joubarbe, f. houseleek.

joue, f. cheek.

jouer, v. a. & n. to play, to sport, to perform || to game || to counterfeit, to deceive || ~ gros jeu, to play high ou deep || se ~, to play, to sport, to amuse oneself, to make a jest of || to baffle || to meddle with || to be played at || to be acted.   [dupe.

jouet, m. plaything, jest, laughing-stock ||

joueur, m. gamester, player, gambler || performer || musician.

joufflu, e, a. chub-faced.

joug, m. yoke.

jouir, v. n. to enjoy, to possess || to use.

jouissance, f. enjoyment, possession || use || luxury.

joujou, m. plaything, toy.

jour, m. day, daylight, light || opening, window || ~s, pl. life || de ~ à autre, from day to day || à ~, open, openly || ~ de l'an, New Year's day || ~ des Rois, Twelfth-day || ~ gras, flesh-day || ~ maigre, fast day || ~ de fête, festival || faux ~, bad light, false appearance.

journal, m. journal, diary, newspaper || day-book.

journalier, m. day-labourer.

journalier, ère, a. daily || changeable.

journaliste, m. journalist.   [inconstant.

journée, f. day, day's work || day's pay ou gain || day's journey || battle || à la ~, by the day || à grandes ~s, by forced marches || à petites ~s, by short stages || homme de ~, day-labourer.

journellement, ad. daily.

joute, f. joust, tilt, tournament || ~ sur l'eau, naumachy.   [dispute.

jouter, v. n. to joust, to tilt, to fight || to

jouteur, m. tilter || antagonist.

jouvence, f. youth.

jouvenceau, m. (fam.) young man.

jouvencelle, f. (fam.) lass, young girl.

jovial, e, a. (-ement, ad.) jovial(ly) || merry.

joyau, m. jewel, gem, locket.

joyouseté, f. jest, joke.

joyeux, se, a. (-sement, ad.) joyful(ly) || cheerful(ly) || glad, merry || merrily.

jubilaire, a. of jubilee.

jubilation, f. jollification || festivity.

jubilé, m. jubilee.

jubiler, v. n. to be joyful, to exult.

jucher, v. n. (se ~), to roost, to perch.

juchoir, m. roosting-place, perch.

judaïque, a. Judaic, Jewish.

judaïser, v. n. to judaise.

judaïsme, m. Judaism.

judas, m. peep-hole.

judicature, f. judicature.

judiciaire, f. judgment.

judiciaire, a. (-ment, ad.) judicial(ly).

judicieux, se, a. (-sement, ad.) judicious(ly).

juge, m. judge || justice || ~ d'instruction, examining magistrate || ~ de paix, Justice of the Peace.

jugement, m. judgment, understanding, sentence || ~ dernier, day of judgment || jour du ~, Doomsday.

juger, v. a. & n. to judge, to discern, to distinguish, to try, to pass sentence || to conjecture, to think, to suppose, to imagine || se ~, to judge ou think oneself || to be tried ou heard.

juguler, v. a. (fam.) to choke || to vex.

juif, ve, m. & f. Jew || Jewess.

juif, ve, a. Jewish.

juillet, m. July.

juin, m. June.   [ward.

juiverie, f. jewry || Jew's trick || Jews'

jujube, f. jujube.

jujubier, m. (bot.) jujube-tree, lotus-tree.

julienne, f. vegetable soup.

jumeau, elle, m. & f. twin.

jumeau, elle, a. twin.   [cheek.

jumelle, f. twin || double opera-glass ||

jument, f. mare.

jungle, m. jungle.

junte, f. junta, council.

jupe, f. petticoat || skirt.

jupon, m. under-petticoat.

juratoire, a. juratory, sworn.

juré, e, m. juryman, juror.

jurement, m. oath, swearing.

jurer, v. a. & n. to swear, to declare, to curse, to blaspheme || to contrast || to clash, to jar.

jureur, m. swearer.

juridiction, f. jurisdiction.

juridique, m. juridical.

juridique, a. (-ment, ad.) juridical(ly).

jurisconsulte, m. jurisconsult, lawyer.

jurisprudence, f. jurisprudence.

juriste, m. jurist.

juron, m. favourite oath || curse.

jury, m. jury, board.

jus, m. juice || gravy.

jusant, m. reflux, ebb, ebb-tide.

jusque, pr. until, till, to, as far as || jusqu'ici, hitherto || jusqu'à present, till now, hitherto || jusqu'à quand? how long? || jusqu'où? how far?

jusquiame, f. henbane.

juste, a. just, equitable, impartial, right, accurate || -ment, au ~, ad. justly, exactly, precisely || exactly right, to the point || ~-milieu, m. moderate party || "the golden mean."

justesse, f. justness, exactness, accuracy, correctness.

justice, f. justice, right || jurisdiction || court of justice || law officers (pl.) || judicial authorities (pl.) || rendre ~ à, to do justice to.

justiciable, a. amenable || devenir le ~ de, to come under the jurisdiction of.

justicier, m. justiciary, judge.

justificatif, ve, a. justificative || documentary.

justifier, v. a. to justify, to vindicate, to exculpate, to verify, to prove, to demonstrate.

jute, m. jute || fil de ~, jute yarn.

juteux, se, a. juicy.

juvenil, e, a. juvenile, youthful.

juxtaposer, v. a. to place side by side.

juxtaposition, f. juxtaposition.

K.

kakatoès, m. cockatoo.

kaléidoscope, m. kaleidoscope.

kanguroo, m. kangaroo.

kaolin, m. (min.) kaolin, China-clay.

keepsake, m. keepsake.

képi, m. military cap.

kermesse, f. parish fair.

kilogramme, m. kilogramme, a thousand grammes (somewhat more than 2 English pounds' weight).   [metres).

kilomètre, m. kilometre (a thousand

kiosque, m. kiosk || news-stall.

knout, m. knout.

kopeck, m. copeck (Russian coin).

kyrielle, f. long and tiresome enumeration || legend.

kyste, m. (méd.) vide cyste.

L.

l' (before on only euphonic) = le.

la, m. (mus.) A || la.

la, art. f. the.

la, pn. her, it || ~ ~, so so, pretty well.

là, ad. there || par ~, by that || ça et ~, par ci par ~, here and there || ~ haut, there above || de ~, thence || dès ~, from that time || jusque-~, so far.

labeur, m. labour, work || toil.

labial, e, a. labial.

laboratoire, m. laboratory.

laborieux, se, a. (~sement, ad.) laborious(ly) || assiduous, sedulous, industrious || hard-working.

labour, m. tillage, ploughing || terres de ~, f. pl. ploughed lands (pl.).

labourable, a. arable.

labourage, m. tillage || husbandry.

labourer, v. a. & n. to till, to plough || to rip || to toil || to drudge || to drag.

laboureur, m. ploughman, husbandman.

labyrinthe, m. labyrinth, maze.

lac, m. lake.

lacer, v. a. to lace.

lacérer, v. a. to lacerate.   [snares (pl.).

lacet, m. lace || springe || braid || -s, pl.

lâche, m. coward.

lâche, a. (~ment, ad.) loose, slack || cowardly || lazy, effeminate || villanous || sluggishly.

lâcher, v. a. & n. to slacken, to unbend, to relax, to let loose, to loose, to abandon, to turn on || to discharge || to give, to slip || to let slip || se ~, to slacken || to get loose || to give utterance || to go off.

lâcheté, f. laxity, slackness || cowardice, cowardliness.

lacis, m. network.

laconique, a. (~ment, ad.) laconic(ally) || brief(ly) || concise(ly).

laconisme, m. laconism.

lacrymal, e, a. lachrymal.

lacs, m. pl. string, snare, noose || knot.

lacté, e, a. lacteal, lacteous, milky || voie -e, f. milky way.   [tion.

lacune, f. gap, deficiency, void, interruplacustre, a. lacustrine.

ladite, f. the said, the same, ditto.

ladre, esse, m. & f. leper || stingy fellow, curmudgeon.

ladre, a. leprous || stingy || unfeeling || measled.   [house.

ladrerie, f. leprosy || stinginess || lazarlagune, f. lagoon.

lai, m. layman.

lai, e, a. lay, clerical.

laiche, f. sedge.

laid, e, a. ugly || naughty || deformed.

laideron, f. ugly girl.

laideur, f. ugliness, deformity.

laie, f. wild sow || lane through a forest.

lainage, m. woollen goods (pl.) || napping || teasing.   [woollen.

laine, f. wool || ~ filée, worsted || de ~,

lainer, v. a. to card (wool).

lainerie, f. woollen goods (pl.) || woolmarket.

laineur, se, m. & f. teaseler.

laineuse, f. gig (machine for carding).

laineux, se, a. woolly, fleecy.

lainier, m. wool-stapler || wool-worker.

laïque, m. layman.

laïque, a. lay, laical.

laisse, f. leash || string || slip.

laisser, v. a. to leave, to let, to forsake, to abandon, to desert || to bequeath, to suffer || to resign || to commit || se ~, to let ou suffer oneself || to be worth || se ~ aller, to let oneself go || to be careless of one's personal appearance || to indulge || to be easily influenced || se ~ aller, m. ease, easiness, freeness, unconstraint || se ~ passer, m. pass, permit.

lait, m. milk || (of eggs) white || ~ coupé, milk mixed with water || ~ de poule, eggflip || petit ~, whey || frère de ~, m. fosterbrother || cochon de ~, m. sucking-pig || vache à ~, f. milch-cow || dents de ~, m. pl. the first teeth that children get (pl.).

laitage, m. milk-food.

laitance, laite, f. soft roe, milt.

laité, e, a. soft-roed.

laiterie, f. dairy, milk-shop, milk-trade.

laitron, m. (bot.) sow-thistle, hare's-lettuce.

laiteux, se, a. milky.

laitier, m. dairyman || dross.

laitière, f. milk-woman, milkmaid || milch-cow.   [brass-wire.

laiton, m. latten, brass || fil de ~, m.

laitue, f. (bot.) lettuce.

laize, f. width (of manufactured stuffs).

lamaneur, m. coasting pilot.

lambeau, m. rag, tatter || shred || scrap.

lambin, m. sluggish person, loiterer || slowcoach.

lambin, e, a. tedious, tardy || loitering.
lambiner, v. n. to loiter || to linger || to
lambourde, f. joist.   [lag.
lambrequin, m. scallop.
lambris, m. ceiling, wainscot.
lambrissage, m. ceiling, wainscoting.
lambrisser, v. a. to wainscot || to panel.
lame, f. blade || sheet || plate || wire || sword ||
lamé, e, a. laminated.   [wave.
lamentable, a. (–ment, ad.) lamentable ||
. lamentably || mournful(ly).
lamentation, f. lamentation, bewailing.
lamenter, v. a. to lament, to mourn, to
bewail.   [ing.
laminage, m. laminating, flattening, roll-
laminer, v. a. to flatten (metals).
laminerie, f. flatting-mill.
laminoir, m. laminating ou flatting-
machine, flattening-mill.
lampadaire, m. lamp-bearer, sconce.
lampas, m. figured silk.
lampe, f. lamp.
lampée, f. tumblerful (of drink).
lamper, v. n. to guzzle || to quaff.
lamperon, m. socket of a lamp, wick-
holder.
lampion, m. illumination-lamp.
lampiste, m. lamp-maker || lamp-lighter.
lamproie, f. lamprey.   [portfire.stick.
lance, f. lance, spear || lancet || – à feu,
lancer, v. a. to fling, to dart, to hurl, to
cast, to throw || to issue || to shoot forth ||
to start || to push || to launch || se –, to
rush upon, to shoot || to venture || to
lancette, f. lancet.   [chance it.
lancier, m. lancer.
lancinant, e, a. shooting || **douleur.–e,**
f. shooting pains (pl.).
landau, m. landau.
lande, f. heath, moor.
langage, m. language || style.
lange, m. swaddling-clothes (pl.).
langoureux, se, a. (–sement, ad.)
languishing(ly) || pining.
langouste, f. large lobster.
langue, f. tongue || speech, language, idiom ||
– de terre, neck of land || coup de –,
backbiting, slander || jeter sa – aux
chiens, to give it up || prendre –, to
get intelligence.   [(mus.) key.
languette, f. tongue || index (of a balance)
langueur, f. languor, faintness, feebleness ||
decline || dullness.
languier, m. smoked pig's-tongue.
languir, v. n. to languish, to linger, to
pine away, to droop || to sigh for.
languissamment, ad. languishingly.
languissant, e, a. languishing, lingering,
pining, languid, faint, feeble.
lanier, m. lanner || shrike (bird).
lanière, f. thong.
lansquenet, m. lansquenet.
lanterne, f. lantern || lantern-tower || sky-
light || flash-pipe || –s, pl. nonsense, trifles ||
– sourde, dark lantern || – magique,
magic-lantern.
lanterner, v. a. & n. to play the fool, to
talk nonsense, to trifle, to dilly-dally || to
bamboozle.

lanternerie, f. idle stories (pl.), nonsensical stuff, trifling.
lanternier, m. lantern-maker, lamp-
lighter || trifler.
laper, v. a. to lap, to lick up.
lapereau, m. young rabbit.
lapidaire, m. lapidary.
lapidaire, a. lapidary.
lapider, v. a. to stone to death || to pelt.
lapin, m. rabbit || coney || famous fellow.
lapine, f. doe rabbit.
lapis-lazuli, m. (min.) lapis-lazuli.
laps, m. lapse.   [petit –, foot-boy.
laquais, m. lackey, footman || flunkey
laque, f. lac, lake, gum-lac || – en feuilles,
shellac.
laque, m. lacquer || japan || lacquer-work ||
lacquered piece of furniture || lacquered
ware.   [lake-coloured.
laqueux, se, a. of gum-lac, like lac ||
laquelle, pn. who, which, that.
laquer, v. a. to lacquer.
larcin, m. larceny, theft, pilfering, robbery.
lard, m. bacon || pig's-fat.
larder, v. a. to lard, to bacon.
lardoire, f. larding-pin.
lardon, m. small slice of bacon, lardoon ||
lare, m. household god.   [rub, jeer, jest.
large, m. breadth, wideness || open sea ||
au –, at large || (mar.) keep off! || au
long et au –, far and wide.
large, a. (–ment, ad.) large(ly) || wide,
broad || liberal(ly) || copious(ly).
largesse, f. liberality.
largeur, f. breadth, width || (rail.) gauge.
larguer, v. a. (mar.) to let loose, to loosen,
to let go, to let run.
larigot, m. flute || flageolet || boire à
tire-–, (fam.) to booze.
larme, f. tear, drop || – batavique, glass-
drop || pleurer à chaudes –s, to weep
bitterly.   [stone.
larmier, m. eaves, drip of a house, drip-
larmoiement, m. watering of the eyes.
larmoyant, e, a. weeping, in tears ||
pathetic.
larmoyer, v. a. to weep.
larron, nesse, m. & f. thief, female thief.
larve, f. larva.
laryngite, f. (méd.) laryngitis.
las, se, a. tired, weary.
lascif, ve, a. (–vement, ad.) lascivious
(ly) || lewd(ly).   [libidinousness.
lascivité, f. lasciviousness, lewdness,
lassant, e, a. tiresome, wearisome.
lasser, v. a. to tire, to weary, to fatigue ||
se –, to grow tired.
latanier, m. (bot.) palm-tree of Mauritius.
latent, e, a. latent, hidden.
latéral, e, a. (–ement, ad.) lateral(ly) ||
sideways.   [dog-Latin.
latin, m. theLatin language || – de cuisine,
latin, e, a. Latin || (mar.) lateen.
latiniser, v. a. to latinise.
latinisme, m. latinism.
latiniste, m. latinist.
latinité, f. latinity.
latitude, f. latitude || climate || freedom.
latitudinaire, m. latitudinarian.

latrines, f. pl. water-closet, privy.
latte, f. lath, shingle.
latter, v. a. to lath.
lattis, m. lath-work.
lauréat, m. prizeman || laureate.
lauréat, a. laureate.
lauréole, m. spurge-laurel.
laurier, m. (bot.) laurel, bay-tree || (fig.)
  glory || ~-rose, rose-laurel || ~-tin,
  laurustine.
lavabo, m. washhand-stand.
lavage, m. washing || slop.
lavande, f. (bot.) lavender. [wagtail (bird).
lavandière, f. washerwoman || water-
lavasse, f. slop, washy mess.
lave, f. lava.
lavé, e, a. washed || (of colours) light.
lavement, m. washing, wash || clyster.
laver, v. a. to wash, to clean || to absolve.
lavette, f. dish-cloth.   [selle, scullion.
laveur, se, m. & f. washer || ~ de vais-
lavis, m. wash, colouring.
lavoir, m. wash-house, sink, scullery.
lavure, f. hogwash, dish-water.
laxatif, m. (méd.) laxative.
laxatif, ve, a. (méd.) laxative.
layer, v. a. to cut a path through a forest.
layetier, m. box-maker, packing-case
layette, f. baby-linen.   [maker.
lazaret, m. lazaretto, pest-house.
lazzi, m. buffoonery || jest.
le, art. m. the.
lé, m. breadth (of cloth).
lèche, f. collop, thin slice.
lèchefrite, f. dripping-pan.
lécher, v. a. to lick || to polish || to finish.
leçon, f. lesson || lecture || reading.
lecteur, trice, m. & f. lecturer, reader.
lecture, f. reading || perusal || cabinet de
  ~, reading-room || en ~, in hand, out.
ledit, m. the said || the same || ditto.
ledit, a. the said || the same || ditto.
légal, e, a. (-ement, ad.) legal(ly) || law-
  ful(ly) || (méd.) forensic.
légaliser, v. a. to legalise.
légalité, f. legality.
légat, m. legate.
légataire, m. & f. legatee.
légation, f. legation, legateship.
lège, a. (mar.) light.
légendaire, m. writer of legends.
légende, f. legend.
léger, ère, a. light, not heavy, nimble ||
  active, slight, fickle || trifling || airy ||
  light-headed || de ~, lightly || à la légère,
  lightly, thinly || rashly, inconsiderately.
légèrement, ad. lightly, swiftly, nimbly ||
  inconsiderately.
légèreté, f. levity, lightness, swiftness,
  nimbleness || slight fault || thoughtlessness ||
  act of levity.
légionnaire, m. legionary soldier || Knight
  of the Legion of Honour.   [legislatress.
législateur, trice, m. & f. legislator ||
législateur, trice, a. legislating.
législatif, ve, a. legislative.
législation, f. legislation, law-giving.
légiste, m. lawyer.
légitimation, f. legitimation || recognition.

légitime, a. (-ment, ad.) legitimate(ly) ||
  lawful(ly) || rightful(ly).   [to justify.
légitimer, v. a. to legitimate || to recognise ||
légitimiste, m. legitimist.
légitimité, f. legitimacy, lawfulness, right-
legs, m. legacy.   [fulness.
léguer, v. a. to leave, to bequeath, to devise.
légume, m. vegetable, greens (pl.);
légumier, m. vegetable-dish.
légumineux, se, a. leguminous.
légumiste, m. & f. vegetarian.
lendemain, m. next day, morrow.
lendore, m. humdrum.
lénitif, ve, a. lenitive, emollient.
lent, e, a. (-ement, ad.) slow(ly) || tardy.
lente, f. nit.
lenteur, f. slowness, tardiness.
lenticulaire, a. lenticular.   [freckles.
lentille, f. lentil || lens || ball, bob || ~s, pl.
lentilleux, se, a. freckled.
lentisque, m. (bot.) lentisk, mastic.
léonin, e, a. leonine.
léopard, m. leopard.
lèpre, f. leprosy.
lépreux, se, m. & f. leper.
lépreux, se, a. leprous.
léproserie, f. hospital for the leprous.
lequel, pn. which, who, that, whom.
les, art. pl. de le, la.
lèse-majesté, f. high treason.
léser, v. a. to wrong, to injure.
lésine, f. stinginess.   [dealing.
lésiner, v. a. to be stingy, to chaffer in
lésinerie, f. stinginess || mean action.
lésineux, se, a. stingy.
lésion, f. wrong, damage, hurt.
lesse, f. hat-band.
lessive, f. lye, lye-washing.
lessiver, v. a. to wash in lye.
lest, m. (mar.) ballast.
lestage, m. (mar.) ballasting.
leste, a. nimble, brisk || free || -ment, ad.
  smartly, nimbly, cleverly || freely.
lester, v. a. (mar.) to ballast.
lesteur, m. ballast-lighter.
léthargie, f. lethargy.
léthargique, a. lethargic.
lettre, f. letter, hand-writing || type, print ||
  ~s patentes, f. pl. patent, letters patent
  (pl.) || à la ~, literally || ~ à cheval, sharp
  letter || ~ de créance, credentials (pl.) ||
  ~ de change, bill of exchange || ~ de
  cachet, arbitrary warrant, lettre-de-cachet
  || ~ recommandée, registered letter || ~
  de voiture, way-bill || homme de -s,
  literary man || belles -s, polite literature.
lettré, e, a. lettered, literate || learned.
lettrine, f. reference || heading.   [literary.
leur, pn. m. & f. pl. their, to them || le ~,
  la ~, les -s, theirs.
leurre, m. lure, enticement.
leurrer, v. a. to lure, to decoy.
levain, m. leaven, yeast, ferment.
levant, m. East || Levant.
levant, e, a. rising.
levé, e, a. raised, lifted up, erect.
levée, f. crop, gathering (of fruits), harvest ||
  bank, causeway || rising, breaking up ||
  levy || removal || trick (at cards).

lever, m. levee || rising || au ~ du soleil, at sunrise.
lever, v. a. & n. to lift, to lift up, to heave, to raise up, to gather || to take off, to take away || to levy || to grow up || se ~, to get up, to rise || to begin to blow.
levier, m. lever || crowbar.
lévitique, a. Levitical.
levraut, m. leveret.
lèvre, f. lip || ~ inférieure, under lip || ~ supérieure, upper lip.
levrette, f. greyhound-bitch || lap-dog.
lévrier, m. greyhound.
levure, f. yeast, barm.
lexicographe, m. lexicographer.
lexique, m. lexicon.
lézard, m. lizard.
lézarde, f. crevice, crack.
se lézarder, to crack, to split.
liais, m. hard freestone.
liaison, f. binding, joining, union, connexion, correspondence, relation, affinity || entanglement.
liane, m. (bot.) tropical creeper.
liant, m. affability || sociability.
liant, e, a. courteous, complaisant, gentle, mild.
liard, m. farthing. [mild.
liarder, v. n. to be sordidly stingy || to haggle.
liasse, f. file || bundle of papers.
libation, f. libation.
libelle, m. libel, lampoon.
libelliste, m. libeller.
libellule, f. dragon-fly.
libéral, e, a. (-ement, ad.) liberal(ly).
libéralisme, m. liberalism || liberals.
libéralité, f. liberality, generosity.
libérateur, trice, m. & f. liberator, deliverer. [exemption.
libération, f. deliverance, discharge ||
libérer, v. a. to free, to rid, to exempt || se ~, to pay one's debts, to clear one's engagements.
libertaire, m. partisan of the anarchists.
liberté, f. liberty, freedom || ~ d'esprit, freedom of the mind || leisure. [truant.
libertin, a. libertine, licentious || idle,
libertinage, m. libertinism, debauchery.
libertiner, v. n. to lead a dissolute life.
libraire, m. bookseller || ~-éditeur, publisher.
librairie, f. book-trade || bookseller's shop.
libre, a. (-ment, ad.) free(ly) || at liberty || unrestrained || licentious || unbecoming, indiscreet, bold || unstamped || open || ~-échange, m. free-trade || ~-échangiste, m. free-trader.
lice, f. list || warp || tilt-yard.
licence, f. licence || licentiousness || degree of licentiate. [Master-of-Arts.
licencié, m. licentiate || -ès-lettres,
licenciement, m. disbanding of soldiers.
licencier, v. a. to disband soldiers.
licencieux, se, a. (-sement, ad.) licentious(ly).
licite, a. (-ment, ad.) lawful(ly).
licorne, f. unicorn.
licou, m. halter, cord.
licteur, m. lictor.

lie, f. lees (pl.), dregs (pl.), grounds (pl.) ||
lié, e, a. tied, united || intimate. [refuse.
liège, m. cork, cork-tree || bouchon de ~, m. cork. [chains (pl.).
lien, m. band, tie, bond, rope || ~s, pl.
lier, v. a. to tie, to bind, to fasten, to unite || se ~, to bind oneself, to enter into a league with, to grow thick, to thicken. [ground-ivy.
lierre, m. (bot.) ivy || ~-terrestre,
liesse, f. joy, mirth.
lieu, m. place, room || cause, reason || -x, pl. premises (pl.) || (~ d'aisance) water-closet || au ~ de, instead of, in place of.
lieue, f. league.
lieur, m. binder.
lieutenance, f. lieutenancy.
lieutenant, m. lieutenant.
lièvre, m. hare || bec de ~, hare-lip.
ligament, m. (an.) ligament, sinew.
lige, m. liege, vassal.
lige, a. liege, vassal.
lignage, m. lineage.
ligne, f. line || path || way || rank || fishing-line || à la ~, in a new line.
ligneux, se, a. ligneous, woody.
ligue, f. league. [to league.
liguer, v. a. to unite in a league || se ~,
ligueur, m. leaguer.
lilas, m. (bot.) lilac.
limace, f. slug, slug-snail.
limaçon, m. snail || escalier en ~, m. spiral staircase.
limaille, f. filings (pl.), file-dust.
limande, f. mud-fish, dab || (mar.) parcel-
limbe, m. limb || ~s, pl. limbo. [ling.
lime, f. file.
limer, v. a. to file, to polish.
limier, m. limehound || spy.
limite, f. limit, boundary, extremity.
limiter, v. a. to limit || to restrain.
limitrophe, a. bordering upon || neighbouring. [shaft (of a cart).
limon, m. lemon, citron || mud, slime ||
limonade, f. lemonade.
limonadier, m., ère, f. lemonade maker ou seller || maid at a coffee-house || coffee-house keeper.
limoneux, se, a. slimy. [horse.
limonier, m. (bot.) lime-tree || shaft-
limonière, f. shaft of a coach.
limousin, m. rough-waller.
limousine, f. waggoner's cloak.
limousinage, m. rough-walling.
limpide, a. limpid, clear.
limpidité, f. limpidness, clearness.
limure, f. filing || filings (pl.). [seed.
lin, m. (bot.) flax || graine de ~, f. lin-
linceul, m. winding-sheet, shroud.
linéaire, a. linear.
linge, m. linen || cloth.
linger, m., ère, f. linendraper || hosier || needlewoman || wardrobe-keeper || seam-stress. [wash-house.
lingerie, f. linendrapery, linen-trade ||
lingot, m. ingot, wedge.
lingotière, f. ingot-mould.
linguiste, m. linguist.
linguistique, f. philology.

linier, ière, a. of flax, flaxen.

linière, f. flax-plantation, flax-field.

linon, m. lawn.   [brained person.

linot, m. cock-linnet || **tête de ~,** f. hare-

linotte, f. hen-linnet.

linteau, m. lintel.

lion, ne, m. & f. lion || lioness || dandy, beau || woman of fashion.

lionceau, m. lion's whelp.

lippe, f. blobber-lip.

lippu, e, a. thick-lipped.

liquéfier, v. a. to liquefy.

liqueur, f. liquor || liquid || spirit || cordial || lusciousness, sweetness || **ce vin a trop de ~,** that wine is too sweet.

liquidation, f. liquidation || settlement ||

liquide, m. liquid || spirit.   [selling off.

liquide, a. liquid || clear.

liquider, v. a. to liquidate || to sell off.

liquoreux, se, a. luscious, sweet.

liquoriste, m. dealer in spirituous liquors.

lire, v. a. ir. to read, to peruse.

lis, m. (bot.) lily || border (of sail-cloth).

lisérage, m. purfling.

liséré, m. embroidering, border.

lisérer, v. a. to embroider, to border.

liseron, m. (bot.) bind-weed.

liseur, se, m. & f. reader.   [legibly.

lisible, a. legible, readable || **-ment,** ad.

lisière, f. list (of cloth), selvage || border, skirt || leading-strings (pl.).

lisse, f. handrail || riband || warp.

lisse, a. sleek, smooth, glossy.

lisser, v. a. to polish, to smoothe, to gloss.

lissoir, m. polisher.

liste, f. list, roll || panel.

lit, m. bed || bedstead || berth || layer || channel || marriage || direction || **~ de douleur,** sick-bed || **~ de parade,** state-bed || **~ de repos,** couch || **~ à roulettes,** truckle-bed || **~ brisé, ~ de camp,** field-bed || **~ en forme d'armoire,** press-bed || **~ de bourre,** flock-bed || **~ de sangle,** folding-bed || **~ à quenouilles, ~ à colonnes,** four-post bed || **~ de veille,** pallet-bed.

litanie, f. endless story || **-s,** pl. litany.

liteau, m. blue stripe (on napkins).

litée, f. lair, haunt.

literie, f. bedding.

lithographe, m. lithographer.

lithographie, f. lithography || lithograph || lithographic printing-office.

lithographier, v. n. to lithograph.

lithographique, a. lithographic.

litière, f. litter, straw.

litige, m. (jur.) litigation, suit at law || issue.

litigieux, se, a. litigious.

litorne, f. field-fare (bird).   [English].

litre, m. litre (somewhat more than 1½ pint

littéraire, a. literary.

littéral, e, a. (-ement, ad.) literal(ly).

littérateur, m. literary man.

littérature, f. literature.

littoral, m. coast, littoral.

littoral, e, a. littoral.

liturgie, f. liturgy.

liure, f. cart-rope, rope.

livide, a. livid, black and blue.

lividité, f. lividness.   [piece || number.

livraison, f. delivery (of goods) || part ||

livre, m. book || **grand ~,** (com.) ledger || **~ classique,** school-book || standard-book || **~ f.** pound || franc.

livrée, f. livery, livery servants (pl.) || marks (pl.) || colours (pl.).

livrer, v. a. to deliver, to give up || to abandon || to betray || to devote.

livresque, a. relating to books.

livret, m. small book || depositor's book || book of the play || multiplication-table, certificate.   [cusp.

lobe, m. (an.) lobe || ear-lap || (arch.) foil ||

local, m. locality || premises (pl.).

local, e, a. local.

localité, f. locality, place.

locataire, m. tenant, lodger || lessee.

location, f. letting out || hiring || renting.

loch, m. (mar.) log || table de ~, f. log-book.

loche, f. loach, groundling (fish).

locher, v. n. to be loose.

lochies, f. pl. (phys.) lochia (pl.), lochial cleansings (pl.).

locomobile, f. portable steam-engine.

locomoteur, trice, a. (an.) of locomotion.

locomotif, ve, a. locomotive.

locomotion, f. locomotion.

locomotive, f. locomotive engine.

locution, f. locution, form of speech, manner of speaking.

lof, m. (mar.) loof, weather-side of a ship.

lofer, v. n. (mar.) to luff.

logarithme, m. logarithm.   [metic.

logarithmique, a. logarithmic, logarith-

loge, f. lodge, box, cabin, cell, hut, booth || kennel || den || **ouvreuse de -s,** f. box-keeper || **premières -s,** pl. first row of boxes.   [convenient.

logeable, a. fit to lodge in, inhabitable,

logement, m. lodging, apartment || ac-commodation || quarters (pl.).

loger, v. a. & n. to lodge, to harbour, to house || to reside, to live || **se ~,** to take a lodging.

logeur, se, m. & f. lodging-house keeper.

logicien, m. logician.

logique, f. logic.

logique, a. (-ment, ad.) logical(ly).

logis, m. home, dwelling, lodging, house || **au ~,** at home.

logogriphe, m. logogriph (riddle).

loi, f. law, rule, precept, command || **~ écrite,** statute-law || **homme de ~,** m. lawyer || **faire la ~,** to give laws, to pre-scribe || **faire ~,** to make law, to be a rule.

loin, ad. & pr. far, far off, at a distance || **~ de, ~ que,** far from || **bien ~, au ~,** very far || **de ~,** at a distance || **de ~ à ~, de ~ en ~,** from distance to distance, at a great distance.

lointain, m. background, distance.

lointain, e, a. far, remote, distant.

loir, m. dormouse.

loisir, m. leisure, spare-time.

lombaire, a. (an.) lumbar, lumbal.

lombes, m. pl. loins (pl.).

londrès, m. regalia (cigar).

long, m. length, long || au ~, tout au ~, diffusely, in all its details || tout du ~, all along, all through || de son ~, tout de son ~, all his length || au ~ et au large, by length and breadth.

long, ue, a. long, large || tedious, long-winded || à la –ue, in time || de –ue main, long since.

longanimité, f. forbearance.

longe, f. thong || loin.

longer, v. a. to go along || to run along.

longévité, f. longevity.

longitude, f. longitude.   [dinal(ly).

longitudinal, e, a. (–ement, ad.) longitu-

longtemps, ad. a long time, a great while || depuis ~, long ago || for a long time now.

longue, f. (gr.) long syllable.   [while.

longuement, ad. long, a long time, a great

longuet, te, a. pretty long.

longueur, f. length || delay, lingering || prolixity.

longue-vue, f. telescope || spy-glass.

looc, looch, m. lock.

lopin, m. bit, morsel.

loquace, a. loquacious, talkative.

loquacité, f. loquacity, talkativeness.

loque, f. rag, tatter.

loquet, m. latch || hasp.

loqueteau, m. small latch.

loquette, f. small bit, little piece.

lorette, f. lady of easy virtue.

lorgner, v. a. to ogle, to leer, to view with side-glances, to quiz.

lorgnerie, f. ogling.

lorgnette, f. spy-glass, opera-glass.

lorgneur, se, m. & f. ogler.

lorgnon, m. quizzing-glass.

loriot, m. gold-hammer (bird).

lors, ad. at the time || dès ~, from that time || pour ~, then, at that time || in that case.

lorsque, c. when, at the time when.

losange, f. lozenge.

lot, m. lot, portion, share, chance || prize.

loterie, f. lottery || raffle.

loti, e, a. portioned out || bien ~, favoured, lucky || in a fine plight.

lotier, m. lotus.

lotir, v. a. to divide into lots.

lotte, f. eel-pout (fish).

lotus, lotos, m. (bot.) lote-tree.

louable, a. praiseworthy.

louage, m. letting out || hiring || à ~, on hire || cheval de ~, m. hack-horse.

louange, f. praise, commendation.

louanger, v. a. to praise, to laud.

louangeur, se, m. & f. praiser.

louangeur, se, a. laudatory.

louche, m. ambiguity || suspicious appearance || something suspicious || ~, f. soup-ladle.   [biguous || suspicious.

louche, a. squinting, squint-eyed || am-

loucher, v. n. to squint.

louer, v. a. to praise, to commend || to hire, to let, to rent || se ~, to hire oneself out, to praise oneself.

loueur, m. praiser, flatterer || letter, hirer.

lougre, m. (mar.) lugger.   [worth.

louis, m. old French coin of 20 francs'

loup, m. wolf || black velvet mask || ~ de mer, tar || entre chien et ~, by twilight || ~-cervier, m. lynx || ~-garou, m. bugbear || surly dog.   [glass.

loupe, f. wen || knob of a tree || magnifying-

lourd, e, a. heavy, weighty, burdensome, dull, stupid || –ement, ad. heavily, clumsily, awkwardly.

lourdaud, m. logger-head.

lourdeur, f. heaviness || dullness.

lousseau, a. (mar.) well.

loustic, m. wag.

loutre, f. otter.

louve, f. she-wolf || sling.

louvet, a. fox-coloured.

louveteau, m. wolf's cub.

louveter, v. n. to whelp (of wolves).

louveterie, f. wolf-hunting.

louvetier, m. wolf-hunter.

louvoyer, v. n. (mar.) to tack || to proceed cautiously.   [ful(ly).

loyal, e, a. (–ement, ad.) loyal(ly) || faith-

loyauté, f. loyalty, fairness, fidelity.

loyer, m. rent (of a house) || wages (pl.).

lubie, f. whim, fancy.

lubricité, f. lewdness.

lubrique, a. lewd.

lucarne, f. skylight, dormer-window.

lucide, a. lucid, clear.

lucidité, f. lucidity.

lucifuge, a. shunning the light.

luciole, f. glow-worm || glow-worm light.

lucratif, ve, a. lucrative.

lucre, m. lucre.

luette, f. (an.) uvula.

lueur, f. gleam, glimmer, glimpse, glare, light.

lugubre, a. (–ment, ad.) mournful(ly) || dismal(ly).

lui, pn. he, him, to him, to her, to it || c'est ~, it is he || ~-même, pn. himself.

luire, v. n. ir. to glitter, to glimmer, to shine, to dawn.

luisant, m. gloss (of a stuff) || polish.

luisant, e, a. glittering, glimmering, bright, shining.

lumière, f. light || candle || flame, fire (fig.) hint || judgment || sense || luminary || touch-hole || sight || knowledge.

lumignon, m. snuff of candles, etc.).

luminaire, m. luminary, light.

lumineux, se, a. luminous.

lunaire, a. lunar.

lunaison, f. lunation.

lunatique, a. moon-struck, whimsical.

lundi, m. Monday || faire le ~, to keep Saint Monday.

lune, f. moon || whim || clair de ~, m. moonshine || ~ de miel, honey-moon || ~ rousse, April moon || faire un trou à la ~, to shoot the moon, to decamp.

lunette, f. glass || seat of a water-closet || (mil.) half-moon battery || merry-thought (bone) || ~ d'approche, telescope || ~ à facettes, multiplying glass || –s, pl. spectacles (pl.).

lunettier, m. spectacle-maker.

lupanar, m. house of ill fame.

lupin, m. (bot.) lupine.
luron, m. jolly fellow || buck, brick || determined dog.
luronne, f. buxom woman || forward *ou* [fast girl.
lustrage, m. glossiness.
lustral, e, a. lustral, holy.
lustre, m. lustre, gloss, brilliancy || sconce || [gaselier.
lustré, e, a. glossy.
lustrer, v. a. to gloss || to glaze.
lustrine, f. lustring (silk-stuff).
lut, f. (chim.) lute.
luter, v. a. (chim.) to lute.
luth, m. (mus.) lute.
luthéranisme, m. Lutheranism.
luthérien, ne, a. Lutheran.
luthier, m. musical instrument-maker.
lutin, m. hobgoblin || wild child.
lutin, e, a. waggish.
lutiner, v. a. to plague, to tease.
lutrin, m. lectern || choristers (pl.).
lutte, f. wrestle || struggle, contest.
lutter, v. n. to wrestle || to struggle || to
lutteur, m. wrestler. [have a match.
luxation, f. dislocation.
luxe, m. luxury || display || **objets de ~**, m. pl. fancy goods.
luxer, v. a. (chir.) to luxate, to disjoint || to dislocate || **se ~**, to get out of joint.
luxueux, se, a. luxurious.
luxure, f. lewdness.
luxuriant, e, a. luxuriant, exuberant.
luxurieux, se, a. lustful, lewd.
luzerne, f. (bot.) lucern-grass.
luzernière, f. lucern-field.
lycée, m. lyceum || (French) college.
lycéen, m. collegian.
lymphatique, a. lymphatic.
lymphe, f. lymph. [house.
lyrique, a. lyrical || **théâtre ~**, m. opera-
lyrisme, m. poetic enthusiasm || dignified and poetic style.

M.

ma, pn. f. my.
macabre, a.; **danse ~**, f. dance of death.
macadamisage, m. macadamising.
macadamiser, v. a. to macadamise.
macaque, m. baboon.
macaron, m. macaroon.
macaronique, a. (poét.) macaronic, affected.
macédoine, f. medley of fruit *ou* vegetables.
macérer, v. a. to macerate.
mâche, f. corn-salad || mash.
mâchefer, m. clinker, iron-dross.
mâchelière, a. of the jaw || **dents -s**, f. pl. grinders, cheek-teeth (pl.).
mâcher, v. a. to chew, to masticate, to mince || to champ. [man.
mâcheur, m. chewer || muncher, trencher-
machicoulis, m. (mil.) machicolation.
machinale, a. (-ment, ad.) mechanical (ly) || instinctive(ly).
machinateur, m. plotter.
machination, f. machination, contrivance.

machine, f. machine, engine || machinery || **~ à vapeur**, steam-engine. [plot.
machiner, v. a. to machinate, to plan, to
machiniste, m. machinist, engineer || engine-man || carpenter.
mâchoire, f. jaw, jaw-bone || block-head.
mâchonner, v. a. to mumble.
mâchurer, v. a. to black, to blacken.
macis, m. mace.
maçon, m. mason, bricklayer. [sonry.
maçonnage, m. bricklayer's work, ma-
maçonner, v. a. to wall up || to bungle.
maçonnerie, f. masonry || stone-work.
maçonnique, a. masonic.
macreuse, f. sea-duck.
maculature, f. waste, waste-paper || wrapper.
macule, f. stain, spot. [per.
maculer, v. a. to spot, to stain.
madame, f. madam, mistress, my lady.
madapolam, m. calico from Madapolam.
mademoiselle, f. miss.
Madère, m. Madeira-wine.
Madone, f. Madonna || image of the Virgin.
madras, m. madras || madras handkerchief.
madré, e, a. spotted, speckled || sharp, cunning.
madrépore, m. madrepore.
madrier, m. joist.
madrigal, m. (mus.) madrigal.
madrure, f. speckle, vein (in wood).
maflé, maflu, e, a. chub-cheeked.
magasin, m. magazine, storehouse, warehouse || wicker-basket *ou* boot of a stage-coach || **garçon de ~**, m. warehouseman.
magasinage, m. warehousing || warehouse-rent. [book.
magasinier, m. warehouse-keeper || stock-
mage, m. magian || **-s**, pl. magi (wise men)
magicien, ne, m. & f. magician. [(pl.).
magie, f. magic || **~ noire**, black art.
magique, a. magical. [ant.
magister, m. country schoolmaster || ped-
magistral, e, a. (-ement, ad.) magisterial(ly).
magistrat, m. magistrate || town-council.
magistrature, f. magistracy.
magnanerie, magnanière, f. silkworm nursery. [grower.
magnanier, m. silkworm breeder, silk-
magnanime, a. (-ment, ad.) magnanimous(ly).
magnanimité, a. magnanimity.
magnésie, f. (chim.) magnesia.
magnétique, a. magnetic.
magnétiser, v. a. to magnetise.
magnétiseur, m. magnetiser.
magnétisme, m. magnetism.
magnificence, f. magnificence, grandeur.
magnifique, a. (-ment, ad.) magnificent (ly) || splendid(ly).
magnolier, m. (bot.) magnolia.
magot, m. hoard of money, hidden treasure || baboon, monkey.
Mahométan, m. Mahometan.
Mahométisme, m. Mahometanism.
mai, m. May || May-pole.
maigre, m. lean || vegetable food.
maigre, a. (-ment, ad.) meagre(ly) || lean || poor(ly) || made without meat.

maigrelet, te, a. thinnish.
maigret, te, a. thin.
maigreur, f. meagreness, leanness.
maigrir, v. n. to grow lean ‖ to fall away.
mail, m. mall.
maille, f. stitch ‖ mesh ‖ link ‖ farthing.
maillechort, m. German silver.
maillet, m. mallet, mall.
mailloche, f. beetle.
maillot, m. swaddling-band, swaddling-clothes (pl.) ‖ tights (pl.) ‖ fleshings (pl.).
main, f. hand ‖ handle ‖ clasper ‖ source ‖ execution ‖ lead (at cards) ‖ trick (at cards) ‖ quire (of paper) ‖ handwriting ‖ power, authority ‖ à deux —s, with both hands ‖ de ~ en ~, from hand to hand ‖ sous ~, clandestinely ‖ à la ~, in hand, at hand ‖ ~-chaude, f. hot cockles ‖ ~-d'œuvre, f. workmanship ‖ manual labour ‖ ~-forte, f. assistance ‖ ~-levée, f. (jur.) replevy ‖ withdrawal.
mainmorte, f. (jur.) mortmain.
maint, e, a. several, many.   [time.
maintenant, ad. now, at present, at this
maintenir, v. a. ir. to maintain, to sustain, to support, to countenance, to protect ‖ to affirm ‖ se ~, to support oneself ‖ to defend oneself ‖ to hold out.
maintien, m. maintenance, support, defence, protection ‖ deportment, carriage, mien.   [countenance.
maire, m. mayor.
mairesse, f. mayoress.
mairie, f. mayoralty, mayor's house, Mansion-House ‖ police-office.
mais, c. but, why ‖ ~ enfin, in a word.
maïs, m. (bot.) maize, Indian corn.
maison, f. house, home, habitation ‖ family ‖ ~ de campagne, country-house, manor ‖ ~ commune, town-hall ‖ ~ rustique, farm ‖ ~ de correction, ~ de force, house of correction ‖ ~ de jeu, gambling-house ‖ ~ meublée, private hotel ‖ ~ publique, house of ill fame ‖ ~ de santé, private hospital ‖ ~ de ville, Guildhall, Town-hall ‖ petites -s, pl. mad-house ‖ faire ~ neuve, to change all one's servants.
maisonnette, f. small house.
maître, m. master, owner, ruler, instructor, director, teacher ‖ ~ de chapelle, bandmaster ‖ ~ d'escrime, ~ d'armes, fencing-master ‖ ~-ès-arts, master-of-arts ‖ ~ de danse, dancing-master ‖ ~ d'étude, usher ‖ ~ de musique, music-master ‖ ~ d'équitation, riding-master ‖ ~ de langues, teacher of languages ‖ ~ d'hôtel, steward.
maîtresse, f. mistress ‖ landlady ‖ governess ‖ chief, head ‖ ~ femme, superior woman.
maîtriser, v. a. to domineer, to govern, to overcome, to subdue, to control.
majesté, f. majesty.   [majestic(ally).
majestueux, se, a. (-sement, ad.)
majeur, e, a. major, of age ‖ greater, superior ‖ force -e, absolute necessity ‖ ton ~, m. (mus.) major key.
majordome, m. major-domo, house-steward.

majorité, f. majority ‖ full age.
majuscule, f. capital letter.
majuscule, a. capital.
mal, m. evil, pain, disease, distemper, sickness ‖ harm, mischief, hurt, trouble ‖ ~ de tête, ~ à la tête, head-ache ‖ ~ de dents, ~ aux dents, tooth-ache ‖ ~ d'enfant, labour ‖ ~ de ventre, gripes ‖ ~ de cœur, sickness ‖ ~ caduc, falling sickness ‖ ~ de mer, sea-sickness ‖ ~ d'aventure, whitlow ‖ en ~, amiss ‖ unfavourably ‖ for the worse.
mal, ad. ill, badly ‖ ~-appris, m. churl ‖ ~-appris, e, a. ill-bred ‖ ~-avisé, e, a. ill-advised, ill-judged ‖ ~-être, m. uneasiness.
malade, m. sick person, patient.
malade, a. sick, ill.
maladie, f. malady, sickness, illness, disease, disorder, distemper ‖ fondness ‖ ~ du pays, home-sickness.
maladif, ve, a. sickly.
maladresse, f. awkwardness, clumsiness, unskilfulness.
maladroit, e, a. (-ement, ad.) awkward (ly) ‖ unhandy ‖ clumsily.
malaise, m. uneasiness, uncomfortableness, restlessness.
malaisé, e, a. difficult, hard, inconvenient ‖ awkward, unhandy ‖ -ment, ad. with difficulty, not easily, hardly.
malbâti, e, a. ill-shaped.
mâle, m. male, cock.
mâle, a. male, stout, manly.
malédiction, f. malediction, curse.
maléfice, m. witchcraft.
maléficié, e, a. bewitched.
malencontre, f. mishap.
malencontreux, se, a. unlucky.   [take.
malentendu, m. misunderstanding, mistake.
malfaisant, e, a. mischievous, noxious.
malfaiteur, trice, m. & f. malefactor, criminal.
malfamé, e, a. ill-famed.
malgré, pr. in spite of, notwithstanding ‖ bon gré ~, whether one will or no.
malhabile, a. (-ment, ad.) unskilful(ly) ‖ awkward(ly).
malhabileté, f. unskilfulness, awkwardness.   [ill-luck ‖ woe.
malheur, m. misfortune ‖ unhappiness ‖
malheureusement, ad. unhappily, unluckily.
malheureux, se, m. & f. poor wretch.
malheureux, se, a. unhappy, unfortunate, unlucky, wretched.
malhonnête, a. (-ment, ad.) dishonest (ly) ‖ uncivil(ly) ‖ rude(ly).
malhonnêteté, f. dishonesty, incivility, rudeness.
malice, f. malice, maliciousness, mischief, wickedness, malicious action, roguishness.
malicieux, se, a. (-sement, ad.) malicious(ly) ‖ mischievous ‖ spiteful(ly).
malignement, ad. maliciously.
malignité, f. malignity.
malin, igne, a. malicious, malignant, mischievous, waggish.
maline, f. (mar.) spring-tide ‖ -s, pl. Mechlin lace.

malingre, a. sickly. [affected.
malintentionné, e, a. ill-disposed, ill-
malitorne, a. (fam.) awkward, gawky.
malle, f. mail ‖ **mail-coach** ‖ **trunk** ‖ **~-
poste,** f. mail.
malléable, a. malleable.
mallette, f. small trunk.
malmener, v. a. to chide, to use ill, to
abuse. [ful.
malotru, e, a. wretched, sorry, sad, piti-
malpeigné, m. shabby fellow.
malpropre, a. (**-ment,** ad.) slovenly ‖
dirty ‖ dirtily.
malpropreté, f. slovenliness, dirtiness.
malsain, e, a. unhealthy, sickly, unwholesome.
malséant, e, a. unbecoming ‖ improper.
malsonnant, e, a. ill-sounding, disagree-
malteur, m. maltster. [able.
maltôte, f. extortion, exaction.
maltôtier, m. extortioner. [ly.
maltraiter, v. a. to ill-treat, to treat harsh-
malveillance, f. malevolence, ill-will.
malveillant, e, a. malevolent, ill-minded.
malversation, f. malversation, malprac-
malverser, v. n. to embezzle. [tice.
malvoisie, m. malmsey.
maman, f. mamma ‖ **bonne ~,** grand-
mamelle, f. (an.) breast ‖ udder. [mamma.
mamelon, m. nipple ‖ (of mountains) pap.
mamelu, e, a. full-breasted.
mammifère, m. mammifer.
mammifère, a. mammiferous.
manant, m. peasant ‖ clown.
manche, m. handle, haft ‖ helve ‖ finger-
board ‖ knuckle-bone ‖ **~,** f. sleeve ‖ (British) Channel ‖ (mar.) hose ‖ game ‖ hit ‖
manchette, f. ruffle, cuff. [bout.
manchon, m. muff. [awkward.
manchot, e, a. a maimed, lame, one-handed,
mandat, m. mandate ‖ commission ‖ money-
order ‖ power of attorney ‖ **~ d'arrêt,**
(jur.) warrant. [torney.
mandataire, m. mandatary, proxy ‖ at-
mandement, m. mandate ‖ charge (of a
bishop to his clergy).
mander, v. a. to order to come, to send
for ‖ to send word, to advise, to inform.
mandibule, f. mandible ‖ jaw. [gora.
mandragore, f. (bot.) mandrake, mandra-
mandrin, m. mandrel ‖ robber ‖ ruffian.
manège, m. manège ‖ horsemanship ‖ rid-
ing-place, riding-school.
mangeable, a. eatable.
mangeaille, f. food, victuals (pl.), eatables
(pl.), meat ‖ grub ‖ creature comforts (pl.).
mangeoire, f. manger, crib.
manger, m. eating ‖ victuals (pl.), food.
manger, v. a. & n. to eat, to consume, to
devour ‖ to spend, to dissipate ‖ **se ~,** to
be eatable ‖ to destroy each other.
mangerie, f. eating, gormandising ‖ exaction, extortion.
mange-tout, m. spendthrift.
mangeur, m., **mangeuse,** f. eater, feeder ‖
trencherman ‖ great eater.
mangeure, f. nibbling, gnawing ‖ place
nibbled by mice, etc. [handy.
maniable, a. tractable, pliable, supple,

maniaque, a. maniacal ‖ eccentric ‖ crotchety, systematic. [fancy, madness.
manie, f. passion, crotchet, eccentricity,
maniement, m. handling, managing,
management, conduct.
manier, v. a. to handle, to feel, to touch ‖
to manage, to rule, to govern ‖ to conduct.
manière, f. manner, way, custom, sort,
kind, style ‖ **de ~ que,** so that.
maniéré, e, a. affected, quaint.
maniérisme, m. mannerism.
maniériste, m. mannerist.
manieur, m. handler.
manifestation, f. manifestation.
manifeste, m. manifesto.
manifeste, a. (**-ment,** ad.) manifest(ly).
manifester, v. a. to manifest.
manigance, f. underhand dealing, intrigue. [to plot.
manigancer, v. a. to contrive, to plan out,
manille, f. manille (game of ombre) ‖
manilla cigar.
manipuler, v. a. to manipulate.
manique, f. hand-leather.
maniveau, m. osier-stand.
manivelle, f. handle, crank ‖ winch.
manne, f. manna ‖ hamper.
mannequin, m. mannikin ‖ dummy ‖ lay-
figure ‖ puppet ‖ hamper.
manœuvre, m. mason's man, hodman ‖
bungler. [tary evolution.
manœuvre, f. manœuvre, conduct ‖ mili-
manœuvrer, v. n. to manœuvre, to work ‖
to act with finesse ‖ to drill.
manoir, m. manor, manor-house, mansion.
manomètre, m. manometer ‖ manoscope ‖
pressure-gauge.
manouvrier, m. workman, labourer.
manque, m. want ‖ **~ de,** for want of.
manqué, e, a. defective ‖ abortive ‖ would-
be. [fault.
manquement, m. miss, omission, failure.
manquer, v. a. & n. to miss, to fail, to do
amiss ‖ to have need of, to want ‖ to
neglect ‖ to miscarry.
mansarde, f. roof, attic, garret ‖ garret-
window.
mansuétude, f. mansuetude.
mante, f. mantle.
manteau, m. cloak ‖ mantel (of a chimney) ‖ **~-Macfarlane,** Inverness-cape ‖
~ de cheminée, chimney-piece ‖ mantelpiece.
mantelet, m. mantlet, small mantle.
mantille, f. mantilla.
manuel, m. manual ‖ hand-book.
manuel, le, a. (**-lement,** ad.) manual(ly) ‖
performed by the hand ‖ from hand to
hand. [ship ‖ manufactory, mill.
manufacture, f. manufacture, workman-
manufacturer, v. n. to manufacture.
manufacturier, ière, a. manufacturing.
manuscrit, m. manuscript.
manuscrit, e, a. manuscript.
manutention, f. management ‖ military
bake-house.
mappemonde, f. map of the world.

maquereau, m. mackerel (fish) || scorch.

maquette, f. sword-mould || small, rough sculpturing model.

maquignon, m. jockey, horse-dealer.

maquignonnage, m. horse-dealing, jockey's trade || underhand work.

maquignonner, v. a. to bishop || to job.

maquiller, v. a. to paint one's face, to make up.　　　　　　　　[ugly person.

marabout, m. marabout || large coffee-pot ||

maraîcher, m. kitchen-gardener.

marais, m. marsh, fen, bog || market-garden || ~ salant, salt-marsh.

marasme, m. marasmus, consumption.

marasquin, m. maraschino.

marâtre, f. stepmother || cruel stepmother.

maraud, e, m. & f. rascal.

maraude, f. marauding.

marauder, v. n. to maraud.

maraudeur, m. marauder.

marbre, m. marble || slab.

marbrer, v. a. to marble.

marbrerie, f. marble-cutting || marble-marbreur, m. marbler.　　　　　　　[mill.

marbrier, m. marble-cutter.

marbrière, f. marble-quarry.

marbrure, f. marbling.

marc, m. half-pound || residuum || grounds (pl.) || grout || grains (pl.) || skins (pl.).

marcassin, m. young wild boar.

marchand, m. merchant, shop-keeper, tradesman, dealer, seller || chapman, customer || ~ en gros, wholesale dealer || ~ en détail, retailer.

marchand, e, a. merchantable, salable || commercial || vaisseau ~, m. merchant vessel || ville -e, f. trading town.

marchandailler, v. a. to biggle and haggle.

marchande, f. trading woman || tradeswoman || ~ de modes, milliner.

marchander, v. a. & n. to cheapen, to haggle, to chaffer || to be in suspense, to hesitate.

marchandeur, m. haggler.　　　　　[hesitates.

marchandise, f. merchandise, goods (pl.) || -s, pl. stock-in-trade.

marche, f. march, journey || step || move (at chess) || borders (pl.) || treadles (pl.) || sailing.

marché, m. market, market-place || bargain || bon ~, cheapness || à bon ~, cheap, cheaply.　　　　　　　　　[step || stretcher.

marchepied, m. foot-stool || foot-board ||

marcher, m. walking || walk || gait.

marcher, v. n. to march, to walk, to go on foot || to move.　　　　　　　[sailer.

marcheur, se, m. & f. walker || (mar.)

marcotte, f. layer, shoot.

marcotter, v. a. to set layers.

mardi, m. Tuesday || ~ gras, Shrove-Tuesday.

mare, f. pool, stagnant water.

marécage, m. marsh, bog.　　　　　　[swampy.

marécageux, se, a. marshy, boggy,

maréchal, m. farrier || blacksmith || (mil.) (field-)marshal || ~ de camp, major-general || ~ ferrant, farrier || ~ de logis, (mil.) quarter-master.

maréchale, f. marshal's wife.

maréchalerie, f. farriery.

marée, f. tide, flux and reflux || fresh seafish || haute ~, high water || basse ~, low water || grande ~, spring-tide || ~ morte, neap-tide || marchand de ~, m.

marelle, f. hop-scotch.　　　　　[fishmonger.

Marengo, m. Oxford gray || à la ~, (culin.) with mushrooms and oil.

margarine, f. (chim.) margarine.

marge, f. margin (of a book).

margelle, f. kerb-stone.

marginal, e, a. marginal.

margot, m. magpie (bird) || (fig.) chatter-margotin, m. small faggot.　　　　　[box.

margouillis, m. puddle || slop, mess.

margoulette, f. (fam.) jaw, whistle.

marguerite, f. (bot.) daisy || (mar.) messenger.

marguillerie, f. churchwardenship.

marguillier, m. churchwarden.

mari, m. husband.

mariable, a. marriageable.

mariage, m. marriage, nuptials (pl.), wedding, wedlock || ~ de convenance, ~ de raison, prudent match.

marié, m. married man || nouveaux -s, pl. newly married couple.

mariée, f. married woman.

marier, v. a. to marry, to match || se ~, to get married.

marie-salope, f. (mar.) mud-boat.

marieur, se, m. & f. matchmaker.

marin, m. mariner, sailor.

marin, e, a. marine || carte ~e, f. sea-chart.

marinade, f. pickle.

marine, f. navigation || navy || seafaring men (pl.) || sea-affairs (pl.) || naval service || (peint.) sea-piece.

mariner, v. a. to marinate, to pickle.

maringouin, m. mosquito.

marinier, m. bargeman.　　　　　　[show.

marionnette, f. puppet || -s, pl. puppet-marital, e, a. (-ement, ad.) marital, matrimonial || like a husband || uxorious

maritime, a. maritime || naval.　　　　[(ly).

maritorne, f. awkward female, dirty marivaudage, m. mannerism.　　　[wench.

marjolaine, f. (bot.) sweet-marjoram.

marmaille, f. brats.　　　　　　　[in a jelly.

marmelade, f. marmalade, jam || en ~,

marmite, f. porridge-pot, flesh-pot, boiler.

marmiton, m. scullion.

marmonner, v. a. to mutter.

marmot, m. large monkey || little boy || croquer le ~, to dance attendance.

marmotte, f. marmot.

marmotter, v. a. to mumble.

marmouset, m. grotesque figure || ugly little fellow || little monkey || andiron.

marne, f. marl.

marner, v. a. to marl.

marneron, m. marl-digger.

marneux, se, a. marly.

marnière, f. marl-pit.

maroquin, m. morocco-leather || roan.

maroquiner, v. a. to dress ou imitate morocco-leather.　　　　　[ou manufacture.

maroquinerie, f. morocco-leather factory

maroquinier, m. morocco-dresser.

marotte, f. fool's bawble || whim, hobby.

maroufle, m. ragamuffin, rascal || clod-
hopper || (peint.) lining-paste.   [markable.
marquant, e, a. marking, conspicuous, re-
marque, f. mark, token || counter || dis-
tinction || ~ de fabrique, trade mark ||
-s, pl. insignia (pl.).
marquer, v. a. & n. to mark, to stamp,
to brand || to appear || to be remarked || to
strike, to show the hour (of clocks, etc.) ||
to create a sensation || to play a con-
spicuous part.   [to checker.
marqueter, v. a. to speckle || to inlay
marqueterie, f. inlaid work || inlaying ||
checker-work || patchwork.
marquetteur, m. inlayer.
marqueur, se, m. & f. marker.
marquis, m. marquis, marquess.
marquisat, m. marquisate.
marquise, f. marchioness || marquee ||
veranda || awning || settee.
marraine, f. godmother.
marri, a. sorrowful || remorseful || afflicted.
marron, m. large chestnut || chestnut-
colour || cracker || runaway slave || ~
d'Inde, horse-chestnut.
marron, ne, a. chestnut-coloured || run-
away || unlicensed.
marronnage, m. running away.
marronner, v. n. to mutter.
marronnier, m. (bot.) chestnut-tree || ~
d'Inde, horse-chestnut tree.
mars, m. March || giboulées de ~, f. pl.
April showers || bière de ~, f. beer brewed
marsouin, m. porpoise.   [in March.
marte, f. marten.
marteau, m. hammer || knocker (of a door).
martel, m. hammer || ~ en tête, uneasi-
ness.   [hammer.
martelage, m. marking of trees with a
marteler, v. a. to hammer || to torment,
to plague.
martelet, m. little hammer.
martial, e, a. martial, warlike.
martinet, m. martin, swift (bird) || flat
candlestick || cat-o'-nine-tails.
martingale, f. martingale || (mar.) mar-
tingale || (at play) double-or-quits.
martin-pêcheur, m. king-fisher (bird).
martre, f. marten.
martyr, e, m. & f. martyr.
martyre, m. martyrdom.
martyriser, v. a. to martyr, to torture.
mascarade, f. masquerade.   [bours).
mascaret, m. eddy of water || bar (of har-
mascaron, m. grotesque head, mask.
masculin, e, a. masculine, male.
masque, m. mask, masker, masquerader.
masquer, v. a. to mask, to disguise with
a mask, to hide || se ~, to put on a mask ||
to disguise oneself.
massacrant, e, a. tormenting || humeur
-e, infernally bad temper.
massacre, m. massacre, butchery, carnage,
slaughter || bungler.
massacrer, v. a. to massacre || to half-
kill || to butcher, to slaughter || to botch,
to spoil.
massacreur, m. murderer || bungler.
massage, m. champooing.

masse, f. mass, lump, heap || sum of one's
earnings || fund || body || whole || estate ||
rammer, large hammer || mace (at bil-
liards) || en ~, in the bulk.
massepain, m. march-pane (cake).
masser, v. a. to stake at play, to lay, to
massier, m. mace-bearer. [set || to mass.
massif, m. massive building || clump of
trees, dead-wood.
massif, ve, a. (-vement, ad.) massive,
massy || bulky, lumpish || (fig.) stupid,
heavy || heavily.
massue, f. club, heavy stick || crowbar.
mastic, mastic, putty.
mastigadour, m. slabbering-bit.
mastiquer, v. a. to cement, to putty.
mastodonte, m. mastodon.
masure, f. decayed house, ruin.   [mate.
mat, m. deadening || dead colour || check-
mat, te, a. unpolished, heavy || dead.
mât, m. (mar.) mast (of a ship) || grand ~,
main-mast.
matamore, m. bully, duellist.
matelas, m. mattress.
matelasser, v. a. to quilt, to stuff.
matelassier, m. mattress-maker.
matelot, m. seaman, sailor || (mar.) consort
matelote, f. fish-stew.   [(ship).
mater, v. a. to checkmate || to subdue, to
bumble || to mortify.
mâter, v. a. (mar.) to mast, to step a mast.
matérialiser, v. a. to materialise.
matérialisme, m. materialism.
matérialiste, m. materialist.
matérialité, f. materiality.
matériaux, m. pl. materials (pl.).
matériel, m. materials (pl.) || apparatus,
implements (pl.).
matériel, le, a. material, corporeal.
matériellement, ad. materially || coarsely.
maternel, le, a. (-lement, ad.) maternal
(ly) || motherly || on the mother's side.
maternité, f. maternity || lying-in hospital.
mâteur, m. (mar.) mast-maker.
mathématicien, m. mathematician.
mathématique, f. mathematics (pl.).
mathématique, a. (-ment, ad.) mathe-
matical(ly).
matière, f. matter, materials (pl.), body,
subject || cause, reason || en ~ de, in
point of.
matin, m. morning || forenoon || prime ||
un de ces quatre -s, one of these days.
matin, ad. early.
mâtin, m. mastiff || clownish fellow || con-
founded fellow || rascal.
mâtin! by Jove!
matinal, e, a. of the morning, early.
matinée, f. morning, forenoon || morning's
occupation, work ou gain || morning per-
matines, f. pl. matins (pl.).   [formance.
matineux, m. early riser.   [early.
matineux, se, a. early rising, matinal
matinier, ère, a. morning matinal.
matir, v. a. to deaden (a surface).
matois, e, a. sharp, cunning, artful.
matou, m. tom-cat.   [weight || womb.
matrice, f. matrix || register || standard
matriculaire, m. matriculate.

matricule, f. matriculation || matriculation-book.

matrimonial, e, a. matrimonial.

matrone, f. matron.

maturation, f. (méd.) maturation, ripening.   [wood for masts.

mâture, f. (mar.) masting || masts (pl.) ||

maturité, f. maturity, ripeness.

maudire, v. a. ir. to curse.   [ecrable.

maudit, e, a. cursed || confounded || exmaugréer, v. n. to swear || to fret and

mausolée, m. mausoleum.   [fume.

maussade, a. sulky, sullen, slovenly, clumsy, dull || -ment, ad. sulkily, in a slovenly manner, peevishly.

maussaderie, f. sulkiness, sullenness, slovenliness.

mauvais, m. (the) bad.

mauvais, e, a. & ad. bad, ill, evil || -e humeur, f. bad humour || ~ plaisant, m. sorry jester || il fait ~, it is bad weather || sentir ~, to have an ill smell || trouver ~, to dislike, to find fault with || faire le ~, to be fractious.

mauve, f. (bot.) mallow || gull (bird).

mauviard, m. thrush (bird).

mauviette, f. field-lark (bird).

mauvis, m. red-wing (bird).

maxillaire, a. (an.) maxillary.

maxime, f. maxim.

mayonnaise, f. (culin.) mayonnaise (sauce).

mazette, f. small, wretched horse || novice || bungler.   [in ou from me.

me, m', pn. me, to me || myself || for, with,

méandre, m. meander || winding.

mécanicien, m. mechanician, machinist || engine-builder || engine-driver.

mécanique, f. mechanics (pl.) || mechanism.

mécanique, a. (-ment, ad.) mechanical

mécanisme, m. mechanism.   [(ly).

mécène, m. patron (of polite literature, etc.).

méchamment, ad. wickedly, maliciously.

méchanceté, f. wickedness, mischievousness, malice, wicked action.

méchant, a. wicked, reprobate.

méchant, e, a. wicked, bad, wretched, mischievous, malicious, peevish || sorry, paltry.

mèche, f. match, wick, link || tinder || auger || lock || lash || plot.

mécher, v. a. to fumigate a wine-cask with burning brimstone.   [mistake.

mécompte, m. misreckoning || miscount,

se mécompter, to misreckon, to miscount, to mistake || to be out.

méconnaissable, a. not to be known again || unrecognisable.

méconnaître, v. a. ir. not to know, not to recognise || to disown || to disregard || to ignore || not to appreciate || to forget.

mécontent, e, a. dissatisfied, ill-satisfied.

mécontentement, m. discontent, dissatisfaction, displeasure.   [please.

mécontenter, v. a. to dissatisfy, to dis-

mécréant, m. miscreant, infidel.

médaille, f. medal || tourner la ~, to turn the tables.

médaillé, e, m. & f. medallist.

médaillé, e, a. with a medal || licensed.

médaillier, m. cabinet of medals.

médailliste, m. medallist.

médaillon, m. medallion || locket.

médecin, m. physician, doctor || docteur ~, m. doctor of medicine.

médecine, f. medicine, physic.

médeciner, v. a. to prescribe medicine || se ~, to take physic.

médiaire, a. intermediate.

médiateur, trice, m. & f. mediator || mediatrix.

médiation, f. mediation, intervention.

médical, e, a. medical, physical.

médicament, m. medicine, medicament,

médicamenter, v. a. to physic.

médicamenteux, se, a. medicinal.

médicinal, e, a. medicinal.

médiocre, m. mediocrity.

médiocre, a. (-ment, ad.) moderate(ly) || middling, tolerable || indifferent(ly).

médiocrité, f. mediocrity || small competency || very ordinary man.

médire, v. n. ir. to slander, to speak ill of.

médisance, f. slander, evil-speaking || scandal.

médisant, e, a. slanderous || scandalous.

méditatif, ve, a. meditative, contemplative.   [ject.

méditer, v. a. & n. to meditate || to pro-

méditerrané, e, a. mediterraneous, midméditum, m. medium.   [land.

méduse, f. medusa, sea-nettle, jelly-fish.

méfait, m. misdeed.

méfiance, f. mistrust, diffidence, distrust.

méfiant, e, a. mistrustful, diffident, distrustful, suspicious.

se méfier, to mistrust, to distrust.

mégarde, f. inadvertency || par ~, inadvertently, by oversight.

mégère, f. shrew, vixen.

mégie, f. tawing, skinning.

mégisserie, f. tawing || white-leather trade.

mégissier, m. tawer, leather-dresser.

mégot, m. (fam.) cigar-end.

meilleur, e, a. better || best.

mélancolie, f. melancholy.

mélancolique, a. melancholic, dull || -ment, ad. in a melancholy manner.

mélange, m. mixture, medley, mixing, mingling || -s, pl. miscellany.

mélanger, v. a. to mix, to mingle, to blend.

mélasse, f. molasses, treacle.

mêlée, f. conflict || fight, scuffle || debate.

mêler, v. a. to mix, to mingle, to blend, to entangle || to interfere || to unite, to join || se ~, to be mixed, to meddle with, to huddle, to intermeddle, to be concerned in.

mélèze, m. (bot.) larch-tree.   [mint.

mélisse, f. (bot.) melissa, balm, balm-

mélodie, f. melody.   [dious(ly).

mélodieux, se, a. (-sement, ad.) melo-

mélodrame, m. melodrama.

mélomane, m. lover of music.

mélomanie, f. excessive fondness for music.

melon, m. (bot.) melon.

melonnière, f. melon-bed.

mélopée, f. (mus.) melopœia.

membrane, f. membrane || film || web.

membre, m. member, limb.

membré, e, a. limbed.

membru, e, a. strong-limbed.

membrure, f. panel-frame.

même, pn. & ad. same, like, self, itself || even, also || very || de ~, tout de ~, in the same way || just so || de ~ que, as well as || à ~, within reach.

mémoire, f. memory, remembrance || de ~, from memory || en ~ de, in memory of, in commemoration of.

mémoire, m. memorandum, memorial, bill, note || -s, pl. memoirs (pl.).

mémorandum, m. memorandum-book.

mémorial, m. memorial to the Roman or Spanish court || waste-book || index.

mémorial, e, a. memorial.

menace, f. menace, threat.

menacer, v. a. to menace, to threaten.

ménage, m. household || house-keeping, housewifery || economy, sparingness || family || pain de ~, m. household-bread || petit ~, baby-house || toile de ~, f. homespun cloth || vivre de ~, to live with economy, to live upon one's means || faire bon ~, to live happily together.

ménagement, m. regard, attention, caution, discretion || conduct.

ménager, v. a. to husband, to preserve, to prepare, to be sparing of || to treat with caution, to manage || se ~, to take care of oneself.

ménager, m. thrifty man, economiser.

ménager, ère, a. saving, sparing, thrifty, parsimonious, frugal || eaux -ères, house-slops (pl.).   [cruet-stand.

ménagère, f. housewife, housekeeper ||

ménagerie, f. menagery || poultry-yard.

mendiant, m. mendicant, beggar || les quatre -s, figs, filberts, raisins, and almonds (pl.).

mendiant, e, a. mendicant, begging.

mendicité, f. mendicity, beggary.

mendier, v. a. & n. to beg.

menée, f. intrigue, secret practice, plot, conspiracy || trace, way.

mener, v. a. to lead, to conduct, to drive, to govern || to steer || to manage || to treat || to deceive.

ménestrel, m. minstrel.   [to deceive.

ménétrier, m. fiddler.

meneur, m. leader || driver || ringleader.

méningite, f. (méd.) meningitis.

menotte, f. small hand || manacle, handcuff.

mense, f. revenue.   [cuff.

mensonge, m. lie, falsehood || error, illusion, vanity.   [counterfeit, illusory.

mensonger, ère, a. false, deceitful,

mensuel, le, a. (-lement, ad.) monthly.

mensuration, f. mensuration.

mental, e, a. (-ement, ad.) mental(ly).

menterie, f. untruth, fib.

menteur, m. liar.

menteur, se, a. deceitful, false, treacherous || delusive.

menthe, f. mint.   [ous || delusive.

mention, f. mention.

mentionner, v. a. to mention.

mentir, v.n. to lie, to fib || sans ~, to tell the truth, truly, indeed.

menton, m. chin.   [truth, truly, indeed.

mentonnière, f. chin-piece, chin-cloth.

French and English.

mentor, m. guide, tutor, mentor.

menu, m. bill of fare || detail || small linen || common folks (pl.).

menu, e, a. slender, small, thin, spare, subtle || vulgar, mean || ~ bois, m. brushwood || -s plaisirs, m. pl. pocket-money, privy purse.

menuaille, f. trash || small money || small

menuet, m. (mus.) minuet.   [fry (pl.).

menuiserie, f. joinery || woodwork || carpentry.   [house-carpenter.

menuisier, m. joiner || ~ en bâtiments,

méphitique, a. mephitic.

méplat, m. flat, flat part || flattish curve || hoop-iron.

méplat, e, a. flat.

se méprendre, to mistake, to be mistaken.

mépris, m. contempt, scorn, disdain || au ~ de, in spite of, in contempt of.

méprisable, a. contemptible, despicable.

méprisant, e, a. contemptuous, scornful, disdainful.

méprise, f. mistake.   [scorn.

mépriser, v. a. to contemn, to despise, to

mer, f. sea || pleine ~, haute ~, main, high seas (pl.) || basse ~, ebb-tide, low water || d'outre ~, oversea.

mercantile, a. mercantile, commercial.

mercenaire, m. hireling || covetous person.

mercenaire, a. mercenary, venal.

mercerie, f. mercery || pedlar's ware ou trade.

merci, m. thanks (pl.) || ~, f. mercy.

merci! thanks! || I dare say! || ~ bien! much obliged! || grand ~, I thank you very much || Dieu ~! thank God!   [dasher.

mercier, ière, m. & f. mercer, haberdasher.

mercredi, m. Wednesday || ~ des Cendres, Ash-Wednesday.

mercure, m. mercury.

mercuriale, f. reprimand, lecture || market-report || (bot.) mercurialis.

mercuriel, le, a. mercurial.

mère, f. mother || dam || cause, occasion || langue ~, f. mother-tongue.

mère, a. primitive || principal || ~ laine, m. finest wool || ~ goutte, f. unpressed

méridien, m. meridian.   [wine.

méridien, ne, a. meridian.   [lounge.

méridienne, f. midday siesta || couch,

méridional, e, a. meridional, southern.

meringue, f. cream-cake.

mérinos, m. Spanish sheep || merino (stuff).

merise, f. (bot.) wild cherry.

merisier, m. (bot.) wild cherry-tree.

mérite, m. merit, worth, desert.

mériter, v. a. & n. to merit, to deserve, to procure, to retrieve || to be worth.

méritoire, a. (-ment, ad.) meritorious(ly).

merlan, m. whiting (fish).

merle, m. blackbird || fin ~, cunning blade.

merlin, m. pole-axe || (mar.) marline.

merluche, f. haddock (fish).

merrain, m. hart's horn || clap-board.

merveille, f. marvel, wonder || à ~, wonderfully, admirably well.

merveilleux, m. coxcomb.

merveilleux, se, a. (-sement, ad.) marvellous(ly) || wonderful(ly).

mes, pn. (pl. de **mon, ma**) my.   [ment.
mésalliance, f. misalliance || disparage-
mésallier, v. a. to undermatch, to dis-
parage || **se ~,** to marry below oneself ||
to degrade oneself.
mésange, f. tom-tit (bird).   [mishap.
mésaventure, f. mischance, misfortune,
mésestimer, v. a. to underrate, to undervalue.   [disagreement.
mésintelligence, f. misunderstanding,
mésinterpréter, v. a. to misinterpret.
mesmérisme, m. mesmerism, animal
magnetism.
mesquin, e, a. (**-ement, ad.**) stingy,
near, shabby, pitiful || niggardly, stingily,
shabbily.   [nearness.
mesquinerie, f. niggardliness, stinginess,
message, m. message, errand.
messager, ère, m. & f. messenger, carrier, runner, forerunner.
messagerie, f. coach-office || stage-coach ||
(rail.) carriage of goods || goods depart-
ment || line of mail steam-packets.
messe, f. mass || **grand' ~,** high-mass.
messéant, e, a. indecent, unseemly, unbecoming.
messeigneurs, m. pl. my lords (pl.).
Messie, m. Messiah.
messieurs, m. pl. messieurs (pl.), gentle-
men (pl.), sirs (pl.).   [surveying.
mesurage, m. measurement, measuring,
mesure, f. measure, rule, proportion ||
limit, boundary || mean, means (pl.) || **à ~
que,** proportionably, in proportion as,
according to || **sans ~,** without measure,
excessively || **outre ~,** beyond all bounds.
mesuré, e, a. measured, circumspect,
cautious, precise.
mesurer, v. a. to measure, to weigh, to
consider, to proportion, to compare || **se
~,** to try one's strength with one.
mesureur, m. measurer, meter.
mésuser, v. n. to misuse, to abuse.
métairie, f. farm-house.
métal, m. metal || **~ blanc anglais,**
Britannia metal.   [gauze.
métallique, a. metallic || **toile ~,** f. wire-
métallurgie, f. metallurgy.
métallurgiste, m. metallurgist.
métamorphose, f. metamorphosis, transformation.   [to transform.
métamorphoser, v. a. to metamorphose,
métaphrase, f. metaphrase.
métaphore, f. metaphor.   [phoric(ally).
métaphorique, a. (**-ment, ad.**) meta-
métaphysicien, m. metaphysician.
métaphysique, f. metaphysics (pl.).
métaphysique, a. (**-ment, ad.**) meta-
physic(ally).
métaphysiquer, v. n. to subtilise.
métaplasme, m. (gr.) metaplasm.
métayer, m. farmer.
métayère, f. farmer's wife.
méteil, m. meslin.
méteil, e, a. mixed with rye.
métempsycose, f. metempsychosis.
météore, m. meteor.
météorique, a. meteoric.
météorologie, f. meteorology.

méthode, f. method, system, way, custom.
méthodique, a. (**-ment, ad.**) methodic
méthodisme, m. methodism.   [(ally).
méthodiste, m. methodist.
méticuleux, se, a. timid || scrupulous.
métier, m. trade, handicraft, employment,
business, profession || loom, frame || **gens
de ~,** pl. tradesmen (pl.), handicraftsmen
métis, m. mongrel.   [(pl.).
métis, e, a. mongrel.
métonymie, f. metonymy.
mètre, m. metre || (poët.) metre.
métré, m. measuring by the metre.
métrer, v. a. to measure.
métrique, a. metrical.
métromane, m. & f. metromaniac.
métronome, m. (mus.) metronome.
métropole, f. chief city || metropolitan
see || mother-church.
métropolitain, m. metropolitan.
métropolitain, e, a. metropolitan.
mets, m. mess, dish || food.
mettable, a. wearable.
mettre, v. a. ir. to put, to set, to lay, to
place, to put on || to deposit || to repose ||
to expose, to deliver || to contribute || to
invest || **~ en pièces,** to cut ou break ou
pull to pieces || **se ~,** to put, to lay, to
place, to set oneself || to sit down.   [rich.
meublant, e, a. for furniture || **bien ~,**
meuble, m. piece of furniture || utensil ||
-s, pl. household-goods (pl.), furniture ||
personal property || **~ à demeure fixe,**
fixture.
meuble, a. movable || personal || mellow.
meubler, v. a. to furnish (a house) || to
stock (a farm) || to adorn, to enrich || **~,**
v. n. to be fit for furniture || **~ bien,** to
be rich, to look well.
meule, f. small heap, rick (of hay) || mill-
stone, grindstone.
meulier, m. millstone-maker.   [stones.
meulière, f. millstone || quarry of mill-
meunier, m. miller || miller's thumb,
river bull-head (fish).
meunière, f. miller's wife.
meurt-de-faim, m. starving wretch.
meurtre, m. murder || (fig.) shame.
meurtrier, ère, m. & f. murderer || mur-
meurtrier, ère, a. murderous.   [deress.
meurtrière, f. loop-hole.
meurtrir, v. a. to bruise.
meurtrissure, f. bruise.
meute, f. pack of hounds.
mi, a. half, mid || **à ~-côte,** half-way up
the hill, half-way up.
mica, m. (min.) mica || glimmer || glist.
miasme, m. (méd.) miasma.
miaulement, m. mewing, caterwauling.
miauler, v. a. to mew.
miche, f. roll of bread, loaf.
Michel-Morin, m. Jack-of-all-trades.
micmac, m. underhand trick.
microscope, m. microscope, magnifying-
microscopique, a. microscopic.   [glass.
midi, m. midday, noon || meridian, South ||
à ~, at noon || **chercher ~ à quatorze
heures,** to look for difficulties where
there are none.

mie, f. crumb of bread || dear, sweetheart.
miel, m. honey || rayon de ~, m. honey-comb || ruche à ~, f. bee-hive.
mielleux, se, a. honeyed || fair-spoken.
mien, ne, pn. mine, my own, of mine || les –s, les –nes, pl. my relations (pl.), my friends (pl.).
miette, f. small crumb, little bit.
mieux, m. best || best way || improvement.
mieux, a. & ad. better, rather || best || de ~ en ~, better and better.
mièvre, a. arch, roguish.
mignard, e, a. (–ement, ad.) delicate || mincing(ly).
mignarder, v. a. to fondle.   [fondling.
mignardise, f. mincing || wheedling ||
mignon, ne, m. & f. darling, fondling || minion.   [(ly) || pretty, dainty, neat.
mignon, ne, a. (–nement, ad.) delicate
mignoter, v. a. to fondle.
migraine, f. (méd.) hemicrania, sick head-
migration, f. migration.   [ache, megrim.
mijaurée, f. affected woman.
mijoter, v. a. to let simmer.
mil, a. thousand.
milan, m. kite, vulture.
milice, f. militia (pl.), train-bands (pl.).
milicien, m. militiaman.
milieu, m. middle, mean || way, expedient || mediocrity || au ~ de, in the middle of, in the midst || au beau ~, in the very middle || le juste ~, the golden mean || ~ de salon, centre ottoman.
militaire, m. soldier.   [tarily.
militaire, a. military || –ment, ad. mili-
militarisme, m. (fig.) stratocracy || [tarism.
militer, v. a. to militate.
mille, m. thousand || mile.
mille, a. thousand || ~-feuille, f. (bot.) milfoil || ~-fleurs, f. all-flower || eau de ~-fleurs, cow's stale || ~-pieds, m. millepede, wood-louse.
millénaire, m. millenium.
millénaire, a. millenary.
millésime, m. date (on coins).
milliaire, m. mile(-stone).
milliard, m. thousand millions.
milliasse, f. ten hundred thousand millions || swarms (pl.), crowds (pl.), a world.
millième, m. thousandth.
millième, a. thousandth.
millier, m. thousand, thousand-weight.
millimètre, m. millimetre, thousandth.
million, m. million.   [part of a metre.
millionième, m. millionth.
millionnaire, m. millionnaire, person worth millions.
milord, m. lord || my lord || (fig.) nabob || cab-phaeton.
mime, m. mime, mimic.
mimique, f. mimic art.
mimique, a. mimic.
minable, a. miserable-looking, wretched.
minaret, m. minaret.   [mince.
minauder, v. n. to smirk, to simper, to
minauderie, f. affected looks (pl.), mincing manners (pl.).   [affected.
minaudier, ère, a. mincing, simpering,
mince, a. thin, slender, small, shallow.

mine, f. mien, look, countenance, figure || wry face, grimace || mine (of minerals) || ore || source || store || plot || secret || de mauvaise ~, ill-looking || avoir bonne ~, to look well.
miner, v. a. to undermine, to make a mine, to excavate || to waste, to consume, to weaken.
minerai, m. ore, unrefined metal.
minéral, m. mineral.
minéral, e, a. mineral.
minéralogie, f. mineralogy.
minéralogiste, m. mineralogist.
minet, te, m. & f. little cat, puss.
mineur, m. minor || miner.   [age.
mineur, e, a. less, lesser || minor, under
miniature, f. miniature || peintre en ~, m. miniature-painter || en ~, miniature, in miniature.
miniaturiste, m. miniature-painter.
minière, f. mining, mine.
minime, a. very little || trifling.
ministère, m. ministry, office, administration || minister's office || ministers (pl.) || agency || ~ public, public prosecutor.
ministériel, le, a. (–lement, ad.) ministerial(ly).
ministre, m. minister || parson.
minois, m. face, pretty face.
minon, m. kitten, puss.
minorité, f. minority.
minoterie, f. meal-store || miller's trade.
minuit, m. midnight || en plein ~, at dead of night.   [copy || (astr.) minute.
minute, f. minute, moment || rough draft.
minuter, v. a. to minute || to rough-draft.
minutie, f. trifles (pl.), minutiæ (pl.).
minutieux, se, a. (–sement, ad.) trifling, insignificant || minute(ly).
mioche, m. brat, urchin.
mi-parti, e, a. of two equal parts.
miracle, m. miracle, wonder || cour des –s, f. den of thieves || à ~, wonderfully well.
miraculeux, se, a. (–sement, ad.) miraculous(ly) || wonderful(ly).
mirage, m. looming || mirage.
mire, f. sight (of a fire-arm) || point de ~, m. object of aim.
mirer, v. a. & n. to aim at, to take one's aim at || (mar.) to loom || se ~, to look at oneself in a looking-glass || to admire oneself.   [self.
mirliflore, m. dandy, coxcomb.
mirliton, m. reed-pipe.
mirmidon, m. myrmidon || shrimp.
mirobolant, e, a. (fam.) wonderful, stunning.
miroir, m. mirror, looking-glass || ~ de toilette, dressing-glass || ~ ardent, burning-glass || œufs au ~, m. pl. fried eggs (pl.).
miroité, a. dapple || shot || shining.
miroiterie, f. looking-glass trade.
miroitier, m. looking-glass-maker.
miroton, m. (culin.) miroton (beef).
mis, e, a. attired || dressed, clad.
misaine, f. (mar.) foresail || mât de ~, m. foremast.
misanthrope, m. misanthrope.
misanthropie, f. misanthropy.

misanthropique, a. misanthropic.
mise, f. laying out of money, expense, disbursement || manner of dressing, fashion || de ~, receivable, current || in fashion || ~ à flot, floating || ~ de fonds, outlay || ~ en accusation, impeachment || ~ en liberté, release || ~ en possession, taking possession || ~ en scène, getting up (of a play) || ~ en train, setting to work || ~ en vente, putting up for sale.
misérable, m. & f. wretch.
misérable, a. (-ment, ad.) miserable || wretched(ly) || wicked || miserably.
misère, f. misery, wretchedness, poverty, want, distress || trouble, plague || trifle.
miséréré, m. (méd.) iliac passion.
miséricorde, f. mercy, pardon.
miséricordieux, se, a. (-sement, ad.) merciful(ly).
missel, m. missal, mass-book.
mission, f. mission.
missionnaire, m. missionary.
missive, f. missive.
mistral, m. violent north-west wind.
mitaine, f. mitten.
mite, f. cheese-mite, tick.
mitiger, v. a. to mitigate.
mitonner, v. a. & n. to fondle || to humour || to prepare || to let simmer || to simmer.
mitoyen, ne, a. middle || vide mur.
mitraillade, f. firing of grape-shot.
mitraille, f. grape-shot || charge à ~, f. case-shot.
mitrailler, v. a. to fire grape-shot.
mitrailleuse, f. mitrailleuse, gatling-gun.
mitre, f. mitre || chimney-top.
mitré, e, a. mitred.
mitron, m. journeyman baker.
mixte, a. mixed.
mixtion, f. mixture.
mixtionner, v. a. to mix, to mingle.
mnémonique, f. mnemonics (pl.).
mnémonique, a. mnemonic.
mobile, m. moving power || spring || motive.
mobile, a. movable, unsteady || quick, lively.
mobiliaire, a. movable, personal.
mobilier, m. furniture || suite.
mobilier, ère, a. movable || of personal property.
mobilisation, m. (mil.) mobilisation.
mobiliser, v. a. to liberate || (mil.) to mobilité, f. mobility.　　　　[mobilise.
mode, m. (gr.) mood || mode.
mode, f. mode, fashion, custom, way, vogue || -s, pl. millinery || fashionable articles of dress (pl.) || à la ~, according to the fashion || in fashion.
modelage, m. modelling.
modèle, m. model, pattern, copy.
modeler, v. a. to model || se ~, to take for one's model.
modeleur, m. modeller.
modérateur, trice, m. & f. moderator || regulator.
modérateur, trice, a. moderating.
modération, f. moderation, temper, abatement.
modéré, e, a. (-ment, ad.) moderate(ly).

modérer, v. a. to moderate, to temper, to abate, to restrain, to cool || se ~, to restrain oneself, to become temperate.
moderne, m. modern style.
moderne, a. modern.
moderniser, v. a. to modernise.
modeste, a. (-ment, ad.) modest(ly).
modestie, f. modesty.
modicité, f. smallness || moderateness.
modification, f. modification, restriction.
modifier, v. a. to modify.
modique, a. (-ment, ad.) moderate(ly).
modiste, m. & f. man-milliner || milliner.
modulation, f. modulation.
moduler, v. a. & n. to modulate || to warble.
moelle, f. marrow || pith (of a tree).
moelleux, m. softness.
moelleux, se, a. (-sement, ad.) full of marrow, pithy || soft(ly) || racy (of wine)
moellon, m. ashlar || rubble.
mœurs, f. pl. manners (pl.), morals (pl.), customs (pl.), ways (pl.).
mofette, f. choke-damp || malaria.
moi, pn. I, me || à ~! help! help! pour ~, quant à ~, as for me, for my part.
moignon, m. stump.
moindre, a. less, lesser || least.
moine, m. monk, friar || warming-pan || ~ bourru, bugbear.
moineau, m. sparrow.
moineau, a. cropped.
moinerie, f. monkhood.
moinillon, m. sorry monk.
moins, ad. less, lesser, except, but || le ~, the least || au ~, pour le ~, at least || à ~, for less || à ~ que, unless.
moirage, m. watering.
moire, f. watered silk || watering.
moiré, e, a. watered.
moirer, v. a. to water.　　　[the month.
mois, m. month || month's pay || au ~, by
moise, f. couple (tool) || brace.
moisi, e, a. mould, mouldiness.
moisi, e, a. mouldy.　　　　　[mouldy.
moisir, v. a. to mould || se ~, to get moisissure, f. mouldiness.
moissine, f. bundle of vine-branches with hanging grapes.
moisson, f. harvest, crop, harvest-time.
moissonner, v. a. to reap corn, to cut corn, to crop || to destroy.
moissonneur, m. reaper, harvest-man.
moissonneuse, f. female reaper || reaping-moite, a. moist, damp.　　　[machine.
moiteur, f. moistness, moisture, dampness.
moitié, f. moiety, half || à ~, by half.
molaire, f. molar tooth.
molaire, a. molar.
môle, m. mole, mound, dike.
molécule, f. particle, atom, molecula.
molester, v. a. to molest.
molette, f. rowel || mullar || windgall.
mollasse, a. flabby, flimsy.
molle, a. f. (de mol) vide mou.
mollement, ad. softly || effeminately || indolently || carelessly || luxuriously.
mollesse, f. softness || effeminacy || flabbiness, laxness.　　　　　　[(fish).
mollet, m. calf (of the leg) || whiting-pout

mollet, te, a. soft ‖ light.
molleton, m. swan-skin.
mollir, v. a. & n. to soften, to grow soft ‖ to give way, to slacken.
mollusque, m. mollusc ‖ shell-fish.
moment, m. moment, instant ‖ dans le ~, immediately, presently ‖ du ~ que, as soon as ‖ à tout ~, every moment ‖ au ~ que, au ~ où, the instant that.
momentané, e, a. momentary ‖ **–ment,** ad. momentarily.
momerie, f. mummery.
momie, f. mummy·‖ sluggard.
mon, pn. m. my.
monacal, e, a. monachal.
monarchie, f. monarchy. (ally).
monarchique, a. (–ment, ad.) monarchic
monarchiste, m. royalist.
monarque, m. monarch.
monastère, m. monastery.
monastique, a. monastic.
monaut, a. one-eared.
monceau, m. heap, pile.
mondain, m. worldling.
mondain, e, a. worldly ‖ worldly-minded.
mondainement, ad. worldly‖mundanely.
mondanité, f. worldliness.
monde, m. world, universe, earth ‖ mankind (pl.), people (pl.), folks (pl.) ‖ menservants (pl.)‖ du ~, in the world ‖fashionable ‖ le grand ~, the court and nobility (pl.) ‖ le beau ~, people of fashion (pl.) ‖ tout le ~, everybody ‖ le demi-monde, fast women (pl.), demi-monde.
monder, v. a. to cleanse, to peel.
mondor, m. man made of money.
monétaire, a. monetary.
moniteur, m. monitor.
monnaie, f. money, coin, mint ‖ de la petite ~, small-coin, change ‖ hôtel de la ~, m. mint ‖ ~ de singe, soft-sawder, blarney.
monnayage, m. coinage of money.
monnayer, v. a. to coin.
monnayeur, m. minter, coiner.
monocle, m. eye-glass.
monocorde, m. (mus.) monochord.
monographie, f. monography.
monolithe, m. monolith.
monologue, m. soliloquy.
monomanie, f. monomania.
monoplan, m. monoplane.
monopole, m. monopoly.
monopoliser, v. a. to monopolise.
monosyllabe, m. (gr.) monosyllable
monosyllabe, a. (gr.) monosyllabic.
monotone, a. monotonous.
monotonie, f. monotony.
monseigneur, m. my Lord ‖ your Lordship ‖ his Lordship ‖ crow-bar.
monsieur, m. sir, master, gentleman.
monstre, m. monster.
monstrueux, se, a. (–sement, ad.) monstrous(ly).
monstruosité, f. monstrosity.
mont, m. mount, mountain‖ ~-de-piété, pawnbroker's office, pawnbrokery.
montage, m. coming up, mounting, setting up, carrying up.

montagnard, e, m. & f. mountaineer, highlander ‖ ultra-revolutionist.
montagnard, e, a. mountain.
montagne, f. mountain ‖ highland ‖ultra-revolutionist party.
montagneux, se, a. mountainous, hilly.
montant, m. amount, sum, sum total ‖ door-post ‖ strength ‖ flavour.
montant, e, a. rising ‖ hilly, steep ‖ (of dresses) high-necked ‖ (of collars) stand-up ‖ (mil.) garde –e, f. relieving-guard.
monte, f. covering ‖ covering season (of horses). (steps pl.).
montée, f. ascent ‖ stairs (pl.), staircase,
monter, v. a. & n. to mount, to go up, to ascend, to get up, to climb ‖ to wind up, to lift up ‖ to carry up ‖ to set up, to establish ‖ to grow up, to amount, to have some height‖ se ~, to come to, to amount‖ to provide oneself ‖ to get excited ‖ to reach.
monteur, m. mounter.
montgolfière, f. fire-balloon.
monticule, m. hillock.
montoir, m. horse-block.
montre, f. watch ‖ sample ‖ muster, review, show, parade ‖ place for showing ‖ ~ à réveil, alarm-watch ‖ ~ à répétition, repeating watch, repeater ‖ ~ à savonnette, hunting watch ‖ en ~, in the window.
montrer, v. a. to show, to exhibit, to let see, to point out‖ to teach ‖ se ~, to show oneself.
montueux, se, a. mountainous, hilly.
monture, f. mount, riding-animal ‖ hackney, nag ‖ mounting. (token ‖ tomb.
monument, m. monument, memorial,
monumental, e, a. monumental, memorial.
se moquer, v. a. to laugh at, to mock, to ridicule, to deride, to scorn, to despise.
moquerie, f. mockery, derision, scorn,
moquette, f. velvet-pile. (scoff.
moqueur, se, m. & f. mocker.
moqueur, se, a. mocking.
morailles, f. pl. (mar.) barnacles (pl.).
moraillon, m. clasp (of a lock).
moral, e, a. (–ement, ad.) moral(ly).
morale, f. morality, morals (pl.), ethics (pl.) ‖ lecture.
moraliser, v. a. to moralise ‖ to lecture.
moraliseur, m. moraliser.
moraliste, m. moralist.
moralité, f. morality, morals (pl.).
morbide, a. morbid.
morbleu! zounds!
morceau, m. bit, morsel, piece, fragment ‖ patch ‖ ~ de pain, (fig.) old song, mere nothing.
morceler, v. a. to parcel, to parcel out.
morcellement, m. parcelling.
mordacité, f. corrosiveness ‖ (fig.) bitterness.
mordant, m. pigment, size. (ness.
mordant, e, a. biting ‖ sharp, satirical, satirical. (snappish.
mordicus, ad. (fam.) doggedly.
mordiller, v. a. to nibble.
mordoré, e, a. reddish-brown.
mordre, v. a. & n. to bite, to gnaw, to corrode, to nibble ‖ to close with, to like ‖ s'en ~ les doigts, to repent of it.

more, m. negro, blackamoor.

moresque, a. moresque, moorish.

morelle, f. (bot.) night-shade.

morfil, m. wire edge || elephants' teeth (pl.).

morfondre, v. a. to chill || se ~, to be chilled || to dance attendance, to wait in vain || to waste one's time.

morfondure, f. cold after heat, morfoundering.

morgue, f. proud look || haughtiness || conceit || dead-house.

morguené ! morguienne ! hang it !

moribond, e, a. dying.

moricaud, e, m. & f. (fam.) blackey, sambo, nigger || black silkworm.

morigéner, v. a. to tutor, to reprimand.

morille, f. (bot.) morel, moril.

morillon, m. black grape || **-s, pl.** rough emeralds (pl.).

morne, m. hillock, mountain.

morne, a. gloomy, dull.

mornifle, f. slap on the cheek.

morose, a. sulky, sullen, sour.

morosité, f. moroseness.

morphine, f. (chim.) morphia.

morpion, m. crab-louse.

mors, m. curb, bit, horse-bit.

morse, m. morse, hippopotamus.

morsure, f. bite, biting.

mort, f. death, decease || ~ **aux mouches,** fly-destroyer || **à ~,** mortally, to death.

mort, e, m. & f. dead person || corpse.

mort, e, a. dead, defunct || stagnant || lying dead || neap || spent || out || lifeless || **ivre-~,** a. dead-drunk || **~-né,** a. still-born.

mortadelle, f. Bologna-sausage.

mortaise, f. mortise.

mortalité, f. mortality.

mortel, m. mortal, man.   [deadly.

mortel, le, a. (-lement, ad.) mortal(ly) ||

mortier, m. mortar || cap || coif.

mortifier, v. a. to mortify || to vex, to humble || to make (meat) tender.

mortuaire, a. mortuary || funeral || **drap ~,** m. pall || **extrait ~,** m. death-certificate || **maison ~,** f. house of the deceased.

morue, f. codfish, cod.

morve, f. glanders (pl.) || snot.

morveux, se, m. & f. brat || slut || **qui se sent ~ se mouche,** let him whom the cap fits wear it.

morveux, se, a. snotty || glandered.

mosaïque, f. marquetry, patch-work.

mosquée, f. mosque.

mot, m. word, saying, sentence || **en un ~,** in a word, in short || **à ces -s,** at those words || **~ à ~, ~ pour ~,** word for word, literally || **bon ~,** jest, joke, witticism || **~ à double entente,** ambiguous word, pun.   [peller || moving power.

moteur, m. motor || mover, author || pro-

moteur, trice, a. motive, moving.

motif, m. motive, incitement, cause, reason.

motiver, v. a. to allege motives ou reasons.

motocycle, m. motor-bicycle.

motte, f. clod || peat || hillock || roll.

motteux, m. white-tail, wheat-ear (bird).

motus ! hush ! mum ! not a word !

mou, m. lights (of animals) (pl.).

mou, (mol), molle, a. soft, mellow || muggy || indolent, weak, effeminate, enervated || **temps ~,** m. close weather.

mouchard, m. spy, eavesdropper.

moucharder, v. a. & n. to spy.

mouche, f. fly || spy, patch || blade || (of foils) cap || loo (game) || little beard on the under-lip || **à miel,** honey-bee || **~e bleue,** blue-bottle (fly) || **une fine ~, a** cunning person.

moucher, v. a. to blow the nose || to snuff a candle || **se ~,** to blow one's nose || **ne pas se ~ du pied,** to be no fool.

moucherolle, f. fly-catcher (bird).

moucheron, m. gnat || snuff (of a candle).

mouchleter, v. a. to spot || to speckle || to cap.

mouchettes, f. pl. snuffers (pl.).

moucheture, f. spot || spottedness || speckle.

mouchoir, m. handkerchief.

mouchure, f. snuffing of a candle.

moudre, v. a. ir. to grind || to mill.

moue, f. pouting, wry face || **faire la ~,** to pout.

muette, f. sea-gull (bird).

moufette, f. choke-damp || malaria.

moufle, m. bloated face.

moufle, f. mitten || tackle.

mouflon, m. mufflon, wild sheep.

mongick, m. (Russian) peasant, **moujik.**

mouillage, m. anchorage.

mouiller, v. a. to wet, to soak, to moisten || to cast anchor || **se ~,** to get wet.

mouillette, f. "finger" of bread.

mouillure, f. wetting.

moulage, m. moulding.

moule, m. mould, cast, model, pattern || netting-rule || **~ à beurre,** butter-print.

moule, f. mussel (fish).

mouler, v. a. to mould, to cast || to print.

mouleur, m. moulder.

moulin, m. mill || **~ à bras,** hand-mill || **~ à eau,** water-mill || **~ à foulon,** fulling-mill || **~ à paroles,** chatterbox || **~ à vent,** windmill || **~ à papier,** paper-mill || **~ à huile,** oil-mill || **~ à poudre,** powder-mill || **~ à café,** coffee-

moulinage, m. silk-throwing.   [grinder.

mouliné, e, a. worm-eaten.

moulinet, m. hand-mill || **faire le ~,** to twirl, to flourish.

moulu, e, a. ground, bruised || aching.

moulure, f. moulding

mourant, e, a. dying, fading, languishing.

mourir, v. n. ir. to die, to expire || **to** perish || **se ~,** to die, to be dying.

mouron, m. chickweed.

mousquet, m. musket.

mousquetaire, m. musketeer.

mousqueterie, f. musketry || **volley of** musketry.

mousqueton, m. musketoon.

mousse, m. cabin-boy.

mousse, f. (bot.) moss || froth, foam || lather.

mousseline, f. muslin.

mousser, v. n. to froth, to foam, to lather, to sparkle || **faire ~,** to puff (one) up.

mousseron, m. (bot.) small white mushroom.   [ling || mossy.

mousseux, e, a. frothy, foaming, spark-

mousson, f. monsoon.
moussu, e, a. mossy.
moustache, f. mustachios (pl.) || (of animals) whisker || **vieille ~,** old soldier.
moustiquaire, f. mosquito-net.
moustique, m. mosquito.
moût, m. must || wort.
moutard, m. little boy, brat.
moutarde, f. mustard || trifles (pl.) || **faire monter la ~ au nez,** to make angry.
moutardier, m. mustard-pot || mustard-maker.
mouton, m. mutton, wether, sheep || sheep-leather || rammer || lamp || prison-spy || **-s,** pl. rolling waves (pl.).
moutonné, e, a. fleecy.
moutonner, v. n. to foam, to whiten.
moutonneux, se, a. fleecy.
moutonnier, a. sheep-like || woolly.
monture, f. grinding || miller's pay || meslin.
mouvant, e, a. moving || shifting || animated || **sable ~,** m. quicksand.
mouvement, m. motion, movement || impulse || (mus.) measure || bustle, agitation || emotion || fit || fluctuation.
mouver, v. a. (hort.) to stir up the mould.
mouvoir, v. a. ir. to move, to stir, to agitate, to incite, to instigate.
moyen, m. means, way, expedient || assistance || power, riches (pl.).
moyen, ne, a. middle, middling, average || middle-sized.
moyennant, pr. for, by means of.
moyenne, f. average.
moyeu, m. nave (of a wheel) || plum.
muable, a. mutable.
mucilage, m. mucilage || gum.
mucilagineux, se, a. muscilaginous.
mucosité, f. mucus.
mue, f. moulting || mewing || moulting-time || slough, cast skin || mew || coop.
muer, v. n. to moult || to mew || to shed the feathers || to change.
muet, te, a. mute, dumb, speechless.
muette, f. mew || shooting-lodge.
mufle, m. muzzle || snout.
muflier, m. snap-dragon.
muge, m. mullet.
mugir, v. n. to roar, to bellow, to low.
mugissement, m. roaring, bellowing.
muguet, m. (bot.) lily of the valley || (méd.) thrush.
muid, m. hogshead.
mulâtre, esse, m. & f. mulatto.
mulâtre, esse, a. mulatto.
mule, f. mule || slipper.
muletier, m. muleteer.
mulot, m. field-mouse.
multinôme, a. (alg.) multinomial.
multipare, a. multiparous.
multiplicateur, m. multiplicator.
multiplicité, f. multiplicity.
multiplier, v. a. to multiply, to increase || to breed || **se ~,** to multiply.
multitude, f. multitude.
municipal, m. municipal guard, constable || municipal officer.
municipal, e, a. municipal.
municipalité, f. municipality || **town-hall.**
munificence, f. munificence.

munir, v. a. to store, to provide with, to furnish with.
munition, f. ammunition || provisions || **pain de ~,** m. ammunition-bread.
munitionnaire, m. commissioner of stores.
muqueux, se, a. (an. & méd.) mucous.
mur, m. wall || **~ mitoyen,** partition-wall || **~ d'appui,** breast-wall || **~ d'enceinte,** walls.
mûr, e, a. ripe, mellow, mature || worn-out || **-ement,** ad. maturely, deliberately.
muraille, f. wall.
muraillement, m. walling.
mural, e, a. a mural.   [blackberry.
mûre, f. (bot.) mulberry || **~ sauvage,**
murène, f. sea-eel (fish).   [dow).
murer, v. a. to wall || to block up (a win-
mûrier, m. (bot.) mulberry-tree || **~ sauvage,** blackberry-bush.
mûrir, v. a. & n. to ripen, to grow ripe.
murmurateur, trice, m. & f. murmurer, grumbler.   [tering.
murmure, m. murmur, grumbling, mut-
murmurer, v. n. to murmur, to grumble || to whisper.
musaraigne, f. shrew-mouse.
musard, m. loiterer.
musard, e, a. loitering.
musarder, v. n. to loiter.
musc, m. musk.
muscade, f. (bot.) nutmeg || juggler's ball || **fleur de ~,** f. (bot. & com.) mace.
muscadel, m. muscatel.
muscadier, m. (bot.) nutmeg-tree.
muscadin, m. musk-lozenge || scented fop.
muscat, m. (bot.) muscatel grape.
muscat, e, a. muscatel.
muscle, m. muscle.
musclé, e, a. musculous.
musculaire, a. muscular.
musculeux, se, m. muscular, brawny.
muse, f. muse || beginning of rutting-time.
museau, m. snout, muzzle, nose.
musée, m. museum.
museler, v. a. to muzzle.
muselière, f. muzzle, nose-band.
muser, v. n. to muse, to loiter, to trifle || to go to rut.
muserolle, f. nose-band of a horse's bridle.
musette, f. bagpipe || nose-bag.
muséum, m. museum.
musical, e, a. (-ement, ad.) musical(ly).
musicien, m. musician.
musique, f. music || band || musical-box || **à ~,** musical.   [flattering.
musqué, e, a. musk-scented || affected ||
musquer, v. a. to perfume with musk.
Musulman, m. Mahometan, Mussulman.
mutabilité, f. mutability.
mutation, f. mutation, change.
mutilateur, m. mutilator.
mutilateur, a. mutilating.
mutiler, v. a. to mutilate, to maim.
mutin, e, m. & f. refractory child || mutinous person || (mil.) mutineer.
mutin, e, a. mutinous, seditious, riotous, headstrong.
se mutiner, to mutiny || to be stubborn.

mutinerie, f. mutiny, sedition || stubbornness, fractiousness.
mutisme, m. dumbness.
mutuel, le, a. (-lement, ad.) mutual(ly) || reciprocal(ly).
myope, m. short-sighted person.
myope, a. short-sighted.
myopie, f. short-sightedness. [not.
myosotis, m. (bot.) myosotis, forget-me-
myriade, f. myriad, ten thousand.
myriamètre, m. ten thousand metres (= 10 kilometres).
myriapode, m. millepede.
myrrhe, f. myrrh.
myrrhis, m. (bot.) myrrh.
myrte, m. (bot.) myrtle.
mystère, m. mystery [mysterious(ly).
mystérieux, se, a. (-sement, ad.)
mysticisme, m. mysticism.
mysticité, f. mysticalness.
mystificateur, m. hoaxer.
mystifier, v. a. to mystify, to hoax.
mystique, a. (-ment, ad.) mystic(ally).
mythe, m. myth, fable.
mythologie, f. mythology.
mythologique, a. mythological.

N.

nabab, m. nabob.
nabot, e, m. & f. shrimp, dwarf.
nacarat, a. nacarat.
nacelle, f. small boat.
nacre, f. mother of pearl.
nage, f. swimming || (mar.) rowlock || à la ~, in swimming || tout en ~, all in a perspiration. [to swim with.
nageoire, f. fin (of a fish) || cork ou bladders
nager, v. n. to swim, to float || (mar.) to row.
nageur, se, m. & f. swimmer || (mar.)
nageur, se, a. swimming. [rower.
naïade, f. naiad, water-nymph.
naïf, ve, a. artless, ingenuous, innocent, unaffected, simple. [(card game).
nain, m. dwarf || ~ jaune, Pope Joan
nain, e, a. dwarfish.
naissance, f. birth, extraction || descent || beginning, rise || spring.
naissant, e, a. rising, coming forth || dawning || incipient || infant || budding.
naître, v. n. ir. to be born, to come into the world || to grow, to arise, to originate.
naïvement, ad. plainly, candidly, ingenuously.
naïveté, f. artlessness, ingenuousness, frankness, native simplicity.
nanan, m. dainties (pl.), goodies (pl.).
nankin, m. nankeen.
nantir, v. a. to give a pledge ou security || être nanti de, to hold as security || se ~, to provide oneself with || to have in hand.
nantissement, m. security, pledge.
naphte, m. (chim.) naphtha. [coin).
Napoléon, m. Napoleon (20 franc gold-
nappe, f. cloth || table-cloth || clap-net.

napperon, m. table-cloth. [daffodil.
narcisse, m. (bot.) narcissus || ~ des prés,
narcotique, m. (méd.) narcotic.
narcotique, a. (méd.) narcotic.
nard, m. (bot.) spikenard. [a fig for...|
nargue, f. spite || (fig.) mockery || ~ de...|
narguer, v. a. to set at defiance.
narine, f. nostril.
narquois, e, a. cunning, sly.
narrateur, m. narrator.
narratif, ve, a. narrative.
narration, f. narration, narrative, recital.
narré, m. narration.
narrer, v. a. to narrate.
nasal, e, a. (-ement, ad.) nasal(ly).
naseau, m. nostril.
nasillard, e, m. & f. snuffler.
nasillard, e, a. snuffling.
nasillement, m. snuffling.
nasiller, v. n. to speak through the nose.
nasilleur, se, m. & f. snuffler. [scrape.
nasse, f. wear (fish) || weir, snare || (fig.)
natal, e, a. natal, native || jour ~, m. birthday || pays ~, m. native country.
natation, f. swimming.
natif, ve, a. native, born.
nation, f. nation, people.
national, e, a. (-ement, ad.) national(ly).
nationaliser, v. a. to nationalise.
nationalité, f. nationality.
nationaux, m. pl. natives (pl.) || native subjects (pl.).
nativité, f. nativity, birth.
natte, f. mat, hassock || plaited hair || plait.
natter, v. a. to mat || to plait the hair.
nattier, m. mat-maker.
naturaliser, v. a. to naturalise.
naturaliste, m. naturalist.
naturalité, f. right of a native || privilege of naturalisation.
nature, f. nature || constitution || kind || d'après ~, from nature || from the life || contre ~, unnatural || payer en ~, to pay in kind.
naturel, m. nature, temper, genius, constitution, disposition of mind || native.
naturel, le, a. natural, easy, ingenuous, plain, sincere || illegitimate.
naturellement, ad. naturally, by nature || easily || frankly || of course.
naufrage, m. shipwreck || faire ~, to be shipwrecked || to be wrecked.
naufragé, e, a. shipwrecked.
naulage, m. freight of passengers.
nauséabond, e, a. nauseous.
nausée, f. nausea || disgust.
nautile, m. nautilus.
nautique, a. nautical.
nautonier, m. mariner, sailor.
naval, e, a. naval.
navée, f. boat-load.
navet, m. (bot.) turnip || (hort.) root.
navette, f. (bot.) rape || rape-seed || rape-oil || netting-needle || weaver's shuttle || faire la ~, to run to and fro.
navigable, a. navigable.
navigateur, m. navigator.
navigateur, a. seafaring.
navigation, f. navigation || voyage.

naviguer, v. n. to navigate, to sail.
navire, m. ship, vessel || ~ marchand, (mar.) merchantman.
navrant, e, a. heartrending.
navrer, v. a. to wound, to rend the heart.
ne, c. no, not || ~ pas, ~ point, not.
né, e, a. born || bien ~, of good birth || well-disposed.
néanmoins, c. nevertheless, however, for all that.
néant, m. nothingness, nothing, nought.
nébuleuse, f. (astr.) cloud, nebula.
nébuleux, se, a. nebulous, cloudy, gloomy.
nébulosité, f. nebulosity, cloudiness.
nécessaire, m. necessaries (pl.) || work-box || dressing-case || canteen.
nécessaire, a. necessary || requisite || -ment, ad. necessarily, needs.
nécessité, f. necessity, exigence, indigence, want || -s, pl. necessaries (pl.).
nécessiter, v. a. to necessitate, to force, to compel.
nécessiteux, se, a. necessaitous, needy.
nec plus ultra, adv. ne plus ultra.
nécrologe, m. obituary.
nécrologie, f. necrology.
nécrologique, a. necrological.
nécromancie, f. necromancy.
nécromancien, m. necromancer.
nécropole, f. necropolis.
nectar, m. nectar.
nef, f. nave (of a church) || (poët.) ship.
néfaste, a. inauspicious, unlucky.
nèfle, f. medlar.
néflier, m. (bot.) medlar-tree.
négatif, ve, a. (-vement, ad.) negative (ly) || in the negative.
négation, f. negation, denial.
négative, f. (gr.) negative || refusal.
négligé, m. negligée, undress, loose dress.
négligemment, ad. negligently, carelessly.
négligence, f. negligence, carelessness.
négligent, e, a. negligent, neglectful || careless.
négliger, v. a. to neglect, to slight || to emit || se ~, to neglect oneself.
négoce, m. trade, trading, commerce.
négociable, a. negotiable.
négociant, m. merchant.
négociateur, m. negotiator.
négociation, f. negotiation.
négocier, v. a. & n. to negotiate, to trade.
nègre, sse, m. & f. negro || negress.
nègrerie, f. negro-yard, barracoon.
négrier, m. slave-dealer || (mar.) slave-ship.
négrillon, ne, m. & f. negro-boy || negro-girl.
neige, f. snow || pelote de ~, f. snow-[ball.
neiger, v. n. to snow.
neigeux, se, a. snowy.
nenni, ad. no, not at all, no forsooth.
nénufar, nénuphar, m. (bot.) water-lily.
néologie, f. neology.
néologisme, m. neologism.
néologiste, néologue, m. neologist.
néophyte, m. neophyte.
néphrétique, a. (an. & méd.) nephritic || renal.

népotisme, m. nepotism.
néréide, f. nereid. [de –s, f. nervous fit.
nerf, m. nerve, strength, sinew || attaque
nerprun, m. (bot.) buck-thorn.
nervé, e, a. nerved.
nerver, v. a. to cord.
nerveux, se, a. nervous, sinewy || vigorous.
nervure, f. nerve, moulding || cording || slips || rib.
net, te, a. neat, clean || clear, pure, innocent, blameless || perspicuous || compte ~, m. clear account || ~, ad. entirely || at once || short || frankly || flatly || -tement, ad. neatly, cleanly, clearly, frankly, plainly.
netteté, f. neatness, cleanness, clearness.
nettoiement, nettoyage, m. cleaning, cleansing, clearing. [scour || to pick.
nettoyer, v. a. to clean, to cleanse, to plainly.
neuf, m. nine || ninth.
neuf, a. nine || ninth.
neuf, m. something new || new clothes || à ~, again, anew || like new.
neuf, ve, a. new, fresh, raw, inexperienced.
neutralement, ad. neutrally.
neutraliser, v. a. to neutralise.
neutralité, f. neutrality.
neutre, a. neuter, neutral. [novena.
neuvaine, f. nine days' devotions (pl.).
neuvième, a. (-ment, ad.) ninth(ly).
neveu, m. nephew.
névralgie, f. (méd.) neuralgia.
névrose, f. (méd.) neurosis.
nez, m. nose || (mar.) bows of a ship (pl.) ||
ni, c. neither, nor. [smell || scent.
niable, a. deniable.
niais, m. simpleton, ninny.
niais, e, a. silly || foolish || -ement, ad. sillily, foolishly.
niaiser, v. n. to paddle, to play the fool.
niaiserie, f. silliness, simplicity, foolery.
niche, f. niche || trick || kennel. [trifle.
nichée, f. nest, brood || crew, set, lot.
nicher, v. n. to nestle || ~, v. a. to put, to
nichet, m. nest-egg. [set.
nichoir, m. breeding-cage.
Nicodème, m. noodle, silly-billy.
nid, m. nest || ~ à rats, rat-hole || wretched hovel.
nielle, f. mildew, blight || cockle.
nieller, v. a. to smut, to blight || to enamel in black.
nier, v. a. to deny, to disown.
nigaud, m. booby, simpleton.
nigaud, e, a. silly, foolish.
nigauder, v. n. to play the fool, to trifle.
nigauderie, f. foolery, silliness, foolish [action.
nihilisme, m. nihilism.
nihiliste, m. nihilist.
nihiliste, a. nihilist, nihilistic.
nille, f. tendril of a vine.
nimbe, f. nimbus, glory.
nipper, v. a. to rig out, to fit out. [(pl.).
nippes, f. pl. clothes (pl.), apparel, things
nique, f.; faire la ~ à qn., to scorn one.
nitouche, f.; sainte ~, demure hypocrite.
nitreux, se, a. (chim.) nitrous.
nitrière, f. saltpetre-bed.
nitrique, a. (chim.) nitric.

niveau, m. level ‖ ~ à bulle d'air, spirit-level ‖ au ~, de ~, level, even with.

niveler, v. a. to level.

niveleur, m. leveller.

nivellement, m. levelling.

nobiliaire, m. peerage(book).

nobiliaire, a. pertaining to the nobility.

noble, m. nobleman.   [ad. nobly.

noble, a. noble, great, illustrious ‖ —ment,

noblesse, f. nobleness, nobility.

noce, noces, f. wedding, nuptials, mar-riage ‖ wedding feast ‖ jollification ‖ drink-ing-bout ‖ comfortable ou pleasant situa-noceur, m. reveller, gay spark.   [tion.

nocher, m. pilot ‖ steersman.

nocturne, a. nocturnal, nightly.

nocuité, f. noxiousness.

nodosité, f. (chir.) node ‖ (bot.) nodosity.

Noël, m. Christmas ‖ Christmas-carol ‖ à la ~, on Christmas Day.

nœud, m. knot, joint, tie ‖ node ‖ rub ‖ knuckle ‖ (fig.) difficulty.

noir, m. black ‖ smudge ‖ bull's-eye ‖ negro ‖ ~ de fumée, lamp-black ‖ faire ~, to be dark.

noir, e, a. black, dark, sable, foul, dirty, gloomy ‖ wicked, base ‖ (of bread, meat, sauces) brown ‖ (of coffee) without milk ‖ ~ animal, bone-black ‖ en ~, on the dark

noirâtre, a. blackish.   [side.

noiraud, m. dark person ‖ blackamoor.

noirceur, f. blackness ‖ heinousness, base-ness, atrocity.   [defame.

noircir, v. a. & n. to blacken, to stain, to

noircissure, f. blackening, black spot.

noire, f. (mus.) crotchet.

noise, f. quarrel ‖ chercher ~ à, to pick a quarrel with.

noisetier, m. (bot.) hazel-tree.

noisette, f. nut, hazel-nut.

noix, f. nut, walnut ‖ tumbler ‖ kernel ‖ pope's eye ‖ knee-cap ‖ ~ de galle, gall-nolis, m. (mar.) freight.   [nut.

noliser, v. a. (mar., com.) to charter (in the Mediterranean).

nom, m. name ‖ noun ‖ fame, reputation, glory ‖ au ~ de, in the name of ‖ de ~, in name ‖ ~ de baptême, christian name ‖ ~ de demoiselle, maiden name ‖ ~ de guerre, assumed name ‖ alias ‖ nick-name.

nomade, a. nomadic, wandering, errant.

nombre, m. number ‖ multitude ‖ harmony.

nombrer, v. a. to number.

nombreux, se, a. numerous ‖ harmonious.

nombril, m. navel ‖ (an.) umbilicus ‖ (bot.) eye ‖ ~ de Vénus, (bot.) navel-wort.

nomenclature, f. nomenclature.

nominal, e, a. nominal.

nominatif, m. (gr.) nominative (case).

nominatif, ve, a. of names, nominative.

nomination, f. nomination, appointment.

nominativement, ad. by name.

nommément, ad. namely, particularly.

nommer, v. a. to name ‖ to call, to ap-point ‖ se ~, to be called.

non, ad. no, not ‖ ~ plus, no more, no longer ‖ ~ seulement, not only.

nonagénaire, m. & f. nonagenarian.

nonagénaire, a. nonagenarian.

nonce, m. nuncio.

nonchalamment, ad. carelessly, supinely.

nonchalance, f. carelessness, supineness.

nonchalant, e, a. negligent, remiss, care-

nonnain, nonne, f. nun.   [less.

nonnette, f. young nun ‖ gingerbread-nut.

nonobstant, pr. notwithstanding.

nonpareille, f. small ribbon ‖ (typ.) non-pareil.   [pareil.

non-sens, m. nonsense.

non-succès, m. failure.

non-usage, m. disuse.

non-valeur, f. unprofitableness, unpro-ductiveness ‖ (com.) outstanding debts

nord, m. North.   ‖ (pl.) ‖ bill of no value.

normal, e, a. normal.

Normand, m. crafty fellow.

normand, e, a. evasive ‖ equivocal.

nos, pn. pl. (de notre) our.

nostalgie, f. home-sickness.

nota, m. note, mark.

notabilité, f. remarkable persons (pl.).

notable, a. notable, of note, remarkable, considerable, eminent ‖ —ment, ad. no-tably ‖ considerably.

notables, m. pl. notables (pl.).

notaire, m. notary, attorney.

notamment, ad. especially, particularly.

notariat, m. notary's office.

note, f. note, mark, remark, annotation.

noter, v. a. to note, to mark, to remark ‖ to brand, to degrade.

noteur, m. music-copier.

notice, f. short account, short memoir, summary.   [to declare.

notifier, v. a. to notify, to make known.

notion, f. notion, idea, conception.

notoire, a. (—ment, ad.) notorious(ly).

notoriété, f. notoriety.

notre, pn. our.

nôtre (le, la), pn. ours ‖ our own ‖ ~s (les), pl. ours (pl.) ‖ our relations (pl.), our friends. (pl.).

noue, f. pantile ‖ gutter-lead ‖ pasture-ground.   [rickety ‖ set.

noué, e, a. tied ‖ (méd.) stiff-connected.

nouer, v. a. & n. to tie, to knit, to join ‖ se ~, (jard.) to knit ‖ to grow rickety.

noueux, se, a. knotty.

nougat, m. almond-cake.

nourrain, m. young fry (pl.).

nourrice, f. wet-nurse, foster-mother ‖ mettre en ~, to put out to nurse.

nourricier, m. foster-father ‖ fosterer.

nourricier, ère, a. nutritive.

nourrir, v. a. & n. to nourish, to nurture, to nurse, to feed ‖ to maintain, to keep ‖ se ~, to live ou feed upon.

nourrissage, m. feeding.

nourrisseur, m. cow-keeper, cattle-feeder.

nourrisson, m. nursling, foster-child, nurse-child.

nourriture, f. nourishment, food, living, livelihood ‖ education.   [ourselves (pl.).

nous, pn. pl. we, us, to us ‖ ~-mêmes, pl.

nouure, f. rickets (pl.).

nouveau, m. new boy (at school) ‖ some-thing new ‖ novelty ‖ de ~, anew ‖ again ‖ also.

nouveau (nouvel), velle, a. new, recent ‖ novel ‖ different ‖ other ‖ further ‖ green ‖ ~, ad. newly.

nouveauté, f. novelty, newness, innovation ‖ marchand de –s, m. linen-draper ‖ magasin de –s, m. fashionable warehouse.

nouvelle, f. news, intelligence, tidings.

nouvellement, ad. newly, recently, freshly, lately.

nouvelliste, m. newsmonger ‖ novelist.

novateur, trice, m. & f. innovator.

novateur, trice, a. innovating.

novembre, m. November.

novice, m. novice, beginner.

novice, a. novice, inexperienced, unskilled.

noviciat, m. novitiate, apprenticeship.

noyade, f. drowning.

noyale, f. sail-cloth.

noyau, m. stone (of a fruit) ‖ noyau (liqueur) ‖ newel of a winding-staircase ‖ nucleus ‖ mould, core.

noyer, m. (bot.) walnut-tree.

noyer, v. a. to drown ‖ **se ~,** to drown oneself, to be drowned.

noyon, m. (at bowls) mark.

nu, m. naked part ‖ (the) nude.

nu, e, a. naked, bare, uncovered ‖ poor, destitute ‖ plain, open ‖ **à ~,** nakedly, openly ‖ without a saddle ‖ **~ pieds,** barefoot ‖ **~-tête,** bareheaded.

nuage, m. cloud ‖ darkness.

nuageux, se, a. cloudy.

nuance, f. shade ‖ gradation of colours.

nuancer, v. a. to shade, to variegate.

nubile, a. marriageable.

nubilité, f. marriageable age.

nudité, f. nudity, nakedness.

nue, f. cloud ‖ –s, pl. skies (pl.).

nuée, f. cloud ‖ storm ‖ (fig.) swarm, multitude.   [to prejudice.

nuire, v. n. to annoy, to wrong, to hurt,

nuisible, a. hurtful, detrimental, prejudicial, noxious, injurious.

nuit, f. night ‖ darkness ‖ **de ~,** in the night ‖ **à la ~ tombante,** at nightfall ‖ **bonne ~,** good night ‖ **faire ~,** to be night *ou* dark ‖ **se faire ~,** to get dark.

nuitamment, ad. in the night, by night.

nuitée, f. night's work ‖ night's lodging.

nul, le, a. null, void, invalid ‖ no, not one, nobody.

nullement, ad. not at all, by no means, in no wise.

nullité, f. nullity, incapacity ‖ flaw ‖ cipher.

nûment, ad. nakedly, plainly.

numéraire, m. cash, specie ‖ bullion.

numéral, e, a. a numeral.

numérique, a. (–ment, ad.) numerical(ly).

numéro, m. number ‖ size.

numérotage, m. numbering.

numéroter, v. a. to number.

numismate, m. numismatologist.

nuptial, e, a. nuptial, bridal.

nuque, f. nape of the neck.

nutritif, ve, a. nutritive, nutritious, nourishing.

nymphe, f. nymph ‖ grub (of insects).

O.

oasis, m. oasis.

obéir, v. n. to obey, **to yield, to comply** with.   [dominion.

obéissance, f. obedience ‖ allegiance ‖

obéissant, e, a. obedient ‖ flexible ‖ dutiful.

obélisque, m. obelisk.

obérer, v. a. to run into debt.

obésité, f. obesity, corpulency.

obituaire, m. obituary.

obituaire, a. an obituary.

objecter, v. a. to object.

objectif, m. object-glass.

objectif, ve, a. objective.

objet, m. object, end, motive ‖ **matter,** business ‖ **~ de risée,** laughing-stock.

objurgation, f. objurgation.

oblation, f. oblation, offering.

obligation, f. obligation, duty, bond.

obligatoire, a. obligatory, compulsory, binding ‖ incumbent ‖ **–ment,** ad. compulsorily.   [pulsorily.

obligé, m. bond, indenture.

obligé, e, a. obliged, bound.

obligeamment, ad. obligingly.

obligeance, f. obligingness.

obliger, v. a. to oblige, to obligate, **to** bind, to compel.

oblique, a. (–ment, ad.) oblique(ly) ‖ indirect(ly) ‖ unfair(ly).

obliquer, v. n. to slant ‖ to turn ‖ to cut.

obliquité, f. obliquity ‖ slant ‖ (fig.) unfairness.   [fairness.

oblitérer, v. a. to obliterate.

oblong, ue, a. oblong.

obole, f. obole ‖ groat ‖ farthing ‖ **straw.**

obscénité, f. obscenity.

obscur, e, a. obscure, dark.

obscurcir, v. a. to obscure, to darken, **to** dim, to sully ‖ **s'~,** to become dark.

obscurcissement, m. darkening ‖ dimness.   [fusedly.

obscurément, ad. obscurely ‖ dimly, con-

obscurité, f. obscurity, obscureness, darkness, gloom.   [sess.

obséder, v. a. to beset ‖ (of spirits) to pos-

obsèques, f. pl. obsequies (pl.).

obséquieux, se, a. (–sement, ad.) obsequious(ly).

observateur, trice, m. & f. observer.

observateur, trice, a. observing.

observation, f. observation, remark ‖ look-out ‖ hint ‖ observance.

observatoire, m. observatory.

observer, v. a. to observe ‖ to examine ‖ to take notice, to mind ‖ **s'~,** to look at each other ‖ to be cautious.

obsession, f. besetting ‖ obsession.

obstacle, m. obstacle.

obstination, f. obstinacy, stubbornness.

obstiné, e, a. (–ément, ad.) obstinate(ly) ‖ stubborn(ly).

obstiner, v. a. to make obstinate ‖ **s'~, to** be obstinately resolved, to insist on.

obstruer, v. a. to obstruct, to stop up.

obtempérer, v. n. to comply, to obey.

obtenir, v. a. ir. to obtain ‖ to acquire.

obtention, f. obtaining, getting.

obtus, e, a. obtuse || dull.
obus, m. (mil.) small bomb, shell.
obusier, m. (mil.) howitzer.
obvier, v. n. to obviate.
occasion, f. occasion, opportunity, occurrence || chance || reason || **par ~,** by chance, incidentally || **d'~,** accidentally, second-hand || **marchandise d'~,** f. second-hand wares (pl.).   [sional(ly).
occasionnel, le, a. (**-lement,** ad.) occa-
occasionner, v. a. to occasion, to cause.
occident, m. Occident, West.
occidental, e, a. occidental, western.
occiput, m. (an.) occiput, back part of the head.
occire, v. a. to slay, to kill.   [the head.
occulte, a. occult.   [possessor.
occupant, e, m. & f. occupier, seizer,
occupation, f. occupation, employment, work.
occuper, v. a. to occupy, to hold, to employ || to take up || to inhabit || to trouble the mind of || to busy || **s'~,** to be busy, to apply oneself to || to think of || to be engaged on || to trouble oneself about.
océan, m. ocean, main sea.
ocre, m. ochre.
octave, f. (mus.) octave || eight.
octobre, m. October.
octogénaire, m. & f. octogenarian.
octogénaire, a. octogenarian.
octroi, m. grant, indult, city-toll.
octroyer, v. a. to grant.
oculaire, a. eye-glass.   [witness.
oculaire, a. ocular || **témoin ~,** m. eye-
oculiste, m. oculist.   [reputation, name.
odeur, f. odour, smell, scent, fragrance ||
odieux, m. odium || odiousness || invidiousness.   [invidious(ly).
odieux, se, a. (**-sement,** ad.) odious(ly) ||
odomètre, m. odometer.   [grant.
odorant, e, a. odorous, odoriferous, fragrant.
odorat, m. smell, smelling.
odoriférant, e, a. fragrant.   [tumour.
œdème, m. (méd.) œdema, œdematose
œil, m. eye || look || hole || bud || lustre || bubble || **à vue d'~,** visibly || **entre quatre yeux,** between two persons || **~-de-bœuf,** m. bull's eye || small oval window || **~-de-perdrix,** m. corn between the toes.
œillade, f. ogling, glance.   [the toes.
œillère, f. eye-flap, blinker || eye-tooth.
œillet, m. (bot.) pink, carnation || eyelet-hole || **~ de poète,** (bot.) sweet-William || **~ d'Inde,** (bot.) marigold.
œilleton, m. offset || layer.
œillette, f. (bot.) black garden-poppy.
œsophage, m. (an.) wind-pipe, gullet.
œuf, m. egg || **~ couvi,** stale egg || **~ rouge, ~ de Pâque,** Easter-egg || **frais,** new-laid egg || **~ poché,** poached egg || **~ à la coque,** soft egg || **~ s à la neige,** whisked eggs (pl.) || **~ s sur le plat,** fried eggs (pl.).
œuvé, e, a. hard-roed.
œuvre, f. work, deed || action.
œuvre, m. (mus.) work || performance || piece of work || **dans ~,** clear, in the clear || **~ s vives,** f. pl. (mar.) keel, bottom || **~ s mortes,** f. pl. (mar.) top-sides (pl.).

offensant, e, a. offensive.
offense, f. offence, injury, trespass, affront
offenser, v. a. to offend, to outrage, to hurt || **s'~ de,** to be offended, angry at.
offenseur, m. offender.
offensif, ve, a. (**-vement,** ad.) offensive
offerte, f. offering, offertory.   [(ly).
offertoire, f. offertory.
office, m. office, function, employment, charge, service, good turn || church-time || **d'~,** officially || **~,** f. pantry, confectionary.
officiel, m. official.   [court.
officialité, f. officiality || ecclesiastical
officiant, m. officiating priest.
officiant, e, a. officiating.
officiel, le, a. (**-lement,** ad.) official(ly).
officier, m. officer.
officier, v. n. to officiate (in a church).
officieux, m. busybody.
officieux, se, a. (**-sement,** ad.) officious(ly) || obliging(ly).
officine, f. laboratory.
offrande, f. offering.
offrant, m. bidder || **au plus ~,** to the highest bidder.
offre, f. offer, tender, proposal.
offrir, v. a. ir. to offer, to tender, to present, to bid.
offusquer, v. a. to offuscate, to dazzle, to darken, to dim, to cloud, to blind.
ogive, f. (arch.) pointed arch.
ognon, m. (bot.) onion, bulb.
ognonnière, f. onion-bed.
ogre, sse, m. & f. ogre || ogress.
ohé! halloo! ho there!
oie, f. goose.
oignon, m. (bot.) onion.
oindre, v. a. ir. to anoint.
oing, m. cart-grease.
oint, e, m. & f. anointed.
oiseau, m. bird, fowl || bricklayer's hod || **~ mouche,** humming-bird.
oiseler, v. a. to bring up birds || to catch birds || to train a hawk.
oiseleur, m. fowler, bird-catcher.
oiselier, m. bird-seller.
oisellerie, f. bird-catching || bird-selling.
oiseux, se, a. idle || trifling.
oisif, ve, a. unoccupied, idle || useless.
oisillon, m. young bird.
oisivement, ad. idly.
oisiveté, f. idleness, sloth, rest.
oison, m. gosling || ninny.
oléagineux, se, a. oily.
oléandre, m. (bot.) oleander, rose-bay.
olfactif, ve, a. olfactory.
olibrius, m. conceited ou meddling fellow.
oligarchie, f. oligarchy.
oligarchique, a. oligarchical.
olivaison, f. olive-season, crop of olives.
olivâtre, a. olive-coloured.
olive, f. (bot.) olive || olive-colour.
olivier, m. (bot.) olive-tree, olive || **jardin des ~ s,** m. Mount of Olives.
olographe, m. holograph.
olographe, a. written with one's own hand.
olympe, m. Olympus, heaven.
ombilical, a. (an. & bot.) umbilic, umbilical.

ombrage, m. shade || umbrage || faire ~, to overshadow || donner de l'~ à, to give umbrage to.

ombrager, v. a. to shade. [skittish.

ombrageux, se, a. suspicious || shy ||

ombre, m. umber, grayling, char (fish).

ombre, f. shade, shadow || ghost || -s chinoises, pl. dissolving views (pl.).

ombrelle, f. parasol.

ombrer, v. a. (peint.) to shade.

ombreux, se, a. shady.

ombromètre, m. rain-gauge.

omelette, f. omelet. [forget.

omettre, v. a. ir. to omit, to leave out, to

omission, f. omission || sauf erreur ou ~, errors excepted. [motor-omnibus.

omnibus, m. omnibus || ~ automobile,

omnivore, a. omnivorous.

omoplate, f. (an.) scapula, shoulder-blade.

on, pn. one, we, they, people, man, men || croire sur un ~-dit, to believe upon hearsay.

onagre, m. wild ass.

once, f. ounce || (fig.) grain.

onchets, m. pl. spellicans (pl.).

oncle, m. uncle.

onction, f. unction, anointing || grace.

onctueux, se, a. unctuous || oily.

onctuosité, f. unctuousness.

onde, f. wave, billow, surge.

ondé, e, a. watered, waved.

ondée, f. shower.

ondine, f. Undine, water genius.

on-dit, m. hearsay, report.

ondoiement, m. private baptism.

ondoyer, v. a. & n. to christen privately || to undulate, to rise in waves.

ondulation, f. undulation.

onduler, v. n. to undulate, to wave || to float. [curly.

onduleux, se, a. undulated, flowing ||

onéraire, a. (jur.) acting.

onéreux, se, a. onerous, burdensome.

ongle, m. nail || hoof || claw || coup d'-s, m. scratch || donner sur les -s, to reprove sharply. [fingers' ends.

onglée, f. hot-ache || numbness at the

onguent, m. ointment.

onomatopée, f. (gr.) onomatopœia.

onze, a. eleven || eleventh.

onzième, a. (-ment, ad.) eleventh(ly).

opacité, f. opacity.

opale, f. (min.) opal.

opéra, m. opera || opera-house.

opérateur, trice, m. & f. operator.

opération, f. operation || performance || transaction.

opérer, v. n. to operate, to work || se faire ~, to undergo an operation.

ophthalmie, f. (méd.) ophthalmia.

opiacé, a. opiate.

opiacé, e, a. (méd.) containing opium.

opiat, m. (méd.) opiate.

opinant, m. speaker.

opiner, v. n. to give one's opinion, to vote, to speak || ~ du bonnet, to nod assent.

opiniâtre, a. obstinate, stubborn.

opiniâtrément, ad. obstinately.

s'opiniâtrer, to persevere stubbornly in one's opinion.

opiniâtreté, f. obstinacy.

opinion, f. opinion, thought, vote || aller aux -s, to put (it) to the vote.

opisthographe, a. written on both sides.

opportun, e, a. opportune, convenient, seasonable, timely. [ably.

opportunément, ad. opportunely, season-

opportunité, f. opportunity, opportuneness, fitness of time.

opposant, m. opponent.

opposant, e, a. opposing.

opposé, e, a. opposite, contrary.

opposer, v. a. to oppose, to go against, to stand against, to hinder, to resist || s'~, to oppose, to be against, to be contrary to.

opposite, m. the opposite, the contrary || à l'~, opposite, facing.

opposition, f. opposition, resistance || stoppage || protestation.

oppresser, v. a. to oppress.

oppresseur, m. oppressor. [sive(ly).

oppressif, ve, a. (vement, ad.) oppres-

oppression, f. oppression, tyranny.

opprimer, v. a. to oppress.

opprobre, m. infamy, shame.

opter, v. a. to choose.

opticien, m. optician.

optimisme, m. optimism.

optimiste, m. optimist.

option, f. option, choice.

optique, f. optics (pl.) || show-box || peep-

optique, a. optic, optical. [show.

opulemment, ad. opulently.

opulence, f. opulence, wealth.

opulent, e, a. opulent, wealthy.

opuscule, m. small treatise.

or, m. gold || ~ moulu, ormolu.

or, c. now, but.

oracle, m. oracle.

orage, m. tempest, storm.

orageux, se, a. stormy, tempestuous.

oraison, f. orison, prayer, speech.

oral, e, a. oral, verbal || "viva voce".

orange, f. orange || orange colour.

orangé, e, a. orange-coloured.

orangeade, f. orangeade.

orangeat, m. candied orange-peel.

oranger, m. (bot.) orange-tree.

orangerie, f. orangery, orange-house.

orateur, m. orator, public speaker.

oratoire, m. oratory.

oratoire, a. oratorical.

orbe, m. orb || orbit || sphere.

orbiculaire, a. orbicular, orbiculate.

orbite, f. orbit.

orcanète, f. (bot.) orchanet.

orchestre, m. orchestra || band || musicians (pl.).

orchestration, f. (mus.) scoring.

ordinaire, m. usual fare || daily board to servants || custom || à l'~, according to custom, as usual || d'~, pour l'~, most often, usually.

ordinaire, a. (-ment, ad.) ordinary || ordinarily || common(ly) || usual(ly).

ordinand, m. candidate for holy orders.

ordinant, m. ordaining bishop.

ordination, f. ordination.

ordonnance, m. (mil.) orderly officer.

ordonnance, f. ordinance, ordering, disposition, prescript, decree || ~ de médecin, prescription. [payment.

ordonnancement, m. written order of

ordonnancer, v. a. to write an order for payment. [disposer, director.

ordonnateur, trice, m. & f. orderer,

ordonnateur, trice, a. ordaining.

ordonner, v. a. to order, to regulate, to direct, to command, to prescribe || to dispose || to confer holy orders.

ordre, m. order, disposition, precept, command || de premier ~, first-rate.

ordure, f. filth, dirt || excrement || filthy thing || corruption || dust, sweepings (pl.).

ordurier, ière, m. & f. ribald, filthy

ordurier, ière, a. filthy. [person.

oreillard, e, a. lap-eared.

oreille, f. ear || ~ de livre, dog's-ear in a book || ~ d'ours, (bot.) auricula || avoir de l'~, to have a good ear || avoir bonne ~, to have a quick ear.

oreiller, m. pillow.

oreillette, f. (an.) auricle || (bot.) ear.

oreillons, m. pl. mumps (pl.).

orfèvre, m. goldsmith, silversmith.

orfèvrerie, f. silversmith's trade, jewel-

orfraie, f. osprey (bird). [lery.

organdi, m. book-muslin.

organe, m. organ || voice || (fig.) means || spokesman || agent.

organeau, m. (mar.) ring for a cable.

organique, a. organic.

organisation, f. organisation.

organiser, v. a. to organise || s'~, to get

organisme, m. organism. [settled.

organiste, m. organist.

organsin, m. organzine, thrown silk.

orge, f. (bot.) barley || ~ perlé, pearl barley.

orgeat, m. sweet barley-water.

orgelet, m. (méd.) stye.

orgie, f. debauch, revelry. [organ.

orgue, m. organ || ~ de Barbarie, street

orgueil, m. pride, haughtiness.

orgueilleux, se, a. (-sement, ad.) proud(ly). [water (of pearls).

orient, m. Orient, East || rising (of the sun) ||

oriental, m. Oriental, eastern || ~e, f. Oriental fashion.

oriental, e, a. Oriental, eastern.

orientaliste, m. orientalist.

orientation, f. (astr.) orientation.

orienter, v. a. to set towards the east || to arrange || s'~, to discover the right road ou way.

orifice, m. orifice, aperture, hole || port.

oriflamme, f. oriflamme. [ad. originally.

originaire, a. originating || native || -ment,

original, m. original, first copy || queer fellow || oddity.

original, e, a. original || odd.

originalité, f. originality.

origine, f. origin, source || beginning || dans l'~, originally. [(ly) || primitive.

originel, le, a. (-lement, ad.) original

orignal, m. elk. [board.

orillon, m. small ear || handle || mould-

oripeau, m. tinsel.

ormaie, f. elm-grove.

orme, m. (bot.) elm.

ormeau, f. (bot.) young elm.

ormille, f. plantation ou hedge of young

orne, m. flowering-ash. [elms.

ornement, m. ornament || d'~, ornamental.

orner, v. a. to adorn, to ornament, to beautify. [track, beaten path.

ornière, f. rut, track (of a wheel) || old

ornithologie, f. ornithology.

orpailleur, m. gold-searcher.

orphelin, e, m. & f. orphan.

orphelinat, m. orphan asylum || orphanage.

orpin, m. (bot.) orpine, stone-crop || (min.)

ort, m. (com.) gross weight. [orpiment.

orteil, m. great toe.

orthodoxe, a. orthodox.

orthodoxie, f. orthodoxy.

orthographe, f. orthography || faute d'~, f. misspelling || misspelt word.

orthographier, v. a. to spell right.

orthopédie, f. (méd.) orthopedy

orthopédiste, m. orthopedist.

ortie, f. (bot.) nettle || rowel (of horses).

orvet, m. slow-worm.

orviétan, m. quack medicine || marchand

os, m. bone. [d'~, m. quack-doctor.

oscillation, f. oscillation || vibration ||

oscillatoire, a. oscillatory. [fluctuation.

osciller, v. n. to oscillate.

osé, e, a. bold, daring.

oseille, f. (bot.) sorrel.

oser, v. a. & n. to dare, to venture.

oseraie, f. osier-plot.

osier, m. (bot.) water-willow, osier.

ossature, f. (an.) skeleton, osseous frame.

osselet, m. huckle-bone.

ossements, m. pl. bones (pl.).

osseux, se, a. bony.

ossifier, v. a. to ossify

ossuaire, m. ossuary

ost, f. army. [ostensibly.

ostensible, a. (-ment, ad.) ostensible ||

ostensoir, m. monstrance.

ostéologie, f. osteology.

ostracisme, m. ostracism.

ostrogot, ostrogoth, m. ostrogoth || barbarian. [barian.

ostrogot, ostrogoth, a. barbarous, barotage, m. hostage.

ôté, pr. except, save, barring.

ôter, v. a. to take away, to take off, to pull off, to deprive of || to remove || s'~, to get away || to be taken away || to deprive oneself of.

ottomane, f. ottoman, sofa.

ou, c. or, either.

où, ad. where, whither || d'~, whence, from.whence || par ~, which way || ~ que, [whithersoever.

ouaille, f. sheep, flock.

ouate, f. cotton-wool || wadding.

ouater, v. a. to stuff with wadding.

oubli, m. oblivion, forgetfulness, neglect.

oublie, f. wafer.

oublier, v. a. to forget, to omit, to leave.

oubliettes, f. pl. secret dungeon, oubliette.

oublieux, se, a. forgetful.

ouest, m. West.

ouf! phew! oh!

oui, ad. yes, ay.

ouï-dire, m. hearsay.
ouïe, f. hearing ‖ –s, pl. gills (of a fish) (pl.).
ouragan, m. hurricane.
ourdir, v. a. to warp ‖ to plot.
ourdissage, m. warping.
ourdisseur, se, m. & f. warper.
ourler, v. a. to hem.
ourlet, m. hem.   [ill-bred man.
ours, m. bear ‖ – mal léché, unlicked cub,
ourse, f. she-bear.
oursin, m. sea-urchin.
ourson, m. bear's cub.
outarde, f. bustard (bird).
outardeau, m. young bustard.
outil, m. tool, implement.
outillage, m. stock of tools.
outiller, v. a. to furnish with tools.
outrage, m. outrage, abuse.
outrageant, e, a. outrageous, abusive.
outrager, v. a. to outrage, to abuse.
outrageux, se, a. (-sement, ad.) outrageous(ly).
outrance, f. utterance ‖ extreme ‖ à ~, à
toute ~, to the utmost, beyond measure.
outre, f. leather-bottle.
outre, ad. & pr. further, beyond, out of,
besides ‖ en ~, moreover, besides ‖ d'~,
en ~, quite through ‖ ~ que, besides that
‖ ~ mesure, beyond measure ‖ passer
~, to go on ‖ ~-mer, ad. beyond seas ‖
~-passer, v. a. to go beyond, to exceed.
outrecuidance, f. presumption.
outremarin, e, a. transmarine.
outremer, m. ultramarine.
outrer, v. a. to overwork, to overload, to
overharass, to provoke, to incense, to exasperate ‖ to exaggerate.
ouvert, e, a. (-ement, ad.) open(ly) ‖
candid(ly) ‖ sincere ‖ à livre ~, at sight.
ouverture, f. opening, aperture, breach ‖
beginning ‖ means, way, advice ‖ (mus.)
overture.   [day.
ouvrable, a. working ‖ jour ~, working-
ouvrage, m. work, piece of work ‖ composition, production ‖ workmanship, performance ‖ job.
ouvragé, e, a. wrought, figured.
ouvré, e, a. wrought ‖ diapered ‖ linge ~,
m. diaper.
ouvrer, v. a. to work ‖ to diaper ‖ to coin.
ouvreur, se, m. & f. opener ‖ box-keeper.
ouvrier, m. labourer, worker, workman ‖
craftsman, artificer, artisan.
ouvrière, f. work-woman.
ouvrir, v. a. ir. to open, to set open ‖ to
unbosom ‖ to sharpen ‖ to start ‖ s'~, to
open ‖ to burst ‖ to open one's mind.
ouvroir, m. working-room.
ovaire, m. (an. & bot.) ovary.
ovale, m. oval.
ovale, a. oval.
ovariotomie, f. (chir.) ovariotomy.
ovation, f. ovation.
ovipare, m. oviparous animal.
ovipare, a. oviparous.
oxyde, m. (chim.) oxide.   [oxidise.
oxyder, v. a. (chim.) to oxidate ‖ s'~, to
oxygène, m. (chim.) oxygen.
oxygéner, v. a. (chim.) to oxygenate.

P.

pacage, m. pasture, pasture-ground.
pacager, v. n. to pasture, to graze.
pachyderme, m. pachydermatous animal, pachyderm.
pacificateur, trice, m. & f. pacificator,
pacifier, peace-maker.
pacificateur, trice, a. pacifying.
pacifier, v. a. to pacify.
pacifique, a. pacific, peaceable, peaceful ‖
mild, gentle ‖ -ment, ad. peaceably,
quietly.
pacotille, f. seaman's venture ou luggage ‖
marchandises de ~, f. pl. slop-made
goods (pl.), slops (pl.), salework.
pacte, m. pact, compact, agreement.
pactiser, v. n. to make an agreement, to
covenant.
Pactole, m. Pactolus ‖ posséder le ~,
to have an endless source of wealth.
padou, m. ferret.
pagaie, f. (mar.) paddle ‖ aller à la ~, to
paganisme, m. paganism, heathenism.
pagayer, v. a. & n. (mar.) to paddle.
page, m. page ‖ tour de ~, schoolboy's
trick ‖ être hors de ~, to be independent ‖ ~, f. page (of a book).
pagination, f. paging (of a book).
paginer, v. a. to page.
pagne, f. cotton drawers, worn by negroes.
pagode, f. pagoda.
paiement, vide payement.
païen, ne, a. pagan, heathen.
paillard, e, a. lecherous, wanton.
paillardise, f. lewdness, libidinousness.
paillasse, f. straw-bed ‖ ~, m. clown.
paillasson, f. straw-mat ‖ garden-matting.
paille, f. straw ‖ flaw (in diamonds) ‖
mote ‖ ~ menue, chaff ‖ tirer à la
courte ~, to draw lots ‖ ~-en-queue,
m. water-wagtail (bird).
pailler, m. farm-yard, heap of straw.
paillet, te, a. pale.
paillette, f. spangle.
pailleter, v. a. to spangle.
pailleux, se, a. made of straw ‖ flawy.
paillon, m. link of a chain ‖ spangle.
pain, m. bread, loaf ‖ livelihood ‖ ~ au
lait, ~ mollet, petit ~, roll ‖ ~ frais,
new bread ‖ ~ bis, brown bread ‖ ~
rassis, stale bread ‖ ~ de munition,
ammunition-bread ‖ ~ bénit, consecrated
bread ‖ ~ de sucre, sugar-loaf ‖ ~ de
bougie, taper ‖ ~ à cacheter, wafer.
pair, m. peer, equal, mate, companion ‖
(com.) par ‖ au ~, at par.
pair, a. even, equal, alike ‖ ~ ou non,
"odds or evens."
paire, f. pair, brace, couple.
pairesse, f. peeress.
pairie, f. peerage.
paisible, a. (-ment, ad.) peaceable ‖
peaceful(ly) ‖ quiet(ly) ‖ peaceably.
paisson, f. pasture, pasturage ‖ stretcher.
paître, v. a. & n. ir. to graze, to feed on,
to crop, to eat.

paix, f. peace, quiet, rest || ~ ! be quiet!
pal, m. stake || pale.
palais, m. palace || court of justice || palate (of the mouth) || taste || gens du ~, f. pl. lawyers (pl.) || terme de ~, m. law-term.
palan, m. (mar.) tackle || amené sous ~, delivered alongside.
palatin, e, a. Palatine || (an.) palatine, of Palatinat, m. Palatinate.
palatine, f. fur-tippet.
pale, f. flood-gate || blade || paddle-board.
pâle, a. pale, wan || tame || —s couleurs, pl. (méd.) chlorosis, green-sickness.
palée, f. row of piles.
palefrenier, m. groom.
palefroi, m. palfrey.
paleron, m. shoulder-bone.
palet, m. quoit.
paletot, m. great-coat.
palette, f. battledore || pallet || paddle || basin.
pâleur, f. paleness, wanness || tameness.
palier, m. landing (of a staircase) || flat.
palinodie, f. recantation || chanter la ~, to recant.
pâlir, v. a. & n. to make pale || to turn pale.
palis, m. pale, stake for a fence.
palissade, f. palisade, paling || stockade.
palissader, v. a. to palisade, to stockade.
palissage, m. paling up.
palissandre, m. rosewood.
palisser, v. a. to nail up (branches) || to pale up.
palliatif, m. (méd.) palliative.
palliatif, ve, a. (méd.) palliative.
pallier, v. a. to palliate.
palme, f. (bot.) palm, palm-tree || ~, m. palm of the hand.
palmé, e, a. (bot.) palmated || webbed.
palmette, f. palm-leaf (as ornament).
palmier, m. (bot.) palm-tree.
palmipède, a. web-footed.
palmiste, m. (bot.) cabbage-palm.
palombe, f. ring-dove (bird).
palonnier, m. spring-bar || whipple-tree.
pâlot, te, a. palish.
palourde, f. cockle.
palpe, f. feeler.
palper, v. a. to feel, to handle gently, to pocket. [finger, to pocket.
palpitation, f. palpitation, panting.
palpiter, v. n. to palpitate, to pant || to quiver, to flutter.
paltoquet, m. clown || churl.
paludéen, ne, a. paludal, of marshes.
(se) pâmer, v. n. & r. to swoon away, to faint away || to be enraptured.
pâmoison, f. (méd.) swoon, fainting-fit.
pamphlet, m. pamphlet.
pamphlétaire, m. pamphleteer.
pamplemousse, f. (bot.) shaddock.
pampre, m. vine-branch || full of leaves.
pan, m. part of a wall || front, fore-part ||
panacée, f. panacea. [lappet, flap.
panache, m. plume, bunch of feathers.
panaché, e, a. plumed || streaky || variegated. [flowers) || to get variegated.
(se) panacher, to break into streaks (of
panachure, f. streak, variegation.
panade, f. (culin.) bread-and-butter soup,
panais, m. (bot.) parsnip. [panada.
panard, a. crook-legged.

panaris, m. whitlow. [ings (pl.).
pancarte, f. placard, toll-table || old writ-
pané, e, a. (culin.) covered with bread-crumbs || beggared || eau—e, f. toast-water.
panégyrique, m. panegyric.
panégyriste, m. panegyrist.
paner, v. a. (culin.) to bread-crumb.
panetière, f. shepherd's crib.
panier, m. basket, pannier, hamper || scuttle || hoop-petticoat || ~ percé, spend-thrift.
panique, f. panic, sudden fright.
panique, a. panic.
panne, f. shag, plush || face of a hammer.
panneau, m. panel, square || trap, gin, snare || pannel (of a saddle).
panneton, m. key-bit.
panonceau, m. scutcheon.
panoplie, f. panoply.
pansage, m. dressing (of a horse).
panse, f. paunch, belly.
pansement, m. (chir.) dressing (of wounds).
panser, v. a. (chir.) to dress (wounds).
pansu, e, a. paunch-bellied.
pantalon, m. pantaloons (pl.) || drawers (pl.) (for ladies) || buffoon.
pantalonnade, f. buffoonery || sham || shuffle. [speak.
pantenne, f. (mar.) topping-yard || en ~,
panthéisme, m. pantheism.
panthéiste, m. pantheist.
panthéon, m. pantheon.
panthère, f. panther.
pantière, f. draw-net.
pantin, m. dancing-jack || guy.
pantographe, m. copying-machine.
pantoufle, f. slipper || en —s, slip-shod || soulier en ~, m. slip-shoe.
paon, ne, a. & f. peacock || peahen.
paonneau, f. young peacock.
papa, m. papa, daddy.
papal, e, a. papal.
papas, m. pope (priest of the Levant).
papauté, f. papacy.
papayer, m. (bot.) papaw-tree.
pape, m. pope.
papegai, m. popinjay (bird).
papelard, e, a. hypocrite, religious hum-
papelardise, f. hypocrisy. [bug.
paperasse, f. old dusty paper, waste paper.
paperasser, v. n. to rummage one's papers || to waste paper.
paperassier, m. waster of paper, scribbler.
papeterie, f. paper-mill || paper-trade || stationery || stationery-case.
papetier, m. paper-maker || stationer.
papier, m. paper || ~ à lettres, note-paper || ~ brouillard, blotting-paper || ~ à cigarettes, cigarette-paper || ~ à calquer, tracing-paper || ~ fort, drawing-paper || ~ gris, brown paper || ~ Joseph, tissue-paper || ~ mâché, papier maché || ~ ministre or tellière, petition-paper || ~-monnaie, paper-money || ~ peint, stained paper || ~ de soie, silver-paper || ~ timbré, stamped paper || ~ de verre, sand-paper || feuille de ~, sheet of paper || main de ~, quire of paper.

papillon, m. butterfly || ~ **de nuit,** moth || ~**s noirs,** pl. blue-devils.
papillonner, v. n. to flirt, to flutter || to hover.   [of the eyes.
papillotage, m. hair in papers || twinkling
papillote, f. curl-paper || spangle || sugarplum || **côtelette en ~,** f. cutlet fried in paper.   [paper the hair || to mackle.
papilloter, v. a. to put hair in paper, **to**
papisme, m. popery.
papiste, m. papist.
papiste, a. popish.
Pâque, f. Passover.
paquebot, m. packet-boat, packet || ~**poste,** mail-packet || ~ **à vapeur,** steampacket.
Pâques, f. pl. Easter || ~ **fleuries,** f. pl. Palm-Sunday || ~ **closes,** f. pl. Low Sunday || **faire ses ~,** to receive the sacrament at Easter.
pâquerette, f. (bot.) Easter-daisy.
paquet, m. bundle, parcel || mail || mass, lump || cluster || slip.
par, pr. by, through, at, in, about, out of, with || ~ **ici,** this way || ~ **là,** that way || ~ **où?** which way? || ~ **delà,** that side, on the other side || ~**dessus,** on, upon, over || ~**dessous,** under, underneath || ~**ci,** ~**là,** here and there.
parabole, f. parable || parabola.   [(ally).
parabolique, a. (–ment, ad.) parabolic
parachute, m. parachute.
paracrotte, m. splasher (of carriages), leather guard to keep one's dress from contact with the wheels.
parade, f. parade, show, state, ostentation || **chambre de ~,** f. state-room || **lit de ~,** m. state-bed.
parader, v. a. to parade || to show a horse.
paradis, m. paradise, heaven || upper gallery (in a play-house).
paradoxal, e, a. paradoxical.
paradoxe, m. paradox.
parafe, etc. *vide* **paraphe, etc.**
parage, m. extraction, descent || sea-coast || latitude, quarter.
paragraphe, m. paragraph.
paraître, v. n. ir. to appear, to seem, to look, to come out || to make a show || **faire ~,** to show, to make appear.
Paralipomènes, m. pl. Chronicles (pl.).
parallèle, m. parallel.
parallèle, a. (–ment, ad.) parallel(ly).
parallélisme, m. parallelism.
parallélogramme, m. parallelogram.
paralogisme, m. paralogism.
paralyser, v. a. to paralyse.
paralysie, f. paralysis, alsy.
paralytique, m. paralytic.
paralytique, a. paralytic.
parangon, m. paragon, pattern, model.
parangon, a. without defect.   [work.
parapet, m. parapet || parapet-wall, breast-
paraphe, m. flourish, initials (pl.), paraph.
parapher, v. a. to sign with a flourish || to put one's initials to.   [wife's property.
paraphernaux, m. pl. paraphernalia (pl.),
paraphrase, f. paraphrase.
paraphraser, v. a. to paraphrase.

paraphraseur, m. amplifier.
parapluie, m. umbrella.
parasite, a. parasitic.
parasol, m. parasol || (bot.) weeping-willow.
paratonnerre, m. conductor, lightning-rod, lightning-conductor.
paravent, m. screen, folding-screen.
parbleu! zounds! forsooth! faith!
parc, m. park || sheep-fold || oyster-bed || **garde de ~,** f. park-keeper.   [cattle).
parcage, m. folding (of sheep) || penning (of
parcelle, f. particle, portion.
parce que, c. because.
parchemin, m. parchment || ~**s,** pl. titles of nobility (pl.).   [parchment-trade.
parcheminerie, f. parchment-factory ||
parcheminier, m. parchment-maker *ou*
parcimonie, f. parsimony.   [seller.
parcimonieux, se, a. parsimonious.
parcourir, v. a. ir. to travel over || to run *ou* go over, to read over || to survey.
parcours, m. right of common || (rail.) ~, **d'une ligne par un convoi,** trip.
pardessus, m. overcoat.
pardi! yes truly!
pardon, m. pardon, forgiveness, mercy || ~ **!** excuse me! I beg your pardon!
pardonnable, a. pardonable, excusable.
pardonner, v. a. to pardon, to forgive, to excuse || to spare.
pareil, le, a. (–lement. ad.) like, alike, equal(ly) || likewise, in like manner.
pareille, f. the like || **rendre la ~,** to give tit for tat.
parement, m. ornament || facings (pl.) (of sleeves) || kerb-stone || altar-cloth || large sticks of a faggot.
parent, m. kinsman, relation || ~**s,** pl. parents (pl.) || family.
parenté, f. relation, kinsfolk (pl.) || relationship || kindred (pl.).
parenthèse, f. (gr.) parenthesis.
parer, v. a. & n. to adorn, to deck || to parry, to ward off, to guard || to stop || to pare, to flesh (the hides) || **se ~,** to make a show, to boast of, to adorn oneself with || to deck oneself, to ward off, to guard against.   [gishness.
paresse, f. idleness, laziness, sloth, slug-
paresser, v. n. to idle.
paresseux, m. idler, lazy fellow.
paresseux, se, a. idle, slothful, lazy, sluggish, heavy.
parfaire, v. a. ir. to complete.
parfait, m. (gr.) preterite, perfect.
parfait, e, a. complete, perfect, finished.
parfaitement, ad. completely, perfectly, exceedingly || ~ **!** all right! certainly! || exactly so!
parfiler, v. a. & n. to unravel, to unweave.
parfois, ad. sometimes, now and then.
parfondre, v. a. to melt, to fuse.
parfum, m. perfume, scent.
parfumer, v. a. to perfume.
parfumerie, f. perfumery.
parfumeur, se, m. & f. perfumer.
pari, m. wager, bet.
paria, m. pariah.   [pair.
pariade, f. pairing-time (for partridges) ||

parier, v. a. to lay a wager, to bet, to wager ‖ to dare say ‖ **il y a à ~**, the odds [are.

pariétaire, f. (bot.) wall-wort.

parieur, se, m. & f. better.

parité, f. parity, equality.

parjure, a. perjured, forsworn. [self.

se parjurer, to perjure ou forswear one-

parlage, m. idle talk, chatter, babble.

parlant, e, a. speaking ‖ chatty ‖ expres- [sive.

parlement, m. parliament.

parlementaire, m. (bearer of a) flag of truce.

parlementaire, a. parliamentary.

parlementer, v. n. to parley.

parler, v. a. & n. to speak, to talk ‖ **se ~**, to speak to each other ‖ to be spoken.

parleur, se, m. & f. talker.

parloir, m. parlour.

parmesan, m. Parmesan cheese.

parmi, pr. among, amongst, amidst.

parodie, f. parody.

parodier, v. a. to parody.

parodiste, m. parodist.

paroi, f. partition, separation, side ‖ wall.

paroisse, f. parish ‖ parish-church ‖ parishioners.

paroissial, e, a. parochial.

paroissien, -ne, m. & f. parishioner ‖ prayer-book.

parole, f. word, speech, saying ‖ promise ‖ book of a play ‖ **homme à deux ~s**, m. insincere man ‖ **sur ma ~**, upon my word ‖ **être homme de ~**, to be as good as one's word ‖ **porter la ~**, to be the spokesman ‖ **prendre sur ~**, to take on credit ‖ **manquer de ~**, to break one's word ‖ **tenir ~**, to keep one's promise ‖ **couper la ~ à qn.**, to cut one short, to interrupt one. [stake double.

paroli, m. paroli (at play) ‖ **faire ~**, to

parolier, m. song-writer.

paronyme, m. (gr.) paronymous word.

paroxysme, m. (méd.) paroxysm, fit.

Parque, f.; **les ~s**, pl. the Fates.

parquer, v. a. to pen up ‖ to park, to fold, to lodge.

parquet, m. bar (in a court of justice) ‖ inlaid floor ‖ chimney-frame ‖ orchestra.

parquetage, m. inlaid work ‖ flooring.

parqueter, v. a. to floor, to inlay.

parqueteur, m. maker of flooring.

parrain, m. godfather ‖ introducer.

parricide, m. parricide (person or crime).

parricide, a. parricidal. [to stud.

parsemer, v. a. to strew, to besprinkle.

part, f. part, portion, share ‖ concern ‖ side, place ‖ **à ~**, aside ‖ exceptional ‖ peculiar ‖ **de ~ et d'autre**, on both sides ‖ **de ~ en ~**, through ‖ **en quelque ~**, wherever ‖ **nulle ~**, nowhere ‖ **quelque ~**, somewhere ‖ **de ma ~**, from me ‖ **faire la ~ à qn.**, to give one his portion ‖ **avoir ~ à**, to be concerned in ‖ **mettre à ~**, to lay aside ‖ **prendre ~ à**, to be concerned in ‖ **prendre en mauvaise ~**, to take ill. [bution.

partage, m. share, portion, division, distri-

partageable, a. divisible.

partageant, m. (jur.) sharer.

partager, v. a. to part, to share, to divide, to parcel ‖ **se ~**, to share ‖ to be divided ‖ to divide one's time.

partance, f. (mar.) sailing from a place ‖ **coup de ~**, m. sailing-gun.

partenaire, m. partner.

parterre, m. flower-garden ‖ pit (in a play-house) ‖ audience, public (in theatres).

parti, m. party, faction, cause ‖ condition, offer ‖ means, expedient ‖ resolution ‖ match ‖ **chef de ~**, m. ring-leader ‖ **esprit de ~**, m. party-spirit.

partial, e, a. (**-ement**, ad.) partial(ly).

partialité, f. partiality.

participe, m. (gr.) participle.

participer, v. n. to participate, to have a share in, to partake.

particulariser, v. a. to particularise.

particularité, f. particularity, peculiarity.

particule, f. particle ‖ (gr.) particle.

particulier, m. individual ‖ private man ‖ fellow.

particulier, ère, a. (**-èrement**, ad.) particular(ly) ‖ peculiar ‖ special(ly) ‖ private, singular ‖ **en ~**, by itself, separately, privately.

partie, f. part, portion, deal ‖ game, sport, diversion ‖ client ‖ **~ carrée**, party of four ‖ **~ civile**, plaintiff ‖ **~ double**, double-entry ‖ **~ fine**, junket ‖ **~ liée**, rubber ‖ **~ simple**, single-entry ‖ **en ~**, in part, partly ‖ **en grande ~**, in a great measure ‖ **tenir bien sa ~**, to act one's part well ‖ **prendre qn. à ~**, to lay a misfortune to one's charge.

partiel, le, a. (**-lement**, ad.) partial(ly).

partir, v. n. ir. to depart, to set out, to go away ‖ to proceed, to flow ‖ **à ~ d'aujourd'hui**, from this day forward.

partisan, m. partisan, adherent.

partitif, ve, a. (gr.) partitive.

partition, f. partition, division ‖ (mus.) parts (pl.), score.

partout, ad. everywhere ‖ **~ où**, wherever.

parure, f. dress, attire, finery, ornament ‖ parings (pl.), shavings (pl.), scrapings (pl.).

parvenir, v. n. ir. to arrive, to reach, to get, to attain, to obtain ‖ to make one's fortune, to come to preferment.

parvenu, e, m. & f. upstart ‖ snob.

parvis, m. parvis (in front of a church).

pas, m. pace, step, footstep ‖ footing ‖ stride ‖ march ‖ furrow (of a screw) ‖ conduct ‖ action ‖ narrow passage, defile ‖ (fig.) precedency ‖ **de ce ~**, immediately ‖ **à petits ~**, with short steps ‖ **~ de charge**, quick pace ‖ **~ de clerc**, blunder ‖ **à ~ de loup**, softly, stealthily ‖ **faux ~**, stumble ‖ slip ‖ fault ‖ **mauvais ~**, scrape, difficulty ‖ **~ à ~**, step by step ‖ **à ~ redoublé**, at double quick pace ‖ **~-d'âne**, m. (bot.) colt's-foot.

pas, ad. no, not ‖ **~ un**, none ‖ **~ du tout**, not at all.

pascal, e, a. paschal.

pasquinade, f. pasquinade.

passable, a. passable, tolerable, support-able, indifferent ‖ **-ment**, ad. passably, tolerably, indifferently. [(in fencing).

passade, f. passing through ‖ fancy ‖ pass

passage, m. passage || passing || gate-way || road, way || passage-money.

passager, ère, m. & f. passenger.

passager, ère, a. transient, not lasting || short-lived. [short time.

passagèrement, ad. transiently, for a

passant, m. passer-by || passenger.

passant, e, a.; chemin ~, m., rue -e, f. thoroughfare || en ~, going along, by the way. [way.

passavant, m. permit, pass || (mar.) gang-

passe, f. pass, thrust || channel || pass-word || odd money || situation || ~-carreau, m. sleeve-board || ~-cheval, m. ferry-boat for horses || ~-debout, m. permit for transit || ~-droit, m. favour || wrong, injustice || ~-lacet, m. bodkin || ~-méteil, m. wheat and rye || ~-parole, m. pass-word || ~-partout, m. pass-key, master-key || passport || ~-passe, m. sleight of hand || tour de ~-passe, m. legerdemain, hocus-pocus || ~-poil, m. edging, braid || ~-temps, m. pastime, amusement, diversion || ~-thé, m. tea-strainer || ~-velours, m. (bot.) amaranth, coxcomb || ~-volant, m. interloper || intruder.

passé, m. past time, things past (pl.).

passé, e, a. past, gone, over.

passement, m. lace, trimming.

passementer, v. a. to lace, to trim.

passementerie, f. lace-making.

passementier, m. lacemaker.

passeport, m. passport.

passer, v. a. & n. to pass, to go over || to exceed, to go beyond, to surpass || to excel || to leave out, to omit || to cease, to fade, to vanish, to disappear || to strain liquors || to happen || se ~, to pass, to happen || to decay, to fade away || to be satisfied.

passereau, m. sparrow. [sengers.

passerelle, f. narrow bridge for foot-pas-

passeur, m. ferryman.

passible, a. passible, liable.

passif, m. passive || (com.) liabilities (pl.).

passif, ve, a. (-vement, ad.) passive(ly).

passion, f. passion || love.

passionné, e, a. (-ment, ad.) passionate (ly) || affectionate(ly) || passionately fond.

passionner, v. a. to impassion, to raise the passions || se ~, to become animated, to fly into a passion.

passiveté, f. passiveness.

passoire, f. strainer.

pastel, m. pastel, crayon.

pastèque, f. (bot.) water-melon.

pasteur, m. shepherd || pastor || parson || [reverend.

pastiche, m. imitative picture.

pastille, f. pastille, lozenge, drop.

pastoral, e, a. (-ement, ad.) pastoral(ly).

pastoureau, elle, m. & f. young shepherd

pat, m. stale-mate. [(ess).

patache, f. packet-boat || stage-coach.

pataquès, pataqu'est-ce, m. awkward

pataraf(f)e, f. scrawl. [mistake.

patate, f. (bot.) kidney-potato.

patatras! I slap! bang!

pataud, m. thick-footed young dog || strapping child.

pataud, e, a. clumsily made || clumsy lout.

patauger, v. a. to tramp in the mud, to splash || to be embarrassed. [pasteboard.

pâte, f. paste, dough || carton de ~, m.

pâté, m. pie, pasty || blot || block.

pâtée, f. paste for poultry || dog's porridge.

patelin, m. wheedler.

patelin, e, a. cajoling || wheedling.

patène, f. patine, chalice-cover.

patenôtre, f. Lord's prayer, paternoster.

patent, e, a. patent || lettres -es, f. pl. letters-patent.

patente, f. license (to sell) || patent.

patenter, v. a. to grant letters-patent.

Pater, m. Lord's prayer || large bead.

patère, f. peg || curtain-pin.

paternel, le, a. (-lement, ad.) paternal (ly). || fatherly.

paternité, f. paternity. [clammy.

pâteux, se, a. doughy, gluish, mealy,

pathétique, a. (-ment, ad.) pathetic(ally).

pathologie, f. pathology.

pathologique, a. pathological.

pathos, m. pathos || bombast.

patibulaire, a. patibulary || hanging || ruffianly.

patiemment, ad. patiently.

patience, f. patience, sufferance, forbearance.

patient, m. patient, sufferer. [ance.

patient, e, a. patient.

patienter, v. n. to have patience.

patin, m. skate, patten.

patinage, m. skating. [skate.

patiner, v. a. & n. to paw, to handle || to

patineur, m. skater. [ing.

patinoir, m. skating-rink, place for skat-

pâtir, v. n. to suffer.

pâtis, m. pasture.

pâtisser, v. a. to make pastry.

pâtisserie, f. pastry-work.

pâtissier, ère, m. & f. pastrycook.

patois, m. country-dialect || jargon.

pâton, m. fattening-ball. [person.

patraque, f. bad watch || rubbish || weakly

pâtre, m. herdsman, shepherd.

patriarcal, e, a. patriarchal.

patriarcat, m. patriarchate.

patriarche, m. patriarch.

patrice, m. patrician, noble.

patriciat, m. patriciate.

patricien, m. patrician.

patricien, ne, a. of noble birth.

patrie, f. native country, native land, birthplace, home.

patrimoine, m. patrimony.

patrimonial, e, a. patrimonial.

patriote, m. patriot.

patriote, a. patriotic. [(ally).

patriotique, a. (-ment, ad.) patriotic

patriotisme, m. patriotism.

patron, m. patron, guardian, defender, protector || (mar.) master of a ship || pattern, sample, model || cockswain.

patronal, e, a. patronal.

patronne, f. patroness.

patronner, v. a. to patronise || to pattern.

patronymique, a. patronymic.

patrouillage, m. paddling.

patrouille, f. patrol.

patrouiller, v. n. to paddle ‖ to paw ‖ to patrol.

patrouillis, m. puddle.

patte, f. paw, foot, claw ‖ foot (of a glass) ‖ flap ‖ tab ‖ end ‖ fluke ‖ à quatre -s, on all fours ‖ ~ d'oie, (fig.) crow's-foot, wrinkle round the eye ‖ cross-roads (pl.)

pattu, e; a. broad-footed ‖ rough-footed.

pâturage, m. pasture, pasture-ground.

pâture, f. pasture, food (for cattle), meat ‖ provender.

pâturer, v. n. to pasture, to feed.

pâturon, m. pastern.

paume, f. palm (of a hand) ‖ tennis (game).

paumer, v. a. to punch.

paumier, m. keeper of a tennis-court.

paupérisme, m. pauperism.

paupière, f. eye-lid ‖ eye-lash.

pause, f. pause, stop, rest.

pauvre, sse, m. & f. poor man, beggar ‖ beggar-woman.

pauvre, a. (-ment, ad.) poor(ly) ‖ needy ‖ needily ‖ indigent ‖ wretched(ly) ‖ beggarly ‖ penuriously.

pauvret, te, m. & f. poor little creature.

pauvreté, f. poverty, want ‖ poor thing.

pavage, m. paving.

se pavaner, to strut, to flaunt.

pavé, m. pavement, paving-stone ‖ carriage-way ‖ road-way ‖ streets (pl.) ‖ haut du ~, m. wall-side ‖ first rank ‖ brûler le ~, to drive ou ride at full speed.

pavement, m. paving, pavement.

paver, v. a. to pave.

paveur, m. pavier.

pavillon, m. pavilion ‖ summer-house ‖ flag ‖ tent.

pavois, m. large shield ‖ (mar.) armour.

pavoisement, m. (mar.) dressing with flags.

pavoiser, v. a. (mar.) to dress ship.

pavot, m. (bot.) poppy.

payable, a. to be paid, payable.

payant, e, m. & f. payer.

paye, f. pay ‖ wages (pl.) ‖ paymaster.

payement, m. payment ‖ jour de ~, m. pay-day.

payer, v. a. & n. to pay, to pay off ‖ to quit, to acquit ‖ se faire ~, to call in one's debts ‖ se ~, to be satisfied with ‖ to, treat oneself to ‖ to be paid for ‖ to be taught.

payeur, m. payer, paymaster.

pays, m. country ‖ countryman, compatriot ‖ ~ bas, lowland ‖ ~ plat, flat country ‖ ~ natal, native country ‖ ~ de cocagne, land of plenty.

paysage, m. landscape.

paysagiste, m. landscape-painter.

paysan, ne, m. & f. peasant ‖ country-woman.

péage, f. toll, turnpike, toll-money, weigh-[bridge ‖ custom-house.

péager, m. toll-collector.

peau, f. skin, hide ‖ pelt ‖ coat, husk.

peausserie, f. peltry ‖ fur-trade.

peaussier, m. skinner, fell-monger, pelt-monger.

pec, a. pickled.

peccadille, f. peccadillo, slight fault.

pêche, f. fishing, fishery ‖ (bot.) peach ‖ ~ à la ligne, angling ‖ ~ de vigne, (bot.) standard peach.

péché, m. sin, trespass ‖ crime.

pêcher, m. (bot.) peach-tree.

pêcher, v. a. & n. to fish ‖ to angle ‖ ~ à la ligne, to angle.

pécher, v. n. to sin, to trespass, to transgress, to be deficient.

pécheresse, f. (female) sinner.

pêcherie, f. fishery, place for fishing.

pêcheur, m. angler, fisherman.

pécheur, m. sinner.   [head.

pécore, f. beast ‖ stupid creature, block-

pectoral, m. breast-piece, breast-plate.

pectoral, e, a. (méd.) pectoral.

péculat, m. peculation ‖ auteur d'un ~, m. peculator.   [earnings (pl.).

pécule, m. stock of money, savings (pl.),

pécuniaire, a. pecuniary.

pécunieux, se, a. monied, having money.

pédagogie, f. pedagogy.

pédagogique, a. pedagogical.

pédale, f. pedal (of an organ) ‖ treadle.

pédaler, v. n. (mus.) to put down the pedal.

pédant, e, m. & f. pedant ‖ pedantic woman.

pédant, e, a. pedantic.

pédanterie, f. pedantry.

pédantesque, a. pedantic.

pédantisme, m. pedantry.   [foot.

pédestre, a. pedestrian ‖ -ment, ad. on

pédicure, m. corn-cutter, chiropodist.

pédon, m. foot-messenger, runner.

Pégase, m. Pegasus.

peignage, m. combing of wool.

peigne, m. comb ‖ brake, hatchel (to dress flax) ‖ ~-fin, small-toothed comb ‖ ~ à démêler, wide-toothed comb.

peignée, f. drubbing ‖ brush.

peigner, v. a. to comb ‖ to drub.

peigneur, m. flax-dresser.

peigneuse, f. combing-machine.

peignier, m. comb-maker.

peignoir, m. dressing-gown ‖ bathing-gown.

peignons, m. pl., peignures, f. pl. combings (pl.).

peindre, v. a. ir. to paint, to draw ‖ to describe ‖ to represent ‖ to adorn ‖ fait à ~, very handsome ‖ se ~, to paint oneself ‖ to be represented.

peine, f. pain, punishment, penalty ‖ labour, toil, torment, difficulty ‖ grief, trouble ‖ à ~, hardly, scarcely ‖ à grand ~, with much difficulty ‖ avec ~, repugnantly ‖ homme de ~, m. working-man ‖ drudge.

peiner, v. a. & n. to afflict, to make uneasy, to trouble ‖ to work hard, to toil.

peintre, m. painter ‖ ~ de portraits, portrait-painter ‖ ~ de paysage, landscape-painter ‖ ~ en miniature, miniature-painter.

peinture, f. painting, picture, colours (pl.).

peintureur, m. dauber.

pékin, m. civilian ‖ cit.

pelage, m. colour of the hair (of animals).

pelard, e, a. barked, peeled (of wood).

pelé, m. bald-headed man || ragamuffin.
pêle-mêle, ad. pell-mell, helter-skelter.
peler, v. a. to make bald || to peel, to pare || to scald (a pig) || se ~, to peel off.
pèlerin, m. pilgrim || traveller.
pèlerinage, m. pilgrimage.
pèlerine, f. cape || tippet.
pelisse, f. pelisse.
pelle, f. shovel, peel || scoop.
pellée, pellerée, pelletée, f. shovelful.
pelleterie, f. furs (pl.), skins (pl.) || furrier's trade.
pelletier, m. furrier, skinner.
pellicule, f. pellicle, cuticle.   [skin.
pelotage, m. putting up into balls || goat-
pelote, f. pin-cushion || ball of snow || round sum || pickings (pl.).
peloter, v. a. & n. to beat, to bang, to cuff || to throw snow-balls.
peloton, m. small ball of worsted, clew of thread, knot || (mil.) platoon.
pelotonner, v. a. to wind up into a ball || se ~, to group together || (mil.) to form in platoons.
pelouse, f. lawn, grass-plot.
pelu, e, a. hairy, woolly.
peluche, f. plush, shag.
peluché, e, a. plushed, shaggy, hairy.
pelucher, v. n. to get shaggy.
pelure, f. paring, peel.
penaillon, m. rag || monk.   [code.
pénal, e, a. penal || code ~, m. criminal
pénalité, f. penalty || penal laws.
pénates, m. pl. household gods, pl.
penaud, e, a. abashed, sheepish || chop-fallen.   -- [pensity, inclination || taste.
penchant, m. declivity, steepness, pro-
penché, e, a. bent, bowed down, prone.
penchement, m. stoop, bend.
pencher, v. a. & n. to bend, to bow down || to incline, to lean.   [inable.
pendable, a. deserving of hanging, abom-
pendaison, f. hanging (on the gallows).
pendant, m. ear-drop, ear-ring || counter-part, fellow || pendant.   [cided.
pendant, e, a. pendent, hanging || unde-
pendant, pr. during || ~ que, while, whilst.
pendard, m. hangdog, rogue, villain.
pendeloques, f. pl. pendants (jewels) (pl.) || ear-drops (pl.) || hanging-rags (pl.).
pendiller, v. n. to dangle, to swing.
pendre, v. a. & n. to hang, to hang up, to suspend || dire pis que ~ de, to fall
pendu, m. hanged person.   [foul of.
pendule, f. clock, time-piece.
pendule, m. pendulum.
pêne, m. bolt (of a lock).
pénétrant, e, a. penetrating, piercing, sharp, acute, sagacious || impressive.
pénétration, f. penetration, acuteness, sagacity.
pénétrer, v. a. & n. to penetrate, to pierce, to move || to search into, to enter into.
pénible, a. (-ment, ad.) painful(ly) || laborious(ly) || difficult || with difficulty.
péninsulaire, a. peninsular.
péninsule, f. peninsula.   [ance.
pénitence, f. penitence, repentance || pen-
pénitencerie, f. penitentiary (place)

pénitencier, m. penitentiary (person).
pénitent, e, a. repentant, contrite.
pénitentiaire, a. penitentiary.
pennage, m. plumage.
pénombre, f. (astr.) penumbra.
pensée, f. thought, idea, sentiment, mean-ing, design, sketch || (bot.) heart's-ease,
penser, m. thought.   [pansy.
penser, v. a. & n. to think, to believe || to reflect, to imagine || to have care || to be near, to be like.
penseur, euse, m. & f. thinker.
penseur, euse, a. thinking.
pensif, ve, a. pensive, thoughtful.
pension, f. pension || annuity || boarding-house, boarding-school || board and lodg-ing || livery (of horses) || ~ bourgeoise, family boarding-house.
pensionnaire, m. boarder, pensioner.
pensionnat, m. boarding-school.
pensionner, v. a. to pension.
pensum, m. task || imposition.
pente, f. declivity, propensity, proneness, inclination || valance (of a bed).
Pentecôte, f. Pentecost, Whitsuntide.
penture, f. hinge || iron-brace.
pér.ultième, f. last syllable but one.
pénultième, a. penultimate.
pénurie, f. penury || scarcity.
pépie, f. pip (disease of birds).
pépier, v. n. to chirp.
pepin, m. kernel || grape-stone.
pépinière, f. (hort.) nursery.
pépiniériste, m. nurseryman.
pépite, f. nugget.
percale, f. cotton cambric.
percaline, f. glazed lining.   [keen, acute.
perçant, e, a. piercing, penetrating || sharp,
perce, ad.; en ~, on tap || mettre en ~, to tap || ~-neige, f. (bot.) snow-drop || ~-oreille, m. earwig (insect).
percé, e, a. pierced, bored, perforated || chaise -e, f. close-stool.   [glade.
percée, f. passage through a wood, vista,
percement, m. piercing, boring || opening.
percepteur, m. tax-gatherer.
perceptible, a. perceivable.   [lectorship.
perception, f. gathering, collection || col-
percevoir, v. a. & n. to pierce, to bore, to broach || to go through || to drill || to stick || to tunnel || to open || to lance || to wet through || to grieve || to thrill || to burst || to cut || to penetrate || to force || to enter || to appear.   [to receive || to perceive.
percevoir, v. a. ir. to gather, to collect.
perche, f. perch, pole.
percher, v. n. to perch, to roost.
perchoir, m. perching-stick, roost.
perclus, e, a. crippled.
perçoir, m. piercer.
percussion, m. percussion.
percuter, v. a. to tap, to strike || (méd.) to sound (the chest, etc.).
perdre, v. a. & n. to lose || to undo, to ruin, to debauch, to corrupt, to put out of the way || to suffer a loss || se ~, to lose oneself, to be lost || to lose one's way, to ruin oneself || to disappear || to hole one's own ball.

perdreau, m. young partridge.
perdrix, f. partridge.
perdu, e, a. lost, ruined, reprobate, bewildered || undone || thrown away || spoilt || wild || leisure || advanced || random || over head and ears in || invisible || dry || **enfants -s,** m. pl. (mil.) forlorn hope.
père, m. father || -s, pl. forefathers (pl.).
pérégrination, f. peregrination.
péremptoire, a. peremptory || **-ment,** ad. peremptorily.
perfectibilité, f. perfectibility.
perfectible, a. susceptible of perfection.
perfection, f. perfection || **en ~,** perfectly.
perfectionnement, m. improvement.
perfectionner, v. a. to perfect, to improve.
perfide, m. & f. perfidious person.
perfide, a. (**-ment,** ad.) perfidious(ly).
perfidie, f. perfidy.
perforer, v. a. to perforate.
péricliter, v. n. to be in danger, to be threatened with ruin.
péril, m. peril, danger, risk.
périlleux, se, a. (**-sement,** ad.) perilous(ly) || dangerous(ly).
périmer, v. n. to pass out of date, to fall into abeyance.
périmètre, m. (géom.) perimeter.
périnée, m. (an.) perineum.
période, f. period.
période, m. pitch, summit.
périodicité, f. periodicity.
périodique, a. (**-ment,** ad.) periodic(ally).
périostite, f. (méd.) periostitis.
péripatéticien, m. peripatetic.
péripatéticien, ne, a. peripatetic.
péripétie, f. sudden turn of fortune.
périphérie, f. (géom.) periphery.
périphrase, f. periphrasis, circumlocution.
périphraser, v. n. to periphrase.
périr, v. n. to perish, to die, to be destroyed, to fall, to be lost.
périssable, a. perishable.
péristyle, m. (arch.) peristyle.
péritoine, m. (an.) peritonium.
perlasse, f. pearl-ashes (pl.).
perle, f. pearl, bead.
perlé, e, a. pearled || pearly || (mus.) brilliant.
perler, v. n. to bead.   [liant.
perlier, 1ère, a. pearl, of pearl.
permanence, f. permanence.
permanent, e, a. permanent, lasting.
perméable, a. permeable, pervious.
permettre, v. a. ir. to permit, to allow || to suffer || **se ~,** to take the liberty.
permis, m. permit, licence.
permis, e, a. allowed, lawful.   [leave.
permission, f. permission, allowance,
permutation, f. exchange.
permuter, v. a. to exchange.
pernicieux, se, a. (**-sement,** ad.) pernicious(ly) || noxious(ly).
péronnelle, f. silly chattering jade.
péroraison, f. peroration.
pérorer, v. n. to harangue || to speechify.
péroreur, m. speechifier.
perpendiculaire, a. (**-ment,** ad.) perpendicular(ly).
perpétration, f. (jur.) perpetration.

perpétuel, le, a. (**-lement, ad.**) perpetual(ly) || everlasting(ly).
perpétuer, v. a. to perpetuate.
perpétuité, f. perpetuity.
perplexe, a. perplexed || perplexing.
perplexité, f. perplexity.
perquisition, f. search.
perron, m. flight of steps (before a house) || (rail.) platform.   [sail.
perroquet, m. parrot || (mar.) top-gallant-
perruche, f. hen-parrot, paroquet.
perruque, f. wig, periwig || fogy.
perruquier, 1ère, m. & f. wig-maker.
pers, e, a. bluish || greenish-blue.
perse, f. chintz.   [some.
persécutant, e, a. importuning, trouble-
persécuter, v. a. to persecute, to importune.
persécuteur, trice, m. & f. persecutor.
persécuteur, trice, a. persecuting.
persévérer, v. n. to persevere.
persienne, f. Venetian-blind, outside shutter-blind.   [irony.
persiflage, m. quizzing || banter, keen
persifler, v. a. & n. to quiz.
persifleur, m. banterer, quiz.
persil, m. (bot.) parsley.   [parsley.
persillade, f. cold meat with vinegar and
persillé, e, a. spotty, green.
persistance, f. persistance.
persister, v. n. to persist.
personnage, m. personage || character,
personnalisme, m. egotism.   [part.
personnalité, f. personality || personal remark || self-love.
personne, f. person.
personne, pn. nobody, none, not anybody.
personnel, m. persons (pl.) || people employed (pl.) || staff || attendants (pl.).
personnel, le, a. (**-lement, ad.**) personal(ly) || selfish || in person.
personnifier, v. a. to personify.
perspectif, ve, a. perspective.
perspective, f. prospect, view || vista || perspective.
perspicace, a. perspicacious.
perspicacité, f. perspicacity.
perspicuité, f. perspicuity.
perspiration, f. perspiration.
persuader, v. a. to persuade, to induce, to advise, to prevail || **se ~,** to persuade oneself || to believe, to imagine.
persuasif, ve, a. persuasive.
persuasion, f. persuasion, conviction, firm belief.
perte, f. loss, damage, ruin || **à ~,** at a loss, with loss || **en pure ~,** to no purpose.
pertinemment, ad. pertinently.
pertuis, m. defile, narrow pass.
pertuisane, f. partisan (halberd).
perturbateur, trice, m. & f. disturber.
perturbateur, trice, a. disturbing.
perturbation, f. perturbation, disturbance.
pervenche, f. periwinkle.
pervers, e, a. perverse.
perversion, f. perversion.
perversité, f. perverseness.
pervertir, v. a. to pervert.
pervertissement, m. perversion.

pesage, m. weighing.

pesamment, ad. heavily.

pesant, m. weight.

pesant, e, a. heavy, weighty, ponderous || dull, stupid || (mus.) slow.

pesanteur, f. weight, heaviness || unwieldiness, dulness, stupidity.

pesée, f. weighing || weigh.

pèse ; ~lettres, m. letter-weight || ~liqueur, m. hydrometer, areometer.

peser, v. a. & n. to weigh, to ponder, to be heavy, to dwell upon, to be a burden to.

peseur, m. weigher.

peson, m. steel-yard.

pessimisme, m. pessimism.

pessimiste, m. pessimist.

peste, f. pest, plague, pestilence || mischievous child, nuisance.   [to bluster.

pester, v. n. to fret and fume || to storm,

pestiféré, m. person infected with the plague.

pestiféré, e, a. pestiferous.   [plague.

pestilence, f. pestilence, plague.

pestilentiel, le, a. pestilential.

pétale, m. (bot.) petal, flower-leaf.

pétarade, f. vain boast || noise of crackers.

pétard, m. petard || cracker.

pétarder, v. a. to blow up with a petard.

Pétaud, m.: la cour du roi ~, f. Bedlam broke loose || scene of confusion.

pétaudière, f. bear-garden.   [to bounce.

péter, v. n. to break wind behind, to fart ||

pétillement, m. sparkling, crackling.

pétiller, v. n. to sparkle, to crackle || to be full || to long || to be boiling.

petit, e, m. & f. little one || little boy ou girl || little thing || darling || cub || whelp || grands et ~s, pl. young and old (pl.), high and low (pl.).

petit, e, a. small, little, short || young || petty, low, inconsiderable || ~ à ~, by degrees || en ~, on a small scale !! ~-fils, m. grandson || ~-gris, m. minever || Russian squirrel || ~-maître, m. coxcomb, dandy.

petitement, ad. meanly, poorly, sparingly.

petitesse, f. smallness, littleness, meanness, lowness.

pétition, f. petition, demand.

pétitionnaire, m. petitioner.

pétitionner, v. n. to petition.

peton, m. pettitoe.

pétoncle, f. scollop (fish).

pétrée, a. (f.) stony || (an.) petrous.

pétrel, m. petrel (bird) || ~ de tempête, stormy petrel.

pétrifier, v. a. to petrify || (fig.) scrape,

pétrin, m. kneading-trough   [mess.

pétrir, v. a. to knead.

pétrissage, m. kneading.

pétrole, m. petroleum.   [of petroleum.

pétroleur, se, m.& f. incendiary by means

pétulant, e, a. petulant, pert, saucy.

peu, ad. little, few || ~ à ~, by degrees || à ~ près, nearly, thereabout || pour ~ que, ever so little, however so little may be || dans ~, in a short time.

peuplade, f. people || colony || tribe.

peuple, m. people, nation || le bas ~, le menu ~, the mob.   [to stock (a pond).

peupler, v. a. & n. to people || to multiply ||

peuplier, m. (bot.) poplar.

peur, f. fear, fright, dread || de ~ de, de ~ que, lest, for fear that, for fear of || sans ~, fearless.

peureux, se, a. timorous, fearful || starting.

peut-être, a. perhaps.

phaéton, m. phaeton.

phalange, f. phalanx.

phalène, f. night-fly, moth.

pharaon, m. pharo (game).

phare, m. (mar.) beacon, light, light-house.

pharisien, m. pharisee, hypocrite.

pharmaceutique, a. pharmaceutical.

pharmacie, f. pharmacy || chemist's shop || medicine-chest || dispensary.

pharmacien, m. chemist || dispenser.

pharmacopée, f. dispensatory.

pharynx, m. (an.) pharynx.

phase, f. phase || phasis || stage.

phébus, m. bombast, bombastic style.

phénix, m. phœnix.

phénomène, m. phenomenon.

philanthrope, m. philanthropist.

philanthropie, f. philanthropy.

philanthropique, a. philanthropic.

philharmonique, a. philharmonic.

philippique, f. philippic.

philologie, f. philology.

philologique, a. philological.

philologue, m. philologer.

philomatique, a. philomatic.

philosophal, e, a.; pierre ~e, f. philosopher's stone.

philosophe, m. philosopher.

philosophe, a. philosophical.

philosopher, v. n. to philosophise.

philosophie, f. philosophy.   [sophic(ally).

philosophique, a. (-ment, ad.) philosophique, a. (-ment, ad.) philosophical.

philotechnique, a. philotechnic, art-loving.

philtre, m. love-potion.   [ing.

phonographe, m. phonograph.

phoque, m. seal.

phosphore, m. phosphorus.

phosphoreux, se, a. phosphorous.

phosphorique, a. phosphoric.

photographe, m. photographer.

photographie, f. photography || photograph.

photographier, v. a. to photograph.

photographique, a. photographic.

phrase, f. phrase, sentence.

phraséologie, f. phraseology.

phraser, v. n. to make phrases, to phrase.

phraseur, phrasier, m. phrase-maker.

phrénologie, f. phrenology.

phthisie, f. (méd.) phthisis, consumption.

phthisique, a. (méd.) phthisical, consumptive.   [perimentalist.

physicien, m. natural philosopher || experimentalist.

physiologie, f. physiology.

physiologique, a. physiological.

physiologiste, m. physiologist.

physionomie, f. physiognomy, countenance, face, look.

physionomiste, m. physiognomist.

physique, f. physics (pl.), natural philosophy.

physique, m. natural constitution.

physique, a. (-ment, ad.) physical(ly).

piaffer, v. n. to strut, to prance, to paw.

piailler, v. n. to bawl, to squall.

piaillerie, f. shrill scolding.

piailleur, m. squaller, bawler.

pianiste, m. & f. pianoforte-player, pianist.

piano, m. piano || ~ carré, square piano || ~ droit, cottage-piano || ~ à queue, [grand piano.

piaulard, m. whiner.

piaulard, e, a. whining.

piauler, v. n. to pule, to whine. [larly.

pic, m. pick-axe || peak || à ~, perpendicu-

picaillon, m. old Piedmontese copper coin, worth rather less than 1 centime || avoir des ~s, (fam.) to be rich ou well off.

pichenette, f. fillip.

picorée, f. marauding || plundering.

picorer, v. n. to pilfer.

picot, m. splinter || purl (of lace).

picoté, e, a. pitted, marked.

picoter, v. a. to prick || to peck (of birds) || to stimulate.

picoterie, f. bickering, teasing.

picotin, m. peck (measure). [shrew.

pie, f. magpie (bird) || ~-grièche, shrike |

pie, a. pious || piebald.

pièce, f. piece, fragment, part, bit, parcel, patch || room (in a house) || ~ à ~, by degrees || en ~s, in pieces, peacemeal || ragged || ~ de conviction, circumstantial evidence || ~ de drap, piece of cloth || ~ d'eau, piece of ornamental water || ~ de résistance, large joint, piece to cut and come again || ~ de vingt-quatre, 24-pounder || ~ de vin, hogshead of wine || ~ d'artillerie, piece of ordnance.

pied, m. foot || à ~, on foot || ~ à ~, by degrees, by little and little || sur le ~ de, at the rate of || au ~ de la lettre, literally || à ~ sec, without wetting one's feet || d'arrache-~, without intermission || coup de ~, m. kick || valet de ~, m. footman || petits ~s, pl. small birds (pl.) || ~ plat, dirty fellow || marcher à ~, to go on foot || avoir un ~ de nez, to look foolish, to look blank || ~-à-terre, m. temporary lodging || country-box || small box.

piédestal, m. pedestal.

piège, m. snare, gin, trap. [(pl.).

pierraille, f. heap of pebbles, broken stones

pierre, f. stone || flint || gem || ~ angulaire, corner-stone || ~ d'attente, stepping-stone || ~ infernale, caustic || ~ à fusil (~ à briquet), gun-flint || ~ à rasoir, ~ à repasser, whetstone || ~ de taille, shaped stone, free-stone || ~ de touche, touch-stone.

pierreries, f. pl. precious stones (pl.).

pierreux, se, a. stony. [jewels (pl.).

pierrier, m. swivel-gun.

pierrot, m. house-sparrow || clown.

piété, f. piety || godliness.

piétinement, m. stamping, kicking.

piétiner, v. n. to tap on the ground with one's feet, to drum.

piétiste, m. pietist. [walker.

piéton, m. foot-passenger, pedestrian,

piètre, a. (fam.) paltry, sorry, mean || -ment, ad. sorrily, wretchedly, pitifully.

piètrerie, f. (fam.) paltry stuff, sorry

pieu, m. stake, pile. [goods (pl.).

pieux, se, a. (-sement, ad.) pious(ly) |

pif, m. nose, nozzle. [godly.

piffre, m., **piffresse,** f. glutton.

pigeon, m. pigeon, dove || ~ culbutant, tumbler || ~ ramier, ring-dove || ~ voyageur, carrier-pigeon.

pigeonneau, m. young pigeon.

pigeonnier, m. pigeon-house.

pigment, m. (an.) pigment.

pignocher, v. n. to nibble.

pignon, m. gable-end || pinion (of a watch) || kernel || avoir ~ sur rue, to have a house of one's own.

pilastre, m. pilaster.

pilau, m. stewed rice.

pile, f. pile, heap || pier || whacking, licking || ~ ou face, head or tail || ~ de Volta, Voltaic battery.

piler, v. a. to pound.

pilier, m. pillar, post || (fig.) ~ de cabaret, tippler || fixture.

pillage, m. pillage, plunder.

pillard, e, m. & f. plunderer.

pillard, e, a. pillaging, thievish.

piller, v. a. to pillage, to plunder.

pillerie, f. robbery, extortion.

pilleur, m. plunderer, robber.

pilon, m. pestle || drum-stick (of a fowl).

pilorier, v. a. to pillory || to expose.

pilot, m. heap of salt.

pilotage, m. pilotage || pile-work || timber for stakes.

pilote, m. pilot, steersman.

piloter, v. a. & n. (mar.) to pilot || to drive [in piles.

pilotin, m. pilot-boy.

pilotis, m. pl. piles (pl.), pile-work.

pilule, f. pill, pillule || (fig.) anger, trouble.

pimbêche, f. pert minx.

piment, m. (bot.) alspice, pimento.

pimpant, e, a. smart, dashing.

pimprenelle, f. (bot.) burnet.

pin, m. (bot.) pine, pine-tree || pomme de ~, f. fir-cone.

pinacle, m. pinnacle.

pinasse, f. (mar.) pinnace.

pince, f. lever, handspike, pincers (pl.), nippers (pl.) || claws (pl.) || ~-maille, m. pinchpenny, stingy fellow || ~-nez, m. double eye-glass, pince-nez.

pincé, e, a. affected, stiff.

pinceau, m. hair-pencil, brush.

pincée, f. pinch.

pincer, v. a. to pinch || to nip hard, to satirise || to catch (one) || (mus.) to play.

pincettes, f. pl. pincers (pl.), tongs (pl.), nippers (pl.).

pinçon, m. pinch (mark made by pinching).

pingouin, m. penguin (bird).

pingre, m. skin-flint.

pingre, a. stingy, close-fisted.

pinson, m. chaffinch (bird).

pintade, f. Guinea-fowl.

pinte, f. pint.

pioche, f. pick-axe, mattock || hard work.

piocher, v. a. to dig with a pick-axe || to fag, to work hard, to study hard.

piocheur, m. digger || hard worker.

pion, m. man (at draughts) || pawn (at chess) || usher. [away.

pioncer, v. n. (fam.) to snooze, to snooze

pionner, v. n. to take pawns (at chess).

pionnier, m. (mil.) pioneer.

pipe, f. pipe, tobacco-pipe || pipe(cask).

pipeau, m. pipe (to play on) || bird-call || lime-twig || snare.

pipée, f. catching of birds (with bird-lime).

pipelet, m. (fam.) porter, doorkeeper.

piper, v. a. to catch birds with a bird-call || to cheat at play || to excel.

piperie, f. cheat, trick, sleight.

pipeur, m. cheat, sharper.

piquant, m. prickle || sting || quill || pungency || point || fun.

piquant, e, a. prickling, prickly, stinging, biting, sharp, tart, smart, bitter.

pique, f. pike, lance || quarrel, bickering || ~, m. spade (at cards) || ~-assiette, m. parasite, spunger || ~-bœuf, m. drover || ~-nique, m. picnic, party.

piquer, v. a. & n. to prick, to sting || to quilt || to stimulate || to exasperate, to pique || to be poignant, to be sharp || se ~, to be piqued, to be displeased at, to be angry with, to be offended at.

piquet, m. picket, stake, peg || piquet (game) || (mil.) picket.

piquette, f. bad wine || washy stuff || swipes (pl.).

piqueur, m. pricker || whipper-in || riding-master || huntsman || overseer.

piquier, m. pikeman.

piqûre, f. pricking, prick, puncture, sting || worm-hole || quilting, stitching.

pirate, m. pirate, freebooter.

pirater, v. n. to pirate.

piraterie, f. piracy.

pire, a. worse || le ~, the worst.

piriforme, a. pear-shaped.

pirogue, f. pirogue (native canoe).

pirouette, f. whirligig || rapid whirling round upon one foot, pirouette || short appearance || subterfuge || jest.

pirouetter, v. a. to whirl, to pirouette.

pis, m. teat, udder, breast.

pis, a. worse || le ~, the worst || de ~ en ~, worse and worse || au ~, au ~-aller, at the worst || ~-aller, m. last resource, last shift.

pisciculture, f. fish-culture.

piscine, f. pool, pond, reservoir.

pisé, m. pise, clay.

pissenlit, m. piss-a-bed || dandelion.

pisser, v. n. to piss, to pass water.

pissoir, m. urinal.

pistache, f. (bot.) pistachio(-nut).

pistachier, m. (bot.) pistachio-tree.

piste, f. track, trace, footstep.

pistil, m. (bot.) pistil.

pistolet, m. pistol || ~ à répétition, revolver || ~ d'arçon, horse-pistol.

piston, m. piston || sucker of a pump || stopper.

pitance, f. pittance.

piteux, se, a. (-sement, ad.) piteous(ly).

pitié, f. pity, compassion || disdain, contempt. [tempt.

piton, m. screw-ring || peak.

pitoyable, a. (-ment, ad.) pitiful(ly) || piteous(ly) || wretched(ly).

pittoresque, a. (-ment, ad.) picturesque || in a picturesque manner.

pivert, m. woodpecker (bird).

pivoine, f. (bot.) peony.

pivot, m. pivot, spindle || hinge || (hort.) tap-root.

pivoter, v. a. & n. to turn on a pivot || (hort.) to shoot a perpendicular root.

placage, m. veneering || plating || patchwork.

placard, m. placard || cupboard (in a wall), slip. [libel.

placarder, v. a. to placard, to post up || to

place, f. place, room, space || post, office, condition, employment || fortress || exchange || stand for hackney-coaches || ~ d'armes, parade || parade-ground || stronghold.

placement, m. placing, putting out money || bureau de ~, m. registry-office.

placer, v. a. to place, to set, to dispose, to rank || to put out at interest || se ~, to get a situation || to sit down in a place.

placet, m. petition.

placeur, se, m. & f. registry-office keeper.

placier, ère, m. & f. agent.

plafond, m. ceiling, floor.

plafonnage, m. ceiling.

plafonner, v. a. to ceil, to roof.

plafonneur, m. ceiling-maker.

plage, f. flat and low sea-shore || climate, region.

plagiaire, m. plagiary. [region.

plagiat, m. plagiarism.

plaider, v. a. & n. to plead, to argue || to litigate || to be at law, to go to law.

plaideur, se, m. & f. pleader, litigious man, litigious woman.

plaidoirie, f. pleading, law-suit.

plaidoyer, m. lawyer's address in court, plea. [defence.

plaie, f. wound, sore || plague. [defence.

plaignant, m. (jur.) plaintiff.

plaignant, e, a. complaining, plaintive.

plain, e, a. plain, even, flat || ~-chant, f. church-music, chant.

plaindre, v. a. ir. to pity, to compassionate, to commiserate, to grudge || se ~, to complain || to make complaints.

plaine, f. plain, field.

plainte, f. complaint, groan, deep sigh.

plaintif, ve, a. (-vement, ad.) plaintive (ly) || doleful(ly).

plaire, v. n. ir. to please, to be agreeable, to give pleasure || plaît-il ? your pleasure? || s'il vous plaît, if you please || plût à Dieu I would to God! || à Dieu ne plaise ! God forbid! || se ~, to please one another || to be pleased, to delight in || to flatter oneself. [strangely.

plaisamment, ad. pleasantly, ludicrously ||

plaisance, f. pleasure || lieu de ~, m., maison de ~, f. country-house.

plaisant, m. jester, joker || **mauvais ~,** sorry jester || humbug.

plaisant, e, a. pleasant, humorous, ludicrous, ridiculous, jocose, comical.

plaisanter, v. a. & n. to jest, to joke, to banter || pour ~, in jest, jesting.

plaisanterie, f. pleasantry, joke, jest, jesting, joking, banter.

plaisir, m. pleasure, delight, joy, sport, diversion || kindness, favour, courtesy || excursion || wafer || -s, pl. rolled wafers (pl.) || à ~, at one's ease, carefully.

plan, m. plane, level, surface || plan || draught, design, project || **premier ~**, foreground.

plan, e, a. plain, even, smooth, flat.

planche, f. plank, board || (copper-)plate || bed || ~ à bouteilles, bottle-rack || ~ à débarquer, (mar.) gangboard of a ship.

planchéier, v. a. to board || to floor.

plancher, m. floor, ceiling.

plançon, m. shoot, twig, set || plank-timber. ,   [hover (of birds) || to sail.

planer, v. a. & n. to plane, to smoothe || to

planétaire, m. orrery.

planétaire, a. planetary.

planète, f. planet.

planeur, m. planisher.

planisphère, m. planisphere.

plant, m. plant, twig, set || **plantation** || jeune ~, vineyard newly set.

plantage, m. plantation.

plantard, m. (hort.) slip.

plantation, f. planting || plantation || colony.

plante, f. plant || sole (of the foot).

planter, v. a. to plant, to fix, to settle || to place || **se ~**, to be planted || to put ou

planteur, m. planter.   [stick oneself.

plantoir, m. dibbler.

planton, m. orderly soldier || **de ~**, on duty.

plantureux, se, a. abundant, fertile.

planure, f. shavings (pl.).   [veneer.

plaque, f. plate (of metals) || slab || badge ||

plaqué, m. plated metal.

plaquer, v. a. to plate, to lay on || to veneer.

plaqueur, m. plater || veneerer.

plasticité, f. plasticity.

plastique, a. plastic.

plastron, m. fencing-pad || butt.

plat, m. dish, mess || scale || flat (of a sword) || ~-bord, m. (mar.) gunwale.

plat, e, a. (-ement, ad.) flatly || smooth || level || dull || dead || mean.

platane, m. (bot.) plane-tree.

plate, f. plate || ~-bande, f. border || flower-bed || ~-forme, f. platform || (rail.) turn-table.

plateau, m. tray, tea-board || platform, table-land || ~ à découper, butler's tray || ~ de carafe, decanter-stand.

platée, f. dishful.

platine, m. platina.   [plate.

platine, f. round copper-plate || gunlock

platitude, f. flatness, dulness, meanness || platitude.

platonique, a. Platonic || sentimental.

plâtrage, m. plaster-work.

plâtras, m. rubbish of plaster.

plâtre, m. plaster || plaster cast.

plâtrer, v. a. to plaster, to parget || to daub over, to palliate.

plâtreux, se, a. chalky.

plâtrier, m. plasterer.

plâtrière, f. plaster-quarry.

plausibilité, f. plausibility.

plausible, a. plausible.

plèbe, f. the Plebs (pl.), common people (pl.).

plébéien, m. plebeian.

plébéien, ne, a. plebeian.

Pléiades, f. pl. Pleiads (pl.).

plein, m. full space.

plein, e, a. & ad. full, abounding, entire, complete || tout ~, plentifully, abundantly || à ~, fully || ~e lune, f. full moon.

pleinement, ad. fully.

plénière, f. plenary.

plénière, a. plenary.

plénipotentiaire, m. plenipotentiary.

plénipotentiaire, a. plenipotentiary.

pléonasme, m. pleonasm.

pléthore, f. (méd.) plethora.

pleurard, m. blubberer.

pleurer, v. a. & n. to weep, to lament || to cry || (of vines) to bleed || to grudge.

pleurésie, f. (méd.) pleurisy.

pleureur, se, m. & f. weeper || mourner.

pleureur, se, a. weeping.

pleurnicher, v. n. to whine.

pleurnicheur, m. whiner.

pleurs, m. pl. tears (pl.) || weeping || (of vines) weeping.

pleutre, m. coward, ignoramus.

pleuvoir, v. n. ir. to rain.

pleyon, m. twig, twine, osier.

pli, m. plait, fold, bent, wrinkle || undulation || wave || tuck || recess.

pliable, a. flexible, bending, supple.

pliage, m. folding, fold.

pliant, m. folding-chair.

pliant, e, a. pliant, pliable, flexible, docile.

plier, v. n. to fold, to fold up, to bend, to bow || to warp, to yield, to submit || **se ~**, to bend || to conform oneself to.

plieur, se, m. & f. folder.   [board.

plinthe, f. (arch.) plinth, skirting || wash-

ploir, m. folder, folding-knife, folding-

plissement, m. plaiting.   [stick.

plisser, v. a. to plait, to crimple, to fold.

plissure, f. plaiting, folding.

plomb, m. lead || plummet, plumb-line || bullets (pl.), shot (pl.) || à ~, perpendicularly || fil à ~, m. plumb-line.

plombage, m. lead-work || leading || stopping || sealing || pressing.

plombagine, f. (min.) plumbago, black-lead.

plomber, v. a. to lead, to fit with lead || to glaze, to varnish || to stamp with lead.

plomberie, f. plumbery || lead-works (pl.).

plombeur, a.; rouleau ~, m. field-roller.

plombier, m. plumber.

plongeon, m. plungeon, sea-diver (bird).

plonger, v. a. & n. to plunge, to dip, to immerse, to duck.

plongeur, m. diver.

ployer, v. a. to fold.

pluie, f. rain || jour de ~, m. rainy day.

plumage, m. plumage, feathers (pl.).

plumasserie, f. feather-trade.

plumassier, m. feather-seller.

plume, f. plume, feather, quill, pen.

plumeau, m. feather-broom, duster.

plumée, f. penful.

plumer, v. a. to plume, to pluck, to fleece.

plumet, m. plume. [to tambour.
plumetis, m. tambouring || **broder au ~,**
plumeux, se, a. feathery. [red-tapist.
plumitif, m. minute-book || quill-driver ||
plupart, f. most *ou* greatest part || **pour
la ~,** mostly || **la ~ du temps,** generally.
pluralité, f. plurality.
pluriel, m. (gr.) plural.
pluriel, le, a. (gr.) plural.
plus, ad. more, most, over || no more, not
any more || **~ tôt,** sooner || **au ~ tôt,** as
soon as possible || **~ tard,** later || **~ loin,**
further || **le ~,** the most, the utmost || **au
~, tout au ~,** at most || **de ~,** besides.
plusieurs, a. pl. many, several, divers,
sundry. [(tense).
plus-que-parfait, m. (gr.) pluperfect
plutôt, ad. rather, more.
pluvial, e, a.; eau **-e,** f. rain-water.
pluvier, m. plover (bird).
pluvieux, se, a. rainy || wet.
pluviomètre, m. rain-gauge.
pneumatique, a. pneumatic || **machine
~,** f. air-pump.
pneumonie, f. (méd.) pneumonia.
pochade, f. rough sketch.
pochard, m. drunkard || boozer.
pochard, e, a. drunk, groggy, boozy.
(se) pocharder, to get drunk.
poche, f. pocket, bag || crop (of a bird) ||
poke || net || crib || pucker.
pocher, v. a. to bruise || to blot || to poach.
pochette, f. small pocket, small purse,
pouch || kit.
pochon, m. black eye.
podagre, m. (méd.) gout in the feet.
podagre, a. gouty.
poêle, f. frying-pan, pan.
poêle, m. stove || pall || canopy.
poêlée, f. (frying-)panful.
poêlier, m. stove-maker.
poêlon, m. saucepan.
poêlonnée, f. saucepanful.
poème, m. poem.
poésie, f. poesy, poetry.
poète, m. poet.
poétesse, f. poetess.
poétique, f. poetics (pl.).
poétique, a. (-ment, ad.) poetical(ly).
poétiser, v. n. to poetise.
poétriau, m. poetaster, bad poet.
poids, m. weight, heaviness, gravity || (fig.)
importance, consequence.
poignant, e, a. poignant, sharp.
poignard, m. poniard, dagger || **coup de
~,** m. stab.
poignarder, v. a. to poniard, to stab.
poigne, f. grasp, grip.
poignée, f. handful || handle (of a sword).
poignet, m. wrist, wrist-band.
poil, m. hair || nap || filaments (pl.) || **~ de
chèvre,** mohair.
poilu, e, a. hairy || shaggy.
poinçon, m. bodkin, puncheon, punch ||
awl || stiletto.
poinçonner, v. a. to stamp || to punch.
poindre, v. n. ir. to peep, to dawn, to begin, to appear. [blow.
poing, m. fist, hand || **coup de ~,** m. cuff,

point, m. point || period || stitch made with
a needle || mark || case, condition, state ||
height, degree || **au dernier ~,** in the
highest degree || **deux -s,** pl. (gr.) colon.
point, ad. no, not, none || **~ du tout,**
not at all.
pointage, m. pointing, aiming || levelling.
pointe, f. point, sharp end || pointed tool ||
promontory || (fig.) sharpness, tartness ||
high taste || quibble, pun || **en ~,** with a
sharp point || **sans ~,** pointless || **~ du
jour,** break of day || **~ de terre,** fore-
land, promontory || **~ du vin,** flavour of
wine.
pointement, m. pointing || levelling.
pointer, v. a. & n. to point, to stick, to
prick, to sharpen || to level, to take aim ||
to scar || to sprout || (mar.) to prick (a chart).
pointeur, m. (mil.) marker || pricker.
pointillage, m. dotting.
pointiller, v. a. & n. to dot, to prick, to
nip, to touch || to cavil.
pointillerie, f. (fam.) bickering, cavilling,
cavil. [cavilling.
pointilleux, se, a. captious, punctilious,
pointu, e, a. pointed, peaked, sharp.
poire, f. pear || **~ d'angoisse,** choke-pear ||
~ à poudre, powder-horn.
poiré, m. perry.
poireau, m. (bot.) leek || wart.
poirée, f. (bot.) white beet.
poirier, m. (bot.) pear-tree.
pois, m. (bot.) pea || **~ chiche,** chick-pea.
poison, m. poison, venom.
poissard, e, a. low, vulgar.
poissarde, f. fishwife, fish-fag.
poisser, v. a. to pitch, to glue.
poisseux, se, a. pitchy.
poisson, m. fish || **~ d'Avril,** April fool.
poissonnaille, f. small fish (pl.), fry (pl.).
poissonnerie, f. fish-market.
poissonneux, se, a. abounding with fish.
poissonnier, ère, m. & f. fishmonger.
poissonnière, f. fish-kettle.
poitrail, m. breast (of a horse), chest ||
breast-leather.
poitrinaire, m. consumptive person.
poitrine, f. breast, chest, bosom.
poivrade, f. pepper-sauce.
poivre, m. pepper.
poivrer, v. a. to pepper. [box.
poivrier, m. (bot.) pepper-plant || pepper-
poivrière, f. pepper-box.
poix, f. pitch || wax.
polaire, a. polar || **étoile ~,** f. pole-star.
pôle, m. pole || **~ de l'aimant,** magnetic
pole. [war.
polémique, f. polemic, controversy, paper-
polémique, a. (-ment, ad.) polemical(ly).
poli, m. polish, gloss.
poli, e, a. (-ment, ad.) polished || polite
(ly) || elegant.
police, f. police || policy || **~ d'assurance,**
policy of insurance || tribunal **de ~,** m.
police-court || salle **de ~,** f. defaulters'
ou dry-room || bonnet **de ~,** m. foraging-
cap. [polish, to civilise.
policer, v. a. to establish policy in || to
polichinel(le), m. Punch, buffoon.

policier, m. policeman.
poliment, m. polishing.
polir, v. a. to polish.
polissage, m. polishing.
polisseur, m. polisher.
polissoir, m. polishing-iron.
polissoire, f. polishing-brush.
polisson, m. rogue, blackguard.
polissonner, v. n. to play the young
  blackguard.   [gish trick, waggishness.
polissonnerie, f. blackguardism ‖ wag-
polissure, f. polishing, polish.
politesse, f. politeness, elegance of manners, good breeding.
politique, f. politics (pl.), policy.
politique, m. politician, statesman.
politique, a. (-ment, ad.) politic, politic-
  al(ly) ‖ cunning ‖ with policy, artfully.
politiquer, v. a. to talk politics ‖ to play
  a shrewd game.
polker, v. n. to dance the polka.
polluer, v. a. to pollute.
poltron, m. poltroon, coward.
poltron, ne, a. cowardly, dastardly.
poltronnerie, f. poltroonery, cowardice.
polygame, m. & f. polygamist.
polygame, a. polygamous.
polygamie, f. polygamy.
polyglotte, m. polyglot.
polyglotte, a. polyglot.
polygone, m. polygon ‖ artillery-ground ‖
polygone, a. polygonal.   [butt.
polygraphe, m. manifold writer.
polysyllabe, m. polysyllable.
polysyllabe, a. polysyllabic.
polytechnique, a. polytechnic.
polythéisme, m. polytheism.
polythéiste, m. polytheist.
pommade, f. pomade ‖ ointment ‖ salve.
pommader, v. a. to pomade, to anoint.
pomme, f. apple ‖ ball ‖ knob ‖ (mar.)
  truck ‖ ~ de terre, potato.
pommé, e, a. (hort.) grown to a round
  head, cabbaged ‖ downright ‖ egregious.
pommeau, m. pommel.
pommelé, e, a. dappled.
se pommeler, to become dappled.
pommer, v. n. (hort.) to grow to a round
  head, to cabbage.
pommeraie, f. orchard of apple-trees.
pommette, f. small pommel, ball, knob ‖
  cheek-bone.
pommier, m. (bot.) apple-tree.
pomologie, f. training of fruit-trees.
pompe, f. pump ‖ pomp, splendour ‖ ~ à
  feu, steam-waterworks (pl.) ‖ ~ à incendie, fire-engine ‖ ~ aspirante, suc-
  tion-pump ‖ ~s funèbres, pl. funeral
  pomp, burial.
pomper, v. a. to pump ‖ to suck up.
pompeux, se, a. (-sement, ad.) pomp-
  ous(ly).
pompier, m. fireman ‖ pump-maker.
pompon, m. trinket, top-knot.
pomponner, v. a. to adorn with top-knots,
ponçage, m. pumicing.   [to deck.
ponce, f. pounce, pumice-stone.
ponceau, m. (bot.) red poppy, corn-rose ‖
  (rail.) culvert.

ponceau, a. crimson red.
poncer, v. a. to rub with pumice-stone, to
poncis, m. pounced drawing.   [pounce.
ponction, f. tapping ‖ faire la ~, to tap.
ponctualité, f. punctuality.
ponctuel, le, a. (-lement, ad.) punctual
ponctuer, v. a. (gr.) to punctuate.   [(ly).
pondage, m. poundage.
pondération, f. weighing, poise.
pondérer, v. n. to poise.
pondeuse, f. laying hen.
pondre, v. a. & n. ir. to lay eggs.
pont, m. bridge ‖ deck (of a ship) ‖ ~ levis,
  draw-bridge ‖ ~ tournant, swing-bridge ‖
  ~ suspendu, chain-bridge ‖ ~ volant,
  flying bridge ‖ ~s et chaussées, pl.
  civil engineering.
ponte, f. egg-laying, laying-time ‖ ~, m.
  punter (at faro).
ponter, v. a. & n. to deck ‖ to punt.
pontet, m. guard ‖ saddle-tree.
pontife, m. pontiff.
pontificalement, ad. pontifically.
pontificat, m. pontificate.
pontifier, v. n. to pontificate ‖ to talk in
  an unctious or devotional manner.
ponton, m. pontoon ‖ hulk.
pontonnier, m. toll-gatherer ‖ (mil.) pon-
popeline, f. poplin, lustre.   [tonier.
populace, f. populace, mob.
populacier, ère, a. vulgar.
populaire, a. (-ment, ad.) popular(ly).
populariser, v. a. to popularise.
popularité, f. popularity.
population, f. population.
populeux, se, a. populous.
porc, m. hog, pork ‖ ~-épic, m. porcupine.
porcelaine, f. porcelain, china, china-ware.
porcelaine, a. enamelled.
porchaison, f. wild-boar season.
porche, m. porch.
porcher, ère, m. & f. swine-herd.
pornographe, m. pornographic writer or
  painter, delineator of obscenities.
pore, m. pore.
poreux, se, a. porous.
porphyre, m. porphyry.
porreau, m. vide poireau.
port, m. port, haven, wharf, harbour ‖
  postage ‖ tonnage ‖ carriage ‖ deportment,
  port, air ‖ ~ de lettres, postage ‖ ~
  d'armes, port of arms ‖ ~ de voix, compass of the voice ‖ franc de ~, a. post-
  free ‖ à bon ~, safe, safely ‖ prosperously.
portable, a. wearable.
portage, m. carriage, porterage.
portail, m. portal, front gate.
portant, e, a. bearing ‖ bien ~, in good
  health ‖ mal ~, unwell ‖ à bout ~, close,
  point-blank ‖ (of duels) breast to breast.
portatif, ve, a. portable.
porte, f. door, gate ‖ de ~ en ~, from
  door to door ‖ à ~ close, with closed
  doors, secretly ‖ ~ de derrière, back-
  door ‖ ~ à deux battants, folding-door ‖
  fausse ~, postern ‖ ~ vitrée, glass-door ‖
  ~ de dégagement, back-door ‖ ~ d'entrée, street-door ‖ chief-door ‖ ~-croi-
  sée, m. French casement.

porte (de porter); ~-affiches, m. bill-frame, advertisement-frame ǁ board-man ǁ ~-allumettes, m. match-box ǁ ~-assiette, m. plate-rack ǁ plate-stand ǁ ~-balle, m. pedlar ǁ ~-barres, m. pole-ring ǁ ~-bouquet, m. bouquet-holder ǁ ~-bouteilles, m. bottle-rack ǁ ~-carafe, m. decanter-stand ǁ ~-cartes, m. cart-case ǁ ~-chapeaux, m. hat-stand ǁ ~-cigare, m. cigar-tube, mouth-piece ǁ ~-cigares, pl. cigar-case ǁ ~-clef, m. turnkey ǁ key-ring ǁ ~-coquetiers, m. egg-stand ǁ ~-couteau, m. knife-rest ǁ ~-croix, m. cross-bearer ǁ ~-curedents, m. toothpick-case ǁ tooth-pick-holder ǁ ~-drapeau, m. (mil.) standard-bearer, ensign ǁ ~-épée, m. sword-bearer, belt ǁ ~-étendard, m. (mil.) standard-bearer ǁ ~-étrivières, m. pl. stirrup-rings (pl.), square-rings (pl.) ǁ ~-flambeau, m. torch-bearer ǁ ~-fleurs, m. flower-stand ǁ ~-fromage, m. cheese-tray ǁ ~-lettres, m. letter-case ǁ ~-liqueurs, m. liquor-frame ǁ ~-livres, m. book-slide ǁ ~-malheur, m. bringer of ill-luck ǁ ill-omen ǁ ~-mèche, m. wick-holder ǁ ~-monnaie, m. money-bag, purse ǁ ~-montre, m. watch-stand ǁ watch-pocket ǁ ~-mouchettes, m. snuffers-tray ǁ ~-musique, m. canterbury ǁ ~-parapluies, m. umbrella-stand ǁ ~-peigne, m. comb-case ǁ ~-pipe, m. pipe-case ǁ ~-plume, m. pen-holder ǁ ~-plumes, m. pen-case ǁ ~-queue, m. train-bearer ǁ ~-queues, m. cue-rack ǁ ~-respect, m. weapon carried for self-defence ǁ badge of dignity ǁ imposing person ǁ ~-rôties, m. toast-rack ǁ ~-trait, m. trace-strap ǁ ~-vent, m. wind-box of an organ ǁ ~-verge, m. verger, usher, beadle ǁ ~-voix, m. speaking-trumpet.

porté, e, a.; ~ à, inclined.

portecrayon, m. pencil-case ǁ port-crayon.

portée, f. brood, litter ǁ reach, extent ǁ comprehension, capacity, ability, power ǁ line in a page of music ǁ **à une~ de fusil,** within gun-shot.

portefaix, m. street-porter.

portefeuille, m. portfolio, pocket-book ǁ bill-case ǁ post of acting Cabinet-Minister.

portemanteau, m. portmanteau, cloak-bag.

porter, v. a. & n. to carry, to bear, to support ǁ to wear ǁ to bring, to convey ǁ to suffer, to endure ǁ to produce, to induce ǁ to favour ǁ to breed ǁ to show ǁ to measure ǁ to be ǁ to have ǁ to cause ǁ to give ǁ to cast ǁ to turn ǁ to lay, to put ǁ to raise ǁ to state ǁ to propose ǁ to drink ǁ to vote for ǁ to shoulder ǁ to lie ǁ to reach ǁ to take effect ǁ to tell ǁ to act upon ǁ to get into ǁ to aim ǁ to tend ǁ **se ~,** to be ǁ to be inclined, to have an inclination for, to incline, to tend ǁ to be worn ǁ to resort ǁ to flock ǁ to rush ǁ to abandon oneself ǁ to stand forward.

porteur, m. porter, carrier ǁ postillion's horse ǁ (com.) **au ~,** to the bearer.

porteuse, f. basket-woman.

portier, m. porter, door-keeper.

portière, f. porteress ǁ coach-door ǁ door-hangings (pl.), curtain. [ance, pittance.

portion, f. portion, part, piece ǁ allow-

portique, m. portico.

portrait, m. portrait, picture ǁ description.

posage, m. laying, laying down.

pose, f. laying of a stone ǁ (mil.) placing of a sentinel after the evening drum ǁ sitting for one's portrait ǁ posture, attitude.

posé, e, a. (-ment, ad.) placed, laid, set ǁ sedate(ly) ǁ grave(ly) ǁ sober(ly) ǁ composed(ly) ǁ slowly.

poser, v. a. & n. to lay, to set, to put, to place, to lay down, to suppose ǁ to lie, to lean, to rest ǁ to sit for one's portrait ǁ **se ~,** to perch on, to light ǁ to show oneself to take a position ǁ to set up for ǁ to be put **ou** laid. [attitudinarian.

poseur, m. layer of stones, builder ǁ hanger ǁ

positif, m. (gr.) positive ǁ positive, reality ǁ (mus.) choir-organ.

positif, ve, a. (-vement, ad.) positive(ly) ǁ exactly ǁ certain ǁ matter-of-fact.

position, f. position, situation ǁ posture ǁ circumstances (pl.) ǁ station.

possédé, e, m. & f. madman ǁ madwoman.

posséder, v. a. to possess, to enjoy, to hold, to have, to be master of ǁ to understand, to know ǁ **se ~,** to have self-command, to command one's temper.

possesseur, m. possessor, owner.

possessif, ve, a. (gr.) possessive.

possession, f. possession, enjoyment, occupation ǁ estates (pl.) ǁ habit.

possibilité, f. possibility.

possible, m. possibility ǁ utmost ǁ best ǁ

possible, a. possible. [au ~, extremely.

postdater, v. a. to post-date.

poste, f. post ǁ stage ǁ post-house ǁ post-office ǁ mail ǁ post-haste ǁ post-boy ǁ **~ aux chevaux,** post-house ǁ **~ aux lettres,** post ǁ **~ aux paquets,** parcels'-delivery ǁ **grande ~,** general post-office ǁ **petite ~,** receiving-house ǁ (in Paris) two-penny post ǁ **"~ restante",** "to be left till called for". [house.

poste, m. post ǁ berth ǁ station ǁ guard-

poster, v. a. to post, to station, to place.

postérieur, e, a. posterior, later ǁ hind ǁ -ement, ad. afterwards.

postériorité, f. posteriority.

postérité, f. posterity.

posthume, a. posthumous. [added.

postiche, a. fictitious, sham, false ǁ super-

postillon, m. postilion, post-boy.

postscriptum, m. postscript.

postulant, e, m. postulant, candidate.

postuler, v. a. & n. to apply for ǁ to sue.

posture, f. posture, situation ǁ state.

pot, m. pot ǁ **~ à cuire,** seething-pot ǁ **~ de vin,** premium, good-will ǁ **~ aux roses,** (fig.) secret ǁ **faire le ~ à deux anses,** to set one's arms akimbo ǁ **~-au-feu,** m. gravy soup with boiled beef ǁ common necessaries of life (pl.) ǁ **~-de-chambre,** m. chamber-pot ǁ **~-pourri,** m. hotch-potch.

potable, a. drinkable.

potage, m. potage, porridge, soup.

potager, m. stove in a kitchen ‖ kitchen-garden.   [f. pot-herb.

potager, ère, a. culinary ‖ **herbe –ère,**

potasse, f. potash.

poteau, m. post, stake.

potée, f. potful ‖ (fig.) swarm.

potelé, e, a. plump, sleek.

potence, f. gallows, gibbet ‖ crutch ‖ standard ‖ sliding ruler ‖ bracket.

potentat, m. potentate.

poterie, f. pottery ‖ earthenware.

poterne, f. (mil.) postern.

potiche, f. Chinese vase.

potier, m. potter.   [to kick up a row.

potin, m. pinchbeck ‖ **faire du ~,** (fam.)

potion, m. potion, draught.

potiron, m. (bot.) pumpkin.

pou, m. louse.

ponah! fie! fie upon it!

pouce, m. thumb ‖ inch.

poucettes, f. pl. manacles (pl.).

poucier, m. thumb-stall.

pouding, f. pudding.

poudre, f. powder, dust ‖ gunpowder ‖ **~ d'or,** gold-dust.

poudrer, v. a. to powder.

poudrette, f. night-soil, manure.

poudreux, se, a. dusty ‖ powdery.

poudrier, m. sand-box.

poudrière, f. powder-mill ‖ powder-flask ‖ sand-box.

pouf, m. puff ‖ ottoman-seat.

pouf! plump! bang!   [laughter.

pouffer, v. n.; **~ de rire,** to burst out into

pouilles, f. pl.; **chanter ~,** to use abusive language.

pouilleux, se, a. lousy, mean.

poulaille, f. poultry.

poulailler, m. poulterer ‖ hen-house ‖ upper gallery (of a theatre).

poulain, m. colt, foal.

poularde, f. fat pullet.

poule, f. hen ‖ pool, stake (at cards) ‖ **~ d'eau,** moor-hen ‖ **~ d'Inde,** Turkey-hen ‖ **~ faisane,** hen-pheasant ‖ **~ mouillée,** (fig.) milksop.   [love-letter.

poulet, m. chick, chicken ‖ (fam.) darling ‖

poulette, f. young hen, pullet ‖ lassie ‖ **à la ~,** (culin.) with white sauce.

pouliche, f. filly.

poulie, f. pulley ‖ (mar.) block.

pouliner, v. n. to foal.

poulinière, f. brood-mare.

poulinière, a. brood.

poulot, te, m. & f. chick ‖ (fam.) darling ‖

pouls, m. pulse.   [ducky, little child.

poult de soie, m. stout silk.

poumon, m. lungs (pl.).

poupard, m. brat, baby, babe.

poupe, f. poop, stern.

poupée, f. doll ‖ puppet ‖ milliner's block.

poupin, ne, a. a dashing, affected (in dress).

poupon, ne, m. & f. baby, chubby-cheeked child, darling.

pour, pr. for, on account of, instead of, on the side of ‖ **~ que,** in order that, that ‖ **~ peu que,** however little ‖ **~ lors,** at that time, then ‖ **~ le moins,** at least ‖ **~ cet effet,** therefore.

pourboire, m. gratuity, pourboire, tip.

pourceau, m. hog, swine.

pourcentage, m. percentage.

pourchasser, v. a. to pursue.

pourfendeur, m. bully, hector.

pourfendre, v. a. to cleave ‖ to kill.

pourparler, m. parley, conference ‖ conversation.   [versation.

pourpier, m. (bot.) purslain.

pourpre, m. purple, purple colour ‖ (méd.) purples (pl.).

pourpre, f. purple cloth ‖ purple dye.

pourpré, e, a. purple, of a purple colour.

pourquoi, m. reason why.

pourquoi, ad. why, for what ‖ **c'est ~,** therefore, so, that is why.

pourrir, v. a. & n. to rot, to make putrid ‖ to grow rotten.

pourrissage, m. rotting.

pourriture, f. rottenness ‖ brown-rust.

poursuite, f. pursuit, running after, prosecution ‖ **~s,** pl. (jur.) proceedings (pl.), prosecution.

poursuivant, m. suitor ‖ plaintiff.

poursuivre, v. a. ir. to pursue, to follow, to run after, to chase, to hunt ‖ to solicit.

pourtant, c. however, howsoever, nevertheless, notwithstanding, though.

pourtour, m. periphery, circumference.

pourvoi, m. (jur.) appeal.

pourvoir, v. a. ir. to provide, to look to, to furnish, to invest with, to supply ‖ **se ~,** to provide oneself with.

pourvoyeur, m. purveyor.

pourvu, e, c. (**~ que**) provided (that).

pousse, f. pursiness, broken wind ‖ asthma ‖ shoot of trees ‖ cutting of teeth ‖ choke-damp ‖ over-fermentation.

poussée, f. push ‖ growth, shoot.

pousser, v. a. & n. to push, to thrust, to force, to press forward, to urge, to drive ‖ to go as far as ‖ to jut out ‖ to germinate, to shoot ‖ **se ~,** to make one's way in the

poussier, m. coal-dust.   [world.

poussière, f. dust ‖ spray.

poussif, ve, a. pursy, broken-winded.

poussin, m. young chick.

poutre, f. beam ‖ mote.

pouvoir, m. power, authority, ability ‖ force ‖ possession ‖ executive.

pouvoir, v. a. & n. ir. to be able, to be possible.   [possible.

pouzzolane, f. puzzolana.

prairie, f. meadow ‖ (Am.) savannah, prairie.   [prairie.

praline, f. burnt almond.

praliner, v. a. to crisp, to burn (of almonds, etc.).

praticable, a. practicable, feasible, performable, operable ‖ passable.

praticien, m. practitioner (in Law and in Medicine).

praticien, ne, a. practising, practical.

pratique, f. practice, exercise, use, habit ‖ practice of the Law ‖ customer ‖ **par ~,** practically.

pratique, a. (**-ment,** ad.) practical(ly).

pratiquer, v. a. & n. to practise, to exercise ‖ to plot, to cabal ‖ to keep company with, to converse ‖ **se ~,** to be customary.

pré, m. meadow, grass-field.
préalable, m. preliminary.
préalable, a. (–ment, ad.) previous(ly) ||
préambule, m. preamble. [au ~, first.
préau, m. yard in a jail || green.
prébende, f. prebend.
prébendier, m. prebendary.
précaire(ment), ad. precarious(ly).
précaution, f. precaution, caution.
(se) précautionner, to be cautious, to
take one's precautions. [ful.
précautionneux, se, a. cautious, care-
précédemment, ad. precedently, before.
précédent, e, a. precedent, preceding,
going before. [precedence.
précéder, v. a. to precede, to have the
précepte, m. precept.
précepteur, m. preceptor, tutor.
préceptorat, m. tutorship.
prêche, m. sermon || Protestant church.
prêcher, v. a. & n. to preach, to publish,
to teach || to praise, to extol || to forebode |
to complain || to preach.
prêcheur, m. preacher || lecturer.
précieuse, f. affected woman.
précieux, se, a. (–sement, ad.) pre-
cious(ly) || costly, valuable, dear, formal,
préciosité, f. affectation. [prim.
précipice, m. precipice.
précipitamment, ad. precipitately, hur-
riedly, hastily.
précipité, e, m. & f. (chim.) precipitate.
précipiter, v. a. to precipitate, to throw
headlong, to hurry, to quicken || se ~, to
precipitate oneself, to rush upon, to rush
into || (chim.) to be precipitated.
précis, m. abstract, summary, substance ||
epitome.
précis, e, a. precise, exact || formal.
précisément, ad. precisely.
préciser, v. a. to determine, to fix, to
specify || se ~, to be fixed ou determined ||
to become distinct.
précité, e, a. above-mentioned.
précoce, a. precocious, early || forward.
précocité, f. precocity. [to extol.
préconiser, v. a. to preconise || to cry up,
précurseur, m. forerunner, harbinger.
précurseur, a. precursory || premoni-
prédécesseur, m. predecessor. [tory.
prédestiné, m. elect.
prédestiné, e, a. elect. [destinate.
prédestiner, v. a. to predestine, to pre-
prédéterminer, v. a. to predetermine.
prédicant, m. Protestant preacher.
prédicateur, m. preacher.
prédication, f. preaching, sermon.
prédiction, f. prediction || foreboding.
prédilection, f. predilection, partiality.
prédire, v. a. ir. to foretell, to prophesy.
prédisposer, v. a. to predispose.
prédominer, v. n. to predominate, to pre-
prééminent, e, a. pre-eminent. [vail.
préexistant, e, a. pre-existent.
préexister, v. n. to pre-exist.
préface, f. preface, preamble || introduction.
préfecture, f. prefecture || prefectship || pre-
fect's house. [preferably.
préférable, a. preferable || –ment, ad.

préférence, f. preference.
préféré, e, a. favourite.
préférer, v. a. to prefer, to like better.
préfet, m. prefect || ~ de police, chief
of police for Paris.
préfix, e, a. appointed.
préfixe, f. (gr.) prefix. [jury, hurt.
préjudice, m. prejudice, detriment, in-
préjudiciable, a. prejudicial, injurious.
préjudiciel, le, a. (jur.) interlocutory.
préjudicier, v. n. to prejudice, to be injurious to. [precedent.
préjugé, m. prejudice || appearance || (jur.)
préjuger, v. a. to prejudge.
prélart, m. (mar.) tarpaulin.
se prélasser, to strut, to walk about with
a free and easy step || to take it easy || to
indulge oneself.
prélat, m. prelate.
prélature, f. prelacy.
prêle, f. (bot.) horse-tail, shave-grass.
prélèvement, m. previous deduction.
prélever, v. a. to levy || to deduct pre-
viously.
préliminaire, m. preliminary.
préliminaire, a. preliminary || –ment,
ad. previously.
préluder, v. n. to prelude. [(ly).
prématuré, e, a. (–ment, ad.) premature
prématurité, f. prematureness.
préméditer, v. a. to premeditate.
prémices, f. pl. premises (pl.) || first-fruits
(pl.) || beginning.
premier, ère, a. first, former, chief ||
ministre, Prime Minister, premier || ~
né, first-born || ~ en ~ lieu, in the first
place || être le ~, to be the first || monter
au ~, to get up to the first floor.
premièrement, ad. first, in the first place.
prémisses, f. pl. premises (pl.).
prémunir, v. a. to fortify beforehand || to
forewarn, to caution.
prenable, a. to be taken, expugnable.
prendre, v. a. & n. ir. to take, to seize, to
catch, to snatch, to lay hold of || to assume
|| to receive, to accept || to drink, to let in ||
to swallow || to curdle || to freeze || se ~,
to be taken, to be caught || to catch at || to
congeal, to freeze.
preneur, m. taker || (jur.) lessee.
preneur, se, a. capturing.
prénom, m. christian name.
préoccupation, f. preoccupation, prepossession.
préoccupé, e, a. pensive.
préoccuper, v. a. to preoccupy, to pre-
possess, to prejudice || to engross.
préopinant, m. previous speaker.
préparateur, m. assistant || private tutor,
crammer, grinder.
préparatif, m. preparation.
préparation, f. preparation.
préparatoire, a. preparatory.
préparer, v. a. to prepare, to fit, to make
ready || to break to.
prépondérance, f. preponderance, overweight. [casting.
prépondérant, e, a. preponderating ||
préposé, m. overseer, inspector.

préposer, v. a. to set over, to entrust to.
préposition, f. (gr.) preposition.
prérogative, f. prerogative.
près, pr. near, by, nigh to, near, at hand, close || almost, exactly || de ~, near, hard by || plus ~, nearer || à peu ~, almost, nearly.
présage, m. presage, omen.
présager, v. a. to forebode.
présalé, m. salt-marsh sheep ou mutton.
presbyte, m. presbyte, presbyope, long-sighted person.
presbyte, a. long-sighted.
presbytéral, e, a. priestly.
presbytère, m. parsonage, vicarage.
presbytérianisme, m. presbyterianism.
presbytérien, m. presbyterian.
presbytérien, ne, a. presbyterian.
prescience, f. prescience, foresight.
prescrire, v. a. & n. ir. to prescribe, to direct || to get by prescription || (jur.) to be acquired ou lost by prescription || se ~, to prescribe to oneself.
préséance, f. precedence.
présence, f. presence || sight.
présent, m. present, gift || present time || (gr.) present tense.   [presently.
présent, e, a. present || à ~, at present,
présentateur, m. presenter.
présentation, f. presentation.
présentement, ad. now.
présenter, v. a. to present, to make a present, to offer, to expose, to show, to introduce to a person || se ~, to present oneself, to appear, to occur.
préservateur, trice, m. & f. preserver.
préservatif, m. preservative.
préservatif, ve, a. preservative.
préserver, v. a. to preserve, to keep || to préservation.
présidence, f. presidency.   [forbid.
président, m. president, chairman, speaker, presiding judge.
présidente, f. president's wife.
présider, v. n. to preside, to be chairman || to govern, to domineer.   [parent.
présomptif, ve, a. presumptive || apparent.
présomption, f. presumption.
présomptueux, se, a. (-sement, ad.) presumptuous(ly).
presque, ad. almost, very near.
presqu'île, f. peninsula.
pressage, m. pressing.
presse, f. press, crowd || printing-press || press-gang || hurry || ~-papiers, m. paper-weight.   [concise.
pressé, e, a. in a hurry || urgent || anxious ||
pressentiment, m. presentiment, foreboding.   [to foresee, to forebode.
pressentir, v. a. to have a presentiment,
presser, v. a. & n. to press, to squeeze || to urge || to hasten || to importune, to harass, to pursue close || to be urgent, to require haste || se ~, to make haste, to crowd, to hasten.
presseur, m. presser.   [lie close.
pressier, m. press-man.
pression, f. pressure.   [press.
pressoir, m. press, press-house, wine-
pressurage, m. wine-pressing.

pressurer, v. a. to press (grapes) || to squeeze, to extort by force.
pressureur, m. press-man, presser.
prestance, f. deportment, port, air.
prestation, f.; ~ de serment, taking of an oath.   [nimbly.
preste, a. (-ment, ad.) quick(ly) || nimble ||
prestesse, f. nimbleness, agility.
prestidigitateur, m. juggler, conjurer.
prestidigitation, f. sleight of hand, conjuring.   [ment, imposture.
prestige, m. prestige, charm, enchant-
prestigieux, se, a. bewitching.
présumer, v. a. to presume, to suppose.
présupposer, v. a. to presuppose.
présure, f. rennet.
prêt, m. loan, money lent.
prêt, e, a. ready, prepared, disposed, proposed, willing.
prétantaine, f.; courir la ~, to ramble about.   [didate.
prétendant, m. pretender, aspirant, can-
prétendre, v. a. & n. to pretend, to claim, to challenge, to aspire, to intend || to contend, to uphold.
prétendu, e, m. & f. future husband ou wife.   [posed, so-called.
prétendu, e, a. pretended, sham || sup-
prête-nom, m. one who lends his name || ostensible agent.
prétentieux, se, a. affected, assuming.
prétention, f. pretention, claim, demand, affectation.
prêter, m. lending.
prêter, v. a. to lend, to attribute || to afford || to give rise || to take || to stretch. || se ~, to comply || to favour || to tolerate.
prétérit, m. (gr.) preterite (tense).
préteur, m. pretor.
prêteur, m. lender || ~ sur gages, pawn-broker.
prétexte, m. pretext, pretence.   [broker.
prétexter, v. a. to give as an excuse.
prétoire, m. judges' bench || pretorium.
prétorien, ne, a. pretorian.
prêtraille, f. black-coats (pl.), parson.
prêtre, m. priest, parson.
prêtresse, f. priestess.
prêtrise, f. priesthood.
préture, f. pretorship.
preuve, f. proof, evidence, trial, ordeal, argument, reason || proof-glass.
preux, m. gallant knight.
preux, a. gallant, doughty.
prévaloir, v. n. ir. to prevail on || se ~, to avail oneself of, to take advantage of || to glory ou pride in.   [cator.
prévaricateur, trice, m. & f. prevari-
prévaricateur, trice, a. prevaricating.
prévariquer, v. a. to prevaricate.
prévenance, f. kind attention.
prévenant, e, a. preventing || pre-engaging || obliging, pleasing.
prévenir, v. a. ir. to prevent, to go before, to anticipate, to outstrip || to prepossess, to hinder || to inform, to warn || se ~, to be prepossessed, to be prejudiced.
préventif, ve, a. preventive || (of imprisonment) before trial.
prévention, f. prevention, prepossession, prejudice || imputation.

préventivement, ad. on suspicion ‖ presumptively.

prévenu, e, m. & f. (jur.) prisoner.

prévenu, e, a. (jur.) accused.

prévoir, v. a. ir. to foresee, to foreknow.

prévôt, m. provost ‖ fencing master's assistant.

prévôté, f. provostship. [sistant.

prévoyance, f. foresight, forethought.

prévoyant, e, a. provident, wary.

prié, m. guest, person invited.

prie-Dieu, m. faldstool ‖ prie-Dieu, devotion-chair.

prier, v. a. to pray, to implore, to supplicate, to entreat ‖ to invite, to beg, to desire.

prière, f. prayer, entreaty, request.

prieur(e), m. (& f.) prior(ess).

prieuré, m. priory.

primaire, a. primary ‖ preparatory.

primat, m. primate.

primatie, f. primacy.

primauté, f. supremacy.

prime, f. premium ‖ bounty ‖ drawback ‖ de ~ abord, at first sight ‖ ~ sautier, ière, a. inconsiderate, thoughtless.

primer, v. a. & n. to overmaster ‖ to hold the first place, to play first hand ‖ to surpass, to overtop, to excel.

primeur, f. first-fruits (pl.) ‖ early flower ou vegetable ‖ early part of the season.

primevère, f. (bot.) primrose, cowslip.

primitif, ve, a. (-vement, ad.) primitive (ly) ‖ original.

primogéniture, f. birth-right.

primordial, e, a. primordial ‖ primogenital ‖ (jur.) first in order.

prince, m. prince ‖ bon ~, easy ou good-natured fellow.

princeps, a. earliest, first ‖ édition ~, f. [first edition.

princesse, f. princess.

princier, ière, a. princely.

principal, m. principal point, principal, chief, main ‖ head-master ‖ capital sum.

principal, e, a. (-ement, ad.) principal (ly) ‖ prime ‖ chief(ly) ‖ essential.

principalat, m. principalship, headmastership.

principauté, f. principality. [mastership.

principe, m. principle, element, rudiment, beginning ‖ motive, maxim.

printanier, ière, a. belonging to the spring, vernal.

printemps, m. spring ‖ (fig.) bloom (of youth).

priorité, f. priority.

pris, e, a. taken, seized, caught ‖ proportioned ‖ frozen over ‖ cloudy.

prise, f. taking, capture, prize ‖ hold ‖ dose ‖ influence ‖ ~s, pl. close quarters ‖ ~ de bec, quarrel.

prisée, f. upset price, appraising.

priser, v. a. & n. to prize, to appraise, to esteem, to estimate, to value ‖ to take snuff.

priseur, m. snuff-taker. [snuff.

prisme, m. prism. [confinement.

prison, f. prison, jail ‖ imprisonment,

prisonnier, ière, m. & f. prisoner.

privation, f. privation, want ‖ bereavement.

privauté, f. intimacy, familiarity.

privé, e, a. privy, private, particular ‖ tame.

priver, v. a. to deprive ‖ to tame ‖ se ~, to deprive oneself, to abstain.

privilège, m. privilege, immunity, permission, licence. [preference.

privilégié, e, a. privileged ‖ (of shares)

privilégier, v. a. to privilege.

prix, m. price, value, rate, worth, merit ‖ prize, reward ‖ au ~ de, at the expense of ‖ in comparison with ‖ au ~ coûtant, at cost price, at prime cost ‖ hors de ~, uncommonly dear ‖ ~ de fabrique, manufacturers' price ‖ ~ fort, full price ‖ ~ fait, ~ fixe, set price ‖ chose de ~, f. thing of great price.

probabilité, f. probability.

probable, a. (-ment, ad.) probable ‖ probably ‖ likely.

probe, a. honest, upright.

probité, f. probity, honesty.

problématique, a. (-ment, ad.) problematic(ally).

problème, m. problem.

procédé, m. proceeding, procedure ‖ -s, pl. delicate manners (pl.).

procéder, v. n. to proceed, to arise out of, to issue. [procedure.

procédure, f. (jur.) proceedings (pl.), legal

procès, m. process, lawsuit, action ‖ trial ‖ ~ verbal, record ‖ minutes of transactions of a society (pl.) ‖ sans autre forme de ~, without further ceremony.

processif, ve, a. litigious.

processionnellement, ad. in procession.

prochain, m. neighbour, fellow-creature.

prochain, e, a. next, near, nearest, proximate. [next term.

prochainement, ad. (jur.) shortly, at the

proche, a., ad. & pr. near, near at hand, just by, next to, hard by, close to ‖ nearly related ‖ de ~ en ~, from place to place, gradually.

proches, f. pl. relations (pl.).

proclamer, v. a. to proclaim.

proconsulat, m. proconsulship.

procréer, v. a. to procreate, to beget.

procurateur, m. (jur.) procurator, proxy.

procuration, f. (jur.) procuracy, power of attorney.

procurer, v. a. to procure, to get.

procureur, m. proctor, proxy ‖ attorney, solicitor.

prodigalement, ad. prodigally.

prodigalité, f. prodigality, profusion.

prodige, m. prodigy.

prodigieux, se, a. (-sement, ad.) prodigious(ly) ‖ amazing(ly).

prodigue, a. spendthrift.

prodigue, a. prodigal, wasteful, lavish.

prodiguer, v. a. to waste, to lavish, to squander away, to throw away.

producteur, trice, m. & f. producer.

productif, ve, a. productive.

production, f. production ‖ exhibition.

produire, v. a. ir. to produce, to bring forth, to yield, to introduce ‖ se ~, to introduce oneself to notice ‖ to be produced ‖ to occur ‖ to happen, to take place.

produit, m. product, produce.
proéminent, e, a. prominent.
profanateur, m. profaner.
profanation, f. profanation.
profane, m. & f. profane man *ou* woman.
profane, a. profane, unholy.
profaner, v. a. to profane, to desecrate ‖ to pollute.
proférer, v. a. to utter.　　　　[nun.
profès, esse, m. & f. professed monk *ou*
professer, v. a. to profess, to declare publicly, to pronounce, to teach.
professeur, m. professor, teacher.
profession, f. profession, calling, business ‖ declaration ‖ occupation ‖ **de ~**, professionally.
professional, e, a. professorial.
professorat, m. professorship.
profil, m. profile, side-face ‖ side-front ‖
profit, m. profit, gain, interest. [section.
profiter, v. a. to profit, to be a gainer, to gain, to improve ‖ **~ de l'occasion**, to improve the opportunity.
profond, m. depths (pl.), bottom.
profond, e, a. profound ‖ deep ‖ learned ‖ extraordinary. 　　　　[soundly.
profondément, ad. profoundly, deeply ‖
profondeur, f. profoundness, profundity, depth, deepness ‖ length.
profusément, ad. profusely, lavishly.
progéniture, f. progeny, offspring.
prognostic, m. prognostic ‖ (méd.) prognosis. 　　[**~ de spectacle**, play-bill.
programme, m. programme, list, bill ‖
progrès, m. progress, improvement.
progresser, v. n. to progress.
progressif, ve, a. (**-vement**, ad.) progressive(ly).　　　[matical proportion.
progression, f. (math.) progression, mathe-
prohiber, v. a. to prohibit.
prohibitif, ve, a prohibitory, prohibitive.
proie, f. prey, booty.
projectile, m. projectile.
projet, m. project, scheme, design, plan ‖ rough draught.　　　　[contrive, to plan.
projeter, v. a. to project, to scheme, to
prolégomènes, m. pl. prolegomena (pl.).
prolétaire, m. proletary.
prolétaire, a. proletarian.
prolifique, a. prolific.
prolixe, a. prolix, diffuse.
prolixité, f. prolixity.
prologue, a. prologue.
prolongation, f. prolongation, protraction.　　　　　　[ing.
prolongement, m. extension, lengthen-
prolonger, v. a. to prolong, to put off, to protract, to lengthen ‖ (mar.) to lay a ship alongside of another.
promenade, f. promenade, walk, walking-place ‖ walking, walk, airing, pleasure-trip ‖ procession ‖ **~ à cheval**, ride ‖ **~ en bateau**, sail, row ‖ **~ en voiture**, drive ‖ **~ à pied**, walk.
promener, v. a. to walk, to lead about ‖ to take for a walk ‖ to humbug, to bamboozle ‖ to turn ‖ **se ~**, to go *ou* walk about ‖ to take a walk ‖ to ramble ‖ to sail about ‖ to cruise.

promeneur, se, m. & f. walker, pedestrian ‖ rider.
promenoir, m. walk, walking-place.
promesse, f. promise, promissory note.
prometteur, m. promiser.　　　[bond.
promettre, v. a. & n. ir. to promise, to engage ‖ **se ~**, to promise oneself, to hope ‖ to purpose.
promis, e, a. promised ‖ intended, engaged.
promiscuité, f. promiscuousness.
promission, f. promise.
promontoire, m. promontory.
promoteur, m. promoter.
promouvoir, v. a. ir. to promote.
prompt, e, a. (**-ement**, ad.) quick(ly) ‖ ready, speedy ‖ speedily ‖ sudden, passionate.
promptitude, f. promptitude, quickness, hastiness, speed, briskness ‖ passion.
promulguer, v. a. to promulgate.
prône, m. Sunday sermon ‖ lecture.
prôner, v. a. to praise, to cry up, to extol.
prôneur, m. tiresome adviser, lecturer,
pronom, m. pronoun.　　　　[proser.
prononcé, m. (jur.) judge's sentence ‖ judgment delivered.
prononcé, e, a. pronounced, marked ‖ prominent.
prononcer, v. a. to pronounce ‖ to mark distinctly, to articulate ‖ to pass judgment, to deliver judgment ‖ to give prominence ‖ **se ~**, to manifest one's intentions.
prononciation, f. pronunciation, speaking ‖ utterance ‖ (jur.) pronouncing ‖ delivery ‖ giving.
pronostic, m. prognostic.
pronostiquer, v. a. to prognosticate.
pronostiqueur, m. prognosticator.
propagande, f. propaganda.
propagandiste, m. propagandist.
propagateur, m. propagator, spreader.
propagation, f. propagation, spreading.
propager, v. a. to propagate, to spread ‖
propension, f. propensity.　　[to extend.
prophète, m. prophet, seer.
prophétesse, f. prophetess.
prophétie, f. prophecy.
prophétique, a. (**-ment**, ad.) prophetic
prophétiser, v. a. to prophesy.　[(ally).
propice, a. propitious.
propitiatoire, a. propitiatory.
proportion, f. proportion ‖ ratio ‖ **en ~**, in proportion ‖ **compas de ~**, m. proportional compasses (pl.).　[proportional(ly).
proportionnel, le, a. (**-lement**, ad.)
proportionner, v. a. to proportion, to proportionate, to adjust, to fit.
propos, m. discourse, talk, words ‖ design ‖ **à ~**, to the purpose, opportunely, seasonably, pertinently ‖ fit, fitting ‖ **à ~ de**, with regard to ‖ **mal à ~**, **hors de ~**, unseasonably ‖ **à ~ de quoi**? for what reason? ‖ **à ~ de rien**, for nothing at all ‖ **de ~ délibéré**, purposely.
proposable, a. fit to be proposed.
proposer, v. a. to propose, to present, to offer ‖ to suggest, to motion ‖ **se ~**, to propose oneself, to design, to intend, to purpose doing a thing.

proposition, f. proposition, proposal || motion.

propre, m. property || peculiar quality || proper sense || c'est du ~ ! nasty thing!

propre, a. (-ment, ad.) one's own || proper (ly) || fit, suitable, apt || clean(ly) || -s termes, m. pl. very words || termes -s, m. pl. correct expressions || in a strict sense || neatly.

propret, te, a. spruce, dressy.

propreté, f. cleanness, cleanliness, neatness, spruceness, delicacy.

propriétaire, m. & f. proprietor, owner || landlord, landlady.

propriété, f. propriety, property, ownership || copyright || landed interest || landlords (pl.) || peculiar quality.

propulseur, m. propeller.

prorata; (au ~), pr. in proportion to.

prorogation, f. prorogation, delay || continuance || adjournment.

proroger, v.a. to prorogue, to prolong, to put off, to adjourn.

prosaïque, a. prosaic.

prosaïsme, m. prosaic form || prosaic poetry || vulgarity, dulness.

prosateur, m. prose-writer.

proscripteur, m. proscriber.

proscription, f. proscription, outlawry.

proscrire, v.a. ir. to proscribe, to outlaw, to banish.

proscrit, e, m. & f. outlaw || refugee.

prose, f. prose.

prosélyte, m. & f. proselyte, convert.

prosélytisme, m. proselytism.

prosodie, f. prosody.

prosodique, a. prosodical.

prosopopée, f. personification.

prospère, a. prosperous.

prospérer, v. n. to prosper, to thrive.

prospérité, f. prosperity.

se prosterner, to prostrate oneself.

prostituée, f. prostitute.

prostituer, v.a. to prostitute.

prostitution, f. prostitution || whoredom.

prostration, f. prostration || (méd.) prostration. [corrector.

prote, m. printers' foreman || overseer ||

protecteur, trice, m. & f. protector, defender, patron || protectress. [ing.

protecteur, trice, a. protective, patronis-

protection, f. protection, defence, tuition, patronage. [(system).

protectionnisme, m. (com.) Protection

protectionniste, m. (com.) protectionist.

protectorat, m. protectorship.

protée, m. proteus.

protégé, e, m. & f. protégé || protégée.

protéger, v.a. to protect, to patronise.

protestant, e, m. & f. Protestant.

protestantisme, m. Protestantism.

protestation, f. protestation.

protester, v. a. & n. to protest.

protêt, m. protest.

protocole, m. protocol.

prototype, m. prototype.

proue, f. (mar.) prow || stem.

prouesse, f. prowess || feat. [token.

prouver, v. a. to prove, to evince, to be-

provenance, f. production || origin || source || en ~, coming, proceeding.

provenir, v. n. ir. to proceed, to arise from.

proverbe, m. proverb, adage.

proverbial, a. (-ement, ad.) proverbial

providence, f. providence. [(ly).

providentiel, le, a. providential.

provignement, m. layering (of vines).

provigner, v. a. & n. to layer.

provin, m. layer of a vine.

province, f. province, country || gens de ~, f. pl. country-people (pl.).

provincial, e, m. & f. country person.

provincial, e, a. provincial, country-like.

proviseur, m. head-master of a government college.

provision, f. provision || stock, store || par ~, in the mean time.

provisionnel, le, a. (-lement, ad.) provisional(ly). [(ly).

provisoire, a. (-ment, ad.) provisional

provisorat, m. provisorship.

provocateur, trice, m. & f. provoker.

provocateur, trice, a. provoking.

provocation, f. provocation || challenge.

provoquer, v. a. to provoke, to challenge, to incense, to promote || (méd.) to cause.

proxénète, m. & f. pimp, pander.

proximité, f. proximity, nearness.

prude, a. prudish.

prudemment, ad. prudently.

prudence, f. prudence.

prudent, e, a. prudent.

pruderie, f. prudery.

prud'homme, m. skilful man, expert.

prune, f. plum || pour des -s, for nothing.

pruneau, m. dried plum.

prunelaie, f. orchard of plum-trees.

prunelle, f. sloe, wild plum || pupil of the

prunellier, m. (bot.) sloe-tree. [eye.

prunier, m. (bot.) plum-tree.

prurit, m. pruriency. [sic acid.

prussique, a. prussic || acide ~, m. prus-

psalmiste, m. psalmist.

psalmodie, f. psalmody.

psalmodier, v. a. to chant psalms || to drone.

psaume, m. psalm.

psautier, m. psalm-book.

pseudonyme, m. assumed name, pseudonym || writer under a fictitious name.

pseudonyme, a. pseudonymous.

psyché, f. dressing-glass, cheval-glass.

psychologie, f. psychology.

psychologique, a. psychologic.

puant, e, a. fusty || stinking.

puanteur, f. stink, bad smell.

pubère, a. pubescent.

puberté, f. puberty.

public, que, a. (-quement, ad.) public (ly) || notorious(ly) || common, general.

publicain, m. publican.

publiciste, m. publicist, political writer.

publicité, f. publicity || advertising.

publier, v. a. to publish.

puce, f. flea.

puceau, m. youth.

puceau, elle, a. virginal.

pucelle, f. virgin, maid || la ~ d'Orléans, the Maid of Orleans, Joan of Arc.
puceron, m. plant-louse.
pudeur, f. bashfulness, decency.
pudibond, e, a. bashful, modest.
pudicité, f. chastity.
pudique, a. (~ment, ad.) chaste(ly).
puer, v. n. to stink, to smell strong.
puéril, e, a. (~ement, ad.) puerile || childish (ly) || boyish, juvenile.
puérilité, f. puerility, childishness.
pugilat, m. pugilistic art, boxing.
pugiliste, m. pugilist, boxer.
puîné, e, m. & f. younger brother ou sister.
puîné, e, a. younger.
puis, ad. then, afterwards.
puisage, m. drawing of water.
puisard, m. cess-pool.
puisatier, m. well-sinker.
puiser, v. a. to draw up, to fetch up (water) || to imbibe || (mar.) to leak.
puisque, c. since, seeing that, as, inasmuch.
puissamment, ad. powerfully, potently, forcibly.
puissance, f. power || force || dominion.
puissant, e, a. powerful, mighty || very rich || potent, efficacious, forcible.
puits, m. well || ~ artésien, artesian well || ~ à bras, pump-well || ~ d'abondance, (fig.) inexhaustible fountain || ~ d'aérage, air-shaft || ~ d'écoulement, well-drain || ~ de science, (fig.) man of great learning || ~ perdu, drain-well, blind-well.
pulluler, v. n. to multiply || to swarm, to increase.
pulmonaire, a. pulmonary.   [pullulate.
pulmonie, f. (méd.) lung-disease.
pulpe, f. pulp || pap.
pulpeux, se, a. pulpous.
pulsation, f. pulsation, throbbing.
pulvérin, m. priming-powder || mist.
pulvériser, v. a. to pulverise.
pumicin, m. palm-oil.
punais, e, a. affected with ozena.
punaise, f. bug || (jestingly) b-flat.
punir, v. a. to punish.
punissable, a. punishable.
punition, f. punishment.
pupillaire, a. pupillary.
pupillarité, f. pupilage.
pupille, m. & f. pupil || ward.
pupille, f. pupil (of the eye).   [stand.
pupitre, m. desk || davenport || music-
pur, e, a. pure, unmingled, genuine, innocent, mere, clear || ~ et simple, unconditional.
purée, f. pea-soup || mashed potatoes.
purement, ad. purely, merely, harmlessly.
pureté, f. purity.
purgatif, m. (méd.) purgative.
purgatif, ve, a. purgative.
purgation, f. purging.
purgatoire, m. purgatory.
purger, v. a. to purge, to cleanse, to clear || to physic || se ~, to purge, to take medicine || to clear oneself.
purifier, v. a. to purify.
purisme, m. purism, affectation of purity
puriste, m. purist.   [in speach.

puritain, m. Puritan, Calvinist.
puritanisme, m. Puritanism.
purpurin, e, a. purplish.
purpurine, f. purple bronze.
purulent, e, a. purulent.
pus, m. (méd.) pus, matter.
pusillanime, a. pusillanimous.
pusillanimité, f. pusillanimity.
pustule, f. pustule, pimple.
pustuleux, se, a. pustulous.
putatif, ve, a. putative, reputed, supposed.
putois, m. polecat.
putréfaction, f. putrefaction.
putréfier, v. a. to putrify.
putride, a. putrid, rotten.
putridité, f. putridness.
pygargue, m. sea-eagle (bird).
pygmée, m. pigmy, dwarf.
pyramidal, e, a. pyramidal.
pyramide, f. pyramid.
pyramider, v. n. to form a pyramid.
pyrotechnie, f. pyrotechnics (pl.).
pyrotechnique, a. pyrotechnic.
pythagoricien, m. Pythagorean.
pythien, ne, pythique, a. Pythian.
pythonisse, f. pythoness, prophetess || witch.

Q.

quadragénaire, m. & f. person forty years old.
quadragénaire, a. forty years old.
Quadragésime, f. Lent || dimanche de la ~, m. first Sunday in Lent.
quadrangulaire, a. four-cornered.
quadrature, f. (géom. & astr.) quadrature || (peint.) fresco-painting.
quadrilatère, m. (géom.) quadrilateral.
quadrilatère, a. (géom.) quadrilateral.
quadrille, m. quadrille.   [ment.
quadrille, f. troop of horse for a tourna-
quadrisaïeul, e, m. & f. ancestor in the fourth degree.   [handed beast.
quadrumane, m. quadrumane, four-
quadrupède, m. quadruped.
quadrupède, a. four-footed.
quadruple, a. quadruple, fourfold.
quadrupler, v. a. & n. to quadruplicate.
quai, m. quay, wharf || (rail.) platform.
quaiche, f. (mar.) ketch.
qualificatif, m. qualificative.
qualificatif, ve, a. qualifying.
qualification, f. qualification || character || title.   [ing circumstances.
qualifié, e, a. qualified || with aggravat-
qualifier, v. a. to qualify, to call, to entitle, to style.
qualité, f. quality, property, accomplishment, qualification, rank || en ~ de, as.
quand, ad. when, what time, whenever || if || ~, c. although, though, even if || ~ et ~, together with || pour ~? for what time ? || ~ même, even though, though, even if.
quant (à), ad. as to, as for || concerning || ~ à moi, as for me.
quantième, m. day of the month.

quantième, a. what, which.

quantité, f. quantity, abundance, multitude.

quarantaine, f. quarantine, forty days || age of forty || Lent. [Academy.

quarante, a. forty || les ~, the French Academy.

quarantième, m. fortieth part.

quarantième, a. fortieth.

quart, m. quarter, fourth part || (mar.) watch || ~ d'heure, quarter of an hour || present moment || ~ d'heure de Rabelais, time to pay at last || rub.

quart, e, a. quartan.

quartaut, m. octave-cask.

quarte, f. fourth. [part of à hundred.

quarteron, m. quarter (of a pound) || fourth

quarteron, ne, m. & f. quadroon.

quartier, m. quarter, fourth part || hindquarter || ward, quarter (of a town) || ~ général, head-quarters (pl.) || ~maître, m. (mar., mil.) quarter-master.

quasi, ad. almost, as good as.

Quasimodo, m. Low Sunday.

quaterne, m. quarternary.

quatorze, m. fourteenth (at piquet) || fourteenth (of the month).

quatorze, a. fourteen.

quatorzième, m. fourteenth part.

quatorzième, a. fourteenth.

quatre, m. four || figure of fourth.

quatre, a. four || figure four || à ~, four together || with great effort || ~vingtdix, a. ninety || ~vingt(s), a. eighty || Quatre-temps, m. pl. Ember-days (pl.).

quatrième, m. fourth || fourth part.

quatrième, a. (-ment, ad.) fourth(ly).

quatriennal, e, a. quadrennial

quatuor, m. (mus.) quartetto.

quayage, m. wharfage, keyage.

que, c. that, if, when, as, than, till, until, but, only, lest, whether, because, how, how much, how many, why || afin ~, to the end that || de sorte ~, so that.

que, pn. that, whom, which, what, of whom, of which, to whom, to which.

quel, le, pn. what || tel ~, such as it is || ~ qu'il soit, whatever he may be.

quelconque, pn. any, whatever, whatsoever.

quelque, pn., a. & ad. some, any, whatever, whatsoever || however, howsoever || about || ~ chose, something, anything || ~ part, somewhere.

quelquefois, ad. sometimes.

quelqu'un, quelqu'une, pn. somebody, someone || quelqués-uns, pl. some, some people, any.

quémander, v. n. to beg clandestinely.

qu'en-dira-t-on, m. public talk, what people may say.

quenelle, f. (culin.) forcemeat-ball.

quenotte, f. first tooth (of infants).

quenouille, f. distaff || bedpost.

querelle, f. quarrel || row || ~ d'Allemand, quarrel without cause. [to chide.

quereller, v. a. to quarrel with, to scold ||

quérir, v. a. to go and fetch.

querelleur, se, m. & f. quarreler.

querelleur, se, a. quarrelsome.

questeur, m. questor, purser.

question, f. question, interrogation, query || rack for torture || issue. [questions.

questionnaire, m. torturer || book of

questionner, v. a. to question || to put to the question.

questionneur, m. questioner.

questure, f. questorship. [rake.

quête, f. quest, search || collection || (mar.)

quêter, v. a. & n. to go in search of || to be in quest of || to make a collection (for the poor) || to beg. [dicant.

quêteur, m. collector (for the poor) || mendicant.

queue, f. tail || end of a thing || stem, stalk (of a flower) || handle || cue || train, rear || ~ d'aronde, dove-tail. (at billiards).

queuter, v. n. to strike two balls at once

qui, pn. who, that, whom, which || à ~, whose, to whom || ~-vive, (mil.) who goes there? challenge || sur le ~-vive, on the look-out.

quia, m. nonplus. [on the look-out.

quibus, m. cash, "tin", "yellow-boys" (pl.). [those who.

quiconque, pn. whoever, whosoever all

quidam, m., quidane, f. certain person.

quiescent, e, a. quiescent.

quiétisme, m. quietism.

quiétiste, m. & f. quietist.

quignon, m. bunch.

quillage, m. keelage, ship-toll.

quille, f. pin, skittle || keel || nine-pin || shank || stump.

quiller, v. n. to throw at nine-pins.

quillier, m. skittle-ground || skittles.

quincaillerie, f. hardwares, hardwaretrade. [monger.

quincaillier, m. hardware-man, iron-

quinconce, m. quincunx.

quine, m. two fives (at trictrac) || five winning numbers.

quinine, f. (chim.) quinine. [years old.

quinquagénaire, m. & f. person fifty

quinquagénaire, a. fifty years old.

Quinquagésime, f. Quinquagesima Sunday.

quinquennal, e, a. quinquennial. [day.

quinquet, m. Argand lamp.

quinquina, m. Peruvian bark.

quint, m. fifth part.

quint, a. fifth. [kilogrammes.

quintal, m. quintal || ~ métrique, 100

quinte, f. quint (at picket ou at feucing) || (mus.) fifth || fit of coughing, freak, whim.

quintessence, f. quintessence.

quintessencier, v. a. to refine || to subtilise.

quintette, m. quintette.

quinteux, se, a. capricious || restive.

quintuple, a. quintuple, five-fold.

quintupler, v. a. to quintuple, to multiply

quinzaine, f. fifteen || fortnight. [five-fold.

quinze, m. fifteenth (of the month).

quinze, a. fifteen || ~ jours, a fortnight.

quinzième, m. fifteenth part.

quinzième, a. (-ment, ad.) fifteenth(ly).

quiproquo, m. mistake. [ceipt.

quittance, f. acquittance, discharge, re-

quittancer, v. a. to write a receipt.

quitte, a. quit, free, clear, discharged || ~ à ~, fit for tat || jouer à ~ ou double, to play double or quits. [forsake, to resign.

quitter, v. a. to quit, to leave, to let go, to

quoailler, v. n. to shake its tail (of a horse).

quoi, pn. which, that which, what, whatever || ~ qu'il en soit, be it as it may || ~! what! how!

quoique, c. though, although.

quolibet, m. low joke.

quote-part, f. quota, share.

quotidien, ne, a. daily.

quotité, f. quota, share || rating.

R.

rabâchage, m. tiresome repetition.

rabâcher, v. a. & n. to repeat again and again.   [(in discourse).

rabâcheur, se, m. & f. tiresome repeater

rabais, m. abatement, diminution, deduction || vente au ~, f. sale at reduced prices.

rabaissement, m. lessening of price, abatement || humiliation.

rabaisser, v. a. to lower, to put down || to lessen, to undervalue.

rabat, m. abatement of price || band (for the neck) || ~-joie, m. & f. mar-joy || scolding person.

rabattre, v. a. & n. to pull down, to beat down, to lower, to abate, to humble, to lessen || to plait, to flatten || to tip (at nine-pins) || to ward off || to turn, to turn aside || se ~, to come down, to descend, to alight || to leave one's road, to turn aside.

rabbin, m. rabbi.   [like.

rabelaisien, ne, a. humorous || Falstaff-

râble, m. back of a hare ou rabbit || rake.

râblu, e, a. strong-backed.

rabonnir, v. a. & n. to improve.

rabot, m. plane.

rabotage, m. planing.

raboter, v. a. to plane.

raboteur, m. moulding-worker, planer.

raboteux, se, a. knobbed, knotty, rough, uneven, rugged.

rabougrir, v. n. (se ~) to grow stunted.

rabouillère, f. burrow.   [up.

rabrouer, v. a. to scout, to snub, to snap

racahout, m. racahout.

racaille, f. rabble || trash, rubbish.

raccommodage, m. mending, repairing, patching, piecing.

raccommodement, m. reconciliation.

raccommoder, v. a. to mend, to repair, to piece || to adjust, to dress || to reunite, to reconcile.   [patcher || botcher.

raccommodeur, se, m. & f. mender,

raccord, m. joining || accord.

raccordement, m. levelling.

raccorder, v. a. to level, to unite || to reconcile, to make friends again.

raccoupler, v. a. to couple again.

raccourci, m. abridgment || foreshortening || en ~, briefly.

raccourcir, v. a. & n. to shorten, to abbreviate || to foreshorten || to contract || to become shorter || se ~, to shrink.

raccourcissement, m. shortening || foreshortening || contraction.

se raccoutumer, to get accustomed again.

raccroc, m. fluke || coup de ~, m. lucky hit.

raccrocher, v. a. to hook again || to recover, to get again || se ~, to catch at, to lay hold of || to become friends again || to recover oneself.

race, f. race, family, line, breed, cast, tribe, stock || de ~, thoroughbred.

rachat, m. repurchase || redemption || ransom || ~ de bans, marriage-license.

rachetable, a. redeemable.

racheter, v. a. to buy again, to buy back, to purchase || to redeem || to compensate.

rachitique, a. rickety.

rachitis, rachitisme, m. rickets (pl.).

racine, f. root.

raclée, f. licking, hiding.

racler, v. a. to scrape, to grate || to clean.

racleur, m. scraper, bad fiddler.

racloir, m. scraper, grater (instrument).

racloire, f. strickle.

raclure, f. scrapings (pl.).

racolage, m. recruiting.

racoler, v. a. to entice men, to enlist, to kidnap, to crimp.

racoleur, m. recruiting-officer || kidnapper.

raconter, v. a. to relate, to tell, to recount.

raconteur, se, m. & f. relater, teller.

racornir, v. a. to make hard and tough || to shrivel up, to crisp.   [ling.

racornissement, m. hardening || shrivel-

racquit, m. winning back.

racquitter, v. a. to win back || to retrieve

rade, f. (mar.) roadstead.   [a loss.

radeau, m. raft.   [off.

radiation, f. (méd.) irradiation || striking

radical, m. Radical.

radical, e, a. (-ement, ad.) radical(ly).

radicalisme, m. radicalism.

radicule, f. radicle.

radié, e, a. radiated.

radier, v. a. to strike off.

radieux, se, a. radiant, bright, shining.

radis, m. (bot.) turnip || radish.

radotage, m., **radoterie,** f. idle talk || dotage || raving.

radoter, v. n. to dote, to rave.

radoteur, se, m. & f. dotard.

radoub, m. (mar.) refitting of a ship.

radouber, v. a. (mar.) to refit.

radoucir, v. a. to soften, to appease, to pacify || se ~, to relent, to soften, to grow mild, to grow gentle.   [mitigation.

radoucissement, m. softening, allaying,

rafale, m. (mar.) squall.

raffermir, v. a. to fasten, to harden, to strengthen, to fortify, to confirm, to secure || se ~, to grow stronger, to get over one's fear.   [fastening || confirmation.

raffermissement, m. strengthening,

raffinage, m. refining.

raffiné, m. fashionable rake.   [sharp.

raffiné, e, a. refined || clever, keen, subtle,

raffinement, m. refinement || subtilty.

raffiner, v. a. & n. to refine || se ~, to become refined.   [refinery.

raffinerie, f. refinery || refining || sugar-

raffineur, m. refiner || sugar-baker.

raffoler, v. n. to be passionately fond of, to dote on.

raffuter, v. a. to remake a hat.

rafistoler, v. a. to spruce up again || to patch up, to mend.

rafle, f. grape-stalk || raffle (at dice) || faire ~, to take the pool.

rafler, v. a. to sweep away.

rafraîchir, v. a. & n. to refresh, to refrigerate, to cool || to repair, to renew || to cut off || to grow cool || se ~, to grow cool, to cool, to recruit oneself.

rafraîchissant, e, a. refrigerative.

rafraîchissement, m. refreshment, cooling || ~s, pl. provisions (pl.), supplies (pl.).

rafraîchissoir, m. cooler || refrigerator.

ragaillardir, v. a. to cheer up.

rage, f. rage, raging, madness || violent desire || hydrophobia || violent pain.

rager, v. n. to be in ou get into a rage.

rageur, se, m. & f. passionate person.

rageur, se, a. passionate.

ragot, m. tittle-tattle.

ragot, te, a. thick and short.

ragoter, v. n. to grumble.

ragoût, m. (culin.) ragoût || stew || relish.

ragoûtant, e, a. savoury, relishing, agreeable. [cite the taste of.

ragoûter, v. a. to revive appetite || to excite the taste of.

ragrafer, v. a. to clasp again.

ragrandir, v. a. to enlarge again.

ragréer, v. a. to repair a house, to newfront a house.

ragrément, m. finishing off || repairing.

raide, a. stiff || tight || steep || rapid || swift || ~, ad. quickly || hard || sharply, right, outright, down, on the spot || surely.

raideur, f. stiffness || tightness || steepness || [swiftness.

raidillon, m. ascent.

raidir, v. a. & n. to stiffen || to tighten || se ~, to get stiff, to bear up, to resist.

raie, f. line, dash upon writing || stripe, streak, furrow || skate || à ~s, striped.

raifort, m. (bot.) horse-radish.

rail, m. rail || chemin de ~s, m. (mil.) waggon-way.

railler, v. a. & n. to jeer, to banter, to rally, to scoff, to jest, to play upon.

raillerie, f. joke, jest, banter, raillery, mockery || ~ à part, in good earnest.

railleur, m. jeerer, joker, banterer, mocker.

railleur, se, a. jeering, bantering, scoffing.

rainette, f. rennet (apple) || tree-frog.

rainure, f. groove.

raiponce, f. rampion. [stag).

raire, v. n. to shave || to bellow (like a

rais, m. spoke (of a wheel) || ray, beam.

raisin, m. grape || (of paper) royal || grappe de ~s, f. bunch of grapes || ~ sec, raisin, plum || ~ de Corinthe, currant.

raisiné, m. grape and pear jam.

raison, f. reason, cause, motive || justice, equity || proof, argument || à ~ de, en ~ de, at the rate of, in proportion to || en ~, in a ratio || pour ~ de quoi, by reason of which || à plus forte ~, still more so || avec ~, right || sans ~, irrational || comme de ~, as it is fit, of course || ~ sociale, (com.) firm || avoir ~, to be right.

raisonnable, a. reasonable, rational || just, convenient, proper || competent || moderate || ~ment, ad. reasonably, rationally, justly, tolerably, moderately.

raisonné, e, a. founded on reason, supported by reasoning, explaining the reasons || methodical || just || fair, wise || classified || delicate.

raisonnement, m. reasoning, ratiocination, argument.

raisonner, v. a. & n. to reason, to argue, to examine into a question || to answer.

raisonneur, m. reasoner || grumbler || prater || faire le ~, to answer.

rajeunir, v. a. & n. to make young again || to grow young again || to colour (hair) || to shave || to revive || to prune.

rajeunissement, m. growing young again, rejuvenescence.

rajouter, v. a. to aid again ou more.

rajustement, m. readjustment, reconcilement, setting in order. [again.

rajuster, v. a. to readjust, to set in order

râle, m. rattle || rail, crake (bird).

râlement, m. rattling in the throat.

ralentir, v. a. to abate, to slacken, to lessen, to make slower || to relent.

ralentissement, m. slackening, abatement.

râler, v. a. to have a rattling in the throat.

ralliement, m. rallying || point de ~, m. rallying place.

rallier, v. a. to rally || (mar.) to bring a ship to the wind.

rallonge, f. lengthening-piece || leaf || table à ~s, f. telescope-table.

rallongement, m. lengthening || being lengthened. [longer.

rallonger, v. a. to lengthen, to make

rallumer, v. a. to light again, to rekindle || to animate again || se ~, to kindle again, to break out again.

ramage, m. chirping ou warbling of birds || flowering || prattling, prattle || ouvrage à ~, m. flowered work.

ramaigrir, v. a. & n. to make ou grow lean again || to make leaner.

ramas, m. collection, heap.

ramasse, f. mountain-sledge || ~-couvert, m. crumb-tray. [set.

ramassé, e, a. picked up, collected || thickset.

ramasser, v. a. to pick up, to gather, to collect, to re-assemble || to cuff || se ~, to assemble, to be assembled || to roll up.

ramasseur, m. sledge-driver || gatherer.

ramassis, m. confused collection || loppings (pl.) || rakings (pl.). [stick.

rame, f. oar, scull || ream (of paper) || prop, stick.

ramé, e, a. rowed || pois ~s, m. pl. peas that grow upon sticks (pl.) || boulets ~s, m. pl. bar-shot (pl.) || balles ~es, f. pl. chain-shot (pl.), cross-bar shot (pl.).

rameau, m. bough, branch || vein || dimanche des Rameaux, m. Palm-Sunday.

ramée, f. green arbour || boughs ou branches with their leaves (pl.).

ramener, v. a. to bring back, to bring again || to restore || to retrieve || to revive.

ramer, v. a. & n. to prop ‖ to stick (peas) ‖ to row ‖ to ply.

rameur, m. rower.

rameux, se, a. branchy.

ramier, m. ring-dove, wood-pigeon (bird).

se ramifier, to ramify, to branch.

ramilles, f. pl. small branches (pl.).

Raminagrobis, m. Grimalkin.

ramingue, a. restive.   [again.

ramoindrir, v. a. & n.; **se ~,** to lessen

ramoitir, v. a. to moisten, to make damp ‖ **se ~,** to get damp.

ramollir, v. a. to soften.

ramollissant, m. emollient.

ramollissant, e, a. emollient.

ramonage, m. sweeping of a chimney.

ramoner, v. a. to sweep.

ramoneur, m. chimney-sweeper.

rampe, f. flight of stairs ‖ balustrade, hand-rail ‖ slope ‖ foot-lights (of a theatre) (pl.).

ramper, v. n. to creep, to crawl, to cringe.

rampiste, m. baluster-maker.

ramure, f. branches (pl.) ‖ horns (pl.).

ramuscule, m. (bot.) ramuscule.

rancart, m. rubbish ‖ **mettre au ~,** to put aside.

rance, a. rancid, rusty.   [put aside.

rancidité, rancissure, f. rancidity, rankness.

rancir, v. n. to grow rancid.   [ness.

rançon, f. ransom.

rançonnement, m. ransoming ‖ extortion.

rançonner, v. a. to ransom, to extort money ‖ to overcharge.

rançonneur, se, m. & f. extortioner.

rancune, f. rancour, grudge, spite, malice.

rancuneux, se, racunier, ère, a. rancorous, spiteful.

rang, m. row, range ‖ rank, station, class, dignity ‖ number ‖ tier ‖ frame ‖ (mar.) rate.

rangé, e, a. ranged ‖ steady ‖ pitched.

rangée, f. range, row, file.

ranger, v. a. to range, to rank, to put in ranks, to arrange, to set in order ‖ to set to rights ‖ to subdue ‖ to sail close to ‖ **se ~,** to make room, to place oneself ‖ to reform ‖ to embrace ‖ to side with ‖ to amend ‖ to fall in ‖ to veer.

ranimer, v. a. to reanimate, to revive ‖ to cheer up ‖ to stir up.

ranz (des vaches), m. Swiss tune for calling the cattle home.

rapace, a. rapacious.

rapacité, f. rapacity.

râpage, m. rasping.

rapatelle, f. horse-hair cloth.

rapatriage, rapatriement, m. reconciliation ‖ return-voyage, home-voyage.

rapatrier, v. a. to reconcile ‖ to be brought back to one's country ‖ **se ~,** to be reconciled, to become friends again.

râpe, f. rasp, grater ‖ stalk.

râpé, m. rape-wine ‖ rappee.   [worn-out.

râpé, e, a. threadbare, shabby, seedy,

râper, v. a. to rasp, to grate.

rapetasser, v. a. to patch up.

rapetisser, v. a. & n. to lessen, to make less, to shorten ‖ **se ~,** to grow less ‖ to lower oneself.

rapide, a. (-ment, ad.) rapid(ly) ‖ swift (ly).

rapidité, f. rapidity, swiftness.   [(ly).

rapiécer, v. a. to piece ‖ to patch.

rapiécetage, m. piecing, patched work.

rapiéceter, v. a. to botch, to patch, to piece all over.

rapière, f. rapier.   [piece all over.

rapin, m. painter's articled pupil ‖ dauber.

rapine, f. rapine, plunder.

rapiner, v. a. to pilfer, to pillage.

rapinerie, f. rapine, plunder.

rappareiller, v. a. to match.

rapparier, v. a. to match.

rappel, m. recall, calling back, revocation ‖ (mil.) beat to arms.

rappeler, v. a. to recall, to call back, to call home, to call again and again ‖ (mil.) to beat to arms ‖ to call to mind ‖ **se ~,** to remember, to recollect.

rapport, m. produce ‖ report ‖ story, tale ‖ likeness, relation, resemblance ‖ tendency, reference ‖ relation, affinity ‖ dependency ‖ reïmbursement ‖ (of the stomach) rising ‖ **pièces de ~,** f. pl. patchwork ‖ inlaidwork ‖ **par ~ à,** for the sake of, with regard to ‖ **faire un ~,** to make a report, to report ‖ **avoir ~ à,** to refer to, to relate to.

rapporter, v. a. & n. to bring back, to carry back ‖ to report, to refer, to quote ‖ to tell ‖ to yield, to bring forth ‖ to derive ‖ to inlay ‖ to repeal (a law) ‖ **se ~,** to relate, to have a reference to, to concern, to allude to, to resort to.

rapporteur, m. reporter ‖ tell-tale ‖ protractor.

rapporteuse, f. tell-tale.   [tractor.

rapprendre, v. a. ir. to learn again.

rapprochement, m. drawing nearer, junction, reconciliation ‖ bringing together.

rapprocher, v. a. to draw near again, to bring near again, to bring together ‖ to set in opposition, to compare ‖ **se ~,** to come near again, to come nearer to, to draw towards a reconciliation.

rapsodie, f. rhapsody.

rapsodiste, m. rhapsodist.

rapt, m. rape ‖ abduction.

râpure, f. raspings (pl.).

raquette, f. racket, battledore.

raquettier, m. racket-maker.   [slow.

rare, a. rare, thin, scarce ‖ uncommon ‖

raréfaction, f. rarefaction ‖ rarity.

raréfier, v. a. to rarefy.

rarement, ad. rarely, seldom.

rareté, f. rarity, rareness, scarcity ‖ **-s,** pl. curiosities (pl.).

rarissime, a. very rare.

rarité, f. rarity, rarefaction.

ras, m. short-nap cloth ‖ **~ de marée,** (mar.) race.

ras, e, a. shorn, short-haired, bare ‖ plain, smooth ‖ open ‖ flat ‖ **à ~ (de),** close (to).

rasade, f. bumper.

rasement, m. razing.

raser, v. a. to shave ‖ to raze, to rake, to demolish ‖ to glance ‖ to graze ‖ to touch lightly ‖ to sail close to ‖ to lay flat.

rasibus, ad. close to.

rasoir, m. razor ‖ **cuir à ~,** m. razor-strop.

rassade, f. glass bead.
rassasiement, m. satiety.
rassasier, v. a. to satiate, to fill || to satisfy || to cloy || to surfeit || to tire.
rassemblement, m. assembling, assemblage, meeting || crowd, mob.
rassembler, v. a. to reassemble || to collect || to unite || to summon up || se ~, to meet || to assemble || to crowd || to muster.
rasseoir, v. a. ir. to settle, to calm || to replace || to fix, to adjust || se ~, to sit down again, to reseat oneself || to be settled.
rasséréner, v. a. to clear up, to calm.
rassiéger, v. a. to besiege again.
rassis, e, a. settled, sedate, calm || stale.
rassortir, v. a. to resort.
rassurer, v. a. to secure, to encourage || to reassure || se ~, to take courage again, to recover oneself || to clear up.
rasure, f. shaving.
rat, m. rat || whim || ballet-girl || ~ de cave, exciseman, excise-officer.
ratatiné, e, a. shrivelled up, shrunk.
se ratatiner, v. a. to shrink, to shrivel.
ratatouille, f. poor stew, bad stuff.
rate, f. spleen, milt || épanouir la ~, to make merry.
râteau, m. rake.
râtelage, m. raking.
râtelée, f. rakeful.
râteler, v. a. to rake.
râteleur, m. raker.
râtelier, m. rack || gun-rack || set of teeth.
rater, v. a. & n. to miss || to miss fire || to miscarry.
ratière, f. rap-trap.
ratifier, v. a. to ratify.
ratine, f. ratteen.
ratiner, v. a. to frieze.
ration, f. share, portion || allowance.
rationnel, le, a. (–lement, ad.) rational.
rationner, v. a. to allowance.
ratissage, m. scraping, raking.
ratisser, v. a. to scrape, to rake.
ratissoire, f. scraper, iron rake.
ratissure, f. scrapings (pl.).
raton, m. racoon || darling || Mouser.
rattacher, v. a. to tie again, to fasten again || to connect || se ~, to be fastened.
ratte, f. field-mouse.
ratteindre, v. a. ir. to overtake, to catch again.
rattraper, v. a. to overtake, to catch again, to come up with, to retake, to recover || se ~ (à), to catch hold of.
rature, f. erasure.
raturer, v. a. to scratch out, to scrape, to raze.
raucité, f. hoarseness.
rauque, a. hoarse.
ravage, m. ravage, devastation, havoc || damage.
ravager, v. a. to ravage, to pillage, to plunder, to strip.
ravageur, m. ravager.
ravalé, e, a. down at heel.
ravalement, m. roughcasting.
ravaler, v. n. to swallow down again || to vilify, to depreciate || to roughcast || se ~, to humble ou lower oneself.
ravaudage, m. mending, patching, botching || bungling.

ravauder, v. a. to mend, to botch.
ravaudeuse, f. stocking-mender.
rave, f. (bot.) radish || turnip.
ravelin, m. (mil.) ravelin.
ravenelle, f. (bot.) wall-flower.
ravier, m. radish-dish.
ravière, f. radish-bed.
ravigote, f. (culin.) sauce with shallots.
ravigoter, v. a. to revive || to revive the appetite of.
ravilir, v. a. to vilify, to debase, to undervalue.
ravin, m. ravine.
ravine, f. great flood, torrent.
ravir, v. a. to ravish, to tear ou take away || to steal || to enrapture || à ~, admirably.
se raviser, v. to change one's mind, to bethink oneself || to think better of it.
ravissant, e, a. rapacious, ravenous || enrapturing, ravishing.
ravissement, m. ravishment, rape || rapture, ecstasy.
ravisseur, m. ravisher.
ravitaillement, m. re-victualling.
ravitailler, v. a. to re-victual.
raviver, v. a. to revive.
ravoir, v. a. ir. to have ou get again || to recover.
rayer, v. a. to erase, to scratch, to blot out || to streak, to stripe || to rifle.
rayon, m. ray, beam || book-shelf || spoke || radius || furrow || (honey-)comb.
rayonnant, e, a. radiant, beaming.
rayonnement, m. radiation, radiancy.
rayonner, v. n. to radiate, to beam.
rayure, f. stripes (in stuff) (pl.) || grooves (in a rifle) (pl.).
raz, m. (mar.) race.
razzia, f. inroad, raid, foray.
réactif, m. (chim.) reagent || test.
réactif, ve, a. reactive.
réaction, f. reaction.
réactionnaire, m. reactionist.
réactionnaire, a. reactionary.
réadmettre, v. a. ir. to readmit.
réafficher, v. a. to post up again.
réagir, v. n. to react.
réajourner, v. a. to readjourn.
réaliser, v. a. to realise || to convert into money.
réalisme, m. realism.
réalité, f. reality || effective existence || en ~, really, indeed.
réapparition, f. reappearance.
réapposer, v. a. to set on again || to seal up again.
réargenter, v. a. to re-silver.
réassigner, v. a. to summon again.
réassurer, v. a. to reinsure.
réatteler, v. a. to yoke again.
rebaisser, v. a. to lower again.
rebander, v. a. to bind ou bend up again.
rébarbatif, ve, a. cross, peevish, gruff, repulsive.
rebâtir, v. a. to rebuild.
rebattre, v. a. to beat again || to shuffle the cards again || to repeat again and again.
rebattu, e, a. repeated over and over again || hackneyed || trite.
rebelle, m. & f. rebel.
rebelle, a. rebellious, stubborn || (of metals) refractory.
rébellion, f. rebellion, revolt, insurrection.
se rebéquer, (fam.) to be saucy.

se rebiffer, to resist || to kick.

reblanchir, v. a. to wash again, to whiten again.

reboire, v. a. ir. to drink again.

reboisement, m. replanting.

rebondi, e, a. plump, chubby.

rebondir, v. n. to rebound.

rebondissement, m. rebound.

rebord, m. edge, border || à ~, brimmed.

reborder, v. a. to new-border || to new-line || to new-bind.

se rebotter, to put on one's boots again.

reboucher, v. a. to stop up again || se ~, to be stopped up again || to grow blunt || to get filled up.

rebouillir, v. a. ir. to boil again.

rebouiser, v. a. to clean and polish (a hat).

rebours, m. wrong side (of stuff) || reverse, opposite, contrary || à ~, au ~, against the grain || the wrong way || backwards.

rebouteur, m. bone-setter.   [wards.

rebraider, v. a. to bridle again.

rebroder, v. a. to embroider again.

rebrouiller, v. a. to entangle ou perplex again.   [ou grain.

rebrousse-poil, ad.; à ~, against the hair

rebrousser, v. a. to turn back || ~ chemin, to retrace one's steps.

rebroyer, v. a. to grind again.

rebrunir, v. a. to burnish again.

rebuffade, f. rebuke, repulse, rebuff.

rébus, m. rebus || pun.

rebut, m. outcast, trash, rebuff || de ~, waste || bois de ~, m. offal timber || bureau des —s, m. dead-letter office.

rebutant, e, a. repulsive, discouraging, forbidding.

rebuter, v. a. to reject, to repulse, to refuse, to rebuff || to dishearten || se ~, to be disheartened.

recacher, v. a. to hide again.

recacheter, v. a. to seal again.

récalcitrant, e, a. refractory, stubborn.

récalcitrer, v. n. to resist stubbornly.

récapituler, v. a. to recapitulate.

recarder, v. a. to card again.

recarreler, v. a. to new-pave.

recasser, v. a. to break again.

recéder, v. a. to restore again.

recel, m. receiving of stolen goods.

recèlement, m. receiving || concealment.

receler, v. a. to conceal ou receive stolen goods.   [goods, intaker.

receleur, se, m. & f. receiver of stolen

récemment, ad. recently, lately.

recensement, m. census || verification || return.   [examine.

recenser, v. a. to make a census || to

récent, e, a. recent, new, fresh || late.

recepage, m. cutting down || topping.

recepée, f. part of a forest cut down.

receper, v. a. to cut trees down to the ground.

récépissé, m. receipt.

réceptacle, m. receptacle || (bot.) thalamus || (bot.) torus.

réception, f. reception, receipt || admittance || levee || drawing-room.

recercler, v. a. to fit with new hoops.

recette, f. receipt of money || receiver's office || medical prescription.

recevable, a. receivable || allowable, admissible.

receveur, se, m. & f. receiver || collector.

recevoir, v. a. ir. to receive, to accept, to approve, to allow, to admit || to lodge || to entertain || to welcome || to give audience || to hold a drawing-room.

réchampir, v. a. to set off (in house-painting).   [(pl.) || de ~, spare.

rechange, m. re-exchange || spare things

rechanger, v. a. to change again.

rechanter, v. a. to sing again || to repeat.

réchapper, v. n. to escape, to recover.

recharger, v. a. to load again || to charge again.

rechasser, v. a. to drive back again, to turn out again || to hunt again.

réchaud, m. chafing-dish || dish-warmer || warming-apparatus || heater || stove.

réchauffé, m. réchauffé, warmed food.

réchauffé, e, a. warmed up, stale || old.

réchauffer, v. a. to warm up || to heat again || to kindle again || to revive || se ~, to warm oneself again || to grow warm again, to get hot again || to be revived again.

réchauffoir, m. dish-warmer.

rechausser, v. a. to put on stockings ou shoes again || to mould up.

rêche, a. rough, coarse, sour.

recherche, f. search, quest, inquiry, investigation, pursuit || courtship, finery.

recherché, e, a. inquired into || sought after || exquisite, choice, rare || affected || far-fetched.

rechercher, v. a. to seek again, to search, to try, to find || to investigate, to make inquiry || to desire earnestly || to court.

rechigné, e, a. sour, crabbed, grim-faced, sulky.

rechigner, v. n. to look sulky.

rechute, f. relapse.

récidive, f. relapse || (jur.) second offence.   [same offence again.

récidiver, v. n. (jur.) to commit the

récidiviste, m. old offender.

récif, m. reef, shelf of rocks.

récipiendaire, m. candidate for reception, new member.   [cistern.

récipient, m. (chim.) receiver || recipient ||

réciprocité, f. reciprocation, reciprocity.

réciproque, a. (-ment, ad.) reciprocal (ly).   [again.

recirer, v. a. to wax again || to black

récit, m. recital, relation, account, narrative || (mus.) recitative.

récitant, m. (mus.) solo, solo-part.

récitatif, m. (mus.) recitative.

récitation, f. recitation || repetition.

réciter, v. a. to recite, to rehearse, to repeat, to relate.

réclamation, f. claim, claiming, demand || protest || opposition || objection || complaint || rectification.

réclame, f. catch-word || article, advertisement || puff.

réclamer, v. a. & n. to beg, to call for, to call upon, to implore, to claim, to lay claim to || to oppose, to make objection, to protest against || se ~, to make use of a person's name.

reclouer, v. a. to nail again.

reclure, v. a. & n. ir. to shut up.

reclus, e, m. & f. recluse || nun.

reclus, e, a. shut up.

reclusion, f. reclusion, confinement.

recogner, v. a. to knock again.

recoiffer, v. a. to dress the head again.

recoin, m. corner, nook || (fig.) recess.

recoller, v. a. to paste again, to glue again.

récollet, te, m. & f. Recollet, Franciscan friar ou nun.   [growth.

récolte, f. crop || harvest || vintage ||

récolter, v. a. to reap, to gather.

recommandable, a. commendable, praiseworthy.   [esteem, value || (jur.) detainer.

recommandation, f. recommendation.

recommander, v. a. to recommend || to order || to enjoin || se ~, to recommend oneself || se ~ de, to make use of the name of, to say one is known to, to refer to.

recommencer, v. a. & n. to begin again, to renew.

récompense, f. recompense, reward, compensation || return.   [pensate.

récompenser, v. a. to reward || to compenser, v. a. to recompose.

recompter, v. a. to count over again.

réconciliable, a. reconcilable.

réconciliateur, se, m. & f. reconciler.

réconcilier, v. a. to reconcile || se ~, to be reconciled.

reconduire, v. a. ir. to reconduct, to lead back, to attend to the door, to see home.

réconfort, m. consolation.

réconforter, v. n. to comfort, to cheer up || to strengthen.

reconnaissable, a. easy to be known again, easy to be recognised.

reconnaissance, f. recognition, gratitude, thankfulness || recompense, reward || (jur.) recognisance, verification || examination || receipt || ticket || I. O. U. (I owe you) || duplicate || (mil.) reconnoitring, observation.

reconnaissant, e, a. thankful.

reconnaître, v. a. ir. to recognise, to acknowledge || to be grateful, to recompense || to own || to find out, to discover || (mil.) to reconnoitre, to explore || se ~, to know oneself again || to know where one is || to recollect oneself.   [regain.

reconquérir, v. a. ir. to reconquer, to reconstitution, f. (jur.) substitution.

reconstruction, f. rebuilding.

reconstruire, v. a. to rebuild.

reconter, v. a. to relate over again.

recopier, v. a. to copy again.   [up.

recoquillement, m. curling ou shrinking

recoquiller, v. a. to curl up, to turn up, to shrivel up || to cock (one's hat).

recorriger, v. a. to correct again.

recors, m. bailiff's follower.

recoucher, v. a. to put to bed again || se ~, to go to bed again.

recoudre, v. a. ir. to sew again.

recoupe, f. second crop || pollen || chips || rubble of stones.

recouper, v. a. to cut again.

recoupette, f. thirds (coarse meal) (pl.).

recourber, v. a. to bend round, to make crooked.

recourir, v. n. ir. to run again || to have recourse to.

recours, m. recourse, refuge, resource, relief, redress || ~ en grâce, petition for pardon.

recouvrement, m. recovery, recovering, regaining || collection of taxes || overlap.

recouvrer, v. a. to recover, to regain || to collect taxes.

recouvrir, v. a. ir. to cover again || se ~, to cover oneself again || to be hid again.

recracher, v. a. & n. to spit again || to fork out again || to disgorge.

récréatif, ve, a. recreative, amusing.

récréation, f. recreation, refreshment, diversion, amusement.

recréer, v. a. to create anew.

récréer, v. a. to amuse, to divert.

recrépir, v. a. to roughcast again || to paint (one's face) || to dress up.

se récrier, to exclaim, to cry out upon || to protest || to express surprise.

récriminer, v. n. to criminate.

récrire, v. a. ir. to write again || to answer.

recroître, v. n. ir. to grow again.

se recroqueviller, to shrivel, to shrink

recrudescence, f. recrudescence.   [up.

recru, e, m. new growth.

recrue, f. recruit, recruiting, new levy, supply || aller en ~, to go a-recruiting.

recrutement, m. recruiting.

recruter, v. a. to recruit.

recruteur, m. recruiter.

recruteur, a. recruiting.

recta, ad. exactly, punctually, all right.

recteur, m. rector, parson.

rectifier, v. a. to rectify.

rectiligne, a. rectilinear.

rectitude, f. rectitude, rightness, uprightness.

recto, m. right-hand page || first page of a leaf || odd page.

rectorat, m. rectorship.

reçu, m. receipt, acquittance.

reçu, p. received || allowed, admitted || usual || customary.

recueil, m. collection, selection || miscellany.

recueillement, m. recollection, contemplation, reflection || devotion || calmness.

recueillir, v. a. ir. to gather, to collect, to reap, to lay together, to heap together, to compile || to receive, to entertain, to make out || se ~, to recollect oneself, to meditate, to contemplate.

recuire, v. a. ir. to cook again || to anneal.

recuit, e, m. & f. annealing of metals.

recul, m. recoil, recoiling.

reculade, f. drawing backwards of carriages || retrograde movement, retreat.

reculé, e, a. remote, distant.

reculement, m. drawing back || delay.

reculer, v. a. & n. to put back, to pull *ou* draw back ‖ to delay, to put off ‖ to start, to fall back, to give ground ‖ to recoil (of cannons) ‖ to recede ‖ **se ~,** to draw back, to go back, to recede.

à reculons, ad. backwards ‖ worse and worse.

se récupérer, v. a. to retrieve one's losses.

récurer, v. a. to scour ‖ to till a third time.

récusable, a. (jur.) exceptionable.

récusation, f. challenge ‖ exception.

récuser, v. a. (jur.) to challenge, to except against ‖ **se ~,** to decline judging.

rédacteur, trice, m. & f. editor, compiler, author ‖ editress.

rédaction, f. editorship, compiling, compilation ‖ editorial staff ‖ editor's room.

redan, m. (arch.) skew-back ‖ check ‖ (mil.) redan.

reddition, f. surrender ‖ **~ de compte,** giving in of accounts.

redéfaire, v. a. ir. to undo again.

redemander, v. a. to ask again, **to ask back again.**

Rédempteur, m. Redeemer.

redescendre, v. a. & n. to take down ‖ to come *ou* go down.

redevable, m. debtor.

redevable, a. indebted.

redevance, f. ground-rent.

redevenir, v. n. ir. to become again.

redevoir, v. a. ir. to owe still, to remain in debt.

rédiger, v. a. to write down, to reduce to writing ‖ to range methodically.

redingote, f. riding-coat ‖ great-coat ‖ frock-coat.

redire, v. a. ir. to repeat, to tell *ou* say again, to report, to blab, to reveal ‖ **trouver à ~,** to find fault with.

rediseur, se, m. & f. tell-tale.

redite, f. repetition.

rédondance, f. redundancy.

rédonder, v. n. to be redundant.

redonner, v. a. & n. to give again, to give back, to return, to restore ‖ to charge again.

redorer, v. a. to new-gild.

redormir, v. n. ir. to sleep again.

redoublé, e, a. reduplicate ‖ (mil.) **pas ~,** m. double-quick time.

redoublement, m. redoubling, increase.

redoubler, v. a. & n. to redouble, to reiterate, to line again ‖ to increase.

redoutable, a. formidable, dreadful.

redoute, f. redoubt ‖ ridotto.

redouter, v. a. to dread, to fear.

redressement, m. straightening again ‖ redress ‖ relief.

redresser, v. a. to make straight, to set upright, to set up again ‖ to mend, to correct, to reform, to put in the right way ‖ **se ~,** to get up again, to stand erect ‖ to trick up oneself, to correct oneself.

redresseur, m. avenger ‖ cheat.

réduction, f. reduction ‖ abatement.

réduire, v. a. ir. to reduce, to subdue, to conquer, to force, to oblige ‖ to decrease, to lessen, to reform ‖ **se ~,** to reduce oneself ‖ to be reduced, to come to.

réduit, m. small habitation ‖ nook ‖ by-place ‖ miserable hovel ‖ retreat ‖ small   [redoubt.

rééditer, v. a. to publish anew.

réel, m. reality.

réel, le, a. (-lement, ad.) real(ly) ‖ true ‖

rééligibilité, f. re-eligibility.   [indeed.

rééligible, a. re-eligible.

réélire, v. a. ir. to elect again.

réer, v. n. (in hunting) to bell.

réexpédier, v. a. to send back *ou* again.

réexporter, v. a. to re-export.

réfaction, f. (com.) allowance, rebate.

refaire, v. a. ir. to do again ‖ to make again ‖ to mend ‖ to refresh ‖ to recruit ‖ to restore ‖ to deal again ‖ to bamboozle.

refait, m. drawn game.

refait, e, a. done again ‖ amended ‖ cheated, fooled.

réfectoire, m. refectory, dining-room.

refend, m. splitting ‖ **mur de ~,** m. partition-wall, middle wall ‖ **pierre de ~,** f. corner-stone ‖ **bois de ~,** m. sawn timber.

référé, m. (jur.) report ‖ **en ~,** sitting in chambers.

référendaire, m. referendary.

référer, v. a. & n. to refer ‖ to make a report ‖ **se ~,** to refer, to have reference *ou* relation (to).   [up.

refermer, v. a. to shut again ‖ to close

referrer, v. a. to new-shoe (a horse).

refiltrer, v. a. to filter *ou* strain again.

réfléchi, e, a. reflected, done with deliberation, premeditated ‖ **verbe ~,** m. (gr.) reflective verb.

réfléchir, v. a. & n. to reflect, to throw back, to reverberate ‖ to reflect upon, to consider attentively ‖ to be thrown back.

réfléchissement, m. reflection.

réflecteur, m. reflector.

réflecteur, a. reflective.

reflet, m. reflex, reflection.

refléter, v. a. to reflect.

refleurir, v. n. to blossom again.

réflexion, f. reflection ‖ consideration.

refluer, v. n. to reflow, to flow back.

reflux, m. reflux, ebbing ‖ change.

refondre, v. a. to melt again, to cast again, to new-mould, to new-cast, to reform.

refonte, f. new-coining (of money) ‖ recasting ‖ remodelling.

reforger, v. a. to new-forge.

réformateur, trice, m. & f. reformer.

réformateur, trice, a. reforming.

réforme, f. reform, reformation ‖ disbanding of soldiers ‖ half-pay ‖ discharged

réformé, e, m. Protestant.   [horses (pl.).

réformer, v. a. to reform, to improve, to mend, to correct ‖ to put on half-pay ‖ to invalid ‖ to discharge ‖ **se ~,** to amend.

réformiste, m. reformer.

refouiller, v. a. to dig *ou* search again ‖ (sculpture) to sink deeper.

refoulement, m. flowing *ou* ebbing back ‖ ramming (of a gun).

refouler, v. a. & n. to full cloth again, to press again ‖ to ram again ‖ to drive back ‖ (mar.) to ebb, to flow back ‖ **~ la marée,** (mar.) to stem the tide.

refouloir, m. rammer.

réfractaire, m. defaulting recruit.

réfractaire, a. refractory, stubborn, obstinate ‖ fire-proof.

réfracter, v. a. to refract.

réfraction, f. refraction ‖ à ~, refracting.

refrain, m. burden (of a song), refrain.

refrapper, v. a. to strike again, to knock again ‖ to new-stamp money.

refréner, v. a. to restrain, to curb, to bridle. [chine.

réfrigérant, m. refrigerator, freezing machine.

réfrigérant, a. (chim.) refrigeratory ‖ (méd.) refrigerant.

réfringent, a. refracting.

refriser, v. a. to curl again.

refrognement, m. frowning, bending of one's brows ‖ sullen look.

se refrogner, to frown.

refroidir, v. a. & n. to cool, to make cold ‖ to moderate ‖ to grow cool, to grow cold ‖ to lessen. [coldness.

refroidissement, m. cooling, coolness.

refrotter, v. a. to rub again.

refuge, m. refuge, shelter ‖ pretence.

réfugié, e, m. & f. refugee.

se réfugier, to seek shelter, to retire.

refus, m. refusal, denial.

refuser, v. a. to refuse, to deny, to withhold, to reject ‖ (mar.) to scant ‖ se ~, to deny oneself a thing ‖ se ~ à, to be contrary to.

réfuter, v. a. to refute.

regagner, v. a. to regain, to recover, to get again ‖ to return to, to go back again ‖ ~ le dessus, to get the upper hand again.

regaillardir, v. a. to cheer up.

regain, m. second crop ‖ aftermath.

régal, m. feast, entertainment, pleasure ‖ luxury ‖ favourite dish. [fare.

régalade, f. (fam.) entertaining at table ‖

régalant, e, a. pleasant.

régale, f. regale, royal privilege.

régalement, m. assessment ‖ levelling.

régaler, v. a. to regale, to treat, to feast, to entertain, to favour ‖ to assess.

regard, m. look, air ‖ aspect ‖ –s, pl. eyes (pl.) ‖ attention ‖ notice ‖ au ~, in comparison to, with respect to, as-to ‖ en ~, opposite.

regardant, m. looker-on, spectator.

regardant, e, a. (too) saving ‖ too severe.

regarder, v. a. to look at (on, upon), to behold, to see, to consider, to observe, to examine ‖ to concern, to belong to ‖ to face, to stand opposite ‖ se ~, to look at oneself, to look at one another ‖ to examine oneself in a looking-glass ‖ to be opposite one another.

regarnir, v. a. to furnish ou trim again.

régates, f. pl. regatta, boat-race.

regeler, v. n. to freeze again.

régence, f. regency ‖ mastership.

régénérateur, trice, m. & f. regenerator.

régénérateur, trice, a. regenerating.

régénération, f. regeneration, reproduction, reformation.

régénérer, v. a. to regenerate ‖ se ~, to be renewed, to grow again.

régent, e, m. & f. regent ‖ professor ‖ director (of the Bank of France).

régenter, v. a. & n. to govern ‖ to domineer ‖ to lecture.

régicide, m. regicide (person or act).

régicide, a. regicidal.

régie, f. administration, management ‖ excise-office. [resist.

regimber, v. a. to kick (of horses) ‖ to

régime, m. diet, regimen, rule ‖ (gr.) objective case ‖ (jur.) administration, management, discipline.

régiment, m. regiment. [body).

région, f. region, country ‖ part (of the

régional, e, a. local.

régir, v. a. to govern, to rule, to administer, to manage. [steward.

régisseur, m. administrator, manager, registrar.

régistraire, m. keeper of the registers.

régistrateur, m. registrar.

régistre, m. register, record ‖ plate of iron in stoves ‖ damper.

régistrer, v. a. to register.

règle, f. rule ‖ ruler ‖ precept, statute, maxim, method ‖ pattern, model ‖ en ~, regular, right ‖ –s, pl. monthly courses (pl.).

réglé, e, a. ruled, regulated, regular, orderly, punctual, fixed, certain ‖ homme ~, m. orderly man ‖ vent ~, m. tradewind.

règlement, m. regulation, rule, order, statute, law.

réglément, ad. regularly, exactly.

réglementaire, a. regulating.

réglementer, v. a. to regulate.

régler, v. a. to rule, to regulate, to set in order ‖ to settle, to determine, to decide ‖ to discipline ‖ to assign ‖ se ~, to become regular ‖ to regulate oneself ‖ to follow another's example.

réglisse, f. liquorice.

régnant, e, a. reigning, prevailing ‖ present.

règne, m. reign ‖ kingdom ‖ prevalence.

régner, v. n. to reign, to govern, to rule ‖ to be in fashion, to prevail ‖ to run along, to extend along.

regonflement, m. rising of water.

regonfler, v. n. to swell, to overflow.

regorgement, m. overflow.

regorger, v. n. & a. to overflow, to run over, to abound ‖ to be glutted ‖ to disgorge. [gorge.

regoûter, v. a. to taste again.

regratter, v. a. & n. to scratch again, to scrape ‖ to huckster.

regratterie, f. huckster's trade ou goods (pl.).

regrattier, tière, m. & f. huckster ‖ huckstress.

regret, m. regret, grief, sorrow, compunction, lamentation ‖ à ~, with regret, with reluctance, unwillingly ‖ à mon ~, to my sorrow ‖ avoir ~ à, to be sorry for.

regrettable, a. to be regretted.

regretter, v. a. to regret.

régulariser, v. a. to regulate, to render regular ‖ se ~, to become regular.

régularité, f. regularity. [moderator.

régulateur, trice, m. & f. regulator,

régulateur, trice, a. regulating.

régulation, f. regulation.

régule, m. (chim.) regulus.

régulier, ère, a. (-èrement, ad.) regular [(ly). || to redeem.

réhabiliter, v. a. to rehabilitate, to rein-state

réhabituer, v. a. to reaccustom.

rehaussement, m. heightening, raising.

rehausser, v. a. to raise || to enhance || to set off.

rehauts, m. pl. lightest ou brightest parts

réimporter, v. a. to re-import. [(pl.).

réimposer, v. a. to re-assess || to re-impose.

réimpression, f. reprint, new edition.

réimprimer, v. n. to reprint.

rein, m. rein, kidney || -s, pl. reins (pl.), loins (pl.).

reine, f. queen || ~-claude, f. (bot.) greengage.

reinette, f. renette (apple).

réinsérer, v. a. to re-insert.

réinstallation, f. re-installation.

réinstaller, v. a. to re-instal.

reinté, e, a. strong-backed, loined.

réintégrande, f. (jur.) re-integration, re-instating. [ment.

réintégration, f. reinstating, reinstate-

réintégrer, v. a. to reinstate.

réitérer, v. a. to reiterate, to repeat.

rejaillir, v. n. to spout ou gush out, to fly out || to turn back, to be reflected.

rejaillissement, m. starting ou springing back, gushing out, rebounding || reflection.

rejet, m. rejection || young shoot.

rejetable, a. rejectable.

rejeter, v. a. & n. to reject, to throw back, to drive back || to vomit || to grow again || to refuse, to disapprove || se ~, to com-pensate oneself by || to fall back || to excuse oneself. [twig, layer.

rejeton, m. offspring, sucker, young shoot,

rejoindre, v. a. ir. to rejoin, to join again.

rejouer, v. a. to play again.

réjoui, e, a. joyous, jovial, joyful, merry.

réjouir, v. a. to rejoice, to gladden, to give joy, to exhilarate, to divert, to cheer || se ~, to rejoice, to divert oneself, to make oneself merry, to be glad of.

réjouissance, f. rejoicing, merry-making || make-weight, boot, surplus.

réjouissant, e, a. amusing.

relâche, m. intermission, discontinuance, rest || no performance || ~, f. (mar.) put-ting into port. [loose, weak.

relâché, e, a. relaxed, released, yielded,

relâchement, m. relaxation, slackness, looseness, weakness, abatement.

relâcher, v. a. & n. to slacken, to release, to loose, to weaken, to yield, to abate || (mar.) to put into harbour || to sail back.

relais, m. relay, change of horses || stage.

relancer, v. a. to rouse (a wild beast) || to fetch out, to snub, to answer roughly.

relaps, m. relapser.

relaps, e, a. relapsed.

rélargir, v. a. to make wider.

rélargissement, m. widening.

relater, v. a. to relate, to mention.

relatif, ve, a. (-vement, ad.) relative(ly) || relating.

relation, f. relation, reference || account, narrative || relation, acquaintance || com-munication || correspondence.

relaver, v. a. to wash again.

relaxation, f. (jur.) release (of a prisoner) || laxness || remission || (méd.) relaxation.

relaxer, v. a. (jur.) to release (a prisoner) || to enlarge || (méd.) to relax.

relayer, v. a. & n. to relieve || to change [horses.

relégation, f. banishment.

reléguer, v. a. to relegate, to exile, to banish, to consign.

relent, m. musty smell.

relevailles, f. pl. churching (of a woman) || faire ses ~, to be churched.

relevé, m. abstract || extract || statement || (culin.) remove.

relevé, e, a. raised, elevated || noble || (culin.) highly seasoned.

relevée, f. rising again || afternoon.

relèvement, m. raising up again || (nav.) bearing, sheer || setting (of a compass).

relever, v. a. to raise up again, to lift up, to turn up, to take up, to raise || to ease, to free, to relieve || to extol, to heighten, to set off || to quicken || to remark, to notice || se ~, to rise again, to get up, to recover || to retrieve a loss.

reliage, m. hooping (of casks).

relief, m. relief, release || relievo, embossed work || donner du ~, to relieve, to set off, to give rank. [to hoop.

relier, v. a. to tie again || to bind (books) ||

relieur, m. bookbinder.

religieuse, f. nun.

religieusement, ad. religiously || exactly.

religieux, se, m. & f. friar, monk || nun.

religieux, se, a. religious, devotional || strict, punctual, exact || maison -se, f. monastery. [scruple.

religion, f. religion || creed || sacredness ||

reliquaire, m. reliquary. [count.

reliquat, m. (com.) remainder of an ac-

reliquataire, m. (com.) debtor.

relique, f. relic.

relire, v. a. ir. to read over again.

reliure, f. binding (of a book).

relouer, v. a. to let again, to underlet.

reluire, v. n. ir. to shine, to glitter.

reluquer, v. a. (fam.) to ogle || to cast sheep's eyes. [in one's mind || to ruminate.

remâcher, v. a. to chew again || to revolve

remaçonner, v. a. to repair (a building).

remander, v. a. to send word again.

remaniement, m. handling again || over-running || repairing.

remanier, v. a. to handle again, to do over again, to retouch, to repair.

se remarier, to re-marry.

remarquable, a. (-ment, ad.) remark-able || conspicuous(ly) || remarkably.

remarque, f. remark, note.

remarquer, v. a. to remark, to take notice of, to note, to mind || faire ~, to observe || se faire ~, to distinguish oneself.

remballer, v. a. to pack up again.

rembarquement, m. re-embarcation.

rembarquer, v. a. (se ~) to re-embark || to re-engage (in).

rembarrer, v. a. to retort on ‖ to stop at once ‖ to baffle.   [bankment.

remblai, m. filling of a ditch ‖ (rail.) em-

remblayer, v. a. to embank.

remboîtement, m. setting (of a bone).

remboîter, v. a. to set (a bone) again.

rembourrément, m. stuffing up, bolstering.

rembourrer, v. a. to stuff, to bolster up.

remboursable, a. repayable ‖ redeemable.

remboursement, m. reimbursement, repayment.   [to redeem.

rembourser, v. a. to reimburse, to repay ‖

rembruni, e, a. dark(ened) ‖ gloomy.

rembrunir, v. a. to make browner, to darken, to make gloomy ‖ se ~, to get darker, to become gloomy.

rembrunissement, m. darkening, gloominess.

rembûchement, m. (in hunting) return to the wood.

se rembûcher, (in hunting) to run into the wood.

remède, m. remedy.

remédier, v. n. to remedy, to cure.

remêler, v. a. to mix again.

remémorer (se), v. a. to remind, to put in mind.   [lead back.

remener, v. a. to carry ou bring back, to

remercier, v. a. to thank ‖ to send away.

remercîment, m. thanks (pl.).

réméré, m. (jur.) redemption ‖ repurchase.

remettre, v. a. ir. to put again, to set again, to put back, to give back, to put off, to delay, to defer ‖ to give, to entrust with ‖ to forgive, to pardon ‖ to deliver up ‖ se ~, to recover, to become composed, to recover oneself ‖ to fall again to ‖ se ~ à, to begin again.

remeubler, v. a. to furnish again.

réminiscence, f. reminiscence.

remis, e, a. (of games) drawn.

remise, f. delay ‖ remittance ‖ delivery ‖ coach-house ‖ (com.) deduction ‖ allowance ‖ voiture de ~, f. job-carriage ‖ fly.

remiser, v. a. to put in a coach-house.

rémission, f. remission, forgiveness.

remmailler, v. a. to mend by taking up stitches.

remmancher, v. a. to new-handle ‖ to resume ‖ to get on again with.

remmener, v. a. to take back.

remontage, m. new-footing ‖ winding-up.

remonte, f. remounts (pl.).

remonter, v. a. & n. to go up again, to get up again, to take up again ‖ to ascend again ‖ to new-foot ‖ to revive ‖ to cheer ‖ to trace one's origin ‖ faire ~, to carry up ‖ to trace up.

remontoir, m. keyless watch.

remontrance, f. remonstrance.

remontrer, v. a. to remonstrate ‖ to show again‖to demonstrate‖en ~ à quelqu'un, to teach one something he does not know.

remordre, v. a. to bite again.

remords, m. remorse.

remorque, f. (mar.) towing ‖ tow.

remorquer, v. a. (mar.) to tow.

remorqueur, m. (mar.) tug.

remoucher, v. a. to snuff a candle again‖ to wipe another's nose.

remoudre, v. a. ir. to grind again.

remouiller, v. a. & n. to wet again ‖ to anchor again.

rémoulade, f. (culin.) remoulade (sauce).

rémouleur, m. grinder.   [shoot.

remous, m. (mar.) eddy, dead water ‖

rempaillage, m. chair-mending.

rempailler, v. a. to new-bottom.

rempailleur, se, m. & f. chair-bottomer.

rempaqueter, v. a. to pack up again.

rempart, m. rampart, bulwark.

remplaçant, m. (mil.) substitute.

remplacement, m. replacing‖ finding of a substitute ‖ system of substitutes ‖ office de ~, m. office for providing substitutes ‖ en ~ de, in place of, vice.

remplacer, v. a. to replace ‖ to serve as a substitute, to succeed ‖ se faire ~, to get a substitute.

remplage, m. filling up of a wine-cask.

rempli, m. fold, tuck.   [tuck up.

remplier, v. a. to fold in, to turn in ‖ to

remplir, v. a. to fill again, to fill up, to complete ‖ to perform ‖ to answer.

remplissage, m. filling up, leakage ‖ mending of lace ‖ make-weight ‖ surplusage ‖ trash ‖ (mus.) middle parts ‖ (mar.) dead-wood.

remplumer, v. a. to new-feather ‖ se ~, to get new feathers ‖ to re-establish oneself ‖ to thrive.

rempocher, v. a. to pocket up again.

rempoissonnement, m. fresh stocking of a pond with fish.   [fish.

rempoissonner, v. a. to stock again with

remporter, v. a. to carry back, to carry, to get, to obtain.

rempoter, v. a. to pot again.

remprunter, v. a. to borrow again.

remuage, m. stirring.   [busy.

remuant, e, a. stirring, fidgety ‖ restless ‖

remue-ménage, m. moving of household goods, rummage ‖ confusion.

remuement, m. motion ‖ removing ‖ stirring, trouble, disturbance.

remuer, v. a. & n. to move, to stir, to shake ‖ to affect, to work up ‖ se ~, to move, to stir oneself, to bestir oneself.

rémunérateur, trice, m. & f. rewarder.

rémunérateur, trice, a. remunerative.

rémunérer, v. a. to remunerate, to reward.

renâcler, v. n. to snort.

renaissance, f. regeneration ‖ revival (of Letters and Arts in the 15th and 16th century).

renaître, v. n. ir. to be born again, to come to life again, to revive ‖ to appear again, to spring up again.

rénal, e, a. (an.) renal ‖ emulgent.

renard, m. fox ‖ (fig.) cunning fellow.

renarde, f. she-fox, vixen ‖ (fig.) vixen.

renardeau, m. fox's cub.

renardier, m. fox-catcher.

renardière, f. fox's hole.

rencaisser, v. a. to put into a chest again.

renchérir, v. a. & n. to increase in value ‖ to grow dearer.

renchérissement, m. rise in price.

rencogner, v. a. to drive into a corner.

rencontre, f. accidental meeting, encounter, rencounter || engagement || occasion, opportunity || collision || de ~, second-hand || faire la ~ de, to meet.

rencontrer, v. a. & n. to meet, to meet with, to find || to guess, to hit, to make a hit || se ~, to meet together, to agree.

rendement, m. yield, produce.

se rendetter, to run into debt again.

rendez-vous, m. rendezvous, appointed meeting || place appointed to meet at.

rendormir, v. a. ir. to lull to sleep again || se ~, to fall asleep again.   [fold up.

redoubler, v. a. to turn in ou down || to

rendre, v. a. & n. to render, to restore, to give back, to return || to reward || to vomit || to give up, to deliver, to produce, to represent || to translate || to turn (of sounds) || se ~, to render oneself, to make oneself || to become, to turn || to go || to submit, to surrender, to yield.

rendu, m. return || un prêté pour un ~, tit for tat, a Roland for an Oliver.

rendu, a. rendered, exhausted, worn out.

rendurcir, v. a. to harden.

rêne, f. rein.

renégat, e, m. & f. renegade.

reneiger, v. n. to snow again.

renfaîter, v. a. to new-roof.

renfermé, m. mustiness.

renfermer, v. a. to shut up, to confine, to include, to contain, to comprehend || se ~, to shut oneself up, to confine oneself || se ~ en soi, to recollect oneself, to meditate with oneself.

renfiler, v. a. to thread again.

renflé, é, a. swollen, risen.

renflement, m. swelling.

renfler, v. n. to swell again.   [again.

renflouer, renfluer, v. a. to set afloat

renfoncement, m. deepening, hollow || distant prospect || bruise.

renfoncer, v. a. to plunge deeper || to put a new head (to a cask) || to indent.

renforcé, e, a. regular, downright.

renforcement, m. strengthening || reinforcement.   [to increase || to raise.

renforcer, v. a. to reinforce, to strengthen ||

renfort, m. reinforcement, recruit, supply || de ~, extra.   [again, to pawn again.

rengager, v. a. to re-engage, to enlist

rengaîner, v. a. to sheathe, to put up.

rengorgement, m. high demeanour || bridling up.   [hand || to bridle up.

se rengorger, to carry it with a high

rengraisser, v. a. & n. to fatten again || to grow fat again.

reniement, m. denial.

renier, v. a. to deny, to disown, to abjure.

reniflement, m. sniffing.

renifler, v. n. to snuffle, to snivel.

renifleur, se, m. & f. sniffer.

renne, f. reindeer.

renom, m. renown, fame.

renommé, e, a. renowned, famous.

renommée, f. fame, reputation, name, celebrity.

renommer, v. a. to name again || to make famous, to renown.

renonce, f. revoke || want of a suit (at cards).   [denial.

renoncement, m. renunciation || self-

renoncer, v. n. to renounce, to give up.

renonciation, f. renunciation, resignation.

renoncule, f. (bot.) ranunculus || crow-foot.

renouer, v. a. to tie again || to resume || to renew.

renoueur, m. bone-setter.   [to renew.

renouveau, m. springtime.

renouveler, v. a. to renew, to make anew || to refresh, to revive.   [revival.

renouvellement, m. renewal, renovation ||

rénovateur, m. renovator.

rénovateur, trice, a. renovating.

rénovation, f. renovation || renewal.

renseignement, m. information, intelligence, inquiry || reference.

renseigner, v. a. to inform.

rente, f. rent, yearly income, revenue || ~ viagère, life-annuity || ~ foncière, ground-rent.

renter, v. a. to endow with an income.

rentier, ière, m. & f. fund-holder || person of independent means.

rentoiler, v. a. to fit with new linen || to new-canvass.

rentraire, v. a. ir. to finedraw, to darn.

rentraiture, f. finedrawing, darning.

rentrayeur, se, m. & f. finedrawer, darner.

rentré, e, a. (méd.) suppressed.

rentrée, f. re-entrance || re-opening, re-appearance || return of cash || housing.

rentrer, v. a. & n. to put in, to bring in, to get in || to re-enter, to enter again, to go in again, to return to || to buy in (at cards) || (méd.) to be suppressed.

renverse, ad.; à la ~, backwards, upon one's back.

renversement, m. overturning, overthrowing, overthrow, inversion, destruction, ruin.

renverser, v. a. to overthrow, to pull down, to turn upside down || to subvert, to ruin || se ~, to throw oneself backwards || to fall back, to fall down || (mil.) to be thrown into confusion.

renvider, v. a. to wind up, to cop.

renvoi, m. sending back, dismissal || reference (in a book) || rising of the stomach.

renvoyer, v. a. to send again, to send back || to return || to dismiss || to refer || to acquit || to put off || to reverberate.

réorganiser, v. a. to reorganise.

réouverture, f. re-opening.

repaire, m. haunt || den (of a wild beast).

repaître, v. a. & n. ir. to feed, to take food, to bait || se ~, to feed on, to delight in.

répandre, v. a. to spread, to spill, to shed, to diffuse, to scatter || to shed blood || ~ des aumônes, to bestow alms || ~ de l'argent, to distribute money || se ~, to be shed, to be scattered, to overspread || se ~ en invectives ou en louanges, to launch forth in abuse ou praise.

répandu, e, a. spread, spilled, shed || in society || in request || fashionable.

reparaître, v. n. ir. to reappear, to show oneself again.

réparateur, trice, m. & f. repairer, restorer, redresser, mender.

réparateur, trice, a. reparative.

réparation, f. reparation, repairing ‖ amends, satisfaction ‖ en ~, under repair.

réparer, v. a. to repair, to restore ‖ to mend, to redeem ‖ to recover ‖ to retrieve ‖ to make amends for.

repartie, f. repartee, reply.

repartir, v. a. to reply, to answer ‖ to set out again. [to assess.

répartir, v. a. to divide, to distribute ‖

répartiteur, m. assessor (of taxes).

répartition, f. repartition, division ‖ assessment.

repas, m. repast, meal ‖ entertainment.

repassage, m. repassing ‖ ironing ‖ grinding ‖ dressing.

repasser, v. a. & n. to repass, to pass again ‖ to call again ‖ to dress again ‖ to iron (linen) ‖ to grind ‖ to strop ‖ to polish. [linen.

repasseur, se, m. & f. grinder ‖ ironer of

repaver, v. a. to new-pave.

repayer, v. a. to pay a second time.

repêcher, v. a. to fish up again ‖ to take out of the water.

repeindre, v. a. ir. to paint again.

repenser, v. n. to think of again.

repentant, e, a. repentant, penitent.

repentir, m. repentance.

se repentir, to repent, to rue.

répercuter, v. a. to repel, to drive back ‖

reperdre, v. a. to lose again. [to reflect.

repère, m. bench-mark ‖ point de ~, m. point of reference. [table, list, catalogue.

répertoire, f. repertory ‖ stock of plays ‖

repeser, v. a. to weigh again.

répétailler, v. a. to make tedious repetitions. [rehearse.

répéter, v. a. to repeat ‖ to reflect ‖ to

répétiteur, m. tutor ‖ private teacher.

répétition, f. repetition, reiteration, rehearsal ‖ private tuition ‖ (jur.) claim.

repétrir, v. n. to knead ou form again.

repeuplement, m. re-peopling ‖ new-stocking. [(a pond).

repeupler, v. a. to re-people ‖ to new-stock

repic, m. repique (at piquet) ‖ faire qn. ~, to nonplus one utterly.

repiquage, m. re-pitching, re-paving ‖ (hort.) pricking out.

répit, m. respite, delay ‖ rest.

replacer, v. a. to replace ‖ to reinvest.

replaider, v. n. to plead again.

replanchéier, v. a. to new-floor.

replanter, v. a. to replant.

replâtrage, m. re-plastering ‖ botching up ‖ palliation. [up ‖ to palliate.

replâtrer, v. a. to new-plaster ‖ to botch

replet, ète, a. plump, fat.

repleuvoir, v. n. ir. to rain again.

repli, m. fold ‖ plait ‖ coil ‖ recess.

replier, v. a. to fold again, to tuck, to wind, to twist ‖ se ~, to wind oneself round, to fold oneself ‖ (mil.) to fall back.

réplique, f. reply, answer, repartee, rejoinder.

répliquer, v. a. & n. to reply, to answer.

replisser, v. a. to plait again.

replonger, v. a. to plunge again.

repolir, v. a. to polish again.

répondant, m. (jur.) bail, security ‖ respondent ‖ lay clerk (in the church).

repondre, v. a. & n. to lay again.

répondre, v. a. & n. to answer, to reply ‖ to correspond ‖ to be answerable for, to be security for.

répons, m. response.

réponse, f. answer, reply.

report, m. (com.) carrying over ‖ sum brought over. [over ‖ to repeat.

reporter, v. a. to carry back, to carry

repos, m. rest, repose, quiet, tranquillity ‖ landing-place (in a staircase) ‖ au ~, at half-cock ‖ sitting ‖ en ~, at rest ‖ quiet(ly) ‖ alone.

reposé, e, a. refreshed, sedate ‖ à tête —e, with a quiet mind.

reposée, f. lair of a wild beast.

reposer, v. a. & n. to place again, to settle ‖ to rest, to take rest, to sleep ‖ to be still, to lie still, to lie as a corpse ‖ se ~, to repose, to rest, to sleep ‖ to rely, to trust ‖ to settle ‖ to cool.

reposoir, m. resting-place ‖ altar set up in the streets for a procession.

repoussant, e, a. repulsive, forbidding.

repoussement, m. recoil (of fire-arms).

repousser, v. a. to repulse, to repel, to drive back, to rebuff ‖ to recoil ‖ to bud again, to shoot again.

repoussoir, m. setting off ‖ contrast.

répréhensible, a. reprehensible.

reprendre, v. a. & n. ir. to retake, to take again ‖ to recover ‖ to resume, to begin again ‖ to blame, to reprimand, to find fault with, to criticise ‖ to answer, to reply ‖ to sew a rent ‖ to return ‖ se ~, to close again ‖ to recollect oneself ‖ to correct one's mistake. [tion.

représailles, f. pl. reprisals (pl.), retalia-

représentant, e, m. & f. representative.

représentatif, ve, a. representative.

représentation, f. representation, performance ‖ image, likeness ‖ exhibition ‖ maintenance of the dignity of one's station ‖ look, air ‖ official entertainment ‖ portly mien ‖ acting of a play.

représenter, v. a. & n. to represent, to describe, to show, to exhibit, to produce, to bring forth ‖ to act a play ‖ to remonstrate, to put in mind ‖ se ~, to present oneself again ‖ to call to one's mind.

répressif, ve, a. repressive.

reprêter, v. a. to lend again.

réprimande, f. reprimand.

réprimander, v. a. to reprimand, to reprove. [to put down.

réprimer, v. a. to repress, to restrain ‖

reprise, f. retaking ‖ recommencing, renewing ‖ darning ‖ reproduction (of a play) ‖ burden (of a song) ‖ ship retaken ‖ —s perdues, pl. fine-drawing ‖ à plusieurs —s, at different times ‖ by starts.

repriser, v. a. to darn.

réprobateur, trice, m. & f. reprover.

réprobateur, trice, a. reprobatory, reproving.

reproche, m. reproach, shame, infamy || (jur.) objection, exception || sans ~, blameless.

reprocher, v. a. to reproach, to upbraid, to rebuke, to taunt || (jur.) to object.

reproducteur, trice, reproductif, ve, a. reproductive.

reproductibilité, f. reproducibility.

reproduire, v. a. ir. to reproduce || se ~, to come again, to reappear.

réprouvé, e, m. & f. reprobate.

réprouver, v. a. to reprobate || to disapprove of.

reptation, f. reptation, creeping.

reptile, m. reptile.

repu, a. full, surfeited, glutted.

républicain, e, m. & f. republican.

républicain, e, a. republican.

républicaniser, v. a. to republicanise.

républicanisme, m. republicanism.

republier, v. a. to republish.

république, f. republic || commonwealth.

répudier, v. n. to repudiate.

répugnance, f. repugnance, reluctance, dislike.   [contrary.

répugnant, e, a. repugnant || opposite,

répugner, v. n. to be repugnant || to feel reluctant.

répulsion, f. repulsion, aversion.

repurger, v. a. to purge again.

réputation, f. reputation, repute, name, fame || character.

réputer, v. a. to repute, to hold, to account.

requérant, e, m. & f. (jur.) suitor, plaintiff, petitioner.   [to demand.

requérir, v. a. ir. to require, to request,

requête, f. request, petition.

requin, m. shark.   [up.

se requinquer, v. (fam.) to spruce oneself

requis, e, a. requisite, required || due.

réquisitoire, m. (jur.) public prosecutor's address to the Court.

resceller, v. a. to seal again.

rescousse, f. rescue.

rescrit, m. rescript.

réseau, m. net-work, bag-net.

réséda, m. (bot.) mignonette.

réserve, f. reserve, reservation || limitation, exception || modesty || de ~, spare || en ~, in reserve, in store || on the retired list || à la ~ de, excepting, except || se tenir sur la ~, to be on one's guard.

réservé, e, a. reserved, cautious, coy || modest.

réserver, v. a. to reserve, to lay by, to keep in store, to save.

réservoir, m. reservoir, fish-pond || steam-chest.

résidant, e, a. resident, dwelling.

résidence, f. residence, dwelling, resident-

résident, m. resident.   [ship.

résider, v. n. to reside, to live.

résidu, m. sediment, residue || remainder.

résignataire, m. resignee.

resigner, v. a. to sign again.

résigner, v. a. to resign || se ~, to resign oneself, to submit || to put up with it.

résiliation, f. (jur.) cancelling.

résilier, v. a. to cancel.

résille, f. hair-net.

résine, f. rosin, resin.

résineux, se, a. resinous.

résipiscence, f. repentance.

résistance, f. resistance, opposition.

résister, v. n. to resist, to oppose, to withstand.   [minate, bold.

résolu, e, a. resolute, determined, deter-

résoluble, a. resolvable.

résolûment, ad. resolutely.

résolution, f. resolution, determination, firmness || solution || (jur.) annulment.

résonnant, e, a. resonant, sonorous.

résonnement, m. resounding.

résonner, v. n. to resound.

résoudre, v. a. ir. to resolve, to determine, to decree, to conclude || to dissolve || to cancel, to annul || se ~, to be dissolved, to turn to, to be reduced to.

respect, m. respect, reverence || ~ humain, worldly fear, regard for public opinion.

respecter, v. a. to respect, to reverence || to spare.

respectif, ve, a. (~vement, ad.) respective(ly).   [spectful(ly).

respectueux, se, a. (~sement, ad.) re-

respiration, f. respiration, breathing.

respirer, v. a. & n. to breathe || to inhale || ~ après, to long for.

resplendir, v. n. to shine with effulgence.

resplendissant, e, a. resplendent.

resplendissement, m. resplendence.

responsabilité, f. responsibility.

responsable, a. responsible, answerable, accountable.

ressac, m. (mar.) surf.

ressaigner, v. a. & n. to bleed again.

ressaisir, v. a. to seize again || se ~ de, to seize upon again, to take possession of again.   [examine minutely.

ressasser, v. a. to sift again || (fig.) to

ressaut, m. jutting out.

ressauter, v. a. & n. to leap again || (arch.) to project, to jut out.

ressécher, v. a. to dry again.

resseller, v. a. to saddle again.

ressemblance, f. resemblance, likeness.

ressemblant, e, a. resembling, like.

ressembler, v. n. to resemble || se ~, to be like each other.

ressemelage, m. new-soling.

ressemeler, v. a. to new-sole.

ressemer, v. a. to sow again.

ressentiment, m. resentment, feeling || slight return.

ressentir, v. a. to resent, to feel || se ~, to feel, to be affected by || to suffer for.

resserrement, m. tightening, stoppage, obstruction || (de cœur) great heaviness of heart || scarcity.

resserrer, v. a. to tie again, to make tighter, to shut up closer, to compress || to constipate || to restrain, to confine || se ~, to contract itself || to confine oneself || to become closer ou tighter.

ressort, m. spring, elasticity || (fig.) cause, means || jurisdiction || department, province.   [to set off.

ressortir, v. n. to go out again || faire ~,

ressortir, v. n. (jur.) to be under the jurisdiction of.

ressortissant, e, a. (jur.) appealable.

resouder, v. a. to new-solder, to solder again.

ressource, f. resource, shift, expedient.

ressouvenir, m. remembrance, recollection, memory.

se ressouvenir, v. r. ir. to remember, to recollect || faire ~, to remind.

ressuer, v. n. to perspire again, to sweat.

ressui, m. lair of a deer.

ressusciter, v. a. & n. to resuscitate, to raise, to raise ou rise from the dead.

ressuyer, v. a. to wipe again || to dry again.

restant, m. remainder, rest.   [again.

restant, e, a. left, remaining || poste -e, f. "to be left till called for".

restaurant, m. restorative || eating-house.

restaurant, e, a. restorative.

restaurateur, m. restorer || eating-house keeper.   ; [ment || revival.

restauration, f. restoration, re-establishment.

restaurer, v. a. to restore, to retrieve, to revive || se ~, to recover one's strength, to take refreshment.

reste, m. rest, residue, remnant, remainder || relic || au ~, du ~, besides, as for the rest, nevertheless.

rester, v. n. to remain, to be left, to stay, to lodge, to stay behind.

restituable, a. restorable, repayable.

restituer, v. a. to restore, to give back, to re-instate.

restituteur, m. restorer (of passages).

restitution, f. restitution, giving back again.

restreindre, v. a. ir. to restrain, to restrict, to limit, to confine || to stint.

restrictif, ve, a. restrictive.

restriction, f. restriction, limitation || reservation.

résultat, m. result.   [pear.

résulter, v. n. to result || to follow || to appear.

résumé, m. summary, recapitulation || summing up || charge || au ~, en ~, on the whole, after all.

résumer, v. a. to sum up, to recapitulate.

résurrection, f. resurrection.

rétable, m. altar-piece || altar-screen.

rétablir, v. a. to re-establish, to restore, to re-instate || to recover (one's health).

rétablissement, m. re-establishing, restoration || recovery.

retailler, v. a. to cut again || to mend.

retaper, v. a. to comb (hair) the wrong way || to do up (a hat) || to curl (a wig).

retard, m. retardment, delay, stop, hindrance || en ~, backward || too slow || in arrears.

retardataire, m. laggart, one in arrears.

retardataire, a. late, behind time || in arrears.

retardement, m. delay.   [arrears

retarder, v. a. & n. to retard, to delay, to put off || to hinder || to go too slow.

reteindre, v. a. ir. to dye again.

retendre, v. a. to stretch again.

retenir, v. a. ir. to retain, to detain, to keep back, to withhold || to deduct || to prevent, to keep from, to hinder || to bespeak || to remember || se ~, to restrain oneself, to refrain from, to forbear.

retenter, v. a. to reattempt.

rétention, f. retention, reservation, retaining.   [echo.

retentir, v. n. to resound, to ring, to re-

retentissement, m. resounding || echo || report (of a gun) || avoir du ~, to make a noise.   [modest || engaged.

retenu, e, a. retained || cautious || discreet,

retenue, f. discretion, caution, circumspection || moderation, modesty || withholding || stoppage (of payment) || deduction.

réticence, f. concealment, omission.

rétif, ve, a. restive.

rétine, f. retina.

retiré, e, a. retired, solitary, lonesome.

retirement, m. contraction.   ↄ

retirer, v. a. to draw again, to pull again || to draw out || to reap, to get, to obtain, to redeem || to harbour || to shoot again, to fire again || se ~, to retire, to withdraw from, to draw back || to retreat.

retomber, v. n. to fall again || to relapse.

retordre, v. a. to twist again || to twist.

rétorquer, v. a. to retort.

retors, e, a. twisted || cunning || (fig. & fam.) artful, cunning.

rétorsion, f. retorsion.

retouche, f. retouching, touching up.

retoucher, v. a. to retouch.

retour, m. return || coming back || winding || vicissitude || conversion || decline || difference || artifice || reversion || repayment || de ~, on one's return || returned || back || to boot || up || sans ~, for ever || irretrievably || ~ sur soi-même, reflection on one's own conduct.

retourne, f. turned-up card, trump.

retourner, v. a. & n. to turn, to turn up, to return, to go back, to come back || to revert || se ~, to turn round, to turn oneself || to look behind.

retracer, v. a. to retrace, to draw again || se ~, to remember || to recur.

rétracter, v. a. to retract, to recant, to call back || se ~, to retract, to recant.

retraire, v. a. ir. (jur.) to redeem (an estate).

retrait, m. (jur.) redeeming, redemption || [shrinkage.

retraite, f. retreat, retiring || refuge, shelter, sanctuary || den (of thieves) || contraction || superannuation || caisse de ~, f. superannuation fund.   [off.

retraiter, v. a. to treat again || to pension

retranchement, m. retrenchment || abridging || (mil.) intreuchment.

retrancher, v. a. to retrench, to cut off, to curtail, to abridge || to forbid || se ~, to restrain oneself, to confine oneself || to curtail ou diminish one's expenses || (mil.) to intrench oneself.

retravailler, v. a. to work again.

retraverser, v. a. to cross again.

rétréci, e, a. narrow ǁ shrunk.

rétrécir, v. a. & n. to straighten, to make narrower, to contract ǁ to shrink.

rétrécissement, m. narrowing, shrinking, contracting ǁ stricture.

retremper, v. a. to soak again, to temper again ǁ se ~, to recruit one's strength.

rétribuer, v. a. to remunerate.

rétribution, f. retribution, recompense, reward.   [active(ly).

rétroactif, ve, a. (-vement, ad.) retro-

rétrograder, v. a. to go backward.

rétrospectif, ve, a. (-vement, ad.) retrospective(ly).

retroussement, m. tucking up again.

retrousser, v. a. to turn up, to tuck up, to cock up.

retroussis, m. flap (of a hat) ǁ boot-top.

retrouver, v. a. to find again, to refind, to recover ǁ to retrieve ǁ to return again to ǁ se ~, to find one another ǁ to be found ǁ to be oneself again.

rets, m. net, netting.

réunion, f. reunion, reconciliation, junction ǁ meeting, assembly.

réunir, v. a. to reunite, to join again ǁ to reconcile, to combine ǁ se ~, to rejoin, to assemble, to meet ǁ to become friends again ǁ to be agreed, to agree.

réussir, v. n. to have good success, to thrive.

réussite, f. success, issue.

revaloir, v. n. ir. to return like for like.

revanche, f. revenge ǁ turn ǁ retaliation ǁ revenge (at cards).

rêvasser, v. n. to have unquiet dreams.

rêvasserie, f. agitating ou broken dream.

rêvasseur, m. dreamer.

rêve, m. dream.   [cross.

revêche, a. harsh, sharp, untractable ǁ

réveil, m. awaking ǁ alarum ǁ (mil.) morning-call.

réveille-matin, m. alarm-clock ǁ alarm-bell ǁ chanticleer, cock.

réveiller, v. a. to wake, to awaken, to arouse from sleep ǁ to revive.

réveillon, m. midnight revel.

révélateur, m. revealer, discoverer.

révélation, f. revelation ǁ discovery ǁ information.   [close.

révéler, v. a. to reveal, to discover, to dis-

revenant, m. ghost, apparition.

revenant, e, a. pleasing, taking ǁ ~-bon, m. (fam.) neat profit, emolument.

revendeur, se, m. & f. huckster, higgler ǁ -se à la toilette, old clothes woman.

revendication, f. claiming.

revendiquer, v. a. to claim.

revendre, v. a. to sell again ǁ to spare ǁ en ~ à, to outwit.

revenir, v. n. ir. to come again, to come back, to return ǁ to recover ǁ to be like, to come to, to amount to ǁ to take a dislike to ǁ to match, to suit ǁ to arise, to result.

revente, f. re-sale.

revenu, m. revenue, income.

revenue, f. young wood (of a coppice).

rêver, v. a. & n. to dream, to rave ǁ to be delirious ǁ to muse, to think of, to ruminate, to consider.

réverbère, m. reflector ǁ street-lamp.

réverbérer, v. a. to reverberate.

reverdir, v. a. & n. to paint green again ǁ to grow green again.

révérence, f. reverence, bow, curtsey.

révérencieux, se, a. (-sement, ad.) reverential(ly) ǁ always bowing.

révérend, e, a. reverend.

révérendissime, a. most reverend.

révérer, v. a. to revere, to reverence.

rêverie, f. musing ǁ dream ǁ delirium.

revernir, v. a. to varnish over again.

revers, m. back ǁ wrong side ǁ back-stroke ǁ counter-part ǁ reverse ǁ facing ǁ ~ de la médaille, dark side of the picture.

reverser, v. a. to pour again ǁ (mar.) to tranship.   [mainder.

reversibilité, f. (jur.) reversion ǁ re-

reversible, a. (jur.) revertible.

revêtement, m. covering ǁ lining.

revêtir, v. a. to clothe, to coat, to dress ǁ to invest ǁ to bestow ǁ to line, to face.

rêveur, m. dreamer.

rêveur, se, a. thoughtful ǁ pensive.

revient, m. (com.) net cost.

revirement, m. sudden change ǁ (mar.) tacking ǁ (com.) transfer.

revirer, v. n. (mar.) to tack about.

réviser, v. a. to revise, to review ǁ to correct.

réviseur, m. reviser.   [rect.

révision, f. revisal, revision, review.

revisiter, v. a. to revisit.

revivifier, v. a. to revive.

revivre, v. n. ir. to revive, to come to life again.

révocabilité, f. revocableness.

révocation, f. revocation, repeal.

revoici, ad. here again ǁ once more ǁ behold again!

revoilà, ad. there again.   [hold again!

revoir, m. next meeting ǁ au ~, good-bye till our next meeting ou for the present.

revoir, v. a. ir. to see again ǁ to revise, to review, to re-examine, to correct.

revoler, v. n. to fly again, to fly back.

révolte, f. revolt, rebellion.

révolté, m. rebel.

révolter, v. a. to cause to revolt ou rebel, to stir up against, to excite indignation ǁ to offend, to shock, to startle ǁ se ~, to revolt, to mutiny.   [plished.

révolu, e, a. revolved, finished, accom-

révolution, f. revolution ǁ total change.

révolutionnaire, m. revolutionist.

révolutionnaire, a. revolutionary.

révolutionner, v. a. to revolutionise ǁ to upset.   [throw back.

revomir, v. a. to vomit, to throw up, to

révoquer, v. a. to revoke, to recall, to repeal.   [to review, to muster.

revue, f. review, survey ǁ passer en ~,

révulsif, m. (méd.) counter-irritant.

révulsif, a. (méd.) counter-irritant.

révulsion, f. (méd.) counter-irritation.

rez-de-chaussée, m. ground-floor.

rhabillage, m. mending ǁ botching.

rhabiller, v. a. to clothe anew, to dress again ǁ to mend.

rhéteur, rhétoricien, m. rhetorician.

rhétorique, f. rhetoric.

rhubarbe, f. (bot.) rhubarb.

rhum, m. rum.

rhumatique, a. rheumatic.

rhumatismal, e, a. (méd.) rheumatic.

rhumatisme, m. (méd.) rheumatism.

rhume, m. cold || ~ de cerveau, cold in the head. [the head.

rhythme, m. rhythm.

rhythmique, a. rhythmical.

riant, e, a. laughing, smiling, cheerful || pleasing. [pleasing.

ribambelle, f. long string.

ribaud, m. ribald.

ribaud, e, a. lecherous, lewd.

ribote, f. revelling || être en ~, to be boozy.

riboter, v. a. to booze, to revel.

riboteur, m. reveller.

ricanement, m. sneering, sneer.

ricaner, v. n. to sneer, to titter.

ricanerie, f. sneer.

ricaneur, se, m. & f. sneerer, giggler.

ric-à-ric, ad. exactly, neither more nor less. [less.

richard, m. moneyed man.

riche, m. rich man || les ~s, pl. the rich (pl.).

riche, a. rich, wealthy || fertile, copious, abundant || langue ~, f. fertile language.

richement, ad. richly, splendidly.

richesse, f. riches (pl.), richness, wealth || copiousness, abundance.

ricin, m. (bot.) castor-oil plant.

ricocher, v. n. to rebound.

ricochet, m. rebound || duck and drake || par ~, indirectly.

ride, f. wrinkle || ripple.

rideau, m. curtain || veil || screen || blower.

rider, v. a. to wrinkle, to shrivel || to ripple.

ridicule, m. ridiculousness || ridiculous thing.

ridicule, a. (-ment, ad.) ridiculous(ly) || ridicule.

ridiculiser, v. a. to ridicule.

rien, m. nothing, nought, anything.

rien, ad. nothing, nought, anything || pour ~, for nothing, gratis || ~ que, only || alone || en moins de ~, in the twinkling of an eye. [eye.

riour, m. laugher || jeerer, banterer.

rieur, se, a. laughing || mocking.

riflard, m. jack-plane || old umbrella.

rigide, a. (-ment, ad.) rigid(ly) || strict(ly) || harsh(ly). [harshness.

rigidité, f. rigidity, stiffness, severity ||

rigole, f. trench, drain, gutter.

rigoleur, m. jolly fellow, boon companion.

rigorisme, m. austerity || strictness || puritanism.

rigoriste, m. rigid moralist.

rigoriste, a. over-rigid.

rigoureux, se, a. (-sement, ad.) rigorous(ly) || severe(ly) || stern(ly) || harsh(ly).

rigueur, f. rigour, severity, harshness, hardness, precision || à la ~, rigorously, strictly. [strictly.

rillettes, f. pl. minced pork.

rimaille, f. paltry verses.

rimailler, v. n. to make paltry verses.

rimailleur, m. rhymster, poetaster.

rime, f. rhyme, verse.

rimer, v. a. & n. to rhyme.

rimeur, m. rhymer.

rinçage, m. rinsing.

rinceau, m. foliage.

rince-bouche, m. finger-glass.

rincée, f. whacking, dressing, blowing up.

rincer, v. a. to rinse, to wash.

rinçure, f. slops (pl.).

ringard, m. fire-iron || paddle || bar.

rioter, v. n. to giggle, to titter.

rioteur, se, m. & f. titterer.

ripaille, f. junketing || faire ~, to feast.

ripopée, f. medley, slop || slipslop.

riposte, f. repartee, keen reply || parry and thrust.

riposter, v. n. to repartee, to make a smart reply || to parry and thrust.

rire, m. laughing, laughter, smile || ~ moqueur, sneer.

rire, v. n. ir. to laugh, to smile, to jest || éclater de ~, to burst out laughing || crever de ~, to split one's sides with laughing || ~ dans sa barbe, ~ sous cape, to laugh in one's sleeve || ~ à gorge déployée, to laugh immoderately.

ris, m. laugh, smile, laughter || (mar.) reef || ~ de veau, sweetbread.

risée, f. laughter, laughing || mockery, laughing-stock || (nav.) gust.

risette, f. pretty laugh.

risible, a. risible, laughable. [risked.

risquable, a. hazardous || that may be

risque, m. risk, hazard || peril.

risquer, v. a. to risk, to hazard, to venture, to stake. [to stake.

rissole, f. (culin.) rissole.

rissolé, m. (culin.) outside, browned part, crackling.

rissoler, v. a. to roast brown.

rit, rite, m. rite, ceremonies (pl.).

ritournelle, f. (mus.) ritornello, flourish || burden of a song || tedious repetition.

rituel, m. ritual.

rivage, m. bank, shore.

rival, e, m. & f. rival, competitor.

rivaliser, v. n. to rival, to vie with.

rivalité, f. rivalry, competition.

rive, f. bank, shore.

river, v. a. to rivet, to clinch.

riverain, m. river-side || borderer.

riverain, e, a. river-side || border.

rivière, f. river || (of diamonds) stream.

rixe, f. scuffle || conflict.

riz, m. (bot.) rice.

rizière, f. rice-field.

rob, m. (méd.) extract || rubber (at cards).

robe, f. robe, gown || (of animals) coat || husk || peel || magistracy || ~ de chambre, morning-gown.

robin, m. limb of the law (lawyer).

robinet, m. spigot, cock, spout.

robuste, a. robust, strong, stout.

roc, m. rock || castle (at chess).

rocaille, f. rock-work.

rocailleur, m. grotto-maker.

rocailleux, se, a. rocky, stony, pebbly.

rocambole, f. a trite, foolish joke || (bot.) wild garlic.

roche, f. rock || quartz || (fig.) flint, steel || anguille sous ~, f. snake in the grass || de la vieille ~, of the old stock or stamp.

rocher, m. rock.

rochet, m. rochet || bobbin.
rocheux, se, a. rocky.
rococo, m. rococo.
rococo, a. old-fashioned || tasteless.
rôder, v. n. to rove, to roam, to ramble
rôdeur, m. rover, rambler. [about.
rodomont, m. bully, blusterer.
rodomontade, f. boasting.
rogations, f. pl. rogation.
rogatons, m. pl. scraps (pl.) || waste-paper.
Roger bontemps, m. jolly fellow.
rogne, f. mange, scab, scurf.
rogner, v. a. to cut, to pare, to clip, to
prune, to shred.
rogneur, se, m. clipper.
rogneux, se, a. mangy, scabby, scurvy.
rognon, m. kidney.
rognonner, v. n. to growl, to grumble.
rognure, f. clipping, paring || shreds (pl.).
rogomme, m. brandy, dram.
rogue, a. proud, haughty.
roi, m. king || ~ de la fève, Twelfth-night
king || jour des ~s, m. Twelfth-day.
roide, a. vide raide.
roitelet, m. petty king, kinglet || wren (bird).
rôle, m. roll, scroll, list || part, character
(in a play) || sheet of law-writing || à tour
de ~, in one's turn.
romain, m. Roman letter. [of Rome.
romain, e, a. Roman || église —e, f. Church
romaine, f. steelyard || (bot.) coss lettuce.
roman, m. romance, novel.
romance, f. romance || ballad.
romancier, m. novel-writer, novelist.
romanesque, a. romantic || —ment, ad.
in a romantic manner.
romantique, m. romantic style.
romantique, a. romantic, fanciful.
romantisme, m. romanticism.
romarin, m. (bot.) rosemary.
rompre, v. a. & n. to break, to break off,
to break through, to rend, to destroy, to
pull down, to ruin || to train up || to fall
out with || to break the thread of one's
discourse || à tout ~, at the most || fran-
tically. [berry-bush.
ronce, f. (bot.) bramble, briar || black-
ronceraie, f. place full of brambles.
rond, m. round, circle, sphere || ~ à pati-
ner, skating-rink || ~-point, m. place
where several streets meet, circus.
rond, e, a. round, spherical || even || coarse ||
plain-dealing || straight-forward.
ronde, f. (mil.) round, patrol || (mus.) semi-
breve || round hand || à la ~, round, round
rondeau, m. (poët.) roundelay. [about.
rondelet, te, a. plumpish.
rondelle, f. rundle, target.
rondement, ad. roundly, sincerely, frankly,
plainly || briskly, vigorously.
rondeur, f. roundness || rotundity || open-
ness, plain-dealing.
rondin, m. billet for fuel || cudgel.
ronflant, e, a. snoring || sonorous || high-
sounding.
ronflement, m. snoring, snore.
ronfler, v. n. to snore || to roar || to boom ||
to hum || to snort (of horses).
ronfleur, se, m. & f. snorer.

ronge-maille, m. nibbler.
ronger, v. a. to gnaw, to nibble, to pick,
to corrode, to eat || to torment || to ruin
|| ~ le frein, to champ the bit.
rongeur, m. rodent (animal).
rongeur, a. gnawing, biting || ver ~, re-
morse of conscience.
ronron, m. purring || faire ~, to purr.
roquefort, m. Roquefort cheese.
roquer, v. n. to castle (at chess).
roquet, m. pug-dog || puppy.
roquette, f. (bot.) rocket.
rosace, f. (arch.) rose || rose-work.
rosacé, e, a. (bot.) rosaceous.
rosaire, m. rosary.
rosat, a. roseate, of roses.
rosbif, m. roastbeef.
rose, f. (bot.) rose || rose-colour || rose-win-
dow || laurier ~, rose-laurel || ~ pompon,
wild rose || ~ trémière, rose-mallow,
hollyhock || ~ de compas, ~ des vents,
rosé, e, a. rosy, roseate. [compass-card.
roseau, m. (bot.) reed.
rosée, f. dew.
roselière, f. reed-bank. [bushes.
roseraie, f. ground planted with rose-
rosette, f. rosette, rose || red ink || red chalk.
rosier, m. (bot.) rose-tree.
rosière, f. winner of the rose (as the best-
behaved girl of her village).
rosse, f. jade, sorry horse.
rossée, f. thrashing.
rosser, v. a. to thrash.
rossignol, m. nightingale (bird) || pick-
lock || wedge || old shopkeeper.
rossinante, f. jade, hack.
rot, m. belch, belching.
rôt, m. roast-meat.
rotatoire, a. rotatory.
roter, v. n. to belch.
rôti, m. roast-meat. [toast.
rôtie, f. toast || ~ au beurre, buttered
rotin, m. rattan-cane. [to broil.
rôtir, v. a. & n. to roast, to burn, to bake,
rôtisserie, f. cook-shop.
rôtisseur, m. keeper of a cook-shop.
rôtissoire, f. roasting-screen.
rotonde, f. rotunda.
rotondité, f. rotundity || plumpness.
rotule, f. (an.) knee-pan.
roture, f. commonalty || plebeian state.
roturier, ère, m. & f. plebeian, commoner.
roturier, ère, a. plebeian, common.
rouage, m. wheel-work.
rouan, m. roan.
rouanne, f. branding-iron.
rouanner, v. a. to mark wine-casks.
roucoulement, m. cooing.
roucouler, v. n. to coo || ~, v. a. to warble
roue, f. wheel || truck. [out.
roué, m. rake, profligate.
roué, e, a. exhausted with fatigue.
rouelle, f. round slice || fillet of veal.
rouennerie, f. printed cottons (pl.).
rouer, v. a. to break on the wheel || ~ de
coups, to thrash soundly.
rouerie, f. trick of a profligate.
rouet, m. spinning-wheel || faire le ~, to
purr (of cats).

rouge, m. red colour || blush || red paint || red heat.

rouge, a. red || red-hot || **~-gorge,** m. robin-redbreast (bird).

rougeâtre, a. reddish.

rougeaud, e, a. ruddy, red-faced.

rougeole, f. (méd.) measles (pl.).

rouget, m. red mullet (fish) || wheat-worm || gurnet.

rougeur, f. redness, ruddiness || blush.

rougir, v. a. & n. to redden, to make red || to grow red || to blush || to be ashamed || to colour.

roui, m. fustiness.

rouille, f. rust || (bot.) blast, mildew.

rouiller, v. a. to rust, to blight || se ~, to grow rusty.

rouillure, f. rustiness.

rouir, v. a. to ret (hemp ou flax).

roulade, f. rolling || (mus.) quaver, trill.

roulage, m. rolling || land-carriage || transport || maison de ~, f., bureau de ~, m. waggon-office.

roulant, e, a. rolling || (mil.) feu ~, m. running fire.

rouleau, m. roll || roller, rolling-pin || coil || au bout de son ~, at the end of one's tether.

roulée, f. thrashing, whacking.

roulement, m. rolling || rotation || (mus.) trill, quaver.

rouler, v. a. & n. to roll, to roll up || to roll upon wheels || to turn || to thrash, to whack || to ramble.

roulette, f. small wheel || hand-chaise || truckle-bed || caster || ~ d'enfant, go-cart.

roulier, m. waggoner, carter.

roulis, m. (mar.) rolling of a ship.

roupie, f. rupee (coin) || snivel.

roupiller, v. n. to doze.

roupilleur, se, m. & f. dozing person.

roussâtre, a. reddish.

rousseau, m. red-haired man.

rousselet, m. russet (pear).

rousseur, f. reddishness, redness || -s, pl. freckles (pl.).

roussi, m. smell of burning || Russia-leather.

roussin, m. thick-set stallion || ~ d'Arcadie, ass.

roussir, v. a. & n. to make look red, to redden || to grow red || faire ~, to brown.

route, f. route, road, way || track, course of a ship || grande ~, high road || en ~, on one's way ou journey || go on! || faire ~, to travel.

routier, m. stager || road-book.

routier, ère, a. of roads || carte -ère, f. road-map.

routine, f. routine, rote, practice || par ~, by rote.

routinier, m. person acting by routine.

routoir, m. retting-pond.

rouverin, a. m. brittle (of iron).

rouvieux, m. mange.

rouvieux, se, a. mangy.

rouvre, m. (bot.) holm-oak.

rouvrir, v. a. to open again, to reopen.

roux, m. (bot.) sumac.

roux, sse, a. reddish brown, red-haired.

royal, e, a. (-ement, ad.) royal(ly) || regal(ly) || kingly, princely.

royalisme, m. royalism.

royaliste, m. royalist.

royaume, m. kingdom, realm.

royauté, f. royalty.

ru, m. irrigation channel.

ruade, f. kicking, jerking.

ruban, m. ribbon, riband || canon à ~, m. twisted barrel.

rubanerie, f. riband-weaving, riband-trade || ribbons (pl.), finery.

rubanier, m. riband-weaver, riband-seller.

rubéfaction, f. (méd.) rubification.

rubicond, e, a. rubicund.

rubis, m. ruby || jewel.

rubrique, f. rubric || red chalk || trick.

ruche, f. bee-hive || quilling.

ruchée, f. hiveful.

rucher, m. apiary, stand for bees.

rude, a. rough, rugged, hard, severe, sharp || uneven || morose, painful || -ment, ad. roughly, rudely, harshly, sharply, severely, violently.

rudesse, f. rudeness, roughness, harshness, ruggedness.

rudiment, m. rudiment.

rudimentaire, a. rudimentary, elementary.

rudoyer, v. a. to use roughly.

rue, f. street, lane || (bot.) rue.

ruelle, f. narrow lane || bed-side.

ruer, v. n. to kick || se ~ (sur), to rush upon.

rugir, v. n. to roar, to bellow.

rugissement, m. roar, bellowing.

rugosité, f. rugosity, wrinkle.

rugueux, se, a. wrinkled.

ruine, f. ruin, fall, overthrow, decay.

ruiner, v. a. to ruin, to destroy, to demolish, to lay waste || to impoverish || to undo.

ruineux, se, a. ruinous.

ruisseau, m. stream, brook, rivulet || gutter.

ruisseler, v. n. to stream, to gush out.

rumeur, f. rumour, uproar, noise || alarm, report.

ruminant, e, a. ruminating, chewing the cud.

ruminer, v. a. to ruminate || to muse on.

rupture, f. rupture, breaking || bursting, falling out || hernia.

rural, e, a. rural.

ruse, f. ruse, cunning, artifice, trick || stratagem.

rusé, e, a. sly, cunning, crafty, sharp, subtle.

ruser, v. n. to dodge, to use shifts, to play shifting tricks.

rustaud, m. clown, churl.

rustand, e, a. clownish, boorish.

rusticité, f. rusticity, churlishness.

rustique, m. rustic, clown.

rustique, a. (-ment, ad.) rustic(ally) || rural || clownish(ly) || rude(ly).

rustiquer, v. a. to jag out, to rough-cast.

rustre, m. clown, churl, boor.

rustre, a. clownish, boorish.

rut, m. rut.

rutilant, a. shining red, brilliantly red.

S.

sa, pn. f. his, her, its || one's.

sabbat, m. Sabbath || fearful noise || nocturnal meeting || witches' work || row, dust || caterwauling || scolding.

sabéisme, m. Sabeism, Sabianism.

sable, m. sand || gravel || hour-glass.
sabler, v. a. to gravel, to sand || to toss
sableux, se, a. sandy.   [off, to quaff.
sablier, m. hour-glass || egg-glass || sand-
box.   [plate.
sablière, f. sand-pit, gravel-pit || wall-
sablon, m. fine *ou* small sand.
sablonner, v. a. to scour with sand.
sablonneux, se, a. sandy.
sablonnier, m. sandman.
sablonnière, f. sand-pit, gravel-pit.
sabord, m. (mar.) port-hole.
saborder, v. a. (mar.) to scuttle.
sabot, m. wooden shoe || horse's hoof ||
skid, drag || (whipping-top).
saboter, v. n. to bungle.   [bungler.
sabotier, m. maker of wooden shoes ||
sabouler, v. a. to toss about, to worry ||
to blow up.
sabre, m. sabre, broad sword.
sabrer, v. a. to slash about, to sabre || to
botch || to bungle.
sabretache, f. sabretash, belt.
sabreur, m. slasher || bungler.
sac, m. sack, bag || ~ de nuit, travelling-
bag || ~ à vin, drunkard || homme de ~
et de corde, m. villain, regular ruffian.
saccade, f. saccade, ébrillade, sudden jerk.
saccadé, e, a. by jerks || abrupt.
saccader, v. a. to jerk.
saccage, m. confusion || jumble.
saccagement, m. sacking, plundering.
saccager, v. a. to plunder || to overturn.
saccageur, m. sacker.   [tion.
saccharification, f. (chim.) saccharifica-
saccharin, e, a. (chim.) saccharine.
saccharine, f. (chim.) saccharine.
sacerdoce, m. priesthood || sacred char-
acter.
sacerdotal, e, a. sacerdotal, priestly.
sachée, f. sackful, bagful.
sachet, m. satchel, scent-bag.
sacoche, f. saddle-bag || money-bag ||
courier-bag.
sacramentel, le, a. (-lement, ad.) sacra-
mental(ly).
sacre, m. coronation (of a king) || con-
secration (of a bishop).
sacré, e, a. sacred, holy, sainted, in-
violable || confounded.
sacrebleu! by Jove! dash it!
sacrement, m. sacrament.
sacrer, v. a. & n. to anoint, to crown (a
king) || to consecrate (a bishop) || to curse
and swear.
sacrificateur, m. sacrificer.
sacrifice, m. sacrifice, offering.
sacrifier, v. a. to sacrifice || to devote.
sacrilège, m. sacrilege.
sacrilège, a. sacrilegious.
sacripant, m. hector, bully.
sacristain, m. sexton.
sacristan, m. sacristan || sexton.
sacristie, f. vestry.
saducéen, m. Sadducee.
safran, m. (bot.) saffron.
safrané, e, a. saffroned.
safraner, v. a. to saffron.
safranière, f. saffron-plantation.

sagace, a. sagacious, acute.
sagacité, f. sagacity, acuteness.
sage, m. sage, wise man.
sage, a. (-ment, ad.) sage(ly) || wise(ly) ||
rational, sensible||discreet(ly) || prudent(ly) ||
good || quiet (of horses) || gentle || ~-femme,
f. mid-wife.
sagesse, f. sageness, wisdom, knowledge.
sagittaire, m. Sagittarius.
sagou, m. sago.
sagouin, m. & f. slovenly man || slut.
sagoutier, m. (bot.) sago-tree.   [done.
saignant, e, a. bleeding, bloody || under-
saignée, f. bleeding || trench || drain ||
small of the arm || faire une ~, to bleed ||
saignement, m. bleeding.   [to drain.
saigner, v. a. & n. to bleed, to take away
blood, to let blood, to breathe a vein, to
cut a drain || to squeeze (one) || ~ du nez,
to bleed at the nose || to be a coward.
saigneux, se, a. bloody || bout ~, m.
scrag-end.   [striking.
saillant, e, a. jutting out, projecting ||
saillie, f. jutting out, projecture || spurt ||
(fig.) sudden fit, start || sally, flash of wit ||
whim || ledge || spindle || en ~, projecting.
saillir, v. a. & n. to serve || to jut out, to
project, to gush out || to stand out.
sain, e, a. sound, healthy, wholesome,
healthful || ~ et sauf, safe and sound.
saindoux, m. hog's lard.   [ciously.
sainement, ad. sound and well || judi-
sainfoin, m. (bot.) sainfoin || French grass.
saint, m. patron, saint.
saint, e, a. saint, sacred, holy, pious ||
~-simonien, ne, m. & f. communist ||
~-simonien, ne, a. communistic.
sainte-barbe, f. (mar.) powder-room.
saintement, ad. holily, piously.
sainteté, f. sanctity, holiness, sacredness.
saisi, a. seized || struck || thrilled || applied
to || burnt.
saisie, f. (jur.) seizure, distress, distraint.
saisir, v. a. to seize, to catch, to grip, to
lay hold on || (jur.) to distrain || to thrill ||
to understand || to overhear || to avail one-
self of.
saisissable, a. (jur.) seizable, distrainable.
saisissant, e, a. piercing || startling ||
thrilling.   [chill.
saisissement, m. sudden shock, pang ||
saison, f. season || être de ~, to be
seasonable || marchand des quatre -s,
salade, f. salad.   [m. costermonger.
saladier, m. salad-dish || salad-basket.
salage, m. salting.
salaire, m. salary, hire, wages, reward.
salaison, f. salting || salt meat.
salamalec, m. (fam.) profound bow.
salamandre, f. salamander || eft.
salarié, m. hireling.
salarié, e, a. hired.
salarier, v. a. to pay, to salary.
salaud, e, a. slovenly, filthy, nasty.
sale, a. (-ment, ad.) dirty, filthy, nasty ||
foul || in a mess || coarse || dirtily, nastily,
salé, m. salt pork.   [filthily.
salé, e, a. salted || (fig.) sharp, pointed ||
awfully dear.

saler, v. a. to salt ‖ to cure ‖ to overcharge. [obscenity.
saleté, f. dirtiness, nastiness, filthiness ‖
saleur, m. salter.
salicoque, f. shrimp (fish).
salière, f. salt-cellar ‖ salt-box ‖ hollow
(of the shoulder).
saligaud, e, a. nasty, slovenly.
salignon, m. salt loaf.
salin, m. salt-spring.
salin, e, a. saline, brinish, briny.
saline, f. salt-pit, salt-well ‖ salt-fish.
salique, a. Salic (law).
salir, v. a. to dirt, to foul, to soil, to sully.
salissant, e, a. that soils ‖ liable to get
dirty.
salisson, f. young slut. [dirty.
salissure, f. spot of dirt.
salive, f. saliva, spittle.
saliver, v. n. to salivate, to slaver.
salle, f. hall, room, parlour ‖ plantation
of trees ‖ house (theatre) ‖ ~ à manger,
dining-room ‖ ~ à danser, dancing-room ‖
~ de concert, music-room ‖ ~ de billard, billiard-room ‖ ~ d'armes, fencing-
school ‖ ~ d'assemblée, assembly-room.
salmigondis, m. hotch-potch, medley.
salmis, m. (culin.) jugged game, stew of
game.
saloir, m. salt-tub.
salon, m. saloon, drawing-room, parlour ‖
~s, pl. fashionable circles (pl.) ‖ ~ littéraire, reading-room ‖ **homme de** ~,
m. man of fashion.
salope, a. dirty, nasty, slovenly.
saloperie, f. nastiness, slovenliness.
salpêtre, m. saltpetre.
salpêtrier, m. saltpetre-maker.
salpêtrière, f. saltpetre-house.
salsepareille, f. (bot.) sarsaparilla.
salsifis, m. (bot.) goat's beard ‖ salsify.
saltimbanque, m. quack, mountebank.
salubre, a. salubrious, wholesome.
salubrité, f. salubrity, wholesomeness ‖
healthfulness.
saluer, v. a. to salute, to greet, to bow ‖
to present one's compliments to.
salure, f. saltness, brine.
salut, m. salute, bow, salutation, greeting ‖ salvation ‖ welfare, safety ‖ evening
prayers.
salutaire, a. salutary, saving, wholesome,
useful ‖ ~ment, ad. salutarily ‖ bene-
ficially. [curtsey.
salutation, f. salutation, bowing, bow,
salve, f. volley, discharge ‖ (of applause)
round. [eve.
samedi, m. Saturday ‖ ~ saint, Easter
sancir, v. n. (mar.) to founder, to sink.
sanctifier, v. a. to sanctify, to hallow, to
keep holy.
sanctionner, v. n. to sanction, to ratify.
sanctuaire, m. sanctuary.
sandal, m. (bot.) sandal-wood.
sandale, f. sandal ‖ fencing-shoe ‖ foot-
stall.
sandaraque, f. (bot.) sandarac.
sang, m. blood ‖ (fig.) family, birth, extraction ‖ de pur ~, thoroughbred ‖ ~-
froid, m. coolness ‖ de ~-froid, coolly.

sanglade, f. lash.
sanglant, e, a. bloody, cruel, injurious ‖
outrageous.
sangle, f. strap, girth, thong ‖ sacking.
sangler, v. a. to girth ‖ to whip, to lash.
sanglier, m. wild-boar.
sanglot, m. sob, sobbing.
sangloter, v. n. to sob.
sangsue, f. leech ‖ (fig.) blood-sucker.
sanguin, e, a. sanguine, blood-red ‖ full-
blooded, sanguineous.
sanguinaire, a. sanguinary, bloodthirsty
sanguine, f. red-chalk ‖ blood-stone.
sanguinolent, e, a. (méd.) bloody.
sanitaire, a. sanitary.
sans, pr. without, besides ‖ were it not for ‖
~-cœur, m. heartless wretch ‖ ~-culotte,
m. ragamuffin ‖ sans-culotte, ultra republican ‖ ~-culottisme, m. the system
of the sans-culottes ‖ ~-façon, m. roughness ‖ ~-gêne, m. impudence ‖ coolness.
sanscrit, m. Sanscrit.
sansonnet, m. starling.
santé, f. health, healthiness ‖ toast.
sapajou, m. marmoset.
sape, f. sapping, undermining.
saper, v. a. to sap.
saperlotte, vide sapristi.
sapeur, m. sapper ‖ ~-pompier, fireman. [man.
saphir, m. sapphire.
sapin, m. fir-tree, pitch-tree ‖ deal board ‖
coffin ‖ hack.
sapine, f. beam of fir-timber.
sapinière, f. forest of fir-trees.
saponaire, f. (bot.) soapwort.
sapristi! by Jingo! hang it! bless your
soul ‖
sarabande, f. saraband (dance).
sarbacane, f. pea-shooter ‖ tube ‖ trunk.
sarcasme, m. sarcasm.
sarcastique, a. sarcastic.
sarcelle, f. teal (bird).
sarclage, m. weeding.
sarcler, v. a. to weed.
sarcleur, m. weeder.
sarcloir, m. weeding-hook, hoe.
sarclure, f. weedings (pl.).
sarcophage, m. sarcophagus.
sardine, f. anchovy, sardine, sprat.
sardoine, f. (min.) sardonyx.
sardonique, a. sardonic, satirical.
sarigue, m. opossum.
sarment, m. vine-branch.
sarrasin, e, a.; blé ~, m. buck-wheat.
sarrau, m. smock-frock.
sas, m. sieve ‖ bolt.
sasse, f. (mar.) scoop.
sasser, v. a. to sift, to bolt.
sasset, m. little sieve.
sassoire, f. splinter-bar (of a coach).
satané, e, a. wretched, confounded.
satanique, a. Satanic.
satiété, f. satiety.
satinade, f. satinet.
satinage, m. hot-pressing, glossing.
satiné, m. satin-like appearance.
satiné, e, a. satin-like ‖ hot-pressed,
glossed. [press.
satiner, v. a. to make satin-like, to hot-
satire, f. satire, lampoon.

satirique, m. satirist.

satirique, a. (-ment, ad.) satirical(ly).

satisfaction, f. satisfaction, gratification, comfort || atonement.

satisfaire, v. a. & n. ir. to satisfy, to content, to please, to gratify, to discharge.

satisfaisant, e, a. satisfactory.

satrape, m. satrap.

saturer, v. a. (chim.) to saturate.

saturnales, f.pl. saturnalia (pl.) || licentious

satyre, m. satyr.   [festivals (pl.).

sauce, f. sauce.   [to scold.

saucer, v.a. to dip in sauce || to wet through ||

saucière, f. sauce-boat || butter-boat.

saucisse, f. sausage.   [gunpowder.

saucisson, m. thick sausage || train of

sauf, pr. save, saving, except, but.

sauf, ve, a. safe || ~ **conduit,** m. safe-

sauge, f. (bot.) sage.   [conduct.

sagrenu, e, a. absurd, impertinent, pert.

saule, m. (bot.) willow || ~ **pleureur,** weeping willow.

saumâtre, a. brackish, briny.

saumon, m. salmon || pig || block.

saumoneau, m. little salmon.

saumure, f. brine, pickle, souse.

saunage, m. salt-trade.

sauner, v. a. to salt.

saunerie, f. saltern, salt-house.

saunier, m. salter.

saupoudrer, v. a. to sprinkle with salt, to powder, to strew || to intersperse.

saur, a. (m.) smoke-dried || sorrel (of horses).

saurer, v.a. to dry in the smoke, to bloat.

sauriens, m. pl. saurians (pl.) || lizards

saussaie, f. willow-plot.   [(pl.).

saut, m. jump, leap, skip, hop, bound || fall (of water) || ~ **de carpe, ~ périlleux,** somerset || ~ **de mouton,** goat-leap || **leap-frog** || ~ **de loup,** ha-ha.

sauté, e, a. (culin.) sauté || lightly fried.

saute, f. (mar.) shifting of the wind || ~ **en-barque,** m. yachting-jacket || ~ **mouton,** m. leap-frog.

sauter, v. a. to leap, to jump, to skip, to hop, to spring, to rush, to tumble || to omit, to pass over || to blow up || ~ **aux yeux,** to be very obvious.   [frog.

sauterelle, f. locust, grasshopper || leap-

sauteur, se, m. & f. jumper, leaper, tumbler || quack.

sautillement, m. skip, leap, hop.

sautiller, v. a. to skip, to leap, to jump to and fro.

sautoir, m. guard-chain || watch-guard || **en** ~, cross-wise || slung over the shoulder.

sauvage, a. (-ment, ad.) savage || wild (ly) || shy || unsociable || fierce(ly).

sauvageon, m. wildstock || seedling.

sauvagerie, f. wildness, shyness.

sauvagin, m. fishy taste.

sauvagin, e, a. fishy.

sauvagine, f. water-fowl.

sauvegarde, f. safeguard.   [guard.

sauvegarder, v. a. to protect, to safe-

sauver, v. a. to save, to preserve, to rescue, to deliver || to spare || **se** ~, to fly away, to make one's escape || to work one's salvation, to provide for one's safety.

sauvetage, m. salvage || escape || life. . . || **canot de** ~, m. lifeboat.

sauveur, m. deliverer || Saviour.

savamment, ad. learnedly, knowingly.

savane, f. savannah.

savant, m. scholar || scientist.

savant, e, a. learned || clever || well-informed.

savantasse, m. pedantic scholar.

savate, f. old shoe || bungled work || hunt-the-slipper (game).

savaterie, f. old-shoe shop.

saveter, v. a. to cobble, to bungle, to botch.

savetier, m. cobbler, bungler.

saveur, f. savour, flavour, taste, relish.

savoir, m. learning, erudition, science, scholarship.

savoir, v. a. ir. to know, to understand, to have knowledge of, to be skilled, to be able, to be aware, to have in memory || **à** ~, namely, viz. || ~ **vivre,** to know how to behave, to be mannerly || **faire** ~, to acquaint, to give intelligence || **se** ~, to know oneself to be || to get known || ~ **faire,** m. skill, wits (pl.). || ~ **vivre,** m. goodmanners (pl.), goodbreeding.

savon, m. soap || ~ **de toilette,** scented soap.

savonnage, m. washing with soap || soap-suds (pl.).   [(fam.) to lecture.

savonner, v.a. to wash with soap, to lather ||

savonnerie, f. soap-house, soap-manufactory.

savonnette, f. soap-ball || metallic spring-cover of a watch || (montre) hunting-

savonneux, se, a. soapy.   [watch.

savonnier, m. soap-boiler || (bot.) soap-berry tree.

savourer, v. a. to savour, to relish.

savoureux, se, a. savoury ||-sement, ad. savourily || with relish.

savoyard, m. errand-porter || churl.

saxophone, m. saxophone (instrument).

saynète, f. comic play, farce.   [the law.

sbire, m. bailiff || police-officer || tool of

scabieuse, f. (bot.) scabious.

scabreux, se, a. scabrous, rugged, rough || ticklish || dangerous.

scalper, v. a. to scalp.

scandale, m. scandal, offence || exposure || **pierre de** ~, f. stumbling-block.

scandaleux, se, a. (-sement, ad.) scandalous(ly).   [to be scandalised.

scandaliser, v. a. to scandalise || **se** ~,

scander, v. a. to scan.

scaphandre, m. cork-jacket || float for swimming || diving-apparatus.

scarabée, m. beetle.

scaramouche, m. buffoon.

scarificateur, m. scarifier.

scarifier, v. a. to scarify.

scarlatine, f. (méd.) scarlatina, scarlet-

scarlatine, a. scarlet.   [fever.

scarole, f. (bot.) endive.   [tion.

sceau, m. seal || seal-office || stamp || sanc-

scélérat, m. villain, profligate.

scélérat, e, a. flagitious, villanous.

scélératesse, f. villany.

scellé, m. (jur.) seal.

scellement, m. sealing || cramping.
sceller, v. a. to seal || to confirm || to cramp.
scelleur, m. sealer.
scène, f. scene || stage, scenery || occurrence || quarrel || uproar || faire une ~ à qn., to blow one up, to go on at one.
scénique, a. scenic.
scepticisme, m. scepticism.
sceptique, m. sceptic.
sceptique, a. sceptical.
sceptre, m. sceptre || sway.
schabraque, f. (mil.) shabrack.
schako, m. (mil.) shako.
schismatique, m. schismatic.
schismatique, a. schismatical.
schisme, m. schism.
schiste, m. shist, flaky stone.
schlague, f. (mil.) flogging.
schnick, m. dram.
schrapnel, m. shrapnel-shell.
sciage, m. sawing.
sciagraphie, f. (arch.) sciagraphy.
sciatérique, a. sciateric.
sciatique, f. (méd.) sciatica.
sciatique, a. (méd.) sciatic.
scie, f. saw || sawfish || (fig.) bore.
sciemment, ad. knowingly.
science, f. science, knowledge, learning.
scientifique, a. (-ment, ad.) scientific (ally).   [bore || (mar.) to hold water.
scier, v. a. & n. to saw || to reap || (fig.) to
scierie, f. saw-mill.   [wood-sawyer.
scieur, m. sawyer || reaper || ~ de long,
scinder, v. a. (jur.) to rescind || to cut off, to divide.
scintiller, v. n. to scintillate.
scion, m. scion, young shoot.
scission, f. secession, separation.
scissionnaire, m. seceder.
scissionnaire, a. seceding.
scissure, f. fissure.
sciure, f. sawdust.
scolaire, a. scholastic.
scolastique, m. school-divine || ~, f. scholastic divinity.   [(ally).
scolastique, a. (-ment, ad.) scholastic
scoliaste, m. scholiast.
scolie, f. scholium.
scolopendre, f. centipede.
scorbut, m. (méd.) scurvy.
scorbutique, a. scorbutic.   [(pl.).
scorie, f. scoria, dross || -s, pl. clinkers
scorpion, m. scorpion || (astr.) Scorpion || weaver (fish).
scorsonère, f. viper's grass.
scrofules, f. pl. (méd.) scrofula, king's
scrofuleux, se, a. scrofulous.   [evil.
scrupule, m. scruple, scrupulosity, qualm.
scrupuleux, se, a. (-sement, ad.) scrupulous(ly) || nice, rigorous.
scrutateur, m. scrutator, searcher.
scruter, v. a. to scrutinise.
scrutin, m. scrutiny, inquiry || ballot.
sculpter, v. a. to sculpture, to carve.
sculpteur, m. sculptor, carver.
sculpture, f. sculpture, carving, statuary.
S. E., His Eminence || His Excellency.
se, pn. oneself, himself, herself, itself, themselves || each other, one another.

séance, f. sitting || session || seat.
séant, m. sitting posture.
séant, e, a. sitting || decent, becoming.
seau, m. pail, bucket || ~ de toilette, slop-pail.
sébile, f. wooden bowl.
sec, m. dryness || manger-food.
sec, sèche, a. dry, dried, sapless || lean || unfeeling || smart || stiff || ready (of money) || ~, ad. dryly || sharply || (of drinking) hard.
sécateur, m. pruning-shears (pl.).
sécession, f. secession.
sécessioniste, m. secessionist.
séchage, m. drying.
sèche, f. cuttle-fish.   [plainly.
sèchement, ad. dryly, roughly, bluntly ||
sécher, v. a. & n. to dry || to grow dry, to wither || to pine away.
sécheresse, f. dryness, aridness || shortness || plainness.
séchoir, m. clothes-horse || drying-room.
second, m. helper, assistant || en ~, in a subordinate capacity || in the second place || au ~, on the second floor.
second, e, a. (-ement, ad.) second(ly).
secondaire, a. (-ment, ad.) secondary || secondarily.
seconde, f. second || second class || second form || second-tier box || fore-cabin.
seconder, v. a. to second, to help, to assist.
secouer, v. a. to shake, to jolt, to toss, to shake off || se ~, to shake oneself.
secourable, a. helpful, ready to help || (mil.) relievable.
secourir, v. a. ir. to succour, to assist, to help, to relieve.
secours, m. succour, assistance, help, relief || supply || au ~! help! help!
secousse, f. shake, shock, jerk, toss.
secret, m. secret || close confinement || secret spring || secret drawer.
secret, ète, a. (-ètement, ad.) secret(ly) || private(ly) || recondite || close || inwardly.
secrétaire, m. secretary || writing-desk || davenport.
secrétairerie, f. secretary's office.
secrétariat, m. secretaryship.
secrète, f. secret prayer.
sécréter, v. a. to secrete.
sécrétion, f. (méd.) secretion.
sectaire, m. sectarian.
sectateur, m. follower, votary.
secte, f. sect.
section, f. section || water-way.
séculaire, a. secular || venerable || old.
sécularisation, f. secularisation.
séculariser, v. a. to secularise.
sécularité, f. secular jurisdiction.
séculier, m. layman.
séculier, ère, a. secular, worldly.
secundo, ad. secondly.
sécurité, f. security.
sedan, m. Sedan-cloth.
sédatif, ve, a. (méd.) sedative, calming.
sédentaire, a. sedentary || -ment, ad. sedentarily.
sédiment, m. sediment || dregs, lees (pl.).
séditieux, se, a. (-sement, ad.) seditious(ly).

sédition, f. riot, tumult, insurrection.

séducteur, trice, m. & f. seducer, mis-leader, enticer.

séducteur, trice, a. seducing || seductive.

séduction, f. seduction || allurement || bribery.

séduire, v. a. ir. to seduce, to mislead, to delude, to bewitch || to corrupt, to bribe.

séïde, m. fanatical assassin || fanatic.

seigle, m. (bot.) rye.

seigneur, m. lord, nobleman || **Grand Seigneur,** high personage || sultan.

seigneurial, e, a. lordly, magnificent.

seigneurie, f. lordship || manor. [noble.

sein, m. breast, heart, bosom || womb || (fig.) midst, depth.

seine, f. drag-net.

seing, m. sign manual, signature.

seize, a. sixteen || sixteenth (of the month).

seizième, m. sixteenth part.

seizième, a. sixteenth.

séjour, m. abode, sojourn, stay.

séjourner, v. n. to stay, to remain || to dwell, to tarry, to make a stay.

sel, m. salt || (fig.) poignancy, wit.

sélection, f. selection.

selle, f. saddle || stool.

seller, v. a. to saddle.

sellerie, f. saddle-room || saddlery.

sellette, f. culprit's stool || shoe-black's box.

sellier, m. saddler. [box.

selon, pr. agreeably to, according to, pursuant to || ~ **moi,** in my opinion.

semailles, f. pl. sowing-time || seed.

semaine, f. week || week's work || week's gain *ou* wages || pocket-money.

semainier, m. letter-rack || set of seven || officer of the week.

sémaphore, m. semaphore.

semaque, f. fishing smack, boat.

semblable, m. equal, match || fellow-creature || **-s,** pl. kind.

semblable, a. like, alike, such.

semblant, m. appearance || pretence || outside, show.

sembler, v. n. to seem, to look, to appear || **il me semble,** methinks. [step.

semelle, f. sole || foot (of a stocking) || (fig.)

semence, f. seed.

semer, v. a. to sow || to spread, to scatter, to sprinkle, to strew. [plough.

semestre, m. half-year || six months' fur-

semestriel, le, a. half-yearly.

semestrier, m. officer (*ou* soldier) who has leave of absence for six months.

semeur, m. sower || spreader.

semi . . . (**en connexion**) half . . .

semi . . . [active.

sémillant, e, a. brisk, lively, sprightly.

séminaire, m. seminary || priests' college.

semis, m. seed-plot || sowing || seedling.

sémitique, a. a Semitic.

semoir, m. sowing-machine || seed-lip ||

semonce, f. summons || lecture. [drill.

semoncer, v. a. to lecture.

semoule, f. semolina.

sempiternel, le, a. everlasting.

sénat, m. senate, senate-house.

sénateur, m. senator.

sénatorerie, f. senatorship.

sénatorial, e, & **sénatorien, ne,** a. senatorial.

sénatrice, f. senator's lady. [torial.

sénatus-consulte, m. decree of the senate.

séné, m. (bot.) senna.

sénéchal, m. seneschal, high bailiff.

sénéchale, f. seneschal's lady.

sénéchaussée, f. seneschal's court.

séneçon, m. (bot.) groundsel.

sénevé, m. (bot.) mustard-seed || charlock.

sens, m. sense, judgment, understanding, intellect, reason, meaning, signification || wits (pl.) || ~ **dessus dessous,** topsy-turvy, upside down || ~ **devant derrière,** the wrong way round; preposterously.

sensation, f. sensation.

sensé, e, a. (**-ment,** ad.) sensible || sensibly. [feeling.

sensibilité, f. sensibility sensitiveness.

sensible, a. sensible, perceptible || easily affected, sensibly affected || compassionate || grateful || painful || obvious || **-ment,** ad. sensibly, perceptibly || feelingly || obviously.

sensiblerie, f. sentimentality || maudlin.

sensitif, ve, a. sensitive.

sensitive, f. (bot.) sensitive plant.

sensualiste, m. sensualist.

sensualité, f. sensuality.

sensuel, m. sensualist.

sensuel, le, a. (**-lement,** a.) sensual(ly) || voluptuous(ly).

sentencieux, se, a. (**-sement,** ad.) sententious(ly).

senteur, m. scent, odour, perfume || **pois de** ~, m. sweet-scented pea.

sentier, m. path, pathway, footway, road.

sentiment, m. sentiment, sensation || affection, feeling || mind, opinion || inclination.

sentimental, e, a. sentimental. [tion.

sentine, f. sink of a ship || well.

sentinelle, f. sentinel || sentry || **en** ~, to stand sentry.

sentir, v. a. & n. ir. to feel, to perceive || to smell || to scent || to savour || to have a smell, to have a taste, to taste || to smell strong || **ne** ~ **que l'eau,** to be tasteless || **se** ~, to feel oneself, to know oneself, to be sensible of one's condition, to know one's resources, to be felt, to cause pain.

seoir, v. n. to be seated, sitting || to suit, to become, to fit.

séparation, f. separation, parting || divorce || ~ **de corps et biens,** (jur.) judicial separation.

séparé, e, a. (**-ment,** ad.) separate(d) || distinct || separately.

séparer, v. a. to separate, to disjoin, to disunite, to set apart, to sunder, to take asunder || to divide || to divorce || **se** ~, to part from one, to leave || to break up.

sept, m. seventh (of the month) || (number) seven.

sept, a. seven.

septembre, m. September.

septentrion, m. north.

septentrional, e, a. a northern.

septième, m. seventh part.

septième, f. sequence of seven cards.

septième, a. (**-ment,** ad.) seventh(ly).

septuagénaire, m. & f. septuagenarian.
septuagénaire, a. septuagenarian.
Septuagésime, f. Septuagesima.
sépulcral, e, a. sepulchral.
sépulture, f. sepulture, burial || vault.
séquelle, f. gang, set, host. [tration.
séquestre, m. (jur.) sequestrator || seques-
séquestrer, v. a. to sequester || to set apart.
sérail, m. seraglio.
séran, m. flax-comb, hackle.
sérancer, v. a. to dress flax, to hackle.
séraphin, m. seraph.
séraphique, a. seraphic.
serein, m. evening dew.
serein, e, a. serene, clear || calm, quiet.
sérénade, f. serenade.
Sérénissime, a. Most Serene.
sérénité, f. serenity, calmness.
séreux, se, a. (méd.) serous.
serf, m. serf.
serfouette, f. hoe.
serfouir, v. a. to hoe.
sergent, m. sergeant || (mar.) holdfast || ~
de ville, policeman, constable || ~ four-
rier, quarter-master || ~ instructeur,
drill-sergeant. [trade.
sergerie, f. serge-manufactory || serge-
séricicole, a. of silk-husbandry || silk-
série, f. series. [producing.
sérieusement, ad. seriously, in earnest.
sérieux, m. seriousness || au ~, in earnest.
sérieux, se, a. serious, solemn, grave ||
thinking.
serin, e, m. & f. canary-bird || simpleton.
serin, e, a. silly, green.
seriner, v. a. to teach a bird with the bird-
organ || to coach up.
serinette, f. bird-organ.
seringat, m. (bot.) syringa.
seringue, f. syringe, squirt.
seringuer, v. a. to syringe, to squirt.
serment, m. oath, swearing, protestation ||
prêter ~, to take an oath.
sermon, m. sermon || lecture.
sermonner, v. n. to lecture.
sermonneur, se, m. & f. sermoniser.
sérosité, f. (méd.) serosity, wateriness ||
serum.
serpe, f. bill-hook, hedging-bill.
serpent, m. serpent, snake.
serpentaire, m. (astr.) Serpentarius ||
secretary-bird || ~, f. (bot.) snake-root.
serpenteau, m. young serpent || small
serpente, f. tissue-paper. [squib.
serpenter, v. n. to wind about, to meander.
serpentin, m. cock of a musket.
serpentine, f. (bot.) grass-plantain ||(min.)
serpentine-stone.
serpentine, a. serpentine.
serpette, f. pruning-knife.
serpillière, f. packing-cloth.
serpolet, m. (bot.) wild thyme.
serre, f. green-house || conservatory || talon,
claw || grip || ~ chaude, hot-house || ~-
file, m. (mil.) last man in a file || sternmost
ship || ~-nez, m. twitch (for horses) || ~-
papiers, m. paper-holder || letter-clip ||
set of pigeon-holes || ~-tête, m. nightcap-
ribbon.

serré, e, a. & ad. squeezed || tight, close,
compact, fast || concise || locked up || closely,
hard, soundly.
serrement, m. squeezing, pressing || op-
pression || tightness || ~ de cœur, great
grief || heart-burning.
serrer, v. a. to squeeze, to tighten, to
fasten, to bind close || to lock up, to clasp ||
to make costive || se ~, to grow tighter,
to shrink || to sit ou lie close. [lock.
serrure, f. lock || ~ à double tour, double
serrurerie, f. locksmith's work ou trade.
serrurier, m. locksmith.
sertir, v. n. to set in a bezil (of jewels).
servage, m. bondage, slavery.
servant, m. gunner || assistant priest.
servante, f. maidservant || dinner-waggon ||
dumb-waiter.
serviable, a. serviceable, obliging.
service, m. service, divine worship || office,
employment || set of dishes and plates,
course of dishes || de ~, in attendance, on
duty.
serviette, f. napkin || towel.
servile, a. (-ment, ad.) servile(ly).
servilité, f. servility, baseness.
servir, v. a. & n. ir. to serve, to wait upon,
to help at table, to attend || to worship || to
be of use, to be useful || to be instrumental
|| to be in service || to serve in the army ||
se ~, to help oneself || to be used up.
serviteur, m. servant.
servitude, f. servitude || (jur.) easement.
ses, pn. pl. (de son) his, her, its, their.
session, f. session, sitting.
seuil, m. sill, threshold.
seul, e, a. (-ement, ad.) sole(ly) || only,
alone, lonely, self || but, singly.
sève, f. sap, juice, moisture.
sévère, a. (-ment, ad.) severe(ly) || hard,
sharp || stern(ly) || rigorous, austere.
sévérité, f. severity, rigour, austerity,
sternness, strictness.
sévices, m. pl. ill-treatment.
sévir, v. n. to be guilty of severe ou ill-
treatment (towards) || to rage.
sevrage, m. weaning.
sevrer, v. a. to wean || to deprive.
sevreuse, f. dry-nurse.
sexagénaire, m. & f. sexagenarian.
sexagénaire, a. sexagenarian.
Sexagésime, f. Sexagesima.
sexe, m. sex.
sextant, m. (astr.) sextant.
sextupler, v. a. to increase sixfold.
sexuel, le, a. sexual.
shako, m. soldier's cap.
si, c. & ad. if, unless, whether || so || ~ que,
and if || ~ bien que, so that.
sibylle, f. sibyl.
sibyllin, e, a. sibylline.
sicaire, m. hired murderer.
siccatif, m. drying colour.
siccatif, ve, a. drying.
sidéral, e, a. sidereal.
siècle, m. century, age || time || world.
siège, m. seat, chair || tribunal, court of
judicature || see (of a bishop) || siege (of a
town) || coachman's box.

siéger, v. n. to hold a see || to sit || (fig.) to be seated.

sien, m. his own, hers, her own, one's own || les –s, pl. his ou her relations (pl.), one's relations (pl.).

sien, ne, pn. his, her, its.

sieste, f. afternoon's nap.

sieur, m. sir, master.

sifflement, m. whistling, hissing, hiss.

siffler, v. a. to whistle, to hiss || to warble || to damn a play.

sifflet, m. whistle || cat-call || wind-pipe.

siffleur, se, m. & f. whistler, hisser.

siffleur, se, a. whistling.

sigisbé, m. gallant, lover.

signal, m. signal, sign.

signalé, e, a. signalised, signal || notorious.

signalement, m. description.

signaler, v. a. to signalise || to describe || to mark out || (mar.) to make signals.

signaliste, m. signalman.

signataire, m. signer, subscriber.

signature, f. signature || signing.

signe, m. sign, token || signal, mark || nod || wink.

signer, v. a. to sign || se ~, to cross oneself.

signet, m. tassel (for books), marker.

signifiant, e, a. significant.

significatif, ve, a. significative, expressive. ||(jur.) legal notice.

signification, f. signification, meaning ||

signifier, v. a. to signify, to mean, to betoken, to express || to declare.

silence, m. silence, stillness || pause.

silencieux, se, a. (–sement, ad.) silent

silex, m. (min.)flint. ||(ly)|| still.

silhouette, f. silhouette || profile, outline, shadow.

silice, f. silicious earth || flint.

sillage, m. track ou course of a ship.

sillon, m. furrow, ridge || wrinkle || –s, pl. land, fields.

sillonner, v. a. to furrow, to wrinkle.

simagrée, f. grimace || –s, pl. apishness.

simarre, m. night-gown || justices' robe.

similaire, a. similar.

similarité, f. similarity.

similor, m. similor.

simoniaque, a. simoniacal.

simonie, f. simony.

simoun, m. simoon.

simple, a. (–ment, ad.) simple || simply || single, only, bare(ly) || mere(ly) || common, ordinary || silly, foolish || downright || plain(ly) || harmless || private.

simplicité, f. simplicity, plainness || silliness.

simplifier, v. a. to simplify.

simulacre, m. image, idol, phantom || feint. |felt.

simulé, e, a. fictitious, feigned || counterfeit.

simuler, v. a. to pretend, to feign || to sham || to counterfeit.   [taneous(ly).

simultané, e, a. (–ment, ad.) simultaneity, f. simultaneousness.

sinapisme, m. mustard-plaster.

sincère, a. (–ment, ad.) sincere(ly) || true||

sincérité, f. sincerity. |truly.

sinécure, f. sinecure.

singe, m. ape, monkey || imitator || copying-machine.

singer, v. a. to ape, to mimic.

singerie, f. apish trick, grimace || mimicry.

singeur, se, a. apish.

singulariser, v. a. to render singular.

singularité, f. singularity, oddness, peculiarity.

singulier, ère, a. (–èrement, ad.) singular(ly) || peculiar(ly) || particular, strange, odd(ly).

sinistre, m. disaster || damage.

sinistre, a. sinister, unlucky, ominous, inauspicious, unfortunate.

sinon, ad. else, or else, if not.

sinueux, se, a. sinuous, winding.

sinuosité, f. sinuosity, windings (pl.).

sinus, m. (an.) sinus || (géom.) sine.

siphon, m. siphon || bottle of Seltzerwater.

sire, m. sire || squire || fellow || stick.

sirène, f. siren, mermaid.

siroco(o), m. sirocco.

sirop, m. sirup.

siroter, v. n. to sip.

sirupeux, se, a. sirupy.

sis, e, a. (jur.) situate.

site, m. site, position.

sitôt (que), c. as soon as.

situation, f. situation, condition || (mar.) bearing.

situé, e, a. situated.

six, m. sixth (of the month).

six, a. six.

sixain, m. stanza of six verses || six packs

sixième, m. sixth.   (of cards).

sixième, f. sequence of six cards.

sixième, a. (–ment, ad.) sixth(ly).

sixte, f. (mus.) sixth.

ski, m. ski.

sobre, a. (–ment, ad.) sober(ly).

sobriété, f. sobriety, soberness, temperance.

sobriquet, m. nickname.   [ance.

soc, m. share || plough-share.

sociabilité, f. sociability.

sociable, a. (–ment, ad.) sociable || sociably || companionable, tractable.

social, e, a. (–ement, ad.) social(ly) || of the firm ou company.

socialisme, m. socialism.

socialiste, m. socialist.

sociétaire, m. partner, member, associate.

société, f. society || company || club || party || partnership.

socle, m. socle, base.

socque, m. wooden sandal, clog.

sœur, f. sister || ~ de lait, foster-sister.

soi, pn. one, oneself, himself, herself, itself, themselves || de ~, of itself || ~~ même, oneself, himself, herself, itself || ~-disant, e, a. would-be || self-styled || supposed || so-called.

soie, f. silk || bristle || hair || ~ plate, twisted silk. |facture.

soierie, f. silk-stuff || silk-trade, silk-manu-

soif, f. thirst || dryness || avoir ~, to be thirsty || (fig.) to thirst for. |nice.

soigné, e, a. highly finished || elaborate ||

soigner, v. n. to look after, to take care of || to attend, to nurse.

soigneux, se, a. (**-sement,** ad.) careful(ly). [tions (pl.).
soin, m. care ‖ **-s,** pl. attendance ‖ attention (pl.).
soir, m. evening, eve, night, afternoon.
soirée, f. evening, evening party, evening performance.
soit, c. & ad. either, or ‖ ~ I be it so! well!
soixantaine, f. sixty, threescore.
soixante, a. sixty, threescore ‖ **~-dix,**
soixantième, m. sixtieth. [seventy.
soixantième, a. sixtieth.
sol, m. soil, ground.
solaire, a. solar, solary.
soldat, m. soldier.
soldat, a. m. soldierly.
soldatesque, f. soldiery.
soldatesque, a. soldierly.
solde, m. final settlement ‖ balance ‖ surplus stock ‖ **pour ~ de tous comptes,** in full of all demands.
solde, f. soldier's pay.
solder, v. a. to pay (troops) ‖ (com.) to close an account ‖ to sell off.
sole, f. sole ‖ sleeper ‖ break.
solécisme, m. (gr.) solecism.
soleil, m. sun ‖ sunshine ‖ (bot.) sunflower ‖ sun-fish ‖ remonstrance ‖ **il fait du ~,** the sun shines.
solennel, le, a. (**-lement,** ad.) solemn
solenniser, v. a. to solemnise. [(ly).
solennité, f. solemnity.
solfège, m. (mus.) solfeggio.
solfier, v. a. (mus.) to solfa.
solidaire, a. (**-ment,** ad.) (jur.) conjointly answerable.
solidarité, f. (jur.) joint responsibility.
solide, a. (**-ment,** ad.) solid(ly) ‖ not liquid ‖ strong, stable, steadfast ‖ firm(ly) ‖ real ‖ substantial(ly).
solidifier, v. a. to solidify.
solidité, f. solidity ‖ firmness, strength ‖ soundness.
soliloque, m. soliloquy.
soliste, m. (mus.) soloist.
solitaire, m. solitaire (jewel).
solitaire, a. solitary, lonely, desert ‖ **--ment,** ad. solitarily.
solive, f. joist, rafter. [fellow.
soliveau, m. small joist ‖ (fig.) stupid
sollicitation, f. solicitation, entreaty.
solliciter, v. a. to solicit ‖ to entreat, to urge ‖ to petition ‖ to canvass.
solliciteur, euse, m. & f. solicitor ‖ canvasser ‖ solicitress.
sollicitude, f. solicitude, anxiety.
soluble, a. soluble, solvable.
solution, f. solution ‖ break.
solvabilité, f. solvency.
solvable, a. solvent.
sombre, a. dark, dim, dull, cloudy, gloomy, melancholy ‖ **faire ~,** to be dark.
sombrer, v. n. (mar.) to sink, to go down.
sommaire, m. summary, compendium.
sommaire, a. summary, compendious ‖ **-ment,** ad. summarily ‖ compendiously.
sommation, f. summons (pl.).
somme, m. sleep, nap.
somme, f. sum ‖ amount ‖ burden ‖ **en ~,**
sommeil, m. sleep ‖ sleepiness. [finally.

sommeiller, v. n. to slumber.
sommelier, m. butler ‖ cellarman.
sommellerie, f. butlership ‖ pantry.
sommer, v. a. to summon, to challenge ‖ to sum up.
sommet, m. summit, top, ridge ‖ height.
sommier, m. pack-horse ‖ horse-hair mattress ‖ bressumer ‖ wind-box of an organ. [man ou lady.
sommité, f. top, apex, height ‖ eminent
somnambule, m. & f. somnambulist.
somnambule, a. nightwalking.
somnambulisme, m. somnambulism.
somnolent, e, a. somnolent, drowsy.
somptuaire, a. sumptuary.
somptueux, se, a. (**-sement,** ad.) sumptuous(ly).
somptuosité, f. sumptuousness.
son, m. sound ‖ bran ‖ beat (of the drum) ‖
son (pl. **ses**), pr. his, her, its. [ringing.
sonate, f. (mus.) sonata.
sondage, m. sounding.
sonde, f. probe ‖ plummet, fathom-line.
sonder, v. a. to sound, to try the depth of, to plumb ‖ (chir.) to probe (a wound) ‖ to search, to scrutinise.
sondeur, m. sounding-man.
songe, m. dream ‖ dreaming ‖ **~-creux,** m. dreamer, visionary.
songer, v. a. & n. to dream ‖ to think, to muse ‖ to consider.
songeur, se, m. & f. dreamer.
sonnaille, f. bell (of a beast of burden).
sonnailler, m. bell-wether.
sonnailler, v. n. to ring continually.
sonnant, e, a. sounding ‖ striking ‖ sonorous.
sonné, e, a. past ‖ completed, full.
sonner, v. a. & n. to sound, to yield a sound, to ring ‖ to strike ‖ to toll.
sonnerie, f. ring of bells ‖ bells of a church ‖ clockwork.
sonnet, m. sonnet.
sonnette, f. little bell ‖ **serpent à -s,** m. rattle-snake.
sonneur, m. bell-ringer.
sonore, a. sonorous.
sophisme, m. sophism.
sophiste, m. sophist. [to subtilise.
sophistiquer, v. a. to act the sophist ‖
soporifique, a. soporific.
sorbe, f. (bot.) sorb-apple.
sorbet, m. sherbet.
sorbetière, f. ice-box.
sorbier, m. (bot.) sorb ‖ service-tree.
sorcellerie, f. sorcery, witchcraft.
sorcier, ère, m. & f. sorcerer, wizard, enchanter, magician, conjurer, diviner ‖ witch, sorceress, hag.
sordide, a. (**-ment,** ad.) sordid(ly) ‖ mean (ly) ‖ niggard(ly). [thing ‖ trifle.
sornette, f. idle talk, nonsense ‖ silly
sort, m. fate, destiny, lot, chance, hazard, fortune ‖ **jeter au ~, tirer au ~,** to cast
sortable, a. suitable. [lots.
sortant, m. outgoer.
sortant, e, a. going ou coming out ‖ drawn ‖ leaving office ‖ retiring, resigning ‖ outgoing.

sorte, f. sort, kind, species, manner, way, wise, guise ‖ de la ~, thus, in this manner ‖ de ~ que, en ~ que, so that.

sorteur, se, a. fond of going out.

sortie, f. going out, exit, issue, passage, outlet, exportation, export ‖ (mil.) attack ‖ à la ~ de, at the end of ‖ ~ de bal, opera-cloak ‖ droit de ~, m. export-duty.

sortilège, m. sorcery, witchcraft, fascination.

sortir, v. a. & n. ir. to issue, to get out ‖ to come out, to go abroad ‖ to emerge, to rise ‖ to take, to obtain ‖ to bring out.

sosie, f. person exactly resembling another ‖ twin.

sot-l'y-laisse, m. "parson's nose" (of a [fowl).

sot, m. blockhead, dolt, fool.

sot, te, a. (-tement, ad.) stupid(ly) ‖ silly, foolish(ly) ‖ idle ‖ impertinent(ly).

sotte, f. silly woman.

sottise, f. silliness, folly, foolishness, stupidity ‖ foolish trick ‖ —s, pl. abusive language.

sou, m. sou, halfpenny ‖ gros ~, penny-[piece.

soubassement, m. base ‖ valance.

soubresaut, m. start, jolt, shock ‖ gambol.

soubrette, f. chamber-maid ‖ abigail.

souche, f. stump ‖ stem, foundation ‖ (fig.) blockhead.

souchet, m. rag-stone.

souci, m. care, solicitude, anxiety, trouble ‖ (bot.) marigold ‖ sans ~, free from care ‖ sans-~, m. careless fellow.

se soucier, to care, to mind, to regard.

soucieux, se, a. careful, cloudy, uneasy.

soucoupe, f. saucer. [solicitous.

soudage, m. soldering.

soudain, e, a. (-ement, ad.) sudden(ly).

soudaineté, f. suddenness.

soudan, m. sultan.

soudard, m. weather-beaten soldier.

soude, f. (min.) soda ‖ (bot.) glass-wort.

souder, v. a. to solder ‖ to weld ‖ to join, to unite.

soudoyer, v. a. to keep soldiers in pay.

soudure, f. solder, soldering.

soufflage, m. glass-blowing.

souffle, m. breath, blast, whiff ‖ breeze of wind ‖ inspiration.

soufflé, m. puff.

soufflé, e, a. (culin.) soufflé.

souffler, v. a. & n. to blow ‖ to sound (a wind-instrument) ‖ to put out, to extinguish ‖ to huff (at draughts) ‖ to pant, to puff ‖ to whisper, to prompt ‖ to swell, to extol ‖ to deprive ‖ to sheathe (a [ship).

soufflerie, f. bellows-work.

soufflet, m. bellows ‖ box on the ear ‖ affront. [box the ears of.

souffleter, v. a. to slap on the face ‖ to

souffletier, m. bellows-maker.

souffleur, m. blower ‖ prompter ‖ panter ‖ ~ d'orgue, organ-blower.

soufflure, f. flaw (in metals) ‖ bubble.

souffrance, f. suffering, pain, affliction, trouble, torment ‖ jour de ~, m. borrowed light ‖ delay.

souffrant, e, a. suffering, in pain, patient ‖ poorly.

souffre-douleur, m. drudge ‖ laughing stock.

souffreteux, se, a. suffering misery, miserable.

souffrir, v. a. & n. to suffer, to bear, to endure, to tolerate, to undergo, to sustain ‖ to give leave, to let, to permit.

soufre, m. sulphur, brimstone.

soufrer, v. a. to dip in brimstone.

soufrière, f. sulphur-mine.

souhait, m. wish, desire ‖ à ~, according to one's wish.

souhaiter, v. a. to wish, to desire, to long [for.

souille, f. bog, soil ‖ (mar.) bed.

souiller, v. a. to dirty, to stain, to sully ‖ to contaminate, to blemish ‖ to profane.

souillon, m. & f. young sloven ou slut ‖ scullion.

souillure, f. filth, dirt, stain, spot.

soûl, m. one's fill.

soûl, e, a. full, glutted ‖ tipsy, drunk.

soulagement, m. relief, ease, comfort ‖ help.

soulager, v. a. to ease, to relieve, to disburden, to alleviate, to comfort, to assist.

soûlard, e, m. & f. drunkard.

soûler, v. a. to fill, to glut, to cloy, to satiate, to fuddle ‖ se ~, to get drunk.

souleur, f. sudden fright.

soulèvement, m. rising ‖ indignation ‖ insurrection ‖ swelling ‖ qualm.

soulever, v. a. to lift, to heave up, to raise up ‖ to rouse ‖ to stir ‖ to excite indignation, to rise ‖ se ~, to rise, to revolt, to mutiny.

soulier, m. shoe. [to mutiny.

soulignement, m. underlining.

souligner, v. a. to underline.

soulte, f. (com.) balance.

soumettre, v. a. ir. to submit, to subdue ‖ se ~, to submit, to yield.

soumis, e, a. submissive ‖ submitted ‖ humble, dutiful.

soumission, f. submission, submissiveness, obedience ‖ (jur.) contract ‖ tender.

soumissionnaire, m. & f. tendering party.

soumissionner, v. a. to tender (for).

soupape, f. valve ‖ plug.

soupçon, m. suspicion ‖ distrust ‖ conjecture, hint ‖ the mere name of it ‖ merest taste.

soupçonner, v. a. to suspect.

soupçonneux, se, a. suspicious.

soupe, f. soup ‖ porridge ‖ ~ grasse, meat soup ‖ ~ maigre, vegetable soup ‖ ~ au lait, milk-porridge ‖ ~ à la bière, egg-flip.

soupente, f. main-braces (of a coach) (pl.) ‖ loft (for a servant's bed).

souper, m. supper.

souper, v. n. to sup, to eat one's supper.

soupeser, v. a. to weigh by the hand.

soupière, f. soup-tureen.

soupir, m. sigh ‖ gasp ‖ (mus.) crotchet-[rest.

soupirail, m. air-hole.

soupirant, m. lover.

soupirer, v. n. to sigh, to fetch a sigh ‖ ~ après, to pant after.

souple, a. supple, pliant, flexible, complaisant.

souplesse, f. suppleness, flexibility, facility ‖ –s, (pl.) tricks (pl.).

souquenille, f. smock-frock, stable-coat.

souquer, v. a. (mar.) to row *ou* pull hard.

source, f. source, spring, fountain ‖ head ‖ de ~, spring ‖ naturally.

sourcil, m. eye-brow.

sourciller, v. n. to knit the brow, to shrink ‖ to spring ‖ to show the least emotion ‖ to gush out.

sourcilleux, se, a. (poét.) high, lofty, steeped, haughty ‖ supercilious.

sourd, e, m. & f. deaf man *ou* woman.

sourd, e, a. deaf ‖ insensible ‖ secret ‖ underhand ‖ dull ‖ dark ‖ hollow ‖ low confused ‖ dead (of files) ‖ rumbling ‖ –ement, ad. in a dull manner ‖ secretly, without noise ‖ in a low voice.

sourdaud, m. person hard of hearing.

sourdine, f. damper ‖. à la ~, secretly ‖ slily.   [up, to gush out.

sourdre, v. n. (of water) to spring, to well

souriceau, m. little mouse.

souricière, f. mouse-trap.

sourire, v. n. ir. to smile, to simper.

sourire, souris, m. smile, simpering.

souris, f. mouse.

sournois, e, a. sly, cunning.

sous, pr. under, beneath, below, nigh ‖ (in comp.) assistant, sub ‖ ~-affermer, v. a. to underlet ‖ ~-barbe, f. under-lip (of a horse) ‖ ~-outané, a. (an.) subcutaneous ‖ ~-chef, m. second clerk ‖ ~-entendre, v. a. to understand ‖ ~-entente, f. mental reservation ‖ ~-ferme, f. underlease ‖ ~-garde, f. trigger-guard ‖ ~-gorge, f. throat-band ‖ ~-lieutenance, f. sub-lieutenancy, ensigncy ‖ ~-lieutenant, m. sub-lieutenant ‖ ensign ‖ cornet ‖ ~-louer, v. a. to underlet ‖ ~-maître, m. assistant master, usher ‖ ~-maîtresse, f. under-governess ‖ ~-marin, a. submarine ‖ ~-œuvre, f. under-pinning ‖ reprendre en ~-œuvre, to underpin ‖ ~-officier, m. non-commissioned officer ‖ ~-ordre, m. (jur.) under-clerk ‖en ~-ordre, subordinate(ly) ‖ ~-pied, m. strap ‖ ~-sol, m. subsoil ‖ basement ‖ ~-ventrière, f. belly-band.

souscripteur, m. subscriber.

souscrire, v. a. & n. ir. to subscribe, to set one's hand to ‖ to give consent to, to consent.   [signed.

soussigné, e, a. underwritten ‖ undersigned.

soussigner, v. a. to subscribe one's name.

soustraction, f. subtraction ‖ abstraction.

soustraire, v. a. ir. to subtract, to deduct ‖ to purloin, to pilfer ‖ se ~, to forsake one's duty, to avoid, to escape.

soutache, f. braid ‖ **broder en ~**, to braid.

soutane, f. cassock ‖ cloth.

soutanelle, f. short cassock.

soute, f. balance of an account ‖ (mar.) store-room ‖small boat ‖~ aux poudres, powder-room.

soutenable, a. maintainable ‖ sufferable.

soutènement, m. prop.

souteneur, m. bully.

soutenir, v. a. ir. to support ‖ to sustain, to bear, to uphold ‖ to assert ‖ to favour, to help, to assist ‖ to be strengthening *ou* nourishing ‖ se ~, to keep oneself up, to support oneself ‖ to resist.

soutenu, e, a. supported ‖ unflagging ‖ continued ‖ unremitting ‖ elevated.

souterrain, m. subterranean place, underground ‖ tunnel ‖ basement. [terraneous.

souterrain, e, a. subterranean, sub-

soutien, m. support, prop, stay.

soutirage, m. racking (of liquors).

soutirer, v. a. to rack, to draw off ‖ to defecate ‖ to draw from ‖ to extort.

souvenir, m. remembrance, recollection, memory ‖ memorandum.

se souvenir, to remember, to recollect ‖ to bear in mind.

souvent, ad. often, oft, frequently.

souverain, e, m. & f. sovereign.

souverain, e, a. sovereign ‖ supreme ‖ –ement, ad. sovereignly ‖ absolutely, in the highest degree.

souveraineté, f. sovereignty, supremacy.

soyeux, se, a. silken, silky, soft.

spacieux, se, a. (–sement, ad.) spacious (ly) ‖ roomy ‖ wide(ly).

spadassin, m. bully, fighter.

sparadrap, m. cere-cloth ‖ adhesive plaster.

sparte, m. (bot.) rush, mat-weed, Spanish-grass.

sparterie, f. rush-matting ‖ rush-mat ‖

spasme, m. spasm.   [rush.

spasmodique, a. spasmodic.

spatule, f. spatula ‖ spoon-bill (bird).

spécial, e, a. (–ement, ad.) special(ly) ‖ particular(ly) ‖ singular(ly) ‖ peculiar(ly).

spécialité, f. speciality ‖ special study *ou* branch *ou* trade ‖ department.

spécieux, se, a. (–sement, ad.) specious (ly).

spécifier, v. a. to specify.   [(ly).

spécifique, m. specific remedy.

spécifique, a. specific.

spécimen, m. specimen.

spectacle, m. spectacle, show ‖ play, theatrical representation ‖ (fig.) public view ‖ **salle de ~**, f. play-house.

spectateur, m. spectator, looker-on ‖ by-stander ‖ –s, pl. audience.

spectre, m. apparition, ghost, sprite ‖ skeleton ‖ spectrum.

spéculateur, m. speculator, observer ‖ theorist.

spéculatif, ve, a. speculative.

spéculer, v. n. to speculate.

spéculum, m. speculum.

sperme, m. (an.) sperm.

sphère, f. sphere, globe ‖ reach.

sphérique, a. spherical.

sphincter, m. (an.) sphincter.

spinelle, m. spinel ruby.

spiral, e, a. spiral.

spirale, f. spiral line, spire.

spirite, m. spiritualist.

spiritualiser, v. a. (chim.) to spiritualise.

spiritualisme, m. spiritualism.

spiritualité, f. spirituality.

spirituel, m. spirituality ‖ spiritual matters (pl.).

spirituel, le, a. (**-lement,** ad.) spiritual (ly) ‖ incorporeal, ghostly ‖ intellectual ‖ witty ‖ wittily.
spiritueux, ɯ. spirit.
spiritueux, se, a. spirituous.
splendeur, f. splendour, brightness, lustre.
splendide, a. (**-ment,** ad.) splendid(ly).
spoliateur, trice, m. & f. spoiler ‖ despoliateur, trice, a. despoiling. [spoiler.
spolier, v. a. to despoil.
spongieux, se, a. spongy.
spontané, e, a. (**-ment,** ad.) spontane-
spontanéité, f. spontaneity.
sporadique, a. sporadical.
sputation, f. spitting ‖ spittle.
squale, ɯ. dog-fish ‖ shark.
squammeux, se, a. scaly.
squelette, m. skeleton.
squille, f. squill.
squirre, m. (méd.) scirrhus.
S. S. (Sa Sainteté), His Holiness.
stabilité, f. stability, firmness ‖ solidity, fixedness.   [ing, steadfast.
stable, a. stable, firm, solid, steady, last-
stage, m. time of probation, course.
stagiaire, m. (old) outer barrister ‖ student.
stagiaire, a. in one's "stage" (of barristers).
stagnant, e, a. stagnant.
stalle, f. stall (in a church *ou* theatre).
stampe, f. branding-iron ‖ (min.) layer,
stance, f. (poët.) stanza.   [vein.
stathouder, m. stadtholder.
station, f. station, stand, stay, sojourn ‖ ~ **pour l'alimentation de l'eau,** (rail.) watering station.
stationnaire, a. stationary.
stationnement, m. taking up a station ‖ stoppage.   [main at.
stationner, v. n. to make a stay, to re-
statique, f. statics (pl.).
statisticien, m. statistician.
statistique, f. statistics (pl.).
statistique, a. statistical.
statuaire, m. statuary (person) ‖ ~, f. statuary (art).
statuaire, a. statuary.
statue, f. statue, figure.   [cide.
statuer, v. a. to decree ‖ to enact ‖ to de-
statut, m. statute, by-law.
stéarique, a.; **bougie** ~, f. composite
stèle, m. obelisk, monolith.   [candle.
sténographe, m. stenographer, short-hand-writer ‖ reporter.
sténographie, f. stenography, short-hand-writing.   [hand.
sténographier, v. a. to write in short-
sténographique, a. stenographical.
stère, m. cubic metre.
stéréotypage, m. stereotyping.
stéréotype, a. stereotyped.
stéréotyper, v. n. to stereotype.
stéréotypeur, m. stereotyper.
stéréotypie, f. stereotyping ‖ stereotype-foundry.
stérile, a. sterile, barren, unfruitful ‖ vain ‖ farrow ‖ of scarcity ‖ **-ment,** ad. barrenly.
stérilité, f. sterility, barrenness.
sternum, m. (an.) sternum, breast-bone.

sternutatoire, m. sternutatory.
sternutatoire, a. sternutatory.
stéthoscope, m. stethoscope.
stibié, e, a. antimonial.
stigmate, m. stigma, mark, brand.
stigmatiser, v. a. to stigmatise, **to brand.**
stimuler, v. a. to stimulate.
stipendiaire, m. hireling.
stipendiaire, a. hired.
stipendié, m. stipendiary.
stipendier, v. a. to keep in pay.
stipuler, v. a. to stipulate.
stoïcien, m. stoic.
stoïcien, ne, a. stoical.
stoïcisme, m. stoicism.
stoïque, a. (**-ment,** ad.) stoic(ally).
stomachique, m. (méd.) stomachic.
stomachique, a. (an. & méd.) stomachic.
store, m. roller-blind.
strabisme, m. squinting.
strangulation, f. strangulation, strangling.
strapontin, m. bracket-seat.
strass, m. paste (to imitate diamonds).
strasse, f. floss-silk.
stratagème, m. stratagem, trick, artifice.
stratégie, f. (mil.) strategy.
stratégique, a. strategical.
stratégiste, m. strategist.
strict, e, a. (**-ement,** ad.) strict(ly) ‖ precise(ly) ‖ rigorous(ly).
strident, e, a. shrill, creaking, grating.
strié, e, a. striated.
stries, f. pl. flutings (pl.), fillets (pl.), striæ (pl.).
strophe, f. (poët.) strophe.
stuc, m. stucco.
stucateur, m. stucco plasterer.
studieux, se, a. (**-sement,** ad.) studious
stupéfait, e, a. stupified.   [(ly).
stupéfier, v. a. to stupify.
stupeur, f. stupor.
stupide, a. (**-ment,** ad.) stupid(ly).
stupidité, f. stupidity ‖ stupid thing.
style, m. style, language ‖ manner.
styler, v. a. to train, to use.
stylet, m. stiletto ‖ (chir.) probe.
su, m. knowledge.
suaire, m. winding-sheet, shroud.
suave, a. savorous, sweet, soft.
suavité, f. suavity, sweetness.
subalterne, m. & f. subaltern, inferior, subordinate.   [ordinate.
subalterne, a. subaltern, inferior, sub-
subdiviser, v. a. to subdivide.
subdéléguer, v. a. to sub-delegate.
subir, v. a. to undergo, to suffer, to submit to ‖ to be under.
subit, e, a. (**-ement,** ad.) sudden(ly).
subjectif, ve, a. subjective.
subjonctif, m. (gr.) subjunctive (mood).
subjuguer, v. a. to subjugate, to subdue ‖ to govern, to conquer.
sublimé, m. (chim.) sublimate.
sublimer, v. a. (chim.) to sublimate.
sublimité, f. sublimity.
sublunaire, a. sublunary.
submerger, v. a. to submerge, **to sub-**merse, to drown ‖ to overwhelm.
submersion, f. submersion.

subodorer, v. a. to smell at a distance.
subordination, f. subordination.
subordonné, e, m. & f. subordinate.
subordonné, e, a. subordinate.
subordonner, v. a. to subordinate.
suborner, v. a. to suborn, to bribe.
suborneur, se, m. & f. suborner.
subrécargue, m. (com., mar.) supercargo.
subrécot, m. after-reckoning.   (ly.)
subreptice, & (-ment, ad.) subreptitious
subrogé, e, a.; ~ tuteur, m. superior
    guardian and trustee.
subroger, v. a. to surrogate.
subséquemment, ad. subsequently.
subséquent, e, a. subsequent.
subside, m. subsidy.
subsidiaire, a. (jur.) subsidiary, auxiliary ||
    -ment, ad. subsidiarily, in the next place.
subsistance, f. subsistence, maintenance,
    livelihood, competence || -s, pl. provisions
    (pl.), victuals (pl.).
subsister, v. n. to subsist, to exist || to
    last, to continue || to live upon, to have
    means of living.   [ject.
substance, f. substance, real being || sub-
substantiel, le, a. (-lement, ad.) sub-
    stantial(ly).
                              [stantive.
substantif, m. (gr.) substantive || noun sub-
substantif, a. m. (gr.) substantive.
substantivement, ad. (gr.) substantively.
subterfuge, m. subterfuge, evasion.
substituer, v. a. to substitute || (jur.) to
    entail.
substitut, m. substitute.
substitution, f. substitution || (jur.) entail.
subtil, e, a. (-ement, ad.) subtile, subtle,
    thin, fine || quick || sharp(ly) || acute, keen ||
    dexterous || cunningly, smartly.
subtiliser, v. a. & n. to subtilise, to refine ||
    to cheat.
subtilité, f. subtilty, subtileness, rareness ||
    cunningness, sagacity, penetration.
suburbain, e, a. suburban.   [help.
subvenir, v. n. ir. to relieve, to assist, to
subvention, f. subsidy, supply, aid || tax.
subventionner, v. a. to subsidise || to
    support.
subversif, ve, a. subversive.
subvertir, v. a. to subvert, to overthrow.
suc, m. juice, substance.
succédané, m. (méd.) succedaneum.
succédané, e, a. (méd.) succedaneous.
succéder, v. n. to succeed || to inherit || to
    follow in order.
succès, m. success, event, issue, pros-
    perity || ~ d'estime, success owing to
    character || quiet success.
successeur, m. successor.
successif, ve, a. (-vement, ad.) suc-
    cessive(ly).   [estate.
succession, f. succession, inheritance ||
succin, m. yellow amber.
succinct, e, a. succinct, short, concise,
    brief, compendious || -ement, ad. suc-
    cinctly, concisely, briefly.
succion, f. suction.
succomber, v. n. to succumb, to sink
    under, to yield, to be overcome.   [ous.
succulent, e, a. succulent, juicy || nutriti-

succursale, f. chapel of ease || branch.
sucement, m. sucking, suck, suction.
sucer, v. a. to suck || to drain.
suceur, m. sucker.
suçoir, m. sucker.   [sucking.
suçon, m. red spot on the skin caused by
suçoter, v. a. to suck over and over.
sucre, m. sugar || ~ brut, brown sugar ||
    ~ candi, sugar-candy || ~ en pain, loaf-
    sugar, lump-sugar || pain de ~, m. sugar-
    loaf.
sucré, e, a. sugared, sugary || sweet || de-
    mure || (of persons) honeyed, bland.
sucrer, v. a. to sugar, to sweeten.
sucrerie, f. sugar-works (pl.) || -s, pl.
    sweetmeats (pl.).
sucrier, m. sugar-basin.
sucrin, a. m. (of melons) sugary.
sud, m. south || south-wind || ~-est-
    quart-est, m. south-east by east || ~-est-
    quart-~, m. south-east by south || ~-
    ouest, m. south-west || ~-ouest-quart-
    ouest, m. south-west by west || ~-ouest-
    quart-~, m. south-west by south.
sudorifique, a. sudorific.
suée, f. (fig.) fright, "stew".
suer, v. a. & n. to perspire, to sweat, to
    be in a sweat || to toil, to drudge || faire
    ~, (fig.) to try one's patience, to sicken.
suette, f. (méd.) sweating fever.
sueur, f. sweat, perspiration || (fig.) labour,
    toil, pains (pl.).
suffire, v. n. r. to suffice, to be sufficient ||
    to afford, to answer || cela suffit, it is
    enough, that will do || se ~, to provide
    for oneself, to support oneself || to find
    resources in oneself.
suffisamment, ad. sufficiently, abun-
    dantly.
suffisance, f. sufficiency || conceitedness.
suffisant, m. conceited fellow, presump-
    tuous dandy ou puppy.
suffisant, e, a. sufficient, conceited, pre-
suffixe, f. (gr.) suffix.   [sumptuous.
suffocant, e, a. suffocating.
suffoquer, v. a. & n. to suffocate, to choke.
suffragant, m. suffragan.
suffrage, m. suffrage, vote || approbation.
suggérer, v. a. to suggest, to intimate.
suggestion, f. suggestion, hint.
suicide, m. suicide (person or act).
se suicider, to commit suicide.
suie, f. soot.
suif, m. tallow, suet, fat || scolding.
suifer, v. a. to tallow.
suint, m. greasiness.
suintement, m. leaking, running out.
suinter, v. n. to leak, to ooze.
suisse, m. head beadle || porter || Swiss
    guard.
suite, f. consequence, sequel, succession ||
    series || file, line || set || continuation || train,
    attendants (pl.), attendance || rest || retinue ||
    links (pl.) || order || sans ~, unconnected ||
    par la ~, in the course of time || de ~,
    after one another, in order || tout de ~,
    immediately, instantly, all at once.
suivant, m. follower.   [attending.
suivant, e, a. following, subsequent, next,

suivant, pr. according to || ~ **que,** according as.

suivante, f. waiting-maid.

suivi, e, a. followed, connected, coherent || sought after, popular.

suivre, v. a. & n. ir. to follow, to go *ou* come after, to succeed, to pursue || to keep pace with || to keep up || to study || to carry out || to result || to attend, to accompany || to observe, to frequent.

sujet, m. subject || matter, object, cause, occasion, reason, ground, motive || stock || **mauvais ~,** rogue || **au ~ de,** about, for.

sujet, te, a. subject, exposed, bound, obliged, liable, addicted.

sujétion, f. subjection, dependence || constraint.

sujette, f. female subject.

sulfhydrique, a. (chim.) hydro-sulphuric.

sulfureux, se, a. (chim.) sulphurous.

sultan, e, m. & f. sultan || sultana.

superbe, f. pride, vanity, arrogance, vainglory, bragging.

superbe, a. (—**ment,** ad.) superb, proud (ly) || haughty || pompous, splendid, sumptuous(ly) || magnificent || arrogant(ly).

supercherie, f. cheat, fraud, deceit.

superficie, f. superficies, surface, area || superficial knowledge.

superficiel, le, a. (—**lement,** ad.) superficial(ly) || shallow || slightly.

superfin, e, a. superfine.

superflu, e, a. superfluous.

superfluité, f. superfluity.

supérieur, e, m. & f. superior || superioress.

supérieur, e, a. superior, upper, higher, prevalent, preferable || —**ement,** ad. superiorly, in a superior manner, wonderfully well.

supériorité, f. superiority.

superlatif, m. (gr.) superlative degree.

superlatif, ve, a. (—**vement,** ad.) superlative(ly).

superposer, v. a. to place over, to add.

superstitieux, se, a. (—**sement,** ad.) superstitious(ly).

superstition, f. superstition.

supplanter, v. a. to supplant.

suppléant, e, m. substitute, assistant.

suppléer, v. a. & n. to supply, to fill up, to make up, to furnish.

supplément, m. supplement, addition, complement.   [ditional.

supplémentaire, a. supplementary, additional.

suppliant, e, m. & f. supplicant, suppliant.

suppliant, e, a. suppliant.

supplice, m. corporal punishment || pain, torment.   [execute.

supplicier, v. a. to punish capitally, to

supplier, v. a. to supplicate, to entreat, to beseech, to implore.

supplique, f. petition, address.

support, m. support, prop || help, assistance || protection.

supportable, a. supportable, tolerable || sufferable, bearable.

supporter, v. a. to support, to sustain, to uphold, to prop || to bear, to suffer, to tolerate || to help, to assist.

---

supposé, e, a. supposed, substituted, pretended, counterfeit, forged || ~ **que,** supposing that.   [to imply || to forge.

supposer, v. a. to suppose, to put the case,

supposition, f. supposition, hypothesis ||

suppôt, m. agent || tool.   [forgery.

supprimer, v. a. to suppress, to smother, to conceal || to omit || to repeal.

suppression, f. suppression.

suppurer, v. n. (méd.) to suppurate.

supputation, f. computation, calculation.

supputer, v. a. to compute, to reckon, to calculate.

suprématie, f. supremacy.

suprême, a. supreme, highest || last.

sur, e, a. sour, acetous.

sur, pr. on, upon, over, in, by, near, about, towards || ~**-le-champ,** ad. immediately, instantly.

sûr, e, a. (—**ement,** ad.) sure(ly) || certain (ly) || infallible || clear || safe(ly) || steady || to be sure.

surabondamment, ad. superabundantly.

surabondance, f. superabundance.

surabondant, e, a. superabundant.

surabonder, v. a. to superabound.

suraigu, ë, a. (méd.) very acute || (mus.) very high.

surajouter, v. a. to superadd.

suranné, e, a. superannuated, worn with age, old, obsolete.

surard, d. of elder-flower.

surbande, f. fillet.

surcharge, f. surcharge, additional charge, overburden || word written on another.

surcharger, v. a. to surcharge, to overcharge, to overload.

surchauffer, v. a. to overheat.

surcroît, m. addition, increase, surplus ||

surdent, f. gag-tooth.   [de ~, extra.

surdité, f. deafness.

surdorer, v. a. to double-gild.

sureau, m. (bot.) elder, elder-tree.

surémission, f. over-issue.

surenchère, f. outbidding.

surenchérir, v. a. to outbid.

surérogatoire, a. supererogatory.

suret, te, a. sourish.

sûreté, f. surety, security, safety || steadiness || **caisse de ~,** f. iron-safe || **en ~,** safely.

surexcitation, f. over-excitement.

surexciter, v. a. to over-excite.

surface, f. surface.

surfaire, v. a. ir. to overcharge, to oversurfaix,   [rate.

surfaix, m. surcingle.

surfin, e, a. superfine.

surgeon, m. (bot.) sucker.   [land.

surgir, v. n. to arise || to land, to come to

surhausser, v. a. to raise higher, to overrate.

surhumain, e, a. superhuman.

surintendant, m. superintendent.

surjet, m. whip, overcasting || **faire un ~,** to whip (seams).

surjeter, v. a. to whip, to overcast (seams).

surlendemain, m. the day after tomorrow.

surlonge, f. sirloin of beef.   [morrow.

surmener, v. a. to overwork.

surmonter, v. a. to surmount || to rise above || to overcome, to outdo.

surmoût, m. new wort. [survive.

surnager, v. n. to swim on, to float || to

surnaturel, le, a. (-lement, ad.) supernatural(ly) || extraordinary || extraordinarily.

surnom, m. surname. [narily.

surnommer, v. a. to surname.

surnuméraire, m. supernumerary.

surnuméraire, a. supernumerary.

suros, m. splint, knot.

surpasser, v. a. to surpass || to exceed || to excel.

surplis, m. surplice. [to excel.

surplomb, m. slope, overhang.

surplomber, v. n. to slope, to overhang.

surplus, m.; au ~, moreover || yet || but.

surprendre, v. n. ir. to surprise, to take by surprise, to take unawares || to amaze, to astonish || to ensnare, to deceive, to intercept, to catch, to overtake.

surpris, e, a. surprised || of surprise.

surprise, f. surprise || Jack-in-the-box.

sursaut, m. surprise || start || en ~, with a start.

surséance, f. (jur.) suspension.

surseoir, v. a. & n. ir. to put off, to suspend || to postpone || to supersede || (jur.) to respite.

sursis, m. suspension, delay || (jur.) reprieve.

surtaux, m. over-assessment, over-rating || excessive taxation. [extra postage.

surtaxe, f. additional tax || overtaxation ||

surtaxer, v. a. to overtax, to over-assess, to overrate. [epergne.

surtout, m. upper-coat, riding-coat ||

surtout, ad. above all things, chiefly, especially. [guard.

surveillance, f. superintendence, watch,

surveillant, m. surveyor, inspector, overseer || warden.

surveille, f. two days before.

surveiller, v. a. & n. to survey, to overlook, to oversee, to inspect, to superintend, to watch.

survenance, f. (jur.) unexpected birth.

survenant, e, m. chance-comer.

survenir, v. n. ir. to survene, to come unexpectedly || to befall.

survider, v. a. to lighten, to pour away apart.

survie, f. (jur.) survivorship.

survivance, f. reversion.

survivancier, m. reversioner.

survivant, e, m. & f. surviver.

survivre, v. n. ir. to survive, to outlive, to outlast.

sus, pr. upon || ~! come! || en ~, besides, moreover, over and above.

susceptibilité, f. susceptibility, irritability, touchiness. [touchy.

susceptible, a. susceptible, sensitive,

susciter, v. a. to raise up || to create.

suscription, f. superscription, address.

susdit, e, a. aforesaid, said.

sus-nommé, e, a. a said, above-named.

suspect, e, a. suspected, suspicious.

suspecter, v. a. to suspect.

suspendre, v. a. to suspend, to hang, to hang up || to put off, to delay, to hinder.

suspendu, e, a. suspended, pendulous || (of carriages) spring.

suspens, a. m. suspended, interdicted || en ~, in suspense || (of debts) outstanding.

suspense, f. suspension.

suspensoir, m. bandage, truss.

sustentation, f. sustenance.

sustenter, v. a. to sustain, to maintain, to support.

suture, f. (an.) suture.

suzerain, m. lord paramount.

suzerain, e, a. paramount.

suzeraineté, f. suzerainty.

s. v. p. (s'il vous plaît), if you please.

svelte, a. slender, graceful, slim.

sveltesse, f. slenderness, slightness.

sycomore, m. (bot.) sycamore-tree.

sycophante, m. sycophant.

syllabaire, m. spelling-book.

syllabe, f. syllable.

syllabique, a. syllabic.

syllogisme, m. syllogism.

sylphe, m., sylphide, f. sylph, sylphid.

sylvain, m. sylvan.

sylviculteur, m. forester.

sylviculture, f. forestry.

symbole, m. symbol || creed.

symbolique, a. symbolical.

symétrie, f. symmetry. [(ally).

symétrique, a. (-ment, ad.) symmetric

symétriser, v. n. to be in symmetry.

sympathie, f. sympathy.

sympathique, a. sympathetic, congenial.

sympathiser, v. n. to sympathise.

symphonie, f. symphony || instrumental concert.

symphoniste, m. symphonist.

symptôme, m. symptom. [ing fit.

syncope, f. (méd.) syncope || swoon, faint-

syndic, m. syndic || assignee.

syndicat, m. syndicate.

synodal, e, a. synodial.

synode, m. synod.

synonyme, m. synonym.

synonyme, a. synonymous.

synonymie, f. synonymy.

synoptique, a. synoptic.

synovie, f. synovia, joint-oil.

syntaxe, f. (gr.) syntax.

synthèse, f. synthesis. [atic(ally).

systématique, a. (-ment, ad.) system-

systématiser, v. a. to systematise.

système, m. system || scheme, plan.

T.

t, m. T square.

ta, pn. f. thy || ~! tut!

tabac, m. tobacco, snuff || ~ à fumer, tobacco || ~ à priser, snuff.

tabagie, f. tap-room, smoking-house || set of smokers. [block.

tabatière, f. snuff-box || sky-light || breech-

tabellion, m. pettifogger, hedge-lawyer.

tabis, m. tabby.

tabiser, v. a. to tabby.

tablature, f. (mus.) tablature || trouble.

table, f. table || board || index || slab || (mar.) mess || ~ à coulisses, telescope-table || ~ à écrire, writing-table || ~ à manger, dining-table || ~ à rallonges, telescope-table || ~ à volets, Pembroke table || ~ de canapé, occasional table || ~ d'harmonie, sounding-board || ~ d'hôte, ordinary || ~ de jeu, ~ à jouer, card-table || ~ de nuit, bed-side stand || ~ de salon, loo-table || ~-portefeuille, Sutherland table || ~ de cuisine, dresser || aimer la ~, to like good living || tenir ~ ouverte, to keep open house.

tableau, m. picture, painting || description, representation || scenery || scenic effect || black-board || list, catalogue.

tabletier, ère, m. & f. toyman, toywoman.

tablette, f. tablet, small table, shelf || lozenge, cake || tablets, pocket-book.

tabletterie, f. fancy turnery-trade.

tablier, m. draught-board || apron, pinafore || blower || floor.

tabouret, m. stool || footstool.

tabourin, m. chimney-cowl.

tac, m. rot (of the sheep).

tache, f. spot, stain, blot || blemish, fault.

tâche, f. task || job || à la ~, by the piece || prendre à ~, to undertake.

tacher, v. a. to spot, to stain.

tâcher, v. n. to endeavour, to try.

tâcheron, m. task-worker, jobbing-workman. [spots.

tacheter, v. a. to speckle, to mark with

tacite, a. (-ment, ad.) tacit(ly) || implied.

taciturne, a. taciturn, silent.

taciturnité, f. taciturnity.

tact, m. feeling, touch || tact.

tacticien, m. tactician.

tactile, a. tactile || tangible.

tactique, f. tactics (pl.).

taffetas, m. taffeta || ~ gommé, oil-silk || ~ d'Angleterre, court-plaster.

tafia, m. tafia, molasses-rum.

taie, f. pillow-case || web (in the eye) || ~ d'oreiller, pillow-case.

taillade, f. cut, slash, gash.

taillader, v. n. to cut, to slash.

taillanderie, f. edged tools (pl.) || edged tool trade.

taillandier, m. edged tool maker.

taillant, m. edge (of a knife etc.).

taille, f. cut, cutting || edge (of a sword) || tally (stick) || shape, waist, size || deal (at cards) || (mus.) tenor || tax, talliage || de ~ à, big enough to || ~-douce, f. copperplate.

taille (de tailler); ~-crayons, m. pencil-pointer || ~-légumes, m. vegetable-cutter || ~-plumes, m. pen-cutter.

tailler, v. a. to cut, to hew || to carve, to sculpture, to tally || to deal (the cards) || to play || to make (a pen) || to prune, to prime || ~ la vigne.

tailleur, m. tailor || cutter. [dress (the vine).

tailleuse, f. tailoress.

taillis, m. copse, coppice, underwood.

tain, m. tin-plate, foil, silvering.

taire, v. a. & n. ir. to conceal, to keep secret || faire ~, to silence || se ~, to hold one's tongue ou peace, to keep silence.

talent, m. talent, faculty, power, genius, capacity || de ~, talented.

talion, m. (peine du ~, f.) retaliation.

talisman, m. talisman.

talmouse, f. cheese-cake.

taloche, f. rap on the head.

talon, m. heel || stock (at cards).

talonner, v. a. to spur || to urge || to pursue close || to beset || to dun || to bump.

talonnière, f. heel-piece || heel-wing.

talus, m. slope || bank || en ~, sloping.

taluter, v. a. to slope.

tamarin, m. (bot.) tamarind.

tambour, m. drum || drummer || tambour || paddle-box || embroidery-frame || ~ de basque, tambourine || ~-maître, corporal of the drums || ~ battant, with the drums beating || with a high hand, harshly.

tambourin, m. tabour.

tambourinage, m. beating of the drum.

tambouriner, v. a. & n. to beat the drum || to cry.

tambourineur, m. drummer.

tamis, m. sieve, bolter.

tamisage, m. sifting.

tamiser, v. a. to sift.

tamiseur, m. sifter || cinder-sifter.

tampon, m. tampion, bung, stopper || (rail.) buffer, pad.

tamponner, v. a. to a bung, to stop, to plug.

tam-tam, m. tom-tom (Indian drum).

tan, m. tan || oak-bark.

tancer, v. a. to rebuke, to scold.

tanche, f. tench (fish).

tandis que, c. whilst || whereas.

tangage, m. (mar.) pitching.

tangente, f. (math.) tangent.

tangible, a. tangible.

tanguer, v. n. (mar.) to pitch.

tanière, f. den.

tannage, m. tanning.

tanne, f. (méd.) grub.

tanné, e, a. tawny, tan-coloured.

tannée, f. used tan.

tanner, v. a. to tan || to vex.

tannerie, f. tan-yard.

tanneur, m. tanner.

tannin ou tanin, m. (chim.) tannin.

tant, ad. so much, so many, as much, as many || ~ de fois, so often || ~ soit peu, ever so little || ~ pis, so much the worse || ~ mieux, so much the better || ~ s'en faut, far from it || ~ s'en faut que, so far from that || ~ que, as long as, so far as.

tante, f. aunt || (fig.) pawnbroker.

tantinet, m. little bit || little drop.

tantôt, c. & ad. just now, presently, almost, by and by, sometimes || this afternoon ou evening. [breeze.

taon, m. ox-fly, gad-fly || ~ marin, sea-

taonner, v. a. to bore, to plague.

tapage, m. brawl, bustle, great noise.

tapageur, m. blusterer.

tapageur, se, a. noisy.

tape, f. slap, rap, tap || bung || ~-cul, m. swing-gate || jolting-carriage.

tapé, e, a. dried || bien ~, smart, slashing.

tapée, f. lot.

taper, v. a. & n. to tap, to slap, to hit, to pat || to stamp || to get || to be heady.

tapin, m. rap, knock.

en tapinois, ad. silly, by stealth.

se tapir, to squat, to crouch, to cower down.

tapis, m. carpet, tapestry || ~ de lit, rug, bedside carpet || ~ vert, grassplot || gambling-table || ~ de table, table-cover.

tapisser, v. a. to carpet || to hang with tapestry || to paper (a room).

tapisserie, f. tapestry,[6] tapestry-hangings (pl.)||fancy needle-work,fancy-work,carpet.

tapissier, m. upholsterer.

tapissière, f. upholsterer's wife||furniture-van.

tapon, m. bundle (of clothes).

tapoter, v. a. to pat, to tap || to thrum.

taquet, m. angle-block || angle-fillet (mar.) cleat || kevel || whelp || goose-neck || (tech.) catch || peg || notch || picker.

taquin, e, m. & f. tease.

taquin, e, a. teasing.

taquiner, v. a. & n. to tease.

taquinerie, f. teasing.

tarabuster, v. a. to vex, to plague.

tarare, m. winnowing-machine.

tarare! pshaw!

taraud, m. (screw-)tap, borer.

tard, ad. late || plus ~, later || au plus ~, at latest || trop ~, too late || tôt ou ~, sooner ou later || il se fait ~, it grows late.

tarder, v. n. to delay, to put off || to linger, to loiter || to long || il me tarde de . . , I long to . . .

tardif, ve, a. (-vement, ad.) tardy || slow(ly) || slackly || dilatory || backward.

tardiveté, f. lateness, backwardness.

tare, f. (com.) tare, waste || defect.

taré, e, a. damaged, spoiled || ill-famed.

tarentule, f. tarantula (spider).

tarer, v. a. to tare || to damage.

taret, m. teredo || ship-worm.

targe, f. target, shield.

targette, f. flat bolt.

se targuer, to boast.

tarière, f. auger, wimble.

tarif, m. tariff, table of rates.

tarifer, v. a. to tariff, to rate.

tarir, v. a. & n. to drain, to dry up || to exhaust || to be dried up.

tarissable, a. exhaustible.

tarissement, m. draining.

taroté, e, a. spotted like Taroc-cards.

tarots, m. pl. spotted cards (pl.).

tartan, m. tartan || plaid.

tartane, f. (mar.) tartan.

tartanelle, f. linsey-woolsey, winsey.

tartare, m.; à la ~, (culin.) with cold mustard-sauce.

tarte, f. tart.

tartelette, f. small tart.

tartine, f. slice of bread and butter ou jam.

tartre, m. tartar.

tartufe, m. hypocrite.

tartuferie, f. hypocrisy.

tas, m. heap, pile || crew || lot, set.

tasse, f. cup || mug || ~ à café, coffee-cup.

tasseau, m. hand-anvil || bracket || tassel.

tassement, m. settling, heaping up.

tasser, v. a. & n. to heap up || to grow thick.

tâter, v. a. to feel, to fumble, to grope || to try, to taste || to examine || to nurse up.

tâte-vin, m. wine-taster.

tatillon, ne, m. & f. busybody.

tatillonnage, m. meddling.

tatillonner, v. n. to keep meddling.

tâtonnement, m. feeling, groping || hesitation || uncertainty.

tâtonner, v. n. to feel, to grope || to fumble, to waver. [person.

tâtonneur, se, m. & f. groper || irresolute

à tâtons, ad. groping, feeling in the dark || feeling one's way.

tatouage, m. tattooing.

tatouer, v. a. to tattoo.

taudion, taudis, m. hovel, dog-hole.

taupe, f. mole || ~-grillon, mole-cricket.

taupier, m. mole-catcher.

taupière, f. mole-trap.

taupin, e, m. skip-jack.

taupinière, f. mole-hill || little hut.

taureau, m. bull.

tautologie, f. tautology.

taux, m. assize, rate, set price || assessment.

taveler, v. a. to spot, to speckle.

tavelure, f. spots (pl.), speckles (pl.).

taverne, f. ale-house || tavern.

taxation, f. taxation || fixing office.

taxe, f. tax, rate, set rate, impost, duty, assessment.

taxer, v. a. to tax, to set a rate upon, to lay a tax on, to rate || to charge, to accuse.

te, t', pn. thee, to thee || at, for, from, with thee || thyself.

té, m. cross-bar, cross-head || (mil.) T.

technique, a. technical.

technologie, f. technology.

technologique, a. technological.

teck, m. (bot.) teak-wood.

tégument, m. integument, tegument.

teigne, f. scald, scurf (on the head) || scale || tiny moth || tenacious fellow ou thing.

teigneux, se, a. scurfy.

teindre, v. a. ir. to dye, to tinge, to tincture, to colour, to give a colour to || to stain.

teint, m. dye || complexion.

teinte, f. tint, tinge || cast || touch.

teinter, v. a. to tint. [ing.

teinture, f. tincture, dye, dyeing || smatter-

teinturerie, f. dyeing-house || dyer's trade.

teinturier, ère, m. & f. dyer.

tel, le, a. such, like, many a one || ~ quel, such as it is || un ~, such a one || ~ maître ~ valet, like master like man.

télégramme, m. telegram.

télégraphe, m. telegraph, (fam.) wire.

télégraphie, f. telegraphy.

télégraphier, v. a. to telegraph.

télégraphique, a. telegraphic.

téléphone, m. telephone.

télescope, m. telescope.

tellement, ad. so, in such a manner || ~ que, so that. [bold(ly).

téméraire, a. (-ment, ad.) rash(ly)

témérité, f. rashness, boldness.

témoignage, m. testimony, evidence, attestation, certificate, profession ‖ proof, token, mark.   [ence ‖ to show.

témoigner, v. a. to testify ‖ to give evid-

témoin, m. witness, deponent ‖ evidence ‖ ~ **oculaire,** eye-witness.

tempe, f. temple (of the head).

tempérament, m. temper, complexion, constitution, nature ‖ (mus.) temperament.

tempérant, e, a. temperate, frugal, sober.

température, f. temperature, climate.

tempéré, e, a. temperate, moderate.

tempérer, v. a. to temper, to moderate, to cool, to calm.

tempête, f. tempest, storm ‖ whirl-wind ‖

tempêter, v. n. to storm.   [trouble.

temple, m. temple, church ‖ fane.

templier, m. templar.   [temporarily.

temporaire, a. temporary ‖ —**ment,** ad.

temporel, m. temporalities (of a church) (pl.) ‖ temporal power *ou* matters (pl.) [poral(ly).

temporel, le, a. (–lement, ad.) tem-

temporiser, v. n. to temporise, to delay.

temporiseur, m. temporiser.

temps, m. time ‖ season ‖ weather ‖ opportunity, occasion ‖ leisure ‖ (gr.) tense ‖ **du bon ~,** leisure time ‖ enjoyment ‖ **dans le ~,** formerly ‖ **pour un ~,** for a while ‖ **à ~,** in time ‖ **avec le ~,** with time ‖ **de tout ~,** at all times, from time immemorial ‖ **de ~ en ~,** from time to time ‖ **en même ~,** at the same time.

tenable, a. bearable ‖ tenable.

tenace, a. tenacious.

ténacité, f. tenacity

tenailles, f. pl. pincers (pl.), nippers (pl.).

tenancier, ière, m. & f. tenant, occupier, copyholder.

tenant, e, m. challenger ‖ defendant ‖ —**s et aboutissants,** pl. butts and bounds (pl.) ‖ particulars (pl.) ‖ ins and outs (pl.) ‖ connections (pl.) ‖ habits (pl.) ‖ **tout d'un ~,** contiguous.

tenant, e, a.; **séance -e,** forthwith.

tendance, f. tendency.

tendelet, m. awning, tilt (of a boat).

tender, m. (rail.) tender.

tendeur, m. hanger ‖ layer.

tendon, m. tendon, sinew.

tendre, v. a. & n. n. to bend, to bow, to stretch out, to reach out, to hang up (drapery)– ‖ to tend, to be inclined towards ‖ to aim at ‖ to go to ‖ to contribute.

tendre, a. tender, soft ‖ moving, sensible ‖ young ‖ delicate ‖ —**ment,** ad. tenderly ‖ passionately, affectionately.   [ness ‖ delicacy.

tendresse, f. tenderness, affection, kind-

tendron, m. tendril, spring ‖ (fig.) young girl ‖ **–s,** pl. gristle, cartilage.

tendu, e, a. stretched, bent, hung ‖ light, tense ‖ stiff.   [intricacy.

ténèbres, f. pl. darkness, obscurity ‖ doubt ‖

ténébreux, se, a. dark, gloomy ‖ (fig.) underhand.

teneur, f. (jur.) tenor, purport ‖ **terms** ‖ ~ **de livres,** m. book-keeper.

ténia, m. tænia, tape-worm.

---

tenir, v. a. & n. ir. to hold, to keep, to contain ‖ to enjoy, to possess ‖ to maintain ‖ to stop, to hinder ‖ to adhere, to stick, to be contiguous ‖ to withstand, to resist ‖ to be sitting ‖ to side with ‖ to depend upon ‖ ~ **à,** to care about ‖ **en ~,** to be caught ‖ to be a dupe ‖ **se ~,** to stick, to adhere, to hold fast, to lay hold of, to stand, to stay, to remain in a place, to lie ‖ **s'en ~ à,** to rely on ‖ to keep to ‖ to abide by ‖ to stick to ‖ to confine oneself to ‖ to stop with ‖ **se ~ de,** to forbear ‖ **se ~ droit,** to stand upright ‖ **se ~ pour,** to consider oneself ‖ **s'en ~ là,** to stop short ‖ to let it alone ‖ to be satisfied with that ‖ **y ~,** to prize it much.

tension, f. tension ‖ application.

tentateur, trice, m. & f. tempter.

tentation, f. temptation.

tentative, f. attempt, trial.

tente, f. tent ‖ pavilion ‖ awning.

tenter, v. a. to tempt, to try.

tenture, f. hangings (pl.), tapestry.

tenu, e, a. held, kept ‖ bound, obliged.

ténu, e, a. tenuous, thin.

tenue, f. hold, holding, duration ‖ sitting, manner, demeanour ‖ steadiness, firmness ‖ tenure ‖ ~ **des livres,** book-keeping ‖ grande ~, gala ‖ **petite ~,** undress ‖ **tout d'une ~,** contiguous.

ténuité, f. tenuity.

ter, ad. third ‖ (mus.) three times.

tercet, m. (poét.) tiercet.

térébenthine, f. turpentine.

térébinthe, m. (bot.) turpentine-tree.

tergiverser, v. n. to shuffle.

terme, m. term, limit, bound ‖ word, expression ‖ term of time, appointed time ‖ quarter (three months) ‖ rent.

terminaison, f. (gr.) termination, ending.

terminer, v. a. to terminate, to limit, to bound, to end, to complete.

ternaire, a. ternary.   [dice.

terne, m. trey (at a lottery) ‖ two threes (at

terne, a. dull, leaden ‖ wan.

ternir, v. a. to tarnish, to dim ‖ to stain, to sully, to spot, to dull ‖ **se ~,** to tarnish ‖ to grow dull, to fade, to decay.

ternissure, f. tarnishing ‖ dullness ‖ blemish.   [~ **bas,** low lands (pl.).

terrain, m. ground, ground-plot, soil ‖

terrasse, f. terrace, platform.

terrassement, m. earthwork ‖ banking ‖ ballasting.

terrasser, v. a. to terrace, to throw *ou* fling down ‖ to nonplus, to overwhelm ‖ to damp one's spirits, to discourage.

terrassier, m. terrace-maker ‖ ballaster.

terre, f. earth, ground, estate ‖ land ‖ world ‖ ~ **cuite,** terra cotta ‖ ~ **ferme,** continent, mainland ‖ ~ **franche,** mould ‖ ~ **houille,** pit-coal ‖ ~ **promise,** Land of promise ‖ ~ **sacrée,** holy ground ‖ ~ **sainte,** holy Land ‖ consecrated ground ‖ **à ~,** low ‖ prosy ‖ commonplace ‖ **de ~,** earthen ‖ **par ~,** on the ground ‖ **down** ‖ by land ‖ **prendre ~,** to land ‖ ~ **neuvier,** m. Newfoundland fisher ‖ ~ **plein,** m. platform of earth.

terreau, m. leaf-mould, compost.
terrer, v. a. to earth || to clay || se ~, to run to earth || (mil.) to shelter in trenches.
terrestre, a. terrestrial, earthly.
terreur, f. terror, dread, great fear || awe || ~ panique, panic terror.
terreux, se, a. earthy || cadaverous || dull.
terrible, a. (-ment, ad.) dreadful(ly) || awful(ly) || enfant ~, m. child who makes awkward remarks.
terrier, m. terrier || burrow.
terrifier, v. a. to terrify.
terrine, f. earthen pan || pot || dish || potted meat || en ~, potted.
terrir, v. n. to lay eggs in the sand (of tortoises) || to approach land (of fishes) || (mar.) to land.
territoire, m. territory.
territorial, e, a. territorial.
terroir, m. soil, ground.
terrorisme, m. terrorism.
terroriste, m. terrorist.
tertiaire, a. tertiary.
tertre, m. hill, hillock, rising ground.
tes, pn. (pl. of ton, ta), thy.
tesseaux, m. pl. trestle-trees (pl.).
tesson, m. fragment of broken glass ou china || potsherd.
testacé, m. testacean.
testacé, e, a. testaceous.
testament, m. testament, last will.
testamentaire, a. testamentary || héritier ~, m. heir by a will || disposition ~, f. (jur.) devise.
testateur, trice, m. & f. testator || testatrix.
tester, v. n. to make one's will.
têt, m. potsherd || test.
tétanos, m. (méd.) tetanus.
têtard, m. tadpole || (hort.) pollard.
tête, f. head || brains (pl.), mind, wits (pl.), judgment || top || choice, best || faculties || obstinacy || front || ~ baissée, head down || headlong || ~-bêche, ad. head to foot || ~ à perruque, barber's block || ~ de loup, Turk's head || ~-à-tête, m. private interview || ~-à-tête, ad. face to face, cheek by jowl.
téter, v. a. & n. to suck || donner à ~, to suckle. [cap.
têtière, f. headstall of a bridle || infant's
tétin, m. nipple.
tétine, f. cow's udder || dent (of a cuirass).
téton, m. breast of a woman.
tette, f. teat, dug.
têtu, e, a. stubborn, headstrong.
texte, m. text.
textile, a. textile. [word for word.
textuel, le, a. (-lement, ad.) textual(ly) ||
texture, f. texture, weaving.
thaumaturge, m. thaumaturgy.
thé, m. tea || tea-party || ~ bou, bohea.
théâtral, e, a. theatrical.
théâtre, m. theatre, stage, play-house ||
théière, f. tea-pot. [de ~, theatrical.
théisme, m. theism.
théiste, m. theist.
thème, m. theme, exercise, subject.
théocratie, f. theocracy.
théocratique, a. theocratical.

théologal, m. theologist.
théologal, e, a. divine.
théologie, f. theology.
théologien, m. theologian, divine.
théologique, a. theological.
théorème, m. theorem.
théoricien, m. theorist.
théorie, f. theory, speculation.
théorique, a. (-ment, ad.) theoretic(ally).
thérapeutique, f. therapeutics (pl.).
thériaque, f. theriaca, treacle.
thermal, e, a. mineral || eaux -es, pl. hot mineral waters (pl.).
thermes, m. pl. hot baths (pl.).
thermomètre, m. thermometer.
thésauriser, v. n. to treasure ou hoard up.
thésauriseur, m. hoarder.
thèse, f. thesis, proposition, disputation || en ~ générale, as a rule.
thibaude, f. cow-hair cloth.
thon, m. tunny (fish). [pectoral.
thoracique, a. (an.) thoracic || (méd.)
thorax, m. (an.) thorax, chest.
thym, m. (bot.) thyme.
thyrse, m. (bot.) thyrsus.
tiare, f. tiara, triple crown.
tibia, m. shin-bone.
tic, m. (méd.) tick || convulsive motion || ridiculous habit. [cool(ly).
tiède, a. (-ment, ad.) lukewarm(ly) ||
tiédeur, f. lukewarmness.
tiédir, v. n. to grow lukewarm, to cool.
tien, m. thy own, thine || les -s, thine, thy kindred (pl.), thy relations (pl.).
tien, ne, pn. thine.
tierce, f. tierce (in fencing).
tiers, tierce, m. & f. third part || third person || le ~ et le quart, everybody, all the world.
tiers, tierce, a. third || of a third person || tertian || ~ état, m. third state.
tige, f. trunk, stem, body || stalk || shank || shaft || rod.
tignasse, f. paltry wig || mop.
tigre, sse, m. & f. tiger || tigress.
tigré, e, a. spotted, speckled.
tillac, m. deck (of a ship).
tillage, m. stripping.
tille, f. bast of young linden-trees || hari.
tiller, v. a. to peel hemp ou flax.
tilleul, m. (bot.) lime-tree, linden-tree || infusion of lime-tree flowers.
tilleur, se, m. & f. stripper.
timbale, f. kettle-drum || cup || battledore || (culin.) raised pie.
timbalier, m. kettle-drummer.
timbre, m. stamp || bell of a clock, call-bell || sound, ring || stamp-office || stamp-duty || post-mark || postage stamp.
timbré, e, a. stamped || crack-brained.
timbrer, v. a. to stamp.
timbreur, m. stamper. [ous(ly).
timide, a. (-ment, ad.) timid(ly) || timor-
timidité, f. timidity, shyness.
timon, m. beam, pole || shaft || (mar.) helm, tiller || (fig.) helm.
timonerie, f. steerage.
timonier, m. wheel-horse || steersman.
timoré, e, a. timorous.

tin, m. (mar.) block || skid.

tinctorial, e, a. used in dyeing.

tine, f. long tub.

tinette, f. small tub, kit.   [roar.

tintamarre, m. clatter, great noise, up-

tintement, m. tinkling (of a bell) || jing-
ling || ~ d'oreilles, tingling in the ear.

tinter, v. a. & n. to strike ou toll a bell,
to chink || to tingle.

tintouin, m. tingling in the ears || trouble ||
uneasiness.

tique, f. tick.

tiquer, v. n. to have the tick.

tiqueté, e, a. speckled, variegated.

tiqueur, se, a. crib-biting.

tir, m. shooting || range || shooting-ground.

tirade, f. long train ou series of words ||
(mus.) slur.

tirage, m. drawing, pulling || draught ||
printing off || towing-path.

tiraillement, m. pulling || twitching.

tirailler, v. a. & n. to pull about, to haul
about, to tease || to shoot || to skirmish.

tiraillerie, f. sharp-shooting, skirmish.

tirailleur, m. sharp-shooter, rifleman,
skirmisher.

tirant, m. string (of a purse) || shoe-strap,
boot-strap || iron bar, cramp || brace (of a
drum) || (mar.) draught.

tirasse, f. draw-net.

tirasser, v. a. to catch with a draw-net.

tire, f. jerk (of the wing) || tout d'une ~,
at a stretch || ~-d'aile, m. quick jerk ||
à ~ d'aile, at full speed.

tire (de tirer): ~-balle, m. ramrod-
screw || ~-bottes, m. boot-jack || ~-
bouchon, m. cork-screw || ringlet || ~-
bourre, m. worm-screw || ~-bouton, m.
button-hook || ~-clou, m. claw-hammer ||
~-fond, m. (chir.) turrel || ~-lait, m.
breast-glass || (boire à) ~-larigot, m.
(pop.) to drink hard or excessively || ~-
ligne, m. ruling-pen || ~-moelle, m.
marrow-spoon || ~-pied, m. shoemaker's
stirrup || ~-plomb, m. glazier's vice.

tirelire, m. song of the lark || ~, f. money-
box.

tirer, v. a. to draw, to pull, to lug, to
pluck, to take off || to gather, to reap || to
demand, to exact || to discharge, to fire ||
se ~, to get out of.

tiret, m. slip (of parchment) || hyphen.

tireur, m. drawer || drawer of a bill of ex-
change || shooter, rifleman, sharp-shooter ||
sportsman || wire-drawer || fencer || game-
keeper || ~ d'armes, fencing-master.

tireuse, f. lady shooter || ~ de cartes,
fortune-teller.

tiroir, m. drawer || slide.

tisane, f. decoction || herb-tea || ~ de
champagne, light champagne.

tison, m. brand, fire-brand.

tisonner, v. a. to stir the fire.

tisonnier, m. poker (in forges).

tissage, m. weaving.

tisser, v. a. to weave.

tisserand, m. weaver.

tisseranderie, f. weaver's trade.

tissu, m. tissue || texture || ~ métallique,
wire-gauze.

titiller, v. a. to tickle.

titre, m. title || title-page || quality, right,
voucher || document || title-deed || claim ||
standard (of coin) || à ~ de, by right of ||
à ~ d'ami, as a friend || à bon ~, à
juste ~, justly, with reason || au ~,
standard || en ~, on the title || head, chief,
regular.

titrer, v. a. to title.

tituber, v. n. to titubate, to stumble.

titulaire, m. incumbent.

titulaire, a. titular || incumbent.

toast, m. toast || health.

tocsin, m. alarm-bell.

toge, f. toga || robe.

tohu-bohu, m. hurly-burly.

toi, pn. thou, thee || à ~, to thee || toujours
à ~, always yours.

toile, f. cloth, linen-cloth, linen || curtain
(at a theatre) || ~ cirée, oil-cloth || floor-
cloth || ~ métallique, wire-gauze || ~
d'emballage, pack-cloth || ~ vernie,
oil-skin || ~ à sac, sack-cloth || ~ à
matelas, tick || ~ peinte, printed calico ||
~ d'araignée, cobweb.

toilerie, f. linen-cloth trade || linen-drapery
ware.

toilette, f. toilet, dressing-table || wash-
stand || lady's attire || wrapping cloth ||
grande ~, full dress || ~-commode,
pedestal washstand.

toilier, ière, m. & f. linendraper.

toise, f. fathom.

toiser, v. a. to measure with a fathom,
to examine from head to foot.

toison, f. fleece || ~ d'or, golden fleece.

toit, m. roof || house || penthouse.

toiture, f. roofing.

tôle, f. sheet-iron.

tolérable, a. tolerable, endurable || mid-
dling || -ment, ad. tolerably.

tolérance, f. toleration || sufferance.

tolérant, e, a. tolerating.

tolérantisme, m. system of toleration.

tolérer, v. a. to tolerate, to suffer.

tôlerie, f. sheet-iron manufacture.

tolet, m. (mar.) thole || thole-pin.

tollé, m. outcry || hue and cry.

tomaison, f. number of a volume.

tomate, f. (bot.) tomato.

tombant, e, a. falling, drooping || flowing ||
à la nuit ~e, at nightfall.

tombe, f. tomb, tomb-stone, grave.

tombeau, m. tomb, grave, grave-stone.

tombée, f. fall.

tombelier, m. carter.

tomber, v. n. to fall, to fall down, to drop ||
to dwindle, to desist, to sin || ~ à terre,
to fall to the ground || ~ par terre, to
fall down || ~ malade, to fall sick.

tombereau, m. tumbrel, dung-cart || cart-
load.

tombola, f. tombola (lottery).

tome, m. tome, volume.

ton, pn. thy.

ton, m. tune, note, sound, voice || accent,
tone || style || donner le ~, to lead the
fashion || (mus.) to lead the choir.

tondage, m. shearing.

tondeur, m. shearer || clipper.

tondeuse, f. shearing-machine ‖ ~ de gazon, lawn-mower.
tondre, v. a. to shear, to clip ‖ to shave ‖ to crop ‖ to mow ‖ to pare.
tonicité, f. (méd.) tonicity.
tonique, m. tonic.
tonique, f. (mus.) key-note.
tonique, a. tonic.
tonne, f. ton ‖ tun.
tonneau, m. cask ‖ tub ‖ (mar.) ton.
tonnelier, m. cooper. [bower.
tonnelle, f. tunnel-net ‖ green arbour ‖
tonnellerie, f. cooperage.
tonner, v. n. to thunder ‖ (fig.) to inveigh against. [nipple-lump.
tonnerre, m. thunder ‖ (of fire arms)
tonsure, f. tonsure ‖ clergy (pl.).
tonsurer, v. a. to give tonsure to.
tonte, f. shearing ‖ shearing-time ‖ wool ‖
tontine, f. tontine. [crop.
tontisse, f. hangings (pl.) ‖ papier-~, m. flock-paper ‖ **bourre** ~, f. cloth-shearings (pl.). [of trees).
tonture, f. shearing (of cloth) ‖ clipping
topaze, f. topaz.
toper, v. n. to agree ‖ to stake.
topinambour, m. Jerusalem artichoke.
topique, m. topic.
topique, a. topical.
topographie, f. topography.
topographique, a. topographical.
toquade, f. infatuation ‖ mad fancy ‖
toque, f., **toquet,** m. cap, bonnet. [hobby.
toqué, e, a. touched ‖ cracked, infatuated.
torche, f. torch, link.
torcher, v. a. to wipe, to rub clean ‖ to do in haste ‖ to drub.
torchère, f. torch ‖ candelabrum.
torchis, m. mud, loam ‖ loam-coated pit ‖ mur de ~, m. mud-wall.
torchon, m. towel, dish-clout, duster ‖ ~ de cuisine, dish-cloth.
tordage, m. twisting (of silk).
tordre, v. a. ir. to twist, to writhe, to wring ‖ to wrest.
torgniole, f. whitlow ‖ thump, rap.
torpeur, f. torpor, numbness.
torpille, f. torpedo, cramp-fish.
torquette, f. quantity of sea-fish wrapped up in straw ‖ twisted tobacco.
torréfier, v. a. to torrefy.
torrent, m. torrent, violent current ‖ flood.
torrentiel, le, a. torrential, falling in torrents.
torrentueux, se, a. torrent-like.
torride, a. torrid.
tors, e, a. twisted, twined, wrung ‖ wreathed ‖ crooked.
torsade, f. twisted string, torsel.
torse, m. torso, trunk.
torser, v. a. to wreathe, to twist.
torsion, f. twisting.
tort, m. wrong, injury, harm, mischief, detriment ‖ à ~, wrongfully, without a cause ‖ à ~ et à travers, at random, right and left, inconsiderately ‖ **avoir** ~, to be in the wrong.
torticolis, m. (méd.) stiff-neck ‖ hypocrite.
tortillage, m. rigmarole ‖ shuffling.

tortillement, m. twisting ‖ shuffling ‖ wriggle.
tortiller, v. a. & n. to twist, to writhe ‖ to shuffle, to use shifts ‖ to waddle ‖ se ~, to wriggle, to writhe.
tortillon, m. cushion (for the head).
tortin, m. thick twisted tapestry.
tortionnaire, a. unjust ‖ violent.
tortis, m. threads twisted together (pl.).
tortu, e, a. tortuous, crooked ‖ bandy.
tortue, f. turtle, tortoise.
tortuer, v. a. to make crooked ‖ se ~, to grow crooked, to warp.
tortueux, se, a. (—sement, ad.) tortuous (ly) ‖ winding ‖ unfair ‖ crooked(ly).
tortuosité, f. crookedness.
torture, f. torture, rack.
torturer, v. a. to torture ‖ to rack ‖ to wrest. [servative.
tory (pl. **tories**), m. Tory (English Conservative).
tôt, ad. soon, quickly ‖ ~ ou tard, sooner or later ‖ au plus ~, as soon as possible.
total, m. totality, whole sum ‖ au ~, en ~, all in all, upon the whole.
total, e, a. (—ement, ad.) total(ly) ‖ whole ‖ entire(ly) ‖ utter(ly) ‖ complete(ly).
totaliser, v. a. to form a total of.
totalité, f. totality, whole.
toton, m. teetotum.
touage, m. (mar.) towing.
touaille, f. roller-towel, jack-towel.
touchant, e, a. touching, affecting, moving, pathetic ‖ ~, pr. about, concerning.
touche, f. (mus.) stop, key ‖ fret ‖ touch stroke ‖ trial of metals ‖ fescue ‖ tail-piece ‖ pierre de ~, f. touchstone.
toucher, m. touch, feeling.
toucher, v. a. & n. to touch, to feel, to handle ‖ to play (upon a musical instrument) ‖ to ink (type) ‖ to move, to affect, to represent ‖ to speak ‖ to reach, to concern, to relate to, to regard ‖ to meddle with ‖ se ~, to touch (one another).
toue, f. ferry-boat.
touée, f. tow-line, warp.
touer, v. a. (mar.) to tow, to warp.
touffe, f. tuft ‖ bunch ‖ cluster ‖ thicket.
touffu, e, a. tufted, thick, bushy.
toujours, ad. always, ever, evermore, continually ‖ nevertheless ‖ all the same.
toupet, m. tuft of hair ‖ foretop ‖ scalp ‖ wig ‖ front ‖ pluck, "brass".
toupie, f. top ‖ ~ d'Allemagne, humming-top ‖ faire aller une ~, to spin a
toupillon, m. small tuft. [top.
tour, m. turn, turning ‖ revolution, circumference, circuit, compass ‖ excursion ‖ turner's lathe ‖ trick, juggle ‖ turning-box (of convents) ‖ à ~, by turns ‖ en un ~ de main, in an instant ‖ ~, f. tower ‖ (at chess) castle, rook.
tourbe, f. turf, peat ‖ mob.
tourbeux, se, a. turfy, peaty.
tourbière, f. turf-pit.
tourbillon, m. whirlwind ‖ whirl, vortex, tornado ‖ bustle ‖ cloud.
tourbillonner, v. n. to whirl, to go whirling round, to turn round rapidly.
tourelle, f. turret.

touret, m. small turner's lathe || wheel || reel.   [a convent.]

tourière, f. attendant of a turning-box (of

tourillon, m. trunnion || pivot || bearing-

touriste, m. tourist.   [neck.

tourlourou, m. young foot-soldier.

tourment, m. torment, pain, anguish.

tourmentant, e, a. tormenting || trouble-

tourmente, f. tempest, storm.   [some.

tourmenter, v. a. to torment, to torture, to rack, to plague, to trouble, to vex || se ~, to agitate oneself, to be vexed, to tumble, to toss || to warp.

tournailler, v. n. to turn about.

tournant, m. turning || whirlpool.

tourné, e, a. turned || spoiled || sour || bien ~, well-shaped.

tournebride, m. inn near a country-seat for servants and horses.

tournebroche, m. kitchen-jack, turnspit.

tournée, f. round, circuit, walk, turn, visit || visitation || journey.

tourner, v. a. & n. to turn, to turn round, to wind, to tack about, to revolve || to change, to convert || to corrupt || to be spoiled || se ~, to turn, to turn about, to go about || to be changed, to change, to become || se ~ en, to be changed into.

tournesol, m. (bot.) sun-flower

tourneur, m. turner.

tournevis, m. turnscrew, screw-driver.

tourniquet, m. turnstile || (mar.) swivel.

tournoi, m. tournament.

tournoiement, m. turning round, rotation, whirling || (de tête) giddiness.

tournoyer, v. n. to turn round, to turn about, to whirl || to hesitate, to shuffle || to beat about the bush.

tournure, f. turn || turner's work || shape, figure || look || curl || disposition || bustle (of a lady's dress).

tourte, f. tart || pie.   [a lady's dress).

tourteau, m. oil-cake.

tourtereau, m. young turtle-dove.

tourterelle, f. turtle-dove.

tourtière, f. tart-pan, pie-dish.

Toussaint, f. All-Saints'-Day.

tousser, v. n. to cough || to hem.

tousseur, se, m. & f. cougher.

tout, m. whole, all || point du ~, pas du ~, not at all || le ~ ensemble, the whole taken together || jouer le ~, to stake all (at cards).

tout, e, a. & ad. all, whole, whatever, any, every || wholly, quite, all, thoroughly || ~ beau, softly, not so fast || ~ à coup, ad. all of a sudden || ~ à fait, ad. alto-gether, entirely || ~ à l'heure, ad. just now, immediately, instantly || ~ de suite, ad. directly, immediately.

toutefois, c. yet, however, nevertheless.

toute-puissance, f. omnipotence.

toutou, m. bow-wow, doggy.

toux, f. cough || coughing.

toxique, m. poison.

tracas, m. bustle || splutter.

tracasser, v. a. & n. to tease, to plague, to trouble || to bustle.

tracasserie, f. shuffling, shuffle, shift, cavil, bickering || annoyance.

tracassier, ière, m. & f. caviller || trouble-some body.   [some.

tracassier, ière, a. cavilling || trouble-

trace, f. trace, mark, step, footstep.

tracé, m. outline || draught || direction || laying out || faire le ~ de, to lay out.

tracement, m. drawing, delineation || lay-ing out.   [to impress, to sketch.

tracer, v. a. to trace, to draw, to imprint,

trachée-artère, f. (an.) wind-pipe.

trachéotomie, f. (chir.) tracheotomy.

traction, f. traction.   [ditional(ly).

traditionnel, le, a. (-lement, ad.) tra-

traducteur, m. translator.

traduction, f. translation.

traduire, v. a. to translate || to interpret || to transfer.

traduisible, a. translatable.

trafic, m. traffic, trade.

trafiquer, v. n. to traffic, to trade, to deal.

trafiqueur, m. trafficker.

tragédie, f. tragedy.

tragédien, m. tragedian.

tragi-comédie, f. tragi-comedy || ~-co-mique, a. tragi-comical.

tragique, m. tragic art ou style ou char-acter ou author || something tragical.

tragique, a. (-ment, ad.) tragical(ly).

trahir, v. a. to betray || to belie || to frus-trate.

trahison, f. treason, treachery.

traille, f. ferry-boat.

train, m. (rail.) train || rate || pace, footstep || attendants, equipage || bustle, noise || float of wood || ~ de maison, establishment || ~ d'aller, (rail.) down-train || ~ de mar-chandises, (rail.) luggage- ou goods-train || ~ de retour, (rail.) back- ou up-train || ~ omnibus, (rail.) parliamentary-train || ~ poste, (rail.) mail-train || à fond de ~, at full speed || en ~, in spirits || in the act of || about it || busy || on the way to || begun || going, working || aller son ~, to go on || to keep going on || to go on at the old rate || mener grand ~, to live in great style || to drive at a fine rate.

traînard, m. lagger, loiterer, straggler.

traîneau, m. sledge, sled || draw-net.

traînée, f. train || trail || street-walker.

traîner, v. a. & n. to draw, to drag, to trail || to haul || to put off || to languish, to linger || se ~, to crawl, to creep along.

traîneur, m. straggler.

train-train, m. regular course, routine.

traire, v. a. ir. to milk.

trait, e, a. wire-drawn || milked.

trait, m. arrow, shaft, dart, bolt || stroke-dash || touch (of a pencil) || lash, leather-string || thought, fancy, sentiment || be-haviour || action, turn || trick.

traitable, a. tractable.

traitant, m. contractor.

traite, f. distance, journey || trade, trading || draught || transport, exportation || remittance of money || ~ des nègres, slave-trade || tout d'une ~, at a stretch.

traité, m. treaty, agreement || treatise.

traitement, m. treatment, usage || salary, emoluments (pl.).

traiter, v. a. & n. to treat, to negotiate || to manage, to handle, to entertain, to discourse || ~ **de**, to call || to style || to address by the title of || **se ~**, to treat one another || to be treated.

traiteur, m. eating-house keeper.

traître, **sse**, m. & f. traitor || traitress.

traître, **sse**, a. treacherous || **en ~**, treacherously.

traîtreusement, ad. treacherously.

trajet, m. way, passage || distance || journey.

tramail, m. trammel.

trame, f. woof, warp, weft || plot.

tramer, v. a. to weave || to plot, to hatch.

tramontane, f. north-wind || north-star || **perdre la ~**, to get confused.

tramway, m. tramway, tram.

tranchant, m. (sharp) edge.

tranchant, e, a. sharp, cutting || decisive, peremptory.

tranche, f. slice, collop, chop || edge || ~-**lard**, m. slicing-knife || ~-**montagne**, m. bully.

tranchée, f. trench || drain || (rail.) cutting || **-s**, pl. colic || pains (pl.).

tranchefile, f. head-band (of a book).

tranchelard, m. larding-knife.

trancher, v. n. & n. to cut off *ou* into || to decide, to determine, to resolve, to solve a difficulty, to end || to contrast strongly || to cut short, to tell one's mind plainly || ~ **du grand seigneur**, to set up for a great lord.

tranchet, m. paring-knife.

tranchoir, m. trencher.

tranquille, a. (-**ment**, ad.) tranquil(ly) || quiet(ly) || still, peaceful, easy || calmly.

tranquilliser, v. a. to tranquillise, to quiet, to still, to calm || **se ~**, to make oneself easy, to be composed.

tranquillité, f. tranquillity, calmness.

transaction, f. transaction, convention, treaty, agreement.

transalpin, e, a. Transalpine.

transatlantique, a. Transatlantic.

transborder, v. a. to tranship.

transcendant, e, a. transcendent.

transcripteur, m. transcriber.

transcrire, v. a. ir. to copy.

transe, f. apprehension, anxiety.

transfèrement, m. transfer.

transférer, v. a. to transfer || to remove || to postpone.

transfert, m. transfer (of property etc.).

transfiguration, f. transfiguration.

transformer, v. a. to transform.

transfuge, m. fugitive, deserter.

transfusion, f. (chir.) transfusion.

transgresser, v. a. to transgress.

transgresseur, m. transgressor.

transiger, v. n. to come to an agreement.

transir, v. a. & n. to chill, to numb, to make cold || to be frozen || to shiver.

transitif, **ve**, a. (gr.) transitive.

transitoire, a. transitory.

translatif, **ve**, a. translatory.

translation, f. removal, postponement || transfer.

translucide, a. translucent, translucid.

transmettre, v. a. ir. to transmit, to transfer, to convey. [ferable.

transmissible, a. transmissible, transferable.

transmuer, v. a. to transmute.

transparent, m. ruled lines (to put under paper) (pl.) || transparent paper || transparency.

transparent, e, a. transparent.

transpercer, v. a. to pierce through || to run through.

transpirer, v. a. to transpire, to perspire || to get known.

transplanter, v. a. to transplant.

transport, m. transport || exportation, carriage || ecstacy, rapture || **frais de ~**, m. pl. carriage || **au cerveau**, (méd.) delirium, light-headedness.

transporter, v. a. to transport, to transfer, to remove, to rummage || **se ~**, to go, to repair.

transposer, v. a. to transpose. [tiate.

transsubstantier, v. a. to transubstantiate.

transsuder, v. a. to transude, to sweat.

transvasement, m. decanting.

transvaser, v. a. to decant.

transversal, e, a. transverse, crossing || **-ement**, ad. transversely, crosswise.

transvider, v. a. to pour from one vessel into another. [into another.

trantran, m. knack.

trapèze, m. trapeze || (géom.) trapezium || (an.) trapezius muscle.

trappe, f. trap || trap-door || pitfall.

trappiste, m. monk of the order of La Trappe.

trapu, e, a. squat || thick-set, stumpy.

traque, f. beating *ou* enclosing of a wood [for game.

traquenard, m. trap. [for game.

traquer, v. a. to entrap || to surround a wood, to drive game. [wild beasts.

traquet, m. mill-clapper || trap, snare (for

traumatique, a. (méd.) traumatic.

travail, m. labour, toil, work, piece of work || industry || trouble || travise, trave || labour, travail, child-birth || **travaux forcés**, m. pl. penal servitude.

travailler, v. a. & n. to labour, to work, to toil || to disorder, to trouble || to ferment || to polish (one's style) || to warp || to chink || to fatigue || to sophisticate.

travailleur, m. labourer, workman || painstaker || pioneer.

travailleur, **se**, a. industrious.

travée, f. (arch.) bay of joists || triforium.

travers, m. breadth || whim, freak, oddity, caprice || **à ~**, **au ~**, across, athwart, through || **en ~**, across, sidewise || **de ~**, awry, across, crosswise || in a wrong sense.

traverse, f. traverse, cross-piece || cross-road || trench || (rail.) sleeper, cross-sleeper || (fig.) thwarting obstacle || **à la ~**, untowardly. [passage.

traversée, f. (mar.) voyage || crossing ||

traverser, v. a. to traverse, to cross, to get over, to pass over || (fig.) to thwart, to cross, to disturb, to vex.

traversier, **ère**, a. crossing || plying across || favourable for crossing.

traversin, m. bolster || cross-bar || stretcher.

travesti, m. travesty || gentleman's part acted by a lady.

travestir, v. a. to disguise || to misrepresent || to travesty || se ~, to disguise oneself.

travestissement, m. disguise, travesty.

trayon, m. dug, teat.

trébuchant, e, a. of full weight.

trébucher, v. n. to stumble || to trip || to weigh down (of balances).

trébuchet, m. trap, assay-scales (pl.).

tréfiler, v. a. to wire-draw.

tréfilerie, f. wire-drawing mill.

tréfileur, m. wire-drawer.

trèfle, m. trefoil || club.

tréfonds, m. (jur.) subsoil || grounds (pl.) || savoir le fonds et le ~, to know all the ins and outs, to completely understand.

treillage, m. trellis, lattice.

treillageur, m. trellis-maker.

treille, f. vine-arbour, vine.

treillis, m. trellis, lattice || glazed calico || sack-cloth.

treilliser, v. a. to lattice.

treize, m. thirteenth (of the month).

treize, a. thirteen.

treizième, m. thirteenth part.

treizième, a. thirteenth.

tréma, m. (gr.) dieresis.

tremblaie, f. grove of aspen-trees.

tremble, m. (bot.) aspen-tree.

tremblement, m. trembling, shaking, shivering || (mus.) quaver, trill || rattle-trap || ~ de terre, earthquake.

trembler, v. n. to tremble, to shiver, to shake, to shudder || (mus.) to quaver.

trembleur, m. timid man || quaker.

trembloter, v. n. to tremble, to shiver.

trémie, f. mill-hopper.

trémière, a.; rose ~, f. (bot.) holly-hock.

trémoussement, m. fluttering.

(se) trémousser, to flutter || to bestir oneself.

trempe, f. temper (of iron) || constitution || humour || cast, stamp || steeping, wetting (of paper) || (fig.) licking.

tremper, v. a. & n. to dip, to steep, to drench, to soak || to temper (iron) || to wet to soak (paper) || r. to have a hand in.

tremplin, m. springing-board.

trentaine, f. thirty || age of thirty.

trente, m. thirtieth (of the month).

trente, a. thirty || ~ et quarante, "rouge et noir."

trentième, m. thirtieth part.

trentième, a. thirtieth.

trépan, m. (chir.) trepan || trepanning.

trépanation, f. (chir.) trepanning || trephining.

trépaner, v. a. (chir.) to trepan || to trepas.

trépas, m. death, decease.

trépasser, v. n. to pass away, to die.

trépidation, f. trepidation || trembling.

trépied, m. trivet || tripod.

trépignement, m. stamping.

trépigner, v. n. to stamp with the feet.

trépointe, f. welt (of leather).

très, ad. very, most.

trésor, m. treasure, hoard || Exchequer.

trésorerie, f. treasury.

trésorier, m. treasurer.

tressaillement, m. start, starting, startle.

tressaillir, v. n. to start, to start up, to give a sudden leap, to leap, to thrill.

tresse, f. braid || curl || plait || twist.

tresser, v. a. to weave, to plait.

tresseur, m. hair-dresser, plaiter.

tréteau, m. trestle || stage || ~ de meule, treuil, m. windlass. [stack-stand.

trève, f. truce, cessation of hostilities.

triage, m. choice || picking || sorting.

triangulaire, a. (-ment, ad.) triangular

tribord, m. (mar.) starboard. [(ly).

tribu, f. tribe, clan.

tribun, m. tribune.

tribunal, m. tribunal || bench || court of

tribunat, m. tribuneship. [justice.

tribune, f. tribune || gallery || race-stand || parliament || de la ~, parliamentary.

tribut, m. tribute || retribution.

tributaire, m. tributary

tributaire, a. tributary. [trick.

tricher, v. a. & n. to cheat (at play) || to

tricherie, f. cheating (at play) || trickery.

tricheur, se, m. & f. sharper, cheat (at play).

tricolore, a. tricoloured || three-coloured.

tricorne, m. three-cornered hat.

tricot, m. cudgel || network.

tricotage, m. knitting.

tricoter, v. to knit.

tricoteur, se, m. & f. knitter.

trictrac, m. backgammon.

tricycle, m. tricycle.

triennal, e, a. triennial.

trier, v. a. to pick, to sort, to choose out.

trieur, se, m. & f. sorter.

trigaud, e, a. shuffling.

trigonométrie, f. trigonometry.

trille, m. (mus.) trill, shake.

triller, v. a. (mus.) to shake.

trillion, m. billion.

trimbaler, v. a. to drag about.

trimer, v. n. to run up and down.

trimestre, m. quarter, three months.

trimestriel, le, a. quarterly.

tringle, f. curtain-rod || bar, lath.

tringler, v. a. to chalk.

Trinité, f. Trinity.

trinquer, v. n. to toast, to touch glasses || to tipple.

trio, m. (mus.) trio. [to tipple.

triolet, m. triolet || (mus.) triplet.

triomphal, e, a. (-ement, ad.) triumphal || triumphantly.

triomphant, e, a. triumphant.

triomphateur, m. triumpher. [cards).

triomphe, m. triumph || ~, f. trump (at

triompher, v. n. to triumph || to exult.

tripaille, f. garbage.

triperie, f. tripe-house.

tripette, f. small tripe || ne pas valoir ~, not to be worth a fig. [woman.

tripier, ière, m. & f. tripe-man || tripe-

triple, m. treble.

triple, a. triple || -ment, ad. trebly.

tripler, v. a. to treble.

tripoli, m. rotten-stone.

tripolir, v. a. to polish with rotten-stone.

tripot, m. gambling-house, hell.

tripotage, m. jumble, medley, mess ‖ intrigue ‖ jobbery.

tripoter, v. a. & n. to huddle, to make a mess, to mingle things together ‖ to brew mischief ‖ to intermeddle.

tripotier, ère, m. & f. bungler, meddler ‖ intriguer ‖ jobber.

trique, f. cudgel, stick.

triqueballe, f. truck (for cannons).

trisaïeul, e, m. & f. great-great-grand-father ‖ great-great-grand-mother.

trisme, m. (méd.) lock-jaw.

trisyllabe, a. trisyllabic.

triste, a. (-ment, ad.) sad(ly) ‖ sorrowful (ly) ‖ afflicted, afflictive, heavy ‖ melancholy.

tristesse, f. sadness, sorrowfulness, dejection, melancholy.

triturer, v. a. to triturate, to pound.

triumvirat, m. triumvirate.

trivial, e, a. (-ement, ad.) trivial(ly) ‖ vulgar(ly).

trivialité, f. trivialness, vulgarity.

troc, m. truck, exchange.

troène, m. (bot.) privet.

trogne, f. face, phiz ‖ drunkard's face.

trognon, m. core (of an apple etc.) ‖ stump, stalk (of a cabbage) ‖ dear, duck.

trois, m. third (of the month).

trois, a. three ‖ ~-mâts, m. (mar.) three-master ‖ ~-six, m. common brandy.

troisième, m. third part ‖ third person ‖ third floor ‖ ~, f. third class.

troisième, a. (-ment, ad.) third(ly).

trombe, f. waterspout.

trombone, m. (mus.) trombone.

trompe, f. trump, trumpet, horn ‖ trunk.

tromper, v. a. to deceive, to delude, to dupe, to cheat, to divert ‖ se ~, to be mistaken ‖ (de) to mistake the . . ., to miss

tromperie, f. deceit, cheat.   [one's . . .

trompeter, v. a. & n. to proclaim by the sound of a trumpet.

trompette, f. trumpet ‖ ~, m. trumpeter.

trompeur, se, m. & f. deceiver, cheat.

trompeur, a. deceitful ‖ delusive.

tronc, m. trunk, stump, stem ‖ stock (of a family) ‖ poor-box ‖ shaft of a pillar.

tronçon, m. stump, piece, fragment.

tronçonner, v. a. to truncate ‖ to cut in

trône, m. throne.   [pieces.

trôner, v. n. to sit on a throne ou in state ‖ to reign ‖ to be in the ascendant.

tronquer, v. a. to truncate, to mutilate ‖ to curtail ‖ to garble.

trop, ad. too, too much, too many, exceedingly ‖ ~ grand, over-much ‖ ~ peu, too little, too few ‖ pas ~ bien, not very well ‖ ~-plein, m. overflow ‖ fulness ‖

trop, m. excess.   [waste.

trophée, m. trophy.

tropique, m. tropic.

tropique, a. tropical.   [change.

troquer, v. a. to truck, to barter, to exchange.

troqueur, se, m. & f. jobber, barterer.

trot, m. trot ‖ aller au ~, to trot.

trotte, f. trip, way, stretch.

trotter, v. n. to trot ‖ to run.

trotteur, se, m. & f. trotter.

trottiner, v. n. to go at a jog-trot ‖ to trot about.

trottoir, m. foot-way, flag-way, pavement ‖ faire le ~, to walk the streets.

trou, m. hole, peep-hole ‖ gap ‖ ~-madame, troll-madam, nine-holes.

troubadour, m. southern bard.

trouble, m. tumult, agitation, uneasiness ‖ ~-fête, m. trouble-feast, troublesome guest, "wet-blanket."

trouble, a. troubled, thick, muddy.

troubler, v. a. to trouble, to make thick ou muddy ‖ to disorder, to confound, to disconcert, to agitate ‖ to spoil ‖ se ~, to grow thick ou muddy, to turn ‖ to be disturbed, to be confounded.   [torn.

troué, e, a. full of holes ‖ with a hole in it ‖

trouée, f. opening (in a wood), gap.

trouer, v. a. to bore, to make holes ‖ se ~, to have a hole.

troupe, f. troop, company, crew, gang, set, flock, shoal ‖ -s, pl. troops (pl.), soldiers

troupeau, m. flock, herd.   [(pl.).

troupier, m. soldier.

trousse, f. truss ‖ bundle ‖ (dressing-) case ‖ aux -s de, in pursuit of.

troussé, e, a. tucked up ‖ (style) well turned ‖ well shaped.

trousseau, m. bundle, bunch ‖ bride's outfit.

trousser, v. a. to truss, to tuck up, to tie up, to pin up, to turn up.

troussis, m. tuck, folding in.

trouvable, a. to be found.

trouvaille, f. chance find ‖ godsend, piece of good luck.

trouver, v. a. to find, to find out, to meet with ‖ to contrive, to discover ‖ aller ~, to go to see (one) ‖ ~ bon, to approve, to like ‖ ~ mauvais, to disapprove, to dislike, to take ill ‖ ~ à redire, to find fault with ‖ se ~, to find oneself ‖ to be ‖ to be found, to meet ‖ se ~ mal, to be ill, to feel unwell.

trouvère, m. trouvère, old poet of the truand, e, m. & f. vagrant. [North of France

truc, m. truck ‖ machinery ‖ knack, skill ‖

truchement, m. interpreter.   [cunning.

truelle, f. trowel ‖ fish-carver.

truellée, f. trowelful.

truffe, f. (bot.) truffle.

truffer, v. a. to stuff with truffles.

truffière, f. truffle-bed.

truie, f. sow.   [salmon-trout.

truite, f. trout (fish) ‖ ~ saumonée,

truité, e, a. red-speckled.

trumeau, m. leg of beef ‖ pier ‖ pier-glass.

tu, pn. thou.

tuable, a. fit for killing.

tuage, m. killing ‖ slaughter.

tuant, e, a. killing ‖ toilsome, tiresome.

tuber, v. a. to tube.   [(bot.) tubercle.

tubercule, m. (méd.) tubercle, pimple ‖

tubéreuse, f. (bot.) tuberose.

tubéreux, se, a. (bot.) tuberous.

tudesque, a. old Teutonic ‖ rough.

tuer, v. a. to kill, to slaughter, to butcher, to massacre ‖ le temps, to pass away the time ‖ se ~, to kill oneself ‖ to take great trouble ‖ never to cease.

tuerie, f. slaughter || slaughter-house, butchery.
A tue-tête, ad. with all one's might || as loud as one can.
tueur, m. slayer || bully.
tuf, tuffeau, m. chalky substratum || tufa, tuff.
tuile, f. tile || ~ creuse, gutter-tile.
tuileau, m. broken tile.
tuiler, v. a. to prove whether one is a free-mason.
tuilerie, f. tile-kiln || les Tuileries, pl. Palace and public garden in Paris.
tuilier, m. tile-maker.
tulipe, f. (bot.) tulip.
tulipier, m. (bot.) tulip-tree.
tulle, m. net, press-point.
tuméfaction, f. (méd.) tumefaction.
tumeur, f. tumour, swelling.
tumulaire, a. of a grave || pierre ~, f. tomb-stone.
tumulte, m. tumult, riot, uproar.
tumultuaire, a. (-ment, ad.) tumultuary || tumultuarily.   [tuous(ly) || riotous(ly).
tumultueux, se, a.(-sement, ad.) tumul-
tunique, f. tunic, coat.
tunnel, m. tunnel.
turbot, m. turbot (fish).
turbotière, f. turbot-kettle.
turbotin, m. small turbot (fish).
turbulence, f. turbulence || wildness.
turbulent, e, a. turbulent || wild.
turlupin, m. punster.
turlupinade, f. pun, low joke.
turlupiner, v. a. & n. to banter || to pun.
turpitude, f. turpitude, baseness.
turquin, e, a.; bleu ~, deep blue, dark
turquoise, f. turquoise.   [grey.
tussilage, m. (bot.) colt's-foot.
tutélaire, a. tutelar.   [ship || protection.
tutelle, f. guardianship, wardship, trustee-
tuteur, m., tutrice, f. guardian, warden || protector, defender || prop.
tutoiement, m. thouing.
tutoyer, v. a. to thou.
tuyau, m. tube, pipe, conduit, funnel, tunnel || quill, stalk (of corn) || ~ de fontaine, water-pipe || ~ d'une pipe, shank of a tobacco-pipe || ~ de soufflet, nozzle of a bellows || ~ d'échappement de vapeur, blast-pipe || ~ de sortie, delivery-pipe || ~ à vapeur, steam-pipe || ~ d'aspiration, suction-pipe.
tuyauter, v. a. to flute, to gauffer.
tuyère, f. blast-pipe.   [num || spandrel.
tympan, m. (an.) drum of the ear, tympa-
tympaniser, v. a. to slander, to defame.
tympanon, m. dulcimer.
type, m. printing-letter || prototype, model, figure || species, sort.
typhoïde, a. typhoid.
typhon, m. hurricane, whirlwind.
typhus, m. (méd.) typhus fever.
typique, a. typical.
typographe, m. typographer, printer || letterpress printer.
typographie, f. typography, printing.
typographique, a. typographical.
tyran, m. tyrant.
tyrannie, f. tyranny, cruelty.   [(ly).
tyrannique, a. (-ment, ad.) tyrannical
tyranniser, v. a. to tyrannise (over).

U.

ubiquité, f. ubiquity.
udomètre, m. rain-gauge.
ulcère, m. ulcer.   [asperate.
ulcérer, v. a. to ulcerate || (fig.) to ex-
uligineux, se, a. uliginous.
ultérieur, e, a. ulterior, further || sub-sequent || -ement, ad. besides, ultimate-ly, lastly.
ultimatum, m. ultimatum, final decision.
ultramontain, m. ultramontane || papist.
ultramontain, e, a. beyond the moun-tains || ultramontanist.
un, e, a. a, an, any || one, the number one || à ~, one by one || l'~ et l'autre, both, each other || les ~s les autres, each other || l'~ après l'autre, one after an-other || ni l'~ ni l'autre, neither || c'est tout ~, it's all the same.
unanime, a. (-ment, ad.) unanimous(ly).
unanimité, f. unanimity || à l'~, unanim-ously.
uni, e, a. (-ment, ad.) united || smooth(ly) || even(ly) || level || plain(ly) || frank || simply.
unième, a. one, first.
unification, f. unification.
uniforme, m. uniform, regimentals (pl.) || military man.
uniforme, a. uniform, even, regular.
uniformément, ad. uniformly.
uniformité, f. uniformity.
union, f. union, conjunction || unity || trait d'~, (gr.) hyphen || (fig.) connecting link.
unioniste, m. unionist, Union man.
unipersonnel, le, a. (gr.) unipersonal.
unique, a. (-ment, ad.) only || sole(ly) || singular(ly).
unir, v. a. to unite, to join together, to combine || to smooth, to level, to make even.
unisson, m. unison || à l'~, in concert.
unitaire, m. unitarian.
unitaire, a. of unity || unitarian.
unité, f. unity || unit.
univers, m. universe, world.
universalité, f. universality.
universel, le, a. (-lement, ad.) uni-versal(ly).   [versity.
universitaire, a. pertaining to a uni-
université, f. university.
urbain, e, a. urbane.
urbanité, f. urbanity, politeness.
ure, m. aurochs, wild-bull.
urètre, m. (an.) urethra.
urgence, f. urgency.
urgent, e, a. urgent, pressing.
uriner, v. n. to make water, to pass water.
urinoir, m. urinal.
urne, f. urn || ballot-box.
urticaire, f. (méd.) nettle-rash.
us, m. (jur.) way, practice, usage, custom || les ~ et coutumes, pl. the manners and customs (pl.).
usage, m. usage, use, practice, custom, way || fashion.

usé, e, a. worn out || old, stale.
user, m. wear(ing), service || être. d'un bon ~, to wear well.
user, v. a. & n. to wear out, to wear off, to waste, to consume || to use, to make use of || s'~, to wear out *ou* off, to waste, to stale || to lose one's strength.
usine, f. works (pl.), manufactory.
usité, e, a. used, usual, in use.
ustensile, m. utensil || implement || tackle.
usuel, le, a. (-lement, ad.) usual(ly).
usufruit, m. usufruct.
usufructuaire, a. usufructuary.
usufruitier, ière, m. & f. usufructuary.
usuraire, a. (-ment, ad.) usurious(ly).
usure, f. usury, exorbitant, interest, unlawful interest || wearing out.
usurier, ère, m. & f. usurer.
usurpateur, m. usurper, intrudér.
usurpation, f. usurpation, encroachment.
usurper, v. a. to usurp || to encroach.
utérin, e, a. by the mother's side.
utérus, m. (anat.) uterus || matrix || womb.
utile, a. (-ment, ad.) useful(ly) || of use, serviceable, good || advantageous(ly) || profitable || profitably.
utiliser, v. a. to make useful (of horses) || to make use of || to turn to account.
utilité, f. utility, usefulness || profit.
Utopie, f. Utopia.
utopique, a. utopian.
utopiste, m. utopist.

V.

va, ad. be it so! done!
vacance, f. vacancy || ~s, pl. holidays (pl.), vacation.
vacant, e, a. vacant, empty || unoccupied || in abeyance.   [uproar.
vacarme, m. noise, tumult, rout, bustle,
vacation, f. day's time || vacancy || ~s, pl. holidays (pl.), vacation.
vaccin, m. (méd.) vaccine-matter.
vaccine, f. cow-pox || vaccination.
vacciner, v. a. to vaccinate.
vache, f. cow || cow-hide || ~ à lait, ~ laitière, milch-cow || ~ pleine, cow with calf.
vacher, ère, m. & f. cow-herd, cow-keeper.
vacherie, f. cow-house.   [wavering.
vacillation, f. vacillation, staggering,
vaciller, v. n. to vacillate, to reel, to stagger, to totter, to waver.
vacuité, f. emptiness, void.
vade, f. go, stake (in gaming).
vade-mecum, m. vade-mecum, manual.
va-et-vient, m. see-saw || see-saw motion, oscillation.
vagabond, e, m. & f. vagabond, vagrant.
vagabond, e, a. vagabond, rambling, vagrant.
vagabondage, m. vagrancy.
vagabonder, v. n. to be (a) vagabond, to wander.
vagir, v. n. to cry (of infants) || to mewl.
vagissement, m. wailing.

vague, m. vacuum.
vague, f. wave, billow, surge.
vague, a. vague, indefinite, indeterminate, unconfined.
vaguement, ad. in a vague and indeterminate manner.
vaguemestre, m. (mil.) baggage-master.
vaguer, v. n. to wander about, to ramble, to rove.
vaillamment, ad. valiantly, courageously.
vaillance, f. valour, courage, bravery || gallantry.
vaillant, m. whole property.
vaillant, e, a. valiant, courageous || gallant ||
vaillantise, f. prowess.   [brave.
vain, e, a. (-ement, ad.) vain(ly) || in vain || fruitless || frivolous || to no purpose || unprofitable || haughty || en ~, in vain.
vaincre, v. a. ir. to vanquish, to subdue || to master || to outdo || to conquer || se ~, to conquer oneself.
vainqueur, m. conqueror, subduer, victor.
vainqueur, a. conquering, victorious.
vairon, m. minnow (fish).
vairon, e, a. m.; wall-eyed (of horses) || œil ~, m. wall-eye.
vaisseau, m. vessel, ship || vain || artery || ~ d'approvisionnement, store-ship || ~ de guerre, man-of-war, ship of war || ~ de la compagnie des Indes, East Indiaman || ~ de la marine royale, His *ou* Her Majesty's ship || ~ de ligne, ship of the line || ~ d'avis, advice-ship || ~ à deux ponts, two-decker || ~ marchand, merchantman || ~ négrier, Guinea-man.
vaisselle, f. dishes and plates (pl.), table-utensils (pl.) || ~ de terre, earthen-ware || ~ d'étain, pewter || ~ d'argent, silver-plate.
val, m. valley, dale || à ~, down.
valable, a. (-ment, ad.) valid(ly) || lawful || in due form.
valériane, f. (bot.) valerian.
valet, m. valet, manservant, footman, groom || knave (at cards) || holdfast || door-weight || ~ de bourreau, ~ du supplice, assistant executioner || ~ de chambre, valet || ~ de charrue, ploughman || ~ de pied, footman || ~ de place, guide.   [(pl.).
valetaille, f. pack of footmen || menials
valeter, v. n. to drudge || to cringe || to dance attendance.
valétudinaire, m. valetudinarian.
valétudinaire, a. valetudinarian.
valeur, f. value, price, worth || valour, courage, bravery, gallantry || signification, meaning || ~ en compte, value in cash || ~ reçue, value received || ~s, pl. (com.) paper, bills (pl.) || de ~, valuable.
valeureux, se, a. (-sement, ad.) valiant(ly) || brave(ly) || gallant(ly).
valide, a. (-ment, ad.) valid(ly) || good in law, lawful || healthy, able-bodied.
valider, v. a. to render valid.
validité, f. validity.
valise, f. cloak-bag, portmanteau.

vallée, f. valley, vale.

vallon, m. small valley, dale.

valoir, v. a. & n. ir. to procure, to produce, to yield, to bring || to be worth, to be of value || **ne rien ~,** to be good for nothing || **vaille que vaille,** at all events || for better for worse.

valse, f. waltz. ·

valser, v. n. to waltz.

valseur, se, m. & f. waltzer.

value, f. value || **plus-~,** superior value || **moins-~,** inferior value.

valve, f. valve, valvula.

valvule, f. valve || valvule.

vampire, m. vampire, blood-sucker.

van, m. winnowing-basket || fan.

vandalisme, m. vandalism.

vanille, f. (bot.) vanilla.

vanillier, m. (bot.) vanilla-tree.

vanité, f. vanity.

vaniteux, se, a. foolishly vain.

vannage, m. winnowing || ventilation.

vanne, f. flood-gate.

vanneau, m. lapwing, tirwit (bird).

vanner, v. a. to winnow, to fan, to ven- **vannerie,** f. basket-trade.　　　[tilate.

vannette, f. flat basket, server.

vanneur, m. winnower.

vannier, m. basket-maker.

vantail, m. leaf of a folding door *ou* win- **vantard,** m. boaster, braggart.　　[dow.

vantard, e, a. boasting.

vantardise, f. habitual boasting, brag- ging.　　　　　　　　　　　　　　[tol.

vanter, v. a. to cry up, to praise, to ex- **vanterie,** f. boasting, bragging.

va-nu-pieds, m. ragamuffin, tatter- demalion.

vapeur, m. steamer.

vapeur, f. vapour, fume, steam, damp, smoke || (poét.) mist || **imperméable à la ~,** steam-tight || **-s,** pl. (méd.) the vapours (pl.).

vaporeux, se, a. vaporous || aerial.

vaporiser, v. a.; **se ~,** to vaporise.

vaquer, v. n. to be vacant || not to sit || **~ à,** to attend to.

varech, m. (mar.) wreck, wrecks (pl.) || sea- **varenne,** f. waste-land.　　　　　　[weed.

vareuse, f. short coat || sailor's jacket.

variabilité, f. variableness, changeable- **variable,** a. variable, changeable.　[ness.

variant, e, a. changeable, fickle.

variante, f. various reading.

variation, f. variation, alteration.

varice, f. (méd.) varicose vein, varix.

varicelle, f. (méd.) chicken-pox.

varier, v. a. & n. to vary || to variegate, to alter || to be changeable || to differ.

variété, f. variety || **-s,** pl. miscellanies (pl.) || medley || extracts (pl.).

variole, f. small-pox.

variqueux, se, a. varicose.

varlope, f. large plane, jointer.

vase, m. vase, vessel.

vase, f. slime, mud, mire.

vaseux, se, a. muddy, miry.

vasistas, m. small casement in a door *ou* **vasque,** f. centre basin.　　　　[window.

vassal, m. vassal.

vasselage, m. vassalage.

vaste, a. vast, spacious, great.

va-tout, m. (at cards) staking one's all.

vaudeville, m. ballad || play intermingled with songs || a theatre in Paris.

vaudevilliste, m. writer of vaudevilles.

à vau-l'eau, ad. down stream || to wrack and ruin || into thin air.

vaurien, m. good-for-nothing fellow || **vautour,** m. vulture (bird).　　　　[rogue.

se vautrer, to wallow, to welter || to spread oneself.

veau, m. calf || veal || calf's leather.

vedette, f. sentinel on horseback || watch- tower || sentry-box || (mar.) scout-watch.

végétal, m. vegetable.

végétal, e, a. vegetable.

végétarien, ne, m. & f. vegetarian.

végétarien, ne, a. vegetarian.

végéter, v. n. to vegetate.

véhémence, f. vehemency.

véhément, e, a. vehement, violent.

véhicule, m. vehicle.

veille, f. watching, sitting up, watch || eve of the day before || **-s,** pl. night-studies (pl.)

veillée, f. sitting up, watching || evening.

veiller, v. a. & n. to sit up, to watch, to wake || to have an eye upon.

veilleur, m. watcher || watchman.

veilleuse, f. watcher || night-light.

veillotte, f. small hay-cock.

veinage, m. veining.

veine, f. vein || (fig.) luck, good run || **je suis en ~,** I have got my hand in.

veiner, v. a. to vein.

veineux, se, a. veiny.

vêler, v. a. to calve.

vélin, m. vellum || **papier ~,** m. wove paper.

velléité, f. velleity || fancy.

véloceman, vélocipédiste, m. cyclist.

vélocipède, m. velocipede, bicycle.

vélocité, f. velocity, swiftness, speed.

vélodrome, m. cycling-ground, cycling- track.

velours, m. velvet || **~ à côtes,** corduroy || **~ croisé,** velveteen || **~ épinglé,** Terry velvet || **~ façonné,** figured velvet || **~ glacé,** shot velvet || **~ de soie,** silk- velvet || **~ uni,** plain velvet || **faire patte de ~,** to draw in one's claws || to fawn.

velouté, m. velveting || velvet-lace || velvet- down || softness.

velouté, e, a. velvet || velvety || soft and smooth to the palate || deep-coloured || **veloutier,** m. velvet-maker.　　　　[rich.

velu, e, a. hairy, shaggy.

venaison, f. venison.

vénal, e, a. (**-ement,** ad.) venal(ly) || vendible, mercenary.

vénalité, f. venality.

venant, m. comer || **à tout ~,** to the first comer || to anyone.

venant, e, a. coming.

vendable, a. salable.

vendange, f. vintage.　　　　　　[to gather.

vendanger, v. a. & n. to gather in grapes || **vendangeur, se,** m. & f. vintager.

venderesse, f. (jur.) vendor.
vendeur, se, m. & f. seller.
vendre, v. a. to sell, to part with ‖ to betray ‖ **à ~**, to be sold ‖ **se ~**, to be sold, to go off ‖ to sell oneself.
vendredi, m. Friday ‖ **~ saint**, Good Friday. [(of plants).
vénéneux, se, a. poisonous, venomous
vener, v. a. to hunt, to bait.
vénérable, a. venerable, reverend.
vénérer, v. a. to venerate.
vénerie, f. hunting ‖ hunting-train.
vénérien, ne, a. venereal.
venette, f. fright, alarm.
veneur, m. huntsman ‖ **grand ~**, master of the hounds.
venez-y-voir, m. raree-show ‖ fine thing.
vengeance, f. vengeance, revenge.
venger, v. a. to revenge, to avenge ‖ to resent ‖ **se ~**, to revenge oneself.
vengeur, eresse, m. & f. avenger.
vengeur, eresse, a. revengeful.
véniel, le, a. (-lement, ad.) venial(ly).
venimeux, se, a. venomous (of animals).
venin, m. venom, poison ‖ grudge, spite.
venir, v. n. ir. to come, to be coming, to arrive ‖ to chance, to happen ‖ to proceed ‖ **à ~**, to come, future.
vent, m. wind, air ‖ breath ‖ hint ‖ vanity, emptiness ‖ **au ~**, windward ‖ **sous le ~**, leeward.
vente, f. sale ‖ **en ~**, on sale.
venter, v. n. to blow ‖ to be windy.
venteux, se, a. windy.
ventilateur, m. ventilator.
ventiler, v. a. to ventilate, to fan.
ventouse, f. ventilator ‖ cupping-glass ‖ **appliquer des —s**, to cup.
ventouser, v. a. to cup.
ventre, m. belly ‖ abdomen ‖ womb ‖ bulging ‖ **à terre**, at full speed.
ventrée, f. litter, brood.
ventrière, f. belly-band ‖ purlin.
ventriloque, m. ventriloquist.
ventriloquie, f. ventriloquy.
ventru, e, a. big-bellied.
venu, e, m. & f. comer ‖ **le premier ~**, anyone ‖ the first come.
venue, f. coming, arrival ‖ growth ‖ venue ‖ **tout d'une ~**, all at once.
vêpres, f. pl. vespers, evening-prayers (pl.) (at church).
ver, m. worm ‖ maggot ‖ moth ‖ grub ‖ **~ de terre**, earth-worm ‖ wretch ‖ **~ luisant**, glow-worm ‖ **~ solitaire**, tape-worm ‖ **~ à soie**, silk-worm ‖ **~ rongeur**, remorse ‖ **tirer les —s du nez à qn**, to pump one ‖ **~-coquin**, m. vine-fretter ‖ maggot.
véracité, f. veracity.
véranda, f. veranda.
verbal, e, a. (-ement, ad.) verbal(ly).
verbaliser, v. n. to write a verbal statement. [ment.
verbe, m. (gr.) verb.
verbeux, se, a. verbose, wordy.
verbiage, m. idle words (pl.), empty talk.
verbiager, v. n. to be verbose.
verbiageur, se, m. & f. wordy speaker, empty talker, twaddler.

verbosité, f. verbosity.
verdâtre, a. greenish.
verdelet, te, a. tartish ‖ vigorous.
verdeur, f. verdure, greenness, green ‖ sap ‖ tartness ‖ vigour, briskness.
verdict, m. (jur.) verdict, finding.
verdier, m. greenfinch (bird). [green.
verdir, v. a. & n. to paint green ‖ to grow
verdoyant, e, a. verdant, green.
verdoyer, v. n. to be verdant.
verdure, f. verdure, green ‖ greens (pl.).
véreux, se, a. rotten, maggoty, worm-eaten ‖ unsound ‖ suspicious.
verge, f. rod, switch, tipstaff ‖ **—s**, pl. rod, birch, shank ‖ handle.
vergé, e, a. (of paper) laid.
verger, m. orchard.
verger, v. a. to measure with a yard.
vergeté, e, a. streaked.
vergeter, v. a. to dust.
vergette(s), f. (pl.) dusting-brush.
vergeure, f. wire-mark.
verglas, m. glazed frost ‖ **il fait du ~**, the rain freezes as it falls.
vergogne, f. shame.
vergue, f. (mar.) yard.
véricle, f. paste, imitation (of jewels).
véridicité, f. veracity, truthfulness.
véridique, a. veracious, truthful.
vérificateur, m. verifier, examiner.
vérification, f. verification, proving, examining ‖ assay.
vérifier, v. a. to verify ‖ to examine ‖ (jur.) to prove.
véritable, a. true, genuine, real ‖ pure ‖ regular ‖ **-ment**, ad. truly, really, indeed.
vérité, f. verity, truth ‖ **—s**, pl. truths (pl.) ‖ faults told (pl.) ‖ **en ~**, in truth, indeed, truly ‖ **à la ~**, it is true.
verjus, m. verjuice, sour grapes.
vermeil, m. silver-gilt.
vermeil, le, a. vermeil, vermilion, rosy, rubicund, ruddy ‖ **teint ~**, rosy complexion.
vermicelle, m. vermicelli.
vermicellier, m. vermicelli-maker ‖ Italian warehouse-man.
vermiculaire, a. vermicular, worm-like.
vermiforme, a. vermiform, vermicular.
vermifuge, m. vermifuge.
vermiller, v. a. to scratch for worms.
vermillon, m. vermilion.
vermillonner, v. a. & n. to paint red ‖ to grub up the earth for worms.
vermine, f. vermin ‖ (fig.) rabble.
vermisseau, m. small worm.
se vermouler, to grow worm-eaten.
vermoulu, e, a. worm-eaten.
vermoulure, f. worm-hole, rottenness in wood ‖ dust from a worm-hole.
vermout, m. vermouth ‖ bitters (pl.).
verni, e, a. patent ‖ of patent leather.
vernir, v. a. to varnish ‖ to japan ‖ to polish ‖ to glaze.
vernis, m. varnish, gloss ‖ japan.
vernisser, v. a. to varnish ‖ to glaze ‖ to japan. [French polisher.
vernisseur, m. varnisher ‖ japanner ‖

vernissure, f. varnishing || japanning || glazing.

vérole, f. (méd.) pox || **petite ~,** small-pox || **petite ~ volante,** chicken-pox.

véron, m. minnow (fish).

véronique, f. (bot.) veronica, speedwell.

verrat, m. boar.

verre, m. glass || glass-case || glass-shade || lamp || ~ **blanc,** crown-glass || ~ **de roche,** flint-glass || ~ **à boire,** drinking-glass || ~ **à vin,** ~ **à pied,** wine-glass || ~ **de vin,** glass of wine.

verrerie, f. glass-house || glass-making || glass-wares (pl.).   [seller.

verrier, m. glass-maker, glass-man, glass-

verrière, f. glass-stand || hand-glass ||

verrine, f. hand-glass.   [winnow.

verroterie, f. glass-ware || glass-trinket.

verrou, m. bolt || **sous les –s,** under lock and key.

verrouiller, v. a. to bolt.

verrue, f. (méd. & bot.) wart.

verruqueux, se, a. warty || (méd.) ver-rucose || (bot.) warted.

vers, m. verse || line || ~, pl. verses (pl.), poetry || ~ **burlesques,** pl. doggerel.

vers, pr. towards, to || about.

versant, m. water-shed || slope.

versant, e, a. apt to overturn.

versatilité, f. versatility.

à verse, ad. hard || fast (of rain).

versé, e, a. versed, skilful, skilled, ex-perienced.

Verseau, m. (astr.) Aquarius.

versement, m. payment, deposit.

verser, v. a. & n. to pour, to spill, to shed || to decant || to pay, to deposit || to overturn, to overset.

verset, m. verse (of the Bible).

versicule, m. short verse.

versificateur, m. versifier.

versifier, v. n. to versify.

version, f. version, translation.

verso, m. left-hand page, second page, even page.

versoir, m. mould-board of a plough.

vert, m. green colour || grass || tartness || ~ **de mer,** sea-green || ~**-de-gris,** m. verdigris.

vert, e, a. green || unripe || sour || tart || sharp, rough || vigorous || fresh, lusty.

vertébral, e, a. (an.) vertebral || spinal || **colonne –e,** f. spinal column.

vertèbre, f. (an.) vertebra.

vertébrés, m. pl. vertebrate animals (pl.).

vertement, ad. briskly, stoutly, smartly.

vertical, e, a. (–ement, ad.) vertical(ly).

vertige, m. (méd.) dizziness, giddiness || swimming in the head || infatuation.

vertigineux, se, a. vertiginous, giddy.

vertigo, m. maggot, crotchet, whim || staggers (pl.).

vertu, f. virtue, probity, chastity || force, power || courage, boldness || **en ~ de,** by virtue of, on account of.   [tuous(ly).

vertueux, se, a. (–sement, ad.) vir-

verve, f. poetical rapture || fit || fire || spirit || humour || maggot, crotchet.

verveine, f. (bot.) vervain.

vesce, f. (bot.) vetch, fitch.

vésicatoire, m. blistering plaster, vesica-tory || **mouche à ~,** f. blister-fly.

vésicule, f. vesicle, little bladder.

vespasienne, f. (street-)urinal.

vesse-de-loup, f. puff-ball.

vesser, v. n. to fizzle || to break wind [silently.

vessie, f. bladder, blister.

vestale, f. vestal.

veste, f. vest, waistcoat.

vestiaire, m. wardrobe || cloak-room.

vestibule, m. entrance-hall.

vestige, m. vestige || track, trace.

vêtement, m. vestment, clothes (pl.), gar-ment, apparel.

vétéran, m. veteran, old soldier || un-promoted school-boy.

vétérance, f. quality of veteran.

vétérinaire, m. veterinary surgeon, far-rier.

vétille, f. trifle.   [rier.

vétiller, v. n. to trifle, to stand upon trifles, to split hairs.

vétillerie, f. hair-splitting.   [trifler.

vétilleur, se, m. & f. punctilious person,

vétilleux, se, a. minute || punctilious.

vêtir, v. a. to clothe || to invest.

veto, m. veto || **droit de ~,** m. right of refusal.

vêture, f. ceremony of giving ou taking the monastic habit ou the veil.

vétusté, f. ancientness, antiquity.

veuf, ve, m. & f. widower || widow.

veuf, ve, a. widowed.

veule, a. soft || feeble || weak.

veuvage, m. widowhood.

vexatoire, a. vexatious.

vexer, v. a. to vex, to plague, to trouble.

viable, a. (méd.) viable, likely to live.

viaduc, m. viaduct.

viager, m. life-interest.

viager, ère, a. for life.

viande, f. meat, flesh, eatables (pl.), vic-tuals (pl.), food || ~ **blanche,** poultry || ~ **creuse,** unsubstantial food || frothy matter || idle fancy || ~ **noire,** game.

viatique, m. viaticum.

vibrer, v. n. to vibrate.

vicaire, m. curate || vicar.

vicarial, e, a. vicarial.

vicariat, m. curateship || vicarship.

vicarier, v. n. to do a curate's duty, to officiate as vicar.

vice, m. vice || defect, fault || ~**-amiral,** m. vice-admiral || ~**-gérant,** m. deputy manager || ~**-président,** m. vice-presi-dent || deputy chairman || ~**-roi,** m. vice-roy.

vicié, e, a. vitiated, corrupted.   [roy.

vicier, v. a. to vitiate, to corrupt.

vicieux, se, a. (–sement, ad.) vicious (ly) || defective.

vicinal, e, a. parochial, parish (of roads).

vicissitude, f. vicissitude.

vicomte, sse, m. & f. viscount || vis-countess.

vicomté, f. viscountship, viscounty.

victime, f. victim.

victimer, v. a. to victimise.

victoire, f. victory.

victoria, f. park phaeton.

victorieux, se, a. (**-sement,** ad.) victorious(ly).

victuailles, f. pl. victuals (pl.).

vidange, f. clearing, emptying || night-soil.

vidangeur, m. night-man.

vide, m. void, chasm, gap, vacuum, vacancy || vanity || à ~, empty.

vide, a. empty, void, vacant || ~-bouteille, m. small country-box with a garden || ~-poches, m. basket.

vider, v. a. to empty, to make empty, to evacuate, to unlade, to clear || se ~, to empty itself || to be settled.

viduité, f. widowhood.

vidure, f. pinking || open work.

vie, f. life, lifetime, days || livelihood || food, bread || sans ~, without life || à ~, for life || en ~, alive || de ma ~, never in my life.

vieil (vieux), vieille, a. old, aged || out of fashion, obsolete || spoiled, worn out, of old standing.

vieillard, m. old man || -s, pl. old people.

vieille, f. old woman.

vieillerie, f. old clothes, old goods, rubbish, old stuff || trash.

vieillesse, f. old age || oldness || old people.

vieillir, v. a. & n. to make one old, to make one look aged || to grow old, to look old || to become obsolete || to become out of fashion.

vieillissement, m. growing old || old age.

vieillot, te, a. oldish.

vielle, f. hurdy-gurdy.

vierge, f. virgin, maid.

vierge, a. virgin || pure.

vieux, a. pl. *vide* **vieil.** [silver.

vif, m. quick || solid || ~-argent, m. quick-

vif, ve, a. live, alive, living || quick, lively, brisk, vivid, sprightly, fiery || de vive voix, by word of mouth.

vigie, f. (mar.) look-out || look-out man.

vigilamment, ad. watchfully.

vigilance, f. watchfulness.

vigilant, e, a. watchful.

vigile, f. vigil || eve of a holiday.

vigne, f. (bot.) vine, vineyard || ~ vierge, hopplant || ~ sauvage, black-bryony.

vigneron, m. vine-dresser || vine-grower.

vignette, f. engraving, cut || vignette.

vignoble, m. vineyard, vines (pl.).

vignot, m. periwinkle.

vigogne, f. vicunia (sort of Spanish wool).

vigoureux, se, a. (**-sement,** ad.) vigorous(ly) || stout(ly).

vigueur, f. vigour, strength, stoutness, force, energy.

vil, e, a. (**-ement,** ad.) vile(ly) || mean(ly) || low || base(ly) || shabby, despicable, wretched.

vilain, m. villain, miser, niggard.

vilain, e, a. (**-ement,** ad.) villanous(ly) || base(ly) || vile, miserable, pitiful || obscene.

vilebrequin, m. wimble.

vilenie, f. villainy || obscenity || covetousness, niggardliness. [to despise.

vilipender, v. a. to vilify, to undervalue.

village, m. village.

villageois, e, m. & f. villager, country-man || country-woman.

villageois, e, a. countrified.

ville, f. town, city || ~ d'eaux, watering-place || à la ~, in town || en ~, out.

villégiature, f. stay at a country-place.

vin, m. wine || ~ clairet, claret || ~ brûlé, ~ chaud, mulled wine || ~ doux, un-fermented wine || ~ de liqueur, sweet wine || ~ ordinaire, table-wine || ~ de Porto, Port wine || ~ du Rhin, Rhenish

vinaigre, m. vinegar. [wine.

vinaigrer, v. a. to season with vinegar.

vinaigrerie, f. vinegar-manufactory.

vinaigrette, f. sauce with vinegar || Bath chair. [vinegar.

vinaigrier, m. vinegar-merchant || cruet for

vindicatif, ve, a. vindicative, revengeful.

vindicte, f. (jur.) vengeance || punishment

vinée, f. vintage. [of crime.

vineux, se, a. vinous || strong.

vingt, m. twentieth (of the month) || score.

vingt, a. twenty.

vingtaine, f. score.

vingtième, m. twentieth part.

vingtième, a. twentieth.

vinicole, a. vine-growing.

vinosité, f. richness, fruity taste, vinosity.

viol, m. violation, rape.

violacé, e, a. of a violet colour.

violat, a. m. of violets.

violateur, trice, m. & f. violator, transgressor. [breach.

violation, f. violation, transgression,

violâtre, a. violet-coloured.

violemment, ad. violently.

violence, f. violence, vehemence || force.

violent, e, a. violent, vehement.

violenter, v. a. to force, to do violence to.

violer, v. a. to violate, to break

violet, m. violet colour.

violet, te, a. of a violet colour.

violette, f. (bot.) violet.

violon, m. violin, fiddle || fiddler || fiddle-pattern || lock-up.

violoncelle, m. violoncello, bass-viol.

violoniste, m. fiddler.

viorne, f. (bot.) viburnum.

vipère, f. viper || adder.

virago, f. virago. [tacking about.

virement, m. transfer || ~ de bord, (mar.)

virer, v. n. to turn about, to tack about || (mar.) to veer.

vireux, se, a. poisonous.

virginal, e, a. virginal, maidenly.

virginité, f. virginity, maidenhood.

virgule, f. comma || point et ~, semicolon.

viril, e, a. (**-ement,** ad.) virile, male || manly || stout(ly) || age ~, m. manhood.

virilité, f. virility, manhood.

virole, f. ferrule.

virtuel, le, a. (**-lement,** ad.) virtual(ly).

virtuose, m. & f. virtuoso.

virulent, e, a. virulent, venomous.

virus, m. (méd.) virus.

vis, f. screw, male screw || ~ d'Archi-mède, water-snail || screw-propeller.

vis-à-vis, m. person opposite.

vis-à-vis, ad. opposite || face to face.

visa, m. visa, signature on passports.

visage, m. face || countenance || look || reception || **trouver ~ de bois,** to find no one at home.   [trails (pl.).

viscère, m. (an.) vital organ || ~s, pl. entrails (pl.).

viscosité, f. viscosity, sliminess.

visée, f. aim, end, design.

viser, v. a. & n. to aim, to take one's aim, to have in view, to tend, to view, to revise || to examine (an act).

visibilité, f. visibility, conspicuousness.

visible, a. visible, discernible, plain, clear, apparent, evident || **-ment,** ad. visibly.

visière, f. aim, visor, sight.

visigoth, m. barbarian.

vision, f. vision, sight.

visionnaire, m. & f. visionary.

visionnaire, a. visionary.

visite, f. visit || search, searching, visitation || attendance.   [spect, to search.

visiter, v. a. to visit, to go to see || to inspect, to search.

visiteur, m. visitor || searcher.

vison, m. mink.   [clammy.

visqueux, se, a. viscous, slimy, sticky,

visser, v. a. to screw.

visuel, le, a. visual.

vital, e, a. vital || essential.

vitalité, f. vitality.

vite, a. (**-ment,** ad.) quick(ly) || speedy, swift || speedily, fast || **faire ~,** to be quick.

vitelotte, f. (bot.) kidney potato.

vitesse, f. quickness, nimbleness, swiftness, celerity, promptness.

viticulture, f. vine-growing.

vitrage, m. glazing || glass-windows (pl.) || glass-partition.

vitraux, m. pl. church-windows (pl.).

vitre, f. pane of glass, glass, glass-window.

vitrer, v. a. to glass, to glaze || **porte vitrée,** f. glass-door, sash-door.

vitrerie, f. glass-trade, glazier's business || glaziery.

vitreux, se, a. vitreous, glassy.

vitrier, m. glazier.

vitrifier, v. a. to vitrify.   [window.

vitrine, f. glass-case || show-case || shop-

vivace, a. long-lived, perennial.

vivacité, f. vivacity, vivaciousness, liveliness, sprightliness, briskness, heat, ardour, mettle || quickness of apprehension.

vivandier, ière, m. & f. sutler.

vivant, m. living || **bon ~,** jolly fellow, good companion || epicurean.

vivant, e, a. living, lively, alive.

vivat! hurra! huzza!

vive, f. weaver (fish).

vive! long live! hurra!

vivement, ad. briskly, sharply, lively, vigorously, quickly || acutely.

viveur, se, m. & f. gay man, fast man ou woman, man ou woman of pleasure.

vivier, m. pond, fish-pond.

vivifier, v. a. to vivify, to quicken, to revive, to give new life to.

vivipare, a. viviparous.

vivisection, f. vivisection.

vivoter, v. n. to live from hand to mouth.

vivre, m. food, diet || ~s, pl. provisions (pl.).

vivre, v. n. ir. to live, to be alive, to exist || to lead a life, to behave || **~ de, to** live upon || to get one's living by.

vocabulaire, m. vocabulary.

vocal, e, a. vocal, oral.   [tion.

vocation, f. vocation, calling || destina-

vociférer, v. n. to vociferate, to brawl.

vœu, m. vow, wish, desire || vote.

vogue, f. vogue, esteem, repute, fashion.

voguer, v. n. to row, to sail, to pull || **vogue la galère!** come weal, come woe!

voici, ad. behold, here is, this is, here are, there are || **me ~,** here I am || **le ~ qui vient,** here he comes.

voie, f. way, means, road, trace, conveyance || cartload || two pails (pl.), linegauge || leak || **~ ferrée,** railway, railroad || **~s de fait,** pl. (jur.) assault.

voilà, ad. behold, there is, there are, **that** is, those are || **le ~,** there he is.

voile, m. veil || pretence, mask, disguise || ~, f. sail || vessel, ship.

voilé, e, a. (of the eye) soft, gentle || (of the voice) husky.

voiler, v. a. to veil, to give the veil, to cover, to cloak, to hide, to colour || **se ~,** to wear a veil.

voilerie, f. (mar.) sail-loft.

voilette, f. small veil || (mar.) small lateen sail.   [ing vessel).

voilier, m. sail-maker || (good) sailer (sail-

voilure, f. sails (pl.) || sail-making.

voir, v. a. & n. ir. to see, to behold, to look || to perceive, to discern, to consider, to observe, to mind || to be sensible of, to penetrate into || to keep company with || **se ~,** to look at ou upon oneself || to visit one another.

voirie, f. commission of highways || common sewer.

voisin, m., **voisine,** f. neighbour.

voisin, e, a. neighbouring, bordering.

voisinage, m. neighbourhood, vicinity.

voisiner, v. n. to be neighbourly || to visit one's neighbours.

voiture, f. carriage, coach, equipage || fare, loading, load || conveyance, vehicle || **~ cellulaire,** prison-van || **~ de place,** cab || **~ de remise,** glass-coach.

voiturer, v. a. to carry, to convey.

voiturier, m. carrier, waggoner || lighter-

voiturin, m. driver || coach.   [man.

voix, f. voice, cry || vote, suffrage || **à haute ~,** loudly || **aller aux ~,** to put it to the vote.

vol, m. flight || robbery, theft || wings expanded || **~ avec effraction,** burglary || **à ~ d'oiseau,** from a bird's-eye view || **~-au-vent,** m. (culin.) puff-pie.

volable, a. that may be stolen.

volage, a. flighty, fickle || light-headed.

volaille, f. poultry.

volant, e, a. flying, winged.

volatil, e, a. (chim.) volatile.

volatile, m. winged creature.

volatiliser, v. a. to volatilise.

volatilité, f. (chim.) volatility.

volatille, f. fowls (for the table) (pl.).

volcan, m. volcano.

volcanique, a. volcanic.
volcaniser, v. a. to volcanise || to inflame.
volée, f. flight, flying || covey, bevy, flock, company || rank, quality || (mar.) broadside || **tout d'une ~,** at one flight || **à la ~,** rashly, hastily, at random || broadcast.
voler, v. a. & n. to rob, to steal || to fly, to soar, to flutter || to run.
volet, m. shutter || pigeon-house.
voleter, v. n. to flutter, to flicker.
voleur, se, m. & f. thief, robber || **au ~!** thieves! (pl.).
volière, f. aviary || pigeon-house.
volige, f. thin plank of white wood.
volontaire, m. volunteer || obstinate person.
volontaire, a. (**-ment,** ad.) voluntary || voluntarily || spontaneous(ly) || wilful.
volonté, f. will || mind || **à ~,** at will, at pleasure || **de bonne ~,** willingly, heartily.
volontiers, ad. willingly, cheerfully, readily, gladly.
Volt, m. Volt, unit of electromotive power.
volte, f. volt || **~-face,** f. wheeling round, facing about || **faire ~,** (mil.) to face about.
volter, v. n. to shift one's place (in fencing).
voltige, f. slack-rope || tumbling upon a rope *ou* on a horse || vaulting.
voltiger, v. n. to fly about, to flutter about || to vault, to tumble upon a rope.
voltigeur, m. vaulter, tumbler || soldier of light infantry. [vulus.
volubilis, m. (bot.) bind-weed, convol-
volubilité, f. volubility.
volume, m. volume, book || bulk.
volumineux, se, a. voluminous, bulky.
volupté, f. voluptuousness, sensual pleasure, luxury.
voluptueux, a. voluptuary.
voluptueux, se, a. (**-sement,** ad.) voluptuous(ly).
vomique, a. vomic || **noix ~,** f. nux vomica.
vomir, v. a. & n. to vomit.
vomissement, m. vomiting.
vomitif, m. (méd.) emetic.
vomitif, ve, a. emetic.
vorace, a. voracious, ravenous.
voracité, f. voracity.
vos, pn. pl. (de **votre**), your.
votant, m. voter.
voter, v. n. to vote.
votif, ve, a. votive.
votre, pn. your.
vôtre, pn.; **le ~, la ~, les vôtres,** pl. yours (pl.).
vouer, v. a. to devote, to consecrate, to vow || **se ~,** to dedicate oneself.
vouloir, m. will, design, intention.
vouloir, v. a. & n. ir. to will, to be willing, to wish, to be pleased, to have a mind, to intend.
voulu, e, a.; **mal ~,** hated || **bien ~,** loved.
vous, pn. you, ye || **c'est ~,** it is you.
voussoir, m. arch-stone.
voussure, f. bending of a vault.
voûte, f. vault, arched roof. [shouldered.
voûté, e, a. vaulted, crooked || round-
voûter, v. a. to vault, to arch || **se ~,** to stoop, to crook, to grow round-shouldered,

voyage, m. voyage, travel, journey, tour, excursion. [to journey.
voyager, v. n. to travel, to make a voyage,
voyageur, se, m. & f. traveller || voyager || passenger || **commis ~,** m. commercial traveller.
voyant, e, a. seeing || showy, gaudy.
voyelle, f. vowel.
voyer, m. overseer of the highways.
voyou, m. (fam.) street-cad.
vrai, m. truth || **à dire ~,** to tell the truth.
vrai, e, a. & ad. true, real, genuine, sincere, serious || exact, fit || truly, really || sincerely || **au ~,** truly, really.
vraiment, ad. indeed, truly, really.
vraisemblable, a. likely, probable || **-ment,** ad. likely, probably.
vraisemblance, f. likelihood, probability
vrille, f. gimlet || tendril.
vrillette, f. death-watch (beetle).
vu, e, a. seen || **~,** c. seeing, considering || **~ que,** seeing, considering that.
vue, f. sight, eye-sight || view || light, casement, window || aim, design || examination, consideration || prospect || **à ~,** at sight || **à ~ d'œil,** visibly || **à ~ de pays,**
vulcaniser, v. a. to vulcanise. [by guess.
vulgaire, m. vulgar mob, common people (pl.), populace.
vulgaire, a. (**-ment,** ad.) vulgar(ly) || common(ly) || vile, trivial, mean.
vulgariser, v. a. to vulgarise || to popu-
vulgarité, f. vulgarity. [larise.
vulnéraire, f. (bot.) kidney-vetch.
vulnéraire, a. vulnerary, good for wounds.
vultueux, se, a. (méd.) red and swollen (of the face).

W.

wagon, m. railway carriage, wagon || truck, lowry || **~-lit,** m. (rail.) sleeping-car.
Watt, m. Watt, unit of electric energy.

X.

xénomanie, f. mania for travelling.
xérès, m. sherry.
xylographe, m. engraver on wood.
xylographie, f. wood-engraving.
xylographique, a. xylographic.

Y.

y, ad. here, there, thither || **il ~ a,** there is, there are || **vous ~ êtes,** you are right, you have it || **~,** pn. to him, to her, to it, to them, of them, of her, of it, by it, by them, with him, with her, with it, with them || for it, for them.
yack, m. yak.
yatagan, m. yataghan (Turkish sword).
yeuse, f. (bot.) holm-oak || evergreen.

yeux, m. pl. de œil.
yole, f. yawl, very small boat.
youcca, m. (bot.) yucca || Adam's needle.
ypréau, m. (bot.) broad-leaved elm.

Z.

zagaie, f. javelin.
zain, a. m. (of horses) of one colour, whole-coloured.
zani, m. merry-Andrew.
zèbre, m. zebra.
zébu, m. zebu.
zélateur, trice, m. & f. zealot.
zèle, m. zeal, warmth || **avec ~**, zealously.
zélé, e, a. zealous.
zénith, m. zenith, vertex.
zéphyr, m. zephyr.
zéro, m. cipher, nought.
zest! pshaw! crack! || **entre le zist et le ~**, middling || undecided.
zeste, m. zest (of oranges) || (fig.) straw.
zézaiement, m. lisp.

zézayer, v. a. & n. to lisp.
zibeline, f. sable || sable-fur.
zibet, m. civet-cat.
zig, m. fellow, chap, cove.
zigzag, m. zigzag || **faire des ~s, to** stagger.
zinc, m. zinc.
zincage, m. zinc-plating.
zincographie, f. zincography.
zinguer, v. a. to cover with zinc.
zinguerie, f. zinc-works (pl.).
zingueur, m. zinc-worker.
zizanie, f. dissension.
zodiaque, m. (astr.) zodiac.
zona, f. (méd.) zona, shingles (pl.).
zone, f. zone.
zoologie, f. zoology.
zoologique, a. zoological.
zoomagnétisme, m. animal magnetism.
zoophyte, m. zoophyte.
zoosperme, m. zoosperm.
zouave, m. (mil.) zouave.
zut! you be blowed! hang it! I am not going to do it! stuff!

List of such more important modern geographical names, as differ in the two languages.

Abdère, f. Abdera.
les Abruzzes, f. pl. the Abruzzi.
l'Abyssinie, f. Abyssinia.
l'Achaïe, f. Achaia.
les Açores, f. pl. Azores.
adriatique, a. Adriatic.
africain, e, a. African.
l'Afrique, f. Africa.
Aix-la-Chapelle, f. Aachen, Aix-la-Chapelle.
Alep, m. Aleppo.
Alexandrie, f. Alexandria.
les Algarves, f. pl. Algarva.
Alger, m. Algiers.
l'Algérie, f. Algeria.
algérien, ne, a. Algerian.
l'Allemagne, f. Germany.
Allemand, e, m. & f. German.
allemand, e, a. German.
les Alpes, f. pl. Alps.
Américain, e, m. & f. American.
américain, e, a. American.
l'Amérique, f. America.
Ancône, f. Ancona.

l'Andalousie, f. Andalusia.
Anglais, e, m. & f. Englishman || Englishwoman.
anglais, e, a. English.
l'Angleterre, f. England.
anséatiques, f. pl.; **les villes ~**, f. pl. Hanse towns.
les Antilles, f. pl. Caribbee Islands.
Anvers, m. Antwerp.
les Apennins, m. pl. Apennines.
Arabe, m. & f. Arab.
arabe, a. Arabian.
l'Arabie, f. Arabia.
Golfe arabique, m. Arabian Gulf.
aragonais, e, a. Aragonese.
l'Archipel, m. Archipelago.
argien, ne, a. Argive.
l'Argovie, f. Aargau.
l'Arménie, f. Armenia.
Arménien, ne, m. & f. Armenian.
arménien, ne, a. Armenian.
asiatique, a. Asiatic.
l'Asie, f. Asia.
l'Assyrie, f. Assyria.

Assyrien, ne, m. & f. Assyrian.
assyrien, ne, a. Assyrian.
Athènes, f. Athens.
Athénien, ne, m. & f. Athenian.
athénien, ne, a. Athenian.
l'Attique, f. Attica.
l'Autriche, f. Austria.
Autrichien, ne, m. & f. Austrian.
autrichien, ne, a. Austrian.
Azof, m. Azow.

Babylone, f. Babylon.
Babylonien, ne, m. & f. Babylonian.
babylonien, ne, a. Babylonian.
la Bactriane, f. Bactra.
Bade, m. Baden.
Bâle, f. Basle.
la Barbade, f. Barbadoes.
barbaresque, a. Barbarian.
la Barbarie, f. Barbary.
Barthélemy (Saint-),f. St.Bartholomew.
Batave, m. & f. Batavian.
batave, a. Batavian.
la Batavie, f. Batavia.
Bavarois, e, m. & f. Bavarian.
bavarois, e, a. Bavarian.
la Bavière, f. Bavaria.
Belge, m. & f. Belgian.
belge, a. Belgian.
la Belgique, f. Belgium.
le Bengale, f. Bengal.
la Béotie, f. Boeotia.
Bethléem, m. Bethlehem.
la Biscaye, f. Biscay.
la Bohème, f. Bohemia.
Bohémien, ne, m. & f. Bohemian.
bohémien, ne, a. Bohemian.
Bologne, f. Bologna.
Bolonais, e, m. & f. Bolognese.
bolonais, e, a. of Bologna.
Bordeaux, m. Bordeaux.
Bordelais, e, m. & f. native of Bordeaux.
bordelais, e, a. of Bordeaux.
Bosniaque, m. & f. Bosnian.
bosniaque, a. Bosnian.
la Bosnie, f. Bosnia.
le Bosphore, m. Bosphorus.
Bougie, f. Bugia.
la Bourgogne, f. Burgundy.
Bourguignon, ne, m. & f. Burgundian.
bourguignon, ne, a. Burgundian.
Bragance, f. Braganza.
le Brandebourg, m. Brandenburg.
Brandebourgeois, e, m. & f. Brandenburger.
brandebourgeois, e, a. of Brandenburg.
Brême, f. Bremen.
le Brésil, m. Brazil.
Brésilien, ne, m. & f. Brazilian.
brésilien, ne, a. Brazilian.
Bresse, f. Brescia. [Great Britain.
la Bretagne, f. Brittany || la grande ~,
Breton, ne, m. & f. native of Brittany || Briton.
breton, ne, a. of Brittany, Breton || British.
Brindes, m. Brindisi.
Bruxelles, f. Brussels.
Bude, f. Buda.
Bulgare, m. & f. Bulgarian.

bulgare, a. Bulgarian.
la Bulgarie, f. Bulgaria.
Byzance, f. Byzantium.
byzantin, e, a. Byzantine.

Cabre, m. & f. Caffre || Kaffir.
cabre, a. Caffre || Kaffir.
Cadix, m. Cadiz.
les Caffres, pl. Caffres.
la Cafrerie, f. Caffraria.
le Caire, m. Cairo.
Calabrais, e, m. & f. Calabrian.
calabrais, e, a. Calabrian.
la Calabre, f. Calabria.
la Californie, f. California.
Calmouck, m. Calmuck.
Campêche, f. Campeachy.
les Canaries, f. pl. Canary Islands.
la Candie, f. Candia.
Candiot, e, m. & f. Candian.
candiot, e, a. Candian.
Cannes, pl. Cannæ, pl. || Cannes.
Cantorbéry, m. Canterbury.
Cap de Bonne-Espérance, m. Cape of
Capoue, f. Capua.   [Good Hope.
la Cappadoce, f. Cappadocia.
caraïbe, a. Caribbee.
la Carinthie, f. Carinthia.
la Carniole, f. Carniola.
les Carpathes, m. pl. Carpathian Mountains.
Carthagène, f. Carthagena.   [tains.
Carthaginois, e, m. & f. Carthaginian.
carthaginois, e, a. Carthaginian.
la mer Caspienne, f. Caspian Sea.
Castillan, e, m. & f. Castilian.
castillan, e, a. Castilian.
la Castille, f. Castile.
Catalan, e, m. & f. Catalonian.
catalan, e, a. Catalonian.
la Catalogne, f. Catalonia.
Catane, f. Catania.
le Catégat, m. Cattegat.
le Caucase, m. Caucasus.
Césarée, f. Cesarea.
Ceylan, m. Ceylon.
la Chalcédoine, f. Chalcedonia.
la Chaldée, f. Chaldea.
chaldéen, ne, a. Chaldean.
la Champagne, f. Champaign.
Chéronée, f. Cheronea.
la Chine, f. China.
Chinois, e, m. & f. Chinese.
chinois, e, a. Chinese. [Saint Christophe.
Christophe (Saint-), m. Saint Kitts ||
la Chypre, f. Cyprus.
la Cilicie, f. Cilicia.
Cimbres, pl. Cimbri, pl.
la Circassie, f. Circassia.
la Cochinchine, f. Cochin China.
Colchide, f. Colchis.
Cologne, m. Cologne.
la Colombie, f. Columbia.
Côme, m. Como.
Copenhague, f. Copenhagen.
Cordoue, f. Cordova.
la Corée, f. Corea.
Corfou, m. Corfu.
Corinthe, f. Corinth.
Cornouailles, f. Cornwall.

la Corogne, f. Corunna.
la Corse, f. Corsica.
corse, a. Corsican.
Cosaque, m. Cossack.
la Côte d'Or, f. the Gold Coast.
Cracovie, f. Cracow.
Crémone, f. Cremona.
Crémonais, e, m. & f. Cremonese
crémonais, e, a. Cremonese.
la Crète, f. Creta.
Crétois, e, m. & f. Cretan.
crétois, e, a. Cretan.
la Crimée, f. Crimea.
Croate, m. & f. Croatian.
croate, a. Croatian.
la Croatie, f. Croatia.
Cumes, f. Cumœ.
Cypriot, e, m. & f. Cyprian.
cypriot, e, a. Cyprian, Cypriste.
la Cyrénaïque, f. Cyrenaïca.
Cythère, f. Cythera.

Dacie, f. Dacia.
la Dalécarlie, f. Dalecarlia.
Dalmate, m. & f. Dalmatian.
dalmate, a. Dalmatian.
la Dalmatie, f. Dalmatia.
Damas, m. Damascus.
le Danemark, m. Denmark.
Danois, e, m. & f. Dane.
danois, e, a. Danish.
le Dauphiné, m. Dauphiny.
Delphes, m. Delphi.
Domingue (Saint-), m. St. Domingo.
la Dominique, f. Dominica.
la Doride, f. Doris.
dorien, ne, a. Dorian.
Douvres, m. Dover.
Dresde, f. Dresden.
Dunkerque, m. Dunkirk.

Ebre, m. Ebro.
l'Écluse, f. Sluys.
l'Écosse, f. Scotland.
Écossais, e, m. & f. Scotchman ‖ Scotch-
écossais, e, a. Scotch.   ⎣woman.
Édimbourg, m. Edinburgh.
Église (États de l'~), m. ancient States
   of the Church, Papal States.
l'Égypte, f. Egypt.
Égyptien, ne, m. & f. Egyptian.
égyptien, ne, a. Egyptian.
Elbe, f. Elba.
Élide, f. Elis.
Elseneur, m. Elsinore.
l'Éolie, f. Eolia.
éolien, ne, a. Eolian.
Éphèse, f. Ephesus.
Épidaure, m. Epidaurus.
l'Épire, m. Epirus.
l'Escaut, m. Sheldt.
Esclavon, ne, m. & f. Sclavonian.
esclavon, ne, a. Sclavonian.
l'Esclavonie, f. Sclavonia.
l'Espagne, f. Spain.
Espagnol, e, m. & f. Spaniard.
espagnol, e, a. Spanish.
les États-Unis, m. pl. United States.

l'Éthiopie, f. Ethiopia.
l'Étrurie, f. Etruria.
étrusque, a. Etrurian.
Eubée, f. Eubœa.
Euphrate, m. Euphrates.
Euripe, m. Euripus.
l'Europe, f. Europe.
Européen, ne, m. & f. European.
européen, ne, a. European.

Féroé (Iles), f. Faroe Isles.
Finistère (le Cap), m. Land's End.
la Finlande, f. Finland.   ⎡lander.
Finlandais, e, Finnois, e, m. & f. Fin-
finlandais, e, finnois, e, a. Finnish.
Flamand, e, m. & f. Fleming.
flamand, e, a. Flemish.   ⎡Flanders.
la Flandre, f., les Flandres, f. pl.
Flessingue, f. Flushing.
Florentin, m. Florentine.
la Floride, f. Florida.
Formose, f. Formosa.
Français, e, m. & f. Frenchman ‖ French-
français, e, a. French.   ⎣woman.
la France, f. France.
Francfort, m. Frankfort.
la Franconie, f. Franconia.
Fribourg, m. Friburg.
le Frioul, m. Friuli.
la Frise, f. Friesland.
Frison, ne, m. & f. Frieslander.
frison, ne, a. Friesland.

la Galatie, f. Galatia.
la Galice, f. Galicia.
la Galicie, f. Gallicia.
Galles, le pays de ~, m. Wales.
gallois, e, a. Welsh.
Gand, m. Ghent.
le Gange, m. Ganges.
la Gascogne, f. Gascony.
Gascon, ne, m. & f. Gascon.
gascon, ne, a. Gascon.
la Gaule, f., les Gaules, f. pl. Gaul.
Gênes, f. Genoa.
Genève, f. Geneva.
Genevois, e, m. & f. Genevese.
genevois, e, a. Genevese.
Génois, e, m. & f. Genoese.
génois, e, a. Genoese.
la Géorgie, f. Georgia.
Germain, e, m. & f. German.
germain, e, a. German.
la Germanie, f. Germania.
Glaciale, Mer ~, f. Frozen Ocean.
la Gothie, f. Gothland, Gothia.
Gœttingue, f. Göttingen.
Grec, que, m. & f. Greek.
grec, que, a. Grecian.
la Grèce, f. Greece.
Grenade, f. Granada.
le Grœnland, m. Greenland.
Grœnlandais, e, m. & f. Greenlander.
grœnlandais, e, a. Greenlaud.
Groningue, f. Groningen.
Gueldre, f. Guelderland.
Guinée, f. Guinea.

le Hainaut, m. Hainault.

Hambourg, m. Hamburg.
Hambourgeois, e, m. & f. Hamburger.
le Hanovre, m. Hanover.
hanovrien, ne, m. & f. Hanoverian.
hanovrien, ne, a. Hanoverian.
la Hanse, f. Hanse Towns (pl.).
la Havane, f. Havannah.
la Haye, f. Hague.
Hèbre, m. Hebrus.
Hébreu, e, m. & f. Hebrew, Hebrewess.
hébraïque, a. Hebrew.
Hélène (Sainte-), f. Saint Helena.
l'Helvétie, f. Helvetia.
Helvétien, ne, m. & f. Helvetian.
helvétien, ne, a. Helvetian.
l'Hespérie, f. Hesperia.
la Hesse, f. Hessia.
Hessois, e, m. & f. Hessian.
hessois, e, a. Hessian.
l'Hibernie, f. Hibernia.
Hindoustan, m. Hindostan.
Hindou, e, m. & f. Hindoo.
hindou, e, a. Hindoo.
la Hollande, f. Holland. [Dutchwoman.
Hollandais, e, m. & f. Dutchman ||
hollandais, e, a. Dutch.
la Hongrie, f. Hungary.
Hongrois, e, m. & f. Hungarian.
hongrois, e, a. Hungarian.

l'Ibérie, f. Iberia.
Ile de France or Ile Maurice, f. Mau-
    ritius.
illinois, e, a. Illinese.
l'Illyrie, f. Illyricum.
illyrien, ne, a. Illyrian.
l'Inde, f. India.
les Indes, f. pl. Indies || Grandes ~ or ~
    Orientales, East-Indies || ~ Occiden-
    tales, West-Indies.
Indien, ne, m. & f. Indian.
indien, ne, a. Indian.
la Ionie, f. Ionia.
ionien, ne, a. Ionian.
l'Irlande, f. Ireland.
Irlandais, e, m. & f. Irishman || Irish-
    woman.
irlandais, e, a. Irish.
l'Islande, f. Iceland.
l'Istrie, f. Istria.
l'Italie, f. Italy.
Italien, ne, m. & f. Italian.
italien, ne, a. Italian.
Ithaque, f. Ithaca.
Ivoire (Côte d'), m. Ivory-Coast.

la Jamaïque, f. Jamaica.
le Japon, m. Japan.
Japonais, e, m. & f. Japanese.
japonais, e, a. Japanese.
le Jourdain, m. Jordan.
la Judée, f. Judea.

Konigsberg, m. Koningsberg.

Lacédémone, f. Lacedæmonia.
Lacédémonien, ne, m. & f. Lacedæmonian.
lacédémonien, ne, a. Lacedæmonian.
Lancastre, m. Lancaster.

Lapon, ne, m. & f. Laplander.
lapon, ne, a. Lapland.
la Laponie, f. Lapland.
Larrons (Iles des), f. pl. Ladrone Islands.
Lépante, f. Lepanto.
Leyde, f. Leyden.
le Liban, m. Lebanon.
la Libye, f. Libya.
libyen, ne, a. Libyan.
Lille, m. Lisle.
Limbourg, m. Limburg.
Lisbonne, f. Lisbon.
la Lithuanie, f. Lithuania.
Livourne, f. Leghorn.
la Lombardie, f. Lombardy.
Londonien, ne, m. & f. Londoner.
londonien, ne, a. of London.
Londres, m. London.
Lorette, f. Loretto.
la Louisiane, f. Louisiana.
Lucques, f. Lucca.
la Lusace, f. Lusatia.
Luxembourg, m. Luxemburg.
la Lydie, f. Lydia.
lydien, ne, a. Lydian.
Lyon, f. Lyons.

la Macédoine, f. Macedonia.
Macédonien, ne, m. & f. Macedonian.
macédonien, ne, a. Macedonian.
Madère, f. Madeira.   [gellan.
Magellan (détroit de), f. Straits of Ma-
Majorque, f. Majorca.
Malais, e, m. & f. Malay.
malais, e, a. Malay.
Malines, f. Mechlin.
Malouines (Iles), f. pl. Falkland Islands.
Malte, f. Malta.
Maltais, e, m. & f. Maltese.
maltais, e, a. Maltese.
la Manche, f. the British Channel.
Mantoue, f. Mantua.
le Maroc, m. Morocco.
Marocain, e, m. & f. native of Morocco.
Marquises (Iles), f. pl. Marquesas.
la Martinique, f. Martinico.
Mastricht, m. Mæstricht.
Maure, m. Moor.
maure, a. Moorish.
Maurice (l'Ile), f. Mauritius.
la Mauritanie, f. Mauritania.
Mayence, f. Mentz.
le Mecklembourg, m. Mecklemburg.
la Mecque, f. Mecca.
la Médie, f. Media.
Médine, f. Medina.
Méditerranée, f. Mediterranean (Sea).
Mer Egée, f. Ægean Sea.
la Mésopotamie, f. Mesopotamia.
Messine, f. Messina.
la Meuse, f. Meuse.
Mexicain, e, m. & f. Mexican.
mexicain, e, a. Mexican.
le Mexique, m. Mexico.
Milanais, e, m. & f. Milanese.
milanais, e, a. Milanese.
milésien, ne, a. Milesian.
Milet, m. Miletus.
Minorque, f. Minorca.

Modène, f. Modena.
la Moldavie, f. Moldavia.
les Moluques, f. pl. Moluccas, pl.
morave, a. Moravian.
la Moravie, f. Moravia.
la Morée, f. Morea.
la Morlaquie, f. Morlaquia.
Moscou, m. Moscow.
la Moscovie, f. Moscovy.
Mycènes, f. Mycene.

Napolitain, e, m. & f. Neapolitan.
napolitain, e, a. Neapolitan.
Neufchâtel, m. Neufchâtel.
le Nil, m. the Nile.
Nimègue, f. Nimeguen.
Ninive, f. Niniveh.
Normand, e, m. & f. Norman.
normand, e, a. Norman.
la Normandie, f. Normandy.
la Norvège, f. Norway.
Norvégien, ne, m. & f. Norwegian.
norvégien, ne, a. Norwegian.   [land.
la Nouvelle-Angleterre, f. New Eng-
la Nouvelle-Écosse, f. Nova Scotia.
la Nouvelle-Zemble, f. Nova Zembla.
la Nubie, f. Nubia.
Numance, f. Numantia.
Numides, m. pl. Numidæ, pl.
la Numidie, f. Numidia.

Océan Atlantique, m. Atlantic Ocean ǁ
~ Pacifique, m. Pacific.
l'Olympe, m. Olympus.
l'Ombrie, f. Umbria.
les Orcades (Iles), f. pl. the Orkneys.
l'Orénoque, m. the Orinoco.
Osnabruck, m. Osnaburg.
Otahiti, f. Otaheite.
Otrante, f. Otranto.
Quessant, m. Ushant.
Ourals (Monts), m. pl. Uralian Chain.

Padoue, f. Padua.
le Palatinat, m. Palatinate.
Palerme, f. Palermo.
Pampelune, f. Pampeluna.
Paris, m. Paris.
Parisien, ne, m. & f. Parisian.
parisien, ne, a. Parisian.
Parme, f. Parma.
Parmesan, e, m. & f. native of Parma.
le Parnasse, m. Parnassus.
parthe, a. Parthian.
la Parthie, f. Parthia.
le Pas-de-Calais, m. the Straits of Dover.
Pavie, f. Pavia.
les Pays-Bas, m. pl. Netherlands, pl.
le Péloponèse, m. Peloponnesus.
péloponésien, ne, a. Peloponnesian.
la Pensylvanie, f. Pennsylvania.
Pergame, m. Pergamos.
la Perse, f. Persia.
Perse, m. & f. Persian.
perse, persan, e, a. Persian.
le Pérou, m. Peru.
Pérouse, f. Perugia.
Péruvien, ne, m. & f. Peruvian.
péruvien, ne, a. Peruvian.
Pétersbourg, m. Petersburg.

Pharsale, f. Pharsalia.
la Phénicie, f. Phenicia.
Phénicien, ne, m. & f. Phenician.
phénicien, ne, a. Phenician.
Philadelphie, f. Philadelphia.
la Phrygie, f. Phrygia.
Phrygien, ne, m. & f. Phrygian.
phrygien, ne, a. Phrygian.
la Picardie, f. Picardy.
le Piémont, m. Piedmont.
Piémontais, e, m. & f. Piedmontese.
piémontais, e, a. Piedmontese.
le Pinde, m. Pindus.
le Pirée, m. Piræus.
Pisan, e, m. & f. native of Pisa.
Pise, f. Pisa.
Plaisance, f. Placentia.
la Pologne, f. Poland.
Polonais, e, m. & f. Pole.
polonais, e, a. Polish.
le Pont, m. Pontus.
le Pont-Euxin, m. Pont-Euxine.
Pontins (les Marais), m. pl. the Pontine
Marshes.
Portugais, e, m. & f. Portuguese.
portugais, e, a. Portuguese.
le Portugal, m. Portugal.
la Pouille, f. Apulia.
la Prusse, f. Prussia.
Prussien, ne, m. & f. Prussian.
prussien, ne, a. Prussian.   [tains, pl.
les Pyrénées, f. pl. the Pyrenean Moun-

Québec, m. Quebec.

Raguse, f. Ragusa.
Ratisbonne, f. Ratisbon.
Ravenne, f. Ravenna.
la Rhétie, f. Rhetia.
le Rhin, m. the Rhine.   [Mountains, pl.
Rocheux (les Monts), m. pl. the Rocky
Romain, e, m. & f. Roman.
romain, e, a. Roman.
Rome, f. Roma, Rome.
la Roumanie, f. Roumania.
Russe, m. & f. Russian.
russe, a. Russian.
la Russie, f. Russia.

Sagonte, f. Saguntum.
le Sahara, f. the Sahara.   [nose.
Saint-Antoine(leCap),m.St.-Anthony's
Saint-Barthélemy, f. St. Bartholomew.
Saint-Ubes, m. Setubal.
Salamanque, f. Salamanca.
Salamine, f. Salamis.
Salonique, f. Salonica.
Samaritain, e, m. & f. Samaritan.
samaritain, e, a. Samaritan.
Samoyèdes, m. pl. Samoides, pl.
Saragosse, f. Saragossa.
la Sardaigne, f. Sardinia.
Sarde, m. & f. Sardinian.
sarde, a. Sardinian.
Sarrasin, e, m. & f. Saracen.
sarrasin, e, a. Saracen.
Saverne, f. Severn.
la Savoie, f. Savoy.   [Savoyard.
Savoisien, ne, m. native of Savoy,

savoisien, ne, a. of Savoy.
la Saxe, f. Saxony.
Saxon, ne, m. & f. Saxon.
saxon, ne, a. Saxon.
Scandinave, m. & f. Scandinavian.
scandinave, a. Scandinavian.
la Scandinavie, f. Scandinavia.
Scythe, m. & f. Scythian.
scythe, a. Scythian.
la Scythie, f. Scythia.
Sébastien (Saint-), m. Saint Sebastian.
Ségovie, f. Segovia.
la Servie, f. Servia.
siamois, e, a. Siamese.
la Sibérie, f. Siberia.
la Sicile, f. Sicily.
Sicilien, ne, m. & f. Sicilian.
sicilien, ne, a. Sicilian.
la Silésie, f. Silesia.
Silésien, ne, m. & f. Silesian.
silésien, ne, a. Silesian.
Smyrne, f. Smyrna.   [Smyrnian.
Smyrnéen, ne, Smyrniote, m. & f.
Sodome, f. Sodom.   [Islands.
Sonde (Archipel de la), m. Sunda
les Sorlingues, f. pl. the Scilly Isles.
la Squabe, f. Swabia.
Sparte, f. Sparta.
Spartiate, m. & f. Spartan.
spartiate, a. Spartan.
la Stirie, f. Stiria.
Strasbourg, m. Strasburg.
la Sudermanie, f. Sudermanland.
la Suède, f. Sweden.
Suédois, e, m. & f. Swede.
suédois, e, a. Swedish.
Suèves, m. pl. Suevi, pl.
la Suisse, f. Switzerland.
Suisse, sse, m. & f. Swiss.
suisse, a. Swiss.
le Sund, m. the Sound.
Syracusain, e, m. & f. Syracusan.
syracusain, e, a. Syracusan.
Syracuse, f. Syracuse.
la Syrie, f. Syria.
Syrien, ne, m. & f. Syrian.
syrien, ne, a. Syrian.

Table (les Monts de la), f. Table Moun-
Tage, m. Tagus.   [tain.
Tahiti, m. Otaheite.
la Tamise, f. Thames.
Tanger, m. Tangiers.
Tarente, f. Tarentum.
tartare, a. Tartar.
la Tartarie, f. Tartary.
Ténériffe, f. Teneriffe.

Terre-de-Feu, f. Terra del Fuego.
Terre-ferme, f. Terra Firma.
Terre-Magellanique, f. Terra Magella-
Terre-Neuve, f. Newfoundland. [nica.
la Terre-Sainte, f. Holy Land.
Thébain, e, m. & f. Theban.
thébain, e, a. Theban.
les Thermopyles, f. pl. Thermopilæ, pl.
la Thessalie, f. Thessaly.
Thessalien, ne, m. & f. Thessalian.
thessalien, ne, a. Thessalian.
Thessalonique, f. Thessalonica.
Thrace, m. & f. Thracian.
la Thuringe, f. Thuringia.
le Tibre, m. Tiber.
le Tigre, m. Tigris.
Tolède, f. Toledo.
Toledan, e, m. & f. native of Toledo.
Toscan, e, m. & f. Tuscan.
toscan, e, a. Tuscan.
la Toscane, f. Tuscany.
la Transylvanie, f. Transylvania.
Trèves, f. Triers.
la Trinité, f. Trinidad.
la Troade, f. Troas.
Troie, f. Troy.
Troyen, ne, m. & f. Trojan.
troyen, ne, a. Trojan.
Turc, que, m. & f. Turk.
turc, que, a. Turkish.
la Turquie, f. Turkey.

l'Ukraine, f. the Ukraine.

la Valachie, f. Wallachia.
Valence, f. Valencia.
Varsovie, f. Warsaw.
Venise, f. Venice.
Vénitien, ne, m. & f. Venetian.
vénitien, ne, a. Venetian.
Véronais, e, m. & f. Veronese.
Vérone, f. Verona.
le Vésuve, m. Vesuvius.
Vicence, f. Vicenza.
Vienne, f. Vienna.
Viennois, e, m. & f. Viennese.
viennois, e, a. Viennese.
la Virginie, f. Virginia.
la Vistule, f. Vistula.

la Westphalie, f. Westphalia.
Wolfenbuttel, m. Wolfenbuttle.
le Wurtemberg, m. Wurtemberg.

Xanthe, m. Xanthus.

la Zélande, f. Zealand.

List of the more usual christian names, not alike in both languages.

Achille, Achilles.
Adélaïde, Adélaïs, Adelaide.
Adèle, Adela, Adeline.
Adolphe, Adolphus.
Adrien, Adrian.
Agathe, Agatha.
Aimée, Amy.
Alphonse, Alphonso.
Ambroise, Ambrosius.
Amédée, Amadeus.
Amélie, Amelia.
Anastase, Anastasius.
André, Andrew.
Angélique, Angelica.
Anne, Anna.
Antoine, Anthony.
Antoinette, Antonia.
Arabelle, Arabella.
Archambaut, Archibald.
Arnaud, Arnold.
Arthur, Arthur.
Athanase, Athanasius.
Auguste, Augustus || Augusta.
Augustin, Austin.
Aurélien, Aurelian.

Barbe, Barbara.
Barnabé, Barnaby.
Barthélemy, Bartholomew.
Baudouin, Baldwin.
Benoît, Benedict.
Berthe, Bertha.
Bertrand, Bertram.
Blanche, Bianca.
Brigitte, Bridget.

Catherine, Catherine.
Cécile, Cecily, Cecilia.
César, Cæsar.
Charles, Charles.
Chrétien, Christian.
Chrétienne, Christiana, Christina.
Christophe, Christopher.
Claire, Clara.
Claude, Claudius, Claude.
Claudine, Claudia.
Clément, Clement.
Clémentine, Clementina.
Clotilde, Clotilda.
Constance, Constantia.
Corneille, Cornelius.
Crépin, Crispin.
Cyprien, Cyprian.

Denis, Dennis, Dionysius.
Denise, Dionysia.
Dominique, Dominic.
Dorothée, Dorothy.

Edmond, Edmund.
Édouard, Edward.
Élie, Elias.
Élise, Elisa.
Élisée, Elisha.
Émilie, Emily, Emmy.
Emme, Emma.
Étienne, Stephen.
Eugène, Eugene.
Eugénie, Eugenia.
Eustache, Eustace.

Fabien, Fabian.
Fanchon, Fanchette, Fanny.
Félicie, Felicia.
Félicité, Felicity.
Flore, Flora.
François, Francis.
Françoise, Frances.
Frédéric, Frederick.

Gaspard, Jasper.
Gautier, Walter.
Genifrède, Winifred.
Geoffroi, Jeffery, Geoffrey.
Gervais, Gervas.
Gilles, Giles.
Godefroy, Godfrey.
Grâce, Grace.
Grégoire, Gregory.
Guillaume, William.
Gustave, Gustavus.

Hélène, Helena, Helen.
Henri, Henry.
Henriette, Henrietta.
Hilaire, Hilary.
Horace, Horatio, Horace.
Hugues, Hugh.
Humfroy, Humphrey.

Ignace, Ignatius.
Isabelle, Isabel, Isabella.
Isaïe, Isaiah.

Jacques, James.
Jacquot, Jim, Jemmy.
Jean, John.

Jeanne, Jane.
Jeanneton, Jeannette, Janet.
Jeannot, Jack, Johnny.
Jenny, Jenny.
Jérémie, Jeremy.
Jérôme, Jerome.
Jules, Julius.
Julie, Julia.
Julien, Julian.
Julienne, Juliana.
Juliette, Juliet.
Justin, Justin, Justinus.
Justine, Justina.

Laure, Laura.
Laurent, Lawrence.
Lazare, Lazarus.
Léon, Leo.
Lia, Leah.
Lise, Lizzie.
Lisette, Loo.
Louis, Lewis.
Louise, Louisa.
Louison, vide Lisette.
Luc, Luke.
Lucie, Lucy.
Lucien, Lucian.
Lucrèce, Lucretia.

Madeleine, Magdalen, Maud.
Madelon, Maudlin.
Margot, Madge, Marget, Marjory, Meg,
  Peg, Peggy.
Marguerite, Margaret.
Marie, Maria.
Mariette, Marion, Mary.
Marthe, Martha.
Mathilde, Matilda.
Matthieu, Matthew.
Maurice, Morris.
Michel, Michael.
Moïse, Moses.

Nannette, Ninon, Nancy.
Nicolas, Nicholas.
Noé, Noah.
Olivie, Olivia.
Olivier, Oliver.
Onfroy, Humphrey.
Othon, Otho.

Patrice, Patrick.
Paul, Paul.
Pauline, Paulina.
Philippe, Philip.
Philippine, Philippa.
Pie, Pius.
Pierre, Peter.

Randolphe, Randal.
Raoul, Ralph.
Raymond, Raymund.
Régine, Regina.
Renaud, Reynold.
Robin, Bob.
Rodolphe, Ralph.
Roland, Rowland, Orlando.
Rosaline, Rosalind.
Rosamunde, Rosamund.
Rosette, Rosy.

Salomon, Solomon.
Samson, Sampson.
Sébastien, Sebastian.
Sigismond, Sigismund.
Silvain, Silvan.
Silvestre, Silvester.
Sophie, Sophia.
Stanislas, Stanislaus.
Susanne, Susan, Susannah.
Suzette, Suzon, Susy.

Théodose, Theodosius.
Théophile, Theophilus.
Thérèse, Theresa.
Thibaud, Theobald.
Thomas, Thomas.
Timothée, Timothy.
Tobie, Toby.
Toinette, Antonia.

Urbain, Urban.
Ursule, Ursula.

Valentin, Valentine.
Valérie, Valery.
Véronique, Veronica.
Vincent, Vincent.

Wilhelmine, Wilhelmina.

Zacharie, Zachary.
Zachée, Zachæus.

Infinitif	Présent		Imparfait du Subjonctif
	de l'Indicatif	du Subjonctif	
absoudre	j'absous, s, t; nous absolvons, ez, ent	que j'absolve, es, e; vions, iez, ent	—
acquérir	j'acquiers, s, t; nous acquérons, ez, ils acquièrent	que j'acquière, es, e; acquérions, iez, acquièrent	que j'acquisse, s, ît; que nous acquissions, iez, ent
aller	je vais, tu vas, il va; nous allons, vous allez, ils vont	que j'aille, que tu ailles, qu'il aille; que nous allions, que vous alliez, qu'ils aillent	que j'allasse, s, ât; que nous allassions, iez, ent
assaillir	j'assaille, es, e; nous assaillons, ez, ent	que j'assaille, es, e; que nous assaillions, iez, ent	que j'assaillisse, s, ît; que nous assaillissions, iez, ent
asseoir	j'assieds, s, d; nous asseyons, ez, ils asseyent ou j'assois, s, t; nous assoyons, ez, ils assoient	que j'asseye ou que j'assoie, que nous asseyions	que j'assisse, s, ît; que nous assissions
astreindre	se conjugue comme ceindre		
avoir	j'ai, tu as, il a; nous avons, vous avez, ils ont	que j'aie, que tu aies, qu'il ait; que nous ayons, que vous ayez, qu'ils aient	que j'eusse, que tu eusses, qu'il eût; que nous eussions, iez, qu'ils eussent
boire	je bois, s, t; nous buvons, ez, ils boivent	que je boive, s, e; buvions, iez, boivent	que je busse, s, ût; que nous bussions, iez, bussent
bouillir	je bous, tu bous, il bout; nous bouillons, vous bouillez, ils bouillent	que je bouille, s, e; que nous bouillions, iez, ent	que je bouillisse, s, ît; que nous bouillissions, iez, ent
braire	il brait, ils braient	qu'il braille, qu'ils braient	—
bruire	il bruit, ils bruissent	—	—
ceindre	je ceins, s, t; nous ceignons	que je ceigne, s, e; que nous ceignions	que je ceignisse, que nous ceignissions
choir	—	—	—
circoncire	je circoncis, s, t; nous circoncisons, ez, ent	que je circoncise, que nous circoncisions	—
clore	je clos, tu clos, il clôt	—	—
conclure	je conclus, s, t; nous concluons, ez, ent	que je conclue, es, e; que nous concluions, iez, ent	que je conclusse, s, ût; que nous conclussions
conduire	se conjugue comme cuire		
confire	je confis, s, t; nous confisons, ez, ent	que je confise, es, e; que nous confisions, iez, ent	que je confisse, es, ît; que nous confissions
connaître	je connais, s, il connaît; nous connaissons	que je connaisse	que je connusse, qu'il connût
conquérir	se conjugue comme acquérir		
construire	se conjugue comme cuire		
contredire	je contredis, s, t; nous contredisons, ez, ent	le reste comme dire	

irréguliers.

Imparfait	Parfait défini	Futur	Impératif	Participe présent	Participe passé
j'absolvais	—	j'absoudrai	absous, absolvons, absolvez	absolvant	absous
j'acquérais	j'acquis	j'acquerrai	acquiers, acquerons, acquerez	acquérant	acquis
j'allais	j'allai	j'irai	va, allons, allez	allant	allé
j'assaillais	j'assaillis	j'assaillirai	assaille, assaillons, assailliez	assaillant	assailli
j'asseyais ou j'assoyais, nous asseyions	j'assis, nous assîmes	j'assiérai ou j'asseyerai, as, a; nous assiérons	assieds ou assois, asseyons ou assoyons, assoyez	asseyant, assoyant	assis
j'avais	j'eus, tu eus, il eut; nous eûmes, vous eûtes, ils eurent	j'aurai, as, a	aie, ayons, ayez	ayant	eu
je buvais, nous buvions	je bus, nous bûmes	je boirai, nous boirons	bois, buvons, buvez	buvant	bu
je bouillais, nous bouillions	je bouillis, nous bouillîmes	je bouillirai, nous bouillirons	bous, bouillons, ez	bouillant	bouilli
il brayait, ils brayaient	—	il braira, ils brairont	—	brayant	—
il bruissait, ils bruissaient	—	—	—	—	—
je ceignais	je ceignis	je ceindrai	ceins, ceignons, ceignez	ceignant	ceint
—	—	—	—	—	chu
je circoncisais	je circoncis	je circoncirai	circoncis, circoncisons, ez	circoncisant	circoncis
—	—	je clorai	clos	—	clos
je concluais	je conclus, nous conclûmes, vous conclûtes, ils conclurent	je conclurai, nous conclurons	conclus, concluons, ez	concluant	conclu
je confisais	je confis	je confirai	confis, confisons, ez	confisant	confit
je connaissais	je connus	je connaîtrai	connais, connaissons, ez	connaissant	connu

Infinitif	Présent		Imparfait du Subjonctif
	de l'Indicatif	du Subjonctif	
coudre	je couds, ds, d; nous cousons, ez, ent	que je couse	que je cousisse
courir	je cours, s, t; nous courons, ez, ent	que je coure, es, e	que je courusse, qu'il courût
couvrir	je couvre, s, e; nous couvrons	que je couvre	que je couvrisse
craindre	se conjugue comme ceindre		
croire	je crois, s, t; nous croyons, ez, ils croient	que je croie, es, e; nous croyions, iez, qu'ils croient	que je crusse, qu'il crût
croître	je croîs, s, t; nous croissons	que je croisse, que nous croissions	que je crusse, qu'il crût
cueillir	je cueille, es, e; nous cueillons	que je cueille	que je cueillisse
cuire	je cuis, s, t; nous cuisons	que je cuise	que je cuisisse
déchoir	je déchois, s, e; nous déchoyons, vous déchoyez, ils déchoient	que je déchoie, que nous déchoyions, que vous déchoyiez, qu'ils déchoient	que je déchusse
dédire	je dédis, s, t; nous dédisons, vous dédisez, ils dédisent	que je dédise	que je dédisse
défaillir	je défaus, s, t; nous défaillons, vous défaillez, ils défaillent	que je défaille	que je défaillisse
détruire	se conjugue comme cuire		
devoir	je dois, s, t; nous devons, vous devez, ils doivent	que je doive, es, e; que nous devions, que vous deviez, qu'ils doivent	que je dusse
dire	je dis, s, t; nous disons, vous dites, ils disent	que je dise, es, e; que nous disions, iez, ent	que je disse
dissoudre	se conjugue comme absoudre		
dormir	je dors, s, t; nous dormons, ez, ent	que je dorme	que je dormisse
échoir	il échoit	—	que j'échusse
éclore	il éclôt; ils éclosent	qu'il éclose; qu'ils éclosent	—
écrire	j'écris, s, t; nous écrivons, ez, ent	que j'écrive, s, e; que nous écrivions, iez, qu'ils écrivent	que j'écrivisse, s, ît; que nous écrivissions, iez, ent
empreindre	se conjugue comme ceindre		
enduire	se conjugue comme cuire		
enfreindre	se conjugue comme ceindre		
s'enquérir	se conjugue comme acquérir		
épreindre	se conjugue comme ceindre		
être	je suis, tu es, il est; nous sommes, vous êtes, ils sont	que je sois, s, t; que nous soyons, que vous soyez, qu'ils soient	que je fusse, s, ût; que nous fussions, iez, ent
exclure	se conjugue comme conclure		
faillir	je faux, tu faux, il faut	—	—
faire	je fais, s, t; nous faisons, vous faites, ils font	que je fasse, s, e; que nous fassions, iez, ent	que je fisse, s, qu'il fît, que nous fissions, iez, ent
falloir	il faut	qu'il faille	qu'il fallût
feindre	se conjugue comme ceindre		
frire	je fris, s, t	—	—
fuir	je fuis, s, t; nous fuyons, ez, ils fuient	que je fuie, es, e; que nous fuyions, iez, fuient	que je fuisse, s, qu'il fuît; que nous fuissions, iez, ent
gésir	ci-gît, il gît; nous gisons, ez, ent	—	—
haïr	je hais, s, t; nous haïssons, ez, ent	que je haïsse, s, e; que nous haïssons, ez, ent	que je haïsse, s, qu'il haït, que nous haïssions, iez, ent
induire	se conjugue comme cuire		
instruire	se conjugue comme cuire		
interdire	j'interdis, s, t; nous interdisons, ez, ent	le reste comme dire	

Imparfait	Parfait défini	Futur	Impératif	Participe présent	Participe passé
je cousais	je cousis	je coudrai	couds, cousons, ez	cousant	cousu
je courais	je courus	je courrai	cours, courons, ez	courant	couru
je couvrais	je couvris	je couvrirai	couvre, couvrons, ez	couvrant	couvert
je croyais	je crus	je croirai	crois, croyons, ez	croyant	cru
je croissais	je crûs	je croîtrai	croîs, croissons, ez	croissant	crû
je cueillais	je cueillis	je cueillerai	cueille, cueillons, ez	cueillant	cueilli
je cuisais	je cuisis	je cuirai	cuis, cuisons, ez	cuisant	cuit
—	je déchus	je décherrai			déchu
je dédisais	je dédis	je dédirai	dédis, dédisons, ez	dédisant	dédit
je défaillais	je défaillis	je défaudrai	—	défaillant, faillant	défailli, failli
je devais	je dus	je devrai	dois, devons, ez	devant	dû
je disais	je dis	je dirai	dis, disons, dites	disant	dit
je dormais	je dormis	je dormirai	dors, dormons, ez	dormant	dormi
—	j'échus	il écherra	—	échéant	échu
—	—	il éclora; ils écloront	—	—	éclos
j'écrivais	j'écrivis, nous écrivîmes	j'écrirai	écris, écrivons, ez	écrivant	écrit
j'étais	je fus, s, t; nous fûmes	je serai, as, a	sois, soyons, soyez	étant	été
je faillais	je faillis	je faudrai	—	faillant	failli
je faisais	je fis, nous fîmes	je ferai, as, a	fais, faisons, faites	faisant	fait
il fallait	il fallut	il faudra	—	—	[var.] fallu (in-
		je frirai, as, a	fris		frit, e
je fuyais, nous fuyions	je fuis, nous fuîmes	je fuirai, as, a	fuis, fuyons, ez	fuyant	fui
je gisais, nous gisions	—	—	—	gisant	—
je haïssais, nous haïssions	je haïs, nous haïmes	je haïrai	hais, haïssons, ez	haïssant	haï

| Infinitif | Présent | | Imparfait du Subjonctif |
	de l'Indicatif	du Subjonctif	
introduire	se conjugue comme cuire		
joindre	se conjugue comme ceindre		
lire	je lis, s, t; nous lisons, ez, ils lisent	que je lise, es, e; que nous lisions, iez, ent	que je lusse, es, qu'il lût; que nous lussions, iez, ent
luire	je luis, s, t; nous luisons, ez, ent	que je luise, es, e; que nous luisions	—
maudire	je maudis, s, t; nous maudissons, ez, ent	que je maudisse, es, e; maudissions, iez, ent	que je maudisse, es, qu'il maudît; que nous maudissions
médire	se conjugue comme dédire		
mentir	je mens, s, t; nous mentons, ez, ent	que je mente, es, e; que nous mentions	que je mentisse, es, mentît; que nous mentissions, iez, ent
mettre	je mets, s, t; nous mettons, ez, ent	que je mette, es, e; mettions, iez, ent	que je misse, es, ît; missions, iez, ent
moudre	je mouds, s, d; nous moulons, ez, ent	que je moule, es, e; moulions, iez, ent	que je moulusse, es, ût; que nous moulussions
mourir	je meurs, s, t; nous mourons, ez, ent	que je meure, que nous mourions	que je mourusse, que nous mourussions
mouvoir	je meus, s, t; nous mouvons, ez, ent	que je meuve, es, e; que nous mouvions	que je musse, es, qu'il mût, que nous mussions
naître	je nais, s, naît; naissons, ez, ent	que je naisse, es, e; naissions, iez, ent	que je naquisse, es, ît; que nous naquisions
nuir	se conjugue comme cuire		
offrir	se conjugue comme couvrir		
oindre	se conjugue comme ceindre		
ouïr		—	—
ouvrir	se conjugue comme couvrir		
paître	je pais, s, il paît; nous paissons	que je paisse, que nous paissions	—
paraître	je parais, s, il paraît; nous paraissons, ez, ent	que je paraisse, que nous paraissions	que je parusse, s, ût; que nous parussions
partir	je pars, s, t; nous partons, ez, ent	que je parte, es, e; que nous partions, iez, ent	que je partisse, es, qu'il partît; que nous partissions
peindre	se conjugue comme ceindre		
plaindre	se conjugue comme ceindre		
plaire	je plais, s, ît; nous plaisons, ez, ent	que je plaise, es, e; que nous plaisions	que je plusse, s, ût; que nous plussions
pleuvoir	il pleut	qu'il pleuve	qu'il plût
poindre	il point	—	—
pourvoir	je pourvois, s, t; nous pourvoyons, ez, ils pourvoient	que je pourvoie, es, e; que nous pourvoyions, iez, voient	que je pourvusse, es, ût; que nous pourvussions
pouvoir	je puis (peux), tu peux, il peut; nous pouvons, ez, ils peuvent	que je puisse, es, e; que nous puissions	que je pusse, es, pût; que nous pussions
prédire	je prédis, s, t; nous prédisons, vous prédisez, ils prédisent	le reste comme dire	
prendre	je prends, s, d; nous prenons, ez, ils prennent	que je prenne, es, e; que nous prenions	que je prisse, es, ît; que nous prissions
prévoir	se conjugue comme voir		
puer	je pue, es, e; nous puons, ez, ent	que je pue, es, e; que nous puions	que je puasse, es, ât; que nous puassions
réduire	se conjugue comme cuire		
se repentir	se conjugue comme mentir		

Imparfait	Parfait défini	Futur	Impératif	Participe présent	Participe passé
je lisais	je lus	je lirai	lis, lisons, lisez	lisant	lu
je luisais	—	je luirai	luis, luisons, ez	luisant	lui (invariable)
je maudissais	je maudis, nous maudîmes	je maudirai	maudis, maudissons, maudissez	maudissant	maudit
je mentais, nous mentions	je mentis, nous mentîmes	je mentirai	mens, mentons, mentez	mentant	menti
je mettais, mettions	je mis, s, it; nous mîmes	je mettrai	mets, mettons, ez	mettant	mis
je moulais, moulions	je moulus, us, ut; nous moulûmes	je moudrai	mouds, moulons	moulant	moulu
je mourais, mourions	je mourus, nous mourûmes	je mourrai, as, a; nous mourrons	meurs, mourons, ez	mourant	mort
je mouvais, nous mouvions	je mus, nous mûmes	je mouvrai, nous mouvrons	meus, mouvons, ez	mouvant	mu
je naissais, naissions	je naquis, nous naquîmes	je naîtrai	nais, naissons, ez	naissant	né
j'oyais (rare)	j'ouïs (rare)	—	oyons (rare), oyez	—	ouï
je paissais, nous paissions	—	je paîtrai	pais, paissons, ez	paissant	—
je paraissais	je parus, s, ut; parûmes	je paraîtrai	parais, paraissons, ez	paraissant	paru
je partais, nous partions	je partis, s, it; nous partîmes	je partirai	pars, partons, partez	partant	parti
je plaisais, nous plaisions	je plus; s, ut; nous plûmes	je plairai	plais, plaisons, plaisez	plaisant	plu
il pleuvait	il plut	il pleuvra	qu'il pleuve	pleuvant	plu
—	—	il poindra	—	—	—
je pourvoyais	je pourvus	je pourvoirai	pourvois, pourvoyons, ez	pourvoyant	pourvu
je pouvais, nous pouvions	je pus, tu pus, il put; nous pûmes, vous pûtes, ils purent	je pourrai	qu'il puisse	pouvant	pu
je prenais, s, t; nous prenions	je pris, s, t; nous prîmes	je prendrai	prends, prenons, prenez	prenant	pris
je puais		je puerai	qu'il pue (ne s'emploie pas)	puant	—

Infinitif	Présent de l'Indicatif	Présent du Subjonctif	Imparfait du Subjonctif
requérir	se conjugue comme acquérir		
résoudre	je résous, s, t; nous résolvons, ez, ent	que je résolve, es, e; résolvions, iez, ent	que je résolusse, es, ût; que nous résolussions
restreindre	se conjugue comme ceindre		
rire	je ris, s, t; nous rions, iez, ent	que je rie, es, e; que nous riions, iez, ent	que je risse, es, qu'il rît; que nous rissions
saillir *	il saille, ils saillent	qu'il saille	qu'il saillît
savoir	je sais, s, t; nous savons, ez, ent	que je sache, es, e; que nous sachions	que je susse, es, ût; que nous sussions
séduire	se conjugue comme cuire		
sentir	se conjugue comme mentir		
seoir (présider, être placé)	—	—	—
seoir (être convenable)	il sied, ils siéent	qu'il siée, qu'ils siéent	—
servir	je sers, s, t; nous servons, ez, ent	que je serve, es, e; que nous servions	que je servisse, es, ît; que nous servissions
sortir	je sors, s, t; nous sortons, ez, ent	que je sorte, es, e; que nous sortions	que je sortisse, es, ît; que nous sortissions
souffrir	se conjugue comme couvrir		
suffire	je suffis, s, t; nous suffisons, ez, ent	que je suffise, es, e; que nous suffisions, iez, ent	que je suffisse, es, ît; que nous suffissions
suivre	je suis, s, t; nous suivons, ez, ent	que je suive, es, e; que nous suivions	que je suivisse, es, ît; que nous suivissions
surseoir	je sursois, s, t; nous sursoyons, ez, ils sursoient	—	—
taire	je tais, s, t; nous taisons, ez, ent	que je taise, es, e; que nous taisions	que je tusse, s, ût; que nous tussions
teindre	se conjugue comme ceindre		
tenir	je tiens, s, t; nous tenons, ez, ils tiennent	que je tienne, es, e; que nous tenions	que je tinsse, s, qu'il tînt; que nous tinssions
tistre	—	—	—
traduire	se conjugue comme cuire		
traire	je trais, s, t; nous trayons, ez, ils traient	que je traie, es, e; que nous trayions	—
tressaillir	se conjugue comme assaillir		
vaincre	je vaincs, s, c; nous vainquons, ez, ent	que je vainque, es, e; que nous vainquions, iez, ent	que je vainquisse, es, ît; que nous vainquissions
valoir	je vaux, x, t; nous valons, ez, ent	que je vaille, es, e; que nous valions, iez, qu'ils vaillent	que je valusse, es, ût; que nous valussions
venir	se conjugue comme tenir		
vêtir	je vêts, s, t; nous vêtons, ez, ent	que je vête, es, e; que nous vêtions	que je vêtisse, es, ît; que nous vêtissions, iez, ent
vivre	je vis, s, t; nous vivons, ez, ent	que je vive, es, e; que nous vivions	que je vécusse, es, ût; que nous vécussions, iez, ent
voir	je vois, s, t; nous voyons, ez, ils voient	que je voie, es, e; que nous voyions	que je visse, es, qu'il vît; que nous vissions, iez, ent
vouloir	je veux, tu veux, il veut; nous voulons, ez, ils veulent	que je veuille, es, e; que nous voulions	que je voulusse, es, qu'il voulût; que nous voulussions

*) saillir: dans le sens de jaillir est régulier.

Imparfait	Parfait défini	Futur	Impératif	Participe présent	Participe passé
je résolvais, nous résolvions	je résolus, s, t; nous résolûmes, ûtes, urent	je résoudrai	résous, résolvons, résolvez	résolvant	résolu
je riais, nous riions	je ris, s, t; nous rîmes	je rirai	ris, rions, rîez	riant	ri
il saillait, ils saillaient	—	il saillera	—	saillant	sailli
je savais, nous savions	je sus, nous sûmes	je saurai	sache, ons, ez	sachant	su
• —	—	—	—	séant	sis
il seyait, ils seyaient	—	il siéra, ils siéront	qu'il siée, qu'ils siéent	seyant	—
je servais, nous servions	je servis, nous servîmes	je servirai	sers, servons, ez	servant	servi
je sortais, nous sortions	je sortis, nous sortîmes	je sortirai	sors, sortons, sortez	sortant	sorti
je suffisais	je suffis, nous suffîmes	je suffirai	suffis, suffisons, ez	suffisant	suffi
je suivais, nous suivions	je suivis, nous suivîmes	je suivrai	suis, suivons, suivez	suivant	suivi
je sursoyais, nous sursoyions	je sursis, nous sursîmes	je surseoierai, nous surseoierons	—	sursoyant	sursis
je taisais, nous taisions	je tus, nous tûmes	je tairai	tais, taisons, taisez	taisant	tu
je tenais, nous tenions	je tins, s, t; nous tînmes, vous tîntes, ils tinrent	je tiendrai	tiens, tenons, ez	tenant	tenu
—	—	—	—	—	tissu
je trayais, nous trayions	—	je trairai	trais, trayons, ez	trayant	trait
je vainquais, nous vainquions	je vainquis, nous vainquîmes	je vaincrai	vaincs, vainquons, ez	vainquant	vaincu
je valais	je valus, s, ut; nous valûmes	je vaudrai	valons, valez, qu'ils vaillent	valant	valu
je vêtais, nous vêtions	je vêtis, nous vêtîmes	je vêtirai	vêts, vêtons, vêtez	vêtant	vêtu
je vivais, nous vivions	je vécus, nous vécûmes	je vivrai	vis, vivons, ez	vivant	vécu
je voyais	je vis, s, il vit; nous vîmes	je verrai	vois, voyons, ez	voyant	vu
je voulais, nous voulions	je voulus, tu voulus, il voulut, nous voulûmes	je voudrai	veux, veuille, voulons, voulez et veuillez	voulant	voulu

A LIST OF POPULAR WORDS

ENGLISH–FRENCH

aileron, s. aileron, m.
air brake, s. frein à air, m.
airdrome, s. aérodrome, m.
air furnace, s. four à air chaud, m.
airman, s. aviateur, m.
airplane, s. aéroplane, avion, m.
airwoman, s. aviatrice, f.
altimeter, s. altimètre, m. [mètre, m.
ammeter, s. galvanomètre, ampère-
amplifier, s. amplificateur, m.
antenna, s. antenne, f.

biplane, s. biplan, m.
birth control, s. malthusianisme, m.
blimp, s. ballon d'observation, m.,
"saucisse", f. [biles), f.
breakdown, s. panne (of automo-
broadcast, v. a. diffuser; s. diffusion, f. [biles), m.
bumper, s. pare-choc (of automo-
bus, s. autobus, m.

cafeteria, s. "cafétéria", f., restaurant, m.
cam shaft, s. arbre (m.) de distribution, f., arbre à cames, f.
carburetor, s. carburateur, m.
chassis, s. châssis, m.
clutch, s. embrayage (of motors), m.
condenser, s. condensateur, m.
connecting rod, s. bielle, f.
crank shaft, s. arbre principal, m.

detecting tube, s. ampoule (f.) de
détection, f. [(s), m.
dope, s. drogue, f., renseignement
dynamic speaker, s. haut-parleur
électrodynamique, m.

exhaust pipe, s. tuyau d'échappement, m.

fan, s. ventilateur, m.
film, s. film, m.
flight, s. vol (of planes), m.

gasoline, s. essence, f.
gear, s. engrenage (of motors), m.
generator, s. générateur, m.
glider, s. planeur, m.
ground wire, s. prise de terre, f.

hangar, s. hangar, m.

headlight, s. phare, m.
hook-up, s. montage, m. [trompe, f.
horn, s. avertisseur, klaxon, m.,
hydroplane, s. hydroaéroplane, hydravion, m.

ignition, s. ignition, f., allumage (of
automobiles), m.

landing, s. atterrissage (of planes), m.
landing gear, s. chariot (m.) d'atterrissage, m.
loudspeaker, s. haut-parleur, m.

magneto, s. magnéto, f.
mechanic, s. mécanicien, m.
merger, s. association, f.
monkey wrench, s. clé anglaise, f.
monoplane, s. monoplan, m.
moratorium, s. moratoire, m.

parachute, s. parachute, m.
power tube, s. ampoule amplificatrice
(or génératrice), f.
puncture, s. crevaison (of tires), f.

radiator, s. radiateur, m.
radio, s. radiotélégraphie, radiotéléphonie, "radio", f.
radio set, s. poste (m.) de radio, f.
radio tube, s. ampoule de radio, f.
receiver, s. récepteur (telephone), m.
rheostat, s. rhéostat, m.
runners, s. glissoirs (of planes), m.

seaplane, s. hydroaéroplane, hydravion, m.
shock absorber, s. amortisseur, m.
skid, v. a. déraper (of automobiles)
sparkplug, s. bougie, f.
steering wheel, s. volant, m.
stop light, s. feu (signal), m.
street-car, s. tramway, m.

talkie, s. film parlant, m.
tank, s. réservoir (for gasoline), m.
tank (war), s. tank, char de combat, m.
television, s. télévision, f. [m.
tire, s. pneu (of automobiles), m.
tractor, s. tracteur, m. [change, m.
trade acceptance, s. lettre (f.) de
traffic signal, s. signaux (lumineux),
triplane, s. triplan, m. [m. pl.

ENGLISH AND FRENCH.

A.

a, ā, préfixe pour at, in, on, etc.

a, ā, an, ăn, art. un, une.

A1, (mar.) de première classe ‖ (fig.) de première qualité.

A. B. = able-bodied.

aback, ă băk′, ad. par derrière, par surprise ‖ (mar.) sur le mât ‖ to be taken (all) ~, être pris au dépourvu, être dérouté.

abacus, ăb′ă kŭs, s. abacus, abaque, m.

abaft, ă băft′, s. (mar.) poupe, f.

abaft, ă băft′, ad. vers la poupe, en arrière.

abandon, ă băn′ dŭn, v. a. abandonner, se désister de ‖ laisser à l'abandon ‖ to ~ oneself to, s'abandonner, se livrer à.

abandoned, ă băn′ dŭnd, a. abandonné ‖ misérable, infâme.

abandoning, ă băn′ dŭn ing, abandonment, ă băn′ dŭn mĕnt, s. abandon, m. ‖ (fig.) laisser-aller, m. ‖ (com. & mar.) délaissement, m.

abase, ă bās′, v. a. baisser, abaisser ‖ rabaisser.

abasement, ă bās′ mĕnt, s. abaissement, m., humiliation, f.

abash, ă băsh′, v.a. déconcerter, confondre.

abashment, ă băsh′ mĕnt, s. confusion, consternation, f. ‖ honte, f.

abate, ă bāt′, v. a. s'abattre, rabaisser ‖ diminuer, calmer ‖ annuler ‖ v. n. s'abattre, diminuer ‖ s'arrêter ‖ s'anéantir, s'affaiblir.

abatement, ă bāt′ mĕnt, s. diminution, f., affaiblissement, retranchement, m. ‖ (com.) rabais, m., remise, f. ‖ no ~, prix fixe.

abattis, ăb′ ă tis ou ăb′ ă tē, s. (mil.) abatis.

abb, ăb, s. trame de laine, chaîne, f. [m.

abbacy, ăb′ bă si, s. dignité d'abbé, f. ‖ administration d'une abbaye, f. ‖ abbatiale, f. [ăl, a. abbatial.

abbatial, ăb bā′ shăl, abbatical, ăb bā′ tik-

abbess, ăb′ bĕs, s. abbesse, f.

abbey, ăb′ bi, s. abbaye, f., couvent, m.

abbot, ăb′ bŭt, s. abbé, m.

abbotship, ăb′ bŭt ship, s. dignité d'abbé, f.

abbreviate, ăb brē′ vi āt, v. a. abréger, raccourcir. [viation, f.

abbreviation, ăb brē vi ā′ shŭn, s. abréviature, ăb brē′ vi ā tŭr, s. abréviation, f., abrégé, m.

ABC, ā bē sē, s. abc, m. ‖ abécédaire, m.

abdicate, ăb′ di kāt, v. a. abdiquer, renoncer ‖ déposséder. [renonciation, f.

abdication, ăb di kā′ shŭn, s. abdication, f.

abdomen, ăb dō′ mĕn, s. abdomen, ventre, m. ‖ lower part of the ~, bas-ventre, hypogastre, m.

abdominal, ăb dŏm′ i năl, a. abdominal.

abduct, ăb dŭkt′, v. a. enlever.

abduction, ăb dŭk′ shŭn, s. abduction, f. ‖ enlèvement, m. [seigne l'alphabet.

abecedarian, ā bē sē dā′ ri ăn, s. qui enseigne l'alphabet.

abecedary, ā bē sē′ dā ri, a. abécédaire.

abed, ă bĕd′, ad. au lit, couché ‖ en couches.

abernethy, ā bĕr nē′ thi, s. biscuit sec, m.

aberration, ăb ĕr′ răns, aberration, ăb ĕr rā′ shŭn, s. égarement, m., aberration, erreur, f. [tenir.

abet, ă bĕt′, v. a. exciter, encourager ‖ soutenir.

abetment, ă bĕt′ mĕnt, s. instigation, f., appui, m. [fauteur, m.

abetter, abettor, ă bĕt′ tĕr, s. instigateur, fauteur, m.

abeyance, ă bā′ ăns, s. (jur.) vacance, attente, f. ‖ in ~, en suspens ‖ (jacent) ‖ to fall into ~, tomber en désuétude, périmer.

abhor, ăb hŏr′, v. a. abhorrer, avoir en horreur.

abhorrence, ăb hŏr′ rĕns, s. horreur, f.

abhorrent, ăb hŏr′ rĕnt, a. saisi d'horreur, détestant ‖ contraire à ‖ incompatible avec ‖ to be ~ to, répugner à.

abide, ă bīd′, v. a. ir. attendre ‖ souffrir ‖ (by) soutenir ‖ s'en tenir à ‖ résister ‖ ~, v. n. demeurer, habiter ‖ continuer ‖ subir.

abiding, ă bī′ ding, s. stabilité, permanence, f. [stant, inébranlable.

abiding, ă bī′ ding, a. qui subsiste ‖ constant, inébranlable.

abigail, ā′ bi găl, s. douucerette, soubrette, f. ‖ péronnelle, f.

ability, ă bil′ i ti, s. habileté, capacité, f. ‖ abilities, pl. talents, moyens, m. pl. ‖ portée, f. ‖ to the best of one's ~, de son mieux.

abintestate, ăb in tĕs′ tāt, a. ab-intestat.

abject, ăb′ jĕkt, a. abject, vil ‖ -ly, ad. bassement. [sesse, f.

abjection, ăb jĕk′ shŭn, s. abjection, bassesse, f.

abjectness, ăb′ jĕkt nĕs, s. abjection, bassesse, lâcheté, f.

abjuration, ăb′ jōō rā′ shŭn, s. abjuration, f.

---

lāte, hăt, făr, lăw; — hēre, gĕt, hĕr; — mīne, ĭnn; — nō, hŏt, prōve; — hōw; — bŏy; — fŏŏt, tūbe, tŭb. ‖ chair, joy; — game, yes; — soul, zeal; — thing, there.

English and French.

abjure, *ăb jōr′,* v. a. abjurer, renoncer avec serment.

ablative, *ăb′ lă tĭv,* s. ablatif, m.

ablaze, *ă blāz′,* a. en flamme.

able, *ā′ bl,* a. capable, en état, habile, vigoureux || **to be ~ to,** pouvoir || **as far as one is ~,** selon ses moyens || **~-bodied,** a. robuste, vigoureux.

abluent, *ăb′ lŭ ĕnt,* a. détersif, qui nettoie.

ablution, *ăb lū′ shŭn,* s. ablution, f. || lotion, f. || **to perform one's ~s,** faire les ablutions.

ably, *ā′ blĭ,* ad. habilement. [rejeter.

abnegate, *ăb′ nē gāt,* v. a. nier, désavouer.

abnegation, *ăb nē gā′ shŭn,* s. abnégation, résignation, f., refus, m.

abnormal, *ăb nŏr′ măl,* a. (-ly, ad.) irrégulier, anormal, difforme || irrégulièrement, énormément. [difformité, f.

abnormity, *ăb nŏr′ mĭ tĭ,* s. irrégularité, f.

aboard, *ă bōrd′,* ad. à bord || **to go ~,** s'embarquer || **to take ~,** embarquer || (mar.) **to fall ~ of,** aborder.

abode, *ă bōd′,* s. demeure, f., séjour, m. || **to take up one's ~,** établir son séjour.

abolish, *ă bŏl′ ĭsh,* v. a. abolir, anéantir, annuler.

abolishment, *ă bŏl′ ĭsh mĕnt,* s. abolition, f. || anéantissement, m. [abolitioniste, m.

abolition, *ăb ō lĭsh′ ŭn,* s. abolition, f.,

abolitionist, *ăb ō lĭsh′ ŭn ĭst,* s. novateur, détestable. [horreur, exécration, f.

abominable, *ă bŏm′ ĭn ă bl,* a. abominable,

abominableness, *ă bŏm′ ĭn ă bl nĕs,* s.

abominate, *ă bŏm′ ĭn āt,* v. a. abhorrer, détester, avoir en horreur.

abomination, *ă bŏm ĭ nā′ shŭn,* s. détestation, f. || **to hold in ~,** avoir en horreur.

aboriginal, *ăb ō rĭj′ ĭ năl,* a. originaire, primitif. [m. pl.

aborigines, *ăb ō rĭj′ ĭ nēz,* s. pl. aborigènes.

abort, *ă bŏrt′,* v. n. faire une fausse couche.

abortion, *ă bŏr′ shŭn,* s. avortement, m., fausse couche, f.

abortive, *ă bŏr′ tĭv,* a. abortif || (fig.) avorté || échoué || **-ly,** ad. avant terme || (fig.) prématurément.

abound, *ă bŏwnd′,* v. n. abonder en *or* de.

abounding, *ă bŏwnd′ ĭng,* s. abondance, f., débordement, f.

about, *ă bŏwt′,* pr. & ad. autour de, environ, vers || à l'égard de || pour || sur || dans || par || après || à || ci et là || de tous côtés || **all ~,** partout || **~ one,** sur soi || **left ~!** demi-tour à gauche! || **round ~,** tout autour de || **to come ~,** être fini || **se changer, arriver || what are you ~?** que faites-vous ? || **to be ~ to,** être sur le point de, aller.

above, *ă bŭv′,* pr. & ad. au-dessus de, par-dessus, sur || plus que, plus de || en haut || trop fier pour || **~ all,** surtout || **over and ~,** en outre || **~ mentioned,** susdit || **to be ~,** être au-dessus de, surpasser.

abrade, *ă brād′,* v. a. effacer, user en frottant. [f. || frottement, m., écorchure, f.

abrasion, *ăb rā′ zhŭn,* s. rature, abrasion,

abreast, *ă brĕst′,* ad. de front, à côté l'un de l'autre || vis-à-vis de.

abridge, *ă brĭj′,* v. a. abréger, retrancher || restreindre || priver || gêner.

abridgment, *ă brĭj′ mĕnt,* s. abrégé, m., réduction, f. [percer.

abroach, *ă brōsh′,* v. a. mettre en perce,

abroach, *ă brōsh′,* ad. en perce, percé.

abroad, *ă brawd′,* ad. dehors, au dehors, à l'étranger || **to be (all) ~,** (fig.) courir, se répandre || **to walk ~,** se promener || **to set ~,** publier, propager.

abrogate, *ăb′ rō gāt,* v. a. abroger, annuler.

abrogation, *ăb rō gā′ shŭn,* s. abrogation, cassation, f.

abrupt, *ăb rŭpt′,* a. abrupte, précipité || brusque || rocailleux || saccadé || brisé || escarpé || **~,** ad. soudain || **-ly,** ad. brusquement. [rudesse, f. || aspérité, f.

abruptness, *ăb rŭpt′ nĕs,* s. brusquerie,

abscess, *ăb′ sĕs,* a. abcès, m.

abscind, *ăb sĭnd′,* v. a. retrancher, couper en deux, diviser. [m.

abscission, *ăb sĭsh′ ŭn,* s. retranchement,

abscond, *ăb skŏnd′,* v. a. & n. (se) cacher.

absconder, *ăb skŏnd′ ẽr,* s. fugitif, m.

absence, *ăb′ sĕns,* s. absence, f. || distraction f. || **~ of mind,** absence d'esprit, distraction, f.

absent, *ăb′ sĕnt′,* v. a. éloigner || **to ~ oneself from,** s'absenter de. [~, être distrait.

absent, *ăb′ sĕnt,* a. absent, éloigné || **to be**

absentee, *ăb sĕn tē′,* s. absent (de son pays *or* de son poste), m.

absenter, *ăb sĕnt′ ẽr,* s. absent, m.

absentment, *ăb sĕnt′ mĕnt,* s. absence, f.

absinth, *ăb′ sĭnth′,* s. absinthe, f.

absolute, *ăb′ sō lŏt,* a. absolu, illimité, arbitraire || **-ly,** ad. absolument, totalement.

absoluteness, *ăb′ sō lŏt nĕs,* s. pouvoir absolu, despotisme, m.

absolution, *ăb sō lō′ shŭn,* s. absolution, f.

absolutism, *ăb′ sō lō tĭzm,* s. absolutisme, m.

absolutist, *ăb′ sō lō tĭst,* s. absolutiste, m.

absolutory, *ăb′ sōl ŭ tẽr ĭ,* a. absolutoire.

absolve, *ăb zŏlv′,* v. a. absoudre, délier, dégager || finir. [tir || préoccuper.

absorb, *ăb sŏrb′,* v. a. absorber || engloutir.

absorbent, *ăb sŏr′ bĕnt,* s. absorbant, m.

absorbent, *ăb sŏr′ bĕnt,* a. absorbant.

absorption, *ăb sŏrp′ shŭn,* s. absorption, f.

abstain, *ăb stān′,* v. n. s'abstenir, se priver de.

abstaining, *ăb stān′ ĭng,* s. abstinence, f.

abstemious, *ăb stē′ mĭ ŭs,* a. (-ly, ad.) abstinent, sobre(ment).

abstemiousness, *ăb stē′ mĭ ŭs nĕs,* s. abstinence, sobriété, tempérance, f.

abstention, *ăb stĕn′ shŭn,* s. abstinence, privation, f. [abstergent, m.

abstergent, *ăb stẽr′ jĕnt,* s. & a. (méd.)

abstinence, *ăb′ stĭ nĕns,* s. abstinence, privation volontaire, f. || **day of ~,** jour maigre, m.

abstinent, *ăb′ stĭ nĕnt,* a. (-ly, ad.) abstinent || sobre(ment).

abstract, *ăb′străkt,* s. résumé, sommaire, m. || (fig.) relevé, m. || in the ~, par abstraction. [parer, abréger.

abstract, *ăb străkt′,* v. a. abstraire, séparé || —ly, ad. abstractivement || absolument.

abstract, *ăb′străkt,* a. abstrait.

abstracted, *ăb străk′tĕd,* a. abstrait || separé || —ly, ad. abstractivement || absolument.

abstraction, *ăb străk′shŭn,* s. abstraction, f. || distraction, f. || distillation, f.

abstractive, *ăb străk′tĭv,* a. abstractif.

abstractively, *ăb străk′tĭv lĭ,* **abstractly,** *ăb străkt′lĭ,* ad. abstraitement.

abstractness, *ăb străkt′nĕs,* s. abstraction, subtilité, f.

abstruse, *ăb strōs′,* ad. caché, abstrus || —ly, ad. abstractivement, obscurément.

abstruseness, *ăb strōs′nĕs,* s. obscurité, difficulté, f.

absurd, *ăb sĕrd′,* a. absurde || insensé || —ly, ad. irraisonnablement.

absurdity, *ăb sĕr′dĭtĭ,* s. absurdité, f.

abundance, *ă bŭn′dăns,* s. abondance, quantité, f. [ad. abondamment.

abundant, *ă bŭn′dănt,* a. abondant || —ly,

abuse, *ă būs′,* s. abus, outrage, m. || erreur, f. || séduction, f.

abuse, *ă būz′,* v. a. abuser, faire un mauvais usage de || dire des injures, outrager || tromper || séduire. [d′injures, m.

abuser, *ă bū′zĕr,* s. séducteur, m. || diseur

abusive, *ă bū′sĭv,* a. abusif, injurieux, || —ly, ad. abusivement, injurieusement.

abusiveness, *ă bū′sĭv nĕs,* s. outrage, m., insolence, f. [brancher.

abut, *ă bŭt′,* v. n. aboutir, confiner || s′embutment, *ă bŭt′mĕnt,* s. arc-boutant, m. || (of bridges) culée, f. [tissant, m.

abuttal, *ă bŭt′ăl,* s. borne, limite, f., aboutissant, m.

abutting, *a bŭt′tĭng,* s. embranchement, m.

abutting, *ă bŭt′tĭng,* a. saillant. [m.

abysmal, *ă bĭz′măl,* a. sans fond.

abyss, *ă bĭs′,* s. abime, gouffre, m. || enfer,

acacia, *ă kā′shĭ ă,* s. acacia, m. [m.

academian, *ăk ă dē′mĭ ăn,* s. académicien, m.

academic, *ăk ă dĕm′ĭk,* s. académicien, m.

academic(al), *ăk ă dĕm′ĭk(ăl),* a. (—ly, ad. académique(ment).

academy, *ă kăd′ē mĭ,* s. académie, école, f. || pension, f.

acanthus, *ă kăn′thŭs,* s. acanthe, f.

accede, *ăk sēd′,* v. n. accéder, accepter, consentir. [hâter.

accelerate, *ăk sĕl′ĕr āt,* v. a. accélérer,

acceleration, *ăk sĕl ĕr ā′shŭn,* s. accélération, f. [teur.

accelerative, *ăk sĕl′ĕr ā tĭv,* a. accélérateur,

accelerator, *ăk sĕl′ĕr ā tēr′ ʒ,* a. accélérant.

accent, *ăk sĕnt′,* v. a. accentuer, écrire les accents || articuler. [f.

accent, *ăk′sĕnt,* s. accent, ton, m. || parole,

accentuate, *ăk sĕn′tū āt,* v. a. accentuer.

accentuation, *ăk sĕn tū ā′shŭn,* s. accentuation, f.

accept, *ăk sĕpt′,* v. a. accepter, recevoir, agréer || comprendre, entendre.

acceptability, *ăk sĕp tă bĭl′ĭ tĭ,* s. qualité de ce qui est acceptable, admissibilité, f.

acceptable, *ăk sĕp′tăbl,* a. acceptable, agréable. [ment.

acceptably, *ăk sĕp′tă blĭ,* ad. agréable-

acceptance, *ăk sĕp′tăns,* s. acceptation, approbation, f. || to find ~, trouver bon accueil || absolute ~, acceptation complète || qualified ~, acceptation conditionnelle.

acceptation, *ăk sĕp tā′shŭn,* s. acceptation, f. || accueil, m., réception, f. || acception d′un mot, f. [teur, m.

accepter, acceptor, *ăk sĕp′tēr,* s. accepteur,

acception, *ăk sĕp′shŭn,* s. acception, f.

access, *ăk sĕs,* s. accès, m. || abord, m. || entrée, f. || to have ~ to one, avoir accès auprès de qn. || easy of ~, d′un accès facile, abordable. [ment.

accessarily, *ăk sĕs sĕr′ĭ lĭ,* ad. accessoire-

accessariness, *ăk′sĕs sĕr ĭ nĕs,* s. complicité, participation, f.

accessary, *ăk′sĕs sĕr ĭ,* s. complice, m.

accessary, *ăk′sĕs sĕr ĭ,* a. participant, complice. [dable.

accessible, *ăk sĕs′si bl,* a. accessible, abor-

accession, *ăk sĕsh′ŭn,* s. accession, f. || augmentation, f., surcroît, m. || avènement au trône, m.

accessional, *ăk sĕsh′ŭn ăl,* a. additionnel.

accessorily, *ăk′sĕs sĕr ĭ lĭ,* ad. accessoirement, comme complice.

accessory, *ăk′sĕs sĕr ĭ,* s. complice, m. || accessoire, m. [ditionnel.

accessory, *ăk′sĕs sĕr ĭ,* a. accessoire, ad-

accident, *ăk′sĭ dĕnt,* s. accident, cas fortuit, malheur, m. || by ~, par hasard || —s, pl. sinistres, m. pl.

accidental, *ăk sĭ dĕn′tăl,* s. accident, m.

accidental, *ăk sĭ dĕn′tăl,* a. (—ly, ad.) accidentel(lement) || fortuit || par hasard.

accipient, *ăk sĭp′ĭ ĕnt,* s. receveur, m.

acclaim, *ăk klām′,* v. a. acclamer || approuver.

acclamation, *ăk klă mā′shŭn,* s. acclamation, f., applaudissement, m.

acclamatory, *ăk klăm′ ă tēr ĭ,* a. d′acclamation. [acclimatation, f.

acclimatisation, *ăk klī mā tĭ zā′shŭn,* s.

acclimatise, *ăk klī′mā tĭz,* v.a. acclimater.

acclivity, *ăk klĭv′ĭ tĭ,* s. montée, f., penchant d′une colline, m.

acclivous, *ăk klĭv′ vŭs,* a. montant, en pente.

accommodable, *ăk kŏm′mō dă bl,* a. accommodable, conforme à.

accommodate, *ăk kŏm′mō dāt,* v. a. accommoder, ajuster, régler || pourvoir, fournir || ~, v. n. être conforme à, s′accorder, s′ajuster. [nable, propre.

accommodate, *ăk kŏm′mō dāt,* a. conve-

accommodating, *ăk kŏm′mō dā tĭng,* a. accommodant, commode.

accommodation, *ăk kŏm mō dā′shŭn,* s. adaptation, f. || accommodation, f. || ajustement, arrangement, m., convenance, commodité, f. || logement, m. || (com.) facilités, f. pl. || ~-bill, s. billet de complaisance,

m. ‖ **~-ladder,** s. (mar.) échelle de commandement, f. ‖ **-s,** pl. emménagements, m. pl.   [accompagnement, m.

accompaniment, *ăk kŭm′pă ni mĕnt,* s.

accompanist, *ăk kŭm′pă nist,* s. accompagnateur, m.

accompany, *ăk kŭm′pă ni,* v. a. accompagner ‖ ~, v. n. s'associer.

accomplice, *ăk kŏm′plis,* s. complice, m.

accomplish, *ăk kŏm′plish,* v. a. accomplir, exécuter, achever ‖ **to ~ a purpose,** remplir un but.   [pli, parfait, distingué.

accomplished, *ăk kŏm′plisht,* a. accom-

accomplishment, *ăk kŏm′plish mĕnt,* s. accomplissement, m. ‖ perfection, f. talent, m. ‖ **-s,** pl. connaissances, f. pl.

accord, *ăk kawrd′,* s. accord, m., union, f. ‖ convention, f. ‖ consentement, s. **of one's own ~,** de son propre gré, de plein gré ‖ **with one ~,** d'un commun accord.   [convenir.

accord, *ăk kawrd′,* v. a. (& n.) (s')accorder.

accordance, *ăk kŏrd′ăns,* s. conformité, f. ‖ bonne intelligence, f. ‖ **in ~ with,** conformément à.

accordant, *ăk kŏrd′ănt,* a. d'accord.

according, *ăk kŏrd′ing,* pr. (to) selon, suivant ‖ **~ as,** selon que ‖ **-ly,** ad. conformément.

accordion, *ăk kŏr′dĭ′ŏn,* s. accordéon, m.

accost, *ăk kŏst′,* v. a. aborder.

account, *ăk kŏwnt′,* s. compte, calcul, m. ‖ valeur, considération, f. ‖ importance, f. ‖ distinction, f. ‖ note, f. ‖ cas, m. ‖ récit, m. ‖ cause, raison, f. ‖ **on ~ a terme** ‖ **d'à-compte** ‖ **on ~ of, à cause de** ‖ **en considération de** ‖ **pour compte de** ‖ **pour cause de** ‖ **à valoir sur** ‖ **on** ou **on all -s,** en tout point ‖ **sous tous les rapports** ‖ **according to ~,** selon lui ‖ **on no ~,** en aucune manière, sous aucun prétexte ‖ **on that ~,** pour cette raison ‖ **à ce sujet** ‖ **to take ~ of,** prendre note de ‖ **to take into ~,** tenir compte de ‖ **to make no ~ of,** ne faire aucun cas de ‖ **to turn to ~,** mettre à profit ‖ **current** ou **running ~,** compte courant ‖ **to give a good ~ of,** rendre bon compte de ‖ **to have an open ~ with one,** être en compte avec qn. ‖ **to keep -s,** tenir des livres ‖ **~-book,** s. livre de comptes, m. ‖ **~-sales,** s. (com.) compte de vente, m.

account, *ăk kŏwnt′,* v. a. compter, calculer ‖ estimer, considérer ‖ ~, v. n. supputer ‖ rendre compte de, rendre raison de, être responsable.

accountability, *ăk kŏwnt ă bĭl′ĭ tĭ,* s. responsabilité, f.

accountable, *ăk kŏwnt′ăbl,* a. responsable ‖ **to be ~ to one,** devoir compte à.

accountant, *ăk kŏwnt′ănt,* s. calculateur, teneur de livres, m. ‖ **public ~,** expert comptable, m.

accoutre, *ăk kŏ′tĕr,* v. a. équiper.

accoutrement, *ăk kŏ′tĕr mĕnt,* s. équipement, m. ‖ oruement, m.   [diter.

accredit, *ăk krĕd′ĭt,* v. a. croire ‖ accré-

accreditation, *ăk krĕd′ĭ tă′shŭn,* s. lettres de créance, f. pl.   [sement, m.

accretion, *ăk krē shŭn,* s. (phys.) accrois-

accrue, *ăk krŏ′* v. n. accroître ‖ résulter.

accumulate, *ăk kū′mŭ lăt,* v. a. (& n.) (s')accumuler ‖ amasser.

accumulation, *ăk kū mŭ lă′shŭn,* s. accumulation, f., entassement, amas, m.

accumulative, *ăk kŭ′mŭ lă tĭv,* a. qui s'accumule ‖ **-ly,** ad. cumulativement.

accuracy, *ăk′kū ră sĭ,* s. exactitude, justesse, f., soin, m.

accurate, *ăk′kū răt,* a. exact, juste, soigneux ‖ **-ly,** ad. exactement.

accurse, *ăk kĕrs′,* v. a. maudire, anathématiser.   [a. maudit, exécrable.

accursed, *ăk kĕr′sĕd,* **accurst,** *ăk kĕrst′,*

accusable, *ăk kū′săbl,* a. accusable ‖ coupable.   [inculpation, f.

accusation, *ăk kū ză′shŭn,* s. accusation,

accusative, *ăk kū′ză tĭv,* s. accusatif, m.

accusatory, *ăk kū′ză tĕr′ĭ,* a. accusatoire.

accuse, *ăk kūz′,* v. a. accuser, censurer.

accuser, *ăk kū′zĕr,* s. accusateur, m., accusatrice, f.   [habituer.

accustom, *ăk kŭs′tŭm,* v. a. accoutumer,

accustomed, *ăk kŭs′tŭmd,* a. accoutumé, habitué.

ace, *ās,* s. as, m., obole, f. ‖ (fig.) point rien, m. ‖ **to be within an ~ of,** être à deux pas de.   [acéphale.

acephalous, *ă sĕf′ă lŭs,* a. (anat. et bot.)

acerbity, *ă sĕr′bĭ tĭ,* s. acerbité, aigreur ‖ sévérité, f.

acetate, *ăs′ĕ tăt,* s. (chem.) acétate, m.

acetic, *ă sĕt′ĭk,* a. acétique.

acetous, *ă sĕ′tŭs,* a. (chem.) acéteux.

ache, *āk,* s. mal, m., douleur, f.

ache, *āk,* v. n. faire mal, souffrir ‖ **my head** (etc.) **-s,** j'ai mal à la tête (etc.).

achievable, *ă chĕv′ă bl,* a. exécutable.

achieve, *ă chēv′,* v. a. achever, exécuter ‖ acquérir ‖ **to ~ a victory,** remporter une victoire.

achievement, *ă chēv′mĕnt,* f. production, f. ‖ exploit, haut-fait, fait d'armes, m.

aching, *ā′king,* s. peine, souffrance, f.

achor, *ā′kŏr,* s. croûte laiteuse, f.

achromatic, *ăk rō măt′ĭk,* a. (opt.) achromatique.

acid, *ăs′ĭd,* s. acide, m.

acid, *ăs′ĭd,* a. acide, piquant.

acidity, *ă sĭd′ĭ tĭ,* s. acidité, f.

acidulate, *ă sĭd′ū lăt,* v. a. aciduler ‖ **-d drops,** pastilles acidulées, f. pl.

acidulous, *ă sĭd′ū lŭs,* a. acidule, aigrelet.

acknowledge, *ăk nŏl′ĕj,* v. a. reconnaître ‖ avouer ‖ être reconnaissant.

acknowledgment, *ăk nŏl′ĕj mĕnt,* s. reconnaissance, f., aveu, m. ‖ concession, f. ‖ gratitude, f. ‖ **my warmest -s,** mes plus vifs remerciments.

acme, *ăk′mĕ,* s. sommet, m. ‖ apogée, f., comble, m. ‖ (méd.) crise, f.

acolyte, *ăk′ō lĭt,* s. acolyte, m.

aconite, *ăk′ō nīt,* s. (bot.) aconit, m.

acorn, *ā′kăwrn,* s. gland, m.

acoustic, *ă kŏw′stĭk,* a. acoustique.

acoustics, ăkōū'stiks, s. pl. acoustique, f.

acquaint, ăkwănt', v. a. informer, faire savoir, apprendre || to ~ oneself with, s'instruire de.

acquaintance, ăkwănt'ăns, s. connaissance, liaison, f. || upon further ~, après plus ample connaissance || to claim ~ with one, se réclamer de qn. || to improve on ~, gagner à être connu.

acquiesce, ăkwiĕs', v. n. acquiescer, se soumettre.

acquiescence, ăkwiĕs'sĕns, s. acquiescement, m., soumission, f. [tant || soumis.

acquiescent, ăkwiĕs'sĕnt, a. consen-

acquirable, ăkwīr'abl, a. qu'on peut acquérir.

acquire, ăkwīr', v. a. acquérir, obtenir.

acquirement, ăkwīr'mĕnt, s. acquisition, f., talent, m. [tion, f., acquêt, m.

acquisition, ăkwĭzish'ŭn, s. acquisi-

acquisitive, ăkwĭz'ĭtĭv, a. acquis, obtenu.

acquit, ăkwĭt', v. a. acquitter, absoudre, délier || to ~ oneself, s'acquitter.

acquittal, ăkwĭt'tăl, s. acquittement, m.

acquittance, ăkwĭt'tăns, s. quittance, décharge, f. [m.

acre, ā'kĕr, s. acre, arpent, demi-hectare,

acreage, ā'kĕrăj, s. mesure (f.), nombre (m.) d'acres.

acrid, ăk'rĭd, a. âcre. [foncier

acrid, ā'kĕrd, a. propriétaire

acridity, ăkrĭd'ĭtĭ, s. âcreté, f.

acrimonious, ăkrĭmō'nĭŭs, a. acrimonieux, âcre || -ly, ad. avec rancune.

acrimony, ăk'rĭmŏnĭ, s. acrimonie, âcreté, f.

acrity, ăk'rĭtĭ, s. âcreté, sévérité, f.

acrobat, ăk'rōbăt, s. acrobate, m.

acropolis, ăkrŏp'ōlĭs, s. acropole, f.

across, ăkrŏs', ad. de travers || en croix || ~, pr. à travers, au travers de || to come ~, tomber sur.

acrostic, ăkrŏs'tĭk, s. acrostiche, m.

act, ăkt, s. acte, m., action, f., fait, exploit, m. || jeu, m. || coup, m. || titre, m. || thèse, f. || in the very ~, sur le fait || en flagrant délit || ~ of Parliament, loi, f.

act, ăkt, v. a. & n. agir, opérer, faire || se comporter || jouer, représenter || to ~ up to, agir conformément à || to ~ on one's advice, agir d'après le conseil de qn.

acting, ăkt'ĭng, s. action, f. || jeu, m.

acting, ăkt'ĭng, a. actif || remplissant les fonctions de.

action, ăk'shŭn, s. action, f., fait, m. || bataille, f. || procès, m. || to bring into ~, mettre à effet || to enter ou bring an ~, intenter un procès.

actionable, ăk'shŭnăbl, a. sujet à procès.

active, ăk'tĭv, a. actif, agile, vif || in the ~ voice, à l'actif || -ly, ad. activement, promptement.

activeness, ăk'tĭvnĕs, activity, ăktĭv'ĭtĭ, s. activité, vivacité, f.

actor, ăk'tĕr, s. acteur, comédien, m.

actress, ăk'trĕs, s. actrice, comédienne, f.

actual, ăk'tūăl, a. (-ly, ad.) actuel(lement) || réel(lement) || présentement.

actuality, ăktūăl'ĭtĭ, actualness, ăk'tūălnĕs, s. actualité, réalité, f.

actuary, ăk'tūĕrĭ, s. expert-comptable, secrétaire, m. [animer, pousser.

actuate, ăk'tūăt, v. a. mettre en action ||

acumen, ăkū'mĕn, s. pointe, f. || pénétration d'esprit, finesse, f.

acute, ăkūt', a. aigu, pointu || subtil, sensible || violent || very ~, suraigu || ~ accent, s. accent aigu, m. || -ly, ad. en pointe || subtilement.

acuteness, ăkūt'nĕs, s. pointe, f. || subtilité, perspicacité, f. || violence, f.

adage, ăd'ăj, s. adage, proverbe, m.

adagial, ădā'jĭăl, a. proverbial.

adamant, ăd'ămănt, s. diamant, m.

adamantine, ădămăn'tĭn, a. de or en diamant || adamantin.

adapt, ădăpt', v. a. adapter, ajuster, accommoder, proportionner.

adaptability, ădăptăbĭl'ĭtĭ, s. adaptabilité, f. [adapter, applicable.

adaptable, ădăpt'ăbl, a. qu'on peut

adaptation, ădăptā'shŭn, s. convenance, adapted, ădăpt'tĕd, a. propre (à). [f.

add, ăd, v. a. ajouter, joindre || to ~ up, additionner || -ed to which, en outre.

adder, ăd'dĕr, s. vipère, f. || ~'s-wort, s. (bot.) vipérine, f.

addible, ăd'dĭbl, a. qu'on peut ajouter.

addict ăd dĭkt'; (to ~ oneself to), s'adonner à.

addictedness, ăd dĭct'ĕd nĕs, addiction, ăd dĭk'shŭn, s. dévouement, attachement, m. || goût, m. || adjudication, f.

addition, ăd dĭsh'ŭn, s. addition; f., accroissement, m. || in ~, en outre, en sus || in ~ to, eu sus de || compound ~, (ar.) addition des nombres complexes || by the ~ of, en ajoutant.

additional, ăd dĭsh'ŭn ăl, a. additionnel || an ~ proof, une nouvelle preuve || -ly, ad. de plus, en outre.

addle, ăd'dl, a. couvi, infécond || ~-headed, ~-pated, a. écervelé.

addled, ăd'dld, a. gâté, couvi ||(fig.) troublé.

address, ăd drĕs', s. adresse, f. || allocution, f. || pétition, f. || recherche en mariage, f. || profession de foi, f. || supplique, f. || plaidoyer, m. || dextérité, habileté, f. || tenue, démarche, f. || hommage, m., cour, f. || abord, m. || to pay one's ~es, faire sa cour. [aborder.

address, ăd drĕs', v. a. adresser, parler à,

addressee, ăd drĕs sē', s. destinataire, m. & f.

addresser, ăd drĕs'sĕr, s. pétitionnaire, m.

adduce, ăd dūs', v. a. produire || avancer.

adducible, ăd dū'sĭbl, a. qui peut être

adept, ădĕpt', s. adepte, m. [allégué.

adept, ădĕpt', a. habile, savant.

adequacy, ăd'ĕkwăsĭ, s. égalité, proportion, f.

adequate, ăd'ĕkwăt, a. (-ly, ad.) égal || proportionné(ment) || suffisant.

adhere, *ăd hēr'*, v. n. adhérer, s'attacher.
adherence, *ăd hē'rĕns*, s. adhérence, adhésion, f., attachement, m.
adherent, *ăd hē'rĕnt*, s. partisan, m.
adherent, *ăd hē'rĕnt*, a. adhérent, attaché.
adhesion, *ăd hē'zhŭn*, s. adhésion, f. || adhérence, f.
adhesive, *ăd hē'sĭv*, a. adhérent || collant || agglutinatif, visqueux || ~ plaster, s. sparadrap, m.   [f.
adhesiveness, *ăd hē'sĭv nĕs*, s. viscosité.
adieu, *ă dū'*, ad. & s. adieu (m.) || to bid ~ to one, faire ses adieux à qn.   [fini.
ad infinitum, *ăd ĭn fĭ nī'tŭm*, ad. à l'infini.
ad interim, *ăd ĭn tĕ'rĭm*, ad. par intérim.
adipose, *ăd'ĭ pōs*, a. (anat.) adipeux.
adit, *ăd'ĭt*, s. galerie d'écoulement, f.
adjacent, *ăd jā'sĕnt*, a. adjacent, voisin.
adjective, *ăd'jĕk tĭv*, s. adjectif, m.
adjectively, *ăd'jĕk tĭv lĭ*, ad. adjectivement.
adjoin, *ăd jŏyn'*, v. a. joindre à, ajouter || ~, v. n. être contigu à, avoisiner.
adjoining, *ăd jŏyn'ĭng*, a. adjacent, contigu.
adjourn, *ăd jĕrn'*, v. a. ajourner.   [tigu.
adjournment, *ăd jĕrn'mĕnt*, s. ajournement, délai, m.
adjudge, *ăd jŭj'*, v. a. adjuger, condamner.
adjudgment, *ăd jŭj'mĕnt*, s. jugement, m., décision, f., décret, m.
adjudicate, *ăd jŏ'dĭ kāt*, v. a. adjuger.
adjudication, *ăd jŏ dĭ kā'shŭn*, s. adjudication, f.
adjudicator, *ăd jŏ'dĭ kā tŏr*, s. juge, m.
adjunct, *ăd'jŭnkt*, s. accessoire, m. || adjoint, m.   [f. || invocation, f.
adjuration, *ăd jŏ rā'shŭn*, s. adjuration, f.
adjure, *ăd jŏr'*, v. a. adjurer || imposer un serment.   [régler.
adjust, *ăd jŭst'*, v. a. ajuster, arranger.
adjustment, *ăd jŭst'mĕnt*, s. ajustement, accommodement, m.
adjutancy, *ăd'jŏŏ tăn sĭ*, s. grade d'adjudant, m. || agencement, m.
adjutant, *ăd'jŏŏ tănt*, s. adjudant, aide-major, m. || (fig.) second, m.
admeasurement, *ăd mĕzh'ŏŏr mĕnt*, s. mesurage, m. || règlement, m., division, f. || dimension, f.
administer, *ăd mĭn'ĭs tĕr*, v. a. administrer, gouverner, fournir || to ~ consolation, donner des consolations || ~, v. n. subvenir, contribuer.   [ministrer.
administrate, *ăd mĭn'ĭs trāt*, v. a. administration.
administration, *ăd mĭn ĭs trā'shŭn*, s. administration, f., gouvernement, m. || (jur.) gestion, f.   [ministratif.
administrative, *ăd mĭn'ĭs trā tĭv*, a. administrateur, exécuteur, m. || gérant, m. || desservant, m.   [ministratrice, f.
administrator, *ăd mĭn'ĭs trā tŏr*, s. administratrice, f.
administratrix, *ăd mĭn ĭs trā'trĭks*, s. administrateur, exécuteur, m.
admirable, *ăd'mĭ rǎbl*, a. admirable, merveilleux, excellent.   [f.
admirableness, *ăd'mĭ rǎ bl nĕs*, s. beauté.
admirably, *ăd'mĭ rǎ blĭ*, ad. admirablement.

admiral, *ăd'mĭ rǎl*, s. amiral, m. || **Lord high ~**, grand-amiral, m. || **Rear ~**, contre-amiral, m. || **Port ~**, l'amiral commandant de port, préfet maritime, m.
admiralship, *ăd'mĭ rǎl shĭp*, s. amirauté, f.
admiralty, *ăd'mĭ rǎl tĭ*, s. amirauté, f. || **First Lord of the ~**, Ministre de la Marine, m.
admiration, *ăd mĭ rā'shŭn*, s. admiration, surprise, f. || **note of ~**, point admiratif, m. || **to ~**, à ravir || **struck with ~**, saisi d'admiration.
admire, *ăd mīr'*, v. a. & n. admirer || s'étonner || adorer.   [admiratrice, f.
admirer, *ăd mī'rĕr*, s. admirateur, m.
admiringly, *ăd mī'rĭng lĭ*, ad. avec admiration.   [d'être admissible, f.
admissibility, *ăd mĭs sĭ bĭl'ĭ tĭ*, s. qualité
admissible, *ăd mĭs'sĭ bl*, a. admissible, valable.
admission, *ăd mĭsh'ŭn*, s. admission, réception, concession, f. || entrée, f., accès, m. || ~ **by order**, **free ~**, entrée de faveur, f. || **ticket of ~**, billet d'entrée, m. || **to make an ~**, faire un aveu.
admit, *ăd mĭt'*, v. a. admettre, recevoir || accorder, permettre || **to ~ of**, admettre, permettre.
admittance, *ăd mĭt'tăns*, s. accès, m., entrée, f. || concession, f. || **no ~! on n'entre pas!** || **no ~ except on business**, le public n'entre pas ici || **to beg ~**, prier d'être admis || **to refuse one ~**, refuser la porte à qn.   [mélange, m.
admixture, *ăd mĭks'tŭr*, s. mixtion, f.,
admonish, *ăd mŏn'ĭsh*, v. n. avertir, reprendre, exhorter.   [moniteur, m.
admonisher, *ăd mŏn'ĭsh ĕr*, s. avertisseur,
admonition, *ăd mŏ nĭsh'ŭn*, s. exhortation, f., avertissement, m., réprimande, f.
admonitor, *ăd mŏn'ĭ tĕr*, s. moniteur, m. || conseiller, m.
admonitory, *ăd mŏn'ĭ tĕr ĭ*, a. avertissant.
ado, *ă dŏ'*, s. peine, difficulté, f., vacarme, m. || affaires, façons, f. pl. || **to make no more ~**, n'en faire ni une ni deux || **without more ~**, sans plus de façons || **to have much ~ to**, avoir de la peine à || **much ~ about nothing**, beaucoup de bruit pour rien.
adolescence, *ă dŏ lĕs'ĕns*, s. adolescence, f.
adolescent, *ă dŏ lĕs'ĕnt*, a. & s. adolescent, m.
adoors, *ă dŏrz'*, ad. à la porte, dehors.
adopt, *ă dŏpt'*, v. a. adopter.
adopted, *ă dŏpt'ĕd*, a. (des personnes) adoptif || (des choses) d'adoption || **-ly**, ad. par adoption.   [choix, m.
adoption, *ă dŏp'shŭn*, s. adoption, f. ||
adoptive, *ă dŏpt'ĭv*, a. adoptif || d'adoption.
adorable, *ă dōr'ă bl*, a. adorable.
adorably, *ă dōr'ă blĭ*, ad. adorablement.
adoration, *ă dō rā'shŭn*, s. adoration, f., hommage, m.
adore, *ă dōr'*, v. a. adorer.
adorn, *ă dâwrn'*, v. a. orner, décorer, embellir || (fig.) faire l'ornement de.

adornment, *ă dăwrn' mĕnt* s. ornement, m., parure, f. [rive || à l'abandon.
adrift, *ă drĭft'*, ad. à flot || (mar.) en dé-
adroit, *ă drŏȳt'*, a. (-ly, ad.) adroit(ement) ||
habile. [térité, f.
adroitness, *ă drŏȳt' nĕs,* s. adresse, dex-
adulation, *ă dŭ lā' shŭn,* s. adulation, f.
adulator, *ăd' ŭ lā tĕr,* s. adulateur, m.,
adulatrice, f. [teur.
adulatory, *ăd' ŭ lā tŏr ĭ,* a. adulateur, flat-
adulatress, *ăd' ŭ lā trĕs.* s. adulatrice, f.
adult, *ă dŭlt',* s. adulte, m. & f.
adult, *ă dŭlt',* a. adulte, adolescent.
adulterate, *ă dŭl' tĕr āt,* v. a. commettre
un adultère || falsifier || corrompre. [fié.
adulterate, *ă dŭl' tĕr āt,* a. adultéré || falsi-
adulteration, *ă dŭl tĕr ā' shŭn,* s. adultéra-
tion, f. || falsification, f. [m.
adulterator, *ă dŭl tĕr ā' tĕr,* s. falsificateur,
adulterer, *ă dŭl' tĕr ĕr,* s. adultère, m.
adulteress, *ă dŭl' tĕr ĕs,* s. adultère, f.
adulterous, *ă dŭl' tĕr ŭs,* a. adultère || (fig.)
impur || -ly, ad. par l'adultère.
adultery, *ă dŭl' tĕr ĭ,* s. adultère, m.
advance, *ăd văns',* s. avance, f., avance-
ment, m., approche, f. || progrès, m. ||
in ~, d'avance, par avance || -s, pl. (com.)
avances, f. pl. || to make —s, faire des
avances, les premiers pas || ~-guard, s.
garde avancée, f.
advance, *ăd văns',* v. a. avancer || faire
avancer, pousser || approcher || accélérer ||
proposer || hausser || élever || ~, v. n.
s'avancer || faire des progrès.
advanced, *ăd vănst',* a. avancé.
advancement, *ăd văns' mĕnt,* s. avance-
ment, progrès, perfectionnement, m. || (of
money) avance, f.
advantage, *ăd văn' tăj,* s. avantage, m.,
supériorité, f. || profit, m. || ~-ground,
s. position avantageuse, f. || to take ~
of, profiter de || exploiter || abuser de.
advantage, *ăd văn' tăj,* v. a. avantager,
favoriser || profiter.
advantageous, *ăd văn tā' jŭs,* a. avanta-
geux, profitable, convenable || -ly, ad.
avantageusement.
advantageousness, *ăd văn tā' jŭs nĕs,* s.
avantage, profit, m.
advent, *ăd' vĕnt,* s. venue, f. || Avent, m.
adventitious, *ăd vĕn tĭsh' ŭs,* a. accidentel,
casuel, extrinsèque || -ly, ad. par aventure.
adventure, *ăd vĕn' tŭr,* s. aventure, f.,
accident, hasard, m. || spéculation || (mar.)
pacotille, f. || to seek —s, courir les
aventures. [turer, risquer.
adventure, *ăd vĕn' tŭr,* v. a. (& n.) (s')aven-
adventurer, *ăd vĕn' tŭr ĕr,* s. aventurier,
m. [f.
adventuress, *ăd vĕn' tŭr ĕs,* s. aventurière,
adventurous, *ăd vĕn' tŭr ŭs,* a. aventu-
reux, hasardeux || -ly, ad. avec témérité,
courageusement.
adverb, *ăd' vĕrb,* s. adverbe, m.
adverbial, *ăd vĕr' bĭ ăl,* a. (-ly, ad.) ad-
verbial(ement). [ennemi, m.
adversary, *ăd' vĕr sĕr ĭ,* s. adversaire, m. ||

adverse, *ăd' vĕrs,* a. adverse, contraire ||
-ly, ad. d'une manière contraire.
adversity, *ăd vĕr' sĭ tĭ,* s. adversité, infortune, misère, f.
advert, *ăd vĕrt',* v. n. parler de || faire
attention || faire allusion à || considérer ||
observer.
advertence, *ăd vĕr' tĕns,* s. attention, f.
advertise, *ăd vĕr tīz',* v. a. informer,
avertir || afficher.
advertisement, *ăd vĕr' tĭz mĕnt,* s. aver-
tissement, avis, m. || annonce, f. || ré-
clame, f.
advertiser, *ăd vĕr tī zĕr,* s. qui annonce,
m. || journal, m. || réclame, petite affiche, f.
advertising-agent, *ăd vĕr tī' zĭng ā jĕnt,*
s. agent de publicité, m.
advice, *ăd vīs',* s. (piece of ~) avis, con-
seil, m., information, f. || letter of ~,
lettre d'avis || to take one's ~, suivre le
conseil de qn. || ~-boat, aviso, m.
advisability, *ăd vī ză bĭl' ĭ tĭ,* s. prudence,
f. || convenance, f.
advisable, *ăd vī' ză bl,* a. prudent, judi-
cieux || convenable. [libérer.
advise, *ăd vīz',* v. a. & n. conseiller || dé-
advised, *ăd vīzd',* p. & a. avisé || réfléchi ||
be ~ by me! croyez-m'en! || ill-~,
malavisé || -ly, ad. de propos délibéré.
advisedness, *ăd vī' zĕd nĕs,* s. délibération.
adviser, *ăd vī' zĕr,* s. conseiller, m. [f.
advocacy, *ăd' vō kă sĭ,* s. plaidoirie, f. ||
défense, f.
advocate, *ăd' vō kāt,* s. avocat, défenseur,
m. || Judge ~, rapporteur, m. || Lord ~,
(d'Ecosse) procureur général, m.
advocate, *ăd' vō kāt,* v. a. défendre.
advocation, *ăd vō kā' shŭn,* s. plaidoirie,
f. || intercession, f.
advowee, *ăd vow' ē,* s. patron, collateur
(d'un bénéfice), m. [collation, f.
advowson, *ăd vow' sŭn,* s. patronage, m.,
adze, *ădz,* s. doloire, f. || herminette, f.
aegis, *ē' jĭs,* s. égide, f.
aerated-waters, *ā' ĕr ā tĕd waw' tĕrs,* s.
pl. eaux minérales, f. pl.
aerial, *ā ē' rĭ ăl,* a. aérien, d'air.
aeriform, *ăr' ĭ fawrm,* a. aériforme.
aerolite, *ăr' ō līt,* s. aérolithe, f.
aerometer, *ăr ŏm' ĕ tĕr,* s. aéromètre, m
aeronaut, *ăr' ō năwt,* s. aéronaute, m.
aeronautics, *ăr ō năw' tĭks,* s. pl. aéronautique, f.
aeroplane, *ăr' ō plān,* s. aéroplane, m.
aerostat, *ăr' ō stăt,* s. aérostat, m.
aerostatics, *ăr ō stăt' ĭks,* s. aérostation, f.
aesthetic, *ĕs thĕt' ĭk,* a. esthétique.
aesthetics, *ĕs thĕt' ĭks,* s. esthétique, f.
afar, *ă făr',* ad. (de) loin || ~ off, au loin.
affability, *ăf fă bĭl' ĭ tĭ,* s. affabilité, f.
affable, *ăf' fă bl,* a. affable, gracieux.
affably, *ăf' fă blĭ,* ad. avec affabilité.
affair, *ăf făr',* s. affaire, f. || as —s stand,
au point où en sont les affaires, or choses.
affect, *ăf fĕkt',* v. a. affecter, émouvoir,
toucher || aimer || feindre || aspirer à.
affectation, *ăf fĕk tā' shŭn,* s. affectation, f.

affected, ăf′sĕkt′ĕd, a. affecté, précieux || touché || -ly, ad. avec affectation.

affecting, ăf′sĕkt′ĭng, a. pathétique, attendrissant, touchant || -ly, ad. d'une manière touchante.

affection, ăf′sĕk′shŭn, s. affection, passion, f. || tendresse, f. || to set one's –s on, placer ses affections dans.

affectionate, ăf′sĕk′shŭn ăt, a. affectueux, passionné || -ly, ad. affectueusement.

affiance, ăf′ī′ăns, s. fiançailles, f. pl.

affiance, ăf′ī′ăns, v. a. fiancer || se confier à.   [claration sous serment, f.

affidavit, ăf′fĭ dā′vĭt, s. déposition, dé-

affiliate, ăf′fĭl′ĭ āt, v. a. adopter || (fig.) rattacher (à).

affiliation, ăf fĭl lĭ ā′shŭn, s. adoption, f. || reconnaissance légale d'un enfant naturel, f.

affinity, ăf fĭn′ĭ tĭ, s. (chim.) affinité, f. || alliance, f.   [déclarer.

affirm, ăf fĕrm′, v. a. affirmer, confirmer,

affirmation, ăf fĕr mā′shŭn, s. affirmation, assertion, confirmation, f.

affirmative, ăf fĕrm′ă tĭv, s. affirmative, affirmation, f. || in the –, affirmativement.

affirmative, ăf fĕrm′ă tĭv, a. affirmatif || -ly, ad. affirmativement.

affix, ăf fĭks, s. (gr.) affixe, m.   [tacher.

affix, ăf fĭks′, v. a. joindre, annexer, at-

afflatus, ăf flā′tŭs, s. haleine, f. || (fig.) inspiration, f.

afflict, ăf flĭkt′, v. a. affliger.

affliction, ăf flĭk′shŭn, s. affliction, f. || calamité, f.   [llence, f.

affluence, ăf′floō ĕns, s. affluence, opu-

affluent, ăf floō′ĕnt, s. affluent, m.

affluent, ăf floō′ĕnt, a. abondant, riche.

afford, ăf fōrd′, v. a. produire, fournir avoir de quoi || se permettre.

affray, ăf frā′, s. querelle, échauffourée, f., tumulte, m.

affright, ăf frīt′, s. frayeur, épouvante, f.

affright, ăf frīt′, v. s. épouvanter, effrayer.

affrightedly, ăf frīt′ĕd lĭ, ad. avec effroi ou frayeur.

affront, ăf frŭnt′, s. affront, outrage, m., insulte, f. || to brook an –, digérer un affront || to pocket an –, avaler un affront.

affront, ăf frŭnt′, v. a. affronter || insulter.

afield, ă fēld′, ad. au champ.   [braver.

afire, ă fīr′, a. flamme, à flăm′, ad. en feu.

afloat, ă flōt′, ad. à flot, flottant || to set –, mettre à flot.

afoot, ă foōt′, ad. à pied.

afore, ă fōr′, pr. & ad. devant, avant || auparavant || –mentioned, –said, a. susdit || –thought, a. prémédité || with malice –thought, avec préméditation || –time, ad. autrefois.

afraid, ă frād′, a. effrayé, épouvanté || to be – of, avoir peur de || to make one –, faire peur à qn.

afresh, ă frĕsh′, ad. de nouveau.

aft, ăft, ad. (mar.) en poupe.

after, ăf′tĕr, pr. & ad. après, derrière || selon || ensuite || – all, après tout || what are you –? qu'est ce que vous faites? ||

–, a. futur, ultérieur || (mar.) de l'arrière || –ages, s. pl. postérité, f. || –birth, s. arrière-faix, m. || délivre, m. || –crop, s. seconde récolte, f. || regain, m. || –hours, s. pl. heures en sus, f. pl. || –hours, ad. après l'heure habituelle || –part, s. dernière partie, f. || –reckoning, s. révision de compte, f. || nouveau compte, m.

aftermath, ăf′tĕr măth, s. regain, m.

aftermost, ăf′tĕr mōst, a. le dernier de tous.

afternoon, ăf′tĕr nōn, s. après-midi, m. & f.   [théâtre, f.

afterpiece, ăf′tĕr pēs, s. petite pièce de

aftertaste, ăf′tĕr tāst, s. arrière-goût, m.

afterthought, ăf′tĕr thăwt, s. arrière-pensée, réflexion tardive, f., changement d'avis, m.   [après, puis.

afterwards, ăf′tĕr wawrdz, ad. ensuite,

again, ăg ăn′, ad. encore, de nouveau, de plus, d'un autre côté, de retour || over –, encore une fois || as much –, encore une fois autant || – and –, sans cesse.

against, ă gĕnst′, pr. contre, vers, sur || – the grain, à contre-poil, à contre-cœur || over –, vis-à-vis.   [l'attente.

agape, ă găp′, ad. la bouche béante || dans

agate, ăg′āt, s. agate, f.

agave, ăg′ă vē, s. (bot.) agave, m.

age, āj, s. âge, m., génération, vieillesse, f. || to be under –, être mineur, en tutelle || to be of –, être majeur || over–, trop vieux || in the flower of one's –, à la fleur de l'âge || to be ten years of –, avoir dix ans.

age, āj, s. v. n. vieillir.

aged, ā′jĕd, a. vieux || âgé || (of horses) hors d'âge || the –, les vieillards || -ly, ad. en vieillard.   [intermédiaire, m.

agency, ā′jĕn sĭ, s. agence, f. || action, f. ||

agent, ā′jĕnt, s. agent, commissionaire, m.

agglomerate, ăg glŏm′ĕr āt, v. a. (& n.) (s')agglomérer || (s')assembler.

agglomeration, ăg glŏm ĕr ā′shŭn, s. agglomération, f., amas, m.

agglutinate, ăg glŏt′ĭ nāt, v. a. agglutiner, rejoindre.   [tination, f.

agglutination, ăg glŏt ĭ nā′shŭn, s. agglu-

aggrandise, ăg′grăn dīz, v. a. agrandir || augmenter.   [agrandissement, m.

aggrandisement, ăg′grăn dĭs mĕnt, s.

aggravate, ăg′gră vāt, v. a. aggraver || exagérer || agacer.

aggravation, ăg gră vā′shŭn, s. aggravation, circonstance aggravante, f. || exagération, f. || provocation, f.

aggregate, ăg′grĕ gāt, s. agrégé, m. || in the –, en masse, en somme.

aggregate, ăg′grĕ gāt, v. a. rassembler || réunir || recueillir.

aggregate, ăg′grĕ gāt, a. ramassé, rassemblé || -ly, ad. collectivement.

aggregation, ăg grĕ gā′shŭn, s. réunion, f. || assemblage, m. || (chim.) agrégation, f., assemblage, amas, m.

aggress, ăg grĕs′, v. a. attaquer le premier || provoquer au combat.

aggression, *ăg grĕsh'ŭn,* s. agression, première attaque, f. [sif, hostile.

aggressive, *ăg grĕs'ĭv,* a. agressif, offen-

aggressiveness, *ăg grĕs'ĭv nĕs,* s. caractère agressif, hostile, m.

aggressor, *ăg grĕs'ĕr,* s. agresseur, m.

aggrieve, *ăg grēv',* v. a. chagriner || faire tort à || ~, v. n. se chagriner.

aghast, *ă găst',* a. épouvanté, effrayé.

agile, *ăj'ĭl,* agile, léger, actif.

agility, *ă jĭl'ĭ tĭ,* s. agilité, légèreté, souplesse, f.

agio, *ā'jĭ ō,* s. agio, m. [plesse, f.

agitate, *ăj'ĭ tāt,* v. a. agiter, remuer, troubler || discuter.

agitation, *ăj ĭ tā'shŭn,* s. agitation, f., trouble, m. || discussion, f.

agitator, *ăj'ĭ tā tĕr,* s. agitateur, meneur, m.

agnate, *ăg'nāt,* s. (jur.) agnat, m. [m.

ago, *ă gō',* ad. passé || long ~, il y a longtemps || a year ~, il y a un an.

agog, *ă gŏg',* ad. avec empressement || to be ~, avoir la tête montée.

agoing, *ă gō'ĭng,* a. & ad. en action, en agone, *ă gŏn',* ad. *vide* ago. [train.

agonise, *ăg'ō nīz,* v. a. faire souffrir l'agonie || torturer || ~, v. n. être à l'agonie.

agonisingly, *ăg'ō nī zĭng lĭ,* ad. avec une angoisse extrême.

agony, *ăg'ō nĭ,* s. agonie, f.

agrarian, *ă grā'rĭ ăn,* a. agraire.

agree, *ă grē',* v. a. & n. mettre d'accord, réconcilier || s'accorder, consentir, convenir || to have ~d on, être convenu de

agreeable, *ă grē'ă bl,* a. agréable || convenable, conforme à || to be ~ to, vouloir bien.

agreeableness, *ă grē'ă bl nĕs,* s. conformité, f., rapport, m. || agrément, m. || aménité, f.

agreeably, *ă grē'ă blĭ,* ad. agréablement || conformément à.

agreement, *ă grē'mĕnt,* s. accord m., concorde, ressemblance, f., rapport, m. || bonne intelligence, f. || accommodement, marché, m. || to come to an ~, tomber d'accord || by private ~, de gré à gré.

agricultural, *ă grĭ kŭl'tŭr ăl,* a. d'agriculture, agricole, f.

agriculture, *ă grĭ kŭl'tŭr,* s. agriculture, f.

agriculturae(al)ist, *ă grĭ kŭl'tŭr(ăl)ĭst,* s. agronome, m.

agrimony, *ăg'rĭ mŭnĭ,* s. aigremoine, f.

aground, *ă grŏwnd',* ad. (mar.) à terre, échoué || to run ~, (mar.) s'échouer.

ague, *ā'gū,* s. fièvre (intermittente), f. || ~-drops, s. pl. gouttes fébrifuges, f. pl.

aguish, *ā'gū ĭsh,* a. fiévreux.

ah! *ă,* * ha!* *ā hā',* ah! hélas!

ahead, *ă hĕd',* a. (mar.) en avant || (fig.) en tête || to get ~ of, gagner l'avant de.

ahoy! *ă hŏy',* (mar.) ho!

aid, *ād,* s. aide, assistance, f., secours, m. || aide, m. || in ~ of, au profit *or* au bénéfice de || by the ~ of, avec l'aide de || ~-de-camp, aide de camp, m.

aid, *ād,* v. a. aider, assister, secourir.

aider, *ād'ĕr,* s. assistant, m. || allié, m.

ail, *āl,* v. a. inquiéter, chagriner, causer de la peine || what ~s you? qu' avez-vous?

ailing, *āl'ĭng,* a. maladif, souffrant.

ailment, *āl'mĕnt,* s. mal, m., souffrance, f. || incommodité, f.

aim, *ām,* s. point de mire, m., visée, f., but, m. || vue, f., dessein, m. || to miss one's ~, manquer son coup || to take ~ at, viser, coucher en joue.

aim, *ām,* v. a. & n. diriger, viser à || tendre, aimless, *ām'lĕs,* a. sans but. [aspirer.

air, *ăr,* s. air, m. || vent léger, m. || chant, m., chanson, f. || mine, apparence, f. || in the open ~, en plein air || au grand air || to take the fresh ~, prendre le frais || to vanish into thin ~, s'en aller à vau-l'eau || s'en tourner en eau de boudin || to beat the ~, donner un coup d'épée dans l'eau || a castle in the ~, un château en Espagne || to have a change of ~, changer d'air || to give oneself ~s, prendre *or* se donner des airs || ~-ball, s. petit ballon, m. || ~-balloon, s. ballon aérostatique, m. || ~-cushion, s. coussin à air, m. || (mach.) matelas d'air, m. || ~-gun, s. fusil à vent, m. || ~-hole, s. soupirail, m. || ~-pump, s. machine pneumatique, f. || ~-shaft, s. puits d'airage, m. || ~-ship, s. dirigeable, m. || ~-tight, *ăr'ĭt,* a. imperméable à l'air || ~-valve, s. soupape à air, f.

air, *ăr,* v. a. aérer || mettre, exposer à l'air || (of linen) chauffer.

aired, *ărd,* a. (of linen) sec.

airily, *ăr'ĭlĭ,* ad. légèrement.

airiness, *ăr'ĭnĕs,* s. exposition à l'air, f. || (fig.) vivacité, légèreté, f.

airing, *ăr'ĭng,* s. tour de promenade, m. || aérage, m. || to take an ~, prendre l'air.

airless, *ăr'lĕs,* a. privé d'air.

airling, *ăr'lĭng,* s. jeune étourdi, m.

airy, *ăr'ĭ,* a. aérien || aéré || délicat || illusoire || folâtre.

aisle, *īl,* s. aile (d'une église), f.

ajar, *ă jär',* a. entr'ouvert.

akimbo, *ă kĭm'bō,* ad. appuyé sur la hanche || with one's arms ~, les poings sur les hanches.

akin, *ă kĭn',* a. parent || allié.

alabaster, *ăl ă băs'tĕr,* s. & a. albâtre, m. ||

alack! *ă lăk',* hélas! [d'albâtre.

alacrity, *ă lăk'rĭ tĭ,* s. vivacité, gaieté, f. || with ~, avec empressement.

alarm, *ă lärm',* s. alarme, épouvante, f. || réveil, m. || to raise, sound an ~, jeter, sonner l'alarme || ~-bell, s. tocsin, m. || ~-clock, s. réveille-matin, m.

alarm, *ă lärm',* v. a. alarmer, inquiéter.

alarming, *ă lärm'ĭng,* a. inquiétant || -ly, ad. d'une manière alarmante.

alarmist, *ă lärm'ĭst,* s. alarmiste, m.

alarum, *ă lär'ŭn,* s. *vide* alarm.

alas! *ă lăs',* hélas!

alb(e), *ălb,* s. aube, f.

albatross, *ăl'bă trŏs,* s. albatros, m.

albeit, *ŏl bē'ĭt,* ad. quoique, bien que.

albino, *ăl bē'nō,* s. albinos, m.

album, *ăl'bŭm,* s. album, souvenir, m.

albumen, *ăl bū'mĕn,* s. albumine, f.

alburnum, *ăl bĕr'nŭm,* s. aubier, m.

alcaic, *ăl kā'ĭk,* s. alcaïque, m.

alcaic, *ăl kā'ĭk,* a. alcaïque.

alchemist, *ăl'kĕ mĭst,* s. alchimiste, **m.**

alchemy, *ăl'kĕ mĭ,* s. alchimie, f.

alcohol, *ăl'kŏ hŏl,* s. alcool, m.

alcoholic, *ăl kŏ hŏl'ĭk,* a. alcoolique.

alcove, *ăl'kōv,* s. renfoncement, m. || al-
côve, f. || tonnelle, f.   [buisson, m.

alder, *ăl'dĕr,* s. aune (arbre), m. ||~-bush,

alderman, *ăl'dĕr măn,* s. conseiller muni-
cipal, m. || (in Paris) maire d'arrondisse-
ment, m. || (fam.) levier de fer, m.

ale, *āl,* s. ale (sorte de bière forte), f. ||
single ~, petite bière, f. || ~-bench, s.
banc de cabaret, m.

alee, *ă lē',* ad. (mar.) sous le vent.

alehouse, *āl'hŏws,* s. cabaret, m. || ~-
keeper, s. cabaretier, m.

alembic, *ă lĕm'bĭk,* s. alambic, m.

alert, *ă lĕrt',* s. alerte, f. || on the ~, en
al.rte, sur le qui-vive.

alert, *ă lĕrt',* a. alerte || vigilant.

alertness, *ă lĕrt'nĕs,* s. promptitude, f. ||
vivacité, f. || vigilance, f.

alga, *ăl'gă,* s. algue, f.

algebra, *ăl'jĕ bră,* s. algèbre, f.

algebraic(al), *ăl jĕ brā'ĭk(ăl),* a.-(-ly, ad.)
algébrique(ment).

algebraist, *ăl'jĕ brā ĭst,* s. algébriste, m.

alias, *ā'lĭ ăs,* s. nom de guerre, faux nom,

alias, *ā'lĭ ăs,* ad. autrement dit.   [m.

alibi, *ăl'ĭ bĭ,* s. (jur.) alibi, m.

alien, *āl'yĕn,* s. étranger, m. || ~-act, loi
sur les étrangers, f. || ~-office, bureau
des étrangers, m.

alien, *āl'yĕn,* a. étranger.   [poser contre.

alienate, *āl'yĕn ât,* v. a. aliéner || indis-

alienation, *āl yĕn ā'shŭn,* s. aliénation, f. ||
~ of mind, égarement d'esprit, m.

alight, *ă lît',* v. n. descendre, mettre pied
à terre || tomber || (of birds) s'abattre.

alight, *ă lît',* a. allumé.

alike, *ă līk',* a. & ad. semblable || pareil
(lement) || également || de même || à la
fois || they are much ~, ils se ressem-
blent beaucoup.   [ture, f.

aliment, *ăl'ĭ mĕnt,* s. aliment, m., nourri-

alimental, *ăl ĭ mĕn'tăl,* a. nutritif || -ly,
ad. d'une manière nutritive.

alimentary, *ăl ĭ mĕn'tĕr ĭ,* a. alimentaire.

alimentation, *ăl ĭ mĕn tā'shŭn,* s. alimentation, f.   [f.

alimony, *ăl'ĭ mŏn ĭ,* s. pension alimentaire,

aliquot, *ăl'ĭ kwŏt,* a. (math.) aliquote.

alive, *ă lîv',* a. vivant, en vie || gai || no
man ~, personne au monde || to be ~ to
one's faults, être sensible à ses fautes ||
while ~, de son vivant.

alkali, *ăl'kă lî,* s. alcali, m.

alkaline, *ăl'kă lîn,* a. alcalin.

alkaloid, *ăl'kă lŏÿd,* s. (chim.) alcaloïde, m.

all, *ăwl,* s. tout, m., toutes choses, f. pl. ||
my ~, tout ce que je possède || tout pour
moi || mon tout.

all, *ăwl,* a. & ad. tout || entièrement, seule-
ment || ~ the better, tant mieux || ~ of
a sudden, tout à coup || ~ of us, nous
tous || not at ~, point du tout || nothing
at ~, rien du tout || ~ along, tout le long
de || tout le temps || ~ at once, tout d'un
coup || tout à coup || once for ~, une fois
pour toutes || ~ but, excepté || presque ||
by ~ means, à quelque prix que ce soit ||
one and ~, tous sans exception || that
is ~, voilà tout || above ~, surtout || ~ in
~, entièrement || tel quel || ~ the same,
tout de même || if that is ~, s'il ne tient
qu'à cela || ~-accomplished, a. d'une
éducation parfaite || ~-powerful, a. tout-
puissant || ~-sufficient, a. suffisant ||
~-wise, a. d'une sagesse infinie || ~-
Hallowmas, s. la Toussaint || ~-Souls-
day, s. les Morts || ~-Saints-day, s. jour
de la Toussaint, m.   [sement, m.

allay, *ăl lā',* s. alliage m. || (fig.) affaiblis-

allay, *ăl lā',* v. a. apaiser || modérer, tem-
pérer.   [adoucissement.

allayment, *ăl lā'mĕnt,* s. allégement, m. ||

allegation, *ăl lĕ gā'shŭn,* s. allégation, f.

allege, *ăl lĕj',* v. a. alléguer || déclarer.

allegiance, *ăl lĕ'jăns,* s. (jur.) obéissance,
f. || fidélité, f.   [rique.

allegoric(al), *ăl lĕ gŏr'ĭk(ăl),* a. allégo-

allegorist, *ăl'lĕ gō rĭst,* s. allégoriste, **m.**

allegory, *ăl'lĕ gōr ĭ,* s. allégorie, f.

allegro, *ăl lā'grō,* s. (mus.) allégro, **m.**

alleluiah, *ăl lĕ lū'yă,* s. alléluia, m.

alleviate, *ăl lē'vĭ ât,* v. a. alléger || adou-
cir, soulager.   [ment, m.

alleviation, *ăl lē vĭ ā'shŭn,* s. soulage-

alley, *ăl'lĭ,* s. allée, f. || ruelle, f. || blind
~, cul-de-sac, m.   [f.

alliance, *ăl lî'ăns,* s. alliance, f. || parenté,

allied, *ăl lîd',* a. allié || parent.   [m.

alligator, *ăl'lĭ gā tĕr,* s. alligator, caïman,

alliteration, *ăl lĭt ĕr ā'shŭn,* s. allitéra-
tion, f.   [tion, f.

allocation, *ăl lō kā'shŭn,* s. (com.) alloca-

allocution, *ăl lō kū'shŭn,* s. allocution,
harangue, f.

allodial, *ăl lō'dĭ ăl,* a. allodial.

allodium, *ăl lō'dĭ ŭm,* s. franc-alleu, m.

allonge, *ăl lŭnj',* s. (of horses) longe, f. ||
(com.) allonge, f. || botte, f.

allonge, *ăl lŭnj',* v. a. allonger.

allopathic, *ăl lō păth'ĭk,* a. allopathique.

allopathist, *ăl lŏp'ă thĭst,* s. allopathe, m.

allopathy, *ăl lŏp'ă thĭ,* s. allopathie, f.

allot, *ăl lŏt',* v. a. départir, accorder, assigner.   [portion, f.

allotment, *ăl lŏt'mĕnt,* s. répartition, f. ||

allow, *ăl lŏw',* v. a. allouer || accorder,
permettre || autoriser || reconnaître, avouer ||
to ~ of, admettre, tolérer || to ~ for,
avoir égard à.   [mis.

allowable, *ăl lŏw'ă bl,* a. allouable || per-

allowableness, *ăl lŏw'ă bl nĕs,* s. conve-
nance, f. || légitimité, f.

allowably, *ăl lŏw'ă blĭ,* ad. convenable-
ment || légitimement.

---

lāte, hăt, făr, lăw; — hēre, gĕt, hér; — mīne, ĭnn; — nō, hŏt, prōve; — hŏw; —

allowance, ăl lŏw' ăns, s. admission || permission, f., assentiment, m. || ration, f. || pension, f. || indulgence, f. || excuse, f. || (com.) bonification, f. || on short ~, à la ration || to put on short ~, rationner || to make ~(s) for, faire la part de, avoir égard à || to stop an ~, retrancher.

allowance, ăl lŏw' ăns, v. a. rationner.

alloy, ăl lŏy', s. alliage, m.

alloy, ăl lŏy', v. a. allier || altérer || diminuer.

allspice, ăwl' spĭs, s. piment, m. [nuer.

allude, ăl lūd', v. n. faire allusion || avoir trait à.

allure, ăl lŏr', v. a. leurrer, séduire.

allurement, ăl lŏr' mĕnt, s. amorce, f., appât, charme, m.

alluring, ăl lŏ' rĭng, a. attrayant, séduisant || -ly, ad. d'une manière attrayante.

alluringness, ăl lŏ' rĭng nĕs, s. séduction, f. || attrait, m.

allusion, ăl lŏ' zhŭn, s. allusion, f. || in ~ to, par allusion à || to make an ~, faire allusion.

allusive, ăl lŏ' sĭv, a. faisant allusion, figuré || composé d'allusions || -ly, ad. par allusion.

alluvial, ăl lŏ' vĭ ăl, a. d'alluvion.

alluvion, ăl lŏ' vĭ ŭn, **alluvium,** ăl lŏ' vĭ ŭm, s. alluvion, f.

ally, ăl lī', s. allié, m.

ally, ăl lī', v. a. allier, joindre.

almanac, ăl' mă năk, s. almanach, m.

almightiness, ăwl mī' tĭ nĕs, s. toute-puissance, f.

almighty, ăwl mī' tĭ, a. tout-puissant.

almond, ă' mŭnd, s. amande, f. || burnt ~, praline, f. || sugared ~, amande lissée || bitter, sweet ~, amande amère, douce || ~s, pl. (anat.) amygdales, f. pl. || ~-cake, s. nougat, m. || ~-milk, s. lait d'amandes, orgeat, m. || ~-tree, s. amandier, m.

almoner, ăl' mŭn ér, s. aumônier, m.

almonry, ăl' mŏn rĭ, s. aumônerie, f.

almost, ăwl' mŏst, ad. presque || à peu près.

alms, ămz, s. pl. aumône, charité, f. || ~-house, s. maison de charité, f., hospice, m.

alnage, ăl' năj, s. aunage, m. [m.

aloe(s), ăl' ō(z), s. aloès, m.

aloft, ă lŏft', ad. en haut, en l'air.

alone, ă lōn', a. & ad. seul(ement) || let me ~ ! laissez-moi tranquille !

along, ă lŏng', ad. le long de, devant soi || all ~, tout le long de || tout le temps || go ~ with you ! allez-vouz en ! || ~ with, ainsi que.

aloof, ă lŏf', ad. de loin || (mar.) au large, au lof || to hold ou keep ~, se tenir à distance.

aloud, ă lŏwd', ad. à haute voix.

alpaca, ăl păk' ă, s. alpaga, m.

alphabet, ăl' fă bĕt, s. alphabet, m.

alphabetic(al), ăl fă bĕt' ĭk(ăl), a. (-ly, ad.) alphabétique(ment).

alpine, ăl' pĭn, a. alpestre.

already, ăwl rĕd' ĭ, ad. déjà.

also, ăwl' sō, ad. aussi, également, encore.

altar, ăwl' tér, s. autel, m. || high ~, maître

autel, m. || ~-cloth, s. nappe d'autel, f. || ~-piece, s. tableau d'autel, m.

alter, ăwl' tér, v. a. (& n.) (s')altérer || changer.

alterable, ăwl' tér ă bl, a. altérable, changeant. [pouvoir être changé.

alterably, ăwl' tér ă blĭ, ad. de manière à

alteration, ăwl tér ă' shŭn, s. altération, f., changement, m. [f., débat, m.

altercation, ăl tér kă' shŭn, s. altercation.

alternate, ăl tér' năt, v. a. & n. alterner || succéder tour à tour.

alternate, ăl tér' năt, a. alternatif, réciproque || (bot. & géom.) alterne || -ly, ad. alternativement, tour à tour.

alternation, ăl tér nă' shŭn, s. alternation, vicissitude, f.

alternative, ăl tér' nă tĭv, s. alternative, f.

alternative, ăl tér' nă tĭv, a. alternatif || -ly, ad, alternativement.

althea, ăl thē' ă, s. (bot.) althée, f.

although, ăwl thō', c. quoique, bien que.

altitude, ăl' tĭ tūd, s. élévation, hauteur, f.

alto, ăl' tō, s. (mus.) alto, m., viole, f.

altogether, ăwl tŏŏ gĕth' ér, ad. entièrement, tout à fait || tout à la fois. [m.

alto-relievo, ăl' tō-rĭ lē' vō, s. haut-relief,

alum, ăl' ŭm, s. alun, m.

alumina, ă lŏ' mĭ nă, s. (chim.) alumine, f.

aluminium, ă lŏ' mĭ nĭ ŭm, s. (chim.) aluminium, m. [lement.

always, ăwl' wăz, ad. toujours, continuel-

A. M. (ante meridiem), du matin.

amain, ă mān', ad. avec violence.

amalgam, ă măl' găm, s. (chim.) amalgame, m. [(s')amalgamer.

amalgamate, ă măl' gă măt, v. a. (& n.)

amalgamation, ă măl gă mă' shŭn, s. amalgamation, f. || amalgame, m.

amanuensis, ă măn ŭ ĕn' sĭs, s. secrétaire, m. || copiste, m.

amaranth, ăm' ă rănth, s. amarante, f.

amaryllis, ăm' ă rĭl' lĭs, s. (bot.) amaryl.

amass, ă măs', v. a. amasser. [lis, f.

amateur, ăm' ă tér, s. amateur, virtuose, m.

amatory, ăm' ă tér' ĭ, a. d'amour, d'amants.

amaze, ă măz', v. a. épouvanter, surprendre, étonner || émerveiller. [ment.

amazedly, ă mă' zĕd lĭ, ad. avec étonne-

amazement, ă măz' mĕnt, s. étonnement, m., surprise, f.

amazingly, ă mă' zĭng lĭ, ad. étonnamment || (fam.) furieusement.

amazon, ăm' ă zŏn, s. amazone, f.

amazonian, ăm ă zō' nĭ ăn, a. d'amazone || hardi. [deur, m.

ambassador, ăm băs' să dér, s. ambassa-

ambassadress, ăm băs' să drĕs, s. ambassadrice, f.

amber, ăm' bér, s. ambre, m. [sadrice, f.

amber, ăm' bér, a. d'ambre.

ambergris, ăm' bér grĭs, s. ambre gris, m.

ambidextrous, ăm bĭ dĕks' trŭs, a. ambidextre.

ambient, ăm' bĭ ĕnt, a. ambiant, environnant. [équivoque, f.

ambiguity, ăm bĭ gŭ' ĭ tĭ, s. ambiguïté,

ambiguous, ăm bĭg' ŭ ŭs, a. (-ly, ad.) ambigu(ment) || équivoque.

ambit, *ăm'bĭt*, s. circonférence, f., contour, m.

ambition, *ăm bĭsh'ŭn*, s. ambition, f.

ambitious, *ăm bĭsh'ŭs*, a. ambitieux || to be ~ of, ambitionner || -ly, ad. ambitieusement.

amble, *ăm'bl*, s. amble, m.

amble, *ăm'bl*, v. n. aller l'amble || trottiner.

ambler, *ăm'blĕr*, haqdenée, f.

ambling, *ăm'blĭng*, s. amble, m.

ambrosia, *ăm brō'zĭ ā*, s. ambroisie, f.

ambrosial, *ăm brō'zĭ ăl*, a. d'ambroisie || délicieux.

ambsace, *ămz'ās*, s. beset, ambesas, m.

ambulance, *ăm'bū lăns*, s. ambulance, f.

ambury, *ăm'bū rĭ*, s. furoncle, m.

ambuscade, *ăm bŭs kād'*, ambush, *ăm'bŏŏsh*, s. embûche, f. || (mil.) embuscade, f.

ambush, *ăm'bŏŏsh*, v. a. embusquer || -ed, mis en embuscade.

ameliorate, *ă mēl'yŏ rāt*, v. a. améliorer || ~, v. n. se perfectionner.   [ration.

amelioration, *ă mēl yŏ rā'shŭn*, s. amélioration, exagération, f.

amenable, *ă mē'nă bl*, a. responsable || sujet à || justiciable (de) || to be ~ to, relever de.

amend, *ă mĕnd'*, v. a. (& n.) (s')amender (se) corriger.   [réformé.

amendable, *ă mĕnd'ă bl*, a. amendable.

amendment, *ă mĕnd'mĕnt*, s. amélioration, f. || réforme, f.

amends, *ă mĕndz'*, s. pl. compensation, f. || to make ~ for, dédommager de.

amenity, *ă mĕn'ĭ tĭ*, s. aménité, f.

amerce, *ă mĕrs'*, v. a. mettre à l'amende.

americanism, *ă mĕr'ĭ kăn ĭzm*, s. idiotisme américain, m.

amethyst, *ăm'ĕ thĭst*, s. améthyste, m.

amiability, *ă mĭ ă bĭl'ĭ tĭ*, s. amabilité, f.

amiable, *ā'mĭ ă bl*, a. aimable.

amiably, *ā'mĭ ă blĭ*, ad. aimablement.

amianth(us), *ăn'ĭ ănth(ŭs)*, s. amiante, m.

amicable, *ăm'ĭ kă bl*, a. amical, bienveillant.   [l'amiable.

amicably, *ăm'ĭ kă blĭ*, ad. amicalement, à

amice, *ăm'ĭs*, s. amict, m.   [parmi

amid(st), *ă mĭd(st')*, pr. au milieu de,

amidships, *ă mĭd'shĭps*, ad. par le travers.

amiss, *ă mĭs'*, ad. mal, en mal, mal à propos || to come ~, embarrasser || to take ~, prendre en mauvaise part.

amity, *ăm'ĭ tĭ*, s. amitié, f.

ammonia, *ăm mō'nĭ ă*, s. ammoniaque, f.

ammonite, *ăm'mŏn ĭt*, s. ammonite, f.

ammonium, *ăm mō'nĭ ŭm*, s. (chim.) ammonium, m.   [f.

ammunition, *ăm mŭ nĭsh'ŭn*, s. munition,

amnesty, *ăm'nĕs tĭ*, s. amnistie, f.

amnesty, *ăm'nĕs tĭ*, v. a. amnistier.

among(st), *ă mŭng(st')*, pr. parmi, entre.

amorous, *ăm'ŏ rŭs*, a. amoureux || -ly, ad. amoureusement.   [à l'amour, m.

amorousness, *ăm'ŏ rŭs nĕs*, s. penchant

amorphous, *ă mŏr'fŭs*, a. amorphe.

amortisation, *ă mŏr tĭ zā'shŭn*, s. amortissement, m.

amount, *ă mŏŭnt'*, s. montant, total, m. || somme, quantité, f. || résultat, m. || to the ~ of, se montant à.   [duire.

amount, *ă mŏŭnt'*, v. n. se monter || se ré-

amour, *ă'mŏr*, s. amourette, f. || intrigue, f., amours, f. pl.

amphibian, *ăm fĭb'ĭ ăn*, s. amphibie, m.

amphibious, *ăm fĭb'ĭ ŭs*, a. amphibie.

amphitheatre, *ăm fĭ thē'ă tĕr*, s. amphithéâtre, m.

ample, *ăm'pl*, a. ample, large.   [f.

ampleness, *ăm'pl nĕs*, s. ampleur, étendue,

amplification, *ăm plĭ fĭ kā'shŭn*, s. amplification, exagération, f.

amplifier, *ăm'plĭ fī ĕr*, s. amplificateur, m. || panégyriste, m.

amplify, *ăm'plĭ fī*, v. a. & n. amplifier || augmenter || développer || s'étendre.

amplitude, *ăm'plĭ tūd*, s. largeur, f. étendue, f.

amply, *ăm'plĭ*, ad. amplement.

amputate, *ăm'pŭ tāt*, v. a. amputer || élaguer || to ~ one's limb, amputer qn. d'un membre.   [tion, f.

amputation, *ăm pŭ tā'shŭn*, s. amputa-

amuck, *ă mŭk'*, ad. en furieux || to run ~, courir en furieux.

amulet, *ăm'ū lĕt*, s. amulette, f.

amuse, *ă mūz'*, v. a. amuser, divertir || tromper.   [divertissement, m.

amusement, *ă mūz'mĕnt*, s. amusement,

amusing, *ă mūz'ĭng*, a. amusant || -ly, ad. d'une manière amusante.

an, *ăn*, art. un, une || ~, c. si, comme si.

anabaptist, *ă nă băp'tĭst*, s. anabaptiste, m.   [nisme, m.

anachronism, *ăn ăk'rŏ nĭzm*, s. anachro-

anaconda, *ă nă kŏn'dă*, s. (boa) anacande, anacandé, m.

anacreontic, *ă năk rē ŏn'tĭk*, s. poème anacréontique, m.   [tique.

anacreontic, *ă năk rē ŏn'tĭk*, a. anacréon-

anæmia, *ă nē'mĭ ă*, s. (méd.) anémie, f.

anæsthetic, *ăn ĕs thĕt'ĭk*, s. anesthésique, m.

anæsthetic, *ăn ĕs thĕt'ĭk*, a. anesthésique.

anagram, *ăn'ă grăm*, s. anagramme, f.

anal, *ā'năl*, a. (anat.) anal.

analogical, *ă nă lŏj'ĭ kăl*, a. (-ly, ad.) analogique(ment).

analogous, *ă năl'ŏ gŭs*, a. analogue || -ly, ad. par analogie.

analogy, *ă năl'ŏ jĭ*, s. analogie, f.

analyse, *ăn'ă līz*, v. a. analyser, faire l'analyse.

analysis, *ă năl'ĭ sĭs*, s. analyse, f.

analyst, *ăn'ă lĭst*, s. analyste, m.

analytic(al), *ă nă lĭt'ĭk(ăl)*, a. analytique.

anarchic(al), *ăn ăr'kĭk(ăl)*, a. anarchique.

anarchist, *ăn'ăr kĭst*, s. anarchiste, m. & f.

anarchy, *ăn'ăr kĭ*, s. anarchie, f.

anathema, *ă năth'ĕ mă*, s. anathème, m.

anathematise, *ă năth'ĕ mă tīz*, v. a. anathématiser || -d, a. anathème.

anatomical, *ăn ă tŏm'ĭ kăl*, a. (-ly, ad.) anatomique(ment).   [disséquer.

anatomise, *ăn ăt'ŏ mīz*, v. a. anatomiser,

anatomist, *ăn ăt'ŏ mĭst*, s. anatomiste, m.

---

lāte, hăt, făr, lăw; — hēre, gĕt, hĕr; — mīne, ĭnn; — nō, hŏt, prōve; — hŏw; —

anatomy, ă năt′ō mĭ, s. anatomie, f. ‖ squelette, m.

ancestor, ăn′ sĕs tĕr, s. aïeul, m. ‖ **-s,** pl. ancêtres, m. pl. |ditaire.

ancestral, ăn sĕs′ trăl, a. d'ancêtres ‖ héré-

ancestry, ăn′ sĕs trĭ, s. aïeux, m. pl. ‖ extraction, f.

anchor, ăng′ kĕr, s. ancre, f. ‖ **sheet ~,** maîtresse ancre, f. ‖ **bower ~,** ancre de bossoir ‖ **spare ~,** ancre de veille ‖ **to cast ~,** jeter l'ancre ‖ **to weigh ~,** lever l'ancre ‖ **to ride at ~,** être à l'ancre.

anchor, ăng′ kĕr, v. a. ancrer, jeter l'ancre, mouiller ‖ —, v. n. se fixer.

anchorage, ăng′ kĕr ăj, s. ancrage, mouillage, m. ‖ droit de mouillage, m. ‖ ancres, f. pl.

anchoring, ăng′ kĕr ĭng, a. à l'ancre ‖ **~- ground,** s. mouillage, m.

anchorite, ăng′ kĕr ĭt, s. anachorète, m.

anchovy, ăn chō′ vĭ, s. anchois, m.

ancient, ăn′ shĕnt, a. (-ly, ad.) ancien(nement). |famille), f.

ancientry, ăn′ shĕnt rĭ, s. ancienneté (de

and, ănd, c. et ‖ **better ~ better,** de mieux en mieux.

andante, ăn dăn′ tā, s. andante, m.

andiron, ănd′ ĭrn, s. chenet, m.

anecdote, ăn′ ĕk dōt, s. anecdote, f.

anecdotic(al), ăn ĕk dŏt′ ĭ k(ăl), a. anecdotique. |mètre, m.

anemometer, ăn ĕ mŏm′ ĕ tĕr, s. anémo-

anemone, ăn ĕm′ ō nē, s. anémone, f. ‖ **sea~,** s. actinie, f.

anent, ăn ĕnt′, pr. touchant.

aneurism, ăn′ ū rĭzm, s. anévrisme, m.

anew, ă nū′, ad. de nouveau, encore ‖ à neuf.

angel, ān′ jĕl, s. ange, m. ‖ **~-fish,** s. ange de mer, m. ‖ **~-shot,** s. boulet ramé, m.

angelic, ăn jĕl′ ĭk, a. (-ally, ad.) angélique(ment).

angelus, ăn′ jĕl ŭs, s. angélus, m.

anger, ăng′ gĕr, s. colère, f.

anger, ăng′ gĕr, v. a. mettre en colère, aigrir ‖ **to provoke one to ~,** exciter la colère de qn.

angle, ăng′ gl, s. angle, m. ‖ coin, m.

angle, ăng′ gl, v. a. pêcher à la ligne.

angled, ăng′ gld, a. à angles.

anglican, ăng′ glĭ kăn, a. anglican.

anglicise, ăng′ glĭ sīz, v. a. angliciser.

anglicism, ăng′ glĭ sĭzm, s. anglicisme, m.

angling, ăng′ glĭng, s. pêche à la ligne, f. ‖ **~-line,** s. ligne à pêcher, f. ‖ **~-rod,** s. perche à pêcher, f. |manie, f.

anglomania, ăng glō mā′ nĭ ä, s. anglo-

angrily, ăng′ grĭ lĭ, ad. avec colère.

angry, ăng′ grĭ, a. fâché, irrité (**with,** contre). |f. ‖ **—ed,** a. navré de douleur, f.

anguish, ăng′ gwĭsh, s. angoisse, douleur, m.

angular, ăng′ gū lĕr, a. angulaire.

angularity, ăng gū lăr′ ĭ tĭ, s. état angulaire, m.

anhydrous, ăn hī′ drŭs, a. (chim.) anhydre.

anil, ăn′ ĭl, s. (bot.) anil, m.

aniline, ăn′ ĭ lĭn, s. (chim.) aniline, f.

animadversion, ăn ĭ măd vĕr′ shŭn, s. animadversion, censure, f., blâme, m.

animadvert, ăn ĭ măd vĕrt′, v. n. censurer, réprimander, blâmer.

animal, ăn′ ĭ măl, s. animal, m.

animal, ăn′ ĭ măl, a. animal. |m.

animalcule, ăn ĭ măl′ kŭl, s. animalcule,

animality, ăn ĭ măl′ ĭ tĭ, s. animalité, f.

animate, ăn′ ĭ māt, v. a. animer, vivifier ‖ encourager.

animate(d), ăn′ ĭ māt (ĕd), a. animé.

animation, ăn ĭ mā′ shŭn, s. animation, f. ‖ verve, vivacité, f.

animosity, ăn ĭ mŏs′ ĭ tĭ, s. animosité, f.

animus, ăn′ ĭ mŭs, s. volonté, f. ‖ intention, f., but, m.

anise, ăn′ ĭs, s. anis, m. |sette, f.

aniseed, ăn′ ĭ sēd, s. graine d'anis, f. ‖ ani-

anker, ăng′ kĕr, s. quartaut, m. (38 lit.)

ankle, ăng′ kl, s. cheville du pied, f. ‖ **~-bone,** s. astragale, f. |chevilles, f.

ankle-deep, ăng′ kl-dēp, a. jusqu'aux

annals, ăn′ nălz, s. pl. annales, f. pl.

anneal, ăn nēl′, v. a. recuire.

annex, ăn nĕks′, s. annexe, f.

annex, ăn nĕks′, v. a. (& n.) annexer ‖ (se) joindre, (s') attacher. |f.

annexation, ăn nĕks ā′ shŭn, s. annexion, f.

annexed, ăn nĕkst′, a. ci-joint.

annihilate, ăn nī′ hĭ lāt, v. a. annihiler, anéantir. |lation, f.

annihilation, ăn nī hĭ lā′ shŭn, s. annihi-

anniversary, ăn nĭ vĕr′ sĕr ĭ, s. anniversaire, m. |saire.

anniversary, ăn nĭ vĕr′ sĕr ĭ, a. anniver-

annotate, ăn′ nō tāt, v. a. annoter.

annotation, ăn nō tā′ shŭn, s. annotation, note, f.

annotator, ăn nō tā′ tĕr, s. annotateur, m.

announce, ăn nowns′, v. a. annoncer.

announcement, ăn nowns′ mĕnt, s. annonce, f. |molester.

annoy, ăn nŏy′, v. a. ennuyer, troubler ‖

annoyance, ăn nŏy′ăns, s. ennui, m. ‖ tourment, m.

annual, ăn′ nū ăl, s. annuaire, m. ‖ plante annuelle, f. |par an.

annual, ăn′ nū ăl, a. (-ly, ad.) annuel ‖

annuitant, ăn nū′ ĭ tănt, s. propriétaire d'une rente viagère, m.

annuity, ăn nū′ ĭ tĭ, s. rente annuelle, f. ‖ **to settle an ~ upon,** constituer une rente à ‖ **to sink money in an ~,** placer son argent à fonds perdu.

annul, ăn nŭl′, v. n. annuler, casser.

annular, ăn′ nū lĕr, a. annulaire.

annulated, ăn′ nū lā tĕd, a. annelé.

annulet, ăn′ nū lĕt, s. petit anneau, m.

annulment, ăn nŭl′ mĕnt, s. annulation, f.

annunciation, ăn nŭn shĭ ā′ shŭn, s. proclamation, f. ‖ Annonciation, f.

anodyne, ăn′ ō dĭn, s. remède anodin, m.

anodyne, ăn′ ō dĭn, a. anodin.

anoint, ă nŏynt′, v. a. oindre ‖ (vulg.) rosser. |régulier ‖ hétéroclite.

anomalous, ă nŏm′ ă lŭs, a. anomal ‖ ir-

anomaly, ă nŏm′ ă lĭ, s. anomalie, f.

anon, *ă nŏn'*, ad. bientôt, tout-à-l'heure || **ever and ~,** de temps en temps.

anonymous, *ă nŏn'ĭ mŭs*, a. anonyme || **-ly,** adv. en gardant l'anonyme.

another, *ăn ŭth'ĕr*, a. un autre, autrui || **one ~,** l'un l'autre || **just such ~,** un tout pareil || **~ and ~,** et encore d'autres.

answer, *ăn'sĕr*, s. réponse, réplique, f. || **-s,** pl. raisons, f. pl.

answer, *ăn'sĕr*, v. a. & n. repondre (à) || raisonner || réussir || satisfaire || **to ~ for,** répondre, être responsable, de or pour.

answerable, *ăn'sĕr ă bl*, a. responsable, comptable || convenable à, conforme.

answerableness, *ăn'sĕr ă bl nĕs*, s. responsabilité, f. || convenance, f. [ment.

answerably, *ăn'sĕr ă blĭ*, ad. convenablement, *ănt*, s. fourmi, f. || **~-bear, ~-eater,** s. fourmilier, m. || **~-hill,** s. fourmilière, f.

antagonism, *ăn tăg'ō nĭzm*, s. antagonisme, m. [m.

antagonist, *ăn tăg'ō nĭst*, s. antagoniste,

antagonistic, *ăn tăg ō nĭs'tĭk*, a. antagoniste.

antarctic, *ănt ărk'tĭk*, a. antarctique.

antecedence, *ăn tē sē'dĕns*, s. antériorité, priorité, f. [antécédent || antécédemment.

antecedent, *ăn tē sē'dĕnt*, a. (-ly, ad.)

antechamber, *ăn tē chăm'bĕr*, s. antichambre, f.

antedate, *ăn'tē dāt*, v. a. antidater.

antediluvian, *ăn tē dĭ lŏ'vĭ ăn*, a. antédiluvien.

antelope, *ăn'tē lōp*, s. antilope, f. [midi.

antemeridian, *ăn tē mē rĭd'ĭ ăn*, a. avant

antennæ, *ăn tĕn'nē*, s. pl. antennes, f. pl.

antenuptial, *ăn tē nŭp'shăl*, a. d'avant le mariage. [antépénultième, f.

antepenultimate, *ăn tē pĕn ŭl'tĭ māt*, s.

antepenultimate, *ăn tē pĕn ŭl'tĭ māt*, a. antépénultième. [dent.

anterior, *ăn tē rĭ ĕr*, a. antérieur, antécé-

anteriority, *ăn tē rĭ ŏr'ĭ tĭ*, s. antériorité, priorité, f. [salle d'attente, f.

anteroom, *ăn'tē rŏm*, s. vestibule, m.,

anthem, *ăn'thĕm*, s. antienne, f. || hymne,

anther, *ăn'thĕr*, s. (bot.) anthère, f. [m.

anthology, *ăn thŏl'ō jĭ*, s. anthologie, chrestomathie, f.

Anthony's fire, *ăn'tŏn ĭs fīr*, s. érysipèle,

anthracite, *ăn'thră sīt*, s. (min.) anthracite, m. [charbon, m.

anthrax, *ăn'thrăks*, s. (méd.) anthrax,

anthropology, *ăn thrō pŏl'ō jĭ*, s. anthropologie, f. [anthropophage, m.

anthropophagus, *ăn thrō pŏf'ă gŭs*, s.

antic, *ăn'tĭk*, s. bouffon, m. || farce, f.

antic, *ăn'tĭk*, a. antique || grotesque.

antichrist, *ăn'tĭ krĭst*, s. antéchrist, m.

anticipate, *ăn tĭs'ĭ pāt*, v. a. anticiper, prévenir.

anticipation, *ăn tĭs ĭ pā'shŭn*, s. anticipation, f. || avant-goût, m. || **by, in ~,** par avance. [ticipation, anticipé.

anticipatory, *ăn tĭs'ĭ pā tĕr ĭ*, a. par an-

anticlimax, *ăn tĭ klī'măks*, s. gradation inverse, f.

anticonstitutional, *ăn tĭ kŏn stĭ tū'shŭn-ăl*, a. anticonstitutionnel.

antidotal, *ăn'tĭ dō tăl*, a. qui a la propriète d'un antidote.

antidote, *ăn'tĭ dōt*, s. antidote, m.

antifebrile, *ăn tĭ fĕb'rĭl*, a. antifébrile.

antimacassar, *ăn tĭ mă kăs'săr*, s. antimacassar, m.

antimonarchical, *ăn tĭ mŏ năr'kĭ kăl*, a. antimonarchique. [timonial || stibié.

antimonial, *ăn tĭ mō'nĭ ăl*, a. (chim.) an-

antimony, *ăn'tĭ mŏn ĭ*, s. antimoine, m.

antipathetic, *ăn tĭ pă thĕt'ĭk*, a. antipathique.

antipathy, *ăn tĭp'ă thĭ*, s. antipathie, f.

antiphrasis, *ăn tĭph'ră sĭs*,s. antiphrase,f.

antipodes, *ăn tĭp'ō dēz*, s. pl. antipodes, m. pl.

antipope, *ăn'tĭ pōp*, s. antipape, m.

antiquarian, *ăn tĭ kwā'rĭ ăn*, **antiquary,** *ăn'tĭ kwā rĭ*, s. antiquaire, m.

antiquated, *ăn'tĭ kwā tĕd*, a. suranné.

antique, *ăn tēk'*, s. antiquité, f. || antiquaille, f.

antique, *ăn tēk'*, a. antique, ancien.

antiquity, *ăn tĭk'wĭ tĭ*, s. antiquité, f.

antiseptic, *ăn tĭ sĕp'tĭk*, s. antiseptique, m.

antiseptic, *ăn tĭ sĕp'tĭk*, a. antiseptique.

antithesis, *ăn tĭth'ē sĭs*, s. antithèse, f.

antler, *ănt'lĕr*, s. andouiller, m. || **-s, pl.** (horns) bois, m. (du cerf).

anus, *ā'nŭs*, s. (anat.) anus, m. [m.

anvil, *ăn'vĭl*, s. enclume, f. || (fig.) métier,

anxiety, *ăng zī'ē tĭ*, s. anxiété, inquiétude, f. || désir, m.

anxious, *ăngk'shŭs*, a. (-ly, ad.) inquiet, soucieux || avec anxiété || désireux.

any, *ĕn'nĭ*, pn. & a. quelque, quelqu'un, aucun || **-thing,** quelque chose||**-where,** nulle part, partout || **-body,** one, une personne quelconque || **-how,** de quelque manière que ce soit || **scarcely ~,** presque pas || **~ and every,** chaque || **~ more,** encore.

aorta, *ā ŏr'tă*, s. (anat.) aorte, f.

apace, *ă pās'*, ad. à grands pas, vite || **à** vue d'œil.

apart, *ă părt'*, ad. à part, séparément, f.

apartment, *ă părt'mĕnt*, s. appartement, m., chambre, f. || **a suite of -s,** un appartement.

apathetic, *ăp ă thĕt'ĭk*, a. apathique.

apathy, *ăp'ă thĭ*, s. apathie, insensibilité, f.

ape, *āp*, s. singe, m. || imitateur, m.

ape, *āp*, v. a. singer.

apeak, *ă pēk'*, ad. (mar.) à pic, en pantenne.

aperient, *ă pē'rĭ ĕnt*, s. (méd.) apéritif, m.

aperient, *ă pē'rĭ ĕnt*, a. (méd.) apéritif.

aperture, *ăp'ĕr tūr*, s. ouverture, f.

apery, *ā'pĕr ĭ*, s. singerie, f.

apex, *ā'pĕks*, s. sommet, m., pointe, f.

aphorism, *ăf'ō rĭzm*, s. aphorisme, m.

apiary, *ā'pĭ ă rĭ*, s. rucher, m.

apiece, *ă pēs'*, a. par pièce, par tête.

apish, *ā'pĭsh*, a. (-ly, ad.) bouffon ||en singe|| **~-trick,** s. singerie, f. [imitative, f.

apishness, *ā'pĭsh nĕs*, s. singerie, humeur

---

lāte, hăt, fàr, làw; — hēre, gĕt, hĕr; — mīne, ĭnn; — nō, hŏt, prōve; — hŏw; —

Apocalypse, *ă pŏk' ă lĭps*, s. apocalypse, f.
Apocrypha, *ă pŏk' rĭ fă*, s. pl. livres apocryphes, m. pl.
apocryphal, *ă pŏk' rĭ făl*, a. apocryphe.
apogee, *ăp' ŏ jē*, s. apogée, m.
apologetic, *ă pŏl ŏ jĕt' ĭk*, a. (-ally, ad.) apologétique(ment). [logie.
apologise, *ă pŏl' ŏ jīz*, v. n. faire une apologie, *ă pŏl' ŏ jĭst*, s. apologiste, m.
apologist, *ă pŏl' ŏ jĭst*, s. apologiste, m.
apologue, *ăp' ŏ lŏg*, s. apologue, m.
apology, *ă pŏl' ŏ jĭ*, s. apologie, excuse, f.
apo(ph)thegm, *ăp' ŏ(f) thĕm*, s. apophthegme, m. [plectique.
apoplectic(al), *ăp ŏ plĕk' tĭk(ăl)*, a. apoplexy, *ăp' ŏ plĕk sĭ*, s. (méd.) apoplexie, f.
apostasy, *ă pŏs' tă sĭ*, s. apostasie, f. [f.
apostate, *ă pŏs' tāt*, s. apostat, m.
apostatise, *ă pŏs' tă tīz*, v. n. renoncer à sa religion.
apostle, *ă pŏs' sl*, s. apôtre, m.
apostleship, *ă pŏs' sl shĭp*, s. apostolat, m.
apostolic(al), *ăp ŏs tŏl' ĭk(ăl)*, a. apostolique.
apostrophe, *ă pŏs' trŏ fē*, s. apostrophe, f.
apostrophise, *ă pŏs' trŏ fīz*, v. a. apostropher.
apothecary, *ă pŏth' ĕ kăr ĭ*, s. pharmacien, m. ||-'s shop, s. pharmacie, f.
apotheosis, *ă pŏth ē ō' sĭs*, s. apothéose, f.
appal, *ăp pawl'*, v. a. faire pâlir, effrayer || ~, v. n. pâlir, s'épouvanter.
appalling, *ăp pawl' ling*, a. épouvantable || effrayant.
appanage, *ăp' păn ăj*, s. apanage, m. || to endow with an ~, apanager.
apparatus, *ăp pă ră' tŭs*, s. appareil, m. || outils, m. pl.
apparel, *ăp păr' ĕl*, s. vêtement, ajustement, m., habits, m. pl. || wearing-~, s. effets d'habillement, m. pl.
apparel, *ăp păr' ĕl*, v. a. habiller, vêtir || (mar.) équiper.
apparent, *ăp pā' rĕnt*, a. apparent, visible || (of heirs) présomptif || -ly, ad. apparemment, évidemment. [spectre, m.
apparition, *ăp pă rĭsh' ŭn*, s. vision, f., apparitor, *ăp păr' ĭ tĕr*, s. appariteur, bedeau, m.
appeal, *ăp pēl'*, s. appel, m. [deau, m.
appeal, *ăp pēl'*, v. n. appeler || ~, v. a. porter à un tribunal supérieur.
appear, *ăp pēr'*, v. n. apparaître, comparaître || to ~ against one, se présenter contre qn.
appearance, *ăp pēr' ăns*, s. apparition, f. || comparution, f. || probabilité, f. || spectacle, m. || aspect, m. || perspective, f. || at first ~, au premier abord || for ~ sake, pour sauver les apparences || to judge by -s, à en juger d'après les apparences || to keep up -s, garder les apparences || to make one's first ~, faire son début.
appease, *ăp pēz'*, v. a. apaiser, calmer.
appeaser, *ăp pēz' ĕr*, s. pacificateur, m.
appellant, *ăp pĕl' lănt*, s. appellant, m. || provocateur, m. [intimé, m.
appellate, *ăp pĕl' lāt*, s. accusé, m. || (jur.)

appellation, *ăp pĕl lā' shŭn*, s. dénomination, f. [latif.
appellative, *ăp pĕl' lă tĭv*, a. (gr.) appellee, *ăp pĕl lē'*, s. (jur.) intimé, m.
appellor, *ăp pĕl' lŏr*, s. (jur.) appelant, m.
append, *ăp pĕnd'*, v. a. apposer, ajouter.
appendage, *ăp pĕn' dăj*, s. dépendance, f., accessoire, m.
appendix, *ăp pĕn' dĭks*, s. appendice, m.
appertain, *ăp pĕr tān'*, v. n. appartenir à, concerner.
appetence, *ăp' pĕ tĕns*, appetency, *ăp'-pĕ tĕn sĭ*, s. envie, inclination, f., désir, m.
appetiser, *ăp' pĕ tīz ĕr*, s. excitant à l'appétit, m.
appetising, *ăp' pĕ tīz ĭng*, a. appétissant.
appetite, *ăp' pĕ tīt*, s. appétit, m. || désir, m.
applaud, *ăp plawd'*, v. a. applaudir. [m.
applause, *ăp plawz'*, s. applaudissement, apple, *ăp' pl*, s. pomme, f. || pommier, m. || prunelle, f. || crab-~, s. pomme sauvage, m. || oak-~, s. galle, f. || pine-~, s. ananas, m. ||~-dumpling, s. chausson, m. ||~-fritter, s. beignet de pomme, m. ||~-orchard, s. pommeraie, f. ||~-paring, ~-peel, s. pelure de pomme, f. ||~-pie, ~-tart, s. tourte aux pommes, f. ||~-tree, s. pommier, m. ||~-woman, s. marchande de pommes, f.
appliance, *ăp plī' ăns*, s. application, f. || moyen, m. || remède, m.
applicability, *ăp plĭ kă bĭl' ĭ tĭ*, s. adhérence, f. || convenance, f.
applicable, *ăp' plĭ kă bl*, a. applicable.
applicant, *ăp' plĭ kănt*, s. pétitionneur, solliciteur, m.
application, *ăp plĭ kā' shŭn*, s. application, f., emploi, usage, m. || attention, f. || to make an ~ to, s'adresser à.
apply, *ăp plī'*, v. a. & n. appliquer, employer || s'adresser (à), s'appliquer.
appoint, *ăp pŏynt'*, v. a. & n. fixer, nommer, désigner || well (ill) -ed, bien (mal) équipé, en bonne (mauvaise) tenue.
appointment, *ăp pŏynt' mĕnt*, s. décret, ordre, m. || rendez-vous, m. || appointements, m. pl. || équipement, m. || to make (keep) an ~, donner (ne pas manquer à) un rendez-vous.
apportion, *ăp pōr' shŭn*, v. a. répartir, partager.
apportionment, *ăp pōr' shŭn mĕnt*, s. répartition, f., partage, m.
apposite, *ăp' pŏ zĭt*, a. (-ly, ad.) convenable, bien appliqué || à propos.
appositeness, *ăp' pŏ zĭt nĕs*, s. convenance, justesse, f.
apposition, *ăp pŏ zĭsh' ŭn*, s. apposition, f.
appraise, *ăp prāz'*, v. a. apprécier, priser.
appraisement, *ăp prāz' mĕnt*, s. estimation, évaluation, f. || prisée, f. || expertise, f.
appraiser, *ăp prāz' ĕr*, s. estimateur, commissaire-priseur, m.
appreciable, *ăp prē' shĭ ă bl*, a. appréciable.
appreciate, *ăp prē' shĭ āt*, v. a. apprécier, évaluer || ~, v. n. augmenter de prix, hausser de valeur.

appreciation, *ăp prē shǐ ā′ shŭn,* s. appréciation, évaluation, f.

apprehend, *ăp prē hĕnd′,* v. a. appréhender ‖ saisir ‖ concevoir ‖ comprendre ‖ craindre.

apprehension, *ăp prē hĕn′ shŭn,* s. appréhension, crainte, f. ‖ conception, f. ‖ prise, arrestation, f. ‖ **to be dull of ~,** avoir l'intelligence dure.

apprehensive, *ăp prē hĕn′ sǐv,* a. intelligent ‖ susceptible ‖ craintif.

apprehensiveness, *ăp prē hĕn′ sǐv nĕs,* s. facilité, f. ‖ appréhension, f.

apprentice, *ăp prĕn′ tǐs,* s. apprenti, m. ‖ clerc, élève, m. ‖ **to article an ~,** placer comme clerc or élève. [apprentissage.

apprentice, *ăp prĕn′ tǐs,* v. a. mettre en apprentissage.

apprenticeship, *ăp prĕn′ tǐs shǐp,* s. apprentissage, m. ‖ **to serve one's ~,** faire son apprentissage.

apprise, *ăp prīz′,* v. a. apprendre ‖ informer, instruire. [cès, abord, m.

approach, *ăp prōch′,* s. approche, f., accès.

approach, *ăp prōch′,* v. a. & n. approcher ‖ s'approcher de. [abordable.

approachable, *ăp prōch′ ă bl,* a. accessible,

approaching, *ăp prōch′ ǐng,* a. prochain.

approbation, *ăp prō bā′ shŭn,* s. approbation, f., aveu, m. ‖ **one's unqualified ~,** toute son approbation.

approbative, *ăp′ prō bā tǐv,* a. approbatif.

appropriate, *ăp prō′ prǐ āt,* v. a. approprier ‖ **to ~ to oneself,** s'approprier. \

appropriate, *ăp prō′ prǐ ăt,* a. ~ (-ly, ad.) convenable(ment) ‖ approprié ‖ propre (ment).

appropriateness, *ăp prō′ prǐ ăt′ nĕs,* s. convenance, justesse, f. [propriation, f.

appropriation, *ăp prō prǐ ā′ shŭn,* s. approval, f.

approval, *ăp prō′ văl,* s. approbation, f.

approve, *ăp prōv′,* v. a. approuver ‖ améliorer. [(jur.) révélateur, m.

approver, *ăp prō′ vĕr,* s. approbateur, m. ‖

approving, *ăp prō′ vǐng,* a. approbateur ‖ -ly, ad. avec approbation.

approximate, *ăp prŏks′ ǐ māt,* v. a. & n. approcher ‖ s'approcher de. [matif.

approximate, *ăp prŏks′ ǐ măt,* a. approximation, approche, f.

approximation, *ăp prŏks′ ǐ mā′ shŭn,* s. approximation, approche, f.

approximative, *ăp prŏks′ ǐ mā tǐv,* a. approximatif. [tenance, dépendance, f.

appurtenance, *ăp pĕr′ tĕ năns,* s. appartenant. [s. abricotier, m.

appurtenant, *ăp pĕr′ tĕ nănt,* a. (jur.) appartenant.

apricot, *ă′ prǐ kŏt,* s. abricot, m. ‖ ~-tree,

April, *ā′ prǐl,* s. avril, m. ‖ ~-fool, s. dupe du premier avril, f. ‖ ~-shower, s. giboulée de mars, f. [m.

apron, *ā′ prŏn,* s. tablier, m. ‖ garde-vue.

apsis, *ăp′ sǐs,* s. (arch.) apside, f. ‖ (astr.) apside, m.

apt, *ăpt,* a.-(-ly, ad.) apte ‖ propre, enclin à ‖ prompt, porté à ‖ à propos. [tion, f.

aptitude, *ăp′ tǐ tūd,* s. aptitude, disposition, f.

aptness, *ăpt′ nĕs,* s. convenance, f., rapport, m. ‖ disposition, pente, f.

aqua, *ă′ kwă (āk′ wă);* ~ **fortis,** s. eau-forte, f. ‖ ~ **regia,** s. (chim.) eau régale, f. ‖ ~ **vitæ,** s. spiritueux de la première distillation, m. pl.

aquarium, *ă kwā′ rǐ ŭm,* s. aquarium, m.

Aquarius, *ă kwā′ rǐ ŭs,* s. (astr.) Verseau, m.

aquatic, *ă kwăt′ ǐk,* a. aquatique, aquatile.

aqueduct, *ăk′ wē dŭkt,* s. aqueduc, m.

aqueous, *ā′ kwǐ ŭs,* a. aqueux.

aquiline, *ăk′ wǐ līn,* a. aquilin.

arabesque, *ăr ă bĕsk′,* s. arabesque.

arable, *ăr′ ă bl,* a. labourable.

arbalist, *ăr′ bă lǐst,* s. arbalète, f.

arbiter, *ăr′ bǐ tĕr,* s. arbitre, m. [fm.

arbitrament, *ăr bǐt′ ră mĕnt,* s. arbitrage,

arbitrarily, *ăr′ bǐ trā rǐ lǐ,* ad. arbitrairement. [traire, m.

arbitrariness, *ăr′ bǐ trā rǐ nĕs,* s. arbitrary,

arbitrary, *ăr′ bǐ trĕr′ǐ,* a. arbitraire.

arbitrate, *ăr′ bǐ trāt,* v. a. décider, déterminer, juger. [m., décision, f.

arbitration, *ăr bǐ trā′ shŭn,* s. arbitrage,

arbitrator, *ăr bǐ trā′ tĕr,* s. arbitre, juge, m. [transaction, f.

arbitrement, *ăr bǐt′ rĕ mĕnt,* s. décision, f.

arbitress, *ăr′ bǐ trĕs,* s. arbitre, f.

arborescent, *ăr bō rĕs′ ĕnt,* a. arborescent.

arboriculturist, *ăr bŏr′ ǐ kŭl′ tŭr ǐst,* s. arboriculteur, m. [tonnelle, f.

arbour, *ăr′ bŏr,* s. berceau, bosquet, m.

arbute, *ăr′ būt,* arbutus, *ăr′ bū tŭs,* s. arbousier, m. ‖ ~-berry, s. arbouse, f.

arc, *ărk,* s. arc, m. ‖ voûte, arche, f.

arcade, *ăr kād′,* s. arcade f. ‖ galerie, f. ‖ passage, m. [fm.

arcanum, *ăr kā′ nŭm,* s. arcane, m. ‖ secret.

arch, *ărch,* s. arche, f. ‖ voûte, f. ‖ arc, m.

arch, *ărch,* v. a. voûter.

arch, *ărch,* a. fin, rusé, fieffé ‖ (in comp.) archi . . . ‖ -ly, ad. malicieusement.

archæologic(al), *ăr kē ō lŏj′ ǐk(ăl),* a. archéologique. [logue, m.

archæologist, *ăr kē ŏl′ ō jǐst,* s. archéologue, m.

archæology, *ăr kē ŏl′ ō jǐ,* s. archéologie, f.

archaism, *ăr′ kā ǐzm,* s. archaisme, m.

archangel, *ărk ān′ jĕl,* s. archange, m.

archbishop, *ărch bǐsh′ ŏp,* s. archevêque, s. [vêché, m.

archbishopric, *ărch bǐsh′ ŏp rǐk,* s. archevêché.

archdeacon, *ărch dē′ kŏn,* s. archidiacre, m. [archidiaconat, m.

archdeaconship, *ărch dē′ kŏn shǐp,* s.

archducal, *ărch dū′ kăl,* a. archiducal.

archduchess, *ărch dŭch′ ĕs,* s. archiduchesse, f.

archduke, *ărch dūk′,* s. archiduc, m.

archdukedom, *ărch dūk′ dŏm,* s. archiduché, m. [arquê.

arched, *ărch′ ĕd (ărchd),* a. voûté ‖ cintré ‖

archer, *ărch′ ĕr,* s. archer, arbalétrier, m.

archery, *ărch′ ĕr′ĭ,* s. tir à l'arc, m. ‖ art de tirer l'arc, m.

archfiend, *ărch′ fēnd,* s. archidémon, m.

archiepiscopacy, *ăr kǐ ē pǐs′ kō pă sǐ,* s. archiépiscopat, m. [épiscopal.

archiepiscopal, *ăr kǐ ē pǐs′ kō păl,* a. archi-

arching, *ărch′ ǐng,* s. voûte, arche, f.

---

archipelago, *är kĭ pĕl' ă gō,* s. archipel, m.

architect, *är' kĭ tĕkt,* s. architecte, m. ‖ (fig.) auteur, artisan, m.

architecture, *är' kĭ tĕk tūr,* s. architecture, f.

archives, *är' kīvz,* s. pl. archives, f. pl.

archivist, *är' kĭ vĭst,* s. archiviste, m.

archness, *ärch' nĕs,* s. espièglerie, finesse, malice, f.   [guichet, m.

archway, *ärch' wā,* s. voûte, f., arceau,

archwise, *ärch' wīz,* a. en forme de voûte.

arctic, *ärk' tĭk,* a. arctique.

ardency, *är' dĕn sĭ,* s. ardeur, véhémence, f.

ardent, *är' dĕnt,* a. (-ly, ad.) ardent, violent ‖ ardemment, passionnément.   [f.

ardour, *är' dĕr,* s. ardeur, chaleur, passion,

arduous, *är' dū ŭs,* a. (-ly, ad.) ardu ‖ rude ‖ difficile(ment).

area, *ā' rĕā,* s. aire, arène, f. ‖ surface, f. ‖ devant (de maison), m. ‖ parvis, m.

areal, *ā' rĕăl,* a. de superficie.

arena, *ă rē' nă,* s. arène, f.

arenaceous, *ăr ĕ nā' shŭs,* a. arèneux ‖ (min.) friable.

areopagus, *ăr ē ŏp' ă gŭs,* s. aréopage, m.

argent, *är' jĕnt,* a. argenté.   [f.

argentation, *är jĕn tā' shŭn,* s. argenture, f.

argil, *är' jĭl,* s. argile, f.

argonaut, *är' gō nŏut,* s. argonaute, m.

argosy, *är' gō sĭ,* s. galère, f.

argue, *är' gū,* v. a. & n. argumenter, disputer, plaider ‖ accuser ‖ to ~ with oneself, raisonner en soi-même.

arguer, *är' gū ĕr,* s. argumentateur, controversiste, m.

argument, *är' gū mĕnt,* s. argument, m. ‖ discussion, f. ‖ sujet, m. ‖ to hold an ~, soutenir une discussion.

argumentative, *är gū mĕn' tă tĭv,* a. qui contient des arguments ‖ disposé à argumenter ‖ -ly, ad. comme argument.

arian, *ā' rĭ ăn,* s. arien, m.

arid, *är' ĭd,* a. aride, sec.

aridity, *ă rĭd' ĭ tĭ,* s. aridité, sécheresse, f.

arietta, *ä rĭ ĕt' tă,* s. ariette, f.

aright, *ă rīt',* ad. droit, bien.

arise, *ă rīz',* v. n. ir. s'élever, s'élever contre ‖ provenir.

aristocracy, *ă rĭs tŏk' ră sĭ,* s. aristocratie, f.

aristocrat, *ă' rĭs tŏ krăt,* s. aristocrate, m.

aristocratical, *ä rĭs tŏ krăt' ĭk,* a. (-ally, ad.) aristocratique(ment).

arithmetic, *ă rĭth' mĕ tĭk,* s. arithmétique, f. ‖ mental ~, calcul de tête, m.

arithmetical, *ă rĭth mĕt' ĭ kăl,* a.(-ly, ad.) arithmétique(ment).

arithmetician, *ă rĭth mĕ tĭsh' ăn,* s. arithméticien, m.

ark, *ärk,* s. arche, f. ‖ ~ of the covenant, arche d'alliance, f.

arm, *ärm,* s. bras, m. ‖ branche (d'un arbre) ‖ arme, f. ‖ ~ in ~, bras dessous, bras dessous ‖ at ~'s length, à la distance des bras ‖ to fold one's ~s, croiser les bras ‖ to hold out one's ~s, tendre les bras ‖ ~-chair, s. fauteuil, m. ‖ ~-hole, s. aisselle, f. ‖ emmanchure, f.

arm, *ärm,* v. a. (& n.) (s')armer.

Armada, *är mä' dă,* s. armada, f.

armadillo, *är mă dĭl' lō,* s. armadille, f. ‖ tatou, m.

armament, *är' mă mĕnt,* s. armement, m.

armature, *är' mă tūr,* s. armure, f. ‖ (arch.) armature, f.   [one-~, manchot.

armed, *ärmd,* a. armé ‖ qui a les bras ...‖

armful, *ärm' fōŏl,* s. brassée, f.

armillary, *är' mĭl lĕr ĭ,* a. armillaire.

armistice, *är' mĭs tĭs,* s. armistice, trève, f.

armless, *ärm' lĕs,* a. sans bras ‖ sans armes.   [petit bras de mer, m.

armlet, *ärm' lĕt,* s. brassard, bracelet, m. ‖

armorial, *är mō' rĭ ăl,* a. armorial ‖ ~ bearings, s. pl. armoiries, f. pl.

armorist, *är' mō rĭst,* s. armoriste, m.

armour, *är' mĕr,* s. armure, f. ‖ chain ~, cotte d'armes, f. ‖ suit of ~, armure complète ‖ to case in ~, cuirasser ‖ ~-bearer, s. écuyer, m.   [blindé, cuirassé.

armoured, *är' mĕrd,* a. vêtu d'armure ‖

armourer, *är' mĕr ĕr,* s. armurier, m.

armoury, *är' mĕr ĭ,* s. arsenal, m. ‖ salle d'armes, f. ‖ armure, f. ‖ armoiries, f. pl.

arms, *ärmz,* s. pl. armes, f. pl. ‖ men at ~, s. pl. gens d'armes, m. pl. ‖ small-arms menues ‖ fire-~, armes à feu ‖ to beat to ~, battre le rappel ‖ ground ~ ! (re)posez (vos) armes !

army, *är' mĭ,* s. armée, f. ‖ standing ~, armée permanente, f.   [arnique, f.

arnica, *är' nĭ kă,* s. (bot.) arnica, m.

aroma, *ă rō' mă,* s. arome, m.

aromatic, *ăr ō măt' ĭk,* a. aromatique.

around, *ă rŏwnd',* pr. & ad. autour de, en rond, en cercle.   [exciter.

arouse, *ă rŏwz',* v. a. soulever ‖ éveiller,

arpeggio, *är pĕd' jō,* s. (mus.) arpège, arpègement, m.

arquebuse, *är' kĕ bōŏz,* s. arquebuse, f.

arquebusier, *är' kĕ bōŏ zēr',* s. arquebusier, m.   [busier, m.

arrack, *är' răk,* s. arack, m.   [busier, m.

arraign, *är răn',* v. a. arranger, rédiger ‖ accuser.   [f.

arraignment, *är răn' mĕnt,* s. accusation,

arrange, *är rānj',* v. a. arranger, mettre en ordre ‖ ~, v. n. s'arranger.

arrangement, *är rānj' mĕnt,* s. arrangement, m. ‖ disposition, f. ‖ to come to an ~ with, s'arranger avec.

arrant, *är' rănt,* a. insigne, fieffé, infâme.

arras, *är' răs,* s. tapisserie, f.

array, *är rā',* s. ordre de bataille ‖ rang, m., rangée, f. ‖ vêtement, m. ‖ atours, m. pl. ‖ liste des jurés, f.

array, *är rā',* v. a. mettre en ordre de bataille ‖ vêtir.   [tirages, m. pl.

arrear(s), *är rēr'(s),* s. arrière, m. ‖ arrest,

arrest, *är rĕst',* s. arrêt, m., saisie, arrestation, f. ‖ to place under ~, mettre aux arrêts.

arrest, *är rĕst',* v. a. arrêter, saisir, retenir.

arrival, *är rī' văl,* s. arrivée, f. ‖ (mar.) arrivage, m. ‖ list of ~s, liste des étrangers, présence, f.

arrive, *är rīv',* v. n. arriver, parvenir à.

---

arrogance, *ăr′rō găns*, s. arrogance, f.
arrogant, *ăr′rō gănt*, a. arrogant, in-
  solent || -ly, ad. arrogamment.
arrogate, *ăr′rō găt*, v. a. arroger, usurper.
arrogation, *ăr′rō gā′ shŭn*, s. prétention, f.
arrow, *ăr′rō*, s. flèche, f. || ~-grass, s.
  (bot.) troscart, m. || ~-root, s. arrow-
  root, m.
arrowy, *ăr′rō ĭ*, a. en forme de flèche.
arsenal, *ăr′sĕ năl*, s. arsenal, m.
arsenic, *ăr′sĕ nĭk*, s. arsenic, m.
arsenical, *ăr sĕn′ĭ kăl*, a. arsenical. [f.
arson, *ăr′sŏn*, s. incendie par malveillance,
art, *ărt*, s. art, m. || habileté, f., artifice,
  m. || the fine —s, les beaux arts || ~-
  union, s. société d'amis des arts, f.
arterial, *ăr tē′rĭ ăl*, a. artériel.
artery, *ăr′tĕr ĭ*, s. artère, f.
artesian, *ăr tē′zhĭ ăn*, a. artésien.
artful, *ărt′fōōl*, a. (-ly, ad.) fait avec art ||
  artificieux, || rusé || artistement.
artfulness, *ărt′fōōl nĕs*, s. habileté,
  adresse, f.
artichoke, *ăr′tĭ chōk*, s. artichaut, m. ||
  Jerusalem ~, topinambour, m.
article, *ăr′tĭ kl*, s. article, m. || condition,
  stipulation, f. || substance, matière, f. ||
  leading-~, s. (des journaux) article de
  fond, premier Paris, premier Londres, etc.,
  m.
article, *ăr′tĭ kl*, v. a. & n. articuler || en-
  gager || stipuler || mettre comme clerc.
articled, *ăr′tĭ kld*, a. apprenti. [stipuler.
articulate, *ăr tĭk′ū lăt*, v. a. articuler ||
articulate, *ăr tĭk′ū lăt*, a. articulé || -ly,
  ad. distinctement || article par article.
articulation, *ăr tĭk ū lā′shŭn*, s. articula-
  tion f. || jointure des os, f.
artifice, *ăr′tĭ fĭs*, s. artifice, m. || fraude, f.
artificer, *ăr tĭf′ĭ sĕr*, s. artisan, ouvrier, m.
artificial, *ăr tĭ fĭsh′ăl*, a. (-ly, ad.) arti-
  ficiel || avec art.   [ficiel, m.
artificiality, *ăr tĭ fĭsh ĭ ăl′ĭ tĭ*, s. état arti-
artillerist, *ăr tĭl′lĕr ĭst*, artilleryman,
  ăr tĭl′lĕr ĭ măn, s. artilleur, m.
artillery, *ăr tĭl′lĕr ĭ*, s. artillerie, f. ||
  heavy ~, s. grosse artillerie, f. || horse
  ~, s. artillerie à cheval, f. || ~-practice,
  s. cannonade, f.
artisan, *ăr′tĭ zăn*, s. artisan, artiste, m.
artist, *ăr′tĭst*, s. artiste, m.
artistic, *ăr tĭs′tĭk*, a. artistique || -ally,
  ad. artistement.   [naïvement.
artless, *ărt′lĕs*, a. sans art || -ly, ad.
artlessness, *ărt′lĕs nĕs*, s. simplicité,
  naïveté, f.
arum, *ā′rŭm*, s. (bot.) arum, gouet, m.
as, *ăz*, c. comme, aussi, que, selon que,
  suivant, tandis que, puisque || ~ for, ~ to,
  quant à || ~ soon ~, aussitôt que || ~ it
  were, pour ainsi dire || ~ though,
  comme si || ~ yet, jusqu'ici. [fœtida, f.
asafœtida, *ăs à fĕt′ĭ dă*, s. (méd.) assa
asbestos, *ăs bĕs′tŏs*, s. asbeste, amiante, m.
ascend, *ăs sĕnd′*, v. a. & n. monter, s'élever.
ascendant, *ăs sĕnd′ănt*, s. ascendant, m. ||
  dessus, m. || supériorité, f.

ascendant, *ăs sĕnd′ănt*, a. supérieur || (jur.)
  ascendant || to be in the ~, prédominer ||
  s'accroître.
ascendency, *ăs sĕnd′ĕn sĭ*, s. supériorité,
  f., pouvoir, m., hauteur, f. || to gain an
  ~ over, prendre le dessus sur.
ascension, *ăs sĕn′shŭn*, s. ascension, f.
ascent, *ăs sĕnt′*, s. montée, f. || élévation, f.
ascertain, *ăs sĕr tān′*, v. a. assurer, s'assurer de, prouver, constater, reconnaître,
  vérifier || régler.
ascetic, *ăs sĕt′ĭk*, s. ascète, m.
ascetic, *ăs sĕt′ĭk*, a. ascétique.
asceticism, *ăs sĕt′ĭ sĭzm*, s. ascétisme, m.
ascribable, *ăs krī′bă bl*, a. attribuable.
ascribe, *ăs krīb′*, v. a. attribuer.
ash, *ăsh*, s. frène, m. || mountain ~, s.
  sorbier des oiseaux, m. || cigar ~, cendres
  de tabac || ~-hole, s. cendrier, m. || ~-
  pan, ~-pit, s. cendrier, m. || ~-Wednes-
  day, s. mercredi des Cendres, m.
ashamed, *ă shāmd′*, a. honteux, confus.
ashen, *ăsh′ĕn*, a. de frène.
ashes, *ăsh′ĕz*, s. pl. cendres, f.pl., cendre, f.
ashore, *ă shōr′*, ad. à terre || to get ~,
  débarquer || to run ~, (mar.) faire côte.
ashy, *ăsh′ĭ*, a. cendreux || cendré.
aside, *ă sīd′*, ad. de côté, à part || to draw
  ~, tirer à l'écart || to lay, put, set ~,
  mettre de côté || to turn ~, (se) détourner.
asinine, *ăs′ĭ nīn*, a. d'âne.
ask, *ăsk*, v. a. demander, réclamer || inter-
  roger || to ~ out, inviter.
askance, *ăs kăns′*, ad. obliquement, de
askew, *ă skū′*, ad. de biais.   [travers.
aslant, *ă slănt′*, ad. obliquement, de côté.
asleep, *ă slēp′*, ad. endormi || fast ~, pro-
  fondément endormi || to fall ~, s'endormir.
aslope, *ă slōp′*, ad. en pente.
asp, *ăsp*, s. aspic, m. || (bot.) tremble, m.
asparagus, *ăs păr′ă gŭs*, s. asperge, f.
aspect, *ăs′pĕkt*, s. aspect, m., mine, f.,
  air, m. || rapport, m., exposition, f.
aspen, *ăs′pĕn*, s. tremble, m.
aspen, *ăs′pĕn*, a. de tremble.
asperity, *ăs pĕr′ĭ tĭ*, s. aspérité, âpreté, f.
asperse, *ăs pĕrs′*, v. a. asperger || diffamer,
  calomnier.   [diffamation, f.
aspersion, *ăs pĕr′shŭn*, s. aspersion, f. ||
asphalt(um), *ăs făl′t(ŭm)*, s. asphalte, m.
asphodel, *ăs′fō dĕl*, s. (bot.) asphodèle, m.
asphyxia, *ăs fĭk′sĭ ă*, s. asphyxie, f.
asphyxiated, *ăs fĭks′ĭ ā tĕd*, a. (méd.)
  asphyxié.
aspirant, *ăs pī′rănt*, s. aspirant, m.
aspirate, *ăs′pĭ răt*, s. (gr.) esprit rude, m.
aspirate, *ăs′pĭ răt*, v. a. aspirer.
aspiration, *ăs pĭ rā′shŭn*, s. aspiration, f.,
  désir ardent, m.   [prétendre (à).
aspire, *ăs pīr′*, v. n. souhaiter ardemment,
aspiring, *ăs pī′rĭng*, a. ambitieux.
ass, *ăs*, s. âne, m. || lourdaud, m. || she-~,
  ânesse, f. || jack-~, s. bourriquet, m. ||
  ~'s foal, s. ânon, m. || ~-driver, s.
  ânier, m.
assail, *ăs săl′*, v. a. assaillir, attaquer.
assailable, *ăs săl′ă bl*, a. attaquable.

assailant, *ăs săl'ănt*, assailer, *ăs săl'ĕr*, s. assaillant, agresseur, m.

assassin, *ăs săs'sĭn*, s. assassin, m.

assassinate, *ăs săs'sĭ năt*, v. a. assassiner, égorger. [sassinat, m.

assassination, *ăs săs sĭ nā'shŭn*, s. assassinat, m.

assault, *ăs săwlt'*, s. assaut, m., attaque, f. ‖ aggravated ~, ~ and battery, (jur.) voies de fait, f. pl. ‖ to take by ~, (mil.) prendre d'assaut.

assault, *ăs săwlt'*, v. a. attaquer ‖ (jur.) commettre des voies de fait sur.

assay, *ăs să'*, s. essai, examen, m.

assay, *ăs să'*, v. a. essayer, eprouver.

assayer, *ăs să'ĕr*, s. essayeur, m.

assemblage, *ăs sĕm'blăj*, s. assemblage, m.

assemble, *ăs sĕm'bl*, v. a. (& n.) (s')assembler.

assembly, *ăs sĕm'blĭ*, s. assemblée, réunion, f. ‖ collège, m. ‖ ~-room, s. salle de réunion, f. [sanction, f.

assent, *ăs sĕnt'*, s. consentement, m. ‖

assent, *ăs sĕnt'*, v. n. consentir à, approuver. [d'assentiment.

assentingly, *ăs sĕnt'ĭng lĭ*, ad. en signe

assert, *ăs sĕr'*, v. a. affirmer, maintenir, défendre ‖ revendiquer.

assertion, *ăs sĕr'shŭn*, s. assertion, défense, f. [sertif.

assertive, *ăs sĕr'tĭv*, a. confirmatif ‖ as-

assess, *ăs sĕs'*, v. a. taxer, imposer.

assessable, *ăs sĕs'ă bl*, a. imposable.

assessed, *ăs sĕst'*, a. direct (impôts).

assessment, *ăs sĕs'mĕnt*, s. taxe, imposition, f. ‖ recensement, m. ‖ cadastre, m.

assessor, *ăs sĕs'ĕr*, s. assesseur, m.

assets, *ăs'sĕts*, s. pl. (jur.) masse active, f.

asseverate, *ăs sĕv'ĕr ăt*, v. a. affirmer solennellement. [mation solennelle, f.

asseveration, *ăs sĕv ĕr ā'shŭn*, s. affir-

assiduity, *ăs sĭ dū'ĭ tĭ*, s. assiduité, f.

assiduous, *ăs sĭd'ŭ ŭs*, a. assidu, appliqué ‖ -ly, ad. avec assiduité.

assign, *ăs sīn'*, v. a. assigner, désigner, destiner ‖ (jur.) transférer.

assignable, *ăs sīn'ă bl*, a. assignable ‖ cessible ‖ qui peut être determiné.

assignation, *ăs sĭg nā'shŭn*, s. assignation, cession, f. ‖ rendez-vous, m.

assignee, *ăs sĭ nē'*, s. délégué, m. ‖ cessionnaire, m. ‖ (in bankruptcy) syndic, m.

assigner, *ăs sīn'ĕr*, s. commettant, m.

assignment, *ăs sīn'mĕnt*, s. assignation, f. ‖ cession, f. [rendre semblable.

assimilate, *ăs sĭm'ĭ lăt*, v. a. assimiler.

assimilation, *ăs sĭm ĭ lā'shŭn*, s. assimilation, f.

assist, *ăs sĭst'*, v. a. assister, aider. [f.

assistance, *ăs sĭs'tăns*, s. assistance, aide,

assistant, *ăs sĭs'tănt*, s. aide, adjoint, m.

assistant, *ăs sĭs'tănt*, a. assistant, aidant ‖ ~ locomotive, s. locomotive auxiliaire, f.

assize, *ăs sīz'*, v. a. taxer.

assizes, *ăs sīz'ĕz*, s. pl. assises, f. pl. ‖ cour de justice, f. ‖ ordonnance, f.

associate, *ăs sō'shĭ ăt*, s. associé, compagnon, m.

associate, *ăs sō'shĭ ăt*, v. a. (& n.) (s')associer. [fédéré.

associate, *ăs sō'shĭ ăt*, a. associé, confédéré.

association, *ăs sō shĭ ā'shŭn*, s. association, alliance, f. ‖ ~s, pl. idées, notions, f. pl. ‖ souvenirs, m. pl.

assonance, *ăs'sō năns*, s. assonance, f.

assort, *ăs sōrt'*, v. a. assortir. [m.

assortment, *ăs sōrt'mĕnt*, s. assortiment,

assuage, *ăs swāj'*, v. a. (& n.) (s')apaiser.

assuagement, *ăs swāj'mĕnt*, s. adoucissement, soulagement, m.

assume, *ăs sūm'*, v. a. & n. prendre, s'attribuer ‖ être arrogant ‖ it is –d that, il est généralement reçu que.

assuming, *ăs sū'mĭng*, a. prétentieux ‖ tranchant ‖ ~ that, admettons que, posons le cas que. [f. ‖ Assomption, f.

assumption, *ăs sŭm'shŭn*, s. présomption,

assurance, *ă shō'răns*, s. assurance, confiance, sécurité, conviction, f.

assure, *ă shōr'*, v. a. assurer, garantir.

assuredly, *ă shō'rĕd lĭ*, ad. certainement.

aster, *ăs'tĕr*, s. (bot.) aster, m. ‖ China ~, reine-marguerite, f.

asterisk, *ăs'tĕr ĭsk*, s. astérisque, m.

astern, *ă stĕrn'*, ad. (mar.) en poupe ‖ arrière.

asthma, *ăst'mă*, s. asthme, m. [arrière.

asthmatic(al), *ăst măt'ĭk (ăl)*, a. asthmatique.

astir, *ă stĕr'*, ad. agité, en émoi. [tique.

astonish, *ăs tŏn'ĭsh*, v. a. étonner, surprendre. [namment.

astonishingly, *ăs tŏn'ĭsh ĭng lĭ*, ad. étonnamment.

astonishment, *ăs tŏn'ĭsh mĕnt*, s. étonnement, m., surprise, f. [interloquer.

astound, *ă stŏwnd'*, v. a. étonner, ahurir, interloquer.

astraddle, *ă străd'dl*, ad. à califourchon.

astragal, *ăs'trä găt*, s. (arch.) astragale, m.

astral, *ăs'trăl*, a. astral.

astray, *ă strä'*, ad. hors du chemin.

astriction, *ă strĭk'shŭn*, s. (méd.) compression, f. ‖ constriction, f. ‖ astriction, f.

astride, *ă strīd'*, ad. à califourchon ‖ les jambes écarquillées.

astringent, *ă strĭn'jĕnt*, s. astringent, m.

astrolabe, *ăs'trō lăb*, s. (astr.) astrolabe, m.

astrologer, *ăs trŏl'ō jĕr*, s. astrologue, m.

astrologic(al), *ăs trō lŏj'ĭk (ăl)*, a. astrologique.

astrology, *ăs trŏl'ō jĭ*, s. astrologie, f.

astronomer, *ăs trŏn'ō mĕr*, s. astronome, m. [tronomique.

astronomic(al), *ăs trō nŏm'ĭk (ăl)*, a. astronomy, *ăs trŏn'ō mĭ*, s. astronomie, f.

astute, *ăs tūt'*, a. (-ly, ad.) fin, rusé ‖ avec ruse. [deux.

asunder, *ă sŭn'dĕr*, ad. séparément ‖ en

asylum, *ă sī'lŭm*, s. asile, refuge, m. ‖ hospice, m. ‖ lunatic ~, maison d'aliénés, f. ‖ private lunatic ~, maison de santé.

at, at, pr. à, dans ‖ en ‖ sur ‖ après ‖ contre ‖ ~ home, au logis ‖ what are you ~? que faites-vous? ‖ to be hard ~ a thing, travailler ferme à qc. ‖ he is ~ it! l'y voilà !

atheism, *ā'thē ĭzm*, s. athéisme, m. [voilà !

atheist, *ā'thē ĭst*, s. athée, m.

atheistic, *ă thē ĭs' tĭk*, a. athéistique.

Athenæum, *ăth ĕ nē' ŭm*, s. athénée, m.

athirst, *ă thĕrst'*, ad. altéré.

athlete, *ăth' lēt*, s. athlète, m.

athletic, *ăth lĕt' ĭk*, a. athlétique, robuste.

athletics, *ăth lĕt' ĭks*, s. pl. athlétique, f.

athwart, *ă thwaŭrt'*, pr. & ad. à travers ‖ à l'encontre de.

atilt, *ă tĭlt'*, ad. en joutant, en combattant.

atlas, *ăt' lăs*, s. atlas, m. ‖ satin, m.

atmosphere, *ăt' mŏs fēr*, s. atmosphère, f.

atmospheric, *ăt' mŏs fĕr' ĭk*, a. atmosphérique.

atom, *ăt' ŏm*, s. atome, m. [sphérique.

atomic(al), *ă tŏm' ĭk (ăl)*, a. atomique.

atone, *ă tōn'*, v. a. expier ‖ racheter.

atonement, *ă tōn' mĕnt*, s. explation, f.

atop, *ă tŏp'*, ad. au haut, au sommet.

atrabilious, *ăt ră bĭl' ĭ ŭs*, a. atrabilaire, mélancolique. [(ment).

atrocious, *ă trō' shŭs*, a. (-ly, ad.) atroce

atrocity, *ă trŏs' ĭ tĭ*, s. atrocité, cruauté, f.

atrophy, *ăt' rŏ fĭ*, s. (méd.) atrophie, f.

attach, *ăt tăch'*, v. a. attacher ‖ arrêter, saisir, faire prisonnier ‖ **to be -ed to**, se rattacher à.

attachment, *ăt tăch' mĕnt*, s. attachement, m., affection, f. ‖ saisie, f., arrêt, m.

attack, *ăt tăk'*, s. attaque, f., assaut, m. ‖

attack, *ăt tăk'*, v. a. attaquer, assaillir.

attain, *ăt tān'*, v. a. atteindre, obtenir ‖ parvenir. [teindre.

attainable, *ăt tān' ă bl*, a. qu'on peut at-

attainder, *ăt tān' dĕr*, s. conviction d'un crime, f. ‖ mort civile, f. ‖ souillure, f.

attainment, *ăt tān' mĕnt*, s. acquisition, f. ‖ talent, m. ‖ -s, pl. connaissances, f. pl.

attaint, *ăt tānt'*, s. atteinte, f. ‖ tache, flétrissure, f. [souiller.

attaint, *ăt tānt'*, v. a. déclarer coupable ‖

attar *ăt' tär* (of roses), s. essence de roses, f.

attempt, *ăt tĕmt'*, s. essai, m. ‖ attaque, f. ‖ attentat, m. ‖ **to perish in the ~**, mourir à la peine.

attempt, *ăt tĕmt'*, v. a. & n. tenter ‖ attaquer ‖ **to ~ one's life**, attenter à la vie de qn.

attend, *ăt tĕnd'*, v. a. & n. servir, attendre ‖ assister ‖ accompagner ‖ soigner ‖ exaucer ‖ ouvrir ‖ faire attention ‖ s'attacher ‖ **to ~ to business**, vaquer aux affaires.

attendance, *ăt tĕn' dăns*, s. service, m. ‖ soins, m. pl., attention, f. ‖ suite, f. ‖ **in ~**, de service.

attendant, *ăt tĕn' dănt*, s. domestique, m.

attendant, *ăt tĕn' dănt*, a. dépendant(de) ‖ **to be ~ upon**, accompagner.

attention, *ăt tĕn' shŭn*, s. attention, f.

attentive, *ăt tĕn' tĭv*, a. attentif ‖ -ly, ad. avec attention. [diminuer.

attenuate, *ăt tĕn' ū ăt*, v. a. atténuer,

attenuation, *ăt tĕn ū ā' shŭn*, s. atténuation, f.

attest, *ăt tĕst'*, v. a. attester, certifier.

attestation, *ăt tĕs ta' shŭn*, s. attestation, f.

attic, *ăt' tĭk*, s. attique, m., mansarde, f.

attic(al), *ăt' tĭk(ăl)*, a. attique ‖ classique.

attire, *ăt tīr'*, s. vêtement, ornement, m., parure, f.

attire, *ăt tīr'*, v. a. vêtir, parer.

attitude, *ăt' ĭ tūd*, s. attitude, posture, f.

attitudinise, *ăt tĭ dū' dĭ nĭz*, v. n. poser.

attorney, *ăt tĕr' nĭ*, s. procureur, m. ‖ avoué, fondé de pouvoir, m. ‖ **~-general**, s. procureur du roi, f. ‖ **power of ~**, s. procuration, f.

attract, *ăt trăkt'*, v. a. attirer, entraîner.

attraction, *ăt trăk' shŭn*, s. attraction, f. ‖ (fig.) attrait, m.

attractive, *ăt trăk' tĭv*, a. attractif ‖ -ly, ad. d'une manière attractive.

attributable, *ăt trĭb' ū tă bl*, a. attribuable.

attribute, *ăt' trĭ būt*, s. (gr.) attribut, m.

attribute, *ăt trĭb' ūt*, v. a. attribuer.

attrition, *ăt trĭsh' ŭn*, s. attrition, f.

attune, *ăt tūn'*, v. a. accorder.

auburn, *aŭ bĕrn*, a. brun obscur, châtain clair. [l'encan, f.

auction, *aŭk' shŭn*, s. vente à l'enchère, à

auctioneer, *aŭk shŭn ēr'*, s. commissaire-priseur, m.

audacious, *aŭ dā' shŭs*, a. audacieux, effronté ‖ -ly, ad. audacieusement.

audacity, *aŭ dăs' ĭ tĭ*, s. audace, impudence, f. [intelligible.

audible, *aŭ' dĭ bl*, a. qu'on peut entendre,

audibly, *aŭ' dĭ blĭ*, ad. à haute voix.

audience, *aŭ' dĭ ĕns*, s. audience, f. ‖ auditoire, m.

audit, *aŭ' dĭt*, s. audition, déposition, f. ‖ examen d'un compte, m. ‖ **~-office**, s. cour des comptes, f. [apurer.

audit, *aŭ' dĭt*, v. a. examiner des comptes,

auditing, *aŭ' dĭt ĭng*, s. apurement, m.

auditor, *aŭ' dĭ tĕr*, s. auditeur, m.

auditory, *aŭ' dĭ tĕr ĭ*, s. auditoire, m., assemblée, f.

auditory, *aŭ' dĭ tĕr ĭ*, a. auditif.

auger, *aŭ' gĕr*, s. tarière, f., vilebrequin, m.

aught, *aŭt*, pn. quelque chose.

augment, *aŭg mĕnt'*, v. a. & n. augmenter ‖ s'accroître.

augur, *aŭ' gĕr*, v. n. augurer, conjecturer.

augury, *aŭ' gū rĭ*, s. augure, présage, m.

August, *aŭ' gŭst*, s. août, m.

august, *aŭ gŭst'*, a. auguste, majestueux, s.

auk, *aŭk*, s. pingouin, m.

aulic, *aŭ' lĭk*, a. aulique. [f.

aunt, *ănt*, s. tante, f. ‖ (cant.) entremetteuse,

aura, *aŭ' ră*, s. vapeur, f. ‖ (méd.) aura, f.

aureole, *aŭ' rē ōl*, s. auréole, f.

auricle, *aŭ' rĭ kl*, s. auricule, f. ‖ (of the heart), oreillette, f.

auricular, *aŭ rĭk' ū lĕr*, a. (-ly, ad.) auriculaire ‖ à l'oreille.

auriferous, *aŭ rĭf' ĕr ŭs*, a. aurifère.

aurora, *aŭ rō' ră*, s. aurore, f. ‖ **~ borealis**, s. aurore boréale, f.

auscultation, *aŭs kŭl tā' shŭn*, s. (méd.) auscultation, f.

auspices, *aŭ' spĭs ĕz*, s. pl. auspices, m. pl.

auspicious, *aŭ spĭsh' ŭs*, a. propice, favorable ‖ -ly, ad. sous d'heureux auspices.

---

lāte, hăt, fär, laŭ; — hēre, gĕt, hĕr; — mīne, ĭnn; — nō, hŏt, prōve; — hŏŭ; —

austere, *áw̄ stēr'*, a. austère, sévère || -ly, ad. avec austérité. [rigueur, f.
austerity, *áw̄ stēr'ĭ tĭ*, s. austérité, sévérité,
austral, *áw̄s'trăl*, a. austral.
authentic, *áw̄ thĕn'tĭk*, a. (-ally, ad.) authentique(ment) || vrai, véritable.
authenticate, *áw̄ thĕn'tĭ kāt*, v. a. légaliser || constater.
authenticity, *áw̄ thĕn tĭs'ĭ tĭ*, s. authenauthor, *áw̄'thĕr*, s. auteur, m.   [ticité, f.
authoress, *áw̄'thĕr ĕs*, s. femme auteur, f.
authorisation, *áw̄ thŏ rĭ zā'shŭn*, s. autorisation, f., pouvoir, m.
authorise, *áw̄'thŏ rīs*, v. a. autoriser.
authoritative, *áw̄ thŏr'ĭ tā tĭv*, a. autorisé || -ly, ad. avec autorité.
authoritativeness, *áw̄ thŏr'ĭ tā tĭv nĕs*, s. air or ton d'autorité, m.
authority, *áw̄ thŏr'ĭ tĭ*, s. autorité, f. || on good ~, de bonne source.
authorship, *áw̄'thĕr shĭp*, s. qualité or profession d'auteur, f.   [biographie, f.
autobiography, *áw̄ tō bī ŏg'rā fĭ*, s. autoautocracy, *áw̄ tŏk'rā sĭ*, s. autocratie, f.
autocrat, *áw̄'tō krăt*, s. autocrate, m.
autocratic, *áw̄ tō krăt'ĭk*, a. (-ally, ad.) autocratique(ment).
autograph, *áw̄'tō grăf*, s. autographe, m.
autographic, *áw̄ tō grăf'ĭk*, a. autographique || (of letters) autographe.
automatic, *áw̄ tō măt'ĭk*, a. (-ally, ad.) automatique(ment).
automaton, *áw̄ tŏm'ă tŏn*, s. automate, m.
automobile, *áw̄ tō mō bēl*, s. automobile, f.
automobilist, *áw̄ tō mō bē'lĭst*, s. automobiliste, m. & f.
autonomous, *áw̄ tŏn'ō mŭs*, a. autonome.
autopsy, *áw̄'tŏp sĭ*, s. (méd.) autopsie, f.
autumn, *áw̄'tŭm*, s. automne, m.
autumnal, *áw̄ tŭm'năl*, a. automnal, d'automne.   [auxiliaires, f. pl.
auxiliaries, *áwg zĭl'ĭ ă rĭz*, s. pl. troupes
auxiliary, *áwg zĭl'ĭ ă rĭ*, a. auxiliaire, assistant.
avail, *ă văl'*, s. avantage, m.   [sistant.
avail, *ă văl'*, v. a. & n. servir, être utile || to ~ oneself of, profiter de.
available, *ă văl'ă bl*, a. avantageux, profitable || disponible || valable.
avalanche, *ăv'ă länsh*, s. avalanche, f.
avarice, *ăv'ă rĭs*, s. avarice, f.
avaricious, *ă vă rish'ŭs*, a. avaricieux, avare || -ly, ad. avec avarice.
avast! *ă văst'*, (mar.) baste! assez! arrête!
avaunt! *ă văhnt'*, arrière!
avenge, *ă vĕnj'*, v. a. venger, punir.
avenue, *ăv'ĕ nū*, s. avenue, f. || allée, f. ||
aver, *ă vĕr'*, v. a. affirmer.   [entrée, f.
average, *ăv'ĕr ăj*, s. (mar.) avarie, f. || terme moyen, m. || on an ~, en moyenne, l'un dans l'autre.
average, *ăv'ĕr ăj*, v.a. prendre la moyenne.
averse, *ă vĕrs'*, a. contraire || to be ~ to, avoir de l'aversion pour.
aversion, *ă vĕr'shŭn*, s. aversion, f. || to take an ~ to, prendre qn. en aversion.
avert, *ă vĕrt'*, v. a. & n. détourner || s'éloigner de.
aviary, *ā'vĭ ĕ rĭ*, s. volière, f.   [ner de.

aviation, *ā vĭ ā'shŭn*, s. aviation, f.
aviator, *ā'vĭ ā tĕr*, s. aviateur, m.
avidity, *ă vĭd'ĭ tĭ*, s. avidité, f.
avocation, *ăv ō kā'shŭn*, s. occupation, f.
avoid, *ă vŏyd'*, v. a. éviter || (jur.) décliner.
avoidable, *ă vŏyd'ă bl*, a. évitable.
avoirdupois *ă vĕr dū pŏyz'*, s. poids de seize onces à la livre.   [gner || produire.
avouch, *ă vŏwch'*, v. a. affirmer || témoiavow, *ă vŏw'*, v. a. avouer, confesser.
avowal, *ă vŏw'ăl*, s. aveu, m.
avowedly, *ă vŏw'ĕd lĭ*, ad. ouvertement.
avuncular, *ă vŭn'kū lăr*, a. qui a rapport à l'oncle ou à la tante.
await, *ă wāt'*, v. a. attendre.
awake, *ă wāk'*, v. n. ir. s'éveiller.
awake, *ă wāk'*, a. éveillé || vigilant.
awaken, *ă wā'kĕn*, v. a. éveiller || réveiller.
awak(en)ing, *ă wāk'(ĕn)ĭng*, s. réveil, m.
award, *ă wáwrd'*, s. jugement, m.
award, *ă wáwrd'*, v. a. & n. adjuger || prononcer un jugement.
awarder, *ă wáwrd'ĕr*, s. arbitre, m.
aware, *ă wār'*, a. vigilant, attentif || to be ~ that, savoir que.
away, *ă wā'*, a. & ad. absent || loin || ~! hors d'ici! || to carry ~, emporter || to fly ~, s'envoler || to go ~, s'en aller || to take ~, enlever || to send ~, renvoyer.
awe, *áw*, s. crainte, f., respect, m.
awe, *áw*, v. a. inspirer du respect, tenir dans l'assujettissement.
awesome, *áw'sŭm*, awful, *áw'fŏŏl*, a.(-ly, ad.) imposant, respectable || terrible(ment) ||
awfulness, *áw'fŏŏl nĕs*, s. caractère terrible. [(fig.) très.   [rible, m.
awhile, *ă whīl'*, ad. pendant quelque temps.
awkward, *áwk'wĕrd*, a. (-ly, ad.) gauche || grossier || maladroit(ement) || lourdement.   [dresse, gaucherie, f.
awkwardness, *áwk'wĕrd nĕs*, s. maladawl, *áwl*, s. alêne, f.
awn, *áwn*, s. barbe, arête, f.
awning, *áwn'ĭng*, s. tente, f. || banne, f. || bâche, f.
awry, *ă rī'*, ad. de travers, contrefait.
axe, *ăks*, s. hache, cognée, f.   [f.
axiom, *ăk'sĭ ŭm*, s. axiome, m., maxime,
axle(-tree), *ăk'sl(-trē)*, s. essieu, m.
ay(e), *āĭ*, s. voix pour, f. || boule blanche, f.
ay(e), *āĭ*, ad. oui, assurément.
ayah, *ā'yă*, s. bonne d'enfant or femme de chambre indienne, f.
azalea, *ăz ăl'ē ă*, s. (bot.) azalée, f.
azimuth, *ăz'ĭ mŭth*, s. (astr.) azimut, m.
azote, *ăz'ōt*, s. azote, m.
azure, *ā'zhōōr*, s. azur, m.
azure, *ā'zhōōr*, a. azuré.

B.

b, bémol, m. || (fig.) punaise, f. || ~ sharp, bécarre, m.   [ès lettres, m.
B.A. = Bachelor of Arts, s. bachelier
baa, *bá*, v. n. bêler.

babble, *băb' bl*, s. babil, m.
babble, *băb' bl*, v. n. babiller, bavarder, balbutier || (fig.) gazouiller.
babbler, *bab' blŭr*, s. babillard, bavard, m.
babbling, *băb' bling*, s. babil, m || gazouillement, m.
babe, *băb*, s. bambin, m.   [lement, m.
baboon, *băbōn'*, s. babouin, m.
baby, *bā' bĭ*, s. petit enfant, m. || poupon, m. || ~-linen, layette, f.
baby, *bā' bĭ*, a. d'enfant.
babyhood, *bā' bĭ hŏŏd*, s. enfance, f.
babyish, *bā' bĭ ĭsh*, a. enfantin || d'enfant.
bacchanal, *băk' ă năl*, s. bacchanale, f.
bacchanalian, *băk ă nā' lĭ ăn*; a. bacchique.
bachelor, *băch' ĕ lŭr*, s. célibataire, garçon, m. || bachelier, m. || -'s button, s. (bot.) bluet, m.   [m. || baccalauréat, m.
bachelorship, *băch' ĕ lŭr shĭp*, s. célibat, m.
back, *băk*, s. dos, derrière, m. || revers, dossier, m. || fond, m. || ~ of a hare, râble de lièvre, m. || with one's ~ to the engine (horses, etc.), en arrière || to turn one's ~ on one, tourner le dos à qn. || ~-door, s. porte de derrière, f. || ~-number, s. numéro arriéré d'un journal, m. || ~-payment, s. arriéré, m. || ~-rent, s. loyer arriéré, m. || ~-stay, s. (mar.) galhauban, m. || ~-train, s. (rail.) train de retour, m.
back, *băk*, v. a. & n. monter *or* dresser un cheval || appuyer || faire reculer || to ~ out, revenir sur ses pas.
back, *băk*, ad. en arrière || en retour.
backbite, *băk' bĭt*, v. a. calomnier.
backblow, *băk' blō*, s. coup de revers, m.
backboard, *băk' bōrd*, s. dossier, m.
backbone, *băk' bōn*, s. épine du dos, f. || to the ~, (fig.) jusqu'à la moelle des os.
backed, *băkt*, a. soutenu, appuyé.
backer, *băk' ĕr*, s. partisan, second, m. || parieur pour, m.
backgammon, *băk' găm mŭn*, s. trictrac, m.
background, *băk' grŏŭnd*, s. fond, enfoncement, m. || in the ~, à l'ombre.
backhanded, *băk' hănd ĕd*, a. donné avec le revers de la main.
backing, *băk' ĭng*, s. massif, m.
backside, *băk' sĭd*, s. derrière, m.
backslide, *băk' slĭd*, v. n. apostasier.
backslider, *băk' slī dĕr*, m. apostat, m.
backsliding, *băk' slī dĭng*, s. éloignement (du Seigneur), m. || infidélité, apostasie, f.
backstairs, *băk' stărz*, s. pl. escalier dérobé, m.   [pide || -ly, ad. à contre-cœur.
backward, *băk' wĕrd*, a. paresseux, stupide || -ly, ad. à contre-cœur.
backwardness, *băk' wĕrd nĕs*, s. paresse, lenteur, répugnance, f.
backward(s), *băk' wĕrd(z)*, ad. en arrière, à la renverse || ~ and forwards, en long et en large.
backwoodsman, *băk' wŏŏds măn*, s. habitant des fôrets occidentales de l'Amérique,
bacon, *bā' kŭn*, s. lard, m.   [m.
bad, *băd*, a. mauvais, méchant || too ~! trop fort! || to go to the ~, filer un mauvais coton || -ly, ad. mal || grandement.
badge, *băj*, s. marque, f., signe, m.

badger, *băj' ĕr*, s. blaireau, m.
badger, *băj' ĕr*, v. a. harceler || pourchasser.
badness, *băd' nĕs*, s. mauvais état, m. || méchanceté, f.
baffle, *băf' fl*, v. a. déjouer, éluder, frustrer.
bag, *băg*, s. sac, m. || poche, f. || to make a good ~, faire bonne chasse.
bag, *băg*, v. a. & n. mettre dans un sac || blouser (au billard) || s'enfler.
bagatelle-board, *băg' ă tĕl bōrd*, s. table de bagatelle, f.
baggage, *băg' găj*, s. bagage, m. || femme de mauvaise vie, f. || to be off bag and ~, plier bagage.
bagging, *băg' gĭng*, s. tolle à sac, f.
baggy, *băg' ĭ*, a. comme un sac, ample.
bagman, *băg' măn*, s. colporteur, m.
bagnio, *băn' yō*, s. bains, m. pl. || bordel, m.
bagpipe, *băg' pĭp*, s. cornemuse, f.
bagpiper, *băg' pĭp ĕr*, s. joueur de cornemuse, m.
bail, *bāl*, s. caution, f.   [muse, m.
bail, *bāl*, v. a. cautionner.
bailee, *bāl ē'*, s. dépositaire, f.
bailiff, *bāl' ĭf*, s. huissier, m. || garde du commerce, m. || sous-intendant, m. || bailli, m. || water-~, officier de port, m.
bailiwick, *bāl' ĭ wĭk*, s. bailliage, m.
bairn, *bărn*, s. (écossais) enfant, m.
bait, *băt*, s. appât, m., amorce, f. || rafraîchissement, m. || ground-~, s. lotte franche, f.
bait, *băt*, v. a. & n. amorcer || appâter, leurrer || s'arrêter (pour prendre des rafraîchissements).
baiting, *băt' ĭng*, s. amorce, f.
bake, *băk*, v. a. & n. cuire au four || faire le pain, boulanger.
bakehouse, *băk' hŏws*, bakery, *bā' kĕr ĭ*, s. boulangerie, f.
baker, *bā' kĕr*, s. boulanger, m.
balance, *băl' ăns*, s. balance, f. || équilibre, m. || balancier (d'une montre), m. || surplus d'un compte, m., solde d'un compte, f. || to strike a ~, établir la balance || to turn the ~, faire pencher la balance || ~-sheet, s. bilan, m.   [hésiter.
balance, *băl' ăns*, v. a. & n. peser, balancer.
balancing-pole, *băl' ăn sĭng pōl*, s. balancier, m.
balconied, *băl' kō nĭd*, a. garni de balcons.
balcony, *băl' kō nĭ*, s. balcon, m.
bald, *băwld*, a. chauve || (fig.) nu || plat || -ly, ad. nûment.
baldachin, *băl' dă kĭn*, s. baldaquin, m.
balderdash, *băwl' dĕr dăsh*, s. galimatias, coq-à-l'âne, m.
baldness, *băwld' nĕs*, s. calvitie, f.
bale, *bāl*, s. balle, f., paquet, m.
bale, *bāl*, v. a. emballer || (mar.) écoper.
balearic, *băl ē ăr' ĭk*, a. baléare.
baleful, *băl' fŏŏl*, a. (-ly, ad.) triste, funeste, fatal || d'une manière funeste.
balk, *băwk*, s. poutre, f., chevron, m. || (of land) entredeux, m. || désappointement, préjudice, m.
balk, *băwk*, v. a. désappointer, frustrer || laisser échapper, omettre.

ball, *båwl,* s. balle, boule, f. || globe, m. ||
bal, m. || masked ~, bal masqué || fancy
dress ~, bal costumé || to load with ~,
charger à balle || ~ and socket, genou,
m. || ~-cartridge, cartouche à balle, f.

ballad, *bål'låd,* s. ballade, f.

ballast, *bål'låst,* s. lest, m.

ballast, *bål'låst,* v. a. lester. [lerine, f.

ballet, *bål'lĕt,* s. ballet, m. || ~-girl, bal-

balloon, *bål lön',* s. ballon, aérostat, m.

ballot, *bål'lŏt,* s. scrutin, m. || ~-box, s.
urne du scrutin, f.

ballot, *bål'lŏt,* v. n. ballotter.

balm, *bâm,* s. baume, m. || (fig.) soulage-

balmy, *bâm'ĭ,* a. balsamique. [ment, m.

balsam, *bâwl'såm,* s. baume, m. || (bot.)
balsamine, f.

balustrade, *bål ŭs tråd',* s. balustrade, f.

bamboo, *bâm'bô,* s. bambou, m.

bamboozle, *bâm bô'zl,* v. a. ambabouiner,
fourber, tromper. [anathème, m.

ban, *bån,* s. publication de mariage, f.,

banana, *bå nå'nå,* s. banane, f.

band, *bånd,* s. lien, m. || ruban, m. || bande,
f. || bande de musiciens ambulants, f. ||
brass ~, musique d'instruments de cuivre,
f. || ~-box, s. carton, m. || ~-master, s.
(mil.) chef de musique, m.

band, *bånd,* v. a. réunir en troupe.

bandage, *bån'dåj,* s. bandage, f. || ~-
maker, s. bandagiste, m.

bandit, *bån'dĭt,* s. bandit, brigand, m.

bandog, *bån'dŏg,* s. chien d'attache, mâtin,

bandsman, *bånds'mån,* s. musicien, m. [m.

bandy, *bån'dĭ,* v. a. & n. pousser la balle,
discuter || to ~ words with, se prendre
de paroles avec.

bandy, *bån'dĭ,* a. tortu || ~-legged, bancal.

bane, *bån,* s. poison, m. || ruine, f.

baneful, *bån'fôôl,* a. (-ly, ad.) venimeux ||
destructif || mortellement.

banewort, *bån'wĕrt,* s. (bot.) morelle, f.

bang, *bång,* s. coup, m., tape, f.

bang, *bång,* v. a. rosser || fermer avec
bruit || ~ I pan!

bangle, *bång'gl,* s. paillette, f. || bracelet
indien, m. [des Indes, m.

banian-tree, *bån'yån trē,* s. (bot.) figuier

banish, *bån'ĭsh,* v. a. bannir, exiler.

banishment, *bån'ĭsh mĕnt,* s. bannissement, exil, m.

banister, *bån'ĭs tĕr,* s. rampe, f.

banjo, *bån'jō,* s. banjo, m., guitarre des
nègres, f.

bank, *bångk,* s. digue, f. || bord, rivage, m. ||
banc, m. || banque, f. || ~-book, s. carnet
de banque, m. || ~-note, s. billet de
banque, m. || ~ of issue, s. banque à
papier-monnaie, f. || ~-stock, s. action
de la banque, f. || branch ~, s. banque
succursale, f.

bank, *bångk,* v. a. terrasser || mettre de
l'argent dans une banque || to ~ with,
avoir pour banquier.

banker, *bångk'ĕr,* s. banquier, m.

banking-house, *bångk'ing hŏws,* s. maison de banque, f.

bankrupt, *bångk'rŭpt,* s. banqueroutier,
m. || (fig.) ruiné, m.

bankrupt, *bångk'rŭpt,* a. en faillite || (fig.)

bankruptcy, *bångk'rŭpt sĭ,* s. banqueroute,
faillite, f. [de mariage, m. pl.

banns, *bånz,* s. pl. (~ of marriage) bans

banquet, *bång'kwĕt,* s. banquet, festin, m.

banquet, *bång'kwĕt,* v. n. banqueter, se
régaler. [la mort, m.

banshee, *bån'shē,* s. spectre messager de

bantam, *bån'tåm,* s. bantam, m., ban-
tame, f.

banter, *bån'tĕr,* s. raillerie, plaisanterie, f.

banter, *bån'tĕr,* v. a. railler, plaisanter.

bantling, *bånt'ling,* s. poupon, m.

baptise, *båp'tiz,* v. a. baptiser.

baptism, *båp'tizm,* s. baptême, m. || cer-
tificate of ~, s. acte de baptême, extrait
baptistaire, m.

baptismal, *båp tiz'mål,* a. baptismal || ~
record, s. extrait de baptême, m.

baptist, *båp'tist,* s. baptiste, m.

baptistery, *båp'tis tĕr ĭ,* s. baptistère, m.

bar, *bår,* s. barre, barrière, f. || (mus.)
mesure, f || barreau, m. || comptoir de ca-
baret, m. || (fig.) empêchement, m. || to
be called to the ~, être appelé en
justice; passer son droit (se dit des étu-
diants) || ~-iron, s. fer en barres, m.

bar, *bår,* v. a. barrer (le chemin) || empêcher,
prohiber. [de mariage, m.

barb, *bårb,* s. barbe, f. || arête, f. || cheval

barb, *bårb,* v. a. aiguiser || barder.

barbarian, *bår bå'rĭ ån,* a. barbare, sauvage, cruel.

barbarism, *bår'bå rizm,* s. (gr.) barbarisme, m. [f.

barbarity, *bår bår'ĭ tĭ,* s. barbarie, cruauté,

barbarous, *bår'bå rŭs,* a. (-ly, ad.) bar-
bare(ment). [entier.

barbecue, *bår'bĕ kū,* v. a. faire rôtir en

barbel, *bår'bĕl,* s. barbeau, m.

barber, *bår'bĕr,* s. barbier, m. || ~'s block,
s. tête à perruque, f.

barberry, *bår'bĕr rĭ,* s. épine-vinette, f.

barbet, *bår'bĕt,* s. barbet, caniche, m.

barbican, *bår'bĭ kån,* s. barbacane, f.

bard, *bård,* s. barde, poète, m. [pouiller.

bare, *bår,* v. a. mettre à nu, découvrir, dé-

bare, *bår,* a. nu, découvert || simple || ~-ly,
ad. à nu || seulement, simplement || pauvre-
ment || à peine.

bareback, *bår'båck,* ad. à nu, à poil.

barebone, *bår'bōn,* s. squelette, m.

barefaced, *bår'fåst,* a. impudent, effronté.

barefoot(ed), *bår'fôôt(ĕd),* a. nu-pieds.

bareheaded, *bår'hĕd ĕd,* a. nu-tête.

barelegged, *bår'lĕgd,* a. nu-jambes. [f.

bareness, *bår'nĕs,* s. nudité, f. || pauvreté,

bargain, *bår'gĕn,* s. marché, contrat, m. ||
bonne affaire, f. || 'tis-a ~, c'est affaire
faite || dead ~, s. vil prix, prix dérisoire,
m. || into the ~, par dessus le marché ||
to make, strike a ~, conclure un
marché. [chander.

bargain, *bår'gĕn,* v. n. faire marché, mar-

barge, *bårj,* s. bateau, m., barque, f.

bargee, *bâr'jĕ*, bargeman, *bârj'măn*, s. batelier, m.

baritone, *bâr'ĭ tŏn*, s. baryton, m.

bark, *bârk*, s. écorce, f. || barque, f., bateau, m.

bark, *bârk*, v. a. écorcer || ~, v. n. aboyer.

barley, *bâr'lĭ*, s. orge, f. || ~-sick, a. enivré || pearl ~, s. orge perlé, m. || ~-water, tisane d'orge, f.

barm, *bârm*, s. levain, m.

barmaid, *bâr'mād*, s. fille de comptoir, f.

barn, *bârn*, s. grange, f., grenier, m. || ~-floor, s. aire d'une grange, f.

barnacle, *bâr'nă kl*, s. barnache, f. || -s, pl. morailles, f. pl.

barometer, *bă rŏm'ĕ tẽr*, s. baromètre, m.

baron, *băr'ŏn*, s. baron, m. || Lord Chief ~, baron premier juge, m.

baronage, *băr'ŏn ăj*, s. dignité de baron, f.

baroness, *băr'ŏn ĕs*, s. baronne, f.

baronet, *băr'ŏ nĕt*, s. baronnet, m. [pl

baronetage, *băr'ŏ nĕt ăj*, s. baronnets, m.

baronetcy, *băr'ŏ nĕt sĭ*, s. titre (m.) or dignité (f.) de baron, m. [baron.

baronial, *bă rō'nĭ ăl*, a. se rapportant au

barony, *băr'ŏ nĭ*, s. baronnie, f.

barouche, *bă rŏsh'*, s. calèche, f.

barrack, *băr'răk*, s. baraque, f. || -s, pl. caserne, f.

barracoon, *băr'ră kōn*, s. négrerie, f.

barrel, *băr'rĕl*, s. baril, m., barrique, f. || canon (d'un fusil), m. || tambour de l'oreille m. || ~-organ, s. orgue à cylindre, m.

barrel, *băr'rĕl*, v. a. entonner || ~ed, a. à cylindre || bombé || double -ed, à deux canons, à deux coups (fusil).

barren, *băr'rĕn*, a. (-ly, ad.) stérile(ment).

barrenness, *băr'rĕn nĕs*, s. stérilité, aridité, sécheresse, f.

barricade, *băr'rĭ kād'*, s. barricade, f.

barricade, *băr'rĭ kād'*, v. a. barricader.

barrier, *băr'rĭ ẽr*, s. barrière, f. || obstacle, m. [m.

barrister, *băr'rĭs tẽr*, s. avocat plaidant.

barrow, *băr'rō*, s. brouette, f. || tumulus, m.

barrowman, *băr'rō măn*, s. brouettier, m.

barter, *băr'tẽr*, v. a. & n. échanger, troquer. [quer.

basalt, *bă săwlt'*, s. basalte, m.

base, *bās*, s. base, f., piédestal, m. || basse f.

base, *bās*, v. a. baser. [basse-taille, f.

base, *bās*, a. (-ly, ad.) bas || vil(ement) méprisable || illégitime || faux.

basement, *bās'mĕnt*, s. fondation, base, f.

baseness, *bās'nĕs*, s. bassesse, f. || illégitimité, f. || (of sound) gravité, f.

bashaw, *băsh ăw'*, s. pacha, m.

bashful, *băsh'fŏŏl*, a. (-ly, ad.) honteux || pudique(ment).

bashfulness, *băsh'fŏŏl nĕs*, s. timidité, modestie, f.

basilica, *băz ĭl'ĭ kă*, s. basilique, f.

basilisk, *băz'ĭ lĭsk*, s. basilic, m.

basin, *bā'sn*, s. bassin, m. || bol, m. || cuvette, f.

basis, *bā'sĭs*, s. base, f., fondement, m.

bask, *băsk*, v. a. & n. (se)chauffer || (fig.) s'endormir.

basket, *băs'kĕt*, s. panier, m., corbeille, f. || waste-paper ~, s. panier de rebut, m.

bass, *băs*, s. natte, f. || ~, *băs*, s. (mus.) basse, f. [s. basse-de-viole, f.

bass, *băs*, a. (mus.) grave, bas || ~-viol,

bassinette, *băs'sĭ nĕt*, s. barcelonnette, f.

bassock, *băs'sŭk*, s. natte, f.

bassoon, *băs sŏn'*, s. (mus.) basson, m.

bastard, *băs'tẽrd*, s. bâtard, m.

bastard, *băs'tẽrd*, a. bâtard || (méd.) faux.

bastardise, *băs'tẽr dīz*, v. a. déclarer bâtard.

bastardy, *băs'tẽr dĭ*, s. bâtardise, f.

baste, *bāst*, v. a. bâtonner || arroser le rôti || faufiler.

bastinado, *băs tĭ nă'dō*, s. bastonnade, f.

bastinado, *băs tĭ nă'dō*, v. a. donner la bastonnade. [ture, f.

basting, *băst'ĭng*, s. bastonnade, f. || faufi-

bastion, *băst'yŏn*, s. bastion, m.

bat, *băt*, s. chauve-souris, f. || bâton, m. ||

bat, *băt*, v. a. jouer au bâton. [raquette, f.

batch, *băch*, s. fournée, f.

bate, *bāt*, v. a. rabattre.

bath, *băth*, s. bain, m. || foot-~, s. bain de pieds, m. || shower-~, s. douche, f. || sponge ou splash-~, s. baignoire, f. || ~-keeper, s. baigneur, m.

bathe, *băth*, v. a. & n. baigner, étuver || se baigner.

bather, *bā'thẽr*, s. baigneur, m.

bathing, *bā'thĭng*; ~-drawers, s. pl. caleçon de bain, m. || ~-gown, s. peignoir, m. || ~-machine, s. voiture de bain, f. || ~-man, s. baigneur, m. [m.

bathos, *bā'thŏs*, s. pathos, m. || galimatias,

bating, *bā'tĭng*, pr. hormis, excepté.

battalion, *bă tăl'yŭn*, s. bataillon, m.

batten, *băt'n*, s. volige, f.

batten, *băt'n*, v. a. & n. engraisser, fertiliser || s'engraisser || to ~ down the hatches, (mar.) condamner les panneaux.

batter, *băt'tẽr*, s. pâte battue, f.

batter, *băt'tẽr*, v. a. battre, renverser.

battering, *băt'tẽr ĭng*; ~-ram, s. bélier, m. || ~-train, s. artillerie de siège, f.

battery, *băt'tẽr ĭ*, s. batterie, f. || pile, f. || (jur.) voies de fait, f. pl. || galvanic ~, pile galvanique, f.

battle, *băt'tl*, s. bataille, f., combat, m. || pitched ~, bataille rangée, f. || ~-array, s. ordre de bataille, m. || ~-axe, s. hache d'armes, f. [batailler.

battle, *băt'tl*, v. n. livrer bataille || (fam.)

battledore, *băt'tl dōr*, s. raquette, f.

battlement, *băt'tl mĕnt*, s. créneau, m. || -ed, a. crénelé.

bavin, *băv'ĭn*, s. cotret, m.

bawble, *băw'bl*, s. babiole, bagatelle, f., colifichet, m.

bawl, *băwl*, v. n. criailler, brailler.

bawling, *băwl'ĭng*, s. criaillerie, f.

bay, *bā*, s. laurier, m. || baie, f., golfe, m. || at ~, aux abois || ~-window, s. fenêtre en saillie.

bay, *bā*, v. n. aboyer. [en saillie.

bay, *bā*, a. bai.

---

lāte, hăt, fär, làw; — hēre, gĕt, hẽr; — mīne, ĭnn; — nō, hŏt, prōve; — hŏw; —

bayonet, *bā'ŏn ĕt,* s. baïonnette, f. ‖ **to carry at the point of the ~,** enlever à la baïonnette ‖ **~-belt,** s. porte-baïonnette, m. ‖ baïonnette.

bayonet, *bā'ŏn ĕt,* v. a. tuer à coups de baïonnette.

bazaar, *bă zār',* s. bazar, m.

B. C., avant J.-C.

be, *bē,* v. n. ir. être, exister ‖ **so ~ it,** ainsi soit-il ‖ **he is not to know it,** il ne doit pas le savoir ‖ **if I were to ..,** si je venais à .. ‖ **I am warm, cold etc.,** j'ai chaud, froid, etc. ‖ **she is 12 years old,** elle a douze ans ‖ **to let ~,** laisser là.

beach, *bēch,* s. rivage, m.

beacon, *bē'kn,* s. signal, fanal, m.

bead, *bēd,* s. grain de collier, chapelet, m. ‖ **to tell one's ~s,** dire son chapelet.

beadle, *bē'dl,* s bedeau, m.

beagle, *bē'gl,* s. briquet, bigle, m.

beak, *bēk,* s. bec, m. ‖ pic, m. ‖ (mar.) éperon, m.

beaked, *bēkt,* a. à bec. [m.

beaker, *bēk'ĕr,* s. tasse à bec, f., gobelet,

beam, *bēm,* s. poutre, f. ‖ (of machines) balancier, m. ‖ timon, m. ‖ rayon (de soleil), m. ‖ **to be on (her) ~-ends,** (mar.) être sur le côté.

beam, *bēm,* v. n. rayonner.

bean, *bēn,* s. fève, f. ‖ **broad-~,** grosse fève, f. ‖ **French-~,** haricot vert, m.

bear, *bār,* s. ours, m. ‖ **she ~,** ourse, f. ‖ **~-garden,** s. fosse aux ours ‖ pétaudière, f.

bear, *bār,* v. a. & n. ir. porter ‖ supporter, souffrir ‖ produire ‖ faire voir ‖ se porter, se comporter ‖ peser ‖ être situé.

bearable, *bār'ă bl,* a. supportable.

beard, *bērd,* s. barbe, f. ‖ dent (d'une flèche), f. [défier.

beard, *bērd,* v. a. s'opposer ouvertement à ‖

bearded, *bērd'ĕd,* a. barbu.

beardless, *bērd'lĕs,* a. imberbe.

bearer, *bār'ĕr,* s. porteur, m. ‖ support, m.

bearing, *bār'ĭng,* s. situation, f. ‖ mine, f. ‖ (of a coast) hauteur, f. ‖ air, m. ‖ maintien, m. ‖ (of land) gisement, m. ‖ conduite, f. ‖ armoiries, f. pl. ‖ **past ~,** a. insupportable.

beast, *bēst,* s. bête, f., animal, m. ‖ **~s,** pl. bêtes à cornes, f. pl. ‖ **of burden,** bête de somme. [talité, f.

beastliness, *bēst'lĭ nĕs,* s. bestialité, brutalité, f.

beastly, *bēst'lĭ,* a. brutal, bestial.

beat, *bēt,* s. coup, m. ‖ rendez-vous, m. ‖ (rail.) parcours, m.

beat, *bēt,* v. a. & n. ir. battre, frapper ‖ piler, vaincre, défaire ‖ être agité ‖ **to ~ back** *ou* **off,** repousser.

beater, *bēt'ĕr,* s. pilon, battoir, batteur, m.

beatification, *bē ăt ĭ fĭ kā'shŭn,* s. béatification, f. [heureux.

beatify, *bē ăt'ĭ fĭ,* v. a. béatifier, rendre

beating, *bēt'ĭng,* s. coups, m. pl., battement, m. ‖ (of drums) batterie, f.

beatitude, *bē ăt'ĭ tūd,* s. béatitude, f.

beau, *bō,* s. élégant, petit-maître, m.

beauteous, *bū'tĭ ŭs,* a. beau.

beautifier, *bū'tĭ fī ĕr,* s. personne *ou* chose qui embellit, f.

beautiful, *bū'tĭ fŏŏl,* a. beau, agréable ‖ **-ly,** ad. admirablement.

beautify, *bū'tĭ fī,* v. a. embellir.

beauty, *bū'tĭ,* s. beauté, f. ‖ **~-spot,** s. tache de beauté, f. ‖ mouche, f.

beaver, *bē'vĕr,* s. castor, m. ‖ chapeau de castor, m.

becalm, *bē kǎm',* v. a. calmer, apaiser.

because, *bē kǎwz',* c. parce que, à cause de.

beck, *bĕk,* s. signe de tête, m. ‖ petit ruisseau, m. ‖ **to be at one's ~ (and call),** être aux ordres de qn.

beckon, *bĕk'n,* v. a. & n. inviter ‖ faire un signe de tête.

become, *bē kŭm',* v. a. & n. ir. convenir, être propre à ‖ devenir ‖ **to ~ of,** devenir.

becoming, *bē kŭm'ĭng,* a. (-ly, ad.) convenable à, bienséant ‖ convenablement.

becomingness, *bē kŭm'ĭng nĕs,* s. convenance, bienséance, f.

bed, *bĕd,* s. lit, m., couche, f. ‖ carreau, m. ‖ **marriage ~,** lit nuptial, m. ‖ **to put to ~,** mettre au lit ‖ **~-chamber,** s. chambre à coucher, f. ‖ **~-clothes,** s. pl. couverture, f. ‖ **~-head,** s. chevet du lit, m. ‖ **~-post,** s. pied de lit, m. ‖ **~-tick,** s. toiles à matelas, f. ‖ **~-time,** s. temps (m.) *ou* heure (f.) de se coucher.

bed, *bĕd,* v. a. coucher ‖ mettre au lit.

bedaub, *bē dăwb',* v. a. barbouiller, enduire. [f.

bedding, *bĕd'dĭng,* s. fourniture d'un lit,

bedeck, *bē dĕk',* v. a. parer, orner.

bedevil, *bē dĕv'l,* v. a. mettre dans un état du diable ‖ ensorceler.

bedew, *bē dū',* v. a. humecter, arroser.

bedim, *bē dĭm',* v. a. obscurcir.

bedizen, *bē dīz'n,* v. a. attifer, orner.

bedlam, *bĕd'lăm,* s. hospice des aliénés, m.

bedlamite, *bĕd'lăm ĭt,* s. aliéné, forcené, m.

bedridden, *bĕd'rĭd dn,* a. alité. [f.

bedroom, *bĕd'rŏm,* s. chambre à coucher,

bedside, *bĕd'sĭd,* s. bord du lit, m.

bedstead, *bĕd'stĕd,* s. bois de lit, m.

bee, *bē,* s. abeille, f. ‖ **~-hive,** s. ruche d'abeilles, f. ‖ **~-master,** s. éleveur d'abeilles, m. [f.

beech, *bēch,* s. hêtre, m. ‖ **~-nut,** s. faine,

beechen, *bēch'n,* a. de hêtre.

beef, *bēf,* s. viande de bœuf, f., du bœuf ‖ **beeves,** pl., bêtes à cornes, f. pl. ‖ **~-steak,** s. bifteck, m., grillade de bœuf, f. ‖ **~-tea,** s. bouillon de bœuf, m.

beefeater, *bēf'ĕt ĕr,* s. soldat aux gardes, m.

beer, *bēr,* s. bière, f. [m.

beet, *bēt,* s. bette, f.

beetle, *bē'tl,* s. escarbot, m. ‖ battoir, m. ‖ **black~,** blatte des cuisines, f. ‖ **~-browed,** aux sourcils épais.

beetle, *bē'tl,* v. n. surplomber ‖ avancer.

beetroot, *bēt'rŏt,* s. betterave, f.

befall, *bē făwl',* v. n. ir. arriver, survenir.

befit, *bē fĭt',* v. a. convenir à, être propre à.

befitting, *bē fĭt'tĭng,* a. convenable.

befool, *bĕfōl'*, v. a. infatuer || duper.

before, *bĕfōr'*, pr. & ad. avant, devant, auparavant.

beforehand, *bĕfōr'hănd*, ad. d'avance, par avance, auparavant || opulent || to be ~ with one, prendre les devants.

beforetime, *bĕfōr'tĭm*, ad. autrefois, jadis.

befoul, *bĕfōŏl'*, v. a. souiller.

befriend, *bĕfrĕnd'*, v. a. favoriser, traiter en ami.

beg, *bĕg*, v. a. demander, prier || supplier(de) || to go ~ging, demander à être accepté || to go a' ~ging, mendier || ~, v. n. mendier, gueuser.

beget, *bĕgĕt'*, v. a. ir. engendrer.

beggar, *bĕg'gĕr*, s. mendiant, gueux, m. || ~ my neighbour, s. (jeu) bataille, f.

beggar, *bĕg'gĕr*, v. a. réduire à la mendicité.　　　　　　[gueuserie, f.

beggarliness, *bĕg'gĕr lĭ nĕs*, s. mendicité,

beggarly, *bĕg'gĕr lĭ*, a. (& ad.) indigent || pauvre(ment) || misérable.

begin, *bĕgĭn'*, v. a. & n. ir. commencer.

beginner, *bĕgĭn'nĕr*, s. débutant, novice, m.

beginning, *bĕgĭn'nĭng*, s. commencement, m. || origine, f. || ~s, pl. notions préliminaires, f. pl.

begone! *bĕgŏn'*, va-t-en! allez-vous en!

begotten, v. beget.

begrime, *bĕgrĭm'*, v. a. barbouiller.

beguile, *bĕgĭl'*, v. a. tromper, duper || surprendre || amuser.

behalf, *bĕhäf'*, s. faveur, f., part, m. || (com.) profit, m. || on ~ of, au nom de || in ~ of, en faveur de, au profit de.

behave, *bĕhäv'*, v. n. ir. se conduire.

behaviour, *bĕhäv'yĕr*, s. conduite, f. || savoir-vivre, m. || to be on one's best ~, être dans son bon jour.

behead, *bĕhĕd'*, v. a. décapiter.

beheading, *bĕhĕd'ĭng*, s. décapitation, f.

behest, *bĕhĕst'*, s. ordre, m.　　　　[arrière.

behind, *bĕhĭnd'*, pr. & ad. derrière, en

behindhand, *bĕhĭnd'hănd*, a. en arrière, en reste.　　　　[templer || ~! i. voici! voilà!

behold, *bĕhōld'*, v. a. ir. regarder, voir.

beholden, *bĕhōld'ĕn*, a. obligé, redevable.

beholder, *bĕhōld'ĕr*, s. spectateur, observateur, m.

behoof, *bĕhōf'*, s. profit, avantage, m.

behove, *bĕhōv'*, v. n. convenir à.

being, *bĕ'ĭng*, s. être, m., existence, f. || to call into ~, mettre au jour || donner naissance à.　　　　　　[actuel, du moment.

being, *bĕ'ĭng*, p. étant || for the time ~,

belabour, *bĕlä'bĕr*, v. a. battre, rosser.

belated, *bĕlā'tĕd*, a. surpris par la nuit, retardé.

belch, *bĕlsh*, s. rot, m. || foulard bariolé.

belch, *bĕlsh*, v. n. roter.　　　　　　[sorcière, f.

beldame, *bĕl'dām*, s. vieille décrépite, f. ||

beleaguer, *bĕlē'gĕr*, v. a. assiéger.

belfry, *bĕl'frĭ*, s. beffroi, clocher, m.

belie, *bĕlĭ'*, v. a. contrefaire, calomnier || donner un démenti à.

belief, *bĕlēf'*, s. croyance, foi, f. || past

all ~, incroyable || to the best of one's ~, autant qu'on sache || to exceed ~, passer toute croyance || to put one's ~ in, avoir croyance en, ajouter foi à.

believable, *bĕlēv'ă bl*, a. croyable.

believe, *bĕlēv'*, v. a. & n. croire, penser.

believer, *bĕlēv'ĕr*, s. croyant, fidèle, m.

bell, *bĕl*, s. cloche, f. || grelot, m. || to bear the ~, être le premier || ~-cord, s. cordon de sonnette, m. || ~-flower, s. campanule, f. || ~-founder, s. fondeur de cloches, m. || ~-pull, s., ~-rope, s. cordon de sonnette, m. || ~-wether, s. sonnailler, m.　　　　　　[fréer, raire.

bell, *bĕl*, v. n. fleurir en forme de cloche ||

bella-donna, *bĕl'lă dŏn'nă*, s. (bot.) belladone, f.

bellicose, *bĕl'lĭkōs*, a. belliqueux.

belligerent, *bĕl lĭj'ĕr ĕnt*, s. puissance belligérente, f.

belligerent, *bĕl lĭj'ĕr ĕnt*, a. belligérant.

bell-mouthed, *bĕl'mŏuthd*, a. évacué.

bellow, *bĕl'lō*, v. n. beugler, mugir.

bellows, *bĕl'lōz*, s. pl. soufflet, m. || ~-blower, s. souffleur d'orgue, m.

belly, *bĕl'lĭ*, s. ventre, m., panse, f.

belly, *bĕl'lĭ*, v. a. se gonfler, s'enfler.

bellyful, *bĕl'lĭfōl*, s. soûl, rassasiement, m.　　　　　　[cerner.

belong, *bĕlŏng'*, v. n. appartenir à || con-

beloved, *bĕlŭv'ĕd*, a. bien-aimé, chéri.

below, *bĕlō'*, pr. & ad. au-dessous de || en bas, là-bas || ci-dessous, ci-après.

belt, *bĕlt*, s. ceinturon, baudrier, m., ceinture, f. || bandage, m. || ~-maker, s. ceinturier, m.

belt, *bĕlt*, v. a. ceindre.　　　　　　[turier, m.

belvedere, *bĕl'vĕdĕr*, s. belvédère, m.

bemoan, *bĕmōn'*, v. a. déplorer, plaindre.

bench, *bĕnsh*, s. banc, établi, m. || cour de justice, f. || King's ~, Cour royale, f. || prison à Londres, m.

bench, *bĕnsh*, v. a. & n. garnir de bancs || asseoir sur un banc.

bencher, *bĕnsh'ĕr*, s. avocat du parquet, m., conservateur, m.

bend, *bĕnd*, s. courbure, f. || (fig.) inclinaison, f. || côte d'un vaisseau, f.

bend, *bĕnd*, v. a. & n. ir. bander, plier, courber, fléchir || diriger || se plier, s'incliner.

beneath, *bĕnēth'*, pr. & ad. sous, au-dessous de || en bas || ~ one's notice, au-dessous de la considération de qn.

benediction, *bĕnĕdĭk'shŭn*, s. bénédiction, f.　　　　　　[m.

benefaction, *bĕnĕfăk'shŭn*, s. bienfait,

benefactor, *bĕnĕfăk'tĕr*, s. bienfaiteur, m.

benefactress, *bĕnĕfăk'trĕs*, s. bienfaitrice, f.

benefice, *bĕn'ĕfĭs*, s. bénéfice, m.　　　　[f.

beneficence, *bĕnĕf'ĭsĕns*, s. bienfaisance, générosité, f.

beneficent, *bĕnĕf'ĭsĕnt*, a. bienfaisant, généreux || ~ly, ad. avec bienfaisance.

beneficial, *bĕnĕfĭsh'ăl*, a. avantageux, profitable || ~ly, ad. avantageusement.

benefit, *bĕn'ĕfĭt*, s. bienfait, bénéfice, m. || profit, m. || ~-night, s. représentation à bénéfice. f. || ~-society, s. société de secours mutuels, f.

benefit, *bĕn'ĕ̄fit*, v. a. &n. faire du bien à, servir || tirer du profit de.

benevolence, *bĕnĕv'ŏlĕns*, s. bienveillance, faveur, f.

benevolent, *bĕnĕv'ŏlĕnt*, a. bienveillant, bienfaisant || -ly, ad. avec bienveillance.

Bengal-lights, *bĕn'gaŭlŭts*, s. pl. feu de Bengale, m.

benighted, *bĕnīt'ĕd*, a. surpris par la nuit.

benign, *bĕnīn'*, a. (-ly, ad.) bénin, bon || clément || salubre || bénignement, favorablement. [douceur, f.

benignity, *bĕnĭg'nĭtĭ*, s. bénignité, bonté.

bent, *bĕnt*, s. pli, m. || penchant, m. || déclivité, f. || tendance, f.

bent, *bĕnt*, a. courbé || déterminé, résolu.

benumb, *bĕnŭm'*, v. a. engourdir.

benzine, *bĕn zēn'*, s. benzine, f.

benzoin, *bĕn'zŏĭn*, s. benjoin, m.

bepraise, *bĕpräz'*, v. a. louer, louanger.

bequeath, *bĕkwēth'*, v. a. léguer.

bequeather, *bĕkwēth'ĕr*, s. testateur, m.

bequest, *bĕkwĕst'*, s. legs, m.

bereave, *bĕrēv'*, v. a. ir. dépouiller, priver de, enlever à.

bereavement, *bĕrēv'mĕnt*, s. privation, f.

bereft, v. bereave.

bergamot, *bĕr'gămŏt*, s. bergamote, f.

Berlin, *bĕr līn'*, s. berline (voiture), f. || ~ wool, s. laine à broder, f.

berry, *bĕr'rĭ*, s. baie, f., grain, m.

berth, *bĕrth*, s. (mar.) poste, m. || place, f.

beryl, *bĕr'ĭl*, s. béryl, m.

beseech, *bĕsēch'*, v. a. supplier, prier.

beseechingly, *bĕsēch'ĭnglĭ*, ad. en suppliant. [venable.

beseem, *bĕsēm'*, v. n. convenir, être convenable

beset, *bĕsĕt'*, v. a. ir. assiéger, obséder || embarrasser.

besetting, *bĕsĕt'ĭng*, a. habituel.

beside(s), *bĕsīd'(z')*, pr. & ad. à côté de, auprès de || d'ailleurs || ~ oneself, hors

besiege, *bĕsēj'*, v. a. assiéger. [de soi.

besmear, *bĕsmēr'*, v. a. barbouiller, salir.

besom, *bē zŭm*, s. balai, m.

besot, *bĕsŏt'*, v. a. abrutir, stupéfier.

bespangle, *bĕspăng'gl*, v. a. orner de paillettes. [diffamer.

bespatter, *bĕspăt'tĕr*, v. a. éclabousser ||

bespeak, *bĕspēk'*, v. a. ir. demander d'avance || retenir, louer || commander || s'adresser à || montrer.

bespoken, v. bespeak. [asperger.

besprinkle, *bĕsprĭng'kl*, v. a. arroser,

best, *bĕst*, a. & ad. le meilleur, la meilleure || le mieux || at ~, au mieux || the ~ of it is that, ce qu'il y a de mieux, c'est que || to do one's ~, faire de son mieux || to make the ~ of a bad business, faire bonne mine à mauvais jeu.

bestial, *bĕst'yăl*, a. (-ly, ad.) bestial(ement)|| brutal(ement). [talité, f.

bestiality, *bĕs yăl'ĭtĭ*, s. bestialité, brutalité

bestir, *bĕstĕr'*, v. r. se remuer, se mettre en mouvement *or* en action.

bestow, *bĕstō'*, v. a. donner, accorder, dispenser, donner en mariage || employer à || to ~ oneself, s'occuper.

bestowal, *bĕstō'ăl*, s. disposition, f.

bestride, *bĕstrīd'*, v. a. ir. enjamber, trabet, *bĕt*, s. pari, m. [verser

bet, *bĕt*, v. a. parier.

betake, *bĕtāk'*, v. a. ir. livrer || to ~ oneself, se rendre, se réfugier.

bethink, *bĕthĭngk'*, v. n. ir. considérer, réfléchir || to ~ oneself, se rappeler, penser à || s'aviser de.

betide, *bĕtīd'*, v. a. arriver à. [heure.

betimes, *bĕtīmz'*, ad. bientôt, de bonne

betoken, *bĕtō'kn*, v.a. désigner || annoncer, présager. [tromper.

betray, *bĕtrā'*, v. a. trahir, découvrir |

betrayer, *bĕtrā'ĕr*, s. traître, m., traîtresse, f. [en mariage.

betroth, *bĕtrŏth'*, v. a. fiancer, accorder

betrothal, *bĕtrŏth'ăl*, s. fiançailles, f. pl.

better, *bĕt'tĕr*, a. & ad. meilleur, mieux || so much the ~, tant mieux.

better, *bĕt'tĕr*, s. meilleur, m. || supérieur, m. supériorité, f., avantage, m. || -s, pl. supérieurs, m. pl. || for ~, for worse, vaille que vaille || to get the ~ of, prendre le dessus sur || I had ~ go, je ferai mieux de m'en aller.

better, *bĕt'tĕr*, v. a. améliorer || avancer, surpasser || soutenir.

bettering, *bĕt'tĕrĭng*, s. amélioration, f.

betting, *bĕt'tĭng*, s. pari, m.

bettor, *bĕt'tĕr*, s. parieur, m.

between, *bĕtwēn'*, betwixt, *bĕtwĭkst'*, pr. entre, au milieu de || betwixt and ~, entre deux âges || ~ this and . . ., d'ici à . . .

bevel, *bĕv'ĕl*, s. fausse équerre, f.

bevel, *bĕv'ĕl*, v. a. couper à angle || ~, v. n. biaiser.

bevel, *bĕv'ĕl*, a. de biais. [son, f.

beverage, *bĕv'ĕrāj*, s. breuvage, m., boisson, f.

bevy, *bĕv'ĭ*, s. volée (d'oiseaux), f. || compagnie, f.

bewail, *bĕwāl'*, v. a. déplorer, pleurer.

beware, *bĕwār'*, v. n. se garder de, faire attention. [embarrasser.

bewilder, *bĕwil'dĕr*, v. a. embrouiller,

bewilderment, *bĕwil'dĕrmĕnt*, s. embarrassement, m. [chanter.

bewitch, *bĕwich'*, v. a. ensorceler, enbeyond, *bĕyŏnd'*, pr. au delà, par delà, au-dessus de, hors de.

bezel, *bĕz'ĕl*, s. chaton d'une bague, m.

bias, *bī'ăs*, s. biais, m. || ligne oblique, f. || inclinaison, f. || préjugé, m.

bias, *bī'ăs*, v. a. pencher || influencer.

bib, *bĭb*, s. bavette, f.

Bible, *bī'bl*, s. bible, f. || ancien testament, m.

biblical, *bĭb'lĭkăl*, a. biblique. [m.

bibliophile, *bĭb'lĭŏfĭl*, s. bibliophile, m.

bibulous, *bĭb'ŭlŭs*, a. altéré.

bicker, *bĭk'ĕr*, v. n. se quereller, escarmoucher.

bickering, *bĭk'ĕrĭng*, s. escarmouche, f.

bid, *bĭd*, s. offre, f. || enchère, f.

bid, *bĭd,* v. a. ir. commander, ordonner || demander, prier, inviter || offrir (un prix) || **to ~** adieu, faire ses adieux.

bidder, *bĭd'dẽr,* s. offrant, enchérisseur, m. || **highest ~,** dernier enchérisseur, m.

bidding, *bĭd'dĭng,* s. ordre, commandement, m. || invitation, f.

bide, *bīd,* v. a. & n. ir. endurer, souffrir || demeurer, habiter || **to ~** one's time, attendre l'occasion.

biennial, *bĭ ĕn'nĭ ăl,* a. biennal || (bot.) bisannuel.

bier, *bēr,* s. bière, f. || cercueil, m.

biffin, *bĭf'fĭn,* s. pomme tapée, f.

bifurcated, *bīfẽr'kā tĕd,* a. bifurqué, fourchu.

big, *bĭg,* a. gros, grand || enflé, plein || fier, orgueilleux || enceinte.

bigamist, *bĭg'ă mĭst,* s. bigame, m. & f.

bigamy, *bĭg'ă mĭ,* s. bigamie, f.

bight, *bĭt,* crique, f.

bigness, *bĭg'nĕs,* s. grosseur, grandeur, f.

bigot, *bĭg'ŏt,* s. bigot, m., bigote, f. || dévot, m., dévote, f. || (en) cagot.

bigoted, *bĭg'ŭt ĕd,* a. (-ly, ad.) (en) bigot.

bigotry, *bĭg'ŏ trĭ,* s. bigotisme, m., bigoterie, f. || cagotisme, m., cagoterie, f.

bigwig, *bĭg'wĭg,* s. gros bonnet, m.

bilateral, *bĭ lăt'ẽr ăl,* a. bilatéral.

bilberry, *bĭl'bẽr rĭ,* s. mûre de ronce, f.

bile, *bīl,* s. bile, f.

bilge, *bĭlj,* s. (mar.) sentine, f.

bilge, *bĭlj,* v. a. défoncer || **~,** v. n. (mar.) faire eau.

bilious, *bĭl'yŭs,* a. bilieux.

bilk, *bĭlk,* v. a. friponner, tromper, escroquer.

bilk, *bĭlk,* s. attrape, f. || flouerie, f.

bill, *bĭl,* s. bec (d'oiseau), m. || serpe, f. || billet, mémoire, m. || projet de loi, m., note, f. || écriteau, m. || **~ of exchange, s.** lettre de change, f. || **~ of lading, s.** lettre de voiture, f. || (mar.) connaissement, m. || **doctor's ~,** s. ordonnance du médecin, f. || **~ of fare,** s. carte d'un restaurant, f. || **~ of health,** s. patente de santé, f. || **~ of mortality,** s. registre mortuaire, m. || **~ of indictment,** s. acte d'accusation, m. || **~ payable to bearer, s.** billet au porteur, m. || **to find a true ~ against,** prononcer la mise en accusation de || **to honour a ~,** faire honneur à un effet || **stick no -s !** défense d'afficher ! || **~broker,** s. courtier de change, m. || **~p'ster,** **~sticker,** s. afficheur.

billet, *bĭl'lĕt,* s. billet, m. || bûche, f. [m. **billet,** *bĭl'lĕt,* v. a. donner un billet de logement.

billhook, *bĭl'hŏŏk,* s. serpe, f.

billiard, *bĭl'jẽrd ;* **~ball,** s. bille, f. || **~cue,** s. queue de billard, f. || **~pocket,** s. blouse, f. || **~room,** s. salle de billard, f. || **~table,** s. billard, m.

billiards, *bĭl'yẽrds,* s. pl. billard, m. || **game of ~,** s. partie de billard, f.

Billingsgate, *bĭl'lĭngs gāt,* s. langage des halles, m.

billion, *bĭl'yŭn,* s. billion, m.

billow, *bĭl'lō,* s. vague, f., flot, m.

billow, *bĭl'lō,* v. n. s'enfler comme les [vagues. **billowy,** *bĭl'lō ĭ,* a. houleux.

bi-metallism, *bĭ mĕt'ăl ĭzm,* s. bimétallisme, m.

bin, *bĭn,* s. huche, f. [lisme, m.

bind, *bīnd,* v. a. & n. ir. lier || relier || obliger || se lier || **to be bound to,** être tenu de. [bandage, m.

binder, *bīnd'ẽr,* s. relieur (de livres), m.

binding, *bīnd'ĭng,* s. bandage, m. || reliure, f. || bordure, f.

bindweed, *bīnd'wēd,* s. (bot.) liseron, m.

binnacle, *bĭn'nă kl,* s. habitacle, m.

binocle, *bĭn'ō kl,* s. binocle, m.

binocular, *bĭ nŏk'ū lẽr,* a. binoculaire.

binomial, *bĭ nō'mĭ ăl,* s. binôme || **~ theorem,** s. binome de Newton, m.

biographer, *bĭ ŏg'ră fẽr,* s. biographe, m.

biographical, *bī ō grăf'ĭ kăl,* a. biographique.

biography, *bĭ ŏg'ră fĭ,* s. biographie, f.

biology, *bĭ ŏl'ō jĭ,* s. biologie, f.

biped, *bī'pĕd,* s. bipède, m.

biplane, *bī'plān,* s. biplan, m.

birch, *bẽrch,* s. bouleau, m.

bird, *bẽrd,* s. oiseau, m. || **~cage, s.** cage, volière, f. || **~call,** s. appeau, m. || **~catcher,** s. oiseleur, m. || **~catching,** s. oiselerie, f. || **~lime,** s. glu, f.

bird, *bẽrd,* v. n. dénicher des oiseaux.

birdseye, *bẽrdz'ī,* a. à vue d'oiseau.

birdsnest, *bẽrdz'nĕst,* v. a. dénicher des oiseaux.

birth, *bẽrth,* s. naissance, couche, f. || (fig.) enfantement, m., portée, f. || mouillage, m.

birthday, *bẽrth'dā,* s. jour de naissance, m.

birthplace, *bẽrth'plās,* s. lieu natal, m.

birthright, *bẽrth'rīt,* s. droit d'aînesse, m.

biscuit, *bĭs'kĭt,* s. biscuit, m.

bisect, *bĭ sĕkt',* v. a. couper en deux.

bishop, *bĭsh'ŏp,* s. évêque, m. || fou (aux échecs), m.

bishopric, *bĭsh'ŏp rĭk,* s. évêché, m.

bismuth, *bĭz'mŭth,* s. (chem.) bismuth, m.

bison, *bī'sŏn,* s. bison, m.

bit, *bĭt,* s. mors, frein, m. || morceau, m. || bouchée, f. || brin, m. || panneton, m. || **not a ~ of it !** pas le moins du monde !

bit, *bĭt,* v. a. emboucher (un cheval).

bitch, *bĭch,* s. chienne, f. || rosse, f.

bite, *bīt,* s. morsure, bouchée, f. || tromperie, f. [attraper, duper.

bite, *bīt,* v. a. ir. mordre || (fig.) piquer ||

bitter, *bĭt'tẽr,* a. (-ly, ad.) amer || amèrement || mordant || cruel(lement) || satirique || **~sweet,** s. douce-amère, f. || **~wort,** s. (bot.) gentiane, f.

bitterish, *bĭt'tẽr ĭsh,* a. tant soit peu amer.

bittern, *bĭt'tẽrn,* s. butor, m. (oiseau).

bitterness, *bĭt'tẽr nĕs,* s. amertume, f. || malice, animosité, f.

bitters, *bĭt'tẽrz,* s. pl. absinthe, f.

bitumen, *bĭ tū'mĕn,* s. bitume, m.

bituminous, *bĭ tū'mĭ nŭs,* a. bitumineux.

bivalve, *bī'vălv,* s. bivalve, m.

bivouac, *bĭv'ōŏ ăk,* s. bivouac, m.

bivouac, *bĭv'ōŏ ăk,* v. n. bivouaquer.

---

lāte, hăt, fâr, lăw ; — hēre, gĕt, hẽr ; — mīne, ĭnn ; — nō, hŏt, prōve ; — hōw ; —

blab, *blăh*, s. bavard, m.

blab, *blăb*, v. a. & n. bavarder.

black, *blăk*, s. couleur noire, f. ‖ deuil, m.

black, *blăk*, a. noir, sombre ‖ triste ‖ atroce ‖ **to beat ~ and blue**, meurtrir de coups ‖ **~-book**, s. livre de punitions, m. ‖ cahier de rapports, m. ‖ grimoire, m. ‖ **~-eye**, s. œil poché, m. ‖ pochon sur l'œil, m. ‖ **~-lead**, s. mine de plomb, f. ‖ **~-letter**, s. lettre gothique, f. ‖ **~-pudding**, s. boudin, m. ‖ **~-thorn**, s. (bot.) prunellier, m.

black(en), *blăk′(n)*, v. a. noircir ‖ obscurcir ‖ diffamer ‖ devenir noir.

blackamoor, *blăk′ă mōr*, s. nègre m.

blackball, *blăk′bāwl*, s. boule noire, f.

blackball, *blăk′bāwl*, v. a. rejeter.

blackberry, *blăk′bĕr rĭ*, s. mûre de ronce, f. ‖ **~-bush**, s. mûrier sauvage, m.

blackbird, *blăk′bĕrd*, s. merle, m.

blackguard, *blăg′gărd*, s. polisson, m.

blacking, *blăk′ing*, s. cirage, m.

blackish, *blăk′ish*, a. noirâtre. [la grève.

blackleg, *blăk′lĕg*, s. personne (f.) qui romp

blackmail, *blăk′māl*, s. extorsion, f.

blackness, *blăk′nĕs*, s. noirceur, f.

blacksheep, *blăk′shĕp*, s. brebis galeuse, f.

blacksmith, *blăk′smith*, s. forgeron, m.

bladder, *blăd′dĕr*, s. vessie, f. ‖ pustule, f.

blade, *blād*, s. lame, f. ‖ omoplate, f. ‖ (poet.) épée, f. ‖ brin d'herbe, m.

blade, *blād*, v. a. mettre une lame à.

blain, *blān*, s. pustule, tumeur, f.

blamable, *blăm′ă bl*, a. blâmable, coupable.

blame, *blām*, s. blâme, m. ‖ réprimande, f.

blame, *blām*, v. a. blâmer, censurer.

blameless, *blăm′lĕs*, a. (-ly, ad.) irréprochable(ment).

blameworthy, *blām′wĕr thĭ*, a. blâmable.

blanch, *blănsh*, v. a. blanchir ‖ (fig.) pâlir ‖ faire pâlir.

bland, *blănd*, a. doux, flatteur.

blandish, *blăn′dish*, v. a. cajoler. [f.

blandishment, *blăn′dish mĕnt*, s. caresse,

blank, *blăngk*, s. blanc, m. ‖ billet blanc, m. ‖ but, m. [effacer.

blank, *blăngk*, v. a. confondre, déconcerter.

blank, *blăngk*, a. blanc ‖ pâle ‖ sans rime.

blanket, *blăng′kĕt*, s. couverture de lit, f. ‖ blanquette, f. [couverture de lit.

blanket, *blăng′kĕt*, v. a. couvrir d'une

blankness, *blăngk′nĕs*, s. vide, m.

blarney, *blăr′nĭ*, s. eau bénite de cour, f. ‖ monnaie de singe, f. ‖ flagornerie, f. ‖ blague, f.

blaspheme, *blăs fĕm′*, v. a. blasphémer.

blasphemer, *blăs fĕ′mĕr*, s. blasphémateur, m. [toire ‖ -ly, ad. avec impiété.

blasphemous, *blăs′fĕ mŭs*, a. blasphéma-

blasphemy, *blăs′fĕ mĭ*, s. blasphème, m.

blast, *blăst*, s. bouffée de vent, f. ‖ son, m. ‖ souffle destructeur, m. ‖ brouissure, f. ‖ infection, f. ‖ **~-furnace**, s. hautfourneau, m. [sauter.

blast, *blăst*, v. a. brûler ‖ détruire ‖ faire

blasting, *blăst′ing*, s. explosion, f.

blasting, *blăst′ing*, a. destructeur.

blaze, *blāz*, s. flamme, f. ‖ bruit, rapport, m. ‖ étoile d'un cheval, m. [briller.

blaze, *blāz*, v. a. & n. publier ‖ flamber,

blazon, *blā′zn*, v. a. blasonner ‖ célébrer.

blazonry, *blā′zn rĭ*, s. blason, m. ‖ (fig.) éclat, m. [blanc.

bleach, *blēch*, v. a. & n. blanchir, devenir

bleacher, *blēch′ĕr*, s. blanchisseur, m.

bleak, *blēk*, a. pâle, blême ‖ froid.

bleakness, *blēk′nĕs*, s. froid, m. ‖ froidure, f.

blear(-eyed), *blēr′(ĭd)*, a. chassieux.

bleat, *blēt*, s. bêlement, m.

bleat, *blēt*, v. n. bêler. [pandre son sang.

bleed, *blēd*, v. a. & n. ir. saigner ‖ ré-

bleeding, *blēd′ing*, s. saignée, f., saignement, m. [m. ‖ déshonneur, m.

blemish, *blĕm′ish*, s. tache, f. ‖ défaut,

blemish, *blĕm′ish*, v. a. souiller, diffamer.

blend, *blĕnd*, s. blende, f. ‖ mélange, m.

blend, *blĕnd*, v. a. mêler, confondre.

bless, *blĕs*, v. a. bénir, rendre heureux ‖ **~ my soul!** Dieu me bénisse!

blessedness, *blĕs′ĕd nĕs*, s. béatitude, sainteté, f.

blessing, *blĕs′sing*, s. bénédiction, f.

blight, *blīt*, s. bruine, nielle, f.

blight, *blīt*, v. a. nieller, flétrir.

blind, *blīnd*, s. store, m. ‖ (fig.) voile, f. ‖ **Venetian~**, a. persienne, jalousie, f.

blind, *blīnd*, v. a. aveugler ‖ obscurcir, blinder. [aveuglément.

blind, *blīnd*, a. aveugle, obscur ‖ **-ly**, ad.

blindfold, *blīnd′fōld*, v. a. bander les yeux.

blindfold, *blīnd′fōld*, a. les yeux bandés.

blindman's-buff, *blīnd′măns bŭf*, s. colinmaillard, m. [ment, m.

blindness, *blīnd′nĕs*, s. cécité, f., aveugle-

blindworm, *blīnd′wĕrm*, s. orvet, m.

blink, *blĭngk*, s. coup d'œil, m., lueur, f.

blink, *blĭngk*, v. n. clignoter.

blinkers, *blĭngk′ĕrs*, s. pl. œillères, f. pl.

bliss, *blĭs*, s. bonheur, m., félicité, f.

blissful, *blĭs′fōŏl*, a. heureux, bienheureux ‖ **-ly**, ad. heureusement.

blister, *blĭs′tĕr*, s. pustule, f. ‖ (méd.) vésicatoire, m. ‖ **~-ed steel**, s. acier de cémentation, m.

blister, *blĭs′tĕr*, v. a. & n. appliquer des vésicatoires ‖ s'élever en pustules.

blistering, *blĭs′tĕr ing*, s. application de vésicatoires, f.

blithe, *blīth*, a. gai, joyeux.

bloat, *blōt*, v. a. & n. enfler, bouffir ‖ s'enfler ‖ **-ed herring**, vide bloater.

bloatedness, *blōt′ĕd nĕs*, s. enflure, bouffissure, f.

bloater, *blōt′ĕr*, s. hareng saur, m.

block, *blŏk*, s. bloc, billot, m. ‖ obstacle m. ‖ lourdaud, m. ‖ forme de chapeau, f. ‖ tête à perruque, f. ‖ pâté de maisons, m. ‖ **~-house**, s. fort, blockaus, m. ‖ **~-tin**, s. étain en lingot, m. ‖ fer-blanc de qualité supérieure, m.

block, *blŏk*, v. a. bloquer.

blockade, *blŏk kād′*, s. blocus, m. ‖ **to run the ~**, forcer le blocus.

blockade, *blŏk kād'*, v. a. bloquer.
blockhead, *blŏk hĕd*, s. lourdaud, m.
blockship, *blŏk'shĭp*, s. stationnaire, m. ||
garde-côtes, m.
blonde, *blŏnd*, s. blonde, f.
blood, *blŭd*, s. sang, m. || parenté, f. ||
race, f. || loss of ~, s. hémorrhagie, f. ||
to breed ill ~, semer la discorde || to
make one's ~ run cold, glacer le sang ||
~-horse, s. cheval pur sang, m. ||
~-vessel, s. vaisseau sanguin, m.
blood, *blŭd*, v. a. ensanglanter || saigner.
bloodguiltiness, *blŭd'gĭl tĭ nĕs*, s. crime
de meurtre, assassinat, m. [meurtre.
bloodguilty, *blŭd'gĭl tĭ*, a. souillé de
bloodhound, *blŭd'hŏwnd*, s. limier, m.
bloodily, *blŭd'ĭ lĭ*, ad. cruellement.
bloodiness, *blŭd'ĭ nĕs*, s. état sanglant,
m. || disposition sanguinaire, f.
bloodless, *blŭd'lĕs*, a. qui n'a pas de sang.
bloodletter, *blŭd'lĕt tĕr*, s. saigneur, m.
bloodletting, *blŭd'lĕt tĭng*, s. saignée, f.
bloodred, *blŭd'rĕd*, a. rouge come du sang.
bloodshed, *blŭd'shĕd*, s. meurtre, carnage,
m.
bloodshot, *blŭd'shŏt*, a. injecté de sang ||
bloodstained, *blŭd'stānd*, a. ensanglanté.
bloodstone, *blŭd'stōn*, s. sanguine, f.
bloodsucker, *blŭd'sŭk ĕr*, s. sangsue, f. ||
(fig.) meurtrier, m. [de sang, m.
bloodthirstiness, *blŭd'thĕrst ĭ nĕs*, s. soif
bloodthirsty, *blŭd'thĕrst ĭ*, a. sanguinaire.
bloody, *blŭd'ĭ*, a. ensanglanté || sanguinaire ||
~ flux, s. dyssenterie, f.
bloom, *blōm*, s. fleur, f. || (fig.) fraîcheur, f.
bloom, *blōm*, v. n. fleurir.
blossom, *blŏs'sŭm*, s. fleur, f.
blossom, *blŏs'sŭm*, v. n. fleurir.
blot, *blŏt*, s. tache d'encre, f. || tache infa-
mante, f.
blot, *blŏt*, v. a. effacer || tacher.
blotch, *blŏch*, s. pustule, f.
blotch, *blŏch*, v. a. noircir.
blotting, *blŏt'tĭng*, ; ~~-case, s. buvard
m. || ~~-paper, s. papier brouillard, m.
blouse, *blŏws*, s. blouse, f.
blow, *blō*, s. coup, m. || at a ~, d'un coup ||
to come to –s, en venir aux mains, aux
coups || ~-fly, s. mouche à viande, f. ||
~-pipe, s. chalumeau, m. || ~-up, s.
algarade, f. || (scolding) savon, m.
blow, *blō*, v. a. & n. ir. souffler, enfler,
s'épanouir || sonner || fleurir || se moucher
to ~ up, faire sauter || donner un savon à ||
full –n, en pleine fleur.
blowzy, *blŏw'zĭ*, a. échevelé || hâlé.
blubber, *blŭb'bĕr*, s. graisse de baleine, f.
blubber, *blŭb'bĕr*, v. n. s'enfler les joues
à force de pleurer.
blubbering, *blŭb'bĕr ĭng*, s. larmes, f. pl.
bluchers, *blō'chĕrz*, s. pl. brodequins, m.pl.
bludgeon, *blŭj'ŭn*, s. assommoir, m.,
trique, f.
blue, *blō*, s. bleu, m. || –s, s. pl. maladie
blue, *blō*, v. a. teindre en bleu. [noire, f.
blue, *blō*, a. bleu || ~-bell, s. jacinthe des
prés, f. || ~-black, s. noire d'ivoire, m. ||

~-bottle, s. bluet (fleur), m. || mouche
bleue, f. || ~(-coat)-boy, s. orphelin, m. ||
~-devils, s. pl. humeurs noires, f. pl. ||
~-stocking, s. bas-bleu, m.
bluejacket, *blō'jăk ĕt*, s. marin, m.
blueness, *blō'nĕs*, s. couleur bleue, f.
bluff, *blŭf*, a. gros || grossier, arrogant.
bluffness, *blŭf'nĕs*, s. bouffissure, f. || brus-
querie, f.
bluish, *blō'ĭsh*, a. bleuâtre.
blunder, *blŭn'dĕr*, s. bévue, bêtise, f.
blunder, *blŭn'dĕr*, v. a. & n. faire une
bévue || se tromper lourdement.
blunderbuss, *blŭn'dĕr bŭs*, s. espingole, f.
blunt, *blŭnt*, v. a. émousser, épointer.
blunt, *blŭnt*, a. émoussé || grossier, brusque ||
–ly, ad. sans pointe || brusquement.
bluntness, *blŭnt'nĕs*, s. état émoussé, m. ||
grossièreté, f.
blur, *blĕr*, s. tache, flétrissure, f.
blur, *blĕr*, v. a. tacher || effacer. [ment.
blurt, *blĕrt*, v. a. to ~ out, dire étourdi-
blush, *blŭsh*, s. rougeur, pudeur, f.
blush, *blŭsh*, v. n. rougir.
bluster, *blŭs'tĕr*, s. tempête, f. || bruit, m.,
fanfaronnade, f. [fracas, gronder.
bluster, *blŭs'tĕr*, v. n. tempêter, faire du
blusterer, *blŭs'tĕr ĕr*, s. fanfaron, m.
blustering, *blŭs'tĕr ĭng*, a. orageux ·||
bruyant || fanfaron.
boar, *bōr*, s. sanglier, m. || ~'s head, s.
hure de sanglier, f.
board, *bōrd*, s. planche, f. || table, f.,
tableau, m., nourriture, f. || bord, m.
conseil, m. || carton, m., assemblée, f. ||
~ and lodging, la table et le logement,
la pension || on ~, à bord || ~ of trade,
tribunal de commerce, m. || ~-wages, s.
pl. frais de table, m. pl.
board, *bōrd*, v. a. & n. planchéier || nourrir,
mettre en pension || être en pension.
boarder, *bōrd'ĕr*, s. pensionnaire, m. ||
day-~, s. demi-pensionnaire, m. & f. ||
parlour-~, s. pensionnaire en chambre, m.
boarding, *bōrd'ĭng*, ; ~~-house, s. pension
bourgeoise, f. || ~~-school, s. pension, f.,
pensionnat, m.
boast, *bōst*, s. vanterie, ostentation, f.
boast, *bōst*, v. a. vanter, louer, m.
boaster, *bōst'ĕr*, s. fanfaron, m. || (tool)
ébauchoir, m. [avec vanterie.
boastful, *bōst'fŏŏl*, a. (-ly, ad.) vantard ||
boat, *bōt*, s. bateau, m., barque, f. || advice
~, s. aviso, m. || long ~, s. (mar.) grand
canot, m. || ~-hook, s. gaffe, f.
boating, *bōt'ĭng*, s. transport par bateau,
m. || promenade en bateau, f.
boatman, *bōt'măn*, s. batelier, m.
boatswain, *bōt'sn*, s. maître d'équipage,
m. || ~'s mate, s. contre-maître, m.
bob, *bŏb*, s. pendant d'oreilles, m. || refrain,
m. || coup, m. || balancier, m. || perruque
à nœuds, f. || (fam.) shilling, m.
bob, *bŏb*, v. a. & n. battre || tromper,
foltrer || pendiller, balancer.
bobbin, *bŏb'bĭn*, s. bobine, f. || ganse, f.
bobsleigh, *bŏb'slā*, s. luge à cornes, f.

lăte, hăt, făr, lăw; — hēre, gĕt, hĕr; — mīne, ĭnn; — nō, hŏt, prōve; — hōw; —

bobtail, bŏb'tăl, s. courte queue, f. || ~-wig, s. perruque à nœuds, f.

bode, bōd, v. a. & n. présager, pronostiquer.

bodice, bŏd'ĭs, s. corset, corsage, m.

bodiless, bŏd'ĭlĕs, a. incorporel.

bodily, bŏd'ĭlĭ, a. (& ad.) corporel(lement) || réel. |friser, m.

bodkin, bŏd'kĭn, s. poinçon, m. || fer à

body, bŏd'ĭ, s. corps, m. || substance, f. || personne, f. || société, compagnie, f. || ~-clothes, s. pl. housse, f. || ~-servant, s. valet, favori, affidé, m.

body, bŏd'ĭ, v. a. corporifier, donner une forme.   [m. pl.

bodyguard, bŏd'ĭgârd, s. gardes du corps,

bog, bŏg, s. marais, marécage, m.

bog, bŏg, v. a. embourber.

boggle, bŏg'gl, v. a. & n. embrouiller || sauter de peur || hésiter.

boggy, bŏg'gĭ, a. marécageux.

bogy, bŏg'gĭ, s. old ~, croque-mitaine, m.

bohea, bŏhē', s. thé bou, m.

boil, bŏyl, s. furoncle, ulcère, m.

boil, bŏyl, v. a. & n. bouillir, faire bouillir or cuire.   [dière, m.

boiler, bŏyl'ĕr, s. chaudron, m. || chau-

boiling-point, bŏyl'ĭng pŏynt, s. terme d'ébullition, m.   [pétueux || violemment.

boisterous, bŏys'tĕrŭs, a. (-ly, ad.) im-

bold, bōld, a. (-ly, ad.) hardi(ment) || courageux || insolent, effronté || as ~ as brass, hardi comme un page.

boldness, bōld'nĕs, s. hardiesse, effronterie, f.   [m.

bole, bōl, s. tronc m. || bol, m. || fourneau,

bolster, bōl'stĕr, s. chevet, m. || compresse, f.   [presses || (fig.) appuyer.

bolster, bōl'stĕr, v. a. appliquer des com-

bolt, bōlt, s. flèche, f. || foudre, f. || verrou, m. || bluteau, m.   [bluter.

bolt, bōlt, v. a. verrouiller || dire hardiment ||

bolter, bōlt'ĕr, s. bluteau, blutoir, tamis, m.

bolus, bō'lŭs, s. bol, m.

bomb, bŏm, s. bombe, f. || ~-ketch, ~-vessel, s. galiote à bombes, f.

bombard, bŏm bârd', v. a. bombarder.

bombardier, bŏm bâr dēr', s. bombardier, m.

bombardment, bŏm bârd'mĕnt, s. bombardement, m.   [bus, m.

bombast, bŏm'băst, s. boursoufflage, phé-

bombastic, bŏm băs'tĭk, a. boursoufflé, ampoulé.

bombazine, bŏm bā zēn', s. bombasin, m.

bomb-proof, bŏm'prŏf, a. à l'épreuve de la bombe.

bond, bŏnd, s. chaîne, f., lien, m., liaison, f. || obligation, f. || bon, m. || ~-holder, s. porteur d'obligation, m.

bond, bŏnd, v. a. entreposer.

bondage, bŏnd'ăj, s. servitude, f.

bondsman, bŏndz'măn, s. esclave, m. || (jur.) répondant, m.

bone, bōn, s. os, m. || arête, f. || to have a ~ to pick with one, avoir maille à partir avec qn. || to make no ~s about, ne pas se faire scrupule de || ~-black, s. noir animal, m.

bone, bōn, v. a. désosser.

bonesetter, bōn sĕt'tĕr, s. chirurgien, m.

bonfire, bŏn'fīr, s. feu de joie, m.

bonnet, bŏn'nĕt, s. bonnet, chapeau, m. || ~-box, s. carton à chapeau, m.

bonnily, bŏn'nĭlĭ, ad. gaiement, agréablement.

bonny, bŏn'nĭ, a. gai, joli, gentil.

bonus, bō'nŭs, s. boni, m. || pot-de-vin, m.

bony, bō'nĭ, a. osseux, ossu.

booby, bō'bĭ, s. nigaud, m.

book, bŏŏk, s. livre, m. || ~-case, s. bibliothèque, f. || ~-marker, s. signet, m. || ~-shelf, s. rayon, m. || ~-stall, s. étalage de livres, m. || ~-trade, s. librairie, f.

book, bŏŏk, v. a. enregistrer, inscrire.

bookbinder, bŏŏk'bĭn dĕr, s. relieur, m.

bookbinding, bŏŏk'bĭnd ĭng, s. reliure, f.

booking-office, bŏŏk'ĭng ŏffĭs, s. bureau de messagerie, m. || (rail.) bureau de distribution de billets, m.   [livres, m.

bookkeeper, bŏŏk'kĕp ĕr, s. teneur de

bookkeeping, bŏŏk'kĕp ĭng, s. tenue des livres, f.   [bookmaker, m.

bookmaker, bŏŏk'mā kĕr, s. (aux courses)

bookseller, bŏŏk'sĕl lĕr, s. libraire, m. || ~ and publisher, s. libraire-éditeur, m.

bookshop, bŏŏk'shŏp, s. librairie, f.

bookworm, bŏŏk'wĕrm, s. lépisme, m. || (fig.) rat de bibliotèque, m.

boom, bŏŏm, s. (mar.) épart, m.

boom, bŏŏm, v. n. bourdonner.

boon, bŏŏn, s. présent, don, m., faveur, f.

boon, bŏŏn, a. gai, enjoué, joyeux.

boor, bŏŏr, s. paysan, rustre, m.

boorish, bŏŏr'ĭsh, a. rustique, grossier.

boorishness, bŏŏr'ĭsh nĕs, s. rusticité, grossièreté, f.

boot, bŏŏt, s. profit, m. || botte, f. || to ~, par-dessus le marché || ~-jack, s. tire-botte, m.

boot, bŏŏt, v. a. mettre ses bottes.   [m.

booted, bŏŏt'ĕd, a. en bottes.

booth, bŏŏth, s. tente, baraque, f.

bootlace, bŏŏt'lās, s. lacet de bottines, m.

bootless, bŏŏt'lĕs, a. inutile, vain.

bootmaker, bŏŏt'māk ĕr, s. bottier, m.

boots, bŏŏts, s. (fig.) décrotteur, m.

booty, bŏŏt'ĭ, s. butin, m.

booze, bŏŏz, v. n. riboter.

borax, bō'răks, s. borax, m.

border, bâwr'dĕr, s. bord, m., bordure, f. || frontière, f.   [finer.

border, bâwr'dĕr, v. a. & n. border || con-

borderer, bâwr dĕr ĕr, s. habitant des frontières, m.

bore, bŏr, s. trou, m. || perçoir, m., vrille, f. || calibre, m. || personne ennuyeuse, f.

bore, bŏr, v. a. trouer, percer || ennuyer.

boreal, bŏr ē ăl, a. boréal.

borer, bŏr'rĕr, s. perçoir, m. || foret, f.

born, bâwrn, p. & a. né.

borough, bŭr'ō, s. bourg, m. || rotten ~, bourg pourri, m. || pocket-~, s. circonscription électorale inféodée à tel ou tel parti, f.

borrow, bŏr'rō, v. a. emprunter.

bosom, bŏŏz'ŭm, s. sein, m. || cœur, m.

bosom, *bŏŏz'ŭm,* v. a. renfermer dans son sein.   [chef, m.

boss, *bŏs,* s. bosse, saillie, f. || (Am.) maître,

botanic(al), *bŏ tăn'ĭk (ăl),* a. botanique.

botanist, *bŏt'ă nĭst,* s. botaniste, m.

botany, *bŏt'ă nĭ,* s. botanique, f.   [m.

botch, *bŏch,* s. ulcère, m. || raccommodage,

botch, *bŏch,* v. a. rapetasser || saboter.

both, *bŏth,* pn. tous les deux, l'un et l'autre || ~ . . . and . . . , et . . . et . . . , tant . . . que . . . || ~, c. aussi, tant.

bother, *bŏth'ĕr,* s. ennui, m. || ~! peste!

bother, *bŏth'ĕr,* v. a. embarrasser, tracasser.   [s. partisan, m.

bottle, *bŏt'tl,* s. bouteille, f. || ~-holder,

bottle, *bŏt'tl,* v. a. mettre en bouteilles.

bottom, *bŏt'tŏm,* s. fond, fondement, m. || peleton, sédiment, m., lie f. || carène, f. || bâtiment, navire, m.

bottom, *bŏt'tŏm,* v. a. & n. fonder, bâtir sur, baser || se fonder || être assis.

bottomless, *bŏt'tŏm lĕs,* a. sans fond.

bottomry, *bŏt'tŏm rĭ,* s. contrat à la grosse.

bough, *bŏw,* s. rameau, m.   [m.

boughshade, *bŏw'shăd,* f. échauguette, f. (en Australie).

bought, *bawt, vide* buy.   [bloc, m.

boulder, *bōl'dĕr,* s. caillou roulé, m. ||

bounce, *bŏwns,* s. bruit soudain, fracas, m. || vanterie, f.   [bruit || se vanter

bounce, *bŏwns,* v. a. se précipiter avec

bouncing, *bŏwn'sĭng,* a. gros || bruyant || ~ lass, grosse dondon, f.   [élan, m.

bound, *bŏwnd,* s. borne, limite, f. || saut,

bound, *bŏwnd,* v. a. & n. borner, limiter, restreindre || sauter, bondir || homeward, outward ~, (mar.) en retour, en partance.

boundary, *bŏwn'dĕr ĭ,* s. borne, limite, f.

boundless, *bŏwnd'lĕs,* a. sans bornes, illimité.

bounteous, *bŏwn'tĭ ŭs,* **bountiful,** *bŏwn'tĭ fŏŏl,* a. (-ly, ad.) bon, bienfaisant, généreux || libéralement.   [(com.) prime, f.

bounty, *bŏwn'tĭ,* s. bonté, munificence, f. ||

bourne, *bōrn,* s. borne, limite, f.

bout, *bŏwt,* s. fois, f., coup, m. || affaire, f.

bovine, *bō'vĭn,* a. bovine.

bow, *bŏw,* s. salut, m., révérence, f. || (of ships) avant, m.   [cliner.

bow, *bŏw,* v. a. & n. plier, courber, s'in-

bow, *bō,* s. arc, m. || archet, m. || arçon (d'une selle), m. || joug, m. || to draw the long ~, en conter, blaguer || to have two strings to one's ~, avoir plusieurs cordes à son arc || ~-window, s. fenêtre cintrée, f. || demi-cercle, m.

bowels, *bŏw'ĕlz,* s. pl. entrailles, f. pl. || compassion, tendresse, f.

bower, *bŏw'ĕr,* s. tonnelle, f., berceau, m. || boudoir, m. || (mar.) ancre de poste, f.   [m.

bowie-knife, *bō'ĭ nīf,* s. couteau-poignard,

bowl, *bōl,* s. bol, m. || godet, bassin, m. ||

bowl, *bōl,* v. a. jouer à la boule.   [boule, f.

bowline, *bō'lĭn* or *bōw'lĭn,* s. bouline, f.

bowling-green, *bōl'ĭng grēn,* s. boulingrin, parterre de gazon, m.

bowman, *bō'măn,* s. archer, m.

bowsprit, *bō'sprĭt,* s. (mar.) beaupré, m.

bow-wow, *bŏw'wŏw,* s. toutou, m.

box, *bŏks,* s. buis, m. || boîte, f., coffre, carton, m. || siège, m. || loge (de théâtre), f. || ~ on the ear, s. soufflet, m. || ~-keeper, s. ouvreur de loges, m. || ~-office, s. bureau de location, m.

box, *bŏks,* v. a. & n. mettre dans une boîte || souffleter || boxer.

boxer, *bŏks'ĕr,* s. boxeur, m.

boxing, *bŏks'ĭng,* ~-day, (~-night), s. lendemain de Noël, m. || ~-match, s. combat à coups de poing, m.

boy, *bŏy,* s. garçon, enfant, m. || day-~, s. externe, m.

boycott, *bŏy'kŏt,* v. a. boycotter.

boycotting, *bŏy'kŏt ĭng,* s. boycottage, m.

boyhood, *bŏy'hŏŏd,* s. enfance, f.

boyish, *bŏy'ĭsh,* a. enfantin, puéril.

boyishness, *bŏy'ĭsh nĕs,* s. enfantillage, m., puérilité, f.

brace, *brās,* s. bandage, lien, m., paire, f. || soupente, f. || ~-s, pl. bretelles, f. pl.

brace, *brās,* v. a. lier, attacher, serrer, bander || (mar.) brasser.

bracelet, *brās'lĕt,* s. bracelet, m.

brachial, *brā'kĭ ăl,* a. brachial.

bracing, *brā'sĭng,* a. fortifiant, salutaire.

bracken, *brăk'ĕn,* s. (bot.) bruyère, fougère, f.   [m.

bracket, *brăk'ĕt,* s. tasseau, m. || crochet,

bracketed, *brăk'ĕt ĕd,* a. égaux.

brackish, *brăk'ĭsh,* a. salé, saumâtre.

brad, *brăd,* s. clou sans tête, m. || ~-awl, s. poinçon, m.   [chemins de fer anglais, m.

Bradshaw, *brăd'shăw,* s. indicateur des

brag, *brăg,* s. vanterie, f.

brag, *brăg,* v. n. se vanter.

braggadocio, *brăg gă dō'shĭ ō,* s. fanfaron, hâbleur, m.   [fanfaron, m.

braggart, *brăg'gĕrt,* s. vantard, m.

braid, *brād,* s. tresse, tissure, f.

braid, *brād,* v. a. tresser, entrelacer.

brain, *brān,* s. cerveau, m., cervelle, f. || jugement, m. || softening of the ~, s. ramollissement du cerveau, m. || to rack one's ~-s, se casser la tête || ~-pan, s. crâne, m.

brain, *brān,* v. a. faire sauter la cervelle.

brainless, *brān'lĕs,* a. écervelé, étourdi.

braise, *brāz,* v. a. braiser.   [f.

braising-pan, *brāz'ĭng păn,* s. braisière,

brake, *brāk,* s. fougère, f. || buisson, m. || brisoir, m. || bridon, m. || brimbale, f. || (rail.) frein, m. || ~-van, s. (rail.) wagon à frein, m.   [frein, m.

brakesman, *brāks'măn,* s. (rail.) garde-

bramble, *brăm'bl,* s. ronce, f., broussailles,

bran, *brăn,* s. son, m.   [f. pl.

branch, *brănsh,* s. branche, f. || succursale, f. || (rail.) embranchement, m. || ~-house, s. commandite, f. || ~-line, s. (rail.) embranchement, m.

branch, *brănsh,* v. a. & n. diviser en branches || pousser des branches || s'embrancher.

brand, *bránd*, s. brandon, tison, m. ‖ foudre, f. ‖ flétrissure, f. ‖ (com.) marque, f. ‖ ~-new, tout à fait neuf.

brand, *bránd*, v. a. diffamer.

brandied, *brán'díd*, a. mêlé d'eau-de-vie.

brandish, *brán'dish*, v.a. brandir, secouer.

brandy, *brán'di*, s. eau-de-vie, f.

brass, *brás*, s. cuivre jaune, airain, m. ‖ impudence, f. ‖ red ~, s. tombac, m. ‖ ~-founder, s. fondeur de laiton, m. ‖ ~-wares, s. pl. dinanderie, f. ‖ ~-wire, s. fil de laiton, m.

brassy, *brás'si*, a. d'airain ‖ impudent.

brat, *brát*, s. bambin, m.

bravado, *brává'dô*, s. bravade, f.

brave, *bráv*, a. (-ly, ad.) brave(ment) ‖ vaillant ‖ courageusement.

brave, *bráv*, v. a. braver. [f.

bravery, *brá'vér'i*, s. bravoure, vaillance,

bravo, *brá'vô*, s. assassin à gages, m.

bravo! *brá'vô*, bravo! fort bien!

brawl, *bráwl*, s. criaillerie, querelle, f.

brawl, *bráwl*, v. n. criailler, brailler.

brawler, *bráwl'ér*, s. criailleur, querelleur, m. [petit-salé, m.

brawn, *bráwn*, s. force musculaire, f. ‖

brawniness, *bráwn'inés*, s. force, fermeté, dureté, f.

brawny, *bráwn'i*, a. charnu, musculeux.

bray, *brá*, s. braiment, m.

bray, *brá*, v. n. braire.

braze, *bráz*, v. a. souder.

brazen, *brá'zn*, v. n. être impudent ‖ to ~ it out, payer d'effronterie.

brazen, *brá'zn*, a. d'airain ‖ impudent ‖ ~-faced, a. impudent, effronté.

brazenness, *brá'znnés*, s. ressemblance au cuivre, f. ‖ impudence, effronterie, f.

brazier, *brá'zíér*, s. chaudronnier, dinandier, m. [violation, f.

breach, *brêch*, s. brèche, f. ‖ rupture,

bread, *brêd*, s. pain, m., nourriture, f. ‖ brown ~, s. pain bis, m. ‖ household ~, s. pain de ménage, m.

breadstuff, *brêd'stúf*, s. blé, m.

breadth, *brêdth*, s. largeur, f., lé, m.

break, *brák*, s. rupture, ouverture, f. ‖ pause, f. ‖ alinéa, m. ‖ changement, m. ‖ pointe du jour, f. ‖ (rail.) frein, m.

break, *brák*, v. a. & n. ir. rompre, briser, fracasser ‖ dompter ‖ faire banqueroute ‖ casser ‖ violer ‖ intercepter ‖ crever ‖ to ~ with one, se chamailler, s'entre-que-

breakage, *brák'áj*, s. casse, f. [reller.

breakdown, *brák'dôwn*, s. déconfiture, f. ‖ détérioration, f. ‖ insuccès, m. ‖ accident, m.

breaker, *brák'ér*, s. briseur, m. ‖ (fig.) violateur, m. ‖ (nav.) brisant, m. ‖ brise-glace, m. ‖ concasseur, m.

breakfast, *brék'fást*, s. déjeuner, m.

breakfast, *brék'fást*, v. n. déjeuner.

breaking, *brák'ing*, s. fracture, rupture, f. ‖ brisement, m. ‖ ~ up, dissolution, f. ‖ séparation, f. ‖ dispersion, f. ‖ fin, f. ‖ commencement des vacances, m. ‖ (of ice) débâcle, f.

bream, *brêm*, s. brème, f. [m.

breakwater, *brák'wáwtér*, s. brise-mer.

breast, *brést*, s. poitrine, f. ‖ (fig.) âme, f. ‖ conscience, f. ‖ to make a clean ~ of it, en avoir le cœur net ‖ ~-bone, s. brechet, m. ‖ ~-pin, s. épingle, broche, f.

breast, *brést*, v. a. attaquer de front, résister.

breastplate, *brést'plát*, s. cuirasse, f.

breastwork, *brést'wérk*, s. parapet, m.

breath, *brêth*, s. haleine, respiration, f. ‖ souffle, m. ‖ relâche, m. ‖ out of ~, à perte d'haleine ‖ to take ~, reprendre haleine. [exhaler.

breathe, *brêth*, v. a. & n. respirer ‖ souffler ‖

breathing, *brêth'ing*, s. aspiration, f. ‖ souffle, m. ‖ soupirail, m. [essoufflé.

breathless, *brêth'lés*, a. hors d'haleine,

breech, *brêch*, s. derrière, postérieur, m. ‖ ~-es, pl. culotte,f. ‖ knee~es, s.pl. culottes courtes, f. pl. ‖ ~-loader, s. arme à feu se chargeant par la culasse, f.

breed, *brêd*, s. race, espèce, f. ‖ couvée, f.

breed, *brêd*, v. a. & n. ir. engendrer ‖ produire ‖ être enceinte ‖ s'accroître.

breeder, *brêd'ér*, s. producteur, père, m.

breeding, *brêd'ing*, s. éducation, instruction, f.

breeze, *brêz*, s. brise, f. ‖ vent frais, m.

breezy, *brê'zi*, a. rafraîchi par les zéphirs.

brethren, *brêth'rén*, s. pl. (poét.) frères, confrères, m. pl.

breviary, *brê'víérí*, s. bréviaire, m.

brevity, *brév'ití*, s. brièveté, précision, f.

brew, *brô*, v. a. & n. brasser ‖ mélanger ‖ machiner ‖ faire le métier de brasseur.

brewer, *brô'ér*, s. brasseur, m.

brewery, *brô'ér'i*, s. brasserie, f.

bribe, *brib*, s. présent, m. ‖ (fig.) appât, m.

bribe, *brib*, v. a. corrompre.

briber, *brí'bér*, s. corrupteur, suborneur, m.

bribery, *brí'bér'i*, s. corruption, subornation, f.

brick, *brik*, s. brique, f. ‖ ~-kiln, s. four à briques, m., briqueterie, f.

brick, *brik*, v. a. briqueter.

bricklayer, *brik'láér*, s. maçon en briques, [m.

bridal, *brí'dál*, a. & s. nuptial ‖ noces,

bride, *brid*, s. fiancée, épouse, f. [f. pl.

bridegroom, *brid'grôm*, s. fiancé, m. ‖ nouveau marié, époux, m. [f.

bridesmaid, *bridz'mád*, s. fille d'honneur,

Bridewell, *brid'wél*, s. maison de correction.

bridge, *brij*, s. pont, m. [tion, f.

bridge, *brij*, v. a. construire un pont.

bridle, *brí'dl*, s. bride, f. ‖ frein, m. ‖ ~-road, ~-way, s. route cavalière, f.

bridle, *brí'dl*, v. a. mettre la bride ‖ gouverner ‖ to ~ (up), v. n. se redresser.

brief, *brêf*, s. (jur.) dossier, m. ‖ bref, m. ‖ in ~, en bref. [ad. brièvement.

brief, *brêf*, a. bref, court ‖ concis ‖ -ly,

briefless, *brêf'lés*, a. sans cause (avocat).

brier, *brí'ér*, s. ronce, f. ‖ broussailles, f. pl.

brig, *brig*, s. brick, m.

brigade, *brigád'*, s. brigade, f.

brigand, *brig'ánd*, s. brigand, m.

bright, *brīt,* a. luisant, brillant, illustre, éclatant || intelligent || -**ly,** ad. brillamment.

brighten, *brīt'n,* v. a. & n. faire briller, polir || rendre illustre || s'éclaircir.

brightness, *brīt'nĕs,* s. lustre, m., clarté, splendeur, f., éclat, m.

brill, *bril,* s. barbue, f.   [deur, f.

brilliancy, *bril'yánsĭ,* s. éclat, m., splendeur, f.

brilliant, *bril'yánt,* s. brillant, m.

brilliant, *bril'yánt,* a. brillant.

brim, *brim,* s. bord, m. || extrémité, f.

brim, *brim,* v. a. & n. remplir jusqu'au bord || être plein jusqu'au bord.

brimful, *brim'fŏŏl,* a. plein jusqu'au bord.

brimming, *brim'ming,* a. tout plein.

brimstone, *brim'stŏn,* s. soufre, m.

brindled, *brin'dld,* a. tacheté, tavelé.

brine, *brīn,* s. saumure, f. || onde amère, f.

brine, *brīn,* v. a. tremper dans la saumure.

bring, *bring,* v. a. ir. apporter, amener, conduire, prévaloir sur || to ~ forth, produire || to ~ forward, faire avancer || sum brought forward, report, m. || to ~ to, ramener à la raison || (mar.) mettre en panne.

bringing up, *bring'ing up,* s. éducation, f.

brink, *bringk,* s. bord, m. || (fig.) penchant, f.   [m.

briny, *brī'nĭ,* a. amer, salé.

brisk, *brisk,* a. vigoureux, vif, animé, spiritueux || -**ly,** ad. vivement; (com.) activement.   [f.

brisket, *bris'kĕt,* s. poitrine (d'un animal).

briskness, *brisk'nĕs,* s. vivacité, gaieté, vigueur, ardeur, f. || (com.) activité, f.

bristle, *bris'sl,* s. soie de sanglier, f. || (bot.) poil, m.

bristle, *bris'sl,* v. a. & n. (se) hérisser.

bristly, *bris'lĭ,* a. hérissé.

Britannia-metal, *brĭtăn'nĭ ă mĕt'l,* s. métal blanc anglais, m.   [casuel.

brittle, *bril'l,* a. frêle, fragile, cassant ||

brittleness, *bril'l nĕs,* s. fragilité, f.

broach, *brōch,* v. a. mettre à la broche || percer || publier || inventer.

broad, *brāwd,* a. large, vaste, grand || plein, entier, grossier || obscène.

broadcloth, *brāwd'clŏth,* s. drap fin, m.

broadside, *brāwd'sīd,* s. flanc d'un vaisseau, m. || bordée, f.

broadsword, *brāwd'sōrd,* s. espadon, m.

brocade, *brō kād',* s. brocart, m.

broccoli, *brŏk'kŏ lĭ,* s. brocoli, m.

brogue, *brōg,* s. sabot, m. || patois, m.

broider, *brōy'dĕr,* v. a. *vide* embroider.

broil, *brŏyl,* s. brouillerie, dispute, f. || tumulte, m.   [brûler.

broil, *brŏyl,* v. a. & n. griller || se griller ||

broken, *brō'kn,* p. & a. cassé || interrompu || écorché || ~ **week,** s. semaine avec un jour de fête, f. || ~-**winded,** a. poussif.

broker, *brō'kĕr,* s. courtier, m. || fripier, m. || brocanteur, m. || **outside** ~, s. courtier marron.

brokerage, *brō'kĕr ăj,* s. courtage, m.

bronchial, *brŏng'kĭ ăl,* a. bronchial, m.

bronchitis, *brŏng kī'tĭs,* s. bronchite, f.

bronze, *brŏnz,* s. bronze, m.

bronze, *brŏnz,* v. a. bronzer.

brooch, *brōch,* s. broche, f. || camaïeu, m.

brood, *brōd,* s. couvée, f. || race, f. || ~-**hen,** s. couveuse, f.   [couver.

brood, *brōd,* v. a. & n. soigner, nourrir ||

brook, *brōŏk,* s. ruisseau, m.

brook, *brōŏk,* v. a. & n. endurer, souffrir.

brooklet, *brōŏk'lĕt,* s. petit ruisseau, m.

broom, *brōm,* s. (bot.) genêt, m. || balai, m. || ~-**stick,** s. manche à balai, m.

broth, *brăwth,* s. bouillon, m.

brothel, *brŏth'ĕl,* s. bordel, m.

brother, *brŭth'ĕr,* s. frère, m. || ~-**in-law,** s. beau-frère, m.   [f. || confrérie, f.

brotherhood, *brŭth'ĕr hŏŏd,* s. fraternité,

brotherly, *brŭth'ĕr lĭ,* a. & ad. fraternelle (ment) || de frère.

brougham, *brō'ăm,* s. brougham, coupé, m.

brow, *brŏw,* s. sourcil, m. || front, air, m. || to knit one's ~, froncer le sourcil.

browbeat, *brŏw'bēt,* v. a. jeter un regard sévère sur.

brown, *brŏwn,* s. couleur brune, f.

brown, *brŏwn,* v. a. brunir || gratiner.

brown, *brŏwn,* a. brun, de couleur brune || ~ **paper,** s. papier gris, m. || ~ **study,** s. pensées sombres, f. pl. || ~ **sugar,** s. cassonade, f.

brownish, *brŏwn'ish,* a. brunâtre.

brownness, *brŏwn'nĕs,* s. couleur brune, f.

browse, *brŏwz,* v. a. brouter.

bruise, *brōz,* s. meurtrissure, bosse, f.

bruise, *brōz,* v. a. écraser, meurtrir.

bruit, *brō'ĭt,* s. bruit, rapport, m.

bruit, *brō'ĭt,* v. a. ébruiter.

Brummagem, *brŭm'ă jĕm,* a. de mauvais aloi, faux.

brunt, *brŭnt,* s. choc, m., violence, f. || (of fire-arms) feu, m.

brush, *brŭsh,* s. brosse, vergette, f. || queue de renard, f. || attaque, f., assaut, m.

brush, *brŭsh,* v. a. & n. brosser, décrotter || raser || effleurer || décamper || **to** ~ **off,** déserter.   [broussailles, f. pl.

brushwood, *brŭsh'wŏŏd,* s. bourrée, f.

brutal, *brō'tăl,* a. (-ly, ad.) brutal(ement) || cruel(lement).

brutalise, *brō'tă līz,* v. a. (& n.) (s')abrutir.

brutality, *brō tăl'ĭ tĭ,* s. brutalité, cruauté.

brute, *brōt,* s. brute, bête, f.   [f.

brute, *brōt,* a. brutal, sauvage.

brutish, *brō'tĭsh,* a. brut, brutal || sensuel.

bryony, *brī'ō nĭ,* s. (bot.) bryone, f.

bubble, *bŭb'bl,* s. bulle d'air, f. || bagatelle, f. || (fig.) chimère, f. || duperie, f.

bubble, *bŭb'bl,* v. a. & n. duper || bouillonner.   [bustier, m.

buccaneer, *bŭk ă nēr',* s. boucanier, flibuster, m.

buck, *bŭk,* s. daim, chevreuil, f. || luron, f. || lapin, m. || lessive, f. || ~-**shot,** s. chevrotine, f. || ~-**thorn,** s. (bot.) nerprun, m.

bucket, *bŭk'ĕt,* s. seau, m.   [m.

bucking, *bŭk'ing,* s. lessive, f.

buckle, *bŭk'l,* s. boucle, f. || boucle de cheveux, f. || [en boucles] s'appliquer à.

buckle, *bŭk'l,* v. a. & n. boucler, mettre

buckler, *bŭk'lẽr*, s. bouclier, m., arme défensive, f.

buckram, *bŭk'răm*, s. bougran, m.

buckskin, *bŭk'skin*, s. peau de daim || sorte d'étoffe de laine, f. [noir, m.

buckwheat, *bŭk'hwēt*, s. sarrasin, blé

bucolic, *bŭkŏl'ĭk*, a. bucolique.

bud, *bŭd*, s. bouton, bourgeon, jet, m.

buddhist, *bōōd'dĭst*, s. bouddhiste, m.

budge, *bŭj*, v. n. se remuer, frétiller.

budget, *bŭj'ĕt*, s. budget, m. || sac, m.

buff, *bŭf*, s. peau de buffle préparée, f.

buff, *bŭf*, a. de peau de buffle || de couleur chamois.

buffalo, *bŭf'fā lō*, s. buffle, m.

buffer, *bŭf'fẽr*, s. (rail.) tampon, m.

buffet, *bŭf'fĕt*, s. coup de poing, m.

buffet, *bŭf'fĕt*, v. a. (& n.) (se) battre à coups de poing.

buffoon, *bŭf fōōn'*, s. bouffon, m.

buffoonery, *bŭf fōōn'ẽ rĭ*, s. bouffonnerie, f.

bug, *bŭg*, s. punaise, f. [drôlerie, f.

bugbear, *bŭg'bār*, s. loup-garou, épouvantail, m.

buggy, *bŭg'gĭ*, s. américaine, f. (calèche).

bugle, *bŭ'gl*, s. cor de chasse, m.

bugler, *bŭ'glẽr*, s. clairon, m.

buhl, *bŭl*, s. marqueterie (de Boule), m.

build, *bĭld*, s. construction, forme, f.

build, *bĭld*, v. a. & n. ir. bâtir, construire || se reposer, compter sur.

builder, *bĭld'ẽr*, s. entrepreneur de bâtiments, m. || (fig.) fondateur, m.

building, *bĭld'ĭng*, s. bâtiment, m. || édifice, m., construction, f.

bulb, *bŭlb*, s. bulbe, f., oignon, m. || ~ of the eye, s. pupille, f.

bulbous, *bŭlb'ŭs*, a. bulbeux.

bulfinch, *bōōl'fĭnsh*, s. bouvreuil, m.

bulge, *bŭlj*, s. (mar.) fonds, m. pl.

bulge, *bŭlj*, v. n. prendre eau.

bulk, *bŭlk*, s. grosseur, masse, quantité, f. || charge d'un bâtiment, f. || calibre, m. || by the ~, à forfait. [lence, f.

bulkiness, *bŭlk'ĭ nĕs*, s. grosseur, corpulence, f.

bulky, *bŭlk'ĭ*, a. grand, massif || corpulent || volumineux.

bull, *bōōl*, s. taureau, m. || bévue, f. || bêtise, f. || ~-baiting, ~-fight, s. course de taureaux, tauromachie, f., combat de taureaux, m. || ~-dog, s. boule-dogue, m. || ~-frog, s. grenouille mugissante, f. || ~-head, s. lourdaud, m. || ~'s-eye, s. œil-de-bœuf, m. || lanterne à réflecteur, f.

bullet, *bōōl'lĕt*, s. boulet, m., balle, f.

bulletin, *bōōl'lĕ tĭn*, s. bulletin, m.

bullion, *bōōl'yŭn*, s. or, argent en lingots, m.

bullock, *bōōl'ŏk*, s. jeune taureau, m. || bœuf, m.

bully, *bōōl'lĭ*, s. tapageur, faux brave, m.

bully, *bōōl'lĭ*, v. n. faire le fanfaron.

bulrush, *bōōl'rŭsh*, s. jonc, m. [part, f.

bulwark, *bōōl'wẽrk*, s. boulevard, rempart, m.

bulwark, *bōōl'wẽrk*, v. a. fortifier.

bumboat, *bŭm'bōt*, s. bateau de provisions, m.

bump, *bŭmp*, s. bosse, f. || coup, m.

bump, *bŭmp*, v. a. heurter, frapper, (avec force). [m.

bumper, *bŭmp'ẽr*, s. rasade, f., rouge-bord,

bumpkin, *bŭm'kĭn*, s. rustre, lourdaud, m.

bumptious, *bŭm'shŭs*, a. qui fait d'embarras.

bun, *bŭn*, s. baba, m.

bunch, *bŭnsh*, s. bosse, tumeur, f. || faisceau, m. || grappe, f.

bunch, *bŭnsh*, v. n. bomber.

bunchy, *bŭnsh'ĭ*, a. touffu, en grappes || noueux. [poignée, f.

bundle, *bŭn'dl*, s. paquet, m. || fagot, m. ||

bundle, *bŭn'dl*, v. a. empaqueter.

bung, *bŭng*, s. bondon, m. || ~-hole, s. bonde, f. [dienne, f.

bungalow, *bŭng'gā lō*, s. baraque indienne, f.

bungle, *bŭng'gl*, s. bévue, faute, f.

bungle, *bŭng'gl*, v. a. bousiller, massacrer.

bungler, *bŭng'glẽr*, s. sabotier, m.

bunion, *bŭn'yŭn*, s. oignon, m.

bunker, *bŭng'kẽr*, s. soute au charbon, f.

bunting, *bŭn'tĭng*, s. drapeau, m.

buoy, *b(ōō)ŏy*, s. (mar.) bouée, f.

buoy, *b(ōō)ŏy*, v. a. & n. faire flotter || flotter. [surnager, f. || (fig.) légèreté, f.

buoyancy, *b(ōō)ŏy'ăn sĭ*, s. faculté de surnager, f. || (fig.) légèreté, f.

buoyant, *b(ōō)ŏy'ănt*, a. flottant, léger.

burden, *bẽr'dn*, s. fardeau, m., charge, f. || refrain, m. || **beast of ~**, bête de somme, f.

burden, *bẽr'dn*, v. a. surcharger.

burdensome, *bẽr'dn sŭm*, a. pesant, onéreux. [glouteron, m.

burdock, *bẽr'dŏk*, s. (bot.) bardane, f. ||

burgess, *bẽr'jĕs*, s. bourgeois, m. || représentant de bourg, m. [geois, m.

burgher, *bẽrg'ẽr*, s. citoyen, franc bourgeois, m.

burglar, *bẽrg'lẽr*, s. voleur de nuit avec effraction, m.

burglarious, *bẽrg'lār ĭ ŭs*, a. de vol de nuit. [effraction, m.

burglary, *bẽrg'lẽr ĭ*, s. vol de nuit avec effraction, m.

burgomaster, *bẽr'gō mǎs tẽr*, s. bourgmestre, m.

burial, *bẽr'ĭ ăl*, s. enterrement, m., funérailles, f. pl. || ~-ground, s. cimetière, m.

burlesque, *bẽr lĕsk'*, s. burlesque, m. [m.

burlesque, *bẽr lĕsk'*, v. a. tourner en ridicule.

burlesque, *bẽr lĕsk'*, a. burlesque, bouffon.

burly, *bẽr'lĭ*, a. replet, gros et gras, dodu.

burn, *bẽrn*, s. brûlure, f. || cuite, f.

burn, *bẽrn*, v. a. & n. ir. brûler || cautériser || incendier. [m.

burner, *bẽrn'ẽr*, s. brûleur (gas~~) bec,

burning-glass, *bẽrn'ĭng glǎs*, s. miroir ardent, m. [v. n. luire.

burnish, *bẽr'nĭsh*, v. a. brunir, polir || ~,

burrow, *bŭr'rō*, s. lapinière, f.

burrow, *bŭr'rō*, v. n. s'enclotir.

bursar, *bẽr'sẽr*, s. boursier, m. || économe, m.

bursarship, *bẽr'sẽr shĭp*, s. économat, m.

burst, *bẽrst*, s. fracas, éclat, m. || (fig.) mouvement, m. || explosion, f.

burst, *bĕrst,* v. n. ir. crever, se crever, éclater, se briser || **-ing charge,** s. bombe foudroyante, f.

burthen, *bĕr'thn,* s. *vide* **burden.**

bury, *bĕr'ĭ,* v. a. enterrer || cacher.

burying-ground, *bĕr'ĭĭng grŏwnd,* s. [cimetière, m.

bus, *bŭs,* s. omnibus, m.

busby, *bŭs'bĭ,* s. colback, m.

bush, *bŏŏsh,* s. buisson, m. || bouchon de cabaret, m. || **to beat about the ~,** tourner autour du pot.

bushel, *bŏŏsh'ĕl,* s. boisseau, m. (40 litres).

bushy, *bŏŏsh'ĭ,* a. buissonneux, touffu.

busily, *bĭz'ĭlĭ,* ad. avec empressement, ardemment.

business, *bĭz'nĕs,* s. affaire, occupation, f. || **mind your own ~!** mêlez-vous de vos propres affaires!

busk, *bŭsk,* s. busc, m.

buskin, *bŭs'kĭn,* s. cothurne, brodequin, m.

buss, *bŭs,* s. baiser, m. [m.

bust, *bŭst,* s. buste, m.

bustard, *bŭs'tĕrd,* s. outarde, f.

bustle, *bŭs'l,* s. tumulte, fracas, m. || tournure, f. [s'empresser.

bustle, *bŭs'l,* v. a. se remuer beaucoup,

busy, *bĭz'ĭ,* v. a. occuper, employer.

busy, *bĭz'ĭ,* a. occupé, affairé.

busybody, *bĭz'ĭbŏd'ĭ,* s. officieux, m.

but, *bŭt,* c. mais, si ce n'est, sinon, seulement, moins || excepté, hormis.

butcher, *bŏŏch'ĕr,* s. boucher, m.

butcher, *bŏŏch'ĕr,* v. a. massacrer, égorger.

butchery, *bŏŏch'ĕrĭ,* s. boucherie, f., carnage, m.

butler, *bŭt'lĕr,* s. sommelier, m.

butt, *bŭt,* s. butte, f., jouet, plastron, m. || botte, f. || pipe, f., muid, m.

butt, *bŭt,* v. n. cosser.

butter, *bŭt'tĕr,* s. beurre, m. || **-ed eggs,** s. œufs brouillés, m. pl.

butter, *bŭt'tĕr,* v. a. beurrer, étendre du beurre sur. [m.

buttercup, *bŭt'tĕr kŭp,* s. jaunet (fleur),

butterfly, *bŭt'tĕr flĭ,* s. papillon, m.

buttermilk, *bŭt'tĕr milk,* s. babeurre, m.

buttery, *bŭt'tĕrĭ,* a. butireux, beurré.

buttock, *bŭt'tŏk,* s. cimier, m., croupe, f.

button, *bŭt'n,* s. bouton, m. || bourgeon, m. || **~-hole,** s. boutonnière, f. || **~-hook,** s. tire-bouton, m.

button, *bŭt'n,* v. a. (& n.) (se)boutonner.

buttress, *bŭt'trĕs,* s. arc-boutant, m.

buttress, *bŭt'trĕs,* v. a. arc-bouter.

buxom, *bŭk'sŭm,* a. souple, gai, enjoué, amoureux || **-ly,** ad. docilement, amoureusement.

buy, *bĭ,* v. a. ir. acheter. [ment, m.

buzz, *bŭz,* s. bourdonnement, chuchote-

buzz, *bŭz,* v. n. bourdonner.

by, *bĭ,* pr. & ad. près de, auprès de, par, sur || d'après, à part || **~ and ~,** tout à l'heure, bientôt || **~ the bye,** à propos || **~ the way,** en passant || **~ day,** de jour || **~ all means,** à quelque prix que ce soit || **~ no means,** nullement.

by, *bĭ;* **~-blow,** s. coup de hasard, m. ||

~-lane, s. ruelle attenante, f. || **~-law,** s. statut, m. || loi locale, f. || **~-name,** s. surnom, sobriquet, m. || **~-path,** s. sentier détourné, m. || **~-street,** s. rue latérale, f. || **~-way,** s. chemin détourné, m.

bye, *bĭ,* s. adieu, m. || **good ~!** adieu!

bygone, *bĭ'gŏn,* a. passé || **let -s be -s!** que le passé soit passé.

bystander, *bĭ'stănd ĕr,* s. assistant, spectateur, m. [d'injure, m.

byword, *bĭ'wĕrd,* s. proverbe, m. || terme

C.

cab, *kăb,* s. cabriolet, m. || fiacre, m. || **hansom~,** s. cabriolet anglais, m. || **~-stand,** s. station de voitures de place, f.

cabal, *kă băl',* s. cabale, f. || intrigue, f.

cabal, *kă băl',* v. n. cabaler.

cabbage, *kăb'băj,* s. chou, m. || **~-lettuce,** s. laitue pommée, f. [mer.

cabbage, *kăb'băj,* v. a. & n. gratter || pom-

cabby, *kăb'bĭ,* **cab-driver,** *kăb' drī vĕr,* **cabman,** *kăb'măn,* s. cocher, m.

cabin, *kăb'ĭn,* s. cabinet, m., cabane, chaumière, f. || **~-boy,** s. mousse, m. || **~-passenger,** s. passager de première classe, m. [dans une cabane.

cabin, *kăb'ĭn,* v. a. & n. enfermer *or* vivre

cabinet, *kăb'ĭn ĕt,* s. cabinet, m. || **~-Council,** s. conseil privé du roi, m. || **~-maker,** s. ébéniste, m.

cable, *kā'bl,* s. câble, m. || **~-length,** s. encâblure, f.

cable, *kā'bl,* v. a. câbler.

caboose, *kă bŏs',* s. (mar.) cuisine f.

cachou, *kăsh ŏ',* s. cachou, m.

cackle, *kăk'l,* s. caquet, m.

cackle, *kăk'l,* v. n. caqueter || ricaner.

cackler, *kăk'lĕr,* s. caqueteur, m.

cactus, *kăk'tŭs,* s. (bot.) cactus, cactier, m.

cad, *kăd,* s. conducteur d'omnibus, m. || gamin, m.

cadaverous, *kă dăv'ĕr ŭs,* a. cadavéreux.

caddy, *kăd'dĭ,* s. boîte à thé, f.

cadence, *kā'dĕns,* s. (mus.) chute, cadence, f.

cadence, *kā'dĕns,* v. a. cadencer. [f.

cadet, *kă dĕt',* s. cadet, m. || volontaire, m.

cæsura, *sĕ zū'ră,* s. césure, f.

cage, *kāj,* s. cage, f. || prison, f.

cage, *kāj,* v. a. mettre en cage || emprisonner. [m.

caitiff, *kā'tĭf,* s. malheureux, misérable,

cajole, *kă jōl',* v. a. cajoler, caresser.

cajolery, *kăjō'lĕr ĭ,* s. cajolerie, f.

cake, *kāk,* s. gâteau, m.

cake, *kāk,* v. n. se former en croûte.

calabash, *kăl'ă băsh,* s. calebasse, f.

calamitous, *kă lăm'ĭ tŭs,* a. calamiteux || malheureux.

calamity, *kă lăm'ĭtĭ,* s. calamité, misère, f.

calash, *kă lăsh',* s. calèche, f. [f.

calcareous, *kăl kā'rĭ ŭs,* s. calcaire.

calcine, *kăl'sĭn*, v. a. (& n.) (se) calciner.
calculable, *kăl'kŭlăbl*, a. calculable.
calculate, *kăl'kŭlāt*, v. a. calculer, compter (sur) || ajuster.   [propre à, favorable à.
calculated, *kăl'kŭlātĕd*, a. calculé, adapté.
calculation, *kăl'kŭlā'shŭn*, s. calcul, m., supputation, f., compte, m.
calculator, *kăl'kŭlātĕr*, s. calculateur, m.
calculus, *kăl'kŭlŭs*, s. (méd.) calcul, m.
caldron, *kăŭl'drŏn*, s. chaudron, m.
calefactor, *kăl'ĕfăktĕr*, s. digesteur, m.
calendar, *kăl'ĕndĕr*, s. calendrier, almanach, m.
calender, *kăl'ĕndĕr*, s. calandre, f.
calender, *kăl'ĕndĕr*, v. a. calandrer.
calf, *kăf*, s. veau, m. || gras de la jambe, m.
calibre, *kăl'ĭbĕr*, s. calibre, m.
calico, *kăl'ĭkō*, s. calicot, m., indienne, f.
calisthenics, *kăl'ĭsthĕn'ĭks*, s. pl. exercises gymnastiques, m. pl.
calk, *kawk*, v. a. calfater.
call, *kawl*, s. appel, m., invitation, f. || commandement, ordre, m. || **~-bell**, s. timbre (de table), m. || **~-bird**, s. chanterelle, f. || **~-boy**, s. domestique, m.
call, *kawl*, v. a. appeler || nommer || rappeler || citer || assembler || commander || **to ~ for**, réclamer, demander, envoyer chercher, aller prendre || **to ~ on**, passer chez || **within ~**, à portée de la voix.
calligraphy, *kăl'lĭg'răfĭ*, s. calligraphie, f.
calling, *kawl'lĭng*, s. vocation, f. || profession, f., métier, m. || emploi, m.
callosity, *kăl'lŏs'ĭtĭ*, s. callosité, f.
callous, *kăl'lŭs*, a. calleux || insensible.
callow, *kăl'lō*, a. sans plumes || jeune.
calm, *kăm*, s. calme, m. || **dead ~**, calme plat, m.
calm, *kăm*, v. a. calmer.
calm, *kăm*, a. (-ly, ad.) calme(ment) tranquille(ment).   [lité f.
calmness, *kăm'nĕs*, s. calme, m., tranquillité (ment).
calomel, *kăl'ŏmĕl*, s. calomel, m.
caloric, *kăl'ŏr'ĭk*, s. calorique, m.
caltrop, *kăl'trŏp*, s. chausse-trappe, f. || herse, f.
calumniate, *kălŭm'nĭāt*, v. a. calomnier.
calumniation, *kălŭm'nĭā'shŭn*, s. diffamation, f.
calumniatory, *kălŭm'nĭātĕrĭ*, a. calomnieux, diffamant.   [tion, f.
calumny, *kăl'ŭmnĭ*, s. calomnie, diffamation, f.
Calvary, *kăl'vărĭ*, s. le Calvaire, m.
calve, *kăv*, v. n. vêler || (fig.) enfanter.
Calvinism, *kăl'vĭnĭzm*, s. calvinisme, m.
cambric, *kăm'brĭk*, s. toile de Cambrai, batiste, f.
camel, *kăm'ĕl*, s. chameau, m.
cameleopard, *kăm'ĕlĕŏpărd*, s. girafe, f.
camellia, *kămĕl'lĭă*, s. (bot.) camélia, m.
cameo, *kăm'ĕō*, s. camée, m.
camera, *kăm'ĕră*, s. chambre de l'appareil photographique, f.
camomile, *kăm'ŏmīl*, s. camomille, f.
camp, *kămp*, s. camp, m. || **~-follower**, s. soldat du train, m. || **~-stool**, s. pliant, s.
camp, *kămp*, v. n. camper.   [m.

campaign, *kăm pān'*, s. expédition militaire, f.   [pagne.
campaign, *kăm pān'*, v. n. faire une campaigner, *kăm pān'ĕr*, s. vieux soldat.
camphor, *kăm'fĕr*, s. camphre, m.   [m.
camphorated, *kăm'fĕrātĕd*, a. camphré.
can, *kăn*, s. bidon, m.   [savoir.
can, *kăn*, v. n. ir. pouvoir, être capable de,
canal, *kănăl'*, s. canal, conduit, m.
canary(bird), *kănă'rĭbĕrd*, s. canari, serin, m.   [biffer || annuler || résilier.
cancel, *kăn'sĕl*, v. a. canceller || effacer ||
cancer, *kăn'sĕr*, s. cancer, m.
cancerous, *kăn'sĕrŭs*, a. cancéreux.
candelabrum, *kăndĕlă'brŭm*, s. candelabre, m.
candid, *kăn'dĭd*, a. candide, franc || **-ly**, ad. franchement, de *or* en bonne foi.
candidate, *kăn'dĭdāt*, s. candidat, aspirant, m.
candied, *kăn'dĭd*, a. candi, confit.
candle, *kăn'dl*, s. chandelle, f. || **~-end** s. bout de chandelle, m. || **~-light**, s. lumière d'une chandelle, des chandelles, f.
Candlemas, *kăn'dlmăs*, s. la Chandeleur, f.
candlestick, *kăn'dlstĭk*, s. chandelier, m. || flambeau, m. || candélabre, m.
candour, *kăn'dĕr*, s. candeur, franchise, f.
candy, *kăn'dĭ*, s. candi, m.   [loyauté, f.
candy, *kăn'dĭ*, v. a. & n. confire au sucre || se candir.
cane, *kăn*, s. canne, f., roseau, m. || bâton, m. || **~-bottom(ed) chair**, s. chaise nattée, f.
cane, *kăn*, v. a. bâtonner.
canicular, *kănĭk'ŭlĕr*, a. caniculaire.
canine, *kă'nĭn*, a. canin, de chien.
caning, *kă'nĭng*, s. coups de canne, m. pl. || volée de coups de canne, f.
canister, *kăn'ĭstĕr*, s. boîte de fer-blanc || corbeille, boîte à thé, f. || **~-shot**, s. mitraille, f.
canker, *kăng'kĕr*, s. chancre, m. || (fig.) ver rongeur, m.   [fecter || (se) corrompre.
canker, *kăng'kĕr*, v. a. & n. ronger || incankerous, *kăng'kĕrŭs*, a. chancreux.
cannibal, *kăn'nĭbăl*, s. cannibale, anthropophage, m.   [phagie, f.
cannibalism, *kăn'nĭbălĭzm*, s. anthropocannon, *kăn'nŏn*, s. canon, m. || **(at billiards)** carambolage, m. || **~-ball**, s. boulet de canon, m. || **~-shot**, s. coup de canon, m.
cannon, *kăn'nŏn*, v. n. caramboler.
cannonade, *kănnŏnād'*, s. canonnade, f.
cannonade, *kănnŏnād'*, v. n. canonner.
cannoneer, *kănnŏnēr'*, s. canonnier, m.
cannot = can not.
canny, *kăn'nĭ*, a. (Écoss.) prudent.
canoe, *kănō'*, s. canot, m.
canon, *kăn'ŏn*, s. canon, m., règle, f. || chanoine, m. || **~-law**, s. droit canon, m.
canoness, *kăn'ŏnnĕs*, s. chanoinesse, f.
canonical, *kănŏn'ĭkăl*, a. canonique || **-s**, s. pl. habits de cérémonie, m. pl.
canonisation, *kănŏnĭză'shŭn*, s. canonisation, f.

canonise, *kăn'ŏn īz,* v. a. mettre au nombre des saints.   [*shĭp,* s. canonicat, m.
canonry, *kăn'ŏn rĭ,* canonship, *kăn'ŏn-*
canopy, *kăn'ŏ pĭ,* s. dais, baldaquin, m.
cant, *kănt,* s. argot, jargon, m. || hypo-crisie, f.
cant, *kănt,* v. a. & n. parler un jargon || faire le cafard.   [m.
Cantab, *kăn'tăb,* s. étudiant de Cambridge,
cantankerous, *kăn tăng'kĕr ŭs,* a. re-vêche, acariâtre.
canteen, *kăn tēn',* s. cantine, f. || bidon, m.
canter, *kăn'tĕr,* s. faux dévot, hypocrite, m. || petit galop, m.
canter, *kăn'tĕr,* v. n. aller au petit galop.
cantharides, *kăn thăr'ĭ dēz,* s. pl. can-tharides, f. pl.
canticle, *kăn'tĭ kl,* s. cantique, m.
canting, *kănt'ĭng,* a. cafard, hypocrite.
canto, *kăn'tō,* s. chant, m.
canton, *kăn'tŏn,* s. canton, m. || contrée, f.
canton, *kăn'tŏn,* v. a. & n. diviser en can-tons || cantonner.   [ment, m.
cantonment, *kăn tŏn'mĕnt,* s. cantonne-
canvas, *kăn'văs,* s. canevas, m. || sollici-tation de suffrages, candidature, f. || ~-
backed duck, s. canard américain, m.
canvass, *kăn'văs,* v. a. examiner, dé-battre || solliciter les suffrages.   [tateur, m.
canvasser, *kăn'văs ĕr,* s. solliciteur || scru-
caoutchouc, *kō'chook,* s. caoutchouc, m.
cap, *kăp,* s. bonnet, m., casquette, f. || capsule, f. || couvercle, m. || a feather in one's ~, une bague au doigt || to set one's ~ at one, vouloir captiver qn.
cap, *kăp,* v. a. & n. ôter le bonnet || coiffer.
capability, *kā pȧ bĭl'ĭ tĭ,* s. capacité, f.
capable, *kā'pȧbl,* a. capable, propre à.
capacious, *kȧ pā'shŭs,* a. large, spacieux.
capacitate, *kȧ păs'ĭ tāt,* v. a. rendre ca-pable.   [ligence, f.
capacity, *kȧ păs'ĭ tĭ,* s. capacité, intel-
caparison, *kȧ păr'ĭ sŭn,* s. caparaçon, m.
caparison, *kȧ păr'ĭ sŭn,* v. a. caparaçon-ner.   [d'un manteau, m.
cape, *kāp,* s. cap, promontoire, m. || collet
caper, *kā'pĕr,* s. câbriole, f., entrechat, m. || câpre, f.
caper, *kā'pĕr,* v. n. faire des cabrioles.
capillary, *kăp'ĭl lăr ĭ,* a. capillaire.
capital, *kăp'ĭ tȧl,* s. capitale, métropole, f. || majuscule, f. || chapiteau, m. || capi-tal, m.
capital, *kăp'ĭ tȧl,* a. capital, principal || ex-cellent || -ly, ad. criminellement || à mer-veille.
capitalise, *kăp'ĭ tȧl īz,* v. a. capitaliser.
capitalist, *kăp'ĭ tȧl ĭst,* s. capitaliste, m.
capitation, *kăp ĭ tā'shŭn,* s. taxe par tête.
capitol, *kăp'ĭ tŏl,* s. capitole, m.   [f.
capitular, *kȧ pĭt'ū lĕr,* s. membre d'un chapitre, m.
capitulate, *kȧ pĭt'ū lāt,* v. n. capituler.
capitulation, *kȧ pĭt ū lā'shŭn,* s. capitu-lation, f.
capon, *kā'pn,* s. chapon, m.
caprice, *kȧ prēs',* s. caprice, m., bizarrerie,

capricious, *kȧ prĭsh'ŭs,* a. capricieux || -ly, ad. capricieusement.   [corne, m.
Capricorn, *kăp'rĭ kăwrn,* s. (astr.) Capri-
capsize, *kăp sīz',* v. a. renverser, chavirer.
capsule, *kăp'sŭl,* s. capsule, f.
captain, *kăp'tĭn,* s. capitaine, chef, m. || ~ of foot, capitaine d'infanterie, m. || ~ of horse, capitaine de cavalerie, m.
captaincy, *kăp'tĭn sĭ,* s. grade de capi-taine, m. || capitainerie, f.
captainship, *kăp'tĭn shĭp,* s. commande-ment, m. || talent militaire, m.
captious, *kăp'shŭs,* a. captieux, insidieux || chicaneur || -ly ad. captieusement.
captiousness, *kăp'shŭs nĕs,* s. humeur pointilleuse, f. || susceptibilité, f.
captivate, *kăp'tĭ văt,* v. a. captiver || en-chanter.
captive, *kăp'tĭv,* s. captif, m.
captive, *kăp'tĭv,* a. captif || to take ~, faire prisonnier.
captivity, *kăp tĭv'ĭ tĭ,* s. captivité, f.
captor, *kăp'tĕr,* s. auteur d'une prise, m.
capture, *kăp'tūr,* s. capture, prise, f.
capture, *kăp'tūr,* v. a. capturer.
Capuchin, *kăp ū shēn',* s. capucin, m.
car, *kăr,* s. charrette, f. || nacelle, f.
car(a)bineer, *kăr bĭ nēr',* s. carabinier, m.
caramel, *kăr'ȧ mĕl,* s. caramel, m.
carat, *kăr'ăt,* s. carat, m.
caravan, *kăr ȧ văn',* s. caravane, f.
caravansary, *kăr ȧ văn'sĕr ĭ,* s. caravan-sérail, m.   [prés, m.
caraway, *kăr'ȧ wā,* s. carvi, cumin des
carbine, *kăr'bĭn,* s. carabine, f.
carbolic, *kăr bŏl'ĭk,* a. carbolique.
carbon, *kăr'bŏn,* s. (chem.) carbone, m.
carbonate, *kăr'bō nāt,* s. carbonate, m.
carbonise, *kăr'bŏn īz,* v. a. carboniser || ~, v. n. (of lamps) charbonner.
carbuncle, *kăr'bŭng kl,* s. escarboucle, f. || carboncle, m. || -d, orné d'escarboucles || (of the nose) bourgeonné.
carbuncular, *kăr bŭng'kū lĕr,* a. d'escar-boucle || (méd.) charbonneux.   [m.
carcass, *kăr'kăs,* s. carcasse, f., cadavre,
card, *kărd,* s. carte à jouer, f. || carte, adresse, f. || carde, f. || pack of -s, jeu de cartes, m. || marked -s, carte ajustée, f. || ~-rack, s. porte-cartes, m. || ~-sharper, s. grec, tricheur, m. || ~-table, s. table de jeu, f.
card, *kărd,* v. a. & n. peigner (la laine).
cardboard, *kărd'bŏrd,* s. carton fin, m.
carder, *kărd'ĕr,* s. cardeur, m.
cardinal, *kăr'dĭ năl,* a. cardinal, principal.
cardinal, *kăr'dĭ năl,* s. cardinal, m.
care, *kăr,* s. souci, soin, m. || attention, f.
care, *kăr,* v. n. se soucier de, s'inquiéter de.
careen, *kȧ rēn',* v. a. (mar.) caréner.
career, *kȧ rēr',* s. carrière, course, f.
careful, *kăr'fŏŏl,* a. soigneux, attentif || circonspect || -ly, ad. soigneusement.
carefulness, *kăr'fŏŏl nĕs,* s. soin, m.
careless, *kăr'lĕs,* a. insouciant, négligent || -ly, ad. négligemment.

carelessness, *kăr′lĕs nĕs*, s. insouciance, négligence, indifférence, f.

caress, *kă rĕs′*, s. caresse, f.

caress, *kă rĕs′*, v. a. caresser.

cargo, *kăr′gō*, s. cargaison, f.

caricature, *kăr′ĭ kă tūr*, s. caricature, f.

caricature, *kăr′ĭ kă tūr*, v. a. caricaturer.

caricaturist, *kăr′ĭ kă tū′rĭst*, s. faiseur de caricatures, m.

caries, *kā′rĭ ēz*, s. carie, f.

carious, *kā′rĭ ŭs*, a. carieux. [m.

carking(care), *kărk′ĭng (kār)*, s. chagrin,

carman, *kăr′măn*, s. charretier, m. ‖ voiturier, m. [minatif.

carminative, *kăr mĭn′ă tĭv*, a. (méd.) car-

carmine, *kăr′mĭn*, s. carmin, m.

carnage, *kăr′năj*, s. carnage, massacre, m.

carnal, *kăr′năl*, a. (-ly, ad.) charnel-(lement).

carnality, *kăr năl′ĭ tĭ*, s. sensualité, f.

carnation, *kăr nā′shŭn*, s. carnation, f. ‖ incarnat, m. ‖ (bot.) œillet, m.

carnelian, *kăr nē′lĭ ăn*, s. cornaline, f.

carnival, *kăr′nĭ văl*, s. carnaval, m.

carnivorous, *kăr nĭv′ō rŭs*, a. carnivore.

carol, *kăr′ŏl*, s. chanson, f., chant, m

carol, *kăr′ŏl*, v. a. chanter ‖ grisoller.

carousal, *kă rŏw′zăl*, s. carrousel, m.

carouse, *kă rŏw′z*, v. n. riboter.

carp, *kărp*, s. carpe, f.

carp, *kărp*, v. n. critiquer.

carpenter, *kăr′pĕn tĕr*, s. charpentier, m. ‖ ~'s bench, établi, m.

carpentry, *kăr′pĕn trĭ*, s. charpenterie, f.

carper, *kărp′ĕr*, s. gloseur, m.

carpet, *kăr′pĕt*, s. tapis, m. ‖ ~-bag, s. sac de nuit, m. ‖ ~-knight, s. homme de salon, m.

carpet, *kăr′pĕt*, v. a. tapisser.

carpeting, *kăr′pĕt ĭng*, s. tapis m., tapis-serie, f. [malignement.

carping, *kărp′ĭng*, a. critique ‖ -ly, ad.

carriage, *kăr′rĭj*, s. transport, m., voiture f. ‖ wagon, m. ‖ affût de canon, m. ‖ maintien, m., conduite f. ‖ port, m. ‖ ~ and four, s. carrosse à quatre chevaux, m. ‖ ~ and pair, s. voiture à deux chevaux, f. ‖ ~-free, ~ paid, a. franc de port.

carrier, *kăr′rĭ ĕr*, s. porteur, m. ‖ voiturier.

carrion, *kăr′rĭ ŏn*, s. charogne, f. [m.

carrot, *kăr′rŏt*, s. carotte, f.

carroty, *kăr′rŏt ĭ*, a. roux.

carry, *kăr′rĭ*, v. a. & n. porter, mener, conduire ‖ l'emporter sur, obtenir ‖ faire voir ‖ montrer ‖ se comporter ‖ ~-all, s. omnibus, m.

carrying-business, *kăr′rĭ ĭng bĭz′nĕs*, s. commerce d'expédition, m.

cart, *kărt*, s. charrette, voiture, f. ‖ to put the ~ before the horse, mettre la charrue devant les bœufs ‖ ~-horse, s. cheval de charrette, m. ‖ ~-load, s. char-retée, f. ‖ ~-shed, s. hangar, m.

cart, *kărt*, v. a. charrier.

cartage, *kăr′tăj*, s. prix de transport, m.

cartel, *kăr′tĕl*, s. cartel, défi, m.

carter, *kărt′ĕr*, s. charretier, m.

Carthusian, *kăr thū′zhĭ ăn*, s. chartreux, m.

cartilage, *kăr′tĭ lăj*, s. cartilage, m. [m.

cartoon, *kăr tŏn′*, s. carton, m.

cartridge, *kăr′trĭj*, s. cartouche, f. ‖ ~-box, s. cartouchière, f. ‖ (mil.) giberne, f. ‖ ~-paper, s. papier-cartouche, m.

cartwright, *kărt′rīt*, s. charron, m.

carve, *kărv*, v. a. & n sculpter, graver ‖ couper, découper. [écuyer tranchant, m.

carver, *kăr′vĕr*, s. sculpteur, graveur, m.‖

carving, *kărv′ĭng*, s. sculpture, gravure, f. ‖ ~-knife, s. couteau à découper, m. ‖ ~-knife and fork, s. service à dé-couper, f.

case, *kăs*, s. cas, m. ‖ état, m. ‖ boîte, f. étui, écrin, m. ‖ (Am.) caractère original, m. ‖ in ~, en cas que ‖ in the ~ of, à l'égard de ‖ ~-knife, s. couteau de cui-sine, m.

case, *kăs*, v. a. encaisser ‖ envelopper ‖ ~-hardened, a. trempé en paquet (acier).

casemate, *kăs′măt*, s. casemate, f.

casement, *kăs′mĕnt*, s. petite fenêtre, croisée, f.

cash, *kăsh*, s. argent comptant, m. ‖ caisse, f. ‖ to pay ~, payer comptant ‖ ~-book, s. livre de caisse, m. ‖ ~-box, s. caisse

cash, *kăsh*, v. a. escompter. [f.

cashier, *kă shēr′*, s. caissier, m.

cashier, *kă shēr′*, v. a. congédier.

cashmere, *kăsh′mēr*, s. cachemire, m.

cask, *kăsk*, s. baril, tonneau, m.

cask, *kăsk*, v. a. mettre en baril.

casket, *kăsk′ĕt*, s. cassette, petite boîte, f.

casket, *kăak′ĕt*, v. a. mettre en cassette.

cassation, *kăs să′shŭn*, s. cassation, f.

cassock, *kăs′sŏk*, s. soutane, f.

cassowary, *kăs′sō wā rĭ*, s. casoar, m.

cast, *kăst*, s. jet, coup, m. ‖ regard, m. ‖ moule, m., forme, f. ‖ nuance, f. ‖ fonte, f. ‖ distribution (des rôles), f. ‖ apparence, f., caractère, m. ‖ ~-iron, s. fonte, f. ‖ ~-steel, s. acier fondu, m.

cast, *kăst*, v. a. &n. ir. jeter, lancer, répandre ‖ renverser, rejeter ‖ vaincre ‖ calculer ‖ tirer au sort ‖ fondre, modeler ‖ se jeter ‖ juger, considérer ‖ to ~ up, additionner, calculer.

castanet, *kăs′tă nĕt*, s. castagnette, f.

castaway, *kăst′ă wā*, s. réprouvé, m.

caste, *kăst*, s. caste, tribu, f. ‖ to lose ~, déchoir.

castellan, *kăs′tĕl lăn*, s. châtelain, m.

castellated, *kăs′tĕl lă tĕd*, a. encastré ‖ crénelé. [lette, f. ‖ poivrier, m.

caster, *kăs′tĕr*, s. calculateur, m. ‖ rou-

castigate, *kăs′tĭ găt*, v. a. châtier. [m.

castigation, *kăs tĭ gă′shŭn*, s. châtiment,

castings, *kăst′ĭngs*, s. pl. objets de fonte, m. pl. [pondérante, f.

casting-vote, *kăst′ĭng vōt*, s. voix pré-

castle, *kăs′sl*, s. château, fort, m..‖ (at chess) tour, f. ‖ to build ~s in the air, faire des châteaux en Espagne.

castle, *kăs′sl*, v. n. (at chess) roquer.

castled, *kăs′sld*, a. couronné d'un château.

castor, *kâs'tĕr,* s. castor, m. ‖ ~-**oil,** s. huile de ricin, f.

castrate, *kăs'trāt,* v. a. châtrer, m.

castration, *kăs trā'shŭn,* s. castration, f.

casual, *kăz'ū ăl,* a. casuel, accidentel ‖ ~ **ward,** salle d'asyle pour les vagabonds ‖ **-ly** ad. par accident.

casualty, *kăz'ū ăl tĭ,* s. cas fortuit, accident, hasard, m.

casuist, *kăz'ū ĭst,* s. casuiste, m.

casuistry, *kăz'ū ĭst rĭ,* s. casuisme, m.

cat, *kăt,* s. chat, m. ‖ (mar.) ~ o' nine tails, martinet, m. ‖ to let the ~ out of the bag, vendre la mèche, lâcher le secret ‖ to rain ~s and dogs, tomber des hallebardes ‖ ~'s cradle, s. scie, f. ‖ ~-call, s. sifflet, m. ‖ ~'s paw, s. brise, f. ‖ dupe, f.

cataclysm, *kăt'ă klĭzm,* s. cataclysme, m.

catacombs, *kăt'ă kŏms,* s. pl. catacombes, f. pl.

catalepsy, *kăt'ă lĕp sĭ,* s. catalepsie, f.

catalogue, *kăt'ă lŏg,* s. catalogue, m. [m.

catamount, *kăt'ă mŏŭnt,* s. chat sauvage,

cataplasm, *kăt'ă plăzm,* s. cataplasme, f.

catapult, *kăt'ă pŭlt,* s. catapulte, f.

cataract, *kăt'ă răkt,* s. cataracte, f. ‖ to couch a ~, abattre une cataracte.

catarrh, *kă târ',* s. catarrhe, m.

catarrhal, *kă târ'ăl,* a. catarrhal.

catastrophe, *kă tăs'trŏ fĕ,* s. catastrophe, f.

catch, *kăch,* s. capture, prise, f. ‖ crampon, m., griffe, f. ‖ loquet, auberon, m. ‖ profit, m. ‖ court intervalle, m. ‖ ~-**penny,** s. moyen d'attraper de l'argent, m.

catch, *kăch,* v. a. & n. ir. prendre, saisir, attraper, gagner ‖ s'accrocher, s'engager ‖ être contagieux ‖ to ~ cold, s'enrhumer.

catcher, *kăch'ĕr,* s. écornifleur, m.

catching, *kăch'ing,* a. contagieux ‖ séduisant.

catchword, *kăch'wĕrd,* s. réplique, f.

catechise, *kăt'ĕ kīz,* v. a. catéchiser, examiner.

catechism, *kăt'ĕ kĭzm,* s. catéchisme, m.

catechist, *kăt'ĕ kĭst,* s. catéchiste, m.

categorical, *kăt ĕ gŏr'ĭ kăl,* a. (-ly, ad.) catégorique(ment).

category, *kăt'ĕ gŏr'ĭ,* s. catégorie, f.

cater, *kā'tĕr,* v. n. faire des provisions, pourvoir.

caterer, *kā'tĕr ĕr,* s. pourvoyeur, m.

cateress, *kā'tĕr ĕs,* s. pourvoyeuse, f.

caterpillar, *kăt'ĕr pĭl lĕr,* s. chenille, f.

caterwaul, *kăt'ĕr wăwl,* s. sabbat des chats, m. ‖ charivari, m.

catgut, *kăt'gŭt,* s. corde à boyau, f.

Catharine-wheel, *kăth'ĕr in hwēl,* s. fenêtre en rosace, f.

cathedral, *kă thē'drăl,* s. cathédrale, f.

catholic, *kăth'ŏ lĭk,* a. catholique.

catholicism, *kă thŏl'ĭ sizm,* s. catholicisme, m.

catkin, *kăt'kĭn,* s. (bot.) chaton, m.

catlike, *kăt'lĭk,* a. de chat. [pignons, f.

catsup, *kăts'ŭp,* s. saumure de champ-

cattle, *kăt'tl,* s. bétail, m., aumailles, f. pl. ‖

~-**plague,** s. peste bovine, f. ‖ ~-**show,** s. exposition de bétail, f.

caucus, *kăw'kŭs,* s. réunion électorale préparatoire en Amérique, f.

caught, *kăwt,* vide **catch.**

caul, *kăwl,* s. coiffe, f.

cauliflower, *kŏl'ĭ flŏwr,* s. chou-fleur, m.

causal, *kăw'zăl,* a. causal, causatif.

cause, *kăwz,* s. cause, f. ‖ source, raison, f., fondement, m. ‖ procès, m.

cause, *kăwz,* v. a. causer.

causeless, *kăwz'lĕs,* a. (-ly, ad.) sans cause, sans raison.

causeway, *kăwz'wā,* s. chaussée, f.

caustic, *kăws'tĭk,* s. caustique, m. ‖ lunar ~, pierre infernale, f.

caustic, *kăws'tĭk,* a. caustique. [risation, f.

cauterisation, *kăw tĕr ĭ zā'shŭn,* s. cauté-

cauterise, *kăw'tĕr īz,* v. a. cautériser.

caution, *kăw'shŭn,* s. prudence, précaution, f., avertissement, m.

caution, *kăw'shŭn,* v. a. avertir.

cautious, *kăw'shŭs,* a. prudent, vigilant ‖ -ly, ad. avec circonspection.

cavalcade, *kăv ăl kād',* s. cavalcade, f.

cavalier, *kăv ă lēr',* s. cavalier, m.

cavalry, *kăv'ăl rĭ,* s. cavalerie, f.

cave, *kāv,* s. caverne, antre, f.

caveat, *kā'vē ăt,* s. opposition, f.

cavern, *kăv'ĕrn,* s. caverne, f.

cavernous, *kăv'ĕrn ŭs,* a. caverneux.

caviare, *kăv'ĭ ăr,* s. caviar, m.

cavil, *kăv'ĭl,* s. chicane, subtilité, f.

cavil, *kăv'ĭl,* v. n. pointiller, sophistiquer.

caviller, *kăv'ĭl ĕr,* s. chicaneur, ergoteur,

cavity, *kăv'ĭ tĭ,* s. cavité, f., creux, m. [m.

caw, *kăw,* v. n. croasser.

Cayenne-pepper, *kā yĕn' pĕp'pĕr,* s. poivre d'Inde, m.

cayman, *kā'măn,* s. caïman, m.

cease, *sēs,* v. a. & n. cesser.

ceaseless, *sēs'lĕs,* a. (-ly, ad.) continuel, [sans cesse.

cedar, *sē'dĕr,* s. cèdre, m.

cede, *sēd,* v. a. & n. céder.

ceiling, *sēl'ing,* s. plafond, plafonnage, m.

celebrate, *sĕl'ĕ brāt,* v. a. célébrer, solenniser. [f.

celebration, *sĕl ĕ brā'shŭn,* s. célébration,

celebrity, *sĕ lĕb'rĭ tĭ,* s. célébrité, f., renom, m. [promptitude, f.

celerity, *sĕ lĕr'ĭ tĭ,* s. célérité, vitesse, f. ‖

celery, *sĕl'ĕr ĭ,* s. céleri, m. ‖ bundle, head of ~, botte (f.), pied (m.) de céleri.

celestial, *sē lĕst'yăl,* s. habitant du ciel, m.

celestial, *sē lĕst'yăl,* a. céleste.

celibacy, *sĕl'ĭ bă sĭ,* s. célibat, m.

celibate, *sĕl'ĭ băt,* a. célibataire.

cell, *sĕl,* s. cellule, f. ‖ cavité, f., cabanon, m.

cellar, *sĕl'lĕr,* s. cave, f. [m.

cellarage, *sĕl'lĕr ăj,* s. caves, f. pl.

cellaret, *sĕl lĕr ĕt',* s. sommellerie, f.

cellular, *sĕl'lū lĕr,* a. cellulaire.

cellule, *sĕl'ŭl,* s. cellule, f.

celluloid, *sĕl'ū lŏyd,* s. celluloïde, m.

cement, *sĕ mĕnt',* s. ciment, m. ‖ lien, m.

cement, *sĕ mĕnt',* v. a. cimenter ‖ ~, v. n. se cimenter ‖ se réunir.

cemetery, *sĕm'ĕ tĕr ĭ*, s. cimetière, m.
cenotaph, *sĕn'ō tăf*, s. cénotaphe, m.
censer, *sĕn'sĕr*, s. encensoir, m.
censor, *sĕn'sŏr*, s. censeur, critique, m.
censorious, *sĕn sō'rĭ ŭs*, a. critique, caustique || **–ly**, ad. en censeur.
censorship, *sĕn'sŏr shĭp*, s. fonction de censeur, censure, f. ~   [répréhensible.
censurable, *sĕn'shŏŏr ă bl*, a. censurable,
censure, *sĕn'shŏŏr*, s. censure, réprimande, f., blame, m.   [réprimander.
censure, *sĕn'shŏŏr*, v. a. censurer, blâmer,
census, *sĕn'sŭs*, s. recensement, m.
cent, *sĕnt*, s. cent, m. || **per ~**, pour cent.
centaur, *sĕn'tawr*, s. centaure, m.
centenarian, *sĕn tĕ nā'rĭ ăn*, s. centenaire,
centenary, *sĕn'tĕ nĕr ĭ*, s. centaine, f.
centenary, *sĕn'tĕ nĕr ĭ*, a. centenaire.
centennial, *sĕn tĕn'nĭ ăl*, a. de cent ans.
centesimal, *sĕn tĕs'ĭ măl*, s. centième, m.
centipede, *sĕn'tĭ pĕd*, s. scolopendre, f.
central, *sĕn'trăl*, a. (**–ly**, ad.) central (ement).
centralise, *sĕn'trăl īz*, v. a. centraliser.
centre, *sĕn'tĕr*, s. centre, m. || cintre, m.
centre, *sĕn'tĕr*, v. a. (& n.) (se) concentrer.
centric(al), *sĕn'trĭk (ăl)*, a. au centre, central.
centrifugal, *sĕn trĭf'ū găl*, a. centrifuge.
centripetal, *sĕn trĭp'ĕ tăl*, a. centripète.
centuple, *sĕn'tū pl*, v. a. centupler.
centuple, *sĕn'tū pl*, a. centuple.
centurion, *sĕn tū'rĭ ŏn*, s. centurion, m. || (in Scripture), centenier, m.
century, *sĕn'tū rĭ*, s. centaine, f. || siècle, m.
ceramic, *sĕ răm'ĭk*, a. céramique.
cerate, *sē'rāt*, s. cérat, m. '
cereal, *sē'rĭ ăl*, a. céréal || **~ grasses**, s. pl. céréales, f. pl.
cerebral, *sĕr'ē brăl*, a. cérébral.
cerecloth, *sēr'klŏth*, s. toile cirée, f.
cerement, *sēr'mĕnt*, s. suaire, m.
ceremonial, *sĕr'ē mō'nĭ ăl*, s. cérémonial, m., étiquette, f.
ceremonial, *sĕr'ē mō'nĭ ăl*, a. cérémonial || **–ly**, ad. d'après le cérémonial.
ceremonious, *sĕr'ē mō'nĭ ŭs*, a. cérémonieux || **–ly**, ad. avec cérémonie.
ceremony, *sĕr'ē mŏn ĭ*, s. cérémonie, f. || façons, f. pl. || **to stand upon ~**, faire des façons.   [certainement.
certain, *sĕr'tĭn*, a. certain, sûr || **–ly**, ad.
certainty, *sĕr'tĭn tĭ*, s. certitude, assurance, f.   [attestation, f.
certificate, *sĕr tĭf'ĭ kāt*, s. certificat, m.,
certification *sĕr tĭf ĭ kā'shŭn*, s. certification, attestation, f.
certify, *sĕr'tĭ fī*, v. a. certifier, attester.
certitude, *sĕr'tĭ tūd*, s. certitude, f.
cerulean, *sĕ rō'lĭ ăn*, s. bleu, azuré.
cesarian, *sē zā'rĭ ăn*, a. césarien || **section**, s. opération césarienne, f.
cess, *sĕs*, s. impôt, m.
cessation, *sĕs sā'shŭn*, s. cessation, f. || **~ of arms**, suspension d'armes, f.
cessible, *sĕs'ĭ bl*, a. (jur.) cessible.   [m.
cession, *sĕs'shŭn*, s. cession, f., abandon,

cesspool, *sĕs'pŏl*, s. puisard, m. || fosse
cestus, *sĕs'tŭs*, s. ceste, m.   [d'aisance, f.
cetacean, *sē tā'shĭ ăn*, s. cétacé, m.
chad, *shăd*, s. alose, f.
chafe, *chāf*, s. échauffement, m., fureur, f.
chafe, *chāf*, v. a. & n. échauffer || frotter || irriter, mettre en colère || s'échauffer.
chafer, *chā'fĕr*, s. hanneton, m.
chaff, *chăf*, s. paille menue, f. || gausserie, f. || **~-cutter**, s. hache-paille, m.
chaff, *chăf*, v. a. railler.
chaffer, *chăf'fĕr*, v. n. barguigner.
chaffinch, *chăf'fĭnsh*, s. pinson, m.
chagrin, *shă grĭn'*, s. chagrin, m.
chain, *chān*, s. chaîne, f. || **~s**, pl. fers, m. pl. || **~-bridge**, s. pont suspendu, m. || **~-gang**, s. chaîne de forçats, f. || **~-shot**, s. boulet ramé, m. || **~-stitch**, s. broderie au crochet, f.   [une chaîne.
chain, *chān*, v. a. enchaîner, fermer par
chair, *chār*, s. chaise, f. || fauteuil, m. || (rail.) coussinet, m. || **~!** à l'ordre! || **to take the ~**, ouvrir une séance || **Bath~**, s. vinaigrette, f.
chair, *chār*, v. a. porter en triomphe.
chairman, *chār'măn*, s. président, m. || (of a Bath-chair), traîneur de vinaichaise, *shāz*, s. chaise, f.   [grette, m.
chalcedony, *kăl sĕd'ō nĭ*, s. calcédoine, f.
chalice, *chăl'ĭs*, s. calice, m. || coupe, f.
chalk, *chawk*, s. craie, f. || **~-pit**, s. marnière, f. || **~-stone**, s. pierre à chaux, f.
chalk, *chawk*, v. a. marquer avec de la craie || crayonner.
chalky, *chawk'ĭ*, a. plein de craie.
challenge, *chăl'lĕnj*, s. cartel, m. || provocation, f. || prétention, f. || (jur.) récusation, f. || (mil.) qui-vive, m.
challenge, *chăl'lĕnj*, v. a. appeler en duel, défier || réclamer || s'arroger || récuser || crier qui-vive.   [prétendant, m.
challenger, *chăl'lĕnj ĕr*, s. provocateur, m.
chalybeate, *kă lĭb'ĭ āt*, a. ferrugineux.
chamber, *chām'bĕr*, s. chambre, f. || cabinet, m. || **~s**, pl. bureaux, m. pl. || **in ~s**, en référé.   [revolvers).
chambered, *chām'bĕrd*, a. à . . . coups (of
chamberlain, *chām'bĕr lān*, s. chambellan, m.   [chambellanie, f.
chamberlainship, *chām'bĕr lān shĭp*, s.
chambermaid, *chām'bĕr măd*, s. femme de chambre, f.
chameleon, *kă mē'lĭ ŏn*, s. caméléon, m.
chamois, *shăm'wă*, s. chamois, m. || **~ leather**, s. chamois, m.
champ, *chămp*, v. a. & n. mâcher, ronger.
champagne, *shăm păn'*, s. plaine, campagne, f. || vin de Champagne, m.
champagne, *shăm păn'*, a. plat || ouvert.
champion, *chăm'pĭ ŏn*, s. champion, combattant, m.   [cartel.
champion, *chăm'pĭ ŏn*, v. a. donner un
chance, *chăns*, s. hasard, m., chance, f. || accident, m. || **by ~**, par hasard || **~ customer**, s. client d'occasion, m.
chance, *chăns*, v. n. arriver, survenir.
chance, *chăns*, a. accidentel, fortuit.

chancel, *chăn'sĕl*, s. sanctuaire, m.

chancellor, *chăn'sĕlĕr*, s. chancelier, m. || ~ Lord High ~, grand chancelier, m. || ~ of the Exchequer, s. ministre des finances, m. [de chancelier, f.

chancellorship, *chăn'sĕlĕrshĭp*, s. dignité

chancery, *chăn'sĕrĭ*, s. chancellerie, f.

chandelier, *shăndĕlēr'*, s. lustre, candélabre, m. [regrattier, m.

chandler, *chănd'lĕr*, s. chandelier, m. ||

change, *chānj*, s. changement, m., vicissitude, altération, f. || Bourse, f. || petite monnaie, f. || on 'Change, à la Bourse.

change, *chānj*, v. a. & n. changer, troquer, donner la monnaie de. [constant.

changeable, *chānj'ăbl*, a. changeant, in-

changeableness, *chānj'ăblnĕs*, s. inconstance, f. [inconstante.

changeably, *chānj'ăblĭ*, ad. d'une manière

changeless, *chānj'lĕs*, a. invariable.

changeling, *chānj'lĭng*, s. enfant supposé, m. || esprit changeant, m.

changer, *chănj'ĕr*, s. changeur, m.

channel, *chăn'nĕl*, s. canal, m. || lit d'une rivière, m. || cannelure (d'une colonne), f.

channel, *chăn'nĕl*, v. a. canneler.

chant, *chănt*, s. chant, m., mélodie, f.

chant, *chănt*, v. a. & n. chanter.

chanter, *chănt'ĕr*, s. chantre, m.

chanticleer, *chănt'ĭklēr*, s. coq, m.

chaos, *kā'ŏs*, s. chaos, m., confusion, f.

chaotic, *kā'ŏt'ĭk*, a. chaotique, confus.

chap, *chăp*, s. crevasse, gerçure, f. || ~s, pl.

chap, *chăp*, v.a.(& n.) (se)gercer. [mâchoire,f.

chapel, *chăp'ĕl*, s. chapelle, f. || ~ of ease, succursale, f.

chapfallen, *chăp'fawln*, a. à oreilles avalées.

chaplain, *chăp'lĭn*, s. chapelain, m.

chaplaincy, *chăp'lĭnsĭ*, s. chapellenie, f.

chaplet, *chăp'lĕt*, s. chapelet, m., guirlande, f.

chapter, *chăp'tĕr*, s. chapitre, m. || assemblée (de chanoines), f.

char, *chăr*, s. ouvrage à la journée, m.

char, *chăr*, v. a. & n. faire du charbon de bois || travailler à la journée.

character, *kăr'ăktĕr*, s. caractère, m. || écriture, f. || réputation, renommée, f. || rôle, personnage, m. || genre, m. || certificat, m. || condition, f. || description, peinture, f. || renseignements, m. pl. || to take away one's ~, perdre la réputation de qn. [riser, dépeindre.

characterise, *kăr'ăktĕrīz*, v. a. caractériser.

characteristic, *kărăktĕrĭs'tĭk*, a. caractéristique.

charade, *shără̇d'*, s. charade, f.

charcoal, *chăr'kōl*, s. charbon de bois, m. || ~-burner, s. charbonnier, m.

charge, *chărj*, s. charge, f., fardeau, m. || soin, m. || garde, f. || accusation, f. || demande, f. || ordre, m. || emploi, m. || attaque, f. || ~s, pl. frais, m. pl. || ~-sheet, s. livre de consignation, m.

charge, *chărj*, v. a. charger, imposer || confier || grever || enjoindre || accuser || attaquer || demander || attribuer

chargeable, *chărj'ăbl*, a. à charge, dispendieux || accusable.

charger, *chăr'jĕr*, s. grand plat, m. || chargeoir, m. || cheval de bataille, m.

charily, *chār'ĭlĭ*, ad. avec économie, soigneusement.

chariot, *chăr'ĭŏt*, s. chariot, m. || coupé, m.

chariot, *chăr'ĭŏt*, v. n. voiturer.

charioteer, *chărĭŏtēr'*, s. conducteur de chars, m. [faisant.

charitable, *chăr'ĭtăbl*, a. charitable, bien-

charitableness, *chăr'ĭtăblnĕs*, s. charité, f. [ment.

charitably, *chăr'ĭtăblĭ*, ad. charitablement.

charity, *chăr'ĭtĭ*, s. charité, f. || bienveillance, aumône, f. || ~-school, s. école de charité, f.

charlatan, *shăr'lătăn*, s. charlatan, m.

charlatanry, *shăr'lătănrĭ*, s. charlatanerie, f. [grande Ourse, f.

Charles's-Wain, *chărlz'ĕzwān*, s. (astr.)

charm, *chărm*, s. charme, enchantement, m. || breloque, f.

charm, *chărm*, v. a. charmer, enchanter.

charmer, *chăr'mĕr*, s. enchanteur, m., enchanteresse, f.

charming, *chăr'mĭng*, a. (-ly. ad.) charmant || d'une manière charmante.

charnel(-house), *chăr'nĕl(hŏws)*, s. charnier, m.

chart, *chărt*, s. carte, f., carte marine, f.

charter, *chăr'tĕr*, s. charte, f. || (jur.) acte, m. || privilège, m. || ~-party, s. charte-partie, f. [fréter || noliser.

charter, *chăr'tĕr*, v. a. privilégier || (mar.)

chartist, *chăr'tĭst*, s. chartiste, m. & f.

charwoman, *chăr'wŏŏmăn*, s. femme à la journée, f. [économe.

chary, *chăr'ĭ*, a. soigneux, circonspect,

chase, *chās*, s. chasse, f. || poursuite, f. || to give ~ to, donner la chasse à. [ler.

chase, *chās*, v. a. chasser, poursuivre || cise-

chasm, *kăzm*, s. ouverture, f., creux, m.

chaste, *chāst*, a. (-ly. ad.) chaste(ment) || pudique(ment) || honnête || pur(ement)

chasten, *chās'n*, v. a. châtier, punir.

chastise, *chăstīz'*, v. a. châtier, corriger.

chastity, *chăs'tĭtĭ*, s. chasteté, pureté, f.

chasuble, *chăz'ūbl*, s. chasuble, f.

chat, *chăt*, s. caquet, babil, m.

chat, *chăt*, v. n. causer, jaser.

chattel, *chăt'tl*, s. biens mobiliers, m. pl. || goods and -s, biens et effets.

chatter, *chăt'tĕr*, s. babil, caquet, m.

chatter, *chăt'tĕr*, v. n. jaser, babiller, causer || claquer.

chatterbox, *chăt'tĕrbŏx*, chatterer, *chăt'tĕrĕr*, s. babillard, moulin à paroles.

chatty, *chăt'tĭ*, a. causeur. [m.

chaw, *chaw*, s. bajoue, f. || bouchée, f.

chaw, *chaw*, v. a. mâcher.

cheap, *chēp*, a. (-ly, ad.) à bon marché.

cheapen, *chēp'n*, v. a. marchander.

cheapness, *chēp'nĕs*, s. bon marché, bas prix, m. [f.|| fourbe, m. || filou, fripon, m.

cheat, *chēt*, s. fraude, fourberie, tricherie,

cheat, *chēt*, v. a. & n. tromper, filouter, tricher.

cheating, *chēt'ing,* s. fourberie, tromperie, f. ‖ tricherie, f.

check, *chĕk,* s. échec, m. ‖ obstacle, frein, m. ‖ (com.) bon, m. ‖ réprimande, f. ‖ contremarque, f. ‖ assignation, f. ‖ étoffe à carreaux, f. ‖ ~-string, s. cordon (de voiture ou de poste), m. ‖ ~-taker, s. contrôleur, m.

check, *chĕk,* v. a. & n. réprimer, retenir ‖ blâmer ‖ donner échec ‖ s'arrêter, contrôler.

checkmate, *chĕk'māt,* s. échec et mat, m.

checkmate, *chĕk'māt,* v. a. mater.

cheek, *chēk,* s. joue, f. ‖ (fam.) impudence, f. ‖ ~ by jowl, tête-à-tête ‖ ~-strap, s. jouillère, f. [~, avoir du toupet.

cheeky, *chē'ki,* a. hardi, insolent ‖ to be

cheer, *chēr,* s. chère, f., repas, m. ‖ gaieté, f. ‖ applaudissement, m. ‖ ~ up ! courage ! ‖ to be of good ~, ne pas perdre courage.

cheer, *chēr,* v. a. (& n.) (se) réjouir.

cheerful, *chēr'fŏŏl,* a. (-ly, ad.) gai(ement) ‖ joyeux, enjoué.

cheerily, *chēr'i li,* ad. gaiement. [m. pl.

cheering, *chēr'ing,* s. applaudissements.

cheerless, *chēr'lĕs,* a. triste, mélancolique.

cheery, *chēr'i,* a. gai.

cheese, *chēz,* s. fromage, m. ‖ ~-dairy, s. fromagerie, f. ‖ ~-hopper, ~-mite, s. ver de fromage, m. ‖ ~-paring, a. (fig.) avare à se ronger les ongles, pingre, chiche ‖ ~-scoop, ~-taster, s. couteau à fromage, m. [mager, m.

cheesemonger, *chēz'mŭng gẽr,* s. fromager, m.

cheetah, *chē'tā,* s. léopard chasseur, m.

chemical, *kĕm'ĭk ăl,* s. produit chimique, m. [(ment).

chemical, *kĕm'ĭk ăl,* a. (-ly, ad.) chimique

chemise, *shĕ mēz',* s. chemise, f.

chemist, *kĕm'ĭst,* s. chimiste, m.

chemistry, *kĕm'ĭs tri,* s. chimie, f.

cheque, *chĕk,* s. chèque, f. ‖ *vide* check ‖ ~-book, s. carnet de chèques, chéquier, m.

chequer, *chĕk'ẽr,* v. a. marqueter ‖ diaprer ‖ ~-ed, a. varié ‖ (fig.) accidenté.

chequer, *chĕk'ẽr,* s. ~-board, s. damier, m. ‖ ~-work, s. marqueterie, f.

cherish, *chĕr'ĭsh,* v. a. chérir, aimer ‖ protéger ‖ nourrir.

charoot, *shĕ rŏt',* s. bout coupé, m.

cherry, *chĕr'ri,* s. cerise, f. ‖ ~-stone, s. noyau de cerises, m. ‖ ~-tree, s. cerisier, m.

chervil, *chẽr'vĭl,* s. cerfeuil, m. [m.

chess, *chĕs,* s. échecs, m. pl. ‖ ~-board, s. échiquier, m. ‖ ~-man, s. pion, m.

chest, *chĕst,* s. caisse, f., coffre, m. ‖ poitrine, f. ‖ ~-of-drawers, s. commode, f.

chestnut, *chĕs'nŭt,* s. châtaigne, f., marron, m. ‖ ~-tree, s. châtaignier, marronnier, m.

cheval-glass, *shĕ văl' glăs,* s. psyché, f.

chew, *chŏ,* v. a. & n. mâcher ‖ (of tobacco) chiquer ‖ (fig.) méditer.

chicane, *shi kān',* s. chicane, f.

chicane, *shi kān',* v. n. chicaner.

chicanery, *shi kā'nẽr i,* s. chicanerie, tromperie, f.

chick, *chĭk,* v. n. germer, pousser.

chickabiddy, *chĭk'ă bĭd dī,* s. cocote, f.

chick(en), *chĭk'(ĕn),* s. poulet, m., poulette, f. [timide.

chicken-hearted, *chĭk'ĕn härt ĕd,* a.

chicken-pox, *chĭk'ĕn pŏks,* s. petite vérole volante, f.

chickory, *chĭk'ŏr i,* s. chicorée, f.

chick-weed, *chĭk' wēd,* s. (bot.) mouron, m.

chide, *chīd,* v. a. & n. ir. gronder, censurer ‖ (se) quereller.

chief, *chēf,* s. chef, commandant, m. ‖ Lord ~ justice, s. grand-juge, m. ‖ ~ of staff, s. chef de l'état-major, m.

chief, *chēf,* a. (-ly, ad.) principal(ement) ‖ premier ‖ surtout.

chieftain, *chēf'tĭn,* s. chef, capitaine, m.

chilblain, *chĭl'blān,* s. engelure, f.

child, *chīld,* s. enfant, m. (pl. children) ‖ from a ~, dès l'enfance ‖ with ~, enceinte ‖ not to be a ~, ne pas faire des enfantillages ‖ ~-crowing, s. (méd.) croup spasmodique, faux croup, m.

childbed, *chīld'bĕd,* s. couches, f. pl.

childhood, *chīld'hŏŏd,* s. enfance, f.

childish, *chīld'ish,* a. (-ly, ad.) enfantin, puéril(ement) ‖ en enfant.

childless, *chīld'lĕs,* a. sans enfant.

childlike, *chīld'līk,* a. enfantin, puéril.

chill, *chĭl,* s. froid, m. ‖ froidure, f. ‖ frisson, m. ‖ to catch a ~, s'enrhumer.

chill, *chĭl,* v. a. & n. refroidir ‖ faire frissonner ‖ (se) glacer.

chill, *chĭl,* a. froid, frais ‖ insensible.

chilliness, *chĭl'li nĕs,* s. frisson, m., froideur, f.

chilly, *chĭl'li,* a. frileux, sensible au froid.

chime, *chīm,* s. harmonie, f., accord, m. ‖ carillon, m. [corder.

chime, *chīm,* v. a. & n. carillonner ‖ s'accorder.

chimera, *ki mē'rā,* s. chimère, f.

chimerical, *ki mēr'i kăl,* a. (-ly, ad.) chimérique ‖ illusoire(ment).

chimney, *chim'ni,* s. cheminée, f. ‖ cylindre de lampe, m. ‖ ~-corner, s. (fig.) coin du feu, m. ‖ ~-piece, s. cheminée, f. ‖ chambranle de cheminée, m. ‖ ~-pot, s. mitre, f. ‖ ~-sweep, s. ramoneur, m. [m.

chimpanzee, *chim pän'zē,* s. chimpanzé, m.

chin, *chin,* s. menton, m. ‖ ~-tuft, s. impériale, barbiche, f.

china, *chi'nā,* s. porcelaine de Chine, f.

chine, *chīn,* s. échine, épine du dos, f.

chink, *chingk,* s. fente, crevasse, f.

chink, *chingk,* v. a. & n. faire tinter ‖ tinter.

chintz, *chints,* s. toile de Perse, cretonne, f.

chip, *chĭp,* s. copeau, m. ‖ miette, f. ‖ échantillon, m. [hacher ‖ chapeler (du pain).

chip, *chĭp,* v. a. couper en petits morceaux,

chiropodist, *kirŏp'ŏ dĭst,* s. pédicure, m.

chirp, *chẽrp,* **chirrup,** *chẽr'ŭp,* v. a. & n. grilloter, strider ‖ gazouiller, ramager ‖ égayer. [m.

chirp(ing), *chẽrp'(ing),* s. gazouillement.

chirurgeon, *kirẽr'jŭn,* *vide* surgeon.

chisel, *chiz'ĕl,* s. ciseau, cisoir, m.

chisel, *chiz'ĕl,* v. a. ciseler.

---

bŏy ; — fŏŏt, tūbe, tŭb. ‖ chair, joy ; — game, yes ; — soul, zeal ; — thing, there.

chit, *chit*, s. bambin, m. ‖ germe, m. ‖ tache de rousseur, f.   [f.

chit-chat, *chit' chăt*, s. babil, m., causerie.

chitterlings, *chit' tĕr lingz*, s. pl. andouilles, tripes, f. pl.

chivalrous, *shiv' ăl rŭs*, a. chevaleresque.

chivalry, *shiv' ăl ri*, s. chevalerie, f.

chive, *chiv*, s. ciboulette, f.

chloral, *klō' răl*, s. chloral, m.

chloride, *klō' rid*, s. chlorure, f.

chlorine, *k'ō' rĭn*, s. chlore, m.   [m.

chloroform, *klō' rō fǎwrm*, s. chloroforme,

chocolate, *chŏk' ō lăt*, s. chocolat, m.

choice, *chŏỹs*, s. choix, m. ‖ meilleur, plus beau, m. ‖ Hobson's ~, s. choix forcé, m.

choice, *chŏỹs*, a. (-ly, ad.) choisi, rare, excellent ‖ avec choix or soin.

choiceless, *chŏỹs' lĕs*, a. qui n'a pas le choix.   [qualité recherchée, f.

choiceness, *chŏỹs' nĕs*, s. délicatesse,

choir, *kwir*, s. chœur, m.

choke, *chōk*, v. a. suffoquer, étouffer, étrangler ‖ boucher ‖ ~-pear, s. poire d'angoisse, f.   [sans réplique, f.

choker, *chō' kĕr*, s. cravate, f. ‖ raison

choler, *kŏl' ĕr*, s. bile, colère, f.

cholera, *kŏl' ĕr ă*, s. choléra, m.

choleraic, *kŏl ĕr ā' ĭk*, a. cholérique.

choleric, *kŏl' ĕr ĭk*, a. bilieux ‖ colérique.

choose, *chōz*, v. a. & n. ir. choisir, élire ‖ préférer.

chop, *chŏp*, s. côtelette, f. ‖ tranche, f. ‖ fente, f. ‖ gueule, f. ‖ -s, pl. bouche, gueule, f. ‖ embouchure, f.

chop, *chŏp*, v. a. & n. couper en petits morceaux, hacher ‖ gercer ‖ troquer.

chopper, *chŏp' pĕr*, s. couperet, m.

chopping, *chŏp' ping*, a. gros et gras ‖ (of the sea) clapoteux ‖ (of the wind) variable ‖ ~-block, s. hachoir, m. ‖ ~-knife, s. couperet, m.

chopstick, *chŏp' stik*, s. baguette, f.

choral, *kō' răl*, a. (-ly, ad.) de or en chœur.

chord, *kǎwrd*, s. corde d'instrument, f.

chord, *kǎwrd*, v. a. garnir de cordes.

chorister, *kŏr' is tĕr*, s. choriste, m.

chorus, *kō' rŭs*, s. chœur, m.

chouse, *chŏws*, v. a. duper, fourber.

chrism, *krizm*, s. chrême, m.

Christ, *krist*, s. Christ, m.

christen, *kris' n*, v. a. baptiser.

Christendom, *kris' n dŏm*, s. chrétienté, f.

christening, *kris' ning*, s. baptême, m.

Christian, *krist' yăn*, s. chrétien, m.

Christian, *krist' yăn*, a. chrétien ‖ ~ name, s. nom de baptême, m.

Christianity, *kris ti ăn' i ti*, s. christianisme, m.   [chrétien.

christianise, *krist' yăn iz*, v. a. faire

Christmas, *kris' măs*, s. Noël, m. ‖ ~-box, s. étrennes, f. pl.

chromatic, *krō māt' ik*, a. chromatique.

chrome, *krōm*, chromium, *krō' mi ŭm*, s. chrome, m.   [s. chromo-lithographie, f.

chromo-(lithograph), *krō mō(lith' ōgrǎf)*,

chronic, *krŏn' ik*, a. chronique.

chronicle, *krŏn' i kl*, s. chronique, f.

chronicle, *krŏn' i kl*, v. a. enregistrer.

chronicler, *krŏn' i klĕr*, s. chroniqueur, m.

chronological, *krŏn ō lŏj' i kăl*, a. chronologique ‖ -ly, ad. suivant l'ordre chronologique.

chronology, *krō nŏl' ō jĭ*, s. chronologie, f.

chronometer, *krō nŏm' ĕ tĕr*, s. chronomètre, m.   [f.

chrysalis, *kris' ă lĭs*, s. chrysalide, nymphe,

Chrysanthemum, *kris săn' thē mŭm*, s. chrysanthème, m.

chubby, *chŭb' bi*, a. à tête grosse ‖ joufflu.

chuck, *chŭk*, s. gloussement, m.

chuck, *chŭk*, v. a. & n. donner un petit coup sous le menton ‖ glousser.

chuckle, *chŭk' kl*, v. a. & n. caresser ‖ rire aux éclats ‖ rire tout bas.

chum, *chŭm*, s. camarade de chambre, m. ‖ du tabac à mâcher.

chump, *chŭmp*, chunk, *chŭngk*, s. billot, bloc, m. ‖ ~-chop, s. côte coupé du quasi de mouton, f.

church, *chĕrch*, s. église, f., temple, m. ‖ High ~, s. église anglicane, f. ‖ Low ~, s. église puritaine d'Angleterre, f. ‖ ~-ale, s. fête à la dédicace d'une église, f. ‖ ~plate, s. argenterie, f. ‖ ~-service, s. office divin, m.   [chée.

church, *chĕrch*, v. a. relever une accouchuring, *chĕrch' ing*, s. relevailles, f. pl.

churchman, *chĕrch' măn*, s. ecclésiastique, m.   [guillier, m.

churchwarden, *chĕrch' wǎūr dn*, s. marchurchyard, *chĕrch' yǎrd*, s. cimetière, m.

churl, *chĕrl*, s. paysan, m. ‖ manant, m. ‖ avare, m.

churlish, *chĕr' lĭsh*, a. grossier.

churn, *chĕrn*, s. baratte, f.

churn, *chĕrn*, v. a. baratter.

cider, *sī' dĕr*, s. cidre, m.

cigar, *sĭ gǎr'*, s. cigare, f. ‖ ~-case, s. porte-cigares, m. ‖ ~-divan, s. salonfumoir, m. ‖ ~-holder, s. brûle-cigare, m.

cincture, *singk' chōōr*, s. ceinture, f.

cinder, *sin' dĕr*, s. cendre, f.

Cinderella, *sin dĕr ĕl' lă*, s. Cendrillon, f.

cinema(tograph), *sin é mă*, *sin é măt' ō grǎf*, s. cinématographe, m.

cinerary, *sin' ĕr ĕ ri*, a. cinéraire.   [m.

cinnabar, *sin' nă băr*, s. cinabre, vermillon,

cinnamon, *sin' nă mŏn*, s. cannelle, f.

cipher, *sī' fĕr*, s. chiffre, zéro, m.

cipher, *sī' fĕr*, v. a. & n. chiffrer ‖ calculer ‖ écrire en chiffres.

circle, *sĕr' kl*, s. cercle, m. ‖ assemblée, f.

circle, *sĕr' kl*, v. a. & n. entourer ‖ se mouvoir circulairement.

circlet, *sĕr' klĕt*, s. petit cercle, m.

circling, *sĕrk' ling*, a. circulaire, en cercle.

circuit, *sĕrk' it*, s. circuit m., rotation, f. ‖ circonférence, f. ‖ tournée (de juge), f.

circuitous, *sĕr kū' i tŭs*, a. détourné ‖ -ly, ad. d'une manière détournée.

circular, *sĕrk' ū lĕr*, s. circulaire, f.

circular, *sĕrk' ū lĕr*, a. circulaire.

circulate, *sĕrk' ū lāt*, v. a. & n. faire circuler ‖ circuler.

circulating, *sĕrk'ŭ lāt ĭng;* ~-library, s. cabinet de lecture, m. || ~-medium, s. agent monétaire, m. [f.

circulation, *sĕrk ŭ lā'shŭn,* s. circulation.

circulatory, *sĕrk'ŭ lā tĕr ĭ,* a. circulaire || ~ decimal, s. décimale périodique, f.

circumcise, *sĕr' kŭm sīz,* v. a. circoncire.

circumcision, *sĕr kŭm sĭzh'ŭn,* s. circoncision, f. [férence, enceinte, f.

circumference, *sĕr kŭm'fĕ rĕns,* s. circon-

circumflex, *sĕr' kŭm flĕks,* s. accent circonflexe, m. [nant.

circumjacent, *sĕr kŭm jā'sĕnt,* a. environ-

circumlocution, *sĕr kŭm lō kū'shŭn,* s. circonlocution, f.

circumlocutory, *sĕr kŭm lŏk'ū tĕr ĭ,* a. périphrastique, indirect.

circumnavigate, *sĕr kŭm nǎv'ĭ gāt,* v. a. naviguer autour de.

circumnavigation, *sĕr kŭm nǎv ĭ gā'shŭn,* s. navigation autour de, f.

circumnavigator, *sĕr kŭm nǎv'ĭ gā tĕr,* s. circumnavigateur, m.

circumscribe, *sĕr kŭm skrīb',* v. a. circonscrire, limiter. [circonscription, f.

circumscription, *sĕr kŭm skrĭp'shŭn,* s.

circumspect, *sĕr' kŭm spĕkt,* a. circonspect, prudent.

circumspection, *sĕr kŭm spĕk'shŭn,* s. circonspection, prudence, f.

circumstance, *sĕr' kŭm stǎns,* s. circonstance, f., événement, m.

circumstanced, *sĕr' kŭm stǎnst,* a. dans une position, situé || well ~, bien dans ses affaires.

circumstantial, *sĕr kŭm stǎn'shǎl,* a. (-ly, ad.) accidentel(lement) || circonstancié || en détail || ~ evidence, s. preuve tirée d'indices, f.

circumvallation, *sĕr kŭm vǎl lā'shŭn,* s. circonvallation, f.

circumvention, *sĕr kŭm vĕn'shŭn,* s. fraude, imposture, f.

circus, *sĕr'kŭs,* s. cirque, m. || (of thoroughfares), rond-point, m.

cistern, *cĭs'tĕrn,* s. citerne, fontaine, f. || réservoir, m.

citadel, *sĭt'ă dĕl,* s. citadelle, forteresse, f.

citation, *sĭ tā'shŭn,* s. citation, f., ajournement, m.

cite, *sĭt,* v. a. citer || assigner, ajourner.

citizen, *sĭt'ĭ zĕn,* s. bourgeois, citoyen, m.

citizenship, *sĭt'ĭ zĕn shĭp,* s. droit de bourgeoisie, m.

citrine, *sĭt'rĭn,* a. citrin.

citron, *sĭt'rŏn,* s. citron, limon, m.

city, *sĭt'ĭ,* s. ville, f. || ~-article, s. bulletin financier, m.

civet, *sĭv'ĕt,* s. civette, f.

civic, *sĭv'ĭk,* a. civique, du citoyen.

civil, *sĭv'ĭl,* a. (-ly, ad.) civil(ement) || civilisé, honnête.

civilian, *sĭ vĭl'yǎn,* s. légiste, m. || bourgeois, m. [f.

civilisation, *sĭv ĭl ĭ zā'shŭn,* s. civilisation, f.

civilise, *sĭv'ĭ līz,* v. a. civiliser, rendre poli.

civility, *sĭ vĭl'ĭ tĭ,* s. civilité, politesse,

honnêteté, f. || to shew one ~, faire des civilités à qn. [m.

clack, *klǎk,* s. claquet, cliquet d'un moulin.

clack, *klǎk,* v. n. claquer, cliqueter || lâcher.

clad, *klǎd,* a. vêtu, habillé.

claim, *klām,* s. demande, prétention, f.

claim, *klām,* v. a. réclamer, prétendre || to ~ acquaintance with one, se réclamer de qn.

claimant, *klǎm'ănt,* s. prétendant, m.

clam, *klǎm,* v. a. & n. gluer || s'attacher.

clamber, *klǎm'bĕr,* v. n. grimper.

clamminess, *klǎm'mĭ nĕs,* s. viscosité, f.

clammy, *klǎm'mĭ,* a. visqueux, tenace.

clamorous, *klǎm'ĕr ŭs,* a. bruyant, tumultueux || -ly, ad. à grand bruit.

clamour, *klǎm'ĕr,* s. clameur, f., bruit, m.

clamour, *klǎm'ĕr,* v. n. crier, faire du bruit, vociférer. [appui, m.

clamp, *klǎmp,* s. emboîture, f. || support.

clamp, *klǎmp,* v. a. emboîter. [f.

clan, *klǎn,* s. clan, m., famille, race, clique.

clandestine, *klǎn dĕs'tĭn,* a. (-ly, ad.) clandestin(ement) || secret.

clang, *klǎng,* s. son aigu, m. || cliquetis, m.

clang, *klǎng,* v. n. rendre un son aigu.

clangorous, *klǎng'gŏ rŭs,* a. résonnant.

clangour, *klǎng'gĕr,* s. son aigu retentissant, m.

clank, *klǎngk,* s. cliquetis, m. [sant, m.

clank, *klǎngk,* v. n. cliqueter.

clap, *klǎp,* s. coup, m. || éclat, m. || battement des mains, m. || ~-trap, s. coup de théâtre, m. || artifice, m. || attrape-nigaud, m.

clap, *klǎp,* v. a. frapper, battre, applaudir || appliquer || jeter || (of doors) fermer.

clapper, *klǎp'pĕr,* s. claqueur, m. || battant, m. || claquet, m.

clapping, *klǎp'pĭng,* s. battement, applaudissement, m. [scur, m.

clare-obscure, *klār ŏb skūr',* s. clair-obscur, m.

claret, *klār'ĕt,* s. vin de Bordeaux, m. || ~-cup, s. vin de Bordeaux frappé, m. || limonade à la glace, f. || ~-jug, s. carafe à Bordeaux, f. [cation, f.

clarification, *klār ĭ fĭ kā'shŭn,* s. clarification, f.

clarify, *klār'ĭ fī,* v. a. & n. clarifier, purifier || s'éclaircir.

clarinet, *klār'ĭ nĕt,* s. clarinette, f.

clarion, *klār'ĭ ŏn,* s. clairon, m.

clash, *klǎsh,* s. cliquetis, choc, m. || (fig.) contradiction, f.

clash, *klǎsh,* v. a. & n. faire du bruit en frappant, résonner || s'entrechoquer || s'opposer.

clasp, *klǎsp,* s. agrafe, boucle, f. || fermoir (d'un livre), m. || embrassement, m. || ~-knife, s. couteau pliant, m.

clasp, *klǎsp,* v. a. agrafer || embrasser.

class, *klǎs,* s. classe, f., rang, ordre, m. || upper -es, haute classe, f. || middle -es, classe moyenne, f. || lower -es, classe inférieure, f.

class, *klǎs,* v. a. ranger par classes.

classic, *klǎs'sĭk,* s. classique, m. || auteur classique, m.

classic(al), *klǎs'sĭk(ǎl),* a. classique.

---

bōy ; — fŏŏt, tūbe, tŭb. || chair, joy ; — game, yes ; — soul, zeal ; — thing, there.

classification, *klăs sĭ fĭ kā' shŭn,* s. classification, f., ordre, m.

classify, *klăs' sĭ fī,* v. a. classifier.

classing, *klăs' sing,* s. classement, m.

clatter, *klăt' ter,* s. fracas, bruit, m.

clatter, *klăt' ter,* v. a. & n. faire sonner || retentir, résonner || babiller.

clause, *klăwz,* s. clause, sentence, f.

claustral, *klăws' trăl,* a. claustral.

clavicle, *klăv' ĭ kl,* s. clavicule, f.

claw, *klăw,* s. griffe, serre, f. || pince (d'une écrevisse), f.

claw, *klăw,* v. a. égratigner, gratter || flatter.

clawed, *klăwd,* a. onguiculé.

clay, *klā,* s. argile, terre glaise, f. || ~-pit, s. argilière, marnière, f.

clayey, *klā' ĭ,* **clayish,** *klā' ĭsh,* a. argileux.

clean, *klēn,* v. a. nettoyer.

clean, *klēn,* a. (-ly, ad.) propre(ment) || pur, net(tement) || élégant || entièrement.

cleanliness, *klēn' lĭ nĕs,* s. propreté, netteté, pureté, f.

cleanly, *klēn' lĭ,* a. propre, net, élégant.

cleanse, *klĕnz,* v. a. nettoyer, purifier, écurer.

clear, *klēr,* v. a. rendre clair, clarifier, purifier, nettoyer || liquider, absoudre || acquitter || gagner || débarrasser, justifier.

clear, *klēr,* a. & ad. (-ly, ad.) clair(ement) || serein || net || évident || irréprochable || libre || entièrement || évidemment || ~-headed, a. éclairé || ~-sighted, a. clairvoyant, pénétrant || ~-starch, v. a. blanchir à neuf || ~-starcher, s. blanchisseuse de fin, f.

clearance, *klēr' ăns,* s. (com.) acquit, m. || défrichement, m.

clearing, *klēr' ing,* s. justification, f., acquittement, m. || défrichement, m. || ~-house, s. comptoir général de virement, m.

clearness, *klēr' nĕs,* s. clarté, splendeur, f., éclat, m. || évidence, pureté, innocence, f.

cleave, *klēv,* v. a. & n. ir. (se) fendre || se coller, s'attacher à.

cleaver, *klēv' ĕr,* s. couperet, m. || fendeur, m. || plante grimpante, f.

cleft, *klĕft,* s. fente, crevasse, f.

clematis, *klĕm' ă tĭs,* s. (bot.) clématite, f.

clemency, *klĕm' ĕn sĭ,* s. clémence, miséricorde, f. || (fig.) douceur, f.

clement, *klĕm' ĕnt,* a. clément, miséricordieux || -ly, ad. avec clémence.

clench, *klĕnsh,* vide clinch.

clergy, *klēr' jĭ,* s. clergé, m.

clergyman, *klēr' jĭ măn,* s. ecclésiastique, prêtre, m.

clerical, *klēr' ĭk ăl,* a. clérical, ecclésiastique.

clerk, *klărk,* s. ecclésiastique, m. || homme de lettres, savant, m. || commis, secrétaire, m.

clerkly, *klărk' lĭ,* a. lettré, savant.

clerkship, *klărk' shĭp,* s. cléricat, m. || emploi de clerc or de commis, m.

clever, *klĕv' ĕr,* a. (-ly, ad.) habile(ment) || adroit(ement).

cleverness, *klĕv' ĕr nĕs,* s. habileté, dextérité, f.

clew, *klō,* s. peloton, m. || guide, m.

clew, *klō,* v. a. (to ~ up) (mar.) carguer.

click, *klĭk,* s. loquet, m. || cliquet, m.

click, *klĭk,* v. n. faire tic-tac.

client, *klī' ĕnt,* s. client, m.

cliff, *klĭf,* s. rocher escarpé, m. || falaise, f.

climacteric, *klī măk' tĕr ĭk,* s. année climatérique, f.

climate, *klī' māt,* s. climat, m.

climatic, *klī măt' ĭk,* a. de climat.

climb, *klĭm,* v. a. & n. ir. monter, grimper || gravir contre.

clinch, *klĭnsh,* v. a. tenir ferme, serrer les poings || river un clou.

clincher, *klĭnsh' ĕr,* s. crampon, m. || mot sans réplique, m.   [coller à.

cling, *kling,* v. n. ir. se cramponner || se

clinic(al), *klĭn' ĭk(ăl),* a. clinique.

clink, *klĭngk,* s. tintement, m.

clink, *klĭngk,* v. a. & n. faire résonner || résonner, tinter.

clinker, *klĭngk' ĕr,* s. mâchefer, m.

clip, *klĭp,* s. coup de poing, m. || embrassement, m.

clip, *klĭp,* v. a. embrasser || couper || tondre.

clipper, *klĭp' pĕr,* s. rogneur, m. || tondeur, m. || fin voilier, m.

clipping, *klĭp' ping,* s. rognure, f.

cloak, *klōk,* s. manteau, m. || (fig.) masque, f. || ~-room, s. (rail.) dépôt des bagages, m.   [masquer.

cloak, *klōk,* v. a. couvrir d'un manteau ||

clock, *klōk,* s. horloge, pendule, f. || (of stockings) coin, m.

clockmaker, *klōk' māk ĕr,* s. horloger, m.

clockwork, *klōk' wĕrk,* s. mouvement d'une horloge, m. || horlogerie, f. || sonnerie, f. || by ~, par mouvement d'horlogerie.   [m. || ~-hopper, s. rustre, m.

clod, *klŏd,* s. motte de terre, f. || lourdaud,

clod, *klŏd,* v. n. se coaguler.

clog, *klŏg,* s. charge, f. || entraves, f. pl. || sabot, m., galoche, f.

clog, *klŏg,* v. a. & n. embarrasser, charger || s'unir, s'attacher.   [m.

cloister, *klŏys' tĕr,* s. cloître, monastère, m.

close, *klōs,* s. clos, enclos, m. || ruelle, f. || fin, f. || (mus.) pause, f.

close, *klōz,* v. a. & n. fermer, boucher, renfermer, conclure, terminer || consolider || se fermer || s'unir || se consolider.

close, *klōs,* a. & ad. (-ly, ad.) fermé, serré, concis, étroit, solide || retiré, solitaire || visqueux, glutineux || obscur || de près, d'une manière serrée, secrètement || à la dérobée || laconiquement || ~-fisted, a. dur à la détente, avare || ~-hauled, a. (mar.) au plus près (du vent) || ~-set, a. serré, pressé, dru || ~-stool, s. chaise percée, f.

closeness, *klōs' nĕs,* s. clôture, f. || solitude, solidité, f. || secret, m. || avarice, f.

closet, *klŏz' ĕt,* s. cabinet, m.

closet, *klŏz' ĕt,* v. a. enfermer dans un cabinet.

closure, *klō zhōŏr,* s. clôture, cloison, conclusion, f.

clot, *klŏt,* s. concrétion, coagulation, f.

clot, *klŏt,* v. n. se coaguler.

cloth, *klŏth,* s. toile, f. ‖ nappe, f. ‖ drap, m. ‖ habit, m. ‖ tapis, m. ‖ linge, m. ‖ long-~, s. guinée, f. (étoffe).

clothe, *klōth,* v. a. (& n.) ir. (se) vêtir, (s')habiller.

clothes, *klōthz,* s. pl. habits, m. pl. ‖ linge, m. ‖ suit of ~, s. habillement complet, m. ‖ ~-basket, s. panier à linge sale, m. ‖ ~-horse, s. séchoir, m. ‖ ~-peg, s. porte-manteau, m. ‖ ~-pin, s. épingle à linge, f. ‖ ~-press, s. garderobe, f.

clothier, *klōth'i ér,* s. drapier, m.

clothing, *klō'thing,* s. vêtement, m.

cloud, *klowd,* s. nue, f. ‖ (fig.) nuée, f. nuage, m. ‖ cache-nez, m. ‖ ~-capped, a. sourcilleux.

cloud, *klowd,* v. a. (& n.) (se) couvrir de nuages ‖ -ily, ad. obscurément.

cloudiness, *klowd'i nês,* s. obscurité, f., ténèbres, f. pl. [serein.

cloudless, *klowd'lês,* a. sans nuages,

cloudy, *klowd'i,* a. nuageux, obscur ‖ troublé ‖ sombre. [butte, f.

clout, *klowt,* s. torchon, m. ‖ pièce, f. ‖

clout, *klowt,* v. a. rapetasser ‖ garnir de clous. [d'ail, f.

clove, *klōv,* s. clou de girofle, m. ‖ gousse

cloven, *klō'vn,* a. fendu, fourchu.

clover, *klō'vér,* s. trèfle, m. ‖ to live in ~, vivre dans l'abondance. [m.

clown, *klown,* s. paysan, rustre, paillasse,

clownish, *klown'ish,* a. rustique, grossier.

cloy, *kloy,* v. a. enclouer (un canon) ‖ soûler.

club, *klŭb,* s. massue, f., gourdin, m. ‖ trèfle, m. ‖ club, m. ‖ cercle, m. ‖ ~-foot, s. pied bot, m. ‖ ~-law, s. lois du plus fort, f. ‖ ~-room, s. salle d'assemblée, f.

club, *klŭb,* v. n. se réunir ‖ se cotiser.

cluck, *klŭk,* v. n. glousser.

clue, *klū,* s. fil, m. ‖ indice, m. ‖ (mar.) escot (de voile), m.

clump, *klŭmp,* s. bloc de bois, m. ‖ bouquet d'arbres, m. ‖ ~-soles, s. pl. semelles à patins, f. pl.

clumsily, *klŭm'zi li,* a. maladroitement.

clumsiness, *klŭm'zi nês,* s. grossièreté, maladresse, f. [lourd.

clumsy, *klŭm'zi,* a. grossier, maladroit,

cluster, *klŭs'tér,* s. amas, groupe, m., masse, f.

cluster, *klŭs'tér,* v. a. & n. mettre en tas ‖ croître en groupes.

clutch, *klŭch,* s. prise, f. ‖ griffe, patte, f.

clutch, *klŭch,* v. a. tenir ferme dans la main, serrer le poing, saisir.

clyster-pipe, *klis'tér pip,* s. canule, f.

coach, *kōch,* s. carrosse, m., voiture, f. ‖ ~-house, s. remise, f. ‖ ~-office, s. bureau des messageries, m.

coach, *kōch,* v. a. mener en carrosse ‖ (fig.) préparer.

coachman, *kōch'măn,* s. cocher, m.

coadjutor, *kō ăd jō'tér,* s. coadjuteur, associé, m. [guler.

coagulate, *kō ăg'u lāt,* v. a. (& n.) (se)coa-

coagulation, *kō ăg u lā'shŭn,* s. coagulation, f.

coal, *kōl,* s. charbon (de terre), m., houille, f. ‖ ~-deposit, s. dépôt houiller, m. ‖ ~-heaver, s. porteur de charbon, m. ‖ ~-hole, s. charbonnier, m. ‖ ~-mine, s. mine de houille, f. ‖ ~-pit, s. houillère, f. ‖ ~-scuttle, s. seau à charbon, m. ‖ ~-shoot, s. seau à charbon, m. ‖ ~-tar, s. goudron de houille, m.

coalesce, *kō ă lês',* v. n. se coaliser, s'unir en masse.

coalescence, *kō ă lês'êns,* s. union, f.

coalition, *kō ăl ĭsh'ŭn,* s. confédération, f.

coaly, *kō'li,* a. houilleux. [fusion, f.

coarse, *kōrs,* a. grossier, gros, impoli ‖ -ly, ad. grossièrement ‖ impoliment.

coarseness, *kōrs'nês,* s. grossièreté, impolitesse, f.

coast, *kōst,* s. côte, f., rivage, m.

coast, *kōst,* v. a. & n. côtoyer, suivre, ranger la côte.

coaster, *kōst'ér,* s. côtier, caboteur, m.

coastguard, *kōst'gärd,* s. garde-côte, m.

coasting, *kōst'ing,* ~-trade, s. petit cabotage, m. ‖ ~-vessel, s. cabotier, m.

coat, *kōt,* s. habit, justaucorps, m. ‖ jaquette, f. ‖ tunique, f. ‖ poil, m., peau, f. ‖ fourrure, f. ‖ great-~, over-~, s. pardessus, paletot, m. ‖ ~ of mail, cotte de mailles, f. ‖ ~ of arms, écusson, m.

coat, *kōt,* v. a. habiller ‖ revêtir.

coating, *kōt'ing,* s. étoffe pour habits, f. ‖ (paint.) couche, f.

coax, *kōks,* v. a. caresser, cajoler.

cob, *kŏb,* s. bidet, m. ‖ araignée, f. ‖ balle (de maïs), f. ‖ ~-nut, s. grosse noisette, f.

cobble, *kŏb'bl,* s. bateau, m.

cobble, *kŏb'bl,* v. a. saveter.

cobbler, *kŏb'blér,* s. savetier, m.

cobweb, *kŏb'wêb,* s. toile d'araignée, f.

cocentric, *kō sên'trik,* a. concentrique.

cochineal, *kŏch'in êl,* s. cochenille, f.

cock, *kŏk,* s. coq, mâle des oiseaux, m. ‖ girouette, f. ‖ robinet, m. ‖ chien (d'un fusil), m. ‖ meule (de foin), f. ‖ forme (d'un chapeau), f. ‖ style (d'un cadran), m. ‖ aiguille (d'une balance), f. ‖ ~-horse, s. dada, m. ‖ ~-loft, s. grenier, m. ‖ ~-sure, a. (fam.) sûr et certain.

cock, *kŏk,* v. a. & n. relever, retrousser ‖ armer (un fusil) ‖ mettre en meule ‖ faire le fier.

cock, *kŏk,* a. à cheval, triomphant ‖ (of birds) mâle.

cockade, *kŏk kād',* s. cocarde, f.

cock-a-doodle-doo, *kŏk'ă dō'dl dō',* s. coquerico, chant du coq, m.

cockatoo, *kŏk ă tō',* s. cacadou, m.

cockatrice, *kŏk'ă tris,* s. basilic, m.

cockchafer, *kŏk'chā fér,* s. hanneton, m.

cockcrow(ing), *kŏk krō'(ing),* s. chant du coq, m.

cocked, *kŏkt,* a. à cornes ‖ to knock into a ~ hat, rosser qn. d'importance.

cocker, *kŏk'ér,* v. a. choyer, dorloter.

cockerel, *kŏk′ĕr ĕl,* s. cochet, petit coq, m.
cockle, *kŏk′l,* s. (bot.) nielle, f. || coque, palourde, f. || ~-shell, s. coquille, f.
cockle, *kŏk′l,* v. a. & n. plier en spirale || se plisser, se rider || (of the sea) moutonner.
cockney, *kŏk′nĭ,* s. badaud de Londres, m.
cockpit, *kŏk′pĭt,* s. (mar.) poste de malades, m.
cockroach, *kŏk′rōch,* s. blatte, f.
cockscomb, *kŏks′kōm,* s. crête du coq, f. || fat, damoiseau, m.   [m.
cockswain, *kŏk′sn,* s. patron de chaloupe,
cocktail, *kŏk′tāl,* a. & s. métis (m.) || malappris (m.) || boisson américaine composée d'eau-de vie et de diverses ingrédients, f.
cocoa, *kŏ′kō,* s. cocotier, m. || ~-nut, s.
cocoon, *kŏ kōn′,* s. cocon, m. [coco, m.
cod, *kŏd,* s. morue, f. || cosse, f. || -s, pl. (an.) bourses, f. pl. || ~-liver oil, s. huile de
/oie de morue, f.
coddle, *kŏd′dl,* v. a. bouillir || dorloter.
code, *kōd,* s. code, m.
codger, *kŏj′ĕr,* s. bonhomme, m.
codicil, *kŏd′ĭ sĭl,* s. codicille, m.
codify, *kŏd′ĭ fī,* v. a. codifier.
codling, *kŏd′lĭng,* s. pomme hâtive, f. || petite morue, f.
coerce, *kŏ ĕrs′,* v. a. restreindre.
coercion, *kŏ ĕr′shŭn,* s. coercition, contrainte, f.
coercive, *kŏ ĕr′sĭv,* a. coercitif.
coeval, *kŏ ē′văl,* s. contemporain, m.
coeval, *kŏ ē′văl,* a. contemporain.
coexist, *kŏ ĕg zĭst′,* v. n. coexister.
coffee, *kŏf′fĭ,* s. café, m. || ~-grounds, s. pl. marc de café, m. || ~-house, s. café, m. || ~-pot, s. cafetière, f. || ~-roaster, s. brûloir à café, m. || ~-room, s. salon d'hôtel, m. || ~-set, s. service à café, m.   [caisse, f.
coffer, *kŏf′fĕr,* s. coffre, coffre-fort, m. ||
coffin, *kŏf′fĭn,* s. bière, f., cercueil, m. || cornet de papier, m.
coffin, *kŏf′fĭn,* v. a. mettre dans un cercueil.
cog, *kŏg,* s. dent de roue, f., alluchon, m. || ruse, f. || ~-wheel, s. roue dentée, f.
cog, *kŏg,* v. a. & n. garnir de dents || cajoler || piper (les dés).
cogency, *kŏ jĕn sĭ,* s. force, puissance, f.
cogent, *kŏ′jĕnt,* a. fort, puissant || -ly, ad. irrésistiblement.   [méditer.
cogitate, *kŏj′ĭ tāt,* v. n. penser, réfléchir,
cognate, *kŏg′nāt,* a. allié, proche || analogue.
cognation, *kŏg nā′shŭn,* s. parenté, consanguinité, f.   [f. || conviction, f.
cognition, *kŏg nĭ′shŭn,* s. connaissance, f.
cognizance, *kŏg′nĭ zăns,* s. connaissance, f. || compétence, f.|| jugement, m. || marque, enseigne, f.   [compétent.
cognizant, *kŏg′nĭ zănt,* a. instruit || (jur.)
cohabit, *kŏ hăb′ĭt,* v. n. habiter ensemble.
cohabitation, *kŏ hăb ĭ tā′shŭn,* s. cohabitation, f.
coheir, *kŏ âr′,* s. cohéritier, m.
coheiress, *kŏ âr′ĕs,* s. cohéritière, f.

cohere, *kŏ hēr′,* v. n. être attaché, s'accorder, convenir.
coherence, *kŏ hē′rĕns,* s. cohésion, f. || liaison, f., rapport, m.
coherent, *kŏ hē′rĕnt,* a. (-ly, ad.) cohérent, conséquent, suivi || avec cohérence.
cohesion, *kŏ hē′zhŭn,* s. cohésion, adhérence, f., rapport, m., liaison, f.
coif, *kŏŷf,* s. coiffe, calotte, f.
coil, *kŏŷl,* s. corde rouée, f. || tumulte, m.
coil, *kŏŷl,* v. a. mettre en peloton.
coin, *kŏŷn,* s. coin, m. || encoignure, f. || monnaie, f.
coin, *kŏŷn,* v. a. monnayer || inventer.
coinage, *kŏŷn′āj,* s. monnayage, m. || invention, f.   [rapporter.
coincide, *kŏ ĭn sīd′,* v. n. coïncider, se
coincidence, *kŏ ĭn′sĭ dĕns,* s. coïncidence,f.
coincident, *kŏ ĭn′sĭ dĕnt,* a. coïncident, d'accord.
coiner, *kŏŷn′ĕr,* s. monnayeur, m. || fauxmonnayeur, m. || forgeur, m.
coke, *kŏk,* s. coke, m.
colander, *kŭl′ăn dĕr,* s. passoire, f.
cold, *kōld,* s. rhume, m. || froid, m. || to catch ~, s'enrhumer.
cold, *kōld,* a. (-ly, ad.) froid(ement) || indifférent, sérieux || avec indifférence || to be ~, avoir froid || ~-drawn, a. préparé par l'expression à froid.
coldness, *kōld′nĕs,* s. froid, m., froideur, f. || indifférence, f.   [chou vert, m.
cole, *kōl,* s. chou frisé, m. || ~-wort, s.
colic, *kŏl′ĭk,* s. colique, f., tranchées, f. pl.
collaborate, *kŏl lăb′ō rāt,* v. n. collaborer, coopérer.   [laboration, f.
collaboration, *kŏl lăb ō rā′shŭn,* s. collaborateur, m.
collaborator, *kŏl lăb ō rā tĕr,* s. collaborateur, m.
collapse, *kŏl lăps′,* s. rapprochement, m. || (méd.) affaissement, m. || (fig.) écroulement, m.
collapse, *kŏl lăps′,* v. n. tomber l'un sur l'autre || s'affaisser || s'écrouler.
collar, *kŏl′lĕr,* s. collet, m. || collier, m. || col, m. || rouleau, m. || collerette, f. || bricole, f. || ~-bone, s. clavicule, f.
collar, *kŏl′lĕr,* v. a. prendre au collet || mettre un collier à || faire un rouleau de.
collate, *kŏl lāt′,* v. a. comparer || collationner || nommer.
collateral, *kŏl lăt′ĕr ăl,* a. (-ly, ad.) collatéral(ement) || indirect(ement).
collation, *kŏl lā′shŭn,* s. collation, f. || don, m. || goûter, m.   [m.
colleague, *kŏl′lēg,* s. collègue, camarade,
collect, *kŏl′lĕkt,* s. collecte, f.
collect, *kŏl lĕkt′,* v. a. & n. recueillir || quêter || conclure.
collected, *kŏl lĕkt′ĕd,* a. calme, tranquille.
collection, *kŏl lĕk′shŭn,* s. collection, f. || quête, f. || levée des lettres, f. || recueil, amas, m., compilation, f., assemblage, m.
collective, *kŏl lĕk′tĭv,* a. assemblé || (gr.) collectif || -ly, ad. collectivement.
collector, *kŏl lĕk′tĕr,* s. collecteur, percepteur, m.

---

college, *kŏl'lĕj,* s. collège, m. ‖ communauté, f., corps, m. [lège, m.
collegian, *kŏl lē'ji ăn,* s. membre d'un collège, écolier, m.
collegiate, *kŏl lē'ji ăt,* s. membre d'un collège, écolier, m.
collegiate, *kŏl lē'ji ăt,* a. collégial.
collide, *kŏl līd',* v. n. se choquer ‖ s'entre-choquer. [m.
collie, *kŏl'lĭ,* s. chien de berger écossais,
collier, *kŏl'yĕr,* s. charbonnier, m. ‖ bâtiment charbonnier, m.
colliery, *kŏl'yĕr ĭ,* s. mine de charbon, f. ‖ commerce de charbon, m.
collision, *kŏl lĭzh'ŭn,* s. collision, f., choc, froissement, m.
collodion, *kŏl lō'di ŏn,* s. collodion, m.
collop, *kŏl'lŏp,* s. tranche, f., morceau, m.
colloquial, *kŏl lō'kwi ăl,* a. de conversation, familier ‖ ~ powers, s. pl. talent de conversation, m. [férence, conversation, f.
colloquy, *kŏl'lō qui,* s. colloque, m., con-
collum, *kŏl'lŭm,* s. (bot.) collet, m.
collusion, *kŏl lō'shŭn,* s. collusion, connivence, f. [soire(ment).
collusive, *kŏl lō'sĭv,* a. (-ly,.ad.) collu-
colon, *kō'lŏn,* s. (gr.) deux points, m. pl.
colonade, *kŏl ō nad',* s. colonnade, f.
colonel, *kẽr'nĕl,* s. colonel, m. [m.
colonelcy, *kẽr'nĕl sĭ,* s. grade de colonel,
colonial, *kō lō'ni ăl,* a. colonial. [sation, f.
colonisation, *kŏl ō nĭ zā'shŭn,* s. coloni-
colonise, *kŏl'ō nīz,* v. a. coloniser.
colonist, *kŏl'ō nĭst,* s. colon, m.
colony, *kŏl'ō nĭ,* s. colonie, peuplade, f.
colophony, *kŏl ō fōn'ĭ,* s. colophane, f.
colossal, *kō lŏs'săl,* a. colossal.
Colosseum, *kŏl ŏs sē'ŭm,* s. Colisée, m.
colossus, *kō lŏs'sŭs,* s. colosse, m.
colour, *kŭl'ĕr,* s. couleur, f. ‖ teint, m. ‖ prétexte, m. ‖ fast ~, couleur solide ‖ ~-blind, a. affecté de daltonisme ‖ ~-sergeant, s. porte-drapeau, m. ‖ -s, s. pl. étendard, m. ‖ (mar.) pavillon national, m. ‖ with flying -s, enseignes déployées ‖ to strike one's -s, (mar.) amener son pavillon.
colour, *kŭl'ĕr,* v. a. & n. colorer ‖ colorier ‖ pallier ‖ prendre couleur, se colorer, rougir ‖ (se) culotter.
colouring, *kŭl'ĕr ĭng,* s. coloris, m.
colourless, *kŭl'ĕr lĕs,* a. sans couleur, pâle. [dent de lait, m.
colt, *kōlt,* s. poulain, m. ‖ jeune étourdi ‖
colum, *kŏl'ŭm,* s. placenta, m.
columbine, *kŏl'ŭm bĭn,* s. couleur gorge de pigeon, f. ‖ (bot.) ancolie, f.
column, *kŏl'ŭm,* s. colonne, f., pilier, m.
columnar, *kŏ lŭm'nĕr,* a. en forme de colonne. [m.
coma, *kō'mă,* s. coma, assoupissement,
comatose, *kŏm'ă tōs,* a. comateux.
comb, *kōm,* s. peigne, m. ‖ crête (d'un coq), f. ‖ rayon (de miel), m. [cheval).
comb, *kōm,* v. a. peigner ‖ étriller (un
combat, *kŭm'băt,* s. combat, m., lutte, f. ‖ single *or* private ~, duel, m.
combat, v. a. & n. combattre.

combatant, *kŭm'băt ănt,* s. combattant, m.
comber, *kōm'ĕr,* s. cardeur de laine, m.
combination, *kŏm bĭ nā'shŭn,* s. combinaison, f. ‖ complot, m., conspiration, f.
combine, *kŏm bīn',* v. a. & n. combiner, joindre ‖ se liguer. [stible, m.
combustible, *kŏm bŭs'tĭ bl,* s. combu-
combustible, *kŏm bŭs'tĭ bl,* a. combustible.
combustion, *kŏm bŭst'shŭn,* s. combustion, f. ‖ embrasement, m.
come, *kŭm,* v. n. ir. venir, arriver ‖ devenir ‖ procéder ‖ se monter (à) ‖ se réduire ‖ ~! i. allons! venez! ‖ to ~ round, changer de résolution ‖ to ~ about, arriver, se passer ‖ to ~ back, revenir ‖ to ~ down, descendre ‖ to ~ in, entrer ‖ to ~ into a fortune, faire fortune ‖ to ~ off, se détacher ‖ se passer ‖ réussir ‖ to ~ out, sortir ‖ paraître (dans les journeaux) ‖ to ~ to, se remettre ‖ devenir ‖ to ~ up, monter ‖ to ~ up with, atteindre ‖ to ~ upon, trouver, rencontrer ‖ still to ~, toujours à venir ‖ ~ what may, coûte que coûte.
comedian, *kō mē'di ăn,* s. comédien, m.
comedy, *kŏm'ē dĭ,* s. comédie, f.
comeliness, *kŭm'lĭ nĕs,* s. beauté, grâce, f.
comely, *kŭm'lĭ,* a. gracieux ‖ décent, convenable ‖ ~, ad. avec grâce ‖ décemment, honnêtement. [s. nouvel arrivé, m.
comer, *kŭm'ĕr,* s. venant, venu, m. ‖ new-~,
comet, *kŏm'ĕt,* s. comète, f.
comfit, *kŭm'fĭt,* s. confiture sèche, f.
comfort, *kŭm'fĕrt,* s. secours, m., assistance, f. ‖ consolation, f. ‖ agrément, m.
comfort, *kŭm'fĕrt,* v. a. conforter, fortifier, consoler. [consolant, agréable, à son aise.
comfortable, *kŭm'fĕrt ă bl,* a. confortable,
comfortably, *kŭm'fĕrt ă blĭ,* ad. commodément, agréablement.
comforter, *kŭm'fĕrt ĕr,* s. consolateur, m. ‖ cache-nez, m. ‖ Job's ~, triste consolateur. [désagréable.
comfortless, *kŭm'fĕrt lĕs,* a. inconsolable ‖
comic(al), *kŏm'ĭk(ăl),* a. (-ly, ad.) comique(ment) ‖ drôle, facétieux.
coming, *kŭm'ĭng,* s. venue, arrivée, f.
coming, *kŭm'ĭng,* a. futur, à venir.
comma, *kŏm'mă,* s. virgule, f. ‖ inverted ~, guillemet, m.
command, *kŏm mând',* s. commandement, ordre, m. [ordonner ‖ gouverner.
command, *kŏm mând',* v. a. & n. commander,
commandant, *kŏm măn dănt',* s. commandant, m. [dant, général, chef, m.
commander, *kŏm măn'dĕr,* s. comman-
commandment, *kŏm mănd'mĕnt,* s. commandement, ordre, m. ‖ précepte, m.
commemorate, *kŏm mĕm'mō rāt,* v. a. commémorer.
commemoration, *kŏm mĕm mō rā'shŭn,* s. commémoration, f. ‖ célébration, f.
commemorative, *kŏm mĕm'mō rā tĭv,* a. qui rappelle. [débuter (comme), devenir.
commence, *kŏm mĕns',* v. a. & n. commencer ‖
commencement, *kŏm mĕns'mĕnt,* s. commencement, m. ‖ début, m.

commend, *kŏm mĕnd'*, v. a. louer, recommander.

commendable, *kŏm mĕn' dȧ bl*, a. recommandable, louable. [ablement.

commendably, *kŏm mĕn' dȧ blĭ*, ad. louablement.

commendation, *kŏm mĕn dā' shŭn*, s. recommandation, louange, f.

commendatory, *kŏm mĕn' dȧ tĕr ĭ*, a. à la louange de.

commensurable, *kŏm mĕn' sū rȧ bl*, a. commensurable || proportionné.

commensurate, *kŏm mĕn' sū rȧt*, v. a. réduire à une mesure commune.

commensurate, *kŏm mĕn' sū rȧt*, a. proportionné, égal.

comment, *kŏm' mĕnt*, **commentary**, *kŏm' mĕn tĕr ĭ*, s. commentaire, m. [gloser.

comment, *kŏm' mĕnt*, v. n. commenter,

commentator, *kŏm' mĕn tā tĕr*, s. commentateur, m. [négoce, m.

commerce, *kŏm' mĕrs*, s. commerce, trafic,

commercial, *kŏm mĕr' shȧl*, a. commercial, de commerce || ~ **directory**, s. almanach du commerce, m. || ~ **traveller**, s. commis voyageur, m.

comminatory, *kŏm mĭn' ȧ tĕr ĭ*, a. comminatoire || menaçant.

commingle, *kŏm mĭng' gl*, v. a. & n. mêler, mélanger. [compassion, plaindre.

commiserate, *kŏm mĭz' ĕr ȧt*, v. a. avoir

commiseration, *kŏm mĭz ĕr ā' shŭn*, s. commisération, pitié, f.

commissariat, *kŏm mĭs sā' rĭ ȧt*, s. intendance militaire, m.

commissary, *kŏm' mĭs sĕr ĭ*, s. commissaire, m. || délégué, m. || intendant militaire, m.

commission, *kŏm mĭsh' ŭn*, s. commission, charge, f., emploi, brevet, m. || ~ **agent**, s. commissionnaire, m. || on ~, en commission || **to charge a** ~, faire payer commission || **to discharge a** ~, s'acquitter d'une commission.

commission, *kŏm mĭsh' ŭn*, v. a. donner commission, députer, déléguer.

commissioner, *kŏm mĭsh' ŭn ĕr*, s. commissaire, m. || commissionnaire, m.

commit, *kŏm mĭt'*, v. a. commettre, confier || livrer, emprisonner || compromettre || engager || renvoyer à une commission.

committal, *kŏm mĭt' tȧl*, **commitment**, *kŏm mĭt' mĕnt*, s. emprisonnement, m.

committee, *kŏm mĭt' tē*, s. comité, m. || (jur.) curateur, m., commission, f.

commodious, *kŏm mō' dĭ ŭs*, a. (-ly, ad.) commode, propre, convenable(ment) || aisé || à l'aise.

commodity, *kŏm mŏd' ĭ tĭ*, s. commodité, f. || denrée, marchandise, f.

commodore, *kŏm' mō dōr*, s. (mar.) commodore, m. || bâtiment convoyeur, m.

common, *kŏm' mŏn*, s. communaux, m. pl., vaine pâture, f. || ~s, pl. bourgeoisie, f. || **House of Commons**, s. Chambre des Communes, m. || ~-**council**, s. conseil municipal, m. || ~-**hall**, s. hôtel de ville, m. || ~-**law**, s. droit coutumier, m.

common, *kŏm' mŏn*, a. (-ly, ad.) commun (ément) || ordinaire(ment) || vulgaire, public || (unil.) simple. [sie, f.

commonalty, *kŏm' mŏn ȧl tĭ*, s. bourgeoi-

commoner, *kŏm' mŏn ĕr*, s. bourgeois, m. || membre de la Chambre des Communes, m.

commonness, *kŏm' mŏn nĕs*, s. communauté, f.

commonplace, *kŏm' mŏn plȧs*, s. lieu commun, m. || pensée triviale, f.

commonplace, *kŏm' mŏn plȧs*, a. banal.

commonsense, *kŏm' mŏn sĕns*, s. sens commun, m. [nable.

commonsense, *kŏm' mŏn sĕns*, a. raison-

commonwealth, *kŏm' mŏn wĕlth*, s. république, f. [f. || émeute, f.

commotion, *kŏm mō' shŭn*, s. commotion,

communal, *kŏm' mūn ȧl*, a. communal.

commune, *kŏm mūn'*, v. n. converser, conférer || **to** ~ **with** oneself, rentrer en soi-même.

communicable, *kŏm mū' nĭ kȧ bl*, a. communicable. [muniant, m.

communicant, *kŏm mū' nĭ kȧnt*, s. communiquer || communier.

communicate, *kŏm mū' nĭ kȧt*, v. a. & n. communiquer || communier.

communication, *kŏm mū' nĭ kā' shŭn*, s. communication, f.

communicative, *kŏm mū' nĭ kā tĭv*, a. communicatif, ouvert.

communicativeness, *kŏm mū' nĭ kā tĭv nĕs*, s. caractère communicatif, m.

communion, *kŏm mūn' yŭn*, s. communication, f. || relations, f. pl. || communion, sainte Cène, f. || **to take the** ~, recevoir le sacrement || ~-**table**, s. sainte table, f.

communist, *kŏm' mū nĭst*, s. communiste, communautaire, m.

community, *kŏm mū' nĭ tĭ*, s. communauté, société, f. [able.

commutable, *kŏm mū' tȧ bl*, a. commu-

commutation, *kŏm mū tā' shŭn*, s. commutation, f., changement, m. [muer.

commute, *kŏm mūt'*, v. a. & n. (jur.) com-

compact, *kŏm' pȧkt*, s. pacte, contrat, m.

compact, *kŏm pȧkt'*, a. compacte, condensé || bref, concis || -ly, ad. d'une manière compacte. [densité, f.

compactness, *kŏm pȧkt' nĕs*, s. compacité,

companion, *kŏm pȧn' yŭn*, s. compagnon, m., compagne, f. || ~-**ladder**, s. (mar.) grande échelle, f. [ciable.

companionable, *kŏm pȧn' yŭn ȧ bl*, a. so-

companionship, *kŏm pȧn' yŭn shĭp*, s. camaraderie, f. || société, f.

company, *kŭm' pȧ nĭ*, s. compagnie, assemblée, f., cercle, m., troupe, f.

comparable, *kŏm' pȧ rȧ bl*, a. comparable.

comparative, *kŏm pȧr' ȧ tĭv*, a. comparatif || -ly, ad. par comparaison || ~ **degree**, s. comparatif, m. [fronter.

compare, *kŏm pȧr'*, v. a. comparer, con-

comparison, *kŏm pȧr' ĭ sŭn*, s. comparaison, f. || **in** ~ **with**, en comparaison de || **beyond** ~, sans comparaison.

compartment, *kŏm pȧrt' mĕnt*, s. compartiment, m.

compass, *kŭm' păs,* s. cercle, circuit, tour, m. || portée, f. || circonférence, f. || enceinte, f. || boussole, f. || ~card, s. rose des vents, f. || ~es, s. pl. (pair of ~) compas, m.

compass, *kŭm' păs,* v. a. entourer, assiéger, obtenir, comploter.

compassion, *kŏm pàsh' ŭn,* s. compassion, commisération, f.

compassionate, *kŏm pàsh' ŭn ăt,* v. a. avoir compassion, avoir pitié. [patissant.

compassionate, *kŏm pàsh' ŭn ăt,* a. compatibility, *kŏm păt' i bĭl' i ti,* s. compatibilité, convenance, f.

compatible, *kŏm păt' ĭ bl,* a. compatible, convenable. [m.

compatriot, *kŏm pā' tri ŏt,* s. compatriote, compeer, *kŏm pēr',* s. compère, camarade, m. [obliger.

compel, *kŏm pĕl',* v. a. forcer, contraindre, compend(ium), *kŏm pĕn' di ŭm,* s. abrégé, m. [penser || dédommager.

compensate, *kŏm' pĕn sāt,* v. a. & n. compensation, *kŏm pĕn sā' shŭn,* s. compensation, f. || ~~balance, s. compensateur, m. [en concurrence.

compete, *kŏm pēt',* v. a. & n. être or entrer competence, *kŏm' pĕtĕns,* competency, *kŏm' pĕ tĕn si,* s. compétence, f. || nécessaire, m.

competent, *kŏm' pĕ tĕnt,* a. suffisant, convenable || compétent || ~ly, ad. suffisamment.

competition, *kŏm pŏ tĭsh' ŭn,* s. concurrence, rivalité, f. [concurrent, m.

competitor, *kŏm pĕt' i tĕr,* s. compétiteur, compilation, *kŏm pi lā' shŭn,* s. compilation, f. [poser.

compile, *kŏm pĭl',* v. a. compiler, compiler, *kŏm pĭl' lĕr,* s. compilateur, m.

complacence, *kŏm plā' sĕns,* complacency, *kŏm plā' sĕn si,* s. satisfaction, f. || complaisance, f. || civilité, f.

complacent, *kŏm plā' sĕnt,* a. complaisant, civil, poli || ~ly, ad. avec complaisance.

complain, *kŏm plān',* v. n. se plaindre.

complainant, *kŏm plān' ănt,* s. plaignant, m. || plaignante, f. [tivement.

complainingly, *kŏm plān' ing li,* ad. plaincomplaint, *kŏm plānt',* s. plainte, f., sujet de plainte, m. || maladie, f.

complaisance, *kŏm' pla zăns* ou *kŏm plā' zăns,* s. complaisance, f.

complaisant, *kŏm' pla zănt,* a. complaisant || ~ly, ad. complaisamment.

complement, *kŏm' plĕ mĕnt,* s. complément, m. || achèvement, m. || complétement, m. || montant, m.

complete, *kŏm plēt',* v. a. compléter, accomplir || achever.

complete, *kŏm plēt',* a. complet, achevé, parfait || ~ly, ad. complètement.

completion, *kŏm plē' shŭn,* s. accomplissement, achèvement, comble, m. [posé.

complex, *kŏm' plĕks,* a. complexe || complexion, *kŏm plĕk' shŭn,* s. complexion, f., tempérament || teint, m.

complexioned, *kŏm plĕk' shŭnd,* a. de teint. [complication. f.

complexity, *kŏm plĕks' i ti,* s. complexité, compliance, *kŏm plī' ăns,* s. condescendance, complaisance, f. || in ~ with, conformément à.

compliant, *kŏm plī' ănt,* a. complaisant, obligeant || soumis (à). [embrouiller.

complicate, *kŏm' pli kāt,* v. a. compliquer, complication, *kŏm pli kā' shŭn,* s. complication, confusion, f. || mélange, m.

complicity, *kŏm plis' i ti,* s. complicité, f.

compliment, *kŏm' pli mĕnt,* s. compliment, m. || cérémonie, flatterie, f. || to pay a ~, faire un compliment || ~s of the season, vœux de bonne année, m. pl. [plimenter, flatter.

compliment, *kŏm' pli mĕnt,* v. a. complimentary, *kŏm pli mĕn' tĕr i,* a. complimenteur, flatteur.

compline, *kŏm' plĭn,* s. complies, f. pl.

comply, *kŏm plī',* v. n. condescendre, s'accommoder à, se soumettre.

component, *kŏm pō' nĕnt,* s. constituant, m.

component, *kŏm pō' nĕnt,* a. constituant.

comport, *kŏm pōrt',* v. n. s'accorder, convenir.

compose, *kŏm pōz',* v. a. composer || arranger, apaiser, calmer || accommoder.

composed, *kŏm pōzd', kŏm pō' zĕd,* a. (-ly, ad.) calme || tranquille(ment).

composer, *kŏm pō' zĕr,* s. auteur, écrivain, m. || compositeur, m.

composing, *kŏm pō' zing,* a. (méd.) calmant || ~~draught, s. calmant, m. || ~~stick, s. composteur, f.

composite, *kŏm' pōz ĭt,* s. bougie stéarique, composito, *kŏm' pōz ĭt,* a. composé. [f.

composition, *kŏm pō zĭsh' ŭn,* s. composition, f. || nature, f. || (jur.) concordat, m.

compositor, *kŏm pōz' i tĕr,* s. compositeur, m.

compost, *kŏm' pōst,* s. engrais, fumier, m.

composure, *kŏm pō' zhŏŏr,* s. composition, structure, f. || tranquillité, f. || accommodement, arrangement, m.

compound, *kŏm' pŏŏnd,* s. composé, m.

compound, *kŏm pŏŏnd',* v. a. & n. composer, arranger || faire un accord, s'accommoder.

compound, *kŏm' pŏŏnd,* a. composé.

comprehend, *kŏm prĕ hĕnd',* v. a. comprendre, contenir, concevoir. [préhensible.

comprehensible, *kŏm prĕ hĕn' sĭbl,* a. comprehensibly, *kŏm prĕ hĕn' si bli,* ad. d'une manière expressive.

comprehension, *kŏm prĕ hĕn' shŭn,* s. compréhension, f. || sommaire, m. || intelligence, f.

comprehensive, *kŏm prĕ hĕn' sĭv,* a. intelligent || énergique || vaste || ~ly, ad. largement. [nĕs, s. précision, énergie, f.

comprehensiveness, *kŏm prĕ hĕn' sĭv*compress, *kŏm' prĕs,* s. compresse, f.

compress, *kŏm prĕs',* v. a. comprimer, resserrer. [compressibilité, f.

compressibility, *kŏm prĕs si bĭl' i ti,* s.

compressible, *kŏm'prĕs'ĕibl,* a. compressible.   [sion, condensation, f.

compression, *kŏm'prĕsh'ŭn,* s. compression.

comprise, *kŏm'prīz',* v. a. comprendre, contenir.   [promis, m.

compromise, *kŏm'prō'mĭz,* s. (jur.) compromis.

compromise, *kŏm'prō'mĭz,* v. a. faire un compromis, s'arranger.   [f.

compulsion, *kŏm'pŭl'shŭn,* s. contrainte.

compulsory, *kŏm'pŭl'sĕr'ĭ,* a. forcé, obligatoire.   [m., componction, f.

compunction, *kŏm'pŭngk'shŭn,* s. remords.

computation, *kŏm'pŭtā'shŭn,* s. supputation, f., compte, m.

compute, *kŏm'pūt',* v. a. compter, calculer.

comrade, *kŏm'rād,* s. camarade, m.

con, *kŏn,* s. contre, m. || **pros and –s,** le pour et le contre.

con, *kŏn,* v. a. étudier, repasser.

con, *kŏn,* pr. contre.

concatenation, *kŏn'kătĕnā'shŭn,* s. enchaînement, m. || succession, f.

concave, *kŏn'kāv,* a. concave, creux.

concavity, *kŏn'kăv'ĭtĭ,* s. concavité, f.

conceal, *kŏn'sēl',* v. a. céler, cacher, dissimuler.   [teur, m.

concealer, *kŏn'sēl'ĕr,* s. (jur.) non-révélateur.

concealment, *kŏn'sēl'mĕnt,* s. recèlement, m. || retraite, cachette, f.

concede, *kŏn'sēd',* v. a. concéder, accorder.

conceit, *kŏn'sēt',* s. pensée, idée, opinion, f. || vanité, f.   [–ly, ad. avec vanité.

conceited, *kŏn'sēt'ĕd,* a. vain, suffisant || comprendre || penser.

conceivable, *kŏn'sē'vȧbl,* a. concevable, intelligible.

conceive, *kŏn'sēv',* v. a. & n. concevoir.

concentrate, *kŏn'sĕn'trāt,* v. a. concentrer.   [centration, f.

concentration, *kŏn'sĕn'trā'shŭn,* s. concentration.

concentre, *kŏn'sĕn'tĕr,* v. a. (& n.) (se)concentrer.

concentric, *kŏn'sĕn'trĭk,* a. (–ally, ad.) concentrique(ment).   [f. || notion, idée, f.

conception, *kŏn'sĕp'shŭn,* s. conception.

concern, *kŏn'sĕrn',* s. affaire, cause, f. || intérêt, égard, m. || inquiétude, f., trouble, m. || importance, f.

concern, *kŏn'sĕrn',* v. a. concerner, toucher, regarder, appartenir || inquiéter || se mêler de.

concerned, *kŏn'sĕrnd',* a. intéressé, touché, affligé, inquiété || –ly, ad. avec intérêt.

concerning, *kŏn'sĕrn'ĭng,* pr. concernant, touchant.   [phonie, f. || in –, de concert.

concert, *kŏn'sĕrt,* s. concert, m. || symphonie.

concert, *kŏn'sĕrt',* v. a. concerter.

concession, *kŏn'sĕsh'ŭn,* s. concession, chose accordée, f.

conch, *kŏngk,* s. conque, f.

conciliate, *kŏn'sĭl'ĭāt,* v. a. concilier, réconcilier.   [tion, f.

conciliation, *kŏn'sĭl'ĭā'shŭn,* s. conciliation.

conciliatory, *kŏn'sĭl'ĭātĕr'ĭ,* a. conciliant.

concise, *kŏn'sīs',* a. concis, succinct || –ly, ad. succinctement, laconiquement.

conciseness, *kŏn'sīs'nĕs,* s. concision, brièveté, f., laconisme, m.

conclave, *kŏng'klāv,* s. conclave, m., assemblée, f.   [miner, achever || juger, décider.

conclude, *kŏn'klōd',* v. a. conclure, déterminer.

concluding, *kŏn'klō'dĭng,* a. concluant || dernier.   [décision, f.

conclusion, *kŏn'klō'zhŭn,* s. conclusion, f.||

conclusive, *kŏn'klō'sĭv,* a. concluant, décisif || –ly, ad. décisivement.

concoct, *kŏn'kŏkt',* v. a. digérer, mûrir || machiner.

concomitant, *kŏn'kŏm'ĭtȧnt,* s. concomitant, m. || compagnon, m. || accessoire, m.

concomitant, *kŏn'kŏm'ĭtȧnt,* a. concomitant || qui accompagne.

concord, *kŏng'kaŭrd,* s. accord, m., harmonie, f. || convention, f. || (gr.) concordance, f. || (mus.) consonnance, f.   [f.

concordance, *kŏn'kŏr'dȧns,* s. concordance.

concordant, *kŏn'kŏr'dȧnt,* a. s'accordant, harmonieux.   [foule, f.

concourse, *kŏng'kōrs,* s. concours, m., concourir.

concrete, *kŏn'krēt,* v. n. se solidifier.

concrete, *kŏn'krēt,* a. concret || solidifié.

concretion, *kŏn'krē'shŭn,* s. concrétion, f.

concubinage, *kŏn'kū'bĭnāj,* s. concubinage, m.

concubine, *kŏng'kūbĭn,* s. concubine, f.

concupiscence, *kŏn'kū'pĭssĕns,* s. concupiscence, f.   [corder, être d'accord.

concur, *kŏn'kĕr',* v. n. concourir || s'accorder.

concurrence, *kŏn'kŭr'rĕns,* s. concours, m. || consentement, m.   [m.

concurrent, *kŏn'kŭr'rĕnt,* s. compétiteur.

concurrent, *kŏn'kŭr'rĕnt,* a. concourant.

concussion, *kŏn'kŭsh'ŭn,* s. ébranlement, m., secousse, f.   [surer.

condemn, *kŏn'dĕm',* v. a. condamner || censurer.

condemnation, *kŏn'dĕmnā'shŭn,* s. condamnation, f.   [damnatoire.

condemnatory, *kŏn'dĕm'nȧtĕr'ĭ,* a. condensation,

condensation, *kŏn'dĕnsā'shŭn,* s. condensation, compression, f.

condense, *kŏn'dĕns',* v. a. (& n.) (se) condenser || épaissir.

condescend, *kŏn'dĕsĕnd',* v. n. condescendre, se conformer, se soumettre.

condescending, *kŏn'dĕsĕn'dĭng,* a. condescendant.

condign, *kŏn'dīn',* a. mérité, juste.

condiment, *kŏn'dĭmĕnt,* s. assaisonnement, m.   [rang, m.

condition, *kŏn'dĭsh'un,* s. condition, f., état,

conditional, *kŏn'dĭsh'ŭnȧl,* a. (–ly, ad.) conditionnel(lement).

conditioned, *kŏn'dĭsh'ŭnd,* a. conditionné.

condolatory, *kŏn'dō'lătĕr'ĭ,* a. de condoléance.   [pleurer, plaindre.

condole, *kŏn'dōl',* v. a. & n. s'affliger,

condolence, *kŏn'dō'lĕns,* s. condoléance, f.

condone, *kŏn'dōn',* v. a. pardonner.

conducive, *kŏn'dū'sĭv,* a. contribuant à, utile, profitable.

conduct, *kŏn'dŭkt,* s. conduite, f. || escorte, f. || direction, f.   [guider, diriger.

conduct, *kŏn'dŭkt',* v. a. mener, conduire,

conductor, *kŏn'dŭk'tĕr,* s. conducteur, guide, directeur, m. || paratonnerre, m.

conductress, *kŏn dŭk′ trĕs*, s. conductrice.
conduit, *kŭn′ dĭt*, s. conduit, tuyau, m. [f.
cone, *kōn*, s. cône, m.
coney, *kō′ nĭ*, s. lapin, m.
confabulate, *kŏn făb′ ū lāt*, v. n. causer,
deviser.   [serie, f.
confabulation, *kŏn făb ū lā′ shŭn*, s. cau-
confection, *kŏn fĕk′ shŭn*, s. confiture, f. ||
composition, f. || opiat, m.   [m.
confectioner, *kŏn fĕk′ shŭn ĕr*, s. confiseur,
confectionery, *kŏn fĕk′ shŭn ĕr ĭ*, s. confiserie, f.   [tion, alliance, ligue, f.
confederacy, *kŏn fĕd′ ĕr ä sĭ*, s. confédéra-
confederate, *kŏn fĕd′ ĕr ät*, s. confédéré, m.
confederate, *kŏn fĕd′ ĕr ät*, v. n. se confédérer.
confederate, *kŏn fĕd′ ĕr ät*, a. confédéré.
confederation, *kŏn fĕd ĕr ä′ shŭn*, s. confédération, f.
confer, *kŏn fēr′*, v. a. & n. conférer || to
~ . . on one, gratifier qn. de . .
conference, *kŏn′ fĕr ĕns*, s. conférence, f. ||
close ~, conférence intime.
confess, *kŏn fĕs′*, v. a. (& n.) (se) confesser ||
to stand –ed, être reconnu.
confessedly, *kŏn fĕs′ sĕd lĭ*, ad. de son
aveu || sans contredit.
confession, *kŏn fĕsh′ ŭn*, s. confession, f. ||
dying ~, derniers aveux, aveux in ex-
tremis, m. pl.   [sional, m.
confessional, *kŏn fĕsh′ ŭn ăl*, s. confes-
confessor, *kŏn fĕs′ sĕr*, s. confesseur, m.
confidant(e), *kŏn′ fĭ dănt*, s. confident, dé-
positaire, m. || confidente, f.
confide, *kŏn fīd′*, v.a.(& n.) (se) confier (en).
confidence, *kŏn′ fĭ dĕns*, s. confiance, assurance, f.
confident, *kŏn′ fĭ dĕnt*, a. sûr, assuré ||
effronté ||–ly, ad. avec confiance.
confidential, *kŏn fĭ dĕn′ shăl*, a. (–ly, ad.)
confidentiel(lement) || hardi.
confiding, *kŏn fīd′ ĭng*, a. confiant ||–ly,
ad. avec confiance.
configuration, *kŏn fĭg ū rā′ shŭn*, s. configuration, f.   [tière, f.
confine, *kŏn′ fīn*, s. confins, m. pl., fron-
confine, *kŏn fīn′*, v. a. confiner, borner,
limiter || enfermer, emprisonner.
confinement, *kŏn fīn′ mĕnt*, s. contrainte,
f. || emprisonnement, m. || couches, f. pl. ||
solitary ~, s. emprisonnement cellu-
laire, m.   [raffermir || établir.
confirm, *kŏn fērm′*, v. a. confirmer, assurer,
confirmation, *kŏn fĕr mā′ shŭn*, s. confirmation, ratification, évidence, f.
confirmative, *kŏn fĕrm′ ä tĭv*, confirma-
tory, *kŏn fĕrm′ ä tĕr ĭ*, a. confirmatif.
confirmed, *kŏn fĕrmd′*, a. assuré || invé-
téré || fieffé, incorrigible || to be ~, faire sa
première communion || ~ invalid, s. ca-
cochyme, malingre, m. || hypochondre, m.
confiscate, *kŏn′ fĭs kāt*, v. a. confisquer,
saisir.   [tion, f.
confiscation, *kŏn fĭs kā′ shŭn*, s. confisca-
conflagration, *kŏn flā grā′ shŭn*, s. incendie, m.
conflict, *kŏn′ flĭkt*, s. conflit, combat, m.

conflict, *kŏn flĭkt′*, v. n. lutter, combattre.
conflicting, *kŏn flĭkt′ ĭng*, a. en contradiction.   [concours, m.
confluence, *kŏn′ floo ĕns*, s. confluent, m. ||
conform, *kŏn fawrm′*, v. a. & n. rendre
conforme || se conformer, s'accommoder à.
conformable, *kŏn fawrm′ ä bl*, a. conforme,
conséquent.   [formément (à).
conformably, *kŏn fawrm′ ä blĭ*, ad. con-
conformation, *kŏn fŏr mā′ shŭn*, s. con-
formation, f. || arrangement, m.
conformity, *kŏn fŏrm′ ĭ tĭ*, s. conformité,
égalité, f. || in ~ with, conformément à.
confound, *kŏn fownd′*, v. a. confondre.
confraternity, *kŏn frä tĕr′ nĭ tĭ*, s. confrérie, f.   [comparer.
confront, *kŏn frŭnt′*, v. a. confronter ||
confuse, *kŏn fūz′*, v. a. confondre, troubler.
confusedly, *kŏn fū′ zĕd lĭ*, ad. confusément.
confusion, *kŏn fū′ zhŭn*, s. confusion, f. ||
renversement, m., ruine, f. || to put to ~,
confusionner.
confute, *kŏn fūt′*, v. a. réfuter.
congeal, *kŏn jēl′*, v. a. & n. congeler,
glacer || se prendre.   [tion, f.
congelation, *kŏn jĕ lā′ shŭn*, s. congéla-
congenial, *kŏn jē′ nĭ ăl*, a. congénial.
congeniality, *kŏn jē nĭ ăl′ ĭ tĭ*, s. affinité,
f. || conformité, analogie, f.
conger, *kŏng′ gĕr*, s. congre, m.
congest, *kŏn jĕst′*, v. a. amasser || amon-
celer || (méd.) engorger.
congestion, *kŏn jĕst′ shŭn*, s. amas, m. ||
(méd.) congestion, f.   [glutiner.
conglutinate, *kŏn glō′ tĭ nāt*, v. a. con-
congratulate, *kŏn grăt′ ū lāt*, v. a. féliciter.
congratulation, *kŏn grăt ū lā′ shŭn*, s. félicitation, f.   [félicitation.
congratulatory, *kŏn grăt′ ū lä tĕr ĭ*, a. de
congregate, *kŏng′ grĕ gāt*, v. a. (& n.) (se)
rassembler.   [grégation, assemblée, f.
congregation, *kŏng grĕ gā′ shŭn*, s. con-
gregation, f. || assemblée, f.
congress, *kŏng′ grĕs*, s. congrès, m. || as-
semblée, f.   [venance, f.
congruity, *kŏng grō′ ĭ tĭ*, s. congruité, con-
congruous, *kŏn′ grō ŭs*, a. conforme (à) ||
–ly, ad. d'une manière conforme.
conic(al), *kŏn′ ĭk (ăl)*, a. conique.   [pl.
conics, *kŏn′ ĭks*, s. pl. sections coniques, f.
coniferous, *kō nĭf′ ĕr ŭs*, a. (bot.) conifère.
conjectural, *kŏn jĕk′ tū răl*, a. (–ly, ad.)
conjectural(ement) || par conjecture.
conjecture, *kŏn jĕk′ tūr*, s. conjecture, f.
conjecture, *kŏn jĕk′ tūr*, v. a. conjecturer.
conjoin, *kŏn jŏyn′*, v. a. & n. conjoindre ||
se joindre.   [(ement) || joint, uni.
conjoint, *kŏn jŏynt′*, a. (–ly, ad.) conjoint
conjugal, *kŏn′ jŏō găl*, a. (–ly, ad.) con-
jugal(ement).   [juguer.
conjugate, *kŏn′ jŏō gāt*, v. a. (gr.) con-
conjugation, *kŏn jŏō gā′ shŭn*, s. conjugaison, f.   [(gr.) conjonction, f.
conjunction, *kŏn jŭnk′ shŭn*, s. union, f. ||
conjunctive, *kŏn jŭnk′ tĭv*, s. (gr.) con-
jonctif, subjonctif, m.
conjunctive, *kŏn jŭnk′ tĭv*, a. (gr.) con-
jonctif, subjonctif.

conjuncture, *kŏn jŭnk´ tŭr,* s. conjoncture, occasion, f. ‖ liaison, f.

conjuration, *kŏn jōō rā´ shŭn,* s. conjuration, f., complot, m.

conjure, *kŏn jōr´,* v. a. conjurer ‖ conspirer, comploter ‖ évoquer.

conjure, *kŭn´jẽr,* v. n. conjurer, ensorceler, charmer. [teur, m.

conjurer, *kŭn´jẽrẽr,* s. sorcier, escamoteur, m.

connate, *kŏn nāt´,* a. inné ‖ inhérent.

connect, *kŏn nĕkt´,* v. a. joindre, lier ‖ unir.

connectedly, *kŏn nĕk´tĕd li,* ad. avec suite, continûment.

connexion, *kŏn nĕk´shŭn,* s. connexion, union, f. ‖ rapport, m., suite, f.

connivance, *kŏn nī´ văns,* s. connivence, f.

connive, *kŏn nīv´,* v. n. conniver, favoriser, tolérer. [m.

connoisseur, *kŏn´nĭs sẽr,* s. connaisseur, m.

connubial, *kŏn nū´ bĭ ăl,* a. conjugal.

conquer, *kŏng´kẽr,* v. a. & n. conquérir, vaincre. [vainqueur, m.

conqueror, *kŏng´kẽr ẽr,* s. conquérant, s.

conquest, *kŏng´kwĕst,* s. conquête, victoire, f. [de même sang.

consanguineous, *kŏn săng gwĭn´ ĭ ŭs,* a.

consanguinity, *kŏn săng gwĭn´ĭ tĭ,* s. consanguinité, f.

conscience, *kŏn´shĕns,* s. conscience, f. ‖ qualm of ~, cri de conscience, m. ‖ ~~money,** s. argent restitué à l'État pour l'acquit de la conscience, m. ‖~~smitten, ~~stricken,** s. atteint de remords.

conscientious, *kŏn shĭ ĕn´shŭs,* a. consciencieux ‖ ~ly, ad. consciencieusement.

conscientiousness, *kŏn shĭ ĕn´shŭs nĕs,* s. conscience, f.

conscious, *kŏn´shŭs,* a. persuadé (de) ‖ dont on a conscience ‖ ~ly, ad. sciemment.

conscript, *kŏn´skrĭpt,* s. conscrit, m., recrue, f. [tion, f., enrôlement, m.

conscription, *kŏn skrĭp´shŭn,* s. conscription, f.

consecrate, *kŏn´sē krāt,* v. a. consacrer ‖ bénir. [tion, f. ‖ canonisation, f.

consecration, *kŏn sē krā´shŭn,* s. consécra-

consecutive, *kŏn sĕk´ū tĭv,* a. consécutif, successif ‖ ~ly, ad. consécutivement, de suite. [aven, m.

consent, *kŏn sĕnt´,* s. consentement, m. ‖

consent, *kŏn sĕnt´,* v. n. consentir à approuver. [d'accord.

consentient, *kŏn sĕn´shĭ ĕnt,* a. consentant.

consequence, *kŏn´sē kwĕns,* s. conséquence, f. ‖ importance, f. ‖ by ~, in ~, par conséquent ‖ of the greatest, highest ~,** de la dernière conséquence.

consequent, *kŏn´sē kwĕnt,* a. conséquent ‖ ~ly, ad. conséquemment, par conséquent.

consequential, *kŏn sē kwĕn´shăl,* a. important, hautain ‖ ~ly, ad. avec importance. [vation, garde, f.

conservation, *kŏn sẽr vā´shŭn,* s. conservation, f.

conservative, *kŏn sẽr´vā tĭv,* s. (parl.) conservateur, m. [vateur.

conservative, *kŏn sẽr´vā tĭv,* a. conser-

conservator, *kŏn sẽr´vā tẽr,* s. conservateur, protecteur, m.

conservatory, *kŏn sẽr´vā tẽr ĭ,* s. dépôt, cabinet, m. ‖ serre, f. [vant.

conservatory, *kŏn sẽr´vā tẽr ĭ,* a. conservant.

consider, *kŏn sĭd´ẽr,* v. a. & n. considérer ‖ estimer ‖ réfléchir. [rable, important.

considerable, *kŏn sĭd´ẽr ă bl,* a. considérable.

considerably, *kŏn sĭd´ẽr ă blĭ,* ad. considérablement, beaucoup.

considerate, *kŏn sĭd´ẽr āt,* a. circonspect ‖ prudent ‖ attentif ‖ modéré ‖ ~ly, ad. considérément.

consideration, *kŏn sĭd ẽr ā´shŭn,* s. considération, f. ‖ importance, f. ‖ égard, m. ‖ out of ~ for you,** en considération de vous. [que, vu que.

considering, *kŏn sĭd´ẽr ĭng,* c. attendu

consign, *kŏn sīn´,* v. a. & n. (com.) consigner ‖ transférer, confier.

consignee, *kŏn sī nē´,* s. consignataire, m.

consigner, *kŏn sīn´ẽr,* s. consignateur, m.

consignment, *kŏn sīn´mĕnt,* s. expédition, f., consignation, f.

consist, *kŏn sĭst´,* v. n. consister ‖ être, exister ‖ être composé.

consistence, consistency, *kŏn sĭs´tĕns, kŏn sĭs´tĕn sĭ,* s. consistance, substance, f. ‖ permanence, stabilité, f.

consistent, *kŏn sĭs´tĕnt,* a. consistant, fixe ‖ conforme, d'accord ‖ ~ly, ad. conséquemment.

consistory, *kŏn sĭs´tẽr ĭ,* s. consistoire, m.

consolable, *kŏn sō´lă bl,* a. consolable.

consolation, *kŏn sō lā´shŭn,* s. consolation, f. [consolateur.

consolatory, *kŏn sō´lă tẽr ĭ,* a. consolant.

console, *kŏn´sōl,* s. console, f.

console, *kŏn sōl´,* v. a. consoler.

consolidate, *kŏn sōl´ĭ dāt,* v. a. (& n.) (se) consolider.

consolidation, *kŏn sōl ĭ dā´shŭn,* s. consolidation, f. ‖ conjonction, f. ‖ (jur.) réunion, f.

consols, *kŏn´sōlz,* s. pl. consolidés, m. pl.

consonance, *kŏn´sō năns,* s. consonance, conformité, f.

consonant, *kŏn´sō nănt,* s. (gr.) consonne, f.

consonant, *kŏn´sō nănt,* a. d'accord avec, conforme à.

consort, *kŏn´sŏrt,* s. compagnon, m., compagne, f., associé, m. ‖ époux, m., épouse, f.

consort, *kŏn sŏrt´,* v. n. s'associer.

conspicuous, *kŏn spĭk´ū ŭs,* a. (-ly, ad.) visible(ment) ‖ apparent, remarquable.

conspiracy, *kŏn spĭr´ ă sĭ,* s. conspiration, f.

conspirator, *kŏn spĭr´ă tẽr,* s. conspirateur, conjuré, m. [ploter.

conspire, *kŏn spīr´,* v. n. conspirer, com-

constable, *kŭn´stă bl,* s. constable, m. ‖ connétable, m. ‖ chief ~,** commissaire de police, m. [gendarmerie, f.

constabulary, *kŭn stăb´ū lẽr ĭ,* s. police,

constancy, *kŏn´stăn sĭ,* s. constance, persévérance, f. ‖ ~ly, ad. constamment.

constant, *kŏn´stănt,* a. constant, ferme ‖

constellation, *kŏn stĕl lā´shŭn,* s. constellation, f. ‖ réunion brillante, f.

---

lāte, hăt, fär, lăw; — hēre, gĕt, hẽr; — mīne, ĭnn; — nō, hŏt, prōve; — hōw,

consternation, *kŏn stĕr nā' shŭn*, s. consternation, f. [obstruer.

constipate, *kŏn' stĭ pāt*, v. a. condenser ||

constipation, *kŏn stĭ pā' shŭn*, s. resserrement, m. || constipation, f.

constituency, *kŏn stĭt' ü ĕn sĭ*, s. circonscription electorale, f. || corps électoral, m. || commettants, m. pl.

constituent, *kŏn stĭt' ü ĕnt*, s. constituant, commettant, m. [essentiel.

constituent, *kŏn stĭt' ü ĕnt*, a. constituant,

constitute, *kŏn' stĭ tūt*, v. a. constituer.

constitution, *kŏn stĭ tū' shŭn*, s. constitution, f. || tempérament, m.

constitutional, *kŏn stĭ tū' shŭn āl*, a. (-ly, ad.) constitutionnel(lement).

constrain, *kŏn strān'*, v. a. contraindre.

constrainable, *kŏn strān' ā bl*, s. contraignable. [ad. par contrainte

constrained, *kŏn strānd'*, a. gêné || -ly,

constraint, *kŏn strānt'*, s. contrainte, f.

constrict, *kŏn strĭkt'*, v. a. resserrer, contracter. [teur, m.

constrictor, *kŏn strĭk' tĕr*, s. (boa)constric-

constringent, *kŏn strĭn' jĕnt*, a. constringent. [bâtir.

construct, *kŏn strŭkt'*, v. a. construire,

construction, *kŏn strŭk' shŭn*, s. construction, f. || (fig.) interprétation, f. || to put a good ~ on, interpréter en bien.

constructive, *kŏn strŭk' tĭv*, a. (-ly, ad.) par induction || implicitement.

constructor, *kŏn strŭk' tĕr*, s. constructeur, m.

construe, *kŏn' strō*, v. a. construire || expliquer.

consul, *kŏn' sŭl*, s. consul, m. [pliquer.

consular, *kŏn' sŭ lär*, a. consulaire.

consulate, *kŏn' sŭ lāt*, **consulship**, *kŏn' sŭl shĭp*, s. consulat, m.

consult, *kŏn sŭlt'*, v. a. (& n.) (se) consulter.

consultation, *kŏn sŭl tā' shŭn*, s. consultation, f.

consultative, *kŏn sŭl' tā tĭv*, a. consultatif.

consulter, *kŏn sŭl' tĕr*, s. consultant, m.

consumable, *kŏn sū' mā bl*, a. qui peut être consumé.

consume, *kŏn sūm'*, v. a. (& n.) (se) consumer || consommer || dévorer.

consumer, *kŏn sū' mĕr*, s. consommateur, m. || dissipateur, m. [mer, terminer.

consummate, *kŏn sŭm' māt*, v. a. consommer || parfait || complet, fini.

consummate, *kŏn sŭm' māt*, a. (-ly, ad.)

consummation, *kŏn sŭm mā' shŭn*, s. consommation, f., achèvement, m. || fin, f.

consumption, *kŏn sŭm' shŭn*, s. consomption, consommation, f. || dissipation, f. || phthisie, f. [phthisique.

consumptive, *kŏn sŭm' tĭv*, a. destructif ||

contact, *kŏn' tăkt*, s. contact, m. || attouchement, m. [fection, f.

contagion, *kŏn tā' jŭn*, s. contagion, in-

contagious, *kŏn tā' jŭs*, a. contagieux.

contain, *kŏn tān'*, v. a. contenir.

contaminate, *kŏn tăm' ĭ nāt*, v. a. souiller, corrompre.

contaminate, *kŏn tăm' ĭ nāt*, a. souillé.

contamination, *kŏn tăm ĭ nā' shŭn*, s. souillure, f. [daigner.

contemn, *kŏn tĕm'*, v. a. mépriser, dé-

contemplate, *kŏn tĕm' plāt*, v. a. & n. contempler || méditer.

contemplation, *kŏn tĕm plā' shŭn*, s. contemplation, vue, f. || projet, m.

contemplative, *kŏn tĕm' plā tĭv*, a. contemplatif || -ly, ad. en contemplation.

contemporaneous, *kŏn tĕm pŏ rā' nĭ ŭs*, a. (-ly, ad.) contemporain || à la même époque.

contemporary, *kŏn tĕm' pŏ rā rĭ*, s. contemporain, m. || confrère, m.

contemporary, *kŏn tĕm' pŏ rā rĭ*, a. contemporain || contemporain

contempt, *kŏn tĕmt'*, s. mépris, dédain, m. || ~ of court, s. offense à la cour, f.

contemptible, *kŏn tĕm' tĭ bl*, a. méprisable.

contemptibly, *kŏn tĕm' tĭ blĭ*, ad. d'une manière vile.

contemptuous, *kŏn tĕm' tū ŭs*, a. méprisant, dédaigneux || -ly, ad. avec mépris.

contend, *kŏn tĕnd'*, v. a. & n. contester, disputer, combattre || prétendre, maintenir.

content, *kŏn tĕnt'*, s. contentement, m. || voix pour, f. || -s, pl. contenu, m.

content, *kŏn tĕnt'*, a. content.

content(ed), *kŏn tĕnt' (ĕd)*, a. content || -ly, ad. avec contentement.

contentedness, *kŏn tĕnt' ĕd nĕs*, s. contentement, m., satisfaction, f.

contention, *kŏn tĕn' shŭn*, s. contention, dispute, f. || émulation, f., zèle m. || bone of ~, pomme de discorde, m.

contentious, *kŏn tĕn' shŭs*, a. litigieux, querelleur || -ly, ad. contentieusement.

contentiousness, *kŏn tĕn' shŭs nĕs*, s. disposition contentieuse, f. [ment, m.

contentment, *kŏn tĕnt' mĕnt*, s. contente-

contest, *kŏn' tĕst*, s. dispute, f.

contest, *kŏn tĕst'*, v. a. disputer, lutter.

contestable, *kŏn tĕs' tā bl*, a. contestable.

context, *kŏn' tĕkst*, s. contexte, m. || sens, m.

contexture, *kŏn tĕks' tūr*, s. contexture, f., tissu, m.

contiguity, *kŏn tĭ gū' ĭ tĭ*, s. contiguïté, f.

contiguous, *kŏn tĭg' ü ŭs*, a. (-ly, ad.) contigu. [modération, f.

continence, *kŏn' tĭ nĕns*, s. continence, f.

continent, *kŏn' tĭ nĕnt*, s. continent, m., terre ferme, f. [déré || -ly, ad. avec retenue.

continent, *kŏn' tĭ nĕnt*, a. continent, mo-

continental, *kŏn tĭ nĕn' tāl*, a. continental, du continent. [f., hasard, m.

contingency, *kŏn tĭn' jĕn sĭ*, s. éventualité,

contingent, *kŏn tĭn' jĕnt*, s. cas fortuit, m. || contingent, m.

contingent, *kŏn tĭn' jĕnt*, a. contingent, casuel || -ly, ad. fortuitement.

continual, *kŏn tĭn' ü āl*, a. (-ly, ad.) continuel(lement).

continuance, *kŏn tĭn' ü ăns*, s. continuation, continuité, f. || persévérance, durée, f. || séjour, m.

continuation, *kŏn tĭn ü ā' shŭn*, s. continuation, f. || -s, pl. pantalons, m. pl. [durer.

continue, *kŏn tĭn' ü*, v. a. & n. continuer

continuedly, *kŏn tĭn'ū ĕd lĭ,* ad. continuellement.

continuity, *kŏn tĭn ū'ĭ tĭ,* s. continuité, suite, f.   [continu || continûment.

continuous, *kŏn tĭn'ū ŭs,* a. (-ly, ad.)

contort, *kŏn tŏrt',* v. a. tordre.

contortion, *kŏn tŏr'shŭn,* s. contorsion, f.

contour, *kŏn tōr',* s. contour, m., circonférence, f.   [f.

contraband, *kŏn'trä bănd,* s. contrebande,

contraband, *kŏn'trä bănd,* a. de contrebande.   [bandier, m.

contrabandist, *kŏn'trä băn dĭst,* s. contre-

contract, *kŏn träkt,* s. contrat, pacte, m.

contract, *kŏn träkt',* v. a. & n. abréger, raccourcir || contracter || se rétrécir || faire un contrat.   [f. || raccourcissement, s.

contraction, *kŏn träk'shŭn,* s. contraction,

contractor, *kŏn träk'tĕr,* s. contractant, m., || fournisseur, m.   [contrarier.

contradict, *kŏn trä dĭkt',* v. a. contredire,

contradiction, *kŏn trä dĭk'shŭn,* s. contredit, m.   [contradictoirement.

contradictorily, *kŏn trä dĭk'tĕr ĭ lĭ,* ad.

contradictoriness, *kŏn trä dĭk'tĕr ĭ nĕs,* s. contradiction, opposition, f.

contradictory, *kŏn trä dĭk'tĕr ĭ,* s. proposition contradictoire, f.   [tradictoire.

contradictory, *kŏn trä dĭk'tĕr ĭ,* a. con-

contradistinction, *kŏn trä dĭs tĭngk'shŭn,* s. in ~ to, par opposition à.

contralto, *kŏn träl'tō,* s. contralto, m.

contrariety, *kŏn trä rī'ĕ tĭ,* s. contrariété, opposition, f.   [ment.

contrarily, *kŏn'trä rĭ lĭ,* ad. contraire-

contrariness, *kŏn'trä rĭ nĕs,* s. contrariété, f.

contrary, *kŏn'trä rĭ,* s. le contraire, l'opposé || on the ~, au contraire || to the ~, pour le contraire.

contrary, *kŏn'trä rĭ,* a. contraire, opposé || ~ minded, ad. qui est d'un avis contraire, opposé.

contrast, *kŏn'träst,* s. contraste, m.

contrast, *kŏn träst',* v. a. contraster.

contravene, *kŏn trä vēn',* v. a. contrevenir à.   [travention, infraction, f.

contravention, *kŏn trä vĕn'shŭn,* s. con-

contributary, *kŏn trĭb'ū tĕr ĭ,* a. contributaire.   [tribuer, payer.

contribute, *kŏn trĭb'ūt,* v. a. & n. con-

contribution, *kŏn trĭ bū'shŭn,* s. contribution, f.   [tribue.

contributive, *kŏn trĭb'ū tĭv,* a. qui con-

contributor, *kŏn trĭb'ū tĕr,* s. collaborateur, m. || correspondant, m.   [buant.

contributory, *kŏn trĭb'ū tĕr ĭ,* a. contri-

contrite, *kŏn'trĭt,* a. contrit || -ly, ad. avec componction.   [f.

contrition, *kŏn trĭsh'ŭn,* s. componction,

contrivance, *kŏn trī'văns,* s. invention, f., plan, m. || artifice, m.

contrive, *kŏn trīv',* v. a. & n. inventer, projeter, concerter, essayer, venir à bout, trouver des expédients || comploter || to ~ to do, savoir faire.

contriver, *kŏn trī'vĕr,* s. inventeur, m.

control, *kŏn trōl',* s. contrôle, m. || inspection, autorité, f.

control, *kŏn trōl',* v. a. contrôler||gouverner, surveiller || to ~ oneself, être maître de soi, se contenir.   [contrôle.

controllable, *kŏn trōl'lä bl,* a. sujet à

controller, *kŏn trōl'lĕr,* s. contrôleur, m.

controversial, *kŏn trō vĕr'shäl,* a. de controverse.   [verse, f.

controversy, *kŏn'trō vĕr sĭ,* s. contro-

controvert, *kŏn'trō vĕrt,* v. a. débattre, contredire.   [testable.

controvertible, *kŏn trō vĕr'tĭ bl,* a. con-

contumacious, *kŏn tū mä'shŭs,* a. (-ly, ad.) obstiné || opiniâtre(ment).

contumacy, *kŏn'tū mä sĭ,* s. obstination, f. || (jur.) contumace, f.

contumelious, *kŏn tū mē'lĭ ŭs,* a. outrageant, offensant, injurieux ||-ly, ad. d'une manière offensante.   [sulte, f. || dédain, m.

contumely, *kŏn'tū mĕl ĭ,* s. outrage, m., in-

contuse, *kŏn tūz',* v. a. contusionner.

contusion, *kŏn tū'zhŭn,* s. contusion, f.

conundrum, *kō nŭn'drŭm,* s. turlupinade, f.

convalescence, *kŏn vä lĕs'sĕns,* s. convalescence, f.   [valescent.

convalescent, *kŏn vä lĕs'sĕnt,* a. con-

convene, *kŏn vēn',* v. a. & n. assembler, convoquer || s'assembler.

convenience, *kŏn vē'nĭ ĕns,* s. convenance, aise, commodité, f.

convenient, *kŏn vē'nĭ ĕnt,* a. convenable, commode, aisé ||-ly, ad. à son aise || to make it ~ to, s'arranger de manière à.

convent, *kŏn'vĕnt,* s. couvent, m.   [m.

conventicle, *kŏn vĕn'tĭ kl,* s. conventicule,

convention, *kŏn vĕn'shŭn,* s. rassemblement, m. || convention, f. || contrat, m.

conventional, *kŏn vĕn'shŭn äl,* a. (-ly, ad.) conventionnel(lement).

conventionality, *kŏn vĕn shŭn äl'ĭ tĭ,* s. phrase or affaire de convention, f.

conventual, *kŏn vĕn'tū äl,* a. monastique.

convergence, *kŏn vĕr'jĕns,* s. convergence, f.

convergent, *kŏn vĕr'jĕnt,* a. convergent.

conversable, *kŏn vĕr'sä bl,* a. sociable.

conversant, *kŏn vĕr'sănt,* a. familier || versé (dans).

conversation, *kŏn vĕr sä'shŭn,* s. conversation, f., entretien, m. || commerce, m.

conversationalist, *kŏn vĕr sä'shŭn äl ĭst,* s. personne qui converse bien.

conversazione, *kŏn vĕr sät zī ō' nē,* s. réunion, f.   [proque, f.

converse, *kŏn'vĕrs,* s. converse, f. || réci-

converse, *kŏn vĕrs',* v. n. converser, s'entretenir.   [proque(ment).

converse, *kŏn'vĕrs,* a. (-ly, ad.) réci-

conversion, *kŏn vĕr'shŭn,* s. conversion, f.

convert, *kŏn'vĕrt,* s. converti, prosélyte, m.

convert, *kŏn vĕrt',* v. a. (& n.) (se) convertir.

convertibility, *kŏn vĕr tĭ bĭl'ĭ tĭ,* s. convertibilité, f.   [transmutable.

convertible, *kŏn vĕr'tĭ bl,* a. convertible,

convex, *kŏn'vĕks,* a. (-ly, ad.) convexe || de forme or d'une manière convexe.

---

lāte, hăt, fär, làw; — hēre, gĕt, hėr; — mīne, ĭnn; — nō, hŏt, prōve; — hōw; —

convexity, *kŏn vĕks' ĭ tĭ,* s. convexité, f.

convey, *kŏn vā',* v. a. porter, transporter, transmettre || communiquer, énoncer.

conveyance, *kŏn vā' ăns,* s. transport, envoi, m. || transmission, f. || communication, f. || cession, f.

conveyancer, *kŏn vā' ăn sĕr,* s. notaire, m.

convict, *kŏn vĭkt,* s. condamné, m. || forçat, m. || ~-establishment, s. colonie pénitentiaire, f.

convict, *kŏn vĭkt',* v.a. convaincre || trouver coupable.

convict, *kŏn' vĭkt,* a. condamné || forçat.

conviction, *kŏn vĭk' shŭn,* s. conviction, f. || condamnation, f.   [suader.

convince, *kŏn vĭns',* v. a. convaincre, persuader.

convincing, *kŏn vĭn' sĭng,* a. (-ly, ad.) convaincant || d'une manière convaincante.

convivial, *kŏn vĭv' ĭ ăl,* a. sociable, joyeux.

conviviality, *kŏn vĭv ĭ ăl' ĭ tĭ,* s. sociabilité, gaieté, f.   [tion, assemblée, f.

convocation, *kŏn vō kā' shŭn,* s. convocation, f.

convoke, *kŏn vōk',* v. a. convoquer.

convolvulus, *kŏn vŏl' vū lŭs,* s. (bot.) convolvulus, m., belle-de-jour, f.

convoy, *kŏn' vŏy,* s. convoi, m., escorte, f.

convoy, *kŏn vŏy',* v. a. convoyer, escorter.

convulse, *kŏn vŭls',* v. a. convulsionner.

convulsed, *kŏn vŭlst',* a. convulsé, agité.

convulsion, *kŏn vŭl' shŭn,* s. convulsion, f. || **to be taken with ~s,** tomber en convulsions.   [-ly, ad. convulsivement.

convulsive, *kŏn vŭl' sĭv,* a. convulsif ||

coo, *kō,* v. n. roucouler.   [traiteur, m.

cook, *kōŏk,* s. cuisinier, m., cuisinière, f. ||

cook, *kōŏk,* v. a. cuire, faire la cuisine.

cookery, *kōŏk' ĕr ĭ,* s. art du cuisinier, m., cuisine, f. || ~-book, s. livre de cuisine, m.

cool, *kōl,* s. frais, m., fraîcheur, f.   [froidir.

cool, *kōl,* v. a. (& n.) (se) rafraîchir, (se) re-

cool, *kōl,* a. frais || tiède || indifférent || impudent || -ly, ad. fraîchement || froidement, de sang-froid.   [frigérant, m.

cooler, *kōl' ĕr,* s. rafraîchisseur, m. || ré-

coolish, *kōl' ĭsh,* a. un peu frais, presque froid.   [différence, f.

coolness, *kōl' nĕs,* s. fraîcheur, f. || in-

coom, *kōm,* s. suie, f., cambouis, m.

coop, *kōp,* s. tonneau, m., barrique, f. || cage, f., poulailler, m. || mue, f.

coop, *kōp,* v. a. parquer, enfermer, encager.

cooper, *kōōp' ĕr,* s. tonnelier, m.

cooperate, *kō ŏp' ĕr āt,* v. n. coopérer.

cooperation, *kō ŏp ĕr ā' shŭn,* s. coopération, f., concours, m.

cooperative, *kō ŏp' ĕr ā tĭv,* a. coopérant.

cooperator, *kō ŏp' ĕr ā tĕr,* s. coopérateur, m.   [de rang, f.

coordination, *kō ŏr dĭ nā' shŭn,* s. égalité

copaiva, *kō pī' vā,* s. copahu, f.

cope, *kōp,* s. calotte, f. || chape, f.

cope, *kōp,* v. a. & n. couvrir la tête || combattre, lutter.

copier, *kŏp' ĭ ĕr,* s. copiste, m.

coping, *kō' pĭng,* s. faite, m. || ~-stone (of a rampart), s. chape, f. || (of a bridge), cordon, m.

copious, *kō' pĭ ŭs,* a. copieux, abondant, riche || -ly, ad. copieusement.

copiousness, *kō' pĭ ŭs nĕs,* s. abondance, richesse, f.

copper, *kŏp' pĕr,* s. cuivre, m. || monnaie de cuivre, f. || chaudière, f. || -s, pl. batterie de cuisine, f. || monnaie de cuivre, f. || ~-plate, s. taille-douce, estampe, f. || ~-work, s. forge de cuivre, f.

copperas, *kŏp' pĕr ăs,* s. couperose, f.

coppersmith, *kŏp' pĕr smĭth,* s. chaudronnier, m.

coppery, *kŏp' pĕr ĭ,* a. cuivreux, érugineux.

coppice, *kŏp' pĭs,* copse, *kŏps,* s. taillis, m.

copy, *kŏp' ĭ,* s. copie, f. || exemplaire, m. || exemple, f. || **rough ~,** brouillon, m. || **fair ~,** copie au net, m. || ~-book, s. cahier, m.   [contrefaire, imiter.

copy, *kŏp' ĭ,* v. a. & n. copier, transcrire ||

copyhold, *kŏp' ĭ hōld,* s. censive, f., domaine douné en fief, m. (en Angleterre).

copying-press, *kŏp' ĭ ĭng prĕs,* s. presse à copier, f.

copyist, *kŏp' ĭ ĭst,* s. copiste, m.

copyright, *kŏp' ĭ rīt,* s. droit d'auteur, droit de propriété littéraire, droit d'impression, m.

coquet, *kō kĕt',* v. n. coqueter.   [m.

coquetry, *kō kĕt' rĭ,* s. coquetterie, f.

coquettish, *kō kĕt' tĭsh,* a. coquet.

coracle, *kŏr' ă kl,* s. bateau pêcheur, m.

coral, *kŏr' ăl,* s. corail, m. || hochet, m.

coralline, *kŏr' ăl līn,* s. coraline, f.

cord, *kaŭrd,* s. corde, f. || cordon, cordeau, m., ficelle, f. || **spinal ~,** moelle épinière, f.

cord, *kaŭrd,* v. a. lier avec des cordes.

cordage, *kŏr' dĕj,* s. cordage, m.

cordial, *kŏr' dĭ ăl,* s. cordial, m.

cordial, *kŏr' dĭ ăl,* a. (-ly, ad.) cordial (ement).

cordiality, *kŏr dĭ ăl' ĭ tĭ,* s. cordialité, f.

corduroy, *kŏr' dōō rŏy,* s. velours de coton, m.   [d'Espagne, f.

cordwain, *kŏr' dwān,* s. peau de chèvre

core, *kōr,* s. cœur, intérieur, m. || trognon d'un fruit, m.   [accusé(e), -me, & f.

co-respondent, *kō rē spŏn' dĕnt,* s. co-

cork, *kŏrk,* s. liège, bouchon de liège, m. || ~-jacket, s. chemise de liège, f.

cork, *kŏrk,* v. a. boucher.

corkscrew, *kŏrk' skrō,* s. tire-bouchon, m. || ~-staircase, s. escalier enlimaçon, m.

corky, *kŏrk' ĭ,* a. de liège.

cormorant, *kŏr' mō rănt,* s. cormoran, m. || glouton, m.

corn, *kaŭrn,* s. blé, grain, m. || (bunion) cor, m. || ~-brandy, s. eau-de-vie de grains, f. || ~-drill, s. semoir, m. || ~-exchange, s. halle au blé, f. || ~-field, s. champ de blé, m. || ~-floor, s. aire, grange, f. || ~-flour, s. farine nutritive préparée, f. || ~-flower, s. barbeau, bluet, m. || ~-loft, s. grenier, m. || ~-trade, s. commerce des céréales, m.

corn, *kaŭrn,* v. a. saler, saupoudrer || granuler.

corncutter, *kaŭrn' kŭt tĕr,* s. pédicure, m.

cornelian, *kŏr nē' lĭ ăn,* s. cornaline, f.

corner, *kŏr′nĕr*, s. coin, angle, m. || extrémité, f. || ~-house, s. maison du coin, f. || ~-stone, s. pierre angulaire, f.

cornered, *kŏr′nĕrd*, a. à ... coins *or* angles.

cornet, *kŏr′nĕt*, s. cornet, petit cor || cornette, m.						[m.

cornetcy, *kŏr′nĕt sĭ*, s. grade de cornette.

cornice, *kŏr′nĭs*, s. corniche, f.

corollary, *kŏ rŏl′lĕr ĭ*, s. corollaire, m.

coronation, *kŏr ŏ nā′ shŭn*, s. couronnement, m.

coroner, *kŏr′ŏ nĕr*, s. coroner, m.

coronet, *kŏr′ŏ nĕt*, s. petite couronne, f.

corporal, *kŏr′pō răl*, s. caporal, m.

corporal, *kŏr′pō răl*, a. (-ly, ad.) corporel(lement).

corporate, *kŏr′pō rāt*, a. incorporé.

corporation, *kŏr pō rā′shŭn*, s. corporation, communauté, f.			[tériel.

corporeal, *kŏr pō′rĭ ăl*, a. corporel, matériel.

corpse, *kŏrps*, s. cadavre, m.

corpulence, *kŏr′pŭ lĕns*, s. corpulence, f. || embonpoint, m.

corpulent, *kŏr′pŭ lĕnt*, a. corpulent, replet.

corpuscle, *kŏr′pŭs kl*, s. corpuscule, atome, m.				[punir || retoucher || adoucir.

correct, *kŏr rĕkt′*, v. a. corriger || châtier,

correct, *kŏr rĕkt′*, a. (-ly, ad.) correct (ement) || exact.

correction, *kŏr rĕk′shŭn*, s. correction, f., châtiment, amendement, m.

corrective, *kŏr rĕk′tĭv*, s. correctif, m.

corrective, *kŏr rĕk′tĭv*, a. correctif, m.

correctness, *kŏr rĕkt′nĕs*, s. exactitude, correction, pureté de langage, f.

corrector, *kŏr rĕk′tĕr*, s. correcteur, m. || réformateur, m.			[réciproque.

correlative, *kŏr rĕl′ă tĭv*, a. corrélatif,

correspond, *kŏr rĕ spŏnd*, v. n. correspondre.

correspondence, *kŏr rĕ spŏn′dĕns*, s. correspondance, f. || rapport, m. || intelligence, f.				[respondant, m.

correspondent, *kŏr rĕ spŏn′dĕnt*, s. cor-

correspondent, *kŏr rĕ spŏn′dĕnt*, a. correspondant, conforme.			[sable.

corrigible, *kŏr′rĭ jĭ bl*, a. corrigible, punis-

corroborate, *kŏr rŏb′ŏ rāt*, v. a. corroborer.

corroboration, *kŏr rŏb ŏ rā′shŭn*, s. corroboration, f.			[boratif, fortifiant.

corroborative, *kŏr rŏb′ŏ rā tĭv*, a. corro-

corrode, *kŏr rōd′*, v. a. corroder, ronger.

corrodent, *kŏr rō′dĕnt*, a. corrosif.

corrodible, *kŏr rō′dĭ bl*, a. qui peut être corrodé.

corrosion, *kŏr rō′zhŭn*, s. corrosion, f.

corrosive, *kŏr rō′sĭv*, s. corrosif, m.

corrosive, *kŏr rō′sĭv*, a. corrosif.

corrugate, *kŏr′rŏŏ gāt*, v. a. rider, froncer, plisser.

corrupt, *kŏr rŭpt′*, v. a. & n. corrompre, gâter, séduire, suborner || se corrompre, se gâter.

corrupt, *kŏr rŭpt′*, a. corrompu, gâté || séduit, suborné || -ly, ad. par corruption || de mauvaise foi.				[vénal, servile.

corruptible, *kŏr rŭp′tĭ bl*, a. corruptible,

corruption, *kŏr rŭp′shŭn*, s. corruption, dépravation, f. || pourriture, f.

corruptive, *kŏr rŭp′tĭv*, a. corruptif.

corruptness, *kŏr rŭpt′nĕs*, s. corruption, f. || pourriture, f.

corsair, *kŏr′sār*, s. corsaire, m.

corselet, *kŏrs′lĕt*, s. corselet, m.

corset, *kŏr′sĕt*, s. corset, m. || ~ maker, s. corsetier, m.

cosily, *kō′zĭ lĭ*, ad. à l'aise.			[corselet, m.

cosmetic, *kŏz mĕt′ĭk*, s. cosmétique, m.

cosmetic, *kŏz mĕt′ĭk*, a. cosmétique.

cosmopolitan, *kŏz mō pŏl′ĭ tăn*, s. cosmopolite, m.

cosmopolitan, *kŏz mō pŏl′ĭ tăn*, cosmopolite, *kŏz mŏp′ō lĭt*, a. cosmopolite.

Cossack, *kŏs′săk*, s. cosaque, m.

cost, *kŏst*, s. prix, m., frais, m. pl., dépense, f. || -s, pl. dépens, m. pl. || first ~, s. prix coûtant, m.

cost, *kŏst*, v. n. coûter.			[diane, f.

costa, *kŏs′tă*, s. (bot.) côte, nervure médiane, f.

costermonger, *kŏs′tĕr mŭng gĕr*, s. marchand des quatre saisons, m.

costive, *kŏs′tĭv*, a. constipé, serré.

costiveness, *kŏs′tĭv nĕs*, s. constipation, f.

costliness, *kŏst′lĭ nĕs*, s. grande dépense, somptuosité, f.

costly, *kŏst′lĭ*, a. cher, coûteux || somptueux.

costume, *kŏs tūm′ or kŏs′tūm*, s. costume, m.

cosy, *kō′zĭ*, a. à l'aise, comfortable.			[m.

cot, *kŏt*, s. cabane, chaumière, f.

co-trustee, *kō trŭs tē′*, s. curateur, m.

cottage, *kŏt′tĕj*, s. cabane, chaumière, f. || villa, f.			[cabane.

cottager, *kŏt′tĕj ĕr*, s. qui vit dans une

cotton, *kŏt′tn*, s. coton, m. || toile de coton, f. || ~-mill, s. filature de coton, f. || ~-shrub, ~-tree, s. cotonnier, m. || ~-wool, s. ouate, f. || ~-yarn, s. fil de coton, m.			[corder.

cotton, *kŏt′tn*, v. n. se cotonner || s'accoucb, *kŏwch*, s. lit, m., couche, f. || chaise longue, f.

couch, *kŏwch*, v. a. & n. coucher || cacher, renfermer || abaisser la cataracte || se coucher, être couché.		[quinte de toux, f.

cough, *kŏf*, s. toux, f. || fit of -ing, s.

cough, *kŏf*, v. n. tousser.

council, *kŏwn′sĭl*, s. conseil, m. || concile, m. || common ~, conseil municipal, m. || privy ~, conseil privé, m. || ~-board, s. corps des conseillers, m.

counsel, *kŏwn′sĕl*, s. conseil, avis, m. || consultation, f. || dessein, m. || avocat, m.

counsel, *kŏwn′sĕl*, v. a. conseiller.

counsellor, *kŏwn′sĕl lĕr*, s. conseiller, avocat, m. || privy ~, conseiller d'état, m.				[comte, m.

count, *kŏwnt*, s. nombre, compte, m. ||

count, *kŏwnt*, v. a. compter, calculer, supputer || estimer || compter sur.

countenance, *kŏwn′tĕ năns*, s. contenance f., visage, m., mine, f. || air, regard, m. || protection, f. || to put out of ~, faire perdre contenance (à).

countenance, *kŏwn′tĕ năns*, v. a. soutenir, maintenir, favoriser || encourager.

counter, *kŏwn'tĕr,* s. comptoir, m. || calculateur, s. || (at cards) jeton, m. || compteur, m. || (mus.) haute-contre, f.

counter, *kŏwn'tĕr,* ad. contre, en opposition || **~action,** s. opposition, f. || **~balance,** s. contre-poids, m. || v. a. contre-balancer || **~check,** s. opposition, f. || réprimande, f. || v. a. contre-carrer, s'opposer || **~evidence,** s. déposition contradictoire, f. || **~irritant,** s. (méd.) révulsif, m. || **~march,** s. contre-marche, f. || v. a. faire une contre-marche || **~mine,** s. contre-mine, f. || v. a. contre-miner || **~plea,** s. réplique, f.

counteract, *kŏwn'tĕr ăkt',* v. a. contrarier.

counterfeit, *kŏwn'tĕr fĭt,* s. contrefaçon, imitation, fausse monnaie, f. || imposteur, m. [imiter.

counterfeit, *kŏwn'tĕr fĭt',* v. a. contrefaire,

counterfeit, *kŏwn'tĕr fĭt,* a. contrefait, faux.

countermand, *kŏwn'tĕr mănd,* s. contremandement, m. [mander.

countermand, *kŏwn'tĕr mănd',* v. a. contre-

counterpane, *kŏwn'tĕr pān,* s. courtepointe, f.

counterpart, *kŏwn'tĕr pârt,* s. (mus.) contre-partie, f. || pendant, m. || (jur.) double, m.

counterpoint, *kŏwn'tĕr pŏynt,* s. (mus.) contre-point, m.

countersign, *kŏwn'tĕr sīn,* s. contre-seing, m. || (mil.) mot de ralliement, s.

countersign, *kŏwn'tĕr sīn',* v. a. contresigner. [haute-contre, f.

countertenor, *kŏwn'tĕr tĕn'ĕr,* s. (mus.)

countervail, *kŏwn'tĕr văl',* v. a. équivaloir, contre-balancer.

countess, *kŏwn'tĕs,* s. comtesse, f.

counting-house, *kŏwnt'ĭng hŏws,* s. comptoir, m.

countless, *kŏwnt'lĕs,* a. innombrable.

country, *kŏwn'trĭ,* s. pays, m., contrée, campagne, f. || pays natal, m. || **~life,** s. vie champêtre or de province, f. || **~seat,** s. maison de campagne, f., château, m. [grossier.

country, *kŭn'trĭ,* a. rustique, campagnard||

countryman, *kŭn'trĭ măn,* s. campagnard, villageois, m. || compatriote, m.

countrywoman, *kŭn'trĭ wŏŏm ăn,* s. campagnarde, f. || compatriote, f.

county, *kŏwn'tĭ,* s. comté, département, m.

couple, *kŭp'l,* s. couple, paire, f. || laisse, f.

couple, *kŭp'l,* v. a. & n. coupler || s'accoupler. [m. || strophe, f.

couplet, *kŭp'lĕt,* s. distique, m. || couplet,

coupling, *kŭp'lĭng,* s. **~irons, ~chains,** s. pl. chaîne d'attelage, f.

courage, *kŭr'ĭj or kŭr'ĕj,* s. courage, m., valeur, f. || to damp one's ~, glacer le courage de qn.

courageous, *kŭr ā'jŭs,* a. courageux || **~ly,** ad. courageusement.

courier, *kŏŏr'ĭ ĕr,* s. courrier, m.

course, *kŏrs,* s. course, carrière, f., cours, ordre, m., marche, f. || service (nombre de plats), m. || manière de vivre, conduite, f., moyen, m. || of ~, par conséquent || matter of ~, chose qui va sans dire || **~s,** pl. basses voiles || règles des femmes, f. pl.

course, *kŏrs,* v. a. & n. poursuivre, chasser || courir.

courser, *kŏr'sĕr,* s. coursier, m. || chasseur,

coursing, *kŏr'sĭng,* s. chasse (à courre), f.

court, *kŏrt,* s. cour, f. || cour de justice, f. || tribunal, m. || passage, m. || impasse, f. || in open ~, en pleine audience || ~ of high commission, cour prévôtale, f. || **~day,** s. jour d'audience, jour de palais, m. || **~lady,** s. dame de la cour, f. || **~martial,** s. conseil de guerre, m. || **~plaster,** s. taffetas d'Angleterre, m. || **~yard,** s. vestibule, m.

court, *kŏrt,* v. a. faire sa cour, courtiser || flatter, cajoler.

courteous, *kĕrt'yŭs,* a. (-ly, ad.) courtois, affable, civil || poli(ment).

courtesan, *kĕr tĕ zăn,* s. courtisane, f.

courtesy, *kĕr tĕ sĭ,* s. courtoisie, politesse, f. || révérence, f.

courtesy, *kĕr tĕ sĭ,* v. n. faire la révérence.

courtier, *kŏrt'yĕr,* s. courtisan, flatteur, m.

courtliness, *kŏrt'lĭ nĕs,* s. politesse, f. || élégance, f.

courtly, *kŏrt'lĭ,* a. de cour, élégant.

courtship, *kŏrt'shĭp,* s. cour, f. || civilité, complaisance, f.

cousin, *kŭz'n,* s. cousin, m., cousine, f. || first ~, cousin germain, m.

cousinship, *kŭz'n shĭp,* s. parenté, f.

cove, *kōv,* s. crique, f. || abri, m.

cove, *kōv,* v. a. voûter. [m.

covenant, *kŭv'ĕnănt,* s. contrat, accord,

covenant, *kŭv'ĕnănt,* v. n. stipuler, contracter. [tractante, f.

covenanter, *kŭv'ĕnăn tĕr,* s. partie con-

coventry, *kŏv'ĕn trĭ,* s.; to send to ~, mettre au ban.

cover, *kŭv'ĕr,* s. couvert, m., enveloppe, f. || couvercle, m. || abri, m., protection, f. || prétexte, m. || to lay a ~, mettre un couvert. [guiser || couver.

cover, *kŭv'ĕr,* v. a. couvrir, cacher, dé-

covering, *kŭv'ĕrĭng,* s. couverture, f. || vêtement, m.

coverlet, *kŭv'ĕr lĕt,* s. couvre-lit, m.

covert, *kŭv'ĕrt,* s. couvert, abri, gîte, m.

covert, *kŭv'ĕrt,* a. couvert, caché || à l'abri || **~ly,** ad. secrètement.

coverture, *kŭv'ĕr tūr,* s. couverture, défense, f. || (jur.) puissance de mari, f.

covet, *kŭv'ĕt,* v. a. & n. convoiter || désirer ardemment.

covetous, *kŭv'ĕtŭs,* a. avide, ambitieux, avare || **~ly,** ad. avec avarice, sordidement. [avarice, f.

covetousness, *kŭv'ĕtŭs nĕs,* s. convoitise,

covey, *kŭv'ĭ,* s. couvée, volée, f.

cow, *kŏw,* s. vache, f. || **~herd,** s. vacher, m. || **~house,** s. vacherie, étable à vaches, f. || **~pox,** s. vaccine, f.

cow, *kŏw,* v. a. intimider, épouvanter.

coward, *kŏw'ĕrd,* s. poltron, lâche, m.

cowardice, *kŏw'ĕr dĭs*, s. lâcheté, poltronnerie, f.

cowardly, *kŏw'ĕrd lĭ*, a. poltron, lâche || ~, ad. en poltron || lâchement.

cower, *kŏw'ĕr*, v. n. s'accroupir, baisser.

cowl, *kŏwl*, s. capuchon, m.

cowslip, *kŏw'slĭp*, s. (bot.) primevère, brayette, f.　　　　　　　　　[miné, m.

coxa, *kŏks'ă*, s. (anat.) os coxal, os innoxcomb, *kŏks'kŏm*, s. fat, petit-maître, m.

coxswain v. cockswain.

coy, *kŏў*, a. (-ly, ad.) modeste(ment) || réservé.　　　　　　　　　　[pruderie, f.

coyness, *kŏў'nĕs*, s. réserve, modestie, f. ||

coz, *kŭz*, s. (fam.) cousin, m.

cozen, *kŭz'n*, v. a. tromper, duper.

cozenage, *kŭz'ĕn ĭj*, s. fourberie, f.

cozener, *kŭz'ĕn ĕr*, s. fourbe, m.

crab, *krăb*, s. écrevisse de mer, f. || pommier sauvage, m. || personne acariâtre, f.

crabbed, *krăb'bĕd*, a. revêche, bourru || difficile || -ly, ad. durement, d'un air revêche.

crabbedness, *krăb'bĕd nĕs*, s. âpreté, f. || air revêche, m. || difficulté, f.

crack, *krăk*, s. fente, f. || craquement, bruit, m. || défaut, m. || fou, fanfaron, m. || vanterie, f. || folie, f.

crack, *krăk*, v. a. & n. fendre, crevasser || rendre stupide || se fendre, craquer || se vanter || ~-brained, a. timbré, fou.

crack, *krăk*, a. premier || champion || expert, adroit.　　　　[m. || biscuit de mer, m.

cracker, *krăk'ĕr*, s. fanfaron, m. || pétard,

crackle, *krăk'l*, s. craquement, bruit, m.

crackle, *krăk'l*, v. n. craqueter, pétiller.

crackling, *krăk'lĭng*, s. craquement, m.

cracknel, *krăk'nĕl*, s. craquelin, m. || échaudé, m.

cradle, *krā'dl*, s. berceau, m.

cradle, *krā'dl*, v. a. bercer.

craft, *krăft*, s. métier, m., profession, f. || artifice, m., fourberie, f. || barque, f.

craftily, *krăf'tĭ lĭ*, ad. artificieusement, avec ruse.

craftiness, *krăf'tĭ nĕs*, s. ruse, finesse, f., stratagème, m.　　　　　　　　　[m.

craftsman, *krăfts'măn*, s. ouvrier, artisan,

crafty, *krăf'tĭ*, a. rusé, artificieux.

crag, *krăg*, s. rocher escarpé, m. || cou, m.

cragged, *krăg'gĕd*, craggy, *krăg'gĭ*, a. raboteux, escarpé.　　　　　　　　　[m.

cragginess, *krăg'gĭ nĕs*, s. état rocailleux,

crake, *krāk*, s. râle, m.

cram, *krăm*, v. a. & n. fourrer || farcir, engraisser || rassasier.　　　[bouts rimés, m.

crambo, *krăm'bō*, s.; dumb ~, jeu de

crammer, *krăm'mĕr*, s. répétiteur, m.

cramp, *krămp*, s. crampe, f. || obstacle, m., contrainte, f. || crochet, m. || ~-iron, s. crampon, m.

cramp, *krămp*, v. n. donner la crampe || empêcher, restreindre || cramponner.

cramp, *krămp*, a. biscornu.

cranberry, *krăn'bĕr rĭ*, s. airelle, f.

crane, *krān*, s. grue, f. || siphon, m.

cranium, *krā'nĭ ŭm*, s. (anat.) crâne, m.

crank, *krăngk*, s. manivelle, f. || détour, m. || crampon, m.

crannied, *krăn'nĭd*, a. fendu, crevassé.

cranny, *krăn'nĭ*, s. fente, crevasse, f.

crape, *krāp*, s. crêpe (étoffe), m.

crash, *krăsh*, s. craquement, fracas, m.

crash, *krăsh*, v. a. & n. rompre, briser || craquer || faire un grand fracas.

crass, *krăs*, a. grossier.

crate, *krāt*, s. emballage à claire-voie.

crater, *krā'tĕr*, s. cratère, m.

cravat, *krăvăt'*, s. cravate, f.

crave, *krāv*, v. a. implorer, solliciter.

craven, *krā'vn*, s. lâche, m.

craven, *krā'vn*, v. a. intimider.

craving, *krā'vĭng*, s. désir ardent, m.

craving, *krā'vĭng*, a. insatiable.

craw, *krăw*, s. jabot, m.

crawfish, *krăw'fĭsh*, crayfish, *krā'fĭsh*, s. écrevisse (de ruisseau), f.

crawl, *krăwl*, v. n. ramper || (fig.) se traîner.

crayon, *krā'ŏn*, s. pastel, crayon, m.

crayon, *krā'ŏn*, v. a. crayonner.　　　[fou.

craze, *krāz*, v. a. briser, fracasser || rendre

craziness, *krā'zĭ nĕs*, s. imbécillité, f.

crazy, *krā'zĭ*, a. cassé, décrépit, caduc || faible, fou.

creak, *krēk*, v. n. crier, craquer.

creak(ing), *krēk'(ĭng)*, s. cri, m.

cream, *krēm*, s. crème, f. || clotted ~, crème caillée, f. || ~-coloured, a. couleur café au lait || ~-faced, a. pâle || ~-jug, s. crémière, f. || ~-laid, a. vergé blanc.

creamy, *krēm'ĭ*, a. de crème || crémeux || mielleux.

crease, *krēs*, s. pli, faux pli, m.

crease, *krēs*, v. a. faire un faux pli.

create, *krēāt'*, v. a. créer, produire.

creation, *krēā'shŭn*, s. création, f.

creative, *krēā'tĭv*, a. créateur, inventif.

creator, *krēā'tĕr*, s. créateur, m.

creature, *krē'tūr* or *krē chōōr*, s. créature, f., animal, m. || ~-comforts, pl. vivres, m. pl., mangeaille, f.

credence, *krē'dĕns*, s. créance, foi, f.

credentials, *krĕdĕn'shălz*, s. pl. lettres de créance, f. pl.

credibility, *krĕd ĭ bĭl'ĭ tĭ*, s. crédibilité, f.

credible, *krĕd'ĭ bl*, a. croyable, digne de foi.　　　　　　　　　　　[croyable.

credibly, *krĕd'ĭ blĭ*, ad. d'une manière

credit, *krĕd'ĭt*, s. crédit, m. || foi, croyance, f. || témoignage, m. || influence, f. || to be a ~ to, faire honneur à.

credit, *krĕd'ĭt*, v. a. croire, ajouter foi à || donner à crédit || porter au crédit de.

creditable, *krĕd'ĭt ă bl*, a. honorable, estimable.

creditableness, *krĕd'ĭt ă bl nĕs*, s. réputation, estime, f.　　　[ment, honnêtement.

creditably, *krĕd'ĭt ă blĭ*, ad. honorable-

creditor, *krĕd'ĭt ĕr*, s. créancier, m. || ~-side, s. (com.) crédit, avoir, m.

credulity, *krĕ dū'lĭ tĭ*, s. crédulité, f.

credulous, *krĕd'ū lŭs*, a. crédule || -ly, ad. avec crédulité.　　　　　　　[foi, f.

creed, *krēd*, s. croyance, f. || profession de

creek, *krēk,* s. petite baie, f. ‖ (Am.) ruisseau, m.

creel, *krēl,* s. panier de pêche, m.

creep, *krēp,* v. n. ramper ‖ se traîner.

creeper, *krēp'ĕr,* s. plante rampante, f. ‖ reptile, f.

creeping, *krēp'ing,* s. fourmillement, m.

cremate, *krēmāt',* v. a. brûler au four crématoire.

cremation, *krēmā'shŭn,* s. crémation, f.

crenellated, *krĕn'ĕlāt ĕd,* a. entaillé, crénelé.

creosote, *krē'ō sōt,* s. créosote, f. [laire.

crepuscular, *krē pŭs'kū lĕr,* a. crépuscu-

crescent, *krĕs'sĕnt,* a. & s. croissant (figure de la nouvelle lune), m.

cress, *krĕs,* s. cresson, m.

crest, *krĕst,* s. crête, huppe, f. ‖ vivacité, f. ‖ fierté, f. ‖ cimier, m. [d'un cimier.

crested, *krĕst'ĕd,* a. crêté ‖ huppé ‖ orné

crestfallen, *krĕst'fâwln,* a. abattu, découragé.

cretaceous, *krē tā'shŭs,* p. crétacé.

crevice, *krĕv'is,* s. crevasse, fente, f.

crew, *krō,* s. troupe, bande, f. ‖ équipage d'un vaisseau, m.

crewel, *krō'ĕl,* s. laine à broder, f.

crib, *krib,* s. mangeoire, crèche, étable, cabane, f.

crib, *krib,* v. a. prendre, chiper ‖ copier.

cribbage, *krib'bĭg,* s. cribbage (jeu de cartes à deux).

crick, *krik,* s. cric-crac, m. ‖ torticolis, m.

cricket, *krik'ĕt,* s. criquet, grillon ‖ jeu de la crosse.

crier, *krī'ĕr,* s. crieur public, m.

crime, *krīm,* s. crime, m.

criminal, *krim'ĭnăl,* s. criminel, m.

criminal, *krim'ĭnăl,* a. (-ly, ad.) criminel(lement) ‖ coupable.

criminality, *krim ĭ năl'ĭ tĭ,* s. culpabilité, criminalité, f.

crimp, *krimp,* s. (mil.) racoleur, m.

crimp(le), *krim'pl,* v. a. friser ‖ gaufrer.

crimson, *krim'zn,* s. cramoisi, m.

crimson, *krim'zn,* a. cramoisi.

cringe, *krinj,* v. n. ramper, s'abaisser.

crinkle, *kring'kl,* s. pli, m. ‖ sinuosité, f.

crinkle, *kring'kl,* v. a. faire des zigzags.

cripple, *krip'pl,* s. estropié, m.

cripple, *krip'pl,* v. a. estropier. [m.

crisis, *krī'sis,* s. crise, f., moment décisif,

crisp, *krisp,* v. a. & n. friser, denteler ‖ se crêper.

crisp, *krisp,* a. frisé, dentelé ‖ friable.

criterion, *krī tē'rĭŏn,* s. critérium, m.

critic, *krit'ik,* s. critique, f.

critical, *krit'ĭkăl,* a. critique ‖ -ly, ad. en critique, exactement.

criticise, *krit'ĭsiz,* v. a. & n. critiquer, censurer, satiriser.

criticism, *krit'ĭsizm,* s. critique, f.

croak, *krōk,* v. n. coasser ‖ croasser.

croaker, *krōk'ĕr,* s. grognon, Jean-qui-pleure, m.

crockery, *krŏk'ĕrĭ,* s. poterie, f.

crocodile, *krŏk'ō dīl,* s. crocodile, m.

crocus, *krō'kŭs,* s. crocus, safran, m.

croft, *krŏft,* s. petit clos, m.

crofter, *krŏf'tĕr,* s. petit fermier, m.

crony, *krō'ni,* s. ami intime, m.

crook, *krŏŏk,* s. croc, crochet, m. ‖ houlette,

crook, *krŏŏk,* v. a. (& n.) (se) courber. [f.

crooked, *krŏŏk'ĕd,* a. courbe ‖ tortu ‖ de travers ‖ pervers ‖ -ly, ad. tortueusement ‖ (fig.) de travers.

crookedness, *krŏŏk'ĕd nĕs,* s. courbure, f. ‖ état tortu, m.

crop, *krŏp,* s. jabot, estomac d'un oiseau, m. ‖ récolte, moisson, f.

crop, *krŏp,* v. a. & n. couper, écourter ‖ moissonner ‖ bretauder.

cropper, *krŏp'pĕr,* s. pigeon à grosse gorge, m. ‖ moissonneur, m. ‖ **to come a ~** (vulg.) tomber tout à plat, à plate terre.

crosier, *krō'zhĕr,* s. crosse, houlette, f.

cross, *krŏs,* s. croix ‖ (fig.) peine, affliction, f., malheur, m.

cross, *krŏs,* v. a. croiser ‖ faire le signe de la croix ‖ traverser ‖ contredire, contrarier.

cross, *krŏs,* a. oblique ‖ contraire, opposé ‖ pervers ‖ contradictoire ‖ malheureux ‖ **~-beam,** s. traverse, f. ‖ **~-bow,** s. arbalète, f. ‖ **~-breed,** s. race croisée, f. ‖ **~-examine,** v. a. interroger contradictoirement ‖ **~-eyed,** a. louche ‖ **~-fire,** s. (mil.) feu croisé, m. ‖ **~-grained,** a. qui a des fibres irrégulières ‖ pervers ‖ **~-legged,** ad. les jambes croisées ‖ **~-line,** s. (rail.) croisière, f. ‖ **~-purpose,** s. propos interrompu, m. ‖ **-ly,** ad. en travers ‖ malheureusement.

cross, *krŏs,* pr. & ad. au travers de, à travers, de travers.

crossing, *krŏs'sing,* s. endroit où l'on traverse ‖ (rail.) croisement, m. ‖ **level ~,** passage à niveau, m. ‖ **~-sweeper,** s. balayeur des rues, m.

crossness, *krŏs'nĕs,* s. méchanceté, f. ‖ mauvaise humeur, f.

crotchet, *krŏch'ĕt,* s. (mus.) noire, f. ‖ crochet, caprice, m.

crotchety, *krŏch'ĕtĭ,* a. sujet aux lubies, capricieux.

crouch, *krŏuch,* v. n. se baisser, ramper.

croup, *krŏp,* s. croupion, m. ‖ (méd.) croup, m. ‖ croupe (d'un cheval), f.

crow, *krō,* s. corneille, f. ‖ levier, m., barre, f. ‖ chant du coq, m. ‖ **carrion ~,** corneille noire, f. ‖ corbine, f. ‖ **to have a ~ to pluck with one,** avoir maille à partir avec qn. ‖ **as the ~ flies,** à vol d'oiseau.

crow, *krō,* v. n. ir. coqueliner ‖ se vanter.

crowd, *krŏud,* s. foule, presse, populace, f.

crowd, *krŏud,* v. a. & n. presser, fouler, entasser, encombrer ‖ s'attrouper ‖ **to ~ on all sail,** (mar.) faire force de voiles.

crown, *krŏun,* s. couronne, guirlande, f. ‖ sommet, m. ‖ forme (d'un chapeau) ‖ tonsure, f. ‖ (fig.) royauté, f. ‖ pièce de cinq shillings ‖ **~-glass,** s. verre de cristal,

m. ‖ ~~land, s. domaine de la couronne,
m. ‖ ~~prince, s. prince royal, m.

crown, *krōwn*, v. a. couronner ‖ damer
(un pion) ‖ **to ~ all**, pour combler, pour
metire le comble.   (qui met le comble.

crowning *krōwn'ing*, a. (fig.) suprême,

crow's-foot, *krōz-fŏŏt*, s. patte-d'oie, f. ‖
(bot.) corne-de-cerf, f.

crow's nest, *krŏz'nĕst*, s. (mar.) vigie, f.

crucial, *krō'shĭ ăl*, a. (chir.) crucial.

crucible, *krŏ'sĭ bl*, s. creuset, m.

crucifix, *krŏ'sĭ fĭks*, s. crucifix, m.

crucifixion, *krŏ sĭ fĭk'shŭn*, s. crucifiement, m.

crucify, *krŏ'sĭ fī*, v. a. crucifier.

crude, *krōd*, a. cru ‖ âpre ‖ indigeste ‖ imparfait ‖ **-ly**, ad. crûment.   [tion.

crudity, *krō'dĭ tĭ*, s. crudité f. ‖ indiges-

cruel, *krŏ'ĕl*, a. (-ly, ad.) cruel(lement) ‖
inhumain, féroce, sanguinaire.

cruelty, *krŏ'ĕl tĭ*, s. cruauté, barbarie, f. ‖
to be guilty of ~ towards, sévir
contre.   [grier, m.

cruet, *krŏ'ĕt*, s. burette, f., huilier, vinai-

cruise, *krŏz*, s. petite coupe, f. ‖ (mar.)
croisière, f.

cruise, *krŏz*, v. n. (mar.) croiser.

cruiser, *krŏ'zĕr*, s. croiseur (vaisseau), m.

crumb, *krŭm*, s. mie, miette, f. ‖ ~~scoop,
s. ramasse-miettes, m. (brosse ou couteau) ‖ ~~tray, s. ramasse-miettes, m.
(auge).

crumble, *krŭm'bl*, v. a. & n. émietter ‖ réduire en poudre ‖ tomber en poussière,
s'écrouler insensiblement.

crump, *krŭmp*, a. bossu, voûté.

crumple, *krŭm'pl*, v. a. chiffonner.

crunch, *krŭnch*, v. a. gruger.

crupper, *krŭp'pĕr*, s. croupe, croupière, f.

crusade, *krŏ sād'*, s. croisade, f.

crusader, *krŏ sā'dĕr*, s. croisé, m.

crush, *krŭsh*, s. écrasement, m. ‖ choc, m.

crush, *krŭsh*, v. a. & n. écraser ‖ opprimer,
choquer les verres ‖ ruiner ‖ se condenser.

crushing-mill, *krŭsh'ing mĭl*, s. bocard,
m. ‖ concasseur, m.

crust, *krŭst*, s. croûte, f. ‖ incrustation, f. ‖
kissing-~, s. biseau, m., baisure, f.

crust, *krŭst*, v. a. & n. couvrir d'une
croûte ‖ se croûter.

crustaceous, *krŭs tā'shŭs*, a. crustacé.

crustily, *krŭs'tĭ lĭ*, ad. de mauvaise
humeur.

crustiness, *krŭs'tĭ nĕs*, s. dureté, f. ‖
(fig.) mauvaise humeur, f.

crusty, *krŭs'tĭ*, a. couvert d'une croûte ‖
(fig.) de mauvaise humeur.

crutch, *krŭch*, s. béquille, f.

cry, *krĭ*, s. cri, m. ‖ acclamation, f.

cry, *krĭ*, v. a. & n. crier, criailler ‖ proclamer, pleurer ‖ **to ~ one's eyes out**,
pleurer toutes les larmes de son corps ‖
to ~ off, ne plus en être ‖ **to ~ out**,
s'écrier.

crying, *krī'ing*, s. cri, m.   [s'écrier.

crypt, *krĭpt*, s. crypte, voûte, f.

crystal, *krĭs'tăl*, s. cristal, m.

crystal, *krĭs'tăl*, a. de cristal.

crystalline, *krĭs'tăl lĭn*, a. cristallin.

crystallisation, *krĭs tăl lĭ să'shŭn*, s.
cristallisation, f.   [talliser.

crystallise, *krĭs'tăl līz*, v.a. (& n.) (se) cris-

cub, *kŭb*, s. petit d'un animal, m.

cub, *kŭb*, v. n. faire des petits.

cubature, *kŭ'bă tūr*, s. cubage, m.

cube, *kŭb*, s. cube, m.

cube, *kŭb*, v. a. cuber.

cubebs, *kŭ'bĕbs*, s. cubèbe, m.

cubic, *kŭ'bĭk*, a. cubique, cube.

cubicle, *kŭ'bĭ kl*, s. cloison, f. ‖ chambrette
à coucher, f.

cubit, *kŭ'bĭt*, s. coudée, f.

cuckoo, *kŏŏk'kō*, s. coucou, m.

cucumber, *kŭ'kŭm bĕr*, s. concombre, m. ‖
~-frame, s. châssis aux concombres, m.

cud, *kŭd*, s. nourriture, f. ‖ **to chew the
~**, ruminer.

cuddle, *kŭd'l*, v. a. serrer, presser ‖
~, v. n. se serrer ‖ se ramasser.   [m.

cuddy, *kŭd'dĭ*, s. (mar.) coqueron, fougon,

cudgel, *kŭd'jĕl*, s. tricot, bâton, m. ‖ **to
take up the ~s for**, rompre une
lance pour qn. ‖ ~-player, s. bâtonniste

cudgel, *kŭd'jĕl*, v. a. rosser.   [m.

cue, *kŭ*, s. queue, f. ‖ réclame, f. ‖ mot du
guet, m. ‖ avis, m. ‖ humeur, f. ‖ **to
give the ~**, donner la réplique.

cuff, *kŭf*, s. coup de poing, m. ‖ manchette,

cuff, *kŭf*, v. a. & n. donner des coups de
poing ‖ se battre à coups de poing.

cuirass, *kwĭ răs'*, s. cuirasse, f.

cuirassier, *kwĭ răs sēr'*, s. cuirassier, m.

culinary, *kŭ'lĭ nĕr'ĭ*, a. de cuisine, culinaire.

cull, *kŭl*, v. a. cueillir ‖ choisir.

cullender, *kŭl'lĕn dĕr*, s. passoire, f.

culminate, *kŭl'mĭ nāt*, v. n. culminer.

culpability, *kŭl pă bĭl'ĭ tĭ*, s. culpabilité, f.

culpable, *kŭl'pă bl*, a. coupable, blâmable.

culpably, *kŭl'pă blĭ*, ad. d'une manière
coupable.

culprit, *kŭl'prĭt*, s. coupable, accuse, m.

cultivate, *kŭl'tĭ vāt*, v. a. cultiver ‖ améliorer.   [culture, f.

cultivation, *kŭl tĭ vā'shŭn*, s. cultivation,

cultivator, *kŭl'tĭ vā tĕr*, s. cultivateur, m.

culture, *kŭl'tūr* ou *kŭl'chōōr*, s. culture, f.

cumber, *kŭm'bĕr*, v. a. embarrasser, incommoder.

cumbersome, *kŭm'bĕr sŭm*, **cumbrous**,
kŭm'brŭs, a. embarrassant, incommode.

cumin, *kŭm'in*, s. cumin, m.

cunning, *kŭn'ning*, s. ruse, f., artifice, m.

cunning, *kŭn'ning*, a. (-ly, ad.) adroit(e-
ment) ‖ rusé, artificieux ‖ fin ‖ avec ruse.

cup, *kŭp*, s. coupe, tasse, f., gobelet, m. ‖
calice (d'une fleur), m. ‖ godet, m. ‖ ventouse, f. ‖ **in one's ~s**, dans les vignes
du Seigneur.

cup, *kŭp*, v. a. ventouser.

cupboard, *kŭb'bŏrd*, s. armoire, f. ‖ placard, m. ‖ buffet, m.

cupidity, *kŭ pĭd'ĭ tĭ*, s. cupidité, f.

cupola, *kŭ'pŏ lă*, s. coupole, f., dôme, m.

cupping-glass, *kŭp'ping glăs*, s. ventouse, f.   [chien, m.

cur, *kŭr*, s. chien dégénéré, m. ‖ (fig.) vilain

curable, *kū′rȧbl*, a. curable, guérissable.
curacy, *kū′rȧsi*, s. vicairie, f.
curate, *kū′rȧt*, s. vicaire, m.
curative, *kū′rȧtiv*, a. curatif.
curator, *kū′rȧ′tĕr*, s. curateur, m.
curb, *kĕrb*, s. frein, m. ‖ gourmette, m. ‖ restreinte, f.
curb, *kĕrb*, v. a. mettre un frein, gourmer ‖ restreindre.
curd, *kĕrd*, s. lait caillé, m.
curd, *kĕrd*, v. a. cailler.
curdle, *kĕr′dl*, v. a. & n. coaguler ‖ se cailler.
cure, *kūr*, s. cure, f. ‖ guérison, f., traitement, m. ‖ ~of souls, charge d'âmes, f.
cure, *kūr*, v. a. guérir ‖ mariner.
curer, *kū′rĕr*, s. médecin, m. ‖ saleur, m.
curfew, *kĕr′fū*, s. couvre-feu, m.
curing, *kūr′ing*, s. cure, f. ‖ salaison, f.
curiosity, *kū′riŏs′iti*, s. curiosité, rareté, f. ‖ ~-shop, s. magasin d'antiquités, m.
curious, *kū′riŭs*, a. curieux ‖ exact, délicat ‖ -ly, ad. curieusement.
curl, *kĕrl*, s. boucle de cheveux, f. ‖ (fig.) ondulation, f.
curl, *kĕrl*, v. a. & n. boucler, tisser ‖ se boucler ‖ s'entortiller.
curlew, *kĕr′lū*, s. courlis, courlieu, m.
curling-iron, *kĕr′lingĭĕrn*, s. fer à friser, m. [papillote, f.
curl(ing)-paper, *kĕr′l(ing)pā′pĕr*, s.
curly, *kĕr′li*, a. frisé, bouclé.
curmudgeon, *kĕr′mŭj′ŭn*, s. avare, ladre, m. [de Corinthe, m.
currant, *kŭr′rȧnt*, s. groseille, f. ‖ raisin
currency, *kŭr′rĕnsi*, s. circulation, f., cours, m., continuité, f.‖papier-monnaie, m.
current, *kŭr′rĕnt*, s. courant, m.
current, *kŭr′rĕnt*, a. courant, circulant ‖ commun ‖ -ly, ad. généralement.
curricle, *kŭr′rikl*, s. cabriolet à pompe, m.
curriculum, *kŭr′rik′ūlŭm*, s. cours d'études, m.
currier, *kŭr′riĕr*, s. corroyeur, m.
currish, *kŭr′rish*, a. hargneux, brutal.
curry, *kŭr′ri*, s. curry, m. (ragoût) ‖ ~-comb,s. étrille, f.‖ ~-powder, s. curry, m.
curry, *kŭr′ri*, v. a. étriller ‖ maltraiter ‖ to ~ favour with, capter la faveur de.
curse, *kĕrs*, s. malédiction, imprécation, f.
curse, *kĕrs*, v. a. & n. maudire ‖ jurer, blasphémer. [misérablement.
cursedly, *kĕr′sĕdli*, ad. abominablement,
cursorily, *kĕr′sĕrili*, ad. à la hâte ‖ en courant.
cursory, *kĕr′sĕri*, a. précipité ‖ léger.
curt, *kĕrt*, a. court.
curtail, *kĕr′tāl′*, v. a. courtauder, écourter ‖ retrancher, démembrer.
curtain, *kĕr′tĭn*, s. rideau, m., toile, f. ‖ ~-lecture, s. semence conjugale, f.
curtain, *kĕr′tĭn*, v. a. garnir de rideaux.
curts(e)y, *kĕrt′si*, s. révérence, f.
curts(e)y, *kĕrt′si*, v. n. faire la révérence ‖ to drop a ~, tirer sa révérence.
curvated, *kĕr′vātĕd*, a. courbé, courbe.
curvature, *kĕr′vȧtūr*, s. courbure, f.

curve, *kĕrv*, s. courbe, f.
curve, *kĕrv*, v. a. courber.
curvet, *kĕr′vĕt*, s. courbette, f.
curvet, *kĕr′vĕt*, v. n. faire des courbettes.
curvilinear, *kĕr′vilĭn′iĕr*, a. curviligne.
cushion, *kōōsh′ŭn*, s. coussin, m. ‖ coussinet, m. ‖ bande, f.
custard, *kŭs′tĕrd*, s. flan, m.
custodian, *kŭstō′diȧn*, s. gardien, m.
custody, *kŭs′tōdi*, s. garde, f., emprisonnement, m., sûreté, f. ‖ to give one into ~, faire arrêter qn.
custom, *kŭs′tŭm*, s. coutume, habitude, f. ‖ douane, f. ‖ droits d'entrée, m. pl. ‖ clientèle, f. ‖ to pass (through) the ~s, douaner ‖ ~-house, s. douane, f. ‖ ~-house officer, s. douanier, m. ‖ ~s-free, a. exempt de douanes.
customarily, *kŭs′tŭmĕrĭli*, ad. habituellement. [naire.
customary, *kŭs′tŭmĕri*, a. d'usage ordi-
customer, *kŭs′tŭmĕr*, s. chaland, m., pratique, f.
cut, *kŭt*, s. coup, m. ‖ tranche, coupure, f., morceau, m. ‖ blessure, f. ‖ pièce, f. ‖ balafre, f. ‖ estampe, gravure, f. ‖ façon, découpure, f. ‖ chemin de traverse, m.
cut, *kŭt*, v. a. & n. ir. couper, trancher, tailler ‖ fendre ‖ sculpter ‖ traverser ‖ se couper ‖ percer ‖ to ~ one's teeth, faire ses dents ‖ to be ~ to the heart, avoir le cœur percé ‖ to ~ off one's escape, couper la retraite à qn. ‖ ~-and-dry, a. tout prêt ‖ ~-away coat, s. habit à la française, m. ‖ ~-purse, s. coupeur de bourses, m. ‖ ~-throat, s. coupe-jarret, m.
cutaneous, *kūtā′nĕŭs*, a. cutané. [m.
cuticle, *kū′tĭkl*, s. pellicule, f., épiderme
cutlass, *kŭt′lȧs*, s. coutelas, m.
cutler, *kŭt′lĕr*, s. coutelier, m.
cutlery, *kŭt′lĕri*, s. coutellerie, f.
cutlet, *kŭt′lĕt*, s. côtelette, f.
cutter, *kŭt′tĕr*, s. instrument tranchant, m. ‖ dent incisive, f. ‖ (ship) côtre, cutter, m.
cutting, *kŭt′ting*, s. coupe, rognure, déchiqueture, f. ‖ (rail.) tranchée, f. ‖ ~ of teeth, poussée des dents, f.
cuttle, *kŭt′tl*, s. (~-fish) sèche, f.
cutty, *kŭt′ti*, s. brûle-gueule, m.
cycle, *sī′kl*, s. cercle, m. ‖ cycle, m.
cyclone, *sī′klōn*, s. ouragan, typhon, m.
cyclopædia, *sīklōpē′diȧ*, s. encyclopédie, f. [dique.
cyclopædic, *sīklōpē′dĭk*, s. encyclopé-
cygnet, *sĭg′nĕt*, s. jeune cygne, m.
cylinder, *sĭl′indĕr*, s. cylindre, m.
cylindrical, *sĭlĭn′drĭkȧl*, a. cylindrique.
cymbal, *sĭm′bȧl*, s. cymbale, f.
cynic, *sĭn′ĭk*, s. cynique, misanthrope, m.
cynical, *sĭn′ĭkȧl*, a. cynique, m.
cynical, *sĭn′ĭkȧl*, a. cynique ‖ -ly, ad. avec cynisme.
cypress, *sī′prĕs*, s. cyprès, m.
Czar, *zȧr*, s. czar, m.
Czarina, *zȧrē′nȧ*, s. czarine, f.

D.

dab, *dăb*, s. coup léger, m. ‖ éclaboussure, f.

dab, *dăb*, v. a. toucher légèrement, éponger.

dabble, *dăb′l*, v. a. & n. barbouiller, éclabousser ‖ bousiller ‖ se mêler (de).

dabbler, *dăb′lĕr*, s. barboteur, m. ‖ bousilleur, m.   [legs, s. faucheux, m.

dad(dy), *dăd′(dĭ)*, s. papa, m. ‖ ~-long-

daffodil, *dăf′ŏ dĭl*, s. (bot.) asphodèle, nar-

daft, *dăft*, a. idiot, fou.   [cisse des prés, m.

dagger, *dăg′gĕr*, s. poignard, m. ‖ at -s drawn, à couteaux tirés.   [réotype, m.

daguerreotype, *dă gĕr′ĕ ŏ tīp*, s. daguer-

dahlia, *dā′lĭ ă*, s. (bot.) dahlia, m.

daily, *dā′lĭ*, s. (fam.) journal quotidien, m.

daily, *dā′lĭ*, a. & ad. journalier, quotidien ‖ journellement.

daintily, *dān′tĭ lĭ*, ad. délicatement.

daintiness, *dān′tĭ nĕs*, s. délicatesse, friandise, f.

dainty, *dān′tĭ*, s. friandise, délicatesse, f.

dainty, *dān′tĭ*, a. délicieux, délicat, friand ‖ élégant.   [laitière, f.

dairy, *dā′rĭ*, s. laiterie, f. ‖ ~-maid, s.

dais, *dā′is*, s. dais, m.

daisy, *dā′zĭ*, s. (bot.) marguerite, f.

dale, *dāl*, s. vallée, f.

dalliance, *dăl′lĭ ăns*, s. caresses, f. pl., badinage conjugal, m. ‖ délai, m.

dally, *dăl′lĭ*, v. n. badiner, perdre son temps, s'amuser.   [temps, s'amuser.

dam, *dăm*, s. digue, f.

dam, *dăm*, v. a. diguer.

damage, *dăm′ĭj*, s. dommage, m. ‖ préjudice, m. ‖ ~s, pl. dédommagement, m. ‖ (mar.) avaries, f. pl.

damage, *dăm′ĭj*, v. a. endommager.

Damascus, *dăm ăs′kŭs*, s. sabre de Damas.

damask, *dăm′ăsk*, s. damas, m.   [m.

damask, *dăm′ăsk*, **damaskeen**, *dăm′ as kēn*, v. a. damasser ‖ damasquiner.

dame, *dăm*, s. dame, f. ‖ femme, f. ‖ ~'s school, s. petit lycée à directrices, m.

damn, *dăm*, v. a. damner, condamner ‖ siffler.

damnable, *dăm′nă bl*, a. damnable.

damnation, *dăm nă′shŭn*, s. damnation, f. ‖ fiasco, m.

damp, *dămp*, s. humidité, f., brouillard, m., vapeur, f. ‖ découragement, m.

damp, *dămp*, v. a. humecter ‖ abattre.

damp, *dămp*, a. humide, moite ‖ abattu.

damper, *dăm′pĕr*, s. (mus.) sourdine, f. ‖ (fig.) rabat-joie, m. ‖ (de cheminée) registre, m.   [teur, f.

dampness, *dămp′nĕs*, s. humidité, moi-

damsel, *dăm′zĕl*, s. demoiselle, f. ‖ jeune paysanne, f.

damson, *dăm′zn*, s. prune de damas, f.

dance, *dăns*, s. danse, f.   •

dance, *dăns*, v. a. & n. danser.   [f.

dancer, *dăn′sĕr*, s. danseur, m., danseuse, f.

dancing, *dăn′sĭng*; ~-master, s. maître de danse, m. ‖ ~-party, s. soirée dansante, f.

dandelion, *dăn′dĭ lī ŏn*, s. pissenlit, m.

dandle, *dăn′dl*, v. a. bercer, dorloter.

dandruff, *dăn′drŭf*, s. crasse de la tête, rogne, f.

dandy, *dăn′dĭ*, s. petit-maître, élégant, m.

danewort, *dăn′wĕrt*, s. (bot.) hièble, f.

danger, *dăn′jĕr*, s. danger, péril, m.

dangerous, *dăn′jĕr ŭs*, a. dangereux, périlleux ‖ -ly, ad. dangereusement.

dangle, *dăng′gl*, v. n. pendiller, être suspendu.   [lureau, m.

dangler, *dăng′glĕr*, s. damoiseau, godelureau, m.

dank, *dăngk*, a. humide, moite.

dapper, *dăp′pĕr*, a. vif, fringant.

dapple, *dăp′l*, v. a. pommeler.

dapple, *dăp′l*, a. pommelé, bigarré.

dare, *dăr*, s. casse-cou, risque-tout, m.

dare, *dăr*, v. a. & n. ir. défier, provoquer, braver ‖ oser, avoir la hardiesse ‖ ~-devil, a. osé, qui ose tout.

daring, *dăr′ĭng*, a. (-ly, ad.) hardi(ment) ‖ audacieux.   [ignorance, f.

dark, *dărk*, s. obscurité, f., ténèbres, f. pl.

dark, *dărk*, a. sombre, obscur ‖ mélancolique ‖ ignorant ‖ -ly, ad. obscurément.

darken, *dărk′n*, v. a. (& n.)(s')obscurcir.

darkie, *dăr′kĭ*, s. (Am.) noir (nègre), m.

darkness, *dărk′nĕs*, s. obscurité, f. ‖ teinte foncée, f., ténèbres, f. pl.

darksome, *dărk′sŭm*, a. obscur, sombre.

darling, *dăr′lĭng*, s. favori, m., favorite, f.

darling, *dăr′lĭng*, a. favori, mignon.

darn, *dărn*, v. a. raccommoder.

darnel, *dăr′nĕl*, s. (bot.) ivraie, f.

dart, *dărt*, s. dard, trait, javelot, m.

dart, *dărt*, v. a. & n. darder, lancer ‖ jeter ‖ voler comme un trait.

dash, *dăsh*, s. attaque, f. ‖ (of pens) trait, m. ‖ choc, élan, m. ‖ filet, m. ‖ mélange, m. ‖ coup, m. ‖ petit brin, grain, m. ‖ ~-board, s. mantelet d'une voiture, m.

dash, *dăsh*, v. a. & n. heurter ‖ jeter, briser ‖ éclabousser ‖ arroser ‖ mêler, biffer ‖ déconcerter ‖ saillir, s'écouler ‖ ~! crac!

dashing, *dăsh′ĭng*, a. brillant, pimpant ‖ fougueux.

dastard, *dăs′tĕrd*, s. lâche, poltron, m.

dastard(ly), *dăs′tĕrd(lĭ)*, a. poltron, lâche.

data, *dā′tă*, s. données, f. pl.

date, *dāt*, s. date, f. ‖ époque, f. ‖ durée, f. ‖ fin, f. ‖ datte, f. ‖ out of ~, vieilli.

date, *dāt*, v. a. dater.

dative, *dā′tĭv*, s. datif, m.

dative, *dā′tĭv*, a. datif.

daub, *dăwb*, s. barbouillage, m. ‖ croûte, f.

daub, *dăwb*, v. a. barbouiller ‖ enduire ‖ pallier, déguiser ‖ ~, v. n. faire l'hypocrite.

dauber, *dăwb′ĕr*, s. mauvais peintre, m.

daughter, *dăw′tĕr*, s. fille, f. ‖ ~-in-law, s. belle-fille, bru, f.   [soumise.

daughterly, *dăw′tĕr lĭ*, a. & ad. de fille

daunt, *dăwnt*, v. a. effrayer.

dauntless, *dăwnt′lĕs*, a. intrépide.

davenport, *dăv′ĕn pŏrt*, s. bureau, secrétaire, m.

davit, *dā′vĭt*, s. (mar.) davié, davier, m.

daw, *dăw*, s. choucas, m.

dawdle, *dăw′dl*, v. n. muser.

dawn, *dǎwn,* s. point du jour, m., aube, f. ||
dawn, *dǎwn,* v. n. poindre.
day, *dā,* s. jour, m., journée, f. || clarté, f. ||
~**s of grace,** pl. jours de faveur, m. pl. ||
break of ~, point du jour || **by the** ~,
au jour le jour || **from** ~ **to** ~, de jour en
jour || **in broad** ~, en plein jour || ~-
boarder, s. demi-pensionnaire, m. || ~-
blush, s. aurore, f || ~-**book,** s. journal,
m. || ~-**labourer,** s. journalier, m. || ~-
scholar, s. externe, m. || ~-**spring,** s.
point du jour, m. || ~-**star,** s. étoile du
matin, f.
daybreak, *dā'brǎk,* s. point du jour, m.
daydream, *dā'drēm* s. rêve de jour, m.
daylight, *dā'līt,* s. clarté du jour, f. || **in
broad** ~, au grand jour.
daytime, *dā'tīm,* s. jour, m., journée, f.
daze, *dāz,* **dazzle,** *dǎz'l,* v. a. éblouir.
deacon, *dē'kn,* s. diacre, m.
dead, *dĕd,* s. morts, m. pl. || milieu, m. ||
fort, m. || **at the** ~ **of night,** au fort de
la nuit || ~-**house,** s. morgue, f. || ~-
letter office, s. bureau des rebuts, m. ||
~-**march,** s. marche funèbre, f.
dead, *dĕd,* a. mort, inanimé || insensible ||
mélancolique || inhabité || éteint || (of let-
ters) tombé en rebut || plat || blanc || ~
sound ~ **bargain,** s. vil prix, m. || ~-
drunk, a. mort-ivre || ~-**heat,** s. épreuve
nulle, f. || ~-**wood,** s. bois sec, m.
deaden, *dĕd'n,* v. a. amortir || émousser ||
matir.
deadeye, *dĕd'ī,* s. (mar.) cap-de-mouton, m.
deadhead, *dĕd'hĕd,* s. passe-volant, m.
deadlight, *dĕd'līt,* s. (mar.) faux sabord, m.
deadlock, *dĕd'lŏk,* s. arrêt, point d'arrêt, m.
deadly, *dĕd'lĭ,* a. (& ad.) mortel(lement) ||
implacable(ment).
deadness, *dĕd'nĕs,* s. mort, f. || froideur,
langueur, f. || insipidité, f.
deaf, *dĕf,* a. sourd || (fig.) insensible || **stone
~, complètement sourd || ~ **and dumb,**
sourd-muet.
deafen, *dĕf'ĕn,* v. a. rendre sourd || étourdir.
deafness, *dĕf'nĕs,* s. surdité, f.
deal, *dēl,* s. quantité, partie, f. || donne, f. ||
bois de sapin, m. || **a great** ~, **a good**
~, une grande partie, beaucoup || **it is-
your** ~, c'est à vous à donner.
deal, *dēl,* v. a. & n. distribuer || disperser,
répandre || trafiquer, commercer || agir,
s'entremettre || se comporter.
dealer, *dēl'ĕr,* s. marchand, trafiquant, m. ||
qui distribue les cartes || **general** ~, né-
gociant, m. || tripier, m.
dealing, *dēl'ĭng,* s. commerce, négoce, m. ||
conduite, f. || **plain** ~, s. franchise, bonne
foi, f. || **double** ~, s. double jeu, m. ||
duplicité, f.
dean, *dēn,* s. doyen, m.
deanery, *dēn'ĕr ĭ,* s. doyenné, décanat, m.
dear, *dēr,* a. cher || bien aimé || favori ||
coûteux || odieux, nuisible || **oh** ~ ! aïe!
oh, mon Dieu! || ~**ly,** ad. chèrement ||
tendrement.
dearness, *dēr'nĕs,* s. tendresse, f. || cherté,
dearth, *dĕrth,* s. cherté, f. [f.

death, *dĕth,* s. mort, f., trépas, m. ||
~'**s door,** à deux doigts de la mort || **to
do to** ~, occire || **to be in at the** ~,
assister à l'halali || ~-**bed,** s. lit de
mort, m. || ~-**blow,** s. coup de mort, m. ||
~-**penalty,** s. peine capitale, f. || ~-
warrant, s. ordre d'exécution, f.
deathlike, *dĕth'līk,* a. mortel, lugubre ||
léthargique.
debar, *dē bâr',* v. a. exclure || s'opposer.
debarkation, *dē bâr kā'shǔn,* s. vide dis-
embarkation.
debase, *dē bās',* v. n. abaisser, avilir ||
falsifier. [m. || billonnage, m.
debasement, *dē bās'mĕnt,* s. avilissement,
debatable, *dē bā'tā bl,* a. contestable.
debate, *dē bāt',* s. débat, m., controverse,
dispute, f. [disputer.
debate, *dē bāt',* v. a. & n. débattre, discuter,
debater, *dē bā'tĕr,* s. disputeur, m. || ora-
teur parlementaire, m.
debauch, *dē bǎwch',* s. débauche, f.
debauch, *dē bǎwch',* v. a. débaucher, corrompre. [libertinage, m.
debauchery, *dē bǎwch'ĕr ĭ,* s. débauche, f.,
debenture, *dē bĕn'tūr,* s. reconnaissance,
obligation, f. [faiblir.
debilitate, *dē bĭl'ĭ tāt,* v. a. débiliter, af-
debility, *dē bĭl'ĭ tĭ,* s. débilité, faiblesse, f.
debit, *dĕb'ĭt,* s. débit, m.
debit, *dĕb'ĭt,* v. a. débiter.
debouch, *dē bōsh',* v. n. (mil.) déboucher.
debt, *dĕt,* s. dette, f. || **to run, get into**
~, faire des dettes.
debtor, *dĕt'tĕr,* s. débiteur, m.
decade, *dĕk'ād,* s. dizaine, f. || décade, f.
decadence, *dē kā'dĕns,* s. décadence, f.
Decalogue, *dĕk'ā lŏg,* s. Décalogue, m.
decamp, *dē kǎmp',* v. a. décamper.
decant, *dē kǎnt',* v. a. transvaser || (chem.)
décanter.
decanter, *dē kǎn'tĕr,* s. carafe, f. || ~-
stand, s. porte-carafe, m.
decapitate, *dē kǎp'ĭ tāt,* v. a. décapiter.
decapitation, *dē kǎp ĭ tā'shǔn,* s. décapitation, f. [dépérissement, m.
decay, *dē kā',* s. déclin, m., décadence, f.,
decay, *dē kā',* v. n. déchoir, s'user, se
délabrer || dépérir.
decease, *dē sēs',* s. décès, trépas, m.
decease, *dē sēs',* v. n. décéder, mourir.
deceit, *dē sēt',* s. fraude, tromperie, f. ||
artifice, m.
deceitful, *dē sēt'fŏŏl,* a. frauduleux, trom-
peur || ~**ly,** ad. frauduleusement.
deceive, *dē sēv',* v. a. décevoir, tromper.
deceiver, *dē sēv'ĕr,* s. trompeur, fourbe, m.
December, *dē sĕm'bĕr,* s. décembre, m.
decency, *dē' sĕn sĭ,* s. décence, bienséance,
decennial, *dē sĕn'nĭ ǎl,* a. décennal. [f.
decent, *dē' sĕnt,* a. décent, convenable ||
~**ly,** ad. décemment.
decentralise, *dē sĕn' trǎl īz,* v. a. décentraliser. [posture, f.
deception, *dē sĕp'shǔn,* s. déception, im-
deceptive, *dē sĕp'tĭv,* a. trompeur, déceptif.
decide, *dē sīd',* v. a. décider, résoudre.

decidedly, dĕ sī́ dĕd lŭ, ad. assurément.
deciduous, dĕ sid́ ŭ ŭs, a. périssable || (bot.) décident, décidu.
decimal, dĕś ĭ măl, a. décimal.
decimate, dĕś ĭ māt, v. a. décimer.
decimation, dĕs ĭ mā́ shŭn, s. décimation, f. || dîme, f.   [crire, dépeindre.
decipher, dĕ sī́ fĕr, v. a. déchiffrer || dé-
decision, dĕ sizh́ ŭn, s. décision, f. || fer-
meté, f. || to come to a ~, prendre une décision.   [-ly, ad. décisivement.
decisive, dĕ sī́ sĭv, a. décisif || prononcé ||
deck, dĕk, s. tillac, pont (d'un vaisseau), m.
declaim, dĕ klāḿ, v. a. & n. déclamer || haranguer.   [teur, m.
declaimer, dĕ klāḿ ĕr, s. déclamateur, rhé-
declamation, dĕ klă mā́ shŭn, s. déclama-tion, f.   [toire.
declamatory, dĕ klăḿ ă tĕr ĭ, a. déclama-
declaration, dĕk lăr ā́ shŭn, s. déclara-tion, f.
declare, dĕ klāŕ, v. a. (& n.) (se) déclarer.
declension, dĕ klĕń shŭn, s. déclin, m., déclinaison, f.
declinable, dĕ klī́ nă bl, a. (gr.) déclinable.
declination, dĕ klĭ nā́ shŭn, s. déclination, f. || déclin, m., décadence, f. || déviation, f. || (gr.) déclinaison, f.
decline, dĕ klīń, s. déclin, m., décadence, f. || (méd.) marasme, m. || to be in, to go into a ~, être, tomber en langueur.
decline, dĕ klīń, v. a. & n. pencher, bais-ser || éviter || refuser || (gr.) décliner || dé-vier || déchoir, dégénérer || tomber en dé-cadence.   [son, f.
declivity, dĕ klĭv́ ĭ tĭ, s. déclivité, inclinai-
declivous, dĕ klī́ vŭs, a. en pente, déclive.
decoction, dĕ kŏḱ shŭn, s. décoctiou, f.
decollate, dĕ kŏĺ lāt, v. a. décoller.
decompose, dĕ kŏm pōź, v. a. décomposer, analyser.
decomposition, dĕ kŏm pō zish́ ŭn, s. dé-composition, analyse, f.
decorate, dĕḱ ō rāt, v. a. décorer, orner.
decoration, dĕk ō rā́ shŭn, s. décoration, f.
decorative, dĕḱ ō rā tĭv, a. de décoration.
decorator, dĕḱ ō rā tĕr, s. décorateur, m.
decorous, dĕ kṓ rŭs, a. décent, convenable || -ly, ad. décemment.   [cence, f.
decorum, dĕ kṓ rŭm, s. décorum, m., dé-
decoy, dĕ kŏý, s. appât, m., séduction, f. || mouchard, m. || ~bird, s. appeau, m.
decoy, dĕ kŏý, v. a. leurrer.
decrease, dĕ krēś, s. décroissement, m., diminution, f.   [décroître.
decrease, dĕ krēś, v. a. & n. diminuer ||
decree, dĕ krḗ, s. décret, statut, m., loi, f.
decree, dĕ krḗ, v. a. & n. décréter || dé-cerner.
decrepit, dĕ krĕṕ ĭt, a. décrépit.
decrial, dĕ krī́ al, s. décri, m.
decrier, dĕ krī́ ĕr, s. détracteur, m.
decry, dĕ krī́, v. a. décrier, censurer.
dedicate, dĕd́ ĭ kāt, v. a. dédier || dévouer || adresser.   [sécration, f.
dedication, dĕd ĭ kā́ shŭn, s. dédicace, con-
dedicatory, dĕd́ ĭ kā tĕr ĭ, a. dédicatoire.

deduce, dĕ dūś, v. a. déduire, inférer || dériver || transplanter.
deducible, dĕ dū́ sĭ bl, a. qui peut être dé-duit.   [rabattre.
deduct, dĕ dŭkt́, v. a. déduire, défalquer.
deduction, dĕ dŭḱ shŭn, s. conclusion, f. || déduction, f. || (com.) remise, f.
deductive, dĕ dŭḱ tĭv, a. déductif || -ly, ad. conséquemment.
deed, dĕd, s. action, f., acte, fait, exploit, m. || (jur.) titre, m. || contrat, m. || in ~, de fait.
deem, dēm, v. n. juger, penser.
deep, dēp, a. profond, creux || pénétrant, grave, sérieux || foncé (of colours) || rusé, fin || ~-laid, a. profond, secret ~-rooted, a. profondément enraciné -ly, ad. profondément, extrêmement, sé-rieusement || (of sounds) gravement.
deepen, dēṕ n, v. a. approfondir || obscurcir.
deeps, dēps, s. profondeur, f. || océan, m. || abîme, m.
deer, dĕr, s. daim, m., bête fauve, f. || ~-stalking, s. chasse de bêtes fauves, f.
deface, dĕ fāś, v. a. défigurer, détériorer, gâter || ruiner || effacer.   [traire.
defalcate, dĕ fáĺ kāt, v. a. déduire, sous-
defalcation, dĕ fal kā́ shŭn, s. retranche-ment, m. || défalcation, f.
defamation, dĕ fă mā́ shŭn, s. diffamation, calomnie, f.   [toire.
defamatory, dĕ făḿ ă tĕr ĭ, a. diffama-
defame, dĕ fāḿ, v. a. diffamer, décrier.
default, dĕ fáwĺt, s. défaut, m., faute, f. || crime, m.
default, dĕ fáwĺt, v. a. & n. violer, man-quer || faire défaut || to go by ~, (jur.) être condamné par défaut.
defaulter, dĕ fáwĺt ĕr, s. délinquant, m. || (jur.) contumace, m. || retardataire, m.
defeasance, dĕ fḗ zăns, s. contre-lettre, annulation, f.
defeat, dĕ fēt́, s. défaite, déroute, f.
defeat, dĕ fēt́, v. a. défaire, mettre en dé-route || déjouer, frustrer.
defect, dĕ fĕkt́, s. défectuosité, f., défaut, m. || (jur.) vice, m.
defective, dĕ fĕḱ tĭv, a. défectueux || im-parfait || (gr.) défectif.   [apologie, f.
defence, dĕ fĕnś, s. défense, protection,
defenceless, dĕ fĕnś lĕs, a. sans défense, faible.   [interdire.
defend, dĕ fĕnd́, v. a. défendre, protéger
defendant, dĕ fĕń dănt, s. défenseur, m. || (jur.) défendeur, m.   [avocat, m.
defender, dĕ fĕń dĕr, s. défenseur, m. ||
defensible, dĕ fĕń sĭ bl, a. défensible.
defensive, dĕ fĕń sĭv, s. défensive, f.
defensive, dĕ fĕń sĭv, a. défensif || -ly, ad. sur la défensive || pour la défense.
defer, dĕ fĕŕ, v. a. & n. différer, remettre || déférer à.   [spect, m.
deference, dĕ f́ ĕr ĕns, s. déférence, f., re-
defiance, dĕ fī́ ăns, s. défi, cartel, m.
deficiency, dĕ fish́ ĕn sĭ, s. défaut, m., insuffisance, f.   [parfait || insuffisant.
deficient, dĕ fish́ ĕnt, a. défectueux, im-

deficit, *défĭ sĭt*, s. déficit, m. || to cover a ~, couvrir un déficit.
defile, *défīl'*, s. défilé, m.
defile, *défīl'*, v. a. & n. souiller || débaucher || défiler.
definable, *défī'năbl*, a. définissable.
define, *défīn'*, v. a. & n. définir || déterminer || dessiner.
definite, *déf'ĭnĭt*, a. défini, exact, précis || -ly, ad. définitivement.
definition, *défĭnĭsh'ŭn*, s. définition, f.
definitive, *défĭn'ĭtĭv*, a. définitif, positif.
deflect, *déflĕkt'*, v. n. décliner, détourner.
deflection, *déflĕk'shŭn*, s. détour, écart, m. || (of the needle) déclinaison, f.
deflower, *déflŏw'r*, v. a. déflorer.
defoliation, *défōlĭā'shŭn*, s. défeuillaison, f.
deform, *défawrm'*, v. a. défigurer.
deformity, *défŏr'mĭtĭ*, s. difformité, f.
defraud, *défrawd'*, v. a. frauder, tromper.
defrauder, *défraw'dĕr*, s. fraudeur, m.
defray, *défrā'*, v. a. défrayer, payer la dépense.
deft, *déft*, a. (-ly, ad.) convenable || adroit (ement).
deftness, *déft'nĕs*, s. gentillesse, f.
defunct, *défŭngkt'*, a. défunt, feu.
defy, *défī'*, v. a. défier, braver.
degenerate, *déjén'ĕrāt*, v. n. dégénérer.
degenerate, *déjén'ĕrāt*, a. dégénéré.
degeneration, *déjénĕrā'shŭn*, s. dégénération, f.
deglutinate, *déglō'tĭnāt*, v. a. décoller.
degradation, *dégrădā'shŭn*, s. dégradation, f.
degrade, *dégrād'*, v. a. dégrader, avilir.
degree, *dégrē'*, s. degré, m. || qualité, condition, f., ordre, rang, m. || intervalle, m. || in some ~, en quelque sorte || by -s, peu à peu.
deification, *déĭfĭkā'shŭn*, s. déification, f.
deify, *dé'ĭfī*, v. a. déifier, diviniser || louer à l'excès.
deign, *dān*, v. n. daigner, accorder.
deity, *dé'ĭtĭ*, s. déité, divinité, f.
deject, *déjĕkt'*, v. a. affliger, décourager.
dejection, *déjĕk'shŭn*, s. abattement, m. || (méd.) défécage, m.
delay, *délā'*, s. délai, retard, m.
delay, *délā'*, v.a. différer, retarder || frustrer.
delectable, *délĕk'tăbl*, a. délectable.
delectation, *délĕktā'shŭn*, s. délectation, f.
delegate, *dĕl'ĕgāt*, s. délégué, m.
delegate, *dĕl'ĕgāt*, v. a. déléguer, député.
delegation, *dĕlĕgā'shŭn*, s. délégation, f.
deleterious, *dĕlĕtē'rĭŭs*, a. délétère.
delf(t), *dĕlf*, s. faïence (de Delft), f.
deliberate, *délĭb'ĕrāt*, v. n. délibérer.
deliberate, *délĭb'ĕrāt*, a. circonspect, prudent || -ly, ad. avec délibération.
deliberateness, *délĭb'ĕrātnĕs*, s. circonspection, prudence, f.
deliberation, *délĭbĕrā'shŭn*, s. délibération, f.
delicacy, *dĕl'ĭkāsĭ*, s. délicatesse, friandise, f. || élégance, f. || tendresse, f.

delicate, *dĕl'ĭkāt*, a. (-ly, ad.) délicat (ement) || friand || exquis || tendre, doux.
delicious, *délĭsh'ŭs*, a. délicieux, exquis || -ly, ad. délicieusement.
deliciousness, *délĭsh'ŭsnĕs*, s. délices, f. pl., plaisir, m.
delight, *délīt'*, s. délice, m., délices, f. pl., plaisir, m. || charme, m.
delight, *délīt'*, v. a. (& n.) divertir, (se) plaire.
delightful, *délīt'fool*, a. délicieux, charmant || -ly, ad. délicieusement.
delineate, *délĭn'ĕāt*, v. a. tracer, dessiner, décrire.
delineation, *délĭnĕā'shŭn*, s. délinéation, esquisse, f.
delinquency, *délĭng'kwĕnsĭ*, s. délit, m.
delinquent, *délĭng'kwĕnt*, s. délinquant, m.
delirious, *délĭr'ĭŭs*, a. délirant, en délire.
delirium, *délĭr'ĭŭm*, s. délire, m.
deliver, *délĭv'ĕr*, v. a. délivrer, affranchir || remettre, rendre || accoucher || prononcer || s'acquitter de || distribuer (letters) || to be -ed immediately ! pressé.
deliverance, *délĭv'ĕrăns*, s. délivrance, f., affranchissement, m. || accouchement, m. || sauveur, m.
deliverer, *délĭv'ĕrĕr*, s. libérateur, m.
delivery, *délĭv'ĕrĭ*, s. délivrance, f., accouchement, m. || débit, m. || livraison, f. || distribution, f.
dell, *dĕl*, s. vallon, m., vallée, f. || creux, m.
delude, *délōd'*, v. a. tromper, abuser.
deluge, *dĕl'ūj*, s. déluge, m.
deluge, *dĕl'ūj*, v. a. inonder.
delusion, *délō'zhŭn*, s. tromperie, illusion, f.
delusive, *délō'sĭv*, a. trompeur, illusoire.
delve, *dĕlv*, v. a. creuser, fouir.
demagogic(al), *dĕmăgŏ'jĭk(ăl)*, a. démagogique.
demagogue, *dĕm'ăgŏg*, s. démagogue, m.
demand, *démănd'*, s. demande, requête, pétition, f. || question, f. || vente, f. || in great ~, très recherché || (com.) fortement demandé || on —, à présentation.
demand, *démănd'*, v. a. demander, réclamer, exiger || questionner.
demarcation, *démărkā'shŭn*, s. démarcation, f.
demean, *démēn'*, v. r. (oneself) se comporter.
demeanour, *démēn'ĕr*, s. conduite, tenue, f.
demented, *démĕn'tĕd*, a. aliéné || en démence.
demerit, *démĕr'ĭt*, s. démérite, m.
demesne, *démēn'*, s. domaine, m.
demigod, *dĕm'ĭgŏd*, s. demi-dieu.
demijohn, *dĕm'ĭjŏn*, s. dame-jeanne, f.
demise, *démīz'*, s. démission, f. || mort, f., décès, m.
demisemiquaver, *dĕm'ĭsĕmĭkwā'vĕr*, s. triple croche, f.
democracy, *démŏk'răsĭ*, s. démocratie, f.
democrat, *dĕm'ŏkrăt*, s. démocrate, m.
democratic, *dĕmŏkrăt'ĭk*, a. (-ally, ad.) démocratique(ment).
demolish, *démŏl'ĭsh*, v.a. démolir, abattre.
demolition, *dĕmōlĭsh'ŭn*, s. démolition, f.
demon, *dē'mŏn*, s. démon, diable, m.

bŏy; — fŏŏt, tŭbe, tŭb. || chair, joy; — game, yes; — soul, zeal; — thing, there.

demoniac, *dĕmō′nĭăk,* s. démoniaque, m.

demoniac, *dĕmō′nĭăk,* a. démoniaque.

demonstrable, *dĕmŏn′străbl,* a. démontrable.

demonstrably, *dĕmŏn′străblĭ,* ad. par démonstration.　[v.a. démontrer, prouver.

demonstrate, *dĕmŏn′străt* ou *dĕm′ŏnstrăt,*

demonstration, *dĕmŏnstrā′shŭn,* s. démonstration, évidence, f.

demonstrative, *dĕmŏn′strătĭv,* a. démonstratif || **-ly,** ad. démonstrativement.

demoralisation, *dĕmŏrălĭză′shŭn,* s. démoralisation, f.

demoralise, *dĕmŏr′ălĭz,* v. a. démoraliser.

demur, *dĕmĕr′,* s. hésitation, doute, f.

demur, *dĕmĕr′,* v. a. & n. douter || différer || hésiter.

demure, *dĕmūr′,* a. sobre || modeste || prude || **-ly,** ad. en prude.

demureness, *dĕmūr′nĕs,* s. modestie, f.

demurrage, *dĕmŭr′răj,* s. (mar.) frais de surestarie, m. pl.

demurrer, *dĕmŭr′rĕr,* s. (jur.) exception, f.

den, *dĕn,* s. caverne, f., repaire, m. || loge (d'une ménagerie), f.

deniable, *dĕnī′ăbl,* a. niable, reniable.

denial, *dĕnī′ăl,* s. dénégation, f., refus, m.

denizen, *dĕn′ĭzn,* s. citoyen, m.

denizen, *dĕn′ĭzn,* v. a. naturaliser.

denominate, *dĕnŏm′ĭnăt,* v. a. dénommer, nommer.　[mination, f.

denomination, *dĕnŏmĭnā′shŭn,* s. dénomination, f.

denominative, *dĕnŏm′ĭnătĭv,* a. dénominatif.　[nominateur, m.

denominator, *dĕnŏm′ĭnătĕr,* s. (ar.) dénote, désigner.

denote, *dĕnōt′,* v. a. dénoter, désigner.

denounce, *dĕnŏuns′,* v. a. dénoncer, accuser || annoncer.　[m.

denouncer, *dĕnŏun′sĕr,* s. dénonciateur, m.

dense, *dĕns,* a. (**-ly,** ad.) dense || épais.

density, *dĕns′ĭtĭ,* s. densité, compacité, f.

dent, *dĕnt,* s. dent (d'une roue), f. || bosse, f.

dent, *dĕnt,* v. a. bossuer.

dental, *dĕn′tăl,* s. (gr.) dentale, f.

dentifrice, *dĕn′tĭfrĭs,* s. dentifrice, m.

dentist, *dĕn′tĭst,* s. dentiste, m.

dentistry, *dĕn′tĭstrĭ,* s. art du dentiste, m. || guérison des dents, f.

dentition, *dĕntĭsh′ŭn,* s. dentition, f.

denudation, *dĕnūdā′shŭn,* s. dénûment, m.　[dénuder.

denude, *dĕnūd′,* v. a. dénuer, dépouiller ||

denunciation, *dĕnŭnsĭā′shŭn,* s. dénonciation, f.　[noncer, refuser.

deny, *dĕnī′,* v. a. dénier || désavouer, re-

deodorise, *dĕō′dĕrĭz,* v. a. désinfecter.

deodoriser, *dĕō′dĕrĭzĕr,* s. désinfectant, m. || appareil désinfectant, m.

depart, *dĕpărt′,* v. n. partir, s'en aller || quitter || se désister, renoncer || mourir || **to ~ this life,** mourir, décéder || the **~ed,** le défunt.　[m.

department, *dĕpărt′mĕnt,* s. département, f.

departure, *dĕpăr′tūr,* s. départ, m. || mort, f.

depend, *dĕpĕnd′,* v.n. dépendre de || résulter || se reposer, se fier à || **~ upon it,** comptez-y.

dependant, *dĕpĕn′dănt,* s. dépendant, m.

dependence, *dĕpĕn′dĕns,* s. dépendance, f., rapport, m. || confiance, f. || **~ on one,** confiance en qn.

dependency, *dĕpĕn′dĕnsĭ,* s. **foreign ~,** s. colonie, f. || (jur.) dépendance, f.

dependent, *dĕpĕn′dĕnt,* a. dépendant.

depict, *dĕpĭkt′,* v. a. dépeindre, décrire.

depilation, *dĕpĭlā′shŭn,* s. dépilation, f.

depletion, *dĕplē′shŭn,* s. déplétion, f.

deplorable, *dĕplō′răbl,* a. déplorable, lamentable.　[ment.

deplorably, *dĕplō′răblĭ,* ad. déplorable-

deplore, *dĕplōr′,* v. a. déplorer, pleurer, plaindre.

deploy, *dĕplŏy′,* v. a. déployer.

deponent, *dĕpō′nĕnt,* s. déposant, m.

depopulate, *dĕpŏp′ūlăt,* v. a. dépeupler.

depopulation, *dĕpŏpūlā′shŭn,* s. dépopulation, f.

deportation, *dĕpŏrtā′shŭn,* s. déportation, f., exil, m.

deportment, *dĕpōrt′mĕnt,* s. maintien, m. || tenue, f. || conduite, f.

depose, *dĕpōz′,* v. a. déposer || mettre bas || attester.

deposit, *dĕpŏz′ĭt,* s. dépôt, gage, m.

deposit, *dĕpŏz′ĭt,* v. a. déposer || consigner, mettre en gage || **to leave a ~,** déposer des arrhes.

depositary, *dĕpŏz′ĭtĕrĭ,* s. dépositaire, m.

deposition, *dĕpŏzĭsh′ŭn,* s. déposition, f., témoignage, m.

depositor, *dĕpŏz′ĭtĕr,* déposant, m.

depository, *dĕpŏz′ĭtĕrĭ,* s. dépôt, magasin, m.　[tion, corruption, f.

depravation, *dĕprăvā′shŭn,* s. dépravation, corruption, f.

deprave, *dĕprāv′,* v. a. dépraver, corrompre.　[chanceté, f.

depravity, *dĕprăv′ĭtĭ,* s. corruption, mé-

deprecate, *dĕp′rēkăt,* v. a. détourner par la prière, prier contre || s'opposer à.

deprecation, *dĕprēkā′shŭn,* s. déprécation, supplication, f.

deprecatory, *dĕp′rēkătĕrĭ,* a. déprécatif.

depreciate, *dĕprē′shĭăt,* v. a. déprécier || dénigrer.　[ciation, f.

depreciation, *dĕprēshĭā′shŭn,* s. dépré-

depredation, *dĕprēdā′shŭn,* s. déprédation, f., pillage, m.　[m. || pillard, m.

depredator, *dĕp′rēdătĕr,* s. déprédateur,

depress, *dĕprĕs′,* v. a. déprimer, abaisser, mortifier, humilier.

depression, *dĕprĕsh′ŭn,* s. dépression, f. || humiliation, déjection, f.

deprivation, *dĕprĭvā′shŭn,* s. privation, f. || (jur.) révocation, f.

deprive, *dĕprīv′,* v. a. priver || destituer.

depth, *dĕpth,* s. profondeur, f., abîme, m. || milieu, cœur, fort, m. || hauteur, obscurité, f. || **to get out of one's ~,** perdre fond.　[délégation, f.

deputation, *dĕpūtā′shŭn,* s. députation,

depute, *dĕpūt′,* v. a. députer, déléguer.

deputy, *dĕp′ūtĭ,* s. député, délégué, m. || **~-chairman,** s. vice-président, m.

derange, *dĕrānj′,* v. a. déranger.

derangement, *dĕrănj'mĕnt*, s. dérangement, m. ||folie, f. [abandonné en mer, m.
derelict, *dĕr'ĕlĭkt*, s. (mar.) vaisseau
dereliction, *dĕr'ĕlĭk'shŭn*, s. abandonnement, renoncement, m.
deride, *dĕrīd'*, v. a. railler.
derider, *dĕrī'dĕr*, s. moqueur, railleur, m.
derision, *dĕrĭzh'ŭn*, s. dérision, f.
derisive, *dĕrī'sĭv*, a. (-ly, ad.) dérisoire|| par dérision.
derivable, *dĕrī'vā bl*, a. dérivable.
derivation, *dĕrĭvā'shŭn*, s. dérivation, f. || source, f. || détour, m.
derivative, *dĕrĭv'ā tĭv*, s. (gr.) dérivé, m.
derivative, *dĕrĭv'ā tĭv*, a. dérivé de || -ly, ad. par dérivation.
derive, *dĕrīv'*, v. a. & n. dériver || provenir, procéder.
derogate, *dĕr'ōgāt*, v. a. & n. déroger.
derogation, *dĕr'ōgā'shŭn*, s. dérogation || diffamation, f. || atteinte, f.
derogatory, *dĕrŏg'ā tĕr ĭ*, a. dérogatoire.
derrick, *dĕr'rĭk*, s. martinet, m.
dervish, *dĕr'vĭsh*, s. dervis, m.
descant, *dĕs'kănt*, s. contrepoint, m. || chanson, f. [vaguer.
descant, *dĕs kănt'*, v. n. discourir || divaguer.
descend, *dĕsĕnd'*, v. a. & n. descendre || faire une irruption || tirer son origine de.
descendant, *dĕsĕn'dănt*, s. descendant, m.
descendent, *dĕsĕn'dĕnt*, a. issu de.
descent, *dĕsĕnt'*, s. descente, f. || origine, f. || invasion, f. || descendants, m. pl., postérité, f.
describe, *dĕskrīb'*, v. a. décrire, dépeindre.
description, *dĕskrĭp'shŭn*, s. description, f. || to beggar ~, rendre toute description impossible.
descriptive, *dĕskrĭp'tĭv*, a. (-ly, ad.) descriptif || d'une manière descriptive.
descry, *dĕskrī'*, v. a. découvrir, apercevoir.
desecrate, *dĕs'ēkrāt*, v. a. profaner.
desecration, *dĕs ēkrā'shŭn*, s. profanation, f.
desert, *dĕz'ĕrt*, s. désert, m., solitude, f.
desert, *dĕzĕrt'*, s. dessert, m. || mérite, m.
desert, *dĕzĕrt'*, v. a. déserter || abandonner, délaisser.
desert, *dĕz'ĕrt*, a. désert, solitaire.
deserter, *dĕzĕrt'ĕr*, s. déserteur, m.
desertion, *dĕzĕr'shŭn*, s. désertion, f.
deserve, *dĕzĕrv'*, v. a. mériter, être digne.
deservedly, *dĕzĕr'vĕdlĭ*, ad. à juste titre.
deserving, *dĕzĕr'vĭng*, a. méritoire, de mérite. [manquer.
desiderate, *dĕsĭd'ĕrāt*, v. a. avoir besoin,
desideratum, *dĕsĭdĕrā'tŭm*, s. chose nécessaire, f., desideratum, m.
design, *dĕzīn'*, s. dessein, m., intention, f. || plan, motif, m.
design, *dĕzīn'*, v. a. dessiner || se proposer, avoir l'intention || destiner || concevoir.
designate, *dĕz'ĭgnāt*, v. a. désigner, indiquer, distinguer.
designation, *dĕzĭgnā'shŭn*, s. désignation, f. || destination, f. [exprès.
designedly, *dĕzī'nĕdlĭ*, ad. à propos,

designer, *dĕzīn'ĕr*, s. auteur, inventeur, m. || machinateur, m. || dessinateur, m.
designing, *dĕzīn'ĭng*, a. (-ly, ad.) insidieux, fourbe || insidieusement.
desirable, *dĕzī'rā bl*, a. désirable, souhaitable.
desirably, *dĕzī'rā blĭ*, ad. à souhait.
desire, *dĕzīr'*, s. désir, m., envie, f.
desire, *dĕzīr'*, v. a. désirer, souhaiter || prier. [-ly, ad. ardemment.
desirous, *dĕzī'rŭs*, a. désireux, avide ||
desist, *dĕzĭst'*, v. n. se désister de, cesser.
desistance, *dĕzĭst'ăns*, s. cessation, f. || (jur.) désistement, m. [chaire, f.
desk, *dĕsk*, s. pupitre, m. || lutrin, m.
desolate, *dĕs'ōlāt*, v. a. désoler, dépeupler.
desolate, *dĕs'ōlāt*, a. désolé || solitaire || triste || ruiné. [mélancolie, f.
desolation, *dĕs ōlā'shŭn*, s. désolation, f.
despair, *dĕspār'*, s. désespoir, f.
despair, *dĕspār'*, v. n. désespérer (de).
despairingly, *dĕspār'ĭng lĭ*, ad. désespérément.
despatch, *dĕspăch'*, s. expédition, diligence, f. || dépêche, f. || ~-boat, s. aviso, m. || ~-box, s. buvard de voyage, m.
despatch, *dĕspăch'*, v. a. dépêcher, expédier.
desperado, *dĕspĕrā'dō*, s. désespéré, m.
desperate, *dĕs'pĕrāt*, a. (-ly, ad.) désespéré(ment) || téméraire || furieux || terrible(ment) || en furieux.
desperation, *dĕs pĕrā'shŭn*, s. désespoir, m.
despicable, *dĕs'pĭkā bl*, a. méprisable, vil.
despicably, *dĕs'pĭkā blĭ*, ad. dédaigneusement.
despise, *dĕspīz'*, v.a. mépriser, dédaigner.
despite, *dĕspīt'*, s. dépit, m., malice, f.
despite, *dĕspīt'*, pr. (in ~ of) en dépit de.
despoil, *dĕspŏyl'*, v.a. dépouiller, priver de.
despond, *dĕspŏnd'*, v. n. désespérer, perdre courage, s'abattre. [m.
despondency, *dĕspŏn'dĕn sĭ*, s. désespoir,
despot, *dĕs'pŏt*, s. despote, tyran, m.
despotic, *dĕspŏt'ĭk*, a. (-ally, ad.) despotique(ment).
despotism, *dĕs'pōtĭzm*, s. despotisme, m.
dessert, *dĕz zĕrt'*, s. dessert, m. [f.
destination, *dĕs tĭnā'shŭn*, s. destination.
destine, *dĕs'tĭn*, v. a. destiner (à) || désigner, marquer.
destiny, *dĕs'tĭnĭ*, s. destinée, f., destin, m.
destitute, *dĕs'tĭtūt*, a. abandonné || privé de.
destitution, *dĕs tĭtū'shŭn*, s. délaissement, dénûment, m. || indigence, f.
destroy, *dĕstrŏy'*, v. a. détruire, dévaster, exterminer || tuer.
destructible, *dĕstrŭk'tĭ bl*, a. destructible
destruction, *dĕstrŭk'shŭn*, s. destruction, perdition, f.
destructive, *dĕstrŭk'tĭv*, a. destructif, pernicieux || -ly, ad. d'une manière destructive. [rompus.
desultorily, *dĕs'ŭltĕr ĭlĭ*, ad. à bâtons

desultoriness, *dĕs'ŭl tĕr ĭ nĕs,* s. décousu, défaut de méthode || manque d'esprit de suite, m.   [suite.

desultory, *dĕs'ŭl tĕ ĭ,* a. décousu, sans

detach, *dĕ tăch',* v. a. détacher, séparer.

detached, *dĕ tacht',* a. (of houses) entouré de jardins.   [tachement, m.

detachment, *dĕ tăch'mĕnt,* s. (mil.) détachement, m. || –s, pl. particularités,

detail, *dĕ tăl'* ou *dĕ'tăl,* s. détail, m. || (Am.) recrutement, m. || –s, pl. particularités,

detail, *dĕ'tăl',* v. a. détailler.   [f. pl.

detain, *dĕ tăn',* v. a. détenir, retenir, retarder, arrêter.

detect, *dĕ tĕkt',* v. a. découvrir || distinguer.

detection, *dĕ tĕk'shŭn,* s. découverte, f.

detective, *dĕ tĕk'tiv,* s. agent de la police secrète, m.   [emprisonnement, m.

detention, *dĕ tĕn'shŭn,* s. détention, f., **deter,** *dĕ tĕr',* v. a. détourner, éffrayer, décourager.

deterge, *dĕ tĕrj',* v. a. déterger, nettoyer.

deteriorate, *dĕ tē'rĭ ō rāt,* v. a. détériorer.

deterioration, *dĕ tē rĭ ō rā'shŭn,* s. détérioration, f.   [se déterminer.

determinable, *dĕ tĕr'mĭ nă bl,* a. qui peut

determinate, *dĕ tĕr'mĭ nāt,* a. déterminé, décidé, décisif, résolu || –ly, ad. positivement, absolument.

determination, *dĕ tĕr mĭ nā'shŭn,* s. détermination, décision, f.

determinative, *dĕ tĕr'mĭ nā tiv,* a. déterminant.   [miner, fixer, décider.

determine, *dĕ tĕr'min,* v. a. & n. déterminer.

detest, *dĕ tĕst',* v. a. détester, abhorrer.

detestable, *dĕ tĕs'tá bl,* a. détestable, abominable.   [ment

detestably, *dĕ tĕs'tá blĭ,* ad. détestablement.

detestation, *dĕ tĕs tă'shŭn,* s. détestation, exécration, f.

dethrone, *dĕ thrōn',* v. a. détrôner.

dethronement, *dĕ thrōn'mĕnt,* s. détrônement, m.   [fulminer.

detonate, *dĕt'ō năt,* v. n. (chem.) détoner ||

detour, *dĕ tōr',* s. détour, m.

detract, *dĕ trăkt',* v. a. déroger || détracter.

detracter, *dĕ trăk'tĕr,* s. détracteur, médisant, m.

detraction, *dĕ trăk'shŭn,* s. détraction, médisance, f.   [perte, f.

detriment, *dĕt'rĭ mĕnt,* s. détriment, m.,

detrimental, *dĕt rĭ mĕn'tăl,* s. (fam.) parti non avantageux, m.   [ciable, nuisible.

detrimental, *dĕt rĭ mĕn'tăl,* a. préjudi-

deuce, *dūs,* s. deux || diantre, diable, m.

devastate, *dĕv'ás tăt,* v. a. dévaster.

devastation, *dĕv ás tă'shŭn,* s. dévastation, f.

develop, *dĕ vĕl'ŏp,* v. a. développer.

deviate, *dĕ'vĭ āt,* v. n. dévier, s'égarer.

deviation, *dĕ vĭ ā'shŭn,* s. déviation, f., égarement, m.   [projet, m. || devise, f.

device, *dĕ vīs',* s. invention, f., expédient,

devil, *dĕv'l,* s. diable, m. || printer's –, s. galopin de typographie, m. || blue –s, s. pl. spleen, m.

devil, *dĕv'l,* v. a. faire cuire sur le gril avec du poivre et de la moutarde.

---

devilish, *dĕv'l ĭsh,* a. (–ly, ad.) diabolique(ment).

devilment, *dĕv'l mĕnt,* s. importunité, f.

devilry, *dĕv'l rĭ,* s. diablerie, f.

devious, *dĕ'vĭ ŭs,* a. (–ly, ad.) déviant, écarté || dans l'égarement.   [léguer.

devise, *dĕ vīz',* v. a. & n. inventer, imaginer ||

deviser, *dĕ vī'zĕr,* s. inventeur, m.

devisor, *dĕ vī'sĕr,* s. testateur, m.

devoid, *dĕ vŏyd',* a. vide, exempt, privé de.

devolve, *dĕ vŏlv',* v. a. & n. dérouler || transmettre || tomber en partage, échoir.

devote, *dĕ vōt',* v. a. dévouer, dédier || maudire, exécrer.   [ment.

devotedly, *dĕ vō'tĕd lĭ,* ad. avec dévouement, m.

devotedness, *dĕ vō'tĕd nĕs,* s. dévouement, m.

devotee, *dĕv'ō tē,* s. bigot, faux dévot, m.

devotion, *dĕ vō'shŭn,* s. dévotion, f. || offrande, f.   [gieux.

devotional, *dĕ vō'shŭn ăl,* a. dévot, reli-

devour, *dĕ vōŭr',* v. a. dévorer || engloutir.

devout, *dĕ vŏwt',* a. (–ly, ad.) dévot(ement) || pieux, religieux.   [f.

devoutness, *dĕ vŏwt'nĕs,* s. dévotion, piété,

dew, *dū,* s. rosée, f. || evening ~, serein, m. || ~drop, s. goutte de rosée, f.

dewlap, *dū'lăp,* s. fanon, m.

dewy, *dū'ĭ,* a. couvert de rosée.

dexter, *dĕk'stĕr,* a. droit || dextre.   [f.

dexterity, *dĕk stĕr'ĭ tĭ,* s. dextérité, adresse,

dexterous, *dĕk'stĕr ŭs,* a. (–ly, ad.) adroit (ement) || habile, expert.

dextrine, *dĕk'strĭn,* s. amidine, f.

diabetes, *dī ă bē'tēz,* s. diabétès, m.

diabolic(al), *dī ă bŏl'ĭk (ăl),* a. (–ly, ad.) diabolique(ment).

diachylon, *dī ăk'ĭ lŏn,* s. diachylum, m.

diadem, *dī'ă dĕm,* s. diadème, m.

diagnose, *dī ăg nōz',* v. a. diagnostiquer.

diagnosis, *dī ăg nō'sĭs,* s. diagnose, m.

diagnostic, *dī ăg nŏs'tĭk,* s. (méd.) diagnostic, m. || –s, pl. diagnostique, f.

diagonal, *dī ăg'ō năl,* s. diagonale, f.

diagonal, *dī ăg'ō năl,* a. (–ly, ad.) diagonal (ement).   [figure, f.

diagram, *dī'ă grăm,* s. diagramme, m. ||

dial, *dī'ăl,* s. cadran, m. || ~-plate, s. cadran, m.

dialect, *dī'ă lĕkt,* s. dialecte, m.

dialectic(al), *dī ă lĕk'tĭk (ăl),* a. logique.

dialogue, *dī'ă lŏg,* s. dialogue, m.

diameter, *dī ăm'ĕ tĕr,* s. diamètre, m.

diametrical, *dī ă mĕt'rĭ kăl,* a. (–ly, ad.) diamétral(ement).

diamond, *dī'ă mŭnd,* s. diamant, m. || (cards) carreau, m. || ~-cement, s. pâte de porcelaine, f. || ~-cutter, s. diamantaire, m.

diaper, *dī'ă pĕr,* s. linge ouvré, damassé, m.

diaper, *dī'ă pĕr,* v. a. diaprer, damasser.

diaphragm, *dī'ă frăm,* s. diaphragme, m.

diarrhœa, *dī ă rē'ă,* s. diarrhée, f.

diary, *dī'ă rĭ,* s. journal, m.

dibble, *dĭb'l,* v. a. planter (avec le plantoir).

dibbler, *dĭb'lĕr,* s. plantoir, m.

---

lăte, hăt, făr, lăw; — hēre, gĕt, hĕr; — mīne, ĭnn; — nō, hŏt, prōve; — hŏw; —

dice, *dīs,* s. (pl. de die) dés, m. pl. || ~-box, s. cornet à dés, m.

dickens! *dĭk'nz,* (the ~!) diantre!

dicky, *dĭk'ĭ,* s. siége de derrière, m. || chemisette, f.

dictate, *dĭk'tāt,* s. règle, f., précepte, m.

dictate, *dĭk'tāt',* v. a. dicter, prescrire, dé-

dictation, *dĭk'tā'shŭn,* s. dictée, f. [clarer.

dictator, *dĭk'tā'tŏr,* s. dictateur, m.

dictatorial, *dĭk'tā'tō'rĭ al,* a. (-ly, ad.) dictatorial || magistral || en dictateur.

dictatorship, *dĭk'tā'tĕr shĭp,* s. dictature || autorité, f.

diction, *dĭk'shŭn,* s. diction, f., style, m.

dictionary, *dĭk'shŭn ĕr ĭ,* s. dictionnaire, m.

didactic, *dĭ dăk'tĭk,* a. didactique. [m.

diddle, *dĭd'l,* v. n. marcher d'un pas incertain, chanceler.

die, *dī,* s. teinture, f., teint, m. || dé, m. || coin (pour frapper la monnaie), m.

die, *dī,* v. n. ir. mourir || expirer || **défaillir** || s'éteindre.

diet, *dī'ĕt,* s. nourriture, f. || diète, f., régime de vie, m. || assemblée politique, f.

diet, *dī'ĕt,* v. a. mettre à la diète || alimenter || v. n. faire diète.

dietary, *dī'ĕ tĕr ĭ,* a. diététique, m. || régime diététique, m.

dietary, *dī'ĕ tĕr ĭ,* a. diététique.

differ, *dĭf'fĕr,* v. n. différer || être dissemblable.

difference, *dĭf'fĕr ĕns,* s. différence, f. || dispute, f., différend, m. || **to split the** ~, départager le différend.

different, *dĭf'fĕr ĕnt,* a. différent, divers || -ly, ad. différemment. [férencier.

differentiate, *dĭf'fĕr ĕn'shĭ āt,* v. a. dif-

difficult, *dĭf'fĭ kŭlt,* a. difficile || pénible.

difficulty, *dĭf'fĭ kŭl tĭ,* s. difficulté, f., obstacle, embarras, m. || objection, f.

diffidence, *dĭf'fĭ dĕns,* s. défiance, f.

diffident, *dĭf'fĭ dĕnt,* a. défiant || -ly, ad. avec défiance.

diffuse, *dĭf'fūz',* v. a. répandre, étendre.

diffuse, *dĭf'fūs',* a. (-ly, ad.) diffus(ément).

diffusion, *dĭf'fū'zhŭn,* s. diffusion, dispersion, propagation, f.

diffusive, *dĭf'fū'sĭv,* a. répandu, dispersé || -ly, ad. diffusément.

dig, *dĭg,* v. a. creuser, bêcher.

digest, *dĭ jĕst',* v. a. & n. digérer, faire la digestion || ranger || rédiger || suppurer.

digester, *dĭ jĕs'tĕr,* s. (chem.) digesteur || remède digestif, m. [digéré.

digestible, *dĭ jĕs'tĭ bl,* a. susceptible d'être

digestion, *dĭ jĕs'tyŭn,* s. digestion, f.

digestive, *dĭ jĕs'tĭv,* a. digestif, m.

digger, *dĭg'gĕr,* s. piocheur, m.

diggings, *dĭg'gĭngs,* s. pl. exploitation de gisements aurifères, f. pl.

digit, *dĭj'ĭt,* s. doigt (mesure), m. || nombre exprimé par un seul chiffre, m.

dignified, *dĭg'nĭ fīd,* a. plein de dignité, digne. [dignité || honorer.

dignify, *dĭg'nĭ fī,* v. a. élever à quelque

dignitary, *dĭg'nĭ tĕr ĭ,* s. dignitaire, m.

dignity, *dĭg'nĭ tĭ,* s. dignité, f., rang, m.

digress, *dĭ grĕs',* v. n. faire une digression.

digression, *dĭ grĕsh'ŭn* s. digression, f., écart, m.

digressive, *dĭ grĕs'sĭv,* a. digressif.

dike, *dīk,* s. fossé, canal, m., digue, f.

dilapidate, *dĭ lăp'ĭ dāt,* v. a. dilapider || démolir. [tion, f.

dilapidation, *dĭ lăp'ĭ dā'shŭn,* s. dilapida-

dilate, *dĭ lāt',* v. a. & n. dilater, étendre || se dilater, s'étendre. [tards, des délais.

dilatorily, *dĭl'ă tĕr ĭ lĭ,* ad. avec des re-

dilatory, *dĭl'ă tĕr ĭ,* a. dilatoire, temporisateur.

dilemma, *dĭ lĕm'mă,* s. dilemme, m.

dilettante, *dĭl'ĕ tăn tā,* a. d'amateur.

diligence, *dĭl'ĭ jĕns,* s. diligence (also as coach), f.

diligent, *dĭl'ĭ gĕnt,* a. diligent, assidu, prompt || -ly, ad. diligemment.

dilly-dally, *dĭl'lĭ dăl'lĭ,* v. n. lanterner.

dilute, *dĭ lōt',* v. a. délayer, détremper.

dilution, *dĭ lō'shŭn,* s. délayement, m.

dim, *dĭm,* v. a. offusquer, éblouir.

dim, *dĭm,* a. ayant la vue trouble || sombre, obscur || -ly, ad. obscurément, confusément, indistinctement.

dime, *dīm,* s. (Am.) pièce de dix "cents" (environ 50 centimes). [étendue, f.

dimension, *dĭ mĕn'shŭn,* s. dimension,

diminish, *dĭ mĭn'ĭsh,* v. a. & n. diminuer, amoindrir.

diminution, *dĭm'ĭ nū'shŭn,* s. diminution, dégradation, f., dénigrement, m. [m.

diminutive, *dĭ mĭn'ū tĭv,* s. (gr.) diminutif.

diminutive, *dĭ mĭn'ū tĭv,* a. petit, chétif || -ly, ad. en petit || désavantageusement.

dimity, *dĭm'ĭ tĭ,* s. basin, m.

dimness, *dĭm'nĕs,* s. obscurcissement de la vue, m. || couleur terne, f. || faiblesse, f. || stupidité, f.

dimple, *dĭm'pl,* s. fossette, f. [se plisser.

dimple, *dĭm'pl,* v. n. former des fossettes,

din, *dĭn,* s. bruit, tintamarre, m.

din, *dĭn,* v. a. étourdir.

dine, *dīn,* v. a. & n. donner à dîner || dîner.

diner-out, *dī'nĕr ŏwt,* s. habitué de restaurant, m. || repas-assiette, m.

ding-dong, *dĭng'dŏng,* s. din-dan, m.

dingey, *dĭng'gĭ,* s. youyou, cri de guerre,

dingy, *dĭn'jĭ,* a. sombre, sale. [m.

dining, *dī'nĭng;* ~-hall, ~-room, s. salle à manger, f. || réfectoire, m.

dinner, *dĭn'nĕr,* ~-party, s. dîné, dîner, m. || ~-time, s. heure du dîner, f. || ~-waggon, s. servante, f.

dint, *dĭnt,* s. coup, m., force, violence, f. || marque, f. || empreinte, f. || by ~ of, à coups de, à force de.

diocese, *dī'ă sĕs,* s. diocèse, m.

dip, *dĭp,* s. chandelle à la baguette, f. || plumée, f. [foncer, percer.

dip, *dĭp,* v. a. & n. tremper, plonger || s'en-

diphtheria, *dĭf thĕ'rĭ ă,* s. diphthérite, f.

diphthong, *dĭf'thŏng,* s. diphthongue, f.

diploma, *dĭ plō'mă,* s. diplôme, m.

diplomacy, *dĭ plō'mă sĭ,* s. diplomatie, f.

diplomatic, *dĭp lō măt'ĭk,* a. diplomatique.

---

bôy; — fŏŏt, tŭbe, tŭb. || chair, joy; — game, yes; — soul, zeal; — thing, there.

diplomatist, *dĭp´lō mät´ĭst,* s. diplomate.
dipper, *dĭp´pẽr,* s. plongeur, m.   [m.
dire, *dīr,* a. terrible, affreux, hideux.
direct, *dĭ rĕkt´,* v. a. diriger, régler ǁ ordonner ǁ adresser.
direct, *dĭ rĕkt´,* a. (-ly, ad.) direct(ement) ǁ droit ǁ clair ǁ tout de suite.
direction, *dĭ rĕk´shŭn,* s. direction, f., règlement, commandement, m. ǁ but, m. ǁ adresse, f.   [m. ǁ droiture, f.
directness, *dĭ rĕkt´nĕs,* s. caractère direct.
director, *dĭ rĕk´tẽr,* s. directeur, m.
directory, *dĭ rĕk´tẽr ĭ,* s. directoire, m. ǁ livre d'adresses, m.
directress, *dĭ rĕk´trĕs,* s. directrice, f.
direful, *dīr´fŏŏl,* a. *vide* dire.
dirge, *dẽrj,* s. chant funèbre, m.
dirigible, *dĭr´ĭ jĭbl,* a. dirigeable.
dirk, *dẽrk,* s. dague, f.
dirt, *dẽrt,* s. boue, fange, f.
dirtiness, *dẽr´tĭ nĕs,* s. saleté, f. ǁ vilen e, f.
dirty, *dẽr´tĭ,* v. a. crotter, souiller, salir.
dirty, *dẽr´tĭ,* a. sale, crotté ǁ bas, vilain.
disability, *dĭs ă bĭl´ĭ tĭ,* s. incapacité, impuissance, f.
disable, *dĭs ā´bl,* v. a. rendre incapable, énerver ǁ désemparer (un vaisseau).
disabuse, *dĭs ă būz´,* v. a. désabuser, détromper.   [accoutumer.
disaccustom, *dĭs ăk kŭs´tŭm,* v. a. désdisadvantage, *dĭs ăd văn´tāj,* s. désavantage, m.   [avantager.
disadvantage, *dĭs ăd văn´tāj,* v. a. désdisadvantageous, *dĭs ăd văn tā´jŭs,* a. désavantageux ǁ **-ly,** ad. désavantageusement.   [contenter.
disaffect, *dĭs ăf fĕkt´,* v. a. indisposer, médisaffection, *dĭs ăf fĕk´shŭn,* s. désaffection, aversion, f.   [s'accorder avec.
disagree, *dĭs ă grē´,* v. n. différer ǁ ne pas disagreeable, *dĭs ă grē´ă bl,* a. désagréable.   [agréablement.
disagreeably, *dĭs ă grē´ă blĭ,* ad. désdisagreement, *dĭs ă grē´mĕnt,* s. désaccord, m., brouillerie, f.
disallow, *dĭs ăl lŏŭ´,* v. a. & n. défendre ǁ désapprouver, rejeter.
disappear, *dĭs ăp pēr´,* v. n. disparaître.
disappearance, *dĭs ăp pēr´ăns,* s. disparition, f.
disappoint, *dĭs ăp pŏÿnt´,* v. a. désappointer, frustrer, tromper, désillusionner.
disappointment, *dĭs ăp pŏÿnt´mĕnt,* s. désappointement, m., mauvaise réussite, contrariété, f.
disapprobation, *dĭs ăp prŏ bā´shŭn,* disapproval, *dĭs ăp prŏ´văl,* s. désapprobation, f., blâme, m.   [prouver.
disapprove, *dĭs ăp prŏv´,* v. a. désapdisarm, *dĭs ärm´,* v. a. désarmer.
disarmament, *dĭs ärm´ă mĕnt,* s. désarmement, m.
disarrange, *dĭs är rānj´,* v. a. déranger.
disarray, *dĭs är rā´,* s. désordre, m.
disarray, *dĭs är rā´,* v. a. mettre en désordre, déshabiller.   [m.
disaster, *dĭz ăs´tẽr,* s. désastre, malheur,

disastrous, *dĭz ăs´trŭs,* a. désastreux, funeste ǁ **-ly,** ad. désastreusement.
disavow, *dĭs ă vŏŭ´,* v. a. désavouer, dénier.
disavowal, *dĭs ă vŏŭ´ăl,* s. désaveu, m.
disband, *dĭs bănd´,* v. a. & n. licencier, congédier ǁ se disperser.   [avocats.
disbar, *dĭs bär´,* v. a. rayer du tableau des disbelief, *dĭs bĕ lēf´,* s. incrédulité, f.
disbelieve, *dĭs bĕ lēv´,* v. a. ne pas croire.
disbeliever, *dĭs bĕ lē´vẽr,* s. incrédule, m.
disburden, *dĭs bẽr´dn,* v. a. décharger ǁ (fig.) débarrasser.   [penser.
disburse, *dĭs bẽrs´,* v. a. débourser, dédisbursement, *dĭs bẽrs´mĕnt,* s. déboursement, m. ǁ **-s,** pl. déboursés, m. pl.
disc, *dĭsk,* s. disque, m.
discard, *dĭs kärd,* s. carte écartée, f.
discard, *dĭs kärd´,* v. a. congédier, renvoyer ǁ écarter.
discern, *dĭz zẽrn´,* v. a. discerner, découvrir.
discernible, *dĭz zẽrn´ĭ bl,* a. perceptible, visible.
discerning, *dĭz zẽrn´ĭng,* a. judicieux, pénétrant ǁ **-ly,** ad. judicieusement.
discernment, *dĭz zẽrn´mĕnt,* s. discernement, m.
discharge, *dĭs chärj´,* s. décharge, f., affranchissement, m. ǁ élargissement, m. ǁ écoulement, m. ǁ absolution, f. ǁ acquit, congé, m.
discharge, *dĭs chärj´,* v. a. & n. décharger, débarquer ǁ débarrasser ǁ désarmer ǁ délier, acquitter ǁ remplir, exécuter ǁ détruire ǁ congédier ǁ se décharger ǁ se dissiper ǁ **to effect a ~,** opérer une libération.
disciple, *dĭs sī´pl,* s. disciple, élève, m.
disciplinarian, *dĭs´ sĭ plĭn ā´rĭ ăn,* s. personne stricte sur la discipline, f. ǁ (mil.) instructeur, m. ǁ presbytérien, m.
disciplinary, *dĭs´ sĭ plĭn ẽr´ĭ,* a. de discipline.
discipline, *dĭs´ sĭ plĭn,* s. discipline, f., règlement, m., soumission, f. ǁ science, f.
discipline, *dĭs´ sĭ plĭn,* v. a. discipliner, élever.   [nier.
disclaim, *dĭs klām´,* v. a. désavouer, redisclaimer, *dĭs klām´ẽr,* s. dénégation, f.
disclose, *dĭs klōz´,* v. a. découvrir, révéler.
disclosure, *dĭs klō´zhŏŏr,* s. découverte, révélation, f.   [ment de couleur, m.
discoloration, *dĭs kŭl ẽr ā´shŭn,* s. changediscolour, *dĭs kŭl´ẽr,* v. a. décolorer, déteindre ǁ **to become -ed,** se décolorer.
discomfit, *dĭs kŭm´fĭt,* v. a. défaire, mettre en déroute.
discomfiture, *dĭs kŭm´fĭt ŭr,* s. défaite, f.
discomfort, *dĭs kŭm´fẽrt,* s. chagrin, m., affliction, f.   [affliger, chagriner.
discompose, *dĭs kŏm pōz´,* v. a. déranger ǁ discomposure, *dĭs.kŏm pō´zhŏŏr,* s. désordre, dérangement, m. ǁ inquiétude, f.
disconcert, *dĭs kŏn sẽrt´,* v. a. déconcerter, déranger.   [séparer.
disconnect, *dĭs kŏn nĕkt´,* v. a. désunir, disconnection, *dĭs kŏn nĕk´shŭn,* s. désunion, f.

disconsolate, *dĭs kŏn′ sō lät,* a. (-ly, ad.) inconsolable(ment).

disconsolateness, *dĭs kŏn′ sō lät nĕs,* s. désolation, f. [ment, chagrin, m.

discontent, *dĭs kŏn tĕnt′,* s. mécontentement || avec mécontentement

discontented, *dĭs kŏn tĕnt′ĕd,* a. (-ly, ad.) mécontent || interrompre || se désunir.

discontinue, *dĭs kŏn tĭn′ ū,* v. a. & n. discontinuer, interrompre || se désunir.

discord, *dĭs′ kawrd,* **discordance,** *dĭs-kŏr′ dăns,* s. discorde, dissension, f.

discordant, *dĭs kŏr′ dănt,* a. discordant, contraire || -ly, ad. d'une manière discordante. [m.

discount, *dĭs′ kŏwnt,* s. escompte, rabais, [m.

discount, *dĭs kŏwnt′,* v. a. escompter, rabattre.

discourage, *dĭs kŭr′ ĭj,* v. a. décourager, intimider || dissuader.

discouragement, *dĭs kŭr′ ĭj mĕnt,* s. découragement, m. [m. || traité, m.

discourse, *dĭs kŏrs′,* s. discours, entretien,

discourse, *dĭs kŏrs′,* v. a. & n. parler, discuter || discourir, s'entretenir, raisonner.

discursive, *dĭs kŏr′ sĭv,* a. discursif, dialogué. [impoli || incivil(ement).

discourteous, *dĭs kŭr′ tŭs,* a. (-ly, ad.)

discourtesy, *dĭs kŭr′ tĕ sĭ,* s. incivilité, f.

discover, *dĭs kŭv′ ĕr,* v. a. découvrir || divulguer. [découvrir || visible.

discoverable, *dĭs kŭv′ ĕr ă bl,* a. qu'on peut

discoverer, *dĭs kŭv′ ĕr ĕr,* s. qui découvre|| espion, m.

discovery, *dĭs kŭv′ ĕr ĭ,* s. découverte, f.

discredit, *dĭs krĕd′ ĭt,* s. discrédit, m., ignominie, f. [honorer.

discredit, *dĭs krĕd′ ĭt,* v. a. discréditer, déshonorer.

discreditable, *dĭs krĕd′ ĭt ă bl,* a. déshonorant, compromettant. [crètement.

discreet, *dĭs krēt′,* a. discret || -ly, ad. dis-

discrepancy, *dĭs krĕp′ ăn sĭ,* s. différence || opposition, f. [traire.

discrepant, *dĭs krĕp′ ănt,* a. différent, con-

discretion, *dĭs krĕsh′ ŭn,* s. discrétion, f.

discretionary, *dĭs krĕsh′ ŭn ĕr ĭ,* a. discrétionnaire, illimité.

discriminate, *dĭs krĭm′ ĭ nät,* v. a. discerner, distinguer, séparer.

discriminate, *dĭs krĭm′ ĭ nät,* a. distingué, différencié || -ly, ad. distinctement.

discrimination, *dĭs krĭm ĭ nä′ shŭn,* s. distinction, marque distinctive, f.

discriminative, *dĭs krĭm′ ĭ nä tĭv,* a. distinctif.

discrown, *dĭs krŏwn′,* v. a. découronner.

discursive, *dĭs kŏr′ sĭv,* a. vagabond || argumentant || -ly, ad. par voie de raisonnement. [agiter.

discuss, *dĭs kŭs′,* v. a. discuter, examiner,

discussion, *dĭs kŭsh′ ŭn,* s. discussion, f., examen, m.

disdain, *dĭs dān′,* s. dédain, mépris, m.

disdain, *dĭs dān′,* v. a. dédaigner, mépriser. [-ly, ad. avec dédain.

disdainful, *dĭs dān′ fōōl,* a. dédaigneux ||

disease, *dĭz ēz′,* s. maladie, f., mal, m.

diseased, *dĭz ēzd′,* a. malade.

disembarcation, *dĭs ĕm bâr kā′ shŭn,* s. débarquement, m. [quer.

disembark, *dĭs ĕm bârk′,* v. a. & n. débarquer.

disembarrass, *dĭs ĕm bâr′ răs,* v. a. débarrasser. [porer, licencier.

disembody, *dĭs ĕm bŏd′ ĭ,* v. a. désincorporer.

disembowel, *dĭs ĕm bŏw′ ĕl,* v. a. désentrailler. [chanter.

disenchant, *dĭs ĕn chânt′,* v. a. désenchanter.

disenchantment, *dĭs ĕn chânt′ mĕnt,* s désenchantement, m.

disencumber, *dĭs ĕn kŭm′ bĕr,* v. a. débarrasser, dégager.

disencumbrance, *dĭs ĕn kŭm′ brăns,* s. débarrassement, dégagement, m.

disengage, *dĭs ĕn gâj′,* v. a. & n. dégager, débarrasser || se dégager || -d, a. vacant, libre. [ment, m., liberté, f.

disengagement, *dĭs ĕn gâj′ mĕnt,* s. dégagement.

disentangle, *dĭs ĕn tâng′ gl,* v. a. dépêtrer || débrouiller, débarrasser (de).

disfavour, *dĭs fā′ vĕr,* s. défaveur, disgrace, f. [veur sur.

disfavour, *dĭs fā′ vĕr,* v. a. jeter la défaveur.

disfiguration, *dĭs fĭg ū râ′ shŭn,* **disfigurement,** *dĭs fĭg′ ĕr mĕnt,* s. défigurement, m. || difformité, f. [former.

disfigure, *dĭs fĭg′ ĕr,* v. a. défigurer, déformer.

disfranchise, *dĭs frăn′ chĭz,* v. a. ôter la franchise *or* les privilèges. [dégorger.

disgorge, *dĭs gŏrj′,* v. a. vomir || (fig.) se

disgrace, *dĭs grās′,* s. disgrâce, défaveur|| infamie, honte, f. [honorer.

disgrace, *dĭs grās′,* v. a. disgracier || dés-

disgraceful, *dĭs grās′ fōōl,* a. honteux, ignominieux || -ly, ad. honteusement.

disguise, *dĭs gĭz′,* s. déguisement, masque, m., dissimulation, f.

disguise, *dĭs gĭz′,* v. a. déguiser, masquer.

disgust, *dĭs gŭst′,* s. dégoût, m., aversion, f.

disgust, *dĭs gŭst′,* v. a. dégoûter.

dish, *dĭsh,* s. plat, m., assiette, f. || ~-cloth, ~-clout, s. torchon de cuisine, m. || ~-cover, s. couvre-plat, m. || ~-warmer, s. réchaud, m.

dish, *dĭsh,* v. a. (~ up) servir, dresser.

dishearten, *dĭs hâr′ tn,* v. a. décourager.

dishevel, *dĭ shĕv′ ĕl,* v. a. décheveler || -led, échevelé || (fig.) en désordre.

dishful, *dĭsh′ fōōl,* s. plat, m.

dishonest, *dĭs ŏn′ ĕst,* a. (-ly, ad.) malhonnête(ment).

dishonesty, *dĭs ŏn′ ĕs tĭ,* s. improbité, f.

dishonour, *dĭs ŏn′ ĕr,* s. déshonneur, m.

dishonour, *dĭs ŏn′ ĕr,* v. a. déshonorer || (com.) ne pas faire honneur à. [rant.

dishonourable, *dĭs ŏn′ ĕr ă bl,* a. déshonorant.

dishonourably, *dĭs ŏn′ ĕr ă blĭ,* ad. ignominieusement.

disillusion, *dĭs ĭl lō′ zhŭn,* v. a. désillusionner.

disinclination, *dĭs ĭn klī nā′ shŭn,* s. manque d'affection, m., aversion, f.

disincline, *dĭs ĭn klīn′,* v. a. indisposer (pour). [parfumer.

disinfect, *dĭs ĭn fĕkt′,* v. a. désinfecter ||

disinfectant, *dis in fĕk' tănt,* s. désinfectant, m. [tion, f.

disinfection, *dis in fĕk' shŭn,* s. désinfec-

disingenuous, *dis in jĕn' ŭ ŭs,* a. de mauvaise foi, déloyal.

disinherit, *dis in hĕr' it,* v. a. déshériter.

disintegrate, *dis in' tĕ grāt,* v. a. désagréger.

disinter, *dis in tĕr',* v. a. déterrer.

disinterested, *dis in' tĕr ĕs tĕd,* a. désintéressé || —ly, ad. avec désintéressement.

disinterestedness, *dis in' tĕr ĕs tĕd nĕs,* s. désintéressement, m. [mation, f.

disinterment, *din in tĕr' mĕnt,* s. exhumation, f.

disjoin, *dis jŏyn',* v. a. déjoindre, désunir.

disjoint, *dis jŏynt',* v. a. démettre, disloquer, démembrer || **—ed speech,** s. discours décousu, m. [f.

dislike, *dis līk',* s. dégoût, m., répugnance.

dislike, *dis līk',* v. a. ne pas aimer || désapprouver. [placer.

dislocate, *dis' lō kāt,* v. a. disloquer || déplacer.

dislocation, *dis lō kā' shŭn,* s. dislocation, f. || déplacement, m. || **compound ~,** luxation, f.

dislodge, *dis lŏj',* v. a. & n. déplacer || faire sortir de || débucher || (mil.) déloger.

disloyal, *dis lŏy' ăl,* a. (-ly, ad.) déloyal(ement) || perfide.

disloyalty, *dis lŏy' ăl ti,* s. déloyauté, f.

dismal, *diz' măl,* a. triste, funeste, sinistre.

dismantle, *dis măn' tl,* v. a. démanteler || (mar.) désarmer.

dismast, *dis măst',* v. a. démâter.

dismay, *dis mā',* s. épouvante, frayeur, f., découragement, m.

dismay, *dis mā',* v. a. épouvanter || décourager || consterner.

dismember, *dis mĕm' bĕr,* v. a. démembrer || déchirer.

dismiss, *dis mis',* v. a. renvoyer, congédier.

dismissal, *dis mis' săl,* s. démission, f. || renvoi, m.

dismount, *dis mŏwnt',* v. a. & n. démonter, descendre de cheval, mettre pied à terre. [sance, f.

disobedience, *dis ō bē' dĭ ĕns,* s. désobéissance, f.

disobedient, *dis ō bē' dĭ ĕnt,* a. désobéissant.

disobey, *dis ō bā',* v. a. désobéir. [sant.

disoblige, *dis ō blīj',* v. a. désobliger, rendre un mauvais office.

disobliging, *dis ō blī' jing,* a. désobligeant || —ly, ad. désobligeamment.

disobligingness, *dis ō blī' jing nĕs,* s. désobligeance, f. [disposition, f.

disorder, *dis ŏr' dĕr,* s. désordre, m. || indisposition, f.

disorder, *dis ŏr' dĕr* v. a. mettre en désordre, déranger || rendre malade.

disorderly, *dis ŏr' dĕr li,* a. confus, tumultueux || déréglé.

disorganisation, *dis ŏr găn i zā' shŭn,* s. désorganisation, f. [niser.

disorganise, *dis ŏr' găn īz,* v. a. désorganiser.

disown, *dis ōn',* v. a. désavouer, renoncer à.

disparage, *dis păr' āj,* v. a. déprécier, dénigrer || mésallier.

disparagement, *dis păr' āj mĕnt,* s. dés-

bonneur, blâme, m., injure, f. || mésalliance, f. [rence, f.

disparity, *dis păr' i ti,* s. disparité, différence, f.

dispassionate, *dis păsh' ŭn āt,* a. calme || —ly, ad. sans passion.

dispel, *dis pĕl',* v. a. disperser, dissiper.

dispensable, *dis pĕn' să bl,* a. dont on peut se dispenser.

dispensary, *dis pĕn' să ri,* s. dispensaire, m. || **(of hospitals),** pharmacie, f.

dispensation, *dis pĕn să' shŭn,* s. dispensation, f.

dispense, *dis pĕns',* v. a. dispenser, distribuer || exempter || se passer de.

dispeople, *dis pē' pl,* v. a. dépeupler.

disperse, *dis pĕrs',* v. a. disperser, dissiper || distribuer.

dispersion, *dis pĕr' shŭn,* s. dispersion, f.

dispirit, *dis pir' it,* v. a. décourager, intimider.

displace, *dis plās',* v. a. déplacer || destituer.

displant, *dis plănt',* v. a. déplanter, transplanter. [ploiement, étalage, m.

display, *dis plā',* s. exposition, f. || déploiement, étalage, m.

display, *dis plā',* v. a. déployer, étaler || faire parade.

displease, *dis plēz',* v. a. & n. déplaire, fâcher, offenser || —d, fâché, mécontent.

displeasure, *dis plĕzh' ōŏr,* s. déplaisir, m., indignation, f.

disport, *dis pōrt',* v. a. (& n.) (s')amuser.

disposable, *dis pō' ză bl,* a. disponible.

disposal, *dis pō' zăl,* s. disposition, f. || vente, f. || cession, f.

dispose, *dis pōz',* v. a. & n. disposer, diriger, arranger, décider || marchander || contracter || —d, disposé, préparé || porté, incliné || **to be —d of** || à vendre!

disposer, *dis pō' zĕr,* s. dispensateur, m. || ordonnateur, m.

disposition, *dis pō zish' ŭn,* s. disposition, f. || ordre, m., inclination, f. || caractère, m.

dispossess, *dis pŏs ĕs',* v. a. déposséder.

dispraise, *dis prāz',* v. a. blâmer, censurer.

disproof, *dis prōf',* s. réfutation, f.

disproportion, *dis prō pōr' shŭn,* s. disproportion, f.

disproportionate, *dis prō pōr' shŭn āt,* a. (-ly, ad.) disproportionné(ment).

disprove, *dis prōv',* v. a. réfuter, désapprouver. [disputable.

disputable, *dis pū' tă bl* ou *dis' pu tă bl,* a.

disputant, *dis' pu tănt,* s. controvertiste, m.

disputation, *dis pu tā' shŭn,* s. dispute, controverse, f.

disputatious, *dis pu tā' shŭs,* **disputative,** *dis pu' tă tiv,* a. disputeur.

dispute, *dis pūt',* s. dispute, contestation, f.

dispute, *dis pūt',* v. a. & n. disputer || argumenter. [incapacité, f.

disqualification, *dis kwŏl i fi kā' shŭn,* s.

disqualify, *dis kwŏl' i fi,* v. a. rendre incapable. [trouble, m.

disquiet, *dis kwī' ĕt,* s. inquiétude, f.

disquiet, *dis kwī' ĕt,* v. a. inquiéter, troubler.

disquisition, *dis kwi zish' ŭn,* s. recherche, f., examen, m.

disregard, *dĭs rĕ gârd′,* s. manque d'attention, m. ‖ mépris, m.

disregard, *dĭs rĕ gârd′,* v. a. négliger, mépriser.

disregardful, *dĭs rĕ gârd′ fŏŏl,* a. méprisant ‖ -ly, ad. avec mépris.

disrelish, *dĭs rĕl′ĭsh,* s. mauvais goût, dégoût, m.

disrelish, *dĭs rĕl′ĭsh,* v. a. donner un mauvais goût, dégoûter ‖ ne pas aimer.

disrepair, *dĭs rĕ pâr′,* s. délabrement, m.

disreputable, *dĭs rĕp′ ū tă bl,* a. déshonorable. [honneur, f.

disrepute, *dĭs rĕ pūt′,* s. disgrâce, f., déshonneur, m.

disrespect, *dĭs rĕ spĕkt′,* s. manque de respect, m., incivilité, f.

disrespectful, *dĭs rĕ spĕkt′ fŏŏl,* a. irrespectueux ‖ -ly, ad. impoliment.

disrobe, *dĭs rōb′,* v. a. déshabiller, dépouiller. [chirure, f.

disruption, *dĭs rŭp′ shŭn,* s. rupture, déchirure, f.

dissatisfaction, *dĭs săt ĭs făk′ shŭn,* s. mécontentement, m. [fâché.

dissatisfied, *dĭs săt′ ĭs fīd,* a. mécontent,

dissatisfy, *dĭs săt′ ĭs fī,* v. a. mécontenter, déplaire.

dissect, *dĭs sĕkt′,* v. a. disséquer.

dissecting, *dĭs sĕk′ tĭng,* ~-knife, s. scalpel, m. ‖ ~-room, s. amphithéâtre d'anatomie, m. [tomiste, m.

dissector, *dĭs sĕk′ tĕr,* s. disséqueur, anatomiste, m.

dissemble, *dĭs sĕm′ bl,* v. a. & n. dissimuler.

dissembler, *dĭs sĕm′ blĕr,* s. hypocrite, m.

dissemblingly, *dĭs sĕm′ blĭng lĭ,* ad. en hypocrite. [répandre.

disseminate, *dĭs sĕm′ ĭ nāt,* v. a. semer,

dissension, *dĭs sĕn′ shŭn,* s. dissension, discorde, f. [schisme, m.

dissent, *dĭs sĕnt′,* s. dissentiment, m. ‖

dissent, *dĭs sĕnt′,* v. n. différer de sentiment.

Dissenter, *dĭs sĕn′ tĕr,* s. dissident, m.

dissentient, *dĭs sĕn′ shĭ ĕnt,* s. opposant, m. [contraire.

dissentient, *dĭs sĕn′ shĭ ĕnt,* a. différent,

dissertation, *dĭs sĕr tā′ shŭn,* s. dissertation, f. [tacher.

dissever, *dĭs sĕv′ ĕr,* v. a. séparer, dé-

dissidence, *dĭs′ sĭ dĕns,* s. différence d'opinion, f.

dissident, *dĭs′ sĭ dĕnt,* s. dissident, m.

dissimilar, *dĭs sĭm′ ĭ lĕr,* a. dissemblable, hétérogène. [simulation, f.

dissimulation, *dĭs sĭm ū lā′ shŭn,* s. dis-

dissipate, *dĭs′ sĭ pāt,* v. a. dissiper ‖ dépenser. [dispersion, f.

dissipation, *dĭs sĭ pā′ shŭn,* s. dissipation,

dissolubility, *dĭs sŏl ū bĭl′ ĭ tĭ,* s. solubilité, dissolubilité, f.

dissoluble, *dĭs′ sŏl′ ū bl,* a. dissoluble.

dissolute, *dĭs′ sŏ lōt,* a. (-ly, ad.) dissolu (ment) ‖ débauché.

dissolution, *dĭs sŏ lō′ shŭn,* s. dissolution, f. ‖ dérèglement de mœurs, m. ‖ mort, f.

dissolve, *dĭz zŏlv′,* v. a. (& n.) (se) dissoudre ‖ fondre.

dissolving views, *dĭz zŏl′ vĭng vūz,* s. pl. ombres chinoises, f. pl.

dissonance, *dĭs′ sŏ nans,* s. dissonance, f.

dissonant, *dĭs′ sŏ nănt,* a. dissonant.

dissuade, *dĭs swād′,* v. a. dissuader, déconseiller.

dissuasion, *dĭs sŭā′ zhŭn,* s. dissuasion, f.

dissuasive, *dĭs swā′ sĭv,* a. (-ly. ad.) dissuasif ‖ dissuasivement.

dissyllabic, *dĭs sĭl lăb′ ĭk,* a. dissyllabe ‖ dissyllabique.

dissyllable, *dĭs sĭl′ lă bl,* s. dissyllabe, m.

distaff, *dĭs′ tăf,* s. quenouille, f.

distance, *dĭs′ tăns,* s. distance, f., éloignement, m. ‖ respect, m. ‖ réserve, f. ‖ **to keep one's ~,** se tenir à distance ‖ **at a ~,** à quelque distance. [derrière.

distance, *dĭs′ tăns,* v. a. éloigner ‖ laisser

distant, *dĭs′ tănt,* a. éloigné, reculé.

distaste, *dĭs tāst′,* s. dégoût, déplaisir, m. ‖ chagrin, m. [désagréable.

distasteful, *dĭs tāst′ fŏŏl,* a. dégoûtant ‖

distemper, *dĭs tĕm′ pĕr,* s. maladie, f. ‖ mauvaise humeur, f. ‖ détrempe, f.

distemper, *dĭs tĕm′ pĕr,* v. a. rendre malade, déranger.

distend, *dĭs tĕnd′,* v. a. étendre, élargir.

distention, *dĭs tĕn′ shŭn,* s. extension, dilatation, f. ‖ (méd.) distension, f.

distich, *dĭs′ tĭk,* s. distique, m.

distil, *dĭs tĭl′,* v. a. & n. distiller. [f.

distillation, *dĭs tĭl lā′ shŭn,* s. distillation,

distillery, *dĭs tĭl′ lĕr ĭ,* s. distillerie, f.

distinct, *dĭs tĭngkt′,* a. distinct ‖ différent ‖ clair, net.

distinction, *dĭs tĭngk′ shŭn,* s. distinction, f. ‖ différence, f. ‖ séparation, f.

distinctive, *dĭs tĭngk′ tĭv,* a. distinctif ‖ -ly, ad. distinctement. [clarté, f.

distinctness, *dĭs tĭngkt′ nĕs,* s. netteté,

distinguish, *dĭs tĭng′ gwĭsh,* v. a. & n. distinguer, discerner ‖ spécifier.

distinguishable, *dĭs tĭng′ gwĭsh ă bl,* a. qu'on peut distinguer.

distort, *dĭs tôrt′,* v. a. tordre, contourner, défigurer.

distortion, *dĭs tôr′ shŭn,* s. contorsion, grimace, f. ‖ sens forcé, m.

distract, *dĭs trăkt′,* v. a. ir. distraire, détourner ‖ troubler ‖ rendre fou.

distracted, *dĭs trăk′ tĕd,* a. distrait, troublé, fou ‖ **to drive one ~,** rendre qn. fou, faire perdre la tête à qn. ‖ -ly, ad. follement.

distracting, *dĭs trăk′ tĭng,* a. atroce, cruel.

distraction, *dĭs trăk′ shŭn,* s. distraction, f. ‖ dérangement d'esprit, m., folie, f.

distrain, *dĭs trān′,* v. a. saisir ‖ se saisir

distraint, *dĭs trānt′,* s. saisie, f. [de.

distraught, *dĭs trawt′,* a. *vide* distracted.

distress, *dĭs trĕs′,* s. (jur.) saisie, f. ‖ misère, f., malheur, m.

distress, *dĭs trĕs′,* v. a. saisir ‖ réduire à la misère, affliger.

distribute, *dĭs trĭb′ ūt,* v. a. distribuer.

distribution, *dĭs trĭ bū′ shŭn,* s. distribution, f.

distributive, *dĭs trĭb'ŭ tĭv*, a. distributif.

district, *dĭs'trĭkt*, s. district, département, m. || région, f. || ~-office, s. bureau d'arrondissement, m.

distrust, *dĭs trŭst'*, s. méfiance, f., soupçon,

distrust, *dĭs trŭst'*, v. a. se méfier.   [m.

distrustful, *dĭs trŭst'fōŏl*, a. méfiant, défiant || -ly, ad. avec méfiance.

disturb, *dĭs tẽrb'*, v. a. troubler, déranger || empêcher.

disturbance, *dĭs tẽr'băns*, s. trouble, tumulte, m., émeute, f.   [sension, f.

disunion, *dĭs ū'nĭ ŭn*, s. désunion, f. || dis-

disunite, *dĭs ū nīt'*, v. a. & n. désunir || brouiller || se désunir.   [m.

disuse, *dĭs ūs'*, s. désuétude, f., non-usage,

disuse, *dĭs ūz'*, v. a. désaccoutumer.

ditch, *dĭch*, s. fossé, m.

ditch, *dĭch*, v. a. fossoyer.

ditto, *dĭt'tō*, ad. (banque) dito || (com.) idem || ~-suit, complet de même étoffe, m.

ditty, *dĭt'tĭ*, s. chanson, f.

diuretic, *dĭ ū rĕt'ĭk*, a. (med.) diurétique.

diurnal, *dĭ ẽr'năl*, s. journal, m.

diurnal, *dĭ ẽr'năl*, a. diurne, journalier.

divan, *dĭ văn'*, s. divan, m. || conseil, m.

dive, *dĭv*, v. a. & n. plonger, s'enfoncer || ~ into, (fig.) approfondir.

diver, *dī'vẽr*, s. plongeur, m.

diverge, *dĭ vẽrj'*, v. n. diverger.

divergence, *dĭ vẽr'jĕns*, s. divergence, f.

divergent, *dĭ vẽr'jĕnt*, a. divergent.

divers, *dī'vẽrz*, a. divers.

diverse, *dī vẽrs'*, a. (-ly, ad.) divers, différent || en sens divers || différemment.

diversification, *dĭ vẽr sĭ fĭ kā'shŭn*, s. changement, m., variation, f.

diversify, *dĭ vẽr'sĭ fī*, v. a. diversifier, varier.

diversion, *dĭ vẽr'shŭn*, s. diversion, f. || divertissement, m.   [rence, f.

diversity, *dĭ vẽr'sĭ tĭ*, s. diversité, diffé-

divert, *dĭ vẽrt'*, v. a. détourner || divertir, amuser.

divest, *dĭ vĕst'*, v. a. dépouiller.

divide, *dĭ vīd'*, v. a. & n. diviser, partager || se diviser || se désunir.

dividend, *dĭv'ĭ dĕnd*, s. (ar.) dividende, m. || portion, f.   [f.

divination, *dĭv ĭ nā'shŭn*, s. divination,

divine, *dĭ vīn'*, s. ecclésiastique, m.

divine, *dĭ vīn'*, v. a. & n. deviner, présager.

divine, *dĭ vīn'*, a. (-ly, ad.) divin(ement) || céleste.   [plongeur, f.

diving-bell, *dī'vĭng bĕl*, s. cloche de

divining-rod, *dĭ vī'nĭng rŏd*, s. baguette divinatoire, f.

divinity, *dĭ vĭn'ĭ tĭ*, s. divinité, f., dieu, m. || Doctor of ~, docteur en théologie.

divisibility, *dĭ vĭz ĭ bĭl'ĭ tĭ*, s. divisibilité,

divisible, *dĭ vĭz'ĭ bl*, a. divisible.   [f.

division, *dĭ vĭzh'ŭn*, s. division, f. || partage, m. || désunion, f.

divisor, *dĭ vī'zẽr*, s. (ar.) diviseur, m.

divorce, *dĭ vōrs'*, s. divorce, m.

divorce, *dĭ vōrs'*, v. a. divorcer.

divulge, *dĭ vŭlj'*, v. a. divulguer, publier.

dizziness, *dĭz'zĭ nĕs*, s. étourdissement, m.

dizzy, *dĭz'zĭ*, a. étourdi, volage || (things) étourdissant.   [factotum, m.

do, *dō*, s. bruit, vacarme, m. || ~-all, s.

do, *dō*, v. a. & n. ir. faire, agir || terminer, effectuer || to ~ away with, abolir, supprimer, détruire || to ~ good, wrong, faire le bien, le mal || I have done, j'ai fini || to ~ up, plier || empaqueter || to have to ~ with one, avoir à démêler avec || he will have nothing to ~ with it, il n'en veut pas || what's to be done ? que faire ? || how ~ you ~ ? comment vous portez-vous ? || he has done with it, il en a fini || to ~ well by one, en agir bien avec || to ~ for, faire son affaire à || to ~ without, se passer de || ~ I je vous en prie! || will that ~ ? est-ce bien comme cela ? || that will ~, c'est bien.

do, *dō*, ad. *vide* ditto.

docile, *dō'sĭl* ou *dŏs'ĭl*, a. docile.

docility, *dō sĭl'ĭ tĭ*, s. docilité, f.

dock, *dŏk*, s. tronçon, m. || banc des accusés, m. || bassin, m. || chantier, m.

dock, *dŏk*, v. a. écourter.

docket, *dŏk'ĕt*, s. étiquette, f.

docket, *dŏk'ĕt*, v. a. étiqueter.   [m.

dockyard, *dŏk'yārd*, s. arsenal maritime,

doctor, *dŏk'tẽr*, s. docteur, m. || médecin, m. || ~ of laws, docteur en droit, m.

doctor, *dŏk'tẽr*, v. a. médicamenter.

doctorate, *dŏk'tẽr āt*, **doctorship,** *dŏk'tẽr shĭp*, s. doctorat, m.   [tique.

doctrinal, *dŏk'trĭ năl*, a. doctrinal, dogma-

doctrine, *dŏk'trĭn*, s. doctrine, f., enseignement, m., préceptes, m. pl.

document, *dŏk'ū mĕnt*, s. document, m.

dodge, *dŏj*, v. n. tergiverser, biaiser.

dodger, *dŏj'ẽr*, s. chicaneur, m.

doe, *dō*, s. daine, f. || ~-rabbit, s. lapine,

doer, *dō'ẽr*, s. faiseur, m.   [f.

doff, *dŏf*, v. a. ôter, tirer.

dog, *dŏg*, s. chien, m. || chenet, m. || a sad ~, un triste sujet, m. || a sly ~, un fin matois, m. || to go to the ~s, prendre le chemin de l'hôpital || ~-bolt, s. fripon, m. || ~-cart, s. guigue, f. (voiture) || ~-days, s. pl. jours caniculaires, m. pl. || ~-fancier, s. amateur de chiens, m. || ~-fish, s. chien de mer, m. || ~-latin, s. latin de cuisine, m. || ~-rose, s. rose sauvage, églantine, f. || ~'s-ear, s. corne, f., pli, m. || ~-star, s. Canicule, f. || ~-weary, a. très fatigué.

dog, *dŏg*, v. a. guetter, épier.

doge, *dōj*, s. doge, m.

dogged, *dŏg'gĕd*, a. bourru, de mauvaise humeur || -ly, ad. d'un air bourru.

doggedness, *dŏg'gĕd nĕs*, s. mauvaise humeur, f.

doggerel, *dŏg'grĕl*, s. vers burlesques, m. pl.

doggerel, *dŏg'grĕl*, a. mauvais || libre.

doggie, *dŏg'gĭ*, s. toutou, m.

doggish, *dŏg'gĭsh*, a. de chien || brutal.

lāte, hăt, fār, lăw; — hēre, gĕt, hẽr; — mīne, ĭnn; — nō, hŏt, prōve; — hŏw; —

dogma, dŏg'mă, s. dogme, m.
dogmatic(al), dŏg mătʹĭk (ăl), a. (-ly, ad.) dogmatique(ment).
dogmatise, dŏg'mătĭz, v. a. dogmatiser.
doily, dŏyʹlĭ, s. serviette de dessert, f.
doing, dōʹĭng, s. action, f., fait, m., affaire, f.
dole, dōl, s. partage. m. ‖ don, m. [f.
dole, dōl, v. a. distribuer.
doleful, dōlʹfŏŏl, a. (-ly, ad.) triste, lugubre ‖ douloureusement ‖ plaintivement.
doll, dōl, s. poupée, f.
dollar, dŏlʹlĕr, s. dollar, m.
dolphin, dŏlʹfĭn, s. dauphin, m.
dolt, dōlt, s. sot, benêt, m.
doltish, dōltʹĭsh, a. bête, stupide.
domain, dō mānʹ, s. domaine, m.
dome, dōm, s. dôme, m.
domestic, dō mĕsʹtĭk, a. domestique ‖ casanier ‖ intérieur.
domestically, dō mĕsʹtĭ kăl lĭ, ad. dans l'intérieur. [voiser.
domesticate, dō mĕsʹtĭ kāt, v. a. apprivoiser.
domestication, dō mĕs tĭ kāʹshŭn, s. apprivoisement, m.
domicile, dŏmʹĭ sĭl, s. domicile, m.
domicile, dŏmʹĭ sĭl, v. a. domicilier.
domiciled, dŏmʹĭ sĭld, a. domicilié.
domiciliary, dŏmĭ sĭlʹĭ ĕr ĭ, a. domiciliaire. [nante, f.
dominant, dŏmʹĭ nănt, s. (mus.) dominant, dŏmʹĭ nănt, a. (-ly, ad.) (en) dominant.
dominate, dŏmʹĭ nāt, v. a. dominer.
domination, dŏm ĭ nāʹshŭn, s. domination, puissance, f. [triser.
domineer, dŏm ĭ nērʹ, v. n. dominer, maîtriser.
dominion, dō minʹyŭn, s. domination, f. ‖ domaine, territoire, m.
domino, dŏmʹĭ nō, s. domino, m. ‖ camail, m.
Don, dŏn, s. Don (seigneur), m. [m.
don, dŏn, v. a. mettre, vêtir, revêtir.
donation, dō nāʹshŭn, s. donation, f., don, m. [tope!
done, dŭn, v. & a. fait ‖ cuit ‖ ~! soit!
donee, dō nēʹ, s. (jur.) donataire, m.
donkey, dŏngʹkĭ, s. baudet, m.
donor, dōʹnĕr, s. (jur.) donateur, m.
doom, dōm, s. jugement, m. ‖ destin, m.
doom, dōm, v. a. juger, condamner ‖ destiner.
doomsday, dōmzʹdā, s. jour du ~dernier jugement, m. ‖ to wait till ~, attendre sous l'orme.
door, dōr, s. porte, entrée, f. ‖ out of ~s, hors de la maison, dehors ‖ within ~s, à la maison, au logis ‖ folding ~s, porte à deux battants ‖ next ~ to, à la première porte de ‖ next ~ to each other, porte à porte ‖ front ~, street ~, porte d'entrée, de la rue ‖ to turn out of ~s, mettre à la porte ‖ ~-hangings, s. pl. portière, f. ‖ ~-keeper, s. portier, m. ‖ ~-knob, s. bouton de porte fixe, m. ‖ ~-mat, s. paillasson, m. ‖ ~-plate, s. plaque, f. ‖ ~-scraper, s. décrottoir, m.
doorcase, dōrʹkās, s. chambranle, m.
doorstep, dōrʹstĕp, s. seuil, m.

doorway, dōrʹwa, s. renfoncement de porte, portail, m. [secret.
dormant, dōrʹmănt, a. dormant, caché, dormer-window, dōrʹ mĕr wĭnʹ dō, s. lucarne, f. [cimetière, m.
dormitory, dōrʹmĭ tĕr ĭ, s. dortoir, m. ‖
dormouse, dōrʹmŏws, s. marmotte, f.
dorsal, dōrʹsăl, a. dorsal.
dose, dōs, s. prise, f. ‖ portion, f. ‖ dose, f.
dose, dōs, v. a. (méd.) doser.
dot, dŏt, s. point, m.
dot, dŏt, v. a. pointiller, parsemer (de).
dotage, dōʹtāj, s. radotage, m., folie, imbécilité, f.
dotard, dōʹtĕrd, s. vieux radoteur, m.
dotation, dō tāʹshŭn, s. dotation, f.
dote, dōt, v. n. radoter ‖ raffoler ‖ to ~ on, être fou de.
doting, dōʹtĭng, a. passionné, extravagant ‖ -ly, ad. follement, éperdument.
double, dŭbʹl, s. double, m., duplicité, ruse, f. ‖ ~ that, le double de cela ‖ ~-chin, s. double menton, m. ‖ ~-entry, s. tenue des livres en parties doubles, f. ‖ ~-faced, a. faux, à double face ‖ ~-lock, s. serrure à double tour, f. ‖ v. a. fermer à double tour ‖ ~-quick, a. à pas de charge.
double, dŭbʹl, v. a. & n. doubler ‖ devenir double ‖ revenir sur ses pas ‖ jouer double ‖ ruser.
double, dŭbʹl, a. double ‖ faux, dissimulé.
doublet, dŭbʹlĕt, s. pourpoint, m.
doubloon, dŭb lōnʹ, s. doublon, m.
doubly, dŭbʹlĭ, ad. doublement.
doubt, dŏwt, s. doute, m.
doubt, dŏwt, v. a. (& n.) (se) douter.
doubtful, dŏwtʹfŏŏl, a. douteux, incertain ‖ -ly, ad. doutensement.
doubtless, dŏwtʹlĕs, a. & ad. sans doute.
dough, dō, s. pâte, f.
doughty, dŏwʹtĭ, a. preux, vaillant.
doughy, dōʹĭ, a. pâteux.
douse, dŏws, v. a. & n. jeter dans l'eau ‖ tomber dans l'eau.
dove, dŭv, s. pigeon, m. ‖ ~-cot, s. colombier, m. [colombe.
dovelike, dŭvʹlĭk, a. doux comme la
dovetail, dŭvʹtāl, s. queue d'aronde, f.
dowager, dŏwʹājĕr, s. douairière, f.
dowdy, dŏwʹdĭ, s. souillon, m., souillonne, f.
dower, dŏwʹĕr, s. dot, f. ‖ douaire, m.
dowered, dŏwʹĕrd, a. dotée.
down, dŏwn, s. duvet, m., plume menue, f. ‖ plaine, f. ‖ ~-hill, s. pente, f.
down, dŏwn, pr. & ad. vers le bas ‖ en bas, par terre ‖ en descendant ‖ up and ~, çà et là.
downcast, dŏwnʹkăst, a. abattu ‖ baissé.
downfall, dŏwnʹfăwl, s. chute, ruine, f.
downhearted, dŏwn hártʹĕd, a. abattu.
downright, dŏwnʹrĭt, a. évident, ouvert, franc ‖ ~, ad. perpendiculairement ‖ complètement. [pieds.
downtrodden, dŏwn trŏdʹdn, a. foulé aux
downward, dŏwnʹwĕrd, a. incliné, déclive ‖ abattu.

downwards, *dŏun'wĕrdz,* ad. en bas, en descendant || (nav.) en aval.   [doux.
downy, *dŏun'ĭ,* a. couvert de duvet ||
doze, *dōz,* s. assoupissement, m. || somme, m.   [sommeiller.
doze, *dōz,* v. a. & n. assoupir, endormir ||
dozen, *dŭz'n,* s. douzaine, f.
drab, *drăb,* s. drap gris brun, m. || pros-
drab, *drăb,* a. de couleur fauve.   [tituée, f.
drachm, *drăm,* s. drachme, dragme, m.
draft, *drȧft,* s. traite, f., bon, m. || levée des troupes, f.
draft, *drȧft,* v. a. dessiner || (mil.) détacher.
drag, *drăg,* s. drague, f., tramail, m. || crochet, croc, m. || ~-**chain,** s. enrayure, f. || ~-**net,** s. drague, f.   [force.
drag, *drăg,* v. a. & n. traîner, tirer de
draggle, *drăg'l,* v. a. & n. crotter, traîner dans la boue || ~-**tailed,** a. traîné dans la boue.
dragoman, *drăg'ō'măn,* s. drogman, m.
dragon, *drăg'ŏn,* s. dragon, m. || ~-**fly,** s. libellule, f.
dragoon, *drȧ-gŏn',* s. dragon (soldat), m.
drain, *drān,* s. fossé d'écoulement, m.
drain, *drān,* v. a. mettre à sec || égoutter.
drainage, *drān'ȧj,* s. écoulement, m. || dessèchement, m. || égouts, pl. || gadoue, f.
drake, *drāk,* s. canard, m.   [f.
dram, *drăm,* s. dragme, m. || petite quantité, f., un peu, m. || petit verre d'eau-de-vie, m.
dram, *drăm,* v. n. boire des liqueurs fortes.
drama, *drȧ'mȧ,* s, drame, m.
dramatic, *drȧ-măt'ĭk,* a. (-ally, ad.) dramatique(ment).
dramatise, *drăm'ȧ-tīz,* v. a. dramatiser.
dramatist, *drăm'ȧ-tĭst,* s. auteur dramatique, m.
drape, *drāp,* v. n. draper || tendre
draper, *drā'pĕr,* s. drapier, marchand de draps, m.   [facture de draps, f.
drapery, *drā'pĕr-ĭ,* s. draperie, f. || manu-
drastic, *drăs'tĭk,* a. drastique.
draught, *drȧft,* s. trait, coup, breuvage, m. || esquisse, f. || égout, m. || (rail.) tirage, m. || traite, f., bon, m. || surpoids, m. || rédaction, expédition, f. || ~-s, pl. jeu de dames, m. || ~-**board,** s. damier, m. || ~-**horse,** s. cheval de trait, m.   [m.
draughtsman, *drȧfts'măn,* s. dessinateur,
draw, *drȧw,* s. lot tiré, m. || ~-**well,** s. puits profond, m.
draw, *drȧw,* v. a. & n. ir. tirer, traîner || attirer || respirer || ouvrir, découvrir || tracer || dessiner, endurer || vider (une volaille) || se retirer, se diriger.
drawback, *drȧw'băk,* s. prime d'exportation, f. || (fig.) mécompte, m. || obstacle, m.
drawbridge, *drȧw'brĭj,* s. pont-levis, m.
drawer, *drȧw'ĕr,* s. (com.) tireur, m. || garçon de cabaret, m. || tiroir, m. || dessinateur, m. || ~-s, pl. caleçons, m. pl. || chest of ~s, commode, f.
drawing, *drȧw'ĭng,* s. action de tirer, f. || dessin, art de dessiner, m. || ~-**board,** s.

planche à dessiner, f. || ~-**book,** s. cahier de dessin, m. || ~-**master,** s. maître de dessin, m. || ~-**pen**(cil), s. tire-ligne, m. || ~-**room,** s. salon de compagnie, m.
drawl, *drȧwl,* s. débit traînant, m.
drawl, *drȧwl,* v. a. traîner (les paroles).
dray(-**cart**)**,** *drā'(kărt),* s. haquet, traîneau, m.   [frette, m.
drayhorse, *drā'hŏrs,* s. cheval de char-
drayman, *drā'măn,* s. charretier, m.
dread, *drĕd,* s. terreur, f.
dread, *drĕd,* v. a. & n. craindre, redouter.
dread, *drĕd,* a. terrible.   [(ment).
dreadful, *drĕd'fŏŏl,* a. (-ly, ad.) terrible
dreadnought, *drĕd'nȧwt,* s. audacieux, m.
dream, *drēm,* s. rêve, songe, m.
dream, *drēm,* v. a. & n. ir. songer, rêver.
dreamy, *drēm'ĭ,* a. chimérique.
drearily, *drēr'ĭ-lĭ,* ad. tristement.
dreary, *drēr'ĭ,* a. horrible, triste.
dredge, *drĕj,* s. drège, dragué, f.
dredger, *drĕj'ĕr,* s. pêcheur d'huîtres, m. || boîte à farine, f.
dredging, *drĕj'ĭng,* s. dragage, m.
dregs, *drĕgz,* s. pl. lie, f., sédiment, m.
drench, *drĕnsh,* v. a. mouiller, tremper, abreuver.   [m. || breuvage, m.
drench(**ing**)**,** *drĕnsh'(ĭng),* s. trempage,
dress, *drĕs,* s. vêtement, m., parure, f. || full ~, grande toilette, f. || high, low ~, robe montante, décolletée, f. || fancy ~, costume masqué, m.
dress, *drĕs,* v. a. & n. vêtir, habiller, parer || panser (une plaie) || apprêter, accommoder (des viandes) || dresser, rompre (un cheval) || s'habiller || s'aligner.
dresser, *drĕs'ĕr,* s. table de cuisine, f. || (in hospitals) externe, m.
dressing, *drĕs'ĭng,* s. parure, toilette, f. || bandage, m. || ~-**case,** s. nécessaire, m. || ~-**gown,** s. robe de chambre, f. || ~-**room,** s. cabinet de toilette, m. || ~-**table,** s. table à toilette, f.
dressmaker, *drĕs'māk-ĕr,* s. couturière, f.
dressy, *drĕs'ĭ,* a. qui aime la toilette || paré.
dribble, *drĭb'bl,* v. a. & n. égoutter || baver.
driblet, *drĭb'lĕt,* s. petite somme, f. || bagatelle, f.
drift, *drĭft,* s. impulsion, f. || grêle, f. || ondée, f. || amas, m. || but, m. || monceau de neige, m. || tourbillon (de poussière), m. || ~-**ice,** s. glaces flottantes, f. pl. || ~-**wood,** s. bois flotté, m.   [celer.
drift, *drĭft,* v. a. & n. pousser || s'amon-
drill, *drĭl,* s. vrille, f. || (agr.) sillon, m. || semoir, m. || (mil.) exercice, m. || ~-**box,** ~-**plough,** s. semoir, m.
drill, *drĭl,* v. a. vriller || discipliner.
drink, *drĭngk,* s. boisson, f., breuvage, m.
drink, *drĭngk,* v.a. & n. ir. boire || absorber.
drinkable, *drĭngk'ȧ-bl,* a. buvable, potable.
drinker, *drĭngk'ĕr,* s. buveur, biberon, m.
drip, *drĭp,* s. larmier, m.
drip, *drĭp,* v. a. & n. (laisser) tomber goutte à goutte.

dripping, *drĭp′pĭng*, s. graisse du rôti, f. ‖ **~-pan**, s. lèchefrite, f.

drive, *drĭv*, s. promenade en voiture, f. ‖ allée, avenue, f. ‖ course, f.

drive, *drĭv*, v. a. & n. ir. pousser ‖ chasser, poursuivre ‖ conduire, mener ‖ obliger ‖ entraîner ‖ saisir ‖ se diriger ‖ ~ on ! en route ! ‖ **to ~ a good bargain**, faire un bon marché ‖ **to ~ away, back, out, off**, chasser ‖ repousser ‖ **what are you driving at?** où en voulez-vous venir'

drivel, *drĭv′l*, s. bave, salive, f.

drivel, *drĭv′l*, v. n. baver ‖ radoter.

driveller, *drĭv′lĕr*, s. radoteur, m. [m.

driver, *drĭv′ĕr*, s. conducteur, m. ‖ cocher,

driving-wheel, *drī′vĭng hwĕl*, s. roue motrice, f.

drizzle, *drĭz′l*, v. a. & n. faire tomber en petites gouttes ‖ bruiner. [fine, f.

drizzling rain, *drĭz′lĭng rān*, s. pluie

droll, *drŏl*, s. bouffon, m.

droll, *drŏl*, a. drôle, plaisant.

drollery, *drŏl′lĕr*i, s. bouffonnerie, farce, f.

dromedary, *drŭm′ĕdĕr*i, s. dromadaire, m.

drone, *drōn*, s. bourdon, m. ‖ fainéant, m.

drone, *drōn*, v. n. bourdonner ‖ vivre dans l'oisiveté, fainéanter.

droop, *drŏp*, v. a. & n. languir, tomber en défaillance ‖ s'affliger, s'affaiblir ‖ pencher, baisser.

drooping, *drŏp′ĭng*, s. langueur, f.

drop, *drŏp*, s. goutte, f. ‖ pastille, f. ‖ pendant d'oreille, m. ‖ **~-scene**, s. rideau d'entr'acte, m.

drop, *drŏp*, v. a. & n. égoutter, dégoutter, tomber par gouttes ‖ laisser échapper, abandonner, cesser ‖ faire allusion à ‖ s'évanouir ‖ lâcher ‖ tomber dans l'oubli ‖ **to ~ in at a friend's**, entrer chez un ami inopinément.

dropsical, *drŏp′sĭkăl*, a. hydropique.

dropsy, *drŏp′sĭ*, s. hydropisie, f.

dross, *drŏs*, s. scorie, f., immondices, f.pl.

drought, *drŏŭt*, s. sécheresse, f. ‖ soif, f.

drove, *drōv*, s. troupeau, m. ‖ foule, f.

drover, *drō′vĕr*, s. conducteur de bestiaux, m. [plonger.

drown, *drŏŭn*, v. a. & n. noyer, inonder ‖

drowse, *drŏŭz*, v. a. & n. sommeiller ‖ s'assoupir. [chaîment.

drowsily, *drŏŭ′zĭlĭ*, ad. en dormant ‖ non-

drowsiness, *drŏŭ′zĭnĕs*, s. assoupissement, m., indolence, f. [pesant.

drowsy, *drŏŭ′zĭ*, a. assoupi, endormi ‖

drubbing, *drŭb′bĭng*, s. volée de coups de bâton, f. [fortement.

drudge, *drŭj*, v. n. piocher, travailler

drudge(r), *drŭj′(ĕr)*, s. homme de peine, m. [m., corvée, f.

drudgery, *drŭj′ĕr*i, s. travail pénible,

drug, *drŭg*, s. drogue, f. ‖ **a ~ in the market**, dur à la vente.

drug, *drŭg*, v. a. droguer, assaisonner.

drugget, *drŭg′gĕt*, s. droguet, m.

druggist, *drŭg′gĭst*, s. droguiste, m.

Druid, *drō′ĭd*, s. druide, m.

drum, *drŭm*, s. tambour, m., caisse, f. ‖ archure de la meule, f. ‖ **~-head**, s. dessus de tambour, m. ‖ **~-head court-martial**, s. conseil de guerre, m. ‖ **~-major**, s. tambour-major, m. ‖ **~-stick**, s. baguette de tambour, f. ‖ cuisse (de volaille), f.

drum, *drŭm*, v. a. & n. battre le tambour ‖ battre ‖ tinter ‖ (Am.) achalander quelqu'un ‖ **to ~ out of**, chasser au son du tambour. [achalandeur, m.

drummer, *drŭm′mĕr*, s. tambour, m. ‖ (Am.)

drunkard, *drŭngk′ĕrd*, s. ivrogne, m.

drunk(en), *drŭngk(ĕn)*, a. (-ly, ad.) ivre, ivrogne. [rie, f. ‖ ivresse, f.

drunkenness, *drŭngk′ĕnnĕs*, s. ivrogne-

dry, *drī*, v. a. & n. (des)sécher, essuyer ‖ se (des)sécher.

dry, *drī*, a. sec, aride, tari ‖ altéré ‖ **-ly**, ad. caustiquement, satiriquement ‖ **~-dock**, s. (mar.) bassin d'échouage, m. ‖ **~-nurse**, s. bonne d'enfants, f. ‖ v. a. sevrer ‖ élever au biberon ‖ **~-rot**, s. pourriture sèche, f. ‖ carie, f. ‖ **~-salter**, s. épicier, m. ‖ droguiste, m. ‖ **~-shod**, a. à pied sec.

drying, *drī′ĭng*, s. ~lines, s. pl. étendage, m. ‖ **~-room**, s. essui, m. ‖ séchoir, m.

dryness, *drī′nĕs*, s. sécheresse, f.

dual, *dū′ăl*, a. dualiste.

dub, *dŭb*, v. a. donner l'accolade ‖ (**to nickname**) baptiser. [doubtful(ly).

dubious(ly), *dū′bĭŭs(lĭ)*, a. & ad. vide

ducal, *dū′kăl*, a. ducal, de duc.

ducat, *dŭk′ăt*, s. ducat, m.

duchess, *dŭch′ĕs*, s. duchesse, f.

duchy, *dŭch′ĭ*, s. duché, m.

duck, *dŭk*, s. cane, f., canard, m. ‖ (fig.) poulette, f. ‖ plongeon, m. ‖ toile à voile, f. ‖ **-s and drakes**, pl. (jeu d'enfants) ricochets, m. pl. ‖ **to make, play ~ and drakes of**, faire des choux et des raves de ‖ jeter par la fenêtre ‖ **~-shot**, s. dragée au canard, f. ‖ **~-weed**, s. lentille de marais or d'eau, f. [tête.

duck, *dŭk*, v. a. & n. plonger ‖ baisser la

ducking, *dŭk′ĭng*, s. plongeon, m.

duckling, *dŭk′lĭng*, s. caneton, jeune canard, m. [tion), m.

ducky, *dŭk′ĭ*, s. petit chat (terme d'affec-

duct, *dŭkt*, s. conduit, m. ‖ canal, m. ‖ tube, m.

ductile, *dŭk′tĭl*, a. ductile ‖ traitable.

ductility, *dŭk′tĭl′ĭtĭ*, s. (of metals) ductilité, f. ‖ souplesse, docilité, f.

dudgeon, *dŭj′ŭn*, s. brouillerie, f. ‖ mauvaise humeur, f. ‖ **in high ~**, tout en colère. [f. ‖ impôt, m.

due, *dū*, s. dû, droit, m. ‖ juste prétention,

due, *dū*, a. & ad. dû ‖ échu, propre, convenable ‖ juste ‖ exactement.

duel, *dū′ĕl*, s. duel, m.

duel, *dū′ĕl*, v. n. se battre en duel.

duellist, *dū′ĕllĭst*, s. duelliste, m.

duenna, *dū̆ĕn′nă*, s. duègne, f.

duet, *dū̆ĕt*, s. (mus.) duo, m.

duffer, *dŭf′fĕr*, s. attrape, f. ‖ patraque, f. ‖ attrapeur, m., attrapeuse, f. ‖ ganache, f.

dug, *dŭg*) s. mamelle, f., pis, m.

dug-out, *dŭg'ŏwt,* s. (Am.) pirogue, f.

duke, *dūk,* s. duc, m.

dukedom, *dūk'dŭm,* s. duché, m.

dulcet, *dŭl'sĕt,* a. doux. [non, m.

dulcimer, *dŭl'sĭ mér,* s. lyre, f. || tympa-

dull, *dŭl,* v. a. hébéter, affaiblir, rendre obtus.

dull, *dŭl,* a. (-y, *dŭl'lĭ,* ad.) stupide(ment) || émoussé, obtus || pesant, lourd || triste, ennuyeux || sombre, faible || sourd || dur || lentement || as ~ as ditch-water, triste comme un bonnet de nuit || ~-witted, a. lourd.

dullard, *dŭl'lérd,* s. lourdaud, m.

dulness, *dŭl'nĕs,* s. stupidité, bêtise, f. || pesanteur, lenteur, nonchalance, f. || manque d'éclat, m.

duly, *dū'lĭ,* ad. dûment, convenablement.

dumb, *dŭm,* a. muet || ~-bell, s. haltère, m. || ~-waiter, s. porte-assiettes, m.

dumbfound, *dŭm'fŏwnd,* v. a. rendre muet, confondre. [silence, m.

dumbness, *dŭm'nĕs,* s. mutisme, m. ||

dummy, *dŭm'mĭ,* s. muet, m. || mannequin, m. || homme de paille, prête-nom, m. || to play ~, (whist) jouer avec le mort.

dump, *dŭmp,* s. absence d'esprit, f. || -s, pl. mélancolie, f.

dumpling, *dŭmp'lĭng,* s. chausson, m.

dumpy, *dŭm'pĭ,* a. court, épais, ramassé.

dun, *dŭn,* s. créancier importun, m.

dun, *dŭn,* v. a. importuner un débiteur.

dun, *dŭn,* a. brun obscur || obscur || (of horses) isabelle || (fig.) sombre.

dunce, *dŭns,* s. bête, f., ignorant, m.

dung, *dŭng,* s. fumier, m., fiente, crotte, f. || ~-cart, s. tombereau, m. || ~-hill, s. tas de fumier, m.

dungeon, *dŭn'jŭn,* s. cachot, m.

duodecimo, *dū ŏ dĕs'ĭ mō,* a. in-douze.

dupe, *dūp,* s. dupe, f.

dupe, *dūp,* v. a. duper, tromper.

duplicate, *dū'plĭ kāt,* s. duplicata, m., copie, f.

duplicity, *dū plĭs'ĭ tĭ,* s. duplicité, f.

durability, *dū rā bĭl'ĭ tĭ,* s. durabilité, f.

durable, *dū'rā bl,* a. durable, constant.

durably, *dū'rā blĭ,* ad. d'une manière durable. [en cage.

durance, *dū'răns,* s. prison, f. || in ~ vile,

duration, *dū rā'shŭn,* s. durée, f.

duress, *dū'rĕs,* s. contrainte, f.

during, *dū'rĭng,* pr. pendant, durant.

dusk, *dŭsk,* s. brune, f. || couleur foncée, f.

duskily, *dŭsk'ĭ lĭ,* ad. obscurément.

duskiness, *dŭsk'ĭ nĕs,* s. obscurité, f.

dusky, *dŭsk'ĭ,* a. obscur || bruni, bronzé.

dust, *dŭst,* s. poussière, poudre, f. || to trample in the ~, fouler aux pieds || ~-bin, ~-hole, s. trou aux ordures, m. || ~-pan, s. pelle à ordures || ~-shot, s. cendrée, f. [poussière.

dust, *dŭst,* v. a. épousseter || couvrir de

duster, *dŭst'ér,* s. torchon, m. || (for horses) époussette, f.

dustiness, *dŭst'ĭ nĕs,* s. état poudreux, m.

dusting-brush, *dŭst'ĭng brŭsh,* s. vergette, f., plumeau, m.

dusty, *dŭst'ĭ,* a. poudreux.

duteous, *dū'tĭ ŭs,* dutiful, *dū'tĭ fŏŏl,* a. obéissant, respectueux || -ly, ad. respectueusement. [f., respect, hommage, m.

dutifulness, *dū'tĭ fŏŏl nĕs,* s. obéissance,

duty, *dū'tĭ,* s. devoir, m. || taxe, f., impôt, m. || devoirs, m. pl., civilités, f. pl. || on ~, de service || off ~, libre || bounden ~, s. devoir rigoureux, m. || customs ~, s. droit de douane, m. || in ~ to, par respect pour || as in ~ bound, comme c'est de son devoir.

dwarf, *dwawrf,* s. nain, m., naine, f.

dwarf, *dwawrf,* v. a. rapetisser.

dwarf, *dwawrf,* a. nain.

dwarfish, *dwawrf'ĭsh,* a. nain, petit.

dwell, *dwĕl,* v. n. ir. demeurer || s'arrêter

dweller, *dwĕl'lér,* s. habitant, m. [sur.

dwelling(-place), *dwĕl'lĭng (plās),* s. habitation, demeure, f.

dwindle, *dwĭn'dl,* v. a. & n. diminuer, décroître || dégénérer || s'affaiblir.

dye, *dī,* s. teinture, f., teint, m. || matière

dye, *dī,* v. a. teindre, colorer. [tinctoriale, f.

dyeing, *dī'ĭng,* s. teinture, f.

dying, *dī'ĭng,* p. & a. mourant, moribond.

dyke, *dīk,* s. fossé, m. || (géol.) dyke, f.

dynamics, *dī năm'ĭks,* s. pl. dynamique, f.

dynamite, *dīn'ă mīt,* s. dynamite, f.

dynamiter, *dī'năm ĭ tér,* s. dynamitard, dynamiteur, m.

dynamo, *dī'nă mō,* s. dynamo, m., machine dynamo-électrique, f.

dynasty, *dĭn'ăs tĭ,* s. dynastie, f.

dysentery, *dĭs'én tér ĭ,* s. dyssenterie, f.

dyspepsia, *dĭs pĕp'sĭ ă,* s. dyspepsie, f.

dyspeptic, *dĭs pĕp'tĭk,* a. dyspeptique.

E.

each, *ēch,* pn. chacun, chacune, chaque || ~ other, l'un l'autre, les uns les autres.

eager, *ē'gér,* a. (-ly, ad.) désireux, avide (ment) || empressé || vif, ardent, violent || aigre || ardemment.

eagerness, *ē'gér nĕs,* s. empressement, attachement, m. || impétuosité, avidité, f. || aigreur, f.

eagle, *ē'gl,* s. aigle, m. || étendard, m. || pièce d'or (10 dollars), f. || ~-eyed, a. aux yeux d'aigle.

eaglet, *ē'glĕt,* s. aiglon, m.

ear, *ér,* s. oreille, f. || épi de blé, m. || anse, f. || quick, sharp ~, oreille fine, f. || box on the ~, soufflet, m. || to have about one's ~s, avoir sur le dos || to give ~ to, prêter l'oreille à || to set by the ~s, mettre aux prises || to turn a deaf ~, fair la sourde oreille || ~-lap. s. bout de l'oreille, m. || ~-ring, s. boucle d'oreille, f. || ~-trumpet, s. cornet acoustique, m.

earache, *ér'āk,* s. mal d'oreille, m.

eared, *ērd*, a. ayant des oreilles || épié.

earl, *ėrl*, s. comte, m.

earldom, *ėrl'dŭm*, s. dignité de comte, f.

earless, *ėr'lĕs*, a. sans oreilles.

earliness, *ėr'lĭ nĕs*. s. heure peu avancée, f. || précocité, f. [hâtif || de bonne heure.

early, *ėr'lĭ*, a. & ad. matinal || précoce.

earn, *ėrn*, v. a. gagner, obtenir, mériter.

earnest, *ėr'nĕst*, s. sérieux, m., chose sérieuse, m. || gage, m., arrhes, f. pl. || in good ~, sérieusement || ~-money, s. arrhes, f. pl.

earnest, *ėr'nĕst*, a. ardent, brûlant || zélé, empressé || -ly, ad. sérieusement || instamment

earnestness, *ėr'nĕst nĕs*, s. ardeur, véhémence, f. || empressement, m. || zèle, m.

earnings, *ėr'nĭngs*, s. pl. gages, m. pl.

earth, *ėrth*, s. terre, f. || monde, m. || ~-born, a. terrestre || ~-worm, s. ver de terre.

earth, *ėrth*, v. a. (& s.) (s')enterrer.   [m.

earthen, *ėr'thn*, a. de terre, terreux.

earthenware, *ėr'thĕn wār*, s. poterie, f.

earthiness, *ėrth'ĭ nĕs*, s. qualité terrestre, f. || grossièreté, f.

earthliness, *ėrth'lĭ nĕs*, s. mondanité, f.

earthly, *ėrth'lĭ*, a. terrestre, mondain.

earthquake, *ėrth'kwāk*, s. tremblement de terre, m.   [m. || terrasses, f. pl.

earthwork, *ėrth'wėrk*, s. terrassement,

earthy, *ėrth'ĭ*, a. terreux || terrestre, grossier.

earwig, *ėr'wĭg*, s. forficule, f.   [sier.

ease, *ēz*, s. aise, f., repos, m., tranquillité, f. || facilité, f. || at ~, à l'aise.

ease, *ēz*, v. a. soulager, adoucir.

easel, *ē'zl*, s. chevalet, m.

easement, *ēz'mĕnt*, s. soulagement, m. || (jur.) servitude, f.   [volontiers.

easily, *ēz'ĭ lĭ*, ad. aisément, facilement ||

easiness, *ē'zĭ nĕs*, s. aisance, facilité, complaisance, tranquillité, f.

east, *ēst*, s. est, orient, m.

east, *ēst*, a. de l'est, oriental.

Easter, *ēst'ėr*, s. Pâques, m.

easterly, *ēst'ėr lĭ*, a. & ad., eastern, *ēst'ėrn*, a. d'est, oriental || vers l'est.

eastward, *ēzt'vėrd*, ad. vers l'orient.

easy, *ē'zĭ*, a. aisé || facile || disposé, tranquille, content, complaisant.   [ronger.

eat, *ēt*, v. a. & n. ir. manger, dévorer ||

eatable, *ē'tă bl*, a. mangeable.

eatables, *ē'tă blĕs*, s. pl. vivres, m. pl.

eating-house, *ēt'ĭng hŏws*, s. restaurant, m.   [m.

eaves, *ēvz*, s. pl. larmier, égout d'un toit.

eavesdropper, *ēvz'drŏp pėr*, s. écouteur, espion, m

ebb, *ĕb*, s. reflux, m. || décadence, f.

ebb, *ĕb*, v. n. refouler, descendre, décliner.

ebon, *ĕb'ŏn*, s. ébène, f.

ebony, *ĕb'ŏnĭ*, s. ébène, f.

ebullition, *ē bŭl ĭsh'ĭn*, s. ébullition, f., bouillonnement, m. || (fig.) violence, f.

eccentric, *ĕk sĕn'trĭk*, s. (fam.) original, m. || (géom.) cercle excentrique, m.

eccentric, *ĕk sĕn'trĭk*, a. excentrique || bizarre.

eccentricity, *ĕk sĕn trĭs'ĭ tĭ*, s. excentricité, f. || bizarrerie, f.   [tique, m.

ecclesiastic, *ĕk klē zĭ ăs'tĭk*, s. ecclésiastic(al), *ĕk klē zĭ ăs'tĭk(ăl)*, a. ecclésiastique.

echo, *ĕk'ō*, s. écho, m.   [clésiastique.

echo, *ĕk'ō*, v. a. & n. répéter || résonner.

eclectic, *ĕk lĕk'tĭk*, s. éclectique, m.

eclectic, *ĕk lĕk'tĭk*, a. éclectique.

eclipse, *ĭ klĭps'*, s. éclipse, f.

eclipse, *ĭ klĭps'*, v. a. éclipser, offusquer.

ecliptic, *ĕ klĭp'tĭk*, s. écliptique, f.

economic(al), *ē kŏ nŏm'ĭk(ăl)*, a. (-ly, ad.) économique(ment) || ménager.   [f.

economics, *ē kŏ nŏm'ĭks*, s. pl. économique,

economise, *ē kŏn'ō mĭs*, v. a. économiser, ménager.   [économiste, m.

economist, *ē kŏn'ō mĭst*, s. économe, m.

economy, *ē kŏn'ō mĭ*, s. économie, f. || frugalité, f.   [galité, f.

ecstasy, *ĕk'stă sĭ*, s. extase, f.   [galité, f.

eddy, *ĕd'dĭ*, s. tourbillon, m.

eddy, *ĕd'dĭ*, v. n. tourbillonner.

edge, *ĕj*, s. tranchant, m. || bord, m., extrémité, f. || tranche (d'un livre), f. || vivacité d'esprit, sagacité, f. || to set one's teeth on ~, agacer les dents à qn. || ~-tool, s. outil tranchant, m.

edge, *ĕj*, v. a. & n. aiguiser, affiler || border || aigrir || exciter || avancer || to ~ in, introduire difficilement.

edged, *ĕjd*, a. tranchant, aiguisé.

edging, *ĕj'ĭng*, s. bordure, f.

edible, *ĕd'ĭbl*, a. mangeable.

edict, *ē'dĭkt*, s. édit, m., ordonnance, f.

edification, *ĕd ĭ fĭ kā'shŭn*, s. édification, instruction, f.

edifice, *ĕd'ĭfĭs*, s. édifice, bâtiment, m.

edify, *ĕd'ĭfĭ*, v. a. édifier || bâtir, construire || instruire

edit, *ĕd'ĭt*, v. a. éditer, rédiger.   [f.

edition, *ĕ dĭ'shŭn*, s. édition, impression, f.

editor, *ĕd'ĭtėr*, s. éditeur, m. || rédacteur, m. || ~'s office, s. rédaction, f.

editorial, *ĕd ĭ tō'rĭ ăl*, s. article de fond, m.

editorial, *ĕd ĭ tō'rĭ ăl*, a. de la rédaction.

editorship, *ĕd'ĭtėr shĭp*, s. emploi de rédacteur, m.

educate, *ĕd'ŭkāt*, v. a. élever, instruire.

education, *ĕd ŭ kā'shŭn*, s. éducation, instruction, f.   [tion.

educational, *ĕd ŭ kā'shŭn ăl*, a. d'éducation.

educator, *ĕd'ŭkā tėr*, s. éducateur, instituteur, m.

educe, *ĭ dūs'*, v. a. tirer, dégager, extraire.

eel, *ēl*, s. anguille, f. || ~-pot, s. claie aux anguilles, f. || ~-pout, s. barbotte, f. || ~-spear, s. trident, m.

e'en, *ēn*, e'er, *ār*, ad. vide even, ever

efface, *ĕf făs'*, v. a. effacer.

effect, *ĕf fĕkt'*, s. effet, résultat, m., réalité, f. || -s, pl. effets, meubles, biens, m. pl.

effect, *ĕf fĕkt'*, v. a. effectuer, exécuter.

effective, *ĕf fĕk'tĭv*, a. effectif, réel, actif || -ly, ad. effectivement.

effectiveness, *ĕf fĕk'tĭv nĕs*, s. effet (qualité de produire de l'effet), m.

effectives, *ĕf fĕk'tĭvs*, s. pl. effectif m. || troupes de guerre, f. pl

bŏy; — *fŏŏt*, *tūbe*, *tŭb*. || *chair*, *joy*; — *game*, *yes*; — *soul*, *zeal*; — *thing*, *there*.

English and French

effectual, *ĕf fĕk' tū ăl*, a. (-ly, ad.) efficace (ment).   [féminer.

effeminate, *ĕf fĕm' ĭ nāt*, v. a. (& n.) (s')ef-

effeminate, *ĕf fĕm' ĭ nāt*, a. efféminé, voluptueux || -ly, ad. d'une manière efféminée.

effervesce, *ĕf fĕr vĕs'*, v. n. être en effervescence.   [cence, f.

effervescence, *ĕf fĕr vĕs' sĕns*, s. effervescence.

effervescent, *ĕf fĕr vĕs' ĕnt*, a. effervescent || ~ draught, s. poudre effervescente, f.

effete, *ĕf fēt'*, a. stérile, usé.   [faire.

efficacious, *ĕf fĭ kā' shŭs*, a. efficace, salutaire.

efficacy, *ĕf' fĭ kă sĭ*, s. efficacité, vertu, f.

efficiency, *ĕf fĭsh' ĕn sĭ*, s. efficacité, f.

efficient, *ĕf fĭsh' ĕnt*, s. agent, principe, m.

efficient, *ĕf fĭsh' ĕnt*, a. (-ly, ad.) efficace (ment).

effigy, *ĕf' fĭ jĭ*, s. image, représentation, f.

efflorescence, *ĕf flō rĕs' ĕns*, s. (méd. & chim.) efflorescence, f. || fleuraison, f.

effluvium, *ĕf flū' vĭ ŭm*, s. vapeurs, f. pl.

effort, *ĕf' fŏrt*, s. effort, m.

effrontery, *ĕf frŭn' tĕr ĭ*, s. effronterie, impudence.   [éclat, lustre, m.

effulgence, *ĕf fŭl' jĕns*, s. splendeur, f.

effulgent, *ĕf fŭl' jĕnt*, a. éclatant.

effusion, *ĕf fū' zhŭn*, s. effusion, f., épanchement, f.

eft, *ĕft*, s. salamandre (lézard), f.

egg, *ĕg*, s. œuf, m. || new-laid ~, œuf frais || soft-boiled ~s, ~s in the shell, œufs à la coque || poached ~s, œufs pochés || hard-boiled ~s, œufs durs || scrambled ~, buttered ~s, œufs brouillés || ~-boiler, s. cocote, f. || ~-cup, s. coquetier, m. || ~-flip, s. lait de poule, m. || ~-shell, s. coquille d'œuf, f.

eglantine, *ĕg' lăn tĭn*, s. (bot.) églantier, m.

egotism, *ĕg' ō tĭzm*, s. égoïsme, égotisme, m.

egot(ist, *ĕg' ō (t) ĭst*, s. égotiste, égoïste, m.

egotistic(al), *ĕg ō tĭs' tĭk(ăl)*, a. vaniteux || égoïste.

egregious, *ĕ grē' jĭ ŭs*, a. éminent, excellent || énorme || -ly, ad. éminemment.

egress, *ē' grĕs*, s. sortie, f.

egriot, *ē' grĭ ŏt*, s. griotte, f.

egyptology, *ē jĭp tŏl' ō jĭ*, s. égyptologie, f.

eider, *ī' dĕr*, s. eider, m.

eiderdown, *ī' dĕr dŏwn*, s. édredon, m.

eight, *āt*, a. huit.

eightfold, *āt' fōld*, a. octuple, huit fois.

eighteen, *ā' tēn*, a. dix-huit.

eighteenth, *ā' tēnth*, a. dix-huitième.

eighth, *āth*, a. (-ly, ad.) huitième(ment).

eightieth, *ā' tĭ ĕth*, a. quatre-vingtième.

eighty, *ā' tĭ*, a. quatre-vingts.

either, *ē' ther* ou *ī' ther*, ad. non plus || ~, pn. l'un ou l'autre, chaque, chacun || ~, c. soit, ou, soit que.

ejaculation, *ĕ jăk ŭ lā' shŭn*, s. éjaculation, f. || oraison jaculatoire, f.

eject, *ĕ jĕkt'*, v. a. jeter, pousser dehors || (méd.) évacuer.   (méd.) évacuation, f.

ejection, *ĕ jĕk' shŭn*, s. expulsion, f.

eke, *ēk*, v. a. augmenter, accroître || prolonger.

elaborate, *ĕ lăb' ō rāt*, v. a. élaborer.

elaborate, *ĕ lăb' ō rāt*, a. bien fait || -ly, ad. exactement.   [tion, f.

elaboration, *ĕ lăb ō rā' shŭn*, s. élaboration, f.

elapse, *ĕ lăps'*, v. n. s'écouler, s'échapper.

elastic, *ĕ lăs' tĭk*, a. élastique.

elasticity, *ĕ lăs tĭs' ĭ tĭ*, s. élasticité, f.

elate, *ĕ lāt'*, v. a. enorgueillir || -d, fier, enorgueilli.

elation, *ĕ lā' shŭn*, s. fierté, f., orgueil, m.

elbow, *ĕl' bō*, s. coude, m. || angle, m.

elbow, *ĕl' bō*, v. a. & n. coudoyer || faire un coude || ~-chair, s. fauteuil, m. || ~-rest, s. accoudoir, m. || ~-room, s. coudées franches, f. pl.

elder, *ĕl' dĕr*, a. ancien, m. || vieillard, m. || (bot.) sureau, m. || ~-berry, s. graine de sureau, f.

elder, *ĕl' dĕr*, a. aîné, plus âgé.   [sureau, f.

elderly, *ĕl' dĕr lĭ*, a. assez âgé || d'un certain âge.   [ancienneté, f.

eldership, *ĕl' dĕr shĭp*, s. primogéniture || eldest, *ĕl' dĕst*, a. aîné, le premier né.

elect, *ĕ lĕkt'*, v. a. élire, choisir.

elect, *ĕ lĕkt'*, a. élu, choisi.   [m.

election, *ĕ lĕk' shŭn*, s. élection, f., choix, electioneering, *ĕ lĕk shŭn ēr' ĭng*, s. manœuvres électorales, f. pl.

elective, *ĕ lĕk' tĭv*, a. électif || -ly, ad. par choix || ~ affinity, s. (chim.) affinité élective, f.

elector, *ĕ lĕk' tĕr*, s. électeur, m.   [teur.

electoral, *ĕ lĕk' tĕr ăl*, a. électoral || d'électorate, *ĕ lĕk' tĕr ăt*, s. électorat, m.

electric(al), *ĕ lĕk' trĭk(ăl)*, a. électrique || ~ current, s. courant électrique, m.

electricity, *ĕ lĕk trĭs' ĭ tĭ*, s. électricité, f.

electrify, *ĕ lĕk' trĭ fī*, v. a. électriser.

electro, *ĕ lĕk' trō*, ~ gilding, s. dorure au feu, f. || ~-plating, s. galvanoplastie, f. || ~-type, v. a. électrotyper.

electuary, *ĕ lĕk' tū ĕr ĭ*, s. électuaire, m.

eleemosynary, *ĕ lē mŏz' ĭ nĕr ĭ*, a. d'aumône, qui vit d'aumônes.

elegance, *ĕl' ĕ găns*, s. élégance, f.

elegant, *ĕl' ĕ gănt*, a. élégant, gracieux || -ly, ad. élégamment.

elegiac, *ĕ lĕ jī' ăk*, a. élégiaque.

elegist, *ĕl' ĕ jĭst*, s. poète élégiaque, m.

elegy, *ĕl' ĕ jĭ*, s. élégie, f.   [cipe, m.

element, *ĕl' ĕ mĕnt*, s. élément, m. || principe, m.

elemental, *ĕl ĕ mĕn' tăl*, elementary, *ĕl ĕ mĕn' tĕr ĭ*, a. élémentaire.

elephant, *ĕl' ĕ fănt*, s. éléphant, m. || ~-driver, s. cornac, m.   [éléphantin.

elephantine, *ĕl ĕ făn' tĭn*, a. d'éléphant ||

elevate, *ĕl' ĕ vāt*, v. a. élever, hausser || exalter || enorgueillir.

elevation, *ĕl ĕ vā' shŭn*, s. élévation, f. || hauteur, sublimité || dignité, f.

elevator, *ĕl' ĕ vā tĕr*, s. chèvre, f. || élévateur, m. || (Am.) ascenseur, m.

eleven, *ĕ lĕv' n*, a. onze.

eleventh, *ĕ lĕv' nth*, a. onzième.

elf, *ĕlf*, s. lutin, m.

elfin, *ĕl' fĭn*, elfish, *ĕlf' ĭ-ŝ*, a. de lutins || enchanté || des eifes.

elicit, *ĕ lĭs′ ĭt*, v. a. faire jaillir, faire sortir.

eligibility, *ĕl ĭ jĭ bĭl′ ĭ tĭ*, s. éligibilité, f.

eligible, *ĕl′ ĭ jĭ bl*, a. éligible ‖ préférable.

eliminate, *ĕ lĭm′ ĭ nāt*, v. a. éliminer, ex- [pulser.

elk, *ĕlk*, s. élan, m.

ell, *ĕl*, s. aune, f. [lipse, f.

ellipse, *ĕl lĭps′*, ellipsis, *ĕl lĭp′ sĭs*, s. el- [liptique.

elliptical, *ĕl lĭp′ tĭk(ăl)*, a. elliptique.

elm, *ĕlm*, s. orme, m.

elocution, *ĕl ŏ kū′ shŭn*, s. élocution, dic- [tion, f. ‖ déclamation, f.

elocutionist, *ĕl ŏ kū′ shŭn ĭst*, s. profes- [seur de déclamation, f. [étendre.

elongate, *ĕ lŏng′ gāt*, v. a. (& n.) (s′)allonger ‖

elongation, *ĕ lŏng gā′ shŭn*, s. extension, f. ‖ élongation, f. [s′évader.

elope, *ĕ lōp′*, v. a. s′enfuir, s′en aller,

elopement, *ĕ lōp′ mĕnt*, s. fuite, évasion, f.

eloquence, *ĕl′ ŏ kwĕns*, s. éloquence, f.

eloquent, *ĕl′ ŏ kwĕnt*, a. éloquent ‖ -ly, ad. éloquemment.

else, *ĕls*, pn. & ad. autre, autre chose ‖ autrement, sinon ‖ what ~ ? quoi encore ?

elsewhere, *ĕls′ hwār*, ad. ailleurs.

elucidate, *ĕ lō′ sĭ dāt*, v. a. éclaircir, ex- [pliquer. [nent, m., explication, f.

elucidation, *ĕ lō sĭ dā′ shŭn*, s. éclaircisse- [ment, m., explication, f.

elude, *ĕ lōd′*, v. a. éluder, éviter, esquiver.

elusive, *ĕ lō′ sĭv*, a. élusif, évasif.

emaciate, *ĕ māsh′ ĭ āt*, v. a. & n. amaigrir ‖ maigrir. [ment, m., maigreur, f.

emaciation, *ĕ māsh ĭ ā′ shŭn*, s. amaigrisse-

emanate, *ĕm′ ă nāt*, v. n. émaner.

emanation, *ĕm ă nā′ shŭn*, s. émanation, f.

emancipate, *ĕ măn′ sĭ pāt*, v. a. éman- [ciper ‖ (fig.) affranchir (de).

emancipation, *ĕ măn sĭ pā′ shŭn*, s. éman- [cipation, f. [efféminer, énerver.

emasculate, *ĕ măs′ kū lāt*, v. a. châtrer ‖

embalm, *ĕm bäm′*, v. a. embaumer.

embank, *ĕm bāngk′*, v. a. remblayer ‖ en- [caisser. [m. ‖ construction de quais, m.

embankment, *ĕm bāngk′ mĕnt*, s. remblai,

embargo, *ĕm bär′ gō*, s. embargo, m. ‖ to lay an ~, mettre un embargo.

embark, *ĕm bärk′*, v. a. (& n.) (s′)embarquer.

embarkation, *ĕm bär kā′ shŭn*, s. em- [barquement, m.

embarrass, *ĕm bār′ răs*, v. a. embarrasser.

embarrassment, *ĕm bär′ răs mĕnt*, s. em- [barras, m. [message, m.

embassy, *ĕm′ băs sĭ*, s. ambassade, f. ‖

embattle, *ĕm băt′ l*, v. a. ranger en bataille.

embed, *ĕm bĕd′*, v. a. enfouir, emboîter.

embellish, *ĕm bĕl′ lĭsh*, v. a. embellir, orner.

ember, *ĕm′ bĕr*, ~-days, s. pl. Quatre- Temps, m. pl. ‖ ~-week, s. semaine des Quatre-Temps, f. [f. pl., braise, f.

embers, *ĕm′ bĕrz*, s. pl. cendres chaudes,

embezzle, *ĕm bĕz′ l*, v. a. malverser ‖ s′ap- [proprier. [sation, f.

embezzlement, *ĕm bĕz′ l mĕnt*, s. malver-

embitter, *ĕm bĭt′ tĕr*, v. a. rendre amer ‖ (fig.) empoisonner ‖ aigrir.

emblazon, *ĕm blā′ zn*, v. a. b′asonner.

emblem, *ĕm′ blĕm*, s. emblème, m.

emblematic(al), *ĕm blĕ măt′ ĭk(ăl)*, a. em- [blématique. [cation, f.

embodiment, *ĕm bŏd′ ĭ mĕnt*, s. personnifi-

embody, *ĕm bŏd′ ĭ*, v. a. incorporer.

embogue, *ĕm bōg′*, v. n. s′emboucher.

embolden, *ĕm bōl′ dn*, v. a. enhardir, en- [courager. [relief.

emboss, *ĕm bŏs′*, v. a. bosseler ‖ graver en

embossment, *ĕm bŏs′ mĕnt*, s. bosselage, travail en bosse, m. [sement, f.

embrace, *ĕm brās′*, s. étreinte, f. ‖ embras-

embrace, *ĕm brās′*, v. a. embrasser ‖ saisir.

embra ure, *ĕm brā′ zhōōr*, s. embrasure, f.

embrocation, *ĕm brŏ kā′ shŭn*, s. embro- [cation, douche, f. [bellir.

embroider, *ĕm brŏy′ dĕr*, v. a. broder ‖ em-

embroiderer *ĕm brŏy′ dĕr ĕr*, s. brodeur, m., brodeuse, f.

embroidery, *ĕm brŏy′ dĕr ĭ*, s. broderie, f.

embroil, *ĕm brŏyl′*, v. a. embrouiller, con- [fondre. [lerie, confusion, f.

embroilment, *ĕm brŏyl′ mĕnt*, s. brouil-

embryo, *ĕm′ brĭ ō*, s. embryon, m.

embryo, *ĕm′ brĭ ō*, a. d′embryon, en germe.

emendation, *ĕm ĕn dā′ shŭn*, s. amende- [ment, m., correction, f.

emerald, *ĕm′ ĕr ăld*, s. émeraude, f.

emerge, *ĕ mĕrj′*, v. n.- s′élever, sortir de, paraître.

emergency, *ĕ mĕr′ jĕn sĭ*, s. émersion, f. ‖ accident, m. ‖ circonstance critique, f.

emery, *ĕm′ ĕr ĭ*, s. émeri, m.

emetic, *ĕ mĕt′ ĭk*, s. vomitif, m.

emigrant, *ĕm′ ĭ gränt*, s. émigrant, m. ‖ émigré, m.

emigrate, *ĕm′ ĭ grāt*, v. n. émigrer. [f.

emigration, *ĕm ĭ grā′ shŭn*, s. émigration,

eminence, *ĕm′ ĭ nĕns*, s. éminence ‖ célé- [brité, f.

eminent, *ĕm′ ĭ nĕnt*, a. éminent ‖ illustre ‖ most ~, éminentissime ‖ -ly, ad. émi- [nemment.

emissary, *ĕm′ ĭs să rĭ*, s. émissaire, m.

emission, *ĕ mĭsh′ ŭn*, s. émission, f.

emit, *ĕ mĭt′*, v. a. pousser dehors, lancer, jeter ‖ émettre, faire circuler.

emmet, *ĕm′ mĕt*, s. fourmi, f.

emollient, *ĕ mŏl′ lĭ ĕnt*, s. émollient, m.

emollient, *ĕ mŏl′ lĭ ĕnt*, a. émollient.

emolument, *ĕ mŏl′ ŭ mĕnt*, s. émolument, avantage, m. [f.

emotion, *ĕ mō′ shŭn*, s. émotion, agitation,

emperor, *ĕm′ pĕr ĕr*, s. empereur, m.

emphasis, *ĕm′ fă sĭs*, s. force, f. ‖ (in a bad sense) emphase, f.

emphasise, *ĕm′ fă sĭz*, v. a. appuyer sur ‖ prononcer avec force. [phatique(ment).

emphatic, *ĕm făt′ ĭk*, a. (-ally, ad.) em-

empire, *ĕm′ pĭr*, s. empire, m.

empiric, *ĕm pĭr′ ĭk*, s. empirique, m. ‖ charlatan, m. [-ly, ad. en empirique.

empiric(al), *ĕm pĭr′ ĭk(ăl)*, a. empirique ‖

empiricism, *ĕm pĭr′ ĭ sĭzm*, s. empirisme ‖

employ, *ĕm plŏy′*, v. a. employer. [m.

employee, *ĕm plŏy′ ē*, s. employé, m., em- ployée, f.

employer, *em ploy' ĕr,* s. maître, patron, m. ‖ (com.) commettant, m.

employ(ment), *em ploy' (mĕnt),* s. emploi, m. ‖ charge, f. ‖ occupation, f. ‖ condition, f. ‖ **to throw out of ~,** priver d'ouvrage.

emporium, *em po' ri ŭm,* s. entrepôt, m. ville marchande, f.

empower, *em pow' ĕr,* v. a. autoriser, donner pouvoir, commettre.

empress, *ĕm' prĕs,* s. impératrice, f.

emptiness, *ĕm' ti nĕs,* s. vide, m. ‖ (fig.) vanité, f. ‖ nullité, f.

empty, *ĕm' ti,* v. a. vider.

empty, *ĕm' ti,* a. vide ‖ ignorant, frivole.

empyrean, *ĕm pi rē' an,* s. empyrée, m.

emu, *ē' mū,* s. émeu, m.

emulate, *ĕm' ū lāt,* v. a. rivaliser, imiter, égaler.   [rivalité, f.

emulation, *ĕm ū lā' shŭn,* s. émulation, f.

emulous, *ĕm' ū lŭs,* a. émule, ambitieux ‖ **-ly,** ad. avec émulation.

emulsion, *ē mŭl' shŭn,* s. émulsion, f.

enable, *ĕn ā' bl,* v. a. rendre capable, mettre à même.

enact, *ĕn ăkt',* v. a. décréter, exécuter.

enactment, *ĕn ăkt' mĕnt,* s. ordonnance, f., décret, m.

enamel, *ĕn ăm' ĕl,* s. émail, m.

enamel, *ĕn ăm' ĕl,* v. a. émailler.

enamour, *ĕn ăm' ĕr,* v. a. rendre amoureux.

encage, *ĕn kāj',* v. a. encager, enfermer.

encamp, *ĕn kamp',* v. a. & n. camper.

encampment, *ĕn kamp' mĕnt,* s. campement, m.

encaustic, *ĕn kaws' tik,* s. encaustique, f.

encaustic, *ĕn kaws' tik,* a. encaustique.

enchant, *ĕn chănt',* v. a. enchanter, charmer.   [enchantement.

enchantingly, *ĕn chănt' ing li,* ad. par enchantment.   [resse, sorcière, f.

enchantment, *ĕn chănt' mĕnt,* s. enchantement, m.

enchantress, *ĕn chănt' rĕs,* s. enchanteresse, sorcière, f.

enchase, *ĕn chās',* v. a. enchâsser.

encircle, *ĕn sĕr' kl,* v. a. environner, entourer.   [fermer ‖ **-d,** ci-inclus.

enclose, *ĕn klōz',* v. a. enclore, clore, renfermer.

enclosure, *ĕn klō' zhŏŏr,* s. clôture, f. ‖ enclos, m. ‖ contenu, m.

encomiast, *ĕn kō' mi ăst,* s. panégyriste, m.

encomium, *ĕn kō' mi ŭm,* s. panégyrique, éloge, m.   [environner.

encompass, *ĕn kŭm' păs,* v. a. entourer,

encore, *ăŭng kōr',* v. a. redemander, crier

encore, *ăŭng kōr',* ad. encore.   [bis (à).

encounter, *ĕn kŏŭn' tĕr,* s. rencontre, f., accident, m.   [rencontrer ‖ s'attaquer.

encounter, *ĕn kŏŭn' tĕr,* v. a. (& n.) (se)

encourage, *ĕn kŭr' ĕj,* v. a. encourager, exciter, conforter, consoler.

encouragement, *ĕn kŭr' ĕj mĕnt,* s. encouragement, m.   [ser (de) ‖ usurper.

encroach, *ĕn krōch',* v. n. empiéter, abu-

encroachment, *ĕn krōch' mĕnt,* s. empiétement, m., usurpation, f.

encumber, *ĕn kŭm' bĕr,* v. a. encombrer, embarrasser ‖ empêcher.

encumbrance, *ĕn kŭm' brăns,* s. encombrement, m. ‖ embarras, empêchement, m. ‖ charge, f. ‖ enfants, m. pl.

encyclopædia, *ĕn si klō pē' di ā,* s. encyclopédie, f.

end, *ĕnd,* s. bout, m., fin, conclusion, f. ‖ but, dessein, m. ‖ bout, m. ‖ morceau, m. ‖ **at an ~,** fini ‖ **on ~,** debout ‖ **to come to a bad ~,** finir mal ‖ **to make both -s meet,** joindre les deux bouts (de l'année) ‖ **to stand on ~** (hair), se dresser sur la tête.

end, *ĕnd,* v. a. & n. finir ‖ cesser.

endanger, *ĕn dăn' jĕr,* v. a. mettre en danger.   [aimer ‖ caresser.

endear, *ĕn dēr',* v. a. rendre cher, faire

endearing, *ĕn dēr' ing,* a. tendre ‖ aimable.

endearment, *ĕn dēr' mĕnt,* s. tendresse, f. ‖ caresses, f. pl.

endeavour, *ĕn dĕv' ĕr,* s. effort, m.

endeavour, *ĕn dĕv' ĕr,* v. a. s'efforcer, tâcher.

endemic, *ĕn dĕm' ik,* a. endémique.

ending, *ĕn' ding,* s. fin, conclusion, f.

endive, *ĕn' div,* s. endive, chicorée, f.

endless, *ĕnd' lĕs,* a. (-ly, ad.) infini ‖ perpétuel(lement).

endorse, *ĕn dŏrs',* v. a. endosser.

endorsee, *ĕn dŏr sē',* s. endossé, m.

endorsement, *ĕn dŏrs' mĕnt,* s. endossement, m.

endorser, *ĕn dŏr sĕr',* s. endosseur, m.

endow, *ĕn dow',* v. a. doter, douer.

endowment, *ĕn dŏw' mĕnt,* s. dotation, f. ‖ don, m.   [tolérable.

endurable, *ĕn dū' rā bl,* a. supportable,

endurance, *ĕn dū' răns,* s. durée, patience, souffrance, f.   [porter ‖ durer, continuer.

endure, *ĕn dūr',* v. a. & n. endurer, supporter.

endways, *ĕnd' wās,* **endwise,** *ĕnd' wis,* ad. perpendiculairement.   [pompe, m.

enema, *ĕn ē' mā,* s. lavement, m. ‖ clysoenemy,** *ĕn' ĕ mi,* s. ennemi, m.

energetic, *ĕn ĕr jĕt' ik,* a. (-ally, ad.) énergique(ment) ‖ vigoureux.

energy, *ĕn' ĕr ji,* s. énergie, vigueur, efficacité, f.   [énerver, efféminer.

enervate, *ĕn' ĕr vāt* ou *ĕ nĕr' vāt,* v. a. affaiblir, débiliter.

enfeeble, *ĕn fē' bl,* v. a. affaiblir, débiliter.

enfilade, *ĕn fi lād',* s. (mil.) enfilade, f.

enfilade, *ĕn fi lād',* v. a. enfiler.

enfold, *ĕn fōld',* v. a. envelopper ‖ embrasser.

enforce, *ĕn fōrs',* v. a. & n. fortifier ‖ contraindre, obliger ‖ faire sentir ‖ prouver, démontrer.

enforcement, *ĕn fōrs' mĕnt,* s. violence, contrainte, f. ‖ approbation, f.

enfranchise, *ĕn frăn' chiz,* v. a. affranchir ‖ naturaliser.

engage, *ĕn gāj',* v. a. & n. engager ‖ mettre en gage ‖ gagner, combattre, se battre, s'entrechoquer ‖ s'engager ‖ obliger, promettre.

engagement, *ĕn gāj' mĕnt,* s. engagement, m. ‖ obligation, f. ‖ occupation, f. ‖ combat, m. ‖ **to meet one's -s,** remplir ses engagements.

---

lāte, hăt, făr, lăw; — hēre, gĕt, hĕr; — mĭne, ĭnn; — nō, hŏt, prōve; — hŏŏt; —

engaging, *ĕn găʹ ĭng,* a. (-ly, ad.) engageant, d'une manière engageante.

engender, *ĕn jĕnʹ dĕr,* v. a. & n. engendrer, produire, faire naître.

engine, *ĕnʹ jĭn,* s. machine, f. || locomotive, f. || artifice, m., ruse, f. || ~-driver, s. mécanicien, m. || ~-house, s. dépôt de pompes à feu, m. [ficier de génie, m.

engineer, *ĕn jĭ nērʹ,* s. ingénieur, m. || of-

engineering, *ĕn jĭ nērʹ ĭng,* s. génie, m.

engrave, *ĕn grāvʹ,* v. a. graver, buriner.

engraver, *ĕn grāʹ vĕr,* s. graveur, m.

engraving, *ĕn grāʹ vĭng,* s. gravure, estampe, f.

engross, *ĕn grōsʹ,* v. a. engraisser || s'emparer, accaparer || (jur.) grossoyer.

engulf, *ĕn gŭlfʹ,* v. a. engouffrer || engloutir.

enhance, *ĕn hânsʹ,* v. a. enchérir, hausser le prix || augmenter || exagérer.

enigma, *ĕ nĭgʹ mă,* s. énigme, f.

enigmatic(al), *ĕ nĭg mătʹ ĭk(ăl),* a. (-ly, ad.) énigmatique(ment).

enjoin, *ĕn jŏĭnʹ,* v. a. enjoindre, ordonner, prescrire.

enjoy, *ĕn jŏĭʹ,* v. a. & n. jouir de, se réjouir || to ~ oneself, s'amuser.

enjoyment, *ĕn jŏĭʹ mĕnt,* s. jouissance, possession, f., plaisir, m.

enlarge, *ĕn lârjʹ,* v. a. & n. élargir || augmenter || étendre, dilater || s'étendre, se dilater, accroître.

enlargement, *ĕn lârjʹ mĕnt,* s. augmentation, f., élargissement, m. || (méd.) hypertrophie, f. || (fig.) dilatation, f.

enlighten, *ĕn līʹ tn,* v. a. éclairer, illuminer || instruire.

enlist, *ĕn lĭstʹ,* v. a. & n. enrôler, s'enrôler.

enlistment, *ĕn lĭstʹ mĕnt,* s. enrôlement, m.

enliven, *ĕn līʹ vn,* v. a. animer, égayer.

enmity, *ĕnʹ mĭ tĭ,* s. inimitié, haine, f.

ennoble, *ĕn nōʹ bl,* v. a. ennoblir, anoblir.

enormity, *ĕ nŏrʹ mĭ tĭ,* s. énormité, f.

enormous, *ĕ nŏrʹ mŭs,* a. énorme || -ly, ad. énormément.

enough, *ĕ nŭfʹ,* s. quantité suffisante, f.

enough, *ĕ nŭfʹ,* ad. assez, suffisamment.

enquire, *ĕn kwīrʹ,* v. n. s'enquérir || s'informer || to ~ after, demander des nouvelles de || ~ within ! s'adresser ici ! || ~, v. a. demander.

enquiring, *ĕn kwīrʹ ĭng,* a. investigateur || -ly, ad. par voie d'interrogation.

enquiry, *ĕn kwīʹ rĭ,* s. demande, question, f. || investigation, f. || to make enquiries, s'informer || ~-office, s. bureau des renseignements, m.

enrage, *ĕn rājʹ,* v. a. irriter, exaspérer.

enrapture, *ĕn răpʹ tūr,* v. a. ravir, charmer.

enrich, *ĕn rĭchʹ,* v. a. enrichir.

enrol, *ĕn rōlʹ,* v. a. enrôler, enregistrer, inscrire, [fendre || se cacher.

ensconce, *ĕn skŏnsʹ,* v. a. & n. couvrir, dé-

enshrine, *ĕn shrĭnʹ,* v. a. enchâsser.

ensign, *ĕnʹ sĭn,* s. enseigne, f., drapeau, m. || sous-lieutenant (d'infanterie), m. || (mar.) pavillon de poupe, m. || marque, f., signe,

m. || porte-drapeau, m. || ~-bearer, s. porte-drapeau, m.

enslave, *ĕn slāvʹ,* v. a. rendre esclave, opprimer || dégrader.

enslavement, *ĕn slāvʹ mĕnt,* s. asservissement, esclavage, m.

ensnare, *ĕn snârʹ,* v. a. prendre au piège || séduire || surprendre || embarrasser.

ensue, *ĕn sūʹ,* v. n. s'ensuivre.

ensuing, *ĕn sūʹ ĭng,* a. prochain, suivant.

ensure, *ĕn shūrʹ,* v. a. *vide* insure.

entablature, *ĕn tăbʹ lă tūr,* s. entablement, m.

entail, *ĕn tālʹ,* s. substitution, f. || (fig.) transmission, f. || bien substitué, m.

entangle, *ĕn tăngʹ gl,* v. a. embrouiller, embarrasser.

enter, *ĕnʹ tĕr,* v. a. & n. entrer dans || admettre, inscrire, enregistrer || initier, introduire || s'engager, entreprendre || pénétrer || to ~ college, entrer au collège.

enterprise, *ĕnʹ tĕr prīz,* s. entreprise, f.

enterprising, *ĕn tĕr ʹprī zĭng,* a. (-ly, ad.) entreprenant || avec un esprit d'entreprise.

entertain, *ĕn tĕr tānʹ,* v. a. entretenir, traiter, régaler, amuser || concevoir || revoir.

entertainer, *ĕn tĕr tānʹ ĕr,* s. amphytrion, hôte, m. || agréable compagnon, m.

entertainment, *ĕn tĕr tānʹ mĕnt,* s. entretien, m., conversation, f. || régal, m. || accueil, m., réception, f. [jetir.

enthral, *ĕn thrâlʹ,* v. a. asservir || assu-

enthrone, *ĕn thrōnʹ,* v. a. placer, mettre sur le trône || introniser.

enthusiasm, *ĕn thūʹ zĭ ăzm,* s. enthousiasme, m., exaltation, f. [m.

enthusiast, *ĕn thūʹ zĭ ăst,* s. enthousiaste.

enthusiastic, *ĕn thū zĭ ăsʹ tĭk,* a. fanatique, exalté || -ally, ad. en enthousiaste.

entice, *ĕnʹ tĭs,* v. a. attirer, leurrer, exciter, séduire.

enticement, *ĕn tĭsʹ mĕnt,* s. incitation, instigation, tentation, séduction, f. || appas, m. pl.

entire, *ĕn tīrʹ,* a. entier, complet || sincère || -ly, ad. entièrement.

entireness, *ĕn tīrʹ nĕs,* **entirety,** *ĕn tīrʹ tĭ,* s. intégrité, perfection, loyauté, f.

entitle, *ĕn tīʹ tl,* v. a. intituler || donner un droit.

entity, *ĕnʹ tĭ tĭ,* s. entité, f., être, m.

entomb, *ĕn tōmʹ,* v. a. enterrer. [f.

entomology, *ĕn tō mŏlʹ ō jĭ,* s. entomologie.

entrails, *ĕnʹ trālz,* s. pl. entrailles, f. pl.

entrance, *ĕnʹ trăns,* s. entrée, avenue, f., passage, m. || commencement, m. || carriage-~, s. porte-cochère, f. || ~-hall, s. vestibule, m. || ~-money, s. entrée, f., prix d'entrée, m.

entrance, *ĕn trânsʹ,* v. a. ravir, extasier.

entrap, *ĕn trăpʹ,* v. a. prendre au piège, attraper. [stamment.

entreat, *ĕn trētʹ,* v. a. supplier, prier in-

entreaty, *ĕn trēʹ tĭ,* s. requête, prière, supplication, f.

entrust, *ĕn trŭstʹ,* v. a. confier.

entry, *ĕn'trĭ*, s. entrée, f., passage, m. ||
enregistrement, m. || double ~, s. partie
double, f.   [tiller.
entwine, *ĕn twīn'*, v. a. entrelacer, entor-
enumeration, *ĕ nŭ mĕ rā'shŭn*, s. énumé-
ration, f., dénombrement, m.
enunciation, *ĕ nŭn sĭ ā'shŭn*, s. énonciation, déclaration, f.   [vrir.
envelop, *ĕn vĕl'ŏp*, v. a. envelopper, cou-
envelope, *ĕn've lŏp*, s. enveloppe, couverture, f.   [aigrir.
envenom, *ĕn vĕn'ŏm*, v. a. envenimer ||
enviable, *ĕn'vĭ ă bl*, a. digne d'envie.
envious, *ĕn'vĭ ŭs*, a. envieux, jaloux ||
-ly, ad. par envie.
environs, *ĕn vī'rŏnz*, s. pl. environs, m. pl.
envoy, *ĕn'vŏy*, s. envoyé, député, m.
envy, *ĕn'vĭ*, s. envie, jalousie, f.
envy, *ĕn'vĭ*, v. a. envier.
epaulet, *ĕp'aw lĕt*, s. épaulette, f.
epergne, *ĕ pĕrn'*, s. surtout, plateau, m.
ephemeral, *ĕ fĕm'ĕ răl*, a. éphémère.
epic, *ĕp'ĭk*, a. épique, héroïque.   [m.
epicure, *ĕp'ĭ kūr*, s. épicurien, gourmand,
epidemic, *ĕp ĭ dĕm'ĭk*, s. épidémie, f.
epidemic, *ĕp ĭ dĕm'ĭk*, a. épidémique.
epigram, *ĕp'ĭ grăm*, s. épigramme, f.
epilepsy, *ĕp'ĭ lĕp sĭ*, s. épilepsie, f.
epileptic, *ĕp ĭ lĕp'tĭk*, a. épileptique.
Epiphany, *ĕ pĭf'ă nĭ*, s. Épiphanie, f.
Episcopacy, *ĕ pĭs'kŏ pă sĭ*, s. épiscopat, m.
episcopal, *ĕ pĭs'kŏ păl*, a. épiscopal
episode, *ĕp'ĭ sŏd*, s. épisode, m.
epistle, *ĕ pĭs'l*, s. épître, lettre, f.
epistolary, *ĕ pĭs'tŏ lĕr ĭ*, a. épistolaire.
epitaph, *ĕp'ĭ tăf*, s. épitaphe, f.
epitome, *ĕ pĭt'ŏ mĕ*, s. épitome, abrégé, m.
epitomise, *ĕ pĭt'ŏ mĭz*, v. a. faire un abrégé.
epoch, *ĕp'ŏk*, s. époque, f.
equal, *ē'kwăl*, s. égal, compagnon, m.
equal, *ē'kwăl*, v. a. égaler, être égal (à).
equal, *ē'kwăl*, a. (-ly, ad.) égal(ement) ||
uniforme || semblable, impartial, équi-
table || ~ to the situation, à la hauteur
de la situation.   [tion, f.
equalisation, *ē kwăl ĭ zā'shŭn*, s. égalisa-
equalise, *ē'kwăl ĭz*, v. a. égaliser, rendre
égal.   [uniformité, f.
equality, *ē kwăl'ĭ tĭ* ou *ē kwŏl'ĭ tĭ*, s. égalité
equanimity, *ē kwă nĭm'ĭ tĭ*, s. égalité
d'âme, tranquillité d'esprit, f.
equation, *ē kwā'shŭn*, s. équation, f.
equator, *ē kwā'tĕr*, s. équateur, m.
equatorial, *ē kwă tō'rĭ ăl*, a. de l'équateur.
equerry, *ē'kwĕr rĭ*, s. écuyer, m.
equestrian, *ē kwĕs'trĭ ăn*, a. équestre, à
cheval || ~ performer, s. voltigeur à
cheval, m.
equidistant, *ē kwĭ dĭs'tănt*, a. équidistant.
equilibrium, *ē kwĭ lĭb'rĭ ŭm*, s. équilibre,
equine, *ē'kwĭn*, a. de cheval.   [m.
equinoctial, *ē kwĭ nŏk'shăl*, a. équinoxial.
equinox, *ē'kwĭ nŏks*, s. équinoxe, f.
equip, *ē kwĭp'*, v. a. équiper.
equipage, *ĕk'wĭ păj*, s. équipement, équi-
page, m. || suite (de valets etc.), f., train,
m.

equipment, *ē kwĭp'mĕnt*, s. équipement,
armement, m.   [poids, m.
equipoise, *ē'kwĭ pŏyz*, s. équilibre, contre-
equitable, *ĕk'wĭ tă bl*, a. équitable, raisonnable.
equitably, *ĕk'wĭ tă blĭ*, ad. équitablement.
equity, *ĕk'wĭ tĭ*, s. équité, impartialité, f.
equivalence, *ē kwĭv'ă lĕns*, s. égalité de
valeur, f., équivalent, m.
equivalent, *ē kwĭv'ă lĕnt*, s. équivalent, m.
equivalent, *ē kwĭv'ă lĕnt*, a. équivalent,
égal en valeur.
equivocal, *ē kwĭv'ō kăl*, a. (-ly, ad.) équi-
voque || ambigu(ment).
equivocate, *ē kwĭv'ō kāt*, v. n. équivoquer.
equivocation, *ē kwĭv ō kā'shŭn*, s. équi-
voque, f.   [voque, f.
era, *ē'ră*, s. ère, époque, f.
eradicate, *ē răd'ĭ kāt*, v. a. déraciner || ex-
tirper, arracher.   [extirpation, f.
eradication, *ē răd ĭ kā'shŭn*, s. éradication,
erase, *ē răz'*, v. a. raser, raturer.
eraser, *ē rā'zĕr*, s. grattoir, m.
erasure, *ē rā'zhoor*, s. rature, f.
ere, *ār*, ad. & pr. auparavant, avant que,
plutôt que || avant.   [fonder.
erect, *ē rĕkt'*, v. a. ériger, élever || établir,
erect, *ē rĕkt'*, a. droit || élevé, haut.
erection, *ē rĕk'shŭn*, s. élévation, struc-
ture, f. || établissement, m.
ermine, *ĕr'mĭn*, s. hermine, f. || -d, fourré
erotic, *ē rŏt'ĭk*, a. érotique.   [d'hermine.
err, *ĕr*, v. n. errer, s'égarer, se tromper.
errand, *ĕr'rănd*, s. message, m., commis-
sion, f. || ~-boy, s. commissionnaire, m. ||
~-girl, s. coursière, f.
errant, *ĕr'rănt*, erring, *ĕr'rĭng*, a. errant,
vagabond || knight-~, s. chevalerie er-
rante, f.
errantry, *ĕr'răn trĭ*, s. vie errante, f.
errata, *ĕr rā'tă*, s. pl. errata, m. pl.,
fautes d'impression, f. pl.
erratic, *ĕr răt'ĭk*, a. errant, vagabond ||
variable || (méd., astr. & géol.) erratique.
erroneous, *ĕr rō'nĭ ŭs*, a. erroné, errant ||
-ly, ad. par erreur, faussement.
error, *ĕr'rĕr*, s. erreur, faute, f. || -s ex-
cepted, sauf erreur (ou omission).
eructation, *ē rŭk tā'shŭn*, s. (méd.) éruc-
tation, f. || (fam.) rot, m.
erudite, *ĕr'ū dīt*, a. érudit, instruit.
erudition, *ĕr ū dĭsh'ŭn*, s. érudition,
science, f., savoir, m.   [ruption, f.
eruption, *ē rŭp'shŭn*, s. éruption, f. || ir-
erysipelas, *ĕr ĭ sĭp'ĕ lăs*, s. érysipèle, m.
escape, *ĕs kāp'*, s. (of gas) fuite, éva-
sion, f. || (of steam) échappement, m. ||
appareil de sauvetage, m. || to make
one's ~, se sauver, s'échapper || to have
a narrow ~, l'échapper belle.
escape, *ĕs kāp'*, v. a. & n. échapper,
éviter || s'échapper, s'évader.   [m.
escapement, *ĕs kāp'mĕnt*, s. échappement,
eschalot, *ĕs chă lŏt'*, s. (bot.) vide shallot.
escheat, *ĕs chēt'*, s. déshérence, aubaine, f.
eschew, *ĕs chō'*, v. n. éviter.   [lier, m.
escort, *ĕs'kŏrt*, s. escorte, suite, f. || cava-
escort, *ĕs kŏrt'*, v. a. escorter.

esculent, *ĕs'kŭ lĕnt*, a. mangeable.

escutcheon, *ĕs kŭch'ŭn*, s. écusson, m.

especially, *ĕs pĕsh'ăl lĭ*, ad. spécialement.

espousals, *ĕs pŏw'zălz*, s. pl. noces, f. pl.

espouse, *ĕs pŏwz'*, v. a. épouser || marier.

espy, *ĕs pī'*, v. a. épier || découvrir.

esquire, *ĕs kwīr'*, s. écuyer, châtelain, m. || (on letters) Monsieur, m.

essay, *ĕs'sā*, s. essai, m.

essay, *ĕs sā'*, v. a. essayer, tenter, éprouver.

essayist, *ĕs'sā ĭst*, s. auteur d'essais, m.

essence, *ĕs'sĕns*, s. essence, f. || parfum, m.

essential, *ĕs sĕn'shăl*, s. essentiel, m.

essential, *ĕs sĕn'shăl*, a. (-ly, ad.) essentiel(lement).

establish, *ĕs tăb'lĭsh*, v. a. établir, fonder, instituer || affermir, ratifier.

establishment, *ĕs tăb'lĭsh mĕnt*, s. établissement, m., fondation, f. || approbation, f. || base, f.

estate, *ĕs tāt'*, s. état, m., condition, f. || fortune, f. || propriété, terre, f. || ~-agent, s. agent d'affaires, m. || entailed ~, s. propriété substituée, f. || personal ~, s. biens-meubles, m. pl. || real ~, s. biens-immeubles, m. pl.

esteem, *ĕs tēm'*, s. estime, f., respect, m.

esteem, *ĕs tēm'*, v. a. estimer.

estimate, *ĕs'tĭ māt*, estimation, *ĕs tĭ mā'shŭn*, s. estimation, f. || évaluation, f., calcul, m. || jugement, m. [calculer.

estimate, *ĕs'tĭ māt*, v. a. estimer, évaluer.

estrange, *ĕs trānj'*, v. a. éloigner, aliéner || indisposer. [ment, m.

estrangement, *ĕs trānj'mĕnt*, s. éloignement, m.

estuary, *ĕs'tū ă rĭ*, s. embouchure (d'un lac etc.), f. || estuaire, m.

etch, *ĕch*, v. a. graver à l'eau forte.

etching, *ĕch'ĭng*, s. gravure à l'eau forte, f.

eternal, *ē tĕr'năl*, a. (-ly, ad.) éternel (lement).

eternity, *ē tĕr'nĭ tĭ*, s. éternité, f.

ether, *ē'thĕr*, s. éther, m.

ethereal, *ē thē'rĭ ăl*, a. éthéré || céleste.

ethical, *ĕth'ĭ kăl*, a. moral || -ly, ad. selon la morale.

ethics, *ĕth'ĭks*, s. pl. éthique, f.

etymological, *ĕt ĭ mŏ lŏj'ĭ kăl*, a. étymologique.

etymology, *ĕt ĭ mŏl'ŏjĭ*, s. étymologie, f.

eucharist, *ū'kă rĭst*, s. eucharistie, f.

eulogise, *ū'lŏ jīz*, v. a. louer.

eulogistic, *ū lŏ jĭs'tĭk*, a. louangeur.

eulogy, *ū'lŏ jĭ*, s. éloge, m.

eunuch, *ū'nŭk*, s. eunuque, m.

euphony, *ū'fō nĭ*, s. euphonie, f.

evacuate, *ē văk'ū āt*, v. a. évacuer. [f.

evacuation, *ĕ văk ū ā'shŭn*, s. évacuation,

evade, *ē vād'*, v. a. & n. échapper || user de subterfuge. [sant.

evanescent, *ĕ văn ĕs'ĕnt*, a. s'évanouis-

evangelical, *ē văn jĕl'ĭk ăl*, a. (-ly, ad.) évangélique(ment).

evaporate, *ē văp'ō rāt*, v. a. & n. faire évaporer || s'évaporer. [tion, f.

evaporation, *ē văp ō rā'shŭn*, s. évapora-

evasion, *ē vā'zhŭn*, s. subterfuge, m.

evasive, *ē vā'sĭv*, a. évasif || -ly, ad. évasivement.

eve, *ēv*, s. veille, f. || soir, m. [sivement.

even, *ē'vn*, a. a. aplanir, rendre égal.

even, *ē'vn*, a. (-ly, ad.) uni, aplani || égal(ement) || semblable || pair || impartial (ement) || ~-handed, a. impartial.

even, *ē'vn*, ad. même, de même, aussi bien || ~ now, tout à l'heure || ~ so, de même, tout comme || ~ that, en cas || ~ though, bien que.

even(ing), *ē'vn(ĭng)*, s. soir, m., soirée, f.

evenness, *ē'vn nĕs*, s. égalité, f. || impartialité, f. || sérénité, f.

evensong, *ē'vn sŏng*, s. chant du soir, m.

event, *ē vĕnt'*, s. événement, m.|| incident, m.

eventful, *ē vĕnt'fŏŏl*, a. plein d'événements.

eventide, *ē'vn tīd*, s. déclin du jour, m.

eventual, *ē vĕn'tū ăl*, a. (-ly, ad.) éventuel(lement). [à jamais.

ever, *ĕv'ĕr*, ad. toujours, jamais || for ~,

evergreen, *ĕv'ĕr grēn*, s. joubarbe, f.

evergreen, *ĕv'ĕr grēn*, a. toujours vert.

everlasting, *ĕv ĕr lăst'ĭng*, a. éternel, immortel || [nellement]

evermore, *ĕv ĕr mōr'*, ad. toujours, éternellement.

every, *ĕv'ĕr ĭ*, a. chaque, chacun, tout.

everybody, *ĕv'ĕr ĭ bŏd ĭ*, everyone, *ĕv'ĕr ĭ wŭn*, pn. tout le monde, chacun.

everywhere, *ĕv'ĕr ĭ hwār*, ad. partout.

evict, *ē vĭkt'*, v. a. évincer.

eviction, *ē vĭk'shŭn*, s. éviction, f.

evidence, *ĕv'ĭ dĕns*, s. évidence, preuve, f. || déposition, f., témoignage, m. || témoin, m. || circumstantial ~, s. (jur.) inductions, f. pl. || to turn Queen's ~, révéler ses complices.

evidence, *ĕv'ĭ dĕns*, v. a. prouver, montrer.

evident, *ĕv'ĭ dĕnt*, a. évident, manifeste, clair || -ly, ad. évidemment.

evil, *ē'vĭl*, s. mal, m., méchanceté, f., malheur, m. || maladie, f. || ~-doer, s. malfaiteur, m. || ~-speaking, s. médisance, f.

evil, *ē'vĭl*, a. (-ly, ad.) méchant || mauvais || mal || ~-minded, a. mal-intentionné.

evince, *ē vĭns'*, v. a. montrer, prouver, démontrer.

evocation, *ĕv ō kā'shŭn*, s. évocation, f.

evoke, *ē vōk'*, v. a. évoquer, faire apparaître. [f. || développement, m.

evolution, *ĕv ō lū'shŭn*, s. (mil.) évolution,

evolve, *ē vŏlv'*, v. a. & n. développer || s'étendre. [femelle, m.

ewe, *ū*, s. brebis, f. || ~-lamb, s. agneau ewer, *ū'ĕr*, s. aiguière, f. [quer.

exact, *ĕgz ăkt'*, v. a. & n. exiger || extorquer.

exact, *ĕgz ăkt'*, a. (-ly, ad.) exact(ement) || ponctuel, précis || soigneux. [sion, f.

exaction, *ĕgz ăk'shŭn*, s. exaction, extorexactitude, *ĕgz ăk'tĭ tūd*, exactness, *ĕgz ăkt'nĕs*, s. exactitude, ponctualité, f.

exaggerate, *ĕgz ăj'ĕr āt*, v. a. exagérer, amplifier. [tion, f.

exaggeration, *ĕgz ăj ĕr ā'shŭn*, s. exagéra-

exalt, *ĕgz ăwlt'*, v. a. élever || exalter || vanter. [élévation, f.

exaltation, *ĕgz ăl tā'shŭn*, s. exaltation,

examination, *ĕgz ăm ĭ nā' shŭn,* s. examen, m. ‖ interrogatoire, m. ‖ vérification, f. ‖ inspection, f. ‖ **competitive ~,** s. concours, m. ‖ **post-mortem ~,** s. autopsie, f.

examine, *ĕgz ăm' ĭn,* v. a. examiner, interroger, discuter avec soin ‖ peser mûrement.

examiner, *ĕgz ăm' ĭ nêr,* s. examinateur, m.

example, *ĕgz ăm' pl,* s. exemple, modèle, m. ‖ **for ~,** par exemple.

exasperate, *ĕgz ăs' pêr ät,* v. a. exaspérer, irriter, provoquer.

exasperation, *ĕgz ăs pêr ā' shŭn,* s. exaspération, irritation, f.

excavate, *ĕks' kă vät,* v. a. excaver, creuser.

excavation, *ĕks kă vā' shŭn,* s. excavation, f. ‖ fouille, f. ‖ déblai, m.

exceed, *ĕk sēd',* v. a. & n. excéder, dépasser, outrepasser ‖ exceller.

exceeding, *ĕk sēd' ing,* a. excédant, excessif ‖ **-ly,** ad. excessivement, extrêmement.   [passer.

excel, *ĕk sĕl',* v. a. & n. exceller, surpasser.

excellence, *ĕk' sĕl lĕns,* s. excellence, prééminence, f. ‖ supériorité, f. [Excellence.

Excellency, *ĕk' sĕl lĕn sĭ,* s.; **His ~,** Son

excellent, *ĕk' sĕl lĕnt,* a. excellent ‖ éminent ‖ **-ly,** ad. excellemment.

except, *ĕk sĕpt',* v. a. & n. excepter, exclure ‖ récuser.   [mis, hors.

excepting, *ĕk sĕp' ting,* pr. excepté, hormis.

exception, *ĕk sĕp' shŭn,* s. exception, exclusion, f. ‖ répugnance, f. ‖ **with the ~ of,** à l'exception de ‖ **to take ~ at, to,** se formaliser, s'offenser de.

exceptionable, *ĕk sĕp' shŭn ă bl,* a. récusable, reprochable.

exceptional, *ĕk sĕp' shŭn ăl,* a. (-ly, ad.) exceptionnel(lement).

excess, *ĕk sĕs',* s. excès, m., extrémité, f.

excessive, *ĕk sĕs' siv,* a. excessif, démesuré ‖ **-ly,** ad. excessivement.

exchange, *ĕks chänj',* s. échange, contre-échange, m. ‖ bourse, f. ‖ **in ~,** en échange ‖ **bill of ~,** s. lettre de change, f. ‖ **rate of ~,** s. taux du change, m. ‖ **~-office,** s. bureau de change, m.

exchange, *ĕks chänj',* v. a. échanger, changer, faire un échange.   [geable.

exchangeable, *ĕks chänj' ă bl,* a. échan-

exchequer, *ĕks chĕk' êr,* s. Échiquier, trésor royal, m. ‖ **~-bill,** s. bon du trésor, m. ‖ **Chancellor of the ~,** s. chancelier de l'Échiquier, m.   [droit de régie, m.

excise, *ĕk sīz',* s. accise, f. ‖ **~-duty,** s.

exciseman, *ĕk sīz' măn,* s. collecteur de l'accise, m.   [tible.

excitable, *ĕk sī' tă bl,* a. excitable, suscep-

excite, *ĕk sīt',* v. a. exciter, encourager ‖ stimuler.

excitement, *ĕk sīt' mĕnt,* s. excitation, f., encouragement, m. ‖ motif, m.

exclaim, *ĕks klām',* v. a. crier, s'écrier.

exclamation, *ĕks klă mā' shŭn,* s. exclamation, clameur, f.

exclude, *ĕks klōd',* v. a. exclure, excepter.

exclusion, *ĕks klō' zhŭn,* s. exclusion, exception, f.   [ad. exclusivement.

exclusive, *ĕks klō' siv,* a. exclusif ‖ **-ly,**

excommunicate, *ĕks kŏm mū' nĭ kät,* v. a. excommunier.

excommunication, *ĕks kŏm mū nĭ kā' shŭn,* s. excommunication, f.   [f.

excoriation, *ĕks kō rĭ ā' shŭn,* s. écorchure,

excrement, *ĕks' krē mĕnt,* s. excrément, m.

excrescence, *ĕks krĕs' ĕns,* s. excroissance, f. ‖ (fig.) excès, m.   [tion, f.

excretion, *ĕks krē' shŭn,* s. (méd.) excré-

excruciate, *ĕks krō' shĭ ät,* v. a. tourmenter, torturer.   [ad.) atroce ‖ affreusement.

excruciating, *ĕks krō shĭ ā' ting,* a.- ‖ **-ly,**

exculpate, *ĕks kŭl' pät,* v. a. disculper, excuser.   [tion, f.

exculpation, *ĕks kŭl pā' shŭn,* s. disculpa-

exculpatory, *ĕks kŭl' pă tēr ĭ,* a. justificatif.

excursion, *ĕks kêr' shŭn,* s. excursion, digression, f. ‖ **~-ticket,** s. billet de train de plaisir, m.

excursionist, *ĕks kêr' shŭn ĭst,* s. touriste, excursioniste, m.

excusable, *ĕks kū' ză bl,* a. excusable.

excuse, *ĕks kūs',* s. excuse, f.

excuse, *ĕks kūz',* v. a. excuser, disculper, dispenser.   [testable.

execrable, *ĕks' ē kră bl,* a. exécrable, dé-

execrate, *ĕks' ē krät,* v. a. exécrer, abhorrer.

execration, *ĕks ē krā' shŭn,* s. exécration, malédiction.   [tuer, accomplir.

execute, *ĕks' ē kūt,* v. a. exécuter ‖ effec-

execution, *ĕks ē kū' shŭn,* s. exécution, f. ‖ (mil.) effet du feu, m.   [m.

executioner, *ĕks ē kū' shŭn ēr,* s. bourreau,

executive, *ĕgz ĕk' ū tĭv,* s. pouvoir exécutif, m.

executive, *ĕgz ĕk' ū tĭv,* a. exécutif.

executor, *ĕgz ĕk' ū tēr,* s. (jur.) exécuteur testamentaire, m.

exemplary, *ĕgz' ĕm plêr ĭ,* a. exemplaire.

exempt, *ĕgz ĕmpt',* v. a. exempter.

exempt, *ĕgz ĕmpt',* a. exempt.

exemption, *ĕgz ĕm' shŭn,* s. exemption, f.

exercise, *ĕks' êr sīz,* s. exercice (du corps), m. ‖ thème, m. ‖ évolutions militaires, f. pl.

exercise, *ĕks' êr sīz,* v. a. & n. exercer ‖ pratiquer ‖ s'exercer ‖ (mil.) faire l'exercice.

exert, *ĕgz êrt',* v. a. employer ‖ exercer ‖ **to ~ oneself,** faire des efforts.

exertion, *ĕgz êr' shŭn,* s. effort, m.

exfoliate, *ĕks fō' lĭ ät,* v. n. s'exfolier, se peler.   [évaporation, f.

exhalation, *ĕgz hă lā' shŭn,* s. exhalaison, f., s. exhalaison, f.

exhale, *ĕgz hāl',* v. a. & n. exhaler, s'exhaler.

exhaust, *ĕgz hāwst',* v. a. épuiser, diminuer.

exhaustion, *ĕgz hāwst' yŭn,* s. épuisement, m.   [intarissable.

exhaustless, *ĕgz hāwst' lĕs,* a. inépuisable,

exhibit, *ĕgz hĭb' ĭt,* v. a. exhiber, montrer, produire.

exhibition, *ĕks hĭ bĭsh' ŭn,* s. exhibition, exposition, f. ‖ bourse, pension, f.

exhibitioner, *ĕks hĭ bĭsh'ŭn ẽr*, s. boursier, m.

exhibitor, *ĕgz hĭb'ĭ tẽr*, s. exposant, m.

exhilarate, *ĕgz hĭl'ā rāt*, v. a. égayer, réjouir, divertir.

exhilaration, *ĕgz hĭl ā rā'shŭn*, s. réjouissance, gaieté, f.

exhort, *ĕgz hŏrt'*, v. a. exhorter, exciter.

exhortation, *ĕgz hŏr tā'shŭn*, s. exhortation, f.

exhume, *ĕks hūm'*, v. a. déterrer, exhumer.

exigency, *ĕks'ĭ jĕn sĭ*, s. exigence, f., besoin, m.

exigent, *ĕks'ĭ jĕnt*, a. exigeant.

exile, *ĕg'zĭl*, s. exil, m. ‖ exilé, m.

exile, *ĕg'zĭl*, v. a. exiler, bannir.

exist, *ĕgz ĭst'*, v. n. exister, être ‖ -ing, a. actuel.

existence, *ĕgz ĭs'tĕns*, s. existence, f.

existent, *ĕgz ĭs'tĕnt*, a. existant.

exit, *ĕks'ĭt*, s. sortie, f., départ, m.

Exodus, *ĕks'ō dŭs*, s. sortie, f. ‖ exode, m. ‖ Exode, m.

exonerate, *ĕgz ŏn'ẽr āt*, v. a. décharger, débarrasser.

exoneration, *ĕgz ŏn ẽr ā'shŭn*, s. décharge, justification, f.

exorbitance, *ĕgz ŏr'bĭ tăns*, s. énormité, f., excès, m.

exorbitant, *ĕgz ŏr'bĭ tănt*, a. (-ly, ad.) exorbitant, énorme.

exorcise, *ĕks'ŏr sīz*, v. a. exorciser.

exorcism, *ĕks'ŏr sĭzm*, s. exorcisme, m.

exordium, *ĕgz ŏr'dĭ ŭm*, s. exorde, préambule, m.

exotic, *ĕgz ŏt'ĭk*, s. plante exotique, f.

exotic, *ĕgz ŏt'ĭk*, a. exotique, étranger.

expand, *ĕks pănd'*, v. a. étendre.

expanse, *ĕks păns'*, s. expansion, dimension, f.

expansion, *ĕks păn'shŭn*, s. expansion, f. ‖ épanouissement, m.

expansive, *ĕks păn'sĭv*, a. (-ly, ad.) expansif.

ex parte, *ĕks' pär'tē*, a. (jur.) d'une seule partie.

expatiate, *ĕks pā'shĭ āt*, v. n. s'étendre sur.

expatriation, *ĕks pā trĭ ā'shŭn*, s. expatriation, f.

expect, *ĕks pĕkt'*, v. a. attendre, espérer.

expectancy, *ĕks pĕk'tăn sĭ*, s. attente, espérance, f.

expectant, *ĕks pĕk'tănt*, s. aspirant, m.

expectant, *ĕks pĕk'tănt*, a. (-ly, ad.) expectant ‖ en attente.

expectation, *ĕks pĕk tā'shŭn*, s. attente, espérance, f. ‖ -s, pl. prétentions, f. pl. ‖ to be in momentary ~ of, attendre d'un moment à l'autre ‖ to fall short of, to fulfil, one's -s, frustrer, remplir ses espérances.

expectorate, *ĕks pĕk'tō rāt*, v. a. expectorer, cracher.

expectoration, *ĕks pĕk tō rā'shŭn*, s. expectoration, f.

expediency, *ĕks pē'dĭ ĕn sĭ*, s. expédient, m. ‖ convenance, propriété, f.

expedient, *ĕks pē'dĭ ĕnt*, a. expédient, convenable ‖ avantageux ‖ -ly, ad. à propos.

expedite, *ĕks'pē dīt*, v. a. expédier, faciliter, accélérer.

expedition, *ĕks pē dĭsh'ŭn*, s. expédition, f. ‖ diligence, hâte, f.

expeditious, *ĕks pē dĭsh'ŭs*, a. (-ly, ad.) expéditif ‖ prompt(ement) ‖ aisé.

expel, *ĕks pĕl'*, v. a. expulser, rejeter.

expend, *ĕks pĕnd'*, v. a. dépenser, débourser.

expenditure, *ĕks pĕn'dĭ tūr*, s. dépense, f. ‖ consommation, f.

expense, *ĕks pĕns'*, s. dépense, f., frais, m. pl. ‖ free of ~, sans frais ‖ franco.

expensive, *ĕks pĕn'sĭv*, a. prodigue ‖ dispendieux ‖ libéral ‖ -ly, ad. d'une manière dispendieuse, à grands frais.

experience, *ĕks pē rĭ'ĕns*, s. expérience pratique, f., usage, m., coutume, habitude, f. ‖ to speak from ~, parler par expérience.

experience, *ĕks pē rĭ'ĕns*, v. a. expérimenter, essayer ‖ éprouver.

experiment, *ĕks pĕr'ĭ mĕnt*, s. expérience, f., essai, m.

experiment, *ĕks pĕr'ĭ mĕnt*, v. a. expérimenter.

experimental, *ĕks pĕr ĭ mĕn'tăl*, a. expérimental ‖ -ly, ad. par expérience.

experimentalist, *ĕks pĕr ĭ mĕn'tăl ĭst*, s. expérimentateur, m.

expert, *ĕks pẽrt'*, s. expert, m.

expert, *ĕks pẽrt'*, a. (-ly, ad.) expert ‖ habile(ment) ‖ adroit.

expertness, *ĕks pẽrt'nĕs*, s. habileté, adresse, f.

expiate, *ĕks'pĭ āt*, v. a. expier, réparer une faute.

expiation, *ĕks pĭ ā'shŭn*, s. expiation, réparation, f.

expiatory, *ĕks pĭ ā'tẽr ĭ*, a. expiatoire.

expiration, *ĕks pĭ rā'shŭn*, s. expiration, évaporation, f. ‖ dernier soupir, m. ‖ respiration, f.

expire, *ĕks pīr'*, v. a. & n. respirer, exhaler ‖ expirer ‖ mourir.

explain, *ĕks plān'*, v. a. expliquer, éclaircir, commenter.

explanation, *ĕks plă nā'shŭn*, s. explication, f.

explanatory, *ĕks plăn'ā tẽr ĭ*, a. explicatif, en explication (de).

expletive, *ĕks'plē tĭv*, s. (gr.) explétif, m.

explicit, *ĕks plĭs'ĭt*, a. (-ly, ad.) explicite(ment) ‖ clair.

explode, *ĕks plōd'*, v. a. & n. censurer, condamner ‖ faire explosion.

exploit, *ĕks plŏyt'*, s. exploit, m.

exploration, *ĕks plō rā'shŭn*, s. exploration, recherche, f., examen, m.

explore, *ĕks plōr'*, v. a. explorer, rechercher, examiner, sonder.

explorer, *ĕks plō'rẽr*, s. explorateur, m.

explosion, *ĕks plō'zhŭn*, s. explosion, f.

explosive, *ĕks plō'sĭv*, a. explosible ‖ explosif.

exponent, *ĕks pō'nĕnt*, s. exposant, m. ‖ interprète, m. ‖ représentant, m.

export, *ĕks pōrt'*, v. a. exporter ‖ ~-duty, s. droit de sortie, m. ‖ ~-trade, s. commerce d'exportation, m.

export(ation), *ĕks' pōrt (ā'shŭn)*, s. exportation, f.

exporter, *ĕks pōr'tẽr*, s. exportateur, m.

expose, *ĕks pōz'*, v. a. exposer ‖ découvrir ‖ compromettre.

exposition, *ĕks pō zĭsh'ŭn*, s. explication, f.

expositor, *ĕks pŏz'ĭ tẽr*, s. interprète, m.

expostulate, *ĕks pŏs' tū lāt,* v. a. disputer, contester.

expostulation, *ĕks pŏs tū lā' shŭn,* s. débat, m., dispute, f. || plainte, f.

exposure, *ĕks pō' zhōōr,* s. exposition, f. || situation, f. || éclat, scandale, m.

expound, *ĕks pŏŭnd',* v. a. exposer, interpréter.

expounder, *ĕks pŏŭn' dĕr,* s. interprète, m.

express, *ĕks prĕs',* s. exprès, m., dépêche, f. || train express, m.   [senter.

express, *ĕks prĕs',* v. a. exprimer || représentable || —ly, ad. expressément.

expressible, *ĕks prĕs' sĭ bl,* a. exprimable.

expression, *ĕks prĕsh' ŭn,* s. expression, f.

expressive, *ĕks prĕs' sĭv,* a. expressif || —ly, ad. d'une manière expressive.

expropriate, *ĕks prō' prĭ āt,* v. a. exproprier.

expulsion, *ĕks pŭl' shŭn,* s. expulsion, f.

expunge, *ĕks pŭnj',* v. a. effacer, anéantir.

expurgate, *ĕks pẽr' gāt,* v. a. épurer, purger.

exquisite, *ĕks' kwĭ zĭt,* s. homme tiré à quatre épingles, m.

exquisite, *ĕks' kwĭ zĭt,* a. exquis, excellent, élégant || —ly, ad. d'une manière exquise.

exquisiteness, *ĕks' kwĭ zĭt nĕs,* s. excellence, délicatesse, f., goût exquis, m. || violence, f.   [expose.

extant, *ĕks' tănt,* a. s'élevant || existant ||

extemporary, *ĕks tĕm' pō rĕr ĭ,* a. improvisé.   [viste.

extempore, *ĕks tĕm' pō rĕ,* ad. à l'improviste.

extemporise, *ĕks tĕm' pō rīz,* v. a. improviser.

extend, *ĕks tĕnd',* v. a. & n. étendre, élargir || communiquer || s'étendre.

extension, *ĕks tĕn' shŭn,* s. extension, f., allongement, m.

extensive, *ĕks tĕn' sĭv,* a. (-ly, ad.) vaste, spacieux, large || ample(ment).

extent, *ĕks tĕnt',* s. étendue, f., portée, f. || (jur.) saisie, f. || to a certain ~, jusqu'à un certain degré || to a great ~, à un haut degré.   [grir || atténuer.

extenuate, *ĕks tĕn' ū āt,* v. a. exténuer, amaigrir || atténuer.

extenuation, *ĕks tĕn ū ā' shŭn,* s. exténuation, diminution, f. || atténuation, f. || in ~ of, pour atténuer.

exterior, *ĕks tē' rĭ ĕr,* s. extérieur, m.

exterior, *ĕks tē' rĭ ĕr,* a. (-ly, ad.) extérieur(ement) || externe.   [miner.

exterminate, *ĕks tẽr' mĭ nāt,* v. a. exterminer.

extermination, *ĕks tẽr mĭ nā' shŭn,* s. extermination, f.   [extérieur(ement).

external, *ĕks tẽr' năl,* a. (-ly, ad.) externe ||

externals, *ĕks tẽr' nălz,* s. pl. dehors, m. pl. || pratiques extérieures, f. pl.

extinct, *ĕks tĭngkt',* a. éteint || aboli.

extinction, *ĕks tĭngk' shŭn,* s. extinction || abolition, f.   [détruire.

extinguish, *ĕks tĭng' gwĭsh,* v. a. éteindre ||

extinguisher, *ĕks tĭng' gwĭsh ĕr,* s. éteignoir, étouffoir, m.

extirpate, *ĕks' tẽr pāt,* v. a. extirper, détruire.   [tion, destruction, f.

extirpation, *ĕks tẽr pā' shŭn,* s. extirpation.

extol, *ĕks tŏl',* v. a. exalter, prôner.

extort, *ĕks tŏrt',* v. a. extorquer, faire des extorsions.   [tion, f.

extortion, *ĕks tŏr' shŭn,* s. extorsion, exaction, f.

extortioner, *ĕks tŏr' shŭn ĕr,* s. extorqueur, exacteur, m.

extra, *ĕks' trā,* s. extra, m. || ~-charge, ~-postage, s. taxe d'affranchissement supplémentaire, f. || ~-super, a. superfin.

extract, *ĕks' trăkt,* s. extrait, m.

extract, *ĕks trăkt',* v. a. extraire, choisir.

extraction, *ĕks trăk' shŭn,* s. extraction, f. || naissance, f. || of French~, d'origine française.   [tion.

extradition, *ĕks trā dĭsh' ŭn,* s. extradition, f. à étranger.

extraneous, *ĕks trā' nĭ ŭs,* a. étranger.

extraordinarily, *ĕks trŏr' dĭ nĕr ĭ lĭ,* ad. extraordinairement.

extraordinary, *ĕks trŏr' dĭ nĕr ĭ,* a. extraordinaire.

extravagance, *ĕks trăv' ă găns,* s. extravagance, f. || folie, f.

extravagant, *ĕks trăv' ă gănt,* a. extravagant, exorbitant, excessif || fou || —ly, ad. extravagamment, follement.

extreme, *ĕks trēm',* s. extrême, m., extrémité, f. || —s meet, les extrêmes se touchent.

extreme, *ĕks trēm',* a. (-ly, ad.) extrême (ment) || outré.

extremity, *ĕks trēm' ĭ tĭ,* s. extrémité, fin, f., bout, m. || situation désespérante, f.

extricate, *ĕks' trĭ kāt,* v. n. débarrasser, dégager.   [surabondance, f.

exuberance, *ĕgz ū' bĕr ăns,* s. exubérance,

exuberant, *ĕgz ū' bĕr ănt,* a. exubérant, surabondant.

exude, *ĕks ūd',* v. n. exsuder.

exult, *ĕgz ŭlt',* v. n. exulter.

exultation, *ĕgz ŭl tā' shŭn,* s. exultation, f. || triomphe, m.

exultingly, *ĕgz ŭl' tĭng lĭ,* ad. d'un air de triomphe.

eye, *ī,* s. œil, m., vue, f. || bouton, bourgeon, m. || trou d'une aiguille, m. || before one's ~s, sous les yeux de qn. || in the ~s of, aux yeux de || to cast an ~ over, jeter un regard sur || to catch one's ~, frapper les yeux à qn. || black~, œil poché || to have an ~ to, avoir égard à || to make one's ~s water, se faire pleurer les yeux || ~-ball, s. prunelle de l'œil, f. || ~-brow, s. sourcil, m. || ~-glass, s. lorgnette, f. || (opt.) oculaire, m. || ~-hole, s. œillet, m. || ~-lash, s. cil, m. || ~-lid, s. paupière, f. || ~-sight, s. vue, f. || ~-sore, s. chose désagréable à l'œil, f., objet d'aversion, m. || ~-tooth, s. dent œillère, f. || ~-witness, s. témoin oculaire, m.

eye, *ī,* v. a. regarder, avoir l'œil sur.

eyed, *īd,* a. aux yeux ...

eyelet, *ī' lĕt,* s. œillet, m.

eyrie, *ī' rĭ,* s. aire, f.

F.

fable, *fā'bl,* s. fable, f.

fabric, *făb'rĭk,* s. fabrique, f. || bâtiment, m. || ouvrage, m. || tissu, m.

fabricate, *făb'rĭ kāt,* v. a. fabriquer || construire. [construction, f.

fabrication, *făb rĭ kā' shŭn,* s. fabrication.

fabricator, *făb'rĭ kā tẽr,* s. fabricateur, inventeur, m. [fabuleusement.

fabulous, *făb'ū lŭs,* a. fabuleux || -ly, ad.

face, *fās,* s. face, f., visage, m., superficie, f. || façade, f. || hardiesse, f. || grimace, f. || extérieur, m., apparence, f. || to my ~, en ma présence || to put a good ~ on the matter, faire bonne contenance || ~-ache, s. tic-douloureux, m.

face, *fās,* v. a. & n. faire face à, regarder en face || affronter, braver || faire des grimaces || faire l'hypocrite || to ~ it out, payer d'audace.

faced, *fāst,* a. de visage . . .

facer, *fā'sẽr,* s. rasade, f. || soufflet, m. ||

facet, *fās'ĕt,* s. facette, f. [échec, m.

facetious, *fă sē'shŭs,* a. facétieux, plaisant, bouffon, gai || -ly, ad. facétieusement. [complaisant.

facile, *făs'il,* a. facile, aisé || flexible ||

facilitate, *fă sĭl'ĭ tāt,* v. a. faciliter, rendre facile.

facility, *fă sĭl'ĭ tĭ,* s. facilité, f. || crédulité, f. || adresse, affabilité, f.

facing, *fā'sĭng,* s. revers d'une manche, parement, m. || (mil.) front, m. || façade, f.

facing, *fā'sĭng,* a. en face, vis-à-vis.

facsimile, *făk sĭm'ĭ lĕ,* s. fac-simile, m.

fact, *făkt,* s. fait, m., action, réalité, f. || in ~, en effet || as a matter of ~, il est de fait || the ~ is that, le fait est que.

faction, *făk'shŭn,* s. faction, cabale, f.

factionist, *făk'shŭn ĭst,* s. factieux, m.

factious, *făk'shŭs,* a. factieux, mutin.

factitious, *făk tĭsh'ŭs,* a. factice, artificiel

factor, *făk'tẽr,* s. facteur, agent, m.

factory, *făk'tẽr ĭ,* s. factorerie, f., comptoir, m. || manufacture, f. || ~-hand, s. ouvrier de fabrique, m.

faculty, *făk'ŭl tĭ,* s. faculté, f. || pouvoir, m. || talent, m. || privilège, m.

fad, *făd,* s. caprice, m., lubie, boutade, f.

fade, *fād,* v. n. se ternir || se faner, se flétrir. [peine, m. || piocheur, m.

fag, *făg,* s. souffre-douleur, m. || homme de

fag, *făg,* v. n. se lasser || piocher

faggot, *făg'gŏt,* s. fagot, m.

fail, *fāl,* s. faute, f., défaut, manque, m., omission, f. || mort, f.

fail, *fāl,* v. a. & n. abandonner || omettre || manquer || déchoir, périr, dépérir || échouer || faire faillite. [banqueroute, f.

failure, *fāl'ūr,* s. manque, défaut, m. ||

fain, *fān,* a. & ad. obligé, forcé, contraint || volontiers. [perdre courage.

faint, *fānt,* v. n. s'évanouir, disparaître ||

faint, *fānt,* a. (-ly, ad.) languissant || faible (ment) || abattu, timide, lâche|| ~-hearted, a. timide, pusillanime.

fainting, *fānt'ĭng,* s. faiblesse, défaillance, f. || in a ~ fit, in a (dead) faint, évanoui.

faintness, *fānt'nĕs,* s. faiblesse, f.

fair, *fār,* s. beauté, belle femme, f. || foire, f.

fair, *fār,* a. (-ly, ad.) beau || agréable (ment) || convenable(ment) || sans tache, pur, clair || blond || favorable || équitable || honnête(ment) || sincère(ment) || calme || ~, ad. en bonne intelligence || ~-spoken, a. élégant, éloquent.

fairing, *fār'ĭng,* s. foire, f.

fairness, *fār'nĕs,* s. beauté, probité, candeur, f. || couleur blonde, f.

fairy, *fā'rĭ,* s. fée, f.

fairy, *fā'rĭ,* a. féerique, de fée.

faith, *fāth,* s. foi, croyance, f. || fidélité, f. || to pin one's ~ on, jurer par || to put ~ in, avoir foi à. [(ment) || sincère.

faithful, *fāth'fŏŏl,* a. (-ly, ad.) fidèle

faithless, *fāth'lĕs,* a. (-ly, ad.) infidèle || perfide(ment) || déloyal.

falcon, *fāw'kn,* s. faucon, m.

falconer, *fāw'kn ẽr,* s. fauconnier, m.

falconry, *fāw'kn rĭ,* s. fauconnerie, f.

fall, *fāwl,* s. chute, f. || déclivité, f. || décadence, f. || dégradation, f. || baisse, f. || cascade, f. || embouchure (d'une rivière), f. || to speculate on the ~, jouer à la baisse.

fall, *fāwl,* v. a. & n. ir. laisser tomber || abaisser, abattre || mettre bas || diminuer, décroître|| s'apaiser || to ~ behind, rester en arrière || to ~ away, maigrir || to ~ back, (mil.) se replier || to ~ in, (mil.) se ranger || to ~ in with, rencontrer || to ~ out, arriver || se quereller || to ~ to, s'y mettre || to ~ through, manquer.

fallacious, *făl lā'shŭs,* a. faux, captieux || -ly, ad. en sophiste. [sophisme, m.

fallacy, *făl'lă sĭ,* s. tromperie, illusion, f.

fallibility, *făl lĭ bĭl'ĭ tĭ,* s. faillibilité, f.

fallible, *făl'lĭ bl,* a. faillible.

falling, *fāwl'ĭng,* s. chute, f. || désertion, f. || ~-sickness, s. épilepsie, f. || ~-star, s. comète, f.

fallow, *făl'lō,* a. fauve, roussâtre || en jachère || ~-deer, s. daim, m.

false, *fāwls,* a. (-ly, ad.) faux, perfide, traître || faussement.

falsehood, *fāwls'hŏŏd,* s. fausseté, tromperie, imposture, f.

falsification, *fāwl sĭ fĭ kā' shŭn,* s. falsification, contrefaçon, f. [saire, m.

falsifier, *fāwl'sĭ fĭ ẽr,* s. falsificateur, faussaire, m.

falsify, *fāwl'sĭ fĭ,* v. a. falsifier || fausser.

falsity, *fāwl'sĭ tĭ,* s. fausseté, f.

falter, *fāwl'tẽr,* v. n. bégayer, se troubler || échouer || trembler. [nouvelle, f.

fame, *fām,* s. renommée, réputation, f. ||

famed, *fāmd,* a. renommé, célèbre.

familiar, *fă mĭl'yẽr,* s. ami intime, m.

familiar, *fă mĭl'yẽr,* a. familier || domestique || -ly, ad. familièrement.

familiarise, *fă mĭl′ yẽr ĭz,* v. a. familiariser.　　[intimité, f.

familiarity, *fă mĭl ĭ ăr′ ĭ tĭ,* s. familiarité,

family, *făm′ ĭ lĭ,* s. famille, f. ‖ classe, espèce, f. ‖ **in the ~ way,** enceinte ‖ **~-tree,** s. arbre généalogique, m.

famine, *făm′ ĭn,* s. famine, disette, f.

famish, *făm′ ĭsh,* v. a. & n. affamer ‖ mourir de faim.

famous, *fā′ mŭs,* a. fameux, renommé ‖ **-ly,** ad. d'une manière éclatante ‖ (fam.) joliment.　　[m.

fan, *făn,* s. éventail, m. ‖ van, m. ‖ soufflet,

fan, *făn,* v. a. éventer ‖ vanner le grain ‖ **~-tail (pigeon),** s. pigeon paon, m.

fanatic, *fă năt′ ĭk,* s. fanatique, m.

fanatic, *fă năt′ ĭk,* a. fanatique.

fanaticism, *fă năt′ ĭ sĭzm,* s. fanatisme, m.

fancier, *făn′ sĭ ẽr,* s. amateur, m. ‖ marchand de nouveautés, m.

fanciful, *făn′ sĭ fŏŏl,* a. fantasque, bizarre ‖ **-ly,** ad. d'une manière bizarre.

fancy, *făn′ sĭ,* s. imagination, image, fantaisie, f., caprice, m. ‖ **to strike, suit one's ~,** être de son goût ‖ **to take a ~ to,** prendre en affection.

fancy, *făn′ sĭ,* v. a. & n. représenter, s'imaginer, se figurer ‖ penser, estimer ‖ **~-articles,** s. pl. nouveautés, f. pl. ‖ **tabletterie,** f. ‖ **~-ball,** s. bal costumé, m.

fang, *făng,* e. défenses, griffes, serres, f. pl.

fanged, *făngd,* a. armé de dents *or* griffes.

fangled, *făng′ gld,* a., **new-~,** de nouvelle invention ‖ d'un nouveau genre.

fantastic(al), *făn tăs′ tĭk (ăl),* a. (-ly, ad.) fantastique(ment) ‖ imaginaire ‖ bizarre (ment).

fantasy, *făn′ tă sĭ,* *vide* fancy.

far, *fär,* a. & ad. éloigné, lointain ‖ loin, au loin ‖ beaucoup, très ‖ **by ~,** de beaucoup ‖ **how ~?** jusqu'où? ‖ **how ~ is it?** combien y a-t-il? ‖ **so ~ so good,** c'est bien jusqu'ici ‖ **~ and wide,** de tous côtés ‖ **~-fetched,** a. recherché, tiré par les cheveux.

farce, *färs,* s. farce, f.

farcical, *fär′ sĭ kăl,* a. bouffon, drôle.

fare, *fär,* s. passage, m. ‖ course, f. ‖ mets, m. pl. ‖ chère, f. ‖ prix du passage, m. ‖ **bill of ~,** s. menu, m.

fare, *fär,* v. n. passer, voyager ‖ manger,

farewell, *fär wĕl′,* s. adieu, m.　　[vivre.

farewell, *fär wĕl,* a. d'adieu.

farinaceous, *făr ĭ nā′ shŭs,* a. farineux.

farm, *färm,* s. ferme, métairie, f.

farm, *färm,* v. a. donner à ferme ‖ prendre à ferme ‖ bailler ‖ cultiver ‖ **~-house** s. ferme, f. ‖ **~-yard,** s. basse-cour, f.

farmer, *fär′ mẽr,* s. fermier, métayer, m.

farming, *färm′ ĭng,* s. agriculture, f.

farmost, *fär′ mōst,* a. le plus éloigné.

farrago, *făr ră′ gō,* s. farrage, mélange, m.

farrier, *făr′ rĭ ẽr,* s. maréchal, maréchal ferrant, m.

farrow, *făr′ rō,* s. petit cochon, m.

farrow, *făr′ rō,* v. n. cochonner.

farther, *fär′ thẽr,* a. & ad. ultérieur ‖ plus loin, au-delà.　　[au plus loin.

farthest, *fär′ thĕst,* a. & ad. le plus éloigné ‖

farthing, *fär′ thĭng,* s. liard anglais, m.

farthingale, *fär′ thĭng găl,* s. crinoline, f.

fascinate, *făs′ sĭ nāt,* v. a. fasciner, ensorceler.

fashion, *făsh′ ŭn,* s. forme, façon, f. ‖ manière, mode, f. ‖ usage, m. ‖ rang, m. ‖ **out of ~,** passé de mode ‖ **after a ~,** tel quel ‖ **to be the ~,** être en vogue ‖ **to be in the ~,** être du dernier chic.

fashion *făsh′ ŭn,* v. a. façonner.

fashionable, *făsh′ ŭn ă bl,* a. à la mode, de bon ton.

fashionably, *făsh′ ŭn ă blĭ,* ad. à la mode.

fast, *făst,* a. & ad. ferme, imprenable ‖ vite, rapide ‖ fermement ‖ promptement ‖ **~ and loose,** ferme et lâche ‖ **~ train,** s. (rail.) convoi de grande vitesse, m.

fast, *făst,* v. n. jeûner.

fasten, *făs′ n,* v. a. & n. attacher, lier ‖ joindre ‖ fermer ‖ s'attacher ‖ se fixer.

faster, *făst′ ẽr,* s. jeûneur, m.

fastidious, *făs tĭd′ ĭ ŭs,* a. dédaigneux ‖ **-ly,** ad. dédaigneusement.

fastness, *făst′ nĕs,* s. fermeté, f. ‖ fort, m.

fat, *făt,* s. gras, m., graisse, f.

fat, *făt,* v. a. & n. engraisser, devenir gras, s'engraisser.

fat, *făt,* a. gras ‖ grossier ‖ riche.

fatal, *fā′ tăl,* a. fatal ‖ funeste ‖ **-ly, ad.** par fatalité.

fatalism, *fā′ tăl ĭzm,* s. fatalisme, m.

fatalist, *fā′ tăl ĭst,* s. fataliste, m.

fatality, *fă tăl′ ĭ tĭ,* s. fatalité, f., destin, m.

fate, *făt,* s. destin, sort, m. ‖ **-s,** pl. parques, f. pl.

fated, *fā′ tĕd,* a. destiné.

father, *fä′ thẽr,* s. père, m. ‖ **~-in-law,** s. beau-père, m.

fatherhood, *fä′ thẽr hŏŏd,* s. paternité, f.

fatherland, *fä′ thẽr lănd,* s. pays natal, m.

fatherless, *fä′ thẽr lĕs,* s. sans père, orphelin.　　[père.

fatherly, *fä′ thẽr lĭ,* a. & ad. paternel ‖ en

fathom, *făth′ ŭm,* s. brasse, toise, f. ‖ portée, f.　　[pénétrer.

fathom, *făth′ ŭm,* v. a. sonder, approfondir ‖

fathomless, *făth′ ŭm lĕs,* a. sans fond ‖ (fig.) impénétrable.

fatigue, *fă tēg′,* s. fatigue, f.

fatigue, *fă tēg′,* v. a. fatiguer ‖ **~-party,** s. (mil.) corvée, f.

fatling, *făt′ lĭng,* s. bête grasse, f.

fatness, *făt′ nĕs,* s. graisse, f., obésité, f.

fatten, *făt′ n,* v. a. & n. engraisser, devenir gras.

fattening, *făt′ n ĭng,* s. engraissement, m.

fatty, *făt′ tĭ,* a. gras, huileux.

fatuity, *făt ū′ ĭ tĭ,* s. fatuité, f.

fatuous, *făt′ ū ŭs,* a. imbécile, sot.

fault, *fawlt,* s. faute, bévue, f., défaut, délit, m. ‖ **to find ~ with,** trouver à redire à ‖ **~-finder,** s. censeur, critique, m.

faultily, *fawl′ tĭ lĭ,* ad. improprement ‖ à tort.

faultiness, *fawl'tĭ něs*, s. fauté, f., vice, m. || offense, f.

faultless, *fowlt'lĕs*, a. sans défaut, irrépréhensible.

faulty, *fŏwl'tĭ*, a. coupable, blâmable.

fauna, *fawn'ă*, s. faune, f.

favour, *fā'vŭr*, s. faveur, bienveillance, f., bon office, m. || grâce, f., pardon, m. || souvenir, m. || air, m., mine, f. || nœud de rubans, m. || with (under) ~, avec votre permission || to curry ~ with, rechercher la faveur de.

favour, *fā'vŭr*, v. a. favoriser.

favourable, *fā'vŭr ă bl*, a. favorable, convenable.

favourably, *fā'vŭr ă blĭ*, ad. favorablement.

favoured, *fā'vŭrd*, a. favori, favorisé || well-~, à bonne mine.

favourite, *fā'vŭr ĭt*, s. favori, m., favorite, f.

fawn, *fawn*, s. faon, m. || ~-coloured, fauve.

fawn, *fawn*, v.n. faonner || caresser, cajoler.

fay, *fā*, s. fée, f.

fealty, *fē'ăl tĭ*, s. féauté, f. || loyauté, f.

fear, *fēr*, s. frayeur, peur, f. || inquiétude, f.

fear, *fēr*, v. a. & n. craindre || faire peur.

fearful, *fēr'fŏŏl*, a. (-ly, ad.) peureux, craintif || affreux, terrible(ment).

fearless, *fēr'lĕs*, a. intrépide, hardi.

feasibility, *fē zĭ bĭl'ĭ tĭ*, s. chose faisable, f.

feasible, *fē'zĭ bl*, a. faisable, praticable.

feast, *fēst*, s. festin, m., fête, f., repas, m.

feast, *fēst*, v. a. & n. fêter, régaler || banqueter.

feat, *fēt*, s. fait, exploit, m., action, f.

feather, *fĕth'ŭr*, s. plume, f. || ornement, m. || (fig.) espèce, f. || volée, f. || bagatelle, f. || in high ~, en veine de gaîté || to show the white ~, faire le poltron.

feather, *fĕth'ŭr*, v. a. orner de plumes || enrichir || ~-bed, s. lit de plumes, m. || ~-broom, s. plumail, m.

feathery, *fĕth'ŭr ĭ*, a. plumeux || (fig.) léger.

feature, *fē'tŭr*, s. trait, linéament, m.

featured, *fē'tŭrd*, a. aux traits .

febrifuge, *fĕb'rĭ fūj*, s. fébrifuge, m.

febrile, *fēb'rĭl*, a. fébrile.

February, *fĕb'rō ĕr ĭ*, s. février, m.

fecula, *fĕk'ŭ lă*, s. fécule, f. || chlorophylle, f.

fecundation, *fĕk ŭn dā'shŭn*, s. fécondation, f.

fecundity, *fē kŭn'dĭ tĭ*, s. fécondité, fertilité, f.

federal, *fĕd'ĕr ăl*, a. fédéral, fédératif.

federate, *fĕd'ĕr āt*, s. confédéré, ligué, m.

federate, *fĕd'ĕr āt*, a. confédéré, ligué.

federation, *fĕd ĕr ā'shŭn*, s. fédération, ligue, f.

fee, *fē*, s. fief, m. || honoraire, salaire, m.

fee, *fē*, v. a. récompenser, payer || corrompre.

feeble, *fē'bl*, a. faible, débile.

feebleness, *fē'bl něs*, s. faiblesse f || imbécillité, f.

feebly, *fē'blĭ*, ad. faiblement.

feed, *fēd*, s. nourriture, f. || pâture, f. || alimentation, f.

feed, *fēd*, v. a. & n. ir. nourrir || faire paître, paître, repaître || se nourrir, manger || engraisser.

feeder, *fēd'ŭr*, s. mangeur, m. || gourmand, m. || appareil d'alimentation, m.

feeding-bottle, *fēd'ing bŏt l*, s. biberon, m.

feel, *fēl*, s. toucher, tact, m.

feel, *fēl*, v. a. & n. ir. sentir, toucher, éprouver || savoir.

feeler, *fēl'ĕr*, s. antenne, f. || (fig.) ballon d'essai, m.

feeling, *fēl'ing*, s. sentiment, m., sensibilité, f.

feeling, *fēl'ing*, a. (-ly, ad.) touchant || sensible(ment) || avec sentiment.

feign, *fān*, v. a. & n. feindre, inventer || feint, faint, s. feinte, f.

felicitate, *fē lis'ĭ tāt*, v. a. rendre heureux || féliciter.

felicitation, *fē lis ĭ tā'shŭn*, s. félicitation, f.

felicity, *fē lis'ĭ tĭ*, s. félicité, prospérité, f.

feline, *fē'lin*, a. de chat.

fell, *fēl*, s. peau, fourrure, f. || ~-monger, s. pelletier, fourreur, m.

fell, *fēl*, v. a. abattre || renverser || assommer.

fell, *fēl*, a. (-y, ad.) cruel(lement) || sanguinaire || d'une manière féroce.

fellow, *fēl'lō*, s. compagnon, camarade, associé, m. || membre d'un collège etc., m. || gueux, misérable, m. || ~-citizen, s. concitoyen, m. || ~-creature, s. semblable, m. || ~-feeling, s. sympathie, f. || ~-student, s. compagnon d'études, m. || ~-sufferer, s. compagnon d'infortune, m. || ~-traveller, s. compagnon de voyage, m.

fellowship, *fēl'lō ship*, s. compagnie, société, association, égalité, f. || bourse de collège, f.

felly, *fēl'lĭ*, s. jante, f.

felon, *fēl'ŏn*, s. criminel, m.

felonious, *fē lō'nĭ ŭs*, a. (-ly, ad.) cruel traître, perfide || en criminel, en traître.

felony, *fēl'ŏn ĭ*, s. félonie, f.

felt, *fēlt*, s. feutre, m., bourre, f.

felucca, *fē lŭk'kă*, s. felouque, f.

female, *fē'māl*, s. femelle, f. || femme, f.

female, *fē'māl*, a. femelle, féminin, de femme || ~ screw, s. écrou, m.

feminine, *fĕm'ĭ nin*, a. féminin || efféminé, délicat, doux.

fen, *fĕn*, s. marécage, marais, m.

fence, *fĕns*, s. rempart, m., garde, défense, f. || escrime, f.

fence, *fĕns*, v. a. & n. enclore, palissader || faire des armes, escrimer.

fencing, *fĕn'sing*, ~-gloves, s. pl. gants bourrés, m. pl. || ~-jacket, s. plastron d'armes, m. || ~-master, s. maître d'armes, m. || ~-match, s. assaut d'armes, m. || ~-pad, s. plastron, m. || ~-school, s. salle d'armes, f.

fend, *fĕnd*, v. a. parer, détourner || se préfender, *fĕn'dĕr*, s. garde-feu, m.

fennel, *fĕn'nĕl*, s. fenouil, m.

ferment, *fĕr'mĕnt*, fermentation, *fĕr mĕn tā'shŭn*, s. fermentation, f.

ferment, *fĕr mĕnt'*, v. a. & n. faire fermenter || fermenter.

fern, *fĕrn*, s. fougère, f. || ~-plot, s. fougeraie, f.

fernery, *fĕrn'ĕr ĭ*, s. fougeraie, f.

ferocious, *fĕ rŏ' shŭs,* a. féroce, rapace ‖
—ly, ad. avec férocité.

ferocity, *fĕ rŏs' ĭ tĭ,* s. férocité, cruauté, f.

ferret, *fĕr' rĕt,* s. furet, m.

ferret, *fĕr' rĕt,* v. a. fureter, dénicher,
fouiller ‖ to ~ out, traquer.

ferruginous, *fĕr rŏ' jĭn ŭs,* a. ferrugineux.

ferrule, *fĕr' rōōl,* s. virole, f. ‖ (of a stick)
bout, m.

ferry, *fĕr' rĭ,* s. bac, m. ‖ passage d'eau, m.

ferry, *fĕr' rĭ,* v. a. traverser en bac ‖ ~
man, s. bachoteur, m.

fertile, *fĕr' tĭl,* a. fertile, fécond.

fertilise, *fĕr' tĭl ĭs,* v. a. fertiliser.

fertility, *fĕr tĭl' ĭ tĭ,* s. fertilité, fécondité, f.

ferule, *fĕr' ŭl,* s. férule, f.

fervency, *fĕr' vĕn sĭ,* s. ferveur, f., zèle, m.

fervent, *fĕr' vĕnt,* a. fervent, zélé ‖ ~ly,
ad. fervemment.

fervid, *fĕr' vĭd,* a. fervent, ardent, brûlant.

fervour, *fĕr' vĕr,* s. ferveur, ardeur, f.

fester, *fĕs' tĕr,* v. n. se corrompre, pourrir ‖
suppurer.

festival, *fĕs' tĭ văl,* s. fête musicale, f.

festival, *fĕs' tĭ văl,* a. de fête, joyeux.

festivity, *fĕs tĭv' ĭ tĭ,* s. fête, f. ‖ joie, f.

festoon, *fĕs tōn',* s. feston, m.

festoon, *fĕs tōn',* v. a. festonner.

fetch, *fĕch,* v. a. aller chercher, apporter,
produire ‖ arriver ‖ valoir.

fetich, *fē' tĭsh,* s. fétiche.

fetid, *fĕt' ĭd,* a. fétide, puant.

fetidness, *fĕt' ĭd nĕs,* s. puanteur, m.

fetlock, *fĕt' lŏk,* s. fanon, m.

fetter, *fĕt' tĕr,* v. a. enchaîner ‖ (fig.) entraver   [vage, m. ‖ entraves, f. pl.

fetters, *fĕt' tĕrz,* s. pl. fers, m. pl. ‖ escla-

feud, *fūd,* s. fief, m. ‖ querelle, animosité,
f.

feudal, *fū' dăl,* a. féodal.   [f.

feudalism, *fū' dăl ĭzm,* s. féodalisme, m.

feudatory, *fū' dă tĕr ĭ,* s. feudataire, m.

fever, *fē' vĕr,* s. fièvre, f.

feverish, *fē' vĕr ĭsh,* a. fiévreux, ayant la
fièvre ‖ brûlant.

few, *fū,* a. peu ‖ a ~, quelques.

fib, *fĭb,* s. mensonge, conte, m.

fib, *fĭb,* v. n. mentir.

fibre, *fī' bĕr,* s. fibre, f.

fibrin, *fī' brĭn,* s. fibrine, f.

fibrous, *fī' brŭs,* a. fibreux.

fickle, *fĭk' l,* a. volage, inconstant, irrésolu.

fickleness, *fĭk' l nĕs,* s. inconstance, humeur volage, f.

fiction, *fĭk' shŭn,* s. fiction, f.

fictitious, *fĭk tĭsh' ŭs,* a. feint ‖ contrefait,
faux ‖ —ly, ad. par fiction.

fiddle, *fĭd' l,* s. violon, m.

fiddle, *fĭd' l,* v. a. jouer du violon ‖ baguenauder ‖ ~stick, s. archet d'un violon, m. ‖ ~sticks ! bah !

fiddler, *fĭd' lĕr,* s. violoniste, m.

fidelity, *fĭ dĕl' ĭ tĭ,* s. fidélité, honnêteté, f.

fidget, *fĭj' ĕt,* s. mouvement d'impatience,
m., inquiétude, f.

fidget, *fĭj' ĕt,* v. a. remuer, frétiller.

fidgety, *fĭj' ĕt ĭ,* a. remuant, inquiet.

fie ! *fī,* fi ! fi donc !

fief, *fēf,* s. fief, m.

field, *fēld,* s. champ, m. ‖ champ de bataille, m. ‖ ~day, s. jour de revue, m. ‖
~glass, s. lunette de campagne, f. ‖
~mouse, s. mulot, m. ‖ ~officer, s.
officier de l'état-major, m. ‖ ~piece, s.
canon, m. ‖ ~practice, s. grandes manœuvres, f. pl. ‖ ~sports, s. pl. plaisir
de la chasse, m. ‖ ~works, s. pl. tra-
vaux, m. pl.

fieldfare, *fēld' fār,* s. litorne, f.

fiend, *fēnd,* s. démon, ennemi, m.

fiendish, *fēnd' ĭsh,* a. diabolique, infernal.

fierce, *fērs,* a. féroce, cruel ‖ —ly, ad. avec
férocité.   [f.

fierceness, *fērs' nĕs,* s. férocité, cruauté,

fieriness, *fī' ĕr ĭ nĕs,* s. chaleur, f. ‖ fougue, f.

fiery, *fī' ĕr ĭ,* a. de feu ‖ ardent, fougueux.

fife, *fīf,* s. fifre, m.

fifteen, *fĭf' tēn,* a. quinze.

fifteenth, *fĭf' tēnth,* a. quinzième ‖ (of
the month) le quinze.

fifth, *fĭfth,* s. (mus.) quinte, f.

fifth, *fĭfth,* a. (-ly, ad.) cinquième(ment).

fiftieth, *fĭf' tĭ ĕth,* a. cinquantième.

fifty, *fĭf' tĭ,* a. cinquante.

fig, *fĭg,* s. figue, f. ‖ bagatelle, f. ‖ ~leaf,
s. feuille du figuier, f. ‖ ~tree, s. figuier,
m.   [tée, f.

fight, *fīt,* s. bataille, f., combat, m., mê-

fight, *fīt,* v. a. & n. ir. combattre, se
battre contre.   [bretteur, m.

fighter, *fīt' ĕr,* s. combattant, guerrier ‖

figment, *fĭg' mĕnt,* s. fiction, invention, f.

figurative, *fĭg' ŭr ā tĭv,* a. figuratif ‖ figuré ‖ —ly, ad. au figuré.

figure, *fĭg' ĕr,* s. figure, forme, tournure,
f. ‖ (ar.) chiffre, m. ‖ ~ of speech, s.
figure de rhétorique, f.

figure, *fĭg' ĕr,* v. a. figurer, façonner ‖ ~
head, s. (mar.) figure, f.

filament, *fĭl' ă mĕnt,* s. filament, m.
(bot.) filet, m.

filbert, *fĭl' bĕrt,* s. aveline, f.

filch, *fĭlch,* v. a. filouter, voler.

filcher, *fĭlch' ĕr,* s. filou, m.   [liste, f.

file, *fīl,* s. fil, m. ‖ lime, f. ‖ liasse, f. ‖

file, *fīl,* v. a. enfiler ‖ limer ‖ défiler ‖ ~
dust, s. limaille, f. ‖ ~firing, s. feu
de file, m. ‖ ~leader, s. chef de file, m.

filial, *fĭl' ĭăl,* a. (-ly, ad.) filial(ement).

filiation, *fĭl ĭ ā' shŭn,* s. filiation, f.

filibuster, *fĭl' ĭ bŭs tĕr,* s. flibustier, m.

filigree, *fĭl' ĭ grē,* s. filigrane, m.

filings, *fī' lĭngz,* s. pl. limaille, f.

fill, *fĭl,* s. suffisance, f.   [rassasier.

fill, *fĭl,* v. a. & n. emplir, remplir ‖ soûler,

filler, *fĭl' lĕr,* s. remplissage, m.

fillet, *fĭl' lĕt,* s. bande, f., bandeau, m. ‖
tresse (de cheveux), f. ‖ filet, m. ‖ rouelle
de veau, f.

filling, *fĭl' lĭng,* s. (de dents) plombage, m.
‖ remplissage, m. ‖ chargement, m.

fillip, *fĭl' lĭp,* s. chiquenaude, f.

---

lāte, hăt, fär, läw ; — hēre, gĕt, hĕr ; — mīne, ĭnn ; — nō, hŏt, prōve ; — hōw ; —

filly, *fĭl'lĭ,* s. pouliche, f.
film, *film,* s. pellicule, membrane, f.
filter, *fĭl'tĕr,* s. filtre, couloir, m.
filter, *fĭl'tĕr,* v. a. filtrer, purifier.
filth(iness), *filth'(ĭ nĕs),* s. ordure, f. || saleté, f.
filthy, *filth'ĭ,* a. sale, malpropre.
filtrate, *fĭl'trāt,* v. a. filtrer.
fin, *fĭn,* s. nageoire, barbe, f. [décisif.
final, *fī'năl,* a. (-ly, ad.) final(ement) ||
finance(s), *fĭ năn'sĕ(s),* s. (pl.) finances, f.
financial, *fĭ năn'shăl,* a. financiel. [f.pl.
financier, *fĭn ăn'sēr,* s. financier, m.
finch, *finsh,* s. pinson, m.
find, *fīnd,* v. a. & n. ir. trouver || découvrir || inventer || attraper || fournir || se porter.
fine, *fīn,* s. amende, f. || in ~, enfin.
fine, *fīn,* v. a. & n. affiner, purifier || mettre à l'amende.
fine, *fīn,* a. beau, bel, fin, pur || mince || affilé || adroit, gracieux, élégant || exquis || **-ly,** ad. joliment, élégamment || **~-spun,** a. finement filé || délicat, subtil.
finedraw, *fīn'drāw,* v. a. rentraire.
finedrawer, *fīn'drāw ĕr,* s. rentrayeur, m.
fineness, *fīn'nĕs,* s. élégance, délicatesse, f. || finesse, f. || affinerie, f.
finery, *fī'nĕr ĭ,* s. brillante parure, f. || colifichets, m. pl.
finger, *fĭng'gĕr,* s. doigt, m. || **~-board,** s. (mus.) manche, m. || **~-glass,** s. rince-bouche, m. || **~-plate,** s. plaque de propreté, f. || **~-post,** s. poteau indicateur, m. || **~-stall,** s. doigtier, m.
finger, *fĭng'gĕr,* v. a. toucher || (mus.) doigter, jouer.
fingering, *fĭng'gĕr ĭng,* s. maniement, m. || (mus.) doigter, m.
finical, *fĭn'ĭ kăl,* a. fat, affecté.
fining, *fī'nĭng,* s. clarification (du vin), f. || **-s,** s. pl. colle, f. [compléter.
finish, *fĭn'ish,* v. a. finir, achever, terminer.
finite, *fī'nĭt,* a. fini, limité, borné.
fir(-tree), *fẽr('trē),* s. sapin, m. || **~-cone,** s. pigne, f.
fire, *fīr,* s. feu, m. || incendie, m. || **running ~,** feu roulant || **on ~,** en feu || **to hang ~,** faire long feu || **to miss ~,** rater || **to set on ~,** mettre en feu || **~-ball,** s. grenade, f. || météore, m. || **~-box,** s. (rail.) boîte à feu, f. || **~-brand,** s. tison ardent, m. || boute-feu, m. || **~-brick,** s. brique réfractaire, f. || **~-brigade,** s. corps de pompiers, m. || **~-brigade station,** s. caserne de pompiers, f. || **~-damp,** s. grisou, m. || **~-eater,** s. ferrailleur, sacripant, m. || **~-engine,** s. pompe à incendie, f. || **~-escape,** s. appareil *or* sac de sauvetage, m. || **~-fly,** s. lampyre, m. || **~-irons,** s. pl. garniture de feu, f. || **~-office,** s. bureau d'assurance contre l'incendie, m. || **~-plug,** s. bouche d'eau, f. || **~-proof,** a. à l'épreuve d feu || **~-screen,** s. écran, m. || **~-ship,** s. brûlot, m. || **~-water,** s. eau-de-vie, f. || **~-wood,** s. bois de chauffage, m.

fire, *fīr,* v. a. & n. faire feu || enflammer || **to catch ~,** prendre feu, s'enflammer ||
fire! *fīr,* au feu! || (mil.) feu! [tirer.
firelock, *fīr'lŏk,* s. fusil, m.
fireman, *fīr'măn,* s. pompier, m. || chauffeur, m.
fireplace, *fīr'plās,* s. cheminée, f., foyer, m. [du feu, m.
fireside, *fīr'sĭd,* s. foyer domestique, coin
fireworks, *fīr'wẽrks,* s. feu d'artifice, m.
firing, *fīr'ĭng,* s. combustible, m. || chauffage, m. || (mil.) feu, tir, m., fusillade, f.
firkin, *fẽr'kĭn,* s. barillet, m.
firm, *fẽrm,* s. maison de commerce, f.
firm, *fẽrm,* a. (-ly, ad.) ferme(ment) || constant || solide(ment).
firmament, *fẽr'mă mĕnt,* s. firmament, m.
firmness, *fẽrm'nĕs,* s. fermeté, constance, f.
first, *fẽrst,* a. & ad. premier || première-ment, d'abord || **at ~,** d'abord.
first-born, *fẽrst'bawrn,* **firstling,** *fẽrst'-ling,* s. premier-né, m.
firth, *fẽrth,* vide frith.
fiscal, *fĭs'kăl,* s. fiscal, m. || fisc, m.
fiscal, *fĭs'kăl,* a. fiscal || fisc.
fish, *fĭsh,* s. poisson, m. || **(at cards)** fiche, f. || (fig.) individu, m. || **~-bone,** s. arête, f. || **~-carver,** s. truelle à poisson, f. || **~-hook,** s. hameçon, f. || **~-line,** s. ligne, f. || **~-rod,** s. manche de la ligne, m. || **~-market,** s. poissonnerie, f. || **~-pond,** s. étang, vivier, m. || **~-wife,** s. poissonnière, f.
fisher(man), *fĭsh'ĕr(măn),* s. pêcheur, m.
fishery, *fĭsh'ĕr ĭ,* s. pêche, f. || **(place)** pêcherie, f.
fishing, *fĭsh'ĭng,* s. pêche, f.
fishy, *fĭsh'ĭ,* a. poissonneux.
fissure, *fĭsh'ōōr,* s. fente, f.
fist, *fĭst,* s. poing, m. [m. pl.
fisticuffs, *fĭs'tĭ kŭfs,* s. pl. coups de poing.
fistula, *fĭs'tū lă,* s. fistule, f.
fit, *fĭt,* s. attaque, atteinte, f., accès, m. || caprice, m. || **by -s and starts,** par bonds, par élans, par à-coups.
fit, *fĭt,* v. a. & n. ajuster, adapter || accommoder || s'ajuster, convenir à, aller à.
fit, *fĭt,* a. (-ly, ad.) convenable(ment) || propre(ment), à propos || bien.
fitful, *fĭt'fŏŏl,* a. (-ly, ad.) qui vient par accès || incertain(ement). [f.
fitness, *fĭt'nĕs,* s. convenance, bienséance, f.
fitting, *fĭt'tĭng,* s. ajustement, m.
fitting, *fĭt'tĭng,* a. convenable, juste.
five, *fĭv,* a. cinq.
fix, *fĭks,* v. a. & n. fixer, attacher, arrêter || se fixer, se déterminer.
fixed, *fĭkst,* a. (-ly, ad.) fixe(ment) || fixé.
fixture, *fĭks'tŭr,* s. meuble fixe, à demeure, m.
fizz(le), *fĭz'(zl),* v. n. siffler || peter.
flabbiness, *flăb'ĭ nĕs,* s. flaccidité, f.
flabby, *flăb'ĭ,* a. mou, mollasse, flasque.
flaccid, *flăk'sĭd,* a. faible, lâche.
flag, *flăg,* s. rapeau, pavillon, m. || glaïeul, m. || **to strike one's ~,** (mar.) amener son pavillon.

flag, *flăg,* v. a. & n. baisser ‖ daller.‖ s'affaisser ‖ flotter à l'aventure ‖ perdre courage ‖ ~-officer, s. chef d'escadre, m. ‖
~-ship, s. vaisseau amiral, m. ‖ ~-staff,
s. mât de pavillon, m. ‖ ~-stone, s.
dalle, f.   [fustiger.

flagellate, *flăj'ĕl lāt,* v. a. flageller.

flagitious, *flă jĭsh'ŭs,* a. méchant, pervers,
scélérat ‖ -ly, ad. d'une manière infâme.

flagon, *flăg'ŏn,* s. flacon, m.

flagrancy, *flă' grăn sĭ,* s. notoriété, f. ‖
feu, m. ‖ ardeur, f.

flagrant, *flā' grănt,* a. brûlant ‖ patent.

flail, *flāl,* s. fléau, m.

flake, *flāk,* s. flocon, m. ‖ étincelle, f. ‖
couche, f. ‖ lame, f. ‖ glaçon, m.

flake, *flāk,* v. n. s'écailler.

flaky, *flā' kĭ,* a. en flocons ‖ par couches.

flame, *flām,* s. flamme, f., feu, m. ‖ ardeur, f. ‖ amour, m.

flame, *flām,* v. n. flamber.

flaming, *flā' ming,* a. flamboyant, ardent,
enflammé.

flamingo, *flă ming' gō,* s. phénicoptère, m.

flange, *flănj,* s. (rail.) rebord, m.

flank, *flăngk,* s. flanc, côté, m.

flank, *flăngk,* v. a. flanquer ‖ (mil.) prendre
en flanc.

flannel, *flăn'nĕl,* s. flanelle, f.

flap, *flăp,* s. pan, m. ‖ patte, f. ‖ petit
coup, m. ‖ bout d'oreille, m.

flap, *flăp,* v. a. & n. frapper de la main ‖
battre des ailes ‖ pendre.

flare, *flâr,* s. vive clarté, f. ‖ flamme, f.

flare, *flâr,* v. n. étinceler ‖ flamber ‖ (of
lamps) filer ‖ (fig.) briller.

flaring, *flā' ring,* a. éblouissant.

flash, *flăsh,* s. éclat, m. ‖ (lumière) éclair,
m. ‖ jet, m. ‖ feu, m. ‖ clinquant, m. ‖
~ of wit, saillie, f., bon mot, m.

flash, *flăsh,* v. a. faire jaillir ‖ jeter, envoyer ‖ ~, v. n. briller ‖ étinceler ‖ passer
comme un éclair ‖ jaillir.

flash, *flăsh,* a. faux ‖ de bas (mauvais)
aloi ‖ équivoque ‖ interlope.

flashy, *flăsh' ĭ,* a. à effet ‖ frivole, superficiel ‖ insipide.

flask, *flăsk,* s. bouteille, poire à poudre, f.

flat, *flăt,* s. plaine, f. ‖ terrain plat, m. ‖
plat (d'une épée), m. ‖ (mus.) bémol, m. ‖
(d'une maison) étage, m.

flat, *flăt,* a. plat, uni ‖ insipide ‖ découragé ‖ (mus.) bémol ‖ -ly, ad. platement ‖
nettement, franc et net ‖ sans esprit.

flatness, *flăt' nĕs,* s. surface unie, f. ‖ insipidité, fadeur, f. ‖ faiblesse, bassesse, f.

flatten, *flăt'n,* v. a. & n. aplatir, aplanir ‖
affadir ‖ abattre ‖ s'aplatir ‖ s'éventer.

flatter, *flăt' tĕr,* s. laminoir, m.

flatter, *flăt' tĕr,* v. a. flatter, caresser.

flattery, *flăt' tĕr ĭ,* s. flatterie, adulation, f.

flatting-mill, *flăt' ting mĭl,* s. laminoir, m.

flatulency, *flăt' ū lĕn sĭ,* s. flatuosité, f.

flatulent, *flăt' ū lĕnt,* a. flatueux, venteux ‖
vain ‖ ampoulé.   [nence, f.

flaunt, *flăwnt,* s. étalage, m. ‖ imperti-

flaunt, *flăwnt,* v. n. se pavaner ‖ flotter,
voltiger.

flavour, *flā' vĕr,* s. saveur, odeur, f., parfum, m. ‖ bouquet (du vin), m.

flavour, *flā' vĕr,* v. a. donner un parfum.

flaw, *flaw,* s. crevasse, m. ‖ défaut, m. ‖
bouffée de vent, f.   [défaut.

flawless, *flaw' lĕs,* a. (-ly, ad.) (fig.) sans

flax, *flăks,* s. lin, m. ‖ ~-comb, s. séran, m.

flaxen, *flăks' ĕn,* a. de lin, blond.

flay, *flā,* v. a. écorcher.

flea, *flē,* s. puce, f. ‖ ~-bite, s. piqûre de
puce, f. ‖ (fig.) petit mal, m.

fledge, *flĕj,* v. a. donner des ailes ‖ -d, a.
couvert de plumes ‖ en état de voler.

flee, *flē,* v. a. s'enfuir.

fleece, *flēs,* s. toison, f.

fleece, *flēs,* v. a. tondre ‖ dépouiller.

fleecy, *flē' sĭ,* a. laineux.

fleet, *flēt,* s. flotte, f.

fleet, *flēt,* a. véloce, rapide.

fleeting, *flēt' ing,* a. passager, fugitif.

fleetness, *flēt' nĕs,* s. rapidité, vitesse, f.

flesh, *flĕsh,* s. chair, viande, f. ‖ embonpoint, m. ‖ ~-brush, s. brosse à friction, f. ‖ ~-colour, s. couleur de chair,
f. ‖ carnation, f. ‖ ~-coloured, a. de
couleur de chair ‖ incarnat.

flesh, *flĕsh,* v. a. repaître ‖ acharner ‖ essayer ‖ mettre en curée.

fleshings, *flĕsh' ings,* s. pl. maillot, m.

fleshless, *flĕsh' lĕs,* a. décharné.

fleshy, *flĕsh' ĭ,* a. charnu, gras.

flexibility, *flĕks ĭ bĭl' ĭ tĭ,* s. flexibilité, f.

flexible, *flĕks' ĭ bl,* a. flexible, pliant,
souple.

flexion, *flĕk' shŭn,* s. flexion, f.

flicker, *flĭk' ŏr,* v. n. battre des ailes ‖ vaciller ‖ voltiger.

flight, *flīt,* s. fuite, f. ‖ volée, f., transport,
m. ‖ accès, m. ‖ ~-time, s. temps du
passage des oiseaux, m. ‖ to put to ~,
mettre en fuite.

flighty, *flīt' ĭ,* a. volage, fugitif.

flimsiness, *flĭm' zĭ nĕs,* s. légèreté, trivialité, f.

flimsy, *flĭm' zĭ,* a. faible, mollasse ‖ trivial.

flinch, *flĭnsh,* v. n. reculer, hésiter ‖ se désister ‖ biaiser.   [de patte, m.

fling, *fling,* s. coup, m. ‖ trait, m. ‖ coup

fling, *fling,* v. a. & n. ir. lancer, darder ‖
s'élancer, bondir.

flint, *flĭnt,* s. pierre à fusil, f., caillou, m. ‖
~-glass, s. cristal, m.

flinty, *flĭnt' ĭ,* a. pierreux, inexorable.

flippancy, *flĭp' păn sĭ,* s. verbiage, m. ‖
pétulance, f.   [lard.

flippant, *flĭp' pănt,* a. délié, agile ‖ babil-

flirt, *flĕrt,* s. coquette, f. ‖ flirt, m.

flirt, *flĕrt,* v. a. & n. jeter avec vitesse ‖
railler, plaisanter ‖ coqueter.

flirtation, *flĕr tā' shŭn,* s. coquetterie, f.

flit, *flĭt,* v. n. s'enfuir, passer rapidement.

flitch, *flĭch,* s. quartier de lard, m.

float, *flōt,* s. flottage, m. ‖ radeau, m. ‖
(fishing) flotte, f., bouchon, m.

float, *flōt,* v. a. & n. mettre à flot || inonder, flotter.

floating, *flōt'ing,* a. flottant || ~capital, s. capital commercial, m. || ~ debts, s. pl. dettes courantes, f. pl.

flock, *flŏk,* s. troupeau, m. || volée, troupe, f. || flocon, m.

flock, *flŏk,* v. n. s'attrouper.

floe, *flō,* s. glaçon, m.

flog, *flŏg,* v. a. fouetter, fustiger.

flood, *flŭd,* s. déluge, torrent, flux, m. || rivière, f. [écluse, f.

flood, *flŭd,* v. a. inonder || ~~gate, s.

floor, *flōr,* s. plancher, parquet || étage, m.

floor, *flōr,* v. a. planchéier || parqueter || jeter par terre. [parquet, m.

flooring, *flōr'ing,* s. parquetage, m. ||

floral, *flō'ral,* a. floral.

florid, *flŏr'id,* a. fleuri || vermeil.

floridity, *flŏ rid'i ti,* s. teint vermeil, m.

florin, *flŏr'in,* s. florin, m. (2 francs 50 centimes).

florist, *flŏr'ist,* s. fleuriste, m. [times).

floss, *flŏs,* s. bourre, f. || (des métaux) floss, m. || ~~silk, s. filoselle, f. || soie

flotilla, *flŏ til'lä,* s. flottille, f. [plate, f.

flounce, *flŏwns,* s. volant, m.

flounce, *flŏwns,* v. a. & n. garnir de volants || se plonger || se trémousser.

flounder, *flŏwn'dẽr,* s. carrelet, m.

flounder, *flŏwn'dẽr,* v. n. se débattre.

flour, *flŏwr,* s. fleur de farine || farine, f.

flourish, *flŭr'ish,* s. ornement, m. || éclat, m. || fanfare, f. || parafe, m.

flourish, *flŭr'ish,* v. a. & n. orner de fleurs || embellir || prospérer || être florissant || faire des phrases || sonner une fanfare.

flout, *flŏwt,* s. raillerie, moquerie, f.

flout, *flŏwt,* v. n. railler, se moquer.

flow, *flō,* s. flux, m. || (fig.) torrent de paroles, m. [couler.

flow, *flō,* v. a. & n. inonder || couler ||

flower, *flŏw'r,* s. fleur, f. || ornement, m. || farine, f. || (fig.) élite, f.

flower, *flŏw'r,* v. a. & n. orner de fleurs || fleurir || ~~garden, s. jardin fleuriste, m. || ~~girl, s. bouquetière, f. || ~~pot, s. pot à fleurs, m. || ~~show, s. exposition de fleurs, f. || ~~stand, s. porte-fleurs, m.

floweret, *flŏw'r ĕt,* s. fleurette, f.

flowery, *flŏw'r i,* a. fleuri || en fleurs.

flowing, *flō'ing,* a. coulant || flottant || (fig.) facile || (mar.) largue.

fluctuate, *flŭk'tū ät,* v. n. flotter || balancer, hésiter. [f.

fluctuation, *flŭk tū ä' shŭn,* s. fluctuation, f.

flue, *flō,* s. duvet, m. || tuyau (de cheminée), f.

fluency, *flō'ĕn si,* s. fluidité, f. || facilité, f.

fluent, *flō'ĕnt,* a. coulant || abondant || éloquent || ~ly, ad. couramment.

fluid, *flō'id,* s. fluide, m.

fluid, *flō'id,* a. fluide.

fluidity, *flŏ id'i ti,* s. fluidité, f.

fluke, *flōk,* s. flet, fléteau, m. || patte d'ancre, f. || (jeu) raccroc, m.

flummery, *flŭm'ẽr i,* s. bouillie, gelée, f. || (fig.) blague, f. || flagornerie, f.

flunkey, *flŭngk'i,* s. laquais, estafier || plat valet, m. [cipitation, f. || émotion, f.

flurry, *flŭr'ri,* s. bouffée de vent, f. || pré-

flurry, *flŭr'ri,* v. a. troubler, ahurir.

flush, *flŭsh,* s. flux, m. || abondance, f. || incarnat, m. || rougeur, f. || transport, m.

flush, *flŭsh,* v. a. & n. rougir || couler rapidement || monter (of a blush) || exalter.

flush, *flŭsh,* a. frais, vigoureux || (Am.) généreux. [ahurir.

fluster, *flŭs'tẽr,* v. a. exciter, troubler,

flute, *flōt,* s. flûte, f. || cannelure, f.

flute, *flōt,* v. a. canneler.

flutist, *flō'tist,* s. flûtiste, m.

flutter, *flŭt'tẽr,* s. vibration, ondulation, f. || émoi, m.

flutter, *flŭt'tẽr,* v. a. & n. déconcerter || déranger || battre des ailes || flotter.

flux, *flŭks,* s. flux, m. || écoulement, m. || dyssenterie, f.

fly, *flī,* s. mouche, f. || balancier, m. || accélérée (voiture), f. || Spanish~~, s. cantharide, f. || ~~blow, s. chiure de mouche, f. || ~~wheel, s. volant, m.

fly, *flī,* v. a. & n. ir. fuir || quitter || voler, s'envoler || s'échapper, se sauver.

flying-machine, *flī'ing mä shēn',* s. aéroplane, m.

foal, *fōl,* s. poulain, m., pouliche, f.

foal, *fōl,* v. a. pouliner || ânonner.

foam, *fōm,* s. écume, f., bouillon, m.

foam, *fōm,* v. n. écumer, bouillonner.

foamy, *fō'mi,* a. écumeux.

fob, *fŏb,* s. gousset, m., petite poche, f.

focus, *fō'kŭs,* s. foyer, m.

fodder, *fŏd'dẽr,* s. fourrage, m.

foe, *fō,* s. ennemi, antagoniste, m.

fog, *fŏg,* s. brouillard, m. || regain, m.

foggy, *fŏg'gi,* a. brumeux.

fog(e)y, *fō'gi,* s. bonhomme, m. || croûton, m. || perruque, f.

foible, *fŏy'ŏl,* s. faible, m.

foil, *fŏyl,* s. défaite, f. || clinquant, m. || échec, m. || fleuret (sorte d'épée), m. || feuille, f. || monture, f. || contraste, m.

foil, *fŏyl,* v. a. défaire, terrasser, battre.

foist, *fŏyst,* v. a. insérer, interpoler.

fold, *fōld,* s. parc, étable pour les brebis, m. || pli, m. [plier, plisser.

fold, *fōld,* v. a. parquer, fair parquer ||

folding, *fōld'ing,* s. pliage, m. || (of sheep) parcage, m. || ~~bed, s. lit pliant, m. || ~~chair, s. fauteuil pliant, m. || ~~door, s. porte à deux battants, f. || ~~screen, s. paravent, m.

foliage, *fō'li äj,* s. feuillage, m.

folio, *fō'li ō,* s. in-folio, m. || folio, m. || feuillet, m. [m.

folk(s), *fōk(s),* s. gens, f. & m. pl., monde,

follow, *fŏl'lō,* v. a. & n. suivre || accompagner || imiter || observer || s'adonner, s'attacher || s'ensuivre, résulter || to ~ the law, étudier en droit || it does not ~ that, il ne s'ensuit pas que.

follower, fŏl'lō ẽr, s. compagnon, m. || imitateur, m. || sectateur, m. || amoureux, m. || roue motrice, f.

folly, fŏl'lĭ, s. folie, f. || sottise, f.

foment, fō mĕnt', v. a. fomenter || encourager.

fomentation, fō mĕn tā'shŭn, s. fomentation, f.

fond, fŏnd, a. (-ly, ad.) fou, extravagant || passionné || tendre(ment) || indulgent || follement. |aimer à la folie.

fondle, fŏnd'l, v a. & n. caresser, dorloter.

fondness, fŏnd'nĕs, s. tendresse, folie, passion f.

font, fŏnt, s. fonts, m. pl. |sion f.

food, fŏd, s. aliment, m., nourriture, pâture,

fool, fŏl, s. sot, niais, fou, m. |f.

fool, fŏl, v. a. & n. se jouer de || infatuer || faire le plaisant, badiner, folâtrer.

foolery, fŏl'ẽr ĭ, s. folie, bouffonnerie, f.

foolhardiness, fŏl hâr'dĭ nĕs, s. témérité, f.

foolish, fŏl'ĭsh, a. (-ly, ad.) imbécile || ridicule || follement || bête(ment).

foolscap, fŏls'kăp, s. papier-pot, m.

foot, fŏŏt, s. pied, m. || base, f., bas, m. || état, m. || infanterie, f., fantassins, m. pl. || ~ by ~, pied à pied, par degrés || on ~, à pied || ~board, s. marchepied, m. || ~lights, s. pl. rampe, f. || ~pace, s. petit pas, m. || ~print, s. empreinte du pied, f. || ~race, s. lutte à la course, f. || ~soldier, s. fantassin, m. || (to be) ~sore, s. (avoir) les pieds écorchés || ~warmer, s. chauffe-pieds, m.

foot, fŏŏt, v. a. & n. fouler aux pieds || aller à pied, marcher || (a stocking) mettre un pied à.

football, fŏŏt'bâwl, s. (game) ballon, m. || (ball) ballon, m. |le pied, m.

foothold, fŏŏt'hōld, s. espace couvert par

footing, fŏŏt'ĭng, s. pied, m. || base, condition, f. || point d'appui, soutien, m. [m.

footman, fŏŏt'măn, s. piéton, m. || laquais,

footpad, fŏŏt'păd, s. voleur de grand chemin, m. |m.

footpath, fŏŏt'păth, s. sentier, m. || trottoir,

footstep, fŏŏt'stĕp, s. pas, m. || trace, f. || to tread in one's ~s, marcher sur les pas de qn.

footstool, fŏŏt'stōl, s. tabouret, m.

fop, fŏp, s. fat, petit-maître, m.

foppery, fŏp'pẽr ĭ, s. sottise, fatuité, f.

foppish, fŏp'pĭsh, a. fat, sot, vain.

for, fŏr, pr. & c. pour, à cause de || car, aussi bien, eu égard à || as ~, quant à || ~ all that, malgré tout cela.

forage, fŏr'ăj, s. fourrage, m.

forage, fŏr'ăj, v. a. & n. fourrager, aller au fourrage.

forager, fŏr'ăjẽr, s. fourrageur, m.

forbear, fŏr bār', v. a. & n. ir. cesser || s'abstenir de || traiter avec clémence.

forbearance, fŏr bār'ăns, s. abstinence || indulgence, clémence, f.

forbid, fŏr bĭd', v. a. & n. ir. défendre, empêcher, prévenir || God ~, à Dieu ne plaise.

force, fŏrs, s. force, f. || vigueur, efficacité, f. || ~s, s. pl. troupes, f. pl.

force, fŏrs, v. a. & n. forcer, contraindre || violer || emporter || s'efforcer || ~d march, s. marche forcée, f.

forcemeat, fŏrs'mēt, s. viande hachée, f.

forceps, fŏr'sĕps, s. pl. pince, f. || forceps, m.

forcible, fŏr'sĭ bl, a. puissant || violent, forcé.

forcibly, fŏr'sĭ blĭ, ad. fortement, par force.

ford, fŏrd, s. gué, m.

ford, fŏrd, v. a. traverser un gué.

fordable, fŏrd'ăbl, a. guéable.

fore, fŏr, a. & ad. antérieur || antérieurement || avant...

forearm, fŏr'ârm, s. avant-bras, m.

forebode, fŏr bōd', v. a. présager.

forecast, fŏr'kăst, s. projet, m. || prévoyance, f. |projeter, prévoir.

forecast, fŏr kăst', v. a. calculer d'avance ||

forecastle, fŏr'kăs l, s. (mar.) gaillard d'avant, m. |forciore.

foreclose, fŏr klōz', v. a. arrêter || (jur.)

foreclosure, fŏr klō'zhŏŏr, s. (jur.) forclusion, f.

foredoom, fŏr dōm', v. a. prédestiner.

forefather, fŏr'fä thẽr, s. aïeul, grand-père, m.

forefend, fŏr fĕnd', vide forbid.

forefinger, fŏr'fĭng gẽr, s. index, m.

forego, fŏr gō', v. a. & n. ir. précéder || quitter, abandonner, se désister.

foregone, fŏr gŏn', a. passé || anticipé.

foreground, fŏr'grownd, s. devant d'un tableau, m. || premier plan, m. |f.

forehead, fŏr'ĕd, s. front, m. || impudence.

foreign, fŏr'ĭn, a. étranger || ~office, s. ministère des affaires étrangères, m.

foreigner, fŏr'ĭn ẽr, s. étranger, m., étrangère, f. |prévision, f.

foreknowledge, fŏr nŏl'ĕj, s. prescience,

foreland, fŏr'lănd, s. promontoire, m.

forelock, fŏr'lŏk, s. toupet, m.

foreman, fŏr'măn, s. chef, m. || contre-maître, m. || chef d'atelier, m. || premier garçon, m.

foremast, fŏr'măst, s. mât de misaine, m.

forementioned, fŏr mĕn'shŭnd, a. susdit.

foremost, fŏr'mōst, s. le plus avancé.

forenoon, fŏr'nŏn, s. matinée, f.

forensic, fŏ rĕn'sĭk, a. du barreau, judiciaire.

forepart, fŏr'părt, s. devant, m. |ciaire.

forerunner, fŏr rŭn'nẽr, s. avant-coureur, précurseur, m.

foresee, fŏr sē', v. a. prévoir, conjecturer.

foreshadow, fŏr shăd'ō, v. a. représenter d'avance, figurer.

foreshorten, fŏr shŏrt'n, v. a. raccourcir.

foresight, fŏr'sīt, s. prévoyance, f. ||

forest, fŏr'ĕst, s. forêt, f. |guidon, m.

forestall, fŏr stawl', v. a. anticiper, devancer || accaparer.

forester, fŏr'ĕs tẽr, s. garde-forestier, m.

forestry, fŏr'ĕs trĭ, s. sylviculture, f.

foretaste, fŏr'tăst, s. avant-goût, m.

foretell, fŏr tĕl', v. a. ir. prédire, prophétiser. |avant-coureur, m.

foreteller, fŏr tĕl'lẽr, s. prophète, m. || (fig.)

forethought, *fōr'thåut,* s. prévoyance, préméditation, f.

foretop, *fōr'tŏp,* s. toupet, m. || (mar.) hune de misaine, f. |cautionner.

forewarn, *fōr wåwrn',* v. a. prévenir, pré-

forewoman, *fōr'wŏŏm ăn,* s. première ou-vrière, f.

forfeit, *fōr'fĭt,* s. amende, f. || déchéance, f., dédit, m. || -s, s. pl. jeu du gage, m.

forfeit, *fōr'fĭt,* v. a. forfaire, faire con-fisquer, perdre par confiscation.

forfeit, *fōr'fĭt,* a. confisqué, perdu par confiscation.

forfeiture, *fōr'fĭt ūr,* s. forfaiture, amende, f. || confiscation, f. [de.

forfend, *fōr fĕnd',* v. a. prévenir, préserver

forge, *fōrj,* s. forge, f. [faire.

forge, *fōrj,* v. a. forger || imaginer || contre-

forger, *fōr'jĕr,* s. forgeron, m. || forgeur, contrefacteur, f.

forgery, *fōr'jĕr'ĭ,* s. contrefaçon, f. || tra-vaux de la forge, m. pl.

forget, *fōr gĕt',* v. a. ir. oublier, perdre le souvenir de || ~-me-not, s. (bot.) myo-sotis, m. [gent.

forgetful, *fōr gĕt'fŏŏl,* a. oublieux, négli-

forgive, *fōr gĭv',* v. a. ir. pardonner, re-mettre (une dette). [rémission, f.

forgiveness, *fōr gĭv'nĕs,* s. pardon, m.,

fork, *fōrk,* s. fourchette, f. || fourche, f.

forked, *fōrkt,* a. fourchu || en zigzag.

forlorn, *fōr låwrn',* a. abandonné, délaissé.

forlornness, *fōr låwrn'nĕs,* s. délaisse-ment, abandon, m.

form, *fåwrm,* s. forme, figure, f. || modèle, m. || méthode, f. || formalité, f. || classe, f. || banc, m.

form, *fåwrm,* v. a. (& n.) (se) former.

formal, *fōr'măl,* a. (-ly, ad.) formel(le-ment) || régulier.

formality, *fōr măl'ĭ tĭ,* s. formalité, f.

formation, *fōr mā'shŭn,* s. formation, f.

former, *fōr'mĕr,* a. premier, précédent.

formerly, *fōr'mĕr lĭ,* ad. autrefois, jadis, au temps passé. [redoutable.

formidable, *fōr'mĭ dă bl,* a. formidable,

formula, *fōr'mŭ lă,* s. formule, f.

formulary, *fōr'mŭ lĕr'ĭ,* s. formulaire, m.

forsake, *fōr sāk',* v. a. ir. abandonner, quitter.

forsooth, *fōr sŏŏth',* ad. en vérité.

forswear, *fōr swår',* v. a. & n. ir. abjurer, renier || se parjurer.

fort, *fōrt,* s. forteresse, f.

forth, *fōrth,* a. & ad. hors de, en avant, dehors, au dehors || and so ~, et ainsi de suite. [paraître.

forthcoming, *fōrth kŭm'ĭng,* a. prêt à

forthwith, *fōrth wĭth',* ad. sur-le-champ || séance tenante.

fortieth, *fōr'tĭ ĕth,* a. quarantième.

fortification, *fōr tĭ fĭ kā'shŭn,* s. fortifica-tion, f. [solider.

fortify, *fōr'tĭ fĭ,* v. a. fortifier || munir || con-

fortitude, *fōr'tĭ tūd,* s. force d'esprit, f.

fortnight, *fōrt'nĭt,* s. quinze jours, pl.

fortress, *fōr'trĕs,* s. forteresse, f.

fortuitous, *fōr tū'ĭ tŭs,* a. fortuit, casuel || -ly, ad. par hasard.

fortunate, *fōr'tū năt,* a. fortuné, heureux || -ly, ad. heureusement.

fortune, *fōr'tūn,* s. fortune, f. || sort, ha-sard, m., aventure, f. || richesses, f. pl. || (piece of) ill-~, s. mauvaise chance, f., guignon, m. || to come (slip) into a ~, faire un héritage || ~-hunter, s. coureur de fortune, m. || ~-teller, s. diseur de bonne aventure, m.

forty, *fōr'tĭ,* a. quarante.

forward, *fōr'wĕrd,* v. a. avancer, hâter, pousser, favoriser || faire parvenir.

forward, *fōr'wĕrd,* a. empressé, ardent || présomptueux || précoce || -ly, ad. avec empressement

forwardness, *fōr'wĕrd nĕs,* s. empresse-ment, m., ardeur, f., avancement, m. || hardiesse, f. || précocité, f.

forward(s), *fōr'wĕrd(z),* ad. en avant || tout droit.

foss, *fŏs,* s. fosse, f., fossé, m.

fossil, *fŏs'ĭl,* s. fossile, m.

fossil, *fŏs'ĭl,* a. fossile.

foster, *fŏs'tĕr,* v. a. nourrir, élever || pro-téger || ~-brother, s. frère de lait, m. || ~-child, s. nourrisson, m. || ~-mother, s. nourrice, f. || ~-sister, s. sœur de lait, f. || ~-son, s. fils adoptif, m.

fosterer, *fŏs'tĕr ĕr,* s. nourricier, m.

foul, *fŏwl,* v. a. salir, souiller || diffamer || (mar.) aborder.

foul, *fŏwl,* a. (-ly, ad.) sale(ment) || impur || méchant, vilain, inique || orageux || nua-geux || honteusement || injustement

foulness, *fŏwl'nĕs,* s. saleté, f. || impureté, f. || infamie, f. || laideur, f.

found, *fŏwnd,* v. a. fonder, établir || fondre.

foundation, *fŏwn dā'shŭn,* s. fondement, m., fondation, f. || établissement, m. || ~-stone, s. pierre fondamentale, f.

foundationer, *fŏwn dā'shŭn ĕr,* s. bour-sier, m.

founder, *fŏwn'dĕr,* s. fondateur, m. || fon-deur, m. [couler à fond || échouer.

founder, *fŏwn'dĕr,* v. n. rendre fourbu ||

foundered, *fŏwn'dĕrd,* a. solbattu.

foundling, *fŏwnd'lĭng,* s. enfant trouvé, m.

foundry, *fŏwn'drĭ,* s. fonderie, f.

fount(ain), *fŏwnt'(ĭn),* s. fontaine, f. || -s, s. pl. eaux, f. pl. || ~-head, s. source, f.

four, *fōr,* a. quatre || on all -s, à quatre pattes || ~-footed, a. quadrupède.

fourfold, *fōr'fōld,* a. quadruple.

fourscore, *fōr skōr,* vide eighty.

fourteen, *fōr'tēn,* a. quatorze.

fourteenth, *fōr'tēnth,* a. quatorzième.

fourth, *fōrth,* s. quart, m.

fourth, *fōrth,* a. (-ly, ad.) quatrième(ment).

fowl, *fŏwl,* s. volaille, f.

fowler, *fŏwl'ĕr,* s. oiseleur, m.

fowling, *fŏwl'ĭng,* s. chasse aux oiseaux, oisellerie, f. || ~-piece, s. fusil de chasse, m.

fox, *fŏks*, s. renard, m. ‖ (fig.) homme rusé, m. ‖ **~-brush**, s. queue de renard, f. ‖ **~-glove**, s. (bot.) digitale, f. ‖ **~-hound**, s. chien loup, m. ‖ **~-hunt(ing)**, s. chasse au renard, f.

F.P. (**Fire-plug**), "Secours contre l'incendie." [sion, f.

fraction, *frăk'shŭn*, s. fraction, f. ‖ division.

fractional, *frăk'shŭn ăl*, a. (ar.) fractionnaire. [sier.

fractious, *frăk'shŭs*, a. hargneux, tracassier.

fracture, *frăk'tŭr*, s. fracture, rupture, f.

fracture, *frăk'tŭr*, v. a. fracturer, rompre.

fragile, *frăj'ĭl*, a. fragile, frêle.

fragility, *frá jĭl'ĭ ti*, s. fragilité, f. ‖ faiblesse, f.

fragment, *frăg'mĕnt*, s. fragment, m. ‖ débris, m. ‖ petite portion, f. ‖ particule, f.

fragmentary, *frăg'mĕn tĕr i*, a. composé de fragments. [parfum, m.

fragrance, *frā'grăns*, s. bonne odeur, f.,

fragrant, *frā'grănt*, a. odoriférant ‖ **-ly**, ad. suavement, bon.

frail, *frāl*, s. panier de jonc, m.

frail, *frāl*, a. frêle, fragile.

frailty, *frāl'ti*, s. fragilité, f. ‖ faiblesse, f.

frame, *frām*, s. fabrique, construction, f. ‖ forme, f. ‖ cadre, m. ‖ (of mind) disposition, f. ‖ invention, f. ‖ métier, m. ‖ **~-knitter**, s. chaussetier, m. ‖ **~-work**, s. charpente, f. ‖ (for working on) métier, m.

frame, *frām*, v. a. former, façonner, ajuster ‖ imaginer. [teur, m.

framer, *frā'mĕr*, s. constructeur, inventeur.

franchise, *frăn'chĭz*, s. franchise, f. ‖ exemption, f. ‖ droit électoral, m.

frank, *frăngk*, s. franc, m. ‖ lettre affranchie, f.

frank, *frăngk*, v. a. affranchir (une lettre).

frank, *frăngk*, a. franc, généreux ‖ **-ly**, ad. franchement.

frankincense, *frăngk'ĭn sĕns*, s. encens, m.

frankness, *frăngk'nĕs*, s. franchise, sincérité, générosité, f. [furieux ‖ avec frénésie.

frantic, *frăn'tĭk*, a. (-ly, ad.) frénétique,

fraternal, *fra tĕr'năl*, a. (-ly, ad.) fraternel(lement) ‖ de frère ‖ en frère.

fraternity, *frá tĕr'ni ti*, s. fraternité, f.

fratricide, *frăt'ri sĭd*, s. fratricide, m.

fraud, *frŏwd*, s. fraude, tromperie, f.

fraudulent, *frŏw'dū lĕnt*, a. frauduleux, fourbe ‖ **-ly**, ad. frauduleusement.

fraught, *frŏwt*, a. chargé, accablé.

fray, *frā*, s. bataille, f., combat, m. ‖ querelle, f.

freak, *frēk*, s. caprice, m., fantaisie, f.

freckle, *frĕk'l*, s. rousseur, f. ‖ **-d**, plein de taches de rousseur, tacheté.

free, *frē*, v. a. affranchir, mettre en liberté.

free, *frē*, a. (-ly, ad.) libre, licencieux ‖ libéral ‖ franc(hement) ‖ quitte, exempt ‖ **to make ~ with**, prendre des libertés avec ‖ **to set ~**, mettre en liberté ‖ **~-hearted**, a. libéral, généreux ‖ **~-spoken**, a. libre et franc ‖ **~-stone**, s. pierre de taille, f. ‖ **~-trade**, s. libre-

échange, m. ‖ **~-trader**, s. libre-échangiste, m. ‖ **~-will**, s. plein gré, m. ‖ libre arbitre, m. [m.

freebooter, *frē'bŏt ĕr*, s. bandit, flibustier.

freedom, *frē'dŭm*, s. liberté, franchise, f.

freehold, *frē'hōld*, s. franc-alleu, m.

freeholder, *frē'hōld ĕr*, s. franc-tenancier, m.

freemason, *frē'mā'sn*, s. franc-maçon, m.

freemasonry, *frē'mā'sn ri*, s. franc-maçonnerie, f. [m.

freethinker, *frē'thĭngk ĕr*, s. esprit fort,

freeze, *frēz*, v. a. (& n.) ir. (se) geler, (se) glacer. [glacière, f.

freezing-machine, *frēz'ing mă shēn*, s. machine à glace.

freight, *frāt*, s. cargaison, f.

freight, *frāt*, v. a. fréter, charger.

freighter, *frāt'ĕr*, s. affréteur, m.

French, *frĕnsh*, a. français ‖ **~ horn**, s. cor de chasse, m. ‖ cornet à piston, m.

frenchify, *frĕnsh'i fi*, v. a. franciser.

frenzy, *frĕn'zi*, s. frénésie, fureur, f.

frequency, *frē'kwĕn si*, s. fréquence, multitude, f.

frequent, *frē'kwĕnt'*, v. a. fréquenter.

frequent, *frē'kwĕnt*, a. fréquent ‖ **-ly**, ad. fréquemment. [tuel, m.

frequenter, *frē'kwĕnt'ĕr*, s. visiteur habituel, m.

fresco, *frĕs'kō*, s. fresque, f.

fresh, *frĕsh*, a. frais ‖ récent, nouveau ‖ robuste ‖ vif ‖ **-ly**, ad. fraîchement, récemment ‖ **~ water**, s. eau douce, f.

freshen, *frĕsh'n*, v. a. (& n.) (se) rafraîchir.

freshet, *frĕsh'ĕt*, s. étang d'eau douce, m. ‖ cours d'eau, m.

freshness, *frĕsh'nĕs*, s. fraîcheur, f.

fret, *frĕt*, s. agitation, f. ‖ fermentation, f. ‖ détroit, m. ‖ (mus.) touche, f. ‖ **~-saw**, s. scie à vider, à découper, f. ‖ **~-work**, s. ouvrage en bosse, m. ‖ (arch.) grecque, f.

fret, *frĕt*, v. a. & n. frotter ‖ bosseler ‖ tourmenter ‖ fermenter ‖ s'agiter, se tourmenter ‖ se corroder.

fretful, *frĕt'fool*, a. de mauvaise humeur, chagrin ‖ **-ly**, ad. avec chagrin.

friable, *fri'ă bl*, a. friable.

friar, *fri'ĕr*, s. moine, m. [ment, m.

friction, *frĭk'shŭn*, s. friction, f., frotte-

Friday, *fri'dā*, s. vendredi, m. ‖ **Good ~**, s. vendredi saint, m. [m. pl.

friend, *frĕnd*, s. ami, m. ‖ **-s**, s.pl. parents,

friendless, *frĕnd'lĕs*, a. sans ami.

friendliness, *frĕnd'li nĕs*, s. bienveillance, amitié, f.

friendly, *frĕnd'li*, a. aimable, amical ‖ **~ society**, s. société de secours mutuels, f.

friendship, *frĕnd'ship*, s. amitié, f.

frieze, *frēz*, s. frise, f.

frigate, *frĭg'āt*, s. frégate, f.

fright, *frĭt*, s. frayeur, peur, f.

frighten, *fri'tn*, v. a. effrayer, épouvanter.

frightful, *frĭt'fool*, a. (-ly, ad.) effroyable (ment).

frigid, *frĭj'ĭd*, a. (-ly, ad.) froid(ement).

frigidity, *fri jĭd'i ti*, s. frigidité, f. ‖ indifférence, f.

frill, *frtl*, s. jabot, m.

fringe, *frĭnj*, s. frange, crépine, f.

fringe, *frĭnj*, v. a. franger. [m. pl.

frippery, *frĭp'pér ĭ*, s. friperie, f.||haillons,

frisk, *frisk*, v. n. sauter, bondir || frétiller.

frisky, *frĭs'ki*, a. frétillant || fringant || folâtre. [f.

frith, *frĭth*, s. bras de mer, m.||embouchure,

fritter, *frĭt'tér*, s. beignet, m. [gaspiller.

fritter, *frĭt'tér*, v. a. morceler || anéantir ||

frivolity, *frĭ vŏl'ĭ tĭ*, s. frivolité, f.

frivolous, *frĭv'õ lŭs*, a. frivole, vain || -ly, ad. d'une manière frivole.

frizzle, *frĭz'l*, v. a. friser.

fro, *frō*, ad. en arrière || to and ~, çà et là.

frock, *frŏk*, s. blouse, f. || robe, f. || ~coat, m.

frog, *frŏg*, s. grenouille, f. [redingote, f.

frolic, *frŏl'ĭk*, s. gaieté, f. || fantaisie, folie,

frolic, *frŏl'ĭk*, v. n. folâtrer, badiner. [f.

frolicsome, *frŏl'ĭk sŭm*, a. gai, folâtre, joyeux à l'excès.

from, *frŏm*, pr. de, par, dès, depuis, d'après.

frond, *frŏnd*, s. (bot.) fronde, frondaison, f. || feuillage, m.

front, *frŭnt*, s. front, m. || façade, f.

front, *frŭnt*, v. a. attaquer de front || affronter || faire face à. [ture, f.

frontage, *frŭnt'áj*, s. façade, f. || devan-

frontal, *frŭnt'ăl*, s. frontal, fronton, m.

frontier, *frŏn'tér*, s. frontière, limite, f.

frontispiece, *frŏn'tis pés*, s. frontispice, m.

frontlet, *frŭnt'lét*, s. frontal, m.

frost, *frŏst*, s. gelée, f. || **glazed ~**, s. verglas, m. || **hoar~**, **white~**, s. frimas, givre, m., gelée blanche, f. || **~-bite**, s. engourdissement causé par le froid, m. || **~-bitten**, a. gelé || **~-flower**, s. cristaux de glace aux fenêtres, m. pl.

frost, *frŏst*, v. a. glacer || **(in cutlery)** damasquiner. [deur glaciale.

frostily, *frŏs'tĭ lĭ*, ad. (fig.) avec une froi-

frosty, *frŏs'tĭ*, a. gelé, glacé || (fig.) froid.

froth, *frŏth*, s. écume, mousse, f.

froth, *frŏth*, v. n. écumer, mousser.

frothy, *frŏth'ĭ*, a. écumeux || frivole.

frousy, *frŏw'zĭ*, a. sale, moisi, vilain.

froward, *frō'wérd*, a. chagrin, opiniâtre, revêche || -ly, ad. de mauvaise humeur.

frowardness, *frō'wérd nés*, s. mauvaise humeur, f. [ment.

frown, *frŏwn*, s. froncement des sourcils,

frown, *frŏwn*, v. n. froncer le sourcil, se refrogner || **to ~ down**, atterrer par un regard.

frozen, *frō'zn*, a. gelé, glacé.

fructify, *frŭk'tĭ fĭ*, v. a. & n. fertiliser || fructifier. [économe.

frugal, *frŏ'găl*, a. (-ly, ad.) frugal(ement) ||

frugality, *frŏ găl'ĭ tĭ*, s. frugalité, f.

fruit, *frŏt*, s. fruit, m. || produit, m. || **~-bearer**, s. arbre fruitier, m. || **~-dish**, s. coupe à fruits, f. || **~-grower**, s. pomiculteur, jardinier pépiniériste, m. || **~-tree**, s. arbre fruitier, m.

fruiterer, *frŏt'ér ér*, s. fruitier, m. || **~'s shop**, s. fruiterie, f.

fruitful, *frŏt'fŏŏl*, a. (-ly, ad.) fertile, fécond || abondamment, fructueusement.

fruition, *frŏ ĭsh'ŭn*, s. jouissance, f.

fruitless, *frŏt'lés*, a. infructueux, stérile.

frump, *frŭmp*, s. vieille ratatinée, f.

frustrate, *frŭs'trát*, v. a. frustrer, annuler

frustration, *frŭs trä'shŭn*, s. désappointement, non-succès, m.

fry, *frĭ*, s. (of fish) frai, m. || fretin, m. || multitude, f. || friture, f.

fry, *frĭ*, v. a. & n. frire || **small ~**, s. menu fretin, m.||**Lamb's ~**, s. fraise d'agneau, f || **frying-pan**, *frĭ'ĭng pän*, s. poêle à frire, f. || **out of the ~ into the fire**, tomber de Charybde en Scylla, de fièvre en chaud mal.

fuchsia, *fū'shĭd*, s. (bot.) fuchsia, f.

fuddle, *fŭd'l*, v. a. (& n.) (s')enivrer.

fudge, *fŭj*, s. blague, craque, f.

fudge! *fŭj*, sottise! bah!

fuel, *fū'él*, s. chauffage, combustible, m.

fugitive, *fū'jĭ tĭv*, s. fugitif, m.

fugitive, *fū'jĭ tĭv*, a. fugitif.

fugue, *fūg*, s. (mus.) fugue, f.

fulcrum, *fŭl'krŭm*, s. support, soutien, m. || point fixe, m. || point d'appui, m.

fulfil, *fŏŏl fĭl'*, v. a. accomplir, remplir.

fulfilment, *fŏŏl fĭl'mént*, s. accomplissement, m. [m.

full, *fŏŏl*, a. plein, m., plénitude, f. || total, rempli || entier || plein(ement) || exactement || tout à fait || **chook ~**, comble tout plein || **to the ~**, surabondamment || **~-blown**, a. épanoui || **~-bodied**, a. gros, replet || **~-compass**, a. à sept octaves || **~-dress**, s. grande tenue, f. || **~-dress ball**, s. bal paré, m. || **~-dress dinner**, s. dîner de cérémonie, m. || **~-length**, s. grandeur naturelle, f.

fuller, *fŏŏl'tér*, s. foulon, m. || **~'s earth**, s. (min.) terre à foulon, f. [foulon, m.

fulling-mill, *fŏŏl'ling mĭl*, s. moulin à

fulminate, *fŭl'mĭ nát*, v. a. & n. fulminer.

fulness, *fŏŏl'nés*, s. plénitude, f. || satiété, f. || largeur, f.

fulsome, *fŏŏl'sŭm*, a. (-ly, ad.) dégoûtant, fastidieux || d'une manière nauséabonde.

fumble, *fŭm'bl*, v. a. & n. tâter, tâtonner || agir maladroitement. [ment.

fumblingly, *fŭm'bling lĭ*, ad. maladroite-

fume, *fūm*, s. fumée, vapeur, f. || colère, f. || vanité, f.

fume, *fūm*, v. a. & n. fumer || parfumer || s'exhaler en vapeur || être en colère.

fumigate, *fū'mĭ gát*, v. n. faire des fumigations. [f.

fumigation, *fū mĭ gä'shŭn*, s. fumigation,

fumigator, *fū mĭ gä'tér*, s. boîte fumigatoire, m.

fun, *fŭn*, s. badinage, m., gaieté, f.

function, *fŭngk'shŭn*, s. fonction, f. || faculté, f.

functional, *fŭngk'shŭn ăl*, a. fonctionnel.

functionary, *fŭngk'shŭn ér ĭ*, s. fonctionnaire, m.

---

fund, *fŭnd,* s. fonds, bien, m. ‖ **sinking ~,** s. caisse d'amortissement, f. ‖ **—s,** s. pl. fonds, m. pl., capital, m.

fund, *fŭnd,* v. a. placer dans les fonds publics ‖ **to have property in the —s,** avoir des rentes sur l'Etat.

fundament, *fŭn'dă mĕnt,* s. fondement, m.

fundamental, *fŭn dă mĕn'tăl,* s. fondement, m. ‖ fondamental(ement).

fundamental, *fŭn dă mĕn'tăl,* a. (-ly, ad.)

funded, *fŭnd'ĕd,* a. consolidé. [f. pl.

funeral, *fū'nĕr ăl,* s. funérailles, obsèques,

funereal, *fū nē'rĭ ăl,* a. funèbre, lugubre, triste.

fungous, *fŭng'gŭs,* a. fongueux, spongieux.

fungus, *fŭng'gŭs,* s. champignon, m. ‖ (méd.) fongus, m.

funk, *fŭngk,* s. venette, f.

funnel, *fŭn'nĕl,* s. entonnoir, m. ‖ tuyau, m.

funny, *fŭn'nĭ,* a. drôle.

fur, *fĕr,* s. fourrure, pelleterie, f. ‖ (méd.) saburres, f. pl. ‖ **—cap,** s. bonnet fourré, m. ‖ **~-clad,** a. à fourrure.

fur, *fĕr,* v. a. fourrer.

furbelow, *fĕr'bĕ lō,* s. falbala, f.

furbish, *fĕr'bish,* v. a. fourbir, polir.

furious, *fū'rĭ ŭs,* a. furieux ‖ **-ly,** ad. violemment.

furl, *fĕrl,* v. a. ployer ‖ (mar.) ferler, serrer.

furlong, *fĕr'lŏng,* s. huitième partie d'un mille anglais, f.

furlough, *fĕr'lō,* s. congé d'absence, m.

furnace, *fĕr'năs,* s. fourneau, m.

furnish, *fĕr'nish,* v. a. fournir, pourvoir de ‖ meubler ‖ équiper.

furnisher, *fĕr'nish ĕr,* s. fournisseur, pourvoyeur, m.

furniture, *fĕr'nĭ tūr,* s. ameublement, m. ‖ équipage, appareil, m. ‖ **~-broker,** s. brocanteur, m.

furrier, *fŭr'rĭ ĕr,* s. fourreur, pelletier, m.

furrow, *fŭr'rō,* s. sillon, m. ‖ ride, f. ‖ guéret, m.

furrow, *fŭr'rō,* v. a. sillonner ‖ rider.

furry, *fĕr'rĭ,* a. fourré, de fourrures.

further, *fĕr'thĕr,* v. a. avancer, aider.

further, *fĕr'thĕr,* a. & ad. de plus, en outre ‖ plus avant, au delà ‖ outre cela.

furtherance, *fĕr'thĕr ăns,* s. avancement, m., protection, aide, f.

furtherer, *fĕr'thĕr ĕr,* s. promoteur, m.

furthermore, *fĕr'thĕr mōr,* ad. encore ‖ de plus ‖ outre cela, d'ailleurs.

furthest, *fĕr'thĕst,* a. le plus éloigné ‖ ~, ad. le plus loin ‖ à la distance ‖ (à l'époque) la plus eloignée. [furtivement.

furtive, *fĕr'tĭv,* a. furtif, dérobé ‖ **-ly,** ad.

fury, *fū'rĭ,* s. furie, frénésie, rage, fureur, f.

furze, *fĕrz,* s. (bot.) ajonc, m. [f.

fuse, *fūz,* v. a. (& n.) (se) fondre.

fusee, *fū zē',* s. fusée d'une montre, f. ‖ fusil, m.

fusel-oil, *fū'sĕl ŏjl,* s. huile empyreumatique de l'eau-de-vie de grains, f.

fusilier, *fū zi lēr',* s. fusilier, fantassin, m.

fusion, *fū'zhŭn,* s. fusion, fonte, f.

fuss, *fŭs,* s. fracas, embarras, m.

fussy, *fŭs'sĭ,* a. faiseur d'embarras.

fustian, *fŭst'ĭ ăn,* s. futaine, f. ‖ boursouflure, f. [teur, f.

fustiness, *fŭs'tĭ nĕs,* s. moisissure, puanfasty, *fŭs'tĭ,* a. sentant le moisi.

futile, *fū'til,* a. futile, frivole.

futility, *fū til'ĭ tĭ,* s. futilité, frivolité, f.

future, *fū'tūr,* s. avenir, m. ‖ **for the ~, in ~,** à l'avenir.

future, *fū'tūr',* a. futur, à venir.

futurity, *fū tū'rĭ tĭ,* s. futur, avenir, m.

fy(e)! *fī,* fi! fi donc!

G.

gab, *găb,* s. bouche, f. ‖ maudite langue, f. ‖ bavardage, m. ‖ **to have the gift of the ~,** avoir la langue bien pendue.

gabardine, *găb'ĕr dēn,* s. gaban, m.

gabble, *găb'l,* s. bourdonnement, m. ‖ babil, m.

gabble, *găb'l,* v. n. bourdonner ‖ bavarder

gabbler, *găb'lĕr,* s. bavard, m.

gabion, *gā'bĭ ŭn,* s. (mar.) gabion, m.

gable(-end), *gā'bl (ĕnd),* s. pignon, m.

gaby, *gā'bĭ,* s. jeannot, badaud, m.

gad, *găd,* s. acier en lingots, m. ‖ baguette, f.

gad, *găd,* v. n. courir çà et là. ‖ **~-fly,** s. taon, m.

gaff, *găf,* s. harpon, crochet, m.

gag, *găg,* s. bâillon, m.

gag, *găg,* v. n. bâillonner. [m.

gage, *gāj,* s. gage, m. ‖ (jur.) nantissement,

gaiety, *gā'itĭ,* s. gaieté, joie, f. ‖ parure, f.

gaily, *gā'lĭ,* ad. gaiement.

gain, *gān,* s. gain, avantage, m.

gain, *gān,* v. a. & n. gagner ‖ profiter.

gainer, *gān'ĕr,* s. gagnant, m.

gainless, *gān'lĕs,* a. sans gain, inutile.

gainsay, *gān'sā,* v. a. contredire ‖ nier.

'gainst, *'gĕnst,* pr. contre (*vide* against).

gait, *gāt,* s. chemin, m., démarche, allure.

gaiters, *gā'tĕrz,* s. pl. guêtres, f. pl.

galaxy, *găl'ăks ĭ,* s. voie lactée, f.

gale, *gāl,* s. brise, f.

galiot, *găl'ĭ ŏt,* s. (mar.) galiote, f.

gall, *gawl,* s. fiel, m., bile, f. ‖ rancune, malice, f. ‖ **~-nut,** s. (bot.) noix de galle, f. [ner.

gall, *gawl,* v. a. & n. écorcher ‖ se chagri-

gallant, *găl'lănt,* a. vaillant, brave, m. ‖ élégant, galant, m.

gallant, *găl lănt',* a. vaillant, brave ‖ **-ly,** ad. vaillamment ‖ galamment.

gallantry, *găl'lăntrĭ,* s. vaillance, f. ‖ pompe, f. ‖ galanterie, f.

galleon, *găl'lĕ ŏn,* s. (mar.) galion, m.

gallery, *găl'lĕr ĭ,* s. galerie, f. ‖ corridor, m. ‖ **picture-~,** s. galerie de tableaux, f.

galley, *găl'lĭ,* s. galère, f. ‖ **~-slave,** s. galérien, forçat, m.

Gallic, *găl'lĭk,* a. gaulois.

galling, *gawl' ling,* a. choquant || (feu d'artillerie) bien nourri.

gallipot, *gäl' li pŏt,* s. gallipot, m.

gallon, *gäl' lŭn,* s. gallon, m.

gallop, *gäl' lŭp,* s. galop, m.

gallop, *gäl' lŭp,* v. a. & n. galoper || aller au galop.

gallows, *gäl' lōz,* s. gibet m., potence, f.

galvanic, *gäl văn' ĭk,* a. galvanique || ~ battery, s. (phys.) pile de Volta, f.

galvanise, *gäl' vă nīz,* v. a. galvaniser.

galvanism, *gäl' văn ĭzm,* s. (phys.) galvanisme, m.

gamble, *găm' bl,* v. n. jouer.

gambler, *găm' blĕr,* s. joueur de profession, m.

gamboge, *găm' bōj',* s. gomme-gutte, f.

gambol, *găm' bŏl,* s. gambade, f.

gambol, *găm' bŏl,* v. n. gambader.

game, *găm,* s. divertissement, jeu, m., partie, f. || gibier, m.

game, *găm,* v. a. jouer || black-~, s. coq de bruyère, m., gélinotte des bois f. || ~-bag, s. carnassière, f. || ~-cock, s. coq dressé au combat, m. || ~-keeper, s. garde-chasse, m. || ~-laws, s. pl. règlements de chasse, m. pl. || ~-leg, s. jambe boiteuse, f. || ~-ly, ad. gaiement.

gamesome, *găm' sŭm,* a. badin, folâtre ||

gamester, *găm' stĕr,* s. joueur, m.

gammon, *găm' mŭn,* s. jambon, m. || trictrac, m.

gammon, *găm' mŭn,* v. a. baliverner.

gamut, *găm' ŭt,* s. (mus.) gamme, f.

gander, *găn' dĕr,* s. jars, m.

gang, *găng,* s. troupe, bande, f.

ganger, *găng' ĕr,* s. chef de brigade, m.

ganglion, *găng' glĭ ŏn,* s. ganglion, m.

gangrene, *găng' grēn,* s. gangrène, f.

gangway, *găng' wā,* s. passage étroit, m. || (nav.) passe-avant, m. || f. (pélican).

gannet, *găn' nĕt,* s. fou, dodo, m. || boubie,

gantlet, gauntlet, *gawnt' lĕt,* s. gantelet, m. || (mil.) baguettes, f. pl.

gaol, *jāl,* s. prison, f. || ~-bird, s. pendard, gibier de potence, m.

gap, *găp,* s. ouverture, fente, brèche, f. || lacune, f. || trou, m. || ~-toothed, a. brèche-dent.

gap, *găp,* v. n. bâiller || se fendre.

gape, *găp,* v. n. bâiller.

garage, *gă răzh',* s. garage, m.

garb, *gärb,* s. habit, vêtement, m. || air, m.

garbage, *gär' băj,* s. tripailles, f. pl.

garble, *gär' bl,* v. a. choisir || cribler.

garden, *gär' dn,* s. jardin, m.

garden, *gär' dn,* v. a. cultiver un jardin || ~-engine, s. pompe d'arrosement, f. || ~-plot, s. parterre, m. || ~-stuff, s. plantes potagères, f. pl.

gardener, *gär' dn ĕr,* s. jardinier, m.

gardening, *gär' dn ing,* s. jardinage, m.

garfish, *gär' fĭsh,* s. orphie, f., brochet de mer, m.

gargle, *gär' gl,* s. gargarisme, m.

gargle, *gär' gl,* v. a. se gargariser.

gargoyle, *gär' gŏyl,* s. (arch.) gargouille, f.

garish, *gär' ĭsh,* a. éclatant, brillant.

garland, *gär' länd,* s. guirlande, f.

garlic, *gär' lĭk,* s. ail, m. [ment, m.

garment, *gär' mĕnt,* s. habillement, vête-

garner, *gär' nĕr,* v. a. mettre en grenier ||

garnet, *gär' nĕt,* s. grenat, m. [amasser.

garnish(ing), *gär' nĭsh(ing),* s. garniture, f., ornement, m.

garnish, *gär' nĭsh,* v. a. garnir, parer, orner.

garotter, *gă rŏt' tĕr,* s. étrangleur, m.

garret, *gär' rĕt,* s. mansarde, f. || grenier, galetas, m.

garrison, *gär' rĭ sŭn,* s. garnison, f.

garrison, *gär' rĭ sŭn,* v. a. mettre en garnison || mettre garnison dans || ~ed, a. à garnison.

garrulity, *gär rŏ' lĭ tĭ,* s. babil, caquet, m.

garrulous, *gär' rŏ lŭs,* a. babillard.

garter, *gär' tĕr,* s. jarretière, f.

gas, *găs,* s. gaz, m. || ~-burner, s. bec à gaz, m. || ~-fitter, s. gazier, m. || ~-light, s. éclairage au gaz, m. || ~-meter, s. compteur à gaz, m. || ~-pipe, s. conduite de gaz, f. || tuyau à gaz, gazifère, m. || ~-store, s. calorifère à gaz, m. || ~-works, s. pl. usine à gaz, f.

gaseous, *gā' zĕ ŭs,* a. gazeux.

gash, *găsh,* s. balafre, cicatrice, f.

gash, *găsh,* v. a. balafrer.

gasometer, *găs ŏm' ĕ tĕr,* s. gazomètre, m.

gasp, *găsp,* s. essoufflement, m. || to the last ~, jusqu'à son dernier soupir.

gasp, *găsp,* v. n. ouvrir la bouche pour respirer || respirer avec peine.

gastric, *găs' trĭk,* a. gastrique.

gastritis, *găs trī' tĭs,* s. gastrite, f.

gastronomist, *găs trŏn' ŏ mĭst,* s. gastronome, m. [mie, f.

gastronomy, *găs trŏn' ŏ mĭ,* s. gastrono-

gate, *găt,* s. porte, f., portail, m., barrière, f. || ~-way, s. porte cochère, f.

gather, *găth' ĕr,* s. froncis, pli, m.

gather, *găth' ĕr,* v. a. & n. cueillir || ramasser || assembler, réunir || choisir || conclure || s'accumuler, s'assembler || (méd.) former un abcès, suppurer.

gatherer, *găth' ĕr ĕr,* s. collecteur, m. || vendangeur, m.

gathering, *găth' ĕr ing,* s. action de cueillir, f. || récolte, f. || tumeur, f.

gaudily, *gaw' dĭ lĭ,* ad. avec faste.

gaudiness, *gaw' dĭ nĕs,* s. clinquant, papillotage, m.

gaudy, *gaw' dĭ,* a. somptueux, éclatant.

gauffer, *gŏf' fĕr,* v. a. gaufrer || tuyauter.

gauge, *gāj,* s. jauge, f. || (rail.) largeur, voie, f.

gauge, *gāj,* v. a. jauger || mesurer.

gaunt, *gawnt,* a. (-ly, ad.) maigre, décharné || élancé.

gauntlet, *gawnt' lĕt,* s. gantelet, m.

gauze, *gawz,* s. gaze, f.

gavot, gavotte, *gă vŏt',* s. gavotte, f.

gawky, *gaw' kĭ,* a. gauche, niais, lourd.

gay, *gā*, a. gai, joyeux.

gaze, *gāz*, s. regard fixe, m.

gaze, *gāz*, v. a. & n. regarder fixement, contempler, fixer.

gazelle, *gā zĕl'*, s. gazelle, f.

gazer, *gā' zér*, s. spectateur, m.

Gazette, *gā zĕt'*, s. gazette, f.

gazette, *gā zĕt'*, v. a. publier officiellement || déclarer en faillite.

gazetteer, *gāz ĕt tēr'*, s. dictionnaire bibliographique, m. || journaliste, m.

gear, *gēr*, s. accoutrement, appareil, habillement, m. || trait, m.

gelatin, *jĕl' ā tĕn*, s. gélatine, f.

gelatinous, *jĕ lăt' i nŭs*, a. gélatineux.

geld, *gĕld*, v. a. ir. châtrer. [m.

gelding, *gĕld' ing*, s. castration, f. || hongre,

gem, *jĕm*, s. pierre précieuse, f, bijou, m. || (bot.) bourgeon, m.

gender, *jĕn' dér*, s. genre, sexe, m.

genealogical, *jĕn ĕ ā lŏj' i kăl*, a. généalogique.

genealogy, *jĕ nĕ ăl' ō jĭ*, s. généalogie, f.

general, *jĕn' ér ăl*, s. général, m. || générale, f.

general, *jĕn' ér ăl*, a. général, universel, commun, public || -ly, ad. en général.

generalise, *jĕn' ér ăl iz*, v. a. généraliser.

generality, *jĕn ér ăl' i tĭ*, s. généralité, f. || plupart, f. [m.

generalship, *jĕn' ér ăl ship*, s. généralat,

generate, *jĕn' ér āt*, v a. engendrer, produire. [race, f.

generation, *jĕn ér ā' shŭn*, s. génération,

generic, *jĕn ér' ik*, a. générique.

generosity, *jĕn ér ŏs' i tĭ*, s. générosité, f.

generous, *jĕn' ér ŭs*, a. généreux, bienfaisant || -ly, ad. généreusement.

genial, *jēn' i ăl*, a. (-ly, ad.) génératif || naturel(lement) || natif || joyeux || gaiement

geniality, *jĕ nĭ ăl' i tĭ*, s. caractère naturel, m. || gaieté, f.

genitive, *jĕn' i tĭv*, s. génitif, m.

genius, *jē' nĭ ŭs*, s. génie, démon, m. || dieu tutélaire, m.

genteel, *jĕn tēl'*, a. (-ly, ad.) honnête, poli(ment) || civil || élégant || élégamment.

gentian, *jĕn' shi ăn*, s. (bot.) gentiane, f.

gentile, *jĕn' til*, s. gentil, païen, m.

gentility, *jĕn til' i tĭ*, s. naissance distinguée, f. || politesse, f. || élégance, f.

gentle, *jĕn' tl*, a. doux, bénin, bénévole, paisible. [m. pl.

gentlefolk, *jĕn' tl fōk*, s. gens de condition,

gentleman, *jĕn' tl măn*, s. gentilhomme, homme honorable, m.

gentlemanlike, *jĕn' tl măn līk*, gentlemanly, *jĕn' tl măn lĭ*, a. de bon ton, bien né, distingué, comme il faut.

gentleness, *jĕn' tl nĕs*, s. noblesse, naissance, f. || urbanité, f.

gentlewoman, *jĕn' tl wŏŏm ăn*, s. dame, femme de bonne famille, f. || dame d'honneur, f. [honnêtement.

gently, *jĕn' tlĭ*, ad. doucement, avec soin ||

gentry, *jĕn' trĭ*, s. haute bourgeoisie, f.

genuflection, *jĕn ū flĕk' shŭn*, s. génuflexion, f.

genuine, *jĕn' ū in*, a. (-ly, ad.) véritable, réel || naturel(lement) || pur, de bon aloi.

genuineness, *jĕn' ū in nĕs*, s. pureté, sincérité, f.

genus, *jē' nŭs*, s. genre, m., espèce, f.

geographer, *jē ŏg' ră fér*, s. géographe, m.

geographic(al), *jē ŏ grăf' ik (ăl)*, a. géographique.

geography, *jē ŏg' răf ĭ*, s. géographie, f.

geological, *jē ŏ lŏ' jik ăl*, a. géologique.

geologist, *jē ŏl' ō jist*, s. géologue, m.

geology, *jē ŏl' ō jĭ*, s. géologie, f.

geometric(al), *jē ŏ mĕt' rik (ăl)*, a. géométrique. [mètre, m.

geometrician, *jē ŏ mĕ trish' ăn*, s. géo-

geometry, *jē ŏm' ĕ trĭ*, s. géométrie, f.

germ, *jérm*, s. germe, bourgeon, m.

german, *jér' măn*, a. germain || allemand.

germander, *jér măn' dér*, s. (bot.) germandrée, f. [pousser.

germinate, *jér' mi năt*, v. n. germer.

gesticulate, *jĕs tik' ū lāt*, v. n. gesticuler.

gesticulation, *jĕs tik ū lā' shŭn*, s. gesticulation, f. [mouvement, m.

gesture, *jĕs' tūr*, s. geste, m., action, f.

get, *gĕt*, v. a. & n. ir. obtenir, gagner || saisir, s'emparer || engager, induire || apprendre || s'attirer || répandre, publier || chasser, bannir, engendrer || arriver, survenir || to ~ with child, devenir enceinte || to ~ by heart, apprendre par cœur || to ~ into a bad habit, contracter, prendre une mauvaise habitude || to ~ along, avancer || to ~ away, se sauver || to ~ off, se tirer d'embarras || to ~ over (it), se remettre, faire son deuil de qc. || to ~ up, arranger || se lever.

getter-up, *gĕt tér ŭp'*, s. promoteur, m.

gewgaw, *gū' gaw*, s. joujou, colifichet, m.

ghastliness, *găst' li nĕs*, s. air sombre, m., pâleur, f. [affreux.

ghastly, *găst' lĭ*, a. horrible, terrible, pâle,

gherkin, *gér' kin*, s. cornichon, m.

ghost, *gōst*, s. âme, f., esprit, fantôme, m.

ghostly, *gōst' lĭ*, a. spirituel.

giant, *jī' ănt*, s. géant, m.

giant, *jī' ănt*, a. de géant.

giantess, *jī' ăn tĕs*, s. géante, f.

gibberish, *gib' bér ish*, s. baragouin, jargon, m

gibbet, *jib' bĕt*, s. gibet, m., potence, f.

gibbet, *jib' bĕt*, v. a. pendre.

gibe, *jib*, s. raillerie, moquerie, f.

gibe, *jib*, v. a. & n. railler, se moquer de.

giblets, *jib' lĕts*, s. pl. abattis d'oie, m., petite-oie, f.

giddily, *gid' di lĭ*, ad. par étourderie, f.

giddiness, *gid' di nĕs*, s. vertige, étourdissement, m. || inconstance, f.

giddy, *gid' dĭ*, a. étourdi || inconstant.

gift, *gift*, s. don, présent, m. || talent, m.

gifted, *gift' ĕd*, a. doué, inspiré, illuminé.

gig, *gig*, s. cabriolet, m. || gigue, f. || touple, f.

gigantic, jĭgăn'tĭk, a. gigantesque.
giggle, gĭg'gl, v. a. ricaner.
gild, gĭld, v. a. ir. dorer.
gilder, gĭld'ẽr, s. doreur, m. || florin, m.
gilding, gĭld'ĭng, s. dorure, f.   [ouïes, f.pl.
gill, jĭl, s. canon (a measure), m.||–s, s.pl.
gilliflower, jĭl'ĭflŏŭr, s. girofée, f.
gilt, gĭlt, s. dorure, f. || or, m.
gimcrack, jĭm'krăk, s. mauvais méca-
   nisme, m. || colifichet, m.
gimlet, gĭm'lĕt, s. vrille, f.   [f.
gimp, gĭmp, s. brandebourg, m. || lézarde,
gin, jĭn, s. trappe, f., trébuchet, m. || ge-
   nièvre, m. || machine pour séparer le coton
   de la graine, f. || chèvre, f. || ~–palace,
   s. assommoir, m., buvette, f.
gin, jĭn, v. a. égrener.
ginger, jĭn'jẽr, s. gingembre, m. || ~–
   bread, s. pain d'épice, m. || ~–beer, s.
   liqueur gazeuse au gingembre, f.
gingerly, jĭn'jẽr lĭ, ad. doucement, crain-
   tivement.
Gipsy, jĭp'sĭ, s. Bohémien(ne), m. (& f.)
giraffe, jĭrăf', s. girafe, f.
girandole, jĭr'ăndōl, s. girandole, f.
gird, gẽrd, v. a. & n. ir. ceindre, attacher
   autour || environner || railler, se moquer.
girder, gẽrd'ẽr, s. solive, poutre, f.
girdle, gẽr'dl, s. ceinture, f.
girdle, gẽr'dl, v. a. ceindre.
girl, gẽrl, s. fille, f.
girlhood, gẽrl'hŏŏd, s. état de fille, m.
girlish, gẽr'lĭsh, a. de jeune fille.
girth, gẽrth, s. sangle, f. || circonférence, f.
gist, jĭst, s. fin mot, m. || fond, m., sub-
   stance, f.
give, gĭv, v. a. & n. ir. donner || prononcer,
   pousser || abandonner, remettre || s'adonner
   à || prêter || rendre || se radoucir, s'amollir ||
   I'll – it to you ! je vous donnerai votre
   compte! || to – in or up, se rendre,
   céder || to – over, cesser.
giving, gĭv'ĭng, s. don, m.
gizzard, gĭz'zẽrd, s. gésier, m.
glacier, glā'sĭẽr, s. glacier, m.
glad, glăd, a. aise, joyeux, réjoui, gai ||
   –ly, ad. avec plaisir.
gladden, glăd'n, v. a. (& n.) (se) réjouir.
glade, glăd, s. clairière, avenue, f. || (Am.)
   verglas, m.
gladiator, glăd'ĭātẽr, s. gladiateur, m.
gladness, glăd'nĕs, s. joie, f., plaisir, m.
glamour, glăm'ẽr, s. illusion d'optique, f.
glance, glăns, s. éclat, trait de lumière,
   m. || coup d'œil, m.
glance, glăns, v. a. & n. jeter un éclat ||
   jeter un coup d'œil || raser, friser, frôler ||
   gland, glănd, s. glande, f.   [censurer.
glanders, glăn'dẽrz, s. pl. morve, f.
glare, glâr, s. éclat de lumière éblouissant,
   m. || regard fixe or féroce, m.
glare, glâr, v. a. & n. éblouir, briller || re-
   garder d'un œil terrible.
glaring, glā'rĭng, a. lueur || –ly, ad.
   brillamment || manifestement.

glass, glâs, s. verre, m. || glace, f., miroir,
   m. || vitre, f., télescope, m. || lorgnon, m. ||
   baromètre, m. || sablier, m. || magnify-
   ing ~, s. microscope, m. || burning–~,
   s. verre ardent, m. || stained–~, s. verre
   de couleur, m. || –es, s. pl. lunettes, f. pl.
glass, glâs, a. de verre || ~–door, s. porte
   vitrée, f. || ~–house, s. verrerie, f. || ~–
   shade, s. globe, cylindre, m.
glassy, glâs'sĭ, a. de verre, vitreux.
glaze, glāz, s. vernis, m.
glaze, glāz, v. a. vitrer || vernisser, glacer.
glazier, glā'zhẽr, s. vitrier, m.   [f.
gleam, glēm, s. rayon, lustre, m., clarté,
gleam, glēm, v. n. rayonner, briller.
gleaming, glēm'ĭng, a. étincelant, brillant.
glean, glēn, v. a. glaner || recueillir.
gleanings, glēn'ĭngs, s. pl. glanage, m. ||
   recueil, m.   [de la cure, f.
glebe-land, glēb'lănd, s. terre dépendant
glee, glē, s. joie, allégresse, f. || chanson à
   plusieurs voix, f.
gleeful, glē'fŏŏl, a. joyeux, gai || –ly, ad.
   joyeusement.
glen, glĕn, s. vallée, f., vallon, m.
glib, glĭb, s. coulant, glissant || (~ of the
   tongue) délié || –ly, ad. coulamment.
glide, glīd, v. n. couler, glisser, se glisser.
glimmer, glĭm'mẽr, s. lueur faible, f.
glimmer, glĭm'mẽr, v. n. jeter une faible
   lueur, reluire.
glimpse, glĭmps, s. lueur, f., éclat, m.
glimpse, glĭmps, v. n. apercevoir.
glint, glĭnt, glitter, glĭt'tẽr, s. étincelle-
   ment, m. || trait de lumière || oripeau, m. ||
   lueur, f.
glisten, glĭs'n, glitter, glĭt'tẽr, v. n.
   briller, éclater, luire, étinceler.
gloaming, glōm'ĭng, s. crépuscule, m., fin
   du jour, brune, f.
gloat, glōt, v. n. jeter des œillades.
globe, glōb, s. globe, m. || sphère, f.
globular, glŏb'ūlẽr, a. globuleux.
globule, glŏb'ūl, s. globule, m.
gloom, glōm, gloominess, glōm'ĭnĕs, s.
   obscurité, f. || tristesse, f.
gloomily, glōm'ĭlĭ, ad. tristement.
gloomy, glōm'ĭ, a. obscur, sombre || triste.
glorification, glōrĭfĭkā'shŭn, s. glorification, f.
glorify, glō'rĭfī, v. a. glorifier, vanter.
glorious, glō'rĭŭs, a. glorieux, illustre ||
   –ly, ad. glorieusement.
glory, glō'rĭ, s. gloire, f., honneur, m.,
   célébrité, f. || admiration, f. || auréole, f.
glory, glō'rĭ, v. n. se glorifier, s'enorgueillir.   [prêt, déguisement, m.
gloss, glŏs, s. glose, f. || lustre, éclat, ap-
gloss, glŏs, v. a. & n. gloser || lustrer,
   vernir || déguiser.
glossary, glŏs'ărĭ, s. glossaire, m.
glossy, glŏs'sĭ, a. poli, reluisant.
glove, glŭv, s. gant, m.
glover, glŭv'ẽr, s. gantier, m.
glow, glō, s. éclat, m. || chaleur, f. || ~–
   worm, s. ver luisant, m.

glow, *glō*, v. n. briller, luire || brûler || rougir || être enflammé.

gloze, *glōz*, v. n. flatter.

glue, *glō*, s. colle forte, f.

glue, *glō*, v. a. coller.

glum, *glŭm*, a. chagrin, sombre.

glut, *glŭt*, s. abondance. f. || satiété, f.

glut, *glŭt*, v. a. avaler, engloutir || rassasier. [queux.

glutinous, *glŏ'tĭ nŭs*, s. glutineux, visqueux.

glutton, *glŭt'n*, s. glouton, gourmand, m.

gluttony, *glŭt'n ĭ*, s. gourmandise, gloutonnerie, f.

glycerine, *glĭs'ĕr ĕn*, s. glycérine, f.

gnarled, *när'ld*, a. noueux. [dents.

gnash, *năsh*, v. a. & n. grincer || grincer des

gnat, *năt*, s. moucheron, m.

gnaw, *nåw*, v. a. & n. ronger, corroder.

gnome, *nōm*, s. gnome, esprit, m.

go, *gō*, s. mode, f. || énergie, f.

go, *gō*, v. n. ir. aller, marcher, passer, partir || mourir || compter || contribuer || tendre à || se conduire, se régler || **~ to** || allons! allez! || **to ~ away**, s'en aller || **to ~ by**, passer par || **it won't ~ down with me!** je ne peux pas digérer cela! || **to ~ off** (d'un fusil), partir || **~ on!** continuez! || **to ~ on at one**, faire une scène à qn. || **to ~ out**, sortir || s'éteindre || **to ~ through with**, pousser à bout || **to ~ without**, se passer de || **who ~es there?** qui vive? || **~-between**, s. médiateur, courtier, entremetteur, m. || **~-cart**, s. chariot, m., roulette d'enfants, f.

goad, *gōd*, s. aiguillon, m.

goad, *gōd*, v. a. aiguillonner, piquer, exciter [m.

goal, *gōl*, s. borne de la carrière, f. || but,

goat, *gōt*, s. chèvre, f. || **he-~**, s. bouc, m.

goblet, *gŏb'lĕt*, s. gobelet, m., coupe, f.

goblin, *gŏb'lĭn*, s. esprit malin, spectre, m.

God, god, *gŏd*, s. Dieu, dieu, m. || **~-child**, s. filleul, m., filleule, f. || **~-daughter**, s. filleule, f. || **~-father**, s. parrain, m. || compère, m. || **~-mother**, s. marraine, f. || **~-son**, s. filleul, m

goddess, *gŏd'dĕs*, s. déesse, f.

godhead, *gŏd'hĕd*, s. divinité, f.

godless, *gŏd'lĕs*, a. athée.

godliness, *gŏd'lĭ nĕs*, s. piété, dévotion, f.

godly, *gŏd'lĭ*, a. & ad. pieux, religieux || religieusement.

godsend, *gŏd'sĕnd*, s. bonne aubaine, f.

goer, *gō'ĕr*, s. marcheur, m. || homme d'énergie, m. [m.

goggle-eye, *gŏg'lĭ*, s. œil à fleur de tête,

going, *gō'ing*, s. allure, démarche, f. || **~s-and comings**, s. allées et venues, f. pl. || **~s on**, s. train, m.

gold, *gōld*, s. or, m. || **as good as ~**, de l'or en barre || **~-digger**, s. mineur à la recherche de gisements aurifères, m. || **~-fish**, s. poisson rouge, m. || **~-leaf**, s. or en feuille, m. || **~-plated**, a. doublé en or

gold(en), *gōld'(n)*, a. d'or.

goldfinch, *gōld'fĭnsh*, s. chardonneret, m.

goldsmith, *gōld'smĭth*, s. orfèvre, m.

golosh, *gŏlŏsh'*, s. galoche, f.

gondola, *gŏn'dŏ lä*, s. gondole, f.

gondolier, *gŏn dŏ lēr'*, s. gondolier, m.

gone, *gŏn*, p. passé || parti || avancé || perdu || mort || adjugé.

gonorrhœa, *gŏn ŏr rē'ä*, s. (méd.) gonorrhée, chaude-pisse, f.

good, *gŏŏd*, a. bon, bienveillant || solide convenable, favorable || **~ I bien! bon!** || **~-bye**, ad. adieu!

goodly, *gŏŏd'lĭ*, a. beau, agréable.

goodness, *gŏŏd'nĕs*, s. bonté, f.

goods, *gŏŏds*, s. pl. meubles, effets, m. pl. || marchandises, f. pl. || **~-department**, s. (rail.) messagerie, f. || **~-office**, s. (rail.) bureau de messagerie, m. [m.

goose, *gŏŏs*, s. oie, f. || carreau de tailleur,

gooseberry, *gŏŏz'bĕr ri*, s. groseille verte, f. || **~-bush**, s. groseiller épineux, m. || **~-fool**, s. groseilles à la crème, f. pl.

gordian-knot, *gŏr dĭ ăn nŏt'*, s. (fig.) nœud gordien, m. [pointe, f.

gore, *gōr* s. sang caillé, m. || boue, f. ||

gore, *gōr*, v. a. percer, piquer, blesser.

gorge, *gŏrj*, s. gorge, f., gosier, m.

gorge, *gŏrj*, v. a. gorger, soûler, rassasier.

gorgeous, *gŏr'jĭ ŭs*, a. (-ly, ad.) splendide(ment) || fastueux.

Gorgon, *gŏr'gŏn*, s. Gorgone, f.

gorilla, *gŏ ril'lä*, s. gorille, f.

gormandise, *gŏr'măn diz*, v. n. goinfrer.

gorse, *gŏrs*, s. ajonc, m.

gory, *gō'ri*, a. ensanglanté.

goshawk, *gŏs'hăwk*, s. autour, m.

gosling, *gŏz'ling*, s. oison, m.

Gospel, *gŏs'pĕl*, s. Évangile, m. [m. pl.

gossamer, *gŏs'să mĕr*, s. fils de la Vierge,

gossamer, *gŏs'să mĕr*, a. ténu.

gossip, *gŏs'sip*, s. commère, causeuse, f. || commérage, m.

gossip, *gŏs'sip*, v. n. bavarder.

gothic, *gŏth'ĭk*, a. gothique.

gouge, *gŏŭj*, s. gouge, f.

gouge, *gŏŭj*, v. a. arracher (en pressant en rond avec le doigt).

gourd, *gŏrd*, s. calebasse, f. [f. || goût, m.

gout, *gŏŭt*, s. goutte, f. || goutte sciatique,

gouty, *gŏŭt'i*, a. goutteux.

govern, *gŭv'ĕrn*, v. a. & n. gouverner || diriger, régler

governable, *gŭv'ĕr nă bl*, a. traitable.

governess, *gŭv'ĕr nĕs*, s. gouvernante, f.

government, *gŭv'ĕrn mĕnt*, s. gouvernement, m. || régime, m. || empire, m. || administration, f. || **~-annuity**, s. rente sur l'État, f. [vernement.

governmental, *gŭv ĕrn mĕn'tăl*, a. du gou-

governor, *gŭv'ĕr nĕr*, s. gouverneur, m. || patron, m. || régulateur, m.

gown, *gŏwn*, s. robe, f. [m.

gownsman, *gŏwnz'măn*, s. homme de robe,

grab, *grăb*, v. a. (**to make a ~ at**) saisir soudainement.

grace, *grās*, s. grâce, faveur, f., bienfait, m., agréments, m. || **~ grâces**, f. pl. ||

Graces, s. pl. les Grâces, f. pl.

grace, *grās*, v. a. donner de la grâce, orner, favoriser.
graceful, *grās'fool*, a. gracieux, élégant || -ly, ad. gracieusement.
graceless, *grās'lĕs*, a. sans grâce || désagréable || impie.
gracious, *grā'shŭs*, a. gracieux, favorable || -ly, ad. gracieusement.
gradation, *grā'dā'shŭn*, s. gradation, f.
grade, *grād*, s. grade, rang, m. [m.
gradient, *grā'dĭ ĕnt*, s. (rail.) relèvement, par degrés. [voir des degrés.
gradual, *grād'ū ăl*, a. graduel || -ly, ad.
graduate, *grād'ū āt*, v.a.&n. graduer || recevoir.
graduation, *grād ū ā'shŭn*, s. graduation.
graft, *grāft*, v. a. & n. greffer, enter. [f.
grain, *grān*, s. grain, blé, m. || (of wood) fil, m. || graine, f. || disposition, inclination, f. || -s, s. pl. drèche, f.
grain, *grān*, v. a. grener || (leather) greneler || peindre en décors || cross -ed, a. (fig.) rebarbatif, revêche || to go against the ~, (fig.) répugner.
grammar, *grăm'măr*, s. grammaire, f.
grammarian, *grăm mā'rĭ ăn*, s. grammairien, m. [grammatical(ement).
grammatical, *grăm măt'ĭk ăl*, a. (-ly, ad.)
grampus, *grăm'pŭs*, s. épaulard, m.
granary, *grăn'ă rĭ*, s. grenier, m.
grand, *grānd*, a. (-ly, ad.) grand(ement), sublime, illustre || ~-child, s. petit-fils, m., petite-fille, f. || ~-daughter, s. petite-fille, f. || ~-father, s. grand-père, aïeul, m. || ~-mother, s. grand'mère, aïeule, f. || ~-son, s. petit-fils, m.
grandam, *grăn'dăm*, s. vieille, f.
grandee, *grăn dē'*, s. grand, m.
grandeur, *grānd'yĕr*, s. grandeur, magnificence, f. [peux, emphatique.
grandiloquent, *grăn dĭl'ō kwĕnt*, a. pompeux, emphatique.
grange, *grānj*, s. ferme, métairie, f.
granite, *grăn'ĭt*, s. granit, m. [man, f.
granny, *grăn'nĭ*, s. grand'mère, bonne maman, f.
grant, *grānt*, s. concession, f.
grant, *grānt*, v. a. accorder || céder, concéder || convenir || to ~ a charter, octroyer une charte || to take for ~ed, admettre, convenir de.
granular, *grăn'ū lĕr*, a. grenelé, grenu, granulaire. [granuler.
granulate, *grăn'ū lāt*, v. a. (& n.) (se)
grape, *grāp*, s. raisin, m. || ~ bunch of -s, s. grappe de raisins, f. || ~-shot, s. mitraille, f. || ~-stone, s. pépin, m.
graphic, *grăf'ĭk*, a. (-ally, ad.) graphique (ment) || pittoresque.
grapnel, *grăp'nĕl*, s. grappin, m.
grapple, *grăp'pl*, s. lutte, f. || grappin, m.
grapple, *grăp'pl*, v.a.&n. grappiner, accrocher || en venir aux mains.
grappling-iron, *grăp'plĭng ī'rn*,s. (mar.) grappin d'abordage, m. [f. pl.
grasp, *grāsp*, s. poignée, prise, f. || griffes,
grasp, *grāsp*, v. a. & n. empoigner, saisir.
grasping, *grāsp'ĭng*, a. cupide, avide, ambitieux.

grass, *grās*, s. herbe, f., gazon, m. || ~-plot, s. gazon, boulingrin, tapis vert, m.
grasshopper, *grās hŏp'ĕr*, s. sauterelle, cigale, f.
grassy, *grās'sĭ*, a. herbeux. [m.
grate, *grāt*, s. grille, f., treillis, m. || foyer,
grate, *grāt*, v. a. & n. gratter, frotter || choquer || fermer d'une grille || grincer.
grateful, *grāt'fool*, a. (-ly, ad.) reconnaissant || agréable(ment) || avec reconnaissance.
grater, *grāt'ĕr*, s. racloir, m.
gratification, *grăt ĭ fĭ kā'shŭn*, s. gratification, récompense, f.
gratify, *grăt'ĭ fĭ*, v. a. gratifier, récompenser || satisfaire.
grating, *grā'tĭng*, s. grille, f.
grating, *grā'tĭng*, a. choquant.
gratis, *grā'tĭs*, ad. gratuitement.
gratitude, *grăt'ĭ tūd*, s. reconnaissance, f.
gratuitous, *grā tū'ĭ tŭs*, a. (-ly, ad.) gratuit(ement) || volontaire.
gratuity, *grā tū'ĭ tĭ*, s. présent, m., gratification, récompense, f.
gratulate, *grăt'ū lāt*, v. a. féliciter.
gratulatory, *grăt'ū lā tĕr ĭ*, a. congratulatoire.
grave, *grāv*, s. fosse, f., tombeau, m.
grave, *grāv*, v. a. & n. graver, ciseler || sculpter.
grave, *grāv*, a. (-ly, ad.) grave(ment) || sérieux || ~-clothes, s. pl. linceul, m. || ~-digger, s. fossoyeur, m. || ~-stone, s. pierre tumulaire, f.
gravel, *grăv'ĕl*, s. gravier, m. || (méd.) gravelle, f. || ~-pit, s. sablonnière, f. || ~-walk, s. allée sablée, f.
graveless, *grāv'lĕs*, a. sans sépulture.
gravelly, *grăv'ĕl lĭ*, a. graveleux.
gravitate, *grăv'ĭ tāt*, v. n. graviter.
gravitation, *grăv ĭ tā'shŭn*, s. gravitation, f.
gravity, *grăv'ĭ tĭ*, s. gravité, pesanteur, f.
gravy, *grā'vĭ*, s. suc de la viande, jus, m.
gray, *grā*, s. couleur grise, f.
gray, *grā*, a. gris || grison || ~-beard, s. barbe grise, f. || vieillard, m. || ~-haired, a. aux cheveux gris.
grayish, *grā'ĭsh*, a. grisâtre.
grayness, *grā'nĕs*, s. couleur grise, f.
graze, *grāz*, v. a. & n. faire paître || paître || effleurer, raser.
grazier, *grā'zhĕr*, s. herbager, m.
grease, *grēs*, s. graisse, f.
grease, *grēs*, v. a. graisser.
greasy, *grē'zĭ*, a. graisseux, crasseux.
great, *grāt*, a. (-ly, ad.) grand(ement) || gros || éminent || enceinte || fort || beaucoup || ~-grand-father (-mother), s. bisaïeul, m., bisaïeule, f. || ~-grand-father, s. trisaïeul, m. || ~-grandson (-daughter), s. arrière-petit-fils, m., arrière-petite-fille, f.
greatness, *grāt'nĕs*, s. grandeur, dignité, f., pouvoir, m. || magnificence, f.
greedily, *grē dĭ lĭ*, ad. goulûment, avidement.

greediness, *grē'dĭ nĕs,* s. gloutonnerie, avidité, f. ‖ désir ardent, m.

greedy, *grē'di,* a. vorace, avide.

greek, *grēk,* s. langue grecque, f. ‖ ~-fire, s. feu grégeois, m.

green, *grēn,* s. couleur verte, f. ‖ verdure, f. ‖ --s, s. pl. légumes verts, m. pl.

green, *grēn,* a. vert, frais, récent ‖ jeune ‖ novice ‖ pâle ‖ ~-room, s. foyer des acteurs, m. ‖ ~-sickness, s. pâles couleurs, f. pl.

greenback, *grēn'băk,* s. grenouille verte, f. ‖ --s, s. pl. (Am.) papier-monnaie, m.

greengage, *grēn'gāj,* s. reine-claude, f.

greengrocer, *grēn'grō sĕr,* s. fruitier, m.

greenhorn, *grēn'hŏrn,* s. blanc-bec, m.

greenhouse, *grēn'hŏws,* s. serre, f.

greenish, *grēn'ĭsh,* a. verdâtre.

greenness, *grēn'nĕs,* s. verdure, f. ‖ verdeur, fraîcheur, f.

greensward, *grēn'swŏrd,* s. pelouse, f.

greet, *grēt,* v. a. & n. saluer.

greeting, *grēt'ĭng,* s. salutation, f., salut, m.

gregarious, *grē gā'rĭ ŭs,* a. en troupe, par troupes, grégaire.

grenade, *grē nād',* s. grenade, f.

grenadine, *grĕn'ă dĭn,* s. grenadine, f.

grey, *grā,* vide gray.

greyhound, *grā'hŏwnd,* s. lévrier, m.

gridiron, *grid'ĭrn,* s. gril, m. ‖ grille-pain, m.

grief, *grēf,* s. chagrin, regret, m., affliction, douleur, f. ‖ **to come to ~,** tomber dans le malheur.   [abus, m.

grievance, *grē văns,* s. grief, tort, m. ‖

grieve, *grēv,* v. a. (& n.) (se) chagriner.

grievous, *grēv'ŭs,* a. grave, affligeant ‖ horrible ‖ -ly, ad. grièvement ‖ cruellement.

griffin, *grif'fin,* s. griffon, m.   [ment.

grig, *grig,* s. petite anguille, f. ‖ égrillard, m. ‖ **merry as a ~,** gai comme un pinson.

grill, *gril,* v. a. faire griller.   [son.

grim, *grim,* a. refrogné, hideux, effrayant ‖ -ly, ad. d'un air refrogné.

grimace, *grĭ mās',* s. grimace, f. ‖ affectation, f. ‖ **to make a ~,** faire une grimace.

grimalkin, *grĭ măl kĭn,* s Raminagrobis, m. ‖ vieux chat, m.

grime, *grim,* s. crasse, f.

grime, *grim,* v. a. barbouiller ‖ noircir.

grimness, *grim'nĕs,* s. regard affreux, m., horreur, f.

grimy, *grĭ'mĭ,* a. noirci, sale.

grin, *grin,* s. grimace, f., grincement de dents, m.   [dents.

grin, *grin,* v. n. grimacer ‖ grincer des

grind, *grĭnd,* v. a. ir. moudre ‖ broyer ‖ aiguiser ‖ (students) préparer ‖ grincer.

grinder, *grĭnd'ĕr,* s. émouleur, broyeur, m. ‖ répétiteur, m. ‖ meule à aiguiser, f. ‖ dent molaire, f.   [ser, f.

grindstone, *grĭnd'stōn,* s. pierre à aiguiser, f.

grinning, *grin'nĭng,* s. grimacier.

grip(e), *grip, grīp,* s. empoignement, m., griffe, f. ‖ prise, f. ‖ affliction, f. ‖ -s, s. pl. colique, f.

grip(e), *grip, grīp,* v. a. & n. empoigner, saisir ‖ serrer.

griskin, *gris'kin,* s. grillade de porc, f.

grisly, *griz'li,* a. horrible, hideux.

grist, *grist,* s. blé à moudre, m. ‖ profit, m. ‖ **to bring ~ to the mill,** faire le compte de qn., être d'un grand profit.

gristle, *gris'l,* s. cartilage, m. ‖ --s, s. pl. tendrons, m. pl.

gristly, *gris'li,* a. cartilagineux.

grit, *grit,* s. recoupe, f., gruau d'avoine, m. ‖ gravier, m.

gritty, *grit'ti,* a. graveleux.

grizzle, *griz'l,* s. couleur grise, f., gris, m.

grizzled, *griz'ld,* **grizzly,** *griz'li,* a. grisâtre ‖ ~ **bear,** s. ours gris, m.

groan, *grōn,* s. gémissement, m.

groan, *grōn,* v. n. gémir, soupirer.

groat, *grōt,* s. huit sous, m. pl.

groats, *grōts,* s. gruau d'avoine, m.

grocer, *grō'sĕr,* s. épicier, m. ‖ marchand droguiste, m.   [f.

grocery, *grō'sĕr ĭ,* s. épicerie, f. ‖ droguerie, f.

grog, *grŏg,* s. grog, m.

groggy, *grŏg'gĭ,* a. ivre, gris, pochard.

groin, *grŏyn,* s. aine, f. ‖ brise-lames, m. ‖ arête, f.

groom, *grōm,* s. palefrenier, m. ‖ ~ **of the chamber,** s. valet de chambre royal, m.

groom, *grōm,* v. n. panser.

groove, *grōv,* s. caverne, f. ‖ rainure, f.

groove, *grōv,* v. a. faire une rainure ‖ canneler.   [tâtons.

grope, *grōp,* v. a. & n. tâtonner, aller à

gross, *grōs,* s. gros, m. ‖ grosse, f.

gross, *grōs,* a. gros, épais ‖ grossier, rude, lourd ‖ -   ad. grossièrement.

grossness, *grōs'nĕs,* s. grosseur, f. ‖ grossièreté, f.

grotesque, *grō tĕsk',* a. grotesque.

grotto, *grŏt'tō,* s. grotte, f.

ground, *grŏwnd,* s. terrain, champ, m., terre, f., pays, m. ‖ fond, m. ‖ lieu, m. ‖ raison, f. ‖ -s, s. pl. lie, f. ‖ principes, m. pl. ‖ **above ~,** qui appartient à la surface de la terre ‖ **below ~,** s. souterrain, m. ‖ **to give ~,** céder ‖ ~-**floor,** s. rez-de-chaussée, m. ‖ ~-**ivy,** s. lierre terrestre, m. ‖ ~-**plot,** s. terrain, m. ‖ plan d'un bâtiment, m. ‖ ~-**rent,** s. rente foncière, f. ‖ ~-**tackle,** s. (mar.) garniture des ancres, f. ‖ ~-**work,** s. fond, fondement, m.

ground, *grŏwnd,* v. a. mettre à terre ‖ fonder ‖ enseigner.

groundless, *grŏwnd'lĕs,* a. (-ly, ad.) sans fondement or raison.   [lité, f.

groundlessness, *grŏwnd'lĕs nĕs,* s. futilité, f.

group, *grōp,* s. groupe, m.

group, *grōp,* v. a. grouper.

grouse, *grŏws,* s. coq de bruyère, m.

grove, *grōv,* s. bocage, bosquet, m.

grovel, *grŏv'l,* v. n. ramper ‖ se vautrer.

grow, *grō,* v. n. ir. cultiver ‖ croître, se faire, devenir ‖ **he is much ~n,** il a beaucoup grandi ‖ **to ~ in knowledge,** croître en sagesse ‖ **to ~ upon one,** gagner

dé l'ascendant sur qn. || **to ~ old,** vieillir, se faire vieux || **to ~ up (to be -n up),** grandir (être parvenu à l'âge adulte) || **full -n,** adulte.
grower, *grō'ėr,* s. cultivateur, m.
growl, *growl,* s. grognement, m.
growl, *growl,* v. n. gronder, murmurer.
growth, *grōth,* s. croissance, f.
grub, *grŭb,* s. larve, f. || ver, m. || puceron, m. || nain, m. || boustifaille, f.
grub, *grŭb,* v. a. défricher, bêcher.
grudge, *grŭj,* s. haine, f. || rancune, f. || envie, f. || **to owe one a ~,** garder rancune à qn., la garder bonne à qn. [fuser.
grudge, *grŭj,* v. a. & n. porter envie || re-
gruel, *grō'ĕl,* s. gruau, m., bouillie de gruau, f. [brusque(ment).
gruff, *grŭf,* a. (**-ly,** ad.) refrogné, rechigné ||
gruffness, *grŭf'nĕs,* s. brusquerie, f.
grumble, *grŭm'bl,* v. n. grogner, grom-
grunt, *grŭnt,* s. grognement, m. [meler.
grunt, *grŭnt,* v. n. grogner (comme un cochon).
guano, *gōō ā'nō or gwâ'nō,* s. guano, m.
guarantee, *găr ăn tē',* s. garant, m., caution, f.
guarantee, *găr ăn tē',* v. a. garantir.
guard, *gârd,* s. garde, défense, f. || garde, m., sentinelle, f. || (rail.) conducteur, m. || **foot-~,** s. garde à pied, m. || **horse-~,** s. garde à cheval, m. || **life-~,** s. garde du corps, m. || **rear-~,** s. arrière-garde, f. || **to be on one's ~,** être sur ses gardes || **to be off one's ~,** être imprudent || **~-house,** s. corps de garde, m. || **~-room,** s. salle des gardes, f.
guard, *gârd,* v. a. & n. garder, protéger || se tenir sur ses gardes.
guarded, *gârd'ĕd,* a. gardé || circonspect.
guardian, *gâr'dĭ ăn,* s. gardien, m. || tuteur, m.
guardian, *gâr'dĭ ăn,* a. gardien || tuteur.
guardianship, *gâr'dĭ ăn ship,* s. tutelle, f.
guava, *gwâ'vă,* s. goyave, f.
gudgeon, *gŭj'ŭn,* s. goujon, m. || dupe, f., affront, m.
guerdon, *gėr'dŏn,* s. récompense, f.
guerilla warfare, *gė rĭl'lă wawr'fâr,* s. guerre de guérillas, f.
guess, *gĕs,* s. conjecture, f.
guess, *gĕs,* v. a. & n. deviner, conjecturer.
guesser, *gĕs'sėr,* s. qui devine || qui conjecture.
guest, *gĕst,* s. hôte, convive, m.
guidance, *gī'dăns,* s. conduite, f.
guide, *gīd,* s. guide, conducteur, m. || **~-book,** s. guide, m. || **~-post,** s. poteau indicateur, m.
guide, *gīd,* v. a. guider, conduire, mener.
guild, *gĭld,* s. société, compagnie, f.
guildhall, *gĭld'hawl,* s. hôtel de ville à Londres, m.
guile, *gīl,* s. fourberie, tromperie, f.
guileful, *gīl'fōōl,* a. fourbe, trompeur.
guileless, *gīl'lĕs,* a. (**-ly,** ad.) sans artifice || sincère(ment).
guillotine, *gĭl ō tēn',* v. a. guillotiner.
guilt, *gĭlt,* s. crime, m., culpabilité, faute,
guiltless, *gĭlt'lĕs,* a. innocent. [f.
guilty, *gĭl'tĭ,* a. coupable, criminel || **to bring one in (not) ~, to bring in a verdict of (not) ~,** déclarer coupable *ou* non coupable (se dit du jury).
guinea, *gĭn'ĭ,* s. guinée, f. || **~-hen,** s. poule de Guinée, f.
guise, *gīz,* s. manière, coutume, f. || ex-
guitar, *gĭ târ',* s. guitare, f. [térieur, m.
gulf, *gŭlf,* s. golfe, m. || abîme, m. || **~-stream,** s. courant du golfe, m.
gull, *gŭl,* s. fourbe, m. || dupe, f. || mouette,
gull, *gŭl,* v. a. fourber, duper. [f.
gullet, *gŭl'lĕt,* s. gosier, m., gorge, f.
gullibility, *gŭl lĭ bĭl'ĭ tĭ,* s. bonhomie, crédulité, f.
gullible, *gŭl'lĭ bl,* a. facile à duper, crédule.
gully, *gŭl'lĭ,* s. ravin, m.
gulp, *gŭlp,* s. gorgée, f. || trait, m.
gulp, *gŭlp,* v. a. avaler (avec avidité).
gum, *gŭm,* s. gomme, f. || gencives, f. pl. || **~-tree,** s. gommier, m.
gum, *gŭm,* v. a. gommer || (Am.) endenter.
gummy, *gŭm'mĭ,* a. gommeux. [velle, f.
gumption, *gŭm'shŭn,* s. esprit, m., cer-
gun, *gŭn,* s. fusil, m. || **-s,** s. pl. artillerie, f. || **~-barrel,** s. canon de fusil, m. || **~-carriage,** s. affût, m. || **~-cotton,** s. coton-poudre, m. || **~-deck,** s. (mar.) pont (d'un vaisseau), m. || **~-metal,** s. métal de fonte, m. || **~-port,** s. (mar.) sabord, m. || **~-practice,** s. (mil.) exercice à feu, m. || **~-room,** s. sainte-barbe, f. || **~-shot,** s. portée de fusil, f. || **within, out of ~-shot,** à portée de fusil, hors de portée || **~-stock,** s. fût, m.
gunboat, *gŭn'bōt,* s. chaloupe canonnière, f.
gunner, *gŭn'nėr,* s. canonnier, m.
gunnery, *gŭn'nėr ĭ,* s. science de l'artillerie, f.
gunpowder, *gŭn'pow dėr,* s. poudre à canon, f. || **~ plot,** s. conspiration des poudres, f.
gunsmith, *gŭn'smĭth,* s. armurier, m.
gunwale, *gŭn'nl,* s. (mar.) plat-bord, m.
gurgle, *gėr'gl,* v. n. murmurer.
gurnet, *gėr'nĕt,* s. rouget, m.
gush, *gŭsh,* s. écoulement, flux, m.
gush, *gŭsh,* v. n. jaillir, ruisseler.
gushing, *gŭsh'ĭng,* a. torrentiel.
gusset, *gŭs'sĕt,* s. gousset, m.
gust, *gŭst,* s. goût, m. || bouffée de vent, f.
gusto, *gŭs'tō,* s. goût, m.
gusty, *gŭs'tĭ,* a. orageux.
gut, *gŭt,* s. boyau, intestin, m. || gloutonnerie, f.
gut, *gŭt,* v. a. éventrer.
gutter, *gŭt'tėr,* s. gouttière, f.
gutter, *gŭt'tėr,* v. a. & n. canneler || couler.
guttural, *gŭt'tėr ăl,* a. guttural.
guy, *gī,* s. pantin, m., caricature, f.
guzzle, *gŭz'zl,* v. a. & n. avaler || bâfrer.
gymnasium, *jĭm nā'zĭ ŭm,* s. gymnase, m.
gymnastic, *jĭm năs'tĭk,* a. gymnastique.

gymnastics, *jĭm năs'tĭks,* s. pl. gymnastique, f.

gyrate, *ji'rāt,* v. n. tourner en rond.

gyration, *ji rā'shŭn,* s. mouvement giratoire, m.

H.

haberdasher, *hăb'ẽr dăsh ẽr,* s. mercier, m.   [cerie, f.

haberdashery, *hăb'ẽr dăsh ẽr ĭ,* s. mercerie, f.

habiliment, *hă bil'ĭ mĕnt,* s. habillement, habit, m.

habit, *hăb'ĭt,* s. habitude, coutume, f. || disposition, f. || habit, habillement, vêtement, m. || riding-~, s. costume de cheval, m., amazone, f. || to get into a ~, contracter, prendre une habitude.

habitable, *hăb'ĭ tă bl,* a. habitable.

habitat, *hăb'ĭ tăt,* **habitation,** *hăb ĭ tā' shŭn,* s. habitation, demeure, f.

habited, *hăb'ĭ tĕd,* a. accoutumé.

habitual, *hă bĭt'ū ăl,* a. (~ly, ad.) habituel || d'habitude || ordinaire(ment) || par habitude.   [coutumer.

habituate, *hă bĭt'ū ăt,* v. a. habituer, accoutumer.

habitude, *hăb'ĭ tūd,* s. habitude, coutume, f.

hack, *hăk,* s. entaille, f. || cheval de louage, m. || mercenaire, m. & f.   [langue.

hack, *hăk,* v. a. hacher, écorcher une

hackle, *hăk'l,* s. soie écrue, f. || séran, m.

hackle, *hăk'l,* v. a. sérancer (du lin).

hackney, *hăk'nĭ,* s. cheval de louange or de fatigue, m. || mercenaire, m. & f. || ~coach, s. fiacre, m.

haddock, *hăd'dŏk,* s. merlu*he, f.

haft, *hăft,* s. manche, m., poignée, f.

hag, *hăg,* s. sorcière, f. || furie, f.

haggard, *hăg'gẽrd,* a. hagard, farouche.

haggle, *hăg'gl,* v. a. & n. hacher || barguigner.

haggler, *hăg'glẽr,* s. barguigneur, m.

ha-ha, *hä'hä,* s. saut de loup, m.

hail, *hāl,* s. grêle, f. || santé, f. || ~fellow, s. ami intime, m.

hail, *hāl,* v. a. & n. saluer || grêler.

hail! *hāl,* salut!

hailstone, *hāl'stōn,* s. grêlon, m.

hair, *hâr,* s. cheveu, m. || poil, m. || fil, m. || gré, m. || ~breadth, s. épaisseur d'un cheveu, f. || ~brush, s. brosse à cheveux, f. || ~cutting, s. coupe de cheveux, f. || ~dresser, s. coiffeur, m. || ~net, s. filet à cheveux, m. || ~splitting, s. pointillerie, f.

hairless, *hâr'lĕs,* a. sans cheveux, chauve.

hairpin, *hâr'pĭn,* s. épingle à cheveux, m.

hairy, *hâr'rĭ,* a. chevelu, poilu.

halberd, *hăl'bẽrd,* s. hallebarde, f.

halberdier, *hăl bẽr dēr',* s. hallebardier, m.

halcyon, *hăl'sĭ ŏn,* s. alcyon, m.   [m.

halcyon, *hăl'sĭ ŏn,* a. serein, heureux.

hale, *hāl,* a. sain, vigoureux.

half, *hăf,* s. moitié, f.

half, *hăf,* a. & ad. demi, à demi, imparfaitement || by halves, par moitié || ~blood, s. demi-frère, m. || demi-sœur, f. || ~bred, a. métis || lâche.

halfpenny, *hā'pĕn nĭ,* s. sou, m.

halfway, *hăf'wā,* ad. à mi-chemin.

hall, *hawl,* s. salle, f. || vestibule, collège, m.

hallo! *hăl lō',* holà ho!

halloo, *hăl lō',* v. n. crier, huer.

hallow, *hăl'lō,* v a. consacrer, bénir || All ~s, la Toussaint.

halo, *hā'lō,* s. halo, m., auréole, f.

halt, *hawlt,* s. halte, f.   [hésiter.

halt, *hawlt,* v. n. fair halte || boiter || clocher||

halt, *hawlt,* a. estropié, boiteux.

halter, *hawl'tẽr,* s. corde, f. || licou, m.

halve, *hăv,* v. a. diviser en deux parties.

ham, *hăm,* s. jarret, m. || jambon, m.

hamlet, *hăm'lĕt,* s. hameau, m.

hammer, *hăm'mẽr,* s. marteau, m. || (of a gun) chien, m.

hammer, *hăm'mẽr,* v. a. & n. marteler || forger || travailler || bégayer || to come to the ~, être vendu à l'encan || ~cloth, s. housse, f.

hammock, *hăm'mŏk,* s. hamac, m.

hamper, *hăm'pẽr,* s. panier, m.

hamper, *hăm'pẽr,* v. a. embarrasser, empêtrer, impliquer.

hamstring, *hăm'strĭng,* s. tendon du jarret, m.   [jarret.

hamstring, *hăm'strĭng,* v. a. couper le

hand, *hănd,* s. main, f. || paume, f. || côté, m. || talent, m., partie, f. || écriture, f. || ouvrier, m. || aiguille (d'une montre), f. || at ~, à la portée de, près, auprès || by ~, à la main || ~ in ~, la main dans la main, en se donnant la main || to ~, corps à corps || out of ~, sur l'heure, sur-le-champ || money out of ~, argent payé comptant || to be ~ in glove with one, être en bons termes avec qn. || on ~, en magasin || on one's ~s, à la charge de qn. || to lay violent ~s on, mettre la main sur qn. || ~barrow, s. civière, f. || ~bell, s. clochette, f. || ~bill, s. prospectus, m. || affiche, f. || ~gallop, s. petit galop, m.

hand, *hănd,* v. a. donner avec la main, remettre || conduire par la main || manier || to ~down, transmettre.

handbook, *hănd'bŏŏk,* s. manuel, m. || livret, m.   [f. pl.

handcuffs, *hănd'kŭfs,* s. pl. menottes,

handful, *hănd'fŏŏl,* s. poignée, f., petit nombre, m.

handicap, *hăn'dĭ kăp,* s. handicap, m.

handicap, *hăn'dĭ kăp,* v. a. handicaper.

handicraft, *hăn'dĭ krăft,* s. métier, m.

handily, *hăn'dĭ lĭ,* ad. adroitement.

handiness, *hăn'dĭ nĕs,* s. adresse, dextérité, f.   [ft., ouvrage, m.

handiwork, *hăn'dĭ wẽrk,* s. main-d'œuvre,

handkerchief, *hăn'kẽr chĭf,* s. mouchoir, m.

handle, *hăn'dl,* s. manche, m., anse, f. || queue (d'une poële), f. || poignée, f.

handle, *hăn' dl*, v. a. manier, traiter ‖ s'exercer sur.

handling, *hănd' ling*, s. maniement, m.

handmaid, *hănd' măd*, s. servante, soubrette, f.

handrail, *hănd' răl*, s. rampe, f.

handsome, *hănd' sŭm*, a. beau, élégant, gentil, généreux ‖ **—ly**, a. élégamment ‖ joliment.   (mar.) anspect, m.

handspike, *hănd' spīk*, s. levier, m. ‖

handwriting, *hănd' rīt ing*, s. écriture, f.

handy, *hăn' di*, a. manuel, adroit, habile.

hang, *hăng*, v. a. & n. ir. pendre, suspendre ‖ tapisser ‖ être pendu, être suspendu ‖ balancer ‖ être en suspens.   ‖maillère, f.

hanger, *hăng' ĕr*, s. coutelas, m. ‖ cré-

hanger-on, *hăng' ĕr ŏn*, s. dépendant, parasite, m.   ‖f. pl., tenture, f.

hangings, *hăng' ings*, s. pl. tapisseries,

hangman, *hăng' măn*, s. bourreau, m.

hank, *hăngk*, s. (of skeins) botte, f.

hanker, *hăngk' ĕr*, v. n. soupirer après.

hansom, *hăn' sŭm*, s. cabriolet de place, m.

hap, *hăp*, s. hasard, sort, destin, m. ‖ at **—hasard**, à l'aventure.

hapless, *hăp' lĕs*, a. malheureux, infortuné.

haply, *hăp' li*, ad. peut-être, par hasard.

happen, *hăp' n*, v. n. arriver, avoir lieu, se passer.

happily, *hăp' pi li*, ad. heureusement.

happiness, *hăp' pi nĕs*, s. bonheur, m., félicité, f.

happy, *hăp' pi*, a. heureux ‖ propice.

harangue, *hă răng'*, v. a. haranguer, faire un discours.

harass, *hăr' ăs*, v. a. harasser, tourmenter ‖ (mil.) harceler.

harbinger, *hăr' bin jĕr*, s. avant-coureur,

harbour, *hăr' bĕr*, s. auberge, f. ‖ asile, m. ‖ port, m.   ‖réfugier.

harbour, *hăr' bĕr*, v. a. & n. héberger ‖ se

hard, *hărd*, a. & ad. (-ly, ad.) dur, solide ‖ difficile(ment) ‖ pénible(ment) ‖ affligeant, cruel ‖ durement ‖ vigoureusement, fortement ‖ ~ of hearing, dur d'oreille ‖ **—hearted**, a. insensible, inhumain.

harden, *hăr' dn*, v.a. & n. durcir ‖ s'endurcir.

hardihood, *hăr' di hŏŏd*, s. hardiesse, f., courage, m.   ‖geusement.

hardily, *hăr' di li*, ad. hardiment, courageusement.

hardiness, *hăr' di nĕs*, s. peine, f. ‖ hardiesse, f., courage, m., effronterie, f.

hardness, *hărd' nĕs*, s. dureté, fermeté, f. ‖ rigueur, cruauté, f. ‖ avarice, f.

hardship, *hărd' ship*, s. peine, f. ‖ tribulation, f. ‖ injustice, f.

hardware, *hărd' wăr*, s. quincaillerie, f.

hardy, *hăr' di*, a. hardi, brave, courageux ‖ robuste.

hare, *hăr*, s. lièvre, m. ‖ **—brained**, a. écervelé, étourdi ‖ **~-lip**, s. bec-de-lièvre,

hark! *hărk*, écoute! écoutez!   [m.

harlequin, *hăr' lĕkwin*, s. arlequin, m.

harlequinade, *hăr' lĕ kwin' ăd'*, s. arlequinade, pasquinade, bouffonnerie, f.

harlot, *hăr' lŏt*, s. prostituée, f.

harm, *hărm*, s. tort, dommage, malheur, m. ‖ to keep out of ~'s way, se préserver de malheur.

harm, *hărm*, v. a. faire du mal à.

harmful, *hărm' fŏŏl*, a. malfaisant, nuisible ‖ **-ly**, ad. dangereusement.

harmless, *hărm' lĕs*, a. (-ly, ad.) innocent, sain et sauf ‖ innocemment.

harmonic, *hăr mŏn' ik*, a. harmonique.

harmonics, *hăr mŏn' iks*, s. pl. doctrine des sons, f.

harmonious, *hăr mō' ni ŭs*, a. harmonieux ‖ -ly, ad. harmonieusement.

harmonise, *hăr' mō nīz*, v. a. & n. rendre harmonieux ‖ accorder ‖ être d'accord.

harmony, *hăr' mō ni*, s. harmonie, f.

harness, *hăr' nĕs*, s. harnais, m.

harness, *hăr' nĕs*, v. a. enharnacher.

harp, *hărp*, s. harpe, f.   [sur, rabâcher.

harp, *hărp*, v. n. pincer la harpe ‖ revenir

harpist, *hărp' ist*, s. joueur de harpe, m.

harpoon, *hăr pōn'*, s. harpon, m.

harpoon, *hăr pōn'*, v. a. harponner.

harpsichord, *hărp' si kaŭrd*, s. clavecin,

harpy, *hăr' pi*, s. harpie, f.   [m.

harridan, *hăr' ri dăn*, s. vieille guenon, f.

harrier, *hăr' ri ĕr*, s. lévrier, m.

harrow, *hăr' rō*, s. herse, f.

harrow, *hăr' rō*, v. a. herser ‖ torturer.

harsh, *hărsh*, a. (-ly, ad.) rude(ment) ‖ âpre ‖ sévère(ment) ‖ rigoureux ‖ offensant ‖ austèrement.

harshness, *hărsh' nĕs*, s. âpreté, aigreur, f. ‖ rudesse, dureté, sévérité, f.

hart, *hărt*, s. cerf, m.

harvest, *hăr' vĕst*, s. moisson, récolte, f. ‖ **~-home**, s. fête après la moisson, f.

harvest, *hăr' vĕst*, v. a. moissonner.

hash, *hăsh*, s. hachis, m.

hash, *hăsh*, v. a. hacher.

hasp, *hăsp*, s. crochet, loquet, m.

hasp, *hăsp*, v. a. agrafer, accrocher.

hassock, *hăs' sŏk*, s. agenouilloir, m.

haste, *hăst*, s. hâte, diligence, f. ‖ in ~, à la hâte.   [se dépêcher.

hasten, *hăs' n*, v. a. & n. hâter, précipiter ‖

hastily, *hă sti li*, ad. à la hâte ‖ passionnément.   [f. ‖ emportement, m.

hastiness, *hă' sti nĕs*, s. hâte, précipitation,

hasty, *hă' sti*, a. hâtif, précoce ‖ prompt, précipité ‖ violent ‖ **~-pudding**, s. bouillie, f.

hat, *hăt*, s. chapeau, m. ‖ **-s off!** chapeaux bas! ‖ opera-~, s. chapeau claque gibus, m. ‖ **~-box**, ~-case, s. étui à chapeau, m. ‖ **~-reviver**, s. brosse à chapeau, m.

hatch, *hăch*, s. couvée, f. ‖ découverte, f. ‖ guichet, m. ‖ (mar.) panneau, m.

hatch, *hăch*, v. a. & n. couver, produire ‖ tramer ‖ faire des hachures.

hatchet, *hăch' ĕt*, s. hachette, f.

hatchment, *hăch' mĕnt*, s. écusson funèbre,

hate, *hăt*, s. haine, f.   [m.

hate, *hăt*, v. a. haïr.

hateful, *hāt′fŏŏl*, a. haïssable, odieux ‖ -ly, ad. odieusement.

hater, *hāt′tĕr*, s. ennemi, m.

hatred, *hā′trĕd*, s. haine, détestation, f.

hatter, *hăt′tĕr*, s. chapelier, m.

haughtily, *haw′ti lĭ*, ad. fièrement.

haughtiness, *haw′tĭ nĕs*, s. hauteur, f., orgueil, m.

haughty, *haw′tĭ*, a. hautain, orgueilleux.

haul, *hawl*, s. action de tirer, f., trait, m.

haul, *hawl*, v. a. tirer, traîner ‖ (mar.) hâler.

haunch, *hawnsh*, s. hanche, f.

haunt, *hawnt*, s. lieu fréquenté, m. ‖ retraite, f.   [siter.

haunt, *hawnt*, v. a. hanter, fréquenter, visiter.

haunter, *hawnt′ĕr*, s. habitué, m.

hautboy, *hō′boy*, s. hautbois, m.

have, *hăv*, v. a. ir. avoir, posséder, con tenir ‖ désirer, souhaiter ‖ savoir ‖ to ~ by heart, savoir par cœur.

haven, *hā′vn*, s. port, m.

haversack, *hăv′ĕr săk*, s. havresac, m.

havock, *hăv′ŏk*, s. ravage, dégât, m.

haw, *haw*, s. cenelle, f. ‖ clos, n.

hawk, *hawk*, s. faucon, m. ‖ épervier, m. ‖ sparrow ~, s. épervier, m.

hawk, *hawk*, v. u. chasser au faucon ‖ colporter ‖ cracher.

hawker, *hawk′ĕr*, s. colporteur, m.

hawse, *haws*, hawser, *haw′sĕr*, s (mar.) haussière, f., grelin, m.

hawthorn, *haw′thawrn*, s. aubépine, f.

hay, *hā*, s. foin, m. ‖ ~cock, s. meulon, m. ‖ ~loft, s. grange à foin, f. ‖ ~maker, s. faneur, m. ‖ ~rick, ~stack, s. meule de foin, f.

hazard, *hăz′ĕrd*, s. hasard, risque, m., chance, f.

hazard, *hăz′ĕrd*, v. a. hasarder, risquer.

hazardous, *hăz′ĕrd ŭs*, a. hasardeux, dangereux ‖ -ly, ad. hasardeusement.

haze, *hāz*, s. brouillard, m., brume, f.

hazel, *hā′zĕl*, s. noisetier, coudrier, m. ‖ ~nut, s. noisette, f.

hazy, *hā′zĭ*, a. nébuleux, sombre.

he, *hē*, pn. il, lui ‖ celui.

head, *hĕd*, s. tête, f. ‖ chef, m. ‖ sommet, m. ‖ titre, point, m. ‖ source, f. ‖ sujet, m. ‖ hure (d'un sanglier), f. ‖ to come to a ~, mûrir ‖ suppurer ‖ to get into one's ~, se mettre, se fourrer dans l'esprit.

head, *hĕd*, v. a. être à la tête, commander, conduire ‖ étêter

head, *hĕd* (in comp.), a. principal, en chef.

headache, *hĕd′āk*, s. mal de tête, m.

headdress, *hĕd′drĕs*, s. coiffure, coiffe, f.

header, *hĕd′ĕr*, s. chef de parti, m. ‖ demiboutisse, f. ‖ to take a ~, piquer de la tête.

headiness, *hĕd′ĭ nĕs*, s. témérité, obstination, f.   [m.

headland, *hĕd′lănd*, s. cap, promontoire, m.

headless, *hĕd′lĕs*, a. sans tête ‖ sans chef ‖ étourdi.

headlong, *hĕd′lŏng*, a. & ad. téméraire, étourdi, emporté ‖ imprudemment, en étourdi.

headmost, *hĕd′mōst*, a. le plus en avant.

headquarters, *hĕd′kwawr′tĕrz*, s. pl. quartier-général, m.

headship, *hĕd′ship*, s. primauté, autorité, f.

headsman, *hĕd′măn*, s. bourreau, m.

headstall, *hĕd′stawl*, s. têtière, f.

headstrong, *hĕd′strŏng*, a. têtu, entêté, obstiné   [teux.

heady, *hĕd′ĭ*, a. violent, emporté ‖ capiteux.

heal, *hāl*, v. a. (& n.) (se) guérir.

healer, *hēl′ĕr*, s. moyen curatif, m.

health(iness), *hĕlth′(ĭ nĕs)*, s. santé, f.

healthy, *hĕlth′ĭ*, a. sain ‖ salutaire.

heap, *hēp*, s. tas, amas, m. ‖ foule, f.

heap, *hēp*, v. a. entasser.

hear, *hēr*, v. a. & n. ir. entendre, écouter ‖ donner audience ‖ apprendre.

hearer, *hēr′ĕr*, s. auditeur, m.

hearing, *hēr′ĭng*, s. ouïe, f. ‖ audience, f. ‖ hard of ~, un peu sourd ‖ to obtain a ~, obtenir audience.

hearken, *hăr′kn*, v n. écouter, entendre.

hearsay, *hēr′sā*, s. ouï-dire, bruit, m.

hearse, *hĕrs*, s. char funèbre, m.

heart, *hărt*, s. cœur, courage, m., vigueur, f. ‖ intérieur, centre, m. ‖ by ~, par cœur ‖ to lose ~, perdre courage ‖ to set one's ~ on, prendre goût à qc. ‖ to take to ~, prendre à cœur ‖ ~ache, s. maux de cœur, m. pl. ‖ (fig.) remords cuisant, m ‖ ~breaking, a. accablant ‖ ~broken, a. qui a le cœur navré‖~burn, s. cardialgie, f. ‖ haine, f.

heartfelt, *hărt′fĕlt*, a. senti au fond du cœur, sincère.

hearth, *hărth*, s. âtre, foyer, m.

hearthstone, *hărt′stōn*, s. foyer de cheminée, f.   [ment.

heartily, *hăr′ti lĭ*, ad. sincèrement, ardemment.

heartiness, *hăr′tĭ nĕs*, s. sincérité, cordialité, f.

heartless, *hărt′lĕs*, a. (-ly. ad.) sans cœur ‖ lâche(ment).

heartrending, *hărt′rĕnd ĭng*, a. désolant, affligeant

heart's ease, *hărts′ēz*, s. (bot.) pensée, f.

hearty, *hăr′tĭ*, a. sincère, intime ‖ en bonne santé   [sité, f.

heat, *hēt*, s. chaleur, f. ‖ vivacité ‖ animo-

heat, *hēt*, v a. chauffer, échauffer.

heath, *hēth*, heather, *hĕth′ĕr*, s. (bot.) bruyère, érice, f. ‖ bruyère, f. ‖ friche, f.

heathen, *hē′thn*, s. païen, m.

heathen, *hē′thn*, a. païen.

heathenish, *hē′thn ish*, a. païen, barbare.

heave, *hēv*, s. soulèvement, m. ‖ soupir, m. ‖ secousse, f.

heave, *hēv*, v. a. & n. ir. élever, soulever, pousser ‖ s'élever, s'enfler ‖ palpiter ‖ respirer avec difficulté ‖ jeter.

heaven, *hĕv′n*, s. ciel, m.

heavenly, *hĕv′n lĭ*, a. & ad. céleste, divin ‖ divinement.   [ment.

heavily, *hĕv′i lĭ*, ad. pesamment, lentement.

heaviness, *hĕv′ĭ nĕs*, s. pesanteur, langueur, f., ennui, m., affliction, f. ‖ (of roads) difficulté, f.

---

tāte, hăt, făr, lăw; — *hēre, gĕt, hĕr*; — *mīne, ĭnn*, — *nō. hŏt, prōve*; — *hŏw*; —

heavy, *hĕv'ĭ,* a. pesant, lourd ‖ abattu, fâcheux ‖ indolent, paresseux ‖ importun, pénible.

hebrew, *hē'brō,* s. hébreu, juif, m.

hecatomb, *hĕk'ă tōōm,* s. hécatombe, f.

heck, *hĕk,* s. ratelier, m. ‖ loquet, m.

hectic, *hĕk'tĭk,* a. étique.

hector, *hĕk'tēr,* v. n. faire le fanfaron.

hedge, *hĕj,* s. haie, f.

hedge, *hĕj,* v. a. entourer d'une haie ‖ **to ~ in,** enfermer ‖ parier pour et contre ‖ **~-hog,** s. hérisson, m. ‖ **~-row,** s. haie,

heed, *hēd,* s. soin, m., attention, f. [f.

heed, *hēd,* v. a. prendre garde, observer, écouter. [**-ly,** ad. attentivement.

heedful, *hēd'fŏŏl,* a. attentif, soigneux ‖

heedless, *hēd'lĕs,* a. négligent, étourdi, distrait ‖ **-ly,** ad. négligemment.

heel, *hēl,* s. talon, m. ‖ **to be out at -s,** avoir les bas percés ‖ **to kick one's -s,** se croiser les bras.

heel, *hēl,* v. n. danser ‖ mettre des talons.

heifer, *hĕf'ēr,* s. génisse, f.

height, *hĭt,* s. hauteur, élévation, f., sommet, m., grandeur, f.

heighten, *hī'tn,* v. a. rehausser ‖ perfectionner, embellir. [ad. odieusement.

heinous, *hā'nŭs,* a. haineux, odieux ‖ **-ly,**

heir, *ār,* s. héritier, m. ‖ **~ apparent,** s. héritier direct, m. ‖ **~ at law,** s. héritier légitime, m. ‖ **~ presumptive,** héritier présomptif, m.

heiress, *ār'ĕs,* s. héritière, f.

heirloom, *ār'lōm,* s. effet hérité, m.

heirship, *ār'shĭp,* s. qualité d'héritier, f. ‖ hérédité, f. [m., fleur des dames, f.

heliotrope, *hē'lĭ ō trōp,* s. (bot.) tournesol,

hell, *hĕl,* s. enfer, m. ‖ **~-cat,** s. furie, f. ‖ **~-hound,** s. Cerbère, m. ‖ (fig.) tison d'enfer, m. [(ement), d'enfer.

hellish, *hĕl'lĭsh,* a. (**-ly,** ad.) infernal

helm, *hĕlm,* s. casque, m. ‖ gouvernail, m. ‖ **to answer the ~,** (mar.) obéir à la barre.

helmet, *hĕl'mĕt,* s. casque, m.

helmsman, *hĕlms'măn,* s. timonier, m.

help, *hĕlp,* s. aide, f. ‖ **~ !** au secours !

help, *hĕlp,* v. a. & n. ir. aider, assister ‖ (at table) servir, présenter ‖ s'empêcher, éviter ‖ **not if I can ~ it !** je n'y puis rien !

helper, *hĕlp'ēr,* s. aide, assistant, m.

helpful, *hĕlp'fŏŏl,* a. utile, secourable.

helpless, *hĕlp'lĕs,* a. (**-ly,** ad.) sans secours ‖ sans ressource ‖ faible.

helpmate, *hĕlp'māt,* s. aide, m. & f.

helter-skelter, *hĕl'tēr skĕl'tēr,* ad. à la hâte, pêle-mêle.

hem, *hĕm,* s. ourlet, bord, m.

hem, *hĕm,* v. a. & n. ourler, border ‖ tousser légèrement ‖ **~ !** hem !

hemisphere, *hĕm'ĭ sfēr,* s. hémisphère, f.

hemlock, *hĕm'lŏk,* s. ciguë, f. [f.

hemorrhage, *hĕm'ŏr rāj,* s. hémorrhagie,

hemorrhoids, *hĕm'ŏr rŏŷdz,* s. pl. hémorrhoïdes, f. pl.

hemp, *hĕmp,* s. chanvre, m.

hempen, *hĕm'pn,* a. de chanvre.

hemstich, *hĕm'stĭch,* s. hémistiche, m.

hen, *hĕn,* s. poule, f. ‖ (of birds) femelle, f. ‖ **~-coop,** s. cage à poules, f. ‖ **~-house,** s. poulailler, m.

henbane, *hĕn'bān,* s. (bot.) jusquiame, f.

hence, *hĕns,* ad. d'ici ‖ de là.

henceforth, *hĕns'fōrth,* **henceforward,** *hĕns'fŏr wĕrd,* ad. désormais, dorénavant.

henchman, *hĕnsh'măn,* s. valet affidé, m.

henpeck, *hĕn'pĕk,* v. a. maîtriser, maltraiter, m. ‖ pn. son, sa, ses, elle. [ter.

herald, *hĕr'ăld,* s. héraut, m.

heraldic, *hĕr ăl'dĭk,* a. héraldique.

heraldry, *hĕr'ăl drĭ,* s. blason, m. ‖ science héraldique, f. [m. pl.

herb, *hĕrb,* s. herbe, f. ‖ **-s,** s. pl. légumes,

herbaceous, *hĕr bā'shŭs,* a. herbacé.

herbage, *hĕr'bāj,* s. herbage, pâturage, m.

herbalist, *hĕr'băl ĭst,* s. herboriste, m.

herbivorous, *hĕr bĭv'ō rŭs,* a. herbivore.

Herculean, *hĕr kū'lē ăn,* a. herculéen.

herd, *hĕrd,* s. troupeau, m., troupe, f.

herd, *hĕrd,* v. n. vivre en troupes.

herdsman, *hĕrdz'măn,* s. pâtre, m.

here, *hĕr,* ad. ici ‖ que voici.

hereabout, *hēr'ă bŏŭt,* ad. aux environs, près d'ici. [mais.

hereafter, *hēr ăf'tēr,* ad. à l'avenir, désormais.

hereat, *hēr ăt',* ad. à ceci, à cela.

hereby, *hēr bī',* ad. par ce moyen.

hereditary, *hĕ rĕd'ĭ tĕr ĭ,* a. héréditaire.

herein, *hēr in',* ad. en ceci.

hereof, *hēr ŏf',* ad. de ceci, d'où.

hereon, *hēr ŏn',* ad. là-dessus, sur quoi.

heresy, *hĕr'ĕ sĭ,* s. hérésie, f. [sur cela.

heretic, *hĕr'ĕ tĭk,* s. hérétique, m. & f.

heretical, *hĕ rĕt'ĭ kăl,* a. hérétique.

heretofore, *hēr tō fōr',* ad. jusqu'ici.

hereupon, *hēr ŭp ŏn',* ad. là-dessus.

herewith, *hēr wĭth',* ad. avec ceci ‖ ci-joint.

heritage, *hĕr'ĭ tāj,* s. héritage, m.

hermetic, *hĕr mĕt'ĭk,* a. (**-ally,** ad.) hermétique(ment).

hermit, *hĕr'mĭt,* s. ermite, m.

hermitage, *hĕr'mĭ tāj,* s. ermitage, m.

hernia, *hĕr'nĭ ă,* s. (méd.) hernie, f.

hero, *hē'rō,* s. héros, m. [(ment).

heroic, *hē rō'ĭk,* a. (**-ally,** ad.) héroïque

heroine, *hĕr'ō ĭn,* s. héroïne, f.

heroism, *hĕr'ō ĭzm,* s. héroïsme, m.

heron, *hĕr'ŭn,* s. héron, m.

heronry, *hĕr'ŭn rĭ,* s. héronnière, f.

herpes, *hĕr'pēz,* s. (méd.) herpès, dartre, serpigo, m.

herring, *hĕr'rĭng,* s. hareng, m.

hers, *hĕrz,* pn. le sien, la sienne ‖ les siens.

herself, *hĕr sĕlf',* pn. elle-même ‖ soi-même ‖ se.

hesitate, *hĕz'ĭ tāt,* v. n. hésiter, balancer.

hesitation, *hĕz ĭ tā'shŭn,* s. hésitation, incertitude, f.

heterodox, *hĕt'ēr ō dŏks,* a. hétérodoxe.

heterogeneous, *hĕt ēr ō jē'nĭ ŭs,* a. hétérogène.

hew, *hū*, v a. ir. couper, tailler.

hexagon, *hĕks'ă gŏn*, s. hexagone, m.

hexagonal, *hĕks ăg'ŏ năl*, a. hexagonal.

heyday, *hā'dā*, s. gaieté, f. || ~ of youth, gaieté folle de la jeunesse.

hiatus, *hī ā'tŭs*, s. hiatus, m. || (fig.) lacune.

hibernate, *hī'bĕr nāt*, v n. hiverner　[f.

hiccough, *hĭk'ŭp*, s. hoquet, m.

hiccough, *hĭk'ŭp*, v n. avoir le hoquet.

hickory, *hĭk'ô rĭ*, s. noyer américain, m.

hide, *hīd*, s. peau, f., cuir, m

hide, *hīd*, v. a. (& n. ir.) (se) cacher || (vulg.) rosser.

hideous, *hĭd'ĭ ŭs*, a. (-ly. ad.) hideux, effroyable || horrible(ment).

hiding-place, *hī'dĭng plăs* s. retraite, cachette, f.

hieroglyph, *hī'ĕr ō glĭf*, s. hiéroglyphe, m.

higgle, *hĭg'l*, v. n. revendre, marchander

higgledy-piggledy, *hĭg'l dĭ pĭg'l dĭ*, ad. pêle-mêle, sens dessus-dessous.

higgler, *hĭg'glĕr*, s. regrattier, m.

high, *hī*, a. haut, élevé || fier, altier || sublime, grand || complet || violent || -ly, ad. hautement, fort || it is ~ time, le moment est venu || ~born, a. de haute naissance || ~-flown, a. fier || enflé, outré || ~-minded, a. magnanime || fier || ~-pressure, a. à haute pression.

highland, *hī'lănd*, s. pays montagneux, m. || montagne, haute terre, f.

highlander, *hī'lăn dĕr*, s. montagnard, m.

highness, *hī'nĕs*, s. hauteur, f. || Highness, (titre) Altesse, f.

highwater, *hī'wăw'tĕr*, s. hautes eaux, m. pl. || ~-mark, s. niveau des hautes eaux, m.

highway, *hī'wā*, s. grand chemin, m.

highwayman, *hī'wā măn*, s voleur de grands chemins, bandit, m

hilarious, *hĭ lā'rĭ ŭs*, a. gai, joyeux

hilarity, *hĭ lăr'ĭ tĭ*, s. gaieté, f.

hill, *hĭl*, s. colline, f.

hillock, *hĭl'lŏk*, s. petite colline, f.

hilly, *hĭl'lĭ*, a. montagneux.

hilt, *hĭlt*, s, poignée (d'une épée), f.

him, *hĭm*, pn. lui, le.

himself, *hĭm sĕlf'*, pn. soi-même, lui-même || se.

hind, *hīnd*, s. biche, f. || rustre, m

hind(er), *hīnd'(ĕr)*, a. postérieur, de derrière.　　　　　|ser, troubler

hinder, *hĭn'dĕr*, v a. empêcher, embarrasser

hind(e)rance, *hĭn'd(ĕ)r ăns*, s. empêchement, obstacle, m.

hind(er)most, *hīnd'(ĕr)mŏst*, a. dernier

hinge, *hĭnj*, s gond, m. || pivot, m. || charnière, f.

hinge, *hĭnj*, v n. tourner || dépendre

hint, *hĭnt*, s. suggestion, insinuation, f., avis, demi-mot, m., donnée, f. || to give or drop a ~, donner un bienveillant avis || to take a ~, accepter un conseil.

hint, *hĭnt*, v a. donner à entendre, suggérer.　　　　　[bath, s. bain de siège, m.

hip, *hĭp*, s. hanche, f. || églantine, f. || ~-hipped, *hĭpt*, a. abattu, triste.

hippodrome, *hĭp'pō drōm*, s. hippodrome, m., arène, f.　　　　[potame, m.

hippopotamus, *hĭp'pō pŏt'ă mŭs*, s. hippo-

hire, *hīr*, s. louage, m. || prix de location, m. || salaire, m.

hire, *hīr*, v. a. louer, donner à louage.

hireling, *hīr'lĭng*, s. mercenaire, m.

hireling, *hīr'lĭng*, a. mercenaire.

hirer, *hī'rĕr*, s. loueur, m.

hirsute, *hĕr sūt'*, a. hérissé || poilu.

his, *hĭz*, pn. son, sa || le sien, la sienne, les siens.

hiss, *hĭs*, v. a. & n. siffler || se moquer de

hist! *hĭst*, chut! paix!

historian, *hĭs tō'rĭ ăn*, s. historien, m.

historic(al), *hĭs tŏr'ĭk (ăl)*, a. (-ly. ad.) historique(ment).

history, *hĭs'tō rĭ*, s. histoire, f

histrionic, *hĭs trĭ ŏn'ĭk*, a. du comédien, scénique.

hit, *hĭt*, s. coup, m., atteinte, f. hasard, m. || à propos, m. || lucky ~, s. chance, bonne rencontre, bonne aubaine, f.

hit, *hĭt*, v. a. & n. ir. frapper, donner un coup, atteindre || donner contre, se choquer, rencontrer, arriver.

hitch, *hĭch*, s. entrave, f.

hitch, *hĭch*, v a. se démener || accrocher

hither, *hĭth'ĕr*, a. & ad. citérieur || ici, y.

hitherto, *hĭth'ĕr tō*, ad. jusqu'ici.

hive, *hīv*, s. ruche, f

hive, *hīv*, v a. & n. mettre dans une ruche || vivre ensemble.

hoar, *hōr*, a. blanc || blanchi || gris.

hoard, *hōrd*, s. amas, trésor, m.

hoard, *hōrd*, v. a. amasser, thésauriser

hoarding, *hōrd'ĭng*, s. amassement, m., thésaurisation, f.　　　[d'une voix rauque.

hoarse, *hōrs*, a. rauque, enroué || -ly, ad.

hoarseness, *hōrs'nĕs*, s. enrouement, m.

hoary, *hō'rĭ*, a. blanc, blanchâtre || moisi || couvert de gelée.

hoax, *hōks*, s. mystification, f.

hoax, *hōks*, v a. mystifier.

hob, *hŏb*, s. paysan, m. || lutin, m

hobble, *hŏb'l*, v. n. clocher, boiter

hobbledehoy, *hŏb'l dĕ hŏy*, s. jeune homme qui n'a pas encore jeté sa gourme, m.

hobby, *hŏb'bĭ*, s. benêt, m. || dada, m. || ~-horse, s. cheval d'enfant, m. || marotte, f.　　　　　[m.

hobgoblin, *hŏb gŏb'lĭn*, s. fantôme, spectre,

hobnail, *hŏb'nāl*, s. caboche, f.

hob-nob, *hŏb'nŏb*, v n. trinquer.

hock, *hŏk*, s. jarret, m. || vin du Rhin, m.

hockey-stick, *hŏk'ĭ stĭk*, s. crosse, f.

hocus, *hō'kŭs*, v n. filouter

hocus-pocus, *hō'kŭs pō'kŭs*, s. jonglerie, f., tour de passe-passe, m.

hodge-podge, *hŏj'pŏj*, s. salmigondis, m.

hodman, *hŏd'măn*, s. aide-maçon, m.

hoe, *hō*, s. houe, f.

hoe, *hō*, v a. bouer

hog, *hŏg*, s. cochon, porc, m. || to go the whole ~, ne pas s'arrêter à moitié chemin.

hoggish, *hŏg'gĭsh*, a. (-ly. ad.) de cochon || en cochon.

---

lāte, hăt, făr, lăw, — hēre, gĕt, hĕr, — mīne, ĭnn, — nō, hŏt, prōve, — hŏw, —

hogshead, *hŏgz'hĕd,* s. muid, m.
hoist, *hŏÿst,* v. a. lever, hausser.
hold, *hōld,* s. prise, f. ‖ serre, f. ‖ appui, m. ‖ prison, t., fort, m. ‖ pouvoir, m., influence, f. ‖ to take or seize ~ of, saisir, empoigner, se saisir de.
hold, *hōld,* v. a. & n. ir. tenir, retenir, prendre ‖ détenir, arrêter ‖ maintenir ‖ soutenir ‖ posséder ‖ célébrer ‖ estimer ‖ croire ‖ continuer, durer ‖ se soutenir, se maintenir ‖ s'attacher, dépendre, dériver ‖ to ~ one's own, se maintenir ‖ to ~ back, retenir ‖ to ~ forth, haranguer ‖ to ~ good, être valable ‖ se confirmer ‖ to ~ in, s'arrêter ‖ arrêter un cheval ‖ to ~ out, résister, tenir bon ‖ ~! arrêtez! ‖ ~-all, s. nécessaire de voyage, m.
holder, *hōl'dər,* s. locataire, fermier, m. ‖ propriétaire, m.   [détention, f.
holding, *hōld'ing,* s. (jur.) possession, f. ‖
hole, *hōl,* s. trou, m., caverne, f.
holiday, *hŏl'i dā,* s. jour de fête, m. ‖ -s, s. pl. vacances, f. pl.
holily, *hō'li li,* ad. saintement.
holiness, *hō'li nĕs,* s. sainteté, f.
hollow, *hŏl'lō,* s. creux, trou, m., cavité, f.
hollow (out), *hŏl'lō,* v. a. creuser, évider.
hollow, *hŏl'lō,* a. creux, enfoncé ‖ faux, hypocrite.   [fidélité, f.
hollowness, *hŏl'lō nĕs,* s. cavité, f. ‖ in-
holly, *hŏl'li,* s. (bot.) houx, m.
hollyhock, *hŏl'li hŏk,* s. (bot.) rose trémière, passe-rose, f.
holster, *hōl'stər,* s. fourreau de pistolet, m.
holy, *hō'li,* a. saint, religieux ‖ ~-water, s. eau bénite, f. ‖ ~-week, s. semaine sainte, f.
homage, *hŏm'āj,* s. hommage, m.   [sainte, f.
home, *hōm,* s. maison, f., logis, m., demeure, f. ‖ patrie, f. ‖ at ~, chez soi ‖ ~-bred, a. du pays, natif ‖ simple ‖ ~-farm, s. maison principale d'une ferme, f. ‖ ~-made, a. fait à la maison ‖ ~-sick, a. qui a le mal du pays ‖ ~-sickness, s. mal du pays, m. ‖ ~-thrust, s. coup qui porte, m. ‖ ~-department, s. ministère de l'intérieur, m.
home, *hōm,* a. domestique ‖ ~, ad. chez soi ‖ à la maison.
homeless, *hōm'lĕs,* a. sans demeure.
homeliness, *hōm'li nĕs,* s. simplicité, f. ‖ grossièreté, f.   [grossier.
homely, *hōm'li,* a. sans ornement, simple,
homespun, *hōm'spun,* a. filé à la maison ‖ grossier.   [vers son pays.
homeward(s), *hōm'wərd(s),* ad. chez soi ‖
homicide, *hŏm'i sīd,* s. homicide, m. ‖ meurtrier, m.
homily, *hŏm'i li,* s. homélie, f.
homœopathic, *hō mē ŏp'ă thik,* a. homéopathique.   [pathie, f.
homœopathy, *hō mē ŏp'ă thi,* s. homéo-
homogeneous, *hō mō jē'ni ǔs,* a. homogène.
hone, *hōn,* s. pierre à rasoir, f.   [gène.
honest, *ŏn'ĕst,* a. (-ly, ad.) honnête(ment) ‖ sincère(ment) ‖ loyal ‖ chaste.
honesty, *ŏn'ĕs ti,* s. honnêteté, probité, sincérité, f. ‖ chasteté, f.

honey, *hŭn'i,* s. miel, m. ‖ douceur, f. ‖ douce amie, f. ‖ ~-comb, s. rayon de miel, m.
honeymoon, *hŭn'i mŏn,* s. lune de miel, f.
honeysuckle, *hŭn'i sŭ kl,* s. (bot.) chèvrefeuille, f.
honied, *hŭn'id,* a. enmiellé.   [feuille, f.
honorarium, *hŏn'ō rā ri ŭm,* s. honoraires, m. pl., salaire, m.
honorary, *ŏn'ĕr ā ri,* a. honoraire.
honour, *ŏn'ĕr,* s. honneur, m. ‖ dignité, f.
honour, *ŏn'ĕr,* v. a. honorer, révérer.
honourable, *ŏn'ĕr ă bl,* a. honorable.
honourably, *ŏn'ĕr ă bli,* ad. honorablement.   [peron, m.
hood, *hŏŏd,* s. coiffe de femme, f. ‖ chahood, *hŏŏd,* v. a. encapuchonner.
hoodwink, *hŏŏd'wink,* v. a. bander les yeux ‖ tromper.
hoof, *hŏf,* s. sabot, m. ‖ corne du pied, f. ‖ ~-bound, a. encastelé.
hook, *hŏŏk,* s. crochet, crampon, m. ‖ hameçon, m. ‖ ~ and eye, agrafes, f. pl. ‖ by ~ or by crook, de toute façon, per fas et nefas.   [à l'hameçon.
hook, *hŏŏk,* v. a. accrocher, agrafer ‖ prendre
hooked, *hŏŏkt,* a. crochu, recourbé.   [m.
hoop, *hŏp,* s. cercle, m. ‖ panier, m. ‖ cri, hoop, *hŏp,* v. a. & n. cercler ‖ pousser des cris.
hoopoo, *hō'pō,* s. huppe, f.
hoot, *hŏt,* s. huée, f.
hoot, *hŏt,* v. n. huer.
hop, *hŏp,* s. houblon, m. ‖ saut, bond, m. ‖ ~-picker, s. cueilleur de houblon, m. ‖ ~-pole, s. échalas, m.
hop, *hŏp,* v. a. & n. houblonner ‖ sauter.
hope, *hŏp,* s. espérance, f., espoir, m.
hope, *hŏp,* v. a. & n. espérer.
hopeful, *hŏp'fŏŏl,* a. plein d'espérances ‖ ~-ly, ad. avec espérance.
hopeless, *hŏp'lĕs,* a. (-ly, ad.) sans espérance ‖ sans espoir.   [d'un moulin, f.
hopper, *hŏp'pĕr,* s. sauteur, m. ‖ trémie
horde, *hōrd,* s. horde, troupe, f.
horizon, *hŏ rī'zŭn,* s. horizon, m.
horizontal, *hŏr i zŏn'tăl,* a. (-ly, ad.) horizontal(ement).
horn, *hŏrn,* s. corne, f. ‖ cor, m. ‖ to draw in one's ~s, (fig.) rentrer les cors.
horned, *hŏrnd,* a. cornu ‖ à cornes.
hornet, *hŏr'nĕt,* s. frelon, m.
hornpipe, *hŏrn'pīp,* s. cornemuse, f.
horny, *hŏr'ni,* a. fait de corne.
horrible, *hŏr'ri bl,* a. horrible, terrible.
horribly, *hŏr'ri bli,* a. horriblement.
horrid, *hŏr'rid,* a. (-ly, ad.) horrible (ment) ‖ affreux.
horrific, *hŏr rif'ik,* a. effrayant.
horror, *hŏr'rĕr,* s. horreur, f. ‖ ~-struck, a. frappé d'épouvante.
horse, *hŏrs,* s. cheval, m. ‖ cavalerie, f. ‖ chevalet, m. ‖ ~-box, s. wagon-écurie, m. ‖ ~-breaker, s. dompteur de chevaux, m. ‖ ~-chestnut, s. marron d'Inde, m. ‖ ~-fly, s. taon, m. ‖ ~-guard, s. garde à cheval, f. ‖ ~-hair, s. crin, m. ‖ ~-laugh, s. gros rire, m. ‖ ~-leech, s.

grosse sangsue, f. ‖ maréchal ferrant, m. ‖ artiste vétérinaire, m. ‖ ~~pond, s. abreuvoir, m. ‖ ~~power, s. puissance en chevaux, f. ‖ ~~race (~~racing), s. course de chevaux, f. ‖ ~~radish, s. raifort, m. ‖ ~~shoe, s. fer à cheval, m. ‖ ~~whip, s. cravache, f. ‖ ~~whip, v. a. donner des coups de cravache (à).

horse, *hŏrs,* v. a. monter.

horseback, *hŏrs'băk,* ad. on ~, à cheval.

horseman, *hŏrs'măn,* s. cavalier, m.

horsemanship, *hŏrs'măn ship,* s. équitation, f. [cheval, cavalière, f.

horsewoman, *hŏrs'wŏŏm ăn,* s. femme à cheval.

horticultural, *hŏr ti kŭl'tū răl,* a. se rapportant au jardinage.

horticulture, *hŏr ti kŭl'tŭr,* s. jardinage, m.

horticulturist, *hŏr ti kŭl'tū rist,* s. horticulteur, m.

hose, *hŏz,* s. haut-de-chausse, m., chaussure, f.; bas, m. pl. ‖ ~~garden~~, s. fleuriste, jardinier fleuriste, m.

hosier, *hŏ zhĕr,* s. marchand de bas, bonnetier, m.

hosiery, *hŏ zhĕr i,* s. bonneterie, f.

hospitable, *hŏs'pi tă bl,* a. hospitalier.

hospitably, *hŏs'pi tă bli,* ad. avec hospitalité.

hospital, *hŏs'pi tăl,* s. hôpital, m.

hospitality, *hŏs pi tăl'i ti,* s. hospitalité, f.

host, *hŏst,* s. hôte m. ‖ hôtelier, m. ‖ armée, f. ‖ hostie, f.

hostage, *hŏs'tăj,* s. otage, m.

hostel(ry), *hŏs'tĕl ri, vide* hotel.

hostess, *hŏst'ĕs,* s. hôtelière, f.

hostile, *hŏs'til,* a. (-ly, ad.) hostile(ment).

hostility, *hŏs til'i ti,* s. hostilité, f.

hot, *hŏt,* a. (-ly, ad.) chaud(ement) ‖ ardent, violent ‖ échauffé ‖ violemment ‖ ~~headed, a. emporté, fougueux ‖ ~~house, s. serre chaude, f.

hotbed, *hŏt'bĕd,* s. couche, f. [podge.

hotchpotch, *hŏch'pŏch,* s. *vide* hodge-

hotel, *hŏ tĕl',* s. hôtel, m., auberge, f.

hotspur, *hŏt'spĕr,* s. homme violent, m., tête chaude, f.

hound, *hŏwnd,* s. chien de chasse, m.

hour, *ŏwr,* s. heure, f. ‖ to keep late ~s, rentrer tard dans la nuit ‖ ~~glass, s. sablier, m.

hourly, *ŏwr'li,* a. & ad. d'heure en heure.

house, *hŏws,* s. maison, habitation, f. ‖ famille, f. ‖ ménage, f. ‖ to keep open ~, tenir table ouverte ‖ ~~agent, s. agent de location, m. ‖ ~~breaker, s. qui vole avec effraction ‖ ~~dog, s. chien de basse cour, m. ‖ ~~warming, s. régal d'entrée, m.

house, *hŏwz,* v. a. & n. loger ‖ abriter ‖ (the harvest) rentrer ‖ (the cattle) faire rentrer.

household, *hŏws'hŏld,* s. famille, f., ménage, m. ‖ ~~bread, s. pain de ménage, m. [famille, m.

householder, *hŏws'hŏld ĕr,* s. chef de

housekeeper, *hŏws'kĕp ĕr,* s. chef de famille, m. ‖ femme de ménage, f.

housekeeping, *hŏws'kĕp ing,* s. ménage, m.

houseless, *hŏws'lĕs,* a. sans abri *or* asile.

housemaid, *hŏws'măd,* s. servante, f.

housewife, *hŏws'wif* ou *hŭz'if,* s. mère de famille, ménagère, f.

housing, *hŏwz'ing,* s. magasinage, m. ‖ ~s, s. pl. bousse, f.

hovel, *hŏv'ĕl,* s. hutte, f. ‖ baraque, f.

hover, *hŏv'ĕr,* v. n. voltiger ‖ hésiter.

how, *hŏw,* ad. comment, comme ‖ ~ much? combien?

how(so)ever, *hŏw(sŏ)ĕv'ĕr,* ad. cependant, pourtant, de quelque manière que.

howitzer, *hŏw'it sĕr,* s. obusier, m.

howl, *hŏwl,* v. n. hurler.

howl(ing), *hŏwl'(ing),* s. hurlement, m.

hoyden, *hŏy'dĕn,* s. jeune étourdie, f.

hub, *hŭb,* s. moyeu, m. [f.

hubbub, *hŭb'bŭb,* s. tumulte, m., émeute,

huckster, *hŭk'stĕr,* s. revendeur, m.

huddle, *hŭd'dl,* v. a. brouiller, confondre.

hue, *hū,* s. couleur, teinte, f. ‖ ~ and cry, huée, f. [m. ‖ orgueilleux, m.

huff, *hŭf,* s. accès de colère, emportement.

huff, *hŭf,* v. a. & n. enfler ‖ traiter avec arrogance.

hug, *hŭg,* s. embrassement, f.

hug, *hŭg,* v. a. embrasser ‖ caresser

huge, *hūj,* a. (-ly, ad.) vaste ‖ énorme (ment).

hugeness, *hūj'nĕs,* s. grandeur énorme, f.

hulk, *hŭlk,* s. carène, f. ‖ ~s, s. pl. pontons, m. pl.

hull, *hŭl,* s. cosse, coque, f. ‖ pellicule, f.

hum, *hŭm,* s. bourdonnement, m.

hum, *hŭm,* v. a. & n. bourdonner ‖ marmoter ‖ fredonner ‖ to ~ and haw, bégayer, balbutier ‖ hésiter.

hum ! *hŭm,* hem ! [(ement).

human, *hū'măn,* a. (-ly, ad.) humain

humane, *hū măn',* a. (-ly, ad.) affable, gracieux, bienveillant.

humanise, *hū'măn iz,* v. a. humaniser, rendre humain. [bon naturel, m.

humanity, *hu măn'i ti,* s. humanité, f.

humankind, *hū'măn kind,* s. genre humain, m.

humble, *hŭm'bl,* v. a. humilier, abattre.

humble, *hŭm'bl,* a. humble, modeste ‖ ~~bee, s. bourdon, m.

humbleness, *hŭm'bl nĕs,* s. humilité, f.

humbly, *hŭm'bli,* ad. humblement.

humbug, *hŭm'bŭg,* s. charlatan, m. ‖ blague, duperie, f.

humbug, *hŭm'bŭg,* v. a. duper, tromper.

humdrum, *hŭm'drŭm,* a. hébété, stupide ‖ ennuyeux.

humid, *hū'mid,* a. humide, moite.

humidity, *hū mid'i ti,* s. humidité, moiteur, f.

humiliate, *hū mil'i āt,* v. a. humilier.

humiliation, *hū mil i ā'shŭn,* s. humiliation, f., abaissement, m. [sion, f.

humility, *hū mil'i ti,* s. humilité, soumis-

humming, *hŭm'ing,* s. ~~bird, s. colibri, m. ‖ ~~top, s. toupie d'Allemagne, f.

humorous, *(h)ṻ́mĕr ŭs*, a. plaisant ‖ capricieux, fantasque, bizarre ‖ —ly, ad. capricieusement ‖ plaisamment.

humour, *(h)ṻ́mĕr*, s. humeur, f. ‖ disposition du caractère, f. ‖ mauvaise humeur, f. ‖ verve comique, f., caprice, m.

humour, *(h)ṻ́mĕr*, v. a. faire ses volontés à ‖ complaire. [plaisant, m.

humourist, *(h)ṻ́mĕr ĭst*, s. humoriste.

hump, *hŭmp*, s. bosse, f. ‖ ~-backed, a. bossu.

hunch, *hŭnsh*, s. coup de coude, m. ‖ bosse, f. ‖ morceau, m. ‖ ~-backed, a. bossu.

hunchback, *hŭnsh´băk*, s. bossu, m.

hundred, *hŭn´drĕd*, a. cent, m., centaine, f.

hundred, *hŭn´drĕd*, a. cent.

hundredfold, *hŭn´drĕd fōld*, a. centuple.

hundredth, *hŭn´drĕdth*, a. centième.

hundredweight, *hŭn´drĕd wāt*, s. quintal, m. (50 kilogrammes).

hung-beef, *hŭng´bēf*, s. bœuf fumé, m.

hunger, *hŭng´gĕr*, s. faim, f.

hunger, *hŭng´gĕr*, v. n. avoir faim.

hungrily, *hŭng´gri lĭ*, ad. de bon appétit ‖ avidement.

hungry, *hŭng´grĭ*, a. affamé.

hunt, *hŭnt*, v. a. & n. chasser ‖ poursuivre.

hunting, *hŭnt´(ĭng)*, s. chasse, f.

hunter, *hŭnt´ĕr*, s. chasseur, m. ‖ chien de chasse, m. ‖ cheval de chasse, m.

hunting, *hŭnt´ĭng*; ~-box, s. rendez-vous de chasse, m. ‖ ~-horn, s. cor de chasse, m. ‖ ~-watch, s. montre à savonnette, f.

huntress, *hŭn´trĕs*, s. chasseresse, f.

huntsman, *hŭnts´măn*, s. chasseur, veneur, piqueur, m. [course de haies, f.

hurdle, *hŭr´dl*, s. claie, f. ‖ ~-race, s.

hurdy-gurdy, *hŭr´dĭ gĕr dĭ*, s. vielle, f.

hurl, *hĕrl*, v. a. lancer, précipiter.

hurly-burly, *hĕr´lĭ bĕr lĭ*, s. tohu-bohu, tintamarre, m.

hurricane, *hŭr´ri kăn*, s. ouragan, m.

hurry, *hŭr´rĭ*, s. hâte, précipitation, f. ‖ tumulte, m. ‖ to be in a ~, être pressé ‖ there is no ~, cela ne presse pas, il n'y a pas péril en la demeure.

hurry, *hŭr´rĭ*, v. a. & n. hâter, précipiter, presser ‖ se hâter. [dommage, m.

hurt, *hĕrt*, s. mal, m., blessure, f. ‖ tort,

hurt, *hĕrt*, v. a. faire tort à ‖ blesser.

hurtful, *hĕrt´fōōl*, a. nuisible, dangereux, pernicieux ‖ -ly, ad. pernicieusement.

husband, *hŭz´bănd*, s. mari époux, m.

husband, *hŭz´bănd*, v. a. ménager ‖ cultiver. [cultivateur, m.

husbandman, *hŭz´bănd măn*, s. laboureur,

husbandry, *hŭz´bănd rĭ*, s. agriculture, f. ‖ économie, f.

hush, *hŭsh*, s. silence, m.

hush, *hŭsh*, v. a. & n. faire taire ‖ se taire ‖ to ~ up, étouffer ‖ ~-money, s. argent donné pour se taire, m.

hush! *hŭsh*, chut! silence!

husk, *hŭsk*, s. cosse, gousse, peau, f.

huskiness, *hŭs´kĭ nĕs*, s. enrouement, m.

husky, *hŭs´kĭ*, a. cossu ‖ rude ‖ enroué.

hussar, *hŏŏz zăr´*, s. hussard, m.

hussy, *hŭz´zĭ*, s. gueuse, coquine, f.

hustle, *hŭs´l*, v. a. pousser ‖ bousculer.

hut, *hŭt*, s. hutte, cabane, f.

hutch, *hŭch*, s. huche, f., clapier, m.

hyacinth, *hī´ă sinth*, s. jacinthe, f.

hybrid, *hī´brĭd*, s. hybride, m.

hybrid, *hī´brĭd*, a. hybride.

hydrant, *hī´drănt*, s. bouche à eau, bouche d'incendie, f.

hydraulic, *hī drāŭ´lĭk*, a. hydraulique.

hydraulics, *hī drāŭ´lĭks*, s. pl. hydraulique, f.

hydrogen, *hī´drŏ jĕn*, s. (chem.) hydrogène, f.

hydropathic, *hī drŏ păth´ĭk*, a. hydropathique.

hydropathy, *hī drŏp´ă thĭ*, s. (méd.) hydropathie, f. [phobie, f.

hydrophobia, *hī drŏ fō´bĭ ă*, s. hydrophobie, f.

hydrostatics, *hī drŏ stăt´ĭks*, s. pl. hydrostatique, f.

hyena, *hī ē´nă*, s. hyène, f. [statique, f.

hygiene, *hī´jĭ ĕn*, s. hygiène, f.

hymeneal, *hī mĕ nē´ăl*, a. de l'hyménée, nuptial. [livre d'hymnes, m.

hymn, *hĭm*, s. hymne, m. ‖ ~-book, s.

hyperbole, *hī pĕr´bō lē*, s. hyperbole, f.

hyperbolic, *hī pĕr bŏl´ĭk*, a. (-ally, ad.) hyperbolique(ment).

hypercritical, *hī pĕr krĭt´ĭ kăl*, a. critique jusqu'à l'excès.

hyphen, *hī´fĕn*, s. trait d'union, m.

hypnotic, *hĭp nŏt´ĭk*, a. hypnotique.

hypnotism, *hĭp´nŏt ĭzm*, s. hypnotisme, m.

hypochondriac, *hĭp ŏ kŏn´drĭ ăk*, s. hypocondriaque, m.

hypocrisy, *hī pŏk´rĭ sĭ*, s. hypocrisie, f.

hypocrite, *hĭp´ō krĭt*, s. hypocrite, m.

hypocritical, *hĭp ō krĭt´ĭ kăl*, a. hypocrite.

hypothesis, *hī pŏth´ĕ sĭs*, s. hypothèse, f.

hypothetic, *hī pŏ thĕt´ĭk*, a. (-ally, ad.) hypothétique(ment) ‖ par hypothèse.

hyssop, *hĭs´sŭp*, s. hyssope, f.

hysterical, *hĭs tĕr´ĭk ăl*, a. (-ly, ad.) hystérique(ment).

hysterics, *hĭs tĕr´ĭks*, s. pl., hysteria, *hĭs tĕr´ĭ ă*, s. hystérie, f., spasmes, m. pl.

I.

I, ī, pn. je, moi ‖ it is ~, c'est moi.

iambic, *ī ăm´bĭk*, a. iambique.

ice, *īs*, s. glace, f.

ice, *īs*, v. a. glacer ‖ ~-berg, s. glacier, m., montagne de glace, f. ‖ ~-bound, a. arrêté par les glaces ‖ ~-cream, s. glace, f. ‖ ~-house, ~-safe, s. glacière, f.

ichneumon, *ĭk nū´mŏn*, s. ichneumon, rat de Pharaon, m.

icicle, *ī´sĭk l*, s. glaçon, m.

iciness, *ī´sĭ nĕs*, s. froid glacial, m.

icy, *ī´sĭ*, a. glacé, glacial.

idea, *ī dē´ă*, s. idée, notion, f.

ideal, *ī dē´ăl*, s. idéal, m.

ideal, *ĭ dē'ăl,* a. (**-ly,** ad.) idéal(ement) ‖ non réel ‖ en idée.   [identique(ment).

identic(al), *ĭ dĕn'tĭk(ăl),* a. (**-ly,** ad.)

identify, *ĭ dĕn'tĭ fī,* v. a. identifier.

identity, *ĭ dĕn'tĭ tĭ,* s. identité, f.

idiocy, *ĭd'ĭ ō sĭ,* s. idiotisme, m., idiotie, f.

idiom, *ĭd'ĭ ŭm,* s. idiome, m.

idiomatic, *ĭd ĭ ō măt'ĭk,* a. idiomatique.

idiosyncrasy, *ĭd ĭ ō sĭng'krä sĭ,* s. idiosyncrasie, f.

idiot, *ĭd'ĭ ŏt,* s. idiot, benêt, m.

idiotic, *ĭd ĭ ŏt'ĭk,* a. fou, stupide, idiot.

idle, *ī'dl,* v. n. être oisif, fainéanter.

idle, *ī'dl, ɔ.* paresseux, oisif ‖ vain ‖ ~ talk, s. verbiage, m.

idleness, *ī'dl nĕs,* s. oisiveté, paresse, f.

idler, *ī'dlĕr,* s. oisif, fainéant, m.

idly, *ī'dlĭ,* ad. oisivement.

idol, *ī'dŏl,* s. idole, f.

idolater, *ĭ dŏl'ā tĕr,* **idolatress,** *ĭ dŏl'ā trĕs,* s. idolâtre, m. & f.

idolatrous, *ĭ dŏl'ā trŭs,* a. idolâtre.

idolatry, *ĭ dŏl'ā trĭ,* s. idolâtrie, f.

idolise, *ī'dŏl ĭz,* v. a. idolâtrer.

idyl, *ī'dĭl,* s. idylle, f.

if, *ĭf,* c. si, pourvu que.

igneous, *ĭg'nĭ ŭs,* a. de feu, en feu.

ignite, *ĭg nīt',* v. a. mettre en feu.

ignoble, *ĭg nō'bl,* a. ignoble, vil.

ignobly, *ĭg nō'blĭ,* ad. ignoblement.

ignominious, *ĭg nō mĭn'ĭ ŭs,* a. ignominieux ‖ **-ly,** ad. ignominieusement.

ignominy, *ĭg'nō mĭnĭ,* s. ignominie, infamie, f.

ignoramus, *ĭg nō rā'mŭs,* s. ignorantin, m.

ignorance, *ĭg'nō răns,* s. ignorance, f. ‖ **to plead** ~, s'excuser sur son ignorance.

ignorant, *ĭg'nō rănt,* a. ignorant ‖ **-ly,** ad. par ignorance.   [rer.

ignore, *ĭg nōr',* v. a. ne pas savoir ‖ igno-

ilex, *ī'lĕks,* s. (bot.) yeuse, f., chêne vert,

ill, *ĭl,* s. mal, malheur, m.   [m.

ill, *ĭl,* a. (**-ly,** ad.) mauvais, méchant ‖ mal ‖ **to be taken** ~, **to fall** ~, tomber malade ‖ ~**-bred,** a. mal élevé ‖ ~**-natured,** a. malin, malicieux ‖ ~**-omened,** a. de mauvais augure ‖ ~**-treat,** ~**-use,** v. a. maltraiter

illegal, *ĭl lē'găl,* a. (**-ly,** ad.) illégal(ement)‖ illicite.

illegality, *ĭl lē găl'ĭ tĭ,* s. illégalité, f.

illegible, *ĭl lĕj'ĭ bl,* a. illisible.   [mité, f

illegitimacy, *ĭl lē jĭt'ĭ mā sĭ,* s. illégiti-

illegitimate, *ĭl lē jĭt'ĭ māt,* a. (**-ly,** ad.) illégitime(ment).

illiberal, *ĭl lĭb'ĕr ăl,* a. (**-ly,** ad.) illibéral, sordide ‖ sans libéralité.

illicit, *ĭl lĭs'ĭt,* a. illicite, défendu.

illimitable, *ĭl lĭm'ĭ tā bl,* a. illimitable.

illiterate, *ĭl lĭt'ĕr ăt,* a. illettré, ignorant.

illness, *ĭl'nĕs,* s. maladie, indisposition, f.

illogical, *ĭl lŏj'ĭ kăl,* a. illogique.

illuminate, *ĭl lū'mĭ nāt,* **illumine,** *ĭl lū' mĭn,* v. a. illuminer, éclairer.

illumination, *ĭl lū mĭ nā'shŭn,* s. illumination, f.

illusion, *ĭl lō'zhŭn,* s. illusion, erreur, f.

illusive, *ĭl lō'sĭv,* **illusory,** *ĭl lō'sĕr ĭ,* a. illusoire.   [illustrer ‖ expliquer, éclaircir.

illustrate, *ĭl'lŭs trāt* ou *ĭl lŭs'trāt,* v. a.

illustration, *ĭl lŭs trā'shŭn,* s. explication, f., éclaircissement, m.

illustrative, *ĭl lŭs'trā tĭv,* a. explicatif.

illustrious, *ĭl lŭs'trĭ ŭs,* a. (**-ly,** ad.) illustre, célèbre ‖ glorieusement.

image, *ĭm'ĭj,* s. image, f. ‖ portrait, m.

image, *ĭm'ĭj,* v. a. se représenter ‖ imaginer.

imagery, *ĭm'ĭj ĕr ĭ,* s. images, fantômes, m. pl.   [concevable.

imaginable, *ĭ măj'ĭ nā bl,* a. imaginable.

imaginary, *ĭ măj'ĭn ĕr ĭ,* a. imaginaire, idéal.   [tion, f. ‖ pensée, idée, f.

imagination, *ĭ măj ĭ nā'shŭn,* s. imagina-

imaginative, *ĭ măj'ĭ nā tĭv,* a. imaginatif.

imagine, *ĭ măj'ĭn,* v. a. imaginer, s'imaginer ‖ inventer.

imbecile, *ĭm'bĕ sĕl,* a. imbécile, idiot, m.

imbecile, *ĭm'bĕ sĕl,* a. imbécile, idiot.

imbecility, *ĭm bē sĭl'ĭ tĭ,* s. imbécillité, faiblesse, f.

imbibe, *ĭm bīb',* v. a. absorber ‖ (fig.) puiser.

imbue, *ĭm bū',* v. a. imbiber ‖ inspirer.

imitate, *ĭm'ĭ tāt,* v. a. imiter.

imitation, *ĭm ĭ tā'shŭn,* s. imitation, f. ‖ **in** ~ **of,** à l'exemple de.

imitative, *ĭm'ĭ tā tĭv,* a. imitatif.

imitator, *ĭm'ĭ tā tĕr,* s. imitateur, m.

immaculate, *ĭm măk'ū lāt,* a. immaculé, pur.

immaterial, *ĭm mă tē'rĭ ăl,* a. immatériel.

immature, *ĭm mā'tūr',* a. vert, qui n'est pas mûr   [commensurable.

immeasurable, *ĭm mĕzh'ōōr ā bl,* a. in-

immeasurably, *ĭm mĕzh'ōōr ā blĭ,* ad. immensément.

immediate, *ĭm mē'dĭ āt,* a. immédiat ‖ (**on letters**) pressé ‖ **-ly,** ad. tout de suite.   [rial, très-ancien.

immemorial, *ĭm mē mō'rĭ ăl,* a. immémo-

immense, *ĭm mĕns',* a. immense, vaste ‖ **-ly,** ad immensément.

immensity, *ĭm mĕn'sĭ tĭ,* s. immensité, f.

immerse, *ĭm mĕrs',* v. a. immerger, plonger.

immersion, *ĭm mĕr'shŭn,* s. immersion, f.

immigrant, *ĭm'mĭ grănt,* s. immigrant, m.

imminence, *ĭm'mĭ nĕns,* s. imminence, f.

imminent, *ĭm'mĭ nĕnt,* a. imminent, menaçant.

immobility, *ĭm mō bĭl'ĭ tĭ,* s. immobilité, f.

immoderate, *ĭm mŏd'ĕr āt,* a. (**-ly,** ad.) immodéré(ment) ‖ excessif.

immodest, *ĭm mŏd'ĕst,* a. (**-ly,** ad.) immodeste(ment).

immodesty, *ĭm mŏd'ĕs tĭ,* s. immodestie, f.

immolate, *ĭm'mō lāt,* v. a. immoler, sacrifier   [f.

immolation, *ĭm mō lā'shŭn,* s. immolation, f.

immoral, *ĭm mŏr'ăl,* a. immoral.

immorality, *ĭm mō răl'ĭ tĭ,* s. immoralité, dépravation, f.

immortal, *ĭm mŏr'tăl,* a. immortel.

immortalise, *ĭm mŏr'tăl ĭz,* v. a. immortaliser   [lité, f.

immortality, *ĭm mŏr tăl'ĭ tĭ,* s. immorta-

immovable, *ĭm mōv'ă bl,* a. immobile.
immovably, *ĭm mōv'ă blĭ,* ad. inébran-
  lablement. [privilége, m.
immunity, *ĭm mū'nĭ tĭ,* s. immunité, f.,
immure, *ĭm mūr',* v. a. entourer de murailles. [tabilité, f.
immutability, *ĭm mū tă bĭl'ĭ tĭ,* s. immu-
immutable, *ĭm mū'tă bl,* a. immuable, invariable. [ment.
immutably, *ĭm mū'tă blĭ,* ad. invariable-
imp, *ĭmp,* s. rejeton, m. || diablotin, m. ||
  petit drôle, m. [m.
impact, *ĭm'păkt,* s. coup porté en poussant,
impair, *ĭm păr',* v. a. détériorer, diminuer.
impalpable, *ĭm păl'pă bl,* a. impalpable.
impart, *ĭm părt',* v. a. donner, commu-
  niquer. [tial(ement).
impartial, *ĭm păr'shăl,* a. (-ly, ad.) impar-
impartiality, *ĭm păr shĭ ăl'ĭ tĭ,* s. impartialité, f.
impassable, *ĭm păs' să bl,* a. impraticable.
impassibility, *ĭm păs sĭ bĭl'ĭ tĭ,* s. insensibilité, f.
impassioned, *ĭm păsh'ŭnd,* a. passionné.
impassive, *ĭm păs'sĭv,* a. insensible.
impatience, *ĭm pā'shĕns,* s. impatience, f.
impatient, *ĭm pā'shĕnt,* a. impatient ||em-
  pressé || -ly, ad. impatiemment.
impeach, *ĭm pēch',* v. a. accuser. [tion, f.
impeachment, *ĭm pēch'mĕnt,* s. accusa-
impecuniosity, *ĭm pē kū nĭ ŏs'ĭ tĭ,* s. pé-
  nurie d'argent, indigence, f.
impede, *ĭm pēd',* v. a. empêcher, arrêter.
impediment, *ĭm pĕd'ĭ mĕnt,* s. empêchement, obstacle, m
impel, *ĭm pĕl',* v. a. pousser.
impend, *ĭm pĕnd',* v. n. pencher, menacer.
impenetrable, *ĭm pĕn'ĕ tră bl,* a. impénétrable. [nétrablement.
impenetrably, *ĭm pĕn'ĕ tră blĭ,* ad. impé-
impenitence, *ĭm pĕn'ĭ tĕns,* s. impénitence, f.
impenitent, *ĭm pĕn'ĭ tĕnt,* a. impénitent.
imperative, *ĭm pĕr'ă tĭv,* a. impératif ||
  -ly, ad. impérativement.
imperceptible, *ĭm pĕr sĕp'tĭ bl,* a. imperceptible. [perceptiblement.
imperceptibly, *ĭm pĕr sĕp'tĭ blĭ,* ad. im-
imperfect, *ĭm pĕr'fĕkt,* s. imparfait, m.
imperfect, *ĭm pĕr'fĕkt,* a. imparfait || -ly,
  ad. imparfaitement. [tion, f.
imperfection, *ĭm pĕr fĕk'shŭn,* s. imperfec-
imperial, *ĭm pē'rĭ ăl,* a. (beard) impériale, f. [jésus (of paper).
imperial, *ĭm pē'rĭ ăl,* a. impérial || grand
imperil, *ĭm pĕr'ĭl,* v. a. mettre en danger.
imperious, *ĭm pē'rĭ ŭs,* a. impérieux, exi-
  geant || -ly, ad. impérieusement.
imperishable, *ĭm pĕr'ĭsh ă bl,* a. impérissable. [méable.
impermeable, *ĭm pĕr'mē ă bl,* a. imper-
impersonal, *ĭm pĕr'sŏn ăl,* a. (-ly, ad.)
  (gr.) impersonnel(lement).
impersonality, *ĭm pĕr sŏn ăl'ĭ tĭ,* s. im-
  personnalité, f., caractère impersonnel, m.

impersonate, *ĭm pĕr'sŏn āt,* v. a. person-
  nifier. [m. || réprésentation, f.
impersonation, *ĭm pĕr sŏn ā'shŭn,* s. rôle,
impertinence, *ĭm pĕr'tĭ nĕns,* s. impertinence, f.
impertinent, *ĭm pĕr'tĭ nĕnt,* a. imperti-
  nent || déplacé || -ly, ad. impertinemment.
imperturbability, *ĭm pĕr tĕr'bă bĭl'ĭ tĭ,* s.
  imperturbabilité, f. [turbable.
imperturbable, *ĭm pĕr tĕr'bă bl,* a. imper-
impervious, *ĭm pĕr'vĭ ŭs,* a. impénétrable,
  inaccessible. [f.
impetuosity, *ĭm pĕt ŭ ŏs'ĭ tĭ,* s.impétuosité,
impetuous, *ĭm pĕt'ŭ ŭs,* a. impétueux ||
  -ly, ad. impétueusement.
impetus, *ĭm'pē tŭs,* s. impulsion, force
  motrice, f.
impiety, *ĭm pī'ĕ tĭ,* s. impiété, f.
impinge, *ĭm pĭnj',* v. a. heurter || to ∼ on,
  enfreindre. [impiété.
impious, *ĭm'pĭ ŭs,* a. impie || -ly, ad. avec
implacable, *ĭm plā'kă bl,* a. implacable.
implacably, *ĭm plā'kă blĭ,* ad. inexorablement. [primer.
implant, *ĭm plănt',* v. a. implanter || im-
implement, *ĭm'plĕ mĕnt,* s. outil, ustensile, m.
implicate, *ĭm'plĭ kāt,* v. a. impliquer.
implication, *ĭm plĭ kā'shŭn,* s. implication, f. [cite(ment).
implicit, *ĭm plĭs'ĭt,* a. (-ly, ad.) impli-
implore, *ĭm plōr',* v. a. implorer, supplier.
imply, *ĭm plī',* v. a. impliquer, enlacer ||
  inférer. [discrétion, f.
impolicy, *ĭm pŏl'ĭ sĭ,* s. inconvenance, in-
impolite, *ĭm pō līt',* a. (-ly, ad.) impoli
  (ment) || malhonnête. [f.
impoliteness, *ĭm pō līt'nĕs,* s. impolitesse,
impolitic, *ĭm pŏl'ĭ tĭk,* a. impolitique.
import, *ĭm'pŏrt,* s. importation, f. || im-
  portance, f. || sens, m., valeur, f. || ∼-
  duty, s. droit d'entrée, m. || ∼-trade, s.
  commerce d'importation, m.
import, *ĭm pŏrt',* v. a. importer.
importance, *ĭm pŏr'tăns,* s. importance, f.
important, *ĭm pŏr'tănt,* a. important.
importation, *ĭm pŏr tā'shŭn,* s. importation, f. [importun(ément).
importunate, *ĭm pŏr'tŭ năt,* a. (-ly, ad.)
importune, *ĭm pŏr'tūn',* v. a. importuner.
importunity, *ĭm pŏr tŭ'nĭ tĭ,* s. importunité, f.
impose, *ĭm pōz',* v. a. imposer || tromper.
imposer, *ĭm pō zĕr',* s. qui impose || trom-
  peur, m. [peur, imposteur.
imposing, *ĭm pō'zĭng,* a. imposant || trom-
imposition, *ĭm pō zĭsh'ŭn,* s. imposition,
  f. || tromperie, f. || impôt, m.
impossibility, *ĭm pŏs sĭ bĭl'ĭ tĭ,* s. impossibilité, f.
impossible, *ĭm pŏs'sĭ bl,* a. impossible.
impost, *ĭm'pōst,* s. impôt, m., imposition
impostor, *ĭm pŏs'tĕr,* s. trompeur, m. [f.
imposture, *ĭm pŏs'tūr,* s. fourberie, fraude,
impotence, *ĭm'pō tĕns,* s. impuissance, f. [f.
impotent, *ĭm'pō tĕnt,* a. impotent, im-
  puissant || -ly, ad. faiblement.

impound, *ĭm pŏwnd'*, v. a. confisquer ‖ mettre en fourrière.

impoverish, *ĭm pŏv'ĕr ĭsh*, v. a. appauvrir.

impracticability, *ĭm prăk'tĭ kă bĭl'ĭ tĭ*, s. impossibilité, f. [ticable.

impracticable, *ĭm prăk'tĭ kă bl*, a. impra-

imprecate, *ĭm'prē kāt*, v. a. maudire.

imprecation, *ĭm prē kā'shŭn*, s. malédiction, f.

impregnable, *ĭm prĕg'nă bl*, a.imprenable.

impregnate, *ĭm prĕg'nāt*, v.a. imprégner ‖ féconder. [f.

impress, *ĭm'prĕs*, s. empreinte, impression,

impress, *ĭm prĕs'*, v. a. imprimer, empreindre, graver ‖ enrôler par force.

impression, *ĭm prĕsh'ŭn*, s. impression, f. ‖ empreinte, f. ‖ to have an ~, se retracer à l'esprit ‖ avoir un souvenir confus.

impressionable, *ĭm prĕsh'ŭn ă bl*, a. impressionable.

impressive, *ĭm prĕs'sĭv*, a. frappant ‖ impressionable ‖ -ly, ad. fortement.

imprint, *ĭm prĭnt'*, v. a. empreindre, imprimer, graver.

imprison, *ĭm prĭz'n*, v. a. emprisonner.

imprisonment, *ĭm prĭz'n mĕnt*, s. emprisonnement, m. [babilité, f.

improbability, *ĭm prŏb ă bĭl'ĭ tĭ*, s. impro-

improbable, *ĭm prŏb'ă bl*, a. improbable.

improbably, *ĭm prŏb'ă blĭ*, ad.improbablement. [propre(ment) ‖ non convenable.

improper, *ĭm prŏp'ĕr*, a. (-ly, ad.) im-

impropriety, *ĭm prō prī'ĕ tĭ*, s. impropriété, f. ‖ inconvenance, f.

improve, *ĭm prŏv'*, v. a. & n. améliorer, perfectionner ‖ s'améliorer, faire des progrès ‖ to ~ upon acquaintance, gagner à être vu de près.

improvement, *ĭm prŏv'mĕnt*, s. amélioration, perfection, f., progrès, m.

improvidence, *ĭm prŏv'ĭ dĕns*, s. imprévoyance, f.

improvident, *ĭm prŏv'ĭ dĕnt*, a. imprévoyant ‖ -ly, ad. avec imprévoyance.

improvisation, *ĭm prŏ vĭ sā'shŭn*, s. improvisation f.

improvise, *ĭm'prŏ vīs*, v. a. & n. improviser. [f.

imprudence, *ĭm prŏʹdĕns*, s. imprudence.

imprudent, *ĭm'prŏ dĕnt*, a. imprudent ‖ -ly, ad. imprudemment.

impudence, *ĭm'pū dĕns*, s. impudence, f.

impudent, *ĭm'pū dĕnt*, a. impudent ‖ -ly, ad. impudemment.

impugn, *ĭm pūn'*, v. a. attaquer ‖ contester.

impulse, *ĭm'pŭls*, impulsion, *ĭm pŭl'shŭn*, s. impulsion, incitation, f.

impulsive, *ĭm pŭl'sĭv*, a. impulsif, moteur.

impunity, *ĭm pū'nĭ tĭ*, s. impunité, f.

impure, *ĭm pūr'*, a.(-ly,ad.)impur(ement) souillé ‖ impudique. [pudicité, f.

impurity, *ĭm pū'rĭ tĭ*, s. impureté, f. ‖ im-

imputation, *ĭm pū tā'shŭn*, s. imputation, f., reproche, m.

impute, *ĭm pūt'*, v. a. imputer, attribuer.

in, *ĭn*, pr. & ad. en, dans ‖ sous, sur ‖ dedans ‖ to be ~, être chez soi.

inability, *ĭn ă bĭl'ĭ tĭ*, s. incapacité, f.

inaccessible, *ĭn ăk sĕs'sĭbl*, a. inaccessible. [f.

inaccuracy, *ĭn ăk'kŭrd sĭ*, s. inexactitude

inaccurate, *ĭn ăk'kū rāt*, a. (-ly, ad.) inexact(ement).

inaction, *ĭn ăk'shŭn*, s. inaction, f.

inactive, *ĭn ăk'tĭv*, a. inactif, oisif.

inactivity, *ĭn ăk tĭv'ĭ tĭ*, s. inactivité, f.

inadequacy, *ĭn ăd'ĕ kwă sĭ*, s. insuffisance, f.

inadequate, *ĭn ăd'ĕ kwāt*, a. insuffisant, incomplet, disproportionné. [sible.

inadmissible, *ĭn ăd mĭs'sĭ bl*, a. inadmis-

inadvertence, *ĭn ăd vĕr'tĕns*, s. inadvertance, f. [sidérément.

inadvertently, *ĭn ăd vĕr'tĕnt lĭ*, ad.incon-

inalienable, *ĭn ăl'yĕn ă bl*, a. inaliénable.

inanimate, *ĭn ăn'ĭ māt*, a. inanimé ‖ mort.

inanition, *ĭn ăn'ĭsh'ŭn*, s. inanition, f.

inapplicable, *ĭn ăp'plĭ kă bl*, a. inapplicable.

inapposite, *ĭn ăp'pŏ zĭt*, a. sans rapport déplacé ‖ qui n'est pas à propos.

inappreciable, *ĭn ăp prē'shĭ ă bl*, a. inappréciable.

inaptitude, *ĭn ăp'tĭ tūd*, s. inaptitude, f.

inarticulate, *ĭn ăr tĭk'ū lāt*, a. inarticulé ‖ -ly, ad. sans articulation. [que.

inasmuch, *ĭn ăz mŭch'*, ad. vu que, attendu

inattention, *ĭn ăt tĕn'shŭn*, s. inattention, négligence, f.

inattentive, *ĭn ăt tĕn'tĭv*, a. inattentif.

inaudible, *ĭn ăw'dĭ bl*, a. qui ne peut pas être entendu.

inaugural, *ĭn ăw'gū răl*, a. inaugural ‖ ~ address, s. discours d'inauguration, m.

inaugurate, *ĭn ăw'gū răt*, v. a. inaugurer.

inauguration, *ĭn ăw gū rā'shŭn*, s. inauguration, f.

inauspicious, *ĭn ăw spĭsh'ŭs*, a. (-ly, ad.) de or sous mauvais augure.

inborn, *ĭn'bŏrn*, inbred, *ĭn'brĕd*, a. inné.

incalculable, *ĭn kăl'kū lă bl*, a. incalculable. [descent.

incandescent, *ĭn kăn dĕs'sĕnt*, a. incan-

incantation, *ĭn kăn tā'shŭn*, s. enchantement, m.

incapability, *ĭn kă pă bĭl'ĭ tĭ*, s. incapacité, impuissance, f.

incapable, *ĭn kā'pă bl*, a. incapable.

incapacitate, *ĭn kă păs'ĭ tāt*, v. a. rendre incapable, affaiblir.

incapacity, *ĭn kă păs'ĭ tĭ*, s. incapacité, f.

incarcerate, *ĭn kăr'sĕr āt*, v. a. incarcérer.

incarnate, *ĭn kăr'nāt*, a. incarné.

incarnation, *ĭn kăr nā'shŭn*, s. incarnation, f.

incase, *ĭn kās'*, v. a. encaisser, enfermer.

incautious, *ĭn kăw'shŭs*, a. négligent, imprudent ‖ -ly, ad. imprudemment.

incendiary, *ĭn sĕn'dĭ ă rĭ*, s.incendiaire, m.

incendiary, *ĭn sĕn'dĭ ă rĭ*, a. incendiaire.

incense, *ĭn'sĕns*, s. encens, parfum, m.

incense, *ĭn sĕns'*, v.a. encenser ‖ exaspérer.

incentive, *ĭn sĕn'tĭv*, s. aiguillon, stimulant, encouragement, m.

incessant, *in sĕs' sănt*, a. (-ly, ad.) continuel(lement).
incest, *in' sĕst*, s. inceste, m.
incestuous, *in sĕs' tŭ ŭs*, a. incestueux ‖ -ly, ad. incestueusement.
inch, *insh*, s. pouce (3 centimètres), m. ‖ petite quantité, f. ‖ ~ by ~, peu à peu ‖ by -es, pied à pied, à petit feu.
incident, *in' si dĕnt*, s. incident, m.
incident, *in' si dĕnt*, a. accidental, casuel ‖ ~ to, attaché à, appartenant.
incidental, *in si dĕn' tăl*, a. accidentel, fortuit, accessoire ‖ -ly, ad. par hasard, accessoirement.
incipient, *in sĭp'ĭ ĕnt*, a. commençant.
incise, *in sīz'*, v. a. inciser.
incision, *in sizh' ŭn*, s. incision, f.
incite, *in sīt'*, v. a. inciter, exciter.
incivility, *in sĭ vĭl' ĭ tĭ*, s. incivilité, f.
inclemency, *in klĕm' ĕn sĭ*, s. inclémence, sévérité, dureté, f. [goureux, dur.
inclement, *in klĕm' ĕnt*, a. inclément, rigoureux, dur.
inclination, *in kli nā' shŭn*, s. inclination, f., penchant, m. ‖ inclinaison, f.
incline, *in' klīn*, s. pente, f. ‖ rampe, f.
incline, *in klīn'*, v. a. & n. incliner, pencher ‖ s'incliner ‖ être porté à.
include, *in klōd'*, v. a. renfermer, comprendre.
including, *in klō' dĭng*, pr. y compris.
inclusion, *in klō' zhŭn*, s. inclusion, f.
inclusive, *in klō' sĭv*, a. (-ly, ad.) inclus (ivement) ‖ y compris. [f.
incoherence, *in kō hē' rĕns*, s. incohérence.
incoherent, *in kō hē' rĕnt*, a. incohérent ‖ -ly, ad. sans liaison.
incombustible, *in kŏm bŭs tĭ bĭl' ĭ tĭ*, s. incombustibilité, f. [bustible.
incombustible, *in kŏm bŭs' tĭ bl*, a. incombincome, *in' kŭm*, s. revenu, m., rentes, f. pl. ‖ ~ tax, s. impôt sur le revenu, m.
incoming, *in' kŭm ĭng*, a. rentant.
incommensurable, *in kŏm mĕn' shŏŏ rā bl*, a. incommensurable. [der.
incommode, *in kŏm mōd'*, v. a. incommoincommodious, *in kŏm mō' dĭ ŭs*, a. incommode, importun, gênant.
incomparable, *in kŏm' pă rā bl*, a. incomparable. [comparaison.
incomparably, *in kŏm' pă rā blĭ*, ad. sans incompatibility, *in kŏm păt ĭ bĭl' ĭ tĭ*, s. incompatibilité, f. [tible.
incompatible, *in kŏm păt' ĭ bl*, a. incompaincompetence, *in kŏm' pĕ tĕns*, s. incompétence, f.
incompetent, *in kŏm' pĕ tĕnt*, a. incompétent ‖ incapable ‖ -ly, ad. incompétemment.
incomplete, *in kŏm plēt'*, a. incomplet, imparfait ‖ -ly, ad. imparfaitement.
incompleteness, *in kŏm plēt' nĕs*, s. état incomplet, m., défectuosité, f.
incomprehensibility, *in kŏm prē hĕn sĭ bĭl' ĭ tĭ*, s. incompréhensibilité, f.
incomprehensible, *in kŏm prē hĕn' sĭ bl*, a. incompréhensible. [vable.
inconceivable, *in kŏn sē' vā bl*, a. inconce-

inconclusive, *in kŏn klō' sĭv*, a. inconcluant. [inconvenance, f.
incongruity, *in kŏn grō' ĭ tĭ*, s. incongruité,
incongruous, *in kŏn' grō ŭs*, a. (-ly, ad.) incongru(ment). [séquent.
inconsequent, *in kŏn' sē kwĕnt*, a. inconinconsiderable, *in kŏn sĭd' ĕr ā bl*, a. insignifiant. [inconsidéré(ment).
inconsiderate, *in kŏn sĭd' ĕr āt*, a. (-ly, ad.)
inconsistency *in kŏn sĭs' tĕn sĭ*, s. incompatibilité, inconsistance, incongruité, f.
inconsistent, *in kŏn sĭs' tĕnt*, a. inconsistant, incompatible ‖ -ly, ad. contradictoirement. [lable.
inconsolable, *in kŏn sō' lā bl*, a. inconsoinconstancy, *in kŏn' stăn sĭ*, s. inconstance, f.
inconstant, *in kŏn' stănt*, a. inconstant.
incontestable, *in kŏn tĕs' tā bl*, a. incontestable. [testablement.
incontestably, *in kŏn tĕs' tā blĭ*, ad. inconincontinence, *in kŏn' tĭ nĕns*, s. incontinence, f.
incontinent, *in kŏn' tĭ nĕnt*, a. incontinent‖ -ly, ad. avec incontinence.
incontrovertible, *in kŏn trō vĕr' tĭ bl*, a. vide incontestable.
inconvenience, *in kŏn vē' nĭ ĕns*, s. incommodité, f., désagrément, m.
inconvenience, *in kŏn vē' nĭ ĕns*, v. a. troubler, déranger.
inconvenient, *in kŏn vē' nĭ ĕnt*, a. (-ly, ad.) incommode(ment).
incorporate, *in kŏr' pō rāt*, v. a. (& n.) (s')incorporer.
incorporate, *in kŏr' pō rāt*, a. incorporé.
incorporation, *in kŏr pō rā' shŭn*, s. incorporation, f.
incorporeal, *in kŏr pō' rĭ ăl*, a. incorporel.
incorrect, *in kŏr rĕkt'*, a. incorrect ‖ -ly, ad. d'une manière incorrecte.
incorrigible, *in kŏr' rĭ jĭ bl*, a. incorrigible.
incorruptibility, *in kŏr rŭp tĭ bĭl' ĭ tĭ*, s. incorruptibilité, f. [ruptible.
incorruptible, *in kŏr rŭp' tĭ bl*, a. incorincrease, *in' krēs*, s. accroissement, m. ‖ propagation, f. ‖ produit, m.
increase, *in krēs'*, v. a. & n. augmenter, accroître ‖ s'augmenter, s'agrandir.
incredibility, *in krĕd ĭ bĭl' ĭ tĭ*, s. incrédibilité, f.
incredible, *in krĕd' ĭ bl*, a. incroyable.
incredibly, *in krĕd' ĭ blĭ*, ad. incroyablement. [f.
incredulity, *in krĕ dū' lĭ tĭ*, s. incrédulité,
incredulous, *in krĕd' ū lŭs*, a. incrédule.
incremation, *in krē mā' shŭn*, s. crémation, f. [surcroît, m.
increment, *in' krē mĕnt*, s. accroissement,
incriminate, *in krim' ĭ nāt*, v. a. inculper.
incrust, *in krŭst'*, v. a. incruster.
incubate, *in' kū bāt*, v. a. couver des œufs.
incubus, *in' kū bŭs*, s. cauchemar, m. ‖ (fig.) lourd fardeau, m.
inculcate, *in kŭl' kāt*, v. a. inculquer.
incumbency, *in kŭm' bĕn sĭ*, s. possession d'un bénéfice, f.

incumbent, *ĭn kŭm' bĕnt*, s. bénéficier, m.
incumbent, *ĭn kŭm' bĕnt*, a. imposé, enjoint, obligatoire.
incur, *ĭn kẽr'*, v. a. encourir, s'attirer.
incurability, *ĭn kū rá bĭl' ĭ tĭ*, s. incurabilité, f.
incurable, *ĭn kū' rá bl*, a. incurable.
incurably, *ĭn kū' rá blĭ*, ad. sans remède.
incursion, *ĭn kẽr' shŭn*, s. irruption, f.
incurvation, *ĭn kẽr vā' shŭn*, s. courbure, f.
indebted, *ĭn dĕt' tĕd*, a. endetté || redevable.
indecency, *ĭn dē' sĕn sĭ*, s. indécence, f.
indecent, *ĭn dē' sĕnt*, a. indécent || -ly, ad. indécemment.
indecision, *ĭn dē' sĭzh' ŭn*, s. indécision, f.
indecisive, *ĭn dē sī' sĭv*, a. indécis.
indecorous, *ĭn dē kō' rŭs*, a. indécent, inconvenant || -ly, ad. indécemment.
indeed, *ĭn dēd'*, ad. en vérité, réellement.
indefatigable, *ĭn dē făt' ĭ gä bl*, a. infatigable.
indefensible, *ĭn dē fĕn' sĭ bl*, a. indéfensable.
indefinite, *ĭn dĕf' ĭ nĭt*, a. (-ly, ad.) indéfini(ment) || illimité.
indelible, *ĭn dĕl' ĭ bl*, a. indélébile, ineffaçable.
indelicacy, *ĭn dĕl' ĭ kä sĭ*, s. indélicatesse, grossièreté, f.
indelicate, *ĭn dĕl' ĭ kät*, a. indélicat, grossier.
indemnification, *ĭn dĕm nĭ fĭ kā' shŭn*, s. dédommagement, m. || indemnité, f.
indemnity, *ĭn dĕm' nĭ tĭ*, s. dédommagement, m. || indemnité, f.
indemnify, *ĭn dĕm' nĭ fĭ*, v. a. indemniser.
indent, *ĭn dĕnt'*, v. a. denteler.
indentation, *ĭn dĕn tā' shŭn*, s. dentelure, f.
indenture, *ĭn dĕn' tūr*, s. contrat d'apprentissage, m.
independence, *ĭn dē pĕn' dĕns*, s. indépendance, f.
independent, *ĭn dē pĕn' dĕnt*, a. indépendant || -ly, ad. indépendamment.
indescribable, *ĭn dē skrī' bä bl*, a. indescriptible.
indestructible, *ĭn dē strŭk' tĭ bl*, a. indestructible.
indeterminate, *ĭn dē tẽr' mĭ nät*, a. indéterminé, indécis || -ly, ad. indéfiniment.
index, *ĭn' dĕks*, s. table des matières, f. || index, m. || aiguille, f.
India, *ĭn' dĭ ä*; ~man, s. vaisseau des Indes, m.||~rubber, s. gomme élastique, f.
Indian summer, *ĭn' dĭ än sŭm' mẽr*, s. (Am.) été tardif, m.
indicate, *ĭn' dĭ kāt*, v. a. indiquer.
indication, *ĭn dĭ kā' shŭn*, s. indication, f., symptôme, m.
indicative, *ĭn dĭk' ä tĭv*, s. (gr.) indicatif.
indicative, *ĭn dĭk' ä tĭv*, a. (gr.) indicatif || ~ of, qui indique.
indictment, *ĭn dīt' mĕnt*, s. acte d'accusation, m.
indifference, *ĭn dĭf' fẽr ĕns*, s. indifférence, f.
indifferent, *ĭn dĭf' fẽr ĕnt*, a. indifférent, impartial || -ly, ad. indifféremment || médiocrement.
indigenous, *ĭn dĭj' ē nŭs*, a. indigène || naturel.
indigent, *ĭn' dĭ jĕnt*, a. indigent, pauvre.
indigestible, *ĭn dĭ jĕs' tĭ bl*, a. qui ne peut se digérer.
indigestion, *ĭn dĭ jĕst' yŭn*, s. indigestion, f.

indignant, *ĭn dĭg' nänt*, a. indigné.
indignation, *ĭn dĭg nā' shŭn*, s. indignation, f.
indignity, *ĭn dĭg' nĭ tĭ*, s. indignité, injure, f., affront, m.
indigo, *ĭn' dĭ gō*, s. indigo, m. || indigotier, m.
indirect, *ĭn dĭ rĕkt'*, a. (-ly, ad.) indirect(ement), f. || détour, m.
indirectness, *ĭn dĭ rĕkt' nĕs*, s. déloyauté, f. || détour, m.
indiscreet, *ĭn dĭs krēt'*, a. indiscret || -ly, ad. indiscrètement.
indiscretion, *ĭn dĭs krēsh' ŭn*, s. indiscrétion, f.
indiscriminate, *ĭn dĭs krĭm' ĭ nät*, a. indistinct, confus || -ly, ad. sans distinction.
indispensable, *ĭn dĭs pĕn' sä bl*, a. indispensable.
indispensably, *ĭn dĭs pĕn' sä blĭ*, ad. indispensablement.
indispose, *ĭn dĭs pōz'*, v. a. indisposer || fâcher.
indisposition, *ĭn dĭs pō zĭsh' ŭn*, s. indisposition, maladie, f.
indisputably, *ĭn dĭs pū' tä blĭ*, ad. incontestablement.
indissoluble, *ĭn dĭs' ō lū bl*, a. indissoluble || -ly, ad. indissolublement.
indistinct, *ĭn dĭs tĭngkt'*, a. (-ly, ad.) indistinct(ement).
indite, *ĭn dīt'*, v. a. écrire, composer.
individual, *ĭn dĭ vĭd' ū äl*, s. individu, m.
individual, *ĭn dĭ vĭd' ū äl*, a. (-ly, ad.) individuel(lement).
individuality, *ĭn dĭ vĭd ū äl' ĭ tĭ*, s. individualité, f.
indivisible, *ĭn dĭ vĭz' ĭ bl*, a. indivisible, inséparable.
indivisibly, *ĭn dĭ vĭz' ĭ blĭ*, ad. indivisiblement.
indolence, *ĭn' dō lĕns*, s. indolence, f.
indolent, *ĭn' dō lĕnt*, a. indolent || -ly, ad. avec indolence.
indorse, *ĭn dōrs'*, v. a. *vide* endorse.
indubitable, *ĭn dū' bĭ tä bl*, a. indubitable.
indubitably, *ĭn dū' bĭ tä blĭ*, ad. indubitablement.
induce, *ĭn dūs'*, v. a. induire, persuader, engager, causer.
inducement, *ĭn dūs' mĕnt*, s. induction, f., motif, m.
inductive, *ĭn dŭk' tĭv*, a. inductif.
indue, *ĭn dū'*, v. a. vêtir, habiller.
indulge, *ĭn dŭlj'*, v. a. & n. avoir de l'indulgence || s'abandonner.
indulgence, *ĭn dŭl' jĕns*, s. indulgence, tendresse, f.
indulgent, *ĭn dŭl' jĕnt*, a. indulgent || -ly, ad. avec indulgence.
indurate, *ĭn' dū rāt*, v. a. durcir, endurcir || s'endurcir.
industrial, *ĭn dŭs' trĭ äl*, a. industriel || ~ exhibition, s. exposition industrielle, f.
industrious, *ĭn dŭs' trĭ ŭs*, a. industrieux, laborieux || -ly, ad. industrieusement.
industry, *ĭn' dŭs trĭ*, s. industrie, f.
inebriate, *ĭn ē' brĭ ät*, v. a. *vide* intoxicate.
ineffable, *ĭn ĕf' fä bl*, a. ineffable, inexprimable.
ineffective, *ĭn ĕf fĕk' tĭv*, ineffectual, *ĭn ĕf fĕk' tū äl*, a. inefficace, inutile || -ly, ad. sans effet.
inefficacious, *ĭn ĕf fĭ kā' shŭs*, a. inefficace.
inefficiency, *ĭn ĕf fĭsh' ĕn sĭ*, s. inefficacité, f.
inefficient, *ĭn ĕf fĭsh' ĕnt*, a. inefficace, impuissant.
inelegant, *ĭn ĕl' ē gänt*, a. inélégant, grossier.

inequality, *ĭn ē kwŏl' ĭ tĭ,* s. inégalité, différence, f.

ineradicable, *ĭn ē răd' ĭ kă bl,* a. inextirpable.   [—ly, ad. lourdement.

inert, *ĭn ẽrt',* a. inerte, inactif || pesant ||

inertness, *ĭn ẽrt' nĕs,* s. inertie, f.

inestimable, *ĭn ĕs' tĭ mă bl,* a. inestimable.

inevitable, *ĭn ĕv' ĭ tă bl,* a. inévitable.

inexcusable, *ĭn ĕks kū' ză bl,* a. inexcusable.   [cuse.

inexcusably, *ĭn ĕks kū' ză blĭ,* ad. sans excuse.

inexhaustible, *ĭn ĕgz hawst' ĭ bl,* a. inépuisable.

inexorable, *ĭn ĕks' ō ră bl,* a. inexorable.

inexorably, *ĭn ĕks' ō ră blĭ,* ad. inexorablement.   [venance, f.

inexpedience, *ĭn ĕks pē' dĭ ĕns,* s. incon-

inexperience, *ĭn ĕks pē' rĭ ĕns,* s. manque d'expérience, m.

inexpiable, *ĭn ĕks' pĭ ă bl,* a. inexpiable.

inexplicable, *ĭn ĕks' plĭ kă bl,* a. inexplicable.   [primable.

inexpressible, *ĭn ĕks prĕs' sĭ bl,* a. inexprimable.

inextricable, *ĭn ĕks' trĭ kă bl,* a. inextricable.   [lité, f.

infallibility, *ĭn făl lĭ bĭl' ĭ tĭ,* s. infaillibi-

infallible, *ĭn făl' lĭ bl,* a. infaillible, certain.

infallibly, *ĭn făl' lĭ blĭ,* ad. infailliblement.

infamous, *ĭn' fă mŭs,* a. infâme, honteux || —ly, ad. avec infamie, honteusement.

infamy, *ĭn' fă mĭ,* s. infamie, f.   [f.

infancy, *ĭn' făn sĭ,* s. enfance, f. || minorité,

infant, *ĭn' fănt,* s. enfant, m. || mineur, m. || infant, m. || ~ school, s. salle d'asile, f.

infanta, *ĭn făn' tă,* s. infante, f.

infanticide, *ĭn făn' tĭ sĭd,* s. infanticide, m.

infantine, *ĭn' făn tĭn,* a. enfantin, puéril.

infantry, *ĭn' făn trĭ,* s. infanterie, f.

infatuate, *ĭn făt' ū ăt,* v. a. infatuer, rendre fou.   [f.

infatuation, *ĭn făt ū ā' shŭn,* s. infatuation, f.

infect, *ĭn fĕkt',* v. a. infecter.

infection, *ĭn fĕk' shŭn,* s. infection, contagion, f.

infectious, *ĭn fĕk' shŭs,* a. infecté || —ly, ad. par contagion.

infer, *ĭn fẽr',* v. a. conclure.

inference, *ĭn' fẽr ĕns,* s. conclusion, f.

inferior, *ĭn fē' rĭ ẽr,* s. inférieur, m.

inferior, *ĭn fē' rĭ ẽr,* a. inférieur.

inferiority, *ĭn fē rĭ ŏr' ĭ tĭ,* s. infériorité, f.

infernal, *ĭn fẽr' năl,* a. infernal || —ly, ad. d'une manière infernale.   [tourmenter.

infest, *ĭn fĕst',* v. a. infester, troubler,

infidel, *ĭn' fĭ dĕl,* s. infidèle, m.

infidelity, *ĭn fĭ dĕl' ĭ tĭ,* s. infidélité, f.

infinite, *ĭn' fĭ nĭt,* a. (—ly, ad.) infini(ment).

infinitesimal, *ĭn fĭ nĭ tĕs' ĭ măl,* a. infinitésimal.

infinitive, *ĭn fĭn' ĭ tĭv,* s. (gr.) infinitif, m.

infirm, *ĭn fẽrm',* a. infirme, faible.

infirmary, *ĭn fẽr' mă rĭ,* s. infirmerie, f.

infirmity, *ĭn fẽr' mĭ tĭ,* s. infirmité, faiblesse, f.   [culquer.

infix, *ĭn fĭks',* v. a. fixer, enfoncer || in-

inflame, *ĭn flăm',* v. a. & n. enflammer || irriter || s'enflammer.

inflammable, *ĭn flăm' mă bl,* a. inflammable.   [flammation, f.

inflammation, *ĭn flăm mă' shŭn,* s. in-

inflammatory, *ĭn flăm' mă tẽr ĭ,* a. inflammatoire || (of speeches) incendiaire.

inflate, *ĭn flāt',* v. a. enfler, souffler.

inflation, *ĭn flā' shŭn,* s. enflure, f.

inflect, *ĭn flĕkt',* v. a. fléchir || décliner, conjuguer.

inflection, *ĭn flĕk' shŭn,* s. inflexion, f. || modulation (de la voix), f.

inflexible, *ĭn flĕks' ĭ bl,* a. inflexible.

inflexibly, *ĭn flĕks' ĭ blĭ,* ad. inflexiblement.

inflict, *ĭn flĭkt',* v. a. infliger, imposer.

infliction, *ĭn flĭk' shŭn,* s. infliction, f.

influence, *ĭn' floo ĕns,* s. influence, f.

influence, *ĭn' floo ĕns,* v. a. influencer.

influential, *ĭn floo ĕn' shăl,* a. influent.

influenza, *ĭn floo ĕn' ză,* s. influenza, f.

influx, *ĭn' flŭks,* s. flux, m., affluence, f.

inform, *ĭn fŏrm',* v. a. informer, instruire.

informal, *ĭn fŏr' măl,* a. informe, irrégulier || insolite || —ly, ad. sans les formalités requises.   [formes, m.

informality, *ĭn fŏr măl' ĭ tĭ,* s. manque de

informant, *ĭn fŏr' mănt,* s. accusateur, m. || correspondant, m.

information, *ĭn fŏr mā' shŭn,* s. avis, m., instruction, f. || accusation, f. || **to lodge ~ against,** dénoncer.

informer, *ĭn fŏr' mẽr,* s. dénonciateur, m.

infrequent, *ĭn frē' kwĕnt,* a. (—ly, ad.) rare(ment).   [gresser, violer.

infringe, *ĭn frĭnj',* v. a. enfreindre, trans-

infuriate, *ĭn fū' rĭ ăt,* v. a. rendre furieux.

infuse, *ĭn fūz',* v. a. infuser || inspirer.

infusion, *ĭn fū' zhŭn,* s. infusion, suggestion, inspiration, f.

ingathering, *ĭn găth' ẽr ĭng,* s. récolte, f.

ingenious, *ĭn jē' nĭ ŭs,* a. ingénieux, inventif || —ly, ad. ingénieusement.

ingenuity, *ĭn jē nū' ĭ tĭ,* s. ingénuité, naïveté, f. || génie, m.

ingenuous, *ĭn jĕn' ū ŭs,* a. ingénu, naïf || généreux || —ly, ad. naïvement.

ingle, *ĭng' gl,* s. feu, m., flamme, f. || cheminée, f.

inglorious, *ĭn glō' rĭ ŭs,* a. inglorieux || honteux || —ly, ad. ignominieusement.

ingot, *ĭn' gŏt,* s. lingot, m.   [primer.

ingraft, *ĭn grăft',* v. a. greffer, enter || im-

ingrained, *ĭn grānd',* a. teint en poil || fig. pur sang.

ingrate, *ĭn' grāt,* s. ingrat, m., ingrate, f.

ingrate, *ĭn' grāt,* a. antipathique, repoussant.   [faveur.

ingratiate, *ĭn grā' shĭ āt,* v. a. mettre en

ingratitude, *ĭn grăt' ĭ tūd,* s. ingratitude, f.

ingredient, *ĭn grē' dĭ ĕnt,* s. ingrédient, m.

ingress, *ĭn' grĕs,* s. entrée, f.

ingulf, *ĭn gŭlf',* v. a. engloutir, engouffrer.

inhabit, *ĭn hăb' ĭt,* v. a. habiter.

inhabitant, *ĭn hăb' ĭt ănt,* s. habitant, m.

inhale, *ĭn hāl',* v. a. inspirer, aspirer.

inharmonious, *ĭn hăr mō' nĭ ŭs,* a. inharmonieux.

inherent, *inhĕ'rĕnt*, a. inhérent || –ly, ad. par inhérence.

inherit, *in hĕr'it*, v. a. hériter.

inheritance, *in hĕr'it ăns*, s. héritage, patrimoine, m.

inheritor, *in hĕr'it ẽr*, s. héritier, m.

inhibit, *in hib'it*, v. a. prohiber. [taller.

inhospitable, *in hŏs'pi tă bl*, a. inhospitalier.

inhospitality, *in hŏs'pi tăl'i ti*, s. inhospitalité, f. [humain(ement).

inhuman, *in hū'măn*, a. (–ly, ad.) inhumain.

inhumanity, *in hū măn'i ti*, s. inhumanité, f.

inhume, *in hūm'*, v. a. inhumer. [f.

inimical, *in im'i kăl*, a. (–ly, ad.) ennemi || hostile(ment) || en ennemi.

inimitable, *in im'i tă bl*, a. inimitable.

iniquitous, *in ik'wi tŭs*, a. inique, injuste.

iniquity, *in ik'wi ti*, s. iniquité, injustice.

initial, *in ish'ăl*, s. initiale, f. [f.

initial, *in ish'ăl*, a. (–ly, ad.) initial(ement) || au commencement.

initiate, *in ish'i at*, v. a. initier.

initiation, *in ish i ā'shŭn*, s. initiation, f.

inject, *in jĕkt'*, v. a. injecter || entasser.

injection, *in jĕk'shŭn*, s. injection, f. || lavement, m.

injudicious, *in jŏŏ dish'ŭs*, a. injudicieux || –ly, ad. sans jugement.

injunction, *in jŭngk'shŭn*, s. injonction, f.

injure, *in'jŏŏr*, v. a. faire tort, injurier, nuire || –d (in one's feelings), outragé.

injurious, *in jŏ'ri ŭs*, a. injurieux || nuisible || –ly, ad. injurieusement.

injury, *in'jŏŏ ri*, s. injustice, f. || tort, m. || atteinte, f. [f.

injustice, *in jŭs'tis*, s. injustice, iniquité,

ink, *ingk*, s. encre, f.

ink, *ingk*, v. a. tacher d'encre.

inkling, *ingk'ling*, s. avis, vent, m.

inkstand, *ingk'stănd*, s. encrier, m.

inky, *ingk'i*, a. d'encre || taché d'encre || noir comme de l'encre.

inlaid, *in lād'*, a. marqueté, parqueté.

inland, *in'lănd*, s. intérieur, m. || intérieur du pays, m.

inland, *in'lănd*, a. intérieur || ~ duty, s. octroi, m. || ~ revenue, s. revenus de l'intérieur, m. pl. || ~ trade, s. commerce intérieur, m.

inlay, *in lā'*, v. a. te marqueter.

inlet, *in'lĕt*, s. entrée, f., passage, m., voie, f. [m.

inmate, *in'māt*, s. pensionnaire, locataire,

inmost, *in'mōst*, a. le plus intérieur.

inn, *in*, s. auberge, hôtellerie, f. || ~ of court, collège d'avocats, m. || ~-keeper, s. hôtelier, aubergiste, m.

innate, *in năt'*, a. inné, naturel.

innavigable, *in năv'i gă bl*, a. innavigable.

inner, *in'nẽr*, a. intérieur.

inning, *in'ning*, s. (of grain) rentrée, f. || –s, s. pl. (at cricket) tour, m.

innocence, *in'nō sĕns*, s. innocence, f.

innocent, *in'nō sĕnt*, s. innocent, m. || pur, m. || idiot, m.

innocent, *in'nō sĕnt*, a. innocent || pur || idiot || –ly, ad. innocemment, niaisement.

innocuous, *in nŏk'ū ŭs*, a. innocent || –ly, ad. sans nuire. [f.

innovation, *in nō vā'shŭn*, s. innovation,

innovator, *in'nō vā tẽr*, s. novateur, m.

innuendo, *in nū ĕn'dō*, s. allusion, insinuation, f. [brable.

innumerable, *in nū'mẽr ă bl*, a. innombrable.

inoculate, *in ŏk'ū lāt*, v. a. inoculer.

inoculation, *in ŏk ū lā'shŭn*, s. inoculation, f.

inodorous, *in ō'dẽr ŭs*, a. inodore.

inoffensive, *in ŏf fĕn'siv*, a. inoffensif.

inoperative, *in ŏp'ẽr ā tiv*, a. inefficace.

inopportune, *in ŏp'pŏr tūn*, a. (–ly, ad.) mal à propos.

inordinate, *in ŏr'di năt*, a. (–ly, ad.) déréglé || irrégulier || irrégulièrement.

inorganic, *in ŏr găn'ik*, a. inorganique.

inquire, *in kwīr'*, v. a. & n. s'enquérir, s'informer, examiner || to ~ after, se renseigner sur, s'informer de.

inquiry, *in kwī'ri*, s. enquête, recherche, f., examen, m. || ~-office, s. bureau de renseignements, m. || to make inquiries, faire des recherches.

inquisition, *ing kwi zish'ŭn*, s. perquisition, f. || inquisition, f.

inquisitive, *in kwiz'i tiv*, a. curieux || –ly, ad. avec curiosité.

inroad, *in'rōd*, s. incursion, invasion, f.

insane, *in sān'*, a. insensé, fou || –ly, ad. follement || en aliéné.

insanity, *in săn'i ti*, s. folie, démence, f.

insatiable, *in sā'shi ă bl*, a. insatiable || vorace.

inscribe, *in skrīb'*, v. a. inscrire, dédier.

inscription, *in skrip'shŭn*, s. inscription, f.

inscrutable, *in skrō'tă bl*, a. inscrutable.

insect, *in'sĕkt*, s. insecte, m. || ~-destroyer, s. insecticide, m. [vora-

insectivorous, *in sĕk tiv'ō rŭs*, a. insectivore.

insecure, *in sē kūr'*, a. pas or peu sûr.

insecurity, *in sē kū'ri ti*, s. insécurité, incertitude, f., danger, m.

insensate, *in sĕn'sāt*, a. insensé.

insensibility, *in sĕn si bil'i ti*, s. insensibilité, f. || stupidité, f.

insensible, *in sĕn'si bl*, a. insensible.

insensibly, *in sĕn'si bli*, ad. insensiblement.

inseparable, *in sĕp'ăr ă bl*, a. inséparable.

inseparably, *in sĕp'ăr ă bli*, ad. inséparablement.

insert, *in sẽrt'*, v. a. insérer.

insertion, *in sẽr'shŭn*, s. insertion, f.

inside, *in'sid*, s. intérieur, m.

inside, *in'sid*, a. intérieur.

insidious, *in sid'i ŭs*, a. insidieux || –ly, ad. insidieusement. [profonde, f.

insight, *in'sit*, s. inspection, connaissance

insignia, *in sig'ni ă*, s. insignes, m. pl.

insignificant, *in sig nif'i kănt*, a. insignifiant || –ly, ad. sans importance.

insincere, *in sin sēr'*, a. peu sincère || faux, trompeur || –ly, ad. sans sincérité.

insincerity, *in sin sĕr'i ti*, s. manque de sincérité, m.

insinuate, *in sin'ū ăt,* v. a. insinuer, suggérer. [tion, f.
insinuation, *in sin ū ā'shŭn,* s. insinuation.
insipid, *in sip'id,* a. (-ly, ad.) insipide (ment) || fade.
insipidity, *in sip id'i ti,* s. insipidité, f.
insist, *in sist',* v. n. insister, persister.
insolence, *in'sō lĕns,* s. insolence, f.
insolent, *in'sō lĕnt,* a. insolent || -ly, ad. insolement. [lité, f.
insolbility, *in sŏl'ū bil i ti,* s. insolubilité, f.
insoluble, *in sŏl'ū bl,* a. insoluble. [f.
insolvency, *in sŏl'vĕn si,* s. insolvabilité, f.
insolvent, *in sŏl'vĕnt,* a. insolvable.
insomuch, *in sō mŭch',* ad. tellement, de sorte que. [veiller, examiner.
inspect, *in spĕkt',* v. a. inspecter, surveiller.
inspection, *in spĕk'shŭn,* s. inspection, surveillance, f.
inspector, *in spĕk'tĕr,* s. inspecteur, m.
inspiration, *in spi rā'shŭn,* s. inspiration, f. || respiration, f. [respirer.
inspire, *in spir',* v. a. inspirer, suggérer ||
inspirit, *in spir'it,* v. a. animer, encourager.
instability, *in stă bil'i ti,* s. instabilité, f.
install, *in stăŭl',* v. a. installer.
installation, *in stăŭl lā'shŭn,* **instalment,** *in stăŭl'mĕnt,* s. installation, f. || payement à terme, m.
instance, *in'stăns,* s. sollicitation, f. || circonstance, f. || for ~, par exemple || at the ~ of, à la requête de.
instance, *in'stăns,* v. n. citer pour exemple.
instant, *in'stănt,* s. moment, m.
instant, *in'stănt,* a. pressant || courant || -ly, ad. instamment. [ad.] instantané(ment).
instantaneous, *in stăn tā'ni ŭs,* a. (-ly, ad.)
instead, *in stĕd',* pr. au lieu de.
instep, *in'stĕp,* s. coude-pied, m.
instigate, *in'sti găt,* v. a. instiguer, exciter.
instigation, *in sti gā'shŭn,* s. instigation, f.
instigator, *in'sti gā tĕr,* s. instigateur, m.
instil, *in stil',* v. a. instiller || inculquer.
instinct, *in'stingkt,* s. instinct, m.
instinct, *in stingkt',* a. animé.
instinctive, *in stingk'tiv,* a. instinctif || -ly, ad. par instinct. [cepte, m.
institute, *in'sti tūt,* s. institut, m. || pré-
institute, *in'sti tūt,* v. a. instituer, établir, fonder.
institution, *in sti tū'shŭn,* s. institution, f.
instruct, *in strŭkt',* v. a. instruire, enseigner. [f., enseignement, m.
instruction, *in strŭk'shŭn,* s. instruction,
instructive, *in strŭk'tiv,* a. instructif || -ly, ad. d'une manière instructive.
instructor, *in strŭk'tĕr,* s. instituteur, m. || (mil.) instructeur, m.
instrument, *in'strŏ mĕnt,* s. instrument, m. || outil, m. || (jur.) acte, m.
instrumental, *in strŏ mĕn'tăl,* a. instrumental. [instrumentiste, m.
instrumentalist, *in strŏ mĕn'tăl ist,* s.
instrumentality, *in strŏ mĕn tăl'i ti,* s. moyen, m. || agence, f. || cause, f. || action, f. || coopération, f.

insubordinate, *in sŭb ŏr'di năt,* a. insubordonné. [insubordination, f.
insubordination, *in sŭb ŏr di nā'shŭn,* s.
insufferable, *in sŭf'fĕr ă bl,* a. intolérable, insupportable.
insufferably, *in sŭf'fĕr ă bli,* ad. d'une manière insupportable. [fisance, f.
insufficiency, *in sŭf fish'ĕn si,* s. insuffisance, f.
insufficient, *in sŭf fish'ĕnt,* a. insuffisant || -ly, ad. insuffisamment.
insular, *in'sū lĕr,* a. insulaire.
insulate, *in'sū lăt,* v. a. isoler.
insult, *in'sŭlt,* s. insulte, f.
insult, *in sŭlt',* v. a. insulter. [sulte, m.
insulter, *in sŭlt'ĕr,* s. auteur d'une insulte.
insultingly, *in sŭlt'ing li,* a. insolemment.
insuperable, *in sū'pĕr ă bl,* a. insurmontable. [ciblement.
insuperably, *in sū'pĕr ă bli,* ad. invinciblement.
insupportable, *in sŭp pŏr'tă bl,* a. insupportable. [supportablement.
insupportably, *in sŭp pŏr'tă bli,* a. insupportablement.
insurance, *in shō'răns,* s. assurance, f. || marine ~, assurance sur la vie, f. || fire ~, assurance contre l'incendie || to effect an ~, assurer, faire assurer.
insure, *in shŏr',* v. a. assurer. [m.
insurgent, *in sĕr'jĕnt,* s. insurgé, révolté,
insurmountable, *in sĕr mŏwn'tă bl,* a. insurmontable. [tion, f.
insurrection, *in sĕr rĕk'shŭn,* s. insurrection.
insurrectionary, *in sĕr rĕk'shŭn ĕr i,* a. insurrectionnel.
intact, *in tăkt',* a. intact.
intangible, *in tăn'ji bl,* a. intangible.
integral, *in'tĕ grăl,* s. totalité, f.
integral, *in'tĕ grăl,* a. intégral, entier || (chim.) intégrant || -ly, ad. intégralement. [f.
integrity, *in tĕg'ri ti,* s. intégrité, probité,
integument, *in tĕg'ū mĕnt,* s. tégument, f.
intellect, *in'tĕl lĕkt,* s. intellect, m. [m.
intellectual, *in tĕl lĕk'tū ăl,* a. intellectuel.
intelligence, *in tĕl'li jĕns,* s. intelligence, nouvelle, f., avis, rapport, m. || ~ office, s. bureau de renseignements.
intelligencer, *in tĕl'li jĕn sĕr,* s. nouvelliste, m.
intelligent, *in tĕl'li jĕnt,* a. intelligent.
intelligible, *in tĕl'li ji bl,* a. intelligible, clair. [ment.
intelligibly, *in tĕl'li ji bli,* ad. intelligiblement.
intemperate, *in tĕm'pĕr ăt,* a. immodéré || -ly, ad. avec intempérance.
intend, *in tĕnd',* v. a. se proposer.
intended, *in tĕnd'ĕd,* a. projeté || intentionnel.
intense, *in tĕns',* a. intense, véhément || fort, excessif || -ly, ad. intensivement.
intensify, *in tĕn'si fi,* v. a. renforcer.
intensity, *in tĕn'si ti,* s. grande attention, intensité, f. [s. intention, f.
intent, *in tĕnt',* **intention,** *in tĕn'shŭn,*
intent, *in tĕnt',* a. appliqué, attentif || to be ~ on, être acharné à || -ly, ad. très attentivement.

intentional, *ĭn tĕn′ shŭn ăl,* a. intentionnel || **-ly,** ad. avec intention.

intentioned, *ĭn tĕn′ shŭnd,* a. intentionné.

inter, *ĭn tẽr′,* v. a. enterrer.

intercede, *ĭn tẽr sēd′,* v. n. passer entre || intercéder. [arrêter.

intercept, *ĭn tẽr sĕpt′,* v. a. intercepter.

intercession, *ĭn tẽr sĕsh′ŭn,* s. intercession, médiation, f.

intercessor, *ĭn tẽr sĕs′ sẽr,* s. médiateur, m.

interchange, *ĭn′ tẽr chānj,* s. change, échange, m.

interchange, *ĭn′ tẽr chānj,* v. a. échanger.

intercourse, *ĭn′ tẽr kōrs,* s. commerce, m. || communication, f.

interdict, *ĭn tẽr dĭkt′,* v. a. interdire.

interdiction, *ĭn tẽr dĭk′ shŭn,* s. interdit, m. || interdiction, f.

interest, *ĭn′ tẽr ĕst,* s. intérêt, profit, m. || intérêts, m. pl. || crédit, m. || influence, f. || **to be to one's ~,** agir dans l'intérêt de qn. || **~-ticket,** s. coupon, m.

interest, *ĭn′ tẽr ĕst,* v. a. intéresser || (com.) être intéressé dans || toucher, émouvoir.

interesting, *ĭn′ tẽr ĕst ĭng,* a. intéressant.

interfere, *ĭn tẽr fēr′,* v. a. s'entremêler || contrarier. [tion, f.

interference, *ĭn tẽr fē′ rĕns,* s. interven

interim, *ĭn′ tẽr ĭm,* s. intérim, entre-temps.

interior, *ĭn tē′ rĭ ẽr,* s. intérieur, m. [m.

interior, *ĭn tē′ rĭ ẽr,* a. intérieur.

interjection, *ĭn tẽr jĕk′ shŭn,* s. (gr.) interjection, f.

interlard, *ĭn tẽr lärd′,* v. a. entrelarder.

interlocution, *ĭn tẽr lō kū′ shŭn,* s. interlocution, f., dialogue, m.

interloper, *ĭn′ tẽr lō pẽr,* s. (com.) courtier-marron, m.

interlude, *ĭn′ tẽr lūd,* s. intermède, m.

intermarriage, *ĭn tẽr măr′ rĭj,* s. intermariage, m.

intermarry, *ĭn tẽr măr′ rĭ,* v. n. s'unir par un double mariage || ~, v. a. contracter un second mariage.

intermediate, *ĭn tẽr mē′ dĭ ăt,* a. intermédiaire || ~ space, s. (rail.) entre-voie, f.

interment, *ĭn tẽr′ mĕnt,* s. enterrement, m.

interminable, *ĭn tẽr′ mĭn ăbl,* a. illimité.

intermingle, *ĭn tẽr mĭng′ gl,* v. a. & n. (s')entremêler || se mêler.

intermission, *ĭn tẽr mĭsh′ ŭn,* s. intermission, interruption, f. [tent.

intermittent, *ĭn tẽr mĭt′ tĕnt,* a. intermit

internal, *ĭn tẽr′ năl,* a. interne || **-ly,** ad. intérieurement. [pellation, f.

interpellation, *ĭn tẽr pĕl lā′ shŭn,* s. inter

interpolate, *ĭn tẽr′ pō lāt,* v. a. interpoler, intercaler. [polation, f.

interpolation, *ĭn tẽr pō lā′ shŭn,* s. inter

interpose, *ĭn tẽr pōz′,* v. a. & n. interposer || s'interposer, intervenir.

interposition, *ĭn tẽr pō zĭsh′ ŭn,* s. interposition, intervention, f.

interpret, *ĭn tẽr′ prĕt,* v. a. interpréter.

interpretation, *ĭn tẽr prĕ tā′ shŭn,* s. interprétation, f.

interpreter, *ĭn tẽr′ prĕ tẽr,* s. interprète, m.

interregnum, *ĭn tẽr rĕg′ nŭm,* s. interrègne, m. [roger.

interrogate, *ĭn tẽr′ rō gāt,* v. a. & n. inter

interrogation, *ĭn tẽr rō gā′ shŭn,* s. interrogation, question, f.

interrogative, *ĭn tẽr rŏg′ ă tĭv,* a. interrogatory, *ĭn tẽr rŏg′ ă tẽr,* a. interrogatif. [rogatoire, m.

interrogatory, *ĭn tẽr rŏg′ ă tẽr i,* s. inter

interrupt, *ĭn tẽr rŭpt′,* v. a. interrompre.

interruptedly, *ĭn tẽr rŭp′ tĕd lĭ,* ad. avec interruption.

interruption, *ĭn tẽr rŭp′ shŭn,* s. interruption, f. [tion, f.

intersect, *ĭn tẽr sĕkt′,* v. a. & n. entrecouper || se croiser.

intersection, *ĭn tẽr sĕk′ shŭn,* s. intersec

intersperse, *ĭn tẽr spẽrs′,* v. a. entremêler.

interstice, *ĭn tẽr stĭs,* s. interstice, intervalle, m.

intertwine, *ĭn tẽr twīn′,* v. a. entrelacer.

interval, *ĭn′ tẽr văl,* s. intervalle, m. || **at ~s,** par intervalles.

intervene, *ĭn tẽr vēn′,* v. n. intervenir, survenir. [tion, médiation, f.

intervention, *ĭn tẽr vĕn′ shŭn,* s. interven

interview, *ĭn′ tẽr vū,* s. entrevue, f.

intestate, *ĭn tĕs′ tāt,* a. intestat.

intestinal, *ĭn tĕs′ tĭ năl,* a. intestinal.

intestine, *ĭn tĕs′ tĭn,* s. intestin, m.

intestine, *ĭn tĕs′ tĭn,* a. intestin.

inthral, *ĭn thrăwl′,* v. a. assujettir.

inthralment, *ĭn thrăwl′ mĕnt,* s. esclavage, m.

intimacy, *ĭn′ tĭ mă sĭ,* s. intimité, f.

intimate, *ĭn′ tĭ māt,* s. ami intime, m.

intimate, *ĭn′ tĭ māt,* v. n. donner à entendre. [(ment.

intimate, *ĭn′ tĭ māt,* a. (-ly, ad.) intime

intimation, *ĭn tĭ mā′ shŭn,* s. avis, m.

intimidate, *ĭn tĭm′ ĭ dāt,* v. a. intimider.

into, *ĭn′ tŏ,* pr. en, dans, dedans, entre.

intolerable, *ĭn tŏl′ ẽr ăbl,* a. intolérable ||

intolerably, *ĭn tŏl′ ẽr ă blĭ,* ad. intolérablement.

intolerance, *ĭn tŏl′ ẽr ăns,* s. intolérance, f.

intolerant, *ĭn tŏl′ ẽr ănt,* a. intolérant.

intonation, *ĭn tō nā′ shŭn,* s. intonation, f.

intone, *ĭn tōn′,* v. a. entonner.

intoxicate, *ĭn tŏks′ ĭ kāt,* v. a. enivrer.

intoxication, *ĭn tŏks ĭ kā′ shŭn,* s. ivresse, f. || enivrement, m. [indocile.

intractable, *ĭn trăk′ tă bl,* a. intraitable ||

intransitive, *ĭn trăn′ sĭ tĭv,* a. (gr.) intransitif. [retrancher.

intrench, *ĭn trĕnsh′,* v. a. envahir || (mil.)

intrenchment, *ĭn trĕnsh′ mĕnt,* s. retranchement, m.

intrepid, *ĭn trĕp′ ĭd,* a. intrépide || **-ly,** ad. avec intrépidité.

intrepidity, *ĭn trĕ pĭd′ ĭ tĭ,* s. intrépidité, hardiesse, f. [ficulté, f.

intricacy, *ĭn′ trĭ kă sĭ,* s. embarras, m., dif

intricate, *ĭn′ trĭ kāt,* a. embrouillé, compliqué || **-ly,** ad. d'une manière embrouillée.

intrigue, *ĭn trēg′,* s. intrigue, f.

intrigue, *ĭn trēg′,* v. n. intriguer.

---

lāte, hăt, fār, lăw; — hēre, gĕt, hẽr; — mīne, ĭnn; — nō, hŏt, prōve; — hōw; —

intrinsic, *in trin'sik*, a. (-ally, ad.) intrinsèque(ment).

introduce, *in trō dūs'*, v. a. introduire.

introduction, *in trō dŭk'shŭn*, s. introduction, préface, f. [naire.

introductory, *in trō dŭk'tĕr ĭ*, a. préliminaire.

intrude, *in trŏd'*, v. n. s'ingérer, se fourrer.

intruder, *in trŏ'dĕr*, s intrus, importun, m.

intrusion, *in trŏ'zhŭn*, s. importunité, f.

intrust, *in trŭst'*, v. a. confier.

intuition, *in tū ish'ŭn*, s. intuition, f.

intuitive, *in tū'ĭ tĭv*, a. intuitif, contemplatif || -ly, ad. par intuition.

inundate, *in'ŭn dāt* ou *in ŭn'dāt*, v. a. inonder, submerger.

inundation, *in ŭn dā'shŭn*, s. inondation, f., débordement, m.

inure, *in ūr'*, v. a. accoutumer || endurcir.

inutility, *in ū til'ĭ tĭ*, s. inutilité, f.

invade, *in vād'*, v. a. envahir, attaquer.

invader, *in vā'dĕr*, s. envahisseur, f.

invalid, *in vă lēd'*, s. invalide, m.

invalid, *in văl'ĭd*, a. invalide, faible || invalable, nul. [valide || annuler.

invalidate, *in văl'ĭ dāt*, v. a. rendre invalidity, *in vă lid'ĭ tĭ*, s. invalidité, f. || nullité, f.

invaluable, *in văl'ŭ ā bl*, a. inestimable.

invariable, *in vā'rĭ ā bl*, a. invariable.

invariablement, *in vā'rĭ ā blĭ*, ad. invariablement. [tion, f.

invasion, *in vā'zhŭn*, s. invasion, irruptive, *in vĕk'tĭv*, s. invective, f.

inveigh, *in vā'*, v a. invectiver.

inveigle, *in vē'gl*, v. a. enjôler, séduire.

invent, *in vĕnt'*, v. a. inventer.

invention, *in vĕn'shŭn*, s. invention, f.

inventive, *in vĕn'tĭv*, a. inventif.

inventory, *in'vĕn tĕr ĭ*, s. inventaire, m.

inverse, *in vĕrs'*, a. (-ly, ad.) inverse (ment).

inversion, *in vĕr'shŭn*, s. inversion, f.

invert, *in vĕrt'*, v. a. renverser.

invertebrate, *in vĕr'tĕ brāt*, a. invertébré.

invest, *in vĕst'*, v. a. revêtir || investir || placer. [examiner.

investigate, *in vĕs'tĭ gāt*, v. a. chercher,

investigation, *in vĕs tĭ gā'shŭn*, s. investigation, f. || perquisition, f.

investiture, *in vĕs'tĭ tūr*, s. investiture, f.

investment, *in vĕst'mĕnt*, s. vêtement, m. || placement, m. [m.

inveteracy, *in vĕt'ĕr ā sĭ*, s. mal invétéré.

inveterate, *in vĕt'ĕr āt*, a. invétéré.

invidious, *in vid'ĭ ŭs*, a. envieux, odieux || -ly, ad. odieusement. [ranimer.

invigorate, *in vig'ō rāt*, v. a. fortifier,

invincible, *in vin'sĭ bl*, a. invincible.

invincibly, *in vin'sĭ blĭ*, ad. invincibleement.

inviolable, *in vī'ō lā bl*, a. inviolable.

inviolate, *in vī'ō lāt*, a. intact.

invisibility, *in viz ĭ bil'ĭ tĭ*, s. invisibilité,

invisible, *in viz'ĭ bl*, a. invisible. [f.

invisibly, *in viz't blĭ*, ad. invisiblement.

invitation, *in vĭ tā'shŭn*, s. invitation, f.

invite, *in vīt'*, v. a. inviter.

inviting, *in vī'ting*, a. séduisant.

invocation, *in vō kā'shŭn*, s. invocation, f.

invoice, *in'vŏys*, s. (com.) facture, f. || second ~, solde, m.

invoice, *in'vŏys*, v. a. facturer.

involuntarily, *in vŏl'ŭn tăr ĭ lĭ*, ad. involontairement. [taire.

involuntary, *in vŏl'ŭn tăr ĭ*, a. involontaire.

involve, *in vŏlv'*, v. a. envelopper || comprendre || impliquer. [nérable.

invulnerable, *in vŭl'nĕr ā bl*, a. invulnérable.

inward, *in'wĕrd*, a. interne, intérieur.

inward(ly), *in'wĕrd(lĭ)*, inwards, *in'wĕrdz*, ad. intérieurement, en dedans.

iota, *ī ō'tă*, s. iota, m.

irascible, *ĭ răs'sĭ bl*, a. irascible.

ire, *ir*, s. colère, f., courroux, m.

iridescent, *ĭ rĭ dĕs'sĕnt*, a. iridescent || ~ ore, s. métal iridescent, m.

iris, *ī'rĭs*, s. iris, m. || arc-en-ciel, m.

irk, *ĕrk*, v. a. fâcher.

irksome, *ĕrk'sŭm*, a. fâcheux, ennuyeux.

iron, *ī'rn*, s. fer, m. || fer à repasser, m. || -s, s. pl. chaînes, f. pl. || cast-~, fer de fonte, m.

iron, *ī'rn*, v. a. repasser || mettre aux fers.

iron, *ī'rn*, a. de fer || sévère || ~-ware, s. quincaillerie, f. || ~-works, s. pl. fonderie de fer, f. || forge, f.

ironclad, *ī'rn klăd*, s. (mar.) cuirassé, blindé, m.

ironic(al), *ī rŏn'ik (ăl)*, a. || -ly, ad. ironique(ment). [taillaudier, m.

ironmonger, *ī'rn mŭng gĕr*, s. ferronnier,

irony, *ī'rŏn ĭ*, s. ironie, f. [éclairer.

irradiate, *ir rā'dĭ āt*, v. a. rayonner,

irrational, *ir răsh'ŭn ăl*, a. irraisonable.

irreclaimable, *ir rē klām'ā bl*, a. irréformable, irréparable. [cable.

irreconcilable, *ir rĕk ŏn sĭl'ā bl*, a. implacable.

irrecoverable, *ir rē kŭv'ĕr ā bl*, a. irréparable. [tissable.

irredeemable, *ir rē dēm'ā bl*, a. non amortissable.

irrefragable, *ir rĕf'rā gā bl*, a. irréfragable.

irrefutable, *ir rē fū'tā bl*, a. incontestable.

irregular, *ir rĕg'ū lĕr*, a. irrégulier || -ly, ad. irrégulièrement. [rité, f.

irregularity, *ir rĕg ū lăr'ĭ tĭ*, s. irrégularité, f.

irrelevant, *ir rĕl'ĕ vănt*, a. inapplicable.

irreligion, *ir rē lĭj'ŭn*, s. irréligion, impiété, f.

irreligious, *ir rē lĭj'ŭs*, a. irréligieux || -ly, ad. irréligieusement. [diable.

irremediable, *ir rē mē'dĭ ā bl*, a. irremédiable.

irremediably, *ir rē mē'dĭ ā blĭ*, a. irremédiablement. [sible.

irremissible, *ir rē mĭs'sĭ bl*, a. irrémissible.

irremovable, *ir rē mōv'ā bl*, a. inamovible.

irreparable, *ir rĕp'ā rā bl*, a. irréparable.

irreproachable, *ir rē prŏch'ā bl*, a. irréprochable.

irresistible, *ir rē zĭs'tĭ bl*, a. irrésistible.

irresistibly, *ir rē zĭs'tĭ blĭ*, ad. irrésistiblement. [(ment).

irresolute, *ir rĕz'ō lŏt*, a. (-ly, ad.) irrésolu

irresolution, *ir rĕz ō lō'shŭn*, s. irrésolution, f.

irrespective, ĭr rĕ spĕk' tĭv, a. sans égard à.
irresponsibility, ĭr rĕ spŏn sĭ bŭ' ĭ tĭ, s. irresponsabilité, f.
irresponsible, ĭr rĕ spŏn' sĭ bl, a. irresponsable. |rable.
irretrievable, ĭr rĕ trē vă bl, a. irréparable.
irretrievably, ĭr rĕ trē vă blĭ, ad. irréparablement. |f.
irreverence, ĭr rĕv' ĕr ĕns, s. irrévérence, f.
irreverent, ĭr rĕv' ĕr ĕnt, a. irrévérent |
  -ly, ad. irrévéremment.
irrevocable, ĭr rĕv' ō kă bl, a. irrévocable.
irrigate, ĭr' rĭ gāt, v. a. arroser.
irrigation, ĭr rĭ gā' shŭn, s. arrosement, m.
irritability, ĭr rĭ tă bĭl' ĭ tĭ, s. irritabilité, f.
irritable, ĭr' rĭ tă bl, a. irritable.   [m.
irritant, ĭr' rĭ tănt, s. irritant, stimulant
irritate, ĭr' rĭ tāt, v. a. irriter.   [sion, f.
irruption, ĭr rŭp' shŭn, s. irruption, invasion, f.
isinglass, ī' zing glâs, s. colle de poisson, f.
island, ī' lănd, s. île, f.
islander, ī' lănd ĕr, s. insulaire, m.
isle, ĭl, s. île, f.
islet, ī' lĕt, s. îlot, m.
isolate, ī' sō lāt, v. a. isoler.
isolation, ī sō lā' shŭn, s. isolement m.
issue, ĭsh' ū, s. issue, sortie, f. || conclusion, f. || émission, f. || publication, f. || succès, événement, m. || cautère, m. || postérité, f. || to die without -, mourir sans postérité || to join -, être d'un avis contraire.
issue, ĭsh' ū, v. a. & n. publier, distribuer, envoyer || sortir, provenir, émettre || descendre de.
isthmus, ĭsth' mŭs ou ĭs' mŭs, s. isthme, m.
it, ĭt, pn. il, elle, le, la, cela.
Italian warehouse, ĭ tăl' yăn wâr' hŏŭs, s. magasin de pâtes d'Italie, m. || charcuterie, f. || -man, s. marchand de comestibles fins, m.
italic, ĭ tăl' ĭk, s. caractère italique, m. || -s, s. pl. italiques, m. pl.
italic, ĭ tăl' ĭk, a. italique.
itch, ĭch, s. gale, f. || démangeaison, f.
itch, ĭch, v. n. démanger.
item, ī' tĕm, s. article, m.
item, ī' tĕm, ad. item, de plus.
itinerant, ī tĭn' ĕr ănt, a. ambulant.
itinerary, ī tĭn' ĕr ĕr ĭ, s. itinéraire, m.
itinerary, ī tĭn' ĕr ĕr ĭ, a. voyageant.
its, ĭts, pn. son, sa, ses.
itself, ĭt sĕlf', pn. soi-même, elle-même || to go of -, aller tout seul.
ivory, ī' vō rĭ, s. ivoire, m. || -black, s. noir d'ivoire, m.
ivory, ī' vō rĭ, a. d'ivoire.
ivy, ī' vĭ, s. (bot.) lierre, m.

J.

jabber, jăb' bĕr, v. n. bavarder, babiller.
jabberer, jăb' bĕr ĕr, s. bavard, m.
jack, jăk, s. tourne-broche || tire-botte, m. || jeune brochet, m. || chevalet, m. || outre,

f. || broc, m. || cochonnet, m. || cric, m. || matelot, m. || (mar.) pavillon de beaupré, m. || Union-Jack, le pavillon anglais
  ~ in the box, s. boîte à surprise, f.
  ~ of all trades, s. maître Jacques, m.
  ~ o'lantern, s. feu follet, m. || ~-tar, s. (fam.) loup de mer, m.
jackal, jăk' ăŭl, s. chacal, m.   [sot, m.
jackanapes, jăk' ă năps, s. singe, m. |
jackass, jăk' ăs, s. âne, baudet, m. || ~-boots, s. pl. grosses bottes, f. pl.
jackdaw, jăk' dăw, s. choucas, m.
jacket, jăk' ĕt, s. jaquette, veste, f.
jade, jād, s. rosse, f.
jaded, jā' dĕd, a. éreinté, aux abois.
jag, jăg, s. denteleur, f.
jag, jăg, v. a. denteler, ébrécher.
jagged, jăg' gĕd, a. dentelé.
jail, jāl, s. prison, f., donjon, m. || ~-bird, s. prisonnier, gibier de potence, m.
jailor, jāl' ĕr, s. geôlier, m.
jam, jăm, s. marmelade, f.
jam, jăm, v. a. serrer, presser.
jangle, jăng' gl, v. n. quereller.
janissary, jăn' ĭs sĕr ĭ, s. janissaire, m.
janitor, jăn' ĭ tĕr, s. appariteur(d'université)
January, jăn' ū ĕr ĭ, s. janvier, m.   [m.
japan, jă păn', s. laque, m.
japan, jă păn', v. a. vernir, vernisser.
jar, jăr, s. cliquetis, m. || contestation, dispute, f. || cruche, f. || bouteille électrique, f., pot, m.
jar, jăr, v. n. cliqueter || se quereller.
jargon, jăr' gŏn, s. jargon, baragouin, m.
jasmine, jăs' mĭn, s. (bot.) jasmin, m.
jasper, jăs' pĕr, s. jaspe, m.
jaundice, jăwn' dĭs, s. jaunisse, f.
jaundiced, jăwn' dĭst, a. atteint de jaunisse
jaunt, jăwnt, s. excursion, f.
javelin, jăv' lĭn, s. javelin, m.
jaw, jăw, s. mâchoire, f. || ~-bone, s. mâchoire, f. || ~-tooth, s. dent mâchelière, f.
jay, jā, s. geai, vautrot, m.   [lière, f.
jealous, jĕl' ŭs, a. jaloux, envieux.
jealousy, jĕl' ŭs ĭ, s. jalousie, f.
jeer, jēr, s. raillerie, moquerie, f.
jeer, jēr, v. a. & n. railler, moquer.
jelly, jĕl' lĭ, s. gelée, f. || ~-broth, s. consommé, m.   [risquer.
jeopardise, jĕp' ĕr dĭs, v. a. hasarder,
jeopardy, jĕp' ĕr dĭ, s. coup d'audace, m.
jerk, jĕrk, s. saccade, secousse, f.
jerk, jĕrk, v. a. secouer, jeter, saccader.
jessamine, jĕs' ă mĭn, s. jasmin, m.
jest, jĕst, s. raillerie, plaisanterie, f.
jester, jĕst' ĕr, s. railleur, plaisant, m.
jestingly, jĕst' ĭng lĭ, ad. pour plaisanter.
Jesuit, jĕz' ū ĭt, s. jésuite, m. || ~'s-bark, s. (bot.) écorce du Pérou, f.
jesuitical, jĕs ū ĭt' ĭk ăl, a. jésuitique.
jet, jĕt, s. jais, m. || jet d'eau, m. || ~-black, a. noir comme du jais.
jetsome, jĕt' sŭm, s. épaves maritimes, f. pl.
jetty, jĕt' ĭ, s. jetée, f.   [barde, f.
Jew, jō, s. juif, m. || ~'s harp, s. guimbarde, f.
jewel, jō' ĕl, s. joyau, bijou, m. || ~-case, s. écrin, m.

jeweller, *jŏ'ĕl ĕr,* s. bijoutier, m.

jewelry, *jŏ'ĕl ri,* s. joaillerie, f.

Jewess, *jŏ'ĕs,* s. juive, f.

Jewish, *jŏ'ish,* a. judaïque.

jewry, *jŏ'ri,* s. juiverie, f.

Jezebel, *jĕz'ĕ bĕl,* s. (fig.) pie-grièche, f.

jib, *jĭb,* s. (mar.) foc, m. ‖ gigue (danse), f. ‖ ~-boom, s. (mar.) bâton de foc, m.

jig, *jĭg,* s. gigue, f.

jilt, *jĭlt,* s. coquette, f.

jilt, *jĭlt,* v. a. & n. duper ‖ coqueter.

jingle, *jĭng'gl,* s. tintement, m. ‖ clochette, f. [tinter, cliqueter.

jingle, *jĭng'gl,* v. a. & n. faire tinter ‖

job, *jŏb,* s. affaire, besogne, f., ouvrage, m., entreprise, f.

job, *jŏb,* v. a. & n. frapper ‖ tripoter ‖ agioter ‖ ~-master, s. loueur de voitures or de chevaux, m. ‖ ~-work, s. travail à forfait, à la tâche, m.

jobber, *jŏb'bĕr,* s. agioteur, m. ‖ ouvrier à la tâche, m. ‖ (fig.) faiseur, m. ‖ tripotier, m. [m. ‖ fripon, m.

jockey, *jŏk'ĭ,* s. jockey, m. ‖ maquignon,

jockey, *jŏk'ĭ,* v. a. tromper, duber.

jocose, *jō kōs',* a. (-ly, ad.) plaisant, jovial ‖ en plaisantant.

jocoseness, *jō kōs'nĕs,* **jocosity,** *jō kŏs'ĭ tĭ,* s. gaieté, plaisanterie, f.

jocular, *jŏk'ū lĕr,* a. (-ly, ad.) gai(ement), plaisant.

jocund, *jŏk'ŭnd,* a. gai, enjoué.

jog, *jŏg,* s. secousse, f. ‖ agitation, f. ‖ obstacle, m. ‖ ~-trot, s. petit trot, m.

jog, *jŏg,* v. a. & n. pousser, secouer, se mouvoir par secousses ‖ aller tout doucement.

John Dory, *jŏn dō'rĭ,* s. zée, m. (poisson).

join, *jŏyn,* v. a. & n. joindre, unir ‖ s'unir, s'accorder ‖ être contigu, toucher.

joiner, *jŏyn'ĕr,* s. menuisier m.

joinery, *jŏyn'ĕr ĭ,* s. menuiserie, f.

joint, *jŏynt,* s. jointure, articulation, f. ‖ charnière, f., pièce de viande ‖ out of ~, en désordre, dérangé ‖ to put one's . . out of ~, se disloquer le . . .

joint, *jŏynt,* v. a. couper dans la jointure ‖ joindre.

joint, *jŏynt,* a. réuni ‖ (in comp.) co . . ‖ -ly, ad. conjointement ‖ ~-stock, a. par actions ‖ anonyme ‖ ~-stock-company, s. société par actions, f.

jointure, *jŏyn'tūr,* s. (jur.) douaire, m.

joist, *jŏyst,* s. solive, f.

joke, *jōk,* s. raillerie, plaisanterie, f. ‖ to crack a ~, plaisanter ‖ to take a ~, se prêter à la plaisanterie ‖ he cannot take a ~, il n'entend pas raillerie ‖ practical ~, mauvaise plaisanterie.

joke, *jōk,* v. n. railler, plaisanter.

jollification, *jŏl lĭ fĭ kā'shŭn,* s. jubilation, noce, f.

jollity, *jŏl'lĭ tĭ,* s. gaieté, joie, f.

jolly, *jŏl'lĭ,* a. gai, enjoué ‖ ~-boat, s. petit canot, m.

jolt, *jōlt,* s. cahot, m., secousse, f.

jolt, *jōlt,* v. a. & n. cahoter.

jorum, *jōr'ŭm,* s. écuelle, jatte, f.

jostle, *jŏs'l,* v. a. pousser, heurter.

jot, *jŏt,* s. point, iota, m. ‖ brin, m.

jot, *jŏt,* v. a. (to ~ down) prendre note de.

journal, *jĕr'nāl,* s. journal, m.

journalism, *jĕr'nāl izm,* s. journalisme, m.

journalist, *jĕr'nāl ist,* s. journaliste, m.

journalistic, *jĕr'nāl is'tik,* a. de journaliste.

journey, *jĕr'ni,* s. voyage, m. ‖ to go on (come off) a ~, aller en (revenir de) voyage ‖ a pleasant ~! bon voyage!

journey, *jĕr'ni,* v. n. voyager.

journeyman, *jĕr'ni măn,* s. ouvrier, m. ‖ garçon, m.

joust, *jŏst,* s. joute, f.

joust, *jŏst,* v. n. jouter.

jovial, *jō'vĭ āl,* a. (-ly, ad.) jovial(ement).

joviality, *jō vĭ ăl'ĭ tĭ,* s. jovialité, gaieté, f.

joy, *jŏy,* s. joie, f., plaisir, m. ‖ to wish one ~, féliciter. [joyeusement.

joyful, *jŏy'fŏŏl,* a. (-ly, ad.) joyeux ‖

joyless, *jŏy'lĕs,* a. triste.

joyous, *jŏy'ŭs,* a. (-ly, ad.) *vide* **joyful.**

jubilant, *jō'bĭ lănt,* a. triomphant.

jubilation, *jō bĭ lā'shŭn,* s. jubilation, f.

jubilee, *jō'bĭ lē,* s. jubilé, m.

judaic, *jō dā'ik,* a. judaïque.

Judaism, *jō'dā izm,* s. judaïsme, m.

judge, *jŭj,* s. juge, m. ‖ arbitre, m.

judge, *jŭj,* v. a. & n. juger.

judg(e)ment, *jŭj'mĕnt,* s. jugement, avis, m. ‖ sens, m. ‖ to pass a ~, passer sentence ‖ to the best of my ~, à mon avis.

judicature, *jō dĭ kā tūr,* s. judicature, f.

judicial, *jō dish'āl,* a. (-ly, ad.) judiciaire (ment) ‖ juridique(ment).

judicious, *jō dish'ŭs,* a. judicieux, sensé ‖ -ly, ad. judicieusement.

jug, *jŭg,* s. cruche, f., pot, broc, m. ‖ ~-ged hare, s. civet de lièvre, m.

juggle, *jŭg'gl,* s. jonglerie, f.

juggle, *jŭg'gl,* v. n. faire le jongleur ‖ ~, v. a. duper ‖ tromper.

juggler, *jŭg'glĕr,* s. jongleur, m.

juice, *jōs,* s. jus, suc, m.

juiciness, *jō'sĭ nĕs,* s. abondance de jus, f.

juicy, *jō'sĭ,* a. juteux, succulent.

jujube, *jō'jōb,* s. jujube, m.

July, *jō lī',* s. juillet, m.

jumble, *jŭm'bl,* s. mélange confus, m.

jumble, *jŭm'bl,* v. a. confondre ‖ brouiller.

jump, *jŭmp,* s. saut, m. ‖ corset, m.

jump, *jŭmp,* v. n. sauter, franchir ‖ s'accorder ‖ to ~ up, se lever en sursaut.

junction, *jŭngk'shŭn,* s. jonction, union, f. ‖ (rail.) bifurcation, f.

juncture, *jŭngk'tūr,* s. jointure, conjoncture, f.

June, *jōn,* s. juin, m.

jungle, *jŭn'gl,* s. fourré, m.

junior, *jō'nĭ ĕr,* s. cadet, m.

junior, *jō'nĭ ĕr,* a. le plus jeune.

juniper, *jō'nĭ pĕr,* s. genièvre, m.

junk, *jŭngk,* s. jonque, f.

junket, *jŭng'kĕt,* s. régal en cachette, m.

junket, *jŭng'kĕt,* v. n. se régaler en cachette.

---

bŏy; — fŏŏt, tūbe, tŭb. ‖ chair, jŏy; — game, yes; — soul, zeal; — thing, there. English and French.

junketings, *jŭng'kĕt ings*, s. pl. bonne chère, f. || **to be on one's ~,** faire bonne chère || faire shoppage (**chiefly of la- dies).**

junta, *jŭn'tä* ou *jŏōn'tä*, s. junte, f.

juridical, *jŏ rĭd'ĭk ăl*, a. (**-ly,** ad.) juri- dique(ment).

jurisdiction, *jŏ rĭs dĭk'shŭn*, s. jurisdic- [tion, f.

jurisprudence, *jŏ rĭs prŏ'dĕns*, s. juris- prudence, f.

jurist, *jŏ'rĭst*, s. juriste, jurisconsulte, m.

juror, *jŏ'rĕr*, s. juré, m.

jury, *jŏ'rĭ*, s. jury, m. || **~-box,** s. banc du jury, m. || **~-mast,** s. mât de fortune,

juryman, *jŏ'rĭ măn*, s. juré, m.   [m.

just, *jŭst*, a. & ad. (**-ly,** ad.) juste(ment) || équitable || vertueux || exactement || **~ as,** tout comme || **~ now,** tout à l'heure || **~ so,** précisément || **~ yet,** tout de suite || pour le moment || **~ tell me,** dites-moi donc.

justice, *jŭs'tĭs*, s. justice, f. || droiture, f. || juge, m.

justifiable, *jŭs'tĭ fĭ ä bl*, a. justifiable.

justifiably, *jŭs'tĭ fĭ ä blĭ*, ad. justement.

justification, *jŭs tĭ fĭ kā'shŭn*, s. justifi- cation, f.   [catif.

justificative, *jŭs tĭf'ĭ kā tĭv*, a. justifi-

justifier, *jŭs'tĭ fĭ ĕr*, s. défenseur, m.

justify, *jŭs'tĭ fĭ*, v. a. justifier.

justle, *jŭs'l*, v. a. (& n.) pousser || (se) heurter.   [exactitude, f.

justness, *jŭst'nĕs*, s. justice, équité, f. ||

jut, *jŭt*, v. n. (**to ~ out**) bomber, saillir, avancer.

jute, *jŏt*, s. jute, chanvre de l'Inde, m.

juvenile, *jŏ'vĕ nīl*, a. jeune, de jeunesse || **~ ball,** s. bal d'enfants, m.

juvenility, *jŏ vĕ nĭl'ĭ tĭ*, s. jeunesse, f.

juxtaposition, *jŭks tä pŏ zĭsh'ŭn*, s. juxta- position, f.

K.

kale, *kāl*, s. chou frisé, m. || **sea~,** s. chou marin, m.   [scope, m.

kaleidoscope, *kā lī'dŏ skōp*, s. kaléido-

kalender, *kăl'ĕn dĕr*, s. *vide* **calender**.

kangaroo, *kăng gä rŏ'*, s. kanguroo, m.

kedge, *kĕj*, s. (mar.) ancre à touer, f.

keel, *kēl*, s. carène, f. || quille, f.

keen, *kēn*, a. aigu, affilé || sévère || véhé- ment || mordant, perçant, pénétrant || **-ly,** ad. âprement, ardemment || **~-sighted,** a. à la vue perçante.

keenness, *kēn'nĕs*, s. pointe aiguë, f. || aigreur, acrimonie, f.

keep, *kēp*, s. garde, f. || entretien, m. || donjon, m.

keep, *kēp*, v. a. & n. ir. tenir, garder, con- server || protéger || dĕtenir, retenir || main- tenir, accomplir || observer, célébrer || entretenir || se tenir, se retenir || rester, de- meurer || **to ~ silence,** garder le silence ||

to ~ one's promise, accomplir sa pro- messe || **to ~ on,** continuer || **to ~ up,** soutenir, maintenir || **to ~ to oneself,** garder pour soi || se tenir sur la réserve || se retirer.

keeper, *kēp'ĕr*, s. gardien, m. || conserva- teur, m. || (com.) teneur, m.

keeping, *kēp'ing*, s. garde, f., entretien, m. || accord, m. || **in ~ with,** en har- monie avec.   [bum, m.

keepsake, *kēp'sāk*, s. souvenir, m. || al-

keg, *kĕg*, s. caque, f., baril, m.

ken, *kĕn*, s. vue, portée de la vue, f.

kennel, *kĕn'nĕl*, s. chenil, m. || meute, f. ||

kept, *kĕpt*, a. entretenu.   [terrier, m.

kerb(-stone), *kĕrb'(stŏn)*, s. bordure de trottoir, f. || margelle, f.

kerchief, *kĕr'chĭf*, s. fichu, m.

kernel, *kĕr'nĕl*, s. glande, f. || pepin, m. || grain, m.

kerseymere, *kĕr'zĭ mēr*, s. casimir, m.

kestrel, *kĕs'trĕl*, s. autour, m. (oiseau).

ketch, *kĕch*, s. quaiche, f.

ketchup, *kĕch'ŭp*, s. *vide* **catsup.**

kettle, *kĕt'tl*, s. chaudron, m., chaudière, f. || **tea~,** bouilloire, f. || **to put the ~ on,** mettre la bouilloire au feu || **~- drum,** s. timbale, f.

key, *kē*, s. clef, f. || touche, f. || ton, m. || **skeleton-~,** crochet, m. || **~-board,** s. clavier, m. || **~-hole,** s. trou de la ser- rure, m. || **~-note,** s. tonique, f. || **~- ring,** s. trousseau de clefs, m. || **~-stone,** s. clef de voûte, f.

keyless, *kē'lĕs*, a. (**of watches**) à re- montoir sans clef.   [recul, m.

kick, *kĭk*, s. coup de pied, m., ruade, f. ||

kick, *kĭk*, v. a. & n. donner des coups de pied, ruer || **to ~ up a row,** faire une esclandre.

kickshaw, *kĭk'shăw*, s. colifichet, m.

kid, *kĭd*, s. cabri, chevreau, m. || **~-gloves,** s. pl. gants de cabron, m. pl.

kidnap, *kĭd'năp*, v. a. voler des enfants.

kidnapper, *kĭd'năp pĕr*, s. voleur d'en- fants, m.   [(fig.) race, f.

kidney, *kĭd'nĭ*, s. rein, m. || rognon, m. ||

kilderkin, *kĭl'dĕr kĭn*, s. petit baril, m.,

kill, *kĭl*, v. a. tuer || abattre.   [caque, f.

killer, *kĭl'lĕr*, s. tueur, meurtrier, m.

killing, *kĭl'ling*, a. (fam.) charmant.

kiln, *kĭl*, s. four, m. || **~-dry,** v. a. sécher au four.   [m.

kilt, *kĭlt*, s. pli, m. || tablier des Écossais,

kimbo, *kĭm'bō*, a. crochu || **to set one's arms a'~,** faire le pot à deux anses.

kin, *kĭn*, s. parent, allié, m. || **next of ~,** plus proche parent, m. || **to be of ~,** être de la famille.

kind, *kīnd*, s. genre, m., espèce, sorte, f. || manière, f. || **to pay in ~,** payer en nature || **~-hearted,** a. bienveillant.

kind, *kīnd*, a. bienfaisant, obligeant, af- fable, complaisant.

kindle, *kīnd'l*, v. a. & n. allumer || prendre feu.   [bontĕ, f.

kindliness, *kīnd'lĭ nĕs*, s. bienveillance,

kindly, *kīnd'lĭ,* a. bienfaisant, doux || favorable || ~, ad. avec bienveillance || ~ go there, ayez la bonté d'y aller

kindness, *kīnd'nĕs,* s. bienveillance, bonté, faveur, f. [renté, f.

kindred, *kīn'drĕd,* s. parents, m. pl., parenté, f.

kindred, *kīn'drĕd,* a. parent.

kine, *kīn,* s. pl. vaches, f. pl.

king, *kīng,* s. roi, m. || ~'s bench, s. cour du banc du roi, f. || ~'s evil, s. écrouelles, f. pl. || ~-cup, s. (bot.) bouton d'or, m.

kingcraft, *kīng'krăft,* s. art de régner, m. || politique astucieuse, f.

kingdom, *kīng'dŭm,* s. royaume, règne, m. || to ~ come, "ad patres."

kingfisher, *kīng'fĭshẽr,* s. Martinpêcheur, m. (oiseau).

kink, *kīngk,* s. coque, f. [parenté, f.

kinsfolk, *kīnz'fōk,* s. parents, m. pl. ||

kinsman, *kīnz'măn,* s. parent, allié, m.

kinswoman, *kīnz'wŏŏmăn,* s. parente [sœur, f.

kiosk, *kēōsk',* s. kiosque, m.

kipper(ed herring), *kĭp'pẽr (ĕd hẽr'rĭng),* s. hareng après le relouage, m.

kirtle, *kẽr'tl,* s. camisole, f., gilet de flanelle || s. baiser, m. [nelle, m.

kiss, *kĭs,* s. baiser || s. baiser, m. [nelle, m.

kiss, *kĭs,* v. a. baiser || to ~ one's hand to a person, envoyer un baiser à qn

kissing, *kĭs'ĭng,* s. baisement, m.

kit, *kĭt,* s. violon de poche, m. || petit baril, m. || tinette, f.

kitchen, *kĭch'ĕn,* s. cuisine, f. || ~-dresser, s. table de cuisine, f. || ~-garden, s. jardin potager, m. || ~-maid, s. fille de cuisine, f. || ~-range, s. cuisine anglaise, f. || ~-stuff, s. graisses de cuisine, f. pl.

kite, *kīt,* s. milan, m. || cerf-volant, m.

kith and kin, *kĭth ănd kĭn,* s. parents et amis, m. pl.

kitten, *kĭt'tn,* s. chaton, m.

kitten, *kĭt'tn,* v. n. chatter.

kleptomania, *klĕp'tō mā'nĭ ă,* s. cleptomanie, f. [mane, m. & f.

kleptomaniac, *klĕp tō mā'nĭ ăk,* s. cleptomane.

knack, *năk,* s. colifichet, m. || habileté, f. || to have the ~ of, connaître le truc.

knacker, *năk'ẽr,* s. écarrisseur, m.

knapsack, *năp'săk,* s. havresac, m.

knave, *năv,* s. fourbe, coquin, m. || valet (aux cartes), m. [nerie, f.

knavery, *nā'vẽr ĭ,* s. fourberie, friponnerie, f.

knavish, *nā'vĭsh,* a. fourbe || ~ly, ad. en fripon || malicieusement

knead, *nēd,* v. a. pétrir.

kneading-trough, *nēd'ĭng trŏf,* s. pétrin, m., huche, f.

knee, *nē,* s. genou, m. || coude, m. || (mar.) courbe, f. || ~-cap, ~-pan, s. rotule, f. || ~-deep, ad. jusqu'aux genoux.

kneed, *nēd,* a. à genoux . . . || coudé || knock-~, a. cagneux.

kneel, *nēl,* v. n. ir. s'agenouiller. [f.

knell, *nĕl,* s. glas, m., sonnerie mortuaire,

knickerbockers, *nĭk'ẽr bŏk ẽrz,* s. pl. culotte bretonne, f.

knicknacks, *nĭk'năks,* s. pl. babioles, f. pl.

knife, *nīf,* s. couteau, m. || paper-~, couteau à papier, m. || carving-~, couteau à découper, m. || clasp-~, couteau pliant, m. || pen-~, canif, m. || pruning-~, serpette, f. || a ~ and fork, un couvert, m. || ~-grinder, s. repasseur de couteaux, m. || ~-rest, s. porte-couteau, m. || ~-tray, s. panier à couteaux, m. [cavalier, m.

knight, *nīt,* s. chevalier, m. || (at chess)

knight, *nīt,* v. a. faire chevalier.

knighthood, *nīt'hŏŏd,* s. chevalerie, f.

knightly, *nīt'lĭ,* ad. en chevalier, de chevalier, chevaleresque.

knit, *nīt,* v. a. tricoter || unir, nouer || (the brow) froncer. [f.

knitter, *nīt'tẽr,* s. tricoteur, m., tricoteuse,

knitting, *nīt'ĭng,* s. tricotage, m. || ~-needle, s. aiguille à tricoter, f. [m.

knob, *nŏb,* s. bosse, f., nœud, m. || bouton,

knock, *nŏk,* s. coup, m. || coup de marteau, m.

knock, *nŏk,* v. a. & n. frapper, heurter, cogner || se heurter || to ~ about, frapper de tous côtés || to ~ down, abattre || adjuger || to ~ up, éreinter || réveiller.

knocker, *nŏk'ẽr,* s. marteau de la porte, m.

knocking, *nŏk'ĭng,* s. coups, m. pl.

knoll, *nōl,* s. monticule, m.

knot, *nŏt,* s. nœud, m. || difficulté, f. || troupe, f. [ser || bourgeonner.

knot, *nŏt,* v. a. & n. nouer, lier || embarrasser.

knotty, *nŏt'tĭ,* a. noueux || raboteux || difficile.

knout, *nŏwt,* s. knout, m. [ficile.

know, *nō,* v. a. & n. ir. connaître, savoir || distinguer, discerner, apercevoir || reconnaître.

knowing, *nō'ĭng,* a. habile, éclairé, savant, intelligent || rusé || ~ly, ad. sciemment || avec finesse.

knowledge, *nŏl'ĕj,* s. connaissance, science, f. || habileté, f. [veau), m.

knuckle, *nŭk'l,* s. jointure, f. || jarret (de

knuckle, *nŭk'l,* v. n. (to ~ under) se soumettre.

L.

la! *lä,* là voici! || mon Dieu!

label, *lā'bĕl,* s. écriteau, m., étiquette, f.

label, *lā'bĕl,* v. a. étiqueter.

labial, *lā'bĭ ăl,* a. labial.

laboratory, *lăb'ō rā tẽr ĭ,* s. laboratoire, m.

laborious, *lă bō'rĭ ŭs,* a. laborieux || pénible || ~ly, ad. laborieusement.

labour, *lā'bẽr,* s. travail, ouvrage, m. || peine, f. || (méd.) travail d'enfant, m.

labour, *lā'bẽr,* v. a. & n. travailler || être tourmenté || être en travail. [lier, m.

labourer, *lā'bẽr ẽr,* s. manœuvre, journa-

laburnum, *lă bẽr'nŭm,* s. faux-ébénier, m.

labyrinth, *lăb'ĭ rĭnth,* s. labyrinthe, m.

lac, *lăk,* s. laque, f. [dentelle, f.

lace, *lās,* s. lacet, cordon, m. || galon, m. ||

lace, *lās*, v. a. lacer ‖ galonner, garnir de dentelle.

lacerate, *lăs'ĕr āt*, v. a. lacérer, déchirer.

lack, *lăk*, s. manque, besoin, m.　　　[de.

lack, *lăk*, v. a. & n. avoir besoin, manque

lackadaisical, *lăk'ă dā zĭ kăl*, a. sentimental.

lackey, *lăk'ĭ*, s. laquais, m.　　　[mental.

laconic, *lă kŏn'ĭk*, a. (–ally, ad.) laconique

lacquer, *lăk'ĕr*, s. laque, m.　　　　[(ment).

lacquer, *lăk'ĕr*, v. a. laquer.

lad, *lăd*, s. jeune garçon, m.

ladder, *lăd'dĕr*, s. échelle, f.

lade, *lād*, v. a. ir. charger.

lading, *lā'dĭng*, s. chargement, m. ‖ bill of ~, lettre de voiture, f.

ladle, *lā'dl*, s. louche, grande cuiller, f.

lady, *lā'dĭ*, s. dame, f. ‖ young ~, demoiselle, f. ‖ my ~, madame, f. ‖ ~-bird, s. bête à Dieu, f. ‖ ~-day, s. fête de l'Annonciation, f. ‖ ~-killer, s. homme à bonnes fortunes, m. ‖ col de chemise (effilé en pointe), m. ‖ ~-love, s. maîtresse, f.　　　　　　　　　[élégant.

ladylike, *lā'dĭ līk*, a. de dame ‖ délicat,

ladyship, *lā'dĭ shĭp*, s. qualité de dame, f. ‖ madame, f.

lag, *lăg*, v. n. tarder, traîner.

laggard, *lăg'gĕrd*, s. traînard, m.

lagoon, *lă gōn'*, s. lagune, f., marais, m.

laic(al), *lā'ĭk(ăl)*, a. laïque, séculier.

lair, *lār*, s. repaire, gîte, réduit, m.

laird, *lārd*, s. laird (lord écossais), m.

laity, *lā'ĭ tĭ*, s. laïques, m. pl.

lamb, *lăm*, s. agneau, m.

lamb, *lăm*, v. n. agneler.

lambkin, *lăm'kĭn*, s. agnelet, m.　[doux.

lamblike, *lăm'līk*, a. comme un agneau,

lame, *lām*, v. a. estropier.

lame, *lām*, a. (–ly, ad.) boiteux ‖ imparfait(ement) m en boitant.

lameness, *lām'nĕs*, s. boitement, m. ‖ imperfection, f.

lament, *lă mĕnt'*, s. complainte, f.

lament, *lă mĕnt'*, v. a. & n. se lamenter, plaindre.

lamentable, *lăm'ĕn tă bl*, a. déplorable.

lamentation, *lăm ĕn tā'shŭn*, s. lamentation, f.

lamented, *lă mĕnt'ĕd*, a. regretté.

lamp, *lămp*, s. lampe, f. ‖ ~-black, s. noir de fumée, m. ‖ ~-lighter, s. allumeur, m. ‖ ~-oil, s. huile à brûler, f. ‖ ~-post, s. candélabre, lampadaire, m. ‖ ~-shade, s. abat-jour, m.

lampoon, *lăm pōn'*, s. pasquinade, f.

lampoon, *lăm pōn'*, v. a. satiriser.

lamprey, *lăm'prĭ*, s. lamproie, f.

lance, *lăns*, s. lance, f.　　　[de lancette.

lance, *lăns*, v. a. percer ‖ donner un coup

lancer, *lăn'sĕr*, s. lancier, m.

lancet, *lăn'sĕt*, s. lancette, f.

land, *lănd*, s. pays, m., contrée, f. ‖ terrain, m. ‖ ~-fall, s. héritage, m. ‖ (mar.) attérage, m. ‖ ~-flood, s. inondation, f. ‖ ~-force, s. armée de terre, f. ‖ ~-holder, s. propriétaire foncier, m. ‖ ~-league, s. landligue en Irlande, f. ‖ ~-owner, s.

propriétaire foncier, m. ‖ ~-tax, s. impôt foncier, m.

land, *lănd*, v. a. & n. débarquer.

landau, *lăn dăw'*, s. landau (voiture), m.

landed, *lăn'dĕd*, a. foncier ‖ ~ property, s. biens-fonds, m. pl.　[débarcadère, m.

landing, *lănd'ĭng*, s. débarquement, m. ‖

landlady, *lănd'lā dĭ*, s. propriétaire, f. ‖ hôtesse, f.

landless, *lănd'lĕs*, a. sans terre.

landlocked, *lănd'lŏkt*, a. enfermé entre des terres, m.　　　　　　　　　　[hôte, m.

landlord, *lănd'lŏrd*, s. propriétaire, m. ‖

landlubber, *lănd'lŭb bĕr*, s. (mar.) marin d'eau douce, m. ‖ vagabond, m.

landmark, *lănd'mărk*, s. frontière, f.

landscape, *lănd'skāp*, s. paysage, m. ‖ ~-gardener, s. architecte-paysagiste, m. ‖ ~-painter, s. peintre de paysage, m.　　　　　　　　　　　　　　　[terre, m.

landslip, *lănd'slĭp*, s. éboulement de

lane, *lān*, s. ruelle, allée, f.

language, *lăng'gwĭj*, s. langage, m.; langue, f. ‖ style, m. ‖ bad ~, grossièretés, f. pl.

languid, *lăng'gwĭd*, a. (–ly, ad.) languissant ‖ faible(ment) ‖ lentement.

languish, *lăng'gwĭsh*, v. n. languir.

languor, *lăng'g(w)ĕr*, s. langueur, f.

lanky, *lăngk'ĭ*, a. maigre, décharné ‖ lâche, plat.

lankness, *lăngk'nĕs*, s. maigreur, f.

lantern, *lăn'tĕrn*, s. lanterne, f. ‖ fanal, m. ‖ magic ~, lanterne magique, f.

lap, *lăp*, s. giron, m. ‖ patte, f. ‖ bout d'oreille, m. ‖ ~-dog, s. chien de chasse, m.

lap, *lăp*, v. a. & n. plier, envelopper ‖ laper, lécher ‖ to ~ over, recouvrir, retomber sur.

lapful, *lăp'fŏŏl*, a. plein son tablier.

lapidary, *lăp'ĭ dĕr'ĭ*, s. lapidaire, m.

lapis lazuli, *lăp'ĭs lăz'ū lī*, s. lapis-lazuli, f.

lappet, *lăp'pĕt*, s. pan, m.　　　　　[m.

lapse, *lăps*, s. écoulement, laps, m. ‖ bévue, f.

lapse, *lăps*, v. n. couler doucement, s'écouler ‖ tomber ‖ faillir ‖ déchoir.

lapwing, *lăp'wĭng*, s. vanneau, m.

larboard, *lăr'bōrd*, s. (mar.) bâbord, m.

larceny, *lăr'sĕnĭ*, s. larcin, vol, m.

larch(-tree), *lărch'(trē)*, s. larix, m.

lard, *lărd*, s. lard, m.

lard, *lărd*, v. a. larder, piquer.

larder, *lăr'dĕr*, s. garde-manger, m.

larding-pin, *lăr'dĭng pĭn*, s. lardoire, f.

large, *lărj*, a. (–ly, ad.) gros ‖ large(ment) ‖ copieux ‖ at ~, amplement, en général ‖ en liberté ‖ diffusément ‖ abondamment.

largeness, *lărj'nĕs*, s. grosseur, grandeur, largeur, f.

largess, *lăr'jĕs*, s. largesse, f.

lark, *lărk*, s. alouette, f. ‖ to have a ~, faire une escapade ‖ what a ~! ça doit être amusant!

lark, *lărk*, v. n. jouer des tours.

larkspur, *lărk'spŭr*, s. pied-d'alouette, m.

larva, *lör'vă,* s. larve, f.
laryngitis, *lăr ĭn jī'tĭs,* s. (méd.) laryngite, f.
larynx, *lă'rĭngks,* s. larynx, m. [m.
lascar, *lăs'kăr,* s. lascar, matelot indien.
lascivious, *lăs sĭv'ĭ ŭs,* a. lascif ‖ -ly, ad. lascivement.
lasciviousness, *lăs sĭv'ĭ ŭs nĕs,* s. lasciveté, impudicité, f.
lash, *lăsh,* s. coup de fouet, m. ‖ coup, m. ‖ sarcasme, m. ‖ cil, m. ‖ laisse, f.
lash, *lăsh,* v. a. & n. fouetter ‖ satiriser ‖
lass, *lăs,* s. (jeune) fille, f. [lancer.
lassitude, *lăs'sĭ tūd,* s. lassitude, f.
lasso, *lăs'sō,* s. lasso, lazo, m.
last, *lăst,* s. forme pour les chaussures, f. ‖
last, *lăst,* v. n. durer. [(mar.) lest, m.
last, *lăst,* a. & ad. dernier ‖ la dernière fois ‖ at ~, enfin ‖ at the ~, en tout dernier lieu ‖ -ly, ad. enfin. [(lement).
lasting, *lăst'ĭng,* a. (-ly, ad.) perpétuel
latch, *lăch,* s. loquet, m. ‖ ~-key, s. passe-partout, m.
late, *lăt,* a. & ad. tard, lent, tardif ‖ feu, défunt ‖ dernièrement ‖ of ~, dernièrement ‖ -ly, ad. depuis peu.
lateen-rigged, *lă tēn'rĭgd,* a. (mar.) gréé en latine. [retard, m.
lateness, *lăt'nĕs,* s. temps très-avancé,
latent, *lă'tĕnt,* a. caché, secret. [ment).
lateral, *lăt'ĕr ăl,* a. (-ly, ad.) latéral(e-
lath, *lăth,* s. latte, f., lattis, m.
lathe, *lăth,* s. tour de tourneur, m.
lather, *lăth'ĕr,* s. mousse de savon, f.
lather, *lăth'ĕr,* v. a. & n. savonner ‖ mousser.
Latin, *lăt'ĭn,* s. langue latine, f.
Latin, *lăt'ĭn,* a. latin.
Latinity, *lă tĭn'ĭ tĭ,* s. latinité, f.
latitude, *lăt'ĭ tūd,* s. étendue, f. ‖ latitude, f.
latitudinal, *lă tĭ tū'dĭ năl,* a. (-ly, ad.) latitudinal(ement). [esprit fort, m.
latitudinarian, *lăt ĭ tū dĭ nă'rĭ ăn,* s.
latten, *lăt'tn,* s. fer-blanc, laiton, m.
latter, *lăt'tĕr,* a. dernier, postérieur ‖ the ~, celui-ci, celle-ci ‖ -ly, ad. dernièrement.
lattice, *lăt'tĭs,* s. treillis, treillage, m.
lattice, *lăt'tĭs,* v. a. treillisser.
laud, *lăwd,* v. a. louer, célébrer.
laudable, *lăwd'ă bl,* a. louable.
laudably, *lăwd'ă blĭ,* ad. louablement.
laudatory, *lăwd'ă tĕr ĭ,* a. louangeur.
laugh, *lăf,* s. rire, m.
laugh, *lăf,* v. n. rire ‖ to ~ in one's sleeve, rire sous barbe ‖ broad ~, s. gros rire, m. ‖ to have the ~ on one's side, avoir les rieurs de son côté.
laughable, *lăf'ă bl,* a. risible. [risible.
laughably, *lăf'ă blĭ,* ad. d'une manière
laugher, *lăf'ĕr,* s. rieur, m.
laughingly, *lăf'ĭng lĭ,* ad. en riant.
laughing-stock, *lăf'ĭng stŏk,* s. risée, f., objet de risée, m.
laughter, *lăf'tĕr,* s. rire, ris, m.
launch, *lănsh,* s. (mar.) mise à l'eau, f., lançage, m. [se jeter à l'eau.
launch, *lănsh,* v. a. & n. lancer à l'eau ‖

laundress, *lăn'drĕs,* s. blanchisseuse, f.
laundry, *lăn'drĭ,* s. lavanderie, f. ‖ lavage, m.
laureate, *lăw'rē ăt,* a. lauréat. [m.
laurel, *lŏr'ĕl,* s. laurier, m.
laurelled, *lŏr'ĕld,* a. couronné de laurier.
lava, *lă'vă,* s. lave, f.
lavatory, *lăv'ă tĕr ĭ,* s. lavoir, m.
lavender, *lăv'ĕn dĕr,* s. lavande, f.
lavish, *lăv'ĭsh,* v. a. prodiguer.
lavish, *lăv'ĭsh,* a. prodigue ‖ -ly, ad. prodigalement.
law, *lăw,* s. loi, f. ‖ droit, m. ‖ procès, m. ‖ jurisprudence, f. ‖ ~-breaker, s. transgresseur de la loi, m. ‖ ~-giver, ~maker, s. législateur, m.
lawful, *lăw'fŏŏl,* a. (-ly, ad.) légal(ement) ‖ légitime. [légitimité, f.
lawfulness, *lăw'fŏŏl nĕs,* s. légalité, f. ‖
lawless, *lăw'lĕs,* a. illégal ‖ déréglé.
lawlessness, *lăw'lĕs nĕs,* s. illégalité, f.
lawn, *lăwn,* s. pelouse, f. ‖ linon, m. ‖ ~-mower, s. faucheur, m. ‖ ~-tennis, s. lawn-tennis, jeu de paume, m.
lawsuit, *lăw'sūt,* s. procès, m.
lawyer, *lăw'yĕr,* s. avocat, m. ‖ légiste, m.
lax, *lăks,* a. lâche ‖ relâché.
laxative, *lăks'ă tĭv,* s. laxatif, m.
laxative, *lăks'ă tĭv,* a. laxatif.
laxity, *lăks'ĭ tĭ,* s. relâchement, m.
lay, *lă,* s. couche, rangée, f. ‖ parl, m., mise, f. ‖ chant, m.
lay, *lă,* v. a. & n. ir. mettre, placer ‖ coucher ‖ apaiser ‖ former, tramer ‖ imputer ‖ pondre (of birds) ‖ parier ‖ to ~ by, mettre de côté, réserver ‖ to ~ down, déposer, mettre bas ‖ to ~ out, arranger ‖ ensevelir (a corpse) ‖ dépenser (money) ‖ to ~ to, (mar.) tenir au vent ‖ to ~ oneself out to, aspirer à qc.
lay, *lă,* a. laï, laïque, laïc ‖ ~-figure, s. mannequin, m.
layer, *lă'ĕr,* s. couche, f. ‖ marcotte, f.
laying, *lă'ĭng,* s. mise, f. ‖ ponte, f.
layman, *lă'măn,* s. laïque, m.
lazar-house, *lă'zăr hŏŏs,* s. lazaretto, *lăz ăr rĕt'tō,* s. lazaret, m.
lazily, *lă'zĭ lĭ,* ad. nonchalamment.
laziness, *lă'zĭ nĕs,* s. fainéantise, f.
lazy, *lă'zĭ,* a. fainéant
lea, *lē,* s. prairie, f., pré, clos, m.
lead, *lĕd,* s. plomb, m. ‖ interligne, m. ‖ to heave the ~, (mar.) jeter la sonde ‖ ~s, s. pl. toiture, f. ‖
lead, *lĕd,* s. conduite, f. ‖ (at cards) main, f. ‖ acquit, m. ‖ to have the ~, avoir la main, être le premier en cartes.
lead, *lĕd,* v. a. plomber ‖ interligner.
lead, *lĕd,* v. a. & n. ir. conduire, mener, diriger, entraîner ‖ to ~ off, emmener, détourner ‖ to ~ on, entraîner, attirer.
lead(en) *lĕd'(n),* a. de plomb ‖ lourd ‖ ~-pencil, s. crayon, m.
leader, *lĕd'ĕr,* s. guide, chef, m. ‖ article de fond, m. ‖ cheval de volée, m.
leading, *lĕd'ĭng;* ~-article, s. article de fond, m., premier Paris, premier Londres, etc. ‖ ~-strings, s. pl. lisières, f. pl.

leaf, *lēf*, s. feuille, f. || feuillet, m. || battant (d'une porte), m. || **to turn over a new ~**, changer de gamme.

leafless, *lēf' lĕs*, a. sans feuilles || effeuillé.

leafy, *lēf' ĭ*, a. feuillu.

league, *lēg*, s. ligue, f. || lieue, f.

league, *lēg*, v. n. se liguer.

leaguer, *lē' gĕr*, s. confédéré, m.

leak, *lēk*, s. (mar.) voie d'eau, f. || **to spring a ~**, (mar.) faire eau, faire une voie d'eau.

leak, *lēk*, v. n. faire eau || **to ~ out**, se répandre || percer.

leakage, *lēk' āj*, s. coulage, m.

leaky, *lēk' ĭ*, a. faisant eau.

lean, *lēn*, v. n. s'appuyer, (se)pencher.

lean, *lēn*, a. maigre.

leanness, *lēn' nĕs*, s. maigreur, f.

leap, *lēp*, s. saut, m. || **to take a ~**, faire un saut || **~-year**, s. année bissextile, f.

leap, *lēp*, v. a. & n. ir. sauter, franchir.

leapfrog, *lēp' frŏg*, s. cheval fondu (jeu d'enfants), m.

learn, *lĕrn*, v. a. & n. apprendre, s'instruire.

learned, *lĕrn' ĕd*, a. savant, érudit || **-ly**, ad. savamment.

learning, *lĕrn' ĭng*, s. science, érudition, étude, f.

lease, *lēs*, s. bail, m. || **~-holder**, s. locataire par bail, m.

lease, *lēs*, v. a. donner à bail.

leaser, *lēs' ĕr*, s. glaneur, m.

leash, *lēsh*, s. laisse, f.

leash, *lēsh*, v. a. mener en laisse.

least, *lēst*, a. & ad. le plus petit, le moindre || moins || **at ~**, **at the ~**, au moins, du moins || **not in the ~**, pas le moins du monde.

leather, *lĕth' ĕr*, s. cuir, m. || peau, f. || **patent-~**, cuir verni, m. || **~-dresser**, s.

leathern, *lĕth' ĕrn*, a. de cuir. tanneur, m.

leathery, *lĕth' ĕr ĭ*, a. qui ressemble au cuir.

leave, *lēv*, s. liberté, permission, f. || congé, m. || **ticket of ~**, s. exeat, m. || **to take one's ~**, prendre congé || **to take French ~**, prendre la permission sous son bonnet || **by your ~**, avec votre permission || ne vous en déplaise || gare!

leave, *lēv*, v. a. ir. quitter, abandonner || laisser || **"to be left till called for,"** poste restante (of letters).

leaved, *lēvd*, a. feuillu.

leaven, *lĕv' n*, s. levain, m.

leaven, *lĕv' n*, v. a. faire lever.

leavings, *lēv' ĭngz*, s. pl. restes, m. pl.

lecherous, *lĕch' ĕr ŭs*, a. débauché.

lection, *lĕk' shŭn*, lecture, *lĕk' tūr* ou *lĕk' chŏŏr*, s. lecture, f., discours, sermon, m. || réprimande, f. || **curtain-~**, semonce conjugale, f. || **~-hall**, s. salle de lecture.

lecture, *lĕk' tūr* ou *lĕk' chŏŏr*, v. a. & n. faire un cours (de) || enseigner || réprimander. fesseur, m.

lecturer, *lĕk' tūr ĕr*, s. lecteur, m. || prolegde, *lĕj*, s. bord, m. || couche, f.

ledger, *lĕj' ĕr*, s. (com.) grand livre de compte, m.

led-horse, *lĕd' hŏrs*, s. cheval de main, m.

lee(-side), *lē' (sīd)*, s. (mar.) bord de sous-le-vent, m. || **~-way**, s. (mar.) dérive, f.

leech, *lēch*, s. sangsue, f. || (mar.) ralingue, f. || **horse-~**, vétérinaire, m.

leek, *lēk*, s. poireau, m.

leer, *lēr*, s. œillade, f.

leer, *lēr*, v. n. regarder du coin de l'œil.

lees, *lēz*, s. pl. lie, f.

leeward, *lē' ĕrd*, a. & ad. sous le vent.

left, *lĕft*, a. gauche || **on the ~**, à gauche || **~-handed**, a. gaucher || **(marriages)** de la main gauche || **~-luggage-office**, s. bureau des bagages en dépôt, m. || **~-off**, a. de rebut. cuisse, f.

leg, *lĕg*, s. jambe, f., pied, m. || gigot, m.

legacy, *lĕg' ā sĭ*, s. legs, m.

legal, *lē' găl*, a. (-ly, ad.) légal(ement).

legalise, *lē' găl ĭz*, v. a. légaliser.

legality, *lē găl' ĭ tĭ*, s. légalité, f.

legate, *lĕg' āt*, s. légat, m.

legatee, *lĕg ā tē'*, s. légataire, m.

legation, *lĕ gā' shŭn*, s. ambassade, f.

legend, *lĕj' ĕnd*, s. légende, f.

legendary, *lĕj' ĕn dĕr ĭ*, a. de légende.

legerdemain, *lĕj' ĕr dē mān*, s. tour de passe-passe, m. ft. pl.

leggings, *lĕg' ĭngz*, s. pl. grandes guêtres,

legibility, *lĕj ĭ bĭl' ĭ tĭ*, s. lisibilité, netteté d'écriture, f.

legible, *lĕj' ĭ bl*, a. lisible.

legibly, *lĕj' ĭ blĭ*, ad. lisiblement.

legion, *lē' jŭn*, s. légion, f.

legislation, *lĕj ĭs lā' shŭn*, s. législation, f.

legislative, *lĕj' ĭs lā tĭv*, a. législatif.

legislator, *lĕj' ĭs lā tĕr*, s. législateur, m.

legislature, *lĕj' ĭs lā tūr*, s. législature, f.

legitimacy, *lĕ jĭt' ĭ mă sĭ*, s. légitimité, f.

legitimate, *lĕ jĭt' ĭ măt*, v. a. légitimer.

legitimate, *lĕ jĭt' ĭ măt*, a. (-ly, ad.) légitime(ment). mation, f.

legitimation, *lĕ jĭt ĭ mā' shŭn*, s. légititeguminous, *lĕ gū' mĭ nŭs*, a. légumineux.

leisure, *lē' zhŏŏr* ou *lĕ' zhŏŏr*, s. loisir, m. || **at ~**, à loisir. loisir, peu à peu.

leisurely, *lē' zhŏŏr lĭ* ou *lĕ' zhŏŏr lĭ*, ad. à

lemon, *lĕm' ŏn*, s. limon, m. || citron, m. || **~-peel**, s. écorce de citron, f.

lemonade, *lĕm' ŏn ād*, s. limonade, f.

lend, *lĕnd*, v. a. ir. prêter.

length, *lĕngth*, s. longueur, étendue, distance, f. || **at ~**, au long || enfin || **at full ~**, tout de son long || **to go**, **carry to great ~s**, aller, porter bien loin.

lengthen, *lĕngth' n*, v. a. & n. allonger, prolonger, s'allonger.

lengthy, *lĕngth' ĭ*, a. détaillé, prolongé.

lenient, *lē' nĭ ĕnt*, a. lénitif.

lenitive, *lĕn' ĭ tĭv*, s. lénitif, calmant, émollient, m.

lenitive, *lĕn' ĭ tĭv*, a. adoucissant.

lenity, *lĕn' ĭ tĭ*, s. douceur, indulgence, f.

lens, *lĕnz*, s. lentille, f., verre lenticulaire, m.

Lent, *lĕnt*, s. Carême, m.

lentil, *lĕn' tĭl*, s. lentille, f.

leonine, *lē' ō nĭn*, a. léonin.

leopard, *lĕp'ĕrd*, s. léopard, m.
leper, *lĕp'ĕr*, s. lépreux, m.
leprosy, *lĕp'rŏ si*, s. lèpre, f.
leprous, *lĕp'rŭs*, a. lépreux, ladre.
lesion, *lē'zhn*, s. lésion, f.
less, *lĕs*, a. & ad. moindre, plus petit ‖ moins ‖ **to grow ~**, diminuer ‖ **none the ~**, d'autant moins.
lessee, *lĕs sē'*, s. fermier, m.
lessen, *lĕs'sn*, v. a. & n. rapetisser, amoindrir ‖ s'amoindrir.   [moins.
lesser, *lĕs'sĕr*, a. & ad. plus petit, moindre ‖
lesson, *lĕs'sn*, s. leçon, f. ‖ réprimande, f.
lessor, *lĕs'sĕr*, s. bailleur, m.
lest, *lĕst*, c. de peur que, de crainte que.
let, *lĕt*, v. a. & n. ir. laisser, permettre, souffrir ‖ louer ‖ empêcher ‖ **to ~ one into a secret**, initier qn. à un secret ‖ **to ~ be or alone**, laisser tranquille ‖ **to ~ down**, faire descendre ‖ **to ~ off**, laisser échapper ‖ décharger (une arme à feu).
lethargic, *lē thär'jĭk*, a. léthargique.
lethargy, *lĕth'är ji*, s. léthargie, f.
letter, *lĕt'tĕr*, s. lettre, f. ‖ caractère d'imprimerie, m. ‖ épître, f. ‖ **~-box**, s. boîte aux lettres, f. ‖ **~-carrier**, s. facteur de la poste, m. ‖ **~-case**, s. portelettres, m. ‖ **~-press**, s. impression typographique, f. ‖ **~-rack**, s. semainier, m. ‖ **~-writer**, s. épistolaire, m. ‖ polygraphe, m.   [ture imprimée.
lettered, *lĕt'tĕrd*, a. lettré ‖ avec couverlettering, *lĕt'tĕr ing*, s. titre, m ‖ caractère d'écriture, m.
lettuce, *lĕt'tis*, s. laitue, f.
Levant, *lē vănt'*, s. levant, orient, m.
levant, *lē vănt'*, v. n. brûler la politesse à qn. ‖ lever le pied.   [levantin.
Levantine, *lē văn'tīn ou lē văn'tĭn*, a.
levee, *lĕv'ē*, s. lever (du roi), m.
level, *lĕv'ĕl*, s. niveau, m., égalité, f. ‖ visée, f.   [tionner ‖ viser.
level, *lĕv'ĕl*, v. a. niveler ‖ diriger ‖ proporlevel, *lĕv'ĕl*, a. uni ‖ horizontal, de niveau.
lever, *lē'vĕr*, s. levier, m.   [mécanique).
leverage, *lēv'ĕr ĭj*, s. moment, m. (en leveret, *lĕv'ĕr ĕt*, s. lévraut, m.
leviathan, *lē vī'ă thăn*, s. léviathan, m.,
Levite, *lē'vīt*, s. lévite, m.   [baleine, f.
levitical, *lē vĭt'ĭ kăl*, a. de lévite.
levity, *lĕv'ĭ ti*, s. légèreté, f.
levy, *lĕv'i*, s. levée, f.
levy, *lĕv'i*, v. a. lever ‖ imposer ‖ enrôler.
lewd, *lūd ou lōd*, a. débauché, dissolu ‖ -ly, ad. lascivement.   [bauche, f.
lewdness, *lūd'nĕs ou lōd'nĕs*, s. délexicographer, *lĕks ĭ kŏg'răf ĕr*, s. lexicographe, m.   [m.
lexicon, *lĕks'ĭ kŏn*, s. lexique, dictionnaire.
liability, *lī ă bĭl'ĭ ti*, s. responsabilité, f. ‖ liabilities, pl. (com.) passif, m.
liable, *lī'ă bl*, a. responsable, exposé à.
liar, *lī'ĕr*, s. menteur, m.
libation, *lī bā'shŭn*, s. libation, f.
libel, *lī'bĕl*, s. libelle, m., satire, f.
libel, *lī'bĕl*, v. a. diffamer.
libeller, *lī'bĕl lĕr*, s. libelliste, m.

libellous, *lī'bĕl lŭs*, a. diffamatoire.
liberal, *lĭb'ĕr ăl*, a. (-ly, ad.) libéral (ement) ‖ généreux, honnête ‖ généreusement.
liberalism, *lĭb'ĕr ăl izm*, s. libéralisme, m.
liberality, *lĭb ĕr ăl'ĭ ti*, s. libéralité, générosité, f.
liberate, *lĭb'ĕr āt*, v. a. affranchir, libérer.
liberation, *lĭb ĕr ā'shŭn*, s. libération, f.
libertine, *lĭb'ĕr tin*, s. libertin, m.
libertine, *lĭb'ĕr tin*, a. libertin.   [m.
libertinism, *lĭb'ĕr tin izm*, s. libertinage,
liberty, *lĭb'ĕr ti*, s. liberté, f., privilège, m. ‖ **at ~**, libre ‖ **to set at ~**, délivrer, affranchir ‖ **to be at ~ to**, avoir la permission de.   [dineux.
libidinous, *lĭ bĭd'ĭ nŭs*, a. libertin, libilibrarian, *lī brā'rĭ ăn*, s. bibliothécaire, m.
library, *lī'brā ri*, s. bibliothèque, f. ‖ **circulating ~**, cabinet de lecture, m.
lice, *līs*, pl. de louse.
licence, *lī'sĕns*, s. licence, f. ‖ permission, f. ‖ patente, f. ‖ **marriage ~**, dispense de bans, f.
licence, *lī'sĕns*, v. a. permissionner ‖ patenter ‖ **-d physician**, s. médecin légalement admis à l'exercice, m.
licentiate, *lī sĕn'shĭ āt*, s. licencié, m.
licentious, *lī sĕn'shŭs*, a. licencieux ‖ -ly, ad. licencieusement.
lichen, *lī'kĕn ou līch'ĕn*, s. lichen, m.
lick, *lĭk*, v. a. lécher ‖ rosser.
licking, *lĭk'ĭng*, s. rossée, f.
licorice, *lĭk'ĕr ĭs*, s. *vide* **liquorice**.
lictor, *lĭk'tĕr*, s. licteur, m.
lid, *lĭd*, s. couvercle, m. ‖ paupière, f.
lie, *lī*, s. mensonge, m. ‖ **to give the ~ to**, démentir.
lie, *lī*, v. n. ir. être couché, reposer ‖ rester, demeurer ‖ être situé ‖ mentir ‖ **here ~s**, ci-gît ‖ **as much as in me**, autant qu'il dépend de moi ‖ **to ~ low**, se tenir coi.   [tapi.
liege, *lēj*, a. lige.
lien, *lī'ĕn*, s. droit de saisie, m.
lieu, *lū*, s. lieu, m. ‖ **in ~ of**, au lieu de.
lieutenancy, *lĕf tĕn'ăn si*, s. lieutenance, f.
lieutenant, *lĕf tĕn'ănt*, s. lieutenant, m.
life, *līf*, s. vie, existence, f. ‖ vivacité, f. ‖ manière de vivre, f. ‖ **for ~**, à vie ‖ **to the ~**, d'après nature ‖ **~-belt**, s. ceinture de sauvetage, f. ‖ **~-boat**, s. canot de sauvetage, m. ‖ **~-buoy**, s. bouée de sauvetage, f. ‖ **~-estate**, s. propriété à vie, f. ‖ **~-guard**, s. garde du corps, m. ‖ **~-office**, **~-policy**, s. bureau d'assurance sur la vie, m. ‖ **~-preserver**, s. appareil de sauvetage, m. ‖ casse-tête, m. ‖ **~-size**, s. grandeur naturelle, f.
lifeless, *līf'lĕs*, a. sans vie.
lifelong, *līf'lŏng*, a. de toute la vie.
lifetime, *līf'tīm*, s. durée de la vie, f.
lift, *lĭft*, s. effort, m. ‖ cric, m. ‖ escalier mécanique, m. ‖ (Am.) treillis, m. ‖ **dead ~**, peine perdue, f. ‖ **to give one a ~**, soulever qn., donner un coup d'épaule à qn.
lift, *lĭft*, v. a. ir. lever, soulever, hausser ‖ élever ‖ voler.

ligament, *lig'ă mĕnt*, s. ligament, lien, m.

ligature, *lig'ă tŭr*, s. ligature, f., bandage, m.

light, *lit*, s. lumière, lueur, f. ‖ clarté, f.; jour, m. ‖ feu, m. ‖ allumette, f. ‖ fenêtre, f. ‖ intelligence, f. ‖ **to come to ~, paraître au grand jour, se révéler ‖ to set ~ to**, mettre le feu à ‖ **to stand in one's own ~**, se cacher à soi-même le jour.

light, *lit*, v. a. & n. ir. allumer, éclairer ‖ arriver ‖ s'enflammer ‖ descendre.

light, *lit*, a. léger ‖ facile, aisé ‖ inconstant, agile ‖ clair ‖ blond ‖ éclatant ‖ **-ly**, ad. légèrement ‖ facilement, superficiellement ‖ gaiement ‖ **~-fingered**, a. fripon, qui a les doigts crochus ‖ **to make ~ of**, ne tenir aucun compte de.

lighten, *lit'n*, v. a. & n. éclairer, luire ‖ faire des éclairs ‖ soulager.

lighter, *lit'ĕr*, s. allumeur, m. ‖ allège, f.

lighterman, *lit'ĕr măn*, s. gabarier, m.

lighthouse, *lit'hŏws*, s. phare, m.

lighting, *lit'ing*, s. éclairage, m.

lightness, *lit'nĕs*, s. légèreté, f.

lightning, *lit'ning*, s. foudre, f. ‖ **forked ~**, foudre, f. ‖ fulguration, f. ‖ **heat ~, sheet ~**, éclairs de chaleur, m. pl. ‖ **~-rod**, s. paratonnerre, m.

lights, *lits*, s. pl. poumons, m. pl.

lightsome, *lit'sŭm*, a. léger ‖ clair, gai, ligneux, *lig'nĕŭs*, a. ligneux. [joyeux.

like, *lik*, s. pareil, m. ‖ pareille, f.

like, *lik*, v. a. & n. aimer, trouver bon, approuver, goûter.

like, *lik*, a. & ad. semblable, pareil, égal ‖ comme ‖ probablement ‖ **that is just ~ him!** c'est bien lui! [probabilité, f.

likelihood, *lik'lĭ hŏŏd*, s. vraisemblance,

likely, *lik'lĭ*, a. & ad. vraisemblable, probable ‖ (Am.) probablement.

liken, *li'kn*, v. a. comparer.

likeness, *lik'nĕs*, s. ressemblance, f. ‖ portrait, m. ‖ **to have one's ~ taken**, faire faire son portrait.

likewise, *lik'wiz*, ad. de même, aussi.

liking, *li'king*, s. goût, m. ‖ gré, n. ‖ embonpoint, m. ‖ amitié, f. ‖ **to take a ~ to**, prendre goût à.

lilac, *li'lăk*, s. lilas, m. [prendre goût à.

lilliputian, *li li pū'shăn*, a. liliputien.

lily, *lil'ĭ*, s. (bot.) lis, m. ‖ **~ of the valley**, s. [(bot.) muguet, m.

limb, *lim*, s. membre, m. ‖ (bot.) muguet, m.

limber, *lim'bĕr*, a. flexible, souple ‖ **-s**, s. pl. (mil.) avant-train, m.

limbo, *lim'bō*, s. limbes, m. pl.

lime, *lim*, s. glu, m. ‖ pierre calcaire, chaux, f. ‖ tilleul, m. ‖ **slaked ~**, chaux éteinte, f. ‖ **~-kiln**, s. chaufour, m. ‖ **~-pit**, s. carrière de chaux, f.

lime, *lim*, v. a. engluer.

limit, *lim'it*, s. limite, frontière, f.

limit, *lim'it*, v. a. restreindre ‖ **-ed company**, s. (com.) compagnie anonyme, f.

limitation, *lim i tā'shŭn*, s. restriction, f.

limn, *lim*, v. a. peindre, dessiner.

limner, *lim'nĕr*, s. peintre, m.

limp, *limp*, s. clochement, m.

limp, *limp*, v. n. clocher.

limp, *limp*, a. flexible, souple.

limpid, *lim'pid*, a. clair, transparent.

linch-pin, *linsh'pin*, s. esse, f.

linden, *lin'dn*, s. tilleul, m.

line, *lin*, s. ligne, f. ‖ rangée, f. ‖ chemin de fer, m. ‖ retranchement, m. ‖ alignement, m. ‖ vers, m. ‖ famille, f. ‖ linéament, m. ‖ dessein, m. ‖ ressort, m. ‖ équateur, m. ‖ **~-keeper**, s. (rail.) cantonnier, m. ‖ **of the ~**, (mil.) de ligne.

line, *lin*, v. a. doubler, garnir ‖ entourer.

lineage, *lin'ĕ ăj*, s. lignée, f.

lineal, *lin'ĕ ăl*, linear, *lin'ĕ ĕr*, a. linéaire ‖ héréditaire ‖ **-ly**, ad. en ligne directe.

lineament, *lin'ĕ ă mĕnt*, s. trait, m.

linen, *lin'ĕn*, s. toile, f. ‖ linge, m. ‖ **~-draper**, s. marchand de toile *or* de nouveautés, m. ‖ **~-press**, s. armoire à linge, f. [linge, f.

linger, *ling'gĕr*, v. n. tarder ‖ languir ‖ hésiter.

linguist, *ling'gwist*, s. linguiste, m.

linguistic, *ling gwis'tik*, a. linguistique.

lining, *li'ning*, s. doublure, f. ‖ coiffe (d'un chapeau), f.

link, *lingk*, s. chaînon, anneau, m. ‖ lien, m. ‖ flambeau, m. ‖ **~-boy**, s. porteflambeau, m.

link, *lingk*, v. a. enchaîner, joindre.

linnet, *lin'nĕt*, s. linotte, f.

linseed, *lin'sēd*, s. graine de lin, f. ‖ **~-oil**, s. huile de lin, f. [nelle, f.

linsey-woolsey, *lin'zi wŏŏl'zi*, s. tartalint, *lint*, s. filasse, f. ‖ charpie, f.

lintel, *lin'tĕl*, s. linteau, m.

lion, *li'ŏn*, s. lion, m.

lioness, *li'ŏn ĕs*, s. lionne, f.

lip, *lip*, s. lèvre, f. ‖ bord, m. ‖ **~-salve**, s. pommade pour les lèvres, f.

liquefy, *lik'wĕ fi*, v. a. (& n.) liquéfier ‖ (se) fondre.

liquid, *lik'wid*, s. liquide, m. [(se) fondre.

liquid, *lik'wid*, a. liquide.

liquidate, *lik'wi dāt*, v. a. liquider.

liquidation, *lik wi dā'shŭn*, s. liquidation, f.

liquor, *lik'ĕr*, s. liqueur, f. [f.

liquorice, *lik'ĕr is*, s. réglisse, f.

lisp, *lisp*, s. bégaiement, m.

lisp, *lisp*, v. n. parler du bout des dents (fig.) bégayer. [désir, m., envie, f.

list, *list*, s. liste, f. ‖ lisière, f. ‖ bord, m. ‖

list, *list*, v. a. & n. enrôler ‖ garnir de lisières ‖ désirer.

listen, *lis'n*, v. a. écouter, prêter l'oreille.

listless, *list'lĕs*, a. inattentif, nonchalant ‖ **-ly**, ad. négligemment.

litany, *lit'ăn i*, s. litanie, f.

literal, *lit'ĕr ăl*, a. (**-ly**, ad.) littéral [(ement).

literary, *lit'ĕr ă ri*, a. littéraire ‖ **~ man**, s. littérateur, m.

literature, *lit'ĕr ă tŭr*, s. littérature, f.

lithe, *lith*, a. souple, pliant, flexible.

lithograph, *lith'ō grăf*, s. lithographie, f.

lithograph, *lith'ō grăf*, v. a. lithographier.

lithographer, *lith ŏg'ră fĕr*, s. lithographe, m. [phique.

lithographic, *lith ō grăf'ik*, a. lithographi-

lithography, *lith ŏg'ră fi*, s. lithographi litigant, *lit'i gănt*, s. plaideur, m. [f.

litigate — looking-glass 137

litigate, *lĭt'ĭgāt*, v. a. & n. plaider, être en procès.

litigation, *lĭtĭgā'shŭn*, s. procès, m.

litigious, *lĭtĭj'ŭs*, a. litigieux, processif.

litter, *lĭt'tĕr*, s. litière, f. || paillasson, m. || portée, f.

litter, *lĭt'tĕr*, v. a. mettre bas (des animaux) || mettre en désordre || ~. v. n. se coucher.

little, *lĭt'tl*, s. bagatelle, f.

little, *lĭt'tl*, a. & ad. petit, peu || ~ by ~, peu à peu.

littleness, *lĭt'tlnĕs*, s. petitesse, f.

liturgy, *lĭt'ĕrjĭ*, s. liturgie, f.

live, *lĭv*, v. n. vivre, exister || se conduire, se comporter.

live, *lĭv*, a. vivant, en vie, vif || ~-stock, s. bétail, m., bestiaux, m. pl. (d'une ferme) || ~ coal, s. braise, f., charbons ardents, m. pl.

livelihood, *lĭv'lĭhŏŏd*, s. nourriture, f.

liveliness, *lĭv'lĭnĕs*, s. vivacité, gaieté, f.

livelong, *lĭv'lŏng*, a. durable, permanent, éternel. [tuel.

lively, *lĭv'lĭ*, a. éveillé, gai || riant || spirituel.

liver, *lĭv'ĕr*, s. foie, m. || good ~, s. gourmand, m.

livery, *lĭv'ĕrĭ*, s. livrée, f. || pension pour les chevaux, f. || corps municipal, m. || ~-company, s. corps de métier (de Londres), m. || ~-man, s. laquais, m.

livid, *lĭv'ĭd*, a. livide.

living, *lĭv'ĭng*, s. entretien, m., subsistance, f.

living, *lĭv'ĭng*, a. vivant || vif. [f.

lizard, *lĭz'ĕrd*, s. lézard, m.

lo! *lō*, voyez! voilà!

loach, *lōch*, s. loche, f.

load, *lōd*, s. fardeau, m., charge, f. || ~-star, s. étoile du Nord, f.

load, *lōd*, v. a. charger.

loadstone, *lōd'stōn*, s. aimant, m.

loaf, *lōf*, s. pain (de sucre), m.

loam, *lōm*, s. terre grasse, marne, f.

loan, *lōn*, s. prêt, m. || emprunt, m. || to raise a ~, faire, contracter un emprunt.

loan, *lōn*, v. s. prêter.

lo(a)th, *lōth*, a. récalcitrant || nothing ~, bien disposé à. [goût pour.

loathe, *lōth*, v. a. détester, avoir du dégoûtant.

loathing, *lōth'ĭng*, s. dégoût, m.

loathly, *lōth'lĭ*, loathsome, *lōth'sŭm*, a. dégoûtant, odieux.

lobby, *lŏb'bĭ*, s. vestibule, f.

lobe, *lōb*, s. lobe, m.

lobelia, *lōbē'lĭä*, s. (bot.) lobélie, f.

lobster, *lŏb'stĕr*, s. homard, m. || ~-salad, s. salade de homard, f.

local, *lō'kăl*, a. local.

localise, *lō'kălīz*, v. a. localiser.

locality, *lōkăl'ĭtĭ*, s. localité, f.

locate, *lō'kāt*, v. a. (Am.) placer, établir, fixer. [looch, m.

loch, *lŏk*, s. lac, m. || (in pharmacy)

lock, *lŏk*, s. serrure, f. || platine (d'un fusil), f. || boucle, f., flocon, m. || écluse, f. || étreinte, f. || bagarre, f.

lock, *lŏk*, v. a. & n. fermer à clef || accrocher || se fermer || to ~ in, enfermer, renfermer || to ~ out, fermer la porte à qn. || to ~ up, serrer, enfermer, tenir sous clef || ~-jaw, s. trisme, m. || ~-out, s. grève des patrons, f.

locker, *lŏk'ĕr*, s. tiroir, m., armoire, f.

locket, *lŏk'ĕt*, s. petite serrure, f., bracelet, m.

locksmith, *lŏk'smĭth*, s. serrurier, m. [m.

locomotion, *lōkōmō'shŭn*, s. locomotion, f.

locomotive, *lōkōmō'tĭv*, s. locomotive, f.

locomotive, *lōkōmō'tĭv*, a. locomotif.

locust, *lō'kŭst*, s. sauterelle, f.

lode, *lōd*, s. filon, m., veine, f.

lodge, *lŏj*, s. cabane, f. || loge, f.

lodge, *lŏj*, v. a. & n. loger, placer, fixer || loger.

lodger, *lŏj'ĕr*, s. locataire, m. [demeure.

lodging-house, *lŏj'ĭng hŏŭs*, s. hôtel meublé, m. [(money) dépôt, m.

lodgment, *lŏj'mĕnt*, s. logement, m. || (of

loft, *lŏft*, s. grenier, m. || soupente, f.

loftiness, *lŏf'tĭnĕs*, s. élévation, sublimité, hauteur, f. || fierté, f.

lofty, *lŏf'tĭ*, a. élevé, haut || sublime || fier.

log, *lŏg*, s. bûche, f., billot, bloc, m. || (mar.) loc, m. || ~-book ou ship's ~, s. (mar.) casernet, m.

loggerhead, *lŏg'gĕrhĕd*, s. lourdaud, sot, m. || to be at ~s, être brouillés || to fall to ~s, en venir aux mains.

logic, *lŏj'ĭk*, s. logique, f.

logical, *lŏj'ĭkăl*, a. logique.

logician, *lōjĭsh'ăn*, s. logicien, m. [m.

logwood, *lŏg'wŏŏd*, s. bois de Campêche,

loin, *lŏyn*, s. longe, f. || ~s, s. pl. reins, m. pl.

loiter, *lŏy'tĕr*, v. n. flâner, fainéanter.

loll, *lŏl*, v. a. & n. tendre, allonger || s'étendre nonchalamment.

lollipop, *lŏl'lĭpŏp*, s. sucre d'orge, m.

lone(ly), *lōn'(lĭ)*, a. solitaire, seul.

loneliness, *lōn'lĭnĕs*, s. solitude, f.

long, *lŏng*, v. n.; to ~ to, avoir envie || to ~ for, désirer ardemment.

long, *lŏng*, a. & ad. long || longuement, longtemps || the ~ and short of it is, en somme, tout compte fait || how ~? combien de temps? || ~-suffering, s. endurant, patient.

longevity, *lŏnjĕv'ĭtĭ*, s. longévité, f.

longing, *lŏng'ĭng*, s. désir ardent, m., impatience f. [longitude, f.

longitude, *lŏn'jĭtūd*, s. longueur, f. ||

longitudinal, *lŏnjĭtū'dĭnăl*, a. (-ly, ad.) longitudinal(ement). [apparence, f.

look, *lŏŏk*, s. regard, m. || coup d'œil, m.

look, *lŏŏk*, v. a. & n. regarder, voir || sembler, paraître || avoir l'air || to ~ after, soigner, veiller à || chercher || to ~ on, (des maisons etc.) donner sur || regarder || ~ out ! prenez-garde ! gare ! || to ~ down upon one, regarder qn. du haut en bas || to ~ forward to, s'attendre à || to ~ one up, passer chez qn. || to ~ up to one, considérer qn. || to ~ up to one, (comme supérieur) || ~-out, s. lieu d'observation, m. || to keep a good ~-out, avoir l'œil au guet. [m., glace, f.

looking-glass, *lŏŏk'ĭng glăs*, s. miroir,

bŏy; — fŏŏt, tube, tŭb. || chair, joy; — game, yes; — soul, zeal; — thing, there.

loom, *lôm*, s. métier de tisserand, m.

loom, *lôm*, v. n. (mar.) paraître sur l'horizon.

loop, *lôp*, s. bride, f. || ~-hole, s. trou, m. || meurtrière, f.

loose, *lôs*, a. délié, détaché || relâché, libre, diffus || lascif || lâche || -ly, ad. lâche-ment || négligemment || lascivement.

loosen, *lô'sn*, v. a. relâcher.

looseness, *lôs'nĕs*, s. relâchement, m. ||

loot, *lôt*, s. butin, m.   [diarrhée, f.

loot, *lôt*, v. a. piller.

lop, *lôp*, v. a. ébrancher, élaguer, émonder || ~-eared, a. à oreilles pendantes.

loquacious, *lôkwā'shŭs*, a. babillard.

loquacity, *lôkwăs'ĭtĭ*, s. loquacité, f.

Lord, lord, *lawrd*, s. seigneur, mari, lord, m. || Dieu, m. || my ~, monseigneur.

lord, *lawrd'*, v. n. to ~ it, dominer. [f.

lordliness, *lawrd'lĭnĕs*, s. dignité, hauteur,

lordling, *lawrd'lĭng*, s. gentillâtre, m.

lordly, *lawrd'lĭ*, a. & ad. seigneurial, de lord, hautain, insolemment, arrogamment.

lordship, *lawrd'shĭp*, s. seigneurie, f.

lore, *lôr*, s. leçon, doctrine, f. || science, f.

lose, *lôz*, v. a. & n. ir. perdre, être privé de, laisser échapper || ruiner || dépenser

loser, *lô'zĕr*, s. perdant, m.   [follement.

loss, *lôs*, s. perte, f. || dead ~, perte sèche, f.

lot, *lôt*, s. lot, sort, m. || quote-part, f. (Am.) terre, f. || to cast ~s, tirer au sort.

loth, *lôth*, a. *vide* lo(a)th.

Lothario, *lôthā'rĭô*, s. (fig.) lovelace, m.

lotion, *lô'shŭn*, s. lotion, f.

lottery, *lôt'tĕrĭ*, s. loterie, f.   [haute voix.

loud, *lowd*, a. (-ly, ad.) haut, fort || à

loudness, *lowd'nĕs*, s. bruit, m., force de

lounge, *lownj*, v. n. flâner.   [la voix.

louse, *lows*, s. pou, m.

lousy, *low'zĭ*, a. pouilleux.

lout, *lowt*, s. rustre, lourdaud, m.

loutish, *lowt'ĭsh*, a. grossier, rustique.

love, *lŭv*, s. amour, m. || amie, f. || in ~, amoureux || to make ~, faire l'amour to play (a game) for ~, jouer pour rien || ~-letter, s. billet-doux, m. || ~-match, s. mariage d'inclination, m. || ~-sick, a. languissant d'amour.

love, *lŭv*, v. a. aimer, chérir.

loveliness, *lŭv'lĭnĕs*, s. amabilité, f.

lovely, *lŭv'lĭ*, a. aimable, charmant.

lover, *lŭv'ĕr*, s. amant, m., amante, f. || amateur, m.   [affectueusement.

loving, *lŭv'ĭng*, a. aimant, tendre || -ly, ad.

low, *lô*, v. n. beugler, mugir.

low, *lô*, a. & ad. bas || de peu de valeur || abattu || vil || bassement || à bas prix || à voix basse || ~-water, s. marée basse, f.

lower, *lô'ĕr*, v. a. & n. baisser, abaisser, abattre, diminuer || s'abaisser.

lower, *lowĕr*, v. n. devenir sombre || s'as-sombrir || s'obscurcir || menacer.

lower, *lô'ĕr*, a. inférieur.

lowering, *low'ĕrĭng*, a. sombre, menaçant.

lowland, *lô'lănd*, s. terrain bas, m. || plaine, f.

lowliness, *lô'lĭnĕs*, s. humilité, f.

lowly, *lô'lĭ*, a. (& ad.) humble(ment).

lowness, *lô'nĕs*, s. bassesse, f.

loyal, *lôy'al*, a. (-ly, ad.) loyal(ement).

loyalty, *lôy'altĭ*, s. loyauté, fidélité, f.

lozenge, *lôz'ĕnj*, s. losange, f. || pastille, f.

lubber, *lŭb'bĕr*, s. lourdaud, m.

lubberly, *lŭb'bĕrlĭ*, a. gros et paresseux.

lubricate, *lô'brĭkăt*, v. a. lubrifier.

lucid, *lô'sĭd*, a. (-ly, ad.) lucide(ment) || lumineux || limpide.   [parence, f.

lucidity, *lôsĭd'ĭtĭ*, s. lucidité, f. || trans-lucifer(-match), *lô'sĭfĕr (măch)*, s. allu-mette chimique, f.

luck, *lŭk*, s. hasard, m., fortune, f., bonheur,

luckily, *lŭk'ĭlĭ*, ad. heureusement   [m.

luckless, *lŭk'lĕs*, a. malheureux.

lucky, *lŭk'ĭ*, a. heureux.

lucrative, *lô'krătĭv*, a. lucratif.

lucre, *lô'kĕr*, s. lucre, gain, m.

lucubration, *lôkūbrā'shŭn*, s. élucubra-tion, f.   [(ment).

ludicrous, *lô'dĭkrŭs*, a.(-ly, ad.) burlesque

luff, *lŭf*, v. n. (mar.) tenir au lof.

lug, *lŭg*, v. a. tirer, traîner.

luggage, *lŭg'găj*, s. bagage, m.|| ~-office, s. bureau des bagages, m. || ~-ticket, s. bulletin de bagages, m. || ~-train, s. train de bagages, m. || ~-van, s. voiture de bagages, f.

lugger, *lŭg'gĕr*, s. lougre, m.

lukewarm, *lôk'wawrm*, a. tiède || -ly, ad. avec tiédeur.

lull, *lŭl*, s. moment de calme, m.

lull, *lŭl*, v. a. & n. endormir || se calmer.

lullaby, *lŭl'lăbĭ*, s. berceuse, f.

lumber, *lŭm'bĕr*, s. vieillerie, f.|| ~-room, s. garde-meuble, m.   [naire, m.

luminary, *lô'mĭnĕrĭ*, s. lumière, f. || lumi-luminous, *lô'mĭnŭs*, a. lumineux, luisant, éclairé.   [ou in the ~, en gros.

lump, *lŭmp*, s. masse, f., bloc, m. || by

lumpy, *lŭmp'ĭ*, a. grumeleux.

lunacy, *lô'năsĭ*, s. folie lunatique, f.

lunar, *lô'nĕr*, a. lunaire.

lunatic, *lô'nătĭk*, s. lunatique, m. || fou, m. || ~-asylum, s. hospice des aliénés, m.

lunatic, *lô'nătĭk*, a. lunatique.

lunch(eon), *lŭnsh'(ŭn)*, s. goûter, m. || second déjeuner, m.

lunch, *lŭnsh*, v. n. déjeuner.   [escrime).

lunge, *lŭnj*, v. a. porter une botte (en

lungs, *lŭngz*, s. pl. poumon, m.

lurch, *lĕrch*, s. embarras, m.

lurcher, *lĕrch'ĕr*, s. chien de chasse, m.

lure, *lôr*, s. leurre, m.

lure, *lôr*, v. a. leurrer.

lurk, *lĕrk*, v. n. se cacher || être aux aguets.

luscious, *lŭsh'ŭs*, a. trop doux || liquoreux.

lust, *lŭst*, s. convoitise, luxure, f.

lust, *lŭst*, v. n. convoiter.

lustful, *lŭst'fool*, a. luxurieux || -ly, ad. luxurieusement.

lustily, *lŭst'ĭlĭ*, ad. vigoureusement.

lustiness, *lŭst'ĭnĕs*, s. vigueur, force, f.

lustre, *lŭs'tĕr*, s. lustre, m. || éclat, m.

lusty, *lŭst'ĭ*, a. robuste, vigoureux.

lute, *lôt*, s. luth, m. || (chim.) lut, m.

lûte, hât, fâr, lâw; — hēre, gĕt, hĕr; — mīne, ĭnn; — nō, hŏt, prōve; — hŏw; —

Lutheran, *lŏ'thĕr ăn,* s. luthérien, m.

luxuriance, *lŭg zū'ri ăns,* s. exubérance, f.

luxuriant, *lŭg zū'ri ănt,* a. abondant, exubérant ‖ **-ly,** ad. abondamment.

luxuriate, *lŭg zū'ri āt,* v.n. être trop fertile.

luxurious, *lŭg zū'ri ŭs,* a. luxurieux, voluptueux ‖ **-ly,** ad. luxurieusement.

luxury, *lŭks'ū ri,* s. luxure, f. ‖ mollesse, f. ‖ objet de luxe, m.

lyceum, *li sē'ŭm,* s. lycée, m.

lye, *līi,* s. lessive, f.

lying, *lī'ing,* s. mensonge, m. ‖ **~-in,** s. couches, f.pl. ‖ **~-in-hospital,** s. hôpital de la Maternité, m.

lymph, *limf,* s. lymphe, f.

lymphatic, *lim făt'ik,* a. lymphatique.

lynch, *ltnsh,* v. a. (Am.) lyncher.

lynx, *lingks,* s. lynx, m.

lyre, *lir,* s. lyre, f.

lyric(al), *lir'ik (ăl),* a. lyrique.

M.

macadamize, *măk ăd'ăm īz,* v. a. macadamiser.

macaroni, *mă kă rō'ni,* s. macaroni, m.

macaroon, *măk ă rōn',* s. macaron, m.

mace, *mās,* s. masse, f. ‖ macis, m., fleur de muscade, f. ‖ **~-bearer,** s. massier, m.

macerate, *măs'ĕr āt,* v. a. macérer ‖ mortifier.

machicolate, *mă chik'ō lāt,* v. a. pratiquer des mâchecoulis au haut des tours fortifiées. [tion, f.

machination, *măk ĭ nă'shŭn,* s. machinamachine, *mă shēn',* s. machine, f. ‖ voiture, f. ‖ **~-made,** a. fait à la mécanique.

machinery, *mă shēn'ĕr i,* s. mécanisme, m.

machinist, *mă shēn'ist,* s. machiniste, m.

mackerel, *măk'ĕr ĕl,* s. maquereau, m.

mad, *măd,* a. fou, furieux, enragé ‖ **-ly,** ad. follement ‖ furieusement ‖ **~-cap,** s. fou, m. ‖ **~-house,** s. Charenton, m.

madam, *măd'ăm,* s. madame, f.

madden, *măd'dn,* v. a. rendre fou.

madder, *măd'dĕr,* s. garance, f.

madman, *măd'măn,* s. fou, insensé, m.

madness, *măd'nĕs,* s. démence, fureur, f.

magazine, *măg ă zēn',* s. magasin, m. ‖ journal, m.

maggot, *măg'gŏt,* s. mite, f. ‖ caprice, m.

magic, *măj'ik,* s. magie, f. [par magie.

magic, *măj'ik,* a. magique ‖ **-ally,** ad.

magician, *mă jish'ăn,* s. magicien, m.

magisterial, *măj is tē'ri ăl,* a. de magistrat ‖ magistral ‖ **-ly,** ad. impérieusement. [f.

magistracy, *măj'is tră si,* s. magistrature, f.

magistrate, *măj'is trāt,* s. magistrat, m. ‖ juge, m. [nimité, f.

magnanimity, *măg năn im'i ti,* s. magnamagnanimous, *măg năn'i mŭs,* a. (-ly, ad.) magnanime(ment).

magnet, *măg'nĕt,* s. aimant, m.

magnetic, *măg nĕt'ik,* a. magnétique, d'aimant.

magnetise, *măg'nĕt īz,* v. a. magnétiser ‖ aimanter. [m.

magnetism, *măg'nĕt izm,* s. magnétisme,

magnificence, *măg nif'i sĕns,* s. magnificence, f. [magnifique(ment).

magnificent, *măg nif'i sĕnt,* a. (-ly, ad.)

magnify, *măg'ni fi,* v. a. grossir ‖ louer excessivement ‖ **-ing-glass,** s. verre grossissant, m.

magnitude, *măg'ni tūd,* s. grandeur, f. ‖ importance, f.

magnolia, *măg nō'li ă,* s. magnolier, m.

magpie, *măg'pī,* s. pie, f.

mahogany, *mă hŏg'ă ni,* s. acajou, m.

maid, *mād,* s. fille, f. ‖ servante, f. ‖ **~ of all work,** s. bonne à tout faire, f.

maiden, *mā'dn,* s. fille, vierge, f.

maiden, *mā'dn,* a. virginal ‖ frais, neuf ‖ **~ lady,** s. demoiselle, f. ‖ **~ speech,** s. premier discours, début, m.

maidenhood, *mā'dn hŏŏd,* s. virginité, f.

maidenly, *mā'dn li,* a. virginal, modeste.

mail, *māl,* s. maille, f. ‖ armure, f. ‖ malle, f. ‖ **~-coach,** s. malle-poste, f. ‖ **~-packet,** **~-steamer,** s. paquebot-poste, m. ‖ **~-train,** s. train-poste, m.

maim, *mām,* v. a. estropier, mutiler.

main, *măn,* s. principal, m. ‖ total, m. ‖ océan, m. ‖ continent, m. ‖ vigueur, f. ‖ **in the ~,** en général.

main, *măn,* a. (-ly, ad.) principal(ement) ‖ capital, essentiel ‖ **by ~ strength,** de haute lutte ‖ **~-land,** s. terre ferme, f. ‖ **~-line,** s. (rail.) voie principale, f. ‖ **~-mast,** s. grand mât, m. ‖ **~-spring,** s. grand ressort, m.

maintain, *măn tăn',* v. a. & n. maintenir ‖ entretenir, nourrir ‖ soutenir.

maintainance, *măn'tăn ăns,* s. entretien, soutien, m. ‖ moyens d'existence, m. pl. ‖ pension alimentaire, f.

maize, *māz,* s. maïs, m.

maizena, *mă zē'nă,* s. maïzéna, m.

majestic, *mă jĕs'tik,* a. majestueux ‖ **-ally,** ad. majestueusement.

majesty, *măj'ĕs ti,* s. majesté, f.

majolica, *mă jŏl'i kă,* s. majolique, f.

major, *mā'jĕr,* s. (mil.) major, m. ‖ majeure, f. ‖ **~-domo,** s. maître d'hôtel, m. ‖ **~-general,** s. général de brigade, m. [plus grand.

major, *mā'jĕr,* a. majeur, d'âge majeur ‖

majority, *mă jŏr'i ti,* s. majorité, f. ‖ grade du major, m.

make, *māk,* s. façon, f. ‖ construction, f.

make, *māk,* v. a. & n. ir. faire, fabriquer ‖ rendre ‖ gagner ‖ (com.) confectionner ‖ s'avancer vers, tendre ‖ contribuer ‖ **to ~ a bed,** faire un lit ‖ **to ~ much (no-thing) of,** faire grand cas (peu de cas) de ‖ **to ~ up** (a quarrel), accommoder, arranger ‖ **to ~ up to one,** amadouer qn. ‖ **~-believe,** s. feinte, f.

makepeace, *măk′ pēs,* s. médiateur, m.

maker, *măk′ ẽr,* s. créateur, m. ‖ faiseur, auteur, m.

makeshift, *māk′ shĭft,* s. pis-aller, m.

makeweight, *māk′ wāt,* s. supplément, m. ‖ (fig.) remplissage, m.

making, *māk′ ing,* s. façon, f. ‖ fabrication, f. ‖ **to be the ~ of one,** faire la fortune de qn.

maladministration, *măl ăd mĭ nĭ strā′ shŭn,* s. mauvaise administration, f.

malady, *măl′ ă dĭ,* s. maladie, f.

malapert, *măl′ ă pẽrt,* a. impertinent.

malaria, *măl ā′ rĭ ă,* s. air infect, m.

malcontent, *măl′ kŏn tĕnt,* s. mécontent, m.

malcontent, *măl′ kŏn tĕnt,* a. mécontent.

male, *māl,* s. mâle, m. [broche à vis, f.

male, *māl,* a. masculin ‖ **~ screw,** s.

malediction, *măl ē dĭk′ shŭn,* s. malédiction, f.

malefactor, *măl ē făk′ tẽr,* s. malfaiteur, m.

maleficent, *măl lĕf′ ĭ sĕnt,* a. malfaisant.

malevolence, *mă lĕv′ ŏ lĕns,* s. malveillance, f.　　　　　　[—ly, ad. malicieusement.

malevolent, *mă lĕv′ ŏ lĕnt,* a. malveillant ‖

malformation, *măl fŏr mā′ shŭn,* s. vice de conformation, m.

malice, *măl′ ĭs,* s. malice, méchanceté, f.

malicious, *mă lĭsh′ ŭs,* a. malicieux ‖ **-ly,** ad. méchamment.　　　　[famer ‖ maltraiter.

malign, *mă līn′,* v. a. envier ‖ nuire ‖ dif-

malign, *mă līn′,* a. malin, malfaisant.

malignance, *mă lĭg′ năns,* **malignity,** *mă lĭg′ nĭ tĭ,* s. malignité, f.

malignant, *mă lĭg′ nănt,* a. malin ‖ **-ly,** ad. malignement.　　　　　　　　[maladie.

malinger, *mă lĭng′ gẽr,* v. n. simuler une

malleability, *măl lē ă bĭl′ ĭ tĭ,* s. malléabilité, f.

malleable, *măl′ lē ă bl,* a. malléable.

mallet, *măl′ lĕt,* s. maillet, m. ‖ (for playing) mail, m.

mallow(s), *măl′ lō(z),* s. (bot.) mauve, f.

malmsey, *măm′ zĭ,* s. vin de malvoisie, m.

malpractice, *măl prăk′ tĭs,* s. malversation, f. ‖ action illicite, f. ‖ mauvais traitement, m.

malt, *mawlt,* s. malt, m. ‖ drêche, f. ‖ **~ liquor,** s. boisson d'orge brassée, f.

maltreat, *măl trēt′,* v. a. maltraiter.

mamma, *măm mă′,* s. maman, f. [pare, m.

mammal, *măm′ măl,* s. mammifère, vivi-

man, *măn,* s. homme, m. ‖ valet, m. ‖ ouvrier, m. ‖ (at chess) pion, m. ‖ **to a ~,** l'un comme l'autre ‖ **~-of-war,** s. vaisseau de guerre, m. ‖ **best ~,** s. garçon d'honneur, m. ‖ **~-eater,** s. anthropophage, m. ‖ **~-trap,** s. chausse-trape, f.

man, *măn,* v. a. armer ‖ garnir de soldats.

manacle, *măn′ ă kl,* v. a. mettre des menottes.

manacles, *măn′ ă klz,* s. pl. menottes, f. pl.

manage, *măn′ āj,* v. a. & n. conduire, mener, manier ‖ administrer, diriger ‖ ménager ‖ dresser, gouverner.

manageable, *măn′ āj ă bl,* a. maniable, traitable.

management, *măn′ āj mĕnt,* s. ménagement, m., administration, f. ‖ conduite habile, f.

manager, *măn′ āj ẽr,* s. directeur, administrateur, m. ‖ ménager, économe, m.

managing, *măn′ āj ing,* a. (com.) gérant.

mandamus, *măn dā′ mŭs,* s. (jur.) ordre royal, m.

mandate, *măn′ dāt,* s. mandat, précepte, m.　　　　　　　　　　　　　　　　　[m.

mandatory, *măn′ dă tẽr ĭ,* s. mandataire, ‖

mandragora, *măn drăg′ ŏ ră,* **mandrake,** *măn′ drāk,* s. mandragore, f.

mane, *măn,* s. crinière, f.

maned, *mănd,* a. ayant une crinière.

manes, *mā′ nēz,* s. pl. mânes, m. pl.

manful, *măn′ fŏŏl,* a. courageux ‖ **-ly,** ad. courageusement.　　　　　　　　[ganèse, m.

manganese, *măn′ găn ēz,* s. (chim.) man-

mange, *mānj,* s. gale, f.

mangle, *măng′ gl,* s. calandre, f. ‖ **~-wurzel,** s. racine du manglier, f.

mangle, *măng′ gl,* v. a. mutiler ‖ calandrer.

mango, *măng′ gō,* s. mangue, m. ‖ **~-tree,** s. manguier, m.

mangy, *măn′ jĭ,* a. galeux.

manhood, *măn′ hŏŏd,* s. virilité, f., âge viril, m. ‖ humanité, f.

mania, *mā′ nĭ ă,* s. manie, folie, f.

maniac, *mā′ nĭ ăk,* s. maniaque, m.

maniac(al), *mā′ nĭ ăk(ăl),* a. maniaque.

manifest, *măn′ ĭ fĕst,* s. manifeste, m.

manifest, *măn′ ĭ fĕst,* v. a. manifester.

manifest, *măn′ ĭ fĕst,* a. manifeste.

manifestation, *măn ĭ fĕs tā′ shŭn,* s. manifestation, f.

manifesto, *măn ĭ fĕs′ tō,* s. manifeste, m.

manifold, *măn′ ĭ fōld,* a. nombreux, varié ‖ **~-writer,** s. polygraphe, m.

manikin, *măn′ ĭ kĭn,* s. nabot, m. ‖ mannequin, m.　　　　　　　　　　　[manipuler.

manipulate, *mă nĭp′ ŭ lāt,* v. a. manier,

manipulation, *mă nĭp ŭ lā′ shŭn,* s. manipulation, f.

mankind, *măn kīnd′,* s. genre humain, m., hommes, m. pl.

manlike, *măn′ līk,* a. d'homme ‖ brave.

manliness, *măn′ lĭ nĕs,* s. air mâle, m. ‖ bravoure, f.　　　　　　　　　　　[homme.

manly, *măn′ lĭ,* a. & ad. mâle ‖ brave ‖ en

manner, *măn′ nẽr,* s. manière, méthode, habitude, f., genre, m., façon, f. ‖ **-s,** pl. politesse, f.　　　　　　　　　　　　　　[m.

mannerism, *măn′ nẽr ĭzm,* s. maniérisme,

mannerist, *măn′ nẽr ĭst,* s. maniériste, m.

mannerly, *măn′ nẽr lĭ,* a. (& ad.) poli(ment).

manœuvre, *măn ŏ′ vẽr,* s. évolution, f., stratagème, m.

manœuvre, *măn ŏ′ vẽr,* v. n. manœuvrer.

manor, *măn′ ẽr,* s. manoir, m., seigneurie, f.

mansion, *măn′ shŭn,* s. demeure, f. ‖ château, m. ‖ **~-house,** s. mairie, f.

manslaughter, *măn′ slaw tẽr,* s. homicide (involontaire), m.

mantle, *măn′ tl,* s. manteau, m.

mantle, *măn′ tl,* v. a. couvrir, déguiser ‖ **~,** v. n. s'étendre ‖ (of wine) écumer.

---

lāte, hăt, fâr, lăw; — hēre, gĕt, hẽr; — mīne, ĭnn; — nŏ, hŏt, prŏve; — hŏw; —

mantlepiece, *măn'tl pēs,* s. manteau de cheminée, m.

manual, *măn'ū ăl,* s. manuel, m.

manual, *măn'ū ăl,* a. manuel. ~

manufactory, *măn ū făk'tĕr ĭ,* s. manufacture, fabrique, f.

manufacture, *măn ū făk'tūr,* s. manufacture, fabrique, f. ‖ facturer, fabriquer.

manufacture, *măn ū făk'tūr,* v. a. manufacturer.

manufacturer, *măn ū făk'tū rĕr,* s. manufacturier, fabricant, m.

manure, *mă nūr',* s. engrais, m.

manure, *mă nūr',* v. a. engraisser, cultiver.

manuscript, *măn'ū skrĭpt,* s. manuscrit, m.

many, *měn'ĭ,* a. plusieurs, beaucoup ‖ **how ~ ?** combien ? ‖ **as ~ as,** autant que.

map, *măp,* s. carte géographique, f.

map, *măp,* v. a. (to ~ out) tracer.

maple, *mā'pl,* s. érable, m.

mar, *mär,* v. a. gâter, détruire, troubler ‖ **~plot,** s. brouillon, m.

marauder, *mă raŭd'ĕr,* s. maraudeur, m.

marauding, *mă raŭ'ding,* s. maraudage, m.

marble, *mär'bl,* s. marbre, m. ‖ bille, f.

marble, *mär'bl,* v. a. marbrer.

marble, *mär'bl,* a. de marbre, marbré.

March, *märch,* *märch,* s. mars, m. ‖ marche, f. ‖ pas, m. [marcher.

march, *märch,* v. a. & n. faire marcher ‖

marchioness, *mär'shŏn ĕs,* s. marquise, f.

mare, *mär',* s. jument, f. ‖ **~'s nest,** s. merle blanc, m. [rine, f.

margarine, *mär' gä rĭn,* s. (chim.) marga-

margin, *mär'jĭn,* s. bord, m., marge, f.

marginal, *mär'jĭ năl,* a. marginal.

marigold, *mär'ĭ gōld,* s. (bot.) souci, m. ‖ œillet d'Inde, m.

marine, *mă rēn',* s. marine, f. ‖ marin, m.

marine, *mă rēn',* a. marin ‖ **~ stores,** s. pl. bric-à-brac, m.

mariner, *mär'ĭ nĕr,* s. matelot, m. ‖ **~'s card,** s. rose des vents, f.

marital, *mär'ĭ tăl,* a. marital, de mari.

maritime, *mär'ĭ tĭm,* a. maritime, naval.

marjoram, *mär'jŏr ăm,* s. marjolaine, f.

mark, *märk,* s. marque, f., signe, m. ‖ but, blanc, m. ‖ **to make one's ~ (in the world),** se distinguer.

mark, *märk,* v. a. & n. marquer, remarquer.

marker, *märk'ĕr,* s. garçon de billard, m.

market, *mär'kĕt,* s. marché, m., place, f. ‖ cours, prix, m. ‖ **in the ~,** (com.) sur la place ‖ **~gardener,** s. maraîcher, m.

marketable, *mär'kĕt ă bl,* a. marchand, de bonne vente.

marksman, *märks'măn,* s. bon tireur, m.

marl, *märl,* s. marne, f. ‖ **~pit,** s. marnière, f.

marl, *märl,* v. a. marner.

marlingspike, *mär'ling spĭk,* s. (mar.) épissoir, m.

marly, *mär'lĭ,* a. marneux.

marmalade, *mär'mă lād,* s. marmelade, f.

marmoset, *mär'mō zĕt,* s. marmot, m.

marmot, *mär'mŏt,* s. marmotte, f.

maroon, *mă rōn',* s. marron, m.

marquee, *mär kē',* s. tente d'officier, f.

marquess, *mär'kwĕs,* s. marquise, f.

marquetry, *mär'kĕt rĭ,* s. marqueterie, f.

marquis, *mär'kwĭs,* s. marquis, m.

marquisate, *mär'kwĭz ăt,* s. marquisat, m.

marriage, *mär'rĭj,* s. mariage, m. ‖ noces, f. pl. ‖ **~articles** (**~settlement**), s. pl. contrat de mariage, m.

marriageable, *mär'rĭj ă bl,* a. nubile.

married, *mär'rĭd,* a. marié, conjugal.

marrow, *mär'rō,* s. moelle, f. ‖ **spinal ~,** moelle épinière, f. ‖ **~fat pea,** s. pois carré, m.

marry, *mär'rĭ,* v. a. (& n.) (se) marier.

marsh, *märsh,* s. marais, m. ‖ **~mallow,** s. (bot.) guimauve, f.

marshal, *mär'shăl,* s. maréchal, m.

marshal, *mär'shăl,* v. a. arranger.

marshy, *märsh'ĭ,* a. marécageux.

mart, *märt,* s. marché, m., foire, f. ‖ vente, f. ‖ entrepôt, m. [m.

marten, *mär'tĕn,* s. martre, f. ‖ martinet,

martial, *mär'shăl,* a. martial, guerrier, belliqueux ‖ **~law,** s. loi militaire, f.

martin, *mär'tĭn,* s. hirondelle domestique, f.

Martinmas, *mär'tĭn măs,* s. la Saint-Martin. [tin.

martyr, *mär'tĕr,* s. martyr, m.

martyrdom, *mär'tĕr dŏm,* s. martyre, m.

marvel, *mär'vĕl,* s. merveille, f.

marvel, *mär'vĕl,* v. n. s'étonner.

marvellous, *mär'vĕl lŭs,* a. merveilleux ‖ **~ly,** ad. merveilleusement.

masculine, *măs'kū lĭn,* s. masculin, m.

masculine, *măs'kū lĭn,* a. masculin, mâle.

masculinity, *măs kū lĭn'ĭ tĭ,* s. virilité, f.

mash, *măsh,* s. mélange, tripotage, m. ‖ (bot.) mâche, f. [brasser.

mash, *măsh,* v. a. mélanger ‖ écraser ‖

mask, *măsk,* s. masque, m. ‖ bal masqué, m. ‖ subterfuge, m.

mask, *măsk,* v. a. (& n.) (se) masquer.

masker, *măsk'ĕr,* s. personne masquée, f.

mason, *mā'sn,* s. maçon, m.

masonry, *mā'sn rĭ,* s. maçonnerie, f.

masquerade, *măs kĕr ād',* s. mascarade, f.

masquerader, *măs kĕr ā'dĕr,* s. personne masquée, f. [book, s. missal, m.

mass, *măs,* s. masse, f. ‖ messe, f. ‖ **~book,** s. missal, m.

massacre, *măs'să kĕr,* s. massacre, m.

massacre, *măs'să kĕr,* v. a. massacrer.

massive, *măs'sĭv,* a. massif. [f.

mast, *măst,* s. mât, m. ‖ gland, m. ‖ faîne,

master, *măs'tĕr,* s. maître, m. ‖ monsieur, m. ‖ chef, m. ‖ patron (d'un vaisseau), m. ‖ professeur, m. ‖ **~key,** s. passe-partout, m. ‖ **~stroke,** s. coup de maître, m.

master, *măs'tĕr,* v. a. maîtriser, dompter, vaincre ‖ exécuter en maître.

masterful, *măs'tĕr fōōl,* a. impérieux ‖ de main de maître.

masterly, *măs'tĕr lĭ,* a. & ad. en maître, de maître ‖ impérieux. [m.

masterpiece, *măs'tĕr pēs,* s. chef d'œuvre,

mastership, *măs'tĕr shĭp,* s. maîtrise, supériorité, f.

mastery, *măs'tĕr ĭ,* s. puissance, supériorité, f., savoir, m.

masticate, *măs'tĭ kāt*, v. a. mâcher.

mastiff, *măs'tĭf*, s. mâtin, m.

mat, *măt*, s. natte, f., paillasson, m.

mat, *măt*, v. a. natter.

match, *măch*, s. allumette, mèche, f. || mariage, parti, m. || partie, f. || lutte, f. || pareil, m. || pari, m. || ~-box, s. porte-allumettes, m.

match, *măch*, v. a. & n. égaler, proportionner || marier, appareiller, apparier.

matchless, *măch'lĕs*, a. incomparable, unique.

matchmaker, *măch'māk ĕr*, s. faiseur de mariages, m.

mate, *māt*, s. mari, compagnon, camarade, m. || aide, m. || (at chess) mat, m. || compagne, f.

mate, *māt*, v. a. marier || mater.

material, *mă tē'rĭ ăl*, s. matière, f. || –s, s. pl. matériaux, m. pl.

material, *mă tē'rĭ ăl*, a. (-ly, ad.) matériel(lement) || essentiel(lement) || important.

materialise, *mă tē'rĭ ăl ĭz*, v. a. matérialiser.

materialism, *mă tē'rĭ ăl ĭzm*, s. matérialisme, m.

materialist, *mă tē'rĭ ăl ĭst*, s. matérialiste, m.

materiality, *mă tē rĭ ăl'ĭ tĭ*, s. matérialité, f.

maternal, *mă tĕr'năl*, a. maternel.

maternity, *mă tĕr'nĭ tĭ*, s. maternité, f.

mathematical, *măth ĕ măt'ĭk ăl*, a. (-ly, ad.) mathématique(ment).

mathematician, *măth ĕ mă tĭsh'ăn*, s. mathématicien, m.

mathematics, *măth ĕ măt'ĭks*, s. pl. mathématiques, f. pl.

matins, *măt'ĭns*, s. pl. matines, f. pl.

matricide, *măt'rĭ sĭd*, s. matricide, m.

matriculate, *mă trĭk'ū lāt*, v. a. immatriculer.

matriculation, *mă trĭk ū lā'shŭn*, s. immatriculation, f.

matrimonial, *măt rĭ mō'nĭ ăl*, a. matrimonial, conjugal.

matrimony, *măt'rĭ mŏn ĭ*, s. mariage, m.

matron, *mā'trŏn*, s. matrone, f.

matronly, *mā'trŏn lĭ*, a. âgée, vénérable.

matter, *măt'tĕr*, s. matière, f. || sujet, m. || objet, m. || affaire, f. || importance, f. || manuscrit, m. || pus, m. || what's the ~ ? qu'y a-t-il ? || ~-of-fact, a. positif, pratique.

matter, *măt'tĕr*, v. n. imp. importer.

mattock, *măt'tŭk*, s. pioche, f.

mattress, *măt'rĕs*, s. matelas, m.

mature, *mă tūr'*, v. a. & n. mûrir.

mature, *mă tūr'*, a. (-ly, ad.) mûr(ement).

maturity, *mă tū'rĭ tĭ*, s. maturité, f. || (of bills) échéance, f.

maudlin, *măwd'lĭn*, a. ivre || larmoyant.

maul, *măwl*, v. a. meurtrir, froisser || battre, étriller || ~-stick, s. baguette de (peintre), f.

maunder, *măwn'dĕr*, v. n. gronder || ra-

Maundy-Thursday, *măwn'dĭ thŭrz'dā*, s. jeudi saint, m.

mausoleum, *măw sō lē'ŭm*, s. mausolée, m.

maw, *măw*, s. panse, f. || jabot, m.

mawkish, *măwk'ĭsh*, a. dégoûtant, fade.

maxim, *măks'ĭm*, s. maxime, f.

May, may, *mă*, s. mai, m. || (bot.) aubépine, f. || ~-bug, s. hanneton, m. || ~-day, s. premier mai, m. || ~-pole, s. mai (arbre), m.

may, *mă*, v. n. ir. pouvoir.

maybe, *mă'bē*, ad. peut-être.

mayor, *mā'ĕr*, s. maire, m.

mayoralty, *mā'ĕr ăl tĭ*, s. mairie, f.

mayoress, *mā'ĕr ĕs*, s. femme du maire, mairesse, f.

maze, *māz*, s. labyrinthe, m., perplexité, f.

mazy, *mā'zĭ*, a. labyrinthique || confus.

me, *mē*, pn. moi, me.

mead, *mēd*, s. hydromel, m.

meadow, *mĕd'ō*, s. prairie, f. || pré, m, pâturage.

meagre, *mē'gĕr*, a. (-ly, ad.) maigre(ment) || pauvre(ment).

meagreness, *mē'gĕr nĕs*, s. maigreur, pauvreté, f.

meal, *mēl*, s. repas, m. || farine, f.

mealy, *mēl'ĭ*, a. farineux || ~-mouthed, a. timide.

mean, *mēn*, s. médiocrité, f. || moyen, m. || –s, s. pl. manière, f. || moyens, m. pl. || by all –s, sans contredit.

mean, *mēn*, v. a. & n. vouloir dire || signifier || penser || se proposer.

mean, *mēn*, a. (-ly, ad.) bas(sement) || vil || médiocre(ment) || in the ~ while (time), en attendant.

meander, *mē ăn'dĕr*, v. a. serpenter.

meaning, *mēn'ing*, s. signification, pensée, f.

meanness, *mēn'nĕs*, s. médiocrité, f. || bassesse de sentiments, lâcheté, f.

meantime, *mēn tim'*, meanwhile, *mēn hwil'*, ad. en attendant.

measles, *mē'zlz*, s. pl. rougeole, f.

measurable, *mĕzh'ŏŏr ă bl*, a. mesurable.

measure, *mĕzh'ŏŏr*, s. mesure, f. || portion, f. || (fig.) portée, f.

measure, *mĕzh'ŏŏr*, v. a. mesurer || arpenter || prendre mesure à.

measurement, *mĕzh'ŏŏr mĕnt*, s. mesurage, m.

meat, *mēt*, s. viande, f. || nourriture, f. || ~-ball, s. boulette de viande, f.

mechanic, *mē kăn'ĭk*, s. ouvrier, artisan, m.

mechanical, *mē kăn'ĭ kăl*, a. (-ly, ad.) mécanique(ment).

mechanician, *mĕk ă nĭsh'ăn*, mechanist, *mĕk'ăn ĭst*, s. mécanicien, m.

mechanics, *mē kăn'ĭks*, s. pl. mécanique, f.

mechanism, *mĕk'ă nĭzm*, s. mécanisme, m.

medal, *mĕd'ăl*, s. médaille, f.

medallion, *mē dăl'yŭn*, s. médaillon, m.

meddle, *mĕd'l*, v. n. se mêler de.

meddler, *mĕd'lĕr*, s. intrigant, m. || tatillon, m.

mediæval, *mĕd ĭ ē'văl*, a. du moyen-âge.

mediate, *mē'dĭ āt*, v. n. s'interposer.

mediation, *mē dĭ ā'shŭn*, s. médiation, entremise, f.

mediator, *mē dĭ ā'tĕr*, s. médiateur, m.

medical, *mĕd'ĭ kăl*, a. médical, médicinal || -ly, ad. en médecine.

medicament, *mĕd'ĭ kă mĕnt*, s. médicament, m.

medicate, *mĕd'ĭ kāt*, v. a. imprégner de drogues || (wine) frelater.

medicine, *mĕd'ĭ sĭn*, s. médecine, f. || médicament, m. || ~-chest, s. droguier, m.

mediocrity, *mē dǐ ŏk' rǐ tǐ,* s. médiocrité, f.
meditate, *měd' ǐ tāt,* v. a. & n. méditer.
meditation, *měd ǐ tā' shǔn,* s. méditation.
meditative, *měd' ǐ tā tǐv,* a. méditatif. [f.
mediterranean, *měd' ǐ těr rā' nē ǎn,* a. méditerranné.
medium, *měd' ǐ ǔm,* s. médium, milieu, m. || moyen, m. || doigt du milieu, m.
medium, *měd' ǐ ǔm,* a. moyen.
medlar, *měd' lẽr,* s. nèfle, f.
medley, *měd' lǐ,* s. mélange, m.
meed, *mēd,* s. récompense, f.
meek, *mēk,* a. (-ly, ad.) doux, paisible || avec douceur. [f.
meekness, *mēk' něs,* s. douceur, modestie,
meet, *mēt,* s. rendez-vous de chasse, m.
meet, *mēt,* v. a. & n. ir. rencontrer || éprouver, recevoir || aller à la rencontre || se rencontrer || se joindre || to ~ one halfway, (fig.) faire des avances à qn.
meet, *mēt,* a. (-ly, ad.) propre || convenable(ment).
meeting, *mēt' ǐng,* s. rencontre, f. || assemblée, f., congrès, m., entrevue, f. || ~-house, s. oratoire, m.
melancholy, *měl' ǎng kǒl ǐ,* s. mélancolie, f.
melancholy, *měl' ǎng kǒl ǐ,* a. mélancolique.
mellifluous, *měl lǐf' lōō ǔs,* a. melliflu.
mellow, *měl' lō,* v. a. & n. mûrir || amollir, s'adoucir. [feux || ivre.
mellow, *měl' lō,* a. mûr || mou, doux, moelleux || (fig.) faux.
mellowness, *měl' lō něs,* s. maturité, f. douceur, f. [-ly, ad. mélodieusement.
melodious, *měl ō' dǐ ǔs,* a. mélodieux ||
melody, *měl' ō dǐ,* s. mélodie, f.
melon, *měl' ǔn,* s. melon, m. || ~-bed, ~-pit, s. melonnière, f.
melt, *mělt,* v. a. & n. ir. fondre, liquéfier || attendrir || se liquéfier, s'attendrir.
melting, *mělt' ǐng,* a. touchant || étouffant.
member, *měm' bẽr,* s. membre, sociétaire, m.
membership, *měm' bẽr shǐp,* s. qualité de membre *ou* de sociétaire, f.
memoir, *měm' wǎwr,* s. mémoire, m.
memorable, *měm' ō rǎ bl,* a. mémorable.
memorably, *měm' ō rǎ blǐ,* ad. digne de mémoire. [souvenir, m. || carnet, m.
memorandum, *měm ō rǎn' dǔm,* s. note, f.||
memorial, *mě mō' rǐ ǎl,* s. mémorial, mémoire, placet, m.
memorial, *mě mō' rǐ ǎl,* a. commémoratif.
memory, *měm' ō rǐ,* s. mémoire, f.. souvenir, m.
menace, *měn' ās,* s. menace, f.
menace, *měn' ās,* v. a. menacer.
menagery, *měn ǎj' ẽr ǐ,* s. ménagerie, f.
mend, *měnd,* v. a. & n. raccommoder || améliorer || se corriger.
mendacious, *měn dā' shǔs,* a. mensonger.
mendacity, *měn dǎs' ǐ tǐ,* s. mensonge, m., fausseté, f.
mendicant, *měn' dǐ kǎnt,* s. mendiant, m.
mendicant, *měn' dǐ kǎnt,* a. mendiant.
mendicity, *měn dǐs' ǐ tǐ,* s. mendicité, f.
menial, *mē' nǐ ǎl,* s. domestique, m.
menial, *mē' nǐ ǎl,* a. domestique || servile.

meningitis, *měn ǐn jī' tǐs,* s. (méd.) méningite, f. [m.
mensuration, *měn sū rā' shǔn,* s. mesurage
mental, *měn' tǎl,* a. (-ly, ad.) mental (ement).
mention, *měn' shǔn,* s. mention, f.
mention, *měn' shǔn,* v. a. faire mention || don't ~ it! il n'y a pas de quoi! || to receive honourable ~, (mil.) être mis à l'ordre du jour.
mephitic, *mě fǐt' ǐk,* a. méphitique.
mercantile, *mẽr' kǎn tǐl,* a. mercantile, marchand.
mercenary, *mẽr' sē nā rǐ,* s. mercenaire, m.
mercenary, *mẽr' sē nā rǐ,* a. mercenaire.
mercer, *mẽr' sẽr,* s. mercier, m.
merchandise, *mẽr' chǎn dǐz,* s. marchandise, f.
merchant, *mẽr' chǎnt,* s. négociant, m. || ~-service, s. marine marchande, f.
merchantman, *mẽr' chǎnt mǎn,* s. vaisseau marchand, m.
merciful, *mẽr' sǐ fōōl,* a. miséricordieux || -ly, ad. miséricordieusement.
merciless, *mẽr' sǐ lěs,* a. (-ly, ad.) impitoyable(ment).
mercurial, *mẽr kū' rǐ ǎl,* a. mercuriel || vif.
mercury, *mẽr' kū rǐ,* s. vif-argent, m.
mercy, *mẽr' sǐ,* s. miséricorde, f.||pardon, m.
mere, *mẽr,* a. (-ly, ad.) seul(ement) || unique || pur. [sane || (fig.) faux.
meretricious, *mẽr ě trǐsh' ǔs,* a. de courtisane || (fig.) faux.
merge, *mẽrj,* v. a. plonger. [dien, m.
meridian, *mě rǐd' ǐ ǎn,* s. midi, m. || méridien, m.
meridional, *mě rǐd' ǐ ō nǎl,* a. méridional.
merit, *mẽr' ǐt,* s. mérite, m.
merit, *mẽr' ǐt,* v. a. mériter.
meritorious, *mẽr ǐ tō' rǐ ǔs,* a. (-ly, ad.) méritoire(ment).
mermaid, *mẽr' mād,* s. sirène, f.
merrily, *mẽr' rǐ lǐ,* ad. gaiement.
merriment, *mẽr' rǐ měnt,* s. joie, jouissance, f.
merry, *mẽr' rǐ,* a. gai, joyeux, enjoué || ~-go-round, s. carrousel, m.
mesh, *měsh,* s. maille, f.
mesmerise, *měz' mẽr ǐz,* v. a. mesmériser.
mesmerism, *měz' mẽr ǐzm,* s. mesmérisme, m. [m.
mess, *měs,* s. mets, plat, m.
message, *měs' sǎj,* s. message, m., commission, f. || dépêche, f.
messenger, *měs' sěn jẽr,* s. messager, m.
metal, *mět' ǎl (mět' l),* s. métal, m. || Britannia-~, métal blanc anglais, titane, m. || gun-~, métal de canon, m.
metallic, *mě tǎl' lǐk,* a. métallique.
metallurgy, *mět' ǎl lẽr jǐ,* s. métallurgie, f.
metamorphose, *mět ǎ mōr' fōs,* v. a. métamorphoser. [morphose, f.
metamorphosis, *mět ǎ mōr' fō sǐs,* s. méta-
metaphor, *mět' ǎ fǒr,* s. métaphore, f.
metaphysical, *mět ǎ fǐz' ǐk ǎl,* a. (-ly, ad.) métaphysique(ment). [sique, f.
metaphysics, *mět ǎ fǐz' ǐks,* s. pl. métaphy-
mete, *mēt,* v. a. mesurer.
meteor, *mē' tē ǒr,* s. météore, m.
meteoric, *mē tē ǒr' ǐk,* a. météorique.

meteorological, *mētēŏr ō lŏj'ĭ kăl,* a. météorologique.   [logie, f.

meteorology, *mē tēŏr ŏl'ŏ jĭ,* s. météorologie.

methinks, *mē thĭngks',* v. imp. il me semble, je pense.

method, *mĕth'ŏd,* s. méthode, f.

methodical, *mē thŏd'ĭk ăl,* a. (-ly, ad.) méthodique(ment).   [méthode.

methodise, *mĕth'ō dīz,* v. a. arranger avec Methodist. *mĕth'ō dĭst,* s. méthodiste, m.

methought, *mē thawt',* v. imp. il m'a semblé, j'ai pensé.

metre, *mē'tēr,* s. mètre, m.

metrical, *mĕt'rĭk ăl,* a. métrique.

metropolis, *mĕt rŏp'ō lĭs,* s. métropole, f.

metropolitan, *mĕt rō pŏl'ĭ tăn,* s. archevêque, m.

mettle, *mĕt'l,* s. vivacité, ardeur, f., courage, m. ‖ to put one on one's ~, enflammer le courage de qn.

mettled, *mĕt'ld,* **mettlesome,** *mĕt'l sŭm,* a. fougueux.   [enfermer.

mew, *mū,* v. n. miauler ‖ to ~ up, v. a.

mews, *mūz,* s. pl. écuries, f. pl.

Michaelmas, *mĭk'ĕl măs,* s. la Saint-Michel, f.

microscope, *mī'krō skŏp,* s. microscope.

microscopic(al), *mī krō skŏp'ĭk (ăl),* a. (-ly, ad.) microscopique(ment).

mid, *mĭd,* a. mi, milieu ‖ ~-course, s. moitié du chemin, f. ‖ ~-way, s. & ad. à moitié chemin.

midday, *mĭd'dā,* s. midi, m.

middle, *mĭd'dl,* s. milieu, m.

middle, *mĭd'dl,* a. moyen, du milieu.

middleman, *mĭd'l măn,* s. intermédiaire, m. ‖ fermier des revenus, m.

middling, *mĭd'lĭng,* a. moyen, médiocre.

midland, *mĭd'lănd,* a. intérieur.

midnight, *mĭd'nĭt,* s. minuit, m.

midnight, *mĭd'nĭt,* a. de minuit.   [m.

midship, *mĭd'shĭp,* s. milieu du vaisseau.

midshipman, *mĭd'shĭp măn,* s. élève de

midst, *mĭdst,* s. milieu, m.   [marine, m.

midsummer, *mĭd'sŭm nĕr,* s. milieu de l'été, m. ‖ la Saint-Jean.

midwife, *mĭd'wīf,* s. sage-femme, f.

midwifery, *mĭd'wĭf rĭ* ou *mĭd'wĭf rĭ,* s. art d'accoucher, m. ‖ accouchement, m.

mien, *mēn,* s. mine, f., air, m.

might, *mĭt,* s. puissance, force, f.

mightily, *mīt'ĭ lĭ,* ad. puissamment.

mightiness, *mīt'ĭ nĕs,* s. puissance, f.

mighty, *mīt'ĭ,* a. puissant.

mignonette, *mĭn yŏn nĕt',* s. réséda, m.

migrate, *mī'grāt,* v. n. émigrer.

migration, *mī grā'shŭn,* s. migration, f.

migratory, *mī'grā tĕr ĭ,* a. migratoire ‖ passager.

milch, *mĭlch,* a. donnant du lait.

mild, *mīld,* a. doux, tendre ‖ -ly, ad.

mildew, *mĭl'dū,* s. nielle, f.   [doucement.

mildness, *mīld'nĕs,* s. douceur, f.

mile, *mĭl,* s. mille, m. ‖ ~-stone, s. borne milliaire, f.   [f.

mileage, *mīl'āj,* s. indemnité kilométrique,

milfoil *mĭl'fŏyl,* s. millefeuille, f.

militant, *mĭl'ĭ tănt,* a. militant, combattant.   [militaires, m. pl.

military, *mĭl'ĭ tĕr ĭ,* s. militaire, m. ‖

military, *mĭl'ĭ tĕr ĭ,* a. militaire.

militate, *mĭl'ĭ tāt,* v. n. combattre.

militia, *mĭ lĭsh'ă,* s. milice, f.

milk, *mĭlk,* s. lait, m.

milk, *mĭlk,* v. a. traire.   [voie lactée, f.

milky, *mĭlk'ĭ,* a. laiteux ‖ doux ‖ ~-way, s.

mill, *mĭl,* s. moulin, m. ‖ filature, f. ‖ moulinet, m. ‖ that's grist to his ~, cela lui va, cela fait son compte ‖ to have been through the ~, avoir passé par de rudes épreuves ‖ ~-dam, s. écluse, f. ‖ ~-hopper, s. trémie, f. ‖ ~-stone, s. meule de moulin, f.   [fouler.

mill, *mĭl,* v. a. moudre ‖ faire mousser

millennium, *mĭl lĕn'nĭ ŭm,* s. millénaire, m. ‖ to put one on one's ~.

miller, *mĭl'ĕr,* s. meunier, m.   [m.

millet, *mĭl'lĕt,* s. millet, mil, m.

milliner, *mĭl'lĭn ĕr,* s. marchande de modes, f.   [mode, f. pl.

millinery, *mĭl'lĭ nĕr ĭ,* s. marchandises de

million, *mĭl'yŭn,* s. million, m. ‖ the ~, la multitude, f.

millionth, *mĭl'yŭnth,* a. millionième.

mime, *mĭm,* s. mime, bouffon, m.

mimic, *mĭm'ĭk,* v. a. imiter.

mimic, *mĭm'ĭk,* a. imitatif ‖ mimique.

mimicry, *mĭm'ĭk rĭ,* s. bouffonnerie, f.

minaret, *mĭn'ă rĕt,* s. minaret, m.

minatory, *mĭn'ă tĕr ĭ,* a. comminatoire.

mince, *mĭns,* v. a. & n. hacher ‖ atténuer ‖ parler avec affectation ‖ not to ~ matters, avoir son franc parler ‖ ~-meat, s. hachis, m., viande hachée, f. ‖ ~-pie, s. pâté au jus, petit four au jus, m.

mincingly, *mĭn'sĭng lĭ,* ad. légèrement ‖ avec affectation.

mind, *mĭnd,* s. esprit, entendement, m. ‖ désir, m. ‖ opinion, f. ‖ mémoire, f. ‖ to change one's ~, se raviser, changer d'avis ‖ to my ~, à mon avis ‖ of the same ~, du même avis ‖ presence of ~, s. présence d'esprit, f. ‖ turn of ~, s. tour d'esprit, m. ‖ to give one a piece of one's ~, donner carrément son avis à qn. ‖ to give one's ~ to, prêter toute son attention à ‖ out of-one's ~, ahuri ‖ interdit, ébahi, tout penaud ‖ to have a great ~ (two-s) to, avoir grande envie de ‖ to make up one's ~, se décider.

mind, *mĭnd,* v. a. & n. prendre garde ‖ penser ‖ rappeler au souvenir ‖ être enclin à ‖ I don't ~, je m'en moque.

minded, *mĭnd'ĕd,* a. disposé, incliné.

mindful, *mĭnd'fŏŏl,* a. attentif, diligent ‖ -ly, ad. attentivement.

mine, *mĭn,* s. mine, f.

mine, *mĭn,* v. a. & n. miner.

mine, *mĭn,* pn. le mien, la mienne ‖ les miens, les miennes.

miner, *mī'nĕr,* s. mineur, m.

mineral, *mĭn'ĕr ăl,* a. minéral, m.

mineral, *mĭn'ĕr ăl,* a. minéral ‖ ~-spring, s. source d'eaux minérales, f.   [logue, m.

mineralogist, *mĭn ĕr ăl'ō jĭst,* s. minéra-

mineralogy, *mĭn ĕr ăl′ ŏ jĭ,* s. minéralogie, f. [mêler.

mingle, *mĭng′ gl,* v. a. & n. mélanger ‖ se

miniature, *mĭn′ ĭ ā tŭr,* s. niniature, f.

minim, *mĭn′ ĭm,* s. pygmée, m. ‖ (mus.) blanche, f.

mining, *mĭn′ ĭng,* s. exploitation des mines, f. ‖ ~share, s. part ou action de mine, f.

minion, *mĭn′ yŭn,* s. mignon, m.

minister, *mĭn′ ĭs tĕr,* s. ministre, m.

minister, *mĭn′ ĭs tĕr,* v. a. & n. administrer, fournir ‖ servir ‖ secourir.

ministerial, *mĭn ĭs tē′ rĭ ăl,* a. ministériel.

ministration, *mĭn ĭs trā′ shŭn,* s. ministère, service, m.

ministry, *mĭn′ ĭs trĭ,* s. ministère, m.

mink, *mĭnk,* s. vision, m.

minnow, *mĭn′ nō,* s. véron, m.

minor, *mī′ nĕr,* s. mineur, m.

minor, *mī′ nĕr,* a. moindre, petit.

minority, *mĭ nŏr′ ĭ tĭ,* s. minorité, f.

minster, *mĭn′ stĕr,* s. cathédrale, f.

minstrel, *mĭn′ strĕl,* s. ménétrier, m.

mint, *mĭnt,* s. monnaie, f. ‖ forge, f. ‖ menthe, f. ‖ hôtel des monnaies, m.

mint, *mĭnt,* v. a. monnayer ‖ forger.

mintage, *mĭnt′ āj,* s. monnayage, m.

minuet, *mĭn′ ū ĕt,* s. menuet, m.

minus, *mī′ nŭs,* ad. moins ‖ en perte.

minute, *mĭn′ ĭt,* s. minute, f. ‖ moment, m. ‖ ~book, s. agenda, n. ‖ ~hand, s. aiguille des minutes, f.

minute, *mĭn′ ĭt,* v. a. écrire sommairement.

minute, *mĭ nūt′,* a. menu, mince ‖ -ly, ad. minutieusement. [nutie, f.

minuteness, *mĭ nūt′ nĕs,* s. petitesse, mi-

minutiae, *mĭ nū′ shĭ ē,* s. pl. particularités, f. pl. [cieuse, f.

minx, *mĭngks,* s. minaudière, petite pré-

miracle, *mĭr′ ă kl,* s. miracle, m., merveille, f.

miraculous, *mĭ răk′ ū lŭs,* a. miraculeux ‖ -ly, ad. miraculeusement.

mirage, *mĭ răzh′,* s. mirage, m.

mire, *mīr,* s. boue, fange, f.

mirkiness, *mĕrk′ ĭ nĕs,* s. obscurité, f.

mirky, *mĕrk′ ĭ,* a. obscur, sombre.

mirror, *mĭr′ rĕr,* s. miroir, m.

mirth, *mĕrth,* s. gaieté, joie, f.

mirthful, *mĕrth′ fŏŏl,* a. joyeux, enjoué.

miry, *mī′ rĭ,* a. bourbeux, fangeux.

misadventure, *mĭs ăd vĕn′ tŭr,* s. mésaventure, f. [f.

misalliance, *mĭs ăl lī′ ăns,* s. mésalliance, f.

misanthrope, *mĭs′ ăn thrŏp,* s. misanthrope, m. [thropie, f.

misanthropy, *mĭs ăn′ thrŏ pĭ,* s. misan-

misapply, *mĭs ăp plī′,* v. n. employer mal à propos.

misapprehension, *mĭs ăp prē hĕn′ shŭn,* s. malentendu, m. [porter mal.

misbehave, *mĭs bē hāv′,* v. n. ir. se com-

misbehaviour, *mĭs bē hāv′ yĕr,* s. mauvaise conduite, f.

miscalculation, *mĭs kăl kū lā′ shŭn,* s. mécompte, m., erreur de calcul, f.

miscarriage, *mĭs kăr′ rĭj,* s. mauvais succès, m. ‖ fausse couche, f.

miscarry, *mĭs kăr′ rĭ,* v. n. échouer ‖ avoir un mauvais succès ‖ avorter.

miscellaneous, *mĭs sĕl lā′ nē ŭs,* a. mêlé, mélangé ‖ divers.

miscellany, *mĭs′ sĕl lā nĭ* ou *mĭs sĕl′ lă nĭ,* s. mélange, m., œuvres mêlées, f. pl.

mischance, *mĭs chăns′,* s. malheur, m., infortune, f.

mischief, *mĭs′ chĭf,* s. mal, dommage, m.

mischievous, *mĭs′ chĭv ŭs,* a. (-ly, ad.) nuisible ‖ méchant ‖ méchamment.

misconception, *mĭs kŏn sĕp′ shŭn,* s. fausse notion, f.

misconduct, *mĭs kŏn′ dŭkt,* s. mauvaise conduite, f. [mal.

misconduct, *mĭs kŏn dŭkt′,* v. a. conduire

misconstruction, *mĭs kŏn strŭk′ shŭn,* s. fausse interprétation, f.

miscreant, *mĭs′ krē ănt,* s. mécréant, m. ‖ scélérat, m. [ĭng, s. méfait, m.

misdeed, *mĭs dēd′,* misdoing, *mĭs dŏ′-*

misdemeanour, *mĭs dē mēn′ ĕr,* s. (jur.) délit, m. [douter de.

misdoubt, *mĭs dŏŭt′,* v. a. se méfier de,

miser, *mī′ zĕr,* s. avare, m.

miserable, *mĭz′ ĕr ă bl,* a. misérable, malheureux ‖ vil. [vilement.

miserably, *mĭz′ ĕr ă blĭ,* ad. misérablement‖

miserly, *mī′ zĕr lĭ,* a. avare.

misery, *mĭz′ ĕr ĭ,* s. misère, f. ‖ malheur, m., disgrâce, f. ‖ pauvreté, f.

misfit, *mĭs fĭt′,* s. mauvaise façon d'un habit, f. ‖ tout ce qui est déplacé.

misfortune, *mĭs fŏr′ tŭn,* s. malheur, m.

misgive, *mĭs gĭv′,* v. a. ir. faire soupçonner, inspirer de la méfiance.

misgiving, *mĭs gĭv′ ĭng,* s. soupçon, m., défiance, f. [verner.

misgovern, *mĭs gŭv′ ĕrn,* v. a. mal gou-

misguided, *mĭs gĭd′ ĕd,* a. mal dirigé ‖ mal inspiré ‖ égaré.

mishap, *mĭs hăp′,* s. accident fâcheux, m.

misinform, *mĭs ĭn fŏrm′,* v. a. mal informer ‖ tromper.

misinterpretation, *mĭs ĭn tĕr prē tā′ shŭn,* s. fausse interprétation, f.

misjudge, *mĭs jŭj′,* v. a. mal juger.

mislay, *mĭs lā′,* v. a. ir. mal placer.

mislead, *mĭs lēd′,* v. a. ir. égarer ‖ induire en erreur ‖ séduire. [mal.

mismanage, *mĭs măn′ āj,* v. a. administrer

misname, *mĭs nām′,* v. a. nommer improprement. [nom peu approprié, m.

misnomer, *mĭs nō′ mĕr,* s. faux nom, m. ‖

misogamy, *mĭ sŏg′ ă mĭ,* s. misogamie, f.

misogynist, *mĭ sŏg′ ĭ nĭst,* s. misogyne, m.

misplace, *mĭs plās′,* v. a. mal placer.

misprint, *mĭs prĭnt′,* s. faute d'impression, f. [prononcer.

mispronounce, *mĭs prō nŏŭns′,* v. a. mal

misquote, *mĭs kwōt′,* v. a. citer à faux.

misrepresent, *mĭs rĕp rē zĕnt′,* v. a. mal représenter.

misrule, *mĭs rŏl′,* s. tumulte, m., confusion, f. ‖ tyrannie, f.

miss, *mis*, s. manque, m. || perte, f. ||
Miss . . . (titre), mademoiselle.
miss, *mis*, v. a. & n. manquer || perdre ||
omettre || se tromper de || s'apercevoir du
manque de.
missal, *mis'săl*, s. missel, m.
misshapen, *mis-shāp'n*, a. difforme.
missile, *mis'sil*, s. projectile, m.
missing, *mis'sing*, a. qui manque.
mission, *mish'ŭn*, s. mission, f. || ~-
house, s. maison de mission, f. || ~-
station, s. station de missionnaires, f.
missionary, *mish'ŭn·ĕr·ĭ*, s. missionnaire, m.
missionary, *mish'ŭn·ĕr·ĭ*, a. des missions.
missive, *mis'siv*, s. lettre missive, f.
misspell, *mis·spĕl'*, v. a. épeler mal ||
écrire mal.
misspend, *mis·spĕnd'*, v. a. gaspiller.
misstatement, *mis·stāt'mĕnt*, s. faux rapport, m.
mist, *mist*, s. brouillard, m.
mistakable, *mis·tā'kă·bl*, a. susceptible
d'être mal compris.
mistake, *mis·tāk'*, s. méprise, f. || erreur,
f. || faute, f. || by ~, par mégarde || and
no ~ ! j'en réponds !
mistake, *mis·tāk'*, v. a. & n. ir. se méprendre, faire une bévue, se tromper.
mistaken, *mis·tā'kn*, a. mal entendu ||
Mister, *mis'tĕr*, (titre) monsieur.　[faux.
mistiness, *mis'ti·nĕs*, s. brouillard, m.
mistletoe, *mis'l·tō*, s. gui, m.
mistress, *mis'trĕs*, s. maîtresse, f. || in-
stitutrice, f. || ~, (*mis'sis*), (titre) Madame.
mistrust, *mis·trŭst'*, s. méfiance, f.
mistrust, *mis·trŭst'*, v. a. se méfier.
mistrustful, *mis·trŭst'fŏol*, a. défiant.
misty, *mist'i*, a. nébuleux.
misunderstand, *mis·ŭn·dĕr·stănd'*, v. a. ir.
mal comprendre.
misunderstanding, *mis·ŭn·dĕr·stănd'-
ing*, s. malentendu, m. || mésintelligence,
misuse, *mis·ūs'*, s. abus, m.　　　　[f.
misuse, *mis·ūz'*, v. a. abuser de.
mite, *mīt*, s. mite, f || légère offrande, f.
mitigate, *mit'i·gāt*, v. a. mitiger, adoucir.
mitigation, *mit·i·gā'shŭn*, s. adoucisse-
mitre, *mī'tĕr*, s. mitre, f.　　[ment, m.
mitten, *mit'n*, s. mitaine, f.
mix, *miks*, v. a. mêler, mélanger.
mixture, *miks'tŭr* ou *miks'chŏor*, s. mixtion, f., mélange, m.　　　　[d'artimon, m.
mizen(-mast), *miz'n(·măst)*, s. (mar.) mât
moan, *mōn*, s. lamentation, f.
moan, *mōn*, v. a. & n. lamenter, déplorer.
moat, *mōt*, s. fossé, m.
moated, *mō'tĕd*, a. entouré d'un fossé.
mob, *mŏb*, s. populace, foule, canaille, f.
mob, *mŏb*, v. a. houspiller.
mobilisation, *mŏb·ĭl·ĭ·zā'shŭn*, s. (mil.)
mobilisation, mise sur pied de guerre, f.
mobilise, *mŏb'il·īz*, v. a. (mil.) mobiliser.
mobility, *mŏ·bil'i·ti*, s. mobilité, f.
moccasin, *mŏk'ă·sin*, s. mocassin, m.
mock, *mŏk*, v. a. & n. se moquer de ||
tromper.

mock, *mŏk*, a. faux, contrefait.
mocker, *mŏk'ĕr*, s. moqueur, railleur, m.
mockery, *mŏk'ĕr·ĭ*, s. moquerie, raillerie, f.||
jouet, m. || to make a mock (*ou* ~) of,
se moquer, se railler de qn.
mocking-bird, *mŏk'ing·bĕrd*, s. oiseau
moqueur, m.　　　　　　　　[manière, f.
mode, *mōd*, s. (gr.) mode, m. || mode, façon,
model, *mŏd'ĕl*, s. modèle, m.
model, *mŏd'ĕl*, v. a. modeler, former.
modeller, *mŏd'ĕl·ĕr*, s. modelleur, m. ||
dessinateur, m.
moderate, *mŏd'ĕr·āt*, v. a. modérer.
moderate, *mŏd'ĕr·āt*, a. (-ly, ad.) modéré
(ment) || médiocre(ment).　　　　　[f.
moderation, *mŏd·ĕr·ā'shŭn*, s. modération.
modern, *mŏd'ĕrn*, a. moderne, nouveau.
modernise, *mŏd'ĕrn·īz*, v. a. moderniser ||
modest, *mŏd'ĕst*, a. modeste.　　[moderner.
modesty, *mŏd'ĕs·ti*, s. modestie, f.
modicum, *mŏd'i·kŭm*, s. un tout petit peu,
un tant soit peu.　　　　　　　[cation, f.
modification, *mŏd·i·fi·kā'shŭn*, s. modifi-
modify, *mŏd'i·fī*, v. a. modifier.
modishness, *mō'dish·nĕs*, s. asservissement à la mode, m.
modulate, *mŏd'ū·lāt*, v. a. (mus.) moduler.
modulation, *mŏd·ū·lā'shŭn*, s. (mus.) modulation, f.　　　　　　　　　[mohair, m.
mohair, *mō·hār*, s. poil de chèvre, m. ||
moiety, *moy'ti*, s. moitié, f.
moist, *moyst*, a. humide, moite.
moisten, *moy'sn*, v. a. humecter.
moisture, *moys'tŭr*, s. humidité, moiteur,
molar, *mō'lĕr*, a. molaire.　　　　[f.
molasses, *mŏ·lăs'sĕz*, s. mélasse, f.
mole, *mōl*, s. môle, m. || grain de beauté,
m. || taupe, f. || ~-hill, s. taupinière, f.
molecule, *mŏl'ĕ·kūl*, s. molécule, f.
moleskin, *mōl'skin*, s. moleskin, m.
molest, *mŏ·lĕst'*, v. a. molester, vexer.
molestation, *mŏl·ĕs·tā'shŭn*, s. vexation,
importunité, f.
mollify, *mŏl'li·fī*, v. a. amollir, ramollir.
mollusk, *mŏl'lŭsk*, s. mollusque, m.
molten, *mōl'tn*, a. fondu || ~ calf, s. le
veau d'or.　　　　　　　　　[portance, f.
moment, *mō'mĕnt*, s. moment, m. || im-
momentarily, *mō'mĕn·tĕr·ĭ·li*, ad. de moment en moment.
momentary, *mō'mĕn·tĕr·ĭ*, a. momentané.
momentous, *mō·mĕn'tŭs*, a. important.
momentum, *mō·mĕn'tŭm*, s. (mec.) moment, m. (de force, d'inertie).
monarch, *mŏn'ărk*, s. monarque, souverain, m.　　　　　　　　　　[chique.
monarchical, *mŏ·när'kik·ăl*, a. monar-
monarchy, *mŏn'ĕr·ki*, s. monarchie, f.
monastery, *mŏn'ă·stĕr·ĭ*, s. monastère, m.
monastic, *mŏ·năs'tik*, a. monastique.
Monday, *mŭn'dā*, s. lundi, m.
money, *mŭn'ĭ*, s. argent, m. || monnaie, f. ||
ready ~, ~ in hand, argent comptant,
m. || pocket-~, menus plaisirs, m. pl. ||
to make ~, ramasser de l'argent || to
raise ~, se procurer de l'argent || ~-box,
s. coffre-fort, m. || ~-grubber, s. har-

pagon, ladre, m. ‖ ~-lender, s. prêteur à intérêt, m. ‖ ~-market, s. marché monétaire *ou* financier, m., la Bourse ‖ ~-order, s. bon, chèque, m. ‖ mandat postal, m.

moneyed, monied, *mŭn'ĭd*, a. riche.

mongrel, *ming'grĕl*, a. métis.

monitory, *mŏn'ĭ tĕr ĭ*, a. d'avertissement ‖ monitorial.

monk, *mŭngk*, s. moine, religieux, m. ‖ ~'s hood, s. (bot.) aconit, m.

monkey, *mŭng'kĭ*, s. singe, babouin, m. ‖ ~-trick, s. singerie, f.

monkish, *mŭngk'ĭsh*, a. monacal. [m.

monogamist, *mŏn ŏg'ă mist*, s. monogame.

monogamy, *mŏ nŏg'ăm ĭ*, s. monogamie, f.

monogram, *mŏn'ŏ grăm*, s. monogramme, m. [mane, m. & f.

monomaniac, *mŏn ŏ mā' nĭ ăk*, s. mono-

monoplane, *mŏn'ŏ plān*, s. monoplan, m.

monopolise, *mŏ nŏp'ŏ lĭz*, v. a. monopoliser ‖ accaparer.

monopolist, *mŏ nŏp'ŏ list*, s. monopoleur, m. ‖ accapareur, m.

monopoly, *mŏ nŏp'ŏ lĭ*, s. monopole, m.

monosyllabic, *mŏn ŏ sil lăb'ik*, a. monosyllabique, m. [labe, m.

monosyllable, *mŏn ŏ sil'lă bl*, s. monosyl-

monotonous, *mŏ nŏt'ŏ nŭs*, a. monotone.

monotony, *mŏ nŏt'ŏ nĭ*, s. monotonie, f.

monsoon, *mŏn sōn'*, s. mousson, f.

monster, *mŏn'stĕr*, s. monstre, m.

monstrosity, *mŏn strŏs'ĭ tĭ*, s. monstruosité, f. [~-ly, ad. monstrueusement.

monstrous, *mŏn'strŭs*, a. monstrueux ‖

month, *mŭnth*, s. mois, m.

monthly, *mŭnth'lĭ*, a. & ad. mensuel ‖ tous les mois ‖ par mois.

monument, *mŏn'ū mĕnt*, s. monument, m.

monumental, *mŏn ū mĕn'tăl*, a. monumental.

mood, *mōd*, s. humeur, f. ‖ (gr.) mode, m.

moodiness, *mōd'ĭ nĕs*, s. mauvaise humeur, f.

moody, *mōd'ĭ*, a. de mauvaise humeur.

moon, *mōn*, s. lune, f. ‖ ~-beam, s. rayon lunaire, m. ‖ ~-struck, a. lunatique.

moonlight, *mōn'līt*, s. clair de lune, m.

moonlight, *mōn'līt*, a. au clair de lune.

moonshine, *mōn'shīn*, s. clair de lune, m. ‖ (fig.) blague, f. ‖ faux brillant, m.

moor, *mōr*, s. marais, m. ‖ bruyère, f. ‖ nègre,

moor, *mōr*, v. a. (& n.) (s')amarrer. [m.

moorish, *mōr'ish*, a. moresque.

moorland, *mōr'lănd*, s. pays marécageux,

moot, *mōt*, v. a (jur.) discuter. [m.

moot, *mōt*, a. contestable, discutable. [f.

mop, *mŏp*, s. torchon, faubert, m. ‖ tignasse,

mop, *mŏp*, v. a. laver ‖ éponger.

mope, *mōp*, v. n. se séquestrer ‖ rêver ‖ s'ennuyer. [-s, s. pl. mœurs, f. pl.

moral, *mŏr'ăl*, s. morale, moralité, f. ‖

moral, *mŏr'ăl*, a. (-ly, ad.) moral(ement).

moralise, *mŏr'ăl ĭz*, v. a. moraliser.

moralist, *mŏr'ăl ĭst*, s. moraliste, m.

morality, *mŏ răl'ĭ tĭ*, s. morale, moralité, f.

morass, *mŏ răs'*, s. marais, m. [f.

morbid, *mŏr'bĭd*, a. maladif.

more, *mŏr*, ad. plus, plus grand, davantage ‖ once ~, encore une fois ‖ no ~, ne .... plus ‖ so much the ~, d'autant plus, à plus forte raison.

moreen, *mō rēn'*, s. serge moirée, f.

moreover, *mŏr ō'vĕr*, ad. de plus, en outre.

morganatic, *mŏr găn ăt'ik*, a. morganatique.

morning, *mŏrn'ing*, s. matin, m., matinée, f. ‖ ~-performance, s. matinée, f. ‖ ~-gown, s. robe de chambre, f.

morocco(-leather), *mō rŏk'kō(lĕth'ĕr)*, s. maroquin, m. [(ment).

morose, *mō rōs'*, a. (-ly, ad.) maussade

morphine, *mŏr'fēn*, morphia, *mŏr'fĭ ă*, s. (chim.) morphine, f.

morrow, *mŏr'rō*, s. lendemain, jour, m.

morsel, *mŏr'sĕl*, s. morceau, m.

mortal, *mŏr'tăl*, s. mortel, homme, m.

mortal, *mŏr'tăl*, a. (-ly, ad.) mortel(lement).

mortality, *mŏr tăl'ĭ tĭ*, s. mortalité, f.

mortar, *mŏr'tĕr*, s. mortier, m.

mortgage, *mŏr'găj*, s. hypothèque, f.

mortgage, *mŏr'găj*, v. a. hypothéquer.

mortgagee, *mŏr găjē'*, s. créancier hypothécaire, m. [hypothèque, m.

mortgager, *mŏr'găjĕr*, s. débiteur sur

mortification, *mŏr tĭ fĭ kā'shŭn*, s. mortification, f. ‖ gangrène, f. ‖ pénitence, f.

mortify, *mŏr'tĭ fī*, v. a. (& n.) humilier ‖ (se) mortifier ‖ se gangrener.

mortise, *mŏr'tĭs*, s. mortaise, f.

mortmain, *mŏrt'mān*, s. (jur.) mainmorte,

mosaic, *mō zā'ik*, a. mosaïque. [f.

mosque, *mŏsk*, s. mosquée, f.

mosquito, *mŏs kē'tō*, s. moustique, m. ‖ ~-net, s. moustiquaire, cousinière, f.

moss, *mŏs*, s. mousse, f. ‖ ~-grown, a. moussu ‖ ~-rose, s. rose moussue, f.

mossy, *mŏs'ĭ*, a. moussu.

most, *mōst*, s. la plupart.

most, *mōst*, a. & ad. le plus, au plus haut degré ‖ -ly, ad. la plupart ‖ le plus souvent.

mote, *mōt*, s. atome, m. ‖ paille, f.

moth, *mŏth*, s. teigne, mite, f.

mother, *mŭth'ĕr*, s. mère, f. ‖ ~-in-law, s. belle-mère, f. ‖ ~ of pearl, s. nacre de perle, f. ‖ ~-country, s. pays natal, m. ‖ ~-tongue, s. langue maternelle, f.

motherhood, *mŭth'ĕr hŏŏd*, s. maternité, f.

motherless, *mŭth'ĕr lĕs*, a. sans mère.

motherly, *mŭth'ĕr lĭ*, a. maternel, de mère.

motion, *mō'shŭn*, s. mouvement, m. ‖ motion, f. ‖ proposition, f. [une motion.

motion, *mō'shŭn*, v. a. proposer ‖ faire

motionless, *mō'shŭn lĕs*, a. immobile.

motive, *mō'tĭv*, s. motif, m.

motive, *mō'tĭv*, a. moteur ‖ motif ‖ ~-power, s. force motrice, f.

motley, *mŏt'lĭ*, mottled, *mŏt'tld*, a. bigarré ‖ (soap) marbré ‖ mêlé.

motor, *mō'tŏr*, s. moteur, m. ‖ ~-bicycle, s. motocycle, m. ‖ ~-car, s. automobile, f. ‖ ~-omnibus, s. omnibus automobile, m.

motto, *mŏt'tō*, s. devise, f.

mould, *mōld,* s. moule, m., forme, f. ||
moisissure, f. || terreau, m.
mould, *mōld,* v. a. & n. mouler, former ||
pétrir || se moisir.   [en poussière.
moulder, *mōld'ẽr,* v. a. (& n.) (se) réduire
mouldiness, *mōld'i nĕs,* s. moisissure, f.
moulding, *mōld'ĭng,* s. moulure, f.
mouldy, *mōld'ĭ,* a. moisi.
moult, *mōlt,* v. n. muer.   [m. || levée, f.
mound, *mownd,* s. rempart, retranchement,
mount, *mownt,* s. mont, m., montagne, f.
mount, *mownt,* v. a. monter, élever || s'élever.
mountain, *mown'tin,* s. montagne, f. ||
to make a ~ out of a mole-hill, faire
d'une mouche un éléphant.   [m.
mountaineer, *mown tin ēr',* s. montagnard,
mountainous, *mown'tin ŭs,* a. mon-
tagneux || énorme.
mountebank, *mown'tĕ băngk,* s. charlatan, saltimbanque, m.   [le deuil.
mourn, *mōrn,* v. a. & n. déplorer || porter
mourner, *mōrn'ẽr,* s. qui porte le deuil,
m. || malheureux, m. || **(hired-)** pleu-
reur, m.   [triste(ment).
mournful, *mōrn'fōōl,* a. (-ly, ad.) lugubre
mourning, *mōrn'ĭng,* s. lamentation, f.
mouse, *mows,* s. souris, f.   [deuil, m.
mouser, *mow'zẽr,* s. preneur de souris, m.
moustache, *mōōs tash',* moustache,
mōōs tash'i ō, s. moustaches, f. pl.
mouth, *mowth,* s. bouche, gueule, f. ||
voix, f. || embouchure, f. || **by word of
~,** de vive voix.
mouth, *mowth,* v. a. & n. gueuler, mâcher.
mouthful, *mowth'fōōl,* s. bouchée, f.
mouthing, *mowth'ĭng,* s. criaillerie, déclamation, f.
mouthpiece, *mowth'pēs,* s. embouchure, f.
move, *mōv,* s. mouvement, m. || **(at chess)**
coup, m.
move, *mōv,* v. a. & n. mouvoir, agiter ||
proposer, persuader, attendrir, toucher ||
exciter || se mouvoir || avancer.
mov(e)able, *mōv'ă bl,* a. mobile.
mov(e)ables, *mōv'ă blz,* s. pl. meubles,
biens meubles, m. pl.
movement, *mōv'mĕnt,* s. mouvement, m.
mover, *mōv'ẽr,* s. rapporteur, m. || **prime
~,** s. principe moteur, m.
moving, *mōv'ĭng,* s. mouvement, m. || atten-
drissement, m.   [d'une manière touchante.
moving, *mōv'ĭng,* a. émouvant || -ly, ad.
mow, *mō,* s. fauchée, f. || meule de foin, f.
mow, *mō,* v. a. & n. faucher, moissonner ||
engranger||—ing machine, s. faucheuse, f.
Mr., Mrs. (= Mister, Mistress), Monsieur, Madame.
much, *mŭch,* a. & ad. beaucoup || très,
fort, bien || **so ~ for!** voilà pour! || **as ~
as,** autant que.
mucilage, *mū'si lāj,* s. mucilage, m.
muck, *mŭk,* s. fumier, m. || boue, f.
mucous, *mū'kŭs,* a. muqueux.
mucus, *mū'kŭs,* s. mucus, m., mucosité, f.
mud, *mŭd,* s. boue, f. || vase, f. || **~-cart,**
s. tombereau, m. || **~-wall,** s. muraille de
terre, f.

muddle, *mŭd'l,* s. embrouillamini, m.
muddle, *mŭd'l,* v. a. troubler, hébéter ||
enivrer à demi || **~,** v. n. barboter.
muddy, *mŭd'dĭ,* a. trouble, bourbeux.
muff, *mŭf,* s. manchon, m. || jobard, m. ||
tasse, f. || gueule, f.
muffle, *mŭf'l,* v. a. envelopper || emmi-
toufler || bander || voiler || assourdir.
mug, *mŭg,* s. gobelet, m. || pot, m.
mulberry, *mŭl'bĕr rĭ,* s. mûre, f. || **~-
tree,** s. mûrier, m.
mulct, *mŭlkt,* v. a. mettre à l'amende.
mule, *mūl,* s. mulet, m., mule, f. || **~-
driver,** s. muletier, m.
muleteer, *mūl'tēr,* s. muletier, m.
mull, *mŭl,* s. brioche, f., four, m.
mull, *mŭl,* v. a. faire chauffer || brûler.
mulled, *mŭld,* a. chaud et épicé.
mullet, *mŭl'lĕt,* s. mulet, m. || muge, m.
multifarious, *mŭl tĭ fā'rĭ ŭs,* a. varié,
divers.
multiple, *mŭl'tĭ pl,* s. (ar.) multiple, m.
multiplicand, *mŭl tĭ plĭ kănd',* s. (ar.)
multiplicande, m.
multiplication, *mŭl tĭp lĭ kā'shŭn,* s.
multiplication, f. || **~-table,** s. table de
Pythagore, f.   [cité, f.
multiplicity, *mŭl tĭ plĭs'ĭ tĭ,* s. multipli-
multiplier, *mŭl'tĭ plĭ ẽr,* s. (ar.) multiplicateur, m.
multiply, *mŭl'tĭ plī,* v. a. multiplier.
multitude, *mŭl'tĭ tūd,* s. multitude, f.
multitudinous, *mŭl tĭ tū'dĭ nŭs,* a. nombreux.   [breux.
mum, *mŭm,* a. silencieux.
mumble, *mŭm'bl,* v. a. & n. marmotter ||
mâchonner.
mummer, *mŭm'mẽr,* s. masque, m., per-
sonne masquée, f. || bouffon, m.
mummery, *mŭm'mẽr ĭ,* s. mascarade, f.
mummy, *mŭm'mĭ,* s. momie, f. || pâte, f.
mumps, *mŭmps,* s. mauvaise humeur, f. ||
(méd.) oreillons, m. pl.
munch, *mŭnsh,* v. a. & n. mâcher
mundane, *mŭn'dān,* a. du monde.
municipal, *mū nis'ĭ păl,* a. municipal.
municipality, *mū nis ĭ păl'ĭ tĭ,* s. munici-
palité, f.   [f.
munificence, *mū nif'ĭ sĕns,* s. munificence
munificent, *mū nif'ĭ sĕnt,* a. libéral ||-ly,
ad. avec munificence.
muniment, *mū'nĭ mĕnt,* s. titre, m., charte,
f. || **~-house,** s. archives, f. pl.
munition, *mū nish'ŭn,* s. munition, f.
murder, *mẽr'dẽr,* s. meurtre, m.
murder, *mẽr'dẽr,* v. a. assassiner, tuer ||
massacrer.
murderer, *mẽr'dẽr ẽr,* s. meurtrier, m.
murderess, *mẽr'dẽr ĕs,* s. meurtrière, f.
murderous, *mẽr'dẽr ŭs,* a. homicide,
sanguinaire.   [hydrique.
muriatic, *mū rĭ ăt'ĭk,* a. (chim.) chlor-
murky, *mẽr'kĭ,* a. obscur, sombre.
murmur, *mẽr'mẽr,* s. murmure, m.
murmur, *mẽr'mẽr,* v. a. & n. murmurer.
murmuringly, *mẽr'mẽr ĭng lĭ,* ad. en
murmurant.
murrain, *mŭr'rān,* s. clavelée, f.

muscatel, *mŭs'kă tĕl*, s. muscat, m.
muscle, *mŭs'l*, s. muscle, m. || moule, f.
Muscovite, *mŭs'kō vīt*, s. Moscovite, m.
muscular, *mŭs'kū lĕr*, a. musculaire || musculeux.
muse, *mūz*, s. muse, f. || rêverie, f.
muse, *mūz*, v. n. méditer, rêver.
museum, *mū zē'ŭm*, s. musée, m.
mushroom, *mŭsh'rŏm*, s. champignon, m.
music, *mū'zĭk*, s. musique, f. || ~-room, s. salle de concerts, f. || ~-stand, s. pupitre à musique, m. || ~-stool, s. tabouret de piano, m.
musical, *mū'zĭ kăl*, a. (-ly, ad.) musical (ement) || harmonieusement.
musician, *mū zĭsh'ăn*, s. musicien, m.
musing, *mū'zĭng*, s. méditation, f.
musk, *mŭsk*, s. musc, m.
musket, *mŭs'kĕt*, s. mousquet, fusil, m.
musketeer, *mŭs kĕt ēr'*, s. mousquetaire, m. [mousqueterie, f.
musketry, *mŭs'kĕt rĭ*, s. fusillade, f. ||
muslin, *mŭs'lĭn*, s. mousseline, f.
mussel, *mŭs'ĕl*, s. moule, f.
must, *mŭst*, v. n. imp. falloir, devoir.
mustache, *mŏŏ stâsh'*, s. *vide* moustache.
mustard, *mŭs'tĕrd*, s. moutarde, f. || ~-seed, s. graine de moutarde, f.
muster, *mŭs'tĕr*, s. revue, f. || troupe, f. || rôle, m. || ~-roll, s. (mar.) rôle d'équipage, m. || (mil.) tableaux du recensement, m. pl.
muster, *mŭs'tĕr*, v. a. faire la revue, assembler || passer en revue || s'assembler.
musty, *mŭs'tĭ*, a. moisi.
mutability, *mū tă bĭl'ĭ tĭ*, s. mutabilité, variabilité, f.
mutation, *mū tā'shŭn*, s. changement, m.
mute, *mūt*, s. muet, m. || fiente d'oiseaux, f.
mute, *mūt*, a. muet, silencieux || -ly, ad. en silence.
mutilate, *mū'tĭ lāt*, v. a. mutiler, estropier.
mutilation, *mū tĭ lā'shŭn*, s. mutilation, f.
mutineer, *mū tĭn ēr'*, s. rebelle, m.
mutinous, *mū'tĭn ŭs*, a. (-ly, ad.) (en) mutiny, *mū'tĭ nĭ*, s. émeute, f. [mutin.
mutiny, *mū'tĭ nĭ*, v. n. se révolter.
mutter, *mŭt'tĕr*, s. murmure, m.
mutter, *mŭt'tĕr*, v. a. & n. murmurer, marmotter.
mutton, *mŭt'n*, s. mouton, m. || ~-chop, s. côtelette de mouton, f. || neck, shoulder of ~, s. gigot, m. [(ment).
mutual, *mū'tū ăl*, a. (-ly, ad.) réciproque
muzzle, *mŭz'l*, s. museau, m. || muselière, f. || gueule, f. || bout, m.
muzzle, *mŭz'l*, v. a. museler.
my, *mĭ*, pn. mon, ma, mes.
myosotis, *mĭ ō sō'tĭs*, s. (bot.) myosotis, gremillet, pensez-à-moi, ne-m'oubliez-pas, myriad, *mĭr'ĭ ăd*, s. myriade, f. [m.
myrrh, *mĕr*, s. myrrhe, f.
myrtle, *mĕr'tl*, s. myrte, m.
myself, *mĭ sĕlf'*, pn. moi-même || me, moi.
mysterious, *mĭs tē'rĭ ŭs*, a. mystérieux || -ly, ad. mystérieusement.
mystery, *mĭs'tĕr ĭ*, s. mystère, m.

mystic(al), *mĭs'tĭk(ăl)*, a. (-ly, ad.) mystique(ment). [fication, f.
mystification, *mĭs tĭ fĭ kā'shŭn*, s. mystimystify, *mĭs'tĭ fī*, v. a. mystifier.
myth, *mĭth*, s. mythe, m. [logique.
mythological, *mĭth ō lŏj'ĭk ăl*, a. mythomythology, *mĭ thŏl'ō jĭ*, s. mythologie, f.

N.

nab, *năb*, v. a. happer, attraper, saisir.
nabob, *nā'bŏb*, s. nabab, richard fastueux,
nag, *năg*, s. bidet, m. [m.
nail, *nāl*, s. clou, m. || ongle, m. || ~-brush, s. brosse à ongles, f.
nail, *nāl*, v. a. clouer.
naked, *nā'kĕd*, a. (-ly, ad.) nu || simple (ment) || nûment.
nakedness, *nā'kĕd nĕs*, s. nudité, f.
namby-pamby, *năm'bĭ păm'bĭ*, a. musqué, prétentieux.
name, *nām*, s. nom, m. || réputation, f. in one's ~, au nom de qn.
name, *nām*, v. a. nommer, appeler.
nameless, *nām'lĕs*, a. anonyme.
namely, *nām'lĭ*, ad. savoir, à savoir.
namesake, *nām'sāk*, s. homonyme, m.
nankeen, *năng kēn'*, s. nankin, m.
nap, *năp*, s. sommeil léger, m. || poil, m.
nape, *nāp*, s. nuque, f.
naphtha, *năp'thă*, s. naphte, f.
napkin, *năp'kĭn*, s. serviette, f. || ~-ring, s. rond de serviette, m.
narcissus, *năr sĭs'ŭs*, s. (bot.) narcisse, m.
narcotic, *năr kŏt'ĭk*, s. narcotique, m.
narcotic, *năr kŏt'ĭk*, a. narcotique.
narrate, *năr'rāt*, v. a. raconter.
narration, *năr rā'shŭn*, narrative, *năr'rā tĭv*, s. narration, f.
narrative, *năr'rā tĭv*, a. narratif.
narrator, *năr rā'tĕr*, s. narrateur, m.
narrow, *năr'rō*, s. passage étroit, m. || ~-s, s. pl. (mar.) détroit, m.
narrow, *năr'rō*, v. a. (& n.) resserrer || (se) rétrécir.
narrow, *năr'rō*, a. (-ly, ad.) étroit(ement) || petit || avare || exact || mesquinement || de près. [pauvreté, f.
narrowness, *năr'rō nĕs*, s. étroitesse, f. ||
nasal, *nā'zăl*, a. nasal.
nastily, *năs'tĭ lĭ*, ad. salement.
nastiness, *năs'tĭ nĕs*, s. saleté, f.
nasturtium, *năs tĕr'shĭm*, s. (bot.) capunasty, *năs'tĭ*, a. sale || obscène. [cine, f.
natal, *nā'tăl*, a. natal.
natation, *nā tā'shŭn*, s. natation, f.
nation, *nā'shŭn*, s. nation, f.
national, *năsh'ŭn ăl*, a. (-ly, ad.) national (ement) || ~-debt, s. dette publique, f.
nationalise, *năsh'ŭn ăl īz*, v. a. rendre national.
nationality, *năsh ŭn ăl'ĭ tĭ*, s. nationalité, f.
native, *nā'tĭv*, s. natif, m.
native, *nā'tĭv*, a. natif, naturel, originaire,

nativity, *nă'tiv'ĭtĭ*, s. nativité, f. ‖ naissance, f.
natural, *năt'ūrăl* ou *năch'ŏŏrăl*, s. (mus.) bécarre, m. ‖ imbécile, idiot, m.
natural, *năt'ūrăl* ou *năch'ŏŏrăl*, a. (-ly, ad.) naturel(lement) ‖ naïf, simple.
naturalisation, *năt'ūrălĭză'shŭn*, s. naturalisation, f.
naturalise, *năt'ūrălīs*, v. a. naturaliser.
naturalist, *năt'ūrălĭst*, s. naturaliste, m.
nature, *nā'tūr* ou *nā'chŏŏr*, s. nature, f. ‖ tempérament, m., espèce, f. ‖ . . . -d, a. de . . . nature.
naught, *nawt*, s. rien, m.
naughtily, *nawt'ĭlĭ*, ad. méchamment.
naughtiness, *nawt'ĭnĕs*, s. méchanceté, f. ‖ [vilain.
naughty, *nawt'ĭ*, a. mauvais, méchant,
nausea, *naw'sĭă*, s. nausée, f.
nauseate, *naw'sĭāt*, v. a. & n. avoir des nausées ‖ rejeter avec dégoût.
nauseous, *naw'shĭŭs*, a. nauséabond, dégoûtant ‖ -ly, ad. avec dégoût.
nautical, *naw'tĭkăl*, naval, *nā'văl*, a. naval ‖ marin ‖ de la marine.
nautilus, *naw'tĭlŭs*, s. nautile, m.
naval, *nā'vl*, a. naval, maritime ‖ de la marine. ‖(d'une église), f.
nave, *nāv*, s. moyeu (d'une roue), m. ‖ nef
navel, *nā'vl*, s. nombril, m.
navigable, *năv'ĭgăbl*, a. navigable.
navigate, *năv'ĭgāt*, v. a. & n. naviguer ‖ gouverner.
navigation, *năv'ĭgā'shŭn*, s. navigation, f.
navigator, *năv'ĭgātĕr*, s. navigateur, m.
navvy, *năv'vĭ*, s. terrassier, m.
navy, *nā'vĭ*, s. marine, f. ‖ ~-board, s. conseil de la marine, m. ‖ ~-office, s. bureaux de la marine, m. pl.
nay, *nā*, ad. non, même, de plus.
nay! *nā*, eh bien! erreur!
neap, *nēp*, a. bas, mort.
near, *nēr*, v. n. s'approcher.
near, *nēr*, a., ad. & pr. (-ly, ad.) proche, voisin, intime ‖ parsimonieux ‖ presque, à peu près, (au) près de ‖ de près ‖ mesquinement ‖ that was a ~ thing, il l'a échappé belle.
nearness, *nēr'nĕs*, s. proximité, mesquinerie, f.
neat, *nēt*, s. gros bétail, m. [nerie, f.
neat, *nēt*, a. (-ly, ad.) net(tement) ‖ propre(ment) ‖ élégant ‖ (of drinks) sec, non trempé.
neatness, *nēt'nĕs*, s. netteté, propreté, f.
nebula, *nĕb'ūlă*, s. (astr.) nébuleuse, f.
nebulous, *nĕb'ūlŭs*, a. nébuleux.
necessaries, *nĕs'ĕsĕrĭz*, s.pl. nécessaire, m., besoins de la vie, m. pl. [ment.
necessarily, *nĕs'ĕsĕrĭlĭ*, ad. nécessaire-
necessary, *nĕs'ĕsĕrĭ*, ad. nécessaire.
necessitate, *nĕsĕs'ĭtāt*, v. a. nécessiter.
necessitous, *nĕsĕs'ĕtŭs*, a. indigent.
necessity, *nĕsĕs'ĭtĭ*, s. nécessité, f.
neck, *nĕk*, s. cou, m. ‖ partie allongée, f. ‖ manche, m. ‖ to fall ~ and crop, tomber de tout son long ‖ to run ~ and ~, se tenir de près, serrés, en ligne ‖ a

stiff ~, torticolis, m. ‖ stiff--ed, a. qui a le cou raide ‖ ~-cloth, s. fichu, m. ‖ ~-tie, s. cravate, f.
neckerchief, *nĕk'ĕrchĭf*, s. fichu, m.
nectarine, *nĕk'tĕrĭn*, s. nectarine, f.
need, *nēd*, s. besoin, m., nécessité, f. ‖ in case of ~, en cas de besoin.
need, *nēd*, v. a. & n. avoir besoin de, manquer ‖ être nécessaire, falloir, être dans le besoin. [(ment).
needful, *nēd'fŏŏl*, a. (-ly, ad.) nécessaire
needily, *nēd'ĭlĭ*, ad. pauvrement.
neediness, *nēd'ĭnĕs*, s. pauvreté, f.
needle, *nē'dl*, s. aiguille, f. ‖ boussole, f. ‖ ~-case, s. étui à aiguilles, m. ‖ ~-gun, s. fusil à aiguille, m. ‖ ~-woman, s. couturière, f. ‖ ~-work, s. ouvrage à l'aiguille, m. ‖ couture, f. ‖ broderie, f.
needless, *nēd'lĕs*, a. (-ly, ad.) inutile (ment).
needs, *nēdz*, ad. nécessairement.
needy, *nē'dĭ*, s. nécessiteux, pauvre.
nefarious, *nĕfā'rĭŭs*, a. abominable.
negation, *nĕgā'shŭn*, s. négation, f.
negative, *nĕg'ătĭv*, s. négative, négation, f.
negative, *nĕg'ătĭv*, v. a. réfuter.
negative, *nĕg'ătĭv*, a. négatif ‖ -ly, ad. négativement.
neglect, *nĕglĕkt*, s. négligence, f.
neglect, *nĕg'lĕkt*, v. a. négliger.
neglectful, *nĕglĕkt'fŏŏl*, a. vide negligent. [chalance, f.
negligence, *nĕg'lĭjĕns*, s. négligence, non-
negligent, *nĕg'lĭjĕnt*, a. négligent, nonchalant ‖ -ly, ad. négligemment.
negotiable, *nĕgō'shĭăbl*, a. négociable.
negotiate, *nĕgō'shĭāt*, v. n. négocier.
negotiation, *nĕgōshĭā'shŭn*, s. négociation, f.
Negress, *nē'grĕs*, s. négresse, f. [tion, f.
Negro, *nē'grō*, s. nègre, m.
neigh, *nā*, neighing, *nā'ĭng*, s. hennissement, m.
neigh, *nā*, v. n. hennir. [ment, m.
neighbour, *nā'bĕr*, s. voisin, m. ‖ prochain, m.
neighbour, *nā'bĕr*, v. a. avoisiner.
neighbourhood, *nā'bĕrhŏŏd*, s. voisinage, m. [civil, en voisin.
neighbourly, *nā'bĕrlĭ*, a. & ad. bon,
neither, *nē'thĕr* ou *nī'thĕr*, c. & pn. ni, non plus ‖ ni l'un ni l'autre.
neology, *nēŏl'ōjĭ*, s. néologie, f.
neophite, *nē'ōfĭt*, s. néophyte, m.
nepenthe, *nĕpĕn'thē*, s. (bot.) nepenthe, m.
nephew, *nĕv'ū*, s. neveu, m.
nepotism, *nĕp'ōtĭzm*, s. népotisme, m.
nerve, *nĕrv*, s. nerf, m. ‖ vigueur, f.
nerveless, *nĕrv'lĕs*, a. énervé, sans vigueur.
nervous, *nĕr'vŭs*, a. nerveux ‖ fort, vigoureux.
nest, *nĕst*, s. nid, m. ‖ nichée, f. ‖ repaire, m. ‖ ~-egg, s. nichet, m. ‖ (fam.) pistole volante, f. ‖ ~-ing-time, s. (of birds) temps de la nichée, m., nidification, f.
nestle, *nĕs'l*, v. a. & n. se nicher, se loger.
nestling, *nĕs'lĭng*, s. petit oiseau au nid, m.
net, *nĕt*, s. filet, rets, m. ‖ landing-~, m., trubleau, m.

net, *nĕt,* v. a. faire un filet.

net, *nĕt,* a. (com.) net, pur.

nether, *nĕth'ĕr,* a. bas, inférieur. [f.

netting-needle, *nĕt'ting nē'dl,* s. navette,

nettle, *nĕt'l,* s. ortie, f.

nettle, *nĕt'l,* v. a. piquer, irriter.

neuralgia, *nūrăl'jĭ ă,* s. névralgie, f.

neurotic, *nūrŏt'ĭk,* a. névrotique.

neuter, *nū'tĕr,* a. neutre, impartial.

neutral, *nū'trăl,* a. neutre ‖ indifférent ‖ -ly, ad. neutralement. [mitiger.

neutralise, *nū'trălĭz,* v. a. neutraliser,

neutrality, *nū trăl'ĭ tĭ,* s. neutralité, f.

never, *nĕv'ĕr,* ad. jamais ‖ ~ mind ! n'importe ! [jamais.

nevermore, *nĕv'ĕr mōr',* ad. au grand

nevertheless, *nĕv'ĕr thĭ lĕs',* c. néanmoins, cependant, pourtant.

new, *nū,* a. & ad. (-ly, ad.) neuf, nouveau ‖ nouvellement ‖ depuis peu ‖ brand ~, tout battant neuf, flambant neuf ‖ ~-fangled, a. nouvellement inventé.

newness, *nū'nĕs,* s. nouveauté, f.

news, *nūz,* s. nouvelle, f., nouvelles, f. pl. ‖ ~-boy, s. colporteur de journaux, m. ‖ ~-room, s. cabinet de lecture, m.

newsagent, *nūz'ā jĕnt,* s. commissionnaire pour les journaux, m. [journal, m.

newspaper, *nūz'pā pĕr,* s. gazette, f.,

next, *nĕkst,* a. & ad. proche, prochain, voisin ‖ ensuite, puis, après ‖ ~ to, presque.

nib, *nĭb,* s. bec d'un oiseau, m. ‖ pointe d'une plume, f.

nibble, *nĭb'bl,* v. a. & n. becqueter ‖ ronger ‖ mordre à l'hameçon ‖ épiloguer (sur).

nibbler, *nĭb'blĕr,* s. épiloguer, m.

nice, *nis,* a. (-ly, ad.) exact(ement) ‖ soigneux ‖ délicat(ement) ‖ joli, agréable, recherché ‖ difficile ‖ soigneusement ‖ avec goût.

niceness, *nis'nĕs,* **nicety,** *ni'sĕ tĭ,* s. exactitude, f. ‖ subtilité, f., raffinement, m. ‖ **niceties,** s. pl. friandises, f. pl.

niche, *nĭch,* s. niche, f.

nick, *nĭk,* s. entaille, f. ‖ ~ of time, moment convenable or précis, m.

nick, *nĭk,* v. a. rencontrer à propos.

nicknack, *nĭk'năk,* s. *vide* knicknack.

nickname, *nĭk'nām,* s. sobriquet, m.

nickname, *nĭk'nām,* v. a. donner un sobriquet.

nicotine, *nĭk'ō tĭn,* s. (chim.) nicotine, f.

niece, *nēs,* s. nièce, f.

niggard, *nĭg'gĕrd,* s. avare, harpagon, m.

niggardliness, *nĭg'gĕrd lĭ nĕs,* s. avarice, f. [vilain, en avare.

niggardly, *nĭg'gĕrd lĭ,* a. & ad. avare,

nigger, *nĭg'gĕr,* s. moricaud, m., moricaude, f. [près, près de, presque.

nigh, *ni,* a., pr. & ad. proche, voisin ‖

night, *nit,* s. nuit, f. ‖ obscurité, f. ‖ to-~, cette nuit, ce soir ‖ ~-cap, s. bonnet de nuit, m. ‖ ~-light, s. veilleuse, f. ‖ ~-stool, s. chaise percée, f. ‖ ~-walker, s. somnambule, m. & f.

nightgown, *nit'gown,* **nightdress,** *nit'drĕs,* s. déshabillé, négligé, m. (des femmes).

nightingale, *nit'in gāl,* s. rossignol, m.

nightly, *nit'lĭ,* a. & ad. nocturne, de nuit, chaque nuit. [belle-dame, f.

nightshade, *nit'shăd,* s. (bot.) belladonna,

nightshirt, *nit'shĕrt,* s. (des hommes) chemise de nuit, f.

nimble, *nĭm'bl,* a. agile, actif, prompt.

nimbly, *nĭm'blĭ,* ad. agilement, vivement.

nimbus, *nĭm'bŭs,* s. nimbe, m.

nine, *nin,* a. neuf.

ninefold, *nin'fōld,* a. neuf fois autant.

ninepins, *nin'pĭnz,* s. pl. jeu de quilles, m.

nineteen, *nin'tēn,* a. dix-neuf ‖ -th, a. dix-neuvième ‖ (of months) dix-neuf.

ninetieth, *nin'tĭ ĕth,* a. quatre-vingt-dixième.

ninety, *nin'tĭ,* a. quatre-vingt-dix.

ninny, *nĭn'nĭ,* s. niais, benêt, m.

ninth, *ninth,* a. (-ly, ad.) neuvième(ment).

nip, *nĭp,* v. a. pincer, égratigner ‖ piquer, vexer ‖ flétrir.

nippers, *nĭp'pĕrz,* s. pl. pincettes, f. pl.

nipple, *nĭp'pl,* s. mamelon, pis, m.

nitrate, *ni'trăt,* s. nitrate, m.

nitre, *ni'tĕr,* s. nitre, salpêtre, m.

nitric, *ni'trĭk,* a. nitrique.

nitrous, *ni'trŭs,* a. nitreux.

no, *nō,* s. voix contre, f.

no, *nō,* a. & ad. aucun, nul, pas un ‖ non.

nobility, *nō bĭl'ĭ tĭ,* s. noblesse, f. ‖ patent of ~, lettres de noblesse, f. pl.

nobleman, *nō'bl(măn),* s. noble, m.

noble, *nō'bl,* a. noble, illustre, généreux.

nobleness, *nō'bl nĕs,* s. noblesse, f.

nobly, *nō'blĭ,* ad. noblement.

nobody, *nō'bŏd'ĭ,* s. personne, f.

nocturnal, *nŏk tĕr'năl,* a. nocturne.

nod, *nŏd,* s. signe de tête, m. ‖ inclination de tête, f. [assoupi.

nod, *nŏd,* v. n. faire un signe de tête ‖ être

noise, *nŏyz,* s. bruit, fracas, m.

noise, *nŏyz,* v. a. (to ~ abroad) répandre.

noisily, *nŏyz'ĭ lĭ,* ad. bruyamment.

noisiness, *nŏy'zĭ nĕs,* s. grand bruit, tumulte, m. [dégoûtant.

noisome, *nŏy'sŭm,* a. nuisible ‖ malsain,

noisy, *nŏy'zĭ,* a. bruyant, turbulent.

nolens-volens, *nō'lĕnz vō'lĕnz,* ad. de gré ou de force.

nominal, *nŏm'ĭ năl,* a. nominal, titulaire ‖ -ly, ad. de nom, nommément.

nominate, *nŏm'ĭ năt,* v. a. nommer, désigner ‖ (at elections) proposer. [f.

nomination, *nŏm'ĭ nā'shŭn,* s. nomination,

nominative, *nŏm'ĭ nă tĭv,* s. nominatif, m.

nominative, *nŏm'ĭ nă tĭv,* a. nominatif.

nominee, *nŏm ĭ nē',* s. personne dénommée, f. [mée, f.

nonage, *nŏn'ăj,* s. minorité, f. [mée, f.

nonagenarian, *nŏn ă jĕn ā'rĭ ăn,* s. nonagénaire, m. [défaut, m.

non-appearance, *nŏn ăp pē'răns,* s. (jur.)

non-attendance, *nŏn ăt tĕn'dăns,* s. (jur.) absence, f.

nonce, *nŏns,* s. for the ~, pour le moment.

nonconformist, *nŏn kŏn fărm'ĭst,* s. non-conformiste, m. [. . . pas.

none, *nŭn,* a. aucun, nul, personne ‖ ne

nonentity, *nŏn ĕn' tĭ tĭ*, s. nonexistence, f., non-être, m.   [observation, f.
non-observance, *nŏn ŏb zēr' văns*, s. inexécution, f.
non-performance, *nŏn pĕr fawrm' ăns*, s. inexécution, f.
nonplus, *nŏn' plŭs*, v. a. embarrasser.
nonsense, *nŏn' sĕns*, s. nonsens, m., absurdité, f. || baliverne, f. || ~! laissez donc!
nonsensical, *nŏn sĕn' sĭ kăl*, a. absurde.
nonsuit, *nŏn' sūt*, s. (jur.) perte de cause, f.
nonsuit, *nŏn' sūt*, v. a. (jur.) débouter.
noodle, *nŏŏ' dl*, s. niais, benêt, m.
nook, *nŏŏk*, s. coin, enfoncement, m.
noon, *nŏn*, s. midi, m. || mmuit, m.
noonday, *nŏn' dā*, s. midi, m.
noose, *noz*, s. nœud coulant, m. || piège, m.
noose, *nŏz*, v. a. attacher avec un nœud coulant, prendre dans un piège.
nor, *nŏr*, c. ni, ne.
normal, *nŏr' măl*, a. normal.
north, *nŏrth*, s. nord, m. || ~-star, s. étoile polaire, f.
northerly, *nŏr' thĕr lĭ*, **northern**, *nŏr' thĕrn*, a. septentrional || ~ lights, s. pl. aurore boréale, f.   [nord.
northward(s), *nŏrth' wĕrd(z)*, ad. vers le nord.
nose, *nŏz*, s. nez, m. || tuyau, m. || bout, m. || to be led by the ~, être mené par le bout du nez, être berné || to put one's ~ out of joint, damer le pion à qn., couper l'herbe sous le pied à qn. || to turn up one's ~, rechigner, faire la grimace || ~-bag, s. musette, f. || ~-band, s. muserolle, f.
nosegay, *nŏz' gā*, s. bouquet, m.
nostalgia, *nŏs tăl jĭ ă*, s. (méd.) nostalgie, f., mal du pays, m.
nostril, *nŏs' trĭl*, s. narine, f. || naseau, m.
nostrum, *nŏs' trŭm*, s. remède secret, m. || poudre de perlimpinpin, f.
not, *nŏt*, ad. non, ne point || ~ at all, point du tout.
notability, *nō tă bĭl' ĭ tĭ*, s. notabilité, f.
notable, *nō' tă bl*, a. remarquable.
notably, *nō' tă blĭ*, ad. notablement.
notarial, *nō tā' rĭ ăl*, a. du notaire || notarié.
notary, *nō' tă rĭ*, s. notaire, m.
notation, *nō tā' shŭn*, s. notation, f.   [m.
notch, *nŏch*, s. entaille, f. || dent, f. || cran, m.
notch, *nŏch*, v. a. entailler || ébrécher.
note, *nŏt*, s. note, marque, f. || avis, billet, m. || observation, f. || note de musique, f. || (gr.) point, m. || distinction, importance, f. || bank-~, billet de banque, m. || to make a ~ of, prendre note de.
note, *nŏt*, v. a. noter, remarquer.
noted, *nō' tĕd*, a. remarquable, célèbre.
nothing, *nŭth' ing*, s. néant, rien, m.   [m.
nothingness, *nŭth' ing nĕs*, s. néant, rien, m.
notice, *nō' tĭs*, s. notice, f., avis, m., nouvelle, f. || connaissance, f. || on, at short ~, à bref délai, à courte échéance || to give ~ to quit, donner congé à || to take ~, prendre || to take no ~ of, ne se soucier de || to attract ~, attirer l'attention.
notice, *nō' tĭs*, v. a. remarquer, observer.

noticeable, *nō' tĭs ă bl*, a. perceptible || digne de remarque.   [tion, f.
notification, *nō tĭ fĭ kā' shŭn*, s. notification, f.
notify, *nō' tĭ fī*, v. a. notifier, faire savoir.
notion, *nō' shŭn*, s. notion, pensée, opinion, f.   [dence, f.
notoriety, *nō tō rī' ĕ tĭ*, s. notoriété, évidence, f.
notorious, *nō tō' rĭ ŭs*, a. (-ly, ad.) notoire (ment) || fameux.
notwithstanding, *nŏt with stănd' ing*, c. nonobstant, néanmoins.
nought, *nawt*, s. rien, néant, m. || zéro, m.
noun, *nŏwn*, s. (gr.) nom, substantif, m.
nourish, *nŭr' ish*, v. a. nourrir, entretenir.
nourishment, *nŭr' ish mĕnt*, s. nourriture, f., aliment, m.
novel, *nŏv' ĕl*, s. roman, m., nouvelle, f.
novel, *nŏv' ĕl*, a. neuf || nouveau || étrange.
novelist, *nŏv' ĕl ist*, s. romancier, m.
novelty, *nŏv' ĕl tĭ*, s. nouveauté, f.
November, *nō vĕm' bĕr*, s. novembre, m.
novice, *nŏv' ĭs*, s. novice, commençant, m.
novitiate, *nō vish' ĭ āt*, s. noviciat, m.
now, *nŏw*, ad. à présent, maintenant || ~ and then, ~ and again, de temps en temps || ~ then! eh bien! et après? || just ~, tout à l'heure.
nowadays, *nŏw' ă dāz*, ad. de nos jours.
nowhere, *nō' hwār*, ad. nulle part.
nowise, *nō' wiz*, ad. nullement.
noxious, *nŏk' shŭs*, a. nuisible || coupable || -ly, ad. pernicjeusement.   [tuyau, m.
nozzle, *nŏz' l*, s. nez (des animaux), m. ||
nucleus, *nū' klĕ ŭs*, s. noyau, m.
nude, *nūd*, a. nu.
nudge, *nŭj*, s. coup de coude, m.
nudge, *nŭj*, v. a. pousser du coude.
nudity, *nū' dĭ tĭ*, s. nudité, f.
nugatory, *nū' gă tŏr ĭ*, a. futile, frivole.
nugget, *nŭg' gĕt*, s. pépite, f.
nuisance, *nū' săns*, s. incommodité, plaie, f. || commit no ~! défense d'uriner!
null, *nŭl*, a. nul, non valide.
nullify, *nŭl' lĭ fī*, v. a. annuler.
nullity, *nŭl' lĭ tĭ*, s. nullité, f.
numb, *nŭm*, a. engourdi, glacé.
numb, *nŭm*, v. a. engourdir.
number, *nŭm' bĕr*, s. nombre, m., quantité, f. || numéro, m. || broken ~, fractional ~, (ar.) nombre fractionnaire, m. || odd ~, nombre impair, m. || (ar.) fraction, f.   [numéroter.
number, *nŭm' bĕr*, v. a. nombrer, compter.
numberless, *nŭm' bĕr lĕs*, a. innombrable.
numbness, *nŭm' nĕs*, s. engourdissement, m.   [chiffre, m.
numeral, *nū' mĕr ăl*, s. lettre numérale, f. ||
numeral, *nū' mĕr ăl*, a. numéral, numérique.   [tion, f.
numeration, *nū mĕr ā' shŭn*, s. numération, f.
numerator, *nū' mĕr ā tĕr*, s. (ar.) numérateur, m.   [numérique(ment).
numerical, *nū mĕr' ĭk ăl*, a. (-ly, ad.)
numerous, *nū' mĕr ŭs*, a. nombreux || -ly, ad. en grand nombre.   [matique, f.
numismatics, *nū mĭs măt' ĭks*, s. pl. numismatique, f.
numskull, *nŭm' skŭl*, s. sot, lourdaud, m.

nun, *nŭn,* s. nonne, religieuse, f.

nuncio, *nŭn′shī ō,* s. nonce, m. [m.

nunnery, *nŭn′nĕr ĭ,* s. couvent de nonnes,

nuptial, *nŭp′shăl,* a. nuptial.

nuptials, *nŭp′shălz,* s. pl. noces, f. pl.

nurse, *nĕrs,* s. nourrice, f. ‖ garde-malade, f. ‖ wet-~, nourrice, f. ‖ dry-~, bonne d'enfants, f.

nurse, *nĕrs,* v. a. nourrir, élever.

nursery, *nĕrs′ĕr ĭ,* s. chambre des enfants, f. ‖ pépinière, f. ‖ ~-maid, s. bonne d'enfants, f. [m.

nursling, *nĕrs′lĭng,* s. nourrisson, mignon,

nurture, *nĕr′tŭr,* v. a. nourrir, élever.

nut, *nŭt,* s. noix, f. ‖ écrou, m. ‖ a hard ~ to crack, un problème épineux, difficile ‖ ~-crackers, s. casse-noisettes, m. ‖ ~-gall, s. noix de galle, f. ‖ ~-shell, s. coquille de noix, f. ‖ ~-tree, s. noisetier,

nut, *nŭt,* v. n. cueillir des noix. [m.

nutmeg, *nŭt′mĕg,* s. muscade, f.

nutriment, *nū′trĭ mĕnt,* s. nourriture, f., aliment, m.

nutrition, *nū trĭsh′ŭn,* s. nutrition, f. ‖ nourriture, f. ‖ aliment, m.

nutritious, *nū trĭsh′ŭs, * **nutritive,** *nū′trĭ tĭv,* a. nourrissant.

nutty, *nŭt′tĭ,* a. qui a un goût de noisette.

nux vomica, *nŭks′vŏm′ĭ kă,* s. (méd.) noix vomique, f.

nymph, *nĭmf,* s. nymphe, f.

O.

oaf, *ōf,* s. sot, benêt, m.

oak, *ōk,* s. chêne, m. ‖ ~-apple, s. galle, f. ‖ pomme de chêne, f. ‖ ~-gall, s. noix

oaken, *ō′kn,* a. de chêne. [de galle, f.

oakum, *ō′kŭm,* s. (mar.) étoupe, f.

oar, *ōr,* s. rame, f., aviron, m. ‖ to put in one's ~, (fig.) placer son mot.

oarsman, *ōrz′măn,* s. rameur, m.

oasis, *ō ā′sĭs,* s. oasis, f.

oat(s) *ōt(s),* s. avoine, f. ‖ to sow one's wild ~, jeter sa gourme.

oath, *ōth,* s. serment, jurement, m. ‖ to be under an ~, être lié par son serment.

oatmeal, *ōt′mēl,* s. gruau (d'avoine), m.

obduracy, *ŏb′dū rā sĭ,* s. endurcissement, m. ‖ insensibilité, f.

obdurate, *ŏb′dū rāt,* a. endurci ‖ obstiné ‖ -ly, ad. inflexiblement.

obedience, *ō bē′dĭ ĕns,* s. obéissance, f.

obedient, *ō bē′dĭ ĕnt,* a. obéissant ‖ -ly, ad. avec obéissance ‖ Yours -ly, votre tout dévoué serviteur.

obeisance, *ō bā′săns,* s. salut, m.

obelisk, *ŏb′ē lĭsk,* s. obélisque, m.

obese, *ō bēs′,* a. obèse, ventru, ventripotent, replet. [point excessif, m.

obesity, *ō bĕs′ĭ tĭ* ou *ō bēs′ĭ tĭ,* s. embonpoint excessif, m.

obey, *ō bā′,* v. a. obéir à ‖ ~, v. n. obéir.

obituary, *ō bĭt′ū ĕr ĭ,* s. obituaire, f.

object, *ŏb′jĕkt,* s. objet, m., matière, f., sujet, m.

object, *ŏb jĕkt′,* v. a. objecter.

objection, *ŏb jĕk′shŭn,* s. objection, f. ‖ reproche, f. ‖ difficulté, f. [à objection.

objectionable, *ŏb jĕk′shŭn ă bl,* a. sujet

objective, *ŏb jĕk′tĭv,* a. (gr.) objectif ‖ ~ case, s. (gr.) régime direct, m. [f.

oblation, *ŏb lā′shŭn,* s. oblation, offrande,

obligation, *ŏb lĭ gā′shŭn,* s. obligation, f.

obligatory, *ŏb′lĭ gā tĕr ĭ,* a. obligatoire.

oblige, *ō blīj′,* v. a. obliger ‖ contraindre ‖ I will be -d if, je vous serai obligé de.

obliging, *ō blī′jĭng,* a. (-ly, ad.) obligeant ‖ obligeamment. [f.

obligingness, *ō blī′jĭng nĕs,* s. obligeance,

oblique, *ŏb lēk′,* a. (-ly, ad.) oblique (ment) ‖ indirect.

obliquity, *ŏb lĭk′wĭ tĭ,* s. obliquité, f.

obliterate, *ŏb lĭt′ĕr āt,* v. a. oblitérer, effacer. [oblitération, f.

obliteration, *ŏb lĭt ĕr ā′shŭn,* s. rature, f. ‖

oblivion, *ŏb lĭv′ŭn,* s. oubli, m.

oblivious, *ŏb lĭv′ĭ ŭs,* a. oublieux.

oblong, *ŏb′lŏng,* a. oblong. [m.

obloquy, *ŏb′lō kwĭ,* s. censure, f., reproche,

obnoxious, *ŏb nŏk′shŭs,* a. sujet or exposé à ‖ nuisible. coupable.

obscene, *ŏb sēn′,* a. obscène, impudique.

obscenity, *ŏb sĕn′ĭ tĭ,* s. obscénité, f.

obscuration, *ŏb skū rā′shŭn,* s. obscurcissement, m.

obscure, *ŏb skŭr′,* v. a. obscurcir.

obscure, *ŏb skŭr′,* a. (-ly, ad.) obscur (ément).

obsequies, *ŏb′sē kwĭz,* s. pl. obsèques, f. pl.

obsequious, *ŏb sē′kwĭ ŭs,* a. obéissant ‖ servile ‖ -ly, ad. avec obéissance ‖ complaisamment.

observable, *ŏb zĕr′vă bl,* a. remarquable.

observance, *ŏb zĕr′văns,* s. observation, f. ‖ respect, m., soumission, f.

observant, *ŏb zĕr′vănt,* a. (-ly, ad.) attentif ‖ respectueux ‖ exact ‖ attentivement. [f.

observation, *ŏb zĕr vā′shŭn,* s. observation,

observatory, *ŏb zĕr′vă tĕr ĭ,* s. observatoire, m. [remarquer, faire observer.

observe, *ŏb zĕrv′,* v. a. & n. observer ‖

observer, *ŏb zĕr′vĕr,* s. observateur, m.

obsolete, *ŏb′sō lēt,* a. inusité ‖ hors de mode.

obstacle, *ŏb′stă kl,* s. obstacle, m. [f.

obstetrics, *ŏb stĕt′rĭks,* s. pl. obstétrique,

obstinacy, *ŏb′stĭ nă sĭ,* s. opiniâtreté, f.

obstinate, *ŏb′stĭ nāt,* a. (-ly, ad.) obstiné (ment).

obstruct, *ŏb strŭkt′,* v. a. encombrer, obstruer ‖ mettre obstacle à.

obstruction, *ŏb strŭk′shŭn,* s. obstruction, f. ‖ empêchement, m. [tenir.

obtain, *ŏb tān′,* v. a. & n. obtenir ‖ se main-

obtainable, *ŏb tān′ă bl,* a. qu'on peut obtenir.

obtrude, *ŏb trōd′,* v. a. introduire ‖ forcer.

obtuse, *ŏb tūs′,* a. obtus, émoussé ‖ stupide.

obviate, *ŏb′vĭ āt,* v. a. obvier à ‖ prévenir.

obvious, *ŏb′vĭ ŭs,* a. clair, évident ‖ -ly, ad. évidemment.

occasion, *ŏk kā' zhŭn*, s. occasion, f., incident, m. ‖ besoin, m. ‖ motif, m., cause, f.
occasion, *ŏk kā' zhŭn*, v. a. occasionner, causer, donner lieu à.
occasional, *ŏk kā' zhŭn ăl*, a. occasionnel, casuel ‖ -ly, ad. fortuitement.
occidental, *ŏk sĭ dĕn' tăl*, a. occidental.
occult, *ŏk kŭlt'*, a. occulte. [sion, f.
occupancy, *ŏk' kŭ păn sĭ*, s. prise de possession, m.
occupant, *ŏk' kŭ pănt*, s. occupant, possesseur, m.
occupation, *ŏk kŭ pā' shŭn*, s. occupation, f., emploi, m. ‖ possession, f.
occupy, *ŏk' kŭ pĭ*, v. a. occuper, employer ‖ habiter ‖ prendre possession de.
occur, *ŏk kŭr'*, v. n. se présenter, se rencontrer ‖ venir à l'esprit ‖ arriver.
occurrence, *ŏk kŭr' rĕns*, s. accident, événement, m. ‖ to be of actual ~, être plein d'actualité.
ocean, *ō' shŭn*, s. océan, m.
oceanic, *ō shē ăn' ĭk*, a. océanien, océanique.
ochre, *ō' kĕr*, s. ocre, f. [nique.
octagon, *ŏk' tă gŏn*, s. octogone, m.
octagonal, *ŏk tăg' ō năl*, a. octogonal.
octave, *ŏk' tăv*, s. octave, f. ‖ ~-cask, s. quartaut, m.
octavo, *ŏk tā' vō*, a. in-octavo.
October, *ŏk tō' bĕr*, s. octobre, m.
ocular, *ŏk' ū lĕr*, a. oculaire.
oculist, *ŏk' ū lĭst*, s. oculiste, m.
odd, *ŏd*, a. impair ‖ de reste ‖ singulier, étrange, bizarre ‖ dépareillé, déparié ‖ -ly, ad. bizarrement.
oddity, *ŏd' dĭ tĭ*, oddness, *ŏd' nĕs*, s. bizarrerie, singularité, originalité, f.
odds, *ŏdz*, s. inégalité, f. ‖ avantage, m., supériorité, f. ‖ dispute, f. [ment.
odious, *ō' dĭ ŭs*, a. odieux ‖ -ly, ad. odieusement.
odium, *ō' dĭ ŭm*, s. haine, f.
odorous, *ō' dĕr ŭs*, a. parfumé.
odour, *ō' dĕr*, s. odeur, f. ‖ bouquet, m.
of, *ŏv*, pr. de, du, de la, des.
off, *ŏf*, a. & pr. éloigné ‖ loin, loin de ‖ distant ‖ contre ‖ to be well (badly) ~, être bien (mal) dans ses affaires ‖ ~ foot, (des chevaux) pied droit, m. ‖ ~-side, s. hors main, m. [m. ‖ carcasse, f.
offal, *ŏf' făl*, s. reste de viande, m. ‖ rebut,
offence, *ŏf fĕns'*, s. offense, f. ‖ faute, f., crime, m. ‖ affront, outrage, m.
offend, *ŏf fĕnd'*, v. a. & n. offenser, irriter ‖ transgresser, violer. [m.
offender, *ŏf fĕnd' ĕr*, s. offenseur, criminel,
offensive, *ŏf fĕn' sĭv*, a. offensant, injurieux ‖ -ly, ad. offensivement.
offer, *ŏf' fĕr*, s. offre, f.
offer, *ŏf' fĕr*, v. a. & n. offrir, présenter ‖ sacrifier ‖ proposer ‖ se présenter ‖ s'efforcer ‖ when occasion ~s, dès que l'occasion s'en présente.
offering, *ŏf' fĕr ĭng*, s. offrande, f., sacrifice, m. ‖ peace-~, sacrifice expiatoire, m.
offertory, *ŏf' fĕr tĕr ĭ*, s. offertoire, m. ‖ quête, f.
office, *ŏf' fĭs*, s. office, m., charge, fonc-

tion, dignité, f. ‖ service, m. ‖ bureau, comptoir, m. ‖ commodités, f. pl.
officer, *ŏf' fĭ sĕr*, s. officier, m.
officer, *ŏf' fĭ sĕr*, v. a. pourvoir d'employés ou d'officiers.
officered, *ŏf' fĭ sĕrd*, a. commandé.
official, *ŏf fĭsh' ăl*, s. employé, m.
official, *ŏf fĭsh' ăl*, a. (-ly, ad.) officiel (lement) ‖ public. [officier.
officiate, *ŏf fĭsh' ĭ āt*, v. a. & n. administrer.
officious, *ŏf fĭsh' ŭs*, a. officieux ‖ -ly, ad. officieusement. [au large.
offing, *ŏf' fĭng*, s. pleine mer, f. ‖ in the ~,
offscouring, *ŏf skŏŭr' ĭng*, s. rebut, m.
offset, *ŏf' sĕt*, s. compensation, f. ‖ (hort.) rejeton, m. ‖ (géom.) ordonnée, f.
offshoot, *ŏf' shŏt*, s. (hort.) rejeton, m. ‖ œilleton, m.
offspring, *ŏf' sprĭng*, s. propagation, f., descendants, m. pl. ‖ lignée, f. ‖ rejeton, m.
oft, *ŏft*, often, *ŏf' n*, oftentimes, *ŏf' n tĭmz*, ad. souvent ‖ often and often, maintes fois ‖ how ~? combien de fois?
ogle, *ō' gl*, v. a. lorgner, regarder à la dérobée.
oh! *ō*, oh! *ō*, ah! ‖ ah! hélas! ouf! aïe! [robée.
oil, *ŏyl*, s. huile, f. ‖ ~-cloth, s. toile cirée, f. ‖ ~-colour, s. couleur à l'huile, f. ‖ ~-painting, s. peinture à l'huile, f. ‖ ~-silk, s. taffetas gommé, m. ‖ ~-skin, s.
oil, *ŏyl*, v. n. huiler. [toile vernie, f.
oiliness, *ŏyl' ĭ nĕs*, s. qualité huileuse, f.
oily, *ŏyl' ĭ*, a. huileux, onctueux. [m.
ointment, *ŏynt' mĕnt*, s. onguent, baume,
old, *ōld*, olden, *ōl' dĕn*, a. vieux, ancien, antique ‖ as ~ as the hills, archi-vieux ‖ séculaire ‖ how ~ are you? quel âge avez-vous? ‖ I am ten years ~, j'ai dix ans ‖ ten years ~, âgé de dix ans.
oldish, *ōld' ĭsh*, a. vieillot. [f.
oldness, *ōld' nĕs*, s. vieillesse, f. ‖ antiquité,
oleaginous, *ō lē ăj' ĭn ŭs*, a. huileux.
oleander, *ō lē ăn' dĕr*, s. laurier-rose, m.
olfactory, *ŏl făk' tĕr ĭ*, a. olfactif.
olive, *ŏl' ĭv*, s. olivier, m. ‖ olive, f.
omelet, *ŏm' ĕ lĕt* ou *ŏm' lĕt*, s. omelette, f.
omen, *ō' mĕn*, s. présage, augure, m.
omened, *ō' mĕnd*, a. augural.
ominous, *ŏm' ĭn ŭs*, a. (-ly, ad.) de mauvais augure, omineux.
omission, *ō mĭsh' ŭn*, s. omission, f.
omissive, *ō mĭs' sĭv*, a. qui commet des omissions. [oublier.
omit, *ō mĭt'*, v. a. omettre ‖ négliger ‖
omnibus, *ŏm' nĭ bŭs*, s. omnibus, m.
omnifarious, *ŏm nĭ fā' rĭ ŭs*, a. multiple.
omnipotence, *ŏm nĭp' ō tĕns*, s. toute-puissance, f.
omnipotent, *ŏm nĭp' ō tĕnt*, a. tout-puissant.
on, *ŏn*, pr. & ad. sur ‖ en avant ‖ après ‖ and so ~, et ainsi de suite ‖ go ~! avancez! ‖ ~ the contrary, au contraire.
once, *wŭns*, ad. une fois ‖ autrefois ‖ at ~, à la fois ‖ ~ upon a time, there was... il était, il y avait une fois... ‖ ~ for all, une fois pour toutes ‖ ~ and again, maintes fois.

one, *wŭn*, a. & pn. un, une || on || ~ an-
other, l'un l'autre, les uns les autres ||
~ by ~, un à un || ~'s, son, sa, ses || ~-
horse, a. attelé d'un seul cheval || (fig.)
tiré par les cheveux, médiocre.
onerous, *ŏn'ĕr ŭs*, a. onéreux.
oneself, one's self, *wŭn sĕlf'*, pr. soi-
même || soi || se || to come to ~, re-
prendre ses esprits, revenir à soi || beside
~ with anger, outré de colère.
onion, *ŭn'yŭn*, s. oignon, m.
only, *ŏn'lĭ*, a. (& ad.) seul(ement) || if ~,
pour peu que.   [assaut, m., attaque, f.
onset, *ŏn'sĕt*, onslaught, *ŏn'slāwt*, s.
onward, *ŏn'wĕrd*, ad. en avant.
onyx, *ŏ'nĭks*, s. onyx, m.
ooze, *ōz*, s. vase, bourbe, f.
ooze, *ōz*, v. n. filtrer || suinter || s'écouler.
oozy, *ō'zĭ*, a. fangeux.
opacity, *ŏ pås'ĭ tĭ*, s. opacité, f.
opal, *ŏ'pål*, s. opale, f.
opalescent, *ŏ pål ĕs'ĕnt*, a. opalescent.
opaque, *ŏ pāk'*, a. opaque.
open, *ŏ'pn*, v. a. & n. ouvrir, découvrir ||
expliquer || commencer || s'ouvrir.
open, *ŏ'pn*, a. (-ly, ad.) ouvert(ement) ||
apparent || franc, sincère || clair || franche-
ment|| ~-handed, a.libéral|| ~-hearted,
a. franc || ~-work, s. ouvrage à jour, m.
opening, *ŏ'pn ĭng*, s. ouverture, f. || début,
m. || débouché, m.   [deur, f.
openness, *ŏ'pn nĕs*, s. évidence, f. || can-
opera, *ŏp'ĕr å*, s. opéra, m. || ~-cloak, s.
sortie de bal, f. || ~-glass, s. lorgnette,
f. || jumelles, f. pl. || ~-hat, s. claque, m. ||
~-house, s. opéra, m. || théâtre lyrique, ||
operate, *ŏp'ĕr āt*, v. n. opérer, agir.   m.
operatio, *ŏp ĕr āt'ĭk*, a. d'opéra.
operating-room, *ŏp'ĕr āt ĭng rōm*, s. (of
hospitals) amphithéâtre, m.
operation, *ŏp ĕr ā'shŭn*, s. opération, f.,
effet, m.
operative, *ŏp'ĕr å tĭv*, s. ouvrier, m.
operative, *ŏp'ĕr å tĭv*, a. efficace.
operator, *ŏp'ĕr ā tĕr*, s. opérateur, m.
ophthalmy, *ŏf'thål mĭ*, s. ophthalmie, f.
opiate, *ŏ'pĭ āt*, s. opiat, m.
opine, *ŏ pīn'*, v. a. opiner.   [ment, m.
opinion, *ŏ pĭn'yŭn*, s. opinion, f., senti-
opinionated, *ŏ pĭn'yŭn ā tĕd*, opiniona-
tive, *ŏ pĭn'yŭn å tĭv*, a. opiniâtre.
opossum, *ŏ pŏs'ŭm*, s. opossum, m.
opponent, *ŏp pō'nĕnt*, s. antagoniste, adversaire, m.   [ad. à propos.
opportune, *ŏp'pŏr tūn*, a. opportun || -ly,
opportuneness, *ŏp'pŏr tūn nĕs*, s. opportunité, f.   [occasion, f.
opportunity, *ŏp pŏr tū'nĭ tĭ*, s.opportunité,
oppose, *ŏp pōz'*, v. a. (& n.) (s')opposer.
opposite, *ŏp'pō sĭt*, s. opposé, m.
opposite, *ŏp'pō sĭt*, a. (-ly, ad.) vis-à-vis ||
en sens opposé.   [résistance, f.
opposition, *ŏp pō zĭsh'ŭn*, s. opposition,
oppress, *ŏp prĕs'*, v. a. opprimer.
oppression, *ŏp prĕsh'ŭn*, s. oppression, f.
oppressive, *ŏp prĕs'sĭv*, a. oppressif || ac-
cablant.

oppressor, *ŏp prĕs'sĕr*, s. oppresseur, m.
opprobrious, *ŏp prō'brĭ ŭs*, a. infamant
opprobrium, *ŏp prō'brĭ ŭm*, s.opprobre, m.
optic(al), *ŏp'tĭk (ăl)*, a. optique, visuel.
optician, *ŏp tĭsh'ăn*, s. opticien, m.
optics, *ŏp'tĭks*, s. pl. optique, f.
option, *ŏp'shŭn*, s. option, f., choix, m.
optional, *ŏp'shŭn ăl*, a. facultatif.
opulence, *ŏp'ū lĕns*, s. opulence, f.
opulent, *ŏp'ū lĕnt*, a. opulent || -ly, ad.
opulemment.   [autrement.
or, *ŏr*, c. ou || soit || ni || ~ else, ou bien,
oracle, *ŏr'åkl*, s. oracle, m.
oracular, *ŏ răk'ū lĕr*, a. (-ly, ad.) d'un
ton d'oracle (énigmatique, obscur).
oral, *ŏ'răl*, a. oral || -ly, ad. de vive voix.
orange, *ŏr'ănj*, s. orange, f.
orangeade, *ŏr ĭnj åd'*, s. orangeade, f.
oration, *ŏ rā'shŭn*, s. oraison, harangue, f.
orator, *ŏr'å tĕr*, s. orateur, m.
oratorical, *ŏr ā tŏr'ĭ kăl*, a. oratoire.
oratory, *ŏr'å tŏr ĭ*, s. art oratoire, m., élo-
quence, f. || oratoire, m.
orb, *ŏrb*, s. orbe, m., sphère, f. || globe, m.
orbit, *ŏr'bĭt*, s. orbite, m.
orchard, *ŏr'chĕrd*, s. verger, m.
orchestra, *ŏr'kĕs trå*, s. orchestre, m.
orchestral, *ŏr kĕs'trăl*, a. d'orchestre.
ordain, *ŏr dān'*, v. a. ordonner || établir.
ordeal, *ŏr'dē ăl*, s. ordalie, f.
order, *ŏr'dĕr*, s. ordre, rang, m. || règle-
ment, m. || précepte, commandement, m. ||
billet, m. || mandat, m. || décoration, f. ||
(com.) demande, f. || to make to ~, faire
sur commande || to take holy ~s, prendre
la soutane || to call to ~, (parl.) rappeler
à l'ordre || in ~ to, afin de, afin que ||
payable to one's ~, (com.) payable à
l'ordre de qn.   [ner, commander.
order, *ŏr'dĕr*, v. a. régler, disposer, ordon-
orderer, *ŏr'dĕr ĕr*, s. ordonnateur, m.
ordering, *ŏr'dĕr ĭng*, s. arrangement, m.
orderly, *ŏr'dĕr lĭ*, s. ordonnance, f.
orderly, *ŏr'dĕr lĭ*, a. & ad. régulier, bien
réglé || par ordre.
ordinance, *ŏr'dĭ năns*, s. ordonnance.
ordinarily, *ŏr'dĭ nå rĭ lĭ*, a. ordinairement
ordinary, *ŏr'dĭ nå rĭ*, s. table d'hôte, f. ||
aumônier, m.   [ordinaire.
ordinary, *ŏr'dĭ nå rĭ*, a. ordinaire || in ~,
ordination, *ŏr dĭ nā'shŭn*, s. ordination,
ordnance, *ŏrd'năns*, s. artillerie, f.   [f.
ore, *ŏr*, s. mine, f., minéral, m.
organ, *ŏr'găn*, s. organe, m. || orgue, m. ||
~-loft, s. tribune d'orgue, f. || ~-pipe,
s. tuyau d'orgue, m. || ~-stop, s. jeu
d'orgue, m.
organic, *ŏr găn'ĭk*, a. organique.
organisation, *ŏr găn ĭ zā'shŭn*, s. organisation, f.
organise, *ŏr'găn ĭz*, v. a. organiser.
organism, *ŏr'găn ĭzm*, s. organisme, m.
organist, *ŏr'găn ĭst*, s. organiste, m.
orgie, *ŏr'jĭ*, s. orgie, f.
orient, *ŏ'rĭ ĕnt*, s. orient, m.
oriental, *ŏ rĭ ĕn'tăl*, a. oriental.

orifice, ŏr'ĭ fĭs, s. orifice, m., ouverture, f.

origin, ŏr'ĭ jĭn, s. origine, source, f. || commencement, m.

original, ō rĭj'ĭ năl, s. original, m.

original, ō rĭj'ĭ năl, a. (-ly, ad.) originel (-lement).

originality, ō rĭj ĭ năl'ĭ tĭ, s. originalité, f.

originate, ō rĭj'ĭ năt, v. a. & n. faire naître, produire || provenir.

ormolu, ŏr'mō lō, s.or moulu, m.

ormolu, ŏr'mō lō, a. d'or moulu.

ornament, ŏr'nă mĕnt, s. ornement, m. || décoration, f.

ornament, ŏr'nă mĕnt, v. a. orner, parer.

ornamental, ŏr nă mĕn'tăl, a. ornemental || -ly, ad. pour ornement.

ornate, ŏr'năt', a. orné.

orphan, ŏr'făn, s. orphelin, m., orpheline, f. || ~-asylum, s. orphelinat, m.

orphan, ŏr'făn, a. orphelin.

orphanage, ŏr'făn ăj, s. orphelinage, m. || orphelinat, m.

orrery, ŏr'rĕr'ĭ, s. planétaire, m.

orthodox, ŏr'thō dŏks, a. orthodoxe.

orthodoxy, ŏr'thō dŏks ĭ, s. orthodoxie, f.

orthographical, ŏr thō grăf'ĭ kăl, a. orthographique.   [f.

orthography, ŏr thŏg'ră fĭ, s. orthographe, graphique.

oscillate, ŏs'sĭl lăt, v. n. osciller.

oscillation, ŏs sĭl lā'shŭn, s. oscillation, f.

osier, ō'zhĭ ĕr, s. osier, m.

osprey, ŏs'prā, s. orfraie, f.   [tion, f.

ossification, ŏs sĭf ĭ kā'shŭn, s. ossification, f.

ossify, ŏs'sĭ fĭ, v. a. (& n.) (s')ossifier.

ossuary, ŏs'sū ĕr ĭ, s. charnier, m.

ostensible, ŏs tĕn'sĭ bl, a. ostensible, visible.

ostensibly, ŏs tĕn'sĭ blĭ, ad. ostensiblement.   [f.

ostentation, ŏs tĕn tā'shŭn, s. ostentation, f.

ostentatious, ŏs tĕn tā'shŭs, a. fastueux || -ly, ad. par ostentation.

ostler, ŏs'lĕr, s. valet d'écurie, m.

ostracise, ŏs'tră sīs, v. a. ostraciser.

ostrich, ŏ'trĭch, s. autruche, f.

other, ŭth'ĕr, pn. autre || each ~, l'un l'autre || one ~, encore un.

otherwise, ŭth'ĕr wīs, ad. autrement.

otter, ŏt'tĕr, s. loutre, f.   [d'ailleurs.

ottoman, ŏt'tō măn, s. ottomane, f. || ~-seat, s. pouf, m.

ought, ăwt, v. imp. devoir, falloir.

ounce, ŏwns, s. once (30 grammes), f.

our, ŏwr, pn. notre, nos || ~s, le nôtre, la nôtre, les nôtres.

ourselves, ŏwr sĕlvz', pn. nous-mêmes.

oust, ŏwst, v. a. déloger || (jur.) évincer.

out, ŏwt, pr. & ad. hors, dehors || sorti externe || à haute voix || vide || expiré fini.   [sur.

outbalance, ŏwt băl'ăns, v. a. l'emporter

outbid, ŏwt bĭd', v. a. ir. enchérir sur.

outbidder, ŏwt bĭd'dĕr, s. enchérisseur, m.

outbreak, ŏwt'brāk, s. éruption, f.

outbuilding, ŏwt bĭld'ĭng, s. annexe d'un bâtiment, f.

outburst, ŏwt'bĕrst, s. explosion, f.

outcast, ŏwt'kăst, s. exilé, m. || rebut, m.

outcast, ŏwt'kăst, a. rejeté || banni.

outcry, ŏwt'krī, s. cri, m., clameur, f.

outdo, ŏwt dō', v. a. ir. exceller, surpasser.

outer, ŏwt'ĕr, a. extérieur || de dessus.

outermost, ŏwt'ĕr mōst, a. le plus en dehors or avancé.

outfit, ŏwt'fĭt, s. équipement, m.

outfitter, ŏwt'fĭt tĕr, s. confectionneur, m.

outflank, ŏwt flănjk', v. a. déborder.

outgoing, ŏwt'gō ĭng, s. sortie, f. || -s, s. pl. dépenses, f. pl.

outgrow, ŏwt grō', v. a. ir. surpasser en croissance || to ~ one's clothes, grandir de manière qu'un vêtement devient trop petit.   [hangar, appentis, m.

outhouse, ŏwt'hŏws, s. dépendance, f.

outing, ŏwt'ĭng, s. excursion, f.

outlandish, ŏwt lănd'ĭsh, a. étranger.

outlast, ŏwt lăst', v. a. surpasser en durée.

outlaw, ŏwt'lăw, s. proscrit, m.

outlaw, ŏwt'lăw, v. a. proscrire.   [ban, m.

outlawry, ŏwt'lăw rĭ, s. proscription, f.,

outlay, ŏwt'lā, s. dépense, f., déboursé, m.

outlet, ŏwt'lĕt, s. sortie, f. || (com.) débouché, m.   [f.

outline, ŏwt'līn, s. contour, m. || esquisse,

outline, ŏwt'līn, v. a. faire les contours.

outlying, ŏwt lā'ĭng, a. éloigné, extérieur.

outmanœuvre, ŏwt mă nō'vĕr, v. a. (mil.) tourner l'ennemi.

outmarch, ŏwt mărch', v. a. devancer.

outnumber, ŏwt nŭm'bĕr, v. a. surpasser en nombre.

outpost, ŏwt'pōst, s. (mil.) avant-poste, m.

outrage, ŏwt'răj, s. outrage, m.

outrage, ŏwt'răj, v. a. outrager.

outrageous, ŏwt rā'jŭs, a. outrageant || outré || scandaleux || -ly, ad. outrageusement.

outrider, ŏwt'rī dĕr, s. piqueur, m.   [ment.

outrigger, ŏwt'rĭg gĕr, s. bateau à rames, à tolets extérieurs, m.

outright, ŏwt rīt', ad. sur-le-champ, tout de suite || parfaitement.

outrun, ŏwt rŭn', outsail, ŏwt săl', v. a. gagner de vitesse, dépasser à la course, à la voile.   [m.

outset, ŏwt'sĕt, s. commencement, début,

outshine, ŏwt shīn', v. a. ir. surpasser en éclat.

outside, ŏwt'sīd, s. dehors, m., surface, f., extérieur, m. || -rs, s. pl. public, m.

outstare, ŏwt stăr', v. a. décontenancer.

outstrip, ŏwt strĭp', v. a. devancer à la course.

outwalk, ŏwt wăwk', v. a. devancer.

outwall, ŏwt wăwl, s. mur extérieur, m.

outward, ŏwt'wĕrd, a. & ad. (-ly, ad.) extérieur(ement) || au dehors || ~-bound, a. & ad. (mar.) en destination pour l'étranger.

outweigh, ŏwt wā', v. a. peser plus que || l'emporter sur.

outwit, ŏwt wĭt', v. a. surpasser en finesse.

outwork, ŏwt'wĕrk, s. ouvrage avancé, m.

oval, ŏ'văl, s. ovale, m.

oval, ŏ'văl, a. ovale.

ovary, ŏ'vă rĭ, s. ovaire, m.

ovation, ŏ vā'shŭn, s. ovation, f.

oven, ŭv'n, s. four, r .

over, ŏ'vĕr, pr. & ad. sur, au-dessus de, par-dessus || au-delà || de l'autre côté || fini entièrement, passé || ~ and above, en outre || all ~, passé, fini || partout || entièrement || ~ against, en face || ~ and ~ again, plusieurs fois.

overabound, ŏ'vĕr å bŏ̆ŭnd', v. n. surabonder.

overact, ŏ'vĕr ăkt', v. a. outrer.

overall, ŏ'vĕr ăⁱl', s. surtout, m.

overarch, ŏ'vĕr ărch', v. a. envoûter, couvrir d'une voûte.

overawe, ŏ'vĕr ăⁱ', v. a. tenir dans la crainte, en imposer. [sur.

overbalance, ŏ'vĕr băl'ăns, v. a. l'emporter

overbear, ŏ'vĕr băr', v. a. ir. vaincre, subjuguer || accabler, dompter.

overbearing, ŏ'vĕr băr'ĭng, a. arrogant, impérieux || -ly, ad. impérieusement.

overbid, ŏ'vĕr bĭd', v. a. ir. enchérir || dépasser || offrir trop pour.

overburden, ŏ'vĕr bĕr'dn, v. a. surcharger.

overcast, ŏ'vĕr kăst', v. a. ir. obscurcir || évaluer trop haut || surjeter.

overcharge, ŏ'vĕr chărj', s. prix exorbitant, m. || surtaxe, f.

overcharge, ŏ'vĕr chărj', v. a. surcharger, accabler || faire payer trop cher.

overcloud, ŏ'vĕr klŏ̆ŭd', v. a. obscurcir.

overcoat, ŏ'vĕr kŏt', s. surtout, m.

overcome, ŏ'vĕr kŭm', v. a. & n. ir. dompter, vaincre || obtenir la victoire.

over-confidence, ŏ'vĕr kŏn'fĭ dĕns, s. excès de hardiesse, m.

over-confident, ŏ'vĕr kŏn'fĭ dĕnt, a. confiant à l'excès || présomptueux.

over-credulous, ŏ'vĕr krĕd'ū lŭs, a. crédule à l'excès.

overdo, ŏ'vĕr dŏ̄', v. a. ir. faire trop, outrer.

overdone, ŏ'vĕr dŭn', a. trop cuit.

overdose, ŏ'vĕr dŏs, s. dose trop forte.

overdraw, ŏ'vĕr drăⁱ', v. a. (one's account) excéder son crédit.

overdress, ŏ'vĕr drĕs', v. a. parer avec excès. [trop vite.

overdrive, ŏ'vĕr drĭv', v. a. ir. faire aller

overdue, ŏ'vĕr dū', a. en retard.

overeat, ŏ'vĕr ēt', v. n. ir. (to ~ oneself) manger trop. [estimer, surfaire.

overestimate, ŏ'vĕr ĕs'tĭ māt, v. a. surfatigue, ŏ'vĕr fă tēg', s. excès de fatigue, épuisement, m. [fatigue.

overfatigue, ŏ'vĕr fă tēg', v. a. s'excéder de

overfeed, ŏ'vĕr fēd', v. a. donner trop à manger || (fig.) rassasier. [trop-plein, m.

overflow, ŏ'vĕr flŏ, s. inondation, f. ||

overflow, ŏ'vĕr flŏ', v. a. & n. ir. remplir outre mesure || inonder || se déborder || surabonder.

over-fond, ŏ'vĕr fŏnd', a. trop passionné.

overgrow, ŏ'vĕr grŏ', v. a. & n. ir. croître trop || grandir trop || couvrir.

overgrown, ŏ'vĕr grŏn', a. excessivement accru, énorme || couvert.

overgrowth, ŏ'vĕr grŏth', s. accroissement excessif, m. [plomber || menacer.

overhang, ŏ'vĕr hăng', v. a. & n. ir. sur-

over-hasty, ŏ'vĕr hăs'tĭ, a. trop pressé || trop ardent || précipité. [larguer.

overhaul, ŏ'vĕr hăⁱl', v. a. réviser || (mar.)

overhead, ŏ'vĕr hĕd', ad. au-dessus de la tête, en haut. [entr'ouïr.

overhear, ŏ'vĕr hēr', v. a. ir. entendre ||

overjoy, ŏ'vĕr jŏⁱ', v. a. ravir, enchanter.

overland, ŏ'vĕr lănd, a. par voie de terre.

overlap, ŏ'vĕr lăp', v. a. couvrir.

over-large, ŏ'vĕr lărj', a. excessivement grand. [fer, surcharger, obscurcir.

overlay, ŏ'vĕr lā', v. a. ir. accabler, étouf-

overleap, ŏ'vĕr lēp', v. a. ir. sauter par-dessus, franchir.

overload, ŏ'vĕr lŏd', v. a. surcharger.

over-long, ŏ'vĕr lŏng', a. trop long.

overlook, ŏ'vĕr lŏ̆ŏk', v. a. surveiller || dominer || parcourir, examiner || passer sous silence, négliger, mépriser.

overmatch, ŏ'vĕr măch', v. a. être trop fort, vaincre.

overmuch, ŏ'vĕr mŭch', ad. trop.

overnight, ŏ'vĕr nĭt', ad. la nuit passée.

overpass, ŏ'vĕr păs', v. a. passer au-delà, franchir. [m.

overplus, ŏ'vĕr plŭs', s. surplus, excédant,

overpower, ŏ'vĕr pŏ̆w'ĕr, v. a. dominer, opprimer, accabler. [surproduction, f.

over-production, ŏ'vĕr prŏ dŭk'shŭn, s.

overrate, ŏ'vĕr răt', v. a. évaluer trop haut.

overreach, ŏ'vĕr rēch', v. a. ir. s'élever au-dessus de, surpasser, duper.

override, ŏ'vĕr rĭd', v. a. ir. surmener.

overrule, ŏ'vĕr rŏ̄l', v. a. gouverner, dominer.

overrun, ŏ'vĕr rŭn', v. a. & n. ir. envahir, ravager || couvrir, inonder || remanier || déborder.

oversee, ŏ'vĕr sē', v. a. ir. surveiller.

overseer, ŏ'vĕr sē'ĕr, s. inspecteur, m.

overset, ŏ'vĕr sĕt', v. a. (& n.) ir. (se) renverser.

overshadow, ŏ'vĕr shăd'ŏ, v. a. ombrager.

overshoe, ŏ'vĕr shŏ', s. galoche, f.

overshoot, ŏ'vĕr shŏt', v. a. & n. ir. porter trop loin || aller au-delà, devancer.

oversight, ŏ'vĕr sĭt, s. surveillance, f. || méprise, erreur, f.

oversleep, ŏ'vĕr slēp', v. n. ir. (to ~ oneself) dormir trop longtemps.

overspent, ŏ'vĕr spĕnt', a. harassé.

overspread, ŏ'vĕr sprĕd', v. a. ir. couvrir, répandre.

overstep, ŏ'vĕr stĕp', v. a. ir. dépasser.

overstrain, ŏ'vĕr strān', v. a. & n. ir. forcer || s'épuiser en efforts. [vertement.

overt, ŏ'vĕrt, a. manifeste || -ly, ad. ou-

overtake, ŏ'vĕr tāk', v. a. ir. atteindre, attraper || surprendre.

overtax, ŏ'vĕr tăks', v. a. surtaxer.

overthrow, ŏ'vĕr thrŏ, s. renversement, m. || défaite, f. [détruire, défaire.

overthrow, ŏ'vĕr thrŏ', v. a. ir. renverser ||

overtime, ŏ'vĕr tīm, s. heures supplémentaires de travail, f. pl. [sus || surpasser.

overtop, ŏ'vĕr tŏp', v. a. s'élever au-des-

overture, ŏ'vĕr'tŭr, s. ouverture, f.

overturn, ō'vẽr tẽrn', v. a. bouleverser.

overvalue, ō'vẽr văl'ū, v. a. évaluer trop haut ‖ estimer trop.　　　　[tueux.

overweening, ō'vẽr wēn'ing, a. présomp-

overweight, ō'vẽr wāt, s. prépondérance, f. ‖ excédant de poids, m.　　　[combler de.

overwhelm, ō'vẽr hwĕlm', v. a. accabler,

overwhelming, ō'vẽr hwĕlm'ing, a. accablant, foudroyant.　　　　[trop.

overwork, ō'vẽr wẽrk', v. a. ir. travailler

overwrought, ō'vẽr rāwt', a. excédé de travail, surmené.

oviparous, ō vĭp'ă rŭs, a. ovipare.

owe, ō, v. a. devoir.　　　[(à) ‖ à l'effet (de).

owing, ō'ing, a. dû ‖ à cause de ‖ grâce

owl, owl, s. hibou, m.

owlet, owl'ĕt, s. chouette, f.

own, ōn, v. a. posséder ‖ réclamer, s'attribuer ‖ reconnaître, avouer, confesser.

own, ōn, a. sien, propre ‖ to hold one's ~, insister sur ses droits.

owner, ōn'ẽr, s. propriétaire, possesseur, m.

ownership, ōn'ẽr ship, s. propriété, f.

ox, ŏks, s. bœuf, m. ‖ ~-fly, s. taon, m.

oxide, ŏks'ĭd, s. oxyde, m.

oxidise, ŏks'ĭ dīz, v. a. oxyder.

oxygen, ŏks'ĭ jĕn, s. oxygène, m.

oyster, oys'tẽr, s. huître, f. ‖ ~-bed, s. banc d'huîtres, m.

ozone, ō'zōn, s. (chim.) ozone, m.

P.

pabulum, păb'ū lŭm, s. nourriture, f., aliment, m.

pace, pās, s. pas, m.

pace, pās, v. a. & n. mesurer ‖ aller au pas ‖ aller l'amble.

pacer, pā'sẽr, s. cheval qui va l'amble, m.

pachydermatous, păk ĭ dẽr'mă tŭs, a. pachyderme.

pacific, pă sĭf'ĭk, a. pacifique.　　　[tion, f.

pacification, pă sĭ f ĭ kā'shŭn, s. pacifica-

pacify, păs'ĭ f ī, v. a. pacifier, apaiser.

pack, păk, s. paquet, ballot, m. ‖ fardeau, m. ‖ jeu, m. ‖ bande, meute, f. ‖ ~-horse, s. cheval de bât, m.

pack, păk, v. a. & n. empaqueter, emballer ‖ (cards) préparer ‖ (off) décamper ‖ comploter ‖ to ~ up, empaqueter ‖ faire ses malles.　　　　　[tage, m. ‖ colis, m.

package, păk'āj, s. emballage, empaque-

packcloth, păk'klŏth, s. toile d'emballage.

packer, păk'ẽr, s. emballeur, m.　　　[f.

packet, păk'ĕt, s. paquet, m. ‖ paquebot, m. ‖ ~-boat, s. paquebot, m.

packing, păk'ing, s. emballage, m. ‖ ~-case, s. caisse d'emballage, f. ‖ ~-cloth, s. toile d'emballage, serpillière, f.

packthread, păk'thrĕd, s. ficelle, f.

pact, păkt, s. pacte, contrat, m.

pad, păd, s. sentier, m. ‖ bourrelet, m. ‖ tampon, m. ‖ cheval qui va l'amble, m. ‖ voleur de grand chemin, m.

pad, păd, v. a. ouater, rembourrer.

paddle, păd'l, s. rame, f. ‖ pagaie, f. ‖ ~-board, s. palette, f. ‖ ~-box, s. tambour, m. ‖ ~-wheel, s. roue à aubes, f.

paddle, păd'l, v. n. pagayer ‖ patrouiller.

paddock, păd'ŏk, s. gros crapaud, m. ‖ enclos, m.

Paddy, păd'dĭ, s. Irlandais, m.

padlock, păd'lŏk, s. cadenas, m.

padlock, păd'lŏk, v. a. cadenasser ‖ mettre au cadenas.

pagan, pā'găn, s. païen, m.

pagan, pā'găn, a. païen.

paganism, pā'găn izm, s. paganisme, m.

page, pāj, s. page, f. ‖ page, m.

page, pāj, v. a. paginer.　　　　　[f.

pageant, pāj'ĕnt, s. spectacle, m., pompe,

pageantry, pāj'ĕn trĭ, s. faste, m., pompe, f. ‖ parade, f. ‖ spectacle, m.

paging, pāj'ing, s. pagination, f.

pail, pāl, s. seau, m.

pain, pān, s. peine, douleur, f. ‖ mal, m. ‖ to be in ~, être en peine ‖ to take great ~s to, se donner de la peine, se donner du mal pour.

pain, pān, v. a. faire de la peine, faire mal.

painful, pān'fool, a. (-ly, ad.) pénible (ment) ‖ douloureux.

painless, pān'lĕs, a. sans peine.

painstaking, pāns'tāk ing, a. laborieux.

paint, pānt, s. couleur, f. ‖ peinture, f. ‖ fard, m.

paint, pānt, v. a. & n. peindre ‖ se farder.

painter, pānt'ẽr, s. peintre, m.

painting, pānt'ing, s. peinture, f.

pair, pār, s. paire, f. ‖ couple, m.

pair, pār, v. a. (& n.) (s')accoupler.

pairing-time, pār'ing tim, s. saison de l'accouplement, époque du rut, f.

palace, păl'ăs, s. palais, m.

palatable, păl'ă tă bl, a. agréable au goût.

palate, păl'ăt, s. palais, m.

palatinate, păl ăt'ĭ nāt, s. palatinat, m.

palatine, păl'ă tin, s. palatin, m.

palatine, păl'ă tin, a. palatin.

palaver, pă lā'vẽr, s. verbiage, m.

palaver, pă lā'vẽr, v. a. & n. flagorner ‖ faire des phrases.

pale, pāl, s. pieu, m. ‖ enceinte, f.

pale, pāl, v. n. pâlir.

pale, pāl, a. pâle, blême.

paleness, pāl'nĕs, s. pâleur, f.

palfrey, pawl'frĭ, s. palefroi, m.

paling, pā'ling, palisade, păl ĭ sād', s. palissade, f.　　　　　[palissader.

paling, pā'ling, palisade, păl ĭ sād', v. a.

palish, pāl'ish, a. un peu pâle, blafard.

pall, pawl, s. manteau, m. ‖ (of funerals) poêle, m.　　　　[affaiblir ‖ devenir insipide.

pall, pawl, v. a. & n. rendre insipide ‖

pallet, păl'lĕt, s. petit lit, gravat, m. ‖ palette, f.

palliate, păl'ĭ āt, v. a. pallier.

palliation, păl ĭ ā'shŭn, s. palliation, f.

palliative, păl'ĭ ă tĭv, s. palliatif, m.

palliative, păl'ĭ ă tĭv, a. palliatif.

pallid, păl'ĭd, a. pâle, blême.

pallor, păl'ẽr, s. pâleur, f.

palm, *pâm*, s. palmier, m., palme, f. || paume, f.

palm, *pâm*, v. a. manier, toucher || duper.

palmated, *păl mā′ tĕd*, a. (bot.) palmé.

palmistry, *păl′mĭs trĭ*, s. chiromancie, f.

Palm-Sunday, *pâm sŭn′ dā*, s. dimanche des Rameaux, m.

palmy, *pâm′ĭ*, a. portant des palmes || (fig.) victorieux.

palpable, *păl′pă bl*, a. palpable.

palpably, *păl′pă blĭ*, ad. palpablement.

palpitate, *păl′pĭ tāt*, v. n. palpiter.

palpitation, *păl pĭ tā′ shŭn*, s. palpitation.

palsied, *pawl′zĭd*, a. paralysé. [f.

palsy, *pawl′zĭ*, s. paralysie, f.

paltriness, *pawl′trĭ nĕs*, s. chétiveté, mesquinerie, f. [chétif.

paltry, *pawl′trĭ*, a. méprisable, bas, vil.

pamper, *păm′pĕr*, v. a. gorger, rassasier || dorloter, choyer. [chure, f.

pamphlet, *păm′flĕt*, s. pamphlet, m. || brochure.

pamphleteer, *păm flĕt ēr′*, s. brochurier, m. || pamphlétaire, m.

pan, *păn*, s. poêle, f. || bassine, terrine, f. || ~-cake, s. crêpe (friture), f.

panacea, *păn ă sē′ă*, s. panacée, f.

Pandemonium, *păn dē mō′ nĭ ŭm*, s. Pan-démonium, m.

pander, *păn′dĕr*, s. maquereau, m.

pander, *păn′dĕr*, v. n. faire le maquereau.

pane, *păn*, s. carreau de vitre, panneau, m.

panegyric, *păn ĕ jĭr′ ĭk*, a. panégyrique.

panegyrist, *păn ĕ jĭr′ ĭst*, s. panégyriste, m. [jurés, f.

panel, *păn′ĕl*, s. panneau, m. || liste des

pang, *păng*, s. angoisse, f.

panic, *păn′ĭk*, s. terreur panique, f.

panic, *păn′ĭk*, a. panique.

pannel, *păn′ĕl*, s. bât, m.

pannier, *păn′nĭ ĕr*, s. panier, m., hotte, f.

pannikin, *păn′nĭ kĭn*, s. poêlon, m., poêlette, f.

panorama, *păn ō rā′mă*, s. panorama, m.

pansy, *păn′zĭ*, s. (bot.) pensée, f. [rer après.

pant, *pănt*, v. n. palpiter, haleter || soupi-

pantechnicon, *păn tĕk′ nĭ kŏn*, s. garde-meubles, m.

panther, *păn′thĕr*, s. panthère, f.

pantomime, *păn′tō mĭm*, s. pantomime, m. & f.

pantry, *păn′trĭ*, s. garde-manger, m.

pap, *păp*, s. mamelle, f. || bouillie, f. ||

papa, *păpă′*, s. papa, père, m. [pulpe, f.

papacy, *pā′pă sĭ*, s. papauté, f.

papal, *pā′păl*, a. papal, du pape.

paper, *pā′pĕr*, s. papier, m. || journal, m. || écrit, m. || -s, pl. (com.) valeurs, f. pl. || ~-credit, (~-currency), s. papier-monnaie, m. || ~-cutter, (~-knife), s. couteau à papier, m. || ~-hanger, s. colleur, décorateur, m. || ~-mill, s. papeterie, f. || ~-weight, s. presse-papiers, m. [m.

paper, *pā′pĕr*, v. a. tapisser.

paper, *pā′pĕr*, a. de papier.

Papist, *pā′pĭst*, s. papiste, m.

Papistry, *pā′pĭs trĭ*, s. Papauté, f.

par, *pâr*, s. valeur égale, f. || at ~, au pair || on a ~, de pair.

parable, *păr′ă bl*, s. parabole, f.

parade, *pă răd′*, s. parade, f., faste, m. || place d'armes, f.

parade, *pă răd′*, v. n. parader.

Paradise, *păr′ă dĭs*, s. paradis, m.

paradox, *păr′ă dŏks*, s. paradoxe, m.

paradoxical, *păr ă dŏks′ ĭ kăl*, a. para-doxal.

paragon, *păr′ă gŏn*, s. modèle parfait, m.

paragraph, *păr′ă grăf*, s. paragraphe, m.

parallel, *păr′ăl ĕl*, s. parallèle, f. || ressemblance, f. [lèle, comparer.

parallel, *păr′ăl ĕl*, v. a. mettre en paral-

parallel, *păr′ăl ĕl*, a. parallèle, égal.

paralyse, *păr′ăl ĭz*, v. a. paralyser.

paralysis, *păr ăl′ĭ sĭs*, s. paralysie, f.

paralytic, *păr ă lĭt′ ĭk*, a. paralytique.

paramount, *păr′ă mŏwnt*, a. supérieur, éminent || lord ~, s. seigneur suzerain, m.

paramour, *păr ă mōr′*, s. amant, m., amante, f.

paraphernalia, *păr ă fĕr nā′ lĭ ă*, s. biens paraphernaux, m. pl. || chiffons, atours, affiquets, m. pl. || attirail, m.

paraphrase, *păr′ă frāz*, v. a. paraphraser.

parasite, *păr′ă sĭt*, s. parasite, m.

parasitic, *păr ă sĭt′ ĭk*, a. (de) parasite.

parasol, *păr ă sŏl′*, s. parasol, m., ombrelle, f. [demi.

parboil, *pâr′ bŏyl*, v. a. faire bouillir à

parcel, *pâr′ sĕl*, s. petit paquet, m. || parcelle, quantité, f.

parcel, *pâr′ sĕl*, v. a. partager, morceller.

parch, *pârch*, v. a. brûler légèrement, griller || dessécher.

parchment, *pârch′ mĕnt*, s. parchemin, m.

pardon, *pâr′dn*, s. pardon, m., grâce, f.

pardon, *pâr′dn*, v. a. pardonner || (law) gracier.

pardonable, *pâr′ dn ă bl*, a. pardonnable.

pare, *pâr*, v. a. rogner, peler.

parent, *pā′rĕnt*, s. père, m., mère, f. || -s, pl. parents, m. pl.

parentage, *pā′rĕnt āj*, s. parenté, f.

parental, *pă rĕn′ tăl*, a. paternel, maternel.

parenthesis, *pă rĕn′thĕ sĭs*, s. parenthèse, f. [parenthèse.

parenthetical, *păr ĕn thĕt′ ĭk ăl*, a. par

parer, *pā′rĕr*, s. boutoir, m.

pariah, *pā′rĭ ă*, s. paria, m.

paring, *pā′ring*, s. rognure, pelure, écorce, f.

parish, *păr′ĭsh*, s. paroisse, f.

parish, *păr′ĭsh*, a. paroissial || ~-clerk, s. sacristain, m. [m.

parishioner, *păr′ĭsh′ŭn ĕr*, s. paroissien,

parity, *păr′ĭ tĭ*, s. parité, f.

park, *pârk*, s. parc, m.

parlance, *pâr′ lăns*, s. langage, m.

parley, *pâr′lĭ*, s. pourparler, m.

parley, *pâr′lĭ*, v. n. discuter || (mil.) par-lementer.

Parliament, *pâr′ lĭ ă mĕnt*, s. parlement, m.

Parliamentary, *pâr lĭ ă mĕnt′ ă rĭ*, a. par-lementaire.

parlour, *păr'lĕr*, s. parloir, m. || petit salon, m.

parochial, *pă rō'kĭ ăl*, a. paroissial.

parody, *păr'ō dĭ*, s. parodie, f.

parody, *păr'ō dĭ*, v. a. parodier.

paroquet, *păr'ō kĕt*, s. perruche, f.

parricidal, *păr rĭ sī'dăl*, a. parricide.

parricide, *păr'rĭ sĭd*, s. parricide (meurtre), m. || parricide (meurtrier), m. & f.

parrot, *păr'rŏt*, s. perroquet, m.

parry, *păr'rĭ*, v. a. parer, éviter || **to ~ and thrust,** riposter.

parse, *pârs*, v. a. (gr.) analyser.

parsimonious, *păr sĭ mō'nĭ ŭs*, a. parcimonieux || **–ly,** ad. avec parcimonie.

parsimony, *păr'sĭ mŏn ĭ*, s. parcimonie, f.

parsley, *pârs'lĭ*, s. persil, m.

parsnip, *pârs'nĭp*, s. panais, m.

parson, *păr'sn*, s. curé, m. || prêtre, m.

parsonage, *păr'snăj*, s. curé, f. || maison du curé, f.

part, *pârt*, s. part, partie, portion, f. || parti, rôle, m. || **–s,** pl. contrées, f. pl. || talents, moyens, m. pl. || **~ and parcel of,** élément, ingrédient, f.

part, *pârt*, v. a. & n. diviser, distribuer || se séparer, partir || **to ~ with,** se défaire de || abandonner || **to ~ from,** se séparer.

partake, *păr tāk'*, v. a. & n. ir. partager, avoir part, participer.

partaker, *păr tā'kĕr*, s. participant, m.

partial, *păr'shăl*, a. (–ly, ad.) partial (ement) || partiel(lement).

partiality, *păr shĭ ăl'ĭ tĭ*, s. partialité, préférence injuste, f.

participate, *păr tĭs'ĭ pāt*, v. n. participer.

participation, *păr tĭs ĭ pā'shŭn*, s. participation, f.

participle, *păr'tĭ sĭ pl*, s. (gr.) participe, m.

particle, *păr'tĭ kl*, s. particule, f.

particular, *păr tĭk'ū lĕr*, s. particularité, f., détail, m. || particulier, m.

particular, *păr tĭk'ū lĕr*, a. particulier || singulier, spécial, intime || exact || **–ly,** ad. surtout.

particularise, *păr tĭk'ū lĕr īz*, v. a. particulariser, spécifier.

particularism, *păr tĭk'ū lĕr ĭzm*, s. particularisme, m.

particularity, *păr tĭk ū lăr'ĭ tĭ*, s. particularité, f.

parting, *pârt'ĭng*, s. séparation, f., départ, adieu, m. || **(of the hair)** raie, f.

partisan, *păr'tĭ zăn*, s. partisan, m. || homme de parti, m.

partition, *păr tĭsh'ŭn*, s. partition, division, f. || **(of rooms)** cloison, f. || **~-wall,** s. mur mitoyen, f.

partition, *păr tĭsh'ŭn*, v. a. diviser en parties.

partitive, *păr'tĭ tĭv*, a. partitif.

partly, *pârt'lĭ*, ad. en partie || **~ . . . ~,** tant . . . que.

partner, *pârt'nĕr*, s. associé, m. || compagnon, m. || partenaire, m. (& f.).

partnership, *pârt'nĕr shĭp*, s. association, société, f.

partridge, *păr'trĭj*, s. perdrix, f.

party, *păr'tĭ*, s. parti, m., partie, f. || intérêt, m. || individu, m. || soirée, f., divertissement, m. || **to be (a) ~ to,** prendre part à, participer à || être complice de || **~-coloured,** a. bigarré || **~-man,** s. factieux, m. || **~-spirit,** s. esprit de parti, m.

paschal, *păs'kăl*, a. pascal.

pass, *pâs*, s. passage étroit, m. || passeport, m., botte, f. || situation, f., état, m. || billet gratuit, m. || billet d'entrée, m. || **~-book,** s. livre de compte particulier, m. || **~-key,** s. passe-partout, m.

pass, *pâs*, v. a. & n. passer, aller au-delà || transmettre || négliger, laisser || surpasser, exceller || se passer || avoir cours, s'écouler || **to ~ (oneself off) for,** se faire passer pour || **to ~ over,** passer légèrement sur qc.

passable, *pâs'să bl*, a. passable || praticable.

passage, *pâs'săj*, s. passage, f. || entrée, f. || traversée, f. || événement, m. || **to work one's ~,** se frayer passage.

passenger, *păs'sĕn jĕr*, s. passager, m. || voyageur, m.

passer-by, *pâs sĕr bī'*, s. passant, m.

passing, *pâs'sĭng*, a. excellent, éminent || passager || **~-bell,** s. glas, m.

passion, *pâsh'ŭn*, s. passion, f. || ardeur, f. || colère, f. || **~-flower,** s. grenadille, f. || **~-week,** s. semaine sainte, f.

passionate, *păsh'ŭn āt*, a. (–ly, ad.) passionné(ment).

passive, *pâs'sĭv*, s. (gr.) passif, m.

passive, *pâs'sĭv*, a. passif || **–ly,** ad. passivement.

passiveness, *pâs'sĭv nĕs*, s. passiveté, f.

Passover, *pâs'ō vĕr*, s. Pâque, f.

passport, *pâs'pōrt*, s. passeport, m.

password, *pâs'wĕrd*, s. mot d'ordre, m.

past, *pâst*, s. passé, m.

past, *pâst*, a. & pr. passé || au-delà de, au-dessus || hors || **half-~ one,** une heure et demie.

paste, *pāst*, s. colle, pâte, f. || strass, m.

paste, *pāst*, v. a. coller.

pasteboard, *pāst'bōrd*, s. carton, m.

pasteboard, *pāst'bōrd*, a. de carton.

pastel, *păs'tĕl*, s. guède, f.

pastil, *păs'tĭl*, s. pastille, f.

pastime, *păs'tĭm*, s. passe-temps, m.

pastor, *păs'tŏr*, s. pasteur, m.

pastoral, *păs'tŏr ăl*, s. pastorale, f.

pastoral, *păs'tŏr ăl*, a. pastoral.

pastry, *păs'trĭ*, s. pâtisserie, f. || **~-cook,** s. pâtissier, m.

pasturable, *păs'tū ră bl*, a. propre au pâturage.

pasturage, *păs'tū răj*, s. pâturage, m.

pasture, *păs'tūr*, s. pâture, f. || viandis, m.

pasture, *păs'tūr*, v. a. & n. faire paître || paître.

pasty, *păs'tĭ*, s. pâté, m.

pat, *păt*, s. petit coup, m., tape, f.

pat, *păt*, v. n. frapper légèrement, taper.

pat, *păt*, a. (–ly, ad.) convenable(ment), propre || à propos || tout juste.

patch, *păch*, s. pièce, f., morceau, m. ‖ mouche (sur le visage), f. ‖ ~-work, s. rapiécetage, m.

patch, *păch*, v. a. rapiécer ‖ mettre des mouches sur le visage.

pate, *păt*, s. (fam.) tête, caboche, f.

paten, *păt'ĕn*, s. patène, f.

patent, *pă'tĕnt*, s. (letters ~) lettres patentes, f. pl. ‖ ~-leather, s. cuir verni, m. ‖ ~-office, s. bureau des brevets d'invention, m. ‖ ~-right, s. législation relative aux brevets d'invention, f. ‖ ~-rolls, s. pl. spécifications de brevet, f. pl. ‖ ~ of nobility, lettre de noblesse, f.

patent, *pă'tĕnt*, a. breveté, public.

patentee, *pătĕntē'*, s. breveté, m.

paternal, *pă'tĕr'năl*, a. ~ (-ly, ad.) paternel (lement).

paternity, *pă'tĕr'nĭtĭ*, s. paternité, f.

path, *păth*, s. sentier, chemin, m.

pathetic, *pă'thĕt'ĭk*, a. ~ (-ally, ad.) pathétique(ment).

pathless, *păth'lĕs*, a. impraticable.

pathological, *păthŏlŏj'ĭkăl*, a. pathologique.

pathology, *pă'thŏl'ŏjĭ*, s. pathologie, f.

pathos, *pā'thŏs*, s. pathétique, m.

pathway, *păth'wā*, s. sentier, m. ‖ bas-côté, m.

patience, *pā'shĕns*, s. patience, f.

patient, *pā'shĕnt*, s. malade, m.

patient, *pā'shĕnt*, a. patient ‖ malade ‖ -ly, ad. patiemment.

patriarch, *pā'trĭărk*, s. patriarche, m.

patriarchal, *pă'trĭărk'ăl*, a. patriarcal.

patrician, *pă'trish'ăn*, s. patricien, m.

patrician, *pă'trish'ăn*, a. patricien.

patrimonial, *păt'rĭmō'nĭăl*, a. patrimonial.

patrimony, *păt'rĭmŏnĭ*, s. patrimoine, m.

patriot, *pā'trĭŏt*, s. patriote, m.

patriotic, *pā'trĭŏt'ĭk*, a. patriotique.

patriotism, *pā'trĭŏtĭzm*, s. patriotisme, m.

patrol, *pă'trōl'*, s. patrouille, f.

patrol, *pă'trōl'*, v. n. faire la ronde.

patron, *pā'trŏn*, s. patron, protecteur, m.

patronage, *păt'rŏnăj*, s. protection, f., patronage, m.

patroness, *pā'trŏnĕs*, s. patronne, f.

patronise, *păt'rŏnīz*, v. a. protéger.

patten, *păt'tĕn*, s. socque, m.

patter, *păt'tĕr*, v. n. piétiner, trépigner ‖ caqueter.

pattern, *păt'tĕrn*, s. patron, modèle, m. ‖ dessin, m.

paucity, *paw'sĭtĭ*, s. petite quantité, f.

paunch, *pawnsh*, s. panse, f.

pauper, *paw'pĕr*, s. pauvre, m.

pauperise, *paw'pĕrīz*, v. a. appauvrir.

pauperism, *paw'pĕrĭzm*, s. paupérisme, m.

pause, *pawz*, s. pause, f. ‖ suspens, m.

pause, *pawz*, v. n. faire une pause ‖ s'arrêter ‖ délibérer.

pave, *pāv*, v. a. paver, frayer ‖ (fig.) préparer.

pavement, *pāv'mĕnt*, s. pavé, m. ‖ trottoir, m.

pavilion, *pă'vĭl'yŏn*, s. pavillon, m., tente, f.

paving, *pā'vĭng*, s. pavage, m. ‖ ~-beetle, s. hie, f. ‖ ~-stone, s. pavé, m.

paw, *paw*, s. patte, f.

paw, *paw*, v. a. & n. frapper du pied ‖ griffer ‖ caresser avec la patte ‖ patiner.

pawed, *pawd*, a. à pattes.

pawn, *pawn*, s. pion, m. ‖ gage, m. ‖ ~-ticket, s. reconnaissance du mont-de-piété, f.

pawn, *pawn*, v. a. engager, mettre en gage.

pawnbroker, *pawn'brōkĕr*, s. prêteur sur gages, m.

pay, *pā*, s. solde, f. ‖ salaire, m. ‖ half-, demi-solde, f. ‖ ~-day, s. jour de payement, m. ‖ ~-master, s. payeur, caissier, m.

pay, *pā*, v. a. payer, acquitter ‖ (com.) rapporter ‖ rendre.

payable, *pā'ăbl*, a. payable.

payee, *pāē'*, s. porteur, m.

payment, *pā'mĕnt*, s. payement, m.

pea, *pē*, s. pois, m. ‖ ~-shooter, s. sarbacane, f. ‖ ~-soup, s. purée de pois, f.

peace, *pēs*, s. paix, f. ‖ justice of the ~, s. juge de paix, m. ‖ to make (one's) ~ with, faire sa paix avec.

peaceable, *pēs'ăbl*, peaceful, *pēs'fool*, a. paisible, tranquille.

peaceably, *pēs'ăblĭ*, ad. paisiblement.

peach, *pēch*, s. pêche, f. ‖ ~-tree, s. pêcher, m.

peacock, *pē'kŏk*, s. paon, m.

peahen, *pē'hĕn*, s. paonne, f.

peak, *pēk*, s. pic, sommet, m., cime, f.

peal, *pēl*, s. carillon, m. ‖ bruit, m. ‖ coup, m. ‖ gronder.

peal, *pēl*, v. a. & n. faire retentir ‖ retentir ‖

pear, *pār*, s. poire, f. ‖ ~-tree, s. poirier, m.

pearl, *pĕrl*, s. perle, f. ‖ parisienne, f. ‖ ~-fishing, s. pêche de perles, f.

pearly, *pĕrl'ĭ*, a. de perle. ‖ a. rustique.

peasant, *pĕz'ănt*, s. paysan, m. ‖ ~-like, peasantry, *pĕz'ăntrĭ*, s. paysans, m. pl.

peat, *pēt*, s. tourbe, houille, f.

pebble, *pĕb'bl*, s. caillou, m.

pebbly, *pĕb'blĭ*, a. caillouteux.

peccadillo, *pĕk'kădĭl'lō*, s. faute légère, f.

peccant, *pĕk'kănt*, a. pécheur, coupable.

peck, *pĕk*, s. picotin, m.

peck, *pĕk*, v. a. becqueter, frapper avec le bec ‖ piocher.

pecker, *pĕk'ĕr*, s. pivert, m.

pectoral, *pĕk'tŏrăl*, s. pectoral, m.

pectoral, *pĕk'tŏrăl*, a. pectoral.

peculate, *pĕk'ūlāt*, v. n. piller le trésor public.

peculation, *pĕk'ūlā'shŭn*, s. péculat, m.

peculator, *pĕk'ūlātĕr*, s. auteur d'un péculat, m.

peculiar, *pĕkū'lĭĕr*, a. particulier, singulier, unique ‖ -ly, ad. particulièrement.

peculiarise, *pĕkū'lĭĕrīz*, v. a. particulariser ‖ détailler.

peculiarity, *pĕkū'lĭăr'ĭtĭ*, s. particularité, singularité, originalité, f.

pecuniary, *pĕkū'nĭĕrĭ*, a. pécuniaire.

pedagogue, *pĕd'ăgŏg*, s. pédagogue, m.

pedal, *pĕd'ăl* ou *pē'dăl*, s. pédale, f.

pedant, *pĕd´ănt,* s. pédant, m.
pedantic, *pĕ dăn´tĭk,* a. pédantesque, pédant.
pedantry, *pĕd´ ănt rĭ,* s. pédanterie, f.
peddle, *pĕd´dl,* v. n. niaiser.
peddler, *pĕd´dlĕr,* s. colporteur, m.
peddling, *pĕd´dlĭng,* a. de peu de valeur, mesquin.
pedestal, *pĕd´ĕs tăl,* s. piédestal, m.
pedestrian, *pĕ dĕs´trĭ ăn,* s. piéton, m.
pedestrian, *pĕ dĕs´ trĭ ăn,* a. à pied.
pedigree, *pĕd´ĭ grē,* s. généalogie, f.
pediment, *pĕd´ĭ mĕnt,* s. fronton, m.
pedlar, *pĕd´ lĕr,* s. colporteur, m.
peel, *pēl,* s. pelure, f. || peau, f. || écorce, f.
peel, *pēl,* v. a. (& n.) (se) peler.
peep, *pēp,* s. première apparition, f. || pointe, f. || œillade, f. || ~-hole, s. judas, m.
peep, *pēp,* v. n. apparaître, poindre || pousser.   [curieux, m.
peeper, *pēp´ĕr,* s. poussin, m. || espion, m. ||
peer, *pēr,* s. pair, m. || compagnon, m.
peerage, *pēr´āj,* s. pairie, f.‚ les pairs, m.pl.
peeress, *pēr´ĕs,* s. pairesse, f.
peerless, *pēr´lĕs,* a. incomparable.
peevish, *pēv´ish,* a. bourru, maussade || -ly, ad. avec mauvaise humeur.   [f.
peevishness, *pēv´ish nĕs,* s. maussaderie,
peewit, *pē´wĭt,* s. vanneau, m.   [m.
peg, *pĕg,* s. cheville, f. || fichoir, m. || fausset,
peg, *pĕg,* v. a. cheviller || marquer.
pelf, *pĕlf,* s. richesses, f. pl. || amour des richesses, m.
pelican, *pĕl´ĭ kăn,* s. pélican, m.
pelisse, *pĕ lēs´,* s. pelisse, f.
pell, *pĕl,* s. peau, f.
pellet, *pĕl´lĕt,* s. boulette, f.
pellicle, *pĕl´lĭ kl,* s. pellicule, f.
pell-mell, *pĕl mĕl´,* ad. pêle-mêle.
pelt, *pĕlt,* s. peau, fourrure, f.
pelt, *pĕlt,* v. a. assaillir (à coups or boules de neige) || jeter || battre.
peltry, *pĕl´trĭ,* s. pelleterie, f.
pen, *pĕn,* s. plume, f. || petit parc, m. || ~-case, s. étui à plumes, m. || ~-knife, s. canif, m. || ~-wiper, s. essuie-plume, m.
pen, *pĕn,* v. a. parquer || écrire.
penal, *pē´năl,* a. pénal || ~-settlement, s. colonie de déportés, f.
penalty, *pĕn´ăl tĭ,* s. peine, amende, f.
penance, *pĕn´ăns,* s. pénitence, f. || to do ~, faire pénitence de.
pence, *pĕns,* pl. de penny.
pencil, *pĕn´sĭl,* s. pinceau, m. || crayon, m. || ~-case, s. porte-crayon, m. || ~-mark, s. marque au crayon, f. || ~-pointer, (~-sharpener), s. taille-crayons, m.
pencil, *pĕn´sĭl,* v. a. peindre || dessiner || écrire au crayon.
pendant, *pĕn´dănt,* s. pendant, m., pendeloque, f. || (mar.) banderolle, f.
pendent, *pĕn´dĕnt,* a. pendant, suspendu || saillant.   [décis.
pending, *pĕnd´ing,* a. (jur.) pendant, indécis.
pendulum, *pĕn´dū lŭm,* s. pendule, balancier, m.
penetrable, *pĕn´ĕ trā bl,* a. pénétrable.

penetrate, *pĕn´ĕ trāt,* v. a. & n. pénétrer.
penetration, *pĕn ĕ trā´shŭn,* s. sagacité, f.
penful, *pĕn´fōol,* s. plumée, f.
penguin, *pĕn´gwĭn,* s. pengouin, m.
penholder, *pĕn´hōld ĕr,* s. porte-plume, m.
peninsula, *pĕ nĭn´sū lă,* s. péninsule, f.
penitence, *pĕn´ĭ tĕns,* s. pénitence, f.
penitent, *pĕn´ĭ tĕnt,* s. pénitent, m.
penitent, *pĕn´ĭ tĕnt,* a. pénitent || -ly, ad. avec pénitence.
penitential, *pĕn ĭ tĕn´shăl,* a. pénitentiel.
penitentiary, *pĕn ĭ tĕn´shă rĭ,* s. pénitencier, m.   [vain, m.
penman, *pĕn´măn,* s. calligraphe, m. || écrivain, m.
penmanship, *pĕn´măn shĭp,* s. écriture, f.
pennant, *pĕn´nănt,* s. banderole, flamme, f.
penny, *pĕn´nĭ,* s. deux sous, m. pl. || ~-a-liner, s. correspondant de journal à deux sous la ligne, m.
pennywise, *pĕn´nĭ wĭz,* a. ménager de bouts de chandelles.
pennyworth, *pĕn´nĕrth,* s. valeur d'un sou, f., pour deux sous || bon marché, m.
pension, *pĕn´shŭn,* s. pension, f. || retraite, f. || ~ off, mettre à la retraite.
pension, *pĕn´shŭn,* v. a. pensionner || to pensioner, *pĕn´shŭn ĕr,* s. pensionnaire, m. || invalide, m.
pensive, *pĕn´sĭv,* a. (-ly, ad.) pensif || triste || d'un air pensif.
pensiveness, *pĕn´sĭv nĕs,* s. mélancolie, f.
Pentecost, *pĕn´tĕ kŏst,* s. Pentecôte, f. [m.
penthouse, *pĕnt´hŏws,* s. appentis, hangar,
penultima, *pĕ nŭl´tĭ mă,* s. pénultième, f.
penultimate, *pĕ nŭl´tĭ măt,* a. pénultième.
penumbra, *pĕ nŭm´ bră,* s. pénombre, f.
penurious, *pĕ nū´rĭ ŭs,* a. chiche || stérile.
penury, *pĕn´ū rĭ,* s. indigence, f.
peony, *pē´ō nĭ,* s. pivoine, f.   [on, pr.
people, *pē´pl,* s. peuple, m., gens, m. pl. ||
people, *pē´pl,* v. a. peupler.
pepper, *pĕp´pĕr,* s. poivre, m. || ~-caster, s. poivrière, f. || ~-corn, s. grain de poivre, m. || bagatelle, f.
pepper, *pĕp´pĕr,* v. a. poivrer || (fig.) rosser.
perambulate, *pĕr ăm´bū lāt,* v. a. parcourir, traverser.
perambulator, *pĕr ăm´bū lā tĕr,* s. compte-pas, m. || voiture d'enfant, f.
perceivable, *pĕr sē´vā bl,* a. perceptible.
perceivably, *pĕr sē´vā blĭ,* ad. sensiblement, clairement.   [voir,
perceive, *pĕr sēv´,* v. a. apercevoir, sentir,
percentage, *pĕr sĕnt´ăj,* s. intérêt (de tant pour cent), m. || proportion, f.
perceptibility, *pĕr sĕp tĭ bĭl´ĭ tĭ,* s. perceptibilité, f.
perceptible, *pĕr sĕp´tĭ bl,* a. perceptible.
perception, *pĕr sĕp´shŭn,* s. perception, f.
perch, *pĕrch,* s. perche, f. || perchoir, m.
perch, *pĕrch,* v. a. (& n.) (se) percher.
perchance, *pĕr chăns´,* ad. par hasard.
percolate, *pĕr kō lāt,* v. a. filtrer.
percussion, *pĕr kŭsh´ŭn,* s. percussion, f., coup, m. || ~-cap, s. capsule, f. || ~-gun, s. fusil à piston, m.   [ruine, f.
perdition, *pĕr dĭsh´ŭn,* s. perdition, f. ||

peremptorily, *pĕr'ĕm tĕr ĭ lĭ*, ad. péremptoirement, absolument.

peremptoriness, *pĕr'ĕm tĕr ĭ nĕs*, s. décision absolue, f. [définitif.

peremptory, *pĕr'ĕm tĕr ĭ*, a. péremptoire.

perennial, *pĕr ĕn'nĭ ăl*, a. perpétuel || (bot.) pérenne, vivace. [ver, compléter.

perfect, *pĕr'fĕkt*, v. a. perfectionner, achever.

perfect, *pĕr'fĕkt*, a. (-ly, ad.) parfait (ement) || accompli || sans défauts.

perfection, *pĕr fĕk'shŭn*, s. perfection, f. || to ~, dans la perfection. [fide(ment).

perfidious, *pĕr fĭd'ĭ ŭs*, a. (-ly, ad.) perfidy, *pĕr'fĭ dĭ*, s. perfidie, f.

perforate, *pĕr'fō rāt*, v. a. perforer || percer.

perforation, *pĕr fō rā'shŭn*, s. perforation, f. || trou, m.

perform, *pĕr fawrm'*, v. a. & n. exécuter, accomplir, faire || réussir.

performance, *pĕr fawrm'ăns*, s. accomplissement, m., exécution, f. || ouvrage, m. || exploit, fait, m., action, f. || représentation, f. || no ~! relâche !

performer, *pĕr fawrm'ĕr*, s. exécuteur, m. || acteur, m. || artiste, m.

perfume, *pĕr'fūm*, s. parfum, m.

perfume, *pĕr'fūm*, v. a. parfumer.

perfumery, *pĕr'fū mĕr ĭ*, s. parfumerie, f.

perhaps, *pĕr hăps'*, ad. peut-être, par hasard.

peril, *pĕr'ĭl*, s. péril, m. [hasard.

perilous, *pĕr'ĭl ŭs*, a. périlleux || -ly, ad. périlleusement.

period, *pē'rĭ ŏd*, s. période, m. || période, f. || époque, f. || to put a ~ to, mettre fin à qc. [périodique, f.

periodical, *pē rĭ ŏd'ĭk ăl*, s. publication periodical, *pē rĭ ŏd'ĭk ăl*, a. (-ly, ad.) périodique(ment). [ticien.

peripatetic, *pĕr ĭ pă tĕt'ĭk*, s. péripatéperiphrasis, *pĕr ĭ frā'sĭs*, s. périphrase, f.

periphrastical, *pĕr ĭ frăs'tĭ kăl*, ad. périphrastique.

perish, *pĕr'ĭsh*, v. n. périr. [phrastique.

perishable, *pĕr'ĭsh ă bl*, a. périssable.

peristyle, *pĕr'ĭ stĭl*, s. péristyle, m.

periwig, *pĕr'ĭ wĭg*, s. perruque, f.

periwinkle, *pĕr'ĭ wĭng kl*, s. vignot, m. || (bot.) pervenche, f.

perjure, *pĕr'jōor*, v. a. se parjurer.

perjured, *pĕr'jōord*, a. parjure.

perjurer, *pĕr'jōor ĕr*, s. parjure, m.

perjury, *pĕr'jōo rĭ*, s. parjure, m.

permanency, *pĕr'mă nĕn sĭ*, s. permanence, f.

permanent, *pĕr'mă nĕnt*, a. (-ly, ad.) permanent || inamovible || d'une manière permanente.

permeable, *pĕr'mē ă bl*, a. perméable.

permeate, *pĕr'mē āt*, v. a. passer à travers.

permission, *pĕr mĭsh'ŭn*, s. permission, f.

permit, *pĕr'mĭt*, s. permis, m. || congé, m.

permit, *pĕr mĭt'*, v. a. permettre.

permutation, *pĕr mū tā'shŭn*, s. permutation, f. [nicieux || pernicieusement.

pernicious, *pĕr nĭsh'ŭs*, a. (-ly, ad.) perperoration, *pĕr ō rā'shŭn*, s. péroraison, f.

perpendicular, *pĕr pĕn dĭk'ū lĕr*, s. perpendiculaire, m.

perpendicular, *pĕr pĕn dĭk'ū lĕr*, a. (-ly, ad.) perpendiculaire(ment). [faire.

perpetrate, *pĕr'pē trāt*, v. a. commettre.

perpetration, *pĕr pē trā'shŭn*, s. exécution, f. || forfait, m.

perpetrator, *pĕr'pē trā tĕr*, s. coupable, criminel, m. || acteur, m.

perpetual, *pĕr pĕt'ū ăl*, a. (-ly, ad.) perpétuel(lement).

perpetuate, *pĕr pĕt'ū āt*, v. a. perpétuer.

perpetuation, *pĕr pĕt ū ā'shŭn*, s. perpétuation, f.

perpetuity, *pĕr pē tū'ĭ tĭ*, s. perpétuité, f.

perplex, *pĕr plĕks'*, v. a. embarrasser || embrouiller. [embarras, m.

perplexity, *pĕr plĕks'ĭ tĭ*, s. perplexité, f.

perquisite, *pĕr kwĭ zĭt*, s. casuel, émolument, m. || petit profit, m.

persecute, *pĕr'sē kūt*, v. a. persécuter, importuner. [tion, f.

persecution, *pĕr sē kū'shŭn*, s. persécution, f.

perseverance, *pĕr sē vē'răns*, s. persévérance, f.

persevere, *pĕr sē vēr'*, v. n. persévérer.

persevering, *pĕr sē vē'rĭng*, a. (-ly, ad.) persévérant || avec persévérance.

persist, *pĕr sĭst'*, v. n. persister. [f.

persistency, *pĕr sĭst'ĕn sĭ*, s. persistance.

persistent, *pĕr sĭst'ĕnt*, a. persistant.

person, *pĕr'sŏn*, s. personne, f. || first singular, (gr.) première personne du singulier, m. || (fam.) soi-même, m. & f.

personage, *pĕr'sŏn ăj*, s. personnage, m.

personal, *pĕr'sŏn ăl*, a. (-ly, ad.) personnel(lement) || mobilier. [f.

personality, *pĕr'sŏn ăl'ĭ tĭ*, s. personnalité, personalty, *pĕr'sŏn ăl tĭ*, s. biens meubles, m. pl. [jouer || feindre.

personate, *pĕr'sŏn āt*, v. a. représenter, personation, *pĕr sŏn ā'shŭn*, s. imitation, f.

personification, *pĕr sŏn ĭ fĭ kā'shŭn*, s. personnification, f.

personify, *pĕr sŏn'ĭ fĭ*, v. a. personnifier.

perspective, *pĕr spĕk'tĭv*, s. perspective, f.

perspective, *pĕr spĕk'tĭv*, a. perspectif.

perspicacious, *pĕr spĭ kā'shŭs*, a. perspicace. [cité, f.

perspicacity, *pĕr spĭ kăs'ĭ tĭ*, s. perspica-

perspicuity, *pĕr spĭ kū'ĭ tĭ*, s. perspicuité, f.

perspicuous, *pĕr spĭk'ū ŭs*, a. (-ly, ad.) clair(ement) || évident. [ration, f.

perspiration, *pĕr spĭ rā'shŭn*, s. transpi-

perspire, *pĕr spīr'*, v. n. transpirer, suer.

persuade, *pĕr swād'*, v. a. persuader, faire croire, exciter, inciter, induire.

persuasion, *pĕr swā'zhŭn*, s. persuasion, conviction, f.

persuasive, *pĕr swā'sĭv*, a. persuasif || -ly, ad. d'une manière persuasive.

pert, *pĕrt*, a. vif, pétulant, impertinent || -ly, ad. avec pétulance or impertinence.

pertain, *pĕr tān'*, v. n. appartenir, concerner. [opiniâtre(ment).

pertinacious, *pĕr tĭ nā'shŭs*, a. (-ly, ad.)

pertinacity, *pĕr tĭ năs'ĭ tĭ*, s. opiniâtreté, f.

pertinency, *pĕr'tĭ nĕn sĭ*, s. convenance, propriété, f.

pertinent, *pĕr'tĭnĕnt*, a. pertinent, convenable || -ly, ad. pertinemment, à propos.

pertness, *pĕrt'nĕs*, s. vivacité, f. || impertinence, f.

perturb, *pĕr'tĕrb'*, v. a. troubler, perturber.

perturbation, *pĕr'tĕr bă'shŭn*, s. perturbation, f., trouble, m., agitation, f.

perusal, *pĕr ö'zăl*, s. lecture, f.

peruse, *pĕr öz'*, v. a. lire, parcourir.

peruser, *pĕr ö'zĕr*, s. lecteur, m.

Peruvian bark, *pĕr ö'vĭ ăn bărk*, s. quinquina, m.

pervade, *pĕr văd'*, v. a. pénétrer.

perverse, *pĕr vĕrs'*, a. pervers || têtu || -ly, ad. avec perversité || malicieusement.

perversion, *pĕr vĕr'shŭn*, s. perversion, f.

perversity, *pĕr vĕr'sĭ tĭ*, s. perversité, f. || méchanceté, f.

pervert, *pĕr vĕrt'*, v. a. pervertir, dépraver.

pervious, *pĕr'vĭ ŭs*, a. perméable || (fig.) accessible.   [m.

pest, *pĕst*, s. peste, f. || ~-house, s. lazaret, m.

pester, *pĕs'tĕr*, v. a. inquiéter, tourmenter.

pestiferous, *pĕs tif'ĕr ŭs*, a. pestilent, contagieux.

pestilence, *pĕs'tĭ lĕns*, s. peste, f.

pestilent, *pĕs'tĭ lĕnt*, pestilential, *pĕs'tĭ lĕn'shăl*, a. pestilentiel.

pestle, *pĕs'tl* ou *pĕs'l*, s. pilon, m.

pet, *pĕt*, dépit, m. || favori(te), m. (& f.) || to be in a ~, être de mauvaise humeur.

pet, *pĕt*, v. a. mignarder, dorloter.

petal, *pĕt'ăl*, s. (bot.) pétale, m.

petard, *pĕ tărd'*, s. pétard, m.

petition, *pĕ tish'ŭn*, s. pétition, supplication, f.   [plier.

petition, *pĕ tish'ŭn*, v. a. pétitionner, supplier.

petitioner, *pĕ tish'ŭn ĕr*, s. pétitionnaire, solliciteur, m.

petrel, *pĕt'rĕl*, s. pétrel, procellaire, m.

petrifaction, *pĕ trĭ făk'shŭn*, s. pétrification, f.

petrify, *pĕt'rĭ fĭ*, v. a. (& n.) (se) pétrifier.

petroleum, *pĕ trö'lĕ ŭm*, s. pétrole, m.

petticoat, *pĕt'tĭ kŏt*, s. jupe, f. || (in jest) cotillon, m. || ~s, pl. jaquette, f.

pettifogger, *pĕt'tĭ fŏg gĕr*, s. avocat insignifiant, m. || chicaneur, m.

pettifogging, *pĕt'tĭ fŏg ging*, s. chicane, f.

pettifogging, *pĕt'tĭ fŏg ging*, a. chicaneur.

pettiness, *pĕt'tĭ nĕs*, s. petitesse, f.

pettish, *pĕt'tish*, a. maussade.

pettitoes, *pĕt'tĭ tōz*, s. pl. pieds de cochon de lait, m. pl. || (of children) petons, m. pl.

petty, *pĕt'tĭ*, a. petit, inférieur, chétif.

petulance, *pĕt'ŭ lăns*, s. pétulance, f.

petulant, *pĕt'ŭ lănt*, a. pétulant || -ly, ad. pétulamment.

pew, *pū*, s. banc d'église, m. || ~-opener, s. sacristain, suisse, bedeau, m.

pewter, *pū'tĕr*, s. étain, m.

phaeton, *fā'ĕ tŏn*, s. phaéton, m. || victoria, f.

phalanx, *făl'ăngks*, s. phalange, f.

phantasmagoria, *făn tăs mă gō'rĭ ă*, s. phantasmagorie, f.

phantom, *făn'tŏm*, s. fantôme, m.

pharisaical, *făr ĭ sā'ĭk ăl*, a. pharisaïque.

Pharisee, *făr'ĭ sē*, s. pharisien, m.

pharmaceutic, *făr mă sū'tĭk*, a. pharmaceutique.   [macopée, f.

pharmacopoeia, *făr mă kŏ pē'ĭ ă*, s. pharmacy, *făr'mă sĭ*, s. pharmacie, f.

phase, *fāz*, s. phase, f.

pheasant, *fĕz'ănt*, s. faisan, m.

phenomenal, *fĕ nŏm'ĕ năl*, a. phénoménal.

phenomenon, *fĕ nŏm'ĕ nŏn*, s. phénomène, m.

phial, *fĭ'ăl*, s. fiole, f.   [m.

philanthropic, *fĭl ăn thrŏp'ĭk*, a. philanthropique.   [thrope, m.

philanthropist, *fĭl ăn'thrŏ pist*, s. philanthropy, *fĭl ăn'thrŏ pĭ*, s. philanthropie, f.   [monique.

philharmonic, *fĭl hăr mŏn'ĭk*, a. philharmonique.

philological, *fĭ lŏ lŏj'ĭ kăl*, a. philologique.

philologist, *fĭ lŏl'ŏ jist*, s. philologue, m.

philology, *fĭ lŏl'ŏ jĭ*, s. philologie, f.

philosopher, *fĭ lŏs'ŏ fĕr*, s. philosophe, m. || ~'s stone, s. pierre philosophale, f.

philosophic(al), *fĭ lŏ sŏf'ĭk(ăl)*, a. (-ly, ad.) philosophique(ment).

philosophise, *fĭ lŏs'ŏ fĭz*, v. n. philosopher.

philosophy, *fĭ lŏs'ŏ fĭ*, s. philosophie, f. || natural ~, physique, f.

philter, *fĭl'tĕr*, s. philtre, m.

phlegm, *flĕm*, s. flegme, m.

phlegmatic, *flĕg măt'ĭk*, a. (-ly, ad.) flegmatique(ment).   [m.

phonograph, *fō'nŏ grăf*, s. phonographe.

phosphate, *fŏs'fāt*, s. phosphate, m.

phosphoric, *fŏs fŏr'ĭk*, a. phosphorique.

phosphorous, *fŏs'fĕr ŭs*, a. phosphoreux.

phosphorus, *fŏs'fĕr ŭs*, s. phosphore, m.

photograph, *fō'tŏ grăf*, s. photographie, f.

photograph, *fō'tŏ grăf*, v. a. photographier.

photographer, *fō tŏg'ră fĕr*, s. photographe, m.   [phique.

photographic, *fō tŏ grăf'ĭk*, a. photographique.

photography, *fō tŏg'ră fĭ*, s. photographie, f.

phrase, *frāz*, s. phrase, expression, f.

phrase, *frāz*, v. a. dénommer.

phraseology, *frā zĕ ŏl'ŏ jĭ*, s. recueil de phrases, m.

phrenology, *frĕ nŏl'ŏ jĭ*, s. phrénologie, f.

phthisis, *tĭs'ĭs*, s. phthisie, f.

physic, *fĭz'ĭk*, s. médecine, f. || -s, pl. physique, f.

physic, *fĭz'ĭk*, v. a. médicamenter.

physical, *fĭz'ĭ kăl*, a. (-ly, ad.) physique (ment).

physician, *fĭ zĭsh'ăn*, s. médecin, m.

physiognomy, *fĭz ĭ ŏn'ŏ mĭ*, s. physionomie, f.   [logique.

physiological, *fĭz ĭ ŏ lŏj'ĭk ăl*, a. physio-

physiologist, *fĭz ĭ ŏl'ŏ jist*, s. physiologiste, m.

physiology, *fĭz ĭ ŏl'ŏ jĭ*, s. physiologie, f.

pianist, *pĭ ăn'ist*, s. pianiste, m.

piano, *pĭ ă'nŏ*, s. piano, m. || grand ~, piano à queue || cottage ~, piano droit || semi-cottage (piccolo) ~, petit piano droit || ~-maker, s. facteur de pianos, m.

pibroch, *pē'brŏk*, s. pibroch, m., cornemuse écossaise. f.

pick, *pik*, (~axe), s. pioche, f.; pic, m.

pick, *pik*, v. a. & n. piquer, becqueter ||
cueillir, glaner, ramasser, éplucher, trier ||
choisir || voler, dérober || manger à petits
morceaux.

picked, *pikt*, a. pointu || choisi.

picker, *pik'ér*, s. cueilleur, m. || (mil.)
épinglette, f.

picket, *pik'ĕt*, s. piquet, m. || vedette, f.

pickings, *pik'ĭngz*, s. pl. épluchures, f. pl.,
petits morceaux, m. pl. || profits, m. pl.

pickle, *pik'l*, s. saumure, f. || to get into
a ~, être dans le pétrin.

pickle, *pik'l*, v. a. mariner.

picklock, *pik'lŏk*, s. crochet, rossignol, m.

pickpocket, *pik'pŏk ĕt*, s. filou, m.

picnic, *pik'nik*, s. pique-nique, m.

pictorial, *pik tō'ri ăl*, a. pittoresque, il-
lustré.

picture, *pik'tŭr* ou *pik'chŏŏr*, s. tableau,
m. || peinture, f.   [représenter.

picture, *pik'tŭr* ou *pik'chŏŏr*, v. a. peindre,

picturesque, *pik tŭ rĕsk'*, a. pittoresque.

pie, *pī*, s. pâte, m., tourte, f. || pie, f. || to
eat humble ~, filer doux.

piebald, *pī'bǎwld*, a. pie.

piece, *pēs*, s. pièce, f., morceau, m., par-
tie, f. || fusil, m. || tableau, m. || to go to
~s, se briser en tombant.

piece, *pēs*, v. a. raccommoder.

piecemeal, *pēs'mēl*, a. & ad. séparé, di-
visé || en pièces.

pied, *pīd*, a. pie, bigarré.

pier, *pēr*, s. pile, f. || trumeau, m. || ~-
glass, s. trumeau, m.   [émouvoir.

pierce, *pērs*, v. a. & n. percer, pénétrer ||

piercingly, *pērs'ing li*, ad. d'une manière
perçante.

piety, *pī'ĕti*, s. piété, dévotion, f.

pig, *pig*, s. cochon, pourceau, m. || lin-
got, m. || to buy a ~ in a poke, ache-
ter chat en poche || ~-headed, a. stupide
|| têtu || ~-sty, s. étable à cochons, f.

pigeon, *pij'ŭn*, s. pigeon, m. || ~-house,
s. colombier, m.   [fleur, f.

pigment, *pig'mĕnt*, s. pigment, m. || cou-

pike, *pīk*, s. pique, f. || pointe, f. || brochet,
m. || pic, m.

piked, *pīkt*, a. pointu, en pointe.

pilaster, *pi lǎs'tĕr*, s. pilastre, m.

pile, *pīl*, s. pieu, pilotis, m. || monceau,
tas, m. || bûcher, m. || édifice, m. || duvet,
m.   [m.

pile, *pīl*, v. a. empiler.

piles, *pīlz*, s. pl. hémorroïdes, f. pl.

pilfer, *pil'fér*, v.a. & n. dérober || grappiller.

pilgrim, *pil'grim*, s. pèlerin, m.

pilgrimage, *pil'grim ăj*, s. pèlerinage, m.

pill, *pil*, s. pilule, f.

pillage, *pil'lāj*, s. pillage, m.

pillage, *pil'lāj*, v. a. piller.

pillager, *pil'lāj ér*, s. pilleur, spoliateur, m.

pillar, *pil'lér*, s. pilier, soutien, support,
m. || ~-(letter-)box, s. borne-boîte, f.

pillion, *pil'yŭn*, s. coussinet, m.

pillory, *pil'lér i*, s. pilori, m.

pillory, *pil'lér i*, v. a. mettre au pilori.

pillow, *pil'lō*, s. oreiller, m. || ~-case, s.
taie d'oreiller, f.

pilot, *pī'lŏt*, s. pilote, m.

pilot, *pī'lŏt*, v. a. piloter.

pilotage, *pī'lŏt ăj*, s. pilotage, m.

pimento, *pi mĕn'tō*, s. piment, m.

pimp, *pimp*, s. maquereau, m.

pimpernel, *pĭm'pér nĕl*, s. pimprenelle, f.

pimple, *pim'pl*, s. bouton, m., pustule, f.

pin, *pin*, s. épingle, f. || cheville, goupille,
f. || quille, f. || style, m. || ~-case, s. étui
à épingles, m. || ~-cushion, s. pelote à
épingles, f. || ~-money, s. épingles, f. pl.

pin, *pin*, v. a. attacher avec une épingle,
cheviller || to ~ down, fixer avec des
épingles || lier, enchaîner, pincer (qn.). [m.

pinafore, *pin'ă fōr*, s. bavette, f. || sarrau,

pincers, *pin'sérz*, s. p.l. pincettes, tenailles,
f. pl.

pinch, *pinsh*, s. pince, f. || prise, f. || op-
pression, difficulté, f., embarras, m.

pinch, *pinsh*, v. a. & n. pincer || serrer ||
piquer, vexer || épargner.

pinchbeck, *pinsh'bĕk*, s. pinchbeck, m.

pine, *pin*, s. pin, m. || ~-apple, s. ana-
nas, m.

pine, *pin*, v. n. languir, soupirer pour.

pinion, *pin'yŭn*, s. aileron, m. || bout
d'aile, m. || pignon, m.

pinion, *pin'yŭn*, v. a. lier les ailes || gar-
rotter || (fig.) enchaîner.

pink, *pingk*, s. œillet, m. || pinque, f. || ~
of politeness, s. la fine fleur de la politesse.   [tesse.

pink, *pingk*, a. rose || petit.

pinnace, *pin'năs*, s. pinasse, f.

pinnacle, *pin'nă kl*, s. pinacle, m.

pint, *pint*, s. demi-litre, m. || chopine, f.

pintail, *pin'tāl*, s. pilet, m.

pioneer, *pī ō nēr'*, s. (mil.) pionnier, m.

pious, *pī'ŭs*, a. pieux || ~-ly, ad. pieuse-
ment.   [m.

pip, *pip*, s. pépie, f. || point sur les cartes,

pipe, *pip*, s. tuyau, m. || brûle-gueule, m. ||
pipe, f. || chalumeau, m. || ~-case, s.
porte-pipe, m. || ~-clay, s. terre de pipe,
f. || v. a. blanchir avec de la terre de pipe
délayée || ~-light, s. cornet de papier, m.

pipe, *pip*, v. n. jouer de la flûte || siffler.

piper, *pī'pér*, s. joueur de cornemuse, m.

piping, *pī'ping*, s. passe-poil, m.

piping, *pī'ping*, a. maladif || ~-hot,
tout chaud.

pipkin, *pip'kin*, s. petit pot de terre, m.

pippin, *pip'pin*, s. reinette, f.

piquancy, *pē'kan si*, s. acidité, f.

piquant, *pē'kant*, a. (-ly, ad.) piquant ||
d'une manière piquante.   [d'honneur, m.

pique, *pēk*, s. pique, brouillerie, f. || point

pique, *pēk*, v. a. piquer, irriter.

piquet, *pē kĕt'*, s. piquet (jeu aux cartes), m.

piracy, *pī'ră si*, s. piraterie, f. || plagiat,
m.

pirate, *pī'rāt*, s. pirate, m. || plagiaire,

pirate, *pī'rāt*, v. a. & n. commettre un
plagiat || pirater.   [contrefaçon.

piratical, *pī răt'ĭ kăl*, a. de pirate || de

pish! *pĭsh,* fi! pouah!

piemire, *pīz'mir,* s. fourmi, f.

piss, *pĭs,* v. n. pisser, uriner.

pistachio, *pĭs tä'shĭō,* s. pistache, f.

pistol, *pĭs'tŏl,* s. pistolet, m. ‖ ~**-gallery,** s. tir au pistolet, m. ‖ ~**-shot,** s. coup de pistolet, m. ‖ portée du pistolet, f.

piston, *pĭs'tŏn,* s. piston, m. ‖ ~**-rod,** s. tige du piston, f.

pit, *pĭt,* s. fosse, carrière, f., tombeau, m. ‖ parterre, creux, m. ‖ ~**-coal,** s. charbon de terre, m. ‖ ~**-fall,** s. trappe, f.

pit, *pĭt,* v. a. faire un creux ‖ to ~ one against another, acharner l'un contre l'autre, les mettre aux prises.

pitapat, *pĭt'ä pät,* ad. en palpitant.

pitch, *pĭch,* s. poix, f. ‖ degré, point, m. ‖ hauteur, f. ‖ portée, f. ‖ ~ and tar, goudron, m. ‖ ~ black, a. noir comme jais.

pitch, *pĭch,* v. a. & n. poisser ‖ fixer, planter, ranger ‖ jeter, lancer ‖ paver ‖ obscurcir ‖ choisir ‖ tomber ‖ (mar.) tanguer ‖ (rail.) plonger ‖ to ~ upon, fixer ‖ to ~ into, donner un galop.

pitcher, *pĭch'ĕr,* s. cruche, f. ‖ pioche, f.

pitchfork, *pĭch'fŏrk,* s. fourche, f. ‖ (mus.) diapason, m.

pitchy, *pĭch'ĭ,* a. de poix, poissé ‖ obscur.

piteous, *pĭt'ĕŭs,* a. (-ly, ad.) piteux, pitoyable(ment) ‖ compatissant.

pith, *pĭth,* s. moelle, f. ‖ énergie, f. ‖ quintessence, f.

pithily, *pĭth'ĭ lĭ,* ad. vigoureusement.

pithiness, *pĭth'ĭ nĕs,* s. énergie, force, f.

pithless, *pĭth'lĕs,* a. sans moelle ‖ sans énergie.　　　　　　　[vigoureux.

pithy, *pĭth'ĭ,* a. moelleux ‖ énergique,

pitiable, *pĭt'ĭ ä bl,* a. digne de pitié.

pitiful, *pĭt'ĭ fŏŏl,* a. déplorable, pitoyable (ment) ‖ méprisable ‖ très-mal ‖ servilement.　　　　　　[f. ‖ état pitoyable, m.

pitifulness, *pĭt'ĭ fŏŏl nĕs,* s. compassion,

pitiless, *pĭt'ĭ lĕs,* a. (-ly, ad.) impitoyable (ment).

pittance, *pĭt'täns,* s. pitance, portion, f.

pitted, *pĭt'tĕd,* a. grêlé, gravé.

pity, *pĭt'ĭ,* s. pitié, compassion, f. ‖ it is a ~, c'est dommage ‖ to take ~ on, prendre en pitié ‖ more's the ~! tant pis!

pity, *pĭt'ĭ,* v. a. & n. avoir pitié, plaindre.

pivot, *pĭv'ŏt,* s. pivot, m.　　　　[tacle, m.

pixie, *pĭks'ĭ,* s. ciboire, m. ‖ (mar.) habi-

placability, *plăk ä bĭl'ĭ tĭ* ou *plä kä bĭl'ĭ tĭ,* s. caractère conciliant, m.　　[liant.

placable, *plăk'ä bl* ou *plä'kä bl,* a. conci-

placard, *plăk'ärd,* s. placard, m.

placard, *plăk'ärd,* v. a. placarder.

place, *plās,* s. place, f., lieu, m. ‖ rang, m. ‖ emploi, m. ‖ demeure, f. ‖ position, f. ‖ in your ~, à votre place ‖ in ~, casé ‖ out of ~, sur le pavé.

place, *plās,* v. a. placer, mettre ‖ établir.

placid, *plăs'ĭd,* a. (-ly, ad.) paisible(ment).

plagiarism, *plă'jĭ ä rĭzm,* s. plagiat, m.

plagiarist, *plă'jĭ ä rĭst,* s. plagiaire, m.

plague, *plāg,* s. peste, contagion, f. ‖ tourment, m.

plague, *plāg,* v. a. infecter de la peste ‖ tourmenter.

plaguily, *plā'gĭ lĭ,* ad. furieusement.

plaice, *plās,* s. carrelet, m.

plaid, *plād* ou *plăd,* s. tartan, plaid, m.

plain, *plān,* s. plaine, f.

plain, *plān,* a. plat, uni ‖ simple, sincère, franc ‖ clair ‖ laid ‖ en bandeaux ‖ ~ dealer, s. honnête homme, m. ‖ homme de bien, m. ‖ ~ work, s. couture, f. ‖ -ly, ad. franchement, distinctement ‖ clairement.

plainness, *plān'nĕs,* s. niveau, m. ‖ simplicité, f. ‖ sincérité, franchise, f.

plainspoken, *plān'spō kn,* a. franc.

plaintiff, *plān'tĭf,* s. (jur.) demandeur, m.

plaintive, *plān'tĭv,* a. plaintif ‖ -ly, ad. plaintivement.

plait, *plāt* ou *plăt,* s. pli, m., tresse, f.

plait, *plāt* ou *plăt,* v. a. plisser ‖ tresser.

plan, *plăn,* s. plan, dessin, m. ‖ projet, m.

plan, *plăn,* v. a. projeter.

plane, *plān,* s. plan, m. ‖ rabot, m. ‖ ~ table, s. table d'arpenteur, f. ‖ ~-tree, s. platane, m.

plane, *plān,* v. a. raboter.

planet, *plăn'ĕt,* s. planète, f.

planetary, *plăn'ĕt ĕr ĭ,* a. planétaire.

plank, *plăngk,* s. planche, f. ‖ (mar.) bordage, m.

plank, *plăngk,* v. a. planchéier.　[dage, m.

plant, *plănt,* s. plante, f. ‖ plant, m. ‖ (com.) fonds, m. ‖ ~-louse, s. puceron, m.

plant, *plănt,* v. a. planter ‖ établir ‖ l'emporter sur.

plantain, *plăn'tĕn,* s. (bot.) plantain, m.

plantation, *plănt ä'shŭn,* s. plantation, f., plantage, m.

planter, *plănt'ĕr,* s. planteur, colon, m.

plaster, *plăs'tĕr,* s. plâtre, m. ‖ emplâtre, m. ‖ adhesive ~, court-~, taffetas d'Angleterre, sparadrap, m. ‖ mustard-~, sinapisme, m. ‖ ~ of Paris, s. stuc, m. ‖ ~-stone, s. gypse, m.

plaster, *plăs'tĕr,* v. a. plâtrer.

plasterer, *plăs'tĕr ĕr,* s. plâtrier, m.

plastic, *plăs'tĭk,* a. plastique.

plasticity, *plăs tĭs'ĭ tĭ,* s. plasticité, f.

plate, *plāt,* s. plaque, f. ‖ assiette, f. ‖ gentes-e, f. ‖ ~-layer, s. poseur de rails, m. ‖ ~-rack, s. porte-assiettes, m. ‖ ~-warmer, s. chauffe-assiettes, m.

plate, *plāt,* v. a. plaquer, laminer ‖ étamer ‖ argenter ‖ blinder.

platform, *plăt'fawrm,* s. plate-forme, f. ‖ (rail.) quai, m. ‖ (Am.) programme politique, m.

platinum, *plăt'ĭ nŭm,* s. platine, m.

platitude, *plăt'ĭ tūd,* s. platitude, f.

platoon, *plă tōn',* s. peloton, m.

platter, *plăt'tĕr,* s. plat, m. ‖ tresseur, m. ‖ (mil. & nav.) gamelle, f.

plaudit, *plaw'dĭt,* s. applaudissement, m.

plausibility, *plaw zĭ bĭl'ĭ tĭ,* s. plausibilité, f.

plausible, *plaw'zĭ bl,* a. plausible.

plausibly, *plaw'zĭ blĭ,* ad. plausiblement.

play, plā, s. jeu, m. ‖ divertissement, spectacle, m. ‖ action, f. ‖ foul ~, filoutage, m., friponnerie, f. ‖ ~-bill, s. programme de spectacle, m. ‖ ~-house, s. théâtre, m.

play, plā, v. a. & n. faire jouer ‖ jouer (de).

player, plā'ēr, s. joueur, m. ‖ acteur, m., actrice, f.

playful, plā'fool, a. enjoué, folâtre ‖ -ly, ad. avec enjouement, en badinant. [m.

playfulness, plā'fool nĕs, s. enjouement.

playmate, plā'māt, s. camarade de jeu, m.

plaything, plā'thing, s. jouet, m.

plea, plē, s. procès, m. ‖ (jur.) exception, f.

plead, plēd, v. a. & n. plaider, défendre ‖ alléguer, prétexter ‖ s'excuser.

pleadable, plēd'ā bl, a. plaidable.

pleader, plēd'ēr, s. avocat, m.

pleadings, plēd'ings, s. pl. débats, m. pl.

pleasant, plĕz'ănt, a. (-ly, ad.) gai(ement), agréable(ment).

pleasantness, plĕz'ănt nĕs, pleasantry, plĕz'ănt rĭ, s. plaisanterie, gaieté, f., agrément, m.

please, plēz, v. a. & n. plaire à, être agréable, contenter ‖ if you ~, s'il vous plaît ‖ ~ God! plût à Dieu!

pleasing, plēz'ing, a. agréable, charmant ‖ (things) riant.

pleasurable, plēzh'ōōr ă bl, a. agréable.

pleasure, plēzh'ōōr, s. plaisir, grĕ. m. ‖ ~-boat, s. barquerolle, f. ‖ ~-ground, s. jardin anglais, m. ‖ ~-van, s. char-à-bancs, m.

plebeian, plē bē'ăn, s. plébéien, m.

plebeian, plē bē'ăn, a. plébéien.

pledge, plĕj, s. gage, m. ‖ caution, f. ‖ toast, m. ‖ vœu de tempérance, m.

pledge, plĕj, v. a. engager ‖ garantir ‖ (in drinking) faire raison à. [fait.

plenary, plē'nă rĭ, a. plein, complet, parfait.

plenipotentiary, plĕn ĭ pō tĕn' shă rĭ, s. plénipotentiaire, m. [plénipotentiaire.

plenipotentiary, plĕn ĭ pō tĕn' shă rĭ, a.

plenitude, plĕn'ĭ tūd, s. plénitude, f.

plentiful, plĕn'tĭ fool, a. abondant.

plenty, plĕn'tĭ, s. abondance, f.

plethora, plĕth'ō ră, s. pléthore, f.

plethoric, plē thŏr'ĭk, a. pléthorique.

pleurisy, plōō'rĭ sĭ, s. pleurésie, f.

pliable, plī'ă bl, pliant, plī'ănt, a. flexible, pliable ‖ docile. [f.

pliancy, plī'ăn sĭ, s. flexibilité, souplesse.

pliers, plī'ērz, s. pl. pincettes, f. pl.

plight, plīt, s. condition, f., état, m.

plight, plīt, v. a. engager.

plod, plŏd, v. n. travailler assidûment ‖ piocher ‖ marcher avec peine.

plot, plŏt, s. morceau de terre, m. ‖ plan, complot, m. ‖ intrigue, f.

plot, plŏt, v. a. & n. comploter, conspirer, machiner ‖ inventer.

plotter, plŏt'tēr, s. conspirateur, m.

plough, plŏw, s. charrue, f. ‖ bouvet, m. ‖ ~-land, s. terre labourable, f.

plough, plŏw, v. a. labourer ‖ sillonner.

ploughman, plŏw'măn, s. laboureur, m.

ploughshare, plŏw'shār, s. soc de charrue, m.

pluck, plŭk, s. action d'arracher, f. ‖ effort, m. ‖ fressure (d'un animal), f. ‖ courage, m.

pluck, plŭk, v. a. arracher, tirer ‖ plumer ‖ dépouiller ‖ déraciner ‖ refuser.

plug, plŭg, s. tampon, m., cheville, f. ‖ piston, m. ‖ robinet, m. ‖ ~-hole, s. bouche d'eau, f.

plug, plŭg, v. a. cheviller.

plum, plŭm, s. prune, f. ‖ raisin sec, m. ‖ French ~, prune de Monsieur ‖ -tree, s. prunier, m.

plumage, plōm'āj, s. plumage, m.

plumb, plŭm, s. plomb, m. ‖ sonde, f. ‖ ~-line, s. niveau, m. ‖ fil à plomb, m.

plumb, plŭm, v. a. mettre à plomb.

plumb, plŭm, ad. à plomb.

plumbago, plŭm bā'gō, s. plombagine, f.

plumber, plŭm'ēr, s. plombier, m.

plume, plŏm, s. plumet, panache, m. ‖ (honour) palme, f.

plume, plŏm, v. a. orner d'une plume ‖ nettoyer. [f.

plummet, plŭm'mĕt, s. plomb, m., sonde.

plump, plŭmp, v. n. s'enfler ‖ tomber lourdement ‖ (parl.) voter pour un seul candidat entre plusieurs.

plump, plŭmp, a. & ad. dodu, potelé, gras ‖ tout d'un coup.

plumper, plŭmp'ēr, s. bourde, f. ‖ (parl.) vote indivis, m.

plumpness, plŭmp'nĕs, s. embonpoint, m.

plunder, plŭn'dēr, s. pillage, butin, m. ‖ (Am.) bagages, m. pl.

plunder, plŭn'dēr, v. a. piller, spolier.

plunderer, plŭn'dēr ēr, s. pillard, m.

plunge, plŭnj, v. a. (& n.) (se) plonger.

plungeon, plŭnj'ŭn, s. plongeon, m.

plunger, plŭnj'ēr, s. plongeur, m. ‖ joueur insouciant, étourdi, m.

pluperfect, plōō'pēr fĕkt, a. (gr.) plusque-parfait, m.

plural, plōō'răl, s. (gr.) pluriel, m.

plural, plōō'răl, a. (gr.) pluriel.

pluralist, plōō'răl ĭst, s. cumulard, m.

plurality, plōō răl'ĭ tĭ, s. pluralité, f.

plush, plŭsh, s. peluche, f.

ply, plī, v. a. & n. travailler avec ardeur ‖ supplier, solliciter ‖ (mar.) bouliner.

P. M. de l'après-midi.

pneumonia, nū mō'nĭ ă, s. pneumonie, f.

poach, pōch, v. a. & n. pocher ‖ piller ‖ braconner.

poacher, pōch'ēr, s. braconnier, m.

pock, pŏk, s. grain de petite vérole, m. ‖ ~-marked, a. marqué de petite vérole, grêlé.

pocket, pŏk'ĕt, s poche, f. ‖ (at billiards) blouse, f. ‖ to be in ~, gagner ‖ to be out of ~, perdre ‖ ~-book, s. portefeuille, m. ‖ ~-knife, s. couteau pliant, m. ‖ jambette, f. ‖ ~-money, s. menus plaisirs, m. pl. [avaler (un affront).

pocket, pŏk'ĕt, v. a. empocher ‖ blouser ‖

pod, pŏd, s. cosse, écale, f.

poem, *pō'ĕm*, s. poème, m.

poesy, *pō'ĕsĭ*, s. poésie, f.

poet, *pō'ĕt*, s. poète, m. ‖ ~ laureate, s. poète couronné, m.

poetaster, *pō'ĕtãstĕr*, s. poétereau, m.

poetess, *pō'ĕtĕs*, s. poétesse, f.

poetic(al), *pōĕt'ĭk (ăl)*, a. (-ly, ad.) poétique(ment).   [vers.

poetise, *pō'ĕtīz*, v. n. poétiser, écrire en

poetry, *pō'ĕtrĭ*, s. poésie, f.   [quant, m.

poignancy, *pōy'nănsĭ*, s. pointe, f., piquant, m.

poignant, *pōy'nănt*, a. piquant, douloureux ‖ satirique.

point, *pōynt*, s. pointe, f. ‖ (rail.) aiguille, f. ‖ cap, m. ‖ point, moment, degré, m. ‖ lieu, m. ‖ but, m. ‖ point capital, m. ‖ nœud de l'affaire, m. ‖ main ~, point capital, m. ‖ nice ~, sujet délicat, m. ‖ in ~ of, en fait de, en matière de ‖ in ~ of fact, en fait ‖ to be on the ~ of, être sur le point de ‖ to come to the ~, aller droit au fait ‖ to stretch a ~, faire plus qu'on n'est obligé de faire ‖ ne pas y regarder de si près ‖ ~-blank, ad. directement, droit au but, de but en blanc.

point, *pōynt*, v. a. aiguiser, affiler ‖ pointer‖ ponctuer ‖ montrer ‖ to ~ out, signaler ‖ to ~ the finger, montrer du doigt.

pointed, *pōynt'ĕd*, a. pointu ‖ mordant ‖ -ly, ad. satiriquement.

pointer, *pōynt'ĕr*, s. index, m. ‖ chien d'arrêt, m. ‖ (rail.) aiguille, f.

pointless, *pōynt'lĕs*, a. sans pointe, obtus ‖ (fig.) plat.

pointsman, *pōynts'măn*, s. aiguilleur, m.

poise, *pōyz*, s. poids, m. ‖ équilibre, m.

poise, *pōyz*, v. a. peser ‖ équilibrer.

poison, *pōy'zn*, s. poison, m.

poison, *pōy'zn*, v. a. empoisonner.

poisoner, *pōy'znĕr*, s. empoisonneur, m.

poisonous, *pōy'znŭs*, a. empoisonné ‖ venimeux.

poke, *pōk*, s. poche, f. ‖ coup de poing, m.

poke, *pōk*, v. a. tâtonner ‖ farfouiller ‖ pousser.   [vantail, m.

poker, *pō'kĕr*, s. fourgon, m. ‖ (Am.) épouvantail, m.

polar, *pō'lĕr*, a. polaire.

polarity, *pōlăr'ĭtĭ*, s. polarité, f.

pole, *pōl*, s. pôle, m. ‖ perche, f. ‖ timon, m. ‖ balancier, m. ‖ ~-axe, s. hache d'armes, f. ‖ (of butchers) merlin, m. ‖ ~-star, s. étoile polaire, f.

polecat, *pōl'kăt*, s. putois, m., fouine, f.

polemic, *pōlĕm'ĭk*, s. écrivain polémique, m.

polemics, *pōlĕm'ĭks*, s. pl. polémique, f.

police, *pōlēs'*, s. police, f. ‖ ~-court, s. tribunal de police, m. ‖ ~-station, s. commissariat *or* poste de police, m.

policeman, *pōlēs'măn*, police-officer, *pōlēs'ŏffĭsĕr*, s. agent de police, m.

policy, *pŏl'ĭsĭ*, s. politique, f. ‖ ruse, f. ‖ police, f. ‖ plan, m.

polish, *pŏl'ĭsh*, s. poli, m. ‖ élégance, f.

polish, *pŏl'ĭsh*, v. a. & n. polir ‖ lustrer ‖ vernir ‖ cirer ‖ policer ‖ se polir.

polisher, *pŏl'ĭshĕr*, s. polisseur, m. ‖ polissoir, m.

polite, *pōlīt'*, a. (-ly, ad.) poli(ment) ‖ civil ‖ galant ‖ ~ literature, s. belles-lettres, f. pl.

politeness, *pōlīt'nĕs*, s. politesse, f.

politic, *pŏl'ĭtĭk*, a. politique ‖ prudent, judicieux.   [tique(ment).

political, *pōlĭt'ĭkăl*, a. (-ly, ad.) politique, m.

politician, *pōlĭtĭsh'ăn*, s. homme politique, m.

politics, *pŏl'ĭtĭks*, s. pl. politique, f.

poll, *pŏl*, s. tête, f. ‖ liste électorale, f. ‖ voix, f. ‖ vote, m. ‖ ~-tax, s. capitation, f.

poll, *pŏl*, v. a. étêter ‖ tondre ‖ voter ‖ inscrire.

pollard, *pŏl'lĕrd*, s. arbre étêté, m.

pollen, *pŏl'lĕn*, s. recoupe, f. ‖ pollen, m.

pollute, *pōllūt'*, v. a. polluer ‖ souiller.

polluter, *pōllū'tĕr*, s. profanateur, m.

pollution, *pōllū'shŭn*, s. pollution, f. ‖ souillure, f.

poltroon, *pŏltrōn'*, s. poltron, lâche, m.

polygamist, *pŏlĭg'ămĭst*, s. polygame, m.

polygamy, *pŏlĭg'ămĭ*, s. polygamie, f.

polyglot, *pŏl'ĭglŏt*, s. polyglotte, f.

polyglot, *pŏl'ĭglŏt*, a. polyglotte.

polygon, *pŏl'ĭgŏn*, s. polygone, m.

polygonal, *pŏlĭg'ōnăl*, a. polygone.

polypus, *pŏl'ĭpŭs*, s. polype, m.

polysyllabic, *pŏlĭsĭllăb'ĭk*, a. polysyllabe.   [nique.

polytechnic, *pŏlĭtĕk'nĭk*, a. polytechnique.

polytheist, *pŏl'ĭthĕĭst*, s. polythéiste, m.

pomade, *pōmăd'*, s. pommade, f.

pomegranate, *pŏm'grănăt*, s. grenade, f. ‖ grenadier, m.

pommel, *pŭm'mĕl*, s. pommeau, m.

pommel, *pŭm'mĕl*, v. a. rosser, frotter.

pomp, *pŏmp*, s. pompe, f., éclat, m.

pompion, *pŏm'pĭŏn*, s. citrouille, f.

pomposity, *pŏmpŏs'ĭtĭ*, s. ostentation, f. ‖ emphase, f.

pompous, *pŏm'pŭs*, a. pompeux ‖ -ly, ad. pompeusement.   [mare, f.

pond, *pŏnd*, s. étang, m. ‖ vivier, m.

ponder, *pŏnd'ĕr*, v. a. & n. peser ‖ méditer.

ponderable, *pŏn'dĕrăbl*, a. pondérable.

ponderingly, *pŏn'dĕrĭnglĭ*, ad. réfléchi.

ponderous, *pŏn'dĕrŭs*, a. pesant ‖ -ly, ad. pesamment.

poniard, *pŏn'yărd*, s. poignard, m.

poniard, *pŏn'yărd*, v. a. poignarder.

pontiff, *pŏn'tĭf*, s. pontife, m.

pontifical, *pŏntĭf'ĭkăl*, a. (-ly, ad.) pontifical(ment).

pontificals, *pŏntĭf'ĭkăls*, s. pl. habits pontificaux, m. pl.

pontificate, *pŏntĭf'ĭkăt*, s. pontificat, m.

pontoon, *pŏntōn'*, s. ponton, m.

pony, *pō'nĭ*, s. poney, m. ‖ (fam.) 25 guinées, f. pl.

poodle, *pō'dl*, s. caniche, f.   [f. pl.

pooh! *pō*, bah! ‖ ~~~! chansons que tout cela! fariboles!   [moquer de.

pooh-pooh, *pō'pō'*, v. a. mépriser, se

pool, *pōl*, s. étang, m. ‖ mare, f. ‖ poule (au billard), f.

poop, *pōp*, s. poupe, f.

poor, *pór*, a. (**-ly**, ad.) pauvre(ment) ‖ chétif ‖ mauvais ‖ mal ‖ **~-box**, s. tronc des pauvres, m. ‖ **~-laws**, s. loi sur l'assistance publique, f. ‖ **~-rate**, s. impôt pour les pauvres, m. [rité, f., refuge, m.

poorhouse, *pór'hóˇes*, s. maison de charité, f. [sesse, f.

poorly, *pór'lï*, a. indisposé.

poorness, *pór'nés*, s. pauvreté, f. ‖ bassesse, f.

pop, *póp*, s. petit coup, m. ‖ **~-gun**, s. canonnière, f. (jouet)

pop, *póp*, v. a. & n. lâcher soudainement, laisser échapper ‖ tirer ‖ survenir ‖ partir ‖ sauter. [qui part]

pop! *póp*, crac! ‖ **~ goes . . . !** voilà . . .

Pope, *póp*, s. pape, m.

Popedom, *póp'dóm*, s. papauté, f.

popery, *pó'pérï*, s. papisme, m. [m.

popinjay, *póp'ïnjâ*, s. papegai, m. ‖ fat, **popish**, *pó'pïsh*, a. (**-ly**, ad.) (en) papiste.

poplar, *póp'lár*, s. peuplier, m.

poplin, *póp'lïn*, s. popeline, f.

poppy, *póp'pï*, s. pavot, m.

populace, *póp'üläs*, s. populace, f.

popular, *póp'ülér*, a. (**-ly**, ad.) populaire (ment).

popularise, *póp'ülär ïz*, v. a. populariser.

popularity, *póp ü lár'ï tï*, s. popularité, f.

populate, *póp'ü lät*, v. a. peupler.

population, *póp ü lä'shün*, s. population, f.

populous, *póp'ü lüs*, a. populeux.

populousness, *póp'ü lüs nés*, s. populosité, f.

porcelain, *pórs'län*, s. porcelaine, f.

porch, *pórch*, s. porche, portique, m.

porcine, *pór'sïn*, a. porcin.

porcupine, *pór'kü pïn*, s. porc-épic, m.

pore, *pór*, s. pore, m.

pore, *pór*, v. n. avoir les yeux fixés (sur) ‖ **to ~ over**, (fig.) dévorer.

pork, *pórk*, s. chair de cochon, f. ‖ **~-butcher**, s. charcutier, m. ‖ **~-chop**, s. côtelette de porc, f.

porker, *pórk'ér*, s. cochon, m.

porosity, *pó rós'ï tï*, s. porosité, f.

porous, *pór'üs*, a. poreux.

porphyry, *pór'fïr ï*, s. porphyre, m.

porpoise, *pór'püs*, s. marsouin, m.

porridge, *pór'rïj*, s. potage, m., soupe, f.

porringer, *pór'rïn jér*, s. écuelle, f.

port, *pórt*, s. port, m. ‖ sabord, m. ‖ vin d'Oporto, m. ‖ **~-fire**, s. fusée, f. ‖ **~-hole**, s. (mar.) sabord, m. ‖ **~-watch**, s. (mar.) garde-port, m.

portable, *pór'tä bl*, a. portatif.

portal, *pór'täl*, s. portail, m., porte, f.

portcullis, *pórt kül'lis*, s. herse, f. ‖ **-ed**, a. à herse.

portend, *pór ténd'*, v. a. présager.

portent, *pór'tént*, s. mauvais augure, m.

portentous, *pór tén'tüs*, a. de mauvais augure ‖ effroyable.

porter, *pór'tér*, s. portier, m. ‖ porteur, portefaix, m. ‖ facteur, m. ‖ garçon, m. ‖ porter, m., bière brune, f.

porterage, *pór'tér äj*, s. frais de transport, m. pl.

porteress, *pór'tér és*, s. femme du concierge, f., (fam.) Madame Pipelet.

portfolio, *pórt fō'lïō*, s. portefeuille, m.

portico, *pór'tï kō*, s. portique, m.

portion, *pór'shün*, s. portion, part, partie, f. ‖ dot, m.

portion, *pór'shün*, v. a. partager ‖ doter.

portionless, *pór'shün lés*, a. sans dot.

portliness, *pórt'lï nés*, s. port majestueux, m., prestance, f.

portly, *pórt'lï*, a. d'un maintien noble.

portmanteau, *pórt män'tō*, s. portmanteau, m.

portrait(ure), *pór'trät(ür)*, s. portrait, m. ‖ **~-painter**, s. peintre de portraits, portraituriste, m.

portray, *pór trä'*, v. a. faire le portrait de.

portrayer, *pór trä'ér*, s. peintre, m.

portress, *pór'trés*, s. portière, f.

pose, *póz*, v. a. embarrasser ‖ interroger.

poser, *pó'zér*, s. examinateur, m. ‖ question embarrassante, f.

position, *pó zish'ün*, s. position, situation, f. ‖ thèse, f. ‖ **in a ~ to**, à même de.

positive, *pó'zï tïv*, s. positif, m.

positive, *pó'zï tïv*, a. (**-ly**, ad.) positif ‖ certain(ement) ‖ absolu(ment) ‖ positivement. [ton décisif, entêtement, m.

positiveness, *pó'zï tïv nés*, s. réalité, f.,

posse, *pós'sé*, s. la force armée.

possess, *póz zés'*, v. a. posséder, jouir de.

possession, *póz zésh'ün*, s. possession, f. ‖ **~ is nine points of the law**, possession vaut titre.

possessive, *póz zés'sïv*, a. (gr.) possessif.

possessor, *póz zés'sér*, s. possesseur, m.

possibility, *pós sï bil'ï tï*, s. possibilité, f. ‖ moyen, m.

possible, *pós'sï bl*, a. possible.

possibly, *pós'sï blï*, ad. peut-être.

post, *póst*, s. poste, f. ‖ courrier, m. ‖ poste, emploi, m. ‖ poteau, m. ‖ pilier, m. ‖ **starting ~**, poteau de départ, m. (dans les courses) ‖ **winning ~**, poteau d'arrivée, m. (dans les courses) ‖ **by return of ~**, par le retour du courrier ‖ **~-boy**, s. postillon, m. ‖ **~-captain**, s. capitaine de vaisseau, m. ‖ **~-card**, s. carte postale, f. ‖ **~-haste**, ad. promptement, en grande diligence ‖ **~-mark**, s. timbre, m. ‖ **~-master**, s. directeur des postes, m. ‖ **~-office**, s. bureau de poste, m. ‖ (**on letters**) poste restante ‖ **~-office directory**, s. almanach des adresses, m. ‖ **~-office order**, s. mandat sur la poste, m. ‖ **~-paid**, a. affranchi ‖ **~-stage**, s. relais de poste, m.

post, *póst*, v. a. & n. jeter à la poste ‖ afficher ‖ placer ‖ porter au grand livre ‖ aller, voyager en poste, courir la poste.

postage, *pós'täj*, s. port de lettre, m. ‖ **~-stamp**, s. timbre-poste, m.

postdate, *póst dät'*, v. a. postdater.

poster, *póst'ér*, s. affiche, f.

posterior, *pós tē'rï ér*, a. postérieur.

posteriority, *pós tē rï ór'ï tï*, s. postériorité, f.

posterity, *pŏs'tēr'ĭtĭ,* s. postérité, f.

postern, *pŏst'ĕrn* ou *pŏs'tĕrn,* s. poterne, f.

posthumous, *pŏst'ūmŭs,* a. posthume.

postilion, *pŏs til'yŭn,* s. postillon, m.

postman, *pŏst'măn,* s. facteur, m.

postpone, *pŏst pōn',* v. a. remettre, différer || estimer moins.   [ment, m.

postponement, *pŏst pōn'mĕnt,* s. ajourne-

postscript, *pŏst'skrīpt,* s. postscriptum, m. || apostille, f.

postulant, *pŏs'tŭlănt,* s. postulant, m.

postulate, *pŏs'tŭlāt,* s. (math.) postulat, m.   [pose, f.

posture, *pŏs'tūr,* s. posture, situation, f. ||

posy, *pō'zĭ,* s. bouquet, m. || devise, f.

pot, *pŏt,* s. pot, m. || ~-bellied, a. ventru, pansu || ~-boy, s. garçon de cabaret, m. || ~-hanger, s. crémaillère, f. || griffonnage, m. || ~-herb, s. herbe potagère, f. || ~-house, s. cabaret, m. || to take ~-luck, courir la fortune du pot.

pot, *pŏt,* v. a. mettre en pot, conserver.

potable, *pō'tăbl,* a. buvable.

potash, *pŏt'ăsh,* potasse, f.   [tions, f. pl.

potation, *pō tā'shŭn,* s. boisson, f. || liba-

potato, *pō tā'tō,* s. patate, pomme de terre, f.

potency, *pō'tĕnsĭ,* s. puissance, force, f.

potent, *pō'tĕnt,* a. puissant, fort.

potentate, *pō'tĕntāt,* s. potentat, m.

potential, *pō tĕn'shăl,* a. (-ly, ad.) virtuel(lement).

pother, *pŏth'ĕr* s. bruit, fracas, m.

potion, *pō'shŭn,* s. breuvage (médicinal), m.

potter, *pŏt'tĕr,* s. potier, m. || ~'s ware, s. poterie, f.

pottery, *pŏt'tĕrĭ,* s. poterie, f.

pouch, *pŏwch,* s. poche, pochette, f.

poulterer, *pōl'tĕr ĕr,* s. poulailler, m.

poultice, *pōl'tĭs,* a. cataplasme, m.

poultry, *pōl'trĭ,* s. volaille, f. || ~-yard, s. basse-cour, f.

pounce, *pŏwns,* s. poudre de pierre de ponce, f. || ~-box, s. poudrier, m.

pounce, *pŏwns,* v. a. poncer || to ~ upon, fondre sur.

pound, *pŏwnd,* s. livre (½ kilogramme), f. || livre sterling, f. || fourrière, f.

pound, *pŏwnd,* v. a. piler, broyer.

pounder, *pŏwnd'ĕr,* s. pilon, m. || billet de ... livres sterling, m. || canon d'un certain calibre, m.

pour, *pōr,* v. a. & n. verser, épancher || pleuvoir à verse || couler rapidement || se précipiter avec violence.

pout, *pŏwt,* v. n. bouder.

poverty, *pŏv'ĕrtĭ,* s. pauvreté, f. || ~-stricken, a. tombé dans l'indigence.

powder, *pŏw'dĕr,* s. poutre, f. || ~-cart, s. caisson, m. || ~-chest, s. caisse d'artifices, f. || ~-flask, ~-horn, s. poire à poudre, f. || ~-mill, s. poudrière, f. || ~-monkey, s. (mil.) valet d'artillerie, m. || (mar.) mousse, m.

powder, *pŏw'dĕr,* v. a. pulvériser, poudrer, saupoudrer.

powdering-tub, *pŏw'dĕr ĭng tŭb,* s. sa-

powdery, *pŏw'dĕrĭ,* a. poudreux, friable.

power, *pŏw'ĕr,* s. pouvoir, m., puissance, faculté, force, f. || force militaire, f. || autorité, f. || to put it out of one's ~ to mettre qn. dans l'impossibilité de.

powerful, *pŏw'ĕrfōōl,* a. puissant || -ly, ad. puissamment.   [sance, f.

powerfulness, *pŏw'ĕr fōōl nĕs,* s. puis-

powerless, *pŏw'ĕr lĕs,* a. impuissant.

powerlessness, *pŏw'ĕr lĕs nĕs,* s. impuissance, f.

pox, *pŏks,* s. vérole, f. || small ~, petite vérole, f. || chicken-~, varicelle, petite vérole volante, f. || cow-~, vaccine, f.

practicability, *prăk tĭ kă bĭl'ĭ tĭ,* s. praticabilité, f.

practicable, *prăk'tĭ kăbl,* a. praticable, faisable.   [manière praticable.

practicably, *prăk'tĭ kă blĭ,* ad. d'une

practical, *prăk'tĭ kăl,* a. (-ly, ad.) (en) pratique.

practice, *prăk'tĭs,* s. pratique, habileté, expérience, f. || coutume, f. || méthode, f. || intrigue, f., artifice, m.

practise, *prăk'tĭs,* v. a. (& n.) pratiquer || (s')exercer.   [m.

practitioner, *prăk tĭsh'ŭn ĕr,* s. praticien.

pragmatic, *prăg măt'ĭk,* a. importun || pragmatique || -ally, ad. impertinemment.

prairie, *prā'rĭ,* s. prairie, f. || ~-dog, s. marmotte des prairies, f.

praise, *prāz,* s. louange, f., éloge, m.

praise, *prāz,* v. a. louer || célébrer.

praiser, *prāz'ĕr,* s. louangeur, m.

praiseworthy, *prāz'wĕr thĭ,* a. louable.

prance, *prăns,* v. a. bondir || piaffer || se pavaner.

prank, *prăngk,* s. folie, f. || farce, f., tour, m.

prate, *prāt,* v. n. caqueter.   [m.

prattle, *prăt'tl,* s. babil, m.

prattle, *prăt'tl,* v. n. babiller, jaser.

prattler, *prăt'lĕr,* s. babillard, m.

prawn, *prăwn,* s. crevette, f.

pray, *prā,* v. a. & n. prier || (jur.) demander.

prayer, *prā'ĕr,* s. prière, f. || demande, f. || Lord's ~, oraison dominicale, f. || ~-book, s. livre de prières, m.

prayerful, *prā'ĕr fōōl,* a. dévot.

preach, *prēch,* v. a. & n. prêcher || to ~ down, dénigrer || to ~ up, prôner.

preacher, *prēch'ĕr,* s. prédicateur, m. || prêcheur, m.

preaching, *prēch'ĭng,* s. prédication, f.

preamble, *prēăm'bl,* s. préambule, m.

prebendary, *prĕb'ĕn dĕr ĭ,* s. prébendier, m.   [précaire(ment).

precarious, *prĕ kā'rĭ ŭs,* a. (-ly, ad.)

precariousness, *prĕ kā'rĭ ŭs nĕs,* s. état précaire, m.

precaution, *prĕ kăw'shŭn,* s. précaution, f.

precautionary, *prĕ kăw'shŭn ĕr ĭ,* a. précautionnel.

precede, *prĕ sēd',* v. a. précéder, devancer.

precedence, *prĕ sē'dĕns,* s. préséance, f. || supériorité, f.

precedent, *prĕ sē'dĕnt,* s. précédent, m.

---

preceding, *prē sēd'ǐng*, a. précédent.
precentor, *prē sěn'tẽr*, s. maître de cha-
pelle, m. || chantre, m.
precept, *prē'sěpt*, s. précepte, m.
preceptor, *prē sěp'tẽr*, s. précepteur, m.
preceptress, *prē sěp'très*, s. maîtresse,
institutrice, f.
precinct, *prē'sǐngt*, s. borne, limite, f.
precious, *prěsh'ǔs*, a. précieux || (fam.)
fier, fameux || —ly, ad. précieusement
preciousness, *prěsh'ǔs něs*, s. prix, m.,
valeur, f.
precipice, *prěs'ǐ pǐs*, s. précipice, m.
precipitancy, *prē sǐp'ǐ tăn sǐ*, s. précipitation.   [cipitamment.
precipitantly, *prē sǐp'ǐ tănt lǐ*, ad. pré-
precipitate, *prē sǐp'ǐ tāt*, s. (chem.) précipité, m.   [piter.
precipitate, *prē sǐp'ǐ tāt*, v. a. & n. préci-
precipitate, *prē sǐp'ǐ tāt*, a. précipité ||
—ly, ad. avec précipitation.
precipitation, *prē sǐp ǐ tā'shǔn*, s. préci-
pitation, f.   [rapide || escarpé.
precipitous, *prē sǐp'ǐ tǔs*, a. précipité,
precise, *prē sīs'*, a. précis, exact || céré-
monieux || scrupuleux || —ly, ad. précisé-
ment, exactement || scrupuleusement.
preciseness, *prē sīs'něs*, s. précision, f. ||
air emprunté, m.
precisian, *prē sǐzh'ǎn*, s. rigoriste, m.
precisianism, *prē sǐzh'ǎn ǐsm*, s. rigo-
risme, m.
precision, *prē sǐzh'ǔn*, s. précision, f.
preclude, *prē klōd'*, v. a. exclure || em-
pêcher.
precocious, *prē kō'shǔs*, a. précoce.
precocity, *prē kǒs'ǐ tǐ*, s. précocité, f.
preconceive, *prē kǒn sēv'*, v. a. concevoir
d'avance.
preconception, *prē kǒn sěp'shǔn*, s. pré-
jugé, m.   [d'avance.
preconcert, *prē kǒn sẽrt'*, v. a. concerter
precursor, *prē kẽr'sẽr*, s. avant-coureur, m.
predatory, *prěd'ā tẽr ǐ*, a. rapace || de
rapine.   [seur, devancier, m.
predecessor, *prē dē sěs'sẽr*, s. prédéces-
predestinate, *prē děs'tǐ nāt*, predestine,
prē děs'tǐn, v. a. prédestiner.
predestination, *prē děs tǐ nā'shǔn*, s. pré-
destination, f.
predicament, *prē dǐk'ā měnt*, s. catégorie,
f. || position, f. || état, m. || cas, m.
predicate, *prěd'ǐ kāt*, s. prédicat, m. || at-
tribut, m.
predicate, *prěd'ǐ kāt*, v a. affirmer.
predict, *prē dǐkt'*, v. a. prédire.
prediction, *prē dǐk'shǔn*, s. prédiction, f.
predilection, *prē dǐ lěk'shǔn*, s. prédilection, partialité, f.   [d'avance.
predispose, *prē dǐs pōz'*, v. a. disposer
predisposition, *prē dǐs pō zǐsh'ǔn*, s. pré-
disposition, f.
predominance, *prē dǒm'ǐ năns*, s. ascen-
dant, m. || (méd.) prédomination, f.
predominant, *prē dǒm'ǐ nănt*, a. préva-
lant.   [dominer.
predominate, *prē dǒm'ǐ nāt*, v. n. pré-

preeminence, *prē ěm'ǐ něns*, s. prééminence, f.
preeminent, *prē ěm'ǐ něnt*, a. prééminent.
preemption, *prē ěm'shǔn*, s. préemption, f.
preengagement, *prē ěn găj'měnt*, s. engagement antérieur, m.
preexamination, *prē ěgz ǎm ǐ nā'shǔn*, s.
examen préalable, m.
preexistence, *prē ěgz ǐst'ěns*, s. préexis-
tence, f.
preface, *prěf'ās*, s. préface, f.
preface, *prěf'ās*, v. a. faire une préface à.
prefatory, *prěf'ā tẽr ǐ*, a. préliminaire.
prefect, *prē'fäkt*, s. préfet, m.
prefecture, *prē'fěk tūr*, s. préfecture, f.
prefer, *prē fẽr'*, v. a. préférer || élever ||
présenter.
preferable, *prěf'ẽr ā bl*, a. préférable.
preferably, *prěf'ẽr ā blǐ*, ad. de préférence.
preference, *prěf'ẽr ěns*, s. préférence, f. ||
~-shares, s. pl. actions privilégiées,
f. pl., le capital-obligations || ~-share-
holder, s. porteur d'actions privilégiées,
m.   [m., promotion, f.
preferment, *prē fẽr'měnt*, s. avancement,
prefix, *prē'fǐks*, s. préfixe, m.
prefix, *prē fǐks'*, v. a. fixer d'avance.
pregnancy, *prěg'nǎn sǐ*, s. grossesse || fer-
tilité, f.
pregnant, *prěg'nănt*, a. enceinte || fertile.
prehensile, *prē hěn'sǐl*, a. (of tails) pre-
nante, préhensile.   [torique.
prehistoric, *prē hǐs tǒr'ǐk*, a. préhis-
prejudge, *prē jǔj'*, v. a. préjuger.
prejudice, *prěj'ōō dǐs*, s. préjugé, m. ||
tort, dommage, m.
prejudice, *prěj'ōō dǐs*, v. a. préoccuper ||
préjudicier.   [ciable.
prejudicial, *prěj ōō dǐsh'ăl*, a. préjudi-
prelacy, *prěl'ā sǐ*, s. prélature, f.
prelate, *prěl'āt*, s. prélat, m.   [naire.
preliminary, *prē lǐm'ǐ něr ǐ*, a. prélimi-
prelude, *prěl'ūd* ou *prē'lūd*, s. prélude, m.
prelude, *prē lūd'*, v. a. préluder.
premature, *prē mā tūr'*, a. (-ly, ad.) pré-
maturé(ment).
prematureness, *prē mā tūr'něs*, s. prématurité, f.   [méditer.
premeditate, *prē měd'ǐ tāt*, v. a. pré-
premeditation, *prē měd ǐ tā'shǔn*, s. préméditation, f.   [m.
premier, *prěm'ǐ ẽr*, s. premier ministre,
premise, *prē mīz'*, v. a. expliquer d'avance.
premises, *prěm'ǐ sěz*, s. pl. prémisses,
f. pl. || (jur.) biens, m. pl.
premium, *prē'mǐ ǔm*, s. prime, f. || récom-
pense, f. || pot-de-vin, m. || at a ~, à prime ||
en prime.
premonition, *prē mǒ nǐsh'ǔn*, s. avertissement préliminaire, m.
premonitory, *prē mǒn'ǐ tẽr ǐ*, a. prémoni-
toire, qui avertit d'avance.
preoccupation, *prē ǒk kū pā'shǔn*, s. oc-
cupation antérieure, f. || prévention, f.
preoccupy, *prē ǒk'kū pǐ*, v. a. préoccuper.
preordain, *prē ǒr dān'*, v. a. ordonner
d'avance.

prepaid, *prē'pād'*, a. payé d'avance || franc de port || ~, ad. franco.   [tion, f.

preparation, *prĕp ă rā'shŭn,* s. prépara-

preparatory, *prē păr' ă tĕr ĭ,* a. prépara-toire, préliminaire.

prepare, *prē pâr'*, v. a. & n. préparer, apprêter || se disposer.

prepay, *prē pā'*, v. a. affranchir.

prepayment, *prē pā' mĕnt,* s. affranchisse-ment, m.

preponderance, *prē pŏn' dĕr ăns,* s. su-périorité, prépondérance, f.   [pondérant.

preponderant, *prē pŏn' dĕr ănt,* a. pré-

preponderate, *prē pŏn' dĕr āt,* v. n. l'em-porter sur.

preposition, *prĕp ŏ zish'ŭn,* s. préposi-tion, f.   [préoccuper.

prepossess, *prē pŏz zĕs'*, v. a. prévenir,

prepossession, *prē pŏz zĕsh'ŭn,* s. pré-jugé, m.

preposterous, *prē pŏs' tĕr ŭs,* a. déplacé, absurde || -ly, ad. à contre-temps, ab-surdement.

prerogative, *prē rŏg' ă tĭv,* s. prérogative, f.

presage, *prĕs' āj,* s. présage, m.   [f.

presage, *prē āj'*, v. a. présager.

presbyterian, *prĕz bǐ tē' rĭ ăn,* a. presby-térien.   [m.

presbytery, *prĕz' bǐ tĕr ĭ,* s. presbytère, f.

prescience, *prē' shĭ ĕns,* s. prescience, f.

prescient, *prē' shĭ ĕnt,* a. doué de pre-science.

prescribe, *prē skrīb'*, v. a. & n. prescrire || ordonner || faire une ordonnance || faire la loi.

prescription, *prē skrĭp' shŭn,* s. (jur.) prescription, f. || ordonnance, f.

presence, *prĕz' ĕns,* s. présence, f. || as-semblée, f. || port, m. || ~-room, s. salon de réception, m.

present, *prĕz' ĕnt,* s. présent, m. || cadeau, m. || -s, pl. (jur.) présentes, f. pl.

present, *prē zĕnt'*, v. a. présenter, offrir || faire un présent || (Am.) accuser.

present, *prĕz' ĕnt,* a. présent || attentif || actif || courant || -ly, ad. à présent || tout à l'heure || bientôt.

presentable, *prē zĕnt' ă bl,* a. présentable.

presentation, *prĕz ĕn tā' shŭn,* s. présen-tation, f. || représentation, f. || ~-copy, s. exemplaire donné, m.   [sentiment, m.

presentiment, *prē sĕn' tĭ mĕnt,* s. pres-

presentment, *prē sĕnt' mĕnt,* s. représen-tation, f. || (Am.) renvoi devant la Cour d'assises, m.

preservation, *prĕs ĕr vā' shŭn,* s. conser-vation, f.   [m.

preservative, *prē zĕrv' ă tĭv,* s. préservatif.

preservative, *prē zĕrv' ă tĭv,* a. préservatif.

preserve, *prē zĕrv'*, s. fruits confits, m. pl. || -s, pl. réserve, f.

preserve, *prē zĕrv'*, v. a. préserver, con-server || confire.

preserver, *prē zĕrv' ĕr,* s. confiseur, m. || (things) préservateur, m. || -s, pl. con-serves (pour les yeux), f. pl.

preside, *prē zīd'*, v. n. présider.

presidency, *prĕz' ĭ dĕn sĭ,* s. présidence, f.

president, *prĕz' ĭ dĕnt,* s. président, chef, m.

press, *prĕs*, s. presse, f. || force, f. || armoire, f. || hand-~, presse à bras, f. || printing-~, presse typographique, f. || in the ~, sous presse, en voie d'impression || to go to ~, être à la veille d'être imprimé || ~-bed, s. lit en armoire, m. || ~-gang, s. (mar.) presse, f.

press, *prĕs*, v. a. & n. presser, serrer || con-traindre || pousser || (mar.) enrôler de force || presser || se presser, se précipiter, venir en foule || to ~ forward, pousser en avant || to ~ out, faire sortir en pressant, ex-primer.

pressing, *prĕs' ĭng,* a. pressant, urgent || -ly, ad. d'une manière pressante.

pressman, *prĕs' măn,* s. pressier, m. || pressureur, m. || journaliste, m.

pressure, *prĕsh' ōōr,* s. pression, impres-sion, f. || violence, f. || pressurage, m.

presumably, *prē zūm' ă blĭ,* ad. probable-ment.

presume, *prē zūm'*, v. a. présumer, sup-poser, s'imaginer, s'aventurer, se fier témérairement à.

presuming, *prē zūm' ĭng,* a. présomp-tueux.   [tion, f.

presumption, *prē zŭm' shŭn,* s. présomp-

presumptive, *prē zŭm' tĭv,* a. présomptif.

presumptuous, *prē zŭm' tū ŭs,* a. pré-somptueux ||-ly, ad. présomptueusement.

presuppose, *prē sŭp pōz'*, v. a. présup-poser.   [position préalable, f.

presupposition, *prē sŭp pŏ zish'ŭn,* s. sup-

pretence, *prē tĕns'*, s. prétention, f. || pré-texte, m.

pretend, *prē tĕnd'*, v. a. & n. prétendre || feindre.   [disant.

pretended, *prē tĕnd' ĕd,* a. prétendu, soi-

pretender, *prē tĕnd' ĕr,* s. prétendant, m.

pretendingly, *prē tĕnd' ĭng lĭ,* ad. avec suffisance.

pretension, *prē tĕn' shŭn,* s. prétention, f.

pretentious, *prē tĕn' shŭs,* a. prétentieux.

preterite, *prĕt' ĕr ĭt,* s. (gram.) parfait, m.

preternatural, *prē tĕr nā' ū răl,* a. sur-naturel || contre nature.

pretext, *prē' tĕkst,* s. prétexte, m.

prettily, *prĭt' tĭ lĭ,* ad. joliment || gentim-ment.   [gance, f.

prettiness, *prĭt' tĭ nĕs,* s. gentillesse, élé-

pretty, *prĭt' tĭ,* a. & ad. joli, gentil || assez.

prevail, *prē vāl'*, v. n. prévaloir, l'empor-ter sur.   [fluence, f.

prevalence, *prĕv' ă lĕns,* s. supériorité, in-

prevalent, *prĕv' ă lĕnt,* a. dominant, puis-sant.   [quer || tergiverser.

prevaricate, *prē văr' ĭ kāt,* v. n. prévari-

prevarication, *prē văr ĭ kā' shŭn,* s. pré-varication, f., subterfuge, m.

prevaricator, *prē văr' ĭ kā tĕr,* s. prévari-cateur, m.   [(de).

prevent, *prē vĕnt'*, v. a. prévenir || empêcher

prevention, *prē vĕn' shŭn,* s. empêche-ment, m.

preventive, *prĕ vĕnt'ĭv*, s. préservatif, m.
preventive, *prĕ vĕnt'ĭv*, a. préservatif.
previous, *prē'vĭ ŭs*, a. (-ly, ad.) préalable
prey, *prā*, s. proie, f. ‖ (ment) ‖ ~ to, avant.
prey, *prā*, v. n. dévorer, piller ‖ victimer ‖ ronger ‖ tourmenter.
price, *prīs*, s. prix, m., valeur, f. ‖ current ~, prix courant ‖ set ~, prix fixe ‖ at cost ~, au prix de revient ‖ to set a ~ on, mettre à prix ‖ high (low) -d, prix élevé, bas prix.
price, *prīs*, v. a. demander le prix de ‖ mettre un prix à. [ciable.
priceless, *prīs'lĕs*, a. sans prix ‖ inappréciable
prick, *prĭk*, s. pointe, f. ‖ piqûre, f. ‖ (of a hare) trace, f.
prick, *prĭk*, v. a. piquer, percer ‖ éperonner ‖ tourmenter ‖ (mus.) noter ‖ to ~ up (one's ears), dresser les oreilles ‖ chauvir des oreilles (se dit des chevaux).
pricker, *prĭk'ẽr*, s. pointe, alêne, f. ‖ (mil.) épinglette, f.
pricking, *prĭk'ĭng*, s. piqûre, f.
prickle, *prĭk'l*, s. piquant, m. [épineux.
prickly, *prĭk'lĭ*, a. plein de piquants
pride, *prīd*, s. orgueil, m. ‖ faste, m. ‖
pride, *prīd*, v. n. se glorifier. [fierté, f.
prier, *prī'ẽr*, s. curieux, espion, m.
priest, *prēst*, s. prêtre, m. ‖ ~-ridden, a. gouverné par les prêtres. [prêtres, f.
priestcraft, *prēst'krăft*, s. imposture des
priestess, *prēst'ĕs*, s. prêtresse, f.
priesthood, *prēst'hōōd*, s. prêtrise, f.
priestlike, *prēst'līk*, priestly, *prēst'lĭ*, a. de prêtre, sacerdotal.
prig, *prĭg*, s. fat, m.
prig, *prĭg*, v. a. (fam.) escamoter, voler.
priggish, *prĭg'gĭsh*, a. suffisant.
prim, *prĭm*, a. affecté, précieux.
primacy, *prī'mȧ sĭ*, s. primatie, f.
primarily, *prī'mẽr'ĭ lĭ*, ad. primitivement ‖ surtout. [principal.
primary, *prī'mẽrĭ*, a. primaire, primitif ‖
primate, *prī'mȧt*, s. primat, primat, m.
prime, *prīm*, s. point du jour, matin, m. ‖ élite, f. ‖ printemps, m. ‖ to be in one's ~, être dans la fleur de l'âge.
prime, *prīm*, v. a. & n. amorcer ‖ préparer.
prime, *prīm*, a. premier ‖ meilleur ‖ -ly, ad. primitivement ‖ excellemment ‖ at ~ cost, au prix coûtant.
primer, *prī'mẽr* ou *prĭm'ẽr*, s. syllabaire,
primeval, *prī mē'văl*, a. primitif. [f.
priming, *prīm'ĭng*, s. amorce, f. ‖ impression, f. [primitivement.
primitive, *prĭm'ĭ tĭv*, a. primitif ‖ -ly, ad.
primness, *prĭm'nĕs*, s. afféterie, f.
primogeniture, *prī mō jĕn'ĭ tūr*, s. primogéniture, f.
primrose, *prĭm'rōz*, s. primevère, f.
prince, *prĭns*, s. prince, souverain, m.
princely, *prĭns'lĭ*, a. & ad. de prince, en prince, en princesse.
princess, *prĭn'sĕs*, s. princesse, f.
principal, *prĭn'sĭ păl*, s. chef, m. ‖ directeur, m. ‖ capital, m. [cipal(ement).
principal, *prĭn'sĭ păl*, a. (-ly, ad.) prin-

principality, *prĭn sĭ păl'ĭ tĭ*, s. principauté, f. [m. ‖ motif, fondement, m.
principle, *prĭn'sĭ pl*, s. principe, élément,
print, *prĭnt*, s. empreinte, impression, estampe, f. ‖ imprimé, journal, m. ‖ out of ~, épuisé.
print, *prĭnt*, v. a. imprimer ‖ empreindre ‖ faire imprimer ‖ inculquer, graver.
printer, *prĭnt'ẽr*, s. imprimeur, m. ‖ ~'s reader, s. correcteur d'imprimerie, m.
printing, *prĭnt'ĭng*, s. imprimerie, f. ‖ impression, f. ‖ ~-house (~-office), s. imprimerie, f. ‖ ~-paper, s. papier d'impression, m.
prior, *prī'ŏr*, s. prieur, m.
prior, *prī'ŏr*, a. antérieur.
prioress, *prī'ŏr ĕs*, s. prieure, f.
priority, *prī ŏr'ĭ tĭ*, s. priorité, f.
priory, *prī'ŏrĭ*, s. prieuré, m.
prism, *prĭzm*, s. prisme, m.
prison, *prĭz'n*, s. prison, f.
prisoner, *prĭz'nẽr*, s. prisonnier, m.
pristine, *prĭs'tĭn*, a. primitif, ancien.
privacy, *prī'vȧ sĭ*, s. secret, m., retraite, solitude, f.
private, *prī'văt*, s. simple soldat, m.
private, *prī'văt*, a. privé, secret, retiré ‖ particulier ‖ domestique ‖ -ly, ad. en particulier ‖ en secret.
privateer, *prī vȧ tēr'*, s. corsaire, m.
privateer, *prī vȧ tēr'*, v. n. aller en course.
privation, *prī vā'shŭn*, s. privation, f.
privet, *prĭv'ĕt*, s. (bot.) troène, f.
privilege, *prĭv'ĭ lĕj*, s. privilège, m.
privilege, *prĭv'ĭ lĕj*, v. a. privilégier.
privily, *prĭv'ĭ lĭ*, ad. en secret.
privy, *prĭv'ĭ*, s. lieux, m. pl.
privy, *prĭv'ĭ*, a. privé, particulier ‖ secret ‖ instruit de.
prize, *prīz*, s. prix, m., récompense, f. ‖ capture, f. ‖ proie, f. ‖ lot, m. ‖ levier, m. ‖ (wind-fall) aubaine, f. ‖ ~-essay, s. ouvrage couronné, m. ‖ ~-fight, s. combat de boxeurs, m. ‖ ~-medal, s. médaille d'honneur, f. ‖ ~-money, s. part de prise, f.
prize, *prīz*, v. a. évaluer, faire cas de ‖ to ~ open, forcer, briser, enfoncer.
prizeman, *prīz'măn*, s. lauréat, m.
pro, *prō*, pr. pour ‖ ~ and con, pour et contre. [f.
probability, *prŏb ȧ bĭl'ĭ tĭ*, s. probabilité,
probable, *prŏb'ȧ bl*, a. probable.
probably, *prŏb'ȧ blĭ*, ad. probablement.
probate, *prō'băt*, s. (jur.) vérification, f.
probation, *prō bā'shŭn*, s. probation, épreuve, f. ‖ noviciat, m. [toire.
probationary, *prō bā'shŭn ẽr ĭ*, a. probaprobationer, *prō bā'shŭn ẽr*, s. candidat,
probe, *prōb*, s. sonde, f. [m.
probe, *prōb*, v. a. sonder.
probity, *prō'bĭ tĭ* ou *prŏb'ĭ tĭ*, s. probité, f.
problem, *prŏb'lĕm*, s. problème, m.
problematical, *prŏb lē măt'ĭk ȧl*, a. (-ly, ad.) problématique(ment).
proboscis, *prō bŏs'sĭs*, s. trompe, f.
procedure, *prō sēd'ūr*, s. procédé, m. ‖ procédure, f.

proceed, *prō sēd'*, v. n. procéder ‖ provenir, poursuivre ‖ continuer ‖ to ~ against one, (jur.) poursuivre qn. en justice.

proceeding, *prō sēd' ing*, s. procédé, m. ‖ procédure, f.   [m.

proceeds, *prō' sēdz*, s. pl. produit, revenu,

process, *prō' sĕs* ou *prŏs' ĕs*, s. progrès, cours, m. ‖ suite, f., procédé, m. ‖ procès, m.

procession, *prō sĕsh' ŭn*, s. procession, f. ‖ cortège, m.   [clarer.

proclaim, *prō klām'*, v. a. proclamer, dé-

proclamation, *prŏk lā mā' shŭn*, s. proclamation, f., édit, m.

proconsul, *prō kŏn' sŭl*, s. proconsul, m.

procrastinate, *prō krăs' tin āt*, v. a. & n. différer, retarder ‖ temporiser.

procrastination, *prō krăs tin ā' shŭn*, s. remise, f., ajournement, m.   [duire.

procreate, *prō' krē āt*, v. a. procréer, pro-

procreation, *prō krē ā' shŭn*, s. procréation, production, f.

proctor, *prŏk' tĕr*, s. avoué, m. ‖ censeur,

proctorship, *prŏk' tĕr ship*, s. fonctions de censeur, f. pl.   [curer.

procurable, *prō kū' rā bl*, a. facile à pro-

procuration, *prŏk ū rā' shŭn*, s. procuration, f.   [reur, m.

procurator, *prŏk' ū rā tĕr*, s. (jur.) procu-

procure, *prō kūr'*, v. a. procurer ‖ causer.

procurement, *prō kūr' mĕnt*, s. entremise, f.   [maquereau, m.

procurer, *prō kūr' ĕr*, s. entremetteur,

prodigal, *prŏd' i găl*, s. prodigue, m.

prodigal, *prŏd' i găl*, a. (-ly, ad.) (en) prodigue.   [f.

prodigality, *prŏd i găl' i tĭ*, s. prodigalité,

prodigious, *prō dĭj' ŭs*, a. prodigieux ‖ -ly, ad. prodigieusement.

prodigy, *prŏd' i jĭ*, s. prodige, m.

produce, *prŏd' ūs*, s. produit, m.

produce, *prō dūs'*, v. a. produire ‖ exhiber.

producer, *prō dū' sĕr*, s. producteur, m.

product, *prŏd' ŭkt*, s. produit, m.

production, *prō dŭk' shŭn*, s. production, f. ‖ produit, m.

productive, *prō dŭk' tĭv*, a. productif ‖ to be ~ of, produire.

productiveness, *prō dŭk' tĭv nĕs*, s. nature productive, f.   [tion, f.

profanation, *prŏf ă nā' shŭn*, s. profana-

profane, *prō făn'*, v. a. profaner.

profane, *prō făn'*, a. (-ly, ad.) (en) profane.

profaneness, *prō făn' nĕs*, **profanity**, *'prō făn' i tĭ*, s. impiété, f.

profaner, *prō făn' ĕr*, s. profanateur, m.

profess, *prō fĕs'*, v. a. professer, faire profession de ‖ se piquer de ‖ to ~ oneself, se dire.   [ment, publiquement.

professedly, *prō fĕs' sĕd lĭ*, ad. ouverte-

profession, *prō fĕsh' ŭn*, s. profession, f., métier, emploi, m. ‖ by ~, de profession ‖ to make ~s, faire profession (de).

professional, *prō fĕsh' ŭn ăl*, a. (-ly, ad.) professionel(lement).

professor, *prō fĕs' sĕr*, s. professeur, m.

professorship, *prō fĕs' ĕr ship*, s. professorat, m.

proffer, *prŏf' fĕr*, s. offre, proposition, f.

proffer, *prŏf' fĕr*, v. a. proposer, offrir.

proficience, *prō fĭsh' ĕns*, s. progrès, m.

proficient, *prō fĭsh' ĕnt*, a. avancé, fort ‖ habile.

profile, *prō' fĕl*, s. profil, m.

profit, *prŏf' ĭt*, s. profit, gain, avantage, m. ‖ produit, revenu, m. ‖ bénéfice, m.

profit, *prŏf' ĭt*, v. a. & n. profiter ‖ faire des progrès ‖ être utile.   [tageux.

profitable, *prŏf' ĭt ă bl*, a. profitable, avan-

profitableness, *prŏf' ĭt ă bl nĕs*, s. utilité, f.

profitably, *prŏf' ĭt ă blĭ*, ad. avantageusement.

profitless, *prŏf' ĭt lĕs*, a. sans profit.

profligacy, *prŏf' lĭ gă sĭ*, s. scélératesse, f.

profligate, *prŏf' lĭ găt*, s. débauché, m.

profligate, *prŏf' lĭ găt*, a. débauché ‖ -ly, ad. sans honte, en infâme.

profound, *prō fŏwnd'*, a. (-ly, ad.) profond(ément).

profundity, *prō fŭnd' ĭ tĭ*, s. profondeur, f.

profuse, *prō fūs'*, a. prodigue ‖ abondant ‖ -ly, ad. profusément.   [abondance, f.

profusion, *prō fū' zhŭn*, s. prodigalité, f. ‖

progeny, *prŏj' ĕ nĭ*, s. descendants, m. pl.

prognosis, *prŏg nō' sĭs*, s. (méd.) prognose, f., pronostic, m.

prognostic, *prŏg nŏs' tĭk*, s. pronostic, m.

prognosticate, *prŏg nŏs' tĭ kāt*, v. a. prognostiquer, prédire.

prognostication, *prŏg nŏs tĭ kā' shŭn*, s. pronostic, présage, m.

programme, *prō' grăm*, s. programme, m.

progress, *prō' grĕs* ou *prŏg' rĕs*, s. progrès, m. ‖ cours, m. ‖ voyage, m.

progress, *prō grĕs'*, v. n. faire des progrès.

progression, *prō grĕsh' ŭn*, s. progression, f. ‖ -ly, ad. par degrés.

progressive, *prō grĕs' sĭv*, a. progressif ‖

progressiveness, *prō grĕs' sĭv nĕs*, s. marche progressive, f.   [fendre.

prohibit, *prō hĭb' ĭt*, v. a. prohiber ‖ dé-

prohibition, *prō hĭ bĭsh' ŭn*, s. prohibition, défense, f.

prohibitory, *prō hĭb' ĭ tĕr ĭ*, a. prohibitif.

project, *prŏj' ĕkt*, s. projet, dessein, m.

project, *prō jĕkt'*, v. a. & n. projeter ‖ saillir.

projectile, *prō jĕk' tĭl*, s. projectile.

projecting, *prō jĕkt' ing*, a. saillant.

projection, *prō jĕk' shŭn*, s. projection, saillie, f.   [jets, m.

projector, *prō jĕkt' ĕr*, s. faiseur de pro-

proletarian, *prō lĕ tā' rĭ ăn*, **proletary**, *prŏl' ĕ tĕr ĭ*, s. prolétaire, m.

prolific, *prō lĭf' ĭk*, a. prolifique, fertile.

prolix, *prō' lĭks*, a. prolixe.

prolixity, *prō lĭks' ĭ tĭ*, s. prolixité, f.

prologue, *prō' lŏg*, s. prologue, m.

prolong, *prō lŏng'*, v. a. prolonger.

prolongation, *prō lŏng gā' shŭn*, s. prolongation, f., prolongement, m.   [f.

prominence, *prŏm' i nĕns*, s. proéminence, f.

prominent, *prŏm' i nĕnt*, a. proéminent ‖ -ly, ad. d'une manière saillante.

promiscuous, *prō mĭs' kū ŭs*, a. (-ly, ad.) mêlé ‖ confus(ément).

promise, *prŏm'ĭs*, s. promesse, f. || espé-
rances, f. pl. || **land of ~**, s. terre promise,
f. || **breach of ~**, s. violation de promesse,
f. || **of great ~**, qui promet beaucoup.

promise, *prŏm'ĭs*, v. a. & n. promettre.

promiser, *prŏm'ĭs ẽr*, s. prometteur, m.

promising, *prŏm'ĭs ĭng*, a. qui promet
beaucoup, qui donne de grandes espérances.   [de promesse.

promissorily, *prŏm'ĭs sẽr ĭ lĭ*, ad. en forme

promissory, *prŏm'ĭs sẽr ĭ*, a. qui contient
une promesse || **~ note**, s. billet à ordre, m.

promontory, *prŏm'ŏn tẽr ĭ*, s. promon-
toire, m.   [cer || élever || encourager.

promote, *prŏ mōt'*, v. a. promouvoir, avan-

promoter, *prŏ mō'tẽr*, s. promoteur, m. ||
faiseur d'affaires, m.

promotion, *prŏ mō'shŭn*, s. promotion, f.,
encouragement, m.

prompt, *prŏmt*, v. a. souffler, suggérer ||
~-book, s. livre du souffleur, m.

prompt, *prŏmt*, a. (-ly, ad.) prompt(ement).

prompter, *prŏmpt'ẽr*, s. souffleur, m.

promptitude, *prŏmt'ĭ tŭd*, **promptness**,
prŏmt'nĕs, s. promptitude, f.

promulgate, *prŏ mŭl'gāt*, v. a. promulguer, publier.   [mulgation, f.

promulgation, *prŏm ŭl gā'shŭn*, s. pro-

prone, *prōn*, a. penché || enclin || couché
le visage contre terre.

proneness, *prōn'nĕs*, s. pente, déclivité,
f. || inclination, f., penchant, m.

prong, *prŏng*, s. fourchon, m. || dent, f.

pronominal, *prŏ nŏm'ĭ năl*, a. pronominal.

pronoun, *prŏ'nŏwn*, s. pronom, m.

pronounce, *prŏ nŏwns'*, v. a. prononcer ||
déclarer.   [nonciation, f.

pronunciation, *prŏ nŭn sĭ ā'shŭn*, s. pro-

proof, *prŏf*, s. preuve, f. || épreuve, f. ||
essai, m.

proof, *prŏf*, a. à l'épreuve || impénétrable ||
to be ~ against, prouver contre.   [m.

prop, *prŏp*, s. appui, soutien, m. || échalas.

prop, *prŏp*, v. a. appuyer || échalasser.

propaganda, *prŏp ă gắn'dä*, s. propa-
gande, f.   [pager || répandre.

propagate, *prŏp'ă gāt*, v. a. & n. (se) pro-

propagation, *prŏp ă gā'shŭn*, s. propagation, f.   [m.

propagator, *prŏp'ă gā tẽr*, s. propagateur,

propel, *prŏ pĕl'*, v. a. pousser en avant ||
-ling-power, s. force motrice, f.

propeller, *prŏ pĕl'lẽr*, s. hélice propulsive,
f. || vapeur à hélice, m.

propensity, *prŏ pĕn'sĭ tĭ*, s. penchant, m.

proper, *prŏp'ẽr*, a. (-ly, ad.) propre(ment),
particulier || naturel, convenable(ment) ||
exact || **-ly speaking**, à la rigueur.

property, *prŏp'ẽr tĭ*, s. propriété, qualité,
f. || possession, f. || **landed ~**, fonds de
terre, domaines, m. pl.

prophecy, *prŏf'ĕ sĭ*, s. prophétie, f.

prophesy, *prŏf'ĕ sī*, v. a. & n. prophétiser.

prophet, *prŏf'ĕt*, s. prophète, m.

prophetess, *prŏf'ĕt ĕs*, s. prophétesse, f.

prophetic, *prŏ fĕt'ĭk*, a. (-ally, ad.) pro-
phétique(ment).

propinquity, *prŏ pĭng'kwĭ tĭ*, s. proximité,
f., voisinage, m.

propitiate, *prŏ pĭsh'ĭ āt*, v. a. rendre propice.   [pitiation, f.

propitiation, *prŏ pĭsh ĭ ā'shŭn*, s. pro-

propitiatory, *prŏ pĭsh'ĭ ā tẽr ĭ*, a. propitiatoire.   [ad. favorablement.

propitious, *prŏ pĭsh'ŭs*, a. propice || -ly,

proportion, *prŏ pōr'shŭn*, s. proportion,
f. || mesure, f. || **in ~ as**, à mesure que ||
in ~ to, en (à) proportion de || **in ~**, en,
à, par proportion.

proportion, *prŏ pōr'shŭn*, v. a. proportionner.

proportionable, *prŏ pōr'shŭn ă bl*, a. proportionné.   [tionnel.

proportional, *prŏ pōr'shŭn ăl*, a. propor-

proportionate, *prŏ pōr'shŭn āt*, a. pro-
portionné || -ly, ad. proportionnellement.

proposal, *prŏ pō'zăl*, s. proposition, offre, f.

propose, *prŏ pōz'*, v. a. proposer.

proposition, *prŏ pŏ zĭsh'ŭn*, s. proposition,
f. || offre, f.   [offrir.

propound, *prŏ pŏwnd'*, v. a. proposer,

proprietary, *prŏ prī'ĕ tẽr ĭ*, s. propriétaire,
m.   [priété.

proprietary, *prŏ prī'ĕ tẽr ĭ*, a. de pro-

proprietor, *prŏ prī'ĕ tẽr*, s. propriétaire,
prŏ prī'ĕ trĕs, s. propriétaire, m. & f.

propriety, *prŏ prī'ĕ tĭ*, s. convenance, f.,
décorum, m.

propulsion, *prŏ pŭl'shŭn*, s. propulsion, f.

pro rata, *prŏ rā'tä*, ad. au prorata de.

prorogation, *prŏ rŏ gā'shŭn*, s. prorogation, f.

prorogue, *prŏ rōg'*, v. a. proroger.

prosaic, *prŏ zā'ĭk*, a. prosaïque.   [f.

proscenium, *prŏ sē'nĭ ŭm*, s. avant-scène,

proscribe, *prŏ skrīb'*, v. a. proscrire.

proscription, *prŏ skrĭp'shŭn*, s. proscription, f.   [prosateur, m.

prose, *prōz*, s. prose, f. || **~-writer**, s.

prosecute, *prŏs'ĕ kūt*, v. a. poursuivre.

prosecution, *prŏs ĕ kū'shŭn*, s. poursuite ||
accusation, f.

prosecutor, *prŏs'ĕ kū tẽr*, s. plaignant, m.

prosecutrix, *prŏs'ĕ kū trĭx*, s. plaignante.

proselyte, *prŏs'ĕ līt*, s. proselyte, m.   [f.

prosody, *prŏs'ŏ dĭ*, s. prosodie, f.

prospect, *prŏs'pĕkt*, s. perspective, f. ||
vue, f., aspect, m. || **to have in ~**, faire
entrer en ligne de compte.

prospective, *prŏ spĕk'tĭv*, a. en perspec-
-tive || prévoyant || d'approche.

prospectus, *prŏ spĕk'tŭs*, s. prospectus, m.

prosper, *prŏs'pẽr*, v.a. & n. faire prospérer,
favoriser || prospérer, réussir.

prosperity, *prŏs pĕr'ĭ tĭ*, s. prospérité, f.

prosperous, *prŏs'pẽr ŭs*, a. prospère,
heureux || -ly, ad. heureusement.

prostitute, *prŏs'tĭ tūt*, s. prostituée, f.

prostitute, *prŏs'tĭ tūt*, v. a. prostituer.

prostitution, *prŏs tĭ tū'shŭn*, s. prostitution, f.

prostrate, *prŏs'trāt*, v. a. renverser,
abattre || **to ~ oneself**, se prosterner.

prostrate, *prŏs'trāt*, a. prosterné.

prostration, *prŏs trā' shŭn,* s. prosternation, f.

prosy, *prōz' ĭ,* a. terre à terre || ennuyeux.

protect, *prō tĕkt',* v. a. protéger, défendre || garantir. [tecteur.

protectingly, *prō tĕkt' ĭng lĭ,* ad. en pro-

protection, *prō tĕk' shŭn,* s. protection, défense, f.

protective, *prō tĕk' tĭv,* a. protecteur.

protector, *prō tĕkt' ẽr,* s. protecteur, m. || défenseur, m.

protest, *prō' tĕst,* s. protestation, f. || protêt, m. || **to enter a ~,** lever un protêt.

protest, *prō tĕst',* v. a. & n. protester, attester.

protestant, *prŏt' ĕs tănt,* s. protestant, m.

protestant, *prŏt' ĕs tănt,* a. protestant.

protestantism, *prŏt' ĕs tănt ĭsm,* s. protestantisme, m. [tion, f.

protestation, *prŏt ĕs tā' shŭn,* s. protesta-

protocol, *prō' tō kŏl,* s. protocole, m.

prototype, *prō' tō tĭp,* s. prototype, m.

protract, *prō trăkt',* v. a. différer, retarder || prolonger. [ff.

protraction, *prō trăk' shŭn,* s. prolongation,

protractor, *prō trăkt' ẽr,* s. rapporteur, m.

protrude, *prō trūd',* v. a. & n. pousser en avant || s'avancer.

protuberance, *prō tū' bẽr ăns,* s. protubérance, tumeur, f. [enflé.

protuberant, *prō tū' bẽr ănt,* a. proéminent ||

proud, *prŏwd,* a. orgueilleux, fier || pompeux ||(inéd.) fongueux ||-ly, ad. fièrement.

prove, *prōv,* v. a. & n. prouver, éprouver, essayer || réussir || devenir || se montrer || **not -n,** (jur.) déclaré non coupable (par les jurés).

provender, *prŏv' ĕn dẽr,* s. fourrage, m.

proverb, *prŏv' ẽrb,* s. proverbe, m.

proverbial, *prō vẽr' bĭ ăl,* a. (-ly, ad.) proverbial(ement).

provide, *prō vĭd',* v. a. & n. pourvoir, se pourvoir, se prémunir. [que.

provided, *prō vĭd' ĕd,* c. (~ that) pourvu

providence, *prŏv' ĭ dĕns,* s. providence, f. || prévoyance, f. || économie, f.

provident, *prŏv' ĭ dĕnt,* a. prévoyant || -ly, ad. avec prévoyance.

providential, *prŏv ĭ dĕn' shăl,* a. (-ly, ad.) providentiel(lement).

province, *prŏv' ĭns,* s. province, f. || emploi, m. || ressort, m.

provincial, *prō vĭn' shăl,* s. provincial, m.

provincial, *prō vĭn' shăl,* a. provincial.

provision, *prō vĭzh' ŭn,* s. provision, f., vivres, m. pl. || précaution, f., préparatif, m. || disposition, f. [slonner.

provision, *prō vĭzh' ŭn,* v. a. approvi-

provisional, *prō vĭzh' ŭn ăl,* a. (-ly, ad.) provisoire(ment).

proviso, *prō vī' zō,* s. clause, condition, f.

provisory, *prō vī' zẽr ĭ,* a. provisoire.

provocation, *prŏv ō kā' shŭn,* s. provocation, f. || défi, m.

provocative, *prō vŏk' ă tĭv,* a. provocateur.

provoke, *prō vŏk',* v. a. provoquer, exciter, irriter || défier.

provokingly, *prō vŏk' ĭng lĭ,* ad. d'une manière agaçante.

provost, *prŏv' ŏst,* s. prévôt, m. || recteur, m. [rectorat, m.

provostship, *prŏv' ŏst shĭp,* s. prévôté, f. ||

prow, *prŏw,* s. proue d'un vaisseau, f.

prowess, *prŏw' ĕs,* s. bravoure, f. || (in jest) prouesse, f.

prowl, *prŏwl,* v. n. rôder çà et là pour piller.

prowler, *prŏwl' ẽr,* s. pillard, m.

proximate, *prŏks' ĭ māt,* a. prochain, proche || -ly, ad. immédiatement.

proximity, *prŏks ĭm' ĭ tĭ,* s. proximité, f.

proxy, *prŏks' ĭ,* s. procuration, f. || fondé de pouvoirs, m.

prude, *prŏd,* s. prude, f.

prudence, *prō' dĕns,* s. prudence, f.

prudent, *prō' dĕnt,* a. prudent, prévoyant.

prudential, *prō dĕn' shăl,* a. dicté par la prudence.

prudery, *prŏd' ẽr ĭ,* s. pruderie, f.

prudish, *prŏd' ĭsh,* a. prude.

prune, *prŏn,* s. pruneau, m., prune, f.

prune, *prŏn,* v. a. émonder, élaguer.

prunello, *prō nĕl' lō,* s. prunelle, f.

pruning, *prŏn' ĭng,* s. serpe, f. || **~-hook, (~-knife),** s. serpe, f. || serpette, f. || **~-shears,** s. sécateur, m. [ff.

pruriency, *prō' rĭ ĕn sĭ,* s. démangeaison, f.

prurient, *prō' rĭ ĕnt,* a. prurigineux.

prussic acid, *prŭs' sĭk ăs' sĭd,* s. acide hydrocyanique, m.

pry, *prī,* v. n. épier, fouiller || se mêler de.

prying, *prī' ĭng,* a. curieux, indiscret.

psalm, *săm,* s. psaume, m.

psalter, *săwl' tẽr,* s. psautier, m.

pseudonym, *sū' dō nĭm,* s. pseudonyme, m.

psychological, *sī kō lŏg' ĭ kăl,* a. psychologique.

psychology, *sī kŏl' ō jĭ,* s. psychologie, f.

ptarmigan, *tär' mĭ gän,* s. gelinotte blanche, f.

puberty, *pū' bẽr tĭ,* s. puberté, f. [ff.

pubescent, *pū bĕs' ĕnt,* a. pubère.

public, *pŭb' lĭk,* s. public, m. || **~-house,** s. cabaret, m. [publiquement.

public, *pŭb' lĭk,* a. public || -ly, ad.

publican, *pŭb' lĭ kăn,* s. publicain, m. || cabaretier, m.

publication, *pŭb lĭ kā' shŭn,* s. publication, édition, f. || **~-price,** s. prix de librairie, prix ordinaire, m.

publicist, *pŭb' lĭs ĭst,* s. publiciste, m.

publicity, *pŭb lĭs' ĭ tĭ,* s. publicité, notoriété, f. [primer.

publish, *pŭb' lĭsh,* v. a. publier, faire im-

publisher, *pŭb' lĭsh ẽr,* s. éditeur, m. || libraire-éditeur, m.

puce, *pūs,* s. couleur de puce, f.

puck, *pŭk,* s. lutin, m.

pucker, *pŭk' ẽr,* s. ride, f. || pli, m.

pucker, *pŭk' ẽr,* v. a. rider, froncer || plisser.

pudding, *pŏŏd' ĭng,* s. pouding, m.

puddle, *pŭd' dl,* s. mare, f.

puddle, *pŭd' dl,* v. a. troubler, salir || puddler.

puddler, m.

puerile, *pū' ẽr ŭ,* a. enfantin.

puff, *pŭf*, s. bouffée, f. || souffle, m. || puff, pouf, m. || ~adder, s. vipère, f. || ~ball, s. vesse-de-loup, f. || ~paste, s. feuilleté, m., pâte feuilletée, f.

puff, *pŭf*, v. a. & n. souffler || lancer des bouffées de tabac || bouffir, enfler, boursoufler || faire mousser || faire la réclame.

puffiness, *pŭf'ĭ nĕs*, s. enflure, f.

puffy, *pŭf'ĭ*, a. bouffi, enflé || boursouflé.

pug, *pŭg*, s. petit singe, m. || petit chien, m. || petit enfant, m. || ~nose, s. nez épaté, m.

pugilism, *pū'jĭl ĭsm*, s. pugilat, m.

pugilist, *pū'jĭl ĭst*, s. boxeur, m.

pugnacious, *pŭg nā'shŭs*, a. querelleur.

puisne, *pū'ne*, a. cadet || inférieur.

pule, *pūl*, v. n. piauler, gémir.

puling, *pūl'ĭng*, s. gémissement, vagissement, m.

pull, *pŏŏl*, s. secousse, f. || lutte, f.

pull, *pŏŏl*, v. a. & n. tirer || arracher || cueillir || déchirer || ruiner || to ~ up, tirer en haut || s'arrêter (voitures).

pullback, *pŏŏl'băk*, s. obstacle, m.

pullet, *pŏŏl'lĕt*, s. poulette, poularde, f.

pulley, *pŏŏl'ĭ*, s. poulie, f. [luxe, f.

Pullmann-car, *pŏŏl'măn kâr*, s. voiture de

pulmonary, *pŭl'mŏn ĕr ĭ*, pulmonic, *pŭl mŏn'ĭk*, a. pulmonaire || phthisique.

pulp, *pŭlp*, s. pulpe, f. || moelle, f.

pulpit, *pŏŏl'pĭt*, s. chaire, f.

pulpous, *pŭlp'ŭs*, pulpy, *pŭlp'ĭ*, a. pulpeux.

pulsation, *pŭl sā'shŭn*, s. pulsation, f.

pulse, *pŭls*, s. pouls, m. || pulsation, f. || légume, f. || to feel one's ~, tâter le pouls à qn. [vérisation, f.

pulverisation, *pŭl vĕr ĭ zā'shŭn*, s. pulverise, *pŭl'vĕr ĭz*, v. a. pulvériser.

pumice, *pŭm'ĭs*, s. pierre-ponce, f.

pumice, *pŭm'ĭs*, v. a. poncer.

pump, *pŭmp*, s. pompe, f. || escarpin, m.

pump, *pŭmp*, v. a. pomper || tirer les vers du nez à.

pumpkin, *pŭmp'kĭn*, s. citrouille, f.

pun, *pŭn*, s. calembour, m.

punch, *pŭnsh*, s. emporte-pièce, m. || polichinelle, m. || punch, ponche, m.

punch, *pŭnsh*, v. a. percer (des trous) || gourmer, donner des bourrades.

puncheon, *pŭnsh'ŭn*, s. poinçon, m. || pièce, f. [m.

punchinello, *pŭn shĭ nĕl'lŏ*, s. polichinelle, m.

punctilio, *pŭngk tĭl'ĭ ŏ*, s. vétille, f.

punctilious, *pŭngk tĭl'ĭ ŭs*, a. pointilleux || -ly, ad. minutieusement.

punctual, *pŭngk'tū ăl*, a. (-ly, ad.) ponctuel(lement) || exact. [tualité, f.

punctuality, *pŭngk tū ăl'ĭ tĭ*, s. ponctuate, *pŭngk'tū ăt*, v. a. ponctuer.

punctuation, *pŭngk tū ā'shŭn*, s. ponctuation, f. [piqûre, f.

puncture, *pŭngk'tūr*, s. ponction, f. ||

pungency, *pŭn'jĕn sĭ*, s. piquant, m. âpreté, f.

pungent, *pŭn'jĕnt*, a. piquant, âpre.

punic, *pū'nĭk*, a. punique || (fig.) traître.

puniness, *pū'nĭ nĕs*, s. petitesse, f.

punish, *pŭn'ĭsh*, v. a. punir, châtier.

punishable, *pŭn'ĭsh ă bl*, a. punissable.

punishment, *pŭn'ĭsh mĕnt*, s. punition, f.

punitive, *pū'nĭ tĭv*, a. punissant || pénal.

punster, *pŭn'stĕr*, s. calembouriste, m.

punt, *pŭnt*, s. ras de carène, pont volant, m.

punt, *pŭnt*, v. n. ponter.

punter, *pŭnt'ĕr*, s. (at play) ponte, m.

puny, *pū'nĭ*, a. jeune || inférieur || chétif.

pup, *pŭp*, s. petit chien, m.

pup, *pŭp*, v. n. chienner.

pupil, *pū'pĭl*, s. pupille, m. & f. || élève, m.

pupilage, *pū'pĭl āj*, s. éducation, f. || minorité, f.

pupillary, *pū'pĭl ĕr ĭ*, a. pupillaire.

puppet, *pŭp'pĕt*, s. marionnette, poupée, f. || ~show, s. marionnettes, f. pl.

puppy, *pŭp'pĭ*, s. petit chien, m. || fat, m.

puppyism, *pŭp'pĭ ĭsm*, s. fatuité, f.

purblind, *pĕr'blĭnd*, a. myope || presque aveugle.

purchase, *pĕr'chās*, s. achat, m., acquisition, f. || (mar.) cabrestan, m.

purchase, *pĕr'chās*, v. a. acheter.

pure, *pūr*, a. (-ly, ad.) pur(ement).

purgation, *pĕr gā'shŭn*, s. purification, f.

purgative, *pĕr'gā tĭv*, s. purgatif, m.

purgative, *pĕr'gā tĭv*, a. purgatif.

purgatory, *pĕr'gā tĕr ĭ*, s. purgatoire, m.

purge, *pĕrj*, v. a. purger || purifier.

purging, *pĕrj'ĭng*, s. purgation, f.

purification, *pū rĭ fĭ kā'shŭn*, s. purification, f., nettoyage, m. || épurement, m.

purify, *pū'rĭ fĭ*, v. a. & n. (se) purifier.

purist, *pū'rĭst*, s. puriste, m.

puritan, *pū'rĭ tăn*, s. puritain, m.

puritanic(al), *pū rĭ tăn'ĭk (ăl)*, a. puritain.

purity, *pū'rĭ tĭ*, s. pureté, f.

purl, *pĕrl*, s. tresse, f. || bière absinthée, f. || murmure, m.

purl, *pĕrl*, v. n. couler en murmurant.

purlieu, *pĕr'lū*, s. lisière, f. || confins, m.pl.

purloin, *pĕr lŏyn'*, v. a. piller.

purple, *pĕr'pl*, s. pourpre, f. || ~s, pl. (méd.) pourpre, m. [pourpre.

purple, *pĕr'pl*, a. de pourpre || (méd.)

purport, *pĕr'pŏrt*, s. sens, m. || contenu, m.

purport, *pĕr'pŏrt*, v. a. & n. montrer, signifier || prétendre.

purpose, *pĕr'pŭs*, s. intention, f., objet, m. || effet, m. || much to the ~, fort à propos || on ~, à dessein || to no ~, en vain || for what ~? à quoi bon ? || to answer the ~, répondre au but.

purpose, *pĕr'pŭs*, v. n. se proposer.

purr, *pĕr*, v. n. faire ronron, ronronner.

purring, *pĕr'ĭng*, s. ronron du chat, m.

purse, *pĕrs*, s. bourse, f. || porte-monnaie, m. || ~net, s. cibadière, f. || ~proud, a. fier de son argent, parvenu.

purse, *pĕrs*, v. a. empocher || froncer.

purser, *pĕrs'ĕr*, s. agent comptable, m.

purslain, *pĕrs'lān*, s. pourpier, poireau, m.

pursuance, *pĕr sū'ăns*, s. poursuite, f. || conséquence, f.

pursuant, *pĕr sū'ănt*, a. en conséquence de, conforme à.

pursue, *pĕr sū′,* v. a. & n. poursuivre || chercher. [f. || –s, pl. occupations, f. pl.

pursuit, *pĕr sūt′,* s. poursuite, f. || recherche,

pursy, *pĕr′sĭ,* a. poussif.

purulence, *pū′rŏŏ lĕns,* s. purulence, f.

purulent, *pū′rŏŏ lĕnt,* a. purulent.

purvey, *pĕr vā′,* v. a. & n. pourvoir.

purveyance, *pĕr vā′āns,* s. provisions, f. pl., vivres, m. pl.

purveyor, *pĕr vā′ĕr,* s. pourvoyeur, m.

pus, *pŭs,* s. (méd.) pus, m., matière purulente, f.

push, *pŏŏsh,* s. poussée, impulsion, f. || effort, m. || moment critique, m. || promotion, f., avancement, m.

push, *pŏŏsh,* v. a. & n. pousser, presser || faire un effort || **to ~ off,** (mar.) pousser au large.

pushing, *pŏŏsh′ĭng,* a. entreprenant.

pusillanimity, *pū sĭl lăn ĭm′ĭ tĭ,* s. pusillanimité, lâcheté, f. [lanime.

pusillanimous, *pū sĭl lăn′ĭ mŭs,* a. pusillanime (des habits) || **to ~**

puss(y), *pŏŏs(ĭ),* s. minon, petit chat, m.

pustule, *pŭs′tŭl,* s. pustule, f.

put, *pŏŏt,* v. a. & n. ir. mettre, poser, placer || employer || supposer || proposer || imputer || mettre sur le compte de || présenter || **to ~ on,** mettre (des habits) || **to ~ by,** mettre de côté (de l'argent) || **to ~ off,** différer, ajourner || **to ~ out,** fâcher, exaspérer || **to ~ out at interest,** mettre à intérêt || **to ~ up with,** supporter, endurer || **to be ~ to it,** se trouver fort embarrassé || **~-off,** s. excuse, blague, f. || **~-on,** s. duperie, colle, farce, rigolade, f.

putative, *pū′tā tĭv,* a. putatif, supposé.

putlog, *pŭt′lŏg,* s. boulin, m. [faction, f.

putrefaction, *pū trē făk′shŭn,* s. putréfaction,

putrefy, *pū′trē fĭ,* v. n. se putréfier. [f.

putrescence, *pū trĕs′sĕns,* s. putréfaction,

putrescent, *pū trĕs′sĕnt,* a. putrescent.

putrid, *pū′trĭd,* a. putride || croupi.

putting-stone, *pŏŏt′ing stōn,* s. pierre qu'on lance pour essayer ses forces, f.

putty, *pŭt′tĭ,* s. potée, f. || mastic, m.

puzzle, *pŭz′zl,* s. embarras, m. || énigme, f.

puzzle, *pŭz′zl,* v. a. embarrasser || (fam.) coller || **(the brain)** alambiquer.

pygmy, *pĭg′mĭ,* s. pygmée, m.

pyramid, *pĭr′ā mĭd,* s. pyramide, f.

pyramidal, *pĭ răm′ĭ dăl,* a. pyramidal.

pyre, *pīr,* s. bûcher, m. [technie, f.

pyrotechnics, *pīr ō tĕk′nĭks,* s. pyro-

python, *pī′thŏn,* s. python, m.

pythoness, *pī′thŏn ĕs,* s. pythonisse, f. || (fig.) devineresse, f.

pyx, *pĭks,* s. ciboire, m.

Q.

quack, *kwăk,* s. charlatan, m.

quack, *kwăk,* v. n. faire le charlatan.

quackery, *kwăk′ĕr ĭ,* s. charlatanerie, f.

quadrangle, *kwŏd′răng gl,* s. carré, m.

quadrant, *kwŏd′rănt,* s. quart de cercle, m.

quadrilateral, *kwŏd rĭ lăt′ĕr ăl,* a. quadrilatère, quadrilatéral.

quadrille, *kă drĭl′,* s. quadrille, m. & f.

quadroon, *kwŏd rōn′,* s. quarteron, m.

quadruped, *kwŏd′rŏŏ pĕd,* s. quadrupède, m.

quadruple, *kwŏd′rŏŏ pl,* a. quadruple.

quaff, *kwăf,* v. a. & n. boire à longs traits || **to ~ off,** sabler.

quaggy, *kwăg′gĭ,* a. marécageux.

quagmire, *kwăg′mīr,* s. fondrière, f.

quail, *kwāl,* s. caille, f.

quail, *kwāl,* v. n. être abattu, faiblir.

quaint, *kwănt,* a. délicat || affecté, prétentieux || **–ly,** ad. d'une manière affectée || bizarrement || adroitement.

quaintness, *kwănt′nĕs,* s. singularité, f.

quake, *kwāk,* v. n. trembler.

quaker, *kwāk′ĕr,* s. quaker, quacre, m.

qualification, *kwŏl ĭ fĭ kā′shŭn,* s. qualification, f. || modification, f. || qualité, f.

qualify, *kwŏl′ĭ fĭ,* v. a. rendre capable or propre, modifier, modérer || (Am.) affirmer par serment

quality, *kwŏl′ĭ tĭ,* s. qualité, f.

qualm, *kwăm,* s. nausée, f. || mal au cœur, m. || scrupule, m.

qualmish, *kwăm′ĭsh,* a. qui a mal au cœur.

quandary, *kwŏn′dā rĭ,* s. incertitude, f.

quantitative, *kwŏn′tĭ tā tĭv,* a. quantitatif.

quantity, *kwŏn′tĭ tĭ,* s. quantité, f.

quantum, *kwŏn′tŭm,* s. total, montant, m.

quarantine, *kwŏr′ăn tēn,* s. quarantaine, f.

quarrel, *kwŏr′rĕl,* s. querelle, dispute, f. || **to pick a ~,** faire une querelle d'Allemand.

quarrel, *kwŏr′rĕl,* v. n. se quereller.

quarrelsome, *kwŏr′rĕl sŭm,* a. querelleur.

quarry, *kwŏr′rĭ,* s. carrière, f. || proie, f. || curée, f. || **~-man,** s. carrier, m.

quart, *kwawrt,* s. (at cards) quatrième, f. || litre, m.

quartan, *kwawr′tăn,* s. fièvre quarte, f.

quarter, *kwawr′tĕr,* s. quartier, m. || quart, m. || trimestre, m. || pardon, m. || **–s,** pl. logement, m. || **to beat to –s,** (mar.) battre la diane || all hands to –s! chacun à son poste! || **~ of an hour,** quart d'heure, m. || **~-deck,** s. gaillard d'arrière, m.

quarter, *kwawr′tĕr,* v. a. écarteler || loger.

quarterly, *kwawr′tĕr lĭ,* a. & ad. trimestriel || par trimestre.

quartern, *kwawr′tĕrn,* s. demi-gallon, m. || **~-loaf,** s. pain de quatre livres, m.

quartet, *kwawr′tĕt′,* s. quatuor, m.

quarto, *kwawr′tō,* s. in-quarto, m.

quarto, *kwawr′tō,* a. in-quarto.

quartz, *kwawrts,* s. quartz, m.

quash, *kwŏsh,* v. a. briser, écraser || dompter || étouffer || annuler.

quasi, *kwā′sī,* ad. quasi. [m.

quatrain, *kwŏt′răn ou kăt′răn,* s. quatrain,

quaver, *kwā′vĕr,* s. (mus.) croche, f. || tremblement de voix, m. || trille, m.

quaver, *kwā′vĕr,* v. n. faire des roulements de voix, triller.

quay, *kē,* s. quai, port, m.

quean, *kwēn,* s. femme de mauvaise vie, f.

queasiness, kwē'zĭ něs, s. faiblesse d'estomac, f., dégoût, m.

queasy, kwē'zĭ, a. qui a mal au cœur ||
fastidieux, dégoûtant.

queen, kwēn, s. reine, f. || (at cards)
dame, f. || to go to ~, (at chess) aller
à dame.

queen, kwēn, v. n. (chess) aller à dame ||
to ~ it, faire, jouer la reine.   [reine.

queenly, kwēn'lĭ, a. de reine, comme une

queer, kwēr, a. (-ly, ad.) bizarre(ment) ||
étrange, drôle || original.

queerness, kwēr'něs, s. bizarrerie, f.

quell, kwĕl, v. a. dompter || étouffer ||
apaiser, réprimer.   [amortir.

quench, kwĕnsh, v. a. éteindre || étancher ||

quenchless, kwĕnsh'lĕs, a. inextinguible.

querist, kwē'rĭst, s. questionneur, m.

querulous, kwĕr'ū lŭs, a. plaintif || -ly,
ad. en se plaignant.

querulousness, kwĕr'ū lŭs něs, s. manie
des procès, f.

query, kwē'rĭ, s. question, demande, f.

query, kwē'rĭ, v. a. questionner || douter de.

quest, kwĕst, s. quête, recherche, f. || in ~
of, à la recherche de.

question, kwĕst'yŭn, s. question, demande,
dispute, f. || doute, m. || torture, f. || open
~, question ouverte || vexed ~, question
controversée || out of the ~, en dehors
de la question || beyond all ~, hors de
doute || to call in ~, mettre en doute ||
beside the ~, à côté de la question || to
put to the ~, mettre à la torture || the
~ is . . ., reste à savoir || there is no ~,
ceci ne fait pas question.

question, kwĕst'yŭn, v. a. & n. question-
ner, interroger || douter de.

questionable, kwĕst'yŭn ă bl, a. douteux.

questor, kwĕs'tĕr, s. questeur, m.

questorship, kwĕs'tĕr shĭp, s. questure, f.

quibble, kwĭb'bl, s. calembour, m.

quibble, kwĭb'bl, v. n. faire des calem-
bours || ergoter.

quick, kwĭk, s. vif, m., chair vive, f. ||
the ~ and the dead, les vivants et les
morts || ~march, s. pas de charge, m. ||
~sighted, a. aux yeux perçants || ~
witted, a. à l'esprit vif, sagace.

quick, kwĭk, a. & ad. vivant || vif, actif,
prompt, habile, alerte || subtil || intelligent ||
-ly, ad. vite, promptement, vivement.

quicken, kwĭk'n, v. a. vivifier, animer ||
hâter, accélérer.

quicklime, kwĭk'līm, s. chaux vive, f.

quickness, kwĭk'něs, s. vitesse, vivacité, f.

quicksand, kwĭk'sănd, s. sable mouvant, m.

quickset hedge, kwĭk'sĕt hĕdj, s. haie
vive, f.

quicksilver, kwĭk'sĭl vĕr, s. vif-argent, m.

quicksilvered, kwĭk'sĭl vĕrd, a. étamé.

quid, kwĭd, s. chique de tabac, f.

quidnunc, kwĭd'nĭngk, s. olibrius, m.

quid-pro-quo, kwĭd'prō kwō', s. quiproquo, m.

quiescent, kwĭ ĕs'sĕnt, a. paisible, calme.

quiet, kwī'ĕt, v. a. calmer, apaiser.

quiet, kwī'ĕt, a. (-ly, ad.) tranquille
(ment) || calme || paisible(ment).

quietness, kwī'ĕt něs, quietude, kwī'ĕ
tūd, s. quiétude, f., repos, m.

quietsome, kwī'ĕt sŭm, a. calme, paisible.

quietus, kwī ē'tŭs, s. repos, m. || mort, f. ||
quittance, f.

quill, kwĭl, s. plume, f. || piquant, m. ||
~driver, s. gratte-papier, plumitif, m.

quill, kwĭl, v. a. plisser, fraiser.

quilt, kwĭlt, s. couvre-pied, m. || courte-
pointe, f.   [point, m.

quilting, kwĭlt'ĭng, s. piqûre, f., arrière-

quince, kwĭns, s. coing, m. || ~tree, s.
cognassier, m.

quincunx, kwĭn'kŭnks, s. quinconce, m.

quinine, kwĭn ēn', s. quinine, f.

quinquagesima, kwĭn kwă jĕs'ĭ mä, s.
quinquagésime, f.   [quennal.

quinquennial, kwĭn kwĕn'nĭ ăl, a. quin-

quinsy, kwĭn'zĭ, s. esquinancie, f.

quint, kwĭnt, s. quinte, f.

quintal, kwĭn'tăl, s. quintal, m.

quintessence, kwĭn tĕs'sĕns, s. quintessence, f.

quintet, kwĭn tĕt', s. quintette, m.

quintuple, kwĭn'tū pl, a. quintuple, m.

quip, kwĭp, s. brocard, lardon, m.

quire, kwīr, s. main de papier, f. || in ~s,
en feuilles.   [f.

quirk, kwĕrk, s. subtilité, chicane, finesse,

quit, kwĭt, v. a. quitter, laisser, tenir
quitte || to give notice to ~, donner
congé au locataire.

quit, kwĭt, a. quitte.

quite, kwĭt, ad. entièrement, tout à fait.

quits ! kwĭts, quitte à quitte !

quittance, kwĭt'tăns, s. quittance, f. ||
revanche, f.

quitter, kwĭt'ĕr, s. abandonneur, m.

quiver, kwĭv'ĕr, s. carquois, m.

quiver, kwĭv'ĕr, v. n. trembler, frissonner ||
~ed, a. armé d'un carquois.

quiz, kwĭz, v. a. mystifier || railler || lorgner.

quoit, kōyt, s. palet, disque, m.

quondam, kwŏn'dăm, a. ancien, ci-devant.

quorum, kwŏr'ŭm, s. nombre suffisant de
juges, m.

quota, kwō'tä, s. quote-part, f.

quotation, kwō'tā'shŭn, s. citation, f. ||
guillemets, m. pl. || (com.) cote, f.

quote, kwōt, v. a. citer || alléguer.

quoth, kwōth, v. def. || ~ he, dit-il.

quotha ! kwōth'ă, holà !   [dienne, f.

quotidian, kwō tĭd'ĭ ăn, s. fièvre quoti-

quotient, kwō'shĕnt, s. (ar.) quotient, m.

R.

R. A., membre de l'académie royale de
peinture, m.

rabbet, răb'bĕt, s. feuillure, râblure, f.

rabbi, răb'bī ou răb'bĭ, s. rabbin, m.

rabbit, răb'bĭt, s. lapin, m. || ~'s nest, s.
rabouillère, f.

rabble, răb'bl, s. canaille, populace, f. ‖ cohue, f.

rabid, răb'ĭd, a. enragé, furieux.

rabies, ră'bĭ ēs, s. (méd.) rage, hydrophobie, f.

race, răs, s. race, lignée, f. ‖ course, carrière, f. ‖ force, f. ‖ bouquet (du vin), m. ‖ ~-horse, s. cheval de carrière, steppeur, m.

race, răs, v. n. courir.

racer, răs'ēr, s. coureur, m. ‖ cheval de course, m.

raciness, ră'sĭ nĕs, s. bouquet (du vin), m. ‖ caractère particulier, m.

rack, răk, s. torture, f. ‖ quenouille, f. ‖ ratelier, m. ‖ grille, f. ‖ arack, m. ‖ ~-rent, s. loyer excessif, f.

rack, răk, v. a. torturer ‖ pressurer ‖ soutirer ‖ to go to ~ and ruin, se perdre, se ruiner.

racket, răk'ĕt, s. raquette, f. ‖ tapage, m.

racket, răk'ĕt, v. n. faire du tapage ‖ faire un tintamarre.

racking, răk'ĭng, a. atroce ‖ fugitif.

racy, ră'sĭ, a. fort, spiritueux.

radial, ră'dĭ ăl, a. radial.

radiance, ră'dĭ ăns, s. éclat, m., splendeur, f.

radiant, ră'dĭ ănt, a. radieux, rayonnant.

radiate, ră'dĭ ăt, v. n. rayonner.

radiation, ră dĭ ā'shŭn, s. rayonnement, m.

radical, răd'ĭ kăl, s. radical, m.

radical, răd'ĭ kăl, a. (-ly, ad.) radical (ement).

radicalism, răd'ĭ kăl ĭsm, s. radicalisme, m.

radish, răd'ĭsh, s. radis, m., rave, f.

radius, ră'dĭ ŭs, s. rayon, m.

raffle, răf'fl s. loterie, f.

raffle, răf'fl, v. n. faire une loterie.

raft, răft, s. radeau, m. ‖ train de bois, m.

rafter, răft'ēr, s. chevron, m.

raftsman, răfts'măn, s. flotteur, m.

rag, răg, s. chiffon, haillon, m. ‖ ~ and bone merchant, s. marchand de chiffons ‖ ~-fair, s. friperie, f. ‖ ~-gatherer (~-picker), s. chiffonnier, m. ‖ ~-stone, s. tuf, m.

ragamuffin, răg ă mŭf'fĭn, s. va-nu-pieds, m.

rage, răj, s. rage, fureur, colère, f.

rage, răj, v. n. être furieux.

ragged, răg'gĕd, a. déchiré ‖ en haillons.

raggedness, răg'gĕd nĕs, s. état déguenillé, dépenaillement, m.

raging, ră'jĭng, s. fureur, f.

ragingly, ră'jĭng lĭ, ad. avec fureur.

ragout, ră gō', s. ragoût, m.

raid, răd, s. incursion, f. ‖ razzia, f.

raider, răd'ēr, s. maraudeur, m.

rail, răl, s. grille, f. ‖ barre, barrière, f., barreau, m. ‖ rail, m. ‖ (mar.) lisse, f. ‖ balustrade, f. ‖ ~-fence, s. barrière, f.

rail, răl, v. a. & n. griller ‖ fermer avec une grille ‖ invectiver.

railer, răl'ēr, s. frondeur, m.

railing, răl'ĭng, s. grille, balustrade, f. ‖ invective, f.

raillery, răl'ēr ĭ, s. raillerie, f.

railroad, răl'rōd, railway, răl'wă, s. chemin de fer, m. ‖ ~-crossing, s. passage à niveau, m. ‖ ~-guard, s. conduc-

teur de train, m. ‖ ~-speed, s. rapidité de la vapeur, f.

raiment, ră'mĕnt, s. vêtement, m.

rain, răn, s. pluie, f. ‖ ~-drop, s. goutte de pluie, f. ‖ ~-gauge, s. pluviomètre, m.

rain, răn, v. n. pleuvoir ‖ to ~ cats and dogs, (fam.) pleuvoir à seaux ‖ to ~ in torrents, pleuvoir à verse.

rainbow, răn'bō, s. arc-en-ciel, m.

rainy, răn'ĭ, a. pluvieux.

raise, răz, v. a. lever, soulever, hausser ‖ élever, ériger, bâtir ‖ faire soulever ‖ faire naître ‖ susciter, exciter ‖ recueillir ‖ contracter ‖ promouvoir ‖ augmenter.

raisin, ră'zn, s. raisin sec, m.

rake, răk, s. râteau, m. ‖ débauché, m.

rake, răk, v. a. râteler, ratisser ‖ to ~-fore and oft, (mar.) faire quête.

rakish, răk'ĭsh, a. dissolu, libertin.

rally, răl'lĭ, v. a. & n. rallier ‖ rallier ‖ se rallier ‖ -ing-point, s. point de ralliement.

ram, răm, s. bélier, m. ‖ hie, f.

ram, răm, v. a. enfoncer ‖ bourrer.

ramble, răm'bl, s. excursion, f.

ramble, răm'bl, v. n. rôder.

rambler, răm'blēr, s. rôdeur, m.

rambling, răm'blĭng, a. vagabond ‖ divaguant.

ramification, răm ĭ fĭ kā'shŭn, s. ramification, f.

ramify, răm'ĭ fĭ, v. n. se ramifier.

rammer, răm'mēr, s. baguette de fusil, f. ‖ hie, f.

ramp, rămp, s. gambade, f.

ramp, rămp, v. n. grimper.

rampant, răm'pănt, a. surabondant ‖ effréné, exubérant.

rampart, răm'părt, s. rempart, m.

rampion, răm'pĭ ŏn, s. raiponce, f.

ramrod, răm'rŏd, s. baguette de fusil, f.

ramshackle, răm'shăkl, a. caduc, délabré.

ranch, rănsh, s. luxation, dislocation, f.

rancid, răn'sĭd, a. rance.

rancidity, răn sĭd'ĭ tĭ, s. rancidité, f.

rancorous, răng'kēr ŭs, a. rancunier.

rancour, răng'kēr, s. rancune, f.

Rand, rănd, s. district aurifère du Transvaal, m.

random, răn'dŏm, s. hasard, m. ‖ at ~, au hasard.

range, rănj, s. rang, m., rangée, f. ‖ classe, f., ordre, m. ‖ portée, f. ‖ étendue, f. ‖ fourneau, m. ‖ échelon, m.

range, rănj, v. a. & n. ranger, arranger ‖ rôder ‖ se ranger, parcourir.

ranger, răn'jēr, s. rôdeur, m. ‖ garde-forestier, m. ‖ chien courant, m.

rank, răngk, s. rang, m. ‖ station, f. ‖ ~ and file, simples soldats, pioupious, m. pl. ‖ to take ~ with, avoir le pas sur.

rank, răngk, v. n. se ranger.

rank, răngk, a. fort, fécond, fertile ‖ rance ‖ grossier.

rankle, răng'kl, v. n. s'envenimer.

rankness, răngk'nĕs, s. surabondance, f. ‖ goût rance, m.

ransack, răn'săk, v. a. piller, saccager.

ransom, răn'sŭm, s. rançon, f.

ransom, răn'sŭm, v. a. rançonner.

rant, rănt, s. phébus, m.

rant, *rănt,* v. n. tempêter || faire des phrases.

ranter, *rănt'ĕr,* s. déclamateur, m. || énergumène, m.

ranunculus, *răn ŭng'kŭ lŭs,* s. renoncule, f.

rap, *răp,* s. coup, m. || tape, f. || **not to care a ~,** (fam.) se moquer pas mal de, se ficher de. [ravir.

rap, *răp,* v. a. frapper avec vitesse || (fig.)

rapacious, *ră pā'shŭs,* a. rapace || **-ly,** ad. avec rapacité.

rapacity, *ră păs'ĭ tĭ,* s. rapacité, f.

rape, *răp,* s. rapt, ravissement, viol, m. || (bot.) navette, f.

rapid, *răp'ĭd,* a. (**-ly,** ad.) rapide(ment).

rapids, *răp'ĭdz,* s. pl. rapides, m. pl.

rapidity, *ră pĭd'ĭ tĭ,* s. rapidité, f.

rapier, *rā'pĭĕr,* s. rapière, f.

rapine, *răp'ĭn* ou *răp'ĭn,* s. rapine, f.

rappee, *răp pē',* s. râpé, m.

rapper, *răp'pĕr,* s. (**on a door**) marteau, m. || bourde, f.

rapt, *răpt,* a. ravi, extasié. [tase, f.

rapture, *răp'tūr,* s. ravissement, m., ex-

rapturous, *răp'tūr ŭs,* a. ravissant || ravi.

rare, *rār,* a. & ad. rare || clairsemé || exquis || **-ly,** ad. rarement || excellemment.

raree-show, *rār'ē shō,* s. spectacle ambulant, m. [tion, f.

rarefaction, *rā rē făk'shŭn,* s. raréfac-

rarefy, *rā'rē fī,* v. a. raréfier.

rarity, *rā'rĭ tĭ,* s. rareté, f.

rascal, *răs'kăl,* s. coquin, fripon, m.

rascality, *răs kăl'ĭ tĭ,* s. coquinerie, f. [m.

rascallion, *răs kăl'yŭn,* s. drôle, malotru,

rascally, *răs'kăl ĭ,* a. bas, vil, infâme.

rase, *rāz,* v. a. raser, effacer || extirper.

rash, *răsh,* s. éruption, f. [inconsidéré.

rash, *răsh,* a. (**-ly,** ad.) téméraire(ment) ||

rasher, *răsh'ĕr,* s. petite tranche, f.

rashness, *răsh'nĕs,* s. témérité, étourderie, f. [rifloir, m.

rasp, *răsp,* s. râpe, f. || **~-file,** s. riflard,

rasp, *răsp,* v. a. râper || chapeler.

raspberry, *răz'bĕr ĭ,* s. framboise, f. || **~-bush,** s. framboisier, m. [lure, f.

rasping, *răs'pĭng,* s. râpure, f. || chapelet.

rat, *răt,* s. rat, m. || transfuge, m. || gâte-métier, m. || **to smell a ~,** (fam.) flairer qc. || **~-trap,** s. ratière, f.

ratable, *rā'tă bl,* a. imposable.

ratably, *rā'tă blĭ,* ad. à proportion.

ratchet, *răch'ĕt,* s. cliquet, déclic, m.

rate, *răt,* s. prix, m., valeur, f. || proportion, f. || taux, m. || compte, m. || ordre, m. || nombre, m. || impôt, m. || cours, m.

rate, *răt,* v. a. évaluer, taxer, réprimander.

rather, *răth'ĕr,* ad. plutôt, mieux || un peu || assez || **I would ~,** j'aimerais mieux. [tion, f.

ratification, *răt ĭ fĭ kā'shŭn,* s. ratifica-

ratify, *răt'ĭ fī,* v. a. ratifier.

ratio, *rā'shĭō,* s. proportion, f.

ration, *rā'shŭn,* s. ration, f.

rational, *răsh'ŭn ăl,* a. (**-ly,** ad.) raisonnable(ment) || rationnel. [lisme, m.

rationalism, *răsh'ŭn ăl ĭsm,* s. rationa-

ratsbane, *răts'bān,* s. mort aux rats, f.

rattan, *răt tăn',* s. rotin, rotang, m.

ratteen, *răt tēn',* s. ratine, f.

rattle, *răt'tl,* s. fracas, m. || **bavardage,** m. || crecelle, f. || **~-snake,** s. serpent à sonnettes, m. [gronder || râter.

rattle, *răt'tl,* v. a. & n. faire du bruit,

ravage, *răv'āj,* s. ravage, m.

ravage, *răv'āj,* v. a. ravager.

ravager, *răv'āj ĕr,* s. destructeur, m.

rave, *răv,* v. n. extravaguer, être en délire || raffoler.

ravel, *răv'ĕl,* v. a. (& n.) (s')embrouiller.

raven, *rā'vn,* s. corbeau, m.

ravenous, *răv'ĕn ŭs,* a. vorace || (fig.) dévorant || **-ly,** ad. avec voracité.

ravenousness, *răv'ĕn ŭs nĕs,* s. voracité, f.

ravine, *ră vēn',* s. ravin, m. || défilé, m.

raving, *răv'ĭng,* a. furieux || **-ly,** ad. en fou. [force.

ravish, *răv'ĭsh,* v. a. ravir || enlever de

ravisher, *răv'ĭsh ĕr,* s. ravisseur, m.

ravishingly, *răv'ĭsh ĭng lĭ,* ad. à ravir.

ravishment, *răv'ĭsh mĕnt,* s. enlèvement, m. || extase, f.

raw, *răw,* a. cru, vert || novice || écorché || froid et humide || pur || **~-boned,** a. maigre || **~-head,** s. loup-garou, m.

rawness, *răw'nĕs,* s. crudité, f. || inexpérience, f.

ray, *rā,* s. rayon, m.

raze, *rāz,* v. n. *vide* **rase.**

razor, *rā'zĕr,* s. rasoir, m.

reach, *rēch,* s. étendue, f. || capacité, f. || portée, f. || pouvoir, m. || **within ~,** à la portée || **out of ~,** hors de la portée.

reach, *rēch,* v. a. & n. atteindre, toucher à, arriver à, obtenir || tendre vers || s'étendre à. [dre à.

react, *rē ăkt',* v. n. réagir.

reaction, *rē ăk'shŭn,* s. réaction, f.

reactionary, *rē ăk'shŭn ĕr ĭ,* a. réactionnaire.

read, *rēd,* v. a. & n. ir. lire, parcourir || étudier, connaître à fond.

read, *rĕd,* a. savant, érudit, habile || **well ~,** qui a de la lecture.

readable, *rēd'ă bl,* a. lisible.

reader, *rēd'ĕr,* s. lecteur, m., lectrice, f. || correcteur, m. [tiers.

readily, *rĕd'ĭ lĭ,* ad. promptement, volontiers.

readiness, *rĕd'ĭ nĕs,* s. promptitude, f. || habileté, f. || bonne volonté, f.

reading, *rēd'ĭng,* s. lecture, f. || leçon, f.

ready, *rĕd'ĭ,* a. (& ad.) prêt, prompt(ement) || empressé || comptant || près, facile || **~-reckoner,** s. barème, m. || **~-made (of clothes),** confectionné, de confection.

real, *rēl,* a. (**-ly,** ad.) réel(lement) || vrai, effectif || **~ estate,** s. immeubles, m. pl.

realisation, *rē ăl ĭ zā'shŭn,* s. réalisation, f.

realise, *rē'ăl ĭz,* v. a. réaliser, effectuer || **to ~ on** ou **from (an investment, etc.),** réaliser des profits dans une entreprise.

reality, *rē ăl'ĭ tĭ,* s. réalité, f.

realm, *rĕlm,* s. royaume, état, m.

ream, *rēm,* s. rame de papier, f.

reanimate, *rē ăn'ĭ māt,* v. a. ranimer.

reap, *rēp,* v. a. & n. moissonner, recueillir.

reaper, *rēp'ĕr*, s. moissonneur, m. || moissonneuse, f.

reaping, *rēp'ĭng*, s. moisson, f. || ~-hook, s. faucille, f. || ~-machine, s. moissonneuse, f. || ~-time, s. moisson, f.

reappear, *rē·ăp'pēr*, v. n. reparaître.

reappearance, *rē·ăp·pēr'ăns*, s. réapparition, f.

reapportion, *rē·ăp·pōr'shŭn*, v. a. répartir de nouveau.

rear, *rēr*, s. arrière-garde, f. || dernière classe, f. || ~-admiral, s. contre-amiral, m. || ~-guard, s. arrière-garde, f.

rear, *rēr*, v. a. & n. élever || se cabrer.

reascend, *rē·ă·sĕnd'*, v. a. & n. remonter.

reason, *rē'zn*, s. raison, f. || argument, m. || by ~ of, en raison de, pour cause de || in ~, comme de juste || to bring to ~, mettre à la raison || to have every ~ to, avoir toutes les raisons du monde pour || it stands to ~, c'est raisonnable.

reason, *rē'zn*, v. a. & n. raisonner || to ~ one into, entraîner qn. à || to ~ one out of, détourner qn. de.

reasonable, *rē'zn·ă·bl*, a. raisonnable.

reasonableness, *rē'zn·ă·bl·nĕs*, s. raison, f. || modération, f.   [ment.

reasonably, *rē'zn·ă·blĭ*, ad. raisonnable-

reasoner, *rē'zn·ĕr*, s. logicien, m.

reasoning, *rē'zn·ĭng*, s. raisonnement, m.

reassume, *rē·ăs·sūm'*, v. a. reprendre.

reassure, *rē·ă·shōr'*, v. a. rassurer || réassurer.

rebaptise, *rē·băp·tīz'*, v. a. rebaptiser.

rebate, *rē·bāt'*, s. rainure, enrayure, mortaise, f.

rebel, *rĕb'ĕl*, s. rebelle, révolté, m.

rebel, *rē·bĕl'*, v. n. se révolter.

rebellion, *rē·bĕl'yŭn*, s. rébellion, f.

rebellious, *rē·bĕl'yŭs*, a. rebelle || ~ly, ad. en rebelle.

rebound, *rē·bōwnd'*, v. n. rebondir.

rebuff, *rē·bŭff'*, s. rebuffade, f. || refus, m.

rebuff, *rē·bŭff'*, v. a. repousser || refuser.

rebuild, *rē·bĭld'*, v. a. ir. rebâtir.

rebuke, *rē·būk'*, s. réprimande, f.

rebuke, *rē·būk'*, v. a. réprimander.

rebus, *rē'bŭs*, s. rébus, m.

rebut, *rē·bŭt'*, v. a. repousser.

recalcitrant, *rē·kăl'sĭ·trănt*, a. récalcitrant.

recall, *rē·kawl'*, s. révocation, f. || past ~, irrévocablement.

recall, *rē·kawl'*, v. a. rappeler, révoquer.

recant, *rē·kănt'* v. a. (& n.) désavouer || (se) rétracter.

recantation, *rē·kăn·tā'shŭn*, s. rétractation, f. || (in irony) palinodie, f.

recapitulate, *rē·kă·pĭt'ū·lāt*, v. a. récapituler.   [capitulation, f.

recapitulation, *rē·kă·pĭt·ū·lā'shŭn*, s. ré-

recapture, *rē·kăp'tūr*, s. (mar.) reprise, rescousse, f.

recapture, *rē·kăp'tūr*, v. a. (mar.) reprendre une prise.   [sister.

recede, *rē·sēd'*, v. n. se retirer || se dé-

receipt, *rē·sēt'*, s. recette, réception, f. ||

reçu, nr., quittance, f. || **to be in ~ of,** avoir reçu.   [missible.

receivable, *rē·sēv'ă·bl*, a. recevable, ad-

receive, *rē·sēv'*, v. a. recevoir || accepter, admettre || éprouver, agréer, accueillir || contenir.   [leur, m. || récipient, m.

receiver, *rē·sēv'ĕr*, s. receveur, m. || recé-

receiving-house, *rē·sēv'ĭng·hōws*, s. petite poste, f. || maison de secours, f.

recent, *rē'sĕnt*, a. récent, nouveau || ~ly, ad. récemment.   [veauté, f.

recentness, *rē'sĕnt·nĕs*, s. récence, nou-

receptacle, *rē·sĕp'tă·kl*, s. réservoir, m. || retraite, f.   [accueil, m.

reception, *rē·sĕp'shŭn*, s. réception, f. ||

receptive, *rē·sĕp'tĭv*, a. réceptif.

recess, *rē·sĕs'*, s. retraite, f. || renfoncement, m. || vacances, f. pl.   [sistement, m.

recession, *rē·sĕs'shŭn*, s. retraite, f. || dé-

recipe, *rĕs'ĭ·pē*, s. (méd.) recette, f.

recipient, *rē·sĭp'ĭ·ĕnt*, s. (chim.) récipient, m.   [proque(ment).

reciprocal, *rē·sĭp'rō·kăl*, a. (-ly, ad.) réci-

reciprocate, *rē·sĭp'rō·kāt*, v. a. rendre la pareille.   [f.

reciprocity, *rĕs·ĭ·prŏs'ĭ·tĭ*, s. réciprocité,

recital, *rē·sī'tăl*, s. récitation, *rĕs·ĭ·tā'-shŭn*, s. récitation, f. || récit, m. || (jur.) exposé, m. || séance, f.

recitative, *rĕs·ĭ·tā·tēv'*, s. (mus.) récitatif,

recitative, *rĕs·ĭ·tā·tēv'*, a. récitant.

recite, *rē·sīt'*, v. a. réciter, raconter, détailler.

reciter, *rē·sīt'ĕr*, s. récitateur, m.

reck, *rĕk*, v. a. & n. avoir soin, se soucier

reckless, *rĕk'lĕs*, a. insouciant.   [de.

reckon, *rĕk'n*, v. a. & n. compter || considérer comme.

reckoner, *rĕk'n·ĕr*, s. calculateur, m.

reckoning, *rĕk'n·ĭng*, s. compte, calcul, m. || **to be out in one's ~,** se tromper dans son calcul, se méconter.

reclaim, *rē·klām'*, v. a. réformer, corriger || réclamer.   [puyer.

recline, *rē·klīn'*, v. a. & n. incliner || s'ap-

recluse, *rē·klōs'*, s. reclus, m.

reclusion, *rē·klō'zhŭn*, s. réclusion, f.

recognisable, *rĕk·ŏg·nī'ză·bl*, a. reconnaissable.

recognisance, *rē·kŏg'nĭ·zăns* ou *rē·kŏn'ĭ·zăns*, s. reconnaissance, f. || **to enter in ~s,** (jur.) être mis sous les verrous.

recognise, *rĕk'ŏg·nīz*, v. a. reconnaître.

recognition, *rĕk·ŏg·nĭsh'ŭn*, s. reconnaissance, f.

recoil, *rē·kŏyl'*, v. n. reculer (devant).

recoin, *rē·kŏyn'*, v. a. refondre la monnaie.

recoinage, *rē·kŏyn'āj*, s. refonte de la monnaie, f.

recollect, *rĕk·ŏl·lĕkt'*, v. a. recueillir || se souvenir || reprendre courage.

recollection, *rĕk·ŏ·lĕk'shŭn*, s. souvenir, m. || **to the best of my ~,** autant que je m'en souviens.

recommence, *rē·kŏm·mĕns'*, v. n. recommencer.   [mander.

recommend, *rĕk·ŏm·mĕnd'*, v. a. recom-

recommendation, rĕk′ŏm mĕn dā′ shŭn, s. recommandation, f. || **letter of ~**, lettre de recommandation, f.

recommendatory, rĕk′ŏm mĕn′ dă tĕr ĭ, a. de recommandation. [commande.

recommender, rĕk′ŏm mĕnd′ ĕr, s. qui recompense.

recompense, rĕk′ ŏm pĕns, s. récompense, f. || compensation, f. || dédommagement, m.

recompense, rĕk′ ŏm pĕns, v. a. récompenser || compenser || dédommager.

recompose, rē kŏm pōz′, v. a. recomposer || tranquilliser.

reconcilable, rĕk′ ŏn sĭ lă bl, a. réconciliable, compatible. [rajuster.

reconcile, rĕk′ ŏn sĭl, v. a. réconcilier.

reconciliation, rĕk ŏn sĭl ĭ ā′ shŭn, s. réconciliation, f. [profond.

recondite, rĕk′ ŏn dīt, a. caché, abstrus.

reconnoitre, rĕk ŏn nŏy′ tĕr, v. a. (mil.) faire une reconnaissance.

reconquer, rē kŏng′ kĕr, v. a. reconquérir.

reconsider, rē kŏn sĭd′ ĕr, v. a. reconsidérer, considérer de, à nouveau.

reconsideration, rē kŏn sĭd ĕr ā′ shŭn, s. rejet d'une motion parlementaire en seconde lecture, m. || **on ~**, toute réflexion faite.

record, rĕk′ ŏwrd, s. registre, m. || maximum de vitesse obtenu par les bicyclistes, etc., m. || **-s**, s. pl. **--office**, s. archives, f. pl.

record, rē kŏwrd′, v. a. enregistrer || célébrer. [m.

recorder, rē kŏwrd′ ĕr, s. archiviste, greffier.

recount, rē kŏwnt′, v. a. raconter.

recoup, rē kŏŏp′, v. a. indemniser || **to ~ oneself (by)**, se rattraper (sur). [m.

recourse, rē kōrs′, s. recours, m. || retour.

recover, rē kŭv′ ĕr, v. a. & n. rétablir la santé || recouvrer, regagner, reprendre || se rétablir || revenir à soi.

recoverable, rē kŭv′ ĕr ă bl, a. recouvrable || guérissable.

recovery, rē kŭv′ ĕr ĭ, s. recouvrement, m. || guérison, f. || **in a fair way of ~**, en convalescence.

recreant, rĕk′ rē ănt, s. lâche, apostat, m.

recreant, rĕk′ rē ănt, a. lâche.

recreate, rĕk′ rē āt, v. a. (& n.) (se) récréer.

recreation, rĕk rē ā′ shŭn, s. récréation, f.

recreative, rĕk′ rē ā tĭv, a. récréatif.

recriminate, rē krĭm′ ĭ nāt, v. a. récriminer.

recrimination, rē krĭm ĭ nā′ shŭn, s. récrimination, f. [m.

recrudescence, rē krŏ dĕs′ sĕns, s. recrudescence, f.

recruit, rē krŏt′, s. recrue, f. || conscrit, m.

recruit, rē krŏt′, v. a. & n. réparer, rétablir || (mil.) recruter.

recruiting, rē krŏt′ ĭng, s. recrutement, m., recrue, f. || **--sergeant**, s. officier recruteur, m.

rectangle, rĕk′ tăng gl, s. rectangle, m.

rectangular, rĕk tăng′ gū lĕr, a. rectangulaire. [fication, f. || distillation réitérée, f.

rectification, rĕk tĭ fĭ kā′ shŭn, s. rectification, f.

rectify, rĕk′ tĭ fī, v. a. rectifier.

rectilineal, rĕk tĭ lĭn′ ē ăl, a. rectiligne.

rectitude, rĕk′ tĭ tūd, s. rectitude, f. || droiture, f.

rector, rĕk′ tĕr, s. recteur, m. || curé, m.

rectorship, rĕk′ tĕr shĭp, s. rectorat, m. || cure, f.

rectory, rĕk′ tĕr ĭ, s. rectorat, m. || cure, f.

recumbent, rē kŭm′ bĕnt, a. penché, couché.

recuperative, rē kū′ pĕr ā tĭv, a. recouvrable. [vrable.

recur, rē kĕr′, v. n. recourir.

recurrence, rē kŭr′ rĕns, s. retour, recours, f.

recurrent, rē kŭr′ rĕnt, a. périodique. [m.

recusant, rĕk′ ŭ zănt, s. dissident, m.

red, rĕd, s. rouge, m., couleur rouge, f.

red, rĕd, a. rouge || **~-haired**, a. roux || **~-hot**, a. tout rouge || ardent || **~-lead**, s. minium, m. || **~-letter day**, fête fêtée, fête obligatoire, f. || **~-tape**, s. (fig.) routine administrative, f. || **~-tapist**, s. bureaucrate, plumitif, m.

redbreast, rĕd′ brĕst, s. rouge-gorge, m.

redden, rĕd′ n, v. a. & n. rougir.

reddish, rĕd′ ĭsh, a. rougeâtre.

redeem, rē dēm′, v. a. racheter, délivrer || dégager, compenser || **to ~ one's promise**, dégager sa parole || **-ing quality**, s. force rédemptrice, f.

redeemable, rē dēm′ ă bl, a. rachetable.

redeemer, rē dēm′ ĕr, s. Rédempteur, m. || libérateur, m.

redemption, rē dēm′ shŭn, s. rédemption, f. || rachat, m., rançon, f.

redistribute, rē dĭs trĭb′ ūt, v. a. redistribuer. [distribution, f.

redistribution, rē dĭs trĭ bū′ shŭn, s. redistribution, f.

redness, rĕd′ nĕs, s. rougeur, f.

redolence, rĕd′ ō lĕns, s. parfum, m.

redolent, rĕd′ ō lĕnt, a. odoriférant.

redouble, rē dŭb′ l, v. a. & n. redoubler.

redoubt, rē dŏwt′, s. redoute, f.

redoubtable, rē dŏwt′ ă bl, a. redoutable.

redound, rē dŏwnd′, v. n. rejaillir || contribuer. [flagement, m.

redress, rē drĕs′, s. réparation, f. || soulagement, m.

redress, rē drĕs′, v. a. redresser, rectifier, corriger, réparer || soulager.

redresser, rē drĕs′ ĕr, s. réformateur, m.

reduce, rē dūs′, v. a. réduire || diminuer || convertir || appauvrir.

reducible, rē dū′ sĭ bl, a. réductible.

reduction, rē dŭk′ shŭn, s. réduction, f.

redundancy, rē dŭn′ dăn sĭ, s. surabondance, redondance, f.

redundant, rē dŭn′ dănt, a. redondant.

reduplicate, rē dū′ plĭ kāt, v. a. redoubler.

reduplication, rē dū plĭ kā′ shŭn, s. réduplication, f. [duplicatif.

reduplicative, rē dū′ plĭ kā tĭv, a. (gr.) rédupliçatif.

redwing, rĕd′ wĭng, s. mauvis, m.

re-echo, rē ĕk′ ō, v. n. résonner, répéter.

reed, rēd, s. roseau, m. || chalumeau, m. || flèche, f.

reedy, rēd′ ĭ, a. couvert de roseaux.

reef, rēf, s. ris d'une voile, m. || récif, m. || **to take in a ~**, (mar.) prendre un ris.

reef, rēf, v. a. prendre un ris || **close -ed**, (mar.) au bas ris.

reek, rēk, s. fumée, f. || vapeur, f.

reek, rēk, v. n. fumer.

reeky, rēk'ĭ, a. enfumé || noir.

reel, rēl, s. dévidoir, m. || bobine, f.

reel, rēl, v. a. & n. dévider || tourner || chanceler.

re-election, rē ĕ lĕk' shŭn, s. réélection, f.

re-engage, rē ĕn gāj', v. a. rengager.

re-engagement, rē ĕn gāj' mĕnt, s. rengagement, m. [gager.

re-enlist, rē ĕn lĭst', v. n. (mil.) se ren-

re-enter, rē ĕn' tĕr, v. a. rentrer.

re-establish, rē ĕs tăb' lĭsh, v. a. rétablir.

re-establishment, rē ĕs tăb' lĭsh mĕnt, s. rétablissement, m.

reeve, rēv, v. a. (to ~ out) éfaufiler.

re-examine, rē ĕgz ăm' ĭn, v. a. réexaminer.

refection, rē fĕk' shŭn, s. rafraîchissement, m. || repas, m. || réfection, f.

refectory, rē fĕk' tŏr ĭ, s. réfectoire, m.

refer, rē fĕr', v. a. & n. référer, remettre || s'en rapporter à || ranger.

referee, rĕf ĕr ē', s. arbitre, m.

reference, rĕf' ĕr ĕns, s. renvoi, rapport, m. || allusion, f. || —s, pl. recommandations, f. pl.

refine, rē fīn', v. a. raffiner, purifier.

refinement, rē fīn' mĕnt, s. raffinage, affinage, m. || raffinement, m.

refinery, rē fīn' ĕr ĭ, s. raffinerie, f.

refit, rē fĭt', v. a. réparer, radouber.

reflect, rē flĕkt', v. a. & n. refléter || rejaillir || réfléchir, considérer || blâmer.

reflection, rē flĕk' shŭn, s. réflexion, f., reflet, m., méditation, reverbération, f. || censure, f.

reflective, rē flĕk' tĭv, a. réfléchissant.

reflector, rē flĕk' tĕr, s. réflecteur, m.

reflex, rē flĕks, a. réflexe.

reform, rē fawrm', s. réforme, f.

reform, rē fawrm', v. a. & n. réformer || corriger. [de nouveau.

re-form, rē fawrm', v. a. reformer, former

reformation, rĕf ŏr mā' shŭn, s. réformation, f. [de correction, f.

reformatory, rē fawrm' ă tĕr ĭ, s. maison

reformer, rē fawrm' ĕr, s. réformateur, m.

reformist, rē fawrm' ĭst, s. réformé, m.

refract, rē frăkt', v. a. réfracter.

refraction, rē frăk' shŭn, s. réfraction, f.

refractoriness, rē frăk' tĕr ĭ nĕs, s. opiniâtreté, f. [obstiné.

refractory, rē frăk' tĕr ĭ, a. réfractaire,

refrain, rē frān', v. n. retenir || s'abstenir de.

refresh, rē frĕsh', v. a. rafraîchir || recréer.

refreshment, rē frĕsh' mĕnt, s. rafraîchissement, m. || ~-bar, s. buffet, m. || ~-room, s. buffet, m.

refrigerator, rē frĭj' ĕr ā tĕr, s. glacière, f., rafraîchissoir, m.

reft, rĕft, a. enlevé, ravi.

refuge, rĕf' ūj, s. refuge, m.

refugee, rĕf ū jē', s. réfugié, m.

refulgent, rē fŭl' jĕnt, a. rayonnant.

refund, rē fŭnd', v. a. restituer, rembourser.

refusal, rē fū' zăl, s. refus, m. || choix, m. || flat ~, refus net, catégorique.

refuse, rē fūs, s. refus, m || rebut, m., camelote, f.

refuse, rē fūz', v. a. & n. refuser.

refutation, rĕf ū tā' shŭn, s. réfutation, f.

refute, rē fūt', v. a. réfuter.

regain, rē gān', v. a. regagner.

regal, rē' găl, a. royal.

regale, rē găl', v. a. régaler. [royauté, m. pl.

regalia, rē gā' lĭ ă, s. pl. insignes de la

regard, rē gärd', s. égard, rapport, m. || considération, f. || with ~ to, à l'égard de.

regard, rē gärd', v. a. regarder, considérer || avoir égard à, estimer || as ~s, quant à.

regardful, rē gärd' fööl, a. attentif || plein d'égards || -ly, ad. avec égards.

regardless, rē gärd' lĕs, a. manquant d'égards, insouciant.

regards, rē gärdz', s. pl. amitiés, f. pl.

regatta, rē găt' tă, s. course en bateau, f.

regency, rē jĕn sĭ, s. régence, f.

regenerate, rē jĕn' ĕr āt, v. a. régénérer.

regenerate, rē jĕn' ĕr ăt, a. régénéré.

regeneration, rē jĕn ĕr ā' shŭn, s. régénération, f.

regent, rē' jĕnt, s. régent, m. [ration, f.

regicide, rē' jĭ sĭd, s. régicide, m.

re-gild, rē gĭld', v. a. redorer.

regimen, rē' jĭ mĕn, s. régime, m., diète, f.

regiment, rē' jĭ mĕnt, s. régiment, m.

regimental, rĕj ĭ mĕn' tăl, a. régimentaire.

regimentals, rĕj ĭ mĕn' tălz, s. pl. uniforme, m.

region, rē' jŭn, s. région, f. [forme, m.

register, rē' jĭs tĕr, s. registre, m.

register, rē' jĭs tĕr, v. a. enregistrer || enrôler || charger (a letter). [taire, m.

registrar, rĕj ĭs trär', s. greffier, secrétaire, m.

registration, rĕj ĭs trā' shŭn, s. enregistrement, m.

registry, rĕj' ĭs trĭ, s. secrétariat, m. || enregistrement, m. || ~-office, s. bureau de placement, m.

regret, rē grĕt', s. regret, m.

regret, rē grĕt', v. a. regretter || se repentir.

regretfully, rē grĕt' fööl lĭ, ad. à contrecœur.

regrettable, rē grĕt' ă bl, a. regrettable.

regular, rē' gū lăr, a. régulier, ordinaire || -ly, ad. régulièrement || -s, s. pl. troupes de ligne, f. pl.

regularity, rĕg ū lăr' ĭ tĭ, s. régularité, f.

regulate, rĕg' ū lāt, v. a. régler, ordonner.

regulation, rĕg ū lā' shŭn, s. règlement, m.

regulator, rĕg' ū lā tĕr, s. régulateur, m. || balancier, m. [liter.

rehabilitate, rē hă bĭl' ĭ tāt, v. a. réhabiliter.

rehabilitation, rē hă bĭ lĭ tā' shŭn, s. réhabilitation, f. [tion, f. || récitation, f.

rehearsal, rē hêrs' ăl, s. récit, m. || répétition, f.

rehearse, rē hêrs', v. a. répéter, réciter, raconter, rapporter.

reign, rān, s. règne, m. || souveraineté, autorité, f. [prévaloir.

reign, rān, v. n. régner, dominer sur || prévaloir.

reimburse, rē ĭm bêrs', v. a. rembourser.

reimbursement, rē ĭm bêrs' mĕnt, s. remboursement, m. [sonner.

reimprison, rē ĭm prĭz' ŏn, v. a. rempri-

rein, *răn,* s. rêne, bride, f. || **to give the ~ to,** lâcher la bride à.

rein, *răn,* v. a. tenir en bride.

reindeer, *răn'dĕr,* s. renne, f.

reinforce, *rē'ĭnfōrs',* v. a. renforcer.

re-insert, *rē'ĭnsĕrt',* v. a. insérer de nouveau. [tablir.

reinstate, *rē'ĭnstāt',* v. a. réintégrer, ré-

re-insure, *rē'ĭnshōr',* v. a. réassurer.

re-issue, *rē'ĭsh'shū,* s. nouvelle émission, f.

reiterate, *rē'ĭt'ĕrāt,* v. a. réitérer. [f.

reiteration, *rē'ĭt'ĕrā'shŭn,* s. réitération,f.

reject, *rējĕkt',* v. a. rejeter.

rejection, *rējĕk'shŭn,* s. rejection, f.

rejoice, *rējōys',* v. a. (& n.) (se) réjouir.

rejoicing, *rējōys'ĭng,* s. réjouissance, f.

rejoin, *rējōyn',* v. a. & n. rejoindre || ré-pliquer.

rejoinder, *rējōyn'dĕr,* s. réplique, f. || **to put in a ~,** (jur.) répliquer.

rejuvenate, *rējō'vĕnāt,* v. a. rajeunir.

rejuvenescence, *rējō'vĕnĕs'sĕns,* s. ra-jeunissement, m.

relapse, *rēlăps',* s. rechute, f.

relapse, *rēlăps',* v. n. retomber.

relate, *rēlāt',* v.a. & n. réciter || se rapporter.

related, *rēlā'tĕd,* a. parent, allié.

relater, *rēlā'tĕr,* s. narrateur, m. [f.

relation, *rēlā'shŭn,* s. relation,f. || parenté,

relationship, *rēlā'shŭn'shĭp,* s. parenté, f.

relative, *rĕl'ătĭv,* s. pronom relatif, m. || parent, m. [lativement.

relative, *rĕl'ătĭv,* a. relatif || -ly, ad. re-

relax, *rēlăks',* v. a. & n. relâcher || délas-ser || se relâcher || se radoucir.

relaxation, *rēlăksā'shŭn,* s. relâchement, f.

relaxing, *rēlăks'ĭng,* a. énervant. [m.

relay, *rēlā',* s. relais, m.

release, *rēlēs',* s. élargissement, m., dé-livrance, quittance, f.

release, *rēlēs',* v. a. relâcher, dégager, décharger || quitter.

relegate, *rĕl'ĕgāt,* v. a. reléguer.

relegation, *rēlēgā'shŭn,* s. relégation, f.

relent, *rēlĕnt',* v. n. s'adoucir || se fondre || céder. [flexible.

relentless, *rēlĕnt'lĕss,* a. impitoyable, in-

relevant, *rĕl'ĕvănt,* a. qui soulage || se rapportant à.

reliance, *rēlī'ăns,* s. confiance, f.

relic, *rĕl'ĭk,* s. reste, m. || relique, f.

relict, *rĕl'ĭkt,* s. veuve, f.

relief, *rēlēf',* s. relief, m. || soulagement, m., aide, f. || pose, f.

relieve, *rēlēv',* v. a. soulager, secourir || délivrer || relever (une sentinelle).

relieving-officer, *rēlēv'ĭngŏf'fĭsĕr,* s. commissaire des pauvres, m.

relievo, *rēlēv'ō,* s. relief, m.

re-light, *rēlīt',* v. a. rallumer.

religion, *rēlĭj'ŭn,* s. religion, f. || dévo-tion, piété, f.

religious, *rēlĭj'ŭs,* a. religieux.|| -ly, ad. religieusement.

religiousness, *rēlĭj'ŭsnĕs,* s. piété, f.

relinquish, *rēlĭng'kwĭsh,* v. a. aban-donner, renoncer.

relinquishment, *rēlĭng'kwĭshmĕnt,* s. abandon, m., cession, f.

reliquary, *rĕl'ĭkwărĭ,* s. reliquaire, m.

relish, *rĕl'ĭsh,* s. goût, m. || plaisir, m.

relish, *rĕl'ĭsh,* v. a. & n. donner du goût, approuver, savourer || avoir bon goût.

relishable, *rĕl'ĭshăbl,* relishing, *rĕl'-ĭshĭng,* a. appétissant, savoureux.

reluctance, *rēlŭk'tăns,* s. répugnance, f.

reluctant, *rēlŭk'tănt,* a. qui agit avec ré-pugnance || peu disposé || -ly, ad. à contre-cœur.

rely, *rēlī',* v. n. compter sur, se reposer sur.

remain, *rēmān',* v. n. rester, s'arrêter, demeurer || durer. [résidu, m.

remainder, *rēmān'dĕr,* s. reste, restant,

remains, *rēmānz',* s. pl. restes, débris, m. pl. || dépouille mortelle, f.

remand, *rēmănd',* v.a. remander, rappeler.

remark, *rēmărk',* s. remarque, f.

remark, *rēmărk',* v.a. remarquer, observer.

remarkable, *rēmărk'ăbl,* a. remarquable.

remarkably, *rēmărk'ăblĭ,* ad. remar-quablement. [marier.

remarry, *rēmăr'rĭ,* v. a. (& n.) (se) re-

remediable, *rēmē'dĭăbl,* a. remédiable.

remedial, *rēmē'dĭăl,* a. réparateur || curatif.

remediless, *rēm'ēdĭlĕs,* a. irrémédiable.

remedy, *rĕm'ĕdĭ,* s. remède, m. || recours, m. [m.

remedy, *rĕm'ĕdĭ,* v. a. remédier.

remember, *rēmĕm'bĕr,* v. a. & n. se sou-venir, se remettre, se rappeler || faire men-tion de || to ~ another kindly to one, rappeler qn. au bon souvenir d'un autre.

remembrance, *rēmĕm'brăns,* s. souvenir, m. || mémoire, f. || kind -s ! mille choses de ma part ! [moire.

remind, *rēmīnd',* v. a. rappeler à la mé-

reminder, *rēmīnd'ĕr,* s. souvenir, m.

reminiscence, *rĕm'ĭnĭs'sĕns,* s. rémi-niscence, f.

remiss, *rēmĭs',* a. négligent, paresseux || -ly, ad. nonchalamment.

remissible, *rēmĭs'sĭbl,* a. rémissible.

remission, *rēmĭsh'ŭn,* s. rémission, f., pardon, m. || indulgence, f. || relâche, m.

remit, *rēmĭt',* v. a. & n. relâcher, adoucir || remettre, faire remettre, envoyer || se re-lâcher, se ralentir.

remittance, *rēmĭt'ăns,* s. (com.) remise, f.

remnant, *rĕm'nănt,* s. reste, restant, m. || coupon (de drap), m. [mer.

remodel, *rēmŏd'ĕl,* v. a. remodeler, réfor-

remonstrance, *rēmŏn'străns,* s. remon-trance, f. [remontrances.

remonstrate, *rēmŏn'strāt,* v. a. faire des

remorse, *rēmōrs',* s. remords, m.

remorseful, *rēmōrs'fŏŏl,* a. déchiré de remords. [cruel.

remorseless, *rēmōrs'lĕs,* a. sans remords.

remote, *rēmōt',* a. éloigné, reculé || -ly, ad. de or au loin || faiblement.

remoteness, *rēmōt'nĕs,* s. éloignement, m. || distance, f.

remount, *rēmŏŭnt',* s. (mil.) remonte, f.

remount, *rēmŏŭnt',* v. a. & n. remonter.

removable, *rēmŏv'ăbl,* a. amovible.

removal, rĕmŏv'ăl, s. déplacement, éloignement, départ, m. || transport, m. || déposition, f.

remove, rĕmŏv', s. déménagement, m. || relevé, m. || départ, m.

remove, rĕmŏv', v. a. & n. déplacer, ôter, éloigner || lever, transférer || s'éloigner || changer de logement, déménager.

remunerate, rĕmŭ'nĕr ăt, v.a. rémunérer.

remuneration, rĕmŭnĕr ă'shŭn, s. rémunération, f.   [nérateur.

remunerative, rĕmŭ'nĕr ă'tĭv, a. rému-

renaissance, rĕnăs'sănz, s. la Renaissance (au 15e siècle).

rencounter, rĕn kŏŭn'tĕr, s. rencontre, f., choc, m. || combat, m.

rend, rĕnd, v. a. déchirer, fendre.

render, rĕn'dĕr, v. a. rendre || traduire.

rendezvous, rĕn'dĕvŏ ou răng'dĕvŏ, v. n. se donner rendez-vous.

renegade, rĕn'ĕgăd, s. renégat, m.

renew, rĕnŭ', v. a. renouveler.

renewal, rĕnŭ'ăl, s. renouvellement, m.

rennet, rĕn'nĕt, s. présure, f.   [savourer.

renounce, rĕnŏŭns', v. a. renoncer, dé-

renovate, rĕn'ŏvăt, v. a. renouveler.

renovation, rĕnŏvă'shŭn, s. renouvellement, m.

renown, rĕnŏŭn', s. renommée, f.

renowned, rĕnŏŭnd', a. renommé, célèbre.   [revenu, loyer, m.

rent, rĕnt, s. déchirure, fente, f. || rente, f.,

rent, rĕnt, v. a. & n. donner à louage, louer.

rentable, rĕnt'ă bl, a. qui peut-être loué.

rental, rĕnt'ăl, s. état de revenus, m.

renter, rĕnt'ĕr, s. locataire, f.

renunciation, rĕnŭn si ă'shŭn, s. renonciation, f.

reoccupy, rĕŏk kū'pĭ, v. a. réoccuper.

reopen, rĕŏ'pn, v. a. & n. rouvrir || (of schools) rentrer.   [écoles, f.

reopening, rĕŏ'pn ĭng, s. rentrée des

reorganisation, rĕŏr găn ĭ ză'shŭn, s. réorganisation, f.

reorganise, rĕŏr'găn ĭz, v. a. réorganiser.

repair, rĕpăr', s. réparation, f. || to keep in ~, entretenir en bon état.

repair, rĕpăr', v. a. & n. réparer, raccommoder || dédommager || se rendre à.

repairer, rĕpăr'ĕr, s. réparateur, raccommodeur, m.

reparable, rĕp'ăr ă bl, a. réparable.

reparation, rĕpă ră'shŭn, s. réparation, f.

repartee, rĕp ăr tĕ', s. réplique prompte et frappante, f.

re-pass, rĕpăs', v. a. repasser.

repast, rĕpăst', s. dîner, m.   [rendre.

repay, rĕpă', v. a. repayer, rembourser.

repayable, rĕpă'ă bl, a. remboursable.

repayment, rĕpă'mĕnt, s. remboursement, m.   [f.

repeal, rĕpĕl', s. révocation, abrogation,

repeal, rĕpĕl', v. a. révoquer, abroger.

repealable, rĕpĕl'ă bl, a. révocable.

repeat, rĕpĕt', v. a. répéter, réitérer, réciter.   [reprises.

repeatedly, rĕpĕ'tĕd lĭ, ad. à plusieurs

repeater, rĕpĕt'ĕr, s. montre à répétition, f.

repel, rĕpĕl', v. a. repousser.

repent, rĕpĕnt', v. a. & n. se repentir.

repentance, rĕpĕnt'ăns, s. repentir, m.

repentant, rĕpĕnt'ănt, a. repentant.

repeople, rĕpĕ'pl, v. a. repeupler.

repercussion, rĕpĕr kŭsh'ŭn, s. répercussion, f.

repertory, rĕp'ĕr tĕr ĭ, s. répertoire, f.

reperusal, rĕpĕrŏ'zl, s. nouvelle lecture, f.

repetition, rĕp ĕ tĭsh'ŭn, s. répétition, f. || (mus.) reprise.

repine, rĕpīn', v. n. s'affliger.

repining, rĕpīn'ĭng, s. murmure, m.

replace, rĕplăs', v. a. replacer, remplacer.

replant, rĕplănt', v. a. replanter.

replantation, rĕplăn tă'shŭn, s. replantation, f.   [achever.

replenish, rĕplĕn'ĭsh, v. a. remplir,

replete, rĕplĕt', a. rempli, plein.

repletion, rĕplĕ'shŭn, s. réplétion, f.

reply, rĕplī', s. réponse, f.

reply, rĕplī', v. a. répliquer, répondre.

report, rĕpŏrt', s. bruit, m. || réputation, f. || récit, rapport, m. || compte-rendu, m. || détonation, f.

report, rĕpŏrt', v. a. rapporter, faire un rapport, rendre compte || to ~ oneself, donner son signalement.

reporter, rĕpŏrt'ĕr, s. rapporteur, m. || correspondant, sténographe, m. || ~-s' gallery, s. tribune des journalistes, f.

reporting, rĕpŏrt'ĭng, s. comptes-rendus de journaux, m., correspondance, f.

repose, rĕpŏz', s. repos, m.

repose, rĕpŏz', v. a. & n. (se) reposer.

repository, rĕpŏz'ĭ tĕr ĭ, s. dépôt, magasin, m.   [session de.

repossess, rĕpŏz zĕs', v. a. rentrer en pos-

reprehensible, rĕp rĕ hĕn'sĭ bl, a. blâmable.   [manière répréhensible.

reprehensibly, rĕp rĕ hĕn'sĭ blĭ, ad. d'une

represent, rĕp rĕ zĕnt', v. a. représenter.

representation, rĕp rĕ zĕn tă'shŭn, s. représentation, f.   [puté, m.

representative, rĕp rĕ zĕnt'ă tĭv, s. dé-

representative, rĕp rĕ zĕnt'ă tĭv, a. représentatif.

repress, rĕprĕs', v. a. réprimer.

repression, rĕprĕsh'ŭn, s. répression, f.

repressive, rĕprĕs'sĭv, a. répressif.

reprieve, rĕprēv', s. sursis, m. || répit, m.

reprieve, rĕprēv', v. a. (jur.) accorder un sursis, surseoir à.

reprimand, rĕp'rĭmănd, s. réprimande, f.

reprimand, rĕp'rĭmănd, v. a. réprimander, blâmer.

reprint, rĕ'prĭnt, s. réimpression, f.

reprint, rĕprĭnt', v. a. réimprimer.

reprisal, rĕprī'zăl, s. repr°saille, f.   [f.

reproach, rĕprŏch', s. reproche, m. || honte,

reproach, rĕprŏch', v. a. reprocher.

reproachable, rĕprŏch'ă bl, a. digne de blâme.

reproachful, rĕprŏch'fŏŭl, a. injurieux || honteux || ~-ly, ad. injurieusement, honteusement.

reprobate, rĕp'rŏbāt, s. réprouvé, m.
reprobate, rĕp'rŏbāt, v. a. réprouver.
reprobate, rĕp'rŏbāt, a. réprouvé.
reprobation, rĕprŏbā'shŭn, s. réprobation, f.
reproduce, rēprŏdūs', v. a. reproduire.
reproduction, rēprŏdŭk'shŭn, s. reproduction, f. [mande, f.
reproof, rēprōf', s. reproche, m., répri-
reprovable, rēprōv'ăbl, a. répréhensible.
reprove, rēprōv', v. a. réprimander.
reprovingly, rēprōv'ĭnglĭ, ad. en guise de reproche.
reptile, rĕp'tĭl, s. reptile, m.
reptile, rĕp'tĭl, reptilian, rĕptĭl'ĭăn, a. reptile || rampant || bas, vil.
republic, rēpŭb'lĭk, s. république, f. [m.
republican, rēpŭb'lĭkăn, s. républicain,
republican, rēpŭb'lĭkăn, a. républicain.
republicanise, rēpŭb'lĭkănīz, v. a. rendre républicain. [publicanisme, m.
republicanism, rēpŭb'lĭkănĭzm, s. ré-
republication, rēpŭb'lĭkā'shŭn, s. nouvelle édition, f.
republish, rēpŭb'lĭsh, v. a. republier.
repudiate, rēpū'dĭāt, v. a. répudier.
repugnance, rēpŭg'năns, s. répugnance, f. || contrariété, f. || résistance, f.
repugnant, rēpŭg'nănt, a. répugnant || -ly, ad. avec répugnance.
repulse, rēpŭls', s. refus, m.
repulse, rēpŭls', v. a. repousser, refuser.
repulsion, rēpŭl'shŭn, s. répulsion, f.
repulsive, rēpŭl'sĭv, a. repoussant || (phys.) répulsif || -ly, ad. d'une manière repoussante || froidement.
repurchase, rēpĕr'chăs, s. rachat, m.
repurchase, rēpĕr'chăs, v. a. racheter.
reputable, rĕp'ūtăbl, a. honorable.
reputably, rĕp'ūtăblĭ, ad. honorablement.
reputation, rĕpūtā'shŭn, s. réputation, f.
repute, rēpūt', s. réputation, f.
repute, rēpūt', v. a. réputer.
request, rēkwĕst', s. requête, demande, prière, f. || réputation, f. [liciter.
request, rēkwĕst', v. a. demander, sol-
requiem, rē'kwĭĕm, s. requiem, m.
require, rēkwīr', v. a. demander || exiger || avoir besoin. [f., besoin, m.
requirement, rēkwīr'mĕnt, s. demande,
requisite, rĕk'wĭzĭt, s. chose nécessaire, f.
requisite, rĕk'wĭzĭt, a. requis, nécessaire.
requisition, rĕkwĭzĭsh'ŭn, s. réquisition, demande, f.
requisitionist, rĕkwĭzĭsh'ŭnĭst, s. signataire d'une convocation (or invitation), m. [pense, f.
requital, rēkwī'tăl, s. revanche, f. || récom-
requite, rēkwīt', v. a. récompenser || se venger || prendre sa revanche.
rescind, rēsĭnd', v. a. rescinder, annuler.
rescript, rē'skrĭpt, s. rescrit, édit, m.
rescue, rĕs'kū, s. délivrance, f. || secours, m.
rescue, rĕs'kū, v. a. délivrer, tirer de.
research, rēsĕrch', s. recherche, f.
reseat, rēsēt', v. a. rasseoir.
re-seize, rēsēz', v. a. ressaisir.

resemblance, rēzĕm'blăns, s. ressemblance, image, f.
resemble, rēzĕm'bl, v. a. ressembler.
resent, rēzĕnt', v. a. ressentir.
resenter, rēzĕnt'ĕr, s. personne animée de ressentiment, f. [catif.
resentful, rēzĕnt'fōōl, a. haineux, vindi-
resentment, rēzĕnt'mĕnt, s. ressentiment, m. [restriction, f. || arrière-pensée, f.
reservation, rēzĕrvā'shŭn, s. réserve,
reserve, rēzĕrv', s. réserve, f.
reserve, rēzĕrv', v. a. réserver.
reservedly, rēzĕr'vĕdlĭ, ad. avec réserve.
reservoir, rēzĕrvăwr', s. réservoir, m. || puisard, m. [diquer de nouveau.
reset, rēsĕt', v. a. reposer, remettre, in-
reship, rēshĭp', v. a. rembarquer.
reshipment, rēshĭp'mĕnt, s. rembarquement, m:
reside, rēzīd', v. n. résider, demeurer.
residence, rĕz'ĭdĕns, s. résidence, f. || domicile, m. [domicile, m.
residency, rĕz'ĭdĕnsĭ, s. résidence, f.,
resident, rĕz'ĭdĕnt, a. résidant, demeurant.
residential, rĕzĭdĕn'shăl, a. de résidence.
residue, rĕz'ĭdū, s. résidu, restant, m.
residuum, rēzĭd'ūŭm, s.(chem.) résidu, m.
resign, rēzīn', v. a. & n. résigner, céder, donner sa démission || se soumettre.
resignation, rēzĭgnā'shŭn, s. résignation, f. || démission, f.
resigner, rēzīn'ĕr, s. démissionnaire, m.
resin, rĕz'ĭn, s. résine, f.
resinous, rĕz'ĭnŭs, a. résineux.
resist, rēzĭst', v. a. résister. [sistance.
resistable, rēzĭst'ăbl, a. capable de ré-
resistance, rēzĭst'ăns, s. résistance, f.
resolute, rĕz'ōlŏt, a. (-ly, ad.) résolu (ment).
resolution, rēzōlŏ'shŭn, s. résolution, f. || to come to a ~, prendre une résolution.
resolvable, rēzŏlv'ăbl, a. résoluble.
resolve, rēzŏlv', v. a. & n. résoudre, décider || se déterminer || se fondre.
resonance, rĕz'ōnăns, s. résonnance, f.
resonant, rĕz'ōnănt, a. résonnant.
resort, rēzŏrt', s. recours, m., assemblée, f. || refuge, m.
resort, rēzŏrt', v. n. recourir || fréquenter.
resound, rēzŏwnd', v. n. résonner.
resource, rēsŏrs', s. ressource, f.
respect, rēspĕkt', s. respect, égard, m., estime, vénération, f. || motif, rapport, m. || -s, pl. devoirs, hommages, m. pl. || in ~ of, par rapport à || with ~ to, à l'égard de.
respect, rēspĕkt', v. a. respecter || regarder.
respectability, rēspĕktăbĭl'ĭtĭ, s. respectabilité, f. [estimable.
respectable, rēspĕkt'ăbl, a. respectable ||
respectably, rēspĕkt'ăblĭ, ad. d'une manière respectable.
respectful, rēspĕkt'fōōl, a. respectueux || -ly, ad. avec respect.
respecting, rēspĕkt'ĭng, prp. à l'égard de.
respective, rēspĕkt'ĭv, a. respectif, relatif || -ly, ad. respectivement, relativement.

respirator, rĕs'pĭ rā'tĕr, s. respirateur, m.

respite, rĕs'pĭt, s. délai, répit, m. || surséance, f., sursis, m.   [surseoir.

respite, rĕs'pĭt, v. a. donner du répit ||

resplendence, rĕ splĕn'dĕns, s. éclat, m.

resplendent, rĕ splĕn'dĕnt, a. resplendissant.

respond, rĕ spŏnd', v. n. répondre.

respondent, rĕ spŏnd'ĕnt, s. (jur.) défendeur, m.   [m.

response, rĕ spŏns', s. réponse, f., écho,

responsibility, rĕ spŏn sĭ bĭl'ĭ tĭ, s. responsabilité, f.

responsible, rĕ spŏn'sĭ bl, a. responsable.

responsive, rĕ spŏn'sĭv, a. (-ly, ad.) qui répond, qui correspond || en réponse.

responsiveness, rĕ spŏn'sĭv nĕs, s. accord, m., correspondance, f.

rest, rĕst, s. repos, m. || (mus.) silence, f. (poet.) césure, f. || arrêt, m. || reste, m. || les autres.

rest, rĕst, v. n. se reposer || se coucher || ~, v. a. reposer, appuyer.   [repos, m.

resting-place, rĕst'ing plās, s. lieu de

restitution, rĕs tĭ tū'shŭn, s. restitution, f.

restive, rĕs'tĭv, a. rétif, opiniâtre.

restless, rĕst'lĕs, a. sans repos, inquiet || -ly, ad. avec inquiétude.

restoration, rĕs tō rā'shŭn, s. restitution, restauration, f.

restorative, rĕ stŏr'ā tĭv, s. restaurant, m.

restorative, rĕ stŏr'ā tĭv, a. restaurant, fortifiant.

restore, rĕ stōr', v. a. restituer || rendre.

restrain, rĕ strān', v. a. retenir || restreindre.

restraint, rĕ strānt', s. contrainte, f. || restriction, gêne, f. || to be under ~, vivre dans la contrainte.

restrict, rĕ strĭkt', v. a. restreindre.

restriction, rĕ strĭk'shŭn, s. restriction, f.

restrictive, rĕ strĭk'tĭv, a. restrictif.

result, rĕ zŭlt', s. résultat, m.

result, rĕ zŭlt', v. n. résulter.

resultant, rĕ zŭlt'ĕnt, s. résultante, f.

resume, rĕ zūm', v. a. reprendre || renouer.

resumption, rĕ zŭm'shŭn, s. reprise, f. || continuation, f.

resurrection, rĕz ĕr rĕk'shŭn, s. résurrection, f. || ~-man, s. voleur de cadavres, m. || ~-pie, s. pâté de restes de viande, m.

resuscitate, rĕ sŭs'sĭ tāt, v. a. faire revivre.

resuscitation, rĕ sŭs sĭ tā'shŭn, s. résurrection, f., retour à la vie, m.

retail, rĕ tāl', s. vente en détail, f.

retail, rĕ tāl', v. a. détailler || vendre en détail.   [débiteur, m.

retailer, rĕ tāl'ĕr, s. (com.) détaillant, m. ||

retain, rĕ tān', v. a. retenir || conserver.

retainer, rĕ tān'ĕr, s. partisan, m. || honoraire, m. || appui, m. || -s, pl. suite, f.

retake, rĕ tāk', v. a. reprendre.   [sailles.

retaliate, rĕ tāl'ĭ āt, v. a. user de repré

retaliation, rĕ tāl ĭ ā'shŭn, s. talion, m.

retaliatory, rĕ tāl'ĭ ā tĕr ĭ, a. en représaille.

retard, rĕ tārd', v. a. retarder.

retardation, rĕ tār dā'shŭn, s. retardement, m.

retch, rĕch, v. n. faire des haut-le-corps.

retell, rĕ tĕl', v. a. redire, répéter.

retention, rĕ tĕn'shŭn, s. conservation, f. || mémoire, f.   [(mémoire).

retentive, rĕ tĕn'tĭv, a. fidèle, tenace

reticence, rĕt'ĭ sĕns, s. réticence, f.

reticent, rĕt'ĭ sĕnt, a. taciturne.

reticle, rĕt'ĭ kl, s. petit filet, m.

reticule, rĕt'ĭ kūl, s. sac, ridicule, m.

retina, rĕt'ĭ nā, s. rétine, f.

retinue, rĕt'ĭ nū, s. suite, f. || cortège, m.

retire, rĕ tīr', v. a. (& n.) (se) retirer.

retired, rĕ tīrd', a. solitaire, secret || ~ list, s. contrôle des personnes (or officiers) en retraite, m.

retirement, rĕ tīr'mĕnt, s. retraite, f.

retiring, rĕ tīr'ing, a. qui fuit le monde || ~ pension, s. pension de retraite, f.

retort, rĕ tŏrt', s. réplique, f. || (chem.) cornue, f.   [la pareille.

retort, rĕ tŏrt', v. a. & n. retorquer, rendre

retouch, rĕ tŭch', v. a. retoucher.

retrace, rĕ trās', v. a. retracer || revenir sur.

retract, rĕ trăkt', v. a. (& n.) (se) rétracter.

retraction, rĕ trăk'shŭn, s. rétractation, f.

retreat, rĕ trēt', s. retraite, f.

retreat, rĕ trēt', v. n. se retirer || (mil.) battre en retraite.   [trancher.

retrench, rĕ trĕnsh', v. a. (& n.) (se) re

retrenchment, rĕ trĕnsh'mĕnt, s. retranchement, m.

retribution, rĕt rĭ bū'shŭn, s. remboursement, m. || récompense, f.   [teur.

retributory, rĕ trĭb'ū tĕr ĭ, a. rémunéra

retrievable, rĕ trēv'ā bl, a. recouvrable.

retrieve, rĕ trēv', v. a. recouvrer || rétablir, réparer, récupérer.   [m.

retriever, rĕ trēv'ĕr, s. bigle, charnaigre.

retroactive, rĕ trō ăk'tĭv, a. rétroactif.

retrograde, rĕ trō grād, v. n. rétrograder, aller en arrière.

retrograde, rĕ trō grād, a. rétrograde.

retrogression, rĕ trō grĕsh'ŭn, s. mouvement rétrograde, m.

retrospect, rĕ trō spĕkt, retrospection, rĕ trō spĕk'shŭn, s. revue du passé, f. || coup d'œil rétrospectif, m.   [spectif.

retrospective, rĕ trō spĕk'tĭv, a. rétro

retry, rĕ trī', v. a. essayer de nouveau.

return, rĕ tĕrn', s. retour, m. || rétrogression, rentrée, f. || récompense, f. || détail, rapport, m., liste, f. || élection, f. || profit, m. || remise, f.

return, rĕ tĕrn', v. a. rendre, restituer || renvoyer || élire || retourner, revenir || répondre || to ~ to Parliament, nommer membre du Parlement.   [(jur.) de renvoi.

returnable, rĕ tĕrn'ā bl, a. restituable ||

reunion, rĕ ūn'yŭn, s. réunion, f.

reunite, rĕ ū nīt', v. a. (& n.) (se) réunir.

reveal, rĕ vēl', v. a. révéler.

revel, rĕv'ĕl, s. orgie, f.

revel, rĕv'ĕl, v. n. bacchanaliser.

revelation, rĕv ĕ lā'shŭn, s. révélation, f. || Book of Revelations, Apocalypse, f.

reveller, rĕv'ĕl ĕr, s. joyeux convive, noceur, m.

revelry, *rĕv′ĕl rĭ*, s. réjouissance tumul-
tueuse, orgie, f. [vanche, f.
revenge, *rĕvĕnj′*, s. vengeance, f. || re-
revenge, *rĕvĕnj′*, v. a. venger.
revengeful, *rĕvĕnj′fōōl*, a. vindicatif ||
-ly, ad. avec vengeance.
revenue, *rĕv′ĕnū*, s. revenu, m., rente, f. ||
~ officer, s. douanier, m.
reverberate, *rĕvĕr′bĕr āt*, v. a. réverbérer,
réfléchir || répercuter.
reverberation, *rĕvĕr bĕr ā′shŭn*, s. ré-
verbération, f. || répercussion, f.
reverberatory, *rĕvĕr′bĕr ā tĕr ĭ*, a. ré-
verbérant. [v. a. révérer, honorer.
revere, *rĕvēr′*, reverence, *rĕv′ĕr ĕns*,
reverence, *rĕv′ĕr ĕns*, s. révérence, f.
reverend, *rĕv′ĕr ĕnd*, s. abbé, m. || pasteur,
m. [Reverend, (titre) Révérendissime.
reverend, *rĕv′ĕr ĕnd*, a. vénérable || Right
reverent, *rĕv′ĕr ĕnt*, reverential, *rĕv-
ĕr ĕn′shăl*, a. (-ly, ad.) révérencieux || re-
apectueux || respectueusement.
reversal, *rĕvĕr′săl*, s. cassation, f.
reverse, *rĕvĕrs′*, s. revers, m. || vicissitude,
f. || contraire, m.
reverse, *rĕvĕrs′*, v. a. renverser || abolir ||
to ~ an engine, changer le sens du
mouvement d'une locomotive.
reversible, *rĕvĕr′sĭ bl*, a. révocable || (of
clothes) à deux endroits.
reversion, *rĕvĕr′shŭn*, s. réversion, f. ||
survivance, f. [réversible.
reversionary, *rĕvĕr′shŭn ĕr ĭ*, a. (jur.)
revert, *rĕvĕrt′*, v. a. retourner, revenir.
revictual, *rĕvĭt′l*, v. a. ravitailler.
review, *rĕvū′*, s. revue, f. || inspection, f.,
examen, m. || critique, f.
review, *rĕvū′*, v. s. faire la revue (des
troupes), passer en revue || revoir, reviser ||
critiquer. [censeur, m.
reviewer, *rĕvū′ĕr*, s. journaliste, critique,
revile, *rĕvīl′*, v. a. injurier, outrager.
revise, *rĕvīz′*, s. seconde épreuve, f.
revise, *rĕvīz′*, v. a. revoir, reviser.
reviser, *rĕvī′zĕr*, s. réviseur, m.
revision, *rĕvĭzh′ŭn*, s. révision, revue, f.
revisit, *rĕvĭz′ĭt*, v. a. visiter de nouveau.
revival, *rĕvī′văl*, s. retour à la vie, m. ||
renaissance, f.
revive, *rĕvīv′*, v. a. & n. faire revivre,
ranimer || revenir en vie || se rétablir.
reviver, *rĕvī′vĕr*, s. restaurateur, m.
revocable, *rĕv′ō kă bl*, a. révocable.
revocation, *rĕv ō kā′shŭn*, s. révocation,
revoke, *rĕvōk′*, v. a. révoquer. [f.
revolt, *rĕvōlt′*, s. révolte, f.
revolt, *rĕvōlt′*, v. n. se révolter.
revolting, *rĕvōlt′ĭng*, a. révoltant.
revolution, *rĕv ō lū′shŭn*, s. révolution, f.
revolutionary, *rĕv ō lū′shŭn ĕr ĭ*, a. révolutionnaire. [lutionnaire, m.
revolutionist, *rĕv ō lū′shŭn ĭst*, s. révo-
revolutionise, *rĕv ō lū′shŭn īz*, v. a. ré-
volutionner. [ter || tourner.
revolve, *rĕvōlv′*, v. a. & n. rouler || médi-
revolver, *rĕvōlv′ĕr*, s. pistolet or fusil à
répétition, m.

revolving, *rĕvōlv′ĭng*, a. tournant || pério-
dique.
reward, *rĕwawrd′*, s. récompense, f.
reward, *rĕwawrd′*, v. a. récompenser.
rewarder, *rĕwawrd′ĕr*, s. rémunérateur, m.
rewrite, *rĕrīt′*, v. a. récrire || rédiger de
nouveau.
rhapsody, *răp′sō dĭ*, s. rapsodie, f.
rhetoric, *rĕt′ō rĭk*, s. rhétorique, f.
rhetorical, *rĕtŏr′ĭ kăl*, a. de rhétorique.
rhetorician, *rĕt ō rĭsh′ăn*, s. rhétoricien,
rhéteur, m.
rheum, *rōm*, s. rhume, m., humeur, f.
rheumatic, *rō măt′ĭk*, a. rhumatique.
rheumatism, *rō′mă tĭzm*, s. rhumatisme,
m., douleurs rhumatismales, f. pl.
rhinoceros, *rĭnŏs′ĕr ŏs*, s. rhinocéros, m.
rhododendron, *rō dō dĕn′drŏn*, s. (bot.)
rhododendron, m.
rhomb, *rŏm*, s. rhombe, m., losange, f.
rhomboid, *rŏm′bŏyd*, s. rhomboïde, m.
rhubarb, *rō′bărb*, s. rhubarbe, f.
rhyme, *rīm*, s. rime, f., vers, m. || with-
out ~ or reason, sans rime ni raison.
rhyme, *rīm*, v. a. & n. rimer || rimailler.
rhym(st)er, *rīm′(st)ĕr*, s. rimailleur, m.
rhythm, *rĭthm*, s. rhythme, m.
rhythmical, *rĭth′mĭ kăl*, a. rhythmique.
rib, *rĭb*, s. côte, f. || nervure, f.
rib, *rĭb*, v. a. garnir de côtes.
ribald, *rĭb′ăld*, a. bas, vil, obscène.
ribaldry, *rĭb′ăld rĭ*, s. obscénités, f. pl.
ribbon, *rĭb′ŏn*, s. ruban, m.
rice, *rĭs*, s. riz, m. || ~-field, s. rizière, f.
rich, *rĭch*, a. (-ly, ad.) riche(ment) || opu-
lent || abondant || précieux || vineux.
riches, *rĭch′ĕs*, s. pl. richesses, f. pl.
richness, *rĭch′nĕs*, s. richesse, f. || abon-
dance, f. || vinosité, f. || succulence, f.
rick, *rĭk*, s. tas, m., meule, f.
rickets, *rĭk′ĕts*, s. pl. rachitis, m.
rickety, *rĭk′ĕt ĭ*, a. rachitique || (of fur-
niture) boiteux.
ricochet, *rĭk′ō shĕt*, v. a. ricocher.
rid, *rĭd*, v. a. ir. délivrer, débarrasser.
riddance, *rĭd′dăns*, s. délivrance, f., débarras, m.
riddle, *rĭd′dl*, s. énigme, f. || crible, m.
riddle, *rĭd′dl*, v. a. cribler.
ride, *rĭd*, s. promenade à cheval or en
voiture, f. || allée, f.
ride, *rĭd*, v. a. & n. ir. aller à cheval or
en voiture || monter || to ~ out a gale,
(mar.) tenir bon sur ses ancres dans un
coup de vent. [annexe, f.
rider, *rī′dĕr*, s. cavalier, m. || écuyer, m. ||
ridge, *rĭj*, s. épine du dos, f. || comble, m.,
faîte, f., sommet, m. || sillon, m. || écueil,
récif, m. [canneler.
ridge, *rĭj*, v. a. hausser, élever || sillonner
ridicule, *rĭd′ĭ kūl*, s. ridicule, m. || to
turn into ~, tourner en ridicule || to
bring ~ on one, ridiculiser qn. [cule.
ridicule, *rĭd′ĭ kūl*, v. a. tourner en ridi-
ridiculous, *rĭ dĭk′ū lŭs*, a. (-ly, ad.) ridi-
cule(ment). [cule, m.
ridiculousness, *rĭ dĭk′ū lŭs nĕs*, s. ridi-

riding, *rī′dĭng*, s. équitation, f. || ~-**coat,** s. redingote (de voyage), f. || ~-**habit,** s. amazone, f. || ~-**horse,** s. cheval de selle, m. || ~-**master,** s. maître d'équitation, m. || ~-**school,** s. manège, m. || ~-**whip,** s.

riding, *rī′dĭng*, a. à cheval. [cravache, f.

rife, *rīf,* a. régnant, commun, abondant.

riffraff, *rĭf′răf,* s. rebut, m. || canaille, f.

rifle, *rī′fl,* s. carabine, f. || ~-**man,** s. carabinier, m. || tirailleur, m. || ~-**pit,** s. (mil.) tranchée-abri, f. || ~-**sword,** s. sabre-baïonnette, m. [gun) rayer.

rifle, *rī′fl,* v. a. piller, voler || vider || (a

riflor, *rī′flĕr,* s. pillard, m.

rig, *rĭg,* s. farce, f.

rig, *rĭg,* v. a. équiper || gréer || attifer || to ~ **the market,** faire hausser les prix || ~-**out,** s. habillement, costume, m.

rigger, *rĭg′ĕr,* s. gréeur, m. [m. pl.

rigging, *rĭg′ĭng,* s. agrès d'un vaisseau,

right, *rĭt,* s. droit, m. || droite, f.

right, *rĭt,* v. a. rendre justice, faire droit à || redresser.

right, *rĭt,* a. & ad. droit || convenable, propre || véritable || juste, honnête || droit || directement, justement, exactement, bien || très || **to set one ~,** remettre qn. à sa place || ~ **and left,** la droite et la gauche || de chaque côté || ~-**ly,** ad. bien || à juste titre.

righteous, *rī′t yŭs* ou *rī′chŭs,* a. (-ly, ad.) juste(ment) || probe. [justice, f.

righteousness, *rī′t yŭs′nĕs,* s. droiture, f. ||

rigid, *rĭj′ĭd,* a. (-ly, ad.) rigide(ment).

rigidity, *rĭ jĭd′ĭ tĭ,* s. rigidité, sévérité, f.

rigmarole, *rĭg′mă rōl,* s. galimatias, m.

rigorous, *rĭg′ĕr ŭs,* a. rigoureux || -ly, ad. rigoureusement.

rigour, *rĭg′ĕr,* s. rigueur, f.

rill, *rĭl,* s. petit ruisseau, ruisselet, m.

rim, *rĭm,* s. bord, m., marge, f.

rime, *rīm,* s. givre, m.

rimy, *rī′mĭ,* a. couvert de givre.

rind, *rīnd,* s. écorce, peau, f. || (of bacon) couenne, f.

ring, *rĭng,* s. anneau, m., bague, f. || cercle, m. || sonnerie, f. || arène, f. || ~-**dove,** s. pigeon ramier, m. || ~-**finger,** s. doigt annulaire, m. || ~-**worm,** s. dartre, f.

ring, *rĭng,* v. a. & n. faire sonner || résonner.

ringing, *rĭng′ĭng,* s. sonnerie, f., son des cloches, m. [m.

ringleader, *rĭng′lēd ĕr,* s. chef d'un parti,

ringlet, *rĭng′lĕt,* s. annelet, m. || boucle, f.

rinse, *rĭns,* v. a. rincer.

riot, *rī′ŏt,* s. vacarme, m. || attroupement, m. || débauche, f. || émeute, f. || ~-**act,** s. loi (anglaise) contre les attroupements de l'année 1817, f.

riot, *rī′ŏt,* v. a. s'abandonner à la débauche || exciter une émeute.

rioter, *rī′ŏt ĕr,* s. débauché, m. || séditieux, m. [bauché) (en) séditieux.

riotous, *rī′ŏt ŭs,* a. (-ly, ad.) (en) débauché.

rip, *rĭp,* v. a. déchirer, fendre || découdre.

ripe, *rĭp,* a. (-ly, ad.) mûr(ement).

ripen, *rī′pn,* v. a. & n. mûrir.

ripeness, *rīp′nĕs,* s. maturité, f.

ripple, *rĭp′pl,* s. ride, f.

ripple, *rĭp′pl,* v. a. (& n.) (se) rider.

rippling, *rĭp′lĭng,* s. bouillonnement, m.

rise, *rĭz,* s. lever, m. || montée, f. || naissance, f. || source, f. || crue, f. || hausse, f.

rise, *rĭz,* v. n. ir. se lever, s'élever || augmenter || paraître, se soulever || venir, provenir de || hausser, renchérir, monter || (of fishes) monter à fleur d'eau pour mordre à l'hameçon.

riser, *rī′zĕr,* s.; **early ~,** personne qui se lève de bon matin, f.

risible, *rĭz′ĭ bl,* a. risible, ridicule.

rising, *rĭz′ĭng,* s. lever, m. || agrandissement, m. || ascension, rébellion, f.

rising, *rĭz′ĭng,* a. levant, naissant || montant || a ~ **man,** un homme qui s'élève.

risk, *rĭsk,* s. risque, péril, m. || **at all ~s,** à tout risque.

risk, *rĭsk,* v. a. risquer. [f.

rite, *rīt,* s. rite, m. || cérémonie religieuse.

ritual, *rĭt′ū ăl,* s. rituel, m.

ritual, *rĭt′ū ăl,* a. rituel.

rival, *rī′văl,* s. rival, m. || émule, m. & f.

rival, *rī′văl,* v. a. rivaliser.

rival, *rī′văl,* a. rival || émule.

rivalry, *rī′văl rĭ,* s. rivalité, f.

rive, *rĭv,* v. a. (& n. ir.) (se) fendre.

river, *rĭv′ĕr,* s. rivière, f., fleuve, m.

rivet, *rĭv′ĕt,* s. rivet, clou rivé, m.

rivet, *rĭv′ĕt,* v. a. river.

rivulet, *rĭv′ū lĕt,* s. petit ruisseau, m.

roach, *rōch,* s. gardon, m. [rade, f.

road, *rōd,* s. route, f., grand chemin, m. ||

roadstead, *rōd′stĕd,* s. rade, f.

roadway, *rōd′wā,* s. chaussée, f.

roam, *rōm,* v. a. & n. rôder, errer.

roan, *rōn,* s. peau maroquinée, f.

roan, *rōn,* a. rouan.

roar, *rōr,* v. n. rugir, mugir || gronder.

roaring, *rōr′ĭng,* s. mugissement, grondement, m. || éclat, m.

roast, *rōst,* v. a. rôtir, griller || brûler (du café) || **to rule the ~,** avoir la haute main.

roast, *rōst,* a. rôti.

roastbeef, *rōst′bēf,* s. du bœuf rôti.

roaster, *rōst′ĕr,* s. rôtissoire, f. || brûloir, m. || rôtisseur, m.

rob, *rŏb,* v. a. voler, dérober.

robber, *rŏb′bĕr,* s. voleur, brigand, m.

robbery, *rŏb′bĕr ĭ,* s. vol, brigandage, m.

robe, *rōb,* s. robe, f. || peau de buffle, f.

robe, *rōb,* v. a. mettre les habits de cérémonie. [rouge-gorge, m.

robin(-redbreast), *rŏb′ĭn (rĕd′brĕst),* s.

robust, *rō bŭst′,* a. robuste, vigoureux.

robustness, *rō bŭst′nĕs,* s. force, vigueur, f.

rock, *rŏk,* s. roc, rocher, m., roche, f. || quenouille, f. || ~-**salt,** s. sel gemme, m. || ~-**work,** s. rocaille, f. || cailloutage, m.

rock, *rŏk,* v. a. & n. branler, bercer || (Am.) lapider || balancer.

rocker, *rŏk′ĕr,* s. berceuse, f.

rocket, *rŏk′ĕt,* s. fusée volante, f.

rocking, *rŏk'ĭng*, s. balancement, m. || ~-**chair**, s. fauteuil à bascule, m., berceuse, f. || ~-**horse**, s. cheval à bascule, m.

rocky, *rŏk'ĭ*, a. rocailleux, caillouteux.

rod, *rŏd*, s. verge, baguette, tringle, f. || tige, f. || canne à pêche, f.

roe, *rō*, s. chevrette, daine, f. || œufs de poisson, m. pl. || ~-**buck**, s. chevreuil, m.

rogation(-week), *rō gā'shŭn (wĕk)*, s. Rogations, f. pl.

rogue, *rōg*, s. fripon, m. || espiègle, m.

roguery, *rō'gĕrĭ*, s. friponnerie, f. || espièglerie, f. [chant.

roguish, *rō'gĭsh*, a. fripon || malin, mé-

roister, *rōys'tĕr*, v. n. faire du tapage.

roll, *rōl*, s. rouleau, m. || roulement, m. || roulade, f. || petit pain, m. || rôle, m., liste, f. || ~s, s. pl. archives, f. pl. || to **strike off the** ~**s**, (mil.) casser || **French** ~, petit pain à café, m. [lindre || tourner.

roll, *rōl*, v. a. & n. rouler || laminer || cy-

roller, *rōl'ĕr*, s. rouleau, cylindre, m. || bandage, m. || roulette, f. || ~-**blind**, s. store, m. [rigoler.

rollick, *rŏl'lĭk*, v. n. faire du tapage ||

rolling, *rōl'ĭng*, s. roulement, roulage, m. || (mar.) roulis, m. || ~-**mill**, s. laminoir, m. || ~-**pin**, s. rouleau, m. || ~-**stock**, s. (rail.) matériel roulant, m.

romance, *rō mäns'*, s. roman, m.

romance, *rō mäns'*, v. n. feindre.

romancer, *rō män'sĕr*, s. romancier, m.

romanist, *rō'män ĭst*, s. catholique romain, m., catholique romaine, f.

romantic, *rō män'tĭk*, a. romanesque.

Romish, *rō'mĭsh*, a. catholique romain.

romp, *rŏmp*, s. garçonnière, f. || jeu brutal, m. [batifoler.

romp, *rŏmp*, v. n. badiner grossièrement,

roof, *rōf*, s. toit, m. || impériale (d'un carrosse), f. || palais, m.

roof, *rōf*, v. a. couvrir d'un toit.

roofing, *rōf'ĭng*, s. toiture, f.

rook, *rōōk*, s. freux, m., grolle, f. || (at chess) tour, f. || tricheur, m.

rook, *rōōk*, v. a. tromper, duper.

rookery, *rōōk'ĕrĭ*, s. lieu habité par des freux, m.

room, *rōm*, s. chambre, f. || espace, m. || (fig.) latitude, f. || **there is no** ~ **for doubt**, il n'y a pas le moindre doute.

roomful, *rōm'fōōl*, a. chambrée, f.

roominess, *rōm'ĭnĕs*, s. grandeur, f.

roomy, *rōm'ĭ*, a. spacieux, vaste.

roost, *rōst*, s. juchoir, m.

roost, *rōst*, v. n. se jucher, se percher.

root, *rōt*, s. racine, f. || origine, f. || (gr.) radical, m.

root, *rōt*, v. n. s'enraciner || **to** ~ **out** ou **up**, déraciner || extirper. [fondément.

rooted, *rōt'ĕd*, a. enraciné || -**ly**, ad. pro-

rope, *rōp*, s. corde, f., câble, m. || ~-**dancer**, s. danseur de corde, f. || ~-**maker**, s. cordier, m. || ~-**walk**, ~-**yard**, s. corderie, f.

rope, *rōp*, v. n. filer.

ropery, *rō'pĕrĭ*, s. corderie, f.

ropy, *rō'pĭ*, a. visqueux.

rosary, *rō'zārĭ*, s. rosaire, m. || roseraie, f.

rose, *rōz*, s. rose, f. || rosette, f. || rosace, f. || **dog**-~, églantier, m. || **damask**-~, rose de Provins || ~-**bed**, s. roseraie, f. || ~-**colour**, s. couleur de rose, f. || ~-**leaf**, s. feuille de rose, f. || ~-**wood**, s. palissandre, m.

roseate, *rō'zĕ ät*, a. de rose || rosé.

rosebud, *rōz'bŭd*, s. bouton de rose, m.

rosemary, *rōz'märĭ*, s. romarin, m.

rosin, *rōz'ĭn*, s. résine, f. || colophane, f.

rosiness, *rō'zĭnĕs*, s. couleur rose, f.

roster, *rōs'tĕr*, s. (mil.) tableau d'ordonnance, m.

rostrum, *rŏs'trŭm*, s. tribune, f.

rosy, *rō'zĭ*, a. couleur de rose.

rot, *rŏt*, s. tac, m. || pourriture, f.

rot, *rŏt*, v. a. & n. pourrir.

rotate, *rō tāt'*, v. n. pivoter, tournoyer.

rotation, *rō tā'shŭn*, s. rotation, f. || ~ **of crops**, assolement, m.

rotatory, *rō tä tĕrĭ*, a. tournant en rond.

rote, *rōt*, s. routine, f. || **by** ~, par routine.

rotgut, *rŏt'gŭt*, s. mauvaise bière, f.

rotten, *rŏt'n*, a. pourri, corrompu, gâté || ~-**stone**, s. tripoli, m. [carie, f.

rottenness, *rŏt'nnĕs*, s. pourriture, f. ||

rotund, *rō tŭnd'*, a. rond.

rotunda, *rō tŭn'dä*, s. rotonde, f.

rotundity, *rō tŭn'dĭtĭ*, s. rondeur, f. || rotondité, f.

rouble, *rō'bl*, s. rouble, m.

rouge, *rōzh*, s. rouge, m.

rouge, *rōzh*, v. n. mettre du rouge.

rough, *rŭf*, s. ostrogoth, m., brute, canaille, f. || ~-**cast**, s. ébauche, f., crépi, m. || ~-**rider**, s. dresseur de chevaux, m. || ~-**shod**, a. ferré à glace.

rough, *rŭf*, v. a. ébaucher || crépir.

rough, *rŭf*, a. (-**ly**, ad.) raboteux || rude (ment) || âpre || grossier || brusque(ment) || ~ **copy**, s. brouillon, m. || **in the** ~, à l'état brut.

roughdraw, *rŭf'drāw*, v. a. ébaucher.

roughen, *rŭf'n*, v. a. rendre raboteux.

roughhew, *rŭf'hū*, v. a. ir. dégrossir || ébaucher.

roughness, *rŭf'nĕs*, s. aspérité, f. || rudesse, âpreté || brusquerie, grossièreté, f.

roughwork, *rŭf'wĕrk*, s. grosse besogne, f.

roughwork, *rŭf'wĕrk*, v. a. travailler grossièrement.

round, *rŏwnd* v. a. & n. arrondir || entourer || s'arrondir.

round, *rŏwnd*, a. (-**ly**, ad.) rond(ement) || circulaire, sphérique || franc(hement) || positif || candide || ~-**house**, s. bureau de police, m. || ~-**robin**, s. pétition revêtue de signatures en rond, f. || ~-**shouldered**, a. voûté. [ronde, autour de.

round, *rŏwnd*, ad. & prp. en rond, à la

roundabout, *rŏwnd'ä bŏwt*, s. manège, m. || jeu de bagues, m. || (Am.) jaquette, f.

roundabout, *rŏwnd'ä bŏwt*, a. détourné.

roundelay, *rŏwn'dĕ lā*, s. rondeau, m.

rounders, *rŏwn'dĕrz*, s. balle au camp, f.

roundhand, *rŏwnd'hănd*, s. ronde, écriture financière, f.
roundhead, *rŏwnd'hĕd*, s. puritain, m.
roundish, *rŏwnd'ĭsh*, a. rondelet.
roundness, *rŏwnd'nĕs*, s. rondeur, f.
rouse, *rŏwz*, v. a. éveiller || réveiller, exciter.
rout, *rŏwt*, s. (mil.) déroute, f.　　　[citer.
rout, *rŏwt*, v. a. mettre en déroute.
route, *rŏt*, s. route, f., chemin, m.
rove, *rŏv*, v. n. rôder.　　　[corsaire, m.
rover, *rŏ'vĕr*, s. rôdeur, vagabond, m. ||
roving, *rŏ'vĭng*, a. vagabond.
row, *rŏ*, s. rang, m., rangée, file, f.
row, *rŏw*, s. tumulte, m. || to have a ~
with one, avoir une querelle avec qn.
row, *rŏ*, v. a. & n. ramer.
rowdy, *rŏw'dĭ*, s. tapageur, m.
rowdyism, *rŏw'dĭ ĭsm*, s. manières des tapageurs, f. pl.
rowel, *rŏw'ĕl*, s. molette (d'éperon), f.
rowing-match, *rŏ'ĭng măch*, s. course à l'aviron, régate, f.
royal, *rŏy'ăl*, a. (-ly, ad.) royal(ement) || ~s, s. pl. (mar.) perroquets volants, m. pl.
royalist, *rŏy'ăl ĭst*, s. royaliste, m.
royalty, *rŏy'ăl tĭ*, s. royauté, f.
rub, *rŭb*, s. frottement, m. || difficulté, f.
rub, *rŭb*, v. a. & n. frotter || frictionner.
rubber, *rŭb'bĕr*, s. frottoir, m. || pierre à aiguiser, f. || lime à bras, f. || partie de whist, f. || ~ball, s. balle élastique, f.
rubbish, *rŭb'bĭsh*, s. décombres, m. pl., ordures, f. pl. || fatras, m. || fadaises, f. pl.
Rubicon, *rŏŏ'bĭ kŏn*, s. Rubicon, m. || to pass the ~, passer le Rubicon, prendre une décision irrévocable.
rubicund, *rŏ'bĭ kŭnd*, a. rubicond, rouge.
ruble, *rŏbl*, s. rouble, m.
rubric, *rŏ'brĭk*, s. rubrique, f.
ruby, *rŏ'bĭ*, s. rubis, m.
ruby, *rŏ'bĭ*, a. rouge, vermeil.
rudder, *rŭd'dĕr*, s. gouvernail, m.
ruddiness, *rŭd'dĭ nĕs*, s. rougeur, f.
ruddy, *rŭd'dĭ*, a. rubicond.　　　[rouge, m.
rude, *rŏd*, a. (-ly, ad.) rude(ment) || dur, raboteux || sévère || grossier, impoli.
rudeness, *rŏd'nĕs*, s. grossièreté, rudesse, brutalité, violence, f.　　　[taire.
rudimentary, *rŏ dĭ mĕnt'ĕr ĭ*, a. rudimen-
rudiments, *rŏ'dĭ mĕnts*, s. pl. rudiments, éléments, m. pl.
rue, *rŏ*, s. (bot.) rue, f.
rue, *rŏ*, v. a. regretter, se repentir de.
rueful, *rŏ'fŏŏl*, a. triste, lamentable.
raff, *rŭf*, s. fraise, f.　　　　　　[pan, m.
ruffian, *rŭf'fĭ ăn*, s. brigand, m. || chena-
ruffian(ly) *rŭf'fĭ ăn (lĭ)*, a. brutal.
ruffle, *rŭf'fl*, s. manchette, f. || trouble, m.
ruffle, *rŭf'fl*, v. a. déranger, troubler || plisser, friser, rider.
rug, *rŭg*, s. petit tapis à haut poil, m.
rugged, *rŭg'gĕd*, a. rude, raboteux || brutal.
ruin, *rŏ'ĭn*, s. ruination, *rŏ ĭ nă shŭn*, s. ruine, perte, f. || débris, m. pl.
ruin, *rŏ'ĭn*, v. a. ruiner, perdre.
ruinous, *rŏ'ĭ nŭs*, a. ruineux || -ly, ad. pernicieusement.

rule, *rŏl*, s. gouvernement, m., domination, f. || règle, f., principe, m.　[régler.
rule, *rŏl*, v. a. & n. gouverner, diriger ||
ruler, *rŏl'ĕr*, s. gouverneur, m. || règle, f.
rum, *rŭm*, s. rhum, m.
rum, *rŭm*, a. drôle, bizarre.
rumble, *rŭm'bl*, v. n. murmurer, gronder.
rumbling, *rŭm'blĭng*, s. bruit sourd, m.
ruminate, *rŏ'mĭ nāt*, v. n. ruminer.　[f.
rumination, *rŏ mĭ nā'shŭn*, s. rumination.
rummage, *rŭm'māj*, v. a. fouiller || bouleverser.　　　　　　　　　　　　[m.
rummer, *rŭm'mĕr*, s. grand verre à patte,
rumour, *rŏ'mĕr*, s. rumeur, f., bruit, m.
rumour, *rŏ'mĕr*, v. a. répandre une nouvelle, faire courir un bruit.
rump, *rŭmp*, s. croupion, m. || croupe, f. || ~steak, s. bifteck Chateaubriand, m.
rumple, *rŭm'pl*, v. a. froisser, chiffonner.
run, *rŭn*, s. course, f. || attaque, f. || cours, ordinaire, m. || vogue, f. || in the long ~, à la longue.
run, *rŭn*, v. a. & n. ir. courir || couler, encourir || percer || forcer, pousser || poursuivre || fondre || aller en avant, passer, se passer, s'écouler, voguer || se précipiter || se sauver || disparaître || être en vogue || to ~ out guns, parquer des canons || to ~ high, (of feelings) bouillonner || to ~ away ou off, s'enfuir, s'échapper || to ~ away with, enlever, détourner une mineure || to ~ a coach, etc., conduire (une voiture, etc.) || to ~ down, renverser (of watches, etc.) être au bas, ne plus aller || (mar. & fig.) couler bas, à fond.
runaway, *rŭn'ă wā*, s. fuyard, m.
rundle, *rŭn'dl*, s. échelon, m.
rundlet, *rŭnd'lĕt*, s. petit baril, m.
runner, *rŭn'nĕr*, s. coureur, m. || courrier, messager, m. || scarlet ~, haricot d'Espagne, m.
running, *rŭn'nĭng*, s. course, f.
running, *rŭn'nĭng*, a. coulant, courant || ~ice, s. glaces flottantes, f. pl.
rupture, *rŭp'tŭr* ou *rŭp'chŏŏr*, s. rupture, f. || hernie, f.　　　　　　[(se) rompre.
rupture, *rŭp'tŭr* ou *rŭp'chŏŏr*, v. a. (& n.)
rural, *rŏ'răl*, a. rural, champêtre || rustique.
rush, *rŭsh*, s. (bot.) jonc, m. || élan, choc, m. || mouvement précipité, m. || ~light, s. veilleuse, f.
rush, *rŭsh*, v. n. se précipiter || se lancer.
rushy, *rŭsh'ĭ*, a. couvert de joncs.
rusk, *rŭsk*, s. biscotte, f.
russet, *rŭs'sĕt*, s. reinette grise, f.
russet, *rŭs'sĕt*, a. roussâtre || rustique.
Russia-leather, *rŭsh'ă lĕth'ĕr*, s. cuir de Russie, m.
rust, *rŭst*, s. rouille, f.
rust, *rŭst*, v. n. se rouiller.
rustic, *rŭs'tĭk*, s. rustaud, m.
rustic, *rŭs'tĭk*, a. rustique.
rusticate, *rŭs'tĭ kāt*, v. a. & n. reléguer à la campagne || habiter la campagne.
rustication, *rŭs tĭ kā'shŭn*, s. vie champêtre, f. || expulsion temporaire, f.
rusticity, *rŭs tĭs'ĭ tĭ*, s. rusticité, f.
rustiness, *rŭs'tĭ nĕs*, s. rouillure, f.

---

lăte, hăt, fär, lăw; — hēre, gĕt, hĕr; — mīne, ĭnn; — nō, hŏt, prōve; — hŏw; —

rustle, *rŭs'l*, v. n. bruire, siffler.
rustling, *rŭst'ling*, s. bruissement, m. ‖ cliquetis, m. ‖ frôlement, m. ‖ frou-frou, m.
rusty, *rŭs'tĭ*, a. rouillé ‖ ranque ‖ moisi.
rut, *rŭt*, s. rut, m. ‖ ornière, f.
rut, *rŭt*, v. n. être en rut.
ruthless, *rŏth'lĕs*, a. impitoyable ‖ -ly, ad. sans pitié.
rye, *rī*, s. seigle, m. ‖ ~-grass, s. ivraie vivace, f. ‖ fromental, m.

S.

Sabbatarian, *săb bă tā'rĭ ăn*, s. sabbatéen, sabbataire, m.
sabbath, *săb'băth*, s. sabbat, m.
sable, *sā'bl*, s. zibeline, f.
sable, *sā'bl*, a. noir (blason) ‖ de zibeline.
sabre, *sā'bĕr*, s. sabre, m.
sabre, *sā'bĕr*, v. a. sabrer.
sacerdotal, *săs ĕr dō'tăl*, a. sacerdotal.
sack, *săk*, s. sac, m. ‖ vin des Canaries, m. ‖ to give one the ~, (fam.) congédier qn. ‖ ~-cloth, s. toile à sac, f. ‖ ~-coat, s. paletot-sac, m.
sack, *săk*, v. a. mettre en sac ‖ saccager.
sacking, *săk'ing*, s. toile à sac, f. ‖ saccagement, sac, m.   [eucharistie, f.
sacrament, *săk'ră mĕnt*, s. sacrement, m.,
sacramental, *săk ră mĕnt'ăl*, a. (-ly, ad.) sacramentel(lement).
sacred, *sā'krĕd*, a. (-ly, ad.) sacré ‖ saint (ement) ‖ consacré.
sacredness, *sā'krĕd nĕs*, s. sainteté, f.
sacrifice, *săk'rĭ fīs*, s. sacrifice, m.
sacrifice, *săk'rĭ fīs*, v. a. & n. sacrifier.
sacrificer, *săk'rĭ fī sĕr*, s. sacrificateur, m.
sacrilege, *săk'rĭ lĕj*, s. sacrilège, m.
sacrilegious, *săk rĭ lē'jŭs*, a. sacrilège.
sad, *săd*, a. (-ly, ad.) triste(ment) ‖ sombre.
sadden, *săd'n*, v. a. attrister.
saddle, *săd'l*, s. selle, f. ‖ side—, selle de dame ‖ ~-bag, s. sacoche, f. ‖ ~-cloth, s. housse, f.
saddle, *săd'l*, v. a. seller.
saddler, *săd'lĕr*, s. sellier, m.
saddlery, *săd'lĕr ĭ*, s. sellerie, f.
sadness, *săd'nĕs*, s. tristesse, f.
safe, *sāf*, s. garde-manger, m. ‖ caisse de sûreté, f. ‖ ~-conduct, s. sauf-conduit, m.
safe, *sāf*, a. sauf, sûr ‖ -ly, ad. en sûreté.
safeguard, *sāf'gărd*, s. sauve-garde, f. ‖ (rail.) chasse-pierres, m.
safeguard, *sāf'gărd*, v. a. sauvegarder.
safety, *sāf'tĭ*, s. sûreté, assurance, f. ‖ ~-valve, s. soupape de sûreté, f.
saffron, *săf'rŏn*, s. safran, m.
saffron, *săf'rŏn*, a. couleur de safran.
sagacious, *să gā'shŭs*, a. sagace, perspicace ‖ -ly, ad. avec sagacité.
sagacity, *să găs'ĭ tĭ*, s. sagacité, f.
sage, *sāj*, s. sage, m. ‖ (bot.) sauge, f.
sage, *sāj*, a. (-ly, ad.) sage(ment).
sago, *sā'gō*, s. sagou, m.

sail, *sāl*, s. voile, f. ‖ aile, f. ‖ vaisseau, m. ‖ to set ~, mettre à la voile ‖ ~-cloth, s. toile à voiles, f. ‖ ~-maker, s. voilier, m. ‖ ~-vessel, s. bâtiment à voiles, m.   [faire voile, nager.
sail, *sāl*, v. a. & n. naviguer, voguer sur ‖
sailer, *sāl'ĕr*, s. voilier, m.
sailing, *sāl'ing*, s. navigation, f. ‖ promenade à la voile, f.
sailor, *sāl'ĕr*, s. marin, matelot, m.
saint, *sānt*, s. saint, m. ‖ béat, m.
saintly, *sānt'lĭ*, ad. saintement.
sake, *sāk*, s. cause, f. ‖ égard, m. ‖ for God's ~, pour l'amour de Dieu.
salad, *săl'ăd*, s. salade, f. ‖ ~-bowl, s. saladier, m. ‖ ~-oil, s. huile d'olives, f.
salamander, *săl'ă măn dĕr*, s. salamandre, f. ‖ fer à gratiner, m.   [ments, m. pl.
salary, *săl'ă rĭ*, s. salaire, m., appointements, *săt*, s. vente, f. ‖ marché, m. ‖ bill of ~, s. contrat d'achat ou de vente, m. ‖ ~-goods, s. pl. marchandises de pacotille, f. pl.   [vente.
saleable, *sā'lă bl*, a. vendable ‖ de bonne
salesman, *sālz'măn*, s. marchand, m. ‖ fripier, m. ‖ marchand de bestiaux, m.
salient, *sā'lĭ ĕnt*, a. saillant.
saline, *sā'līn*, a. salin.
saliva, *să lī'vă*, s. salive, f.
sallow, *săl'lō*, a. blême, jaune.
sally, *săl'lĭ*, s. sortie, saillie, f. ‖ irruption, f. ‖ boutade, f.
sally, *săl'lĭ*, v. n. (mil.) faire une sortie ‖ to ~ forth, jaillir impétueusement, sortir brusquement de.
salmon, *săm'ŭn*, s. saumon, m. ‖ ~-trout, s. truite saumonée, f.
saloon, *să lōn'*, s. salon, m. ‖ (of a vessel) premières, f. pl.
salt, *sawlt*, s. sel, m. ‖ (fig.) trait piquant, m. ‖ ~-box, ~-cellar, s. salière, f. ‖ ~-works, s. saline, f.
salt, *sawlt*, v. a. saler.
salt, *sawlt*, a. salé.
salter, *sawlt'ĕr*, s. saleur, m. ‖ saunier, m.
salting-tub, *sawlt'ing tŭb*, s. saloir, m.
saltless, *sawlt'lĕs*, a. sans sel, insipide.
saltness, *sawlt'nĕs*, s. salure, f.
saltpetre, *sawlt'pē tĕr*, s. salpêtre, m.
salubrious, *să lō brĭ ŭs*, s. salubre.
salubrity, *să lō'brĭ tĭ*, s. salubrité, f.
salutary, *săl'ū tĕr ĭ*, a. salutaire.
salutation, *săl ū tā'shŭn*, s. salutation, f. ‖ salut, m.   [fire a ~, saluer du canon.
salute, *să lōt'*, s. salut, m. ‖ salve, f. ‖ to salute, *să lōt'*, v. a. saluer.
salvage, *săl'văj*, s. sauvetage, m.
salvation, *săl vā'shŭn*, s. salut, m.
salvo, *săv ou săv*, s. onguent, emplâtre, m.
salver, *săl'vĕr*, s. soucoupe, f. ‖ plateau, m.
salvo, *săl'vō*, s. restriction, f. ‖ salve, f.
sambo, *săm'bō*, s. moricaud, m.
same, *sām*, a. même le même ‖ much the ~, à peu près de même ‖ it is all the ~ to me, cela m'est parfaitement égal ‖ all the ~, peu importe.

sameness, *săm′ nĕs,* s. identité, f.

samphire, *săm′ fĕr,* s. (bot.) passe-pierre, f.

sample, *săm′ pl,* s. échantillon, m.

sample, *săm′ pl,* v. a. échantillonner.

sampler, *săm′ plĕr,* s. modèle, m.

sanctification, *săngk tĭ fĭ kā′ shŭn,* s. sanctification, f.

sanctify, *săngk′ tĭ fĭ,* v. a. sanctifier.

sanctimonious, *săngk tĭ mō′ nĭ ŭs,* a. saint || béat || hypocrite || -ly, ad. en hypocrite, avec hypocrisie.

sanctimony, *săngk′ tĭ mŏn ĭ,* s. air de sainteté, f.

sanction, *săngk′ shŭn,* s. sanction, f.

sanction, *săngk′ shŭn,* v. a. sanctionner.

sanctity, *săngk′ tĭ tĭ,* s. sainteté, f.

sanctuary, *săngk′ tŭ ĕr ĭ,* s. sanctuaire, m. || asile, refuge, m.

sand, *sănd,* s. sable, m. || ~-bank, s. banc de sable, m. || ~-box, s. poudrier, m. || ~-glass, s. sablier, m. || ~-paper, s. papier de verre, m. || ~-pit, s. sablière, f. || ~-stone, s. grès, m.

sand, *sănd,* v. a. sabler.

sandal, *săn′ dăl,* s. sandale, f. || santal, m.

sanded, *sănd′ ĕd,* a. sablé || sablonneux.

sandwich, *sănd′ wĭch,* s. sandwich, m.

sandy, *sănd′ ĭ,* a. sablonneux.

sane, *sān,* a. sain.

sanguinary, *săng′ gwĭ nĕr ĭ,* a. sanguinaire.

sanguine, *săng′ gwĭn,* a. sanguin || de couleur de sang || vif.   [sanguine, f.

sanguineness, *săng′ gwĭn nĕs,* s. nature sanguine, f.

sanguineous, *săng gwĭn′ ĕ ŭs,* a. sanguin.

sanitary, *săn′ ĭ tĕr ĭ,* a. sanitaire.

sanitation, *săn ĭ tā′ shŭn,* s. cure, guérison, f.

sanity, *săn′ ĭ tĭ,* s. jugement sain, m.

sap, *săp,* s. sève, f. || sape, f.

sap, *săp,* v. a. & n. saper.   [tissime.

sapient, *sā′ pĭ ĕnt,* a. savantissime, doctissime.

sapless, *săp′ lĕs,* a. sans sève, sec.

sapling, *săp′ lĭng,* s. arbrisseau, m.

sapodilla, *săp ō dĭl′ lă,* s. sapotille, f.

sapper, *săp′ pĕr,* s. sapeur, m.

sapphire, *săf′ fīr,* s. saphir, m.

sappy, *săp′ pĭ,* a. succulent.

sarcasm, *săr′ kăzm,* s. sarcasme, m.

sarcastic, *săr kăs′ tĭk,* a. sarcastique || -ally, ad. d'une manière sarcastique.

sarcenet, *sărs′ nĕt,* s. florence, f.

sarcophagus, *săr kŏf′ ă gŭs,* s. sarcophage, m. || cave à vin, f.

sardine, *săr′ dĕn,* s. sardine, f.

sarsaparilla, *săr să pă rĭl′ lă,* s. (bot.) salsepareille, f.

sash, *săsh,* s. ceinture, f. || châssis, m. || ~-door, s. porte vitrée, f. || ~-frame, s. châssis fixe, m. || ~-window, s. fenêtre à coulisse, f.

Satan, *sā′ tăn,* s. Satan, m.

satanic, *să tăn′ ĭk,* a. satanique.

satchel, *săch′ ĕl,* s. sachet, m. || gibecière, f.

sate, *sāt,* v. a. soûler, rassasier.   [f.

satellite, *săt′ ĕl lĭt,* s. satellite, m.

satiate, *sā′ shĭ āt,* v. a. rassasier.

satiety, *să tī′ ĕ tĭ,* s. satiété, f.

satin, *săt′ ĭn,* s. satin, m. || ~-wood, s. bois de citron, m.

satin, *săt′ ĭn,* a. de satin || satiné.

satinet, *săt ĭn ĕt′,* s. satinade, f.

satire, *săt′ īr,* s. satire, f.   [rique(ment).

satirical, *să tĭr′ ĭk ăl,* a. (-ly, ad.) satirise,

satirise, *săt′ ĭr īz,* v. a. satiriser.

satirist, *săt′ ĭr ĭst,* s. satirique, m.

satisfaction, *săt ĭs făk′ shŭn,* s. satisfaction, f.   [manière satisfaisante.

satisfactorily, *săt ĭs făk tĕr′ ĭ lĭ,* ad. d'une

satisfactory, *săt ĭs făk′ tĕr ĭ,* a. satisfaisant.

satisfy, *săt′ ĭs fĭ,* v. a. & n. satisfaire, contenter.

satrap, *sā′ trăp,* s. satrape, m.

saturate, *săt′ ū rāt,* v. a. (chim.) saturer.

Saturday, *săt′ ĕr dā,* s. samedi, m.

saturnalia, *săt ĕr nā′ lĭ ă,* s. saturnales, f. pl.

saturnalian, *săt ĕr nā′ lĭ ăn,* a. des saturnales.

saturnine, *săt′ ĕr nīn,* a. sombre || taciturne.

satyr, *săt′ ĕr,* s. satyre, m.

sauce, *săws,* s. sauce, f. || (Am.) légume, m.

sauce, *săws,* v. a. assaisonner.

saucer, *săw′ sĕr,* s. saucière, f.

saucily, *săw′ sĭ lĭ,* ad. impertinemment.

sauciness, *săw′ sĭ nĕs,* s. impertinence, f.

saucy, *săw′ sĭ,* a. insolent, impertinent.

saunter, *săwn′ tĕr,* v. n. flâner.

sausage, *săw′ săj,* s. saucisse, f.

savage, *săv′ ăj,* s. sauvage, m.

savage, *săv′ ăj,* a. sauvage || farouche || -ly, ad. d'une manière féroce.

savageness, *săv′ ăj nĕs,* s. férocité, f.

savanna, *să văn′ nă,* s. savane, f.

save, *săv,* v. a. sauver, préserver || épargner || God ~ the king ! vive le roi || ~-all, s. brûle-tout, m.

save, *săv,* pr. excepté, hormis.

saveloy, *săv′ ĕ lŏy,* s. cervelas, m.

saver, *sā′ vĕr,* s. sauveur, m. || économe, m.

saving, *sā′ vĭng,* s. épargne, économie, f.

saving, *sā′ vĭng,* a. ménager, économe || -ly, ad. avec économie.

saving, *sā′ vĭng,* pr. excepté.

savings-bank, *sā′ vĭngz băngk,* s. caisse d'épargne, f.

Saviour, *sā′ vĭ ĕr,* s. Sauveur, m.

savour, *sā′ vĕr,* s. saveur, odeur, f.

savour, *sā′ vĕr,* v. a. & n. savourer, goûter || sentir.

savourily, *sā′ vĕr ĭ lĭ,* ad. savoureusement.

savouriness, *sā′ vĕr ĭ nĕs,* s. bonne saveur, f., bon goût, m.

savoury, *sā′ vĕr ĭ,* a. savoureux.

savoy, *să vŏy′,* s. chou frisé, m.

saw, *săw,* s. scie, f. || old ~, mot banal, m. || adage usé, m. || ~-dust, s. sciure de bois, f. || ~-mill, s. scierie, f.

saw, *săw,* v. a. scier.

sawbones, *săw′ bōnz,* s. frater, m.

sawyer, *săw′ yĕr,* s. scieur de long, m.

saxifrage, *săks′ ĭ frāj,* s. (bot.) saxifrage, f.

say, *sā,* s. mot, dire, m. || to have one's ~, dire son mot.

say, *sā,* v. a. ir. dire, parler, réciter || **it is said,** on dit || **the said . . .,** le dit . . .

saying, *sā′ ĭng,* s. dicton, proverbe, m.

---

lāte, hăt, făr, lăw; — hēre, gĕt, hėr; — mīne, ĭnn; — nō, hŏt, prōve; — hŏw; —

scab, *skăb*, s. croûte || gale, rogne, f.
scabbard, *skăb' bérd*, s. fourreau d'épée, m.
scabbed, *skăb' bĕd*, scabby, *skăb' bĭ*, a. galeux || vil.
scabbiness, *skăb' bĭ nĕs*, s. état galeux, m.
scabious, *skă' bĭ ŭs*, a. scabieux.
scaffold, *skăf' fŏld*, s. échafaud, m. [m.
scaffolding, *skăf' fŏld ĭng*, s. échafaudage,
scald, *skawld*, s. teigne, f. || brûlure, f.
scald, *skawld*, v. a. échauder.
scalding, *skawld' ĭng*, ; ~-hot, a. tout bouillant || ~-house, s. échaudoir, m.
scale, *skāl*, s. écaille, f. || échelle, f. || (mus.) gamme, f. || bassin (of a balance), m. (pair of) —s, s. pl. balance, f.
scale, *skāl*, v. a. (& n.) escalader || (s')écailler.
scaling-ladder, *skā' lĭng lăd dĕr*, s. échelle de siège, f.
scallion, *skăl' yŭn*, s. échalote, f.
scallop, *skŏl' lŏp*, s. feston, m. || dentelure, f. || coquille, f. || pétoncle, m.
scallop, *skŏl' lŏp*, v. a. denteler || festonner || accommoder en coquille.
scalp, *skălp*, s. péricrâne, m.
scalp, *skălp*, v. a. scalper.
scaly, *skā' lĭ*, a. écaillé, écailleux.
scamp, *skămp*, s. vaurien, m.
scamper, *skăm' pĕr*, s. fuite, escapade, f.
scamper, *skăm' pĕr*, v. n. prendre la fuite.
scan, *skăn*, v.a. scander (verses) || scruter.
scandal, *skăn' dăl*, s. scandale, m. || médisance, f. || honte, f. [diffamer.
scandalise, *skăn' dăl ĭz*, v. a. scandaliser,
scandalous, *skăn' dăl ŭs*, a. scandaleux, honteux, infâme || —ly, ad. scandaleusement. [chétif.
scant(y), *skănt(ĭ)*, a. étroit, exigu || mesquin,
scantily, *skănt' ĭ lĭ*, a. étroitement || mesquinement. [mesquinerie, f.
scantiness, *skănt' ĭ nĕs*, s. exiguité, f. ||
scantling, *skănt' lĭng*, s. petite portion, f.
scapegoat, *skāp' gōt*, s. bouc émissaire, m.
scapegrace, *skāp' grās*, s. vaurien, m.
scar, *skăr*, s. cicatrice, f.
scar, *skăr*, v. a. cicatriser.
scarce, *skărs*, a. rare || —ly, ad. à peine, presque pas.
scarcity, *skărs' ĭ tĭ*, s. rareté, f.
scare, *skār*, v. a. épouvanter, effrayer.
scarecrow, *skār' krō*, s. épouvantail, m.
scarf, *skărf*, s. écharpe, f. || cravate longue, f. || ~-pin, s. épingle de cravate, f. || ~-skin, s. épiderme, m.
scarify, *skăr' ĭ fī*, v. a. scarifier.
scarlatina, *skăr lă tē' nă*, s. fièvre scarlatine, f.
scarlet, *skăr' lĕt*, s. écarlate, f. [tine, f.
scarlet, *skăr' lĕt*, a. écarlate || ~-fever, s. fièvre scarlatine, f.
scarp, *skărp*, s. escarpe, f.
scate, *skāt*, vide skate.
scatter, *skăt' tĕr*, v. a. (& n.) (se) disperser || éparpiller || répandre || (of fire-arms) écarter || ~-brained, a. volage.
scattered, *skăt' tĕrd*, a. dispersé.
scavenger, *skăv' ĕn jĕr*, s. boueur, m.
scene, *sēn*, s. scène, f. || décoration, f. || théâtre, m. || ~-shifter, s. machiniste, m.

scenery, *sēn' ĕr ĭ*, s. paysage, m. || vue, f., site, m. || décors, m. pl.
scenic, *sēn' ĭk*, a. scénique.
scent, *sĕnt*, s. odorat, m. || parfum, m. || (fig.) nez, m. || piste, f. || to be on the right ~, être sur la voie || to be on the wrong ~, être en défaut || ~-bag, s. sachet, m. || ~-bottle, s. flacon d'odeurs, m. || ~-box, s. cassolette, f.
scent, *sĕnt*, v. a. sentir, fiairer || parfumer.
scentless, *sĕnt' lĕs*, a. inodore.
scepter, *sĕp' tĕr*, s. sceptre, m. || empire, m.
sceptic, *skĕp' tĭk*, s. sceptique, m.
sceptical, *skĕp' tĭk ăl*, a. sceptique.
scepticism, *skĕp' tĭ sĭzm*, s. scepticisme, m.
schedule, *shĕd' ŭl*, s. liste, f., inventaire, m. || (jur.) bilan, m. [modèle, m.
scheme, *skēm*, s. plan, projet, dessein,
scheme, *skēm*, v. n. projeter.
schemer, *skēm' ĕr*, s. homme à projets, m.
scheming, *skēm' ĭng*, s. manie de faire des projets, f.
schism, *sĭzm*, s. schisme, m.
schismatic, *sĭz măt' ĭk*, s. schismatique, m.
scholar, *skŏl' ĕr*, s. écolier, m. || homme de lettres, m.
scholarship, *skŏl' ĕr shĭp*, s. érudition, f., savoir, m. || bourse (aux collèges), f.
scholastic, *skō lăs' tĭk*, a. scolastique.
scholiast, *skō lĭ ăst*, s. scoliaste, m.
school, *skōl*, s. école, f. || ~-book, s. livre à l'usage des écoles, m. || ~-house, s. école, f.
school, *skōl*, v. a. instruire || réprimander.
schoolboy, *skōl' bŏy*, s. écolier, m.
schooling, *skōl' ĭng*, s. instruction, f. || école, m. || réprimande, f.
schoolmaster, *skōl' măs tĕr*, s. maître d'école, m. [de pension, f.
schoolmistress, *skōl' mĭs trĕs*, s. maîtresse
schooner, *skōn' ĕr*, s. goélette, f.
sciatica, *sĭ ăt' ĭ kă*, s. sciatique, f.
science, *sī' ĕns*, s. science, f.
scientific, *sī ĕn tĭf' ĭk*, a. (–ally, ad.) scientifique(ment).
scimitar, *sĭm' ĭ tĕr*, s. cimeterre, m.
scintillate, *sĭn' tĭl lāt*, v. a. étinceler.
scintillation, *sĭn tĭl lā' shŭn*, s. étincelle- ment, m. [ficielle, f.
sciolism, *sī' ŏ lĭzm*, s. connaissance super-
sciolist, *sī' ŏ lĭst*, s. demi-savant, m.
scion, *sī' ŏn*, s. (bot.) scion, rejeton, m.
scission, *sĭzh' ŭn*, s. scission, division, f.
scissors, *sĭz' zĕrs*, s. pl. ciseaux, m. pl.
scoff, *skŏf*, s. raillerie, moquerie, f.
scoff, *skŏf*, v. n. se moquer de.
scoffer, *skŏf' fĕr*, s. railleur, moqueur, m.
scoffingly, *skŏf' fĭng lĭ*, ad. par moquerie.
scold, *skōld*, s. grondeuse, f.
scold, *skōld*, v. a. & n. gronder.
scollop, *skŏl' lŏp*, vide scallop.
sconce, *skŏns*, s. candélabre, m.
scoop, *skōp*, s. pelle, f. || écope, f. || grande cuiller, f.
scoop, *skōp*, v. a. creuser, évider.
scope, *skōp*, s. but, dessein, m. || espace, lieu, m. || carrière, liberté, f., essor, m.

scorbutic, *skŏr bū′ tĭk*, a. scorbutique.
scorch, *skŏrch*, v. a. & n. griller, brûler.
score, *skōr*, s. coche, f. ‖ taille, f. ‖ ligne, f. ‖ compte, m. ‖ dette, f. ‖ raison, f. ‖ (mus.) partition, f. ‖ vingtaine, f. ‖ on the ~ of, à cause de ‖ en raison de.
score, *skōr*, v. a. entailler ‖ marquer ‖ (mus.) orchestrer ‖ mettre en compte.
scorer, *skōr′ ĕr*, s. marqueur, m.
scoria, *skō′ rĭ ä*, s. scorie, f.
scorn, *skŏrn*, s. dédain, m., moquerie, f.
scorn, *skŏrn*, v. a. & n. dédaigner, mépriser.
scorner, *skŏrn′ ĕr*, s. contempteur, moqueur, m.   [ad. avec dédain.
scornful, *skŏrn′ fŏŏl*, a. dédaigneux ‖ -ly,
scorpion, *skŏr′ pĭ ŭn*, s. scorpion, m.
scot, *skŏt*, s. quote-part, f. ‖ écot, m. ‖ to pay ~ and lot, payer rubis sur l'ongle ‖ ~-free, a. exempt de payement.
scotch, *skŏch*, s. entaille, coche, f. ‖ ~-hopper, s. marelle (jeu d'enfants), f.
scotch, *skŏch*, v. a. entailler ‖ enrayer.
scoundrel, *skŏŏn′ drĕl*, s. gredin, fripon, m.
scoundrelly, *skŏŏn′ drĕl ĭ*, a. fourbe, (de) coquin.
scour, *skŏŏr*, v. a. & n. écurer, nettoyer ‖ purger ‖ raser ‖ écumer ‖ rôder.
scourer, *skŏŏr′ ĕr*, s. dégraisseur, écureur, m. ‖ coureur, m.
scourge, *skĕrj*, s. fouet, m. ‖ châtiment, m.
scourge, *skĕrj*, v. a. fouetter, châtier.
scout, *skŏŏt*, s. espion, m. ‖ garçon, m., vedette, f. ‖ (mar.) corvette, f.
scout, *skŏŏt*, v. a. & n. se moquer de ‖ espionner.
scowl, *skŏwl*, s. air refrogné, m.
scowl, *skŏwl*, v. n. se refrogner.
scowlingly, *skŏwl′ ing lĭ*, ad. d'un air refrogné.   [malgreur, f.
scragginess, *skrăg′ gĭ nĕs*, s. rudesse, f. ‖
scraggy, *skrăg′ gĭ*, a. décharné ‖ raboteux.
scramble, *skrăm′ bl*, s. dispute, f. ‖ gribouilette (jeu d'enfants), f.
scramble, *skrăm′ bl*, v. n. grimper ‖ se traîner ‖ tâcher d'attraper ‖ se battre pour avoir, tâcher d'empoigner.
scrap, *skrăp*, s. fragment, petit morceau, m. ‖ -s, pl. restes, m. pl. ‖ ~-book, s. album, m. ‖ ~-paper, s. papier à brouillons, m.   [penny, s. grippe-sou, m.
scrape, *skrāp*, s. embarras, m. ‖ ~-
scrape, *skrāp*, v. a. & n. ratisser, racler, gratter, effacer.
scraper, *skrā′ pĕr*, s. décrottoir, m. ‖ mauvais violon, m. ‖ avare, m.
scraping, *skrā′ pĭng*, s. ratissure, f. ‖ frottement, m. ‖ grattage, m.
scratch, *skrăch*, s. égratignure, f.
scratch, *skrăch*, v. n. gratter, égratigner ‖ raturer.
scratcher, *skrăch′ ĕr*, s. grattoir, m.
scrawl, *skrawl*, s. griffonnage, m.
scrawl, *skrawl*, v. a. griffonner.
scream, *skrēm*, screech, *skrēch*, s. cri perçant, m. ‖ ~-owl, s. chat-huant, m.
scream, *skrēm*, screech, *skrēch*, v. n. jeter un cri.

screen, *skrēn*, s. paravent, m. ‖ crible, m. ‖ (fig.) abri, m. ‖ folding ~, s. paravent, m.
screen, *skrēn*, v. a. abriter ‖ cribler.
screw, *skrŏ*, s. vis, f. ‖ ~-driver, s. tournevis, m. ‖ ~-nut, s. écrou, m. ‖ ~-propeller, s. (mar.) hélice d'un vapeur, f. ‖ ~-steamer, s. vapeur à hélice, m.
screw, *skrŏ*, v. a. visser ‖ serrer ‖ (fig.) pressurer ‖ to ~ down a lid, fermer à vis un couvercle.
scribble, *skrĭb′ bl*, s. griffonnage, m.
scribble, *skrĭb′ bl*, v. a. griffonner.
scribbler, *skrĭb′ blĕr*, s. griffonneur, m. ‖ écrivailleur, m.
scribe, *skrīb*, s. copiste, m. ‖ écrivain, m.
scrip, *skrĭp*, s. petit sac, m. ‖ chiffon, m. ‖ (com.) scrip, reçu provisoire, m.
scriptural, *skrĭp′ tū rǎl*, a. biblique.
Scripture, *skrĭp′ tūr*, s. Écriture sainte, f.
scrivener, *skrĭv′ ĕn ĕr*, s. notaire, m. ‖ courtier, m.
scrofula, *skrŏf′ ū lǎ*, s. scrofules, f. pl.
scrofulous, *skrŏf′ ū lŭs*, a. scrofuleux.
scroll, *skrŏl*, s. rouleau, m.
scrub, *skrŭb*, s. homme de peine, m. ‖ pauvre diable, m.   [s'éreinter.
scrub, *skrŭb*, v. a. & n. frotter ‖ laver ‖
scrubby, *skrŭb′ bĭ*, a. pauvre, chétif ‖ méchant ‖ rabougri.
scruple, *skrŏ′ pl*, s. scrupule, m.
scruple, *skrŏ′ pl*, v. n. se faire scrupule ‖ hésiter.   [scrupuleuse, f.
scrupulosity, *skrŏ pū lŏs′ ĭ tĭ*, s. humeur
scrupulous, *skrŏ′ pū lŭs*, a. scrupuleux ‖ -ly, ad. scrupuleusement.
scrutineer, *skrŏ tĭ nēr′*, s. scrutateur, m.
scrutinise, *skrŏ′ tĭ nīz*, v. a. scruter, examiner, sonder.   [scrutin, m.
scrutiny, *skrŏ′ tĭn ĭ*, s. recherche exacte, f. ‖
scud, *skŭd*, v. n. s'enfuir à la hâte ‖ (mar.) faire vent arrière.   [mêlée, lutte, f.
scuffle, *skŭf′ fl*, s. querelle, f. ‖ combat, m.,
scuffle, *skŭf′ fl*, v. n. se battre, lutter.
scull, *skŭl*, s. godille, f.
scullery, *skŭl′ lĕr ĭ*, s. lavoir, évier, m.
scullion, *skŭl′ yŭn*, s. marmiton, souillon, m.
sculptor, *skŭlp′ tĕr*, s. sculpteur, m.   [m.
sculpture, *skŭlp′ tūr*, s. sculpture, f.
sculpture, *skŭlp′ tūr*, v. a. sculpter.
scum, *skŭm*, s. écume, f. ‖ crasse, f., rebut, m.
scum, *skŭm*, v. a. écumer.   [m.
scummer, *skŭm′ mĕr*, s. écumoire, f.
scurf, *skĕrf*, s. teigne, f. ‖ croûte, f.
scurfy, *skĕrf′ ĭ*, a. teigneux.   [sière, f.
scurrility, *skŭr rĭl′ ĭ tĭ*, s. raillerie gros-
scurrilous, *skŭr′ rĭl ŭs*, a. bas, vil, grossier ‖ -ly, ad. d'une manière indécente.
scurvily, *skĕr′ vĭ lĭ*, ad. vilement.
scurviness, *skĕr′ vĭ nĕs*, s. bassesse, f.
scurvy, *skĕr′ vĭ*, s. scorbut, m.
scurvy, *skĕr′ vĭ*, a. scorbutique ‖ vil, méprisable ‖ ladre.
scutcheon, *skŭch′ ŭn*, s. écusson, m.
scuttle, *skŭt′ tl*, s. panier large, m.
scuttle, *skŭt′ tl*, v. n. (mar.) saborder ‖ to ~ away, décamper, se sauver.
scythe, *sĭth*, s. faux, f.

sea, *sē*, s. mer, f., océan, m. ‖ main ~, haute mer, f. ‖ heavy ~, mer orageuse, f. ‖ high –s, s. pl. hautes marées, f. pl. ‖ ~-bath, s. bain de mer, m. ‖ ~-breeze, s. brise du large, f. ‖ ~-calf, s. veau marin, m. ‖ ~-card, s. compas de mer, m. ‖ ~-chart, s. carte marine, f. ‖ ~-coal, s. charbon de terre, m. ‖ ~-coast, s. littoral, m. ‖~-fight, s. combat naval, m. ‖ ~-girt, s. isolé au milieu des eaux ‖ ~-green, s. vert d'eau, m. ‖ ~-gull, s. mouette, f. ‖ ~-hog, s. marsouin, m. ‖ ~-horse, s. morse, m. ‖ ~-kale, s. chou marin, m. ‖ ~-legs, s. pl. pied marin, m. ‖ ~-piece, s. tableau de mer, m. ‖ ~-service, s. service de la marine, m. ‖ ~-shore, s. rivage de la mer, m. ‖ ~-term, s. terme de marine, m.

seaboard, *sē'bōrd*, s. bord de la mer, m.
seafaring, *sē'fāriṅg*, a. marin.
seal, *sēl*, s. sceau, m. ‖ cachet, m. ‖ phoque, m.
seal, *sēl*, v. a. sceller, cacheter. [m.
sealing-wax, *sēl'iṅg wäks*, s. cire à cacheter, f.
sealskin, *sēl'skin*, s. peau de phoque, f.
seam, *sēm*, s. couture, f. ‖ suture, f.
seam, *sēm*, v. a. couturer.
seaman, *sē'män*, s. marin, matelot, m.
seamanship, *sē'män ship*, s. art de naviguer, f.
seamstress, *sēm' strès*, s. couturière, f.
seamy, *sēm'i*, a. dont on voit les coutures ‖ the ~ side, revers de la médaille, m.
seaport, *sē'pōrt*, s. port de mer, m.
sear, *sēr*, v. a. brûler ‖ cautériser ‖ faner.
search, *sērch*, s. recherche, f. ‖ perquisition, f. ‖ visite, f. ‖ ~-warrant, s. mandat de perquisition, m.
search, *sērch*, v. a. & n. chercher, faire une recherche ‖ examiner, visiter, sonder.
searcher, *sērch'ér*, s. scrutateur, m. ‖ sonde, f.
seasick, *sē'sik*, a. pris du mal de mer.
seasickness, *sē'sik nès*, s. mal de mer, m.
seaside, *sē'sid*, s. bord de la mer, m.
season, *sē'zn*, s. saison, f., temps propice, moment opportun, m.
season, *sē'zn*, v. a. & n. assaisonner ‖ accoutumer ‖ s'acclimater ‖ se sécher.
seasonable, *sē'zn ā bl*, a. à propos, convenable ‖ de saison.
seasonably, *sē'zn ā bli*, ad. à propos.
seasoning, *sē'zn iṅg*, s. assaisonnement, m.
seat, *sēt*, s. siège, m., chaise, f. ‖ demeure, f. situation, f. ‖ keep your ~s, please! ne vous dérangez pas, messieurs!
seat, *sēt*, v. a. asseoir ‖ placer, poser, fixer, établir.
seated, *sēt'ēd*, a. situé ‖ à ... places ‖ pray be ~! prenez place, s'il vous plaît!
seaweed, *sē'wēd*, s. algue, f.
seaworthiness, *sē'wér thi nès*, s. bon état d'un vaisseau, m.
seaworthy, *sē'wér thi*, a. en état de tenir la mer.
secant, *sē' känt*, s. (geom.) sécante, f.

secede, *sēsēd'*, v. n. se séparer ‖ faire scission.
seceder, *sēsē'dér*, s. scissionnaire, m.
secession, *sēsésh'ün*, s. séparation, f. ‖ scission, f.
seclude, *sēklōd'*, v. a. exclure, éloigner.
seclusion, *sēklō'shün*, s. exclusion, f.
second, *sēk'ünd*, s. second, m. ‖ témoin, m. ‖ seconde, f.
second, *sēk'ünd*, v. a. seconder.
second, *sēk'ünd*, a. (-ly, ad.) second, deuxième(ment). [dairement
secondarily, *sēk'ünd ér i li*, ad. secondairement.
secondary, *sēk'ünd ér i*, a. secondaire ‖ subalterne. [crétion, f.
secrecy, *sē'krēsi*, s. secret, m. ‖ discrétion, f.
secret, *sē'krēt*, s. secret, m. ‖ in ~, en secret ‖ to keep a ~, garder un secret.
secret, *sē'krēt*, a. secret ‖ -ly, ad. secrètement ‖ to keep a thing ~, tenir qc. secret.
secretary, *sēk'rē tér i*, s. secrétaire, m. ‖ Home ~, Secrétaire de l'Intérieur, m.
secretaryship, *sēk'rē tér i ship*, s. secrétariat, m.
secrete, *sēkrēt'*, v. a. sécréter ‖ cacher.
secretion, *sēkrē'shün*, s. sécrétion, f.
sect, *sēkt*, s. secte, f. [s. sectaire, m.
sectarian, *sēk tā'ri än*, sectary, *sēk'tér i*, section, *sēk'shün*, s. section, f.
sectional, *sēk'shün äl*, a. sectionnel.
sector, *sēk'tér*, s. (geom.) secteur, m.
secular, *sēk'u lér*, a. séculier, laïque.
secularisation, *sēk ū lä ri zā'shün*, s. sécularisation, f.
secularise, *sēk'u lā riz*, v. a. séculariser.
secularity, *sēk ü lär'i ti*, s. mondanité, f.
secure, *sēkūr'*, v. a. mettre en sûreté ‖ assurer, confirmer, garantir.
secure, *sēkūr'*, a. (-ly, ad.) sûr(ement) ‖ assuré ‖ en sûreté. [caution, f.
security, *sēkūr'i ti*, s. sécurité, sûreté, f. ‖
sedan, *sēdän'*, s. chaise à porteurs, f.
sedate, *sēdāt'*, a. (-ʼ, ad.) calme ‖ posé (ment).
sedateness, *sēdāt'nès*, s. calme, m.
sedative, *sēd'ā tiv*, a. sédatif.
sedentary, *sēd'én tér i*, a. sédentaire.
sedge, *sēj*, s. glaïeul, jonc, m. ‖ ~-warbler, s. fauvette des roseaux, f. [m.
sediment, *sēd'i mént*, s. sédiment, résidu, m.
sedition, *sēdish'ün*, s. sédition, f.
seditious, *sēdish'üs*, a. séditieux ‖ -ly, ad. séditieusement. [factieux, m.
seditiousness, *sēdish'üs nès*, s. esprit
seduce, *sēdūs'*, v. a. séduire.
seducer, *sēdū'sér*, s. séducteur, m.
seduction, *sēdük'shün*, s. séduction, f.
seductive, *sēdük'tiv*, a. séduisant ‖ -ly, ad. d'une manière séduisante. [assidûment
sedulous, *sēd'ū lüs*, a. assidu ‖ -ly, ad.
see, *sē*, s. siège épiscopal, m.
see, *sē*, v. a. & n. ir. voir, apercevoir, observer ‖ fréquenter ‖ s'informer ‖ être attentif, prendre garde.
seed, *sēd*, s. semence, graine, f. ‖ postérité, f. ‖ ~-bed (~-garden, ~-plot), s. semis, m. ‖ ~-time, s. semailles, f. pl.

seed, *sēd,* v. n. grener, monter en graine.

seedling, *sēd'ling,* s. jeune plante, f.

seedsman, *sēd'z'măn,* s. semeur, m.

seedy, *sēd'ĭ,* a. grenu || plein de graines ||usé.

seeing, *sē'ing,* s. vue, visiou, f. || ~ **is believing,** voir c'est croire || ~ **that,** vu que. [tâcher d'obtenir.

seek, *sēk,* v. a. & n. ir. chercher||demander,

seem, *sēm,* v. n. sembler, paraître.

seeming, *sēm'ing,* s. apparence, f. || **to my ~,** à ce qu'il me semble.

seeming, *sēm'ing,* a. apparent || -ly, ad. apparemment.

seemliness, *sēm'lĭ něs,* s. bienséance, f.

seemly, *sēm'lĭ,* a. bienséant, convenable.

seer, *sē'ér,* s. prophète, m.

see-saw, *sē'sȧw,* s. bascule, f.

see-saw, *sē'sȧw,* v. n. se balancer.

seethe, *sēth,* v. a. & n. ir. bouillir.

segment, *sĕg'mĕnt,* s. segment, m.

segregate, *sē'grĕgāt,* v. a. séparer.

seine, *sēn,* s. (~-net) seine, f.

seizable, *sēz'ȧ bl,* a. saisissable.

seize, *sēz,* v. a. saisir, s'emparer de.

seizure, *sē'zŭr,* s. saisie, prise, f. || accès, m. || (jur.) saisie-arrêt, f.

seldom, *sĕl'dŭm,* ad. rarement.

select, *sĕ lĕkt',* v. a. choisir.

select, *sĕ lĕkt',* a. d'élite.

selection, *sĕ lĕk'shŭn,* s. choix, m.

self, *sĕlf,* pn. même || soi || one's ~, soi-même || ~-**acting,** a. automoteur || ~-**conceit,** s. présomption, f. || ~-**command** (~-**control**), s. empire sur soi-même, m. || ~-**condemned,** a. qui se condamne soi-même || ~-**confident,** a. plein de confiance en soi-même || ~-**conscious,** a. qui a la conscience de sa propre valeur||~-**defence,** s. défense personnelle, f. || ~-**denial,** s. renoncement à soi-même, m. || ~-**esteem,** s. estime de soi-même, f. || ~-**evident,** a. de toute évidence || ~-**government,** s. gouvernement du pays par lui-même, m. || ~-**interest,** s. égoïsme, m. || ~-**interested,** a. égoïste || ~-**love,** s. amour-propre, m. || ~-**made,** a. de ménage || ~-**possessed,** a. qui a l'empire sur soi-même || ~-**possession,** s. empire sur soi-même, m. || ~-**praise,** s. éloge de soi-même, m. || ~-**reliance,** s. confiance en soi-même, f. || ~-**relying,** a. qui a confiance en soi-même || ~-**sacrificing,** a. dévoué || ~-**seeking,** a. égoïste || ~-**styled,** a. soi-disant || ~-**taught,** a. instruit par soi-même || ~-**will,** s. opiniâtreté, f. || ~-**willed,** a. opiniâtre || volontaire.

selfish, *sĕlf'ĭsh,* a. égoïste.

selfishness, *sĕlf'ĭsh něs,* s. égoïsme, m.

selfsame, *sĕlf'sām,* a. même.

sell, *sĕl,* s. duperie, attrape, f.

sell, *sĕl,* v. a. & n. ir. vendre, trafiquer.

seller, *sĕl'ér,* s. vendeur, marchand, m.

selling-off, *sĕl'ing ŏf,* s. vente au rabais, f

Seltzer-water, *sĕlt'zér wȧw tér,* s. eau de Seltz, f.

selvage, *sĕl'vȧj,* s. lisière, f. [Seltz, f.

semaphore, *sĕm'ȧ fōr,* s. sémaphore, m.

semblance, *sĕm'blȧns,* s. ressemblance, apparence, f.

semibreve, *sĕm'ĭ brēv,* s. (mus.) ronde, f.

semicircle, *sĕm'ĭ sér kl,* s. demi-cercle, m.

semicircular, *sĕm'ĭ sér'kŭ lér,* a. demi-circulaire. [m. & f.

semicolon, *sĕm'ĭ kō' lŏn,* s. point et virgule,

seminal, *sĕm'ĭ năl,* a. séminal. [m.

seminarist, *sĕm'ĭ nér ĭst,* s. séminariste,

seminary, *sĕm'ĭ nér ĭ,* s. pépinière, f. || séminaire, m. [double-croche, f.

semiquaver, *sĕm'ĭ kwā vér,* s. (mus.)

semitone, *sĕm'ĭ tōn,* s. demi-ton, m.

semolina, *sĕm ō lē' nȧ,* s. semoule, f.

sempstress, *sĕm'strĕs,* s. couturière, f.

senate, *sĕn'āt,* s. sénat, m. || ~-**house,** s. sénat, m.

senator, *sĕn'ā tér,* s. sénateur, m.

senatorial, *sĕn ā tō'rĭ ăl,* a. sénatorial.

send, *sĕnd,* v. a. ir. envoyer, dépêcher || ~ **away,** renvoyer, congédier || **to ~ off,** expédier.

sender, *sĕnd'ér,* s. expéditeur, m.

seneschal, *sĕn'ĕs chȧl,* s. sénéchal, m.

senile, *sē'nĭl,* a. sénile || vieux, suranné.

senior, *sēn'yér,* s. aîné, ancien, doyen, m.

seniority, *sēn iŏr'ĭ tĭ,* s. ainesse, f. || ancienneté, f.

senna, *sĕn'nȧ,* s. séné, m.

sennight, *sĕn'nĭt,* s. huitaine, f.

sensation, *sĕn sā'shŭn,* s. sensation, f. || ~ **...,** à effet || **to create a ~,** faire sensation, faire de l'éclat.

sense, *sĕns,* s. sens, m. || sensation, f. || raison, f. || sentiment, m. || opinion, f. || signification, f. || **to be in one's right ~s,** être dans son bon sens || **to be out of one's ~s,** être hors de son bon sens, être un peu toqué.

senseless, *sĕns' lĕs,* a. insensible || absurde || -ly, ad. sans raison.

senselessness, *sĕns' lĕs nĕs,* s. absurdité, f.

sensibility, *sĕn sĭ bil'ĭ tĭ,* s. sensibilité, f.

sensible, *sĕn'sĭ bl,* a. sensible, sensé.

sensibly, *sĕn'sĭ blĭ,* ad. sensiblement || sagement, sensément.

sensitive, *sĕn'sĭ tĭv,* a. sensitif || susceptible || ~ **plant,** s. sensitive, f. [f.

sensitiveness, *sĕn'sĭ tĭv nĕs,* s. sensibilité,

sensual, *sĕn'sŭ ăl,* a. (-ly, ad.) sensuel (lement). [sensuel.

sensualise, *sĕn'sŭ ă līz,* v. a. rendre

sensualist, *sĕn'sŭ ă list,* s. sensuel, m. (philos.) sensualiste, m.

sensuality, *sĕn sŭ ăl'ĭ tĭ,* s. sensualité, f.

sentence, *sĕn'tĕns,* s. sentence, f., jugement, m. || phrase, f.

sentence, *sĕn'tĕns,* v. a. condamner.

sententious, *sĕn tĕn'shŭs,* a. sentencieux || -ly, ad. sentencieusement.

sentiment, *sĕn'tĭ mĕnt,* s. sentiment, m.

sentimental, *sĕn tĭ mĕn'tăl,* a. sentimental.

sentimentality, *sĕn tĭ mĕn tăl'ĭ tĭ,* s. sentimentalité, f.

sentinel, *sĕn'tĭ nĕl,* s. sentry, *sĕn'trĭ,* s. sentinelle, f. || ~-**box,** s. guérite, f.

separable, *sĕp'ăr ȧ bl,* a. séparable.

separate, *sĕp´ăr ăt*, v. a. (& n.) (se) séparer.
separate, *sĕp´ăr ăt*, a. separé || **-ly**, ad. à part.
separation, *sĕp ăr ā´ shŭn*, s. séparation, f. || **judicial ~**, divorce, m.
sepia, *sē´pĭ ä*, s. seiche, sèche, f.
sepoy, *sē´pŏÿ*, s. cipaye, m.
September, *sĕp tĕm´bĕr*, s. septembre, m.
septennial, *sĕp tĕn´nĭ ăl*, a. septennal.
septuagenarian, *sĕp tū ă jĕn ā´rĭ ăn*, s. septuagénaire, m. & f. || [Septuagésime.
septuagesima, *sĕp tū ă jĕs´ĭ mă*, s. la
sepulchral, *sĕ pŭl´krăl*, a. sépulcral.
sepulchre, *sĕp´ŭl kĕr*, s. sépulcre, m.
sepulture, *sĕp´ŭl tūr*, s. sépulture, f.
sequacious, *sĕ kwā´shŭs*, a. docile.
sequel, *sē´kwĕl*, s. suite, f.
sequence, *sē´kwĕns*, s. suite, série,`f.
sequester, *sĕ kwĕs´tĕr*, v. a. séquestrer.
sequestration, *sĕk wĕs trā´shŭn*, s. séquestre, m. || isolement, m. [m.
sequestrator, *sĕk wĕs trā´tŏr*, s. séquestre
seraglio, *sĕ răl´yō*, s. sérail, m.
seraph, *sĕr´ăf*, s. séraphin, m.
serenade, *sĕr ĕ nād´*, s. sérénade, f.
serenade, *sĕr ĕ nād´*, v. a. donner une sérénade f.
serene, *sĕ rēn´*, a. serein || most **~**, sérénissime || **-ly**, ad. avec sérénité.
serenity, *sĕ rĕn´ĭ tĭ*, s. sérénité, f.
serf, *sĕrf*, s. serf, esclave, m.
serfdom, *sĕrf´dŏm*, s. esclavage, m.
serge, *sĕrj*, s. serge (étoffe), f.
sergeant, serjeant, *săr´jĕnt*, s. sergent, m. || maréchal des logis, m. || huissier, m. || (of police) brigadier, m. || avocat, m.
serial, *sē´rĭ ăl*, s. œuvre qui paraît par séries, f.
serial, *sē´rĭ ăl*, a. sériel. [séries, f.
series, *sē´rēēz*, s. série, suite, f.
serious, *sē´rĭ ŭs*, a. sérieux || grave || **-ly**, ad. sérieusement.
seriousness, *sē´rĭ ŭs nĕs*, s. sérieux, m.
sermon, *sĕr´mŏn*, s. sermon, m.
sermonise, *sĕr´mŏn ĭz*, v. n. sermonner.
serous, *sĕr´ŭs*, a. séreux. [teau, m.
serpent, *sĕr´pĕnt*, s. serpent, m. || serpentine, f.
serpentine, *sĕr´pĕn tĭn*, s. serpentine, f.
serpentine, *sĕr´pĕn tĭn*, a. serpentant.
serrate, *sĕr´rāt*, v. a. créneler, denteler.
serried, *sĕr´rid*, a. serré, compacte.
serum, *sē´rŭm*, s. sérum, m.
servant, *sĕr´vănt*, s. serviteur, domestique, m. || servante, f. || **your obedient ~ (in letters)**, votre très-humble serviteur.
serve, *sĕrv*, v. a. & n. servir, être subordonné || être utile à, suffire || traiter || s'accommoder à || desservir || être en service, être au service || **that will ~ him right**, cela lui apprendra à vivre.
service, *sĕr´vĭs*, s. service, m. || emploi, office, m. || hommage, m. || utilité, f. || **divine ~**, s. office divin, m. || **dinner-~**, vaisselle de table, f. || **tea ~**, service à thé, m. [futile.
serviceable, *sĕr´vĭs ă bl*, a. serviable ||
servile, *sĕr´vĭl*, a. (-ly, ad.) servile(ment).
servility, *sĕr vĭl´ĭ tĭ*, s. servilité, f.

servitude, *sĕr´vĭ tūd*, s. servitude, f. || penal **~**, travaux forcés, m. pl.
session, *sĕsh´ŭn*, s. session, f. || **~'s hall ou house**, s. chambre de justice, f.
set, *sĕt*, s. assortiment, m. || série, f. || garniture, f. || (at play) partie, f.
set, *sĕt*, v. a. & n. ir. mettre, placer, fixer, poser, ajuster, régler || établir || évaluer || planter || mettre au jeu || parier || encadrer || louer, affermer || aiguiser, affiler, repasser || orner || se coucher (of the sun) || s'affaiblir || se fixer, coaguler || prendre racine, planter || mettre en musique || se mettre en route || attraper (of birds) || s'appliquer || **to ~ aside**, réserver, mettre de côté || **to ~ forth**, montrer || déployer || **to ~ off**, embellir, parer || rehausser || **to ~ on edge**, agacer || **to ~ to**, se chamailler || **to ~ up**, ériger, dresser || **to ~ up for oneself**, se qualifier de || **~-down**, s. mot sans réplique, m. || **~-off**, s. parure, f., ornement, m. || contrepoids, m. || **~-out**, s. étalage, m. || début, m. || **~-to**, s. dispute, querelle, f., chamaillis, m.
set, *sĕt*, a. fixe || réglé.
settee, *sĕt tē´*, s. petit canapé, m.
setter, *sĕt´tĕr*, s. chien couchant, m. || enfourneur, m. || compositeur, m. || instigateur, m.
setting, *sĕt´tĭng*, s. action de placer, f. || coucher du soleil, m.
settle, *sĕt´l*, v. a. & n. fixer, mettre, établir || régler, arranger || clarifier || calmer || se marier || se rasseoir, se fixer, s'établir || se remettre au beau.
settlement, *sĕt´l mĕnt*, s. établissement, règlement, m. || douaire, m. || sédiment, m. || liquidation, f. || colonie, f.
settler, *sĕt´tĕr*, s. colon, m.
seven, *sĕv´n*, a. sept.
seventeen, *sĕv´n tēn*, a. dix-sept.
seventeenth, *sĕv´n tēnth*, a. dix-septième.
seventh, *sĕv´nth*, a. (-ly, ad.) septième (ment). [xième.
seventieth, *sĕv´n tĭ ĕth*, a. soixante-di-
seventy, *sĕv´n tĭ*, a. soixante-dix.
sever, *sĕv´ĕr*, v. a. (& n.) (se) séparer.
several, *sĕv´ĕr ăl*, a. plusieurs, divers, différent || particulier || **-ly**, ad. séparément.
severe, *sĕ vēr´*, a. sévère, rigide, rigoureux, cruel || **-ly**, ad. rigoureusement.
severity, *sĕ vĕr´ĭ tĭ*, s. sévérité, f.
sew, *sō*, v. a. coudre.
sewer, *sō´ĕr*, s. couturier, m., couturière, f.
sewer, *sū´ĕr*, s. égout, cloaque, m.
sew(er)age, *sū´(ĕr)ăj*, s. immondices des égouts, f. pl. || système d'égouts, m.
sewing, *sō´ĭng*, s. couture, f. || **~-cushion**, s. coussin à coudre, m. || **~-machine**, s. couseuse mécanique, f. || **~-needle**, s. aiguille à coudre, f. [sexe.
sex, *sĕks*, s. sexe, m. || **fair ~**, le beau
sexagenarian, *sĕks ă jĕn ā´rĭ ăn*, s. sexagénaire, m. & f. [gésime.
sexagesima, *sĕks ă jĕs´ĭ mă*, s. la Sexa-
sexennial, *sĕks ĕn´nĭ ăl*, a. sexennal.

sexton, *sĕks'tŭn,* s. sacristain, m. || fossoyeur, m.

sextuple, *sĕks'tū pl,* a. sextuple.

sexual, *sĕks'ū ăl,* a. sexuel.

shabbily, *shăb'bĭ lĭ,* ad. mesquinement, pauvrement.   [pauvreté, f.

shabbiness, *shăb'bĭ nĕs,* s. mesquinerie, f.||

shabby, *shăb'bĭ,* a. chiche, chétif || bas, vil || usé || **~-genteel,** a. râpé || chétivement vêtu.   [entraver.

shackle, *shăk'l,* v. a. enchaîner || (fig.)

shackles, *shăk'lz,* s. pl. fers, m. pl.

shad, *shăd,* s. alose, f.

shaddock, *shăd'dŏk,* s. pamplemousse, f.

shade, *shād,* s. ombre, f. || nuance, f., ombrage, m. || abat-jour, m. || (fig.) abri, m.

shade, *shād,* v. a. ombrager || protéger || nuancer || obscurcir.

shadiness, *shā'dĭ nĕs,* s. ombrage, m.

shadow, *shăd'ō,* s. ombre, f.   [ombrer.

shadow, *shăd'ō,* v. a. ombrager || protéger ||

shadowy, *shăd'ō ĭ,* shady, *shā'dĭ,* a. ombragé || obscur, sombre || a ~ character, caractère vaporeux, m.

shaft, *shăft,* s. flèche, f., trait, m. || puits, m. || fût, m., tige, f. || limon, m. || **~-horse,** s. limonier, m.   [caporal (tabac), m.

shag, *shăg,* s. peluche, f. || poil rude, m. ||

shagged, *shăg'gĕd,* **shaggy,** *shăg'gĭ,* a. velu || hérissé.

shagreen, *shā grēn',* s. peau de chagrin, f.

shake, *shāk,* s. secousse, f. || (mus.) trille, f. || ébranlement, m.

shake, *shāk,* v. a. & n. ir. secouer, remuer, agiter || branler, chanceler || (mus.) triller || trembler || **to ~ one's belief,** ébranler la foi de qn.   [ment, m.

shaking, *shā'kĭng,* s. secousse, f., tremble-

shaky, *shā'kĭ,* a. branlant, cassé.

shall, *shăl,* v. n. def. ir. devoir.

shallop, *shăl'lŏp,* s. chaloupe, f.

shallow, *shăl'lō,* s. bas-fond, haut-fond, m.

shallow, *shăl'lō,* a. peu profond, bas || frivole, superficiel.

shallowness, *shăl'lō nĕs,* s. peu de profondeur, m. || frivolité, f.

sham, *shăm,* s. fraude, imposture, f.

sham, *shăm,* v. a. & n. tromper, duper, faire accroire || user de feintes.

sham, *shăm,* a. faux, prétendu, feint.

shambles, *shăm'blz,* s. pl. boucherie, f.

shambling, *shăm'blĭng,* a. lourd.

shame, *shăm,* s. honte, f. || pudeur, f. || **for ~** fi ! fi ! fi donc !

shame, *shăm,* v. a. faire honte à.   [fus.

shamefaced, *shăm'fāst,* a. pudique || con-

shameful, *shăm'fŏŏl,* a. honteux || **-ly,** ad. honteusement.

shameless, *shăm'lĕs,* a. impudent || **-ly,** ad. sans honte.   [f.

shamelessness, *shăm'lĕs nĕs,* impudence,

shammy-leather, *shăm'mĭ lĕth'ĕr,* s. chamois, m.

shampoo, *shăm pŏ',* v. a. masser.

shamrock, *shăm'rŏk,* s. trèfle, m.

shank, *shăngk,* s. jambe, f. || tuyau, m. || verge, f. || tige, f.

shanty, *shăn'tĭ,* s. hutte, baraque, f.

shape, *shāp,* s. forme, figure, f. || taille, stature, f.   [régler, ajuster.

shape, *shāp,* v. a. former || proportionner,

shapeless, *shāp'lĕs,* a. informe.

shapely, *shāp'lĭ,* a. bien fait.

share, *shār,* s. part, portion, f. || action, f., dividende, m. || soc, m. || **preference~,** (com.) action privilégiée, f.

share, *shār,* v. a. & n. partager || avoir part.   [m.

shareholder, *shār'hōld ĕr,* s. actionnaire,

sharer, *shār'ĕr,* s. partageant, m.

shark, *shărk,* s. requin, m. || escroc, m.

sharp, *shărp,* s. (mus.) dièse, m.

sharp, *shărp,* a. (-ly, ad.) aigu, tranchant, pointu || pénétrant, perçant, piquant || spirituel(lement) || sévèrement, vivement || satirique || cruel || vif || violent || éveillé, dégourdi || **look ~** ! attention ! dépêchez-vous ! || **~-shooter,** s. tirailleur, m.

sharpen, *shăr'pn,* v. a. aiguiser, affiler || déniaiser.

sharper, *shărp'ĕr,* s. escroc, filou, m.

sharpness, *shărp'nĕs,* s. tranchant, m., pointe, f. || âpreté, rigueur, pénétration d'esprit, f. || violence, f.   [briser.

shatter, *shăt'tĕr,* v. a. & n. fracasser || se

shave, *shāv,* v. a. ir. raser, faire la barbe || tondre || planer || **to get~d,** se faire raser.

shaver, *shā'vĕr,* s. barbier, m. || usurier, m.

shaving, *shā'vĭng,* s. rognure, f. || **~-s,** s. pl. copeaux, m. pl. || **~-dish,** s. plat à barbe,

shawl, *shăwl,* s. châle, m.   [m.

she, *shē,* s. femelle, f.

she, *shē,* pn. elle || celle.

sheaf, *shēf,* s. gerbe, f.

sheaf, *shēf,* v. a. mettre en gerbes.

shear, *shēr,* v. a. ir. tondre.

shearing, *shēr'ĭng,* s. tonte, tonture, f.

shears, *shērz,* s. pl. ciseaux, m. pl. || cisailles,

sheath, *shēth,* s. fourreau, m.   [f. pl.

sheathe, *shēth,* v. a. rengaîner, mettre dans le fourreau || revêtir de planches.

shed, *shĕd,* s. appentis, hangar, m.

shed, *shĕd,* v. a. ir. répandre, verser || se dépouiller de.

sheep, *shēp,* s. brebis, f., mouton, m. || (fig.) sot, m. || basane, f. || **~-cot,** **~-fold,** s. parc à brebis, m. || **~-hook,** s. houlette, f. || **~'s-eye,** s. (fig.) œillade, f. || **~-skin,** s. basane, f.

sheepish, *shēp'ĭsh,* a. timide, simple || bête.

sheepishness, *shēp'ĭsh nĕs,* s. bêtise, f.

sheer, *shēr,* v. n. s'en aller secrètement || (mar.) embarder || **to ~ off,** (mar.) alarguer || **to ~ up,** (mar.) élonger.

sheer, *shēr,* a. & ad. pur || tout d'un coup.

sheet, *shēt,* s. drap de lit, m. || feuille de papier, f. || lame, f. || (mar.) écoute, f. || main-~, (mar.) écoute de grand perroquet || winding-~, linceul, suaire, m. || **in -s,** en feuilles || **~-almanac,** s. calendrier de comptoir, m. || **~-anchor,** s. maîtresse ancre, f. || **~-iron,** s. tôle, f. || **~-lightning,** s. éclair de chaleur, m. || **~-music,** s. cahiers de musique, m. pl.

sheeting, *shēt'ing*, s. toile pour draps de lit, f. [sable, m.

shelf, *shĕlf*, s. tablette, f. || écueil, banc de

shell, *shĕl*, s. écaille, cosse, f. || coquille, f. || écorce, f. || bombe, f., coquillage, m. || ~-**work,** s. rocaille, f.

shell, *shĕl*, v. a. & n. écaler, écosser || bombarder || s'écailler. [de coquille.

shelly, *shĕl'lĭ*, a. abondant en écailles ||

shelter, *shĕl'tēr*, s. abri, asile, m.

shelter, *shĕl'tēr*, v. a. mettre à couvert, mettre à l'abri || défendre, protéger.

shelterless, *shĕl'tēr lĕs*, a. sans asile.

shelve, *shĕlv*, v. n. aller en pente.

shelving, *shĕlv'ing*, s. pente, f.

shelving, *shĕlv'ing*, a. en pente, en talus.

shepherd, *shĕp'ērd*, s. berger, pâtre, m. || pasteur, m.

shepherdess, *shĕp'ērd ĕs*, s. bergère, f.

sherbet, *shĕr'bĕt*, s. sorbet, m.

sheriff, *shĕr'if*, s. shérif, m.

sherry, *shĕr'rĭ*, s. vin de Xérès, m.

shew, *shō*, s. & v. a. *vide* show.

shield, *shēld*, s. bouclier, m. || (fig.) protection, f.

shield, *shēld*, v. a. défendre.

shift, *shift*, s. ressource, f., expédient, m., défaite, f., subterfuge, m. || chemise de femme, f. || **to make ~ to live,** gagner péniblement sa vie.

shift, *shift*, v. a. & n. changer, déplacer, changer de vêtement || (rail.) changer de voiture || trouver des expédients.

shifter, *shift'ēr*, s. homme rusé, m.

shillelagh, *shil lā'lă*, s. casse-tête, m.

shilling, *shil'ling*, s. 1 franc 25 centimes || **a ~ in the pound,** cinq pour cent.

shilly-shally, *shil'lĭ shăl'lĭ*, v. n. être indécis, irrésolu. [jambe, m.

shin(-bone), *shin'(bōn)*, s. tibia, os de la

shine, *shin*, v. n. ir. luire, reluire, briller.

shingle, *shing'gl*, s. bardeau, m. || ~-**s,** pl. (méd.) zona, zoster, m. [f.

shining, *shi'ning*, s. éclat, m. || splendeur, f.

shining, *shi'ning*, a. luisant, éclatant.

shiny, *shin'ĭ*, a. luisant, éclatant.

ship, *ship*, s. vaisseau, navire, m. || ~-**agent,** s. commissionnaire-expéditeur, m. || ~-**board,** ad. à bord || ~-**boy,** s. mousse, m. || ~-**broker,** s. courtier maritime, m. || ~-**builder,** s. constructeur de navires, m. || ~-**load,** s. cargaison, f. || ~-**owner,** s. armateur, m.

ship, *ship*, v. a. (mar.) embarquer || **(the oars)** armer || **(the helm)** monter || **(a sea)** recevoir, embarquer (une vague).

shipment, *ship'mĕnt*, s. chargement, m.

shipper, *ship'pēr*, s. patron d'un navire, m.

shipping, *ship'ping*, s. vaisseaux, m. pl. || flotte, f. || chargement, m. || ~-**agent,** s. facteur maritime, m.

shipwreck, *ship'rĕk*, s. naufrage, m.

shipwreck, *ship'rĕk*, v. a. & n. naufrager.

shire, *shire*, s. comté, département, m.

shirt, *shĕrt*, s. chemise d'homme, f. || ~-**front,** s. chemisette, f. [f.

shirting, *shĕrt'ing*, s. toile pour chemises,

shiver, *shiv'ēr*, s. éclat, m. || fragment, m. || frissonnement, m.

shiver, *shiv'ēr*, v. a. & n. rompre, mettre en pièces || se briser || frissonner. [m.

shivering, *shiv'ēr ing*, s. frissonnement, m.

shoal, *shōl*, s. foule, f. || banc de sable, m.

shoal, *shōl*, v. n. s'attrouper || (of water)

shoal, *shōl*, a. bas, peu profond. [baisser.

shock, *shŏk*, s. choc, coup, m. || secousse, f. || moyette, f. || ~-**head,** s. chignon, m.

shock, *shŏk*, v. a. choquer, heurter || attaquer || offenser. [geant, horrible.

shocking, *shŏk'ing*, a. choquant, affli-

shoddy, *shŏd'dĭ*, s. shuddy, m. || effiloché, m. || ~-**mill,** s. effilocheuse, f. || fabrique de laine de shuddy, f.

shoe, *shō*, s. soulier, m. || fer à cheval, m. || ~-**black,** ~-**boy,** s. décrotteur, m. || ~-**horn,** s. chausse-pied, m. || ~-**lace,** ~-**string,** s. cordon de soulier, m.

shoe, *shō*, v. a. ir. chausser || ferrer.

shoeing, *shō'ing*, s. ferrage, m.

shoeless, *shō'lĕs*, a. sans souliers.

shoemaker, *shō'māk ēr*, s. cordonnier, m.

shoot, *shōt*, s. rejeton, m. || remous, m.

shoot, *shōt*, v. a. & n. ir. lancer, tirer, décharger || décocher, darder || pousser || bourgeonner || jaillir || passer avec rapidité, s'élancer, s'avancer || provenir.

shooter, *shōt'ēr*, s. tireur, m.

shooting, *shōt'ing*, s. chasse au tir, f. || pousse, f., élancement, m. || ~-**ground,** ~-**gallery,** s. tir, m. || ~-**jacket,** s. habit de chasse, m. || ~-**lodge** (~-**box),** s. rendez-vous de chasse, m.

shooting, *shōt'ing*, a. (of pain) lancinant || (of stars) filant. ·

shop, *shŏp*, s. boutique, f., magasin, atelier, m. || ~-**bill,** s. enseigne, f. || ~-**boy,** s. garçon de magasin, m. || ~-**front,** s. fenêtre d'étalage, f. || ~-**lifter,** s. auteur d'un vol dans un magasin, m.

shop, *shŏp*, v. n. faire des emplettes.

shopkeeper, *shŏp'kēp ēr*, s. boutiquier, m.

shopping, *shŏp'ping*, s. emplettes, f. pl.

shore, *shōr*, s. rivage, m., côte, f. || appui, m. || **to stand in~,** (mar.) courir à terre.

shorn, *shōrn*, a. tondu. [terre.

short, *shōrt*, a. court || bref || concis, serré || inférieur || **to be ~ of money,** être à court d'argent || **to fall ~ of,** être au-dessous de || **to cut ~,** couper court à || **to make ~ work of,** ne pas y aller par quatre chemins || **in ~,** bref, en un mot || **the long and the ~ of it is,** en résumé || ~-**lived,** a. qui vit peu de temps || ~-**sighted,** a. myope || ~-**sightedness,** s. myopie, f. || -**ly,** ad. sous peu, bientôt || brièvement. [sance, f.

shortcoming, *shōrt'kŭm ing*, s. insuffi-

shorten, *shōrt'n*, v. a. (& n.) (se) raccourcir, abréger || couper.

shorthand, *shōrt'hănd*, s. sténographie, f. || ~-**writer,** s. sténographe, m.

shortness, *shōrt'nĕs*, s. peu de longueur, m., brièveté, f. || imperfection, f. || petitesse, f.

shot, *shŏt*, s. coup de feu; m. || trait lancé, m. || boulet de canon, m. || compte, m. || portée, f. || small-~, dragée, cendre de plomb, f. || duck-~, dragée aux canards,

shot, *shŏt*, a. chatoyant.   [f.

shoulder, *shōl'dĕr*, s. épaule, f. || to give one the cold ~, battre froid à qn. || ~-blade, s. omoplate, f. || ~-strap, s. bretelle, f. || broad-~ed, a. aux larges épaules || round-~ed, a. qui a le dos rond.   [sur les épaules || pousser.

shoulder, *shōl'dĕr*, v. a. mettre or porter

shout, *shŏut*, s. cri, m. || acclamation, f. || (of laughter) éclat, m.

shout, *shŏut*, v. n. pousser des cris de joie, faire des acclamations.

shouter, *shŏw'tĕr*, s. acclamateur, m.

shove, *shŭv*, s. coup, m.

shove, *shŭv*, v. a. & n. pousser || fourrer || to ~ off, (mar.) pousser au large.

shovel, *shŭv'l*, s. pelle, f.   [ramasser.

shovel, *shŭv'l*, v. a. jeter avec une pelle ||

show, *shō*, s. spectacle, m. || étalage, m., parade, f. || ~-case, s. montre, f. || ~-room, s. local d'une exposition, m.

show, *shō*, v. a. ir. montrer, faire voir || enseigner, démontrer || publier || exposer || conduire || prouver || paraître, avoir l'air || to ~ off, étaler.

shower, *shŏw'ĕr*, s. ondée, giboulée, f. || (fig.) grêle, f. || ~-bath, s. douche, f.

shower, *shŏw'ĕr*, v. a. & n. inonder || pleuvoir à verse.

showery, *shŏw'ĕr ĭ*, a. pluvieux.

showy, *shō'ĭ*, a. brillant || fastueux.

shrapnel-shell, *shrăp'nĕl shĕl*, s. shrapnel, m.

shred, *shrĕd*, s. morceau, m., rognure, f.

shred, *shrĕd*, v. a. couper en petits morceaux.

shrew, *shrō*, s. pie-grièche, f. || mégère, f.

shrewd, *shrōd*, a. (-ly, ad.) fin(emeut) || rusé.

shrewdness, *shrōd'nĕs*, s. finesse, ruse, f.

shrewish, *shrō'ĭsh*, a. acariâtre || -ly, ad. en criaillant.   [f.

shrewmouse, *shrō'mŏus*, s. musaraigne,

shriek, *shrēk*, s. cri perçant, m.

shriek, *shrēk*, v. n. pousser des cris perçants.   [cants.

shrike, *shrīk*, s. pie-grièche, f.

shrill, *shrĭl*, a. perçant, aigu, grêle.

shrillness, *shrĭl'nĕs*, s. son aigu, m.

shrimp, *shrĭmp*, s. crévette, f. || bout d'homme, m.

shrine, *shrīn*, s. reliquaire, m., châsse, f.

shrink, *shrĭngk*, v. n. ir. se resserrer, se rétrécir, se racourcir || se reculer.   [m.

shrinkage, *shrĭngk'āj*, s. rétrécissement,

shrivel, *shrĭv'l*, v. a. & (n.) (se) rider.

shroud, *shrŏud*, s. abri, m. || linceul, drap mortuaire, m. || (mar.) hauban, m.

shroud, *shrŏud*, v. a. & n. mettre à l'abri || défendre, protéger || couvrir d'un drap mortuaire || se mettre à l'abri.

Shrove, *shrōv*; ~-tide, s. les jours gras, m. pl. || ~-Tuesday, s. mardi gras, m.

shrub, *shrŭb*, s. arbrisseau, arbuste, m.

shrubbery, *shrŭb'bĕr ĭ*, s. plantation d'arbrisseaux, f.

shrubby, *shrŭb'bĭ*, a. d'arbrisseau || plein d'arbrisseaux.

shrug, *shrŭg*, s. haussement d'épaules, m.

shrug, *shrŭg*, v. a. lever, hausser, m.

shudder, *shŭd'dĕr*, s. frissonnement, m.

shudder, *shŭd'dĕr*, v. n. frissonner, frémir || trembler.

shuffle, *shŭf'fl*, s. mélange, m. || artifice, m. || confusion, f. || défaite, f.

shuffle, *shŭf'fl*, v. a. & n. mélanger, mêler || confondre || biaiser, tergiverser || éluder || s'intriguer.

shuffler, *shŭf'flĕr*, s. fourbe, biaiseur, m.

shuffling, *shŭf'flĭng*, s. ruses, f. pl., détours, subterfuges, m. pl.

shuffling, *shŭf'flĭng*, a. évasif || chicaneur.

shun, *shŭn*, v. a. éviter || échapper.

shunt, *shŭnt*, s. voie de garage, f.

shunt, *shŭnt*, v. a. changer de voie.

shut, *shŭt*, v. a. & n. ir. fermer, renfermer || to ~ off, intercepter || to ~ off steam, intercepter la vapeur.

shutter, *shŭt'tĕr*, s. volet de fenêtre, m.

shuttle, *shŭt'tl*, s. navette, f. || ~-cock, s. volant, m.

shy, *shī*, v. n. avoir peur || faire un écart.

shy, *shī*, a. (-ly, ad.) réservé || timide (ment) || soupçonneux.

shyness, *shī'nĕs*, s. réserve, timidité, f.

sibyl, *sĭb'ŭl*, s. sibylle, f.

sick, *sĭk*, a. malade || indisposé || dégoûté || sea-~, qui a le mal de mer || ~-list, s. rôle des malades, m. || ~-ward, s. salle des malades, f.

sicken, *sĭk'n*, v. a. & n. rendre malade, faire mal au cœur || tomber malade || languir.   [goût.

sickening, *sĭk'n ĭng*, a. qui donne du dé-

sickle, *sĭk'kl*, s. faucille, f.

sickliness, *sĭk'lĭ nĕs*, s. état maladif, m.

sickly, *sĭk'lĭ*, a. maladif.

sickness, *sĭk'nĕs*, s. maladie, f., mal au cœur, m. || sea-~, mal de mer, m.

side, *sīd*, s. côté, m. || flanc, bord, m. || parti, m., secte, f. || on one ~, d'un côté || on all ~s, de tous côtés || to take one's ~, prendre le parti de qn. || one-~d, a. qui n'a qu'un côté, qu'une face || ~-dish, s. entremets, m. || hors-d'œuvre, m. || ~-face, s. profil, m. || ~-scene, s. coulisse, f. || ~-walk, s. contre-allée, f.

side, *sīd*, v. n. se joindre à un parti.

side, *sīd*, a. latéral, oblique, de côté.

sideboard, *sīd'bōrd*, s. buffet, m.

sidelong, *sīd'lŏng*, a. (& ad.) oblique(ment)||

sider, *sīd'ĕr*, s. partisan, m.   [de côté.

sideways, *sīd'wāz*, ad. de côté, oblique-ment.   [d'évitement, f.

siding, *sī'dĭng*, s. (rail.) croisière, f. || gare

sidle, *sī'dl*, v. n. marcher de côté.

siege, *sēj*, s. siège, m. || to lay ~ to, mettre le siège à || to raise a ~, lever le siège.   [siège.

sieve, *sĭv*, s. tamis, crible, m.

sift, *sĭft*, v. a. tamiser, cribler || (fig.) sonder.

siftings, *sif'tĭngz*, s. pl. criblures, f. pl.

sigh, *sĭ*, soupir, m.

sigh, *sĭ*, v. n. soupirer, gémir.

sight, *sĭt*, s. vue, faculté de voir, f. || vision, f. || aspect, m. || spectacle, m. || mire d'un fusil, f. || at ~, (com.) à vue || at ... days' ~, (com.) à ... jours de vue || to hate the ~ of one, détester la vue de qn. || out of ~, hors de vue || to lose ~ of, perdre de vue || ~-hole, s. mire, f. || ~-seeing, s. curiosité des foules, f.

sight, *sĭt*, v. a. (mar.) apercevoir, remarquer.

sightless, *sĭt'lĕs*, a. aveugle.

sightly, *sĭt'lĭ*, ad. agréable à la vue, beau.

sign, *sĭn*, s. signe, m., marque, f., symbole, m. || enseigne, f. || souvenir, m. ||~-board, s. enseigne, f. || ~-manual, s. signature royale, f. || ~-post, s. poteau d'enseigne.

sign, *sĭn*, v. a. signer || faire signe.   [m.

signal, *sĭg'năl*, s. signal, signe, m. || ~-light, s. fanal, m.

signal, *sĭg'năl*, v. a. signaler.

signal, *sĭg'năl*, a. signalé, insigne || -ly, ad. d'une manière signalée.

signalise, *sĭg'nălĭz*, v. a. signaler.

signalman, *sĭg'năl măn*, s. signaliste, m.

signature, *sĭg'nă tūr*, s. signature, marque, f.

signer, *sĭn'ĕr*, s. signataire, m.   [f.

signet, *sĭg'nĕt*, s. cachet, m.

significance, *sĭg nĭf'ĭ kăns*, s. signification, f. || importance, f. || énergie, f.

significant, *sĭg nĭf'ĭ kănt*, a. significatif.

signification, *sĭg nĭf ĭ kā'shŭn*, s. signification, f.

signify, *sĭg'nĭ fī*, v. a. & n. signifier.

silence, *sī'lĕns*, s. silence, m.

silence, *sī'lĕns*, v. a. faire taire.

silent, *sī'lĕnt*, a. silencieux, taciturne || -ly.

silex, *sī'lĕks*, s. caillou, m. [ad. en silence.

silhouette, *sĭl hŏ ĕt'*, s. silhouette, f.

silicious, *sĭ lĭsh'ŭs*, a. siliceux.

silk, *sĭlk*, s. soie, f. || ~-goods, s. pl. soieries, f. pl. || ~-mill, s. fabrique de soie, f.

silk, *sĭlk*, a. de soie.   [soyeux.

silken, *sĭlk'n*, silky, *sĭlk'ĭ*, a. de soie,

silkiness, *sĭlk'ĭ nĕs*, s. douceur, f.

silkworm, *sĭlk'wĕrm*, s. ver à soie, m. || ~-nursery, s. magnanerie, f.

sill, *sĭl*, s. seuil, appui, m.

silily, *sĭl'ĭ lĭ*, ad. sottement.

silliness, *sĭl'lĭ nĕs*, s. sottise, f.

silly, *sĭl'lĭ*, a. sot, niais, simple.

silver, *sĭl'vĕr*, s. argent, m. || monnaie blanche, f. || German-~, ruolz, christophle, m. || ~-mounted, a. monté en argent || ~-plate, s. argenterie, f.

silver, *sĭl'vĕr*, v. a. argenter || étamer.

silver, *sĭl'vĕr*, a. d'argent || argentin.

silversmith, *sĭl'vĕr smĭth*, s. orfèvre, m.

silvery, *sĭl'vĕr ĭ*, a. argenté.

similar, *sĭm'ĭ lĕr*, a. semblable || -ly, ad. de la même manière.   [f.

similarity, *sĭm ĭ lăr'ĭ tĭ*, s. ressemblance,

simile, *sĭm'ĭ lē*, similitude, *sĭ mĭl'ĭ tŭd*, s. similitude, f.

simmer, *sĭm'mĕr*, v. n. bouillir doucement.

simony, *sĭm'ŏn ĭ*, s. simonie, f.

simoon, *sĭ mōn'*, s. simoun, m.

simper, *sĭm'pĕr*, s. minauderie, f.

simper, *sĭm'pĕr*, v. n. sourire niaisement.

simple, *sĭm'pl*, a. simple, naïf || pur || ~-minded, a. ingénu.

simpleness, *sĭm'pl nĕs*, s. simplicité, f.

simpleton, *sĭm'pl tŏn*, s. niais, sot, m.

simplicity, *sĭm plĭs'ĭ tĭ*, s. simplicité, f.

simplify, *sĭm'plĭ fī*, v. a. simplifier.

simply, *sĭm'plĭ*, ad. simplement.

simulate, *sĭm'ū lāt*, v. a. feindre.

simulation, *sĭm ū lā'shŭn*, s. dissimulation, f.   [ad.] simultané(ment).

simultaneous, *sĭm ŭl tā'nē ŭs*, a. (-ly,

sin, *sĭn*, s. péché, m. || besetting ~, péché d'habitude, m. || ~-offering, s. sacrifice expiatoire, m.

since, *sĭns*, c. puisque || ~, pr. depuis que || ever ~, depuis lors, dès lors.

sincere, *sĭn sēr'*, a. (-ly, ad.) sincère (ment) || yours -ly, votre très-humble serviteur.

sincerity, *sĭn sĕr'ĭ tĭ*, s. sincérité, f.

sinecure, *sī'nē kūr*, s. sinécure, f.

sine die, *sī'nē dī'ē*, ad. indéfiniment.

sinew, *sĭn'ū*, s. nerf, m. || tendon, m.

sinewy, *sĭn'ū ĭ*, a. nerveux || vigoureux.

sinful, *sĭn'fool*, a. pécheur, criminel || -ly, ad. en pécheur.

sinfulness, *sĭn'fool nĕs*, s. méchanceté, f.

sing, *sĭng*, v. a. & n. ir. chanter || faire ronron || (of the ears) tinter || ~-song, s. chant monotone, m.   [ber, roussir.

singe, *sĭnj*, v. a. brûler légèrement, flamber || ~singeing, *sĭnj'ĭng*, s. roussi, m. || légère brûlure, f.   [teuse.

singer, *sĭng'ĕr*, s. chanteur, m., chanteuse.

singing, *sĭng'ĭng*, s. chant, m. || ~-boy, s. enfant de chœur, m. || ~-master, s. maître de chant, m.

single, *sĭng'gl*, v. a. choisir, distinguer.

single, *sĭng'gl*, a. seul, particulier, singulier, simple || non marié || ~-handed, a. de son propre chef || ~-hearted, a. sincère, franc.   [cérité, f.

singleness, *sĭng'gl nĕs*, s. simplicité, sincérité, f.

singlestick, *sĭng'gl stĭk*, s. gourdin, m.

singly, *sĭng'glĭ*, ad. simplement || en particulier.

singular, *sĭng'gū lĕr*, s. (gr.) singulier, m.

singular, *sĭng'gū lĕr*, a. singulier || -ly, ad. singulièrement.   [f.

singularity, *sĭng gū lăr'ĭ tĭ*, s. singularité, f.

sinister, *sĭn'ĭs tĕr*, a. sinistre || pervers.

sink, *sĭngk*, s. égout, évier, m. [méchant.

sink, *sĭngk*, v. a. & n. ir. couler à fond, enfoncer || creuser || abaisser, dégrader || perdre || plonger, précipiter || cacher || diminuer || amortir || s'enfoncer || devenir creux || s'abaisser, succomber.

sinking-fund, *sĭngk'ĭng fŭnd*, s. caisse d'amortissement, m.   [f.

sinner, *sĭn'nĕr*, s. pécheur, m., pécheresse.

sinuosity, *sĭn ŭ ŏs'ĭ tĭ*, s. sinuosité, f.

sinuous, *sĭn'ŭ ŭs*, a. sinueux.

sinus, *sī'nŭs*, s. baie, f.

sip, *sĭp*, s. petit coup (en buvant), m.

---

sip, *sĭp*, v. a. & n. buvotter, boire à petits coups ‖ siroter.

siphon, *sī´fŭn*, s. siphon, m.

sippet, *sĭp´pĕt*, s. croûton, m.

Sir, *sẽr*, s. (titre) monsieur, m. ‖ (of a knight) le chevalier . . ., m.

sire, *sĭr*, s. père, m. ‖ (to sovereigns) Sire, m.

siren, *sī´rĕn*, s. sirène, f.

sirloin, *sẽr´boyn*, s. aloyau, m.

sirup, *sĭr´ŭp*, s. sirop, m.

sister, *sĭs´tẽr*, s. sœur, f. ‖ religieuse, f. ‖ half-~, demi-sœur, f. ‖ ~-in-law, s. belle-sœur, f.   [de sœurs, f.

sisterhood, *sĭs´tẽr hŏŏd*, s. communauté

sisterly, *sĭs´tẽr lĭ*, ad. en sœur.

sit, *sĭt*, v. n. ir. s'asseoir sur, asseoir ‖ demeurer ‖ siéger ‖ être situé ‖ couver ‖ to ~ for one's portrait, poser ‖ to ~ up (at night), rester levé, veiller.

site, *sīt*, s. situation, contrée, f.

sited, *sī´tĕd*, a. situé.

sitter, *sĭt´tẽr*, s. personne sédentaire, f. ‖ personne qui pose, f.

sitting, *sĭt´tĭng*, s. posture, pose, f. ‖ séance, f. ‖ audience, f.

situated, *sĭt´ū ā tĕd*, a. situé, placé.

situation, *sĭt´ū ā´shŭn*, s. situation, f.

six, *sĭks*, a. six ‖ at -es and sevens, sens dessus dessous.

sixpence, *sĭks´pĕns*, s. 60 centimes, m. pl.

sixteen, *sĭks´tēn*, a. seize.

sixteenth, *sĭks´tēnth*, a. seizième ‖ (of the month) seize.

sixth, *sĭksth*, a. (-ly, ad.) sixième(ment).

sixtieth, *sĭks´tĭ ĕth*, a. soixantième.

sixty, *sĭks´tĭ*, a. soixante.

size, *sĭz*, s. grandeur, taille, f. ‖ grosseur, f. ‖ mesure, f. ‖ calibre, m. ‖ (com.) numéro, m. ‖ état, m., condition, f. ‖ qualité, f. ‖ colle, colle forte, f.

size, *sĭz*, v. a. coller.   [taille . . .

sized, *sĭzd*, a. d'une grandeur de . . ., de

skate, *skāt*, s. patin, m. ‖ (fish) raie, f., ange, m.

skate, *skāt*, v. n. patiner, glisser.

skating-rink, *skāt´ĭng rĭnk*, s. arène ou salle pour patiner, f.

skein, *skān*, s. écheveau, m.

skeleton, *skĕl´ĕ tŏn*, s. squelette, m. ‖ ~-key, s. crochet, m.

sketch, *skĕch*, s. esquisse, f. ‖ ~-block, s. bloc de feuilles de papier à esquisser, m. ‖ ~-book, s. album, m.

sketch, *skĕch*, v. a. esquisser, ébaucher.

skewer, *skū´ẽr*, s. brochette, f.

skewer, *skū´ẽr*, v. a. brocheter.

ski, *shē*, s. ski, m.

skid, *skĭd*, s. sabot à enrayer, m.

skid, *skĭd*, v. a. enrayer.

skiff, *skĭf*, s. esquif, m.

skilful, *skĭl´fŏŏl*, a. (-ly, ad.) adroit (ement) ‖ habile(ment).

skilfulness, *skĭl´fŏŏl nĕs*, s. habileté, f.

skilled, *skĭld*, a. adroit, versé dans.

skillet, *skĭl´lĕt*, s. poêlon, m.

skim, *skĭm*, s. écume, f. ‖ crème, f.

skim, *skĭm*, v. a. & n. écumer, effleurer ‖ écrémer.

skimmer, *skĭm´mẽr*, s. écumoire, f.

skin, *skĭn*, s. peau, f. ‖ pelure, f. ‖ (fig.) écorce, f. ‖ ~-deep, a. superficiel.

skin, *skĭn*, v. a. écorcher, couvrir d'une pellicule.   [grippe-sou, m.

skinflint, *skĭn´flĭnt*, s. fesse-mathieu,

skinned, *skĭnd*, a. couvert d'une peau.

skinner, *skĭn´nẽr*, s. pelletier, m.

skinny, *skĭn´nĭ*, a. décharné, maigre.

skip, *skĭp*, s. saut, m.   [omettre.

skip, *skĭp*, v. a. & n. sautiller, passer ‖

skipper, *skĭp´pẽr*, s. sauteur, m. ‖ (of a ship) patron, m.

skirmish, *skẽr´mĭsh*, s. escarmouche, f.

skirmish, *skẽr´mĭsh*, v. n. escarmoucher.

skirmisher, *skẽr´mĭsh ẽr*, s. tirailleur, m.

skirt, *skẽrt*, s. basque, f., pan, m. ‖ jupe, f. ‖ bord, m., marge, lisière, f.

skirt, *skẽrt*, v. a. border.

skittish, *skĭt´tĭsh*, a. ombrageux ‖ capricieux, volage ‖ -ly, ad. capricieusement.

skittle, *skĭt´tl*, s. quille, f.   [caché.

skulk, *skŭlk*, v. n. guetter qc. ‖ se tenir

skulker, *skŭlk´ẽr*, s. lâche, calin, m.

skull, *skŭl*, s. crâne, m.

sky, *skī*, s. ciel, firmament, m. ‖ ~-light, s. abat-jour, m. ‖ lucarne, f. ‖ (mar.) claire-voie, f. ‖ ~-parlour, s. galetas, m. ‖ ~-rocket, s. fusée volante, f. ‖ ~-scraper, s. (mar.) grand perroquet royal, m. ‖ ~-scrapers, s. pl. maisons de sept à huit étages en Amérique, f. pl.

slab, *slăb*, s. plaque, dalle, f.

slack, *slăk*, a. éteindre (lime).

slack, *slăk*, a. lâche, lent, nonchalant.

slacken, *slăk´kn*, v. a. & n. lâcher, ralentir, diminuer ‖ arrêter, retenir ‖ adoucir ‖ se relâcher, se ralentir ‖ s'amolir.

slackness, *slăk´nĕs*, s. relâchement, m. ‖ négligence, nonchalance, f.

slag, *slăg*, s. scorie, f. ‖ laitier, m.

slake, *slāk*, v. a. (lime) éteindre.

slam, *slăm*, v. a. fermer avec bruit ‖ faire la vole (aux cartes).

slander, *slăn´dẽr*, s. médisance, f.

slander, *slăn´dẽr*, v.a. calomnier, diffamer.

slanderer, *slăn´dẽr ẽr*, s. calomniateur, m.

slanderous, *slăn´dẽr ŭs*, a. calomnieux ‖ -ly, ad. avec calomnie.

slang, *slăng*, s. jargon, argot, m.

slangy, *slăng´ĭ*, a. trivial, d'argot.

slant, *slănt*, v. n. être en pente.

slanting, *slănt´ĭng*, a. (-ly, ad.) oblique ‖ de travers ‖ en écharpe, en talus.

slap, *slăp*, s. claque, tape, f. ‖ soufflet, m.

slap, *slăp*, v. a. taper, claquer.

slap, *slăp*, ad. droit, raide.

slap! *slăp*, crac! pan!

slash, *slăsh*, s. taillade, f.

slash, *slăsh*, v. a. & n. balafrer, taillader.

slate, *slāt*, s. ardoise, f. ‖ ~-pencil, s. crayon d'ardoise.

slate, *slāt*, v. a. couvrir d'ardoise.

slating, *slā´tĭng*, s. toiture en ardoise, f.

slattern, *slăt´tẽrn*, s. souillon, f.

slatternly, *slăt'tẽrn lĭ*, ad. malpropre-ment, négligemment.

slaughter, *slăw'tẽr*, s. carnage, massacre, m. ‖ abattage, m. ‖ ~-house, s. abat-toir, m. [abatre.

slaughter, *slăw'tẽr*, v. a. massacrer ‖

slaughterer, *slăw'tẽr ẽr*, s. abatteur, m.

slave, *slăv*, s. esclave, m. & f. ‖ ~-ship, s. négrier, m. [esclave.

slave, *slăv*, v. n. travailler comme un

slaver, *slā'vẽr*, s. négrier, m.

slaver, *slăv'ẽr*, s. bave, f.

slaver, *slăv'ẽr*, v. n. baver.

slavery, *slā'vẽr ĭ*, s. esclavage, m.

slavish, *slā'vĭsh*, a. (-ly, ad.) servile (ment) ‖ d'esclave ‖ en esclave.

slavishness, *slā'vĭsh nĕs*, s. servilité, f.

slay, *slā*, v. a. ir. tuer.

slayer, *slā'ẽr*, s. meurtrier, m.

sledge, *slĕj*, s. traineau, m. ‖ ~-hammer, s. marteau à deux mains, m.

sleek, *slēk*, v. a. lisser, polir.

sleek, *slēk*, a. lisse, poli.

sleep, *slēp*, s. sommeil, m. ‖ to go to ~, s'endormir ‖ ~-walking, s. somnambu-lisme, m.

sleep, *slēp*, v. n. ir. dormir. [lisme, m.

sleeper, *slēp'ẽr*, s. dormeur, m. ‖ (rail.) traverse, f. [fainéant.

sleepily, *slēp'ĭ lĭ*, ad. en dormant, en

sleepiness, *slēp'ĭ nĕs*, s. assoupissement, m.

sleeping, *slēp'ĭng*, ~-car, s. (rail.) wa-gon-lit, m. ‖ ~-draught, s. potion nar-cotique, f. ‖ ~-room, s. dortoir, m.

sleepless, *slēp'lĕs*, a. sans sommeil.

sleeplessness, *slēp'lĕs nĕs*, s. insomnie, f.

sleepy, *slēp'ĭ*, a. endormi ‖ soporifique ‖

sleet, *slēt*, s. grésil, m. [lourd.

sleet, *slēt*, v. n. grésiller.

sleeve, *slēv*, s. manche, f. ‖ to laugh in one's ~, rire sous cape.

sleight, *slīt*, s. tour d'adresse, m. ‖ ~ of hand, tour de passe-passe, m.

slender, *slĕn'dẽr*, a. mince, svelte ‖ ché-tif ‖ -ly, ad. légèrement ‖ pauvrement ‖ faiblesse, f.

slenderness, *slĕn'dẽr nĕs*, s. médiocrité,

slice, *slīs*, s. tranche, f. ‖ spatule, f.

slice, *slīs*, v. a. trancher.

slick, *slĭk*, a. (Am.) facile, lisse.

slide, *slīd*, s. glissade, glissoire, f. ‖ cou-lisse, f. ‖ (of magic lanterns, etc.) verre, m. ‖ vue, f. [ber.

slide, *slīd*, v. n. ir. glisser, s'écouler, tom-ment, m. ‖ ~-door, s. porte à coulisse, f. ‖ ~-knot, s. nœud coulant, m.

sliding, *slīd'ĭng*, s. glissade, f., coule-

slight, *slīt*, s. dédain, m. ‖ to put a ~ on one, déverser le mépris sur qn.

slight, *slīt*, v. a. dédaigner ‖ manquer à.

slight, *slīt*, a. mince, insignifiant ‖ léger ‖ -ly, ad. légèrement.

slightingly, *slīt'ĭng lĭ*, ad. avec mépris.

slightness, *slīt'nĕs*, s. faiblesse, non-chalance, f. ‖ mépris, m.

slily, *slī'lĭ*, ad. finement.

slim, *slĭm*, a. mince, svelte [bave, f.

slime, *slĭm*, s. limon, m., bourbe, f. ‖

sliminess, *slī'mĭ nĕs*, s. viscosité, f.

slimy, *slī'mĭ*, a. visqueux, vaseux.

sling, *slĭng*, s. ronde, f. ‖ coup, coup de fronde, m. ‖ écharpe, f.

sling, *slĭng*, v. a. ir. lancer avec une fronde.

slink, *slĭngk*, v. n. ir. se dérober, s'é-chapper.

slip, *slĭp*, s. glissade, f. ‖ erreur, f. ‖ barde, f. ‖ écoulement, m. ‖ napperon, m. ‖ (mar.) cale de construction, f. ‖ -s, s. pl. troi-sièmes loges de côté, f. pl. ‖ ~-knot, s. nœud coulant, m.

slip, *slĭp*, v. a. & n. glisser, couler, laisser échapper ‖ échapper, se dérober ‖ se dé-barrasser de ‖ se glisser, s'écouler, s'échap-per ‖ se tromper ‖ fourrer doucement.

slipper, *slĭp'ẽr*, s. pantoufle, f. ‖ mule, f.

slipperiness, *slĭp'ẽr ĭ nĕs*, s. lubricité, f. ‖ incertitude, f.

slippery, *slĭp'ẽr ĭ*, a. lubrique.

slipshod, *slĭp'shŏd*, a. en pantoufles ‖

slit, *slĭt*, s. fente, f. ‖ (fig.) en négligé.

slit, *slĭt*, v. a. fendre en long.

slobber, *slŏb'bẽr*, s. bave, f.

sloe, *slō*, s. prune sauvage, f.

sloop, *slōp*, s. chaloupe, f.

slop, *slŏp*, s. lavaille, rinçure, f. ‖ gâchis, m. ‖ ripopée, f. ‖ ~-basin, s. bol à rinçure, m. ‖ ~-pail, s. seau aux eaux sales, m.

slop, *slŏp*, v. a. laisser tomber.

slope, *slōp*, s. pente, déclivité, f. ‖ talus, m. ‖

slope, *slōp*, v. a. taluter. [échancrure, f.

sloping, *slōp'ĭng*, a. oblique, en pente.

sloppy, *slŏp'ĭ*, a. bourbeux, fangeux.

sloth, *slŏth*, s. paresse, f. ‖ (animal) paresseux, m.

slothful, *slŏth'fŏŏl*, a. fainéant.

slouch, *slŏwch*, v. a. & n. abaisser la tête ‖ rabaisser le chapeau ‖ se dandiner lourde-ment.

slough, *slŏw*, s. bourbier, m. [ment.

sloven, *slŭv'ĕn*, s. personne malpropre, f.

slovenliness, *slŭv'ĕn lĭ nĕs*, s. malpro-preté, saleté, f. [(meut) ‖ sale(ment).

slovenly, *slŭv'ĕn lĭ*, a. (& ad.) malpropre

slow, *slō*, a. (-ly, ad.) lent(ement) ‖ tardif, pesant ‖ (rail.) de petite vitesse.

slowness, *slō'nĕs*, s. lenteur, f.

slowworm, *slō'wẽrm*, s. orvet, m.

slug, *slŭg*, s. fainéant, m., limace, f. ‖ lingot, m.

sluggard, *slŭg'gẽrd*, s. fainéant, m.

sluggish, *slŭg'gĭsh*, a. paresseux, in-dolent ‖ -ly, ad. avec indolence.

sluggishness, *slŭg'gĭsh nĕs*, s. paresse, indolence, f. [écluisière, f.

sluice, *slōs*, s. écluse, f. ‖ ~-gate, s. porte

sluice, *slōs*, v. a. débonder.

slumber, *slŭm'bẽr*, s. sommeil léger, m.

slumber, *slŭm'bẽr*, v. n. sommeiller.

slums, *slŭms*, s. bas quartiers, m. pl.

slur, *slẽr*, s. tache, f. ‖ blâme, m. ‖ (mus.) coulé, m. [(mus.) lier les notes.

slur, *slẽr*, v. a. salir ‖ passer légèrement ‖

slut, *slŭt*, s. salope, guenipe, f.

sly, *slī*, a. (-ly, ad.) fin(ement) ‖ rusé ‖ avec ruse ‖ on the ~, en cachette ‖ furtivement ‖ ~-boots, s. sournois, m. ‖ finaud, m.

smack, *smăk*, s. goût, m. || gros baiser, m. || peu, m. || claque, f. || semaque, m.
smack || claquer || avoir le goût.
small, *smăl*, a. partie la plus mince, f.
small, *smŏl*, a. petit, menu, exigu, faible, léger, minime, délié, fin.
smallish, *smŏl'ish*, a. un peu petit.
smallness, *smŏl'nĕs*, s. petitesse, faiblesse, exiguité, f. || peu d'importance.
smalt, *smălt*, s. émail, m.
smart, *smărt*, s. douleur aiguë, f.
smart, *smărt*, v. n. sentir une cuisante douleur || porter la peine (de).
smart, *smărt*, a. piquant, cuisant, douloureux || vif, éveillé, animé || élégant || brillant || (Am.) beaucoup || —ly, ad. vivement || spirituellement || avec élégance.
smartness, *smărt'nĕs*, s. vivacité, f. || finesse, élégance, coquetterie, f.
smash, *smăsh*, s. fracas, m.
smash, *smăsh*, v. a. briser, écraser.
smattering, *smăt'tĕr'ĭng*, s. connaissance d'odeurs, m. || —salts, s. pl. sels, m. pl.
smear, *smēr*, s. tache, f. || superficielle, f.
smear, *smēr*, v. a. graisser || barbouiller.
smell, *smĕl*, s. odorat, m. || odeur, f.
smell, *smĕl*, v. a. & n. ir. sentir || flairer.
smeller, *smĕl'ĕr*, s. flaireur, m.
smelling, *smĕl'ĭng ;* —bottle, s. flacon d'odeurs, m. || —salts, s. pl. sels, m. pl.
smelt, *smĕlt*, s. éperlan, m.
smelt, *smĕlt*, v. a. fondre.   [derie, f.
smelting-house, *smĕlt'ĭng hŏŭs*, s. fon-
smile, *smīl*, s. sourire, m.
smile, *smīl*, v. n. sourire.
smirch, *smĕrch*, v. a. noircir, salir.
smirk, *smĕrk*, v. n. sourire.
smite, *smīt*, v. a. ir. frapper || enflammer.
smith, *smith*, s. forgeron, m.
smithy, *smith'ĭ*, s. forge, f.
smitten, *smĭt'tn*, a. épris (de).
smock, *smŏk*, s. chemise de femme, f. || —frock, s. blouse, f.
smokable, *smŏk'ă bl*, a. fumable.
smoke, *smŏk*, s. fumée, f. || vapeur, f. || to end in —, s'en aller en eau de boudin || —consumer, s. fumivore, m.||—stack, s. cheminée, f.   [—dry, v. a. boucaner.
smoke, *smŏk*, v. a. & n. fumer, enfumer ||
smokeless, *smŏk'lĕs*, a. sans fumée.
smoking, *smŏ'kĭng ;* —divan, s. salonfumoir, m. || estaminet, m. ||—compartment, s. (rail.) compartiment pour fumeurs, m.
smoky, *smŏ'kĭ*, a. fumeux || enfumé.
smooth, *smŏŏth*, v. a. unir || lisser || apaiser || flatter || dérider.
smooth, *smŏŏth*, a. (-ly, ad.) uni(ment) || poli, lisse, doux || doucement || aisément, f.
smoothing, *smŏŏth'ĭng*, s. aplanissement, m. ||—plane, s. guillaume à recaler, m., varlope, f.   [f. || douceur, f.
smoothness, *smŏŏth'nĕs*, s. surface unie,
smother, *smŭth'ĕr*, s. fumée épaisse, f.
smother, *smŭth'ĕr*, v. a. étouffer, suffoquer.
smoulder, *smŏl'dĕr*, v. n. brûler lentement.
smug, *smŭg*, a. pimpant, élégant.

smuggle, *smŭg'gl*, v. a. faire la contrebande.
smuggler, *smŭg'glĕr*, s. contrebandier, m. || bâtiment de contrebande, m.
smuggling, *smŭg'glĭng*, s. contrebande, f.
smut, *smŭt*, s. tache de suie, f. || nielle, f.
smut, *smŭt*, v. a. noircir || salir.
smuttiness, *smŭt'tĭ nĕs*, s. noirceur, f. || obs énité, f.   [scène.
smutty, *smŭt'tĭ*, a. enfumé, niellé || obsnack, *snăk*, s. part, portion, f.
snaffle, *snăf'fl*, s. caveçon, bridon, m.
snag, *snăg*, s. bosse, f., nœud, m.
snail, *snāl*, s. limaçon, escargot, m. || — paced, a. à pas de tortue.
snake, *snāk*, s. serpent, m. || a — in the grass, quelque anguille sous roche || — moss, s. (bot.) lycopode en massue, m. || —root, s. (bot.) serpentaire, f. || polygala de Virginie, m. || —'s tongue, s. (bot.) lygodie, f. || —weed, s. (bot.) renouée bistorte, f.
snaky, *snā'kĭ*, a. de serpent || tortueux.
snap, *snăp*, s. claquement, m. || coup de dent, m.   [attraper.
snap, *snăp*, v. a. & n. faire claquer|| happer,
snappers, *snăp'pĕrz*, s. pl. castagnettes, f. pl.   [neux || aigre(ment).
snappish, *snăp'pĭsh*, a. (-ly, ad.) harg-
snappishness, *snăp'pĭsh nĕs*, s. aigreur, f.
snare, *snār*, s. piège, m.
snarl, *snărl*, v. n. grogner, gronder.
snarler, *snăr'lĕr*, s. grogneur, m.
snatch, *snăch*, s. prise, f. || accès, m. || morceau, m.   [ment.
snatch, *snăch*, v. a. saisir, arracher violemment.
sneak, *snēk*, s. homme rampant, m.
sneak, *snēk*, v. n. ramper || s'humilier.
sneer, *snēr*, s. ricanement, m., raillerie, f.
sneer, *snēr*, v. n. ricaner || se moquer de.
sneeringly, *snēr'ĭng lĭ*, ad. d'un ton moqueur.
sneeze, *snēz*, v. n. éternuer.   [queur.
snick, *snĭk*, v. a. parer la balle à grand' peine (au jeu de paume).
sniff, *snĭf*, v. n. renifler || —, v. a. aspirer.
snip, *snĭp*, s. coupure, f. petit morceau, m.
snip, *snĭp*, v. a. couper, rogner.
snipe, *snĭp*, s. bécassine, f. || sot, m.
snivel, *snĭv'l*, s. roupie, f.   [et pleurer.
snivel, *snĭv'l*, v. n. avoir la roupie || crier
sniveller, *snĭv'lĕr*, s. pleurnicheur, m.
snob, *snŏb*, s. snob, m. || parvenu, m.|| goujat, m.
snooze, *snŏz*, s. sommeil léger, m.   [m.
snooze, *snŏz*, v. n. roupiller.
snore, *snŏr*, snort, *snŏrt*, s. ronflement, m.
snore, *snŏr*, snort, *snŏrt*, v. n. ronfler.
snout, *snŏŭt*, s. museau, m. || groin, m. || bout, m. || boutoir, m.
snow, *snŏ*, s. neige, f. || —slip, s. avalanche, f. || —storm, s. orage de neige, f.
snow, *snŏ*, v. n. neiger.   [m.
snowball, *snŏ'băŭl*, s. pelote de neige, f.
snowdrift, *snŏ'drĭft*,s.(rail.) amas de neige, m. || tourbillons de neige, m. pl.
snowdrop, *snŏ'drŏp*, s. (bot.) perce-neige, f.
snowflake, *snŏ'flăk*, s. flocon de neige, m.
snowy, *snŏ'ĭ*, a. neigeux.

snub, *snŭb,* v. a. réprimander, reprendre ‖ ~-**nose,** s. nez camus, m.

snuff, *snŭf,* s. tabac à priser, m. ‖ lumignon, m. ‖ mouchure, f. ‖ ~-**box,** s. tabatière, f. ‖ ~-**taker,** s. priseur, m.

snuff, *snŭf,* v. a. moucher ‖ renifler.

snuffers, *snŭf'fèrs,* s. pl. mouchettes, f. pl.

snuffle, *snŭf'fl,* v. n. nasiller.

snug, *snŭg,* a. serré ‖ commode, confortable ‖ caché ‖ **-ly,** ad. commodément.

so, *sō,* ad. ainsi, si ‖ tellement, tant, aussi ‖ comme cela ‖ de même ‖ alors ‖ **I think** ~, je le pense ‖ **if** ~, s'il en est ainsi ‖ **why** ~? pourquoi cela? ‖ ~ **that,** de sorte que.

soax, *sōk,* v. a. & n. tremper ‖ faire tremper ‖ imbiber.

soap, *sōp,* s. savon, m. ‖ ~-**ball,** s. savonnette, f. ‖ ~-**boiler,** s. savonnier, m. ‖ ~-**bubble,** s. bulle de savon, f. ‖ ~-**stone,** s. stéatite, f. ‖ ~-**suds,** s. eau de savon, f. ‖ ~-**works,** s. pl. savonnerie, f.

soap, *sōp,* v. a. savonner.

soapery, *sōp'èr i,* s. savonnerie, f.

soapy, *sōp'i,* a. savonneux.

soar, *sōr,* v. n. prendre l'essor ‖ s'élever.

soaring, *sōr'ing,* s. essor, m.

sob, *sŏb,* s. sanglot, m.

sob, *sŏb,* v. n. sangloter.

sober, *sō'bèr,* a. (**-ly,** ad.) sobre(ment) ‖ de sang-froid ‖ sérieux ‖ modérément.

sobriety, *sō brï'ĕ ti,* s. sobriété, modération, tempérance, f. ‖ sang-froid, m.

sociability, *sō shï ă bïl'ĭ tï,* s. sociabilité, f.

sociable, *sō'shă bl,* s. calèche à bateau, f.

sociable, *sō'shă bl,* a. sociable.

sociably, *sō'shă blï,* ad. d'une manière sociable.

social, *sō'shăl,* a. (**-ly,** ad.) social(ement) ‖ sociable.

socialism, *sō'shăl izm,* s. socialisme, m.

socialist, *sō'shal ist,* s. socialiste, m.

society, *sō sī'ĕ tï,* s. société, f.

sock, *sŏk,* s. chaussette, f. ‖ semelle, f.

socket, *sŏk'ĕt,* s. bobèche, f. ‖ orbite, f. ‖ alvéole, m. ‖ bec, m.

socle, *sō'kl,* s. (arch.) socle, m.

sod, *sŏd,* s. motte de terre, f. ‖ gazon, m.

soda, *sō'dă,* s. soude, f. ‖ ~-**water,** s. eau de Seltz, f. ‖ dium, m.

sodium, *sō'dï'ŭm,* s. (chim.) natrium, so-

soever, *sō ĕv'ĕr,* c. que ce soit.

sofa, *sō'fă,* s. sofa, canapé, m. ‖ ~-**bed** (-**stead**), s. lit-canapé, m.

soft, *sŏft,* a. mou, doux ‖ tendre, faible, facile, délicat ‖ efféminé ‖ **-ly,** ad. mollement ‖ doucement ‖ ~-**hearted,** a. tendre, sensible ‖ ~-**spoken,** a. à voix basse.

soften, *sŏf'n,* v. a. amollir, adoucir, attendrir.

softening, *sŏf'n ing,* s. adoucissement, m.

softness, *sŏft'nĕs,* s. douceur, mollesse, f.

soil, *sŏyl,* s. souillure, f. ‖ fumier, m. ‖ sol, m.

soil, *sŏyl,* v. a. souiller, salir. ‖ terrain, m.

sojourn, *sō'jĕrn* ou *sō jĕrn'* ou *sŏj'ĕrn,* s. séjour, m. ‖ v. n. séjourner.

sojourn, *sō'jĕrn* ou *sō jĕrn'* ou *sŏj'ĕrn,* v. n. séjourner.

solace, *sōl'ăs,* s. consolation, f.

solace, *sōl'ăs,* v. a. consoler.

solan-goose, *sō'lăn gōs,* s. pélican de l'île Bass, m.

solar, *sō'lèr,* a. solaire ‖ du soleil.

solder, *sōl'dèr* ou *sō'dèr,* s. soudure, f.

solder, *sōl'dèr* ou *sō'dèr,* v. a. souder.

soldier, *sōl'jèr,* s. soldat, m. ‖ **to go -ing,** aller en soldat.

soldierlike, *sōl'jèr lïk,* **soldierly,** *sōl'jèr lï,* a. de soldat, militaire.

soldiery, *sōl'jèr i,* s. soldatesque, f. ‖ troupes, f. pl. ‖ sole, f.

sole, *sōl,* s. plante du pied, f. ‖ semelle, f. ‖

sole, *sōl,* v. a. ressemeler.

sole, *sōl,* a. (**-ly,** ad.) seul(ement) ‖ unique (ment) ‖ universel.

solecism, *sōl'ĕ sizm,* s. solécisme, m.

solemn, *sōl'ĕm,* a. (**-ly,** ad.) solennel (lement).

solemnisation, *sōl ĕm nï zā'shŭn,* s. solennisation, célébration, f. ‖ célébrer.

solemnise, *sōl'ĕm nïz,* v. a. solenniser,

solemnity, *sō lĕm'nï tï,* s. solennité, f.

solicit, *sō lis'it,* v. a. solliciter ‖ inviter.

solicitation, *sō lis ï tā'shŭn,* s. sollicitation, f. ‖ excitation, f.

solicitor, *sō lis'ït èr,* s. solliciteur, m. ‖ (jur.) avoué, m. ‖ ~-**general,** s. procureur général, m.

solicitous, *sō lis'ït ŭs,* a. inquiet, plein de souci ‖ **-ly,** ad. avec inquiétude.

solicitude, *sō lis'ï tūd,* s. sollicitude, f.

solid, *sōl'id,* a. (**-ly,** ad.) solide(ment) ‖ massif ‖ réel ‖ grave, profond.

solidify, *sō lid'ï fï,* v. a. solidifier.

solidity, *sō lid'ï tï,* s. solidité, f.

soliloquise, *sō lïl'ō kwïz,* v. n. faire un monologue, monologuer.

soliloquy, *sō lïl'ō kwi,* s. monologue, m.

solitaire, *sōl ï tār',* s. solitaire (diamant monté seul), m.

solitarily, *sōl'ï tèr ï lï,* ad. solitairement.

solitariness, *sōl'ï tèr ï nĕs,* s. retraite, f.

solitary, *sōl'ï tèr ï,* s. ermite, m.

solitary, *sōl'ï tèr ï,* a. solitaire ‖ retiré.

solitude, *sōl'ï tūd,* s. solitude, f.

solo, *sō'lō,* s. (mus.) solo, m.

solstice, *sōl'stis,* s. solstice, m.

soluble, *sōl'ŭ bl,* a. dissoluble.

solution, *sō lō'shŭn,* s. dissolution, f.

solve, *sōlv,* v. a. résoudre.

solvency, *sōl'vĕn sï,* s. solvabilité, f.

solvent, *sōl'vĕnt,* a. dissolvant ‖ solvable.

some, *sŭm,* a. quelque, un peu ‖ du, de la, quelques-uns, certains, les uns, les autres.

somebody, *sŭm'bŏd ï,* **someone,** *sŭm'wŭn,* s. quelqu'un, une personne.

somehow, *sŭm'hŏw,* ad. de façon ou d'autre. ‖ *sŭm'èr sĕt,* s. culbute, f.

somersault, *sŭm'èr sawlt,* **somerset,**

something, *sŭm'thing,* s. & ad. quelque chose, m. ‖ un peu.

sometime, *sŭm'tïm,* ad. autrefois, jadis ‖ ~ **or other,** quelque jour.

sometimes, *sŭm'tïms,* ad. quelquefois, de temps en temps ‖ tantôt.

somewhat, *sŭm'hwŏt,* s. & ad. quelque chose ‖ en quelque sorte, tant soit peu.

somewhere, *sŭm' hwār,* ad. quelque part ‖ ~ **else,** ailleurs ‖ (quelque) autre part.

somnambulism, *sŏm năm' bŭ lizm,* s. somnambulisme, m.

somnambulist, *sŏm năm' bŭ list,* s. somnambule, m. & f.

somnolence, *sŏm' nō lĕns,* s. somnolence, f.

son, *sŭn, r.* fils, m. ‖ descendant, m. ‖ ~-**in-law,** s. gendre, m.

sonata, *sō nä' tä,* s. sonate, f.

song, *sŏng,* s. chanson, f. ‖ chant, m. ‖ (fig.) bagatelle, f.

songster, *sŏng' stĕr,* s. chanteur, m.

songstress, *sŏng' strĕs,* s. chanteuse, f.

sonnet, *sŏn' nĕt,* s. sonnet, m.

sonorous, *sō nō' rŭs,* a. (-**ly,** ad.) sonore (ment).

soon, *sŏn,* ad. bientôt, tôt, de bonne heure ‖ volontiers ‖ **as** ~ **as,** aussitôt que ‖ **how** ~ **?** dans combien de temps ?　　[mieux.

sooner, *sŏn'ĕr,* ad. plus tôt ‖ plutôt,

soonest, *sŏn'ĕst,* ad. le plus tôt ‖ le mieux.

soot, *sŏŏt,* s. suie, f.　　[vérité, ma foi !

sooth, *sŏŏth,* s. vérité, réalité, f. ‖ **in** ~,

soothe, *sŏŏth,* v. a. flatter ‖ apaiser.

soothingly, *sŏŏth'ing li,* ad. d'une manière flatteuse.　　[vineresse, f.

soothsayer, *sŏŏth'sā ĕr,* s. devin, m., de-

sooty, *sŏŏt'i,* a. fuligineux ‖ noir.

sop, *sŏp,* s. morceau trempé, m. ‖ (fig.) os à ronger ‖ cadeau, présent, m.

sop, *sŏp,* v. a. tremper.

sophism, *sŏf' izm,* s. sophisme, m.

sophist, *sŏf' ist,* s. sophiste, m.

sophistical, *sŏ fis' tik äl,* a. sophistique.

sophisticate, *sŏ fis' ti kät,* v. a. sophistiquer, falsifier.

sophistry, *sŏf' is tri,* s. sophismes, m. pl.

soporific, *sō pō rif' ik,* s. soporifique, m.

soporific, *sō pō rif' ik,* a. soporifique.

soprano, *sō prän' ō,* s. (mus.) soprano, m.

sorb, *sŏrb,* s. sorbe, corme, f.

sorcerer, *sŏr' sĕr ĕr,* s. sorcier, m.

sorceress, *sŏr' sĕr ĕs,* s. sorcière, f.

sorcery, *sŏr' sĕr i,* s. sorcellerie, f., sortilège, m.

sordid, *sŏr' dĭd,* a. (-**ly,** ad.) sordide(ment) ‖ vil ‖ bas(sement) ‖ avare.

sordidness, *sŏr' dĭd nĕs,* s. sordidité, f. ‖ mesquinerie, f.

sore, *sōr,* s. ulcère, m., plaie, f.

sore, *sōr,* a. douloureux ‖ écorché ‖ violent ‖ -**ly,** ad. douloureusement, grièvement.

soreness, *sōr' nĕs,* s. douleur, f., mal, m., amertume, peine aiguë, f. ‖ sensibilité, f.

sorrel, *sŏr' rĕl,* s. oseille, f.

sorrel, *sŏr' rĕl,* a. alezan saure.

sorrily, *sŏr' ri li,* ad. châtivement, misérablement ‖ pitoyablement.

sorrow, *sŏr' rō,* s. chagrin, m., affliction, tristesse, f. ‖ **to one's** ~, à sa grande douleur.

sorrow, *sŏr' rō,* v. n. être affligé.

sorrowful, *sŏr' rō fŏŏl,* a.(-**ly,**ad.) chagrin ‖ triste(ment) ‖ affligeant.

sorry, *sŏr' ri,* a. affligé ‖ triste ‖ **I am** ~ **for it,** j'en suis fâché ‖ **I am** ~ **to say,** à mon grand regret.

sort, *sŏrt,* s. sorte, espèce, classe, manière, f., genre, m. ‖ **to be out of** ~**s,** n'être pas dans son assiette.　　[assortir.

sort, *sŏrt,* v. a. séparer, classer, trier,

sorter, *sŏrt' ĕr,* s. trieur, m.

sortie, *sŏr' tĕ,* s. (mil.) sortie, f.

sot, *sŏt,* s. sot, imbécile, m. ‖ ivrogne, m.

sottish, *sŏt' tish,* a. (-**ly,** ad.) sot(tement) ‖ abruti.

soul, *sōl,* s. âme, f., esprit, m. ‖ être, m. ‖ **upon my** ~ **!** par ma foi ! ‖ parole d'honneur ! ‖ ~-**bell,** s. glas, m.

sound, *sŏŭnd,* s. son, bruit, m. ‖ Sund, m. ‖ sonde, f.　　[sonder.

sound, *sŏŭnd,* v. a. & n. sonner ‖ résonner ‖

sound, *sŏŭnd,* a. (-**ly,** ad.) sain(ement) ‖ en bon état, fort, vigoureux ‖ solidement ‖ vigoureusement ‖ bien ‖ ~ **title,** s. titre valable, m.

sounding, *sŏŭnd'ing,* ~-**board,** s. table d'harmonie, f. ‖ abat-voix, m. ‖ sommier, m. ‖ ~-**lead** (~-**line**), s. sonde, f.

soundness, *sŏŭnd' nĕs,* s. santé, f. ‖ solidité, f. ‖ vigueur, pureté, f.

soup, *sŏp,* s. soupe, f., potage, m. ‖ ~-**basin,** ~-**tureen,** s. soupière, terrine, f.

sour, *sŏŭr,* v. a. & n. (s')aigrir.

sour, *sŏŭr,* a. (-**ly,** ad.) aigre(ment) ‖ acide ‖ morose.

source, *sōrs,* s. source, f. ‖ origine, f.

sourness, *sŏŭr' nĕs,* s. aigreur, f.

souse, *sŏŭs,* s. marinade, f.

souse, *sŏŭs,* v. a. mariner ‖ plonger ‖ saucer.

south, *sŏŭth,* s. sud, midi, m. ‖ **South-down sheep ou mutton,** s. pré-salé, m.

south, *sŏŭth,* a. méridional ‖ vers le sud.

southerly, *sŭ thĕr li,* southern, *sŭ thĕrn,* a. méridional, du sud ‖ ~-**wood,** s. citronnelle, f.

southward, *sŏŭth'wĕrd,* ad. vers le sud.

sovereign, *sŏv'ĕr in,* s. souverain, m. ‖ 25 francs.　　[verain(ement).

sovereign, *sŏv'ĕr in,* a. (-**ly,** ad.) sou-

sovereignty, *sŏv'ĕr in ti,* s. souveraineté, f.

sow, *sŏw,* s. truie, f.

sow, *sō,* v. a. ir. semer, ensemencer.

sower, *sō'ĕr,* s. semeur, m.

sowing, *sō'ing,* ~-**machine,** s. semoir, m. ‖ ~-**time,** s. semailles, f. pl.

spa, *spä,* s. source d'eau minérale, f.

space, *spās,* s. espace, m., distance, f., intervalle, m.

space, *spās,* v. a. espacer.

spacious, *spā' shŭs,* a. spacieux, vaste ‖ -**ly,** ad. spacieusement.　　[étendue, f.

spaciousness, *spā' shŭs nĕs,* s. vaste

spade, *spād,* s. bêche, f. ‖ (**at cards**) pique, m.

span, *spăn,* s. empan, m. ‖ paire, f.

span, *spăn,* v. a. mesurer par empans, brasser ‖ s'assortir.

spangle, *spăng' gl,* s. paillette, f.

spangle, *spăng' gl,* v. a. orner de paillettes.

spaniel, *spăn' yĕl,* s. épagneul, m. ‖ flatteur, m. ‖ **water**—, barbet, m.

spanish-fly, *spăn' ish fli,* s. cantharide, f.

---

lāte, hăt, fär, lăw; — hēre, gĕt, hĕr; — mīne, ĭnn; — nō, hŏt, prōve; — hŏw; —

spanker-boom, *spăngk'ĕr bŏm,* s. (mar.) baume, gui, m.

spar, *spär,* s. espars, m. pl. || spath, m.

spar, *spär,* v. n. se quereller.

spare, *spär,* v. a. & n. épargner, ménager, traiter avec indulgence || se dispenser de, se passer || **to have . . . and to ~,** avoir . . . de reste.

spare, *spär,* a. (-ly, ad.) parcimonieux || de réserve || maigre(ment) || **~room,** s. chambre d'ami *or* à donner, f.

sparing, *spä'ring,* a. (-ly, ad.) rare(ment) || frugal || chiche(ment) || modérément. [f.

sparingness, *spä'ring nĕs,* s. parcimonie.

spark, *spärk,* s. étincelle, f. || bluette, f. || petit-maître, m.

sparkle, *spär'kl,* s. étincelle, f.

sparkle, *spär'kl,* v. n. étinceler || mousser.

sparkler, *spär'klĕr,* s. trait d'esprit brillant, m. [mousseux.

sparkling, *spär'kling,* a. étincelant ||

sparrow, *spär'rō,* s. moineau, m. || **~hawk,** s. épervier, m. || **~wort,** (bot.) passerine, f.

spasm, *spăzm,* s. spasme, m.

spasmodic, *spăz mŏd'ik,* a. spasmodique.

spat, *spät,* s. frai des mollusques, m. || taloche, f. [le gril, m.

spatchcock, *spăch'kŏk,* s. poulet rôti sur

spatter, *spät'tĕr,* v. a. éclabousser.

spatula, *spät'ŭlä,* s. spatule, f.

spavin, *spăv'in,* s. éparvin, m.

spawn, *spaŭn,* s. frai, m. || race, f.

spawn, *spaŭn,* v. a. & n. frayer || engendrer.

spawner, *spaŭn'ĕr,* s. poisson femelle, f.

speak, *spēk,* v. a. & n. ir. parler, discourir || prononcer.

speaker, *spēk'ĕr,* s. parleur, orateur, m. || interlocuteur, m. || président, m.

speaking, *spēk'ing,* s. action de parler, f. || discours, m. || **~trumpet,** s. porte-voix, m. || **~tube,** s. cornet acoustique, m.

spear, *spēr,* s. lance, f. || harpon, m. || épieu, m. || **~wort,** s. (bot.) renoncule, f.

spear, *spēr,* v. a. percer à coups de lance || harponner.

special, *spĕsh'ăl,* s. supplément extraordinaire d'un journal, m. || (rail.) train spécial, m.

special, *spĕsh'ăl,* a. (-ly, ad.) spécial (ement) || particulier || principalement.

speciality, *spĕsh i ăl'i tĭ,* s. spécialité, f.

specialty, *spĕsh'ăl tĭ,* s. contrat sous seing privé, m.

specie, *spĕsh'ĭ,* s. argent comptant, m.

species, *spē'shēz,* s. espèce, sorte, f.

specific, *spĕs if'ik,* a. (-ly, ad.) spécifique (ment). [cification, f.

specification, *spĕs ĭ fi kā'shŭn,* s. spéci-

specify, *spĕs'ifi,* v. a. spécifier.

specimen, *spĕs'i mĕn,* s. spécimen, modèle, m. [spécieusement.

specious, *spē'shŭs,* a. spécieux || -ly, ad.

speck, *spĕk,* s. tache, f., point, m.

speck, *spĕk,* v. a. tacher.

speckle, *spĕk'kl,* s. petite tache, bigarrure, f.

speckle, *spĕk'kl,* v. a. tacheter, moucheter.

spectacle, *spĕk'tä kl,* s. spectacle, m. || **-s,** pl. lunettes, f. pl.

spectator, *spĕk tā'tĕr,* s. spectateur, m.

spectre, *spĕk'tĕr,* s. spectre, m., apparition, f.

spectrum, *spĕk'trŭm,* s. spectre solaire, m.

speculate, *spĕk'ŭlāt,* v. n. méditer sur || faire une spéculation.

speculation, *spĕk ŭlā'shŭn,* s. spéculation, méditation, f. [spéculateur.

speculative, *spĕk'ŭlātĭv,* a. spéculatif ||

speculator, *spĕk'ŭlātĕr,* s. spéculateur, m.

speculum, *spĕk'ŭlŭm,* s. miroir, m. || spe-culum, m.

speech, *spēch,* s. discours, m. || langage, m., harangue, f. || plaidoyer, m. || **figure of ~,** s. figure de rhétorique, f.

speechify, *spēch'i fī,* v. n. pérorer.

speechless, *spēch'lĕs,* a. muet || interdit.

speed, *spēd,* s. hâte, f. || succès, m.

speed, *spēd,* v. a. & n. ir. dépêcher, expédier || presser || favoriser || réussir || se hâter, prospérer.

speedily, *spēd'ĭlĭ,* ad. à la hâte.

speediness, *spēd'i nĕs,* s. célérité, hâte, f.

speedy, *spēd'i,* a. prompt, rapide, expé-ditif || **~bound,** a. sous le charme.

spell, *spĕl,* s. charme, m. || histoire, f. ||

spell, *spĕl,* v. a. & n. ir. épeler || ortho-graphier || écrire correctement || enchanter.

spelling, *spĕl'ing,* s. épellation, f. || ortho-graphe, f. || **~book,** s. syllabaire, m.

spelter, *spĕl'tĕr,* s. zinc, m.

spend, *spĕnd,* v. a. & n. ir. dépenser, em-ployer || consommer || passer || prodiguer, dissiper || épuiser || faire la dépense || se perdre.

spendthrift, *spĕnd'thrift,* s. prodigue, m.

sperm, *spĕrm,* s. sperme, m. [leine, m.

spermaceti, *spĕr mä sē'tĭ,* s. blanc de ba-

spew, *spū,* v. a. vomir.

sphere, *sfēr,* s. sphère, f. [(ment).

spherical, *sfēr'ik äl,* a. (-ly, ad.) sphérique

sphinx, *sfingks,* s. sphinx, m.

spice, *spis,* s. épice, f. || petite quantité, légère teinture, f. || atteinte, f.

spice, *spis,* v. a. épicer.

spicy, *spi'si,* a. aromatique.

spider, *spi'dĕr,* s. araignée, f. || **~monkey,** s. atèle, m.

spigot, *spig'ŏt,* s. fausset, m.

spike, *spik,* s. épi de blé, m. || pointe, f. || long clou, m., cheville, f.

spike, *spik,* v. a. clouer. [dien, m.

spikenard, *spik'närd,* s. (bot.) nard in-

spill, *spil,* v. a. & ir. répandre, renverser.

spin, *spin,* v. a. & n. ir. filer || traîner en longueur, tourner.

spinach, *spin'äj,* s. épinards, m. pl.

spinal, *spi'näl,* a. spinal || **~ column,** s. colonne vertébrale, f. || **~ cord,** **~ mar-row,** s. moelle épinière, f. || **~ disease,** s. consomption dorsale, f.

spindle, *spin'dl,* s. fuseau, m., broche, f. || pivot, m. || **~shanks,** s. pl. jambes de fuseaux, jambes de coq, f. pl.

spine, *spin,* s. épine, épine du dos, f.

spinner, *spin'nĕr*, s. fileur, m., fileuse, f.

spinning, *spin'ning*; ~~mill, s. filature, f. ‖ ~~wheel, s. rouet à filer, m.

spinster, *spin'stĕr*, s. fileuse, f. ‖ fille, f.

spiræa, *spī rē'ä*, s. (bot.) spirée, f.

spiral, *spī'răl*, s. spirale, f.

spiral, *spī'răl*, a. (-ly, ad.) spiral ‖ en spirale.

spire, *spīr*, s. spirale, f. ‖ pyramide, f. ‖ aiguille, flèche de clocher, f.

spirit, *spir'it*, s. esprit, m., âme, f. ‖ courage, feu, m. ‖ génie, m. ‖ fantôme, m. ‖ liqueur spiritueuse, f. ‖ to raise one's ~s, remonter le courage de qn. ‖ low ~s, accablement, abattement, m. ‖ proof ~s, esprit de preuve, m. ‖ raw ~s, liqueurs pures, sans eau, f. pl. ‖ ~~lamp, s. réchaud à alcool, m. ‖ ~~level, s. niveau à bulle d'air, m. ‖ ~~rapping, s. jonglerie des esprits frappeurs, f.

spirit, *spir'it*, v. a. animer, encourager ‖ to ~ away, enlever par ruse.

spirited, *spir'it ĕd*, a. animé, vigoureux ‖ -ly, ad. vigoureusement ‖ ardemment.

spiritless, *spir'it lĕs*, a. abattu ‖ sans verve ‖ inanimé.   [tuel(lement).

spiritual, *spir'it ŭ ăl*, a. (-ly, ad.) spiri-

spirituality, *spir'it ŭ ăl'ĭ ti*, s. spiritualité, f., spirituel, m.

spirituous, *spir'it ŭ ŭs*, a. spiritueux.

spirt, *spĕrt*, v. a. & n. (faire) jaillir.

spit, *spit*, s. broche, f.

spit, *spit*, v. a. & n. ir. embrocher ‖ cracher.

spite, *spīt*, s. dépit, m., rancune, f. ‖ in ~ of, en dépit de, malgré.

spite, *spīt*, v. a. dépiter.

spiteful, *spīt'fŏŏl*, a. plein de dépit ‖ méchant ‖ -ly, ad. par dépit ‖ malicieusement ‖ par rancune.

spittle, *spit'tl*, s. salive, f., crachat, m.

spittoon, *spit tōn'*, s. crachoir, m.

splash, *splăsh*, s. éclaboussure, f. ‖ ~~board, s. garde-crotte, m.

splash, *splăsh*, v. a. éclabousser.

splay, *splā*, v. a. épauler (a horse) ‖ ~~foot, a. cagneux.

spleen, *splēn*, s. rate, hypocondrie, f.

splendid, *splĕn'dĭd*, a. (-ly, ad.) splendide(ment) ‖ magnifique, brillant.

splendour, *splĕn'dĕr*, s. splendeur, f. ‖ pompe, f. ‖ éclat, m.

splenetic, *splĕn ĕt'ĭk*, a. atrabilaire.

splice, *splīs*, v. a. joindre à onglet ‖ (mar.) épisser.

splint(er), *splint't(ĕr)*, s. éclat de bois, f. (chir.) éclisse, f. ‖ esquille, f.

splinter, *splin'tĕr*, v. a. & n. briser, fendre, éclisser ‖ voler en éclats.

split, *split*, s. fente, f. ‖ querelle, f. ‖ (Am.) chevauchée à bride abattue, f.

split, *split*, v. a. & n. ir. fendre ‖ briser ‖ partager ‖ se fendre.

splitter, *split'tĕr*, s. fendeur, m.

splutter, *splŭt'tĕr*, s. vacarme, m.

splutter, *splŭt'tĕr*, v. n. bredouiller.

spoil, *spŏyl*, s. pillage, m. ‖ butin, m. ‖ dépouille, f.

spoil, *spŏyl*, v. a. & n. corrompre, gâter, abîmer ‖ ravager, piller ‖ se corrompre, se gâter.

spoiler, *spŏyl'ĕr*, s. spoliateur, voleur, m. ‖ destructeur, m. ‖ personne qui gâte, f.

spoke, *spōk*, s. raie d'une roue, f. ‖ échelon, m.   [parole.

spokesman, *spōks'măn*, s. qui porte la

spoliate, *spō'li ăt*, v. a. dépouiller

spoliation, *spō li ā'shŭn*, s. spoliation, f.

sponge, *spŭnj*, s. éponge, f. ‖ écouvillon, m. ‖ ~~bath, s. bain anglais, m. ‖ ~~cake, s. biscuit de caisse, m.

sponge, *spŭnj*, v. a. & n. éponger ‖ écouvillonner ‖ piquer l'assiette.

sponger, *spŭnj'ĕr*, s. pique-assiette, m.

sponginess, *spŭnj'i nĕs*, s. nature spongieuse, f.

spongy, *spŭnj'i*, a. spongieux.   [ieuse, f.

sponsor, *spŏn'sĕr*, s. garant, m. ‖ parrain, m. ‖ marraine, f.   [f.

spontaneity, *spŏn tă nē'ĭ tĭ*, s. spontanéité,

spontaneous, *spŏn tă'nĕ ŭs*, a. (-ly, ad.) spontané(ment).

spoon, *spōn*, s. cuiller, cuillère, f. ‖ dessert-~~, cuiller à dessert, f. ‖ gravy-~~, cuiller à ragoût, f. ‖ table-~~, cuiller à soupe, f. ‖ tea-~~, cuiller à thé, f.

spoonful, *spōn'fŏŏl*, s. cuillerée, f.

sport, *spōrt*, s. divertissement, amusement, jeu, m. ‖ chasse, f. ‖ pêche, f. sport, m.   [se divertir, badiner.

sport, *spōrt*, v. a. & n. faire parade de

sportive, *spōrt'iv*, a. enjoué, folâtre ‖ plaisant.   [f. ‖ enjouement, m.

sportiveness, *spōrt'iv nĕs*, s. folâtrerie,

sportsman, *spōrts'măn*, s. chasseur, m. ‖ pêcheur, m. ‖ amateur de sport, m.

spot, *spŏt*, s. tache, f. ‖ lieu, m., place, f. ‖ coin, m.   [marquer.

spot, *spŏt*, v. a. tacher ‖ tacheter ‖ (fam.)

spotless, *spŏt'lĕs*, a. sans taches ‖ pur.

spotty, *spŏt'tĭ*, a. taché.

spouse, *spŏwz*, s. époux, m. ‖ épouse, f.

spout, *spŏwt*, s. tuyau de décharge, m. ‖ to put up the ~, (fam.) mettre en gage, au clou, chez ma tante.

spout, *spŏwt*, v. a. & n. jaillir ‖ déclamer.

sprain, *sprān*, s. foulure, entorse, f.

sprain, *sprān*, v. a. se fouler.

sprat, *sprăt*, s. sardine, melette, f.

sprawl, *sprawl*, v. n. s'étaler ‖ se débattre, f.

spray, *sprā*, s. embrun, m.

spread, *sprĕd*, s. étendue, f. ‖ propagation, f.

spread, *sprĕd*, v. a. & n. ir. étendre, déployer ‖ divulguer ‖ s'étendre, se répandre ‖ ~~eagle, s. aigle éployée, f.

spree, *sprē*, s. bamboche, f.

sprig, *sprig*, s. brin, m., brindille, f.

sprightliness, *sprīt'li nĕs*, s. vivacité, gaieté, f., feu, m.

sprightly, *sprīt'li*, a. vif, gai.

spring, *spring*, s. élan, saut, m. ‖ élastique, m. ‖ ressort, m. ‖ printemps, m. ‖ source, f. ‖ fente, f. ‖ hair-~~, spiral, m. ‖ main-~~, grand ressort ‖ ~~tide, m. grande marée, f. ‖ ~~water, s. eau de fontaine, f. ‖ ~~wheat, s. blé de mars, m.

spring, *sprĭng*, v. a. & n. ir. faire lever, faire partir || pousser, croître || paraître, naître, descendre, s'élever, procéder || jaillir, s'élancer, sauter, bondir || se détendre || s'enfuir, s'envoler.

springe, *sprĭnj*, s. piège, filet, m.

springiness, *sprĭng'ĭ nĕs*, s. élasticité, f.

sprinkle, *sprĭng'kl*, v. a. & n. asperger, arroser || (fig.) parsemer.

sprinkler, *sprĭng'klĕr*, s. qui asperge || goupillon, m.

sprinkling, *sprĭng'klĭng*, s. aspersion, f., arrosement, m. || légère teinture, f.

sprit-sail, *sprĭt' sāl*, s. (mar.) civadière, f.

sprite, *sprĭt*, s. esprit, fantôme, m.

sprout, *sprŏwt*, s. jet, rejeton, m. || jeune chou, m. || Brussels—, chou de Bruxelles, m.

sprout, *sprŏwt*, v. n. germer, pousser.

spruce, *sprōs*, v. a. & n. rafistoler || se faire beau.   [recherche.

spruce, *sprōs*, a. pimpant || —ly, ad. avec

spruceness, *sprōs'nĕs*, s. parure affectée.

spume, *spūm*, s. écume, f.   [f.

spume, *spūm*, v. n. écumer, mousser.

spunk, *spŭngk*, s. amadou, m. || (fam.) courage, m.

spur, *spĕr*, s. éperon, m. || aiguillon, m. || ergot, m. || stimulant, m. || hâte, f.

spur, *spĕr*, v. a. donner de l'éperon à || éperonner || instiguer.   [sifié || bâtard.

spurious, *spū'rĭ ŭs*, a. supposé, faux, fal-

spurn, *spĕrn*, v. a. pousser du pied || traiter avec mépris.

sputter, *spŭt'tĕr*, v. a. & n. cracher en parlant || bredouiller, balbutier.

spy, *spĭ*, s. espion, m. || espionne, f.

spy, *spĭ*, v. a. épier, espionner || —glass, s. longue-vue, f.

squab, *skwŏb*, s. coussin, sofa, m.

squab, *skwŏb*, a. (of birds) nouvellement éclos || dodu.   [querelle, f. || bagarre, f.

squabble, *skwŏb'bl*, s. chamaillis, m. ||

squabble, *skwŏb'bl*, v. n. se chamailler.

squad, *skwŏd*, s. escouade, f.   [cadre, f.

squadron, *skwŏd'rŏn*, s. escadron, m. || es-

squalid, *skwŏl'ĭd*, a. sale, malpropre.

squall, *skwâwl*, s. cri alarmant, m. || rafale, f., coup de vent, grain, m.

squall, *skwâwl*, v. n. crier, brailler.

squaller, *skwâwl'ĕr*, s. criard, m.

squally, *skwâwl'lĭ*, a. orageux.   [piller.

squander, *skwŏn'dĕr*, v. a. dissiper, gas-

squanderer, *skwŏn'dĕr ĕr*, s. dissipateur, prodigue, m.

square, *skwâr*, s. carré, m. || équerre, f. || place carrée, f. || carreau, m.

square, *skwâr*, v. a. & n. carrer, équarrir || régler, ajuster || mesurer || cadrer.

square, *skwâr*, a. (—ly, ad.) carré(ment) || convenable || conforme || balancé || juste, honnête || équitable(ment).

squareness, *skwâr'nĕs*, s. quadrature, f.

squash, *skwŏsh*, v. a. écraser.

squat, *skwŏt*, v. n. s'accroupir, se tapir.

squat, *skwŏt*, a. accroupi, blotti.

squatter, *skwŏt'tĕr*, s. colon, m.

squaw, *skwâw*, s. (Am.) femme d'un Indien.

squeak, *skwēk*, s. cri perçant, m.   [f.

squeak, *skwēk*, v. n. jeter des cris perçants.

squeaker, *skwēk'ĕr*, s. criard, m. || cochon de lait, m.

squeal, *skwēl*, v. n. pousser des cris.

squeamish, *skwēm'ĭsh*, a. délicat || dégoûté.   [ment, m.

squeeze, *skwēz*, s. compression, f. || serre-

squeeze, *skwēz*, v. a. presser, serrer.   [f.

squib, *skwĭb*, s. fusée d'artifice, f. || satire, f.

squint, *skwĭnt*, s. regard louche, m. || —eyed, a. louche || méchant.

squint, *skwĭnt*, v. n. loucher.

squire, *skwĭr*, s. écuyer, m. || propriétaire, m. || (of a lady) cavalier, m.

squirrel, *skwĭr'rĕl*, s. écureuil, m.

squirt, *skwĕrt*, s. seringue, f. || jet d'eau, m.

squirt, *skwĕrt*, v. a. seringuer.

stab, *stăb*, s. coup de poignard, m.

stab, *stăb*, v. a. percer || poignarder.   [f.

stability, *stă bĭl'ĭ tĭ*, s. stabilité, constance, f.

stable, *stā'bl*, s. étable, écurie, f. || —yard, s. basse-cour, f. || livery—s, s. pl. pension pour les chevaux, f.

stable, *stā'bl*, v. a. établer.   [ferme.

stable, *stā'bl*, a. stable, fixe || constant,

stabling, *stā'blĭng*, s. écuries, f. pl.

stack, *stăk*, s. meule (de foin, etc.), f. || pile (de bois), f. || souche, f.

stack, *stăk*, v. a. mettre en meule.

stadtholder, *stăd'hōld ĕr*, s. stathouder, m.

staff, *stăf*, s. bâton, m. || échelon, m. || état-major, m. || soutien, m. || corps, m.

stag, *stăg*, s. cerf, m. || —beetle, s. cerf-volant, m. || —hound, s. limier, m.

stage, *stāj*, s. échafaudage, m., estrade, f. || théâtre, m., scène, f. || degré, état, m. || relais, m. || journée, f. || voiture publique, f. || —box, s. loge d'avant-scène, f. || —driver, s. postillon, m. || —whisper, s. chuchotements qu'on peut entendre, m. pl.

stager, *stā'jĕr*, s. comédien, m. || routier, m.

stagger, *stăg'gĕr*, v. a. & n. chanceler || ébranler, étonner || hésiter, vaciller.

staggers, *stăg'gĕrz*, s. pl. vertige des chevaux, m. || étourderie, f.

stagnancy, *stăg'năn sĭ*, s. stagnation, f.

stagnant, *stăg'nănt*, a. stagnant || inactif.

stagnate, *stăg'nāt*, v. n. être stagnant.

stagnation, *stăg nā'shŭn*, s. stagnation, f.

staid, *stād*, a. grave, posé.

staidness, *stād'nĕs*, s. gravité, f.

stain, *stān*, s. tache, souillure, f. || honte, f.

stain, *stān*, v. a. tacher || mettre en couleur || souiller.

stainer, *stān'ĕr*, s. teinturier, m.

stainless, *stān'lĕs*, a. sans tache || pur.

stair, *stâr*, s. marche d'un escalier, m. || —s, s. pl. escalier, m. || —rod, s. tringle d'escalier, f.

staircase, *stâr'kās*, s. escalier, m.

stake, *stāk*, s. poteau, m. || enjeu, m.

stake, *stāk*, v. a. garnir de pieux || mettre au jeu.

stalactite, *stăl'ăk tīt*, s. stalactite, f.

stalagmite, *stăl'ăg mīt*, s. stalagmite, f.

stale, *stāl*, a. vieux, usé, gâté || rassis ||

stalemate, *stāl'māt*, s. pat, m.   [éventé.

stalemate, *stāl'māt*, v. a. faire pat.   [f.

staleness, *stāl'nĕs*, s. vieillesse || platitude,

stalk, *stawk*, s. tuyau, m. || tige, queue, f. || démarche fière, f.

stalk, *stawk*, v. n. marcher fièrement || aller à la dérobée.

stalking-horse, *stawk'ing hŏrs*, s. (hunt.) cheval factice, m. || prétexte, m.

stall, *stawl*, s. écurie, étable, f. || échoppe, f., étalage, étal, m., boutique, f. || stalle, f.

stall, *stawl*, v. a. établer.

stallage, *stawl'āj*, s. étalage, m.

stallion, *stāl'yŭn*, s. étalon, m.

stamen, *stā'mĕn*, s. stamina, *stăm'ĭn ă*, s. pl. (bot.) étamines, f. pl. || base, force, f. || nerf, m.   [tier.

stammer, *stăm'mĕr*, v. n. bégayer, balbutier.

stammerer, *stăm'mĕr ĕr*, s. bègue, m. & f., bredouilleur, m.

stamp, *stămp*, s. poinçon, coin, m. || balancier, m. || empreinte, impression, f. || timbre, cachet, m., estampe, f. || trempe, f. || a man of the right ~, homme de bon aloi, marqué au bon coin, m.

stamp, *stămp*, v. a. & n. fouler aux pieds || piler, broyer || imprimer || estampiller || estamper || affranchir || timbrer || contrôler.

stamper, *stăm'pĕr*, s. timbreur, m. || détritoir, m. || bocard, m.   [rêter.

stanch, *stănch*, v. a. & n. étancher || s'arstanch, *stănch*, a. solide || ferme || (hunt.) sûr.

stand, *stănd*, s. station, f. || place, f. || délai, m. || pause, halte, f. || résistance, f. embarras, m. || guéridon, m., console, f., étalage, m. || to bring, come to a ~, arrêter, s'arrêter.

stand, *stănd*, v. a. & n. ir. endurer, résister, soutenir, maintenir, défendre || être debout, se tenir debout || demeurer ferme || être situé, subsister || s'arrêter || rester tranquille || se défendre || reposer || (at elections) se présenter || to ~ for, représenter, signifier || ~~still, s. arrêt, m. || to come to a ~~still, être dans l'embarras || ~~up, a montant || en règle.

standard, *stănd'ĕrd*, s. étendard, m. || pavillon, m. || étalon, m. || titre, m. || modèle, m. || type, m. || mesure, f. || ~~bearer, s. porte-drapeau, enseigne, m. || porte-étendard, m.   [(gold etc.) au titre.

standard, *stănd'ĕrd*, a. type || classique ||

standing, *stănd'ing*, s. durée, f. || position, place, f., rang, m.

standing, *stănd'ing*, a. établi, fixe, constant || durable || stagnant.

staple, *stā'pl*, s. étape, f., entrepôt, m. || gâche d'une serrure, f.

staple, *stā'pl*, a. établi || principal.

star, *stăr*, s. étoile, f. || astre, m. || astérisque, m. || shooting~, étoile filante, f. || evening-~, étoile du soir, Vénus, f. || ~~fish, s. astérie, f.

star, *stăr*, v. a. étoiler || parsemer || jouer sur un théâtre étranger.

starboard, *stăr'bŏrd*, s. (mar.) tribord, m.

starch, *stărch*, s. empois, m. || amidon, m.

starch, *stărch*, v. a. empeser.

starching, *stărch'ing*, s. empesage, m.

stare, *stăr*, s. regard fixe, m.

stare, *stăr*, v. n. regarder fixement or avec étonnement.

staring, *stăr'ing*, a. éclatant || hérissé.

stark, *stărk*, a. & ad. fort || vrai, pur || tout-à-fait.

starless, *stăr'lĕs*, a. sans étoiles.

starlight, *stăr'līt*, s. lumière des étoiles, f.

starling, *stăr'ling*, s. sansonnet, étourneau, m. || brise-glace, m.

starred, *stărd*, starry, *stăr'rĭ*, a. étoilé, orné d'étoiles.

start, *stărt*, s. tressaillement, m. || saut, m. || élan, m. || premier pas, m. || by (fits and) ~s, par boutades, à bâtons rompus, par sauts et par bonds.

start, *stărt*, v. a. & n. faire tressaillir, troubler || lancer || soulever, mettre sur le tapis, proposer || découvrir, apercevoir || sauter, trembler || partir || hésiter.

starter, *stărt'ĕr*, s. inventeur, auteur, m.

startle, *stăr'tl*, v. n. s'effrayer, tressaillir.

starvation, *stăr vā'shŭn*, s. inanition, f. || mort de faim, f.

starve, *stărv*, v. a. & n. faire mourir de faim, affamer || mourir de faim || mourir de froid.

starveling, *stărv'ling*, s. affamé, m.

state, *stāt*, s. état, m., condition, f. || rang, m., dignité, pompe, f. || State, État, m.

state, *stāt*, v. a. établir, régler || constater, détailler.

statecraft, *stāt'krăft*, s. ruses de la politique, f. pl.   [pompe, f.

stateliness, *stāt'lĭ nĕs*, s. grandeur,

stately, *stāt'lĭ*, a. & ad. majestueux, magnifique || majestueusement.

statement, *stāt'mĕnt*, s. état, m. || détail, procès-verbal, rapport, exposé, m.

statesman, *stāts'măn*, s. homme d'État, m.   [tique, f.

statesmanship, *stāts'măn shĭp*, s. politics, *stāt'ĭks*, s. pl. statique, f.

station, *stā'shŭn*, s. situation, position, condition, f. || poste, m., place, f., emploi, m. || état, rang, m. || (rail.) débarcadère, m., gare, f. || police-~, poste de police, m.

station, *stā'shŭn*, v. a. poster, placer.

stationary, *stā'shŭn ĕr'i*, a. stationnaire, fixé.

stationer, *stā'shŭn ĕr*, s. papetier, marchand de papier, m. || libraire, m. || ~'s hall, s. Chambre des libraires, f.

stationery, *stā'shŭn ĕr i*, s. papeterie, f.

statist, *stā'tĭst*, s. homme d'État, m.

statistical, *stă tĭs'tĭk ăl*, a. statistique.

statistician, *stă tĭs tĭsh'ŭn*, s. statisticien, m.   [f.

statistics, *stă tĭs'tĭks*, s. pl. statistique,

statuary, *stăt'ū ĕr ĭ*, s. statuaire, m. & f.

statue, *stăt'ū*, s. statue, f.

stature, *stăt'ūr*, s. stature, taille, f.

statute, *stăt'ūt*, s. statut, m., loi, f. ~~

fair, s. foire légale, f. || ~-labour, s. corvée, f. || ~-law, s. droit écrit, m.

staunch, stânch, a. *vids* stanch.

stave, stäv, s. douve, f.

stave, stäv, v. a. défoncer.

stay, stä, s. séjour, m. || soutien, m. || stabilité, f. || ~-at-home, a. casanier || ~s, s. pl. corset, m.

stay, stä, v. a. & n. ir. arrêter, empêcher || étayer || rester, demeurer, s'arrêter || attendre, rester immobile.

stead, stěd, s. place, f., lieu, m.

steadfast, stěd'fäst, a. stable, fixe || constant || -ly, ad. avec fermeté, avec constance.   [constance, f.

steadfastness, stěd'fäst něs, s. fermeté,

steadily, stěd'ĭ lĭ, ad. fermement.

steadiness, stěd'ĭ něs, s. fermeté, f. || régularité, f. || conduite rangée, f.

steading, stěd'ing, s. grange, f.

steady, stěd'ĭ, v. a. affermir, assurer.

steady, stěd'ĭ, a. ferme, solide || ~! restez tranquille!

steak, stāk, s. tranche de viande, f.

steal, stēl, v. a. & n. ir. voler || s'échapper.

stealing, stēl'ing, s. vol, m.   [robée.

stealth, stělth, s. vol, m. || by ~, à la dé-

stealthily, stělth'ĭ lĭ, ad. clandestinement.

stealthy, stělth'ĭ, a. furtif.

steam, stēm, s. vapeur, fumée, f. || to get up ~, chauffer la vapeur || to let off ~, stopper || ~-engine, s. machine à vapeur, f. || ~-navigation, s. navigation à vapeur, f. || ~-power, s. force de la vapeur, f.

steam, stēm, v. a. cuire à la vapeur || ~, v. n. jeter de la vapeur || fumer || naviguer à la vapeur.

steamboat, stēm'bōt, steamer, stēm'ěr, s. vapeur, bateau à vapeur, m.

steed, stēd, s. coursier, cheval, m.

steel, stēl, s. acier, m. || briquet, m. || ~-works, s. pl. aciérie, f.

steel, stēl, v. a. acérer, aciérer, endurcir.

steelyard, stēl'yärd, s. romaine, f. || peson, m.   [cipice, m.

steep, stēp, s. descente escarpée, f., pré-

steep, stēp, v. a. tremper, infuser.

steep, stēp, a. escarpé || raide.

steeple, stēp'l, s. clocher, m.

steeplechase, stēp'l chās, s. course au clocher, f.

steepness, stēp'něs, s. pente escarpée, f.

steer, stēr, s. bouvillon, m.

steer, stēr, v. a. & n. gouverner, diriger || (fig.) se diriger || manœuvrer.

steerage, stēr'äj, s. (mar.) gouvernement, m., direction, f. || ~-passenger, s. passager d'entrepôt *or* de troisième classe, m. || ~-way, s. (mar.) sillage, m.

steering, stēr'ing, s. (mar.) gouvernement, m. || ~-gear, s. levier de distribution, m.

steersman, stēr'z män, s. timonier, m.

stem, stěm, s. tronc, m. || tige, queue, f. || pédoncule, m. || race, f.

stem, stěm, v. n. s'opposer à.

stench, stěnsh, s. puanteur, f.

stencil, stěn'sĭl, s. patron découpé, m.

stenographer, stěn ŏg'rä fěr, s. sténographe, m.   [graphique.

stenographic, stěn ŏ gräf'ĭk, a. sténo-

stenography, stěn ŏg'rä fĭ, s. sténographie, f.

step, stěp, s. pas, m., marche, f. || échelon, m. || marchepied, m. || ~-brother, s. beau-frère, m. || ~-daughter, s. belle-fille, f. || ~-father, s. beau-père, m. || ~-mother, s. belle-mère, f. || marâtre, f. || ~-sister, s. belle-sœur, f. || ~-son, s. beau-fils, m.

step, stěp, v. n. faire un pas, marcher.

stepping-stone, stěp'ping stōn, s. marchepied, m.   [m.

stereoscope, stěr'ěŏ skōp, s. stéréoscope,

stereotype, stěr'ěŏ tĭp, s. cliché, m.

stereotype, stěr'ěŏ tĭp, v. a. stéréotyper || [clicher.

sterile, stěr'ĭl, a. stérile.

sterility, stěr'ĭl'ĭtĭ, s. stérilité, f.

sterling, stěr'ling, a. vrai, de bon aloi || one pound ~, une livre sterling.

stern, stěrn, s. (mar.) poupe, f. || ~-post, s. étambot, m. || ~-sheets, s. pl. (mar.) palans de la barre, m. pl.

stern, stěrn, a. (-ly, ad.) sévère(ment) || austère, rude.

sternmost, stěrn'mōst, a. en serre-file.

sternness, stěrn'něs, s. sévérité, dureté, f.

stethoscope, stěth'ŏ skōp, s. stéthoscope, m.

stevedore, stē'vĭ dōr, s. arrimeur, m.

stew, stū, s. étuvée, f. || compote, f. || venette, f. || ~-pan, s. braisière, f.

stew, stū, v. a. étuver.

steward, stū'ěrd, s. intendant, économe, maître d'hôtel, m. || (mar.) commis aux vivres, m.

stewardship, stū'ěrd shĭp, s. charge de maître d'hôtel, f. || administration, f.

stick, stĭk, s. bâton, m. || canne, f. || archet, m.

stick, stĭk, v. a. & n. coller, ficher || saigner, tuer || percer || être collé, s'arrêter, s'attacher || hésiter || to ~ bills, coller des affiches, afficher || to ~ out, faire saillie || to ~ up, dresser, mettre droit || stuck-up, a. vain || ~-up, a. droit || montant || ~-ups, s. pl. faux-col, m. || to ~ at nothing, ne se faire aucun scrupule de.

stickiness, stĭk'ĭ něs, s. viscosité, f.

stickler, stĭk'lěr, s. partisan, champion, m.

sticky, stĭk'ĭ, a. gluant, visqueux.

stiff, stĭf, a. raide || obstiné || gêné, affecté || empesé || -ly, ad. avec opiniâtreté || ~-neck, s. torticolis, m.   [se raidir.

stiffen, stĭf'fn, v. a. & n. raidir, engourdir ||

stiffness, stĭf'něs, s. raideur, f. || opiniâtreté, f. || gêne, f.

stifle, stĭf'fl, v. a. étouffer.   [trissure, f.

stigma, stĭg'mä, s. stigmate, m. || flé-

stigmatise, stĭg'mä tīz, v. a. stigmatiser.

stile, stĭl, s. barrière d'enclos || aiguille d'un cadran solaire, f.

stiletto, stĭ lět'tō, s. poinçon, m. || stylet, m.

still, stĭl, s. silence, m. || alambic, m.

still, *stĭll*, v. a. calmer || distiller.
still, *stĭll*, a. tranquille, calme || ~-born, a. mort-né || ~-life, s. nature inanimée, f.
still, *stĭll*, ad. & c. encore || cependant || toujours. [calme, m.
stillness, *stĭll'nĕs*, s. tranquillité, f.
stilts, *stĭlts*, s. pl. échasses, f. pl.
stimulant, *stĭm'ū lănt*, s. stimulant, m.
stimulate, *stĭm'ū lāt*, v. a. stimuler, piquer.
stimulating, *stĭm'ū lā tĭng*, stimulative, *stĭm'ū lă tĭv*, a. stimulant. [tion, f.
stimulation, *stĭm ū lā'shŭn*, s. stimula-
stimulus, *stĭm'ū lŭs*, s. stimulant, m. || aiguillon, m.
sting, *stĭng*, s. aiguillon, m. || remords, m. [piqûre, f.
sting, *stĭng*, v. a. ir. piquer, percer, mordre.
stingily, *stĭn'jĭ lĭ*, ad. mesquinement
stinginess, *stĭn'jĭ nĕs*, s. mesquinerie, f.
stinging-nettle, *stĭng'ĭng nĕt l*, s. ortie, f.
stingy, *stĭn'jĭ*, a. chiche, avare. [f.
stink, *stĭngk*, s. puanteur, f.
stink, *stĭngk*, v. n. ir. puer.
stint, *stĭnt*, s. limite, f.
stint, *stĭnt*, v. a. borner, limiter.
stipend, *stī'pĕnd*, s. salaire, m., appointements, m. pl. [pointé.
stipendiary, *stī pĕn'dĭ ĕr ĭ*, a. salarié, ap-
stipple, *stĭp'pl*, v. a. pointiller.
stipulate, *stĭp'ū lāt*, v. n. stipuler. [f.
stipulation, *stĭp ū lā'shŭn*, s. stipulation,
stir, *stĕr*, s. tumulte, m., agitation, f.
stir, *stĕr*, v. a. & n. remuer, agiter || inciter, animer || faire naître, provoquer || se remuer, se révolter || apparaître.
stirrup, *stĭr'rŭp*, s. étrier, m. || ~-cup, s. coup, vin de l'étrier || ~-iron, s. étrier, m. || ~-leather, s. étrivière, f.
stitch, *stĭch*, s. point, m. || maille, f. || ~ in one's side, s. point de côté, m.
stitch, *stĭch*, v. a. piquer || coudre || brocher.
stiver, *stī'vĕr*, s. liard, m. [m.
stoat, *stōt*, s. belette, f. || (ermine) roselet,
stock, *stŏk*, s. tronc, m. || bloc, m. || famille, race, f. || capital, m. || cravate, f. || assortiment, m. || bétail, m. || objet, m. || ~s, pl. fonds publics, m. pl. || joint-~ company, s. société anonyme, f. || common ~, actions primitives, f. pl. || preferred ~, actions privilégiées, f. pl. || rolling-~, (rail.) matériel roulant, matériel d'exploitation, m. || live-~, nombre des bestiaux nourris dans une ferme, f. || to take ~ of, faire l'inventaire || ~-in-trade, s. fonds de boutique, m. || ~-exchange, s. bourse des fonds publics, f. || ~-fish, s. morue, f., stockfisch, m. || ~-holder, s. actionnaire, m. || ~-jobber, s. agioteur, m. || ~-still, a. immobile || ~-taking, s. récolement de l'inventaire, m. [assortir.
stock, *stŏk*, v. a. pourvoir, approvisionner,
stockade, *stŏk'ād*, s. palissade, f.
stocking, *stŏk'ĭng*, s. bas, m.
stoic, *stō'ĭk*, s. stoïcien, m. [(ment).
stoical, *stō'ĭk ăl*, a. (-ly, ad.) stoïque
stoicism, *stō'ĭ sĭzm*, s. stoïcisme, m.

stoker, *stō'kĕr*, s. chauffeur, m.
stole, *stōl*, s. étole, f.
stolid, *stŏl'ĭd*, a. stupide, lourd.
stolidity, *stŏ lĭd'ĭ tĭ*, stolidness, *stŏl'ĭd-nĕs*, s. stupidité, f.
stomach, *stŭm'ăk*, s. estomac, m. || appétit, m. || to lie heavy on one's ~, peser sur l'estomac, sur le cœur || to turn one's ~, soulever le cœur || ~-ache, s. mal à l'estomac, m. [porter.
stomach, *stŭm'ăk*, v. a. se fâcher || sup-
stomached, *stŭm'ăkt*, a. courroucé.
stomacher, *stŭm'ăk ĕr*, s. corsage lacé, m.
stomachic, *stō măk'ĭk*, s. stomachique, m.
stomachic, *stō măk'ĭk*, a. stomachique.
stone, *stōn*, s. pierre, f., caillou, m. || pepin, noyau, m. || precious ~, pierre précieuse, f. || ~-breaker, s. tailleur de pierres, m. || ~-blind, a. complètement aveugle || ~-crop, s. (bot.) saxifrage, f. || ~-cutter, s. tailleur de pierre, m. || ~-dead, a. raide mort || ~-fruit, s. fruit à noyau, m. || ~-horse, s. étalon, m. || ~-pit, s. carrière, f. || ~'s-throw, s. jet de pierre, m. || within a ~'s-throw, à deux pas. [les pepins.
stone, *stōn*, v. a. lapider || empierrer, ôter
stone, *stōn*, a. de pierre.
stoneware, *stōn'wâr*, s. grès, m.
stoning, *stōn'ĭng*, s. lapidation, f.
stony, *stōn'ĭ*, a. pierreux, de pierre.
stool, *stōl*, s. tabouret, m. || (méd.) selle, f.
stoop, *stōp*, s. inclination, f. || abaissement, m. || (Am.) cruche, f.
stoop, *stōp*, v. n. se baisser || se tenir courbé || s'humilier || se percher. [tête.
stoopingly, *stōp'ĭng lĭ*, ad. en baissant la
stop, *stŏp*, s. pause, f. || obstacle, m. || ~-watch, s. montre à arrêt, f.
stop, *stŏp*, v. a. & n. arrêter, empêcher || cesser || boucher, obstruer || faire halte, se reposer.
stoppage, *stŏp'păj*, s. obstacle, empêchement, m. || (rail.) temps d'arrêt, m.
stopper, *stŏp'pĕr*, stopple, *stŏp'pl*, s. bouchon, m. || tampon, m. || piston, m.
stopper, *stŏp'pĕr*, v. a. boucher.
store, *stōr*, s. magasin, dépôt, m. || quantité, f. || provisions, f. pl. || to set great ~ by, faire grand cas de || ~-keeper, s. garde-magasin, m. [pourvoir.
store, *stōr*, v. a. fournir, emmagasiner,
storey, *stō'rĭ*, s. étage, m.
storied, *stō'rĭd*, a. historié || à ... étage.
stork, *stŏrk*, s. cigogne, f.
storm, *stŏrm*, s. orage, m., tempête, f. || assaut, m. [tempéter.
storm, *stŏrm*, v. a. & n. donner l'assaut ||
storminess, *stŏrm'ĭ nĕs*, s. état orageux, m.
storming-party, *stŏrm'ĭng păr tĭ*, s. colonne d'assaut, f.
stormy, *stŏrm'ĭ*, a. orageux, violent || ~-petrel, s. pétrel, m., caillette procellaire, f.
story, *stō'rĭ*, s. histoire, f. || fable, f., mensonge, m. || étage, m. (vide storey) || ~-teller, s. conteur, m. || menteur, m.
stout, *stowt*, s. bière brune, f.

stout, *stŏwt*, a. fort || vigoureux || brave || résolu || gros || **-ly**, ad. vigoureusement || fortement || résolûment.

stoutness, *stŏwt'nĕs*, s. vigueur, f. || corpulence, f., courage, m. [m.

stove, *stŏv*, s. étuve, f. || poêle, fourneau,

stow, *stŏ*, v. a. serrer, entasser || (mar.) arrimer. [m. || (mar.) arrimage, m.

stowage, *stŏ'ăj*, s. magasin, magasinage,

stowaway, *stŏ'ă wā*, s. passager de contrebande, lapin, m.

straddle, *străd'dl*, v. n. écarter les jambes || marcher les jambes écartées. [persé.

straggle, *străg'gl*, v. n. rôder || être dis-

straggler, *străg'glĕr*, s. vagabond, m. || (mil.) traînard, m.

straight, *strāt*, a. & ad. droit || directement || sur-le-champ. [dresser.

straighten, *strāt'tn*, v. a. dresser, re-

straightforward, *strāt fŏr'wĕrd*, a. franc, loyal || **-ly**, ad. avec droiture.

straightway, *strāt'wā*, ad. tout de suite.

strain, *strān*, s. effort, m. || entorse, f. || manière, f. || mélodie, f. || style, m.

strain, *strān*, v. a. tendre || filtrer || serrer, forcer || se fouler || s'efforcer.

strainer, *strān'ĕr*, s. couloir, m.

strait, *strāt*, a. détroit, m. || défilé, m., gorge, f. || embarras, m.

strait, *strāt*, a. (**-ly**, ad.) étroit(ement) || sévère, pénible, gênant || intime || **~-laced**, a. lacé étroitement || contraint || **~-waistcoat**, s. camisole de force, f.

straiten, *strā'tn*, v. a. étrécir, resserrer.

straitness, *strāt'nĕs*, s. étroitesse, sévérité, f. || embarras, m.

strand, *strănd*, s. côte, f., rivage, m.

strand, *strănd*, v. n. échouer sur la côte.

strange, *strānj*, a. (**-ly**, ad.) étranger || singulier || étrange(ment).

strangeness, *strānj'nĕs*, s. étrangeté, f. || singularité, f. [connu, m.

stranger, *strān'jĕr*, s. étranger, m. || in-

strangle, *străng'gl*, v. a. étrangler.

strangles, *strān'glz*, s. pl. gourme, f.

strangulation, *străng gŭ lā'shŭn*, s. étranglement, m.

strap, *străp*, s. courroie, bretelle, f. || **shoulder~**, banderole de bricole, f. || sangle de bretelle, f.

strappado, *străp pā'dō*, s. estrapade, f.

strapping, *străp'ping*, s. bande, f.

strapping, *străp'ping*, a. grand, gros.

stratagem, *străt'tăjĕm*, s. stratagème, artifice, m.

strategic, *străt ĕj'ĭk*, a. stratégique.

strategist, *străt'ĕjĭst*, s. stratègue, m.

strategy, *străt'ĕjĭ*, s. stratégie, f.

stratum, *strā'tŭm*, s. couche, f.

straw, *străw*, s. paille, f. || fétu, rien, m. || not to care a **~**, se soucier (de qc.) comme de l'an quarante || **~-bed**, s. paillasse, f. || **~-cutter**, s. coupe-paille, m.

strawberry, *străw'bĕr rĭ*, s. fraise, f. || **~-bed**, s. fraisière, f. || **~-plant**, s. fraisier, m.

stray, *strā*, s. bête épave, f.

stray, *strā*, v. n. rôder, s'égarer.

stray, *strā*, a. égaré.

streak, *strēk*, s. raie, bande, f.

streak, *strēk*, v. a. rayer, bigarrer.

streaky, *strēk'ĭ*, a. rayé, bariolé.

stream, *strēm*, s. courant, torrent, m. || main **~**, fleuve, m. || **tributary ~**, fleuve tributaire. [briller.

stream, *strēm*, v. n. couler, ruisseler ||

streamer, *strēm'ĕr*, s. banderole, f., pavillon, m. || flamme, f.

streamy, *strēm'ĭ*, a. ruisselant || jaillissant || sillonné de ruisseaux.

street, *strēt*, s. rue, f. || **~-door**, s. porte sur la rue, f. || **~-walker**, s. coureuse, prostituée, f. [f. || forces, f. pl.

strength, *strĕngth*, s. force, f. || résistance,

strengthen, *strĕng'thn*, v. a. fortifier, affermir || encourager.

strengthener, *strĕng'thnĕr*, s. corroboratif, m.

strenuous, *strĕn'ū ŭs*, a. vaillant, courageux || zélé, actif || **-ly**, ad. vaillamment || ardemment.

strenuousness, *strĕn'ū ŭs nĕs*, s. zèle, m., ardeur, f., empressement, m.

stress, *strĕs*, s. importance, f. || violence, f. || effort, m. || (gr.) accent, m.

stretch, *strĕch*, s. étendue, f. || tension, f.

stretch, *strĕch*, v. a. & n. étendre, élargir, allonger, exagérer, forcer || s'étendre, s'élargir, se déployer || **to ~ a point**, (fig.) faire plus qu'on n'est obligé de faire.

stretcher, *strĕch'ĕr*, s. brancard, m. || **glove~**, ouvre-gants, m. || baguette, f., étendeuse, f. [et là.

strew, *strō*, v. a. parsemer, répandre çà

striated, *strī'ā tĕd*, a. strié.

strict, *strĭkt*, a. (**-ly**, ad.) strict(ement) || exact(ement) || ponctuel, positif || sévère (ment) || resserré || étroit. [vérité, f.

strictness, *strĭkt'nĕs*, s. exactitude, sévérité, f.

stricture, *strĭk'tŭr*, s. contraction, f., étranglement, m. || critique, f.

stride, *strīd*, s. enjambée, f. || pas, m.

stride, *strīd*, v. a. & n. ir. enjamber.

strife, *strīf*, s. lutte, f. || contestation, f. || différend, m.

strike, *strīk*, s. racloire, f. || (of workmen) grève, f. || **to be on ~**, être en grève.

strike, *strīk*, v. a. & n. ir. frapper, heurter, battre || affliger || étonner, épouvanter || lancer, jeter, pousser || choquer, imprimer, graver || marquer || faire || se mettre en grève, cesser de travailler || causer || se frapper, se heurter, échouer || sonner.

striker, *strī'kĕr*, s. gréviste, m.

striking, *strī'king*, a. frappant.

string, *strĭng*, s. corde, f. || cordon, m., ficelle, attache, f. || fil, m. || fibre, f., tendon, filament, m. || suite, f.

string, *strĭng*, v. a. ir. garnir de cordes || enfiler || tendre || accorder || **-ed instrument**, s. instrument à cordes, m.

stringent, *strĭn'jĕnt*, a. astringent || fort.

stringy, *strĭng'ĭ*, a. fibreux.

strip, *strĭp*, s. bande, f.

strip, *strĭp,* v. a. dépouiller, priver || écorcher || piller.

stripe, *strĭp,* s. raie, f. || coup, m.

stripe, *strĭp,* v. a. rayer.

strive, *strĭv,* v. n. ir. s'efforcer, tâcher || combattre.

striving, *strī'vĭng,* s. effort, m. || lutte, dispute, f.

stroke, *strōk,* s. coup, m. || trait de plume, m. || effort, m. || brassée, f. || **on the ~ of 12,** à midi sonnant.

stroke, *strōk,* v. a. caresser.

stroll, *strōl,* s. promenade, f.

stroll, *strōl,* v. n. rôder.

stroller, *strōl'ĕr,* s. vagabond, m. || comédien ambulant, m.

strong, *strŏng,* a. (**-ly,** ad.) fort(ement) || vigoureux, robuste || puissant, énergique || impétueux || vigoureusement || solidement || **~-box,** s. coffre-fort, m. || **~-minded,** a. à esprit fort.

stronghold, *strŏng'hōld,* s. place forte, f.

strop, *strŏp,* s. cuir à repasser, m.

strop, *strŏp,* v. a. repasser sur le cuir.

strophe, *strŏf'ē,* s. strophe, stance, f.

structural, *strŭk'tūr ăl,* a. de structure.

structure, *strŭk'tūr,* s. construction, f. || édifice, m.   [battre, lutter contre.

struggle, *strŭg'gl,* v. n. s'efforcer, se débattre.

struggling, *strŭg'lĭng,* s. lutte, f. || effort, m. || combat, m.

strum, *strŭm,* v. a. taper || (fig.) massacrer.

strumpet, *strŭm'pĕt,* s. prostituée, f.

strut, *strŭt,* s. démarche fière, f.

strut, *strŭt,* v. n. se pavaner.

strychnine, *strĭk'nēn,* s. strychnine, f.

stub, *stŭb,* s. tronc, tronçon, chicot, m.

stubble, *stŭb'bl,* s. chaume, m.

stubborn, *stŭb'bĕrn,* a. (**-ly,** ad.) obstiné (ment) || entêté || opiniâtrément || **~ fact,** s. fait irréfutable, m.

stubbornness, *stŭb'bĕrn nĕs,* s. opiniâtreté, f., entêtement, m.

stubby, *stŭb'bĭ,* a. trapu || plein de chaume.

stucco, *stŭk'kō,* s. stuc, m.

stud, *stŭd,* s. clou, m., bossette, f. || haras, m. || **~-horse,** s. étalon, m.

stud, *stŭd,* v. a. garnir de clous.

studding-sail, *stŭd'dĭng sāl,* s. (mar.) bonnette, f.

student, *stū'dĕnt,* s. étudiant, m.

studied, *stŭd'ĭd,* a. étudié, savant.

studio, *stū'dĭŏ,* s. atelier, m.

studious, *stū'dĭ ŭs,* a. studieux || diligent, soigneux || **-ly,** ad. studieusement, attentivement.

study, *stŭd'ĭ,* s. étude, attention, méditation, f. || cabinet, m. || **to be in a brown ~,** avoir l'esprit mal tourné.

study, *stŭd'ĭ,* v. a. & n. étudier, méditer sur || s'étudier, s'appliquer.

stuff, *stŭf,* s. matière, étoffe, f. || drap, m. || drogue, f.   [farcir || se bourrer.

stuff, *stŭf,* v. a. & n. remplir, bourrer ||

stuff! *stŭf,* bah!

stuffing, *stŭf'fĭng,* s. farce, f.

stultify, *stŭl'tĭ fī,* v. a. rendre fou, hébéter.

stumble, *stŭm'bl,* s. faux pas, m.

stumble, *stŭm'bl,* v. n. broncher, trébucher, faire un faux pas.

stumbling, *stŭm'blĭng,* s. bronchade, f. || **~-block,** s. pierre d'achoppement, f.

stump, *stŭmp,* s. tronc, tronçon, bout, chicot, m. || moignon, m.

stump, *stŭmp,* v. n. (**to ~ off**) s'en aller.

stumpy, *stŭmp'ĭ,* a. plein de chicots || trapu.

stun, *stŭn,* v. a. étourdir, abasourdir.

stunt, *stŭnt,* v. a. empêcher de croître.

stupefaction, *stū pē fak'shŭn,* s. stupéfaction, f. || stupidité, f.

stupefy, *stū'pē fī,* v. a. hébéter || engourdir.

stupendous, *stū pĕn'dŭs,* a. prodigieux, étonnant.

stupid, *stū'pĭd,* a. (**-ly,** ad.) stupide(ment).

stupidity, *stū pĭd'ĭ tĭ,* s. stupidité, bêtise, f.

stupor, *stū'pŏr,* s. stupeur, f.   [f.

sturdily, *stĕr'dĭ lĭ,* ad. fortement, hardiment || brusquement.

sturdiness, *stĕr'dĭ nĕs,* s. brusquerie, f. || force, f. || vigueur, f. || hardiesse, f.

sturdy, *stĕr'dĭ,* a. brusque, brutal || obstiné, vigoureux, fort.

sturgeon, *stĕr'jŏn,* s. esturgeon, m.

stutter, *stŭt'tĕr,* v. n. bégayer, bredouiller.

sty, *stĭ,* s. étable à cochons, f.   [floriot, m.

stye, *stĭ,* s. orgelet, m. || (fam.) compère.

style, *stĭl,* s. style, m. || diction, f. || raison sociale, titre, m. || goût, genre, m. || poinçon, m. || aiguille, f.

style, *stĭl,* v. a. appeler || donner le titre de.

stylish, *stĭ'lĭsh,* a. de bon ton || élégant || coquet.

suave, *swāv,* a. suave.   [coquet.

suavity, *swāv'ĭ tĭ,* s. suavité, douceur, f.

sub, *sŭb,* **~-editor,** s. rédacteur-gérant, m. || **~-let,** v. a. sous-louer || **~-lieutenant,** s. sous-lieutenant, m. || **~-officer,** s. sous-officier, m.

subaltern, *sŭb'ăl tĕrn,* s. subalterne, m.

subaltern, *sŭb'ăl tĕrn,* a. subalterne.

subcutaneous, *sŭb kū tā'nē ŭs,* a. souscutané.

subdivide, *sŭb dĭ vīd',* v. a. subdiviser.

subdivision, *sŭb dĭ vĭzh'ŭn,* s. subdivision, f.   [assujettir || mortifier.

subdue, *sŭb dū',* v. a. subjuguer || vaincre,

subduer, *sŭb dū'ĕr,* s. vainqueur, m.

subject, *sŭb'jĕkt,* s. sujet, m. || (gr.) nominatif, m.   [juguer, exposer.

subject, *sŭb jĕkt',* v. a. soumettre, sub-

subject, *sŭb'jĕkt,* a. sujet, soumis à.

subjection, *sŭb jĕk'shŭn,* s. sujétion, f. || assujettissement, m.

subjective, *sŭb jĕk'tĭv,* a. subjectif.

subjoin, *sŭb jŏyn',* v. a. joindre, ajouter à.

subjugate, *sŭb'jōō gāt,* v. a. subjuguer, assujettir.   [tissement, m.

subjugation, *sŭb jōō gā'shŭn,* s. assujet-

subjunctive, *sŭb jŭngk'tĭv,* s. (gr.) subjonctif, m.   [m.

sublimate, *sŭb'lĭ māt,* s. (chim.) sublimé,

sublimate, *sŭb'lĭ māt,* v. a. (chim.) sublimer.   [tion, f.

sublimation, *sŭb lĭ mā'shŭn,* s. sublima-

sublime, *sŭb līm',* s. sublime, m.

sublime, *săb lĭm'*, a. sublime || élevé ||-ly, ad. avec sublimité.

sublimity, *săb lĭm'ĭ tĭ*, s. sublimité, élévation, f.   [terrestre.

sublunar(y), *săb lŏ'nĕr(ĭ)*, a. sublunaire.

submarine, *săb mă rēn'*, a. sousmarin.

submerge, *săb mĕrj'*, v. a. submerger.

submersion, *săb mĕr'shŭn*, s. submersion, f.   [f. || résignation.

submission, *săb mĭsh'ŭn*, s. soumission.

submissive, *săb mĭs'sĭv*, a. soumis ||-ly, ad. avec soumission.   [mission, f.

submissiveness, *săb mĭs'sĭv nĕs*, s. soumettre.

submit, *săb mĭt'*, v. a. (& n.) (se) soumettre.   [ordonner, soumettre à.

subordinate, *săb ŏr'dĭ nāt*, v. a. subordonner.

subordinate, *săb ŏr'dĭ nāt*, a. subalterne, inférieur ||-ly, ad. en sous-ordre.

subordination, *săb ŏr dĭ nā'shŭn*, s. subordination, f.

suborn, *săb ŏrn'*, v. a. suborner.

subornation, *săb ŏr nā'shŭn*, s. subornation, f., subornement, f.   [citation, f.

subpœna, *săb pē'nă*, s. (jur.) assignation.

subpœna, *săb pē'nă*, v. a. (jur.) ajourner, citer.   [s'abonner à || consentir.

subscribe, *săb skrīb'*, v. a. & n. souscrire.

subscriber, *săb skrī'bĕr*, s. souscripteur, abonné, m.   [tion, f. || abonnement, f.

subscription, *săb skrĭp'shŭn*, s. souscription.

subsequent, *săb'sĕ kwĕnt*, a. subséquent, suivant ||-ly, ad. ensuite, après.

subserve, *săb sĕrv'*, v. n. servir, être aux ordres de.

subservience, *săb sĕr'vĭ ĕns*, subserviency, *săb sĕr'vĭ ĕn sĭ*, s. utilité, f. || subordination, f. || dépendance, f.

subservient, *săb sĕr'vĭ ĕnt*, a. subordonné || utile.   [seoir, se calmer.

subside, *săb sīd'*, v. n. baisser || se rassubsidiary, *săb sĭd'ĭ ĕr ĭ*, s. auxiliaire, m. || subsidiaire, m.   [subsidiaire.

subsidiary, *săb sĭd'ĭ ĕr ĭ*, a. auxiliaire || subsidiaire.

subsidise, *săb'sĭ dīz*, v. a. subventionner.

subsidy, *săb'sĭ dĭ*, s. subside, m. || subvention, f.

subsist, *săb sĭst'*, v. n. subsister, exister.

subsistence, *săb sĭs'tĕns*, s. subsistance, f., entretien, m.

substance, *săb'stăns*, s. substance, matière, f. || essentiel, corps, m. || réalité, f. || fortune, f.

substantial, *săb stăn'shăl*, a. (-ly, ad.) substantiel(lement) || essentiel || réel(lement) || matériel, fort || solide(ment) || vrai || riche.   [prouver par des faits.

substantiate, *săb stăn'shĭ āt*, v.a. établir ||

substantive, *săb'stăn tĭv*, s. substantif, m.

substantively, *săb stăn'tĭv lĭ*, ad. substantivement.

substitute, *săb'stĭ tūt*, v. a. substituer.

substitution, *săb stĭ tū'shŭn*, s. substitution, f.   [férieure, m. || sous-sol, m.

substratum, *săb strā'tŭm*, s. couche insubterfuge, *săb'tĕr fūj*, s. subterfuge, faux-fuyant, m.   [rain.

subterranean, *săb tĕr rā'nē ăn*, a. souter-

subtile, *săb'tĭl* ou *săt'l*, a. (-ly, ad.) subtil(ement) || délié, menu, fin || délicat || rusé, artificieux.   [tilisation, f.

subtilisation, *săb tĭl ĭ zā'shŭn*, s. subtilise, *săb'tĭl ĭz* ou *săt'l ĭz*, v. a. subtiliser.   [f.

subtility, *săb'tĭl tĭ* ou *săt'l tĭ*, s. subtilité.

subtle, *săt'l*, a. subtil, fin, rusé, adroit.

subtlety, *săt'l tĭ*, s. subtilité, finesse, ruse.

subtract, *săb trăkt'*, v. a. soustraire.   [f.

subtraction, *săb trăk'shŭn*, s. soustraction, f.   [pl. banlieue, f.

suburb, *săb'ĕrb*, s. faubourg, m. || -s, s.

suburban, *săb ĕr'băn*, a. faubourien.

subversion, *săb vĕr'shŭn*, s. subversion, f., renversement, m.

subversive, *săb vĕr'sĭv*, a. subversif.

subvert, *săb vĕrt'*, v. a. subvertir.

subverter, *săb vĕrt'ĕr*, s. destructeur, m.

subway, *săb'wā*, s. galerie souterraine, f.

succeed, *săk sēd'*, v. a. & n. succéder || suivre || réussir.

success, *săk sĕs'*, s. succès, m. || réussite, f.

successful, *săk sĕs'fōōl*, a. heureux, prospère ||-ly, ad. avec succès.

succession, *săk sĕsh'ŭn*, s. succession, suite, f. || postérité, f. || héritage, m.

successive, *săk sĕs'sĭv*, a. successif ||-ly, ad. successivement.

successor, *săk sĕs'sĕr*, s. successeur, m.

succinct, *săk sĭngkt'*, a. concis ||-ly, ad. succinctement, avec concision.

succour, *săk'kĕr*, s. secours, m., aide, f.

succour, *săk'kĕr*, v. a. secourir, aider, assister, seconder.

succulence, *săk'kū lĕns*, s. succulence, f.

succulent, *săk'kū lĕnt*, a. succulent.

succumb, *săk kŭmb'*, v. a. succomber.

such, *săch*, a. tel, pareil, semblable || ~ as, tel que || comme || ceux (celles) qui || ~ a one, un tel.   [absorber.

suck, *săk*, v. a. & n. sucer, teter || respirer ||

sucker, *săk'ĕr*, s. suceur, m. || piston d'une pompe, m. || suçoir, m.

sucking, *săk'ĭng*, ~-pig, s. cochon de lait, m. ||~-pipe, s. tuyau d'aspiration, m. || ~-pump, s. pompe aspirante, f.

suckle, *săk'l*, v. a. allaiter, donner le sein, donner à teter à un enfant.

suckling, *săk'lĭng*, s. enfant à la mamelle, nourrisson, m.   [ment, m.

suction, *săk'shŭn*, s. succion, f., aspirasudden, *săd'dn*, a. (-ly, ad.) soudain (ement) || subit || tout-à-coup || (all) of on a ~, tout-à-coup.

suddenness, *săd'dn nĕs*, s. soudaineté, f.

sudorific, *sū dŏr ĭf'ĭk*, s. sudorifique, m.

sudorific, *sū dŏr ĭf'ĭk*, a. sudorifique.

suds, *sădz*, s. eau de savon, f.

sue, *sū*, v. a. & n. poursuivre en justice || supplier, implorer.

suet, *sū'ĕt*, s. graisse, f. || suif, m.

suffer, *săf'fĕr*, v. a. & n. permettre || souffrir, supporter, endurer, éprouver.

sufferable, *săf'fĕr ă bl*, a. supportable.

sufferance, *săf'fĕr ăns*, s. tolérance, f. || on ~, par tolérance.

sufferer, *sŭf´fėr ėr,* s. qui souffre, m. ‖ victime, f. ‖ patient, m.

suffering, *sŭf´fėr ĭng,* s. souffrance, f.

suffice, *sŭf fīs´,* v. n. suffire.

sufficiency, *sŭf´fĭsh´ėn sĭ,* s. suffisance, f. ‖ capacité, f.   [ad. assez.

sufficient, *sŭf´fĭsh´ėnt,* a. suffisant ‖ -ly,

suffocate, *sŭf´fō kāt,* v.a. suffoquer, étouffer.   [m.

suffocation, *sŭf fō kā´shŭn,* s. étouffement,

suffragan, *sŭf´frā găn,* s. suffragant, m.

suffrage, *sŭf´frāj,* s. suffrage, vote, m.

suffuse, *sŭf fūz´,* v.a. répandre, remplir.

suffusion, *sŭf fū´zhŭn,* s. suffusion, f. ‖ épanchement, m.

sugar, *shŏŏg´ėr,* s. sucre, m. ‖ **barley ~,** sucre d'orge, m. ‖ **brown ~,** sucre brut, m. ‖ **lump ~,** sucre en pain, m. ‖ **moist ~,** cassonade, f. ‖ **sifted ~,** sucre en poudre, m. ‖ **~-baker,** s. confiseur, m. ‖ **~-basin,** s. sucrier, m. ‖ **~-candy,** s. candi, m. ‖ **~-cane,** s. canne à sucre, f. ‖ **~-house,** s. sucrerie, f. ‖ **~-loaf,** s. pain de sucre, m. ‖ **~-mill,** s. moulin à canne à sucre, m. ‖ **~-nippers,** s. pl. pincettes à sucre, f. pl. ‖ **~-plum,** s. dragée, f. ‖ **~-sifter,** s. cuillère à sucre, f. ‖ **~-tongs,** s. pl. pinces à sucre, f. pl.

sugar, *shŏŏg´ėr,* v.a. sucrer ‖ (fig.) adoucir.

sugary, *shŏŏg´ėr ĭ,* a. sucré.

suggest, *sŭj jĕst´,* v.a. suggérer, insinuer.

suggestion, *sŭj jĕst´yŭn,* s. suggestion, insinuation, f. ‖ instigation, persuasion, f.

suicidal, *sū´ĭ sīdl,* a. qui a rapport au suicide.   [mit ~, se suicider.

suicide, *sū´ĭ sīd,* s. suicide, m. ‖ **to commit ~,** suit, *sūt,* s. suite, série, f. ‖ assortiment, m. ‖ pétition, f. ‖ procès, m. ‖ poursuite judiciaire, f. ‖ recherche en mariage, f. ‖ costume complet, m.

suit, *sūt,* v. a. & n. assortir, adapter ‖ s'accorder, correspondre.

suitability, *sūt´ă bĭl´ĭ tĭ,* **suitableness,** *sūt´a bl nĕs,* s. conformité, convenance, f.

suitable, *sūt´ă bl,* a. convenable, conforme, propre.   [conformément.

suitably, *sūt´ă blĭ,* ad. convenablement,

suite, *swēt,* s. suite, f. ‖ train, m.

suitor, *sūt´ėr,* s. suppliant, m. ‖ plaideur, m. ‖ amant, m.   [bouder ‖ faire la mine.

sulk, *sŭlk,* v. n. **to ~, to be in the ~,**

sulkiness, *sŭl´kĭ nĕs,* s. bouderie, f.

sulky, *sŭl´kĭ,* a. bourru, hargneux.

sullen, *sŭl´lĕn,* a. maussade ‖ chagrin ‖ sombre ‖ opiniâtre ‖ -ly, ad. obstinément.

sullenness, *sŭl´lĕn nĕs,* s. humeur chagrine, f. ‖ obstination, f. ‖ malignité, f.

sully, *sŭl´lĭ,* v. a. souiller, tacher.

sulphate, *sŭl´fāt,* s. sulfate, m.

sulphide, *sŭl´fĭd,* s. sulfure, m.

sulphur, *sŭl´fėr,* s. soufre, m.

sulphuric, *sŭl fū´rĭk,* a. sulfurique.

sulphurous, *sŭl´fėr ŭs,* a. sulfureux.

sultan, *sŭl´tăn,* s. sultan, m.

sultana, *sŭl tä´nä,* s. sultane, f. ‖ **-s, ~-raisins,** s. pl. raisins secs sans pepins, m. pl.

sultriness, *sŭl´trĭ nĕs,* s. chaleur étouffante, f.

sultry, *sŭl´trĭ,* a. d'une chaleur étouffante.

sum, *sŭm,* s. somme, f., tout, total, m.

sum, *sŭm,* v. a. additionner ‖ résumer ‖ **to ~ up,** faire le total de ‖ résumer ‖ en résumé.   [ment.

summarily, *sŭm´mėr ĭ lĭ,* ad. sommaire-

summarise, *sŭm´mėr īz,* v. a. résumer.

summary, *sŭm´mėr ĭ,* s. sommaire, m.

summary, *sŭm´mėr ĭ,* a. sommaire.

summer, *sŭm´mėr,* s. été, m. ‖ **~-house,** s. pavillon, m. ‖ habitation d'été, f.

summer, *sŭm´mėr,* a. d'été.

summing-up, *sŭm´mĭng ŭp´,* s. résumé, m.

summit, *sŭm´mĭt,* s. sommet, m.

summon, *sŭm´mŭn,* v. a. sommer, citer, assigner ‖ ordonner, commander ‖ exciter.

summoner, *sŭm´mŭn ėr,* s. huissier, m.

summons, *sŭm´mŭnz,* s. sommation, citation, assignation, f.

sumptuary, *sŭm´tū ėr ĭ,* a. somptuaire.

sumptuous, *sŭm´tū ŭs,* a. somptueux ‖ -ly, ad. somptueusement.   [tuosité, f.

sumptuousness, *sŭm´tū ŭs nĕs,* s. somp-

sun, *sŭn,* s. soleil, m. ‖ **~-beam,** s. rayon du soleil, m. ‖ **~-bright,** a. radieux ‖ **~-burn,** s. hâle, m. ‖ **~-burnt,** a. hâlé, basané ‖ **~-dial,** s. cadran solaire, m. ‖ **~-flower,** s. tournesol, m. ‖ **~-light,** s. lumière du soleil, f.

Sunday, *sŭn´dā,* s. dimanche, m. ‖ **Low ~,** Quasimodo, f.

sunder, *sŭn´dėr,* v. a. séparer, partager.

sundries, *sŭn´drĭz,* s. pl. diverses choses, f. pl. ‖ faux frais, m. pl. ‖ (com.) divers, m. pl.

sundry, *sŭn´drĭ,* a. divers.   [m. pl.

sunless, *sŭn´lĕs,* a. sans soleil.

sunny, *sŭn´nĭ,* a. exposé au soleil, ensoleillé ‖ (fig.) ‖ heureux ‖ riant.

sunrise, *sŭn´rīz,* s. lever du soleil, m.

sunset, *sŭn´sĕt,* s. coucher du soleil, m.

sunshade, *sŭn´shād,* s. en-tout-cas, m.

sunshine, *sŭn´shīn,* s. clarté du soleil, f. ‖ (fig.) bonheur, m.

sunshiny, *sŭn´shīnĭ,* a. de soleil.

sunstroke, *sŭn´strōk,* s. coup de soleil, m.

sup, *sŭp,* s. gorgée, f.

sup, *sŭp,* v. a. humer, avaler ‖ siroter ‖ ~, v. n. souper.   [abonder.

superabound, *sū pėr ă bŏwnd´,* v. n. sur-

superabundance, *sū pėr ă bŭn´dăns,* s. surabondance, f.

superabundant, *sū pėr ă bŭn´dănt,* a. surabondant ‖ -ly, ad. surabondamment.

superadd, *sū pėr ăd´,* v. n. surajouter.

superaddition, *sū pėr ăd dĭsh´ŭn,* s. surcroît, m.   [suranné ‖ retraité.

superannuated, *sū pėr ăn´nū ā tĕd,* a.

superannuation, *sū pėr ăn nū ā´shŭn,* s. mise à la retraite, f. ‖ pension de retraite, f. ‖ **~-fund,** s. caisse de retraite, f.

superb, *sū pėrb´,* a. (-ly, ad.) superbe.   [m.

supercargo, *sū pėr kär´gō,* s. subrécargue,

supercilious, *sū pėr sĭl´ĭ ŭs,* a. hautain, arrogant.

supererogation, *sū pĕr ĕr rŏ gā' shŭn,* s. surérogation, f.

supererogatory, *sū pĕr ĕr rŏg' ă tĕr ĭ,* a. surérogatoire.   [superficiel(lement).

superficial, *sū pĕr fish' ăl,* a. (-ly, ad.)

superficies, *sū pĕr fish' ĭ ēz,* s. superficie, f.

superfine, *sū' pĕr fīn,* a. superfin.

superfluity, *sū pĕr flōō' ĭ tĭ,* s. superfluité, f. || superflu, m.

superfluous, *sū' pĕr flōō ŭs,* a. superflu || -ly, ad. avec superfluité || inutilement.

superhuman, *sū pĕr hū' măn,* a. surhumain.

superintend, *sū pĕr ĭn tĕnd',* v. a. surveiller.   [surveillance, f.

superintendence, *sū pĕr ĭn tĕnd' ĕns,* s.

superintendent, *sū pĕr ĭn tĕnd' ĕnt,* s. surintendant, inspecteur, m. || (rail.) chef de gare, m. || (of police) commissaire, m.

superior, *sŭ pē' rĭ ĕr,* s. supérieur, chef, m.   [signe.

superior, *sŭ pē' rĭ ĕr,* a. supérieur || in-

superioress, *sŭ pē' rĭ ĕr ĕs,* s. supérieure, f.

superiority, *sŭ pē' rĭ ŏr' ĭ tĭ,* s. supériorité, f.

superlative, *sŭ pĕr' lă tĭv,* s. superlatif, m.

superlative, *sŭ pĕr' lă tĭv,* a. suprême || -ly, ad. au suprême degré.

supernatural, *sū pĕr năt' ŭ răl* ou *sū pĕr năt' chŏŏ răl,* a. (-ly, ad.) surnaturel(lement).

supernumerary, *sū pĕr nū' mĕr ĕr ĭ,* s. surnuméraire, m. || comparse, m.

supernumerary, *sū pĕr nū' mĕr ĕr ĭ,* a. surnuméraire || supplémentaire.   [l'adresse.

superscribe, *sū pĕr skrīb',* v. a. mettre la suscription, adresse, f.

superscription, *sū pĕr skrĭp' shŭn,* s. suscription, adresse, f.

supersede, *sū pĕr sēd',* v. a. remplacer || faire supprimer || (law) surseoir à || rejeter.

superstition, *sū pĕr stĭsh' ŭn,* s. superstition, f.

superstitious, *sū pĕr stĭsh' ŭs,* a. superstitieux || -ly, ad. superstitieusement.

superstructure, *sū pĕr strŭk' chŏŏr,* s. édifice, m. || superstructure, f.

supervene, *sū pĕr vēn',* v. n. survenir.

supervise, *sū pĕr vīz',* v. a. surveiller, inspecter.   [lance, f.

supervision, *sū pĕr vĭzh' ŭn,* s. surveil-

supervisor, *sū pĕr vī' zĕr,* s. surveillant, inspecteur, m.

supine, *sū' pīn,* a. couché sur le dos || nonchalant || penché || -ly, ad. nonchalamment.   [f.

supineness, *sū pīn' nĕs,* s. nonchalance,

supper, *sŭp' pĕr,* s. souper, m. || the Lord's ∼, la Sainte Cène.

supplant, *sŭp plănt',* v. a. supplanter.

supple, *sŭp' pl,* a. souple.   [m.

supplement, *sŭp' plĕ mĕnt,* s. supplément,

supplement, *sŭp' plĕ mĕnt,* v. a. (to — with) suppléer || ajouter.

supplemental, *sŭp plĕ mĕnt' ăl,* **supplementary,** *sŭp plĕ mĕnt' ĕr ĭ,* a. supplémentaire.

suppleness, *sŭp' pl nĕs,* s. souplesse, f.

suppliant, *sŭp' plĭ ănt,* **supplicant,** *sŭp' plĭ kănt,* s. suppliant, m.

supplicate, *sŭp' plĭ kāt,* v. a. supplier.

supplication, *sŭp plĭ kā' shŭn,* s. supplication, f.

supplicatory, *sŭp' plĭ kă tĕr ĭ,* a. suppliant.

supplier, *sŭp plī' ĕr,* s. fournisseur, m.

supply, *sŭp plī',* s. fourniture, f. || provision, f. || approvisionnement, m. || secours, m. || demand and ∼, l'offre et la demande || supplies, s. pl. budget des dépenses, m.

supply, *sŭp plī',* v. a. suppléer || procurer, subvenir || approvisionner.

support, *sŭp pōrt',* s. soutien, appui, support, m. || in ∼ of, à l'appui de.

support, *sŭp pōrt',* v. a. supporter || souffrir || soutenir || entretenir || assister.

supportable, *sŭp pōrt' ă bl,* a. supportable.

supporter, *sŭp pōrt' ĕr,* s. soutien, appui, défenseur, m. || partisan, m.

supposable, *sŭp pō' ză bl,* a. supposable.

suppose, *sŭp pōz',* v.a. supposer, imaginer.

suppose, *sŭp pōz',* c. si.   [tion, f.

supposition, *sŭp pō zĭsh' ŭn,* s. supposi-

supposititious, *sŭp pŏz ĭ tĭsh' ŭs,* a. supposé.   [pêcher || étouffer, cacher.

suppress, *sŭp prĕs',* v. a. supprimer, em-

suppression, *sŭp prĕsh' ŭn,* s. suppression, f. || répression, f.

suppurate, *sŭp' pū răt,* v. n. suppurer.

suppuration, *sŭp pū ră' shŭn,* s. suppuration, f.   [supériorité, f.

supremacy, *sŭ prĕm' ă sĭ,* s. suprématie,

supreme, *sŭ prēm',* a. suprême || -ly, ad. au suprême degré.

surcease, *sĕr sēs',* s. arrêt, m., interruption, f.

sure, *shōr,* a. & ad. (-ly, ad.) sûr, certain (ement) || assuré, ferme || to be ∼! assurément! certainement! || I am ∼ I ma foi! || be ∼ to ..., soyez certain, soyez sûr de ...

sureness, *shōr' nĕs,* s. sûreté, f.

surety, *shōr' tĭ,* s. sûreté, f. || caution, garantie, f. || garant, m.

surf, *sĕrf,* s. brisant, ressac, m.

surface, *sĕr' făs,* s. surface, f.

surfeit, *sĕr' fĭt,* s. indigestion, satiété, f., dégoût, m.   [se soûler.

surfeit, *sĕr' fĭt,* v. a. &. n. soûler, rassasier

surge, *sĕrj,* s. vague, f., flot, m., houle, f.

surge, *sĕrj,* v. n. s'élever, s'enfler.

surgeon, *sĕr' jŭn,* s. chirurgien, m. || médecin-chirurgien, m.   [pharmacie, f.

surgery, *sĕr' jĕr ĭ,* s. chirurgie, f. || (place)

surgical, *sĕr' jĭ kăl,* a. chirurgical || de chirurgie.

surlily, *sĕr' lĭ lĭ,* ad. d'un air rechigné.

surliness, *sĕr' lĭ nĕs,* s. morosité, f.

surly, *sĕr' lĭ,* a. hargueux, morose.

surmise, *sĕr mīz',* s. soupçon, m.

surmise, *sĕr mīz',* v. a. soupçonner.

surmount, *sĕr mŏwnt',* v. a. surmonter.

surmountable, *sĕr mŏwnt' ă bl,* a. surmontable.

surname, *sĕr' năm,* s. surnom, m.

surname, *sĕr' năm,* v. a. surnommer.

surpass, *sĕr păs',* v. a. surpasser.

surpassing, *sĕr păs' ĭng,* a. éminent || -ly, ad. éminemment.

surplice, *sẽr'plĭs*, s. surplis, m.

surplus, *sẽr'plŭs*, surplusage, *sẽr'plŭs āj̆*, s. surplus, m. || remplissage, m., superfluité, f. || bouche-trou, m.

surprise, *sẽr'prĭz'*, s. surprise, f.

surprise, *sẽr'prĭz'*, v. a. surprendre.

surprising, *sẽr prī'zĭng*, a. surprenant || -ly, ad. étonnamment.

surrender, *sŭr rĕn'dẽr*, s. reddition, f. || cession, f.　　　　　　　　　　[rendre.

surrender, *sŭr rĕn'dẽr*, v. a. (& n.) (se)

surreption, *sŭr rĕp'shŭn*, s. subreption, f.

surreptitious, *sŭr rĕp tĭsh'ŭs*, a. subreptice || -ly, ad. clandestinement.

surrogate, *sŭr'rō gāt*, s. délégué, m.

surrogate, *sŭr'rō gāt*, v. a. subroger.

surround, *sŭr rŏwnd'*, v. a. environner, entourer || cerner.

surroundings, *sŭr rŏwnd'ĭngs*, s. pl. entourage, m. || environs, m. pl.

survey, *sẽr'vā*, s. coup d'œil, m. || examen, m. || arpentage, m. || inspection, f.

survey, *sẽr vā'*, v. a. surveiller, examiner, observer || arpenter.

surveying, *sẽr vā'ĭng*, s. arpentage, m.

surveyor, *sẽr vā'ẽr*, s. intendant, inspecteur, m. || expert, m. || arpenteur, m. || géomètre, m.　　　　　　　[tion, f.

surveyorship, *sẽr vā'ẽr shĭp*, s. inspection, f.

survival, *sẽr vī'val*, s. survivance, f.

survive, *sẽr vīv'*, v. a. & n. survivre.

survivor, *sẽr vī'vẽr*, s. survivant, m.

survivorship, *sẽr vī'vẽr shĭp*, s. survivance, f.

susceptible, *sŭs sĕp'tĭ bl*, a. susceptible.

suspect, *sŭs'pĕkt*, s. personne suspecte, f.

suspect, *sŭs pĕkt'*, v. a. & n. soupçonner, se douter de.

suspend, *sŭs pĕnd'*, v. a. suspendre || to one's judgment, suspendre son jugement || ~, v. n. (com.) cesser ses payements.

suspender(s), *sŭs pĕn'dẽr(z)*, s. (& pl.) bretelle, f. || suspensoir, m.

suspense, *sŭs pĕns'*, s. suspens, doute, m., incertitude, f. || cessation, f. || in ~, en suspens.

suspension, *sŭs pĕn'shŭn*, s. suspension (de payements), f. || ~-bridge, s. pont suspendu, m. || ~-railway, s. chemin de fer suspendu, m.　　　　　[soir, m.

suspensor(y), *sŭs pĕn'sẽr(ĭ)*, s. suspensuspicion, *sŭs pĭsh'ŭn*, s. soupçon, m. || (jur.) suspicion, f.

suspicious, *sŭs pĭsh'ŭs*, a. soupçonneux, suspect || -ly, ad. avec soupçon || d'une manière suspecte || [meur soupçonneuse, f.

suspiciousness, *sŭs pĭsh'ŭs nĕs*, s. humeur soupçonneuse, f.

sustain, *sŭs tān'*, v. a. soutenir, maintenir || supporter, souffrir || résister || secourir || appuyer.

sustainable, *sŭs tān'ă bl*, a. soutenable.

sustainer, *sŭs tān'ẽr*, s. soutien, appui, m.

sustenance, *sŭs'tĕ năns*, s. subsistance, f., entretien, m.

sutler, *sŭt'lẽr*, s. vivandier, cantinier, m.

suture, *sū'tŭr*, s. suture, f.

swab, *swŏb*, s. faubert, m.

swaddle, *swŏd'dl*, v. a. emmaillotter.

swagger, *swăg'gẽr*, v. n. faire le fanfaron.

swaggerer, *swăg'gẽr ẽr*, s. fanfaron, m.

swaggering, *swăg'gẽr ĭng*, s. fanfaronnade, f.　　　　　　　[m. || amant, m.

swain, *swān*, s. jeune homme, m. || berger.

swallow, *swŏl'lō*, s. hirondelle, f. || gosier, m. || ~-tail, a. en queue d'aronde.

swallow, *swŏl'lō*, v. a. avaler, engloutir, s'approprier.

swamp, *swŏmp*, s. marécage, marais, m.

swamp, *swŏmp*, v. a. plonger, s'enfoncer.

swampy, *swŏm'pĭ*, a. marécageux.

swan, *swŏn*, s. cygne, m. || ~-skin, s. molleton, m.

swap, *swŏp*, v. a. troquer, échanger.

sward, *swăwrd*, s. gazon, m., pelouse, f.

swarm, *swăwrm*, s. essaim, m. || fourmillière, f.

swarm, *swăwrm*, v. n. essaimer || fourmiller de || accourir en foule.

swarthiness, *swăwrth'ĭ nĕs*, s. teint basané, m.　　　　　　　　　　[sombre.

swarthy, *swăwrth'ĭ*, a. basané || noir,

swashbuckler, *swŏsh'bŭk lẽr*, s. fanfaron, m.　　　　　　　　　　　　[m.

swath, *swŏth*, s. andain, m.

swathe, *swăth*, s. maillot, m., langes, m. pl.

swathe, *swăth*, v. a. emmaillotter.

sway, *swā*, s. pouvoir, m., domination, f. || prépondérance, f.

sway, *swā*, v. a. & n. manier, brandir || gouverner, maitriser, influencer.

swear, *swâr*, v. a. & n. ir. faire prêter serment à || jurer, blasphémer.

swearing, *swâr'ĭng*, s. prestation de serment, f. || jurons, m. pl.

sweat, *swĕt*, s. sueur, transpiration, f. || peine, f. || bloody ~, hémorrhagie du

sweat, *swĕt*, v. n. suer.　　　　　[derme, f.

sweep, *swēp*, s. balayage, coup de balai, m. || ramoneur, m. || oscillation, f. || courbe, f. || cambrure, f. || portée, f. || chimney-~, ramoneur, m. || ~-net, s. drège, f.

sweep, *swēp*, v. a. & n. ir. balayer || ramoner || glisser sur || cambrer || frapper || osciller.

sweeper, *swēp'ẽr*, s. balayeur, m. || ramoneur, m. || crossing-~, balayeur, balayeuse de rue, m. & f.

sweeping, *swēp'ĭng*, a. rapide || général.

sweepings, *swēp'ĭngz*, s. pl. balayures, f. pl.　　　　　　　　　　　　[jeux, f.

sweepstake, *swēp'stāk*, s. course par enjeux.

sweet, *swēt*, s. douceur, f., plaisir, m.

sweet, *swēt*, a. doux, savoureux, odorant || mélodieux || gracieux, tendre, aimable, agréable || frais || ~-briar, s. (bot.) églantier odorant, m. || ~-pea, s. pois de senteur, m. || ~-scented, a. odoriférant || ~-stuffs, s. pl. parfums, m. pl. || ~-William, s. (bot.) œillet de poète, m. || -ly, ad. doucement || agréablement || mélodieusement.

sweetbread, *swĕt'brĕd*, s. ris de veau, m.

sweeten, *swēt'n*, v. a. adoucir, sucrer || soulager || purifier.

sweetener, *swēt'n ẽr*, s. adoucissant, m.

sweetening, *swēt'n ĭng,* s. adoucissement, m. || désinfection, f. [amoureuse, f.
sweetheart, *swēt' hârt,* s. amoureux, m.,
sweetmeat, *swēt' mēt,* s. sucrerie, f., bon-bon, m.
sweetness, *swēt' nĕs,* s. douceur, suavité, f.
swell, *swĕl,* s. bombement, m. || élévation, f. || houle, f. || pédale d'expression, f. || gandin, m.
swell, *swĕl,* v. a. & n. ir. enfler, gonfler, augmenter || bouffir d'orgueil || s'enfler, se bouffir, s'augmenter || accroître || s'enor-
swell, *swĕl,* a. à la mode. [gueillir.
swelling, *swĕl' ĭng,* s. enflure, tumeur, f.
swelter, *swĕl' tĕr,* v. a. & n. brûler, griller || étouffer de chaleur.
swerve, *swĕrv,* v. n. rôder, s'écarter.
swift, *swĭft,* s. martinet, m.
swift, *swĭft,* a. (-ly, ad.) vite || prompt (ement) || rapide(ment) || léger.
swiftness, *swĭft' nĕs,* s. vitesse, prompti-
swill, *swĭll,* s. lavure, f. [tude, rapidité, f.
swill, *swĭll,* v. a. boire beaucoup || enivrer.
swim, *swĭm,* s. nageoire, vessie, f. || vessie natatoire (des poissons); f.
swim, *swĭm,* v. n. ir. nager || flotter sur l'eau || passer légèrement.
swimmer, *swĭm' mĕr,* s. nageur, m.
swimming, *swĭm' ĭng,* s. nage, f. || vertige, m. || ~-match, s. pari à la nage, m. || ~-school, s. école de natation, f.
swimmingly, *swĭm' ĭng lĭ,* ad. aisément.
swindle, *swĭn' dl,* v. a. escroquer.
swindler, *swĭn' dlĕr,* s. escroc, m.
swindling, *swĭnd' lĭng,* s. escroquerie, f.
swine, *swĭn,* s. cochon, m. || ~-herd, s. porcher, m.
swing, *swĭng,* s. oscillation, f. || dandine-ment, m. || branle, m. || escarpolette, f. || libre cours, m. || ~-bridge, s. pont tour-nant, m. || ~-door, s. porte battante, f. || ~-glass, s. miroir à bascule, m.
swing, *swĭng,* v. a. & n. ir. balancer, agiter, brandir, brandiller, flotter, se balancer.
swinish, *swi'nĭsh,* a. de cochon || mal-propre || bestial.
swipes, *swĭps,* s. mauvaise bière, f. || abondance, f. || piquette, f.
swish, *swĭsh,* v. a. agiter, remuer.
switch, *swĭch,* s. houssine, baguette, f. || (rail.) aiguille, f.
switch, *swĭch,* v. a. houssiner. [fleur, m.
switchman, *swĭch' măn,* s. (rail.) aiguil-
swivel, *swĭv' l,* s. tourniquet, m. || ~-gun, s. pierrier, m.
swoon, *swŏn,* s. évanouissement, m.
swoon, *swŏn,* v. n. s'évanouir.
swoop, *swŏp,* s. action d'un oiseau qui fond sur la proie, f. || at one ~, d'un seul coup.
sweep, *swŏp,* v. a. fondre sur, s'abattre sur || enlever.
sword, *sŏrd,* s. épée, f. || ~-belt, s. bau-drier, m. || ~-cutler, s. fourbisseur, m. || ~-fish, s. épée-de-mer, f. || ~-knot, s. dragonne, f. || ~-stick, s. canne à épée, f.
swordsman, *sŏrdz' măn,* s. tireur d'armes,
sworn, *swŏrn,* a. juré, assermenté. [m.

Sybarite, *sĭb' ă rīt,* s. sybarite, m.
Sybaritic(al), *sĭb ă rĭt' ĭk (ăl),* a. volup-tueux.
sycamore, *sĭk' ă mōr,* s. (bot.) sycomore, m.
sycophancy, *sĭk' ō făn sĭ,* s. adulation, f.
sycophant, *sĭk' ō fănt,* s. flagorneur, m.
syllabic, *sĭl lăb' ĭk,* a. syllabique.
syllable, *sĭl' lă bl,* s. syllabe, f.
syllabus, *sĭl' lă bŭs,* s. sommaire, pro-gramme, m.
syllogism, *sĭl' lō jĭzm,* s. syllogisme, m.
sylph, *sĭlf,* s. sylphe, m. || sylphide, f.
sylvan, *sĭl' văn,* a. des bois, champêtre.
symbol, *sĭm' bŏl,* s. symbole, m.
symbolic, *sĭm bŏl' ĭk,* a. (-ally, ad.) sym-bolique(ment).
symmetrical, *sĭm mĕt' rĭ kăl,* a. symé-trique || -ly, ad. avec symétrie.
symmetry, *sĭm' mĕ trĭ,* s. symétrie, f.
sympathetic, *sĭm pă thĕt' ĭk,* a. sympa-thique || -ally, ad. par sympathie.
sympathise, *sĭm' pă thīz,* v. n. sympa-thiser, compatir à.
sympathy, *sĭm' pă thĭ,* s. sympathie, f.
symphony, *sĭm' fō nĭ,* s. symphonie, f.
symptom, *sĭm' tŭm,* s. symptôme, indice, m.
symptomatic, *sĭm tō măt' ĭk,* a. symptô-matique.
synagogue, *sĭn' ă gŏg,* s. synagogue, f.
syncope, *sĭn' kō pē,* s. (méd.) syncope, f.
syndic, *sĭn' dĭk,* s. syndic, m.
synod, *sĭn' ŏd,* s. synode, m.
synodal, *sĭn' ō dăl,* synodic, *sĭn ŏd' ĭk,* a. synodal, synodique.
synonym, *sĭn' ō nĭm,* s. synonyme, m.
synonymus, *sĭn ŏn' ĭ mŭs,* a. synonyme.
synonymy, *sĭn ŏn' ĭ mĭ,* s. synonymie, f.
synopsis, *sĭ nŏp' sĭs,* s. synopsis, f.
synoptical, *sĭn ŏp' tĭk ăl,* a. synoptique.
syntax, *sĭn' tăks,* s. syntaxe, f.
synthesis, *sĭn' thĕ sĭs,* s. synthèse, f.
syphilis, *sĭf' ĭ lĭs,* s. (méd.) syphilis, f.
syphilitic, *sĭf ĭ lĭt' ĭk,* a. (méd.) syphili-tique.
syringa, *sĭ rĭng' gă,* s. (bot.) syringa, m.
syringe, *sĭr' ĭnj,* s. seringue, f.
syringe, *sĭr' ĭnj,* v. a. seringuer.
syrup, *sĭr' ŭp,* s. vide sirup.
system, *sĭs' tĕm,* s. système, régime, m., méthode, f. || organisme, m., économie, f.
systematic, *sĭs tĕm ăt' ĭk,* a. (-ally, ad.) systématique(ment).

T.

T.; to a ~, parfaitement, exactement.
tabby, *tăb' bĭ,* a. tabisé, ondé, rayé.
tabernacle, *tăb' ĕr năk l,* s. tabernacle, m.
table, *tā' bl,* s. table, f., tableau, m. || bureau, m. || liste, f. || to clear the ~, desservir la table || to turn the ~s on one, faire tourner les chances contre qn. f. || ~-beer, s. petite bière, f. || ~-cloth, s. nappe, f. || ~-land, s. plateau, m. || ~-spoon, s. cuiller (à bouche), f. || ~-talk,

s. propos de table, m. || ~~wine, s. vin ordinaire, m.
tablet, *tăb'lĕt,* s. carreau, m., tablette, f.
taboo, *tă bŏ',* s. tabou, m.
taboo, *tă bŏ',* v. a. interdire.
tabular, *tăb'ū lĕr,* a. en forme de table.
tabulate, *tăb'ū lāt,* v. a. disposer en forme de table.   [sous-entendu.
tacit, *tăs'ĭt,* a. (-ly, ad.) tacite(ment) ||
taciturn, *tăs'ĭ tẽrn,* a. taciturne.
taciturnity, *tăs ĭ tẽrn'ĭ tĭ,* s. taciturnité, f.
tack, *tăk,* s. petit clou, m., broquette, f. || (mar.) bordée, f. || amure, f.   [louvoyer.
tack, *tăk,* v. a. accrocher, attacher || (mar.)
tackle, *tăk'kl,* s. cordages d'un vaisseau, m. pl. || poulie, f. || ustensiles, m. pl.
tact, *tăkt,* s. tact, m.
tactful, *tăkt'fool,* a. plein de tact, discret.
tactician, *tăk tish'ăn,* s. tacticien, f.
tactics, *tăk'tĭks,* s. pl. tactique, f.
tadpole, *tăd'pōl,* s. petit crapaud, m.
taffeta, *tăf'ĕ tă,* s. taffetas, m.
taffrail, *tăf'rāl,* s. (mar.) couronnement || de la poupe, m.
tag, *tăg,* s. ferret, m.
tag, *tăg,* v. a. ferrer || joindre.
tag-rag, *tăg'răg,* s. canaille, f.
tail, *tāl,* s. queue, f. || culée, f. || ~~piece, s. cul-de-lampe, m.
tailor, *tāl'ĕr,* s. tailleur, m.
tailor, *tāl'ĕr,* v. n. exercer l'état de tailleur.
tailoress, *tāl'ĕr ĕs,* s. tailleuse, f.
tailoring, *tāl'ŏr ĭng,* s. métier ou ouvrage de tailleur, m.   [f.
taint, *tānt,* s. souillure, tache, f. || infection;
taint, *tānt,* v. a. gâter, souiller, infecter || ~ed, gâté.
taintless, *tānt'lĕs,* a. sans tache, pur.
take, *tāk,* s. prise, f. || pêche, f.
take, *tāk,* v. a. & n. ir. prendre, saisir, s'emparer de || arrêter, attraper, prendre, emporter || louer || accepter, recevoir, admettre || tolérer, souffrir, supposer || comprendre, penser, croire || tendre || se diriger vers || avoir effet, réussir || plaire, charmer || **to ~ one for,** prendre qn. pour || **I ~ it,** je pense, ce me semble, m'est avis || **to be much ~n with,** être fort épris de || **to ~ away,** enlever, emporter || **to ~ in,** rentrer || (fig.) comprendre || (fam.) tromper, duper || **to ~ off,** enlever, ôter || (fam.) imiter || **to ~ to,** se mettre à || **to ~ (very much) to one,** prendre qn. en amitié || **~~in,** s. duperie, f. || attrape, f. || ~~off, s. caricature, f.
taker, *tā'kĕr,* s. preneur, m.
taking, *tā'kĭng,* s. prise, f. || **to be in a great ~ about,** être en grande inquiétude au sujet de.
taking, *tā'kĭng,* a. séduisant.
tale, *tāl,* s. conte, m., histoire, f. || compte, m. || ~~bearer, s. rapporteur, m.
talent, *tăl'ĕnt,* s. talent génie, m.
talented, *tăl'ĕnt ĕd,* a. de talent.
talisman, *tăl'ĭs măn,* s. talisman, m.
talk, *tawk,* s. conversation, f., discours, babil, m., causerie, f. || bruit, m.
talk, *tawk,* v. n. parler, causer, jaser ||

raisonner || **to ~ one over,** enjôler qn. || **to ~ one into, out of,** persuader qn. à, dissuader qn. de.
talkative, *tawk'ă tĭv,* a. babillard, jaseur.
talker, *tawk'ĕr,* s. parleur, babillard, vantall, *tawl,* a. grand, haut.   [tard, m.
tallow, *tăl'lō,* s. suif, m. || ~~chandler, s. fabricant de chandelles, m.
tallowy, *tăl'lō ĭ,* a. graisseux.
tally, *tăl'lĭ,* v. a. & n. ajuster, s'accorder || ~~man, s. fripier, m. || ~~system (~~trade), s. commerce à tempérament, m.
talon, *tăl'ŏn,* s. serre, f.
tamable, *tā'mă bl,* a. apprivoisable.
tamarind, *tăm'ă rĭnd,* s. tamarin, m.
tamarisk, *tăm'ă rĭsk,* s. tamarisc, m.
tambour, *tăm'bŏr,* s. tambour de basque, m.
tambour, *tăm'bŏr,* v. a. broder au tambour.
tambourine, *tăm bŏŏr ēn',* s. tambourin, m.
tame, *tām,* v. a. apprivoiser || dompter.
tame, *tām,* a. apprivoisé, dompté, doux, domestique || abattu, humilié || -ly, ad. sans résistance || avec soumission.
tameness, *tām'nĕs,* s. apprivoisement, m. || timidité, f.
tamer, *tā'mĕr,* s. dompteur, m.
tammy, *tăm'mĭ,* s. tamis, filtre, m.
tamper, *tăm'pĕr,* v. a. chercher à corrompre || prendre des remèdes || tremper dans || se mêler || tâtonner.
tan, *tăn,* s. tan, m.   [tannerie, f.
tan, *tăn,* v. a. tanner || hâler || ~~yard, s.
tandem, *tăn'dĕm,* s. tandem, cabriolet à deux chevaux en flèche, m. || bicycle à deux, m.
tangent, *tăn'jĕnt,* s. tangente, f.
tangible, *tăn'jĭ bl,* a. tangible, tactile.
tangle, *tăng'gl,* v. a. embarrasser, embrouiller.
tank, *tăngk,* s. étang, m. || citerne, f.
tankard, *tăng'kĕrd,* s. grand pot à couvercle, m.
tanner, *tăn'nĕr,* s. tanneur, m.
tannery, *tăn'nĕr ĭ,* s. tannerie, f.
tannin, *tăn'nĭn,* s. (chem.) tanin, m.
tansy, *tăn'zĭ,* s. (bot.) tanaisie, f.
tantalise, *tăn'tă līs,* v. a. faire souffrir le supplice de Tantale à, tourmenter.
tantamount, *tănt'ă mŏŭnt,* a. équivalent.
tantivy, *tăn tĭv'ĭ,* ad. à bride abattue.
tantrum, *tăn'trŭm,* s. mauvaise humeur, f.
tap, *tăp,* s. tape, f., coup léger, m. || cannette, f., robinet de bois, m. || cabaret, m. || ~~room, s. cabaret, m. || estaminet, m.
tap, *tap,* v. a. taper, percer un tonneau || faire la ponction.   [s. ver solitaire, m.
tape, *tāp,* s. ruban de fil, m. || ~~worm,
taper, *tā'pĕr,* s. bougie, f.
taper, *tā'pĕr,* v. n. se terminer en pointe.
taper, *tā'pĕr,* a. conique.
tapestry, *tăp'ĕs trĭ,* s. tapisserie, f.
tapis, *tă pē',* s. tapis, m.
tapping, *tăp'pĭng,* s. mise en perce, f. || ponction, f. || incision, f.
tapster, *tăp'stĕr,* s. garçon de cabaret, m.
tar, *tăr,* s. goudron, m. || matelot, m. || **Jack Tar,** s. marin, m.

tar, *tär,* v. a. goudronner. [ment.
tardily, *tär' dĭ lĭ,* ad. tardivement, lente-
tardiness, *tär' dĭ nĕs,* s. lenteur, f.
tardy, *tär' dĭ,* a. tardif, lent ‖ en retard.
tare, *tär,* s. ivraie, f. ‖ (com.) tare, f.
tarentula, *tär ĕn' tū lä,* s. tarentule, f.
target, *tär' gĕt,* s. cible, f. ‖ **~-practice,** s. tir à la cible, m.
tariff, *tär' ĭf,* s. tarif, m.
tarlatan, *tär' lä tän,* s. tarlatane, f.
tarnish, *tär' nĭsh,* v. a. (& n.) (se) ternir.
tarpaulin, *tär pāw' lĭn,* s. toile goudronnée, f.
tarragon, *tär' rä gŏn,* s. estragon, m. ‖ [f.
tarry, *tär' rĭ,* v. n. tarder, attendre.
tarry, *tär' rĭ,* a. goudronné.
tart, *tärt,* s. tarte, f.
tart, *tärt,* a. (-ly, ad.) aigre(ment) ‖ acide.
tartan, *tär' tän,* s. tartan (étoffe), m.
tartar, *tär' tẽr,* s. tartre, m. ‖ **to catch a ~,** s'adresser à plus fort que soi.
tartish, *tärt' ĭsh,* a. aigrelet.
tartness, *tärt' nĕs,* s. aigreur, f.
task, *täsk,* s. tâche, besogne, f., pensum, m. ‖ **to take to ~,** réprimander.
task, *täsk,* v. a. imposer une tâche.
tassel, *tăs' ĕl,* s. gland de soie, m. ‖ tourne-feuille, m.
tasseled, *tăs' ĕld,* a. orné de glands.
taste, *tāst,* s. goût, m. ‖ saveur, odeur, f. ‖ affection, inclination, f. ‖ discernement, m. ‖ échantillon, m.
taste, *tāst,* v. a. & n. goûter ‖ sentir ‖ ap-prouver ‖ avoir du goût, sentir.
tasted, *tāst' ĕd,* a. de . . . goût.
tasteful, *tāst' fŏŏl,* a. savoureux ‖ **-ly,** ad. avec goût.
tasteless, *tāst' lĕs,* a. sans goût, fade.
taster, *tāst' ẽr,* s. dégustateur, m.
tasty, *tāst' ĭ,* a. qui a bon goût.
tatter, *tăt' tẽr,* s. guenille, f., lambeau, m.
tatterdemalion, *tăt tẽr dē māl' yŭn,* s. gueux, va-nu-pieds, m.
tattle, *tăt' tl,* s. babil, caquet, m.
tattle, *tăt' tl,* v. a. babiller, jaser.
tattler, *tăt' tlẽr,* s. babillard, m.
tattoo, *tăt tŏŏ',* s. (mil.) retraite, f. ‖ tatouage
tattoo, *tăt tŏŏ',* v. a. tatouer. [m.
taunt, *tawnt,* s. insulte, f. ‖ réprimande, f. ‖ raillerie, f.
taunt, *tawnt,* v. a. insulter ‖ tourner en ridicule ‖ réprimander. [lence.
tauntingly, *tawnt' ĭng lĭ,* ad. avec inso-
taut, *tawt,* a. raide, fortement tendu.
tautological, *taw tŏ lŏj' ĭ kăl,* a. tautolo-gique.
tautology, *taw tŏl' ō jĭ,* s. tautologie, f.
tavern, *tăv' ẽrn,* s. cabaret, m., auberge, f. ‖ **~-keeper,** s. aubergiste, m.
taw, *taw,* s. bille (à jouer), f.
taw, *taw,* v. a. passer en mégie.
tawdriness, *taw' drĭ nĕs,* s. clinquant, m.
tawdry, *taw' drĭ,* a. clinquant ‖ éclatant.
tawny, *taw' nĭ,* a. tanné ‖ basané.
tax, *tăks,* s. taxe, f., impôt, m. ‖ **~-gatherer,** s. percepteur, m. ‖ **~-payer,** s. contribuable, m. & f. [accuser.
tax, *tăks,* v. a. taxer, imposer une taxe ‖

taxable, *tăks' ä bl,* a. imposable.
taxation, *tăks ä' shŭn,* s. taxation, f.
taxi(cab), *tăks' ĭ (kăb),* s. taximètre, m. [m.
taxidermist, *tăks ĭ dẽr' mist,* s. empailleur,
taxidermy, *tăks ĭ dẽr' mĭ,* s. empaillage, m.
tea, *tē,* s. thé, m. ‖ **~-caddy,** s. boîte à thé, f. ‖ **~-garden,** s. guinguette, f. ‖ **~-kettle,** s. bouilloire, f. ‖ **~-party,** s. thé, m. ‖ **~-plant, ~-shrub,** s. arbre à thé, m. ‖ **~-pot,** s. théière, f. ‖ **~-service, ~-set,** s. ‖ **~-things,** s. pl. service à thé, m. ‖ **~-table,** s. table à thé, f.
teach, *tēch,* v. a. & n. ir. enseigner, ap-prendre ‖ professer.
teachable, *tēch' ä bl,* a. docile.
teacher, *tēch' ẽr,* s. maître, précepteur, qui enseigne, m.
teaching, *tēch' ĭng,* s. instruction, f.
teal, *tēl,* s. sarcelle, f.
team, *tēm,* s. attelage, m. [telage, m.
teamster, *tēm' stẽr,* s. conducteur d'un at-
tear, *tẽr,* s. larme, f.
tear, *tär,* v. a. ir. déchirer, arracher ‖ (rail.) enlever les rails ‖ **~,** v. n. (to **~ along**) courir vite.
tearless, *tẽr' lĕs,* a. sans larmes. [lainer.
tease, *tēz,* v. a. tourmenter, importuner ‖
teasel, *tē' zl,* s. chardon de foulon, m.
teaser, *tē' zẽr,* s. importun, m.
teat, *tēt,* s. tette, f., teton, m.
technical, *tĕk' nĭ kăl,* a. technique.
technicalities, *tĕk nĭ kăl' ĭ tĭz,* s. pl. ter-mes techniques, m. pl.
technology, *tĕk nŏl' ō jĭ,* s. technologie, f.
tedious, *tē' dĭ ŭs,* a. ennuyeux, fatigant ‖ **-ly,** ad. ennuyeusement.
tediousness, *tē' dĭ ŭs nĕs,* s. tedium, *tē' dĭ ŭm,* s. ennui, m. ‖ lenteur, f.
teem, *tēm,* v. a. & n. enfanter, mettre bas ‖ être enceinte.
teeth, *tēth,* s. pl. dents, f. pl.
teethe, *tēth,* v. n. faire les dents.
teething, *tēth' ĭng,* s. dentition, f.
teetotal, *tē tō' tăl,* a. de tempérance.
teetotaler, *tē tō' tăl ẽr,* s. buveur d'eau, m.
teetotalism, *tē tō' tăl ĭzm,* s. tempérance, f.
teetotum, *tē tō' tŭm,* s. toton, m.
tegument, *tĕg' ū mĕnt,* s. tégument, m.
telegram, *tĕl' ē grăm,* s. télégramme, m.
telegraph, *tĕl' ē gräf,* s. télégraphe, m.
telegraph, *tĕl' ē gräf,* v. a. télégraphier.
telegraphic, *tĕl ē gräf' ĭk,* a. télégra-phique.
telegraphy, *tĕl ĕg' rä fĭ,* s. télégraphie, f.
telephone, *tĕl' ē fōn,* s. téléphone, m.
telephonic, *tĕl ē fŏn' ĭk,* a. téléphonique.
telephony, *tĕl' ē fŏn ĭ,* s. téléphonie, f.
telescope, *tĕl' ē skōp,* s. télescope, m. ‖ **~-table,** s. table à rallonges, f.
telescopic, *tĕl ē skŏp' ĭk,* a. télescopique.
telescopy, *tĕl ĕs' kō pĭ,* s. télescopie, f.
tell, *tĕl,* v. a. & n. ir. dire, conter ‖ instruire, informer, annoncer, publier ‖ compter ‖ **~-tale,** s. rapporteur, m. ‖ compteur, m.
teller, *tĕl' lẽr,* s. diseur, rapporteur, narra-teur, m. ‖ compteur, m.

telling, *tĕl'ĭng,* a. expressif ‖ énergique ‖ frappant ‖ mordant.   [f.

temerity, *tĕ mĕr'ĭ tĭ,* s. témérité, hardiesse,

temper, *tĕm'pĕr,* s. caractère, naturel, m. ‖ humeur, f. ‖ combinaison, f. ‖ trempe, f. ‖ sang-froid, m. ‖ **to be in a ~,** être de mauvaise humeur ‖ **to be in a ~ to,** être d'humeur à ‖ **good, bad -ed,** a. qui a le caractère bien fait, mal fait.

temper, *tĕm'pĕr,* v. a. mêler, détremper, délayer ‖ tempérer ‖ modérer.

temperament, *tĕm'pĕr ă mĕnt,* s. tempérament, m.   [modération, f.

temperance, *tĕm'pĕr ăns,* s. tempérance, f.

temperate, *tĕm'pĕr ăt,* a. tempéré, modéré, frugal ‖ **-ly,** ad. avec tempérance.

temperateness, *tĕm'pĕr ăt nĕs,* s. tempérance, f., sang-froid, m.

temperature, *tĕm'pĕr ă tūr,* s. température, f.

tempest, *tĕm'pĕst,* s. tempête, f., orage, m.

tempestuous, *tĕm pĕs'tū ŭs,* a. orageux.

Templar, *tĕm'plĕr,* s. étudiant (anglais) en droit, m. ‖ templier, m.

temple, *tĕm'pl,* s. temple, m. ‖ tempe, f.

temporal, *tĕm'pō răl,* a. (**-ly,** ad.) temporel(lement).   [m.

temporality, *tĕm pō răl'ĭ tĭ,* s. temporel,

temporarily, *tĕm'pō rā rĭ lĭ,* ad. temporairement.   [temporaire, m.

temporariness, *tĕm'pō rā rĭ nĕs,* s. état

temporary, *tĕm'pō rā rĭ,* a. temporaire.

temporise, *tĕm'pō rĭz,* v. n. temporiser.

tempt, *tĕmt,* v. a. tenter ‖ entraîner à.

temptation, *tĕm tā'shŭn,* s. tentation, f.

tempter, *tĕm'tĕr,* s. tentateur, m.

temptress, *tĕm'trĕs,* s. tentatrice, f.

ten, *tĕn,* s. dizaine, f.

ten, *tĕn,* a. dix.

tenable, *tĕn'ă bl,* a. (mil.) tenable.

tenacious, *tĕnā'shŭs,* a. tenace ‖ **-ly,** ad. opiniâtrément.   [f. ‖ entêtement, m.

tenacity, *tĕnăs'ĭ tĭ,* s. ténacité, viscosité,

tenancy, *tĕn'ăn sĭ,* s. usufruit, m.

tenant, *tĕn'ănt,* s. tenancier, fermier, m. ‖ locataire, m. ‖ habitant, m., habitante, f.

tenant, *tĕn'ănt,* v. a. tenir à bail.

tenantless, *tĕn'ănt lĕs,* a. inhabité.

tench, *tĕnsh,* s. tanche, f.

tend, *tĕnd,* v. a. & n. garder, avoir soin ‖ tendre à ‖ contribuer à.

tendency, *tĕn'dĕn sĭ,* s. tendance, f.

tender, *tĕn'dĕr,* s. offre, m. ‖ (rail.) tender, m. ‖ **legal ~,** monnaie légale, f.

tender, *tĕn'dĕr,* v. a. offrir, proposer, présenter ‖ estimer.

tender, *tĕn'dĕr,* a. (**-ly,** ad.) tendre(ment) ‖ sensible ‖ délicat(ement) ‖ jaloux.

tenderness, *tĕn'dĕr nĕs,* s. tendreté, f. ‖ tendresse, affection, f.

tendon, *tĕn'dŏn,* s. tendon, m.

tendril, *tĕn'drĭl,* s. (bot.) vrille, f.

tenement, *tĕn'ĕmĕnt,* s. tènement, m. ‖ maison, f. ‖ **~-house,** s. logement de famille, m.

tenet, *tĕn'ĕt,* s. dogme, principe, m.

tenfold, *tĕn'fōld,* a. décuple.

tennis, *tĕn'nĭs,* s. paume, f. ‖ **~-court,** s. jeu de paume, m.

tenor, *tĕn'ĕr,* s. caractère, m. ‖ style, m. ‖ teneur, f. ‖ (mus.) ténor, m. ‖ viole, f.

tense, *tĕns,* s. (gr.) temps, m.

tense, *tĕns,* a. tendu, raide.

tension, *tĕn'shŭn,* s. tension, f.

tent, *tĕnt,* s. tente, f.

tent, *tĕnt,* v. n. camper.

tentative, *tĕn'tă tĭv,* a. d'essai ‖ expérimental ‖ **-ly,** ad. à titre d'essai.

tenter, *tĕnt'ĕr,* s. crochet, m. ‖ séchoir, m. ‖ **~-hook,** s. clou à crochet, m. ‖ **to be on ~-hooks,** être sur des charbons ardents.   [(of the month) dix.

tenth, *tĕnth,* a. (**-ly,** ad.) dixième(ment) ‖

tenuity, *tĕ nū'ĭ tĭ,* s. ténuité, f.

tenure, *tĕn'ūr,* s. possession, occupation, tenure, f.   [f. ‖ tenure, f.

tepid, *tĕp'ĭd,* a. tiède.

tercentenary, *tĕr sĕn'tĕn ĕr ĭ,* a. triséculaire.   [laire.

teredo, *tĕr ē'dō,* s. perce-bois, f.

tergiversation, *tĕr jĭ vĕr să'shŭn,* s. tergiversation, évasion, f.

term, *tĕrm,* s. terme, m. ‖ limite, f. ‖ -ition, stipulation, f. ‖ expression, f. ‖ inscription, f. ‖ **to be on good ~s with one,** être bien avec qn. ‖ **to come to ~s with one,** s'arranger avec qn. ‖ **to reduce to the lowest ~s,** (math.) réduire à sa plus simple expression.

term, *tĕrm,* v. a. appeler, nommer.

termagant, *tĕr'mă gănt,* s. mégère, f.

terminal, *tĕr'mĭ năl,* a. extrême.

terminate, *tĕr'mĭ nāt,* v. a. (& n.) (se) terminer ‖ mettre un terme à ‖ (fig.) aboutir.

termination, *tĕr mĭ nā'shŭn,* s. borne, limite, f. ‖ conclusion, f. ‖ (gr.) terminaison, f.

terminus, *tĕr'mĭ nŭs,* s. (rail.) embarcadère, m.   [dère, débarcadère, m.

tern, *tĕrn,* s. sterne, m., hirondelle de mer, f.   [à la danse, chorégraphique.

terpsichorean, *tĕrp sĭk ō rē'ăn,* a. relatif

terrace, *tĕr'răs,* s. terrasse, f.

terrace, *tĕr'răs,* v. a. terrasser.

terra-cotta, *tĕr'ră cŏt'tă,* s. terre cuite, f.

terrapin, *tĕr'ră pĭn,* s. tortue de mer, f.

terrestrial, *tĕr rĕs'trĭ ăl,* a. terrestre.

terrible, *tĕr'rĭ bl,* a. terrible.

terribly, *tĕr'rĭ blĭ,* ad. terriblement.

terrier, *tĕr'rĭ ĕr,* s. terrier, m.

terrific, *tĕr rĭf'ĭk,* a. terrible.

terrify, *tĕr'rĭ fī,* v. a. effrayer.

territorial, *tĕr rĭ tō'rĭ ăl,* a. territorial.

territory, *tĕr'rĭ tŏr ĭ,* s. territoire, m.

terror, *tĕr'rĕr,* s. terreur, f. ‖ effroi, m.

terrorise, *tĕr'rŏr ĭz,* v. a. terroriser.

terrorism, *tĕr'rŏr ĭzm,* s. terrorisme, m.

terse, *tĕrs,* a. net ‖ élégant ‖ **-ly,** ad. proprement ‖ élégamment.

terseness, *tĕrs'nĕs,* s. netteté, f.

tertian, *tĕr'shŭn,* a. tiers ‖ **~ fever,** s. fièvre tierce, f.

tertiary, *tĕr'shĭ ĕr ĭ,* a. tertiaire.

tesselate, *tĕs'sĕ lāt,* v. a. marqueter.

test, *tĕst,* s. épreuve, f. ‖ pierre de touche, f. ‖ (chim.) réactif, m. ‖ **~-glass, ~-tube,** s. éprouvette, f.

---

lāte, hăt, fär, läw; — hēre, gĕt, hĕr; — mīne, ĭnn; — nō, hŏt, prōve; — hŏw; —

testacean, *tĕs'tă sē'ăn*, s. testacé, m.
testaceous, *tĕs'tă shŭs*, a. testacé.
testament, *tĕs'tă mĕnt*, s. testament, m.
testamentary, *tĕs tă mĕnt'ĕr ĭ*, a. testamentaire.
testator, *tĕs tā'tĕr*, s. testateur, m.
testatrix, *tĕs tā'triks*, s. testatrice, f.
tester, *tĕs'tĕr*, s. ciel de lit, m.
testifier, *tĕs'tĭ fī ĕr*, s. témoin, m.
testify, *tĕs'tĭ fī*, v. a. témoigner.
testily, *tĕs'tĭ lĭ*, ad. maussadement.
testimonial, *tĕs tĭ mō'nĭ ăl*, s. certificat, m., attestation, f.   [preuve, f.
testimony, *tĕs'tĭ mŭn ĭ*, s. témoignage, m.,
testiness, *tĕs'tĭ nĕs*, s. maussaderie, f.
testing, *tĕst'ĭng*, s. épreuve, f., essai, m. ||
~-house, s. maison d'épreuve, f.
testy, *tĕs'tĭ*, a. maussade, bourru.
tetanus, *tĕt'ă nŭs*, s. tétanos, m.
tether, *tĕth'ĕr*, s. attache (des chevaux), f. ||
to be at the end of one's ~, être au bout de son latin.
tetter, *tĕt'tĕr*, s. dartre, f.
Teutonic, *tū tŏn'ĭk*, a. teutonique.
text, *tĕkst*, s. texte, m. || ~-hand, s.
grosse, f.   [tissu, m.
textile, *tĕks'tĭl*, a. textile || ~ fabric, s.
textual, *tĕks'tū ăl*, a. textuel.
texture, *tĕks'tŭr*, s. tissure, f., tissu, m. ||
combinaison, f.
than, *thăn*, ad. & c. que, de.
thank, *thăngk*, v. a. remercier, rendre grâces || ~s, s. grâces, f. pl. || remerciment, m. || to return ~s, faire ses remerciments || ~-offering, s. sacrifice d'actions de grâces, m.
thankful, *thăngk'fŏŏl*, a. reconnaissant ||
-ly, ad. avec reconnaissance.   [tude, f.
thankfulness, *thăngk'fŏŏl nĕs*, s. gratithankless, *thăngk'lĕs*, a. ingrat.
thanksgiving, *thăngks'gĭv ĭng*, s. action de grâces, m.
that, *thăt*, pn. & c. ce, cet, cette, que, qui ||
afin que, pour que, de manière que || so ~, si bien que, de sorte que.
thatch, *thăch*, s. chaume, m.
thatch, *thăch*, v. a. couvrir de chaume.
thaw, *thaw*, s. dégel, m.
thaw, *thaw*, v. a. & n. dégeler || se fondre.
the, *thē* ou *thĭ*, art. le, la, les.   [m.
theatre, *thē'ā tĕr*, s. théâtre, m. || spectacle,
theatrical, *thē ăt'rĭk ăl*, a. théâtral, scénique || ~s, s. pl. spectacle, m.
thee, *thē*, pn. toi, te.
theft, *thĕft*, s. vol, larcin, m.
their, *thār*, pn. leur, leurs || ~s, le leur ||
la leur || les leurs, à eux, à elles.
theism, *thē'ĭzm*, s. théisme, m.
theist, *thē'ĭst*, s. théiste, m.
them, *thĕm*, pn. eux, elles.
theme, *thēm*, s. thème, m.
themselves, *thĕm sĕlvz'*, pn. eux-mêmes, elles-mêmes || se.
then, *thĕn*, ad. & c. alors, après, ensuite || donc, par conséquent || till ~, jusque là, d'ici là || now and ~, de temps en temps, de temps à autre.

thence, *thĕns*, ad. de là.
thenceforth, *thĕns'fŏrth*, thenceforward, *thĕns fŏr'wĕrd*, ad. dès lors.
theocracy, *thē ŏk'ră sĭ*, s. théocratie, f.
theocratic(al), *thē ō krăt'ĭk (ăl)*, a. théocratique.
theodolite, *thē ŏd'ō līt*, s. théodolite, m.
theologian, *thē ō lō'jĭ ăn*, s. théologien, m.
theologic(al), *thē ō lŏj'ĭk (ăl)*, a. (-ly, ad.) théologique(ment).
theology, *thē ŏl'ō jĭ*, s. théologie, f.
theorem, *thē'ō rĕm*, s. théorème, m.
theoretic(al), *thē ō rĕt'ĭk (ăl)*, a. théorique || -ly, ad. selon la théorie.
theorist, *thē'ō rĭst*, s. théoricien, m.
theory, *thē'ō rĭ*, s. théorie, f.
theosophy, *thē ŏs'ō fĭ*, s. théosophie, f.
therapeutics, *thĕr ă pū'tĭks*, s. pl. thérapeutique, f.
there, *thār*, ad. là, y, en cela || here and ~, çà et là || ~ is, ~ are, il y a.
thereabout(s), *thār'ă bŏŭt(s)*, ad. aux environs || environ, à peu près, presque || là-dessus.
thereafter, *thār āft'ĕr*, ad. ensuite.
thereat, *thăr āt'*, ad. par là.
thereby, *thār bī'*, ad. par là, pour cela.
therefor, *thār fŏr'*, ad. pour cela.
therefore, *thār'fŏr*, ad. c'est pourquoi, pour cela, pour cette raison, aussi.
therefrom, *thār frŏm'*, ad. de cela, d'après cela, en.   [dans, à ce sujet.
therein, *thăr in'*, ad. dans cela, y, là-dethereinto, *thăr in'tŏ*, ad. dans cela, y.
thereof, *thār ŏf'*, ad. de cela, en, y.   [y.
thereon, *thār ŏn'*, ad. sur cela, là-dessus.
thereto, *thār tŏ'*, thereunto, *thār ŭn'tŏ*, ad. à cela, à quoi.   [jadis.
theretofore, *thār tŏ fŏr'*, ad. autrefois,
thereunder, *thār ŭn'dĕr*, ad. là-dessous.
thereupon, *thār ŭp ŏn'*, ad. là-dessus, sur cela, sur ce.
therewith, *thār wĭth'*, ad. avec cela.
therewithal, *thār wĭth ăl'*, ad. au surplus, en outre.
thermal, *thĕr'măl*, a. thermal || ~ waters, s. pl. thermes, m. pl.   [mètre, m.
thermometer, *thĕr mŏm'ĕ tĕr*, s. thermothese, *thēz*, pn. pl. ces, ceux-ci, celles-ci.
thesis, *thē'sĭs*, s. thèse, f.
thew, *thū*, s. force musculaire, f.
they, *thā*, pn. ils, elles, on.
thick, *thĭk*, s. épaisseur, f. || fort, m. || to be in the ~ of it, être au fort de la mêlée.
thick, *thĭk*, a. & ad. épais, gros, grand || touffu || trouble || grossier || fréquent || fréquemment, souvent, profondément || -ly, ad. en foule || through ~ and thin, toujours et partout, quand même || to be as ~ as thieves, être comme les deux doigts de la main || ~-headed, a. lourd, stupide || ~-set, a. épais || trapu || ~-skinned, a. insensible.
thicken, *thĭk'n*, v. a. & n. épaissir || condenser, serrer || grossir || s'épaissir || se resserrer.   [m., condensation, f.
thickening, *thĭk'n ĭng*, s. épaississement,

thicket, *thĭk'ĕt*, s. taillis, fourré, m.

thickness, *thĭk'nĕs*, s. épaisseur, grosseur, dureté, f.

thief, *thēf*, s. voleur, larron, m. || (of candles) champignon, m. || ~-catcher, s. agent de police, m.

thieve, *thēv*, v. n. voler, dérober.

thievish, *thēv'ĭsh*, a. adonné au vol || -ly, ad. en voleur.

thievishness, *thēv'ĭsh nĕs*, s. penchant au vol, m. || habitude du vol, f.

thigh, *thī*, s. cuisse, f.

thimble, *thĭm'bl*, s. dé à coudre, m. || ~-rig, s. tour de gobelet, m. || ~-rigger, s. joueur de gobelets, m.   [nime, f.

thimbleful, *thĭm'bl fool*, a. quantité mi-

thin, *thĭn*, v. a. éclaircir, rendre mince || amaigrir, atténuer, raréfier.

thin, *thĭn*, a. & ad. mince, menu, délié, maigre || clair, rare || -ly, ad. en petit nombre.   [les tiennes, à toi.

thine, *thĭn*, pn. le tien, la tienne, les tiens,

thing, *thĭng*, s. chose, affaire, f. || no such ~ I point du tout ! || in the nature of -s, selon la nature des choses || as -s go, le monde est ainsi fait.

think, *thĭngk*, v. a. & n. ir. penser, méditer, considérer, examiner, juger, observer || croire || s'imaginer, se figurer || s'aviser de || to ~ much of, penser souvent à.

thinker, *thĭngk'ĕr*, s. penseur, m.

thinking, *thĭngk'ĭng*, s. pensée, opinion, f., avis, jugement, m. || to my ~, à mon avis.   [cieux.

thinking, *thĭngk'ĭng*, a. réfléchi, judi-

thinness, *thĭn'nĕs*, s. ténuité, rareté, exiguité, f. || maigreur, f.

third, *thĕrd*, s. tiers, m.

third, *thĕrd*, a. (-ly, ad.) troisième(ment) || the ~ person, (gr.) troisième personne, f.

thirst, *thĕrst*, s. soif, f.

thirst, *thĕrst*, v. n. avoir soif.

thirstily, *thĕrst'ĭ lĭ*, ad. avidement.

thirsty, *thĕrst'ĭ*, a. qui a soif, altéré.

thirteen, *thĕr'tēn*, a. treize || -th, a. treizième || (of the month) treize.

thirtieth, *thĕr'tĭ ĕth*, a. treizième || trente.

thirty, *thĕr'tĭ*, a. trente.

this, *thĭs*, pn. ce, cet, cette || ceci || between ~ and then, d'ici là.

thistle, *thĭs'l*, s. chardon, m.

thither, *thĭth'ĕr*, ad. là, y.

thong, *thŏng*, s. courroie, f.

thorn, *thăwrn*, s. épine, f. || affliction, f., chagrin, m.

thorny, *thăwrn'ĭ*, a. épineux || difficile.

thorough, *thŭr'ŏ*, pr. & a. (-ly, ad.) à travers, au travers de || complet, entier || parfait(ement) || entièrement, complètement || ~-bred, a. de pur sang || vrai || accompli || ~-paced, a. achevé, parfait.

thoroughfare, *thŭr'ŏ fār*, s. lieu de passage, m. || rue fréquentée, f. || no ~ I rue barrée ! on ne passe pas !

those, *thōz*, pn. ces, ceux-là, celles-là.

thou, *thŏw*, pn. tu, toi.

though, *thō*, c. quoique, bien que, quand

même, pourtant, cependant || as ~, comme si || what ou even ~, quand même.

thought, *thăwt*, s. pensée, réflexion, f., sentiment, m. || imagination, f. || dessein, m. || soin, m. || attente, f. || on second -s, après mûre réflexion || to be lost in ~, être absorbé dans la méditation || ~-reader, s. hypnotiseur, m. || ~-reading, s. hypnotisme, m.

thoughtful, *thăwt'fool*, a. pensif, contemplatif, rêveur || -ly, ad. avec réflexion.

thoughtfulness, *thăwt'fool nĕs*, s. méditation profonde, f. || inquiétude, f.

thoughtless, *thăwt'lĕs*, a. (-ly, ad.) étourdi(ment) || insoucieux, inattentif || sans souci.

thoughtlessness, *thăwt'lĕs nĕs*, s. étourderie, inadvertance, f.   [lier, m.

thousand, *thŏw'zănd*, s. mille, m. || millthousand, *thŏw'zănd*, a. mille || millier.

thousandfold, *thŏw'zănd fōld*, a. mille fois autant.

thousandth, *thŏw'zăndth*, a. millième.

thraldom, *thrăwl'dŭm*, s. esclavage, m.

thrall, *thrăwl*, s. esclave, m. & f.

thrash, *thrăsh*, v. a. & n. battre le blé || rosser.

thrashing, *thrăsh'ĭng*, s. battage, m. || ~-floor, s. aire, f. || ~-machine, s. batteuse à blé, f.   [f.

thread, *thrĕd*, s. fil, m. || suite, continuité, f.

thread, *thrĕd*, v. n. enfiler || passer au travers de.   [battu.

threadbare, *thrĕd'bār*, a. râpé || usé || re-

threat, *thrĕt*, s. menace, f. || empty ~, menace en l'air, f.

threaten, *thrĕt'n*, v. a. menacer.

threatening, *thrĕt'nĭng*, s. menace, f.

threateningly, *thrĕt'nĭng lĭ*, ad. en menaçant.

three, *thrē*, a. trois || Rule of ~, (ar.) règle de trois, f. || ~-cornered, a. triangulaire || ~-decker, s. (mar.) troisponts, m. || ~-master, s. (mar.) troismâts, m.

threefold, *thrē'fōld*, a. triple.   [mâts, m.

threepence, *thrĕp'pĕns*, s. trente centimes, m.   [times.

threepenny, *thrĕp'ĕn ĭ*, a. de trente cen-

threescore, *thrē'skōr*, a. soixante.

threshold, *thrĕsh'ōld*, s. seuil, f.

thrice, *thrĭs*, ad. trois fois.

thrift, *thrĭft*, s. gain, profit, m. || frugalité, économie, f.

thriftily, *thrĭft'ĭ lĭ*, ad. frugalement.

thriftiness, *thrĭft'ĭ nĕs*, s. frugalité, économie, f.   [sier.

thriftless, *thrĭft'lĕs*, a. prodigue, dépen-

thrifty, *thrĭft'ĭ*, a. frugal, ménager, économe || prospère.   [m.

thrill, *thrĭl*, s. vrille, f. || tressaillement, m.

thrill, *thrĭl*, v. a. & n. percer || pénétrer || tressaillir, frémir.

thrilling, *thrĭl'ĭng*, a. saisissant, pénétrant || perçant || à sensation.   [croître.

thrive, *thrĭv*, v. n. ir. prospérer, réussir,

thriving, *thrĭv'ĭng*, a. florissant || -ly, ad. d'une manière florissante.

throat, *thrōt*, s. gosier, m., gorge, f. || ~-band, s. sous-gorge, f.

throb, *thrŏb*, s. palpitation, f.

throb, *thrŏb*, v. n. battre, palpiter.

throe, *thrō*, s. douleurs de l'enfantement, f. pl. || agonie, f. || angoisse, f.

throne, *thrōn*, s. trône, m, || to come to the ~, monter au trône.

throng, *thrŏng*, s. foule, presse, f.

throng, *thrŏng*, v. a. & n. presser, venir en foule || accourir.   [métier continu, m.

throstle, *thrŏs't'l*, s. grive commune, f. ||

throttle, *thrŏt'tl*, s. larynx, m.

throttle, *thrŏt'tl*, v. a. étrangler, suffoquer.

through, *thrō*, pr. & ad. à travers, au travers de || par, à cause de || de part en part, jusqu'au bout, jusqu'à la fin || to carry ~, mener à bonne fin || to read anything ~, lire en entier || ~-ticket, s. (rail.) billet direct, m.

throughout, *thrō ŏwt'*, pr. & ad. au travers de || d'un bout à l'autre, partout.

throw, *thrō*, s. jet, m. || coup, m. || élan, m.

throw, *thrō*, v. a. & ir. jeter, lancer || terrasser, renverser.

thrum, *thrŭm*, v. a. jouer mal, racler || (mar.) piquer, larder.   [m. pl.

thrush, *thrŭsh*, s. grive, f. || (méd.) aphthes,

thrust, *thrŭst*, s. coup, m., poussée, f.

thrust, *thrŭst*, v. a. & n. ir. pousser, presser, serrer || forcer || jeter || se mêler, se fourrer, s'ingérer.

thumb, *thŭm*, s. pouce, m. || ~-ring, s. anneau à cacheter, m. || ~-screw, s. poucettes, f. pl.   [feuilleter.

thumb, *thŭm*, v. a. manier gauchement ||

thump, *thŭmp*, s. coup (de poing), m.

thump, *thŭmp*, v. a. battre du poing.

thumping, *thŭmp'ing*, a. gros, épais || lourd.

thunder, *thŭn'dĕr*, s. tonnerre, m., foudre, f. || ~-bolt, s. foudre, f. & m. || ~-clap, s. coup de tonnerre, m. || ~-storm, s. orage accompagné de tonnerre, m.

thunder, *thŭn'dĕr*, v. a. & n. fulminer || tonner.   [tonnant.

thundering, *thŭn'dĕr ing*, a. foudroyant,

thunderstruck, *thŭn'dĕr strŭk*, a. frappé de la foudre || atterré.

Thursday, *thĕrz'dā*, s. jeudi, m.

thus, *thŭs*, ad. ainsi, de cette manière.

thwack, *thwăk*, s. grand coup, m.

thwack, *thwăk*, v. a. battre, frapper.

thwart, *thwawrt*, s. (mar.) banc de nage, m.

thwart, *thwawrt*, v. a. traverser || contrarier.

thy, *thi*, pn. ton, ta, tes. [rier, contrecarrer.

thyme, *tĭm*, s. thym, m. || wild ~, serpolet, m.   [refl. verb) te.

thyself, *thĭsĕlf'*, pn. toi-même || (in a tiara, *tĭ ă'rŭ* ou *tĭ ā'rā*, s. tiare, f.

tick, *tĭk*, s. crédit, m. || tique, f. || coutil, matelas, m., taie, f. || tic-tac, m. || on ~, (fam.) "à l'œil."

ticket, *tĭk'ĕt*, s. billet, m. || étiquette, f. || ~-collector, s. billeteur, m. || ~-office, s. guichet à billets, m. || ~-of-leave-man, s. forçat libéré, m.

ticket, *tĭk'ĕt*, v. a. étiqueter.

ticking, *tĭk'ing*, s. coutil, m. || tic-tac, m.

tickle, *tĭk'kl*, v. a. & n. chatouiller.

tickling, *tĭk'ling*, s. chatouillement, m.

ticklish, *tĭk'klish*, a. chatouilleux || délicat || difficile || chancelant.

ticklishness, *tĭk'klish nĕs*, s. nature chatouilleuse, f. || difficulté, f.   [saison, f.

tide, *tĭd*, s. marée, f. || cours, courant, m.,

tide, *tĭd*, v. n. flotter || to ~ over, franchir une difficulté.

tidewaiter, *tĭd'wāt ĕr*, s. douanier, m.

tidily, *tĭd'ĭ lĭ*, ad. proprement.

tidiness, *tĭd'ĭ nĕs*, s. propreté, f.

tidings, *tī'dingz*, s. pl. nouvelles, f. pl.

tidy, *tĭd'ĭ*, a. propre, net || adroit.

tie, *tī*, s. nœud, m., attache, f. || engagement, m. || course de chevaux indécise, f. || (mus.) barre de jonction, f.

tie, *tī*, v. a. lier || obliger.

tier, *tēr*, s. rang, m., rangée, file, f.

tiff, *tĭf*, s. petit coup (of drink), m. || boutade, f. || bisbille, f.

tiffany, *tĭf'fă nĭ*, s. gaze de soie, f.

tiger, *tī'gĕr*, s. tigre, m. || groom, m.

tight, *tīt*, a. (-ly, ad.) serré, raide || bien fermé || étroit(ement) || sévèrement || proprement.   [serrer.

tighten, *tīt'n*, v. a. tendre || serrer || res-

tightness, *tīt'nĕs*, s. tension, f. || étroitesse, f. || raideur, f. || propreté, f.

tights, *tīts*, s. pl. pantalon collant, m. || mail-

tigress, *tī'grĕs*, s. tigresse, f.   [lot, m.

tilbury, *tĭl'bĕr ĭ*, s. tilbury, m.   [m.

tile, *tīl*, s. tuile, f. || ~-maker, s. tuilier,

tile, *tīl*, v. a. couvrir de tuiles.

tiler, *tīl'ĕr*, s. couvreur en tuile, m.

tiling, *tīl'ing*, s. toit couvert de tuiles, m.

till, *tĭl*, s. tiroir, m.

till, *tĭl*, v. a. cultiver, labourer.

till, *tĭl*, pr. & c. jusqu'à.

tillable, *tĭl'tă bl*, a. labourable.

tillage, *tĭl'lāj*, s. culture, f., labour, m.

tiller, *tĭl'lĕr*, s. laboureur, cultivateur, m. || petit tiroir, m. || gouvernail, m. || rejeton, m.

tilt, *tĭlt*, s. tente, f. || bâche, f., pavillon, m. || joute, f., carrousel, m. || coup de lance, m. || ~-yard, s. champ clos, m.

tilt, *tĭlt*, v. a. & n. couvrir d'une banne || pousser, lancer || jouter || (mar.) ballotter || s. jouteur, m.   [pencher.

tilter, *tĭlt'ĕr*, s. jouteur, m.

tilth, *tĭlth*, s. labourage, m.

timber, *tĭm'bĕr*, s. bois de charpente, m. || ~-work, s. charpente, f. || ~-yard, s. chantier de bois, m.

timber, *tĭm'bĕr*, v. a. boiser.

timbering, *tĭm'bĕr ing*, s. boisage, m.

time, *tĭm*, s. temps, m. || (mus.) mesure, f. || fois, f. || in ~, avec le temps, à temps || to waste ~, perdre le temps || to kill ~, tuer le temps || to have a fine ~, s'amuser rudement || to beat ~, (mus.) battre la mesure || it is high ~, le moment est venu de || to be near one's ~, approcher de son terme (se dit d'une femme enceinte) || ~ and again, de temps en temps || ~s out of mind, temps immémorial || at the same ~, en même temps || **behind**, **before** ~, en retard, en avance || **in the nick of** ~, à point nommé || **in the mean** ~, en attendant || **~honoured**, a. antique et vénérable || **~server**, s. complaisant, m. || **~serving**, s. servilité, f. || **~table**, s. tableau de service, m.

time, *tîm*, v. a. accommoder au temps || régler.

timed, *tîmd*, a. de saison || fait à propos.

timekeeper, *tîm'kêp'êr*, s. chronomètre, m. || montre marine, f.   [portunité, f.

timeliness, *tîm'li nés*, s. à-propos, m. || opportunité, f.

timely, *tîm'li*, a. & ad. opportun || à propos.

timepiece, *tîm'pês*, s. pendule, f.

timid, *tîm'id*, a. (-ly, ad.) craintif || timide(ment).   [nés, s. timidité, f.

timidity, *ti mîd'i ti*, **timidness**, *tîm'id-timorous**, *tîm'êr ús*, a. (-ly, ad.) timide (ment), timoré, craintif.

tin, *tín*, s. étain, m. || fer-blanc, m. || **(cash)** quibus, m. || **~foil**, s. tain, m., étamure, f. || **~plate**, s. fer-blanc, m. || **~tack**, s. plaque d'étain, f. || broquette d'étain, f. || **~ware**, s. ferblanterie, f. || **~worker**, s. ferblantier, m.

tin, *tín*, v. a. étamer.

tincture, *tingk'tûr*, s. teinte, f. || teinture, f. || goût, m.   [preindre de.

tincture, *tingk'tûr*, v. a. teindre || em**tinder**, *tín'dêr*, s. amadou, m., mèche, f.

tinea, *tín'ê ä*, s. (méd.) teigne, f.

tinge, *tínj*, s. teinte, f.

tinge, *tínj*, v. a. teindre.

tingle, *ting'gl*, v. n. tinter || fourmiller.

tingling, *ting'gling*, s. tintement, m. || fourmillement, m.

tinker, *tingk'êr*, s. chaudronnier, m.

tinkle, *ting'kl*, v. a. & n. tinter || faire ré-sonner.

tinkling, *ting'kling*, s. tintement, m.

tinman, *tín'mán*, s. ferblantier, m.

tinner, *tín'nêr*, s. ouvrier, m.

tinsel, *tín'sêl*, s. clinquant, m. || faux brillant, m.

tinsel, *tín'sêl*, a. faux || **(showy)** voyant.

tint, *tínt*, s. teinte, f.

tint, *tínt*, v. a. teinter, nuancer.

tiny, *tî'ni*, a. petit, mince.

tip, *típ*, s. bout, m., pointe, f. || **~toe**, s. pointe du pied, f. || **~top**, s. comble, sommet, m. || **~top**, a. au plus haut degré.   [doucement || donner un pourboire.

tip, *típ*, v. a. garnir le bout || frapper

tippet, *típ'pêt*, s. pèlerine, collerette, f.

tipple, *típ'pl*, s. boisson enivrante, f.

tipple, *típ'pl*, v. n. gobelotter.

tippler, *típ'plêr*, s. ivrogne, biberon, m.

tippling, *típ'pling*, s. ivrognerie, f.

tipstaff, *típ'stäf*, s. verge, f. || huissier à

tipsy, *típ'si*, a. ivre, gris.   [verge, m.

tire, *tîr*, s. parure, f. || attirail, m. || bande de roue, f.

tire, *tîr*, v. a. (& n.) (se) fatiguer.

tiresome, *tîr'súm*, a. fatigant, ennuyeux.

tiresomeness, *tîr'súm nés*, s. lassitude, f. || ennui, m.

tiring-room, *tîr'ing rôm*, s. cabinet de toilette, m.   [papier de soie, m.

tissue, *tísh'ú*, s. tissu, m. || **~paper**, s.

tissue, *tísh'ú*, v. a. entrelacer.

tit, *tít*, s. petit cheval, bidet, m., rosse, f. || ~ **for tat**, donnant donnant || **to give** ~ **for tat**, renvoyer la balle (à qn.).

titbit, *tít'bít*, s. morceau délicat, m. || (fam.) bonne bouche, f.

tithe, *títh*, s. dîme, f.

titillate, *tít'i lât*, v. n. chatouiller.

titlark, *tít'lärk*, s. alouette de pré, f.

title, *tî'tl*, s. titre, m. || **~deed**, s. titre de propriété, f. || **~page**, s. titre d'un livre, m.

title, *tî'tl*, v. a. titrer.

titmouse, *tít'môûs*, s. mésange, f.

titter, *tít'têr*, s. ricanement, m.

titter, *tít'têr*, v. n. ricaner.

tittle, *tít'tl*, s. point, m. || iota, m. || **~tattle**, s. babil, caquet, m.

titular, *tít'ú lêr*, a. titulaire.

to, *tó* ou *tô*, pr. à, au, à la, vers, en, envers, jusque || **as** ~, quant à.   [flagorneur, m.

toad, *tôd*, s. crapaud, m. || **~eater**, s.

toadstool, *tôd'stôl*, s. champignon bâtard, m.   [vilité, f.

toadyism, *tôd'i izm*, s. flagornerie, ser**toast**, *tôst*, s. pain grillé, m. || rôtie, f. || santé, f., toste, toast, m.   [santé.

toast, *tôst*, v. a. rôtir, griller || porter une

toaster, *tôst'êr*, s. rôtissoir, m.   [à rôtie, f.

toasting-fork, *tôst'ing fôrk*, s. fourchette

tobacco, *tó bák'kô*, s. tabac, m. || **~pipe**, s. pipe à fumer, f. || **~pouch**, s. blague à tabac, f.   [de tabac, m.

tobacconist, *tó bák'kô nist*, s. marchand

toboggan, *tó bôg'gn*, s. luge, f.

toboggan, *tó bôg'gn*, v. n. luger.

to-day, *tó dá'*, ad. aujourd'hui.   [trotter.

toddle, *tôd'dl*, v. n. décamper, s'en aller,

toe, *tô*, s. orteil, doigt du pied, m.

toffee, *tôf'fê*, s. sucre brûlé (au beurre), m.

toga, *tô'gä*, s. toge, f.

together, *tó gêth'êr*, ad. ensemble.

toggery, *tôg'gêr i*, s. attifement, m. || nippes, f. pl.

toil, *tôyl*, s. peine, fatigue, f. || travail, m.

toil, *tôyl*, v. n. travailler péniblement, se fatiguer, s'éreinter.

toiler, *tôyl'êr*, s. travailleur, m.

toilet, *tôyl'êt*, s. (table de) toilette, f.

toilsome, *tôyl'súm*, a. pénible, fatigant.

token, *tô'kn*, s. signe, m., marque, f. || preuve, f.

tolerable, *tôl'êr ä bl*, a. tolérable, médiocre.

tolerably, *tôl'êr ä bli*, ad. passablement.

tolerant, *tôl'êr ánt*, a. tolérant.

tolerate, *tôl'êr ât*, v. a. tolérer.

toleration, *tôl êr ä'shún*, s. tolérance, f.

toll, *tôl*, s. péage, m. || **~bar**, **~gate**, s. barrière où l'on paye le péage, f. || **~col-lector**, s. péager, m.

toll, *tôl*, v. a. & n. tinter, sonner.

tomahawk, *tôm'ä hawk*, s. casse-tête, m.

tomato, *tó mä'tó* ou *tô mä'tô*, s. tomate, f. || **~sauce**, s. sauce tomate, f.

tomb, *tôm*, s. tombe, f. || tombeau, m.

tomboy, tŏm'bŏy, s. garçon bruyant, m. ‖
    garçonnière, f.   [tumulaire, f.
tombstone, tŏm'stŏn, s. tombe, pierre
tomcat, tŏm'kăt, s. matou, m.
tomfool, tŏm'fōl', s. niais, m.
tomfoolery, tŏm'fōl'ĕr ĭ, s. niaiseries, f.pl.
to-morrow, tŏ mŏr'rŏ, ad. demain ‖ the
    day after ~, après-demain.
tomtit, tŏm'tĭt, s. mésange, f.
ton, tŭn, s. tonneau, m.
tone, tŏn, s. ton, accent, m. ‖ high –d, a.
tongs, tŏngs, s. pl. pincettes, f. pl.
tongue, tŭng, s. langue, f. ‖ langage, m.,
    parole, f. ‖ languette, f. ‖ aiguille (d'une
    balance), f. ‖ to hold one's ~, se taire ‖
    a slip of the ~, la langue lui a fourché ‖
    ~-tied, a. qui a le filet ‖ (fig.) obligé or
    réduit au silence.
tongueless, tŭng'lĕs, a. muet.   [m. & f.
tonic, tŏn'ĭk, s. (méd. & mus.) tonique,
tonic, tŏn'ĭk, a. tonique, élastique.
tonnage, tŭn'nāj, s. tonnage, m.
tonsil, tŏn'sĭl, s. amygdale, f.
tonsorial, tŏn sō'rĭ ăl, a. relatif au métier
    du barbier.
tonsure, tŏn'shōŏr, s. tonsure, f.
too, tō, ad. trop ‖ aussi.
tool, tōl, s. outil, instrument, m.
tooth, tōth, s. dent, f. ‖ goût, m. ‖ eye–,
    canine, dent œillère, f. ‖ wisdom–~, dent
    de sagesse, f. ‖ to set one's teeth on
    edge, agacer les dents ‖ in one's teeth,
    à la figure, au nez de qn. ‖ to go at it –
    and nail, s'y prendre de toutes ses forces
    ‖ to cast in one's teeth, reprocher à
    qn. ‖ to grind one's teeth, grincer des
    dents ‖ to have a sweet ~, aimer les
    douceurs " ~-ache, s. mal de dents, m. ‖
    ~-drawer, s. dentiste, m. ‖ ~-pick, s.
    cure-dent, m. ‖ ~-powder, s. dentifrice,
tooth, tōth, v. a. denteler, engrener.   [m.
toothless, tōth'lĕs, a. édenté, sans dents.
top, tŏp, s. cime, f., sommet, faîte, comble,
    m. ‖ surface, f., toupie, f., sabot, m. ‖
    hune, f. ‖ from ~ to toe, de pied en cap ‖
    ~-gallant, s. (mar.) perroquet, m. ‖
    ~-hamper, s. (mar.) tout ce qui gêne la
    manœuvre à bord ‖ ~-heavy, a. ivre ‖
    ~-knot, s. huppe, aigrette des oiseaux,
    f. ‖ ~-mast, s. mât de hune, m.
top, tŏp, v. a. & n. couronner ‖ surpasser ‖
    renchérir ‖ tailler ‖ éteter ‖ s'élever, domi-
top, tŏp, a. supérieur, du dessus.   [ner.
topaz, tō'păz, s. topaze, f.
tope, tŏp, v. n. boire avec excès.
toper, tō'pĕr, s. ivrogne, biberon, m.
topic, tŏp'ĭk, s. sujet, m., matière, f. ‖
    topique, m.
topical, tŏp'ĭ kăl, a. topique.
topmost, tŏp'mŏst, a. le plus haut or élevé.
topographic(al), tŏp ō grăf'ĭk(ăl), a. to-
    pographique.
topography, tō pŏg'ră fĭ, s. topographie, f.
topological, tŏp ō lŏj'ĭ kăl, a. topologique.
topple, tŏp'pl, v. n. tomber en avant ‖
    tomber.   [hunier, m.
topsail, tŏp'sāl (mar. tŏp'sl), s. (mar.)

topsy-turvy, tŏp sĭ tĕr'vĭ, ad. sens dessus
    dessous.
torch, tŏrch, s. torche, f., flambeau, m. ‖
    ~-bearer, s. porte-flambeau, m. ‖ ~-
    light, s. lumière de flambeau, f. ‖ ~-
    light-procession, s. promenade aux
    flambeaux, f.   [f., supplice, m.
torment, tŏr'mĕnt, s. tourment, m. ‖ torture,
torment, tŏr mĕnt', v. a. tourmenter.
tormenter, tŏr mĕnt'ĕr, s. bourreau, m.
tornado, tŏr nā'dŏ, s. ouragan, m.
torpedo, tŏr pē'dŏ, s. torpille, f.
torpid, tŏr'pĭd, a. torpide, engourdi.
torpor, tŏr'pŏr, s. torpeur, f.
torrent, tŏr'rĕnt, s. torrent, m.
torrid, tŏr'rĭd, a. torride, brûlant.
tortoise, tŏr'tŭs, s. tortue, f. ‖ ~-shell,
    s. écaille de tortue, f.
tortuous, tŏr'tū ŭs, a. tortueux.
torture, tŏr'tŭr, s. torture, f. ‖ to put to
    the ~, mettre à la torture.
torture, tŏr'tŭr, v. a. torturer.
torturer, tŏr'tū rĕr, s. bourreau, m.
Tory, tō'rĭ, s. tory, royaliste, m.
toss, tŏs, s. secousse, f. ‖ jet, m. ‖ ballotte-
    ment, m. ‖ mouvement de tête, m.
toss, tŏs, v. a. ir. jeter avec la main ‖
    lancer, ballotter ‖ agiter.
total, tō'tăl, s. total, m.   [entier, complet.
total, tō'tăl, a. (–ly, ad.) total(ement)
totality, tō tăl'ĭ tĭ, s. totalité, f., total, m.
totter, tŏt'tĕr, v. n. chanceler, vaciller.
touch, tŭch, s. toucher, m. ‖ tact, at-
    touchement, m. ‖ touche, f., trait, m.,
    teinte, f. ‖ ~-hole, s. lumière, f. ‖ ~-
    stone, s. pierre de touche, f. ‖ ~-wood,
    s. amadou, m.
touch, tŭch, v. a. & n. toucher ‖ toucher
    à, mettre la main à ‖ attaquer ‖ to ~ at,
    (mar.) toucher à, aborder à ‖ ~-me-not,
    s. (méd. & bot.) noli me tangere, m.
touchiness, tŭch'ĭ nĕs, s. susceptibilité, f.
touchy, tŭch'ĭ, ad. susceptible.
tough, tŭf, a. dur, visqueux, tenace.
toughen, tŭf'n, v. n. durcir, se raidir.
toughness, tŭf'nĕs, s. dureté, f. ‖ visco-
    sité, ténacité, f.
tour, tōr, s. tour, voyage, m.
tourist, tōr'ĭst, s. touriste, m.
tournament, tŏr'nă mĕnt, s. tournoi, m.
tout, tŏwt, v. n. s'achalander ‖ to ~ for,
    solliciter.   [m.
touter, tŏwt'ĕr, s. solliciteur, m. ‖ placier,
tow, tō, s. filasse, étoupe, f. ‖ touage, m.,
    remorque, f. ‖ ~-line, s. corde de halage,
tow, tō, v. a. touer, remorquer.   [f.
towage, tō'āj, s. halage, m.
towards, tō'ĕrdz ou tōrdz, ad. vers, envers,
    à l'égard de ‖ environ.
towel, tŏw'ĕl, s. essuie-main, m., serviette,
    f. ‖ ~-horse, s. séchoir, porte-serviettes,
    m.   [viettes, f.
towelling, tŏw'ĕl lĭng, s. toile pour ser-
tower, tŏw'ĕr, s. tour, forteresse, f.
tower, tŏw'ĕr, v. n. s'élever, dominer.
towering, tŏw'ĕr ĭng, a. très-élevé, domi-
    nant.

towing, *tō'ĭng;* ~**boat,** s. bateau remorqueur, m. ‖ ~**path,** s. chemin de halage, m. ‖ ~**rope,** s. corde de halage, f.

town, *toŭn,* s. ville, cité, f. ‖ ~**clerk,** s. greffier de la mairie, m. ‖ ~**crier,** s. crieur public, m. ‖ ~**hall,** ~**house,** s. hôtel-de-ville, m.

township, *toŭn'shĭp,* s. commune, juridiction d'une ville, f.

townsman, *toŭnz'măn,* s. citadin, concitoyen, m.

toxicology, *tŏks ĭ kŏl'ō jĭ,* s. toxicologie, f.

toy, *tōy,* s. joujou, jouet, m. ‖ bagatelle, f. ‖ niaiserie, folâtrerie, f. ‖ ~**man,** s. bimbelotier, marchand de joujoux, m. ‖ ~**shop,** s. boutique de joujoux, f.

toy, *tōy,* v. n. folâtrer, badiner.

trace, *trās,* s. trace, f. ‖ trait, m.

trace, *trās,* v. a. suivre les traces, suivre à la piste ‖ tracer, calquer.

trachea, *trā kē'ă,* s. (an. & bot.) trachée, f.

tracheal, *trā kē ăl,* a. trachéal.

tracheotomy, *trā kē ŏt'ō mĭ,* s. (chir.) trachéotomie, f.   [ingres, m.

tracing, *trā'sĭng;* ~**paper,** s. papier

track, *trăk,* s. trace, f., vestige, m., impression, f. ‖ route, f., sentier, m.

track, *trăk,* v.a. suivre à la piste ‖ traquer.

trackless, *trăk'lĕs,* a. sans traces.

tract, *trăkt,* s. espace de pays, m., contrée, f. ‖ traité, m., brochure, f.

tractable, *trăk'tă bl,* a. traitable, docile.

tractableness, *trăk'tă bl nĕs,* s. docilité, douceur, f.

tractably, *trăk'tă blĭ,* a. docilement.

traction, *trăk'shŭn,* s. traction, f. ‖ ~**engine,** s. machine à vapeur locomobile, f.

trade, *trād,* s. commerce, trafic, négoce, m. ‖ profession, f., métier, m. ‖ état, m., corps de métiers, m. ‖ **Jack of all** ~**s,** s. franc-coureur, m. ‖ ~**mark,** s. marque de fabrique, f. ‖ ~**s-union,** s. association ouvrière, f. ‖ ~**wind,** s. vent alizé, m.

trade, *trād,* v. n. trafiquer, commercer.

trader, *trā'dĕr,* s. marchand, m. ‖ navire de commerce, m.

tradesman, *trādz'măn,* s. boutiquier, m.

tradespeople, *trādz'pē pl,* s. commerçants, fournisseurs, m. pl.

trading, *trā'dĭng,* s. commerce, m.

trading, *trā'dĭng,* a. commerçant.

tradition, *trā dĭsh'ŭn,* s. tradition, f.

traditional, *trā dĭsh'ŭn ăl,* a. (-ly, ad.) traditionnel(lement).

traduce, *trā dūs',* v. a. blâmer, diffamer, calomnier ‖ propager.

traffic, *trăf'ĭk,* s. trafic, négoce, m. ‖ ~**manager,** s. (rail.) chef du mouvement, m.   [cer.

traffic, *trăf'ĭk,* v. n. trafiquer, commercer.

trafficker, *trăf'fĭk ĕr,* s. trafiquant, commerçant, négociant, m.

tragedian, *trăjē'dĭ ăn,* s. tragédien, m.

tragedy, *trăj'ĕ dĭ,* s. tragédie, f.

tragic(al), *trăj'ĭk(ăl),* a. (-ly, ad.) tragique(ment).

tragicalness, *trăj'ĭ kăl nĕs,* s. caractère tragique, m.   [comédie, f.

tragi-comedy, *trăj ĭ kŏm'ĕ dĭ,* s. tragi-

tragi-comical, *trăj ĭ kŏm'ĭ kăl,* a. tragi-comique.   [f.

trail, *trāl,* s. piste, trace, f. ‖ queue, traînée, f.

trail, *trāl,* v. a. suivre à la piste, traîner.

train, *trān,* s. artifice, piège, m. ‖ queue, f. ‖ série, suite, f. ‖ (rail.) train, convoi, m. ‖ méthode, marche, procession, f. ‖ traînée de poudre, f. ‖ **down-**~, (rail.) train descendant, m., train qui part de Londres, m. ‖ **excursion-**~, train de plaisir, m. ‖ **express-**~, express, train express, m. ‖ **mixed** ~, train mixte, m. ‖ **parliamentary** ~, slow-~, train-omnibus, m. ‖ **through-**~, train direct, m. ‖ **up-**~, (rail.) train montant, train qui va à Londres, m. ‖ ~ **of artillery,** train d'artillerie, m. ‖ ~**oil,** s. huile de baleine, f.

train, *trān,* v. a. traîner, entraîner ‖ attirer, instruire, dresser, élever.

trainer, *trān'ĕr,* s. instituteur, m. ‖ dresseur, m.   [cipline, f. ‖ exercice, m.

training, *trān'ĭng,* s. éducation, f. ‖ dis-

traitor, *trā'tĕr,* s. traître, m.

traitorous, *trā'tĕr ŭs,* a. traître, perfide ‖ -ly, ad. en traître.

traitress, *trā'trĕs,* s. traîtresse, f.

tram, *trăm,* s. chariot de roulage, m. ‖ rail plat, m.   [trave, f.

trammel, *trăm'mĕl,* s. tramail, m. ‖ en-

trammel, *trăm'mĕl,* v. a. entraver.

tramp, *trămp,* s. vagabond, m. ‖ bruit des pas, piétinement, m.   [sur.

trample, *trăm'pl,* v. a. fouler ‖ marcher

trampling, *trămp'lĭng,* s. piétinement, m.

tramway, *trăm'wā,* s. tramway, m.

trance, *trăns,* s. extase, f. ‖ (méd.) catalepsie, f.

tranced, *trănst'ŏd,* a. en extase.

tranquil, *trăn'kwĭl,* a. (-ly, ad.) tranquille (ment).   [liser.

tranquillise, *trăn'kwĭl ĭs,* v. a. tranquil-

tranquillity, *trăn kwĭl'ĭ tĭ,* s. tranquillité, f.   [faires.

transact, *trăns ăkt',* v. a. faire ses af-

transaction, *trăns ăk'shŭn,* s. négociation, affaire, f. ‖ ~**s,** pl. mémoires, m. pl.

transactor, *trăns ăk'tĕr,* s. négociateur, m.

transalpine, *trăns ăl'pĭn,* a. transalpin.

transatlantic, *trăns ăt lăn'tĭk,* a. transatlantique.   [monter ‖ exceller.

transcend, *trăn sĕnd',* v. a. surpasser, sur-

transcendency, *trăns sĕn'dĕn sĭ,* s. excellence, f. ‖ exagération, f.

transcendent, *trăn sĕn'dĕnt,* a. transcendant ‖ -ly, ad. par excellence.

transcribe, *trăn skrīb',* v. a. transcrire, copier.

transcriber, *trăn skrī'bĕr,* s. copiste, m.

transcript, *trăn'skrĭpt,* s. copie, f.

transcription, *trăn skrĭp'shŭn,* s. transcription, f.

transept, *trăn'sĕpt,* s. transept, m.

transfer, *trăns'fĕr,* s. transport, m. ‖ cession, f.

transfer, *trăns'fĕr'*, v. a. transférer, transporter || transmettre.

transferable, *trăns'fĕr'ă bl*, a. transférable, transportable.

transferrer, *trăns'fĕr'rĕr*, s. cédant, m.

transfiguration, *trăns fĭg ū'rā'shŭn*, s. transfiguration, f.

transfigure, *trăns'fĭg'ūr*, v. a. transfigurer, transformer.

transfix, *trăns'fĭks'*, v. a. transpercer.

transform, *trăns'fawrm'*, v. a. (& n.) (se) transformer.

transformation, *trăns'fawr mā'shŭn*, s. transformation, métamorphose, f.

transfuse, *trăns'fūz'*, v. a. transvaser.

transgress, *trăns'grĕs'*, v. a. & n. transgresser, violer.

transgression, *trăns grĕsh'ŭn*, s. transgression, violation, f., péché, m.

transgressor, *trăns'grĕs'sĕr*, s. transgresseur, m. || pécheur, m.

transient, *trăns'ĭ ĕnt* ou *trăn'shĕnt*, a. transitoire, passager || -ly, ad. en passant.

transit, *trăns'ĭt*, s. passage, transit, m.

transition, *trăn zish'ŭn*, s. transition, f.

transitive, *trăns'ĭ tĭv*, a. (gr.) transitif.

transitoriness, *trăns'ĭ tĕr ĭ nĕs*, s. courte durée, f.   [passager.

transitory, *trăns'ĭ tĕr ĭ*, a. transitoire.

translatable, *trăns lā' tă bl*, a. traduisable.

translate, *trăns'lāt'*, v. a. traduire || transférer.   [version, f.

translation, *trăns lā'shŭn*, s. traduction, f.

translator, *trăns lā'tĕr*, s. traducteur, m.

translucent, *trăns lū'sĕnt*, a. translucide.

transmarine, *trăns mă rēn'*, a. d'outre-mer.   [transmigration, f.

transmigration, *trăns mĭ grā'shŭn*, s.

transmissible, *trăns mĭs'sĭ bl*, a. transmissible.   [mission, f.

transmission, *trăns mĭsh'ŭn*, s. transmit, *trăns mĭt'*, v. a. transmettre.

transmutation, *trăns mū tā'shŭn*, s. transmutation, f.   [transformer.

transmute, *trăns mūt'*, v. n. transmuer.

transom, *trăn'sŏm*, s. traverse, f.

transparency, *trăns pā'rĕn sĭ*, s. transparence, f. || transparent, m.

transparent, *trăns pā'rĕnt*, a. transparent|| -ly, ad. d'une manière transparente.

transpire, *trăn spīr'*, v. a. transpirer.

transplant, *trăns plănt'*, v. a. transplanter.

transplantation, *trăns plăn tā'shŭn*, s. transplantation, f.   [sant.

transplendent, *trăn splĕn'dĕnt*, a. éblouis-

transport, *trăns'pŏrt*, s. transport, m. || vaisseau de transport, m. || déporté, m.

transport, *trăns pŏrt'*, v. a. transporter || déporter.   [portable.

transportable, *trăns pŏrt'ă bl*, a. transportation, *trăns pŏr tā'shŭn*, s. transportation, f. || transport, m. || déportation, f.

transporting, *trăns pŏrt'ĭng*, a. ravissant.

transpose, *trăns pōz'*, v. a. transposer.

transposition, *trăns pō zish'ŭn*, s. transposition, f.

trans-ship, *trăns ship'*, v. a. transborder.

transubstantiate, *trăn sŭb stăn' shĭ āt*, v. a. transsubstantier.

transubstantiation, *trăn sŭb stăn shĭ ā' shŭn*, s. transsubstantiation, f.

transverse, *trăns vĕrs'*, a. transversal || -ly, ad. de travers.   [s. trappe, f.

trap, *trăp*, s. trappe, f., piège, m. || ~-door,

trap, *trăp*, v. a. prendre au piège.

trapeze, *tră pēz'*, s. trapèze, m.

trappings, *trăp'pĭngs*, s. pl. ornement d'une selle, m. || parure, f.

trappist, *trăp'pist*, s. trappiste, m.

trash, *trăsh*, s. camelote, f., rebut, m., drogue, f.   [méchant.

trashy, *trăsh'ĭ*, a. de rebut || mauvais,

travel, *trăv'ĕl*, s. voyage, m.

travel, *trăv'ĕl*, v. a. & n. voyager || parcourir || être en voyage.

traveller, *trăv'ĕl lĕr*, s. voyageur, m. || commercial ~, commis voyageur, m.

travelling, *trăv'ĕl ĭng*, s. voyages, m. pl.

traverse, *trăv'ĕrs*, v. a. traverser.

travesty, *trăv'ĕs tĭ*, s. travesti, m. || travestissement, m.

travesty, *trăv'ĕs tĭ*, v. a. travestir.

tray, *trā*, s. plateau à rebords, m. || auge, f., baquet, m.

treacherous, *trĕch'ĕr ŭs*, a. traître, perfide || -ly, ad. en traître, avec perfidie.

treachery, *trĕch'ĕr ĭ*, s. trahison, perfidie, f.

treacle, *trē'kl*, s. mélasse, thériaque, f.

tread, *trĕd*, s. pas, m. || (of birds) accouplement, m. || ~-mill, s. moulin de discipline, m. || treuil à tambour, m.

tread, *trĕd*, v. a. & n. ir. marcher sur, fouler || écraser, frayer || cocher || s'accoupler (of birds).   [germe, m.

treadle, *trĕd'l*, s. marche, f. || (of eggs)

treason, *trē'zn*, s. trahison, f. || high ~, lèse-majesté, f.

treasonable, *trē'zn ă bl*, a. traître.

treasure, *trĕzh'ōōr*, s. trésor, m.

treasure, *trĕzh'ōōr*, v. a. thésauriser, amasser, accumuler.

treasurer, *trĕzh'ōōr ĕr*, s. trésorier, m.

treasurership, *trĕzh'ōōr ĕr ship*, s. emploi de trésorier, m.

treasury, *trĕzh'ōōr ĭ*, s. trésorerie, f. || ministère des finances, m.

treat, *trēt*, s. régal, m. || banquet, m.

treat, *trēt*, v. a. & n. traiter || discuter || régaler.

treatise, *trēt'ĭz*, s. traité, ouvrage, m.

treatment, *trēt'mĕnt*, s. traitement, m.

treaty, *trēt'ĭ*, s. traité, m.

treble, *trĕb'l*, s. (mus.) le dessus.

treble, *trĕb'l*, v. a. & n. tripler.

treble, *trĕb'l*, a. triple.

trebly, *trĕb'lĭ*, ad. triplement.

tree, *trē*, s. arbre, m. || pontet, m. || embouchoir, m. || croix, f. || family-~, arbre généalogique, m.

trefoil, *trē'fŏÿl*, s. trèfle, m.

trellis, *trĕl'lĭs*, s. treillis, m.

tremble, *trĕm'bl*, v. n. trembler.

trembling, *trĕm'blĭng*, s. tremblement, m.

trembiingly, *trĕm'blĭng lĭ*, ad. en tremblant.   [terrible(ment).

tremendous, *trĕ mĕn'dŭs*, a. (-ly, ad.)

tremulous, *trĕm'ū lŭs*, a. tremblant.

trench, *trĕnsh*, s. tranchée, f. ǁ rigole, f.

trench, *trĕnsh*, v. a. trancher ǁ creuser.

trencher, *trĕnsh'ĕr*, s. tranchoir, m. ǁ ta'le, f. ǁ ~man, s. ami de table, m. ǁ pique-assiette, m.

trepan, *trĕ păn'*, s. trépan, m.

trepan, *trĕ păn'*, v. a. trépaner.

trespass, *trĕs'păs*, s. violation de propriété, f. ǁ injure, f. ǁ offense, f.

trespass, *trĕs'păs*, v. n. transgresser, convenir à la loi, violer.

trespasser, *trĕs'păs sĕr*, s. délinquant, m. ǁ intrus, m.

tress, *trĕs*, s. tresse, boucle de cheveux, f.

trestle, *trĕs'sl*, s. tréteau, chevalet, m.

trial, *trī'ăl*, s. essai, m., épreuve, tentative, f. ǁ jugement, procès, m. ǁ **to be on one's ~**, être en cause ǁ **to take on ~**, prendre à l'essai.

triangle, *trī'ăng gl*, s. triangle, m.

triangular, *trī ăng gŭ lĕr*, a. triangulaire.

tribal, *trī'băl*, a. qui fait partie d'une tribu.

tribe, *trīb*, s. classe, tribu, famille, f.

tribulation, *trĭb ū lā'shŭn*, s. vexation, f.

tribunal, *trĭ bū'năl*, s. tribunal, m.

tribune, *trĭb'ūn ou trī'būn*, s. tribun, m.

tributary, *trĭb'ū tĕr ĭ*, s. tributaire, m.

tributary, *trĭb'ū tĕr ĭ*, a. tributaire.

tribute, *trĭb'ūt*, s. tribut, m.

trice, *trīs*, s. instant, clin d'œil, m.

trichina, *trĭ kī'nă*, s. trichine, f.

trick, *trĭk*, s. tour d'adresse, artifice, m., fourberie, f. ǁ main, levée, f.

trick, *trĭk*, v. a. tricher, duper ǁ orner, parer.

trickery, *trĭk'ĕr ĭ*, s. tricherie, f., artifice, m., fraude, f.

trickle, *trĭk'kl*, v. n. ruisseler, dégoutter.

trickster, *trĭk'stĕr*, s. fourbe, m. ǁ trompeur, m.   [m.

tricolour, *trī'kŭl ŏr*, s. drapeau tricolore.

tricoloured, *trī'kŭl ŏrd*, a. tricolore.

trident, *trī'dĕnt*, s. trident, m.

triennial, *trī ĕn'nĭ ăl*, a. triennal.

trier, *trī'ĕr*, s. expérimentateur, m. ǁ épreuve, f. ǁ pierre de touche, f.

trifle, *trī'fl*, s. bagatelle, babiole, vétille, f.

trifle, *trī'fl*, v. a. & n. badiner, s'amuser à des riens.

trifler, *trī'flĕr*, s. badin, baguenaudier, m.

trifling, *trī'flĭng*, a. futile, frivole ǁ peu de chose ǁ -ly, ad. légèrement.

triflingness, *trī'flĭng nĕs*, s. futilité, f.

trigger, *trĭg'gĕr*, s. détente, f.

trigonometry, *trĭg ŏn ŏm'ĕ trĭ*, s. trigonométrie, f.

trilateral, *trī lăt'ĕr ăl*, a. trilatéral.

trill, *trĭl*, s. (mus.) trille, f.

trill, *trĭl*, v. a. & n. (mus.) triller.

trim, *trĭm*, s. parure, f., arrimage, m. ǁ attirail, m.

trim, *trĭm*, v. a. & n. ajuster, équiper, orner, parer ǁ nettoyer ǁ raser, couper ǁ

---

arrimer ǁ orienter (sails) ǁ émonder (trees) ǁ hésiter.   [(ment).

trim, *trĭm*, a. (-ly, ad.) bien ajusté ǁ propre

trimmer, *trĭm'mĕr*, s. décorateur, m. ǁ (fig.) girouette, f.   [ornements, m. pl.

trimming, *trĭm'mĭng*, s. garniture, f.,

trinitarian, *trĭn ĭ tā'rĭ ăn*, s. trinitaire, m.

trinity, *trĭn'ĭ tĭ*, s. trinité, f.

trinket, *trĭng'kĕt*, s. bagatelle, f., colifichet, m.

trio, *trē'ō ou trī'ō*, s. trio, m. [fichet, m.

trip, *trĭp*, s. croc-en-jambe, faux pas, m. ǁ excursion, f.

trip, *trĭp*, v. a. & n. supplanter ǁ attraper ǁ trébucher, faire une bévue ǁ se méprendre ǁ faire un petit voyage.

tripartite, *trī par'tĭt*, a. triparti.

tripe, *trĭp*, s. tripes, f. pl.

triple, *trĭp'l*, a. triple.

triplet, *trĭp'lĕt*, s. trio, m. ǁ triolet, m. ǁ tercet, m.

tripod, *trī'pŏd*, s. trépied, m.

tripos, *trī'pŏs*, s. (univ.) grand concours, m.

trireme, *trī'rēm*, s. tirème, f.

trisyllabic, *trĭ sĭl lăb'ĭk*, a. trisyllabe.

trisyllable, *trĭ sĭl'lă bl*, s. trisyllabe, m.

trite, *trīt*, a. (-ly, ad.) usé ǁ trivial(ement).

triteness, *trīt'nĕs*, s. trivialité, f.

triturate, *trĭt'ū rāt*, v. a. triturer, broyer.

trituration, *trĭt ū rā'shŭn*, s. trituration, f.

triumph, *trī'ŭmf*, s. triomphe, m.

triumph, *trī'ŭmf*, v. n. triompher.

triumphal, *trī ŭm'făl*, a. triomphal.

triumphant, *trī ŭm'fănt*, a. triomphant ǁ -ly, ad. en triomphe.   [m.

triumvirate, *trī ŭm'vĭ rāt*, s. triumvirat, m.

trivet, *trĭv'ĕt*, s. trépied, m.

trivial, *trĭv'ĭ ăl*, a. (-ly, ad.) trivial(ement) commun, vulgaire.

triviality, *trĭv ĭ ăl'ĭ tĭ*, s. trivialité, f.

troglodite, *trŏg'lō dĭt*, s. troglodyte, m.

troll, *trōl*, v. a. & n. tourner, rouler.

trolloy, *trŏl'lĭ*, s. tombereau, m.

trollop, *trŏl'lŏp*, s. souillon, f.

troop, *trŏp*, s. troupe, bande, compagnie, f. ǁ ~-horse, s. cheval de troupe, m.

troop, *trŏp*, v. n. marcher par troupes ǁ s'attrouper.   [cavalier, m.

trooper, *trŏp'ĕr*, s. soldat de cavalerie,

trophy, *trō'fĭ*, s. trophée, m.

tropic, *trŏp'ĭk*, s. tropique, m.

tropic(al), *trŏp'ĭk (ăl)*, a. tropique, métaphorique.

trot, *trŏt*, s. trot, m. ǁ jog-~, petit trot, m.

trot, *trŏt*, v. n. trotter.

troth, *trŏth*, s. fidélité, foi, f. ǁ vérité, f.

trotter, *trŏt'tĕr*, s. trotteur, m. ǁ pied de mouton, m.

trouble, *trŭb'l*, s. peine, f., tourment, m., inquiétude, f. ǁ trouble, m.

trouble, *trŭb'l*, v. a. troubler.

troublesome, *trŭb'l sŭm*, a. inquiétant, ennuyeux, pénible, désagréable, importun.

troublesomeness, *trŭb'l sŭm nĕs*, s. ennui, m. ǁ peine, importunité, f.

troublous, *trŭb'lŭs*, a. tumultueux, agité, confus.

---

lūte, hăt, făr, law; — hēre, gĕt, hĕr; — mīne, ĭnn; — nō, hŏt, prōve; — hŏw; —

trough, *trôf,* s. auge, f. || baquet, m. || **in the ~ of the sea,** dans l'entre-deux des lames. [pantalons, f.
trousering, *trŏu'zĕr ĭng,* s. étoffe pour
trousers, *trŏu'zĕrz,* s. pl. pantalon, m.
trout, *trŏut,* s. truite, f.
trove, *trŏv,* s. trouvaille, f. || **treasure-~,** trésor trouvé, m. [m.
trowel, *trŏu'ĕl,* s. truelle, f. || déplantoir,
truant, *trŏ'ănt,* s. fainéant, vagabond, m.
truant, *trŏ'ănt,* a. paresseux, fainéant.
truce, *trôs,* s. trêve, f.
truck, *trŭk,* s. troc, échange, m. || traîneau, camion, m. || wagon, m. || charrette, f. || roue d'affût, f. || (rail.) plate-forme, f.
truck, *trŭk,* v. a. troquer.
truckle, *trŭk'l,* (~-bed), s. roulette, f.
truckle, *trŭk'l,* v. n. se soumettre, ramper.
truculent, *trŭk'ū lĕnt,* a. sauvage, cruel.
trudge, *trŭj,* v. n. marcher avec peine, se traîner || faire route à pied.
true, *trŏ,* a. vrai, véritable, sincère || pur, naturel || fidèle, probe || exact || ~-born, ~-bred, a. de bonne race || ~-hearted, a. honnête, fidèle || ~-love, s. bien-aimé, m. || ~-lovers' knot, s. nœud d'amour, m. (en forme de ∞).
truffle, *trŭf'fl,* s. truffe, f.
truism, *trŏ'ĭzm,* s. vérité évidente, f.
truly, *trŏ'lĭ,* ad. véritablement, réellement, justement. [atout, m.
trump, *trŭmp,* s. trompe, trompette, f. ||
trump, *trŭmp,* v. a. jouer un atout || **to ~ up,** inventer.
trumpery, *trŭmp'ĕr ĭ,* s. fourberie, fausseté, invention, f. || friperie, f.
trumpery, *trŭmp'ĕr ĭ,* a. trompeur, faux.
trumpet, *trŭm'pĕt,* s. trompette, f. || trompette, m. || **speaking-~,** cornet acoustique, m. [clamer || divulguer.
trumpet, *trŭm'pĕt,* v. a. trompeter || pro-
trumpeter, *trŭm'pĕt ĕr,* s. trompette, m. (& [fig.] f.).
truncate, *trŭng kāt',* v. a. tronçonner.
truncheon, *trŭn'shŭn,* s. gros bâton, m.
trundle, *trŭn'dl,* s. roulette, f.
trundle, *trŭn'dl,* v. n. rouler.
trunk, *trŭngk,* s. tronc, m. || malle, f. || coffre, m. || trompe (d'un éléphant), f. || torse, m. || ~-light, s. abat-jour, m. || ~-line, s. ligne principale, f. || ~-maker, s. coffretier, layetier, m.
trunnion, *trŭn'yŭn,* s. tourillon, m.
truss, *trŭs,* s. bandage, m. || trousse, f., paquet, m. || ~-maker, s. bandagiste, m.
truss, *trŭs,* v. a. empaqueter || trousser.
trussel-bed, *trŭs'sĕl bĕd,* s. lit de sangle, m.
trust, *trŭst,* s. confiance, assurance, espérance, f. || dépôt, m. || commission, administration, f., crédit, m. || **breach of ~,** s. (jur.) félonie, f. || parjure, m.
trust, *trŭst,* v. a. & n. se fier à, avoir confiance en, confier, vendre à crédit || espérer, s'attendre à. [teur, tuteur, m.
trustee, *trŭs tē',* s. dépositaire, administra-
trustily, *trŭst'ĭ lĭ,* ad. fidèlement.

trustiness, *trŭs'tĭ nĕs,* s. honnêteté, fidélité, f. [féal.
trusty, *trŭst'ĭ,* a. fidèle, honnête, loyal,
truth, *trŏth,* s. fidélité, réalité, f. || **in ~, of a ~,** en vérité, à vrai dire.
truthful, *trŏth'fŏŏl,* a. plein de vérité.
try, *trĭ,* v. a. & n. essayer, éprouver, tenter || épurer, raffiner || juger || tâcher || mettre en jugement || fatiguer.
trying, *trĭ'ĭng,* a. pénible, cruel || critique.
tryst, *trĭst,* s. rendez-vous, m.
trysting-place, *trĭst'ĭng plās,* s. lieu du rendez-vous, m.
tub, *tŭb,* s. baquet, m., tine, cuve, f.
tube, *tūb,* s. tube, conduit, m.
tubercle, *tū'bĕr kl,* s. tubercule, m.
tuberculosis, *tū bĕr kū lŏ'sĭs,* s. (méd.) tuberculose, f.
tuberose, *tū'bĕr ŏs,* s. tubéreuse, f.
tuberous, *tū'bĕr ŭs,* a. tuberculeux.
tubular, *tū'bū lĕr,* a. tubulaire || ~-bridge, s. pont-tube, m.
tuck, *tŭk,* s. pli, repli, m. || estoc, m.
tuck, *tŭk,* v. a. retrousser, relever || **to ~ up,** trousser, retrousser || **to ~ in,** rentrer.
tucker, *tŭk'ĕr,* s. collerette, f.
Tuesday, *tūz'dā,* s. mardi, m.
tuft, *tŭft,* s. touffe, f. || houppe, f. || (mil.) pompon, m. || ~-hunter, s. plat valet (qui se faufile avec les gens huppés), m.
tufted, *tŭft'ĕd,* a. touffu, peluché.
tug, *tŭg,* s. tiraillement, m., secousse, f. || remorqueur, m.
tug, *tŭg,* v. a. & n. tirer || remorquer || lutter.
tuition, *tū ĭsh'ŭn,* s. enseignement, m., instruction, f. || pension (**price of schooling**), f. [de rose, m.
tulip, *tū'lĭp,* s. tulipe, f. || ~-wood, s. bois
tumble, *tŭm'bl,* s. chute, f. || culbute, f.
tumble, *tŭm'bl,* v. a. & n. jeter par terre, tourner, bouleverser || dégringoler || chiffonner || se jeter, tomber, rouler.
tumbledown, *tŭm'bl dŏwn,* a. délabré, qui menace ruine.
tumbler, *tŭm'blĕr,* s. sauteur, m. || bateleur, m. || grand verre, m. || (**of fire-arms**) gâchette, f. [caisson, m.
tumbril, *tŭm'brĭl,* s. tombereau, m. || (mil.)
tumefy, *tū'mĕ fĭ,* v. a. tuméfier.
tumour, *tū'mĕr,* s. tumeur, f.
tumular, *tū'mū lĕr,* a. tumulaire.
tumult, *tū'mŭlt,* s. tumulte, trouble, m., émeute, f.
tumultuous, *tū mŭl'tū ŭs,* a. tumultueux || -ly, ad. tumultueusement. [m.
tun, *tŭn,* s. tonne, f. || tonneau, m. || ivrogne,
tunable, *tū'nă bl,* a. harmonieux || accordable.
tune, *tūn,* s. ton, son, air, m., harmonie, f., accord, m. || bonne humeur, f. || **in ~,** a. de bonne humeur || **out of ~,** a. de mauvaise humeur.
tune, *tūn,* v. a. accorder.
tuneful, *tūn'fŏŏl,* a. harmonieux.
tuneless, *tūn'lĕs,* a. discordant.
tuner, *tū'nĕr,* s. accordeur, m.
tunic, *tū'nĭk,* s. tunique, f.

tuning, tū´nǐng, s. accord, m. || ~-fork, s. diapason, m. || ~-hammer, s. accordoir, m.   [tunnel, m.

tunnel, tǔn´něl, s. tuyau de cheminée, m. ||

tunnel, tǔn´něl, v. a. percer.

tunny, tǔn´nǐ, s. thon, m.

turban, těr´băn, s. turban, m.

turbid, těr´bǐd, a. trouble, bourbeux.

turbot, těr´bǒt, s. turbot, m.

turbulence, těr´bǔ lěns, s. turbulence, f., tumulte, m., agitation, f.

turbulent, těr´bǔ lěnt, a. turbulent, séditieux, tumultueux || bruyant.

tureen, tū rēn´, s. soupière, saucière, f.

turf, těrf, s. gazon, m. || tourbe, f. || hippodrome, m. || turf, m., courses, f. pl.

turf, těrf, v. a. gazonner.

turfing, těrf´ ǐng, s. gazonnement, m.

turfite, těrf´ ǔt, s. (fam.) amateur du turf, m. || escroc, m.

turgid, těr´jǐd, a. enflé, ampoulé.

Turkey(~-cock, ~-hen), těr´kǐ, s. coq d'Inde, dindon, m. || dinde, f.

turmeric, těr´měr ǐk, s. (bot.) safran des Indes, m.

turmoil, těr´mōyl, s. trouble, vacarme, m.

turn, těrn, s. tour, m. || détour, m. || changement, m. || retour, m. || service, m. || tournure, f. || forme, f., contour, m. || goût, m. || at every ~, à tout bout de champ || to serve one's ~, satisfaire, suffire.

turn, těrn, v. a. & n. tourner, faire tourner, retourner, renverser || changer || faire baisser || façonner au tour, former || traduire || diriger || examiner || se tourner, se retourner || se diriger vers || se transformer, se changer, s'altérer || devenir || to ~ away, renvoyer, congédier || to ~ round, tourner, retourner || to ~ over, tourner || feuilleter || to ~ out, mettre dehors || to ~ up, trousser, remplier || to ~ the tables on one, faire changer la fortune || ~-cock, s. fontainier, m. || ~-off, s. embranchement, m. || ~-out, s. train, équipage, m. || grève, f. || gare d'évitement, f.

turncoat, těrn´kǒt, s. renégat, m.

turner, těrn´ěr, s. tourneur, m.

turning, těrn´ ǐng, s. tournant, détour, coude, m. || rue, f. || ~-in, s. rempli, m. || ~-lathe, s. tour, m.

turnip, těr´nǐp, s. navet, m.

turnkey, těrn´kē, s. porte-clés, m.

turnpike, těrn´pǐk, s. tourniquet, m. || barrière, f.

turnplate, těrn´plāt, turntable, těrn´tābl, s. plaque tournante, f. || ~-keeper, s. garde de plaque tournante, m.

turnscrew, těrn´skrō, s. tournevis, m.

turnspit, těrn´spǐt, s. tourne-broche, m.

turnstile, těrn´stǐl, s. tourniquet, m.

turpentine, těr´pěn tǐn, s. térébenthine, f. || ~-tree, s. térébinthe, m.

turpitude, těr´pǐ tūd, s. turpitude, f.

turquoise, těr´kǒyz ou těr´kwāwz, s. turquoise, f.

turret, tǔr´rět, s. tourelle, f.   [quoise, f.

turreted, tǔr´rět ěd, a. flanqué de tourelles.

turtle, těr´tl, s. tourterelle, f. || tortue, f. || ~-dove, s. tourterelle, f.

tush! tǔsh, bah! taisez-vous donc!

tusk, tǔsk, s. défenses du sanglier, f. pl.

tusked, tǔskt, a. muni de défenses.

tussle, tǔs´sl, s. lutte, f., chamaillis, m.

tut! tǔt, ta!

tutelage, tū´tě lāj, s. tutelle, f.

tutelar, tū´tě lěr, a. tutélaire.   [tuteur, m.

tutor, tū´těr, s. instituteur, précepteur, m.,

tutor, tū´těr, v. a. instruire, enseigner || reprendre.   [communs.

twaddle, twǒd´dl, v. n. débiter des lieux

twain, twān, a. deux.

twang, twǎng, s. son aigu, m. || son nasillard, m.   [rendre un son aigu.

twang, twǎng, v. a. & n. faire résonner ||

tweak, twēk, v. a. pincer.

tweezers, twē´zěrz, s. pl. pincettes, f. pl.

twelfth, twělfth, s. douzième, douze, m.

twelfth, twělfth, a. douzième, douze || ~-night, s. jour des Rois, m.

twelve, twělv, s. douze, m. || midi, m. || minuit, m.

twelve, twělv, a. douze || midi || minuit.

twelvemonth, twělv´mǔnth, s. année, f.

twentieth, twěn´tǐ ěth, a. vingtième.

twenty, twěn´tǐ, a. vingt.

twice, twīs, ad. deux fois.

twiddle, twǐd´dl, v. a. palper, tâter.

twig, twǐg, s. branche, brindille, f.

twilight, twī´līt, s. crépuscule, f.

twill, twǐl, s. croisé, m.

twin, twǐn, s. jumeau, m., jumelle, f.

twine, twǐn, s. entrelacement, m. || ficelle, f.

twine, twǐn, v. a. (& n.) (s')entrelacer || entortiller || serpenter.

twinge, twǐnj, s. élancement, m. || tourment, m. || remords, m.

twinge, twǐnj, v. a. pincer, tourmenter.

twinkle, twǐng´kl, v. n. étinceler, scintiller || clignoter.

twinkling, twǐng´klǐng, s. étincellement, m. || clin d'œil, m., œillade, f.

twirl, twěrl, s. rotation, f.

twirl, twěrl, v. a. & n. tourner, faire tourner || tourner, tournoyer.

twist, twǐst, s. cordon, m. || cordonnet, m. || tortillement, m. || (of tobacco) carotte, f. || (arq.) nervure, f.

twist, twǐst, v. a. & n. retordre, tisser, tresser, entortiller, enlacer || s'entrelacer, s'entortiller.   [procher.

twit, twǐt, v. a. blâmer || to ~ with, re-

twitch, twǐch, s. secousse, f. || contraction spasmodique, f.

twitch, twǐch, v. a. tirailler, tirer, pincer.

twitter, twǐt´těr, s. gazouillement, m.

twitter, twǐt´těr, v. n. gazouiller.

two, tō, a. deux || to walk ~ and ~, aller bras dessus bras dessous.

twofold, tō´fōld, a. & ad. double.

twopence, tō´pěns ou tǔp´ěns, s. vingt centimes.

twopenny, tǔp´ěn ǐ, a. de vingt centimes.

tympan(um), tǐm´păn(ǔm), s. tympan, m.

type, *tĭp,* s. type, caractère (d'imprimerie), m. || ~**-founder,** s. fondeur en caractères d'imprimerie, m. || ~**-foundry,** s. fonderie de lettres, f.

typhoid, *tĭ'fŏjd,* a. typhoïde.

typhoon, *tĭ'fōōn',* s. typhon, m.

typhus, *tĭ'fŭs,* s. typhus, m.

typographer, *tĭ'pŏg'rä'fĕr,* s. typographe, m.   [graphique.

typographic(al), *tĭ'pŏ'gräf'ĭk(ăl),* a. typographique.

typography, *tĭ'pŏg'räfĭ,* s. typographie, f.

tyrannical, *tĭ'răn'nĭk'ăl,* a. tyrannique || -**ly,** ad. en tyran.

tyrannise, *tĭr'ăn'īz,* v. a. tyranniser.

tyranny, *tĭr'ăn'ĭ,* s. tyrannie, f.

tyrant, *tĭ'rănt,* s. tyran, m.

tyro, *tĭ'rō,* s. novice, commençant, m.

U.

ubiquity, *ū'bĭk'wĭtĭ,* s. présence universelle, ubiquité, f.

udder, *ŭd'dĕr,* s. pis, m., tetine, f.

ugliness, *ŭg'lĭnĕs,* s. laideur, difformité, f.

ugly, *ŭg'lĭ,* a. laid, difforme.   [f.

ulcer, *ŭl'sĕr,* s. ulcère, m. || aphthe, m.

ulcerate, *ŭl'sĕr'āt,* v. a. (& n.) (s')ulcérer.

ulceration, *ŭl'sĕr'ā'shŭn,* s. ulcération, f.

ulcerous, *ŭl'sĕr'ŭs,* a. ulcéreux.

ulterior, *ŭl'tĕ'rĭ'ĕr,* a. ultérieur.

ultimate, *ŭl'tĭmāt,* a. dernier, décisif || -**ly,** ad. enfin, à la fin.

ultimatum, *ŭl'tĭ'mā'tŭm,* s. ultimatum, m.

ultimo, *ŭl'tĭ'mō,* ad. du mois dernier.

ultra, *ŭl'trä,* a. extrême.

ultramarine, *ŭl'trä'mä'rēn',* s. outremer, m.   [mer.

ultramarine, *ŭl'trä'mä'rēn',* a. d'outre-

ultramontane, *ŭl'trä'mŏn'tān,* s. ultra-montain, m.

ultramontane, *ŭl'trä'mŏn'tān,* a. ultra-montain.

umber, *ŭm'bĕr,* s. terre d'ombre, f.

umbrage, *ŭm'brāj,* s. ombrage, m. || to take ~, prendre ombrage.

umbrella, *ŭm'brĕl'la,* s. parapluie, m. || to put up an ~, ouvrir le parapluie || ~-case, s. fourreau de parapluie, m. || ~-stand, s. porte-parapluies, m.

umpirage, *ŭm'pĭr'āj,* s. arbitrage, m.

umpire, *ŭm'pĭr,* s. arbitre, m.

unabashed, *ŭn'ā'băsht',* a. sans vergogne.

unabated, *ŭn'ā'bā'tĕd,* a. non affaibli || toujours égal.

unable, *ŭn'ā'bl,* a. incapable || ne pouvant

unaccented, *ŭn'ăk'sĕn'tĕd,* a. sans accent.

unacceptable, *ŭn'ăk'sĕpt'ā'bl,* a. inacceptable, désagréable.

unaccepted, *ŭn'ăk'sĕp'tĕd,* a. refusé.

unaccommodating, *ŭn'ăk'kŏm'mō'dā'tĭng,* a. peu accommodant.

unaccompanied, *ŭn'ăk'kŭm'pän'ĭd,* a. sans compagnons || seul.

unaccomplished, *ŭn'ăk'kŏm'plĭsht,* a. inachevé, incomplet.

unaccountable, *ŭn'ăk'koŭnt'ā'bl,* a. inexplicable || bizarre || irresponsable.

unaccountably, *ŭn'ăk'koŭnt'ā'blĭ,* ad. d'une manière inexplicable.

unaccredited, *ŭn'ăk'krĕd'ĭ'tĕd,* a. non accrédité.

unaccustomed, *ŭn'ăk'kŭs'tŭmd,* a. peu habitué || inaccoutumé.

unacknowledged, *ŭn'ăk'nŏl'ĕjd,* a. non reconnu || non avoué.

unacquainted, *ŭn'ăk'kwānt'ĕd,* a. inconnu || qui ignore.

unadjusted, *ŭn'ăd'jŭst'ĕd,* a. non ajusté || (jur.) en litige.

unadorned, *ŭn'ă'dŏŭrnd',* a. sans parure, simple.

unadulterated, *ŭn'ă'dŭl'tĕr'ā'tĕd,* a. naturel, pur, non frelaté.

unadvisable, *ŭn'ăd'vī'ză'bl,* a. peu sage || mal vu.

unadvised, *ŭn'ăd'vīzd',* a. imprudent, indiscret, malavisé || -**ly,** ad. imprudemment || inconsidérément.

unaffected, *ŭn'ăf'fĕkt'ĕd,* a. sans affectation, simple, sincère || -**ly,** ad. sans affectation.

unaffectedness, *ŭn'ăf'fĕkt'ĕd'nĕs,* s. candeur, ingénuité, f.

unaffecting, *ŭn'ăf'fĕkt'ĭng,* a. peu touchant.

unaided, *ŭn'ād'ĕd,* a. sans aide, sans secours.

unalienable, *ŭn'ā'lyĕn'ā'bl,* a. inaliénable.

unalloyed, *ŭn'ăl'lŏjd',* a. sans alliage, pur.

unalterable, *ŭn'ăŭl'tĕr'ā'bl,* a. inaltérable, immuable.

unaltered, *ŭn'ăŭl'tĕrd,* a. qui n'est point changé.

unambitious, *ŭn'ăm'bĭsh'ŭs,* a. sans ambition.

unanimity, *ū'nă'nĭm'ĭtĭ,* s. unanimité, f.

unanimous, *ū'năn'ĭ'mŭs,* a. (-**ly,** ad.) unanime(ment).

unannounced, *ŭn'ăn'noŭnst',* a. sans se faire annoncer.

unanswerable, *ŭn'ăn'sĕr'ā'bl,* a. irréfutable, incontestable.

unanswerably, *ŭn'ăn'sĕr'ā'blĭ,* ad. d'une manière incontestable.

unanswered, *ŭn'ăn'sĕrd,* a. (resté) sans réplique.

unappalled, *ŭn'ăp'păŭld',* a. sans crainte.

unappeasable, *ŭn'ăp'pēz'ā'bl,* a. implacable.

unappeased, *ŭn'ăp'pēzd',* a. non apaisé.

unappreciated, *ŭn'ăp'prē'shĭ'ā'tĕd,* a. non apprécié || incompris.

unapprehensive, *ŭn'ăp'prē'hĕn'sĭv,* a. sans appréhension || peu intelligent.

unapprised, *ŭn'ăp'prīzd',* a. ignorant (de).

unapproachable, *ŭn'ăp'prōch'ā'bl,* a. inabordable.

unapproved, *ŭn'ăp'prōvd',* a. désapprouvé.

unarmed, *ŭn'ärmd',* a. sans armes.

unasked, *ŭn'äskt',* a. non demandé || sans être invité.

unaspiring, *ŭn'ăs'pī'rĭng,* a. sans ambition.

unassailable, *ŭn ăs săl' ă bl ,* a. inattaquable.

unassisted, *ŭn ăs sĭst' ĕd,* a. sans aide.

unassorted, *ŭn ăs sŏrt' ĕd,* a. non assorti.

unassuming, *ŭn ăs sū' mĭng,* a. sans prétention, modeste.

unassured, *ŭn ă shŏrd',* a. non assuré.

unatoned, *ŭn ă tōnd',* a. non expié.

unattached, *ŭn ăt tăcht',* a. indépendant de ‖ en disponibilité.

unattainable, *ŭn ăt tān' ă bl ,* a. impossible à atteindre.

unattained, *ŭn ăt tānd',* a. manqué.

unattempted, *ŭn ăt tĕm' tĕd,* a. non tenté ‖ non essayé.

unattended, *ŭn ăt tĕnd' ĕd,* a. sans suite, seul, sans être accompagné.

unattested, *ŭn ăt tĕst' ĕd,* a. non attesté.

unattractive, *ŭn ăt trăk' tĭv,* a. peu attrayant.

unauthenticated, *ŭn ăw thĕn' tĭk ă tĕd,* a. non constaté ‖ (jur.) non légalisé.

unauthorised, *ŭn ăw' thŏr ĭzd,* a. sans autorité.

unavailing, *ŭn ă văl' ĭng,* a. inutile, futile.

unavenged, *ŭn ă vĕnjd',* a. non vengé ‖ impuni.

unavoidable, *ŭn ă voÿd' ă bl ,* a. inévitable.

unavoidably, *ŭn ă voÿd' ă blĭ,* ad. inévitablement.

unavowed, *ŭn ă vŏwd',* a. non avoué.

unaware, *ŭn ă wăr' ,* ad. ignorant, inattentif.

unawares, *ŭn ă wărz',* ad. à l'improviste ‖ par mégarde.

unawed, *ŭn ăwd',* a. sans être effrayé.

unbacked, *ŭn băkt',* a. sans appui.

unbaked, *ŭn băkt',* a. non cuit.

unballast, *ŭn băl' lăst,* a. a délester.

unbaptised, *ŭn băp tīzd',* a. non baptisé.

unbar, *ŭn băr',* v. a. débarrer.

unbearable, *ŭn băr' ă bl ,* a. insupportable.

unbecoming, *ŭn bĕ kŭm' ĭng,* a. malséant, peu convenable ‖ -ly, ad. contre la bienséance.

unbecomingness, *ŭn bĕ kŭm' ĭng nĕs,* s. inconvenance, f.

unbefitting, *ŭn bĕ fĭt' tĭng,* a. inconvenant.

unbefriended, *ŭn bĕ frĕnd' ĕd,* a. sans amis.

unbelief, *ŭn bĕ lēf',* s. incrédulité, f. [f.

unbeliever, *ŭn bĕ lēv' ĕr,* s. incrédule, m. &

unbelieving, *ŭn bĕ lēv' ĭng,* a. incrédule.

unbend, *ŭn bĕnd',* v. a. ir. débander, détendre, relâcher ‖ délasser.

unbending, *ŭn bĕnd' ĭng,* a. inflexible.

unbeneficed, *ŭn bĕn' ĕ fĭst,* a. sans bénéfice.

unbiassed, *ŭn bī' ăst,* a. sans préjugés, impartial.

unbidden, *ŭn bĭd' dn,* a. sans invitation, spontané, non sollicité.

unbind, *ŭn bīnd',* v. a. ir. délier, détacher ‖ desserrer.

unbleached, *ŭn blēcht',* a. écru.

unblemished, *ŭn blĕm' ĭsht,* a. sans tache, pur.

unblest, *ŭn blĕst',* a. maudit, misérable.

unblown, *ŭn blōn',* a. non épanoui.

unblushing, *ŭn blŭsh' ĭng,* a. effronté.

unbolt, *ŭn bōlt',* v. a. déverrouiller, ouvrir.

unborn, *ŭn băŭrn',* a. à naître ‖ à venir.

unbosom, *ŭn bŏŏz' ŭm,* v. a. révéler, découvrir, confier.

unbound, *ŭn bŏwnd',* a. délié ‖ desserré ‖ (of books) non relié.

unbounded, *ŭn bŏwnd' ĕd,* a. illimité, infini, immense ‖ -ly, ad. sans bornes.

unbridle, *ŭn brī' dl,* v. a. débrider, ôter le frein ‖ (fig.) déchaîner.

unbridled, *ŭn brī' dld,* a. débridé ‖ effréné.

unbroken, *ŭn brō' kn,* a. non rompu or cassé ‖ non interrompu ‖ non violé ‖ non affaibli ‖ indompté.

unbrotherly, *ŭn brŭth' ĕr lĭ,* ad. indigne d'un frère, peu fraternel.

unbuckle, *ŭn bŭk' kl,* v. a. déboucler.

unbuilt, *ŭn bĭlt',* a. à bâtir.

unburden, *ŭn bĕr' dn,* v. a. décharger ‖ (fig.) soulager.

unburied, *ŭn bĕr' ĭd,* a. sans sépulture.

unburnt, *ŭn bĕrnt',* a. non brûlé.

unbutton, *ŭn bŭt' tn,* v. a. déboutonner.

uncage, *ŭn kāj',* v. a. délivrer.

uncalled, *ŭn kăwld',* a. sans être appelé ~ **for,** mal à propos ‖ inutile ‖ gratuit ‖ immérité.

uncanny, *ŭn kăn' nĭ,* a. sinistre, de mauvais augure.

uncap, *ŭn kăp',* v. a. **(bottles)** décoiffer ‖ **(swords)** démoucheter.

uncared, *ŭn kărd',* a. (~ **for)** dont on ne se soucie pas.

uncarpeted, *ŭn kărp' ĕt ĕd,* a. dépourvu de tapis.

unceasing, *ŭn sēs' ĭng,* a. continuel, perpétuel, incessant.

unceremonious, *ŭn sĕr ĕ mō' nĭ ŭs,* a. sans cérémonie ‖ -ly, ad. sans cérémonie.

uncertain, *ŭn sĕr' tăn* ou *ŭn sĕr' tĭn,* a. incertain.

uncertainty, *ŭn sĕr' tĭn tĭ,* s. incertitude, f.

unchain, *ŭn chān',* v. a. déchaîner.

unchangeable, *ŭn chānj' ă bl,* a. immuable, invariable.

unchangeableness, *ŭn chānj' ă bl nĕs,* s. immutabilité, invariabilité, f.

unchangeably, *ŭn chānj' ă blĭ,* ad. immuablement.

unchanged, *ŭn chānjd',* a. toujours le même, inaltérable.

unchanging, *ŭn chānj' ĭng,* a. qui ne change pas, invariable.

uncharitable, *ŭn chăr' ĭ tă bl,* a. peu charitable.

uncharitableness, *ŭn chăr' ĭ tă bl nĕs,* s. manque de charité, m.

uncharitably, *ŭn chăr' ĭ tă blĭ,* ad. sans charité.

unchaste, *ŭn chăst',* a. incontinent.

unchecked, *ŭn chĕkt',* a. sans retenue, sans frein, non réprimé.

unchristian, *ŭn krĭst' yăn,* a. antichrétien.

uncivil, *ŭn sĭv' ĭl,* a. incivil, impoli.

uncivilised, *ŭn sĭv' ĭl ĭzd,* a. incivilisé.
unclad, *ŭn klăd',* a. sans vêtements, nu.
unclaimed, *ŭn klāmd',* a. non réclamé.
unclasp, *ŭn klăsp',* v. a. dégrafer.
uncle, *ŭng' kl,* s. oncle, m. || (fam. **pawn-broker**) tante, f.
unclean, *ŭn klēn',* a. (-ly, ad.) sale(ment) || malpropre || impur.
uncleanliness, *ŭn klĕn' lĭ nĕs,* **uncleanness,** *ŭn klĕn' nĕs,* s. malpropreté, saleté, f.
uncleansed, *ŭn klĕnzd',* a. non purifié, sale || non nettoyé, non curé.
unclinch, *ŭn klĭnsh',* v. a. ouvrir, desserrer.
unclose, *ŭn klōz',* v. a. ouvrir.
unclouded, *ŭn klŏwd' ĕd,* a. sans nuages, serein.
uncock, *ŭn kŏk',* v. a. débander.
uncoil, *ŭn kŏȳl',* v. a. dérouler.
uncoloured, *ŭn kŭl' ŭrd,* a. non coloré.
uncombed, *ŭn kōmd',* a. non peigné, mal peigné.
uncomeliness, *ŭn kŭm' lĭ nĕs,* s. mauvaise grâce, laideur, f.
uncomely, *ŭn kŭm' lĭ,* a. manquant de grâce || désagréable.
uncomfortable, *ŭn kŭm' fĕrt ă bl,* a. désagréable, incommode || mal à l'aise.
uncomfortableness, *ŭn kŭm' fĕrt ă bl nĕs,* s. désagrément, m., incommodité, f.
uncomfortably, *ŭn kŭm' fĕrt ă blĭ,* ad. mal à l'aise.
uncommon, *ŭn kŏm' mŏn,* a. peu commun, rare || -ly, ad. extraordinairement
uncommonness, *ŭn kŏm' mŏn nĕs,* s. rareté, f.
uncompleted, *ŭn kŏm plē' tĕd,* a. inachevé.
uncompromising, *ŭn kŏm' prō mī zĭng,* a. irréconciliable.
unconcern, *ŭn kŏn sĕrn',* s. indifférence, f.
unconcerned, *ŭn kŏn sĕrnd',* a. indifférent, froid || désintéressé.
unconditional, *ŭn kŏn dĭsh' ŭn ăl,* a. sans condition, absolu || -ly, ad. sans conditions.
unconfined, *ŭn kŏn fīnd',* a. illimité, sans bornes.
unconfirmed, *ŭn kŏn fĕrmd',* a. non confirmé || non fortifié.
unconnected, *ŭn kŏn nĕk' tĕd,* a. décousu, sans liaison, sans rapport.
unconquerable, *ŭn kŏng' kĕr ă bl,* a. invincible || insurmontable.
unconquered, *ŭn kŏng' kĕrd,* a. non conquis || indompté.
unconscionable, *ŭn kŏn' shŭn ă bl,* a. déraisonnable || sans conscience.
unconscionably, *ŭn kŏn' shŭn ă blĭ,* ad. d'une manière déraisonnable || sans conscience.
unconscious, *ŭn kŏn' shŭs,* a. sans la conscience de || ignorant || -ly, ad. à son insu.
unconsciousness, *ŭn kŏn' shŭs nĕs,* s. ignorance, f. [consacré || non bénit.
unconsecrated, *ŭn kŏn' sĕ krā tĕd,* a. non
unconstitutional, *ŭn kŏn stĭ tū' shŭn ăl,* a. inconstitutionnel.

unconstrained, *ŭn kŏn strānd',* a. spontané, volontaire.
unconstraint, *ŭn kŏn strānt',* s. liberté, f. || aisance, f. || laisser aller, m.
uncontaminated, *ŭn kŏn tăm' ĭ nā tĕd,* a. (fig.) pur, sans souillure.
uncontested, *ŭn kŏn tĕs' tĕd,* a. incontesté.
uncontradicted, *ŭn kŏn tră dĭk' tĕd,* a. non contredit, sans démenti, sans contradiction.
uncontrollable, *ŭn kŏn trōl' ă bl,* a. ingouvernable, irrésistible.
uncontrolled, *ŭn kŏn trōld',* a. sans opposition || sans frein.
uncontroverted, *ŭn kŏn' trō vĕrt ĕd,* a. incontesté.
unconversant, *ŭn kŏn' vĕr sănt,* a. peu familier avec || peu versé dans.
unconvinced, *ŭn kŏn vĭnst',* a. non convaincu.
unconvincing, *ŭn kŏn vĭn' sĭng,* a. non convaincant.
uncork, *ŭn kŏrk',* v. a. déboucher.
uncorrected, *ŭn kŏr rĕk' tĕd,* a. non corrigé.
uncorrupted, *ŭn kŏr rŭp' tĕd,* a. non corrompu || pur.
uncouple, *ŭn kŭp' l,* v. a. découpler.
uncourteous, *ŭn kŏrt' yŭs,* a. impoli.
uncourtliness, *ŭn kŏrt' lĭ nĕs,* s. impolitesse, f.
uncourtly, *ŭn kŏrt' lĭ,* a. impoli || étranger au grand monde, à la cour.
uncouth, *ŭn kŏth',* a. (-ly, ad.) bizarre || gauche(ment) || grossier, rude(ment).
uncouthness, *ŭn kŏth' nĕs,* s. bizarrerie, f. || gaucherie, f. || grossièreté, f.
uncover, *ŭn kŭv' ĕr,* v. a. (se) découvrir.
uncropped, *ŭn krŏpt',* a. non cueilli, non moissonné.
uncrowned, *ŭn krŏwnd',* a. découronné || sans couronne.
unction, *ŭngk' shŭn,* s. onction, f.
unctuous, *ŭngk' tū ŭs,* a. onctueux.
uncultivated, *ŭn kŭl' tĭ vā tĕd,* a. inculte.
uncurbed, *ŭn kĕrbd',* a. effréné.
uncured, *ŭn kūrd',* a. non guéri || non fumé (viande).
uncurl, *ŭn kĕrl',* v. a. défriser, déboucler.
uncut, *ŭn kŭt',* a. non coupé || entier.
undamaged, *ŭn dăm' ĭjd,* a. non endommagé or (mar.) avarié.
undaunted, *ŭn dănt' ĕd,* a. intrépide.
undeceive, *ŭn dē sēv',* v. a. détromper, désabuser.
undecided, *ŭn dē sī' dĕd,* a. indécis.
undecipherable, *ŭn dē sī' fĕr ă bl,* a. indéchiffrable.
undecked, *ŭn dĕkt',* a. sans ornements || (mar.) non ponté.
undeclined, *ŭn dē klīnd',* a. invariable.
undefaced, *ŭn dē fāst',* a. non défiguré || non détérioré.
undefended, *ŭn dē fĕnd' ĕd,* a. sans défense || sans avocat.
undefiled, *ŭn dē fīld',* a. pur || sans tache.
undefinable, *ŭn dēf' nă bl,* a. indéfinissable.
undefined, *ŭn dē fīnd',* a. indéfini.

undeformed, *ŭn dē fårmd′*, a. non déformé.

undemonstrative, *ŭn dē mŏn′ strå tĭv*, a. inostensible.

undeniable, *ŭn dē nī′ å bl*, a. incontestable.

undeniably, *ŭn dē nī′ å blĭ*, ad. incontestablement.

undepressed, *ŭn dē prĕst′*, a. non abattu.

under, *ŭn′ dẽr*, pr. & ad. sous, au-dessous de ‖ en bas ‖ **~ such circumstances,** en l'état où sont les choses ‖ **~-clerk,** s. sous-commis, m. ‖ **~-secretary,** s. sous-secrétaire, m.

underbid, *ŭn dẽr bĭd′*, v. a. ir. offrir moins que.

underclothes, *ŭn dẽr klōthz′*, **underclothing,** *ŭn dẽr klō′ thĭng*, s. vêtements de dessous, m. pl.

undercurrent, *ŭn dẽr kŭr rĕnt*, s. courant sous l'eau, m.　　　　　　　　　[m.

undercut, *ŭn′ dẽr kŭt*, s. **(of meat)** filet,

underdone, *ŭn dẽr dŭn′*, a. pas assez cuit.

undergo, *ŭn dẽr gō′*, v. a. ir. souffrir, subir, endurer, essuyer.

undergraduate, *ŭn dẽr grăd′ ū āt*, s. bachelier, m.

underground, *ŭn′ dẽr grŏwnd*, s. sousterrain, sous-sol, m.

underground, *ŭn′ dẽr grŏwnd*, a. sousterrain ‖ **~,** ad. sous terre.　　　　[m.

undergrowth, *ŭn′ dẽr grōth*, s. bois taillis,

underhand, *ŭn dẽr hånd′*, a. clandestin, caché ‖ **~,** ad. sous main, en cachette.

underlay, *ŭn dẽr lā′*, v. a. mettre sous ‖ étayer.

underlet, *ŭn dẽr lĕt′*, v. a. ir. sous-louer.

underlie, *ŭn dẽr lī′*, v. a. être au fond de ‖ être sous.

underline, *ŭn dẽr lĭn′*, v. a. souligner.

underling, *ŭn′ dẽr lĭng*, s. subalterne, m.

undermine, *ŭn dẽr mīn′*, v. a. miner ‖ nuire à.

undermost, *ŭn′ dẽr mōst*, a. le plus bas.

underneath, *ŭn dẽr nēth′*, ad. & pr. dessous, au-dessous.

underpart, *ŭn′ dẽr pårt*, s. accessoire, m.

underpin, *ŭn dẽr pĭn′*, v. a. étayer, supporter ‖ reprendre en sous-œuvre.

underplot, *ŭn′ dẽr plŏt*, s. menée secrète, f. ‖ (théat.) sous-intrigue, f.

underpraise, *ŭn dẽr prāz′*, v. a. ne pas apprécier à sa juste valeur.

underprop, *ŭn dẽr prŏp′*, v. a. soutenir, étayer.

underrate, *ŭn dẽr rāt′*, v. a. déprécier, évaluer au-dessous de sa valeur.

undersell, *ŭn dẽr sĕl′*, v. a. ir. vendre à meilleur marché qu'un autre ‖ vendre à trop bas prix.

undersigned, *ŭn dẽr sīnd′*, a. soussigné ‖ **I, the ~,** je soussigné.

undersized, *ŭn′ dẽr sīzd*, a. au-dessous de la mesure ordinaire.

understand, *ŭn dẽr stånd′*, v. a. & n. ir. comprendre, entendre, concevoir ‖ apprendre ‖ **to give one to ~,** donner à entendre à qn.

understanding, *ŭn dẽr stånd′ ĭng*, s. entendement, m., intelligence, f., jugement, m. ‖ habileté, capacité, f. ‖ accord, m., harmonie, f. ‖ **to come to an ~ with one,** parvenir à une entente avec qn.

understanding, *ŭn dẽr stånd′ ĭng*, a. intelligent, éclairé, habile, entendu.

understate, *ŭn dẽr stāt′*, v. a. dire moins que ‖ amoindrir.

understrapper, *ŭn′ dẽr străp pẽr*, s. agent subalterne, m.

undertake, *ŭn dẽr tāk′*, v. a. & n. ir. entreprendre, se charger de ‖ attaquer ‖ s'aventurer, se hasarder ‖ promettre, s'engager.

undertaker, *ŭn dẽr tā kẽr*, s. entrepreneur, m. ‖ maître-maçon, m. ‖ entrepreneur des pompes funèbres, m.

undertaking, *ŭn dẽr tā′ kĭng*, s. entreprise, f., dessein, m.

undertone, *ŭn′ dẽr tōn*, s. ton bas, m. ‖ **in an ~,** à demi-voix.

undervaluation, *ŭn dẽr văl ū ā′ shŭn*, s. sous-évaluation, f.

undervalue, *ŭn dẽr văl′ ū*, v. a. déprécier, dépriser ‖ mépriser.

underwood, *ŭn′ dẽr wŏŏd*, s. bois menu, m., broussailles, f. pl.

underwork, *ŭn′ dẽr wẽrk*, s. petites affaires, f. pl.

underwork, *ŭn dẽr wẽrk′*, v.a. supplanter ‖ travailler à trop bas prix.

underworker, *ŭn′ dẽr wẽrk ẽr*, s. manœuvre, m. ‖ gâte-métier, m.

underwrite, *ŭn dẽr rīt′*, v. a. ir. écrire dessous, signer ‖ assurer (un vaisseau).

underwriter, *ŭn′ dẽr rĭt ẽr*, s. assureur, m.

undescried, *ŭn dē skrīd′*, a. inaperçu.

undeserved, *ŭn dē zẽrvd′*, a. (-ly, ad.) non mérité ‖ injuste(ment).　　　　[de.

undeserving, *ŭn dē zẽr′ vĭng*, a. indigne

undesigned, *ŭn dē zīnd′*, a. sans dessein, involontaire.

undesigning, *ŭn dē zīn′ ĭng*, a. franc, sincère, sans artifice.

undesirable, *ŭn dē zī′ rå bl*, a. peu désirable.

undetected, *ŭn dē tĕk′ tĕd*, a. non découvert.

undetermined, *ŭn dē tẽr′ mĭnd*, a. indécis, incertain.

undeterred, *ŭn dē tẽrd′*, a. intrépide.

undeviating, *ŭn dē vī ā′ ĭng*, a. droit, régulier, ferme ‖ **-ly,** ad. tout droit, sans dévier.

undigested, *ŭn dĭ jĕs′ tĕd*, a. qui n'est pas digéré, indigeste.　　　　　　　　[bas.

undignified, *ŭn dĭg′ nĭ fīd*, a. sans dignité,

undiminished, *ŭn dĭ mĭn′ ĭsht*, a. non diminué.

undimmed, *ŭn dĭmd′*, a. non obscurci.

undirected, *ŭn dĭ rĕk′ tĕd*, a. sans adresse.

undiscerned, *ŭn dĭz zẽrnd′*, a. non aperçu.

undiscerning, *ŭn dĭz zẽrn′ ĭng*, a. sans discernement.

undisciplined, *ŭn dĭs′ sĭp plĭnd*, a. indiscipliné.

undiscoverable, *ŭn dĭs kŭv′ ẽr å bl*, a. qu'on ne peut découvrir.

...k, ŭn lĭngk', v. a. dérouler || défaire.
...vely, ŭn lĭv'lĭ, a. lourd.
...ad, ŭn lōd', v. a. ir. décharger || alléger.
...ck, ŭn lŏk', v. a. ouvrir.
...ooked (~-for), ŭn lŏŏkt', a. imprévu, ...attendu, inopiné.
...oose, ŭn lōs', v. a. délier, dénouer, dé-...cher, dégager, desserrer.
...luckily, ŭn lŭk'ĭ lĭ, ad. malheureuse-...ment. [infortune, f.
...luckiness, ŭn lŭk'ĭ nĕs, s. malheur m.,
...nlucky, ŭn lŭk'ĭ, a. malheureux, in-...fortuné || de mauvais augure || malin.
...nmade, ŭn mād', a. pas fait || défait.
...nmake, ŭn māk', v. a. ir. défaire.
...nman, ŭn măn', v. a. dégrader, ravaler ...efféminer, amollir, décourager || châtrer ...(mar.) désarmer.
...nmanageable, ŭn măn'āj ă bl, a. indis-...ciplinable, intraitable.
...nmanly, ŭn măn'lĭ, a. indigne d'un ...homme, efféminé.
...nmannered, ŭn măn'nėrd, a. sans ma-...nières, grossier.
...nmannerliness, ŭn măn'nėr lĭ nĕs, s. ...malhonnêteté, grossièreté, f.
...nmannerly, ŭn măn'nėr lĭ, a. mal élevé, ...impoli, grossier.
...nmanured, ŭn mă nūrd', a. sans engrais.
...nmarked, ŭn märkt', a. non marqué || ...inaperçu.
...nmarred, ŭn märd', a. non gâté || non ...troublé. [dans le célibat.
...nmarried, ŭn măr'rĭd, a. non-marié,
...nmarry, ŭn măr'rĭ, v. a. démarier.
...nmask, ŭn măsk', v. a. (& n.) (se) dé-...masquer || dévoiler.
...nmastered, ŭn măs'tėrd, a. indompté.
...nmatched, ŭn măcht', a. sans égal, in-...comparable, sans pareil.
...nmeaning, ŭn mēn'ĭng, a. insignifiant.
...nmeant, ŭn mĕnt', a. involontaire.
...nmeasured, ŭn mĕzh'ōrd, a. immense || ...illimité || sans mesure.
...nmeditated, ŭn mĕd'ĭ tā tĕd, a. non pré-...médité.
...nmeet, ŭn mēt', a. impropre, inconvenant.
...nmentionable, ŭn mĕn'shŭn ă bl, a. dont ...on ne doit pas parler.
...nmentioned, ŭn mĕn'shŭnd, a. non ...mentionné.
...nmerciful, ŭn mėr'sĭ fŏŏl, a. (-ly, ad.) ...impitoyable(ment) || sans miséricorde, in-...humain || sans pitié, barbare.
...nmercifulness, ŭn mėr'sĭ fŏŏl nĕs, s. ...cruauté, dureté, f.
...nmerited, ŭn mėr'ĭt ĕd, a. non mérité.
...nmethodical, ŭn mĕ thŏd'ĭk ăl, a. (-ly, ...ad.) sans méthode.
...nmindful, ŭn mĭnd'fŏŏl, a. négligent, in-...attentif, oublieux.
...nmistakable, ŭn mĭs tā'kă bl, a. clair, ...évident.
...nmistakably, ŭn mĭs tā'kă blĭ, ad. claire-...ment, évidemment.
...nmixed, ŭn mĭkst', a. sans mélange, pur.
...nmolested, ŭn mō lĕst'ĕd, a. non molesté.

unmoor, ŭn mōr', v. a. démarrer.
unmotherly, ŭn mŭth'ėr lĭ, a. non ma-ternel. [à pied.
unmounted, ŭn mŏwnt'ĕd, a. démonté ||
unmoved, ŭn mōvd', a. non mû, non changé, immobile, stable || sans être af-fecté.
unmuffle, ŭn mŭf'l, v. a. désaffubler.
unmusical, ŭn mū'zĭ kăl, a. peu harmo-nieux or musical.
unmuzzle, ŭn mŭz'l, v. a. ôter la muse-lière, démuseler.
unnail, ŭn nāl', v. a. déclouer.
unnamable, ŭn nām'ă bl, a. innommable.
unnatural, ŭn nă'tū răl ou ŭn nă'chŏŏ răl, a. contraire à la nature || dénaturé || -ly, ad. contre nature.
unnecessarily, ŭn nĕs'ĕs ĕr ĭ lĭ, ad. sans nécessité, inutilement.
unnecessary, ŭn nĕs'ĕs sĕr ĭ, a. non né-cessaire, inutile.
unneighbourly, ŭn nā'bėr lĭ, a. non amical, de mauvais voisin.
unnerve, ŭn nėrv', v. a. énerver, affaiblir.
unnoticed, ŭn nō'tĭst, a. non remarqué, inaperçu || négligé.
unnumbered, ŭn nŭm'bėrd, a. innom-brable || non numéroté.
unobjectionable, ŭn ŏb jĕk'shŭn ă bl, a. irréprochable || irrécusable.
unobjectionably, ŭn ŏb jĕk'shŭn ă blĭ, ad. d'une manière irrécusable.
unobservant, ŭn ŏb zėr'vănt, a. inattentif.
unobserved, ŭn ŏb zėrvd', a. inobservé, inaperçu.
unobstructed, ŭn ŏb strŭkt'ĕd, a. non obstrué || sans obstacle.
unobtainable, ŭn ŏb tān'ă bl, a. qui ne peut être obtenu, hors d'atteinte.
unobtrusive, ŭn ŏb trō'sĭv, a. réservé, modeste, discret.
unoccupied, ŭn ŏk'kū pĭd, a. inoccupé || oisif || disponible || inhabité.
unoffending, ŭn ŏf fĕnd'ĭng, a. inoffensif.
unoffered, ŭn ŏf'fėrd, a. non offert.
unofficial, ŭn ŏf fĭsh'ăl, a. inofficieux.
unopened, ŭn ō'pnd, a. fermé.
unopposed, ŭn ŏp pōzd', a. sans oppo-sition.
unornamented, ŭn ŏr'nă mĕnt ĕd, a. sans ornements.
unorthodox, ŭn ŏr'thŏ dŏks, a. hétérodoxe.
unostentatious, ŭn ŏs tĕn tā'shŭs, a. sans ostentation, sans faste.
unpack, ŭn păk', v. a. dépaqueter, déballer.
unpaid, ŭn pād', a. non payé, sans solde || non affranchi.
unpalatable, ŭn păl'ă tă bl, a. désagréable, dégoûtant.
unparalleled, ŭn păr'ăl lĕld, a. incom-parable, sans pareil.
unpardonable, ŭn pär'dn ă bl, a. impar-donnable.
unpardonably, ŭn pär'dn ă blĭ, ad. d'une manière impardonnable.
unparliamentary, ŭn pär lĭ mĕnt'ă rĭ, a. contraire aux usages du parlement.

---

undiscovered, ŭn dĭs kŭv'ėrd, a. inconnu || caché.
undisguised, ŭn dĭs gīzd', a. sans déguise-ment, ouvert, sincère.
undismayed, ŭn dĭs mād', a. sans peur.
undisturbed, ŭn dĭs tėrbd', a. tranquille, calme.
undivided, ŭn dĭ vī'dĕd, a. indivisé, entier.
undivulged, ŭn dĭ vŭljd', a. secret.
undo, ŭn dō', v. a. ir. défaire || rétracter, an-nuler, abroger || ruiner, perdre || changer.
undone, ŭn dŭn', p. & a. défait || inexé-cuté || ruiné.
undoubted, ŭn dŏwt'ĕd, a. (-ly, ad.) in-dubitable(ment).
undoubting, ŭn dŏwt'ĭng, a. convaincu.
undress, ŭn'drĕs, s. négligé, m. || (mil.) petite tenue, f.
undress, ŭn drĕs', v. a. déshabiller.
undressed, ŭn drĕst', a. déshabillé || qui n'est pas préparé.
undried, ŭn drīd', a. non séché || vert.
undue, ŭn dū', a. qui est injuste || méchant.
undulate, ŭn'dū lāt, v. n. ondoyer, on-duler.
undulating, ŭn'dū lāt ĭng, a. (of ground) accidenté. [f.
undulation, ŭn dū lā'shŭn, s. ondulation,
unduly, ŭn dū'lĭ, ad. indûment || trop.
undutiful, ŭn dū'tĭ fŏŏl, a. désobéissant, irrespectueux || -ly, ad. irrespectueuse-ment.
undutifulness, ŭn dū'tĭ fŏŏl nĕs, s. manque de respect, m. || désobéissance, f.
undying, ŭn dī'ĭng, a. immortel.
unearned, ŭn ėrnd', a. non mérité.
unearth, ŭn ėrth', v. a. déterrer.
unearthly, ŭn ėrth'lĭ, a. céleste || infernal.
uneasily, ŭn ē'zĭ lĭ, ad. péniblement.
uneasiness, ŭn ē'zĭ nĕs, s. incommodité, inquiétude, peine, f., déplaisir, m.
uneasy, ŭn ē'zĭ, a. inquiet, pénible, in-commode, mal à son aise || difficile.
unedifying, ŭn ĕd'ĭ fī ĭng, a. peu édifiant.
uneducated, ŭn ĕd'ū kā tĕd, a. sans édu-cation.
unembarrassed, ŭn ĕm băr'răst, a. non embarrassé || à l'aise || libre.
unemployed, ŭn ĕm plŏyd', a. désœuvré, oisif || inactif, dormant (capital).
unencumbered, ŭn ĕn kŭm'bėrd, a. dé-barrassé, non chargé || dégagé, non hypo-théqué, non grevé.
unendowed, ŭn ĕn dŏwd', a. non doué.
unenjoyed, ŭn ĕn jŏyd', a. dont on ne jouit pas.
unenlightened, ŭn ĕn līt'nd, a. qui n'est pas éclairé.
unenterprising, ŭn ĕn'tėr prī zĭng, a. peu entreprenant.
unentertaining, ŭn ĕn tėr tān'ĭng, a. peu amusant, inamusant.
unenviable, ŭn ĕn'vĭ ă bl, a. peu digne d'envie.
unenvied, ŭn ĕn'vĭd, a. peu envié.
unequal, ŭn ē'kwŏl, a. (-ly, ad.) inégal (ement) || inférieur.

unequalled, ŭn ē'kwŏld, a. sans égal, in-comparable.
unequivocal, ŭn ē kwĭv'ō kăl, a. non équi-voque.
unerring, ŭn ėr'rĭng, a. (-ly, ad.) in-faillible(ment).
uneven, ŭn ē'vn, a. (-ly, ad.) inégal (ement) || impair || raboteux.
unevenness, ŭn ē'vn nĕs, s. inégalité, f.
unexampled, ŭn ĕg zăm'pld, a. sans exemple, unique.
unexceptionable, ŭn ĕk sĕp'shŭn ă bl, a. irréprochable.
unexhausted, ŭn ĕg zhăwst'ĕd, a. inépuisé.
unexpected, ŭn ĕks pĕk'tĕd, a. (-ly, ad.) inattendu || inopiné(ment) || à l'improviste.
unexpectedness, ŭn ĕks pĕk'tĕd nĕs, s. arrivée inattendue, f.
unexpired, ŭn ĕks pīrd', a. non expiré.
unexplained, ŭn ĕks plānd', a. inexpliqué.
unexplored, ŭn ĕks plōrd', a. inexploré.
unexposed, ŭn ĕks pōzd', a. non exposé, caché.
unfaded, ŭn fā'dĕd, a. non fané or flétri.
unfading, ŭn fā'dĭng, a. qui n'est pas sujet à se flétrir.
unfailing, ŭn fā'lĭng, a. infaillible, certain.
unfair, ŭn fär', a. (-ly, ad.) injuste(ment) || malhonnête.
unfairness, ŭn fär'nĕs, s. mauvaise foi, injustice, f.
unfaithful, ŭn fāth'fŏŏl, a. (-ly, ad.) in-fidèle(ment).
unfaithfulness, ŭn fāth'fŏŏl nĕs, s. in-fidélité, f.
unfaltering, ŭn fŏwl'tėr ĭng, a. assuré, ferme, hardi.
unfamiliar, ŭn fă mĭl'yėr, a. inaccoutumé, peu commun, peu familier.
unfashionable, ŭn făsh'ŭn ă bl, a. qui n'est pas de mode or à la mode.
unfashionably, ŭn făsh'ŭn ă blĭ, ad. passé de mode.
unfasten, ŭn făs'n, v. a. délier, détacher, défaire || desserrer || relâcher.
unfatherly, ŭn fă'thėr lĭ, a. peu paternel.
unfathomable, ŭn făth'ŭm ă bl, un-fathomed, ŭn făth'ŭmd, a. insondable || sans fond || impénétrable.
unfavourable, ŭn fā'vėr ă bl, a. défavo-rable. [favorablement
unfavourably, ŭn fā'vėr ă blĭ, ad. dé-favorablement.
unfeasible, ŭn fē'zĭ bl, a. impraticable.
unfeathered, ŭn fĕth'ėrd, a. sans plumes.
unfed, ŭn fĕd', a. qui n'est point nourri.
unfeeling, ŭn fēl'ĭng, a. insensible.
unfeigned, ŭn fānd' ou ŭn fān'ĕd, a. (-ly, ad.) sans feinte, sincère(ment) || réel.
unfelt, ŭn fĕlt', a. qui n'est pas senti.
unfeminine, ŭn fĕm'ĭ nĭn, a. peu féminin, qui n'est pas d'une femme.
unfenced, ŭn fĕnst', a. sans clôture, ouvert.
unfermented, ŭn fėr mĕnt'ĕd, a. non fer-menté || sans levain.
unfetter, ŭn fĕt'tėr, v. a. ôter les chaînes, délivrer.
unfilial, ŭn fĭl'ĭ ăl, a. peu filial.
unfilled, ŭn fĭld', a. non rempli, vide.

unfinished, *ŭn fin'isht,* a. imparfait, in-achevé.

unfit, *ŭn fit',* v. a. rendre incapable.

unfit, *ŭn fit',* a. impropre, inconvenant, incapable || —ly, ad. mal à propos.

unfitness, *ŭn fit'nĕs,* s. incapacité, in-aptitude, f.

unfitting, *ŭn fit'ting,* a. inconvenant.

unfix, *ŭn fiks',* v. a. détacher || fondre || rendre indécis.

unfixed, *ŭn fikst',* a. qui n'est point fixé, indéterminé || vagabond.

unflagging, *ŭn flăg'ging,* a. infatigable, persévérant.

unfledged, *ŭn flĕjd',* a. sans plumes || jeune, novice.

unfold, *ŭn fōld',* v. a. déplier, développer, révéler, découvrir, expliquer || exposer (mar.) déparquer (sheep).

unforbidden, *ŭn fŏr bid'n,* a. pernis.

unforced, *ŭn fōrst',* a. libre, aisé, naturel.

unforeseen, *ŭn fōr sēn',* a. imprévu, in-opiné.

unforgiving, *ŭn fŏr giv'ing,* a. impla-cable, inexorable.

unfortified, *ŭn fŏr'ti fid,* a. sans fortifica-tions, non fortifié.

unfortunate, *ŭn fŏr'tū năt,* a. infortuné, malheureux || —ly, ad. malheureusement.

unfounded, *ŭn fŏwnd'ĕd,* a. sans fonde-ment, dénué de fondement.

unframed, *ŭn frămd',* a. non façonné or encadré.

unfrequented, *ŭn frē kwĕnt'ĕd,* a. peu fréquenté.

unfriended, *ŭn frĕnd'ĕd,* a. sans amis.

unfriendliness, *ŭn frĕnd'li nĕs,* s. dis-position peu amicale, f. || froideur, f.

unfriendly, *ŭn frĕnd'li,* a. peu amical || mal disposé.

unfrock, *ŭn frŏk',* v. a. défroquer.

unfrozen, *ŭn frō'zn,* a. non gelé.

unfruitful, *ŭn frōt'fōol,* a. infructueux, in-fertile, stérile. [lité, f.

unfruitfulness, *ŭn frōt'fōol nĕs,* s. stéri-

unfunded, *ŭn fŭnd'ĕd,* a. flottant.

unfurl, *ŭn fĕrl',* v. a. déployer || (mar.) dé-ferler.

unfurnished, *ŭn fĕr'nisht,* a. non meublé || dépourvu de.

ungainly, *ŭn găn'li,* a. & ad. maladroit, gauche.

ungallant, *ŭn găl lănt',* a. peu galant.

ungarnished, *ŭn gär'nisht,* a. dégarni.

ungarrisoned, *ŭn găr'ri sŭnd,* a. sans garnison.

ungenerous, *ŭn jĕn'ĕr ŭs,* a. peu généreux.

ungentle, *ŭn jĕn'tl,* a. rude, dur.

ungentlemanly, *ŭn jĕn'tl măn li,* a. in-digne d'un honnête homme || peu délicat, malhonnête.

ungentleness, *ŭn jĕn'tl nĕs,* s. dureté, rudesse, sévérité, f. || impolitesse, f.

ungently, *ŭn jĕn'tli,* ad. rudement.

ungird, *ŭn gĕrd',* v. a. ir. dessangler || ôter la ceinture.

unglazed, *ŭn glăzd',* a. non vitré, non verni.

ungodliness, *ŭn gŏd'li nĕs,* s. impiété, f.

ungodly, *ŭn gŏd'li,* a. impie.

ungovernable, *ŭn gŭv'ĕrn ă bl,* a. ingou-vernable, intraitable || licencieux.

ungoverned, *ŭn gŭv'ĕrnd,* a. sans lois || effréné.

ungraceful, *ŭn grăs'fōol,* a. (-ly, ad.) dis-gracieux, sans grâce.

ungracefulness, *ŭn grăs'fōol nĕs,* s. manque de grâce, m., gaucherie, f.

ungracious, *ŭn grā'shŭs,* a. désagréable || mal vu || —ly, ad. d'une manière peu gracieuse.

ungrammatical, *ŭn grăm măt'i kăl,* a. contraire aux règles de la grammaire || —ly, ad. contre la grammaire.

ungrateful, *ŭn grāt'fōol,* a. ingrat || dés-agréable || —ly, ad. en ingrat || désagréa-blement.

ungratefulness, *ŭn grāt'fōol nĕs,* s. in-gratitude, f.

ungrounded, *ŭn grŏwnd'ĕd,* a. sans fonde-ment.

ungrudgingly, *ŭn grŭj'ing li,* ad. de bon cœur, volontiers.

unguarded, *ŭn gärd'ĕd,* a. sans défense || indiscret, inconsidéré.

unhallowed, *ŭn hăl'lōd,* a. profane.

unhand, *ŭn hănd',* v. a. lâcher.

unhandsome, *ŭn hănd'sŭm,* a. mal-gracieux, laid, malhonnête || —ly, ad. sans grâce, mal.

unhandy, *ŭn hăn'di,* a. maladroit, gauche.

unhappily, *ŭn hăp'pi li,* ad. malheureuse-ment. [m.

unhappiness, *ŭn hăp'pi nĕs,* s. malheur,

unhappy, *ŭn hăp'pi,* a. malheureux.

unharmed, *ŭn härmd',* a. non blessé, sain et sauf.

unharness, *ŭn här'nĕs,* v. a. déharnacher || dételer || désarmer.

unhatched, *ŭn hăcht',* a. non éclos.

unhealthiness, *ŭn hĕlth'i nĕs,* s. mau-vaise santé, f., état maladif, m.

unhealthy, *ŭn hĕlth'i,* a. maladif || malsain.

unheard, *ŭn hĕrd',* a. non entendu || in-connu, inouï.

unheeded, *ŭn hēd'ĕd,* a. inaperçu || mé-connu, négligé.

unheeding, *ŭn hēd'ing,* a. inattentif || insouciant.

unhelped, *ŭn hĕlpt',* a. sans secours.

unhesitating, *ŭn hĕz'i tā ting,* a. déter-miné || —ly, ad. sans hésitation.

unhewn, *ŭn hūn',* a. brut || non taillé.

unhindered, *ŭn hin'dĕrd,* a. sans ob-stacles || libre.

unhinge, *ŭn hinj',* v. a. mettre hors des gonds || mettre en désordre, troubler.

unholy, *ŭn hō'li,* a. impie, profane.

unhonoured, *ŭn ŏn'ĕrd,* a. non honoré, non respecté.

unhook, *ŭn hōok',* v. a. décrocher.

unhoped, *ŭn hōpt'* (~-for), a. inespéré.

unhorse, *ŭn hŏrs',* v. a. démonter, dés-arçonner.

unhurt, *ŭn hĕrt',* a. sain et sauf || intact.

unicorn, *ū'ni kŏrn,* s. licorne, f.

uniform, *ū'ni fărm,* s. uniforme, m.

uniform, *ū'ni fărm,* a. uniforme || —ly, ad. uniformément.

uniformity, *ū ni fŏr'mi ti,* s. uniformité, f.

unify, *ū'ni fi,* v. a. unifier.

unilateral, *ū ni lăt'ĕr ăl,* a. unilatéral.

unimaginable, *ŭn i măj'in ă bl,* a. in-imaginable.

unimpaired, *ŭn im pārd',* a. non altéré, intact || non usé.

unimpeachable, *ŭn im pēch'ă bl,* a. in-attaquable || irréprochable.

unimpeached, *ŭn im pēcht',* a. incontesté || intact.

unimportant, *ŭn im pōrt'ănt,* a. de peu d'importance, indifférent.

unimpressed, *ŭn im prĕst',* a. non im-primé, inédit || non pénétré.

unimproved, *ŭn im prōvd',* a. non corrigé || non amélioré.

uninfected, *ŭn in fĕkt'ĕd,* a. non infecté de.

uninflammable, *ŭn in flăm'mă bl,* a. in-inflammable.

uninformed, *ŭn in făwrmd',* a. non in-struit || ignorant, sans instruction.

uninhabitable, *ŭn in hăb'it ă bl,* a. in-habitable.

uninhabited, *ŭn in hăb'i tĕd,* a. inhabité.

uninitiated, *ŭn in ish'i āt ĕd,* a. profane.

uninjured, *ŭn in'jōord,* a. non blessé || non endommagé || sain et sauf.

uninspired, *ŭn in spīrd',* a. sans in-spiration, non inspiré.

uninstructed, *ŭn in strŭkt'ĕd,* a. sans instruction, sans culture.

uninstructive, *ŭn in strŭk'tiv,* a. non instructif.

uninsured, *ŭn in shŏrd',* a. non assuré.

unintelligible, *ŭn in tĕl'li ji bl,* a. in-intelligible.

unintelligibly, *ŭn in tĕl'li ji blī,* ad. d'une manière inintelligible.

unintended, *ŭn in tĕnd'ĕd,* a. non inten-tionnel.

unintentional, *ŭn in tĕn'shŭn dl,* a. fait sans dessein || —ly, ad. sans intention.

uninterested, *ŭn in'tĕr ĕst ĕd,* a. désin-téressé || impartial.

uninteresting, *ŭn in'tĕr ĕst ing,* a. peu intéressant.

unintermitted, *ŭn in tĕr mit'tĕd,* **un-intermitting,** *ŭn in tĕr mit'ting,* a. (-ly, ad.) incessant, continu, suivi.

uninterred, *ŭn in tĕrd',* a. sans sépulture.

uninterrupted, *ŭn in tĕr rŭp'tĕd,* a. con-tinu || —ly, ad. sans interruption.

uninvested, *ŭn in vĕs'tĕd,* a. non investi (of money) non placé.

uninvestigated, *ŭn in vĕs'ti gā tĕd,* a. qui n'a pas été examiné.

uninvited, *ŭn in vī'tĕd,* a. sans être invité.

union, *ū'ni ŭn,* s. union, f. || harmonie, f. || trades ~, union industrielle, f. || ~-jack, s. (mar.) pavillon anglais, m.

unionist, *ū'ni yŭn ist,* s. unioniste, m.

uniparous, *ū nip'ă rŭs,* a. unipare.

unique, *ū* ...

unison, *ū'ni* ...

uni... ...

Unitarian, *ŭn* ...

unitarian, *ŭn* ...

unite, *ū nīt',* v. a. ...

unitedly, *ū* ...

unity, *ū'ni ti,* s. ...

universal, *ū ni* ... ad. universellement

universality, *ū ni* ... versalité, f.

universe, *ū'ni vĕrs,* ...

university, *ū ni vĕr's*... ~ man, s. universitai...

unjust, *ŭn jŭst',* a. (-ly, ...

unjustifiable, *ŭn jŭs*... justifiable, inexcusable.

unjustifiably, *ŭn jŭs'ti f*... manière injustifiable.

unkennel, *ŭn kĕn'nĕl,* v. a... busquer || débucher.

unkept, *ŭn kĕpt',* a. non ... accompli || non gardé.

unkind, *ŭn kīnd',* a. (-ly, ad.) ... sans bienveillance, peu aimabl... || durement.

unkindly, *ŭn kīnd'li,* a. ennem... sible || contraire || sans amitié, ...

unkindness, *ŭn kīnd'nĕs,* s. ma... bonté, m., dureté, désobligeance, ...

unknit, *ŭn nit',* v. a. ir. dénouer, ...

unknowable, *ŭn nō'ă bl,* a. impénét... méconnaissable. [sa...

unknowingly, *ŭn nō'ing li,* ad. sa...

unknown, *ŭn nōn',* a. inconnu.

unlace, *ŭn lās',* v. a. délacer, délier.

unlade, *ŭn lād',* v. a. ir. décharger.

unlading, *ŭn lād'ing,* s. déchargement, ...

unladylike, *ŭn lā'di lik,* a. de mauvais ton... indigne d'une dame comme il faut.

unlamented, *ŭn lă mĕnt'ĕd,* a. qui n'est ... pas regretté.

unlatch, *ŭn lăch',* v. a. ouvrir (une porte).

unlawful, *ŭn lăw'fōol,* a. (-ly, ad.) illégal... (ement) || illégitime(ment).

unlawfulness, *ŭn lăw'fōol nĕs,* s. illé-galité, f. || illégitimité, f.

unlearn, *ŭn lĕrn',* v. a. désapprendre.

unlearned, *ŭn lĕrn'ĕd,* a. illettré, ignorant.

unleavened, *ŭn lĕv'nd,* a. sans levain.

unless, *ŭn lĕs',* c. à moins que, à moins de, excepté que.

unlessened, *ŭn lĕs'nd,* a. entier, intégral.

unlettered, *ŭn lĕt'tĕrd,* a. illettré.

unlicensed, *ŭn li'sĕnst,* a. sans patente.

unlicked, *ŭn likt',* a. mal léché, informe.

unlighted, *ŭn lit'ĕd,* a. non allumé || non éclairé.

unlike, *ŭn lik',* a. différent || improbable.

unlikelihood, *ŭn lik'li hŏod,* s. invrai-semblance, improbabilité, f.

unlikely, *ŭn lik'li,* a. & ad. invraisem-blable(ment).

unlikeness, *ŭn lik'nĕs,* s. dissimilitude, f.

unlimited, *ŭn lim'i tĕd,* a. illimité || —ly, ad. sans bornes.

läte, hăt, fär, läw; — hēre, gĕt, hĕr; — mīne, inn; — nō, hŏt, prōve; — hōw; —

bŏy; — fōot, tūbe, tŭb || chair, joy; — game, yes; — soul, zeal; — thing, there.
English and French.

unpatented, *ŭn pā′ tĕnt ĕd,* a. non breveté.

unpatriotic, *ŭn pā trĭ ŏt′ ĭk,* a. peu patriotique.

unpave, *ŭn pāv′,* v. a. dépaver ‖ décarreler.

unpaved, *ŭn pāvd′,* a. non pavé ‖ dépavé.

unpensioned, *ŭn pĕn′ shŭnd,* a. qui ne reçoit pas de pension.

unpeople, *ŭn pē′ pl,* v. a. dépeupler.

unperceived, *ŭn pẽr sēvd′,* a. inaperçu.

unperformed, *ŭn pẽr fārmd′,* a. inexécuté ‖ non accompli.

unpersecuted, *ŭn pẽr′ sē kū tĕd,* a. non poursuivi.

unphilosophical, *ŭn fĭl ō sŏf′ ĭ kăl,* a. contraire aux règles de la philosophie.

unpick, *ŭn pĭk′,* v. a. forcer une serrure.

unpin, *ŭn pĭn′,* v. a. détacher, défaire.

unpitied, *ŭn pĭt′ ĭd,* a. sans être plaint.

unpitying, *ŭn pĭt′ ĭ ĭng,* a. impitoyable.

unplaced, *ŭn plāst′,* a. sans place.

unpleasant, *ŭn plĕz′ ănt,* a. (–ly, ad.) désagréable(ment).

unpleasantness, *ŭn plĕz′ ănt nĕs,* s. désagrément, m. ‖ nature désagréable, f.

unpledged, *ŭn plĕjd′,* a. non engagé.

unploughed, *ŭn plōwd′,* a. non labouré.

unplume, *ŭn plōm′,* v. a. déplumer.

unpoetical, *ŭn pō ĕt′ ĭk ăl,* a. prosaïque.

unpolished, *ŭn pŏl′ ĭsht,* a. non poli, rude, grossier, non civilisé.

unpolluted, *ŭn pŏl lō′ tĕd,* a. pur ‖ sans tache, sans souillure.

unpopular, *ŭn pŏp′ ū lẽr,* a. impopulaire.

unpopularity, *ŭn pŏp ū lăr′ ĭ tĭ,* s. impopularité, f.

unportioned, *ŭn pŏr′ shŭnd,* a. sans dot.

unpracticed, *ŭn prăk′ tĭst,* a. inexpérimenté.

unprecedented, *ŭn prĕs′ ē dĕnt ĕd,* a. sans précédent, sans exemple.

unprejudiced, *ŭn prĕj′ ŏŏ dĭst,* a. sans préjugés, sans prévention.

unpremeditated, *ŭn prē mĕd′ ĭ tā tĕd,* a. non prémédité, improvisé.

unprepared, *ŭn prē pârd′,* a. non préparé, sans être préparé.

unprepossessed, *ŭn prē pŏz zĕst′,* a. sans préjugés, impartial.

unprepossessing, *ŭn prē pŏz zĕs′ ĭng,* a. peu prévenant *or* engageant.

unpresuming, *ŭn prē zūm′ ĭng,* **unpretending,** *ŭn prē tĕnd′ ĭng,* a. sans prétentions, modeste.

unprincely, *ŭn prĭns′ lĭ,* a. indigne d'un prince.

unprincipled, *ŭn prĭn′ sĭ pld,* a. sans principes ‖ sans mœurs.

unproductive, *ŭn prō dŭk′ tĭv,* a. improductif ‖ stérile.

unprofessional, *ŭn prō fĕsh′ ŭn ăl,* a. étranger à une profession.

unprofitable, *ŭn prŏf′ ĭt ă bl,* a. inutile, bon à rien, vain ‖ peu profitable.

unprofitableness, *ŭn prŏf′ ĭt ă bl nĕs,* s. inutilité, f.

unprofitably, *ŭn prŏf′ ĭt ă blĭ,* ad. inutilement, sans profit.

unprolific, *ŭn prō lĭf′ ĭk,* a. infécond.

unpromising, *ŭn prŏm′ ĭs ĭng,* a. qui ne promet rien ‖ qui s'annonce mal.

unpropitious, *ŭn prō pĭsh′ ŭs,* a. défavorable, sinistre.

unprosperous, *ŭn prŏs′ pẽr ŭs,* a. malheureux ‖ –ly, ad. sans succès.

unprotected, *ŭn prō tĕkt′ ĕd,* a. sans protection, non protégé.

unproved, *ŭn prōvd′,* a. non prouvé, sans preuve ‖ non éprouvé.

unprovided, *ŭn prō vī′ dĕd,* a. non pourvu, dépourvu ‖ ~–for, a. non pourvu.

unprovoked, *ŭn prō vōkt′,* a. non provoqué, non irrité.

unpublished, *ŭn pŭb′ lĭsht,* a. non publié, inconnu ‖ inédit.

unpunctual, *ŭn pŭngk′ tū ăl,* a. inexact.

unpunctuality, *ŭn pŭngk tū ăl′ ĭ tĭ,* s. défaut de ponctualité, m.

unpunished, *ŭn pŭn′ ĭsht,* a. impuni.

unpurchased, *ŭn pẽr′ chăst,* a. non acheté.

unpurified, *ŭn pū′ rĭ fīd,* a. non purifié.

unqualified, *ŭn kwŏl′ ĭ fīd,* a. incapable ‖ pas propre à.

unqualify, *ŭn kwŏl′ ĭ fī,* v. a. rendre incapable.

unquenchable, *ŭn kwĕnch′ ă bl,* a. inextinguible, insatiable.

unquenched, *ŭn kwĕnsht′,* a. non éteint.

unquestionable, *ŭn kwĕst′ yŭn ă bl,* a. incontestable.

unquestionably, *ŭn kwĕst′ yŭn ă blĭ,* ad. sans contredit.

unquestioned, *ŭn kwĕst′ yŭnd,* a. non contesté ‖ indisputable ‖ sans être interrogé.

unquiet, *ŭn kwī′ ĕt,* a. inquiet, turbulent.

unransomed, *ŭn răn′ sŭmd,* a. non racheté ‖ non rançonné.

unravel, *ŭn răv′ l,* v. a. effiler, défaire, dénouer ‖ démêler.

unreached, *ŭn rēcht′,* a. qu'on n'a pas atteint.

unread, *ŭn rĕd′,* a. sans être lu ‖ illettré.

unreadable, *ŭn rĕd′ ă bl,* a. illisible.

unready, *ŭn rĕd′ ĭ,* a. non préparé, non prêt ‖ maladroit.

unreal, *ŭn rē′ ăl,* a. feint, vain ‖ faux ‖ imaginaire.

unreality, *ŭn rēăl′ ĭ tĭ,* s. fausses apparences, f. pl.

unreasonable, *ŭn rē′ zn ă bl,* a. irraisonnable, déraisonnable.

unreasonableness, *ŭn rē′ zn ă bl nĕs,* s. déraison, f. ‖ injustice, f.

unreasonably, *ŭn rē′ zn ă blĭ,* ad. déraisonnablement.

unrecalled, *ŭn rē kăwld′,* a. non rappelé.

unreclaimed, *ŭn rē klāmd′,* a. non corrigé, non amendé ‖ non réclamé.

unrecompensed, *ŭn rĕk′ ŏm pĕnst,* a. non récompensé.

unreconcilable, *ŭn rĕk′ ŏn sĭl ă bl,* a. irréconciliable.

unreconciled, *ŭn rĕk′ ŏn sĭld,* a. irrécon-

unrecorded, *ŭn′rĕ ka̤wrd′ĕd*, a. non enregistré || oublié.

unrecovered, *ŭn′rĕkŭv′ĕrd*, a. non recouvré || non guéri.

unredeemed, *ŭn′rĕdēmd′*, a. non racheté || non dégagé.

unredressed, *ŭn′rĕdrĕst′*, a. non réformé.

unrefined, *ŭn′rĕfīnd′*, a. non raffiné (affiné, purifié) || grossier.

unreflecting, *ŭn′rĕflĕkt′ĭng*, a. irréfléchi.

unreformed, *ŭn′rĕfa̤wrmd′*, a. non réformé.

unrefracted, *ŭn′rĕfrăkt′ĕd*, a. qui n'est pas réfléchi.

unrefreshed, *ŭn′rĕfrĕsht′*, a.non rafraîchi.

unregarded, *ŭn′rĕgärd′ĕd*, a. négligé, méprisé, oublié.

unregistered, *ŭn′rĕj′ĭstĕrd*, a. non enregistré || non chargé (lettre).

unrelenting, *ŭn′rĕlĕnt′ĭng*, a. implacable, inexorable, inflexible.

unrelieved, *ŭn′rĕlēvd′*, a. non secouru.

unremarked, *ŭn′rĕmärkd′*, a. inaperçu.

unremedied, *ŭn′rĕm′ĕdĭd*, a.irrémédiable || auquel on n'a pas remédié.

unremitting, *ŭn′rĕmĭt′ĭng*, a. (-ly, ad.) sans relâche, sans cesse.

unremunerative, *ŭn′rĕmū′nĕrătĭv*, a. qui ne rapporte rien || peu lucratif.

unrepealed, *ŭn′rĕpēld′*, a. irrévoqué, non abrogé.

unrepentant, *ŭn′rĕpĕnt′ănt*, **unrepenting**, *ŭn′rĕpĕnt′ĭng*, a. non repentant, impénitent, sans repentir.

unrepining, *ŭn′rĕpīn′ĭng*, a. sans murmurer.

unreproached, *ŭn′rĕprōcht′*, a. non blâmé, non censuré.

unresented, *ŭn′rĕzĕnt′ĕd*, a. non ressenti || pardonné.

unreserved, *ŭn′rĕzĕrvd′*, a. sans réserve, franc, sincère || **-ly**, ad. sans réserve, franchement.

unreservedness, *ŭn′rĕzĕr′vĕdnĕs*, s. franchise, f. || nature expansive, f.

unresisting, *ŭn′rĕzĭst′ĭng*, a. sans résistance, soumis.

unresolved, *ŭn′rĕzŏlvd′*, a. irrésolu, indécis.

unresponding, *ŭn′rĕspŏnd′ĭng*, a. irresponsable.

unrestored, *ŭn′rĕstōrd′*, a. ncn restitué.

unrestrained, *ŭn′rĕstrānd′*, a. sans contrainte, libre || déréglé.

unrestricted, *ŭn′rĕstrĭkt′ĕd*, a. sans restriction.

unrevealed, *ŭn′rĕvēld′*, a. non révélé.

unrevenged, *ŭn′rĕvĕnjd′*, a. non vengé.

unrewarded, *ŭn′rĕwa̤wrd′ĕd*, a. sans être récompensé.

unriddle, *ŭn′rĭd′dl*, v. a. expliquer, résoudre.

unrifled, *ŭn′rī′fld*, a. non rayé, lisse.

unrig, *ŭn′rĭg′*, v. a. dépouiller || débarnacher || (mar.) dégréer.

unrighteous, *ŭn′rī′yŭs* ou *ŭn′rī′chŭs*, a. (-ly, ad.) injuste(ment) || inique.

unrighteousness, *ŭn′rī′chŭsnĕs*, s. injustice, f. || iniquité, f.

unripe, *ŭn′rīp′*, **unripened**, *ŭn′rīp′nd*, a. vert || (fig.) prématuré.

unripeness, *ŭn′rīp′nĕs*, s. défaut de maturité, m., verdeur, crudité, f.

unrivalled, *ŭn′rī′văld*, a. sans rival.

unroll, *ŭn′rōl′*, v. a. dérouler, déplier.

unroof, *ŭn′rōf′*, v. a. enlever le toit.

unruffle, *ŭn′rŭf′fl*, v. n. se calmer.

unruffled, *ŭn′rŭf′fld*, a. calme.

unruliness, *ŭn′rō′lĭnĕs*, s. indiscipline, f. || fougue, f.

unruly, *ŭn′rō′lĭ*, a. intraitable, turbulent, fougueux, sans frein.

unsaddle, *ŭn′săd′dl*, v. a. desseller.

unsafe, *ŭn′sāf′*, a. qui n'est pas sûr || hasardeux || **-ly**, ad. en danger.

unsalable, *ŭn′sāl′ăbl*, a. invendable.

unsalted, *ŭn′sa̤wlt′ĕd*, a. non salé.

unsanctified, *ŭn′săngk′tĭfīd*, a. profane, impie.

unsanctioned, *ŭn′săngk′shŭnd*, a. non sanctionné.

unsatisfactorily, *ŭn′săt′ĭsfăk′tĕr ĭlĭ*, ad. d'une manière peu satisfaisante.

unsatisfactory, *ŭn′săt′ĭsfăk′tĕr ĭ*, a. peu satisfaisant, mécontent (de).

unsatisfied, *ŭn′săt′ĭsfīd*, a. mécontent.

unsavouriness, *ŭn′sā′vĕr ĭnĕs*, s. fadeur, insipidité, f.

unsavoury, *ŭn′sā′vĕr ĭ*, a. insipide, fade.

unsay, *ŭn′sā′*, v. a. ir. rétracter, se dédire.

unscarred, *ŭn′skärd′*, a. non cicatrisé.

unschooled, *ŭn′skōld′*, a. sans éducation.

unscientific, *ŭn′sĭĕntĭf′ĭk*, a. peu scientifique.

unscrew, *ŭn′skrō′*, v. a. dévisser.

unscriptural, *ŭn′skrĭp′tūrăl*, a. non fondé sur l'Écriture.

unscrupulous, *ŭn′skrō′pŭlŭs*, a. non scrupuleux || **-ly**, ad. sans scrupule.

unscrupulousness, *ŭn′skrō′pŭlŭsnĕs*, s. caractère peu scrupuleux, m.

unseal, *ŭn′sēl′*, v. a. décacheter, desceller.

unsearchable, *ŭn′sĕrch′ăbl*, a. inscrutable, impénétrable.

unseasonable, *ŭn′sē′znăbl*, a. hors de saison, à contre-temps, mal à propos, indu.

unseasonableness, *ŭn′sē′znăblnĕs*, s. contre-temps, m.

unseasonably, *ŭn′sē′zr ăblĭ*, a. mal à propos.

unseasoned, *ŭn′sē′znd*, a. non assaisonné.

unseat, *ŭn′sēt′*, v. a. chasser de son siège, détrôner || désarçonner.

unseated, *ŭn′sēt′ĕd*, a. sans siège, debout.

unseconded, *ŭn′sĕk′ŭndĕd*, a. non secondé.

unsecured, *ŭn′sēkūrd′*, a. sans garantie || à découvert.

unseeing, *ŭn′sē′ĭng*, a. aveugle. [f.

unseemliness, *ŭn′sēm′lĭnĕs*, s. indécence,

unseemly, *ŭn′sēm′lĭ*, a. indécent, messéant, malséant, inconvenant.

unseen, *ŭn′sēn′*, a. sans être vu || invisible.

unselfish, *ŭn′sĕlf′ĭsh*, a. désintéressé.

unsent, *ŭn sĕnt'*, a. non envoyé || ~ **for,** qu'on n'a pas envoyé chercher.

unserviceable, *ŭn sĕr' vĭs ă bl*, a. inutile.

unsettle, *ŭn sĕt' tl*, v. a. rendre incertain || déranger || bouleverser.

unsettled, *ŭn sĕt' tld*, a. qui n'est pas fixé, inconstant, volage || irrésolu.

unsettledness, *ŭn sĕt' tld nĕs*, s. irrésolution, incertitude, f.

unsew, *ŭn sō'*, v. a. ir. découdre.

unsex, *ŭn sĕks'*, v. a. priver de sexe, des qualités du sexe.

unshackle, *ŭn shăk' l*, v. a. déchaîner.

unshackled, *ŭn shăk' ld*, a. sans chaînes.

unshaded, *ŭn shā' dĕd*, a. qui n'est point ombragé || découvert.

unshaken, *ŭn shā' kn*, a. inébranlable, ferme.

unshapely, *ŭn shāp' lĭ*, a. difforme.

unshaved, *ŭn shāvd'*, a. sans être rasé.

unsheathe, *ŭn shēth'*, v.a. tirer du fourreau.

unsheltered, *ŭn shĕl' tĕrd*, a. sans abri.

unship, *ŭn shĭp'*, a. v. débarquer || désarmer.   [fers (chevaux).

unshod, *ŭn shŏd'*, a. sans chaussure || sans

unshorn, *ŭn shōrn'*, a. non tondu.

unshrinking, *ŭn shrĭngk' ĭng*, a. intrépide, imperturbable.

unsightliness, *ŭn sīt' lĭ nĕs*, s. laideur, f.

unsightly, *ŭn sīt' lĭ*, a. désagréable à la vue || difforme.

unsilvered, *ŭn sĭl' vĕrd*, a. désargenté || non argenté.

unsisterly, *ŭn sĭs' tĕr lĭ*, a. indigne d'une sœur.

unsized, *ŭn sīzd'*, a. non collé.

unskilful, *ŭn skĭl' fŏŏl*, **unskilled,** *ŭn-skĭld'*, a. (-ly, ad.) maladroit(ement).

unskilfulness, *ŭn skĭl' fŏŏl nĕs*, s. maladresse, inhabileté, f.

unslaked, *ŭn slākt'*, a. non éteint || ~ **lime,** s. chaux vive, f.

unsmoked, *ŭn smōkt'*, a. non fumé || à moitié fumé.

unsociable, *ŭn sō' shă bl*, **unsocial,** *ŭn-sō' shăl*, a. insocial, insociable.

unsoiled, *ŭn sōyld'*, a. non souillé || pur.

unsold, *ŭn sōld'*, a. invendu.

unsolder, *ŭn sŏl' dĕr*, v. a. dessouder.

unsoldierlike, *ŭn sōl' jĕr lĭk*, **unsoldierly,** *ŭn sōl' jĕr lĭ*, a. peu militaire.

unsolicited, *ŭn sō lĭs' ĭ tĕd*, a. sans être sollicité.

unsolved, *ŭn sŏlvd'*, a. non expliqué.

unsophisticated, *ŭn sō fĭs' tĭ kā tĕd*, a. non altéré, p ur.

unsought, *ŭn sáwt'*, a. non examiné, non exploré || spontané.

unsound, *ŭn sŏwnd'*, a. malsain, maladif || gâté, défectif, corrompu, vicieux || hétérodoxe || non réel, non solide.

unsoundness, *ŭn sŏwnd' nĕs*, s. défaut de solidité, m., faiblesse, f. || corruption, f. || erreur, f.

unsown, *ŭn sōn'*, a. sans être semé.

unsparing, *ŭn spăr' ĭng*, a. prodigue, libéral || impitoyable.

unspeakable, *ŭn spēk' ă bl*, a. inexprimable, indicible.

unspeakably, *ŭn spēk' ă blĭ*, ad. d'une manière inexprimable.

unspecified, *ŭn spĕs' ĭ fīd*, a. non spécifié.

unspent, *ŭn spĕnt'*, a. non dépensé, non épuisé.   [spōylt', a. non gâté.

unspoiled, *ŭn spōyld'*, **unspoilt,** *ŭn-*

unsportsmanlike, *ŭn spōrts' măn lĭk*, a. contraire aux règles du sport.

unspotted, *ŭn spŏt' tĕd*, a. sans tache || immaculé.   [irrésolu.

unstable, *ŭn stā' bl*, a. instable, inconstant,

unstained, *ŭn stānd'*, a. sans tache, immaculé || non teint.

unstamped, *ŭn stămpt'*, a. non-timbré || non affranchi (lettre).

unstatesmanlike, *ŭn stāts' măn lĭk*, a. impolitique.

unsteadfast, *ŭn stĕd' fāst*, a. léger, inconstant || non stable.

unsteadily, *ŭn stĕd' ĭ lĭ*, ad. inconsidérément, indiscrètement.

unsteadiness, *ŭn stĕd' ĭ nĕs*, s. légèreté, indiscrétion, inconstance, f.

unsteady, *ŭn stĕd' ĭ*, a. inconstant, irrésolu || changeant, léger, inconséquent.

unstirred, *ŭn stĕrd'*, a. non remué.

unstitch, *ŭn stĭch'*, v. a. découdre, défaire.

unstrengthened, *ŭn strĕngth' nd*, a. non fortifié.

unstring, *ŭn strĭng'*, v. a. ir. ôter les cordes, relâcher, détendre.

unstudied, *ŭn stŭd' ĭd*, a. qui n'est pas étudié, imprémédité, sans apprêt.

unsubdued, *ŭn sŭb dūd'*, a. insoumis || indompté.   [mis.

unsubmissive, *ŭn sŭb mĭs' sĭv*, a. insoumis.

unsubstantial, *ŭn sŭb stăn' shăl*, a. insubstantiel, immatériel || léger || sans corps || peu solide.

unsuccessful, *ŭn sŭk sĕs' fŏŏl*, a. malheureux || -ly, ad. sans succès.

unsuccoured, *ŭn sŭk' kŭrd*, a. sans secours, non secouru.

unsuitability, *ŭn sū tă bĭl' ĭ tĭ*, **unsuitableness,** *ŭn sū' tă bl nĕs*, s. disconvenance, incongruité, f.

unsuitable, *ŭn sū' tă bl*, a. inconvenant.

unsuitably, *ŭn sū' tă blĭ*, ad. d'une manière peu convenable.

unsuited, *ŭn sū' tĕd*, a. non accommodé, non arrangé || mal adapté.

unsullied, *ŭn sŭl' lĭd*, a. qui n'est pas souillé || pur.

unsupplied, *ŭn sŭp plīd'*, a. non pourvu de || non satisfait.

unsupported, *ŭn sŭp pōrt' ĕd*, a. sans soutien, sans appui.

unsurpassed, *ŭn sĕr păst'*, a. non surpassé, transcendant.

unsuspected, *ŭn sŭs pĕkt' ĕd*, a. non suspect || non suspecté.

unsuspicious, *ŭn sŭs pĭsh' ŭs*, a. confiant || non suspect.

unsustained, *ŭn sŭs tānd'*, a. sans soutien, sans appui.

unswathe, *ŭn swăth'*, v. a. démailloter.

unswept, *ŭn swĕpt'*, a. non balayé || non ramoné.

unsymmetrical, *ŭn sĭm mĕt' rĭ kăl*, a. sans symétrie.

unsystematic(al), *ŭn sĭs tĕm ăt' ĭk (ăl)*, a. peu systématique. || gâté.

untainted, *ŭn tănt' ĕd*, a. non taché, non

untamable, *ŭn tā' mă bl*, a. inapprivoisable || indomptable.

untamed, *ŭn tāmd'*, a. non apprivoisé.

untarnished, *ŭn tăr' nĭsht*, a. sans tache.

untasted, *ŭn tāst' ĕd*, a. qu'on n'a pas goûté.

untaught, *ŭn tăwt'*, a. mal élevé, ignorant, illettré || qu'on n'a pas appris.

unteachable, *ŭn tēch' ă bl*, a. indocile.

untenable, *ŭn tĕn' ă bl*, a. insoutenable.

untenanted, *ŭn tĕn' ănt ĕd*, a. inhabité.

untested, *ŭn tĕst' ĕd*, a. non éprouvé.

unthanked, *ŭn thăngkt'*, a. sans remerciement, sans être remercié.

unthankful, *ŭn thăngk' fŏŏl*, a. ingrat || -ly, ad. avec ingratitude.

unthankfulness, *ŭn thăngk' fŏŏl nĕs*, s. ingratitude, f.

unthinking, *ŭn thĭngk' ĭng*, a. irréfléchi.

unthought (of), *ŭn thăwt'*, a. auquel on ne pense pas, oublié || inattendu.

unthrifty, *ŭn thrĭft' ĭ*, a. prodigue, dépensier || qui ne prospère pas.

untidiness, *ŭn tī' dĭ nĕs*, s. malpropreté, f.

untidy, *ŭn tī' dĭ*, a. malpropre || sans goût.

untie, *ŭn tī'*, v. a. dénouer, délier, détacher.

until, *ŭn tĭl'*, pr. & ad. jusqu'à, jusqu'à ce que, jusques à.

untilled, *ŭn tĭld'*, a. inculte, sans culture.

untimely, *ŭn tĭm' lĭ*, a. & ad. hâtif, précoce, prématuré || à contre-temps, prématurément.

untiring, *ŭn tīr' ĭng*, a. infatigable.

unto, *ŭn' tŏŏ*, pr. à, au, dans, envers.

untold, *ŭn tōld'*, a. non compté || passé sous silence || non raconté.

untouched, *ŭn tŭcht'*, a. intact, non affecté.

untoward, *ŭn tō' ĕrd*, a. (-ly, ad.) revêche, pervers || intraitable || gauche(ment) || maladroit(ement) || malgracieux || fâcheux, à contre-temps, malencontreux.

untowardness, *ŭn tō' ĕrd nĕs*, s. perversité, opiniâtreté, f. || malencontre, f.

untraced, *ŭn trāst'*, a. sans trace || (roads) non frayé.

untrained, *ŭn trānd'*, a. non élevé, non instruit || irrégulier || (animals) non dressé.

untranslatable, *ŭn trăns lā' tă bl*, a. intraduisible.

untravelled, *ŭn trăv' ĕld*, a. qui n'a pas voyagé || inexploré.

untried, *ŭn trīd'*, a. non essayé.

untrimmed, *ŭn trĭmd'*, a. sans ornement, sans garniture || simple.

untrod(den), *ŭn trŏd' (n)*, a. non frayé.

untroubled, *ŭn trŭb' ld*, a. calme, tranquille || non tracassé.

untrue, *ŭn trŏŏ'*, a. faux || inexact || perfide.

untruly, *ŭn trŏŏ' lĭ*, ad. faussement.

untrustworthy, *ŭn trŭst' wĕr thĭ*, a. indigne de confiance.

untrustworthiness, *ŭn trŭst' wĕr thĭ nĕs*, s. faible confiance qu'inspire qn.

untrusty, *ŭn trŭst' ĭ*, a. déloyal, infidèle.

untruth, *ŭn trōth'*, s. fausseté, f., mensonge, m. || inexactitude, f.

untunable, *ŭn tū' nă bl*, a. discordant.

untutored, *ŭn tū' tĕrd*, a. sans instruction || ignorant, inculte.

untwine, *ŭn twīn'*, v. a. détordre, détortiller, dérouler.

unused, *ŭn ūzd'*, a. non employé || inusité.

unusual, *ŭn ū' zhū ăl*, a. extraordinaire, étrange, rare || -ly, ad. rarement.

unutterable, *ŭn ŭt' tĕr ă bl*, a. inexprimable, ineffable.

unvalued, *ŭn văl' ūd*, a. non évalué || peu estimé || méprisé.

unvaried, *ŭn vā' rĭd*, unvarying, *ŭn vā' rĭ ĭng*, a. non varié, uniforme || invariable.

unvarnished, *ŭn văr' nĭsht*, a. non vernissé || naturel || simple.

unveil, *ŭn vāl'*, v. a. dévoiler.

unversed, *ŭn vĕrst'*, a. peu versé dans.

unviolated, *ŭn vī' ō lā tĕd*, a. intact || respecté || non violé.

unvisited, *ŭn vĭz' ĭt ĕd*, a. non visité, non fréquenté.

unwakened, *ŭn wā' knd*, a. endormi, non réveillé.

unwarily, *ŭn wā' rĭ lĭ*, ad. inconsidérément, imprudemment.

unwariness, *ŭn wā' rĭ nĕs*, s. imprudence, imprévoyance, étourderie, f.

unwarlike, *ŭn wăwr' lĭk*, a. peu belliqueux.

unwarned, *ŭn wăwrnd'*, a. non averti.

unwarrantable, *ŭn wŏr' rănt ă bl*, a. inexcusable, insoutenable.

unwarranted, *ŭn wŏr' rănt ĕd*, a. non autorisé || incertain || sans garantie.

unwary, *ŭn wā' rĭ*, a. imprudent, inconsidéré, étourdi.

unwashed, *ŭn wŏsht'*, s. crasseux, m.

unwashed, *ŭn wŏsht'*, a. non lavé.

unwasted, *ŭn wāst' ĕd*, a. non consumé.

unwasting, *ŭn wāst' ĭng*, a. ne dépérissant pas || indestructible.

unwatered, *ŭn wăw' tĕrd*, a. non arrosé || (stuffs) non moiré.

unweakened, *ŭn wēk' nd*, a. non affaibli.

unweaned, *ŭn wēnd'*, a. non sevré.

unwearied, *ŭn wēr' ĭd*, a. non fatigué || infatigable.

unwedded, *ŭn wĕd' ĕd*, a. non marié.

unwelcome, *ŭn wĕl' kŭm*, s. mal reçu, mal accueilli || déplaisant, fâcheux.

unwell, *ŭn wĕl'*, ad. indisposé.

unwholesome, *ŭn hōl' sŭm*, a. malsain || insalubre.

unwieldy, *ŭn wēld' ĭ*, a. pesant, lourd.

unwilling, *ŭn wĭl' lĭng*, a. qui ne veut pas || de mauvaise volonté || to be ~ to, n'être pas disposé à || -ly, ad. à contre-cœur.

unwillingness, *ŭn wĭl' lĭng nĕs*, s. mauvais vouloir, m., répugnance, f.

unwind, *ŭn wīnd'*, v. a. ir. débrouiller, démêler, dérouler.

unwise, *ŭn wīz'*, a. pas sage, imprudent.

unwished, *ŭn wisht'*, a. (~ for) non désiré.

unwitnessed, *ŭn wit' nĕst*, a. sans témoin|| inaperçu.

unwittingly, *ŭn wit' tĭng lĭ*, ad. à son insu.

unwonted, *ŭn wŏnt' ĕd*, a. inaccoutumé || rare.

unworn, *ŭn wōrn'*, a. qui n'a pas été porté || non usé. [gâché.

unworkmanlike, *ŭn wĕrk' măn lĭk*, a.

unworthily, *ŭn wĕr' thĭ lĭ*, ad. indignement.

unworthiness, *ŭn wĕr' thĭ nĕs*, s. indignité, f.

unworthy, *ŭn wĕr' thĭ*, a. indigne.

unwounded, *ŭn wŏnd' ĕd*, a. intact, sans blessure.

unwrap, *ŭn răp'*, v. a. développer.

unwrinkled, *ŭn rĭng' kld*, a. sans ride.

unwritten, *ŭn rĭt' tn*, a. non écrit || blanc.

unwrought, *ŭn rāwt'*, a. brut, naturel.

unyielding, *ŭn yēld' ĭng*, a. ferme, inflexible || entêté.

unyoke, *ŭn yōk'*, v. a. dételer.

up, *ŭp*, pr. & ad. haut, en haut, debout, levé || & throw ~, vomir || résigner || to be ~ to it, avoir le fil || to walk ~ and down, se promener en long et en large || ~s and downs, les hauts et les bas de la vie, les vicissitudes humaines.

upbear, *ŭp bār'*, v. a. ir. tenir élevé, soutenir, supporter.

upbraid, *ŭp brād'*, v. a. reprocher.

upbraidingly, *ŭp brād' ĭng lĭ*, ad. avec reproche.

upcast, *ŭp' kăst*, a. lancé en l'air.

upheaval, *ŭp hē' văl*, s. élévation, f.

upheave, *ŭp hēv'*, v. a. ir. soulever, lever.

uphill, *ŭp' hĭl*, a. montant || difficile, pénible.

uphold, *ŭp hōld'*, v. a. ir. lever en haut, soutenir, maintenir.

upholder, *ŭp hōld' ĕr*, s. soutien, appui, fauteur, m. || partisan, m.

upholsterer, *ŭp hōl' stĕr ĕr*, s. tapissier, m.

upholstery, *ŭp hōl' stĕr ĭ*, s. tapisserie, f.

upland, *ŭp' lănd*, s. pays montagneux, m.

upland, *ŭp' lănd*, a. montagneux.

uplift, *ŭ̆, lĭft'*, v. a. élever.

upon, *ŭp ŏn'*, pr. sur, dessus || ~ my word! sur ma parole! parole d'honneur!

upper, *ŭp' pĕr*, a. supérieur, du haut, de dessus || (of Houses, & géog.) haut || ~-cloth, s. napperon, m. || ~-hand, s. avantage, m., supériorité, f.

uppermost, *ŭp' pĕr mŏst*, a. le plus haut.

upraise, *ŭp rāz'*, v. a. élever, exalter.

uprear, *ŭp' rēr*, v. a. lever, soulever.

upright, *ŭp' rĭt*, a. (-ly, ad.) droit || perpendiculaire(ment) || équitable || honnête (ment) || intègre || debout || avec probité.

uprightness, *ŭp' rĭt nĕs*, s. élévation perpendiculaire, droiture, f. || probité, honnêteté, intégrité, f.

uproar, *ŭp' rōr*, s. bruit, tumulte, vacarme, m. || émeute, f.

uproarious, *ŭp rōr' ĭ ŭs*, a. tumultueux, bruyant.

uproot, *ŭp rōt'*, v. a. déraciner.

upset, *ŭp sĕt'*, v. a. ir. renverser.

upshot, *ŭp' shŏt*, s. fin, issue, f.

upside-down, *ŭp' sid dŏwn'*, ad. sens dessus dessous || to turn ~, bouleverser.

upstart, *ŭp' stărt*, s. parvenu, m.

upward, *ŭp' wĕrd*, a. en haut || ascensionnel || ~(s), ad. en haut, plus.

uranian, *ū rā' nĭ ăn*, s. uranide, m.

urban, *ĕr' băn*, a. urbain.

urbane, *ĕr bān'*, a. poli.

urbanity, *ĕr băn' ĭ tĭ*, s. urbanité, f.

urchin, *ĕr' chĭn*, s. hérisson, m. || marmot, m. || gamin, m. || sea—, oursin, hérisson de mer, m.

urethra, *ŭ rē' thrā*, s. urètre, m.

urge, *ĕrj'*, v. a. presser, pousser, solliciter, irriter, importuner, insister sur || s'avancer.

urgency, *ĕr' jĕn sĭ*, s. urgence, f.

urgent, *ĕr' jĕnt*, a. urgent, pressant || -ly, ad. instamment, ardemment.

urinal, *ū' rĭ năl*, s. urinoir, m. || urinal, m.

urinary, *ū' rĭ nĕr ĭ*, a. urinaire.

urine, *ū' rĭn*, s. urine, f.

urn, *ĕrn*, s. urne, f., vase, m.

us, *ŭs*, pn. nous.

usable, *ū' ză bl*, a. dont on peut se servir.

usage, *ū' zăj*, s. usage, m. || traitement, m.

usance, *ū' zăns*, s. usance, f.

use, *ūs*, s. usage, emploi, m. || utilité, f., profit, avantage, m. || coutume, habitude, f. || intérêt, m. || in —, d'usage, en usage || of no ~, inutile || out of ~, hors d'usage, vieilli || to put to a good ~, mettre de l'argent à intérêt.

use, *ūz*, v. a. & n. faire usage de, se servir de, employer || accoutumer, habituer || traiter || exercer || (to be –d to) avoir la coutume de, être accoutumé à || être dans l'usage.

used, *ūzd*, p. & a. employé, usé, consommé, enduré || dressé.

useful, *ūs' fōōl*, a. utile, avantageux, profitable || -ly, ad. utilement.

usefulness, *ūs' fōōl nĕs*, s. utilité, f.

useless, *ūs' lĕs*, a. (-ly, ad.) inutile(ment).

uselessness, *ūs' lĕs nĕs*, s. inutilité, f.

usher, *ŭsh' ĕr*, s. huissier, m. || introducteur, m. || sous-maître, maître d'étude, m.

usher, *ŭsh' ĕr*, v. a. introduire || annoncer || inaugurer.

usual, *ū' zhōō ăl*, a. (-ly, ad.) ordinaire (ment) || commun || d'ordinaire.

usurer, *ū' zhĕr ĕr*, s. usurier, m.

usurious, *ū zhō' rĭ ŭs*, a. usuraire, exorbitant || qui fait l'usure.

usurp, *ū zĕrp'*, v. a. usurper.

usurpation, *ū zĕr pā' shŭn*, s. usurpation, f.

usurper, *ū zĕrp' ĕr*, s. usurpateur, m.

usurpingly, *ū zĕrp' ĭng lĭ*, ad. par usurpation. [tion.

usury, *ū' zhōō rĭ*, s. usure, f.

utensil, *ū tĕn' sĭl*, s. ustensile, m.

uterine, *ū' tĕr ĭn*, a. utérin.

utilise, *ū' tĭl ĭz*, v. a. utiliser.

utility, *ū tĭl' ĭ tĭ*, s. utilité, f.

utmost, *ŭt′mŏst,* a. le plus grand, le plus haut, extrême, dernier.

utopia, *ū tō′pǐ ă,* s. utopie, f.

utopian, *ū tō′pǐ ăn,* a. utopique, imaginaire, chimérique.

utter, *ŭt′tér,* v. a. prononcer, proférer || exprimer || publier || vendre || (jur.) émettre, mettre en circulation.

utter, *ŭt′tér,* a. extérieur, extrême, excessif || entier, complet || **–ly,** ad. entièrement || de fond en comble.

utterable, *ŭt′tér ă bl,* a. exprimable.

utterance, *ŭt′tér ăns,* s. prononciation, articulation, f. || débit, m., vente de marchandises, f.

utterer, *ŭt′tér ér,* s. (jur.) émissionnaire (de fausse monnaie), m.

uvula, *ū′vū lă,* s. uvule, luette, f.

uxorious, *ŭg zō′rǐ ŭs,* a. tendre à l'excès pour sa femme.

uxoriousness, *ŭg zō′rǐ ŭs nés,* s. sotte complaisance pour sa femme, f.

V.

vacancy, *vă′kăn sǐ,* s. vide, m. || place vacante, f. || vacance, f. || loisir, m. || défaut de pensée, m.

vacant, *vă′kănt,* a. vide || de loisir, inactif, libre, dégagé || irréfléchi.

vacate, *vă kāt′,* v. a. vider, quitter || annuler || se démettre de.

vacation, *vă kā′shŭn,* s. vacances, f. pl.

vaccinate, *văk′sǐ nāt,* v. a. vacciner.

vaccination, *văk sǐ nā′shŭn,* s. vaccination, vaccine, f.

vaccine, *văk′sǐn;* **~-lymph, ~-matter,** s. vaccin, m.

vacillate, *văs′ǐl lāt,* v. n. vaciller.

vacillation, *văs ǐl lā′shŭn,* s. vacillation, f.

vacuity, *vă kū′ǐ tǐ,* s. vacuité, f., vide, m. || (fig.) néant, m.

vacuous, *văk′ū ŭs,* a. vide.

vacuum, *văk′ū ŭm,* s. vide, m.

vademecum, *vă dē mē′kŭm,* s. vade-mecum.

vagabond, *văg′ă bŏnd,* s. vagabond, m.

vagabond, *văg′ă bŏnd,* a. vagabond, errant, sans domicile.

vagary, *vă′gă rǐ,* s. caprice, m. || divagation, f.

vagina, *vă jī′nă,* s. vagin, m.

vagrancy, *vă′grăn sǐ,* s. vagabondage, m.

vagrant, *vă′grănt,* s. vagabond, m.

vagrant, *vă′grănt,* a. vagabond, errant.

vague, *văg,* a. (**–ly,** ad.) vague(ment) || indéterminé.

vails, *vāls,* s. pl. douceur (pour les domestiques) || gratification, f.

vain, *văn,* a. vain, orgueilleux || **in ~,** en vain || **–ly,** ad. vainement, en vain, avec vanité.

vainglorious, *văn glō′rǐ ŭs,* a. vaniteux.

vainglory, *văn glō′rǐ,* s. vaine gloire, f.

valance, *văl′ăns,* s. cantonnière, f.

vale, *vāl,* s. vallée, f., vallon, m.

valentine, *văl′én tǐn,* s. amant choisi le jour de la Saint-Valentin, m. || billet de la Saint-Valentin, m.

valerian, *vă lē′rǐ ăn,* s. valériane, f.

valet, *văl′ĕt* ou *vă′lā,* s. valet, domestique, m.

valetudinarian, *văl ē tū dǐ nă′rǐ ăn,* s. valétudinaire, m.

valetudinarian, *văl ē tū dǐ nă′rǐ ăn,* a. valétudinaire.

valiant, *văl′yănt,* a. vaillant, brave || **–ly,** ad. vaillamment.

valid, *văl′ǐd,* a. (**–ly,** ad.) valide(ment) || valable.

validity, *vă lǐd′ǐ tǐ,* s. validité, f.

valise, *vă lēs′,* s. valise, f.

valley, *văl′lǐ,* s. vallée, f., vallon, m.

valorous, *văl′ér ŭs,* a. valeureux.

valour, *văl′ér,* s. valeur, bravoure, f.

valuable, *văl′ū ă bl,* a. précieux || **–s,** s. pl. objets de prix, m. pl.

valuation, *văl ū ā′shŭn,* s. évaluation, f.

value, *văl′ū,* s. valeur, f., prix, mérite, m. || **to set a ~ on,** estimer.

value, *văl′ū,* v. a. évaluer, priser, estimer, faire cas de || honorer.

valueless, *văl′ū lés,* a. sans valeur.

valuer, *văl′ū ér,* s. appréciateur, m. || (jur.) expert, m.

valve, *vălv,* s. soupape, f., clapet, m.

valvular, *văl′vū lăr,* a. valvulaire.

vamp, *vămp,* v. a. rapiécer.

vampire, *văm′pīr,* s. vampire, m.

van, *văn,* s. avant-garde, f. || tarare, m. || voiture, f. || char à bancs, m. || tapissière, f. || (rail.) wagon, m. || **goods–~,** wagon à coulisses, m. || **break–~,** wagon à frein, m. || **cattle–~,** wagon-écurie, m.

Vandal, *văn′dăl,* s. vandale, m.

vandalism, *văn′dăl ĭzm,* s. vandalisme, m.

vane, *văn,* s. girouette, f. || (mar.) flouette, f. || (of machines) registre, m.

vanguard, *văn′gărd,* s. avant-garde, f.

vanilla, *vă nĭl′lă,* s. vanille, f. || vanillier, m.

vanish, *văn′ish,* v. n. s'évanouir || se perdre, disparaître || **–ing line,** s. horizon, m.

vanity, *văn′ĭ tǐ,* s. vanité, f.

vanquish, *văng′kwish,* v. a. vaincre.

vanquisher, *văng′kwish ér,* s. vainqueur, triomphateur, m.

vantage-ground, *văn′tăj grŏŭnd,* s. position supérieure or avantageuse, f.

vapid, *văp′ĭd,* a. fade, insipide || moisi.

vapidness, *văp′ĭd nés,* s. fadeur, f. || (of liquids) évent, m.

vaporous, *vă′pér ŭs,* a. vaporeux || flatueux.

vapour, *vă′pér,* s. vapeur, f.

variable, *vă′rǐ ă bl,* a. variable, inconstant.

variableness, *vă′rǐ ă bl nés,* s. variabilité, inconstance, f.

variably, *vă′rǐ ă blǐ,* ad. d'une manière variable.

variance, *vă′rǐ ăns,* s. variation, f. || désaccord, m. || **at ~,** en désaccord.

variation, *vă rǐ ā′shŭn,* s. variation, f. || déviation, déclinaison, f.

varicose vein, *vă′rǐ kōs văn′,* s. varice, f.

variegate, vā″rĭĕ̆gāt, v. a. varier, bigarrer.

variegation, vā″rĭĕgā″shŭn, s. diversité de couleurs, f.

variety, vā″rī″ĕ̆tĭ, s. variété, f.

variola, vāʳrĭō̆lă̆, s. variole, petite vérole, f.

various, vā″rĭŭs, a. (-ly, ad.) divers (ement) || variable, différent.

varnish, vär″nĭsh, s. vernis, m.

varnish, vär″nĭsh, v. a. vernir, vernisser || déguiser, farder.

varnishing, vär″nĭsh″ĭng, s. vernissure, f.

vary, vā″rĭ, v. a. & n. varier, diversifier || changer || dévier, s'éloigner.

vascular, vă̆s″kŭ̆lär, a. vasculaire.

vase, vā̆z, s. vase, m.

vassal, vă̆s″săl, s. vassal, m.

vassalage, vă̆s″să̆lăj, s. vasselage, m.

vast, vă̆st, a. vaste, immense || -ly, ad. immensément || extrêmement.

vastness, vă̆st″nĕs, s. grande étendue, immensité, f. || énormité, f.

vat, vă̆t, s. cuve, f., cuvier, m.

vault, vă̆wlt, s. voûte, f. || cave, f. || saut, m.

vault, vă̆wlt, v. a. & n. voûter || sauter, voltiger.

vaulter, vă̆wlt″ĕr, s. sauteur, voltigeur, m.

vaulting, vă̆wlt″ĭng, s. voltige, f.

vaunt, vă̆wnt, v. a. & n. vanter, prôner || se vanter, se glorifier, faire parade.

vaunter, vă̆wnt″ĕr, s. fanfaron, m.

veal, vē̆l, s. veau, m. || viande de veau, f. || ~-collop, s. escalope, f. || ~-cutlet, s. côtelette de veau, f.

veer, vē̆r, v. n. tourner || changer de bord.

vegetable, vĕ̆j″ĕ̆tă̆bl, s. végétal, m. || légume, m. || ~-dish, s. légumier, m. || casserole à légumes, f. || ~-garden, s. jardin potager, m.

vegetable,vĕ̆j″ĕ̆tă̆bl, a. végétal || végétable.

vegetarian, vĕ̆j″ĕ̆tā″rĭăn, s. végétarien, m.

vegetarianism, vĕ̆j″ĕ̆tā″rĭăn̄ĭzm, s. végétarianisme, m.

vegetate, vĕ̆j″ĕ̆tāt, v. n. végéter.

vegetation, vĕ̆j″ĕ̆tā″shŭn, s. végétation, f.

vegetative, vĕ̆j″ĕ̆tā″tĭv, a. végétatif.

vehemence, vē̆″hĕ̆mĕn̄s, s. véhémence, violence, force, f. [ad. avec véhémence.

vehement, vē̆″hĕ̆mĕn̄t, a. véhément || -ly,

vehicle,vē̆″hĭkl, s. voiture, f. || véhicule, m.

vehicular, vē̆hĭk″ŭ̆lĕr, a. véhiculaire.

veil, vāl, s. voile, m. || prétexte, m. || déguisement, m.

veil, vāl, v. a. voiler, déguiser, couvrir.

vein, văn, s. veine, f. || couche (de terre, de métal etc.), f. || marque (dans le bois etc.), f. || inclination, humeur, f., génie, m. || to be in the ~ to, être en veine de.

vein, văn, v. a. marquer de veines, jasper.

veined, vănd, veiny, văn″ĭ, a. veiné, veineux || varié.

vellum, vĕ̆l″lŭm, s. vélin, m.

velocipede, vĕ̆lŏs″ĭpĕd, s. vélocipède, m.

velocity, vĕ̆lŏs″ĭtĭ, s. vélocité, f. || vitesse, f.

velodrome, vĕ̆l″ōdrŏm, s. velodrome, m.

velvet, vĕ̆l″vĕt, s. velours, m. || ~-pile, s. moquette, f.

velvet, vĕ̆l″vĕt, a. de velours || velouté.

velveteen, vĕ̆l″vĕtēn′, s. velours croisé, m.

velvety, vĕ̆l″vĕtĭ, a. velouté.

venal, vē̆″năl, a. vénal.

venality, vē̆nă̆l″ĭtĭ, s. vénalité, f.

vend, vĕ̆nd, v. a. vendre, débiter.

vender, vĕ̆nd″ĕr, s. vendeur, m.

veneer, vĕ̆nē̆r′, s. feuille à plaquer, f.

veneer, vĕ̆nē̆r′, v. a. plaquer.

veneering, vĕ̆nē̆r′ĭng, s. placage, m.

venerable, vĕ̆n″ĕră̆bl, a. vénérable.

venerably, vĕ̆n″ĕ̆ră̆blĭ, ad. vénérablement.

venerate, vĕ̆n″ĕ̆rāt, v. a. vénérer, révérer.

veneration, vĕ̆n″ĕ̆rā″shŭn, s. vénération, f.

venereal, vĕ̆nē̆″rē̆ă̆l, a. vénérien.

Venetian-blind, vĕ̆nē̆″shăn blĭnd, s. persienne, f.

vengeance, vĕ̆n″jăns, s. vengeance, f.

venial, vē̆″nĭă̆l, a. véniel.

venison, vĕ̆n″zn, s. venaison, f.

venom, vĕ̆n″ŏm, s. venin, m.

venomous, vĕ̆n″ŏmŭs, a. venimeux || vénéneux. [m.

venomousness, vĕ̆n″ŏmŭsnĕs, s. venin,

vent, vĕ̆nt, s. soupirail, passage, m., lumière, issue, f. || vente, f., débit, m. || to find ~, trouver une issue || to give ~ to, donner carrière à || ~-hole, s. soupirail, m. || trou de bonde, m. || ~-peg, s. fausset, m.

vent, vĕ̆nt, v. a. & n. donner issue, exhaler, éventer, faire sortir || divulguer || vendre, débiter || flairer, sentir.

ventilate, vĕ̆n″tĭlāt, v. a. éventer || vanner || examiner, discuter. [f.

ventilation, vĕ̆n″tĭlā″shŭn, s. ventilation, f.

ventilator, vĕ̆n″tĭlā″tĕr, s. ventilateur, m.

ventricle, vĕ̆n″trĭkl, s. ventricule, m.

ventriloquism, vĕ̆n″trĭl″ōkwĭzm, s. ventriloquie, f. [loque, f.

ventriloquist, vĕ̆n″trĭl″ōkwĭst, s. ventri-

venture, vĕ̆n″tŭr, s. aventure, f., risque, hasard, m. || at a ~, à l'aventure || to put to the ~, risquer.

venture, vĕ̆n″tŭr, v. a. (& n.) risquer || (se) hasarder.

venturous, vĕ̆n″tŭrŭs, a. (-ly, ad.) hardi (ment) || aventureux || hasardeusement.

venturousness, vĕ̆n″tŭrŭsnĕs, s. hardiesse, témérité, f.

venue, vĕ̆n″ū, s. (jur.) siège du tribunal compétent, m. || to change the ~, dessaisir la juridiction ordinaire pour cause de suspicion légitime.

veracious, vĕ̆rā″shŭs, a. (-ly, ad.) véridique(ment) || véritable. [f.

veracity, vĕ̆ră̆s″ĭtĭ, s. véracité, véridicité,

veranda, vĕ̆răn″dă̆, s. véranda, f. || marquise, f.

verb, vĕ̆rb, s. (gr.) verbe, m.

verbal, vĕ̆rb″ă̆l, a. (-ly, ad.) verbal(ement) || littéral(ement).

verbatim, vĕ̆rbā″tĭm, ad. mot pour mot.

verbena, vĕ̆rbē̆″nă̆, s. (bot.) verbène, f.

verbose, vĕ̆rbōs′, a. verbeux, diffus.

verbosity, vĕ̆rbŏs″ĭtĭ, s. verbosité, f.

verdant, vĕ̆r″dănt, a. verdoyant, vert.

verdict, vĕ̆r″dĭkt, s. verdict, m. || arrêt,

m. || opinion, f. || **to bring in a ~ of guilty**, (jur.) déclarer coupable (se dit du jury).

verdigris, *vĕr'dĭ grĭs*, s. vert-de-gris, m.

verdure, *vĕr'dŭr*, s. verdure, f.

verge, *vĕrj*, s. verge, baguette, f. || lisière, f. || bord, m., extrémité, f. || ressort, m., juridiction, f. || **on the ~ of**, à la veille de.

verge, *vĕrj*, v. n. tendre, incliner.

verger, *vĕr'jĕr*, s. porte-verge, m.

verification, *vĕr'ĭ fĭ kā' shŭn*, s. vérification, avération, f.

verify, *vĕr'ĭ fī*, v. a. vérifier.

verily, *vĕr'ĭ lĭ*, ad. en vérité.

verjuice, *vĕr'jŏs*, s. verjus, m.

vermicelli, *vĕr mĭ chĕl'lĭ*, s. vermicelle, m.

vermicular, *vĕr mĭk'ū lĕr*, a. vermiculaire.

vermifuge, *vĕr mĭ fūj*, s. vermifuge, m.

vermilion, *vĕr mĭl'yŭn*, s. vermillon, m.

vermin, *vĕr'mĭn*, s. vermine, f. || **~-destroyer**, s. insecticide, m.

vernacular, *vĕr năk'ū lĕr*, a. du pays || maternel.

vernal, *vĕr'năl*, a. printanier, du printemps.

versatile, *vĕr'să tĭl*, a. versatile, variable, flexible, mobile, inconstant.

versatility, *vĕr să tĭl'ĭ tĭ*, s. versatilité, mobilité, f. || souplesse, f.

verse, *vĕrs*, s. vers, m. || verset, m.

versed, *vĕrst*, a. versé.

versification, *vĕr sĭ fĭ kā' shŭn*, s. versification, f. || [meur, rimailleur, m.

versifier, *vĕr'sĭ fīĕr*, s. versificateur, ri-

versify, *vĕr'sĭ fī*, v. a. versifier.

version, *vĕr'shŭn*, s. version, f.

verst, *vĕrst*, s. verste, f.

versus, *vĕr'sŭs*, pr. contre.

vertebra, *vĕr'tĕ brȧ*, s. vertèbre, f.

vertebral, *vĕr'tĕ brăl*, a. vertébral.

vertebrate, *vĕr'tĕ brăt*, a. vertébré.

vertex, *vĕr'tĕks*, s. sommet de la tête, m.

vertical, *vĕr'tĭ kăl*, a. (**-ly**, ad.) vertical (ement).

vertiginous, *vĕr tĭj'ĭn ŭs*, a. vertigineux || [rotatoire.

vertigo, *vĕr'tĭ gō*, s. vertige, m.

vervain, *vĕr'vān*, s. (bot.) verveine, f.

very, *vĕr'ĭ*, a. & ad. vrai, réel || véritable || seul || très, fort, bien, même.

vesicatory, *vĕs'ĭ kā tŏ rĭ*, s. (chir.) vésicatoire, emplâtre vésicant, m.

vesicle, *vĕs'ĭ kl*, s. vésicule, f.

Vespers, *vĕs'pĕrz*, s. vêpres, f. pl.

vessel, *vĕs'sĕl*, s. vase, m. || vaisseau, m.

vest, *vĕst*, s. veste, f. || gilet, m.

vest, *vĕst*, v. a. habiller, vêtir || orner || revêtir.

vesta, *vĕs'tȧ*, s. allumette-bougie, f.

Vestal, *vĕs'tăl*, s. vestale, f.

vestige, *vĕs'tĭj*, s. vestiges, m. pl., trace, f.

vesting, *vĕst'ĭng*, s. étoffe pour gilets, f.

vestment, *vĕst'mĕnt*, s. vêtement, m.

vestry, *vĕst'rĭ*, s. sacristie, f. || assemblée de la commune, f. || comité de la paroisse, m. || conseil de fabrique, m.

vesture, *vĕs'tŭr* ou *vĕst'chŏor*, s. vêtement, m.

vetch, *vĕch*, s. (bot.) vesce, f.

veteran, *vĕt'ĕr ăn*, s. vétéran, m.

veteran, *vĕt'ĕr ăn*, a. ancien, expérimenté.

veterinarian, *vĕt ĕr ĭ nā'rĭ ăn*, s. r édecin vétérinaire, m.

veterinary, *vĕt'ĕr ĭ nĕr ĭ*, a. vétérinaire || **~-surgeon**, vide veterinarian.

veto, *vē'tō*, s. véto, m. || **to put a ~ on**, mettre le véto à (une loi).

vex, *vĕks*, v. a. vexer, tourmenter.

vexation, *vĕks ā'shŭn*, s. vexation, affliction, f., tourment, chagrin, m.

vexatious, *vĕks ā' shŭs*, a. vexant, contrariant || **-ly**, ad. d'une manière vexatoire.

vexing, *vĕks'ĭng*, a. contrariant, vexant.

viaduct, *vī'ă dŭkt*, s. viaduc, m.

vial, *vī'ăl*, s. fiole, f.

viand, *vī'ănd*, s. viande, f., aliments, m. pl.

viaticum, *vī ăt'ĭ kŭm*, s. viatique, m.

vibrate, *vī'brāt*, v. n. vibrer.

vibration, *vī brā'shŭn*, s. vibration, f.

viburnum, *vī bŭr'nŭm*, s. (bot.) viorne, f.

vicar, *vĭk'ĕr*, s. vicaire, m. || curé, ministre d'une paroisse, m.

vicarage, *vĭk'ĕr āj*, s. vicairie, f., vicariat, m. || cure, f., presbytère, m.

vicarious, *vī kā'rĭ ŭs*, a. de délégation.

vicarship, *vĭk'ĕr shĭp*, s. vicariat, m. || cure, f.

vice, *vīs*, s. vice, m. || étau, m.

vice, *vī'sĕ*, in comp. vice . . .

vicinity, *vĭ sĭn'ĭ tĭ*, s. voisinage, m. || proximité, f. || environs, m. pl.

vicious, *vĭsh'ŭs*, a. vicieux || **-ly**, ad. vicieusement.

viciousness, *vĭsh'ŭs nĕs*, s. nature vicieuse, f. || vice, m.

vicissitude, *vĭ sĭs'sĭ tūd*, s. vicissitude, f.

victim, *vĭk'tĭm*, s. victime, f.

victimise, *vĭk'tĭm īz*, v. a. sacrifier.

victor, *vĭk'tĕr*, s. vainqueur, m.

victorious, *vĭk tō'rĭ ŭs*, a. victorieux || **-ly**, ad. victorieusement.

victory, *vĭk'tĕr ĭ*, s. victoire, f.

victual, *vĭt'l*, v. a. avitailler.

victualler, *vĭt'lĕr*, s. pourvoyeur, m. || **licensed ~**, cabaretier, aubergiste, m.

victualling, *vĭt'lĭng*, s. avitaillement, m.

victuals, *vĭt'lz*, s. pl. vivres, m. pl., nourriture, f. || victuailles, f. pl.

vicuna, *vĭ kōn'yȧ*, s. vigogne, f.

videlicet, *vĭ dĕl'ĭ sĕt*, ad. savoir, c'est-à-dire.   [lutter.

vie, *vī*, v. n. rivaliser avec || disputer ||

view, *vū*, s. vue, f. || faculté de voir, f. || espace qui s'offre à la vue, f. || coup d'œil, regard, m. || perspective, f. || examen, m. || idée, notion, f. || intention, f., dessein, m. || **bird's-eye ~**, plan à vol d'oiseau, m. || **with a ~ to**, dans l'intention de.

view, *vū*, v. a. voir, apercevoir, considérer || regarder || examiner.

vigil, *vĭj'ĭl*, s. vigile, f. || veille, f.

vigilance, *vĭj'ĭl ăns*, s. vigilance, f.

vigilant, *vĭj'ĭl ănt*, a. vigilant, attentif.

vigorous, *vĭg'ĕr ŭs*, a. vigoureux, robuste || **-ly**, ad. vigoureusement.

vigour, *vĭg'ẽr*, s. vigueur, force, f.

vile, *vīl*, a. (-ly, ad.) vil(ement) ‖ bas (sement) ‖ abject.

vileness, *vil'nẽs*, s. bassesse, f.

vilify, *vĭl'ĭ fī*, v. a. avilir, abaisser ‖ diffamer, dénigrer, vilipender. [f.

villa, *vĭl'lä*, s. villa, maison de campagne,

village, *vĭl'lăj*, s. village, m.

villager, *vĭl'lăj ẽr*, s. villageois, m.

villain, *vĭl'lăn*, s. vilain, coquin, m.

villanous, *vĭl'lăn ŭs*, a. (-ly, ad.) vilain (ement) ‖ méchant ‖ bas(sement) ‖ méprisable. [famie, f.

villany, *vĭl'lăn ĭ*, s. scélératesse, f. ‖ in-

vindicate, *vĭn'dĭ kāt*, v. a. justifier, défendre ‖ soutenir, maintenir.

vindication, *vĭn dĭ kā'shŭn*, s. justification, défense, f.

vindicator, *vĭn'dĭ kā tẽr*, s. défenseur, m.

vindicatory, *vĭn'dĭ kā tẽr ĭ*, a. vengeur ‖ justificatif.

vindictive, *vĭn dĭk'tĭv*, a. vindicatif.

vine, *vīn*, s. vigne, f. ‖ ~-arbour, s. treille f. ‖ ~-branch, s. sarment, m. ‖ (poét.) pampre, m. ‖ ~-clad, a. abondant en vignes ‖ ~-dresser, s. vigneron, m. ‖ ~-estate, s. vignoble, m. ‖ ~-growing, s. viticulture, f. ‖ ~-stick, s. échalas, m.

vinegar, *vĭn'ẽgẽr*, s. vinaigre, m. ‖ ~-cruet, s. vinaigrier, m.

vinery, *vĭn'ẽr ĭ*, s. serre à vignes, f.

vineyard, *vĭn'yärd*, s. vigne, f.

vinosity, *vĭ nŏs'ĭ tĭ*, s. qualité vineuse, f.

vinous, *vīn'ŭs*, a. vineux.

vintage, *vĭn'tăj*, s. vendange, f. ‖ vinée, f.

vintager, *vĭn'tā jẽr*, s. vendangeur, m., vendangeuse, f.

vintner, *vĭnt'nẽr*, s. cabaretier, m.

violate, *vī ō lāt*, v. a. violer.

violation, *vī ō lā'shŭn*, s. violation, f. ‖ infraction, f. ‖ viol, m.

violator, *vī ō lā tẽr*, s. violateur, infracteur, m.

violence, *vī'ō lẽns*, s. violence, f. ‖ to do ~ to oneself, attenter à ses jours ‖ to offer ~, sévir.

violent, *vī'ō lẽnt*, a. violent ‖ fort ‖ gros ‖ -ly, ad. violemment, avec violence.

violet, *vī'ō lĕt*, s. violette, f. ‖ ~-colour, s. violet m.

violin, *vī ō lĭn* ou *vī ō lĭn'*, s. violon, m.

violinist, *vī ō lĭn ĭst*, s. violoniste, violon, m. [m.

violoncello, *vī ō lŏn chĕl'lō*, s. violoncelle,

viper, *vī'pẽr*, s. vipère, f.

viperine, *vī'pẽr ĭn*, **viperous**, *vī'pẽr ŭs*, a. de vipère, vipérin. [masse, f.

virago, *vĭ rā'gō*, s. virago, femme hom-

virgin, *vẽr'jĭn*, s. vierge, f.

virgin, *vẽr'jĭn*, a. vierge ‖ virginal.

virginal, *vẽr'jĭn ăl*, a. virginal, pur.

virginity, *vẽr jĭn'ĭ tĭ*, s. virginité, f.

viridity, *vĭ rĭd'ĭ tĭ*, s. verdeur, f.

virile, *vĭr'ĭl* ou *vĭr'īl*, a. viril.

virility, *vĭ rĭl'ĭ tĭ*, s. virilité, f.

virtu, *vẽr tō'*, s. goût des arts, m. ‖ objects of ~, objets d'art, m. pl.

virtual, *vẽr'tū ăl*, a. (-ly, ad.) virtuel(le) ment).

virtue, *vẽr'tū*, s. vertu, f. ‖ by ~ of, en vertu de ‖ in ~ of, conformément à.

virtuoso, *vẽr tū ō'sō*, s. virtuose, m.

virtuous, *vẽr'tū ŭs*, a. vertueux ‖ -ly, ad. vertueusement.

virulence, *vĭr'ū lẽns*, s. virulence, f.

virulent, *vĭr'ū lẽnt*, a. virulent ‖ -ly, ad. malicieusement.

virus, *vī'rŭs*, s. virus, m.

visage, *vĭz'āj*, s. visage, m., figure, f.

viscera, *vĭs'sẽr ă*, s. pl. viscères, m. pl.

viscosity, *vĭs kŏs'ĭ tĭ*, s. viscosité, f.

viscount, *vī'kownt*, s. vicomte, m.

viscountess, *vī'kownt ĕs*, s. vicomtesse, f.

viscounty, *vī'kownt ĭ*, s. vicomté, m.

viscous, *vĭs'kŭs*, a. visqueux.

visibility, *vĭz ĭ bĭl'ĭ tĭ*, s. visibilité, f.

visible, *vĭz'ĭ bl*, a. visible.

visibly, *vĭz'ĭ blĭ*, ad. visiblement, à vue d'œil.

vision, *vĭzh'ŭn*, s. vision, f. ‖ vue, f.

visionary, *vĭzh'ŭn ẽr ĭ*, s. visionnaire, m.

visionary, *vĭzh'ŭn ẽr ĭ*, a. visionnaire.

visit, *vĭz'ĭt*, s. visite, f. ‖ tournée, f. ‖ to be on a ~, être en visite ‖ to pay a ~, rendre visite.

visit, *vĭz'ĭt*, v. a. & n. visiter ‖ faire des visites.

visitant, *vĭz'ĭ tănt*, s. visiteur, m.

visitation, *vĭz ĭ tā'shŭn*, s. visite, f. ‖ tournée, f. ‖ épreuve, f.

visiting, *vĭz'ĭ tĭng*, s. visite, f. ‖ visites, f. pl. ‖ ~-card, s. carte, f.

visitor, *vĭz'ĭ tẽr*, s. visiteur, m. ‖ visiteuse, f.

visor, *vĭz'ẽr*, s. visière, f. ‖ masque, m.

visored, *vĭz'ẽrd*, a. masqué.

vista, *vĭs'tă*, s. vue, perspective, échappée, f. ‖ percée, f.

vital, *vī'tăl*, a. vital ‖ essentiel ‖ -s, s. pl. parties vitales, f. pl.

vitality, *vī tăl'ĭ tĭ*, s. vitalité, f.

vitiate, *vĭsh'ĭ āt*, v. a. vicier, corrompre.

vitreous, *vĭt'rĭ ŭs*, a. vitreux.

vitrifaction, *vĭt rĭ făk'shŭn*, s. vitrification, f.

vitrify, *vĭt'rĭ fī*, v. a. (& n.) (se) vitrifier.

vitriol, *vĭt'rĭ ŏl*, s. vitriol, m.

vituperate, *vĭ tū'pẽr āt*, v. a. blâmer, réprimander.

vivacious, *vĭ vā'shŭs*, a. vif, alerte.

vivacity, *vĭ văs'ĭ tĭ*, s. vivacité, f.

vivarium, *vĭ vā'rĭ ŭm*, s. vivier, parc, m. ‖ garenne, f. [oral.

viva-voce, *vī'vă vō'sĕ*, ad. de vive voix ‖

vivid, *vĭv'ĭd*, a. vif ‖ -ly, ad. vivement.

vividness, *vĭv'ĭd nĕs*, s. vivacité, f.

vivification, *vĭv ĭ fĭ kā'shŭn*, s. vivification, f. ‖ revivification, f.

vivify, *vĭv'ĭ fī*, v. a. vivifier, animer.

viviparous, *vĭ vĭp'ă rŭs*, a. vivipare.

vivisection, *vĭv ĭ sĕk'shŭn*, s. vivisection, f.

vixen, *vĭks'n*, s. renarde, f. ‖ femme querelleuse, f.

viz., *vĭz*, ad. (for videlicet) savoir, c'est-à-dire.

vizier, *vĭz'yẽr*, s. vizir, m.   [m.

vocabulary, *vŏ kăb' ŭ lẽr ĭ*, s. vocabulaire,

vocal, *vŏ' kăl*, a. vocal, de voix || –ly, ad. par la voix || verbalement.

vocalist, *vŏ' kăl ĭst*, s. chanteur, m., chanteuse, cantatrice, f.

vocation, *vŏ kā' shŭn*, s. vocation, f.

vocative, *vŏk' ă tĭv*, s. (gr.) vocatif, m.

vociferate, *vŏ sĭf' ẽr āt*, v. n. vociférer.

vociferation, *vŏ sĭf ẽr ā' shŭn*, s. vociféra-tion, f., cris, m. pl.

vociferous, *vŏ sĭf ẽr ŭs*, a. violent, em-porté || bruyant.

vogue, *vōg*, s. vogue, mode, f. || to be in ~, être en vogue, être à la mode.

voice, *vŏĭs*, s. voix, f. || parole, f. || in a low ~, à voix basse || ~-pipe, s. porte-voix, m.

void, *vŏȳd*, s. vide, m.

void, *vŏȳd*, v. a. vider, évacuer || révoquer.

void, *vŏȳd*, a. vide, vacant || vain, nul, in-valide || dépourvu de.

volatile, *vŏl' ă tĭl*, a. volatil || volage, changeant || léger.

volatilisation, *vŏl ă tĭl ĭ zā' shŭn*, s. (chim.) volatilisation, f.   [C

volatilise, *vŏl' ă tĭl īz*, v. a. volatiliser.

volatility, *vŏl ă tĭl' ĭ tĭ*, s. légèreté, f. || volatilité, f.

volcanic, *vŏl kăn' ĭk*, a. volcanique.

volcano, *vŏl kā' nō*, s. volcan, m.

vole, *vōl*, s. vole, f. || campagnol, m.

volley, *vŏl' lĭ*, s. volée, décharge, salve, f. || acclamation, f. || ~-firing, s. feu de peloton, m.

volt, *vōlt*, s. volte, f.

Volt, *vōlt*, s. (phys.) Volt, m., unité de la force électrique.

voltaic, *vŏl tā' ĭk*, a., ~ pile, s. pile de Volta, f.

volubility, *vŏl ū bĭl' ĭ tĭ*, s. volubilité, f.

voluble, *vŏl' ū bl*, a. mobile, flexible || rou-lant || délié (de la langue).

volubly, *vŏl' ū blĭ*, ad. avec volubilité.

volume, *vŏl' ūm*, s. volume, m., grosseur, f. || tome, m. || (of revolving smoke) tourbillon, m.

voluminous, *vŏ lū' mĭ nŭs*, a. volumineux.

voluntarily, *vŏl' ŭn tẽr ĭ lĭ*, ad. volontaire-ment.

voluntary, *vŏl' ŭn tẽr ĭ*, s. impromptu en musique, m.

voluntary, *vŏl' ŭn tẽr ĭ*, a. volontaire.

volunteer, *vŏl ŭn tēr'*, s. volontaire, m.

volunteer, *vŏl ŭn tēr'*, v. a. (& n.) (s')offrir || (mil.) s'engager comme volontaire.   [m.

voluptuary, *vŏ lŭp' tŭ ẽr ĭ*, s. sensualiste,

voluptuous, *vŏ lŭp' tŭ ŭs*, a. voluptueux || –ly, ad. voluptueusement.

voluptuousness, *vŏ lŭp' tŭ ŭs nĕs*, s. vo-lupté, f.

volute, *vŏ lūt'*, s. volute, f.

vomica, *vŏm' ĭ kă*, s. vomique, f. || nux-~, noix vomique, f.   [tif, m.

vomit, *vŏm' ĭt*, s. vomissement, m. || vomi-

vomit, *vŏm' ĭt*, s. matière des vomisse-ments, f. || vomitif, m.

vomit, *vŏm' ĭt*, v. a. vomir, rendre.

vomiting, *vŏm' ĭt ĭng*, s. vomissement, m.

voracious, *vŏ rā' shŭs*, a. vorace || dévo-rant || –ly, ad. avec voracité.

voracity, *vŏ răs' ĭ tĭ*, s. voracité, f.

vortex, *vŏr' tĕks*, s. tourbillon, m.

votary, *vŏ' tẽr ĭ*, s. adorateur, m. || secta-teur, m. || partisan, m.

votary, *vŏ' tẽr ĭ*, a. votif.

vote, *vōt*, s. vote, m., voix, f. || suffrage, m. || to put to the ~, mettre aux voix.

vote, *vōt*, v. a. voter || élire || déclarer.

voter, *vŏ' tẽr*, s. votant, m.

voting, *vŏ' tĭng*, s. action de voter, f. || ~-paper, s. bulletin, m.

votive, *vŏ' tĭv*, a. votif.

vouch, *vŏwch*, v. a. & n. attester || affirmer, garantir || répondre de.

voucher, *vŏwch' ẽr*, s. garant, m. || garantie, preuve, f. || titre, m.

vouchsafe, *vŏwch săf'*, v. a. & n. accor-der || daigner.

vow, *vŏw*, s. vœu, m.

vow, *vŏw*, v. a. & n. vouer || faire vœu || protester, jurer.

vowel, *vŏw' ĕl*, s. voyelle, f.

voyage, *vŏȳ' ăj*, s. voyage (par mer), m.

voyage, *vŏȳ' ăj*, v. a. & n. traverser || voyager (sur mer).

vulcan, *vŭl' kăn*, s. vulcain, m.

vulcanise, *vŭl' kăn ĭz*, v. a. vulcaniser.

vulcanite, *vŭl' kăn ĭt*, s. (min.) vulcanite, f.

vulgar, *vŭl' gẽr*, s. bas peuple, vulgaire, m., populace, f.

vulgar, *vŭl' gẽr*, a. (–ly, ad.) vulgaire (ment) || bas, vil.

vulgarism, *vŭl' gẽr ĭzm*, s. expression vul-gaire, f.

vulgarity, *vŭl găr' ĭ tĭ*, s. vulgarité, bas-sesse, f.

vulgarise, *vŭl' gẽr ĭz*, v. a. rendre vulgaire.

Vulgate, *vŭl' gāt*, s. Vulgate, f.

vulnerable, *vŭl' nẽr ă bl*, a. vulnérable.

vulnerary, *vŭl' nẽr ẽr ĭ*, s. vulnéraire, m.

vulpine, *vŭl' pĭn*, a. de renard || rusé.

vulture, *vŭl' tŭr* ou *vŭl' chŏŏr*, s. vautour, m.

vulturine, *vŭl' tŭ rĭn*, a. de vautour.   [m.

W.

wad, *wŏd*, s. bourre, f. || paquet, m.

wad, *wŏd*, v. a. bourrer, ouater.

wadding, *wŏd' dĭng*, s. bourre, f. || ouate, f.

waddle, *wŏd' dl*, v. n. se dandiner.

wade, *wād*, v. n. passer à gué || barboter.

wafer, *wā' fẽr*, s. oublie, f., pain à cache-ter, m. || hostie, f.

waffle, *wŏf' fl*, s. gaufre, f.

waft, *wăft*, s. corps flottant, m.

waft, *wăft*, v. a. & n. porter au travers des airs, transporter || soutenir || flotter.

wag, *wăg*, s. plaisant, farceur, m.

wag, *wăg*, v. a. & n. remuer, agiter.

wage, *wāj*, v. a. faire la guerre.

wager, *wā′jẽr*, s. gageure, f., pari, m. ‖ to lay a ~, parier.

wager, *wā′jẽr*, v. a. gager, parier. [m.

wages, *wā′jẽs*, s. pl. gages, m. pl., salaire,

waggery, *wăg′gẽrĭ*, s. espièglerie, f., badinage malin, m.

waggish, *wăg′gĭsh*, a. espiègle. [f.

waggishness, *wăg′gĭsh′nĕs*, s. espièglerie,

waggle, *wăg′gl*, v. n. frétiller, vaciller.

waggon, *wăg′gŏn*, s. fourgon, chariot, m. ‖ (rail.) wagon, m. ‖ baggage-~, fourgon à bagages, m. ‖ ~-master, s. (mil.) vaguemestre, m. ‖ ~-office, s. entreprise de roulage, f. ‖ ~-train, s. (mil.) équipages du train, m. pl.

waggoner, *wăg′gŏn′nẽr*, s. roulier, charretier, m.

waggonette, *wăg′gŏn′nĕt′*, s. (Am.) vide sociable, s. [geronnette, f.

wagtail, *wăg′tāl*, s. hoche-queue, m., ber-

wail, *wāf*, s. chose trouvée et non réclamée, f.

wail, *wāl*, s. lamentation, f., gémissement, m., complainte, f.

wain, *wān*, s. voiture, f. ‖ **Charles′** ~, (astr.) le grand Chariot, m.

wainscot, *wān′skŏt*, s. boiserie, f.

wainscot, *wān′skŏt*, v. a. boiser, lambrisser.

waist, *wāst*, s. taille, ceinture, f. ‖ ~-band, s. ceinture, f., ceinturon, m.

waistcoat, *wĕs′kŏt*, s. gilet, m.

waistcoating, *wĕs′kōt′ĭng*, s. étoffe pour gilets, f. [f.

wait, *wāt*, s. guet-apens, m. ‖ embuscade,

wait, *wāt*, v. a. & n. attendre, être dans l'attente ‖ rester ‖ accompagner.

waiter, *wāt′ẽr*, s. garçon, m. ‖ (tray) plateau, m. ‖ dumb-~, servante, f. (petite table).

waiting, *wāt′ĭng*, s. attente, f. ‖ service, m. ‖ to keep one ~, faire attendre qn. ‖ ~-room, s. salle d'attente, f. ‖ ~-woman (~-maid), s. femme de chambre, f.

waitress, *wāt′rĕs*, s. fille de salle, f.

waits, *wāts*, s. musiciens ambulants de la Noël, m. pl.

waive, *wāv*, v. a. renoncer à ‖ rejeter ‖ remettre, différer.

waiver, *wāv′ẽr*, s. renonciation, f.

wake, *wāk*, s. veille, f. ‖ fête de village, f. ‖ (fig.) trace, f. ‖ (mar.) sillage, m.

wake, *wāk*, v. a. & n. ir. veiller.

wakeful, *wāk′fōōl*, a. éveillé ‖ vigilant.

waken, *wā′kn*, v. a. & n. éveiller, réveiller ‖ exciter ‖ s'éveiller.

waking, *wā′kĭng*, s. veille, f.

wale, *wāl*, s. marque, f. ‖ lisière (du drap), f.

walk, *wăwk*, s. marche, f. ‖ promenade, f., tournée, f. ‖ avenue, f.

walk, *wăwk*, v. a. & n. traverser, passer au travers de ‖ passer par ‖ marcher ‖ se promener ‖ aller le pas ‖ ~ in ! entrez ! ‖ ~ up ! montez !

walker, *wăwk′ẽr*, s. marcheur, promeneur, piéton, m., promeneuse, f.

walking, *wăwk′ĭng*, s. marche, promenade, f. ‖ ~-coat, s. habit de ville, m. ‖ ~-stick, s. canne, f.

wall, *wăwl*, s. mur, m., muraille, f. ‖ (anat.) paroi, f. ‖ haut du pavé, m. ‖ (fig.) rempart, m. ‖ to go to the ~, succomber ‖ to give one the ~, céder le haut du pavé à qn. ‖ ~-creeper, s. grimpereau, m. ‖ ~-eye, s. œil vairon, m. ‖ ~-flower, s. giroflée jaune, f. ‖ violier, m. ‖ ~-fruit, s. fruit d'espalier, m. ‖ ~-tree, s. arbre en espalier, m.

wall, *wăwl*, v. a. entourer de murailles.

wallet, *wŏl′lĕt*, s. bissac, m., besace, valise, f. [dans ‖ nager ‖ croupir.

wallow, *wŏl′lō*, v. n. se vautrer, se rouler

walnut, *wăwl′nŭt*, s. noix, f. ‖ noyer, m. ‖ ~-tree, s. noyer, m.

walrus, *wăwl′rŭs*, s. morse, m.

waltz, *wăwlts*, s. valse, f.

waltz, *wăwlts*, v. n. valser.

wan, *wŏn*, a. blême, pâle.

wand, *wŏnd*, s. baguette, f.

wander, *wŏn′dẽr*, v. n. rôder ‖ s'écarter ‖ to be ~ing, être en délire, délirer.

wanderer, *wŏn′dẽr′ẽr*, s. rôdeur, vagabond, s. [égarement, m.

wandering, *wŏn′dẽr′ĭng*, s. excursion, f. ‖

wane, *wān*, s. décroissance, f., déclin, m.

wane, *wān*, v. n. décroître ‖ décliner.

wanness, *wŏn′nĕs*, s. pâleur, f. [m.

want, *wŏnt*, s. manque, défaut, m. ‖ besoin,

want, *wŏnt*, v. a. & n. avoir besoin de, manquer de ‖ désirer.

wanting, *wŏnt′ĭng*, a. qui manque, absent.

wanton, *wŏn′tŏn*, s. libertin, m.

wanton, *wŏn′tŏn*, v. n. folâtrer, jouer, badiner.

wanton, *wŏn′tŏn*, a. lascif, voluptueux, dissolu ‖ folâtre, gai ‖ fécond ‖ ~ly, ad. lascivement ‖ en folâtrant, gaiement.

wantonness, *wŏn′tŏn′nĕs*, s. lasciveté, impudicité, volupté, f. ‖ badinage, m. ‖ licence, f.

war, *wăwr*, s. guerre, f. ‖ man of ~, vaisseau de guerre, m.

war, *wăwr*, v. n. faire la guerre.

warble, *wăwr′bl*, v. a. gazouiller ‖ fredonner.

warbler, *wăwr′blẽr*, s. chanteur, m. ‖ fauvette, f. [m.

warbling, *wăwr′blĭng*, s. gazouillement,

ward, *wăwrd*, s. pupille, m. ‖ tutelle, f. ‖ quartier, m. ‖ arrondissement, m. ‖ garde, f.

ward, *wăwrd*, v. a. défendre, préserver ‖ parer, éluder.

warden, *wăwrd′ẽn*, s. gardien, garde, gouverneur, m. ‖ geôlier, m., geôlière, f.

warder, *wăwrd′ẽr*, s. garde, gardien, m.

wardmote, *wăwrd′mōt*, s. conseil d'arrondissement, m.

wardrobe, *wăwrd′rōb*, s. garderobe, f.

wardship, *wăwrd′shĭp*, s. tutelle, f.

ware, *wār*, s. marchandise, denrée, f.

warehouse, *wār′hŏws*, s. magasin, m. ‖ ~-man, s. garde-magasin, m. ‖ marchand en gros, m.

warfare, *wåůr'får,* s. vie militaire, f. guerre, f.

warily, *wå'rĭ lĭ,* ad. prudemment.

wariness, *wå'rĭ něs,* s. prudence, f.

warlike, *wåůr'lĭk,* s. belliqueux.

warm, *wåůrm,* v. a. & n. chauffer, échauffer || s'échauffer.

warm, *wåůrm,* a. (-ly, ad.) chaud(ement) || zélé, emporté || chaleureusement || ~-hearted, a. cordial, affectueux.

warmer, *wåůrm'ěr,* s. réchaud, m.

warming, *wåůrm'ĭng,* s. chauffage, m. || ~-pan, s. bassinoire, f.

warmth, *wåůrmth,* s. chaleur, f. || zèle, m.

warn, *wåůrn,* v. a. avertir, prévenir, informer || to ~ against, prévenir contre.

warning, *wåůrn'ĭng,* s. avertissement, avis, m. || congé, m. || (of clocks) avant-quart, m. || to give ~, donner congé.

warp, *wåůrp,* s. chaîne, f. || (mar.) touée, f.

warp, *wåůrp,* v. a. & n. ourdir || détourner, écarter || se déjeter, s'écarter.

warrant, *wŏr'rånt,* s. brevet, m. || mandat d'arrêt, m. || garantie, f. || death-~, ordre d'exécution d'un arrêt de mort, m. || search-~, mandat d'enquête, m.

warrant, *wŏr'rånt,* v. a. garantir, attester || justifier. [soutenable.

warrantable, *wŏr'rånt å bl,* a. justifiable ||

warranty, *wŏr'rånt ĭ,* a. garantie, f.

warren, *wŏr'rěn,* s. garenne, f.

warrior, *wŏr'rĭ ěr,* s. guerrier, soldat, m.

wart, *wåůrt,* s. verrue, f. || poireau, m. || ~-wort, s. (bot.) réveille-matin, m.

wary, *wå'rĭ,* a. prudent.

wash, *wŏsh,* s. lavage, m. || cosmétique, m. || marécage, m. || lavis, m. || lavure, f. || lavasse, f. || (méd.) lotion, f. || ~-hand-basin, s. cuvette, f. || ~-hand-stand, s. lavabo, m. || ~-house, s. lavoir, m. || ~-leather, s. peau de chamois, f. || ~-stand, s. toilette, f.

wash, *wŏsh,* v. a. (& n.) (se) laver.

washerwoman, *wŏsh'ěr wŏŏm ăn,* s. blanchisseuse, f.

washing, *wŏsh'ĭng,* s. lavage, m. || blanchissage, m. || ~-bill, s. note du blanchissage, f. || ~-stand, s. lavabo, m.

washy, *wŏsh'ĭ,* a. humide, mouillé || faible || ~ stuff, s. lavasse, f.

wasp, *wŏsp,* s. guêpe, f.

waspish, *wŏsp'ĭsh,* a. acariâtre.

waste, *wåst,* s. gaspillage, m. || déchet, m. || dégât, m. || folle dépense, f. || désert, m. || to go ou run to ~, se perdre, s'user || ~-book, s. brouillard, m. || ~-pipe, s. tuyau de décharge or de dégorgement, m.

waste, *wåst,* v. a. & n. diminuer, gâter, dissiper, prodiguer || ravager || dépérir || s'user || s'épuiser.

waste, *wåst,* a. inutile, de rebut || ~-paper-basket, s. panier à papier, m. || ~-paper, s. papier de rebut, m.

wasteful, *wåst'fŏŏl,* a. destructeur, prodigue || -ly, ad. prodigalement.

wastefulness, *wåst'fŏŏl něs,* s. prodiga-lité, f. || gaspillage, m.

watch, *wŏch,* s. veille, f., guet, m. || garde, f. || (mar.) quart, m. || surveillance, f. || montre, f. || to keep ~, veiller || ~-dog, s. chien de garde, m. || ~-fire, s. feu de bivouac, m. || ~-light, s. veilleuse, f. || fanal, m. || ~-tower, s. tour d'observation, f.

watch, *wŏch,* v. a. & n. veiller, surveiller, épier || garder || avoir soin de.

watcher, *wŏch'ěr,* s. surveillant, observa-teur, m.

watchful, *wŏch'fŏŏl,* a. vigilant || -ly, ad. vigilamment. [f.

watchfulness, *wŏch'fŏŏl něs,* s. vigilance,

watching, *wŏch'ĭng,* s. insomnie, f.

watchmaker, *wŏch'mā kěr,* s. horloger, m.

watchman, *wŏch'măn,* s. gardien de nuit, m. || garde, homme de guet, m.

watchword, *wŏch'wěrd,* s. mot d'ordre, m.

water, *wåů'těr,* s. eau, f. || to make ~, (mar.) faire eau || to pass ~, (méd.) uriner || of the first ~, de haute volée || to hold ~, être étanche, imperméable || ~-beetle, s. nageur, m., puce aquatique, f. || ~-bucket, s. sceau, m. || ~-closet, s. cabinet d'aisance, m. || ~-colours, s. pl. aquarelle, f. || ~-cress(es), s. pl. cresson, m. || ~-cure, s. hydrothérapie, f. || ~-dog, s. barbet, m. || ~-fowl, s. oiseau aquatique, m. || poule d'eau, f. || ~-gauge, s. flotteur, m. || ~-gruel, s. gruau à l'eau, m. || ~-lily, s. nénuphar, m. || ~-line, s. ligne de flottaison, f. || ~-mark, s. niveau des eaux, m. || filagramme, m. || ~-pipe, s. conduit d'eau, m. || ~-side, s. bord de l'eau, m. || ~-station, s. station à prendre de l'eau, f. || ~-wheel, s. roue hydrau-lique, f. || ~-works, s. pl. ouvrages hydrauliques, m. pl. || machine hydrau-lique, f.

water, *wåů'těr,* v. a. & n. arroser || abreuver || moirer || (mar.) faire de l'eau || pleurer || to make one's mouth ~, faire venir l'eau à la bouche.

waterage, *wåů'těr åj,* s. transport par eau, m. || prix du transport par eau, m.

waterfall, *wåů'těr fåwl,* s. chute d'eau, cascade, f.

watering, *wåů'těr ĭng,* s. arrosement, m. || abreuvage, m. || ~-cart, s. voiture d'ar-rosage public, f. || ~-engine, s. pompe d'irrigation, f. || ~-place, s. abreuvoir, m. || ville d'eaux or maritime, f. || ~-pot, s. arrosoir, m.

waterlogged, *wåů'těr lŏgd,* a. rempli d'eau.

waterman, *wåů'těr măn,* s. batelier, m.

waterproof, *wåů'těr prŏf,* **watertight,** *wåů'těr tĭt,* a. imperméable (à l'eau).

watershed, *wåů'těr shěd,* s. versant, m.

waterspout, *wåů'těr spŏwt,* s. trombe, f.

waterway, *wåů'těr wå,* s. cours d'eau, m. || gouttière, f.

watery, *wåů'těr ĭ,* a. aqueux, liquide || plein d'eau || marin.

wattle, *wŏt'tl,* s. claie, f. || barbe de coq, f.

wattle, *wŏt'tl,* v. a. entourer de claies.

wave, *wāv*, s. vague, onde, f. || ondulation, f.
wave, *wāv*, v. n. ondoyer || flotter, se balancer || tournoyer.
waver, *wā′vẽr*, v. n. vaciller, chanceler.
wavering, *wā′vẽr ing*, s. irrésolution, f.
wavering, *wā′vẽr ing*, a. irrésolu.
wavy, *wā′vĭ*, a. ondoyant.
wax, *wăks*, s. cire, f. || poix, f. || ~-light, s. bougie, f. || ~-taper, s. bougie filée or d'allume, f. || cierge, m. || ~-work, s. figure de cire, f.
wax, *wăks*, v. a. cirer || ~, v. n. croître, s'accroître || se faire.
waxen, *wăks′n*, a. de cire.
waxy, *wăks′ĭ*, a. cireux.
way, *wā*, s. voie, f. || chemin, m., route, f. || passage, m. || expédient, m. || the right, wrong ~, la bonne, la mauvaise voie || to be in the ~, embarrasser, gêner || out-of-the~, a. extraordinaire || to be in the family ~, être enceinte || to get under ~, (mar.) se mettre en route || to lose one's ~, s'égarer || to get out of the ~, emporter, enlever || to make one's (own) ~, faire à sa guise || to make the best of one's ~, hâter le pas || any-~, ad. de manière ou d'autre || to work one's ~, se faire jour || ~-bill, s. itinéraire de voiture publique, m.
wayfarer, *wā′fā rẽr*, s. voyageur, m.
wayfaring, *wā′fā ring*, a. en voyage.
wayward, *wā′wẽrd*, a. têtu, maussade.
we, *wē*, pn. nous.
weak, *wēk*, a. (-ly, ad.) faible(ment) || débile.
weaken, *wēk′n*, v. a. affaiblir.
weakening, *wēk′n ing*, s. affaiblissement, m., débilitation, f.
weakness, *wēk′nĕs*, s. faiblesse, f. || faible, m.
weal, *wēl*, s. bien, m., prospérité, f. || contusion, meurtrissure, f.
wealth, *wĕlth*, s. bien, m., richesses, f. pl.
wealthily, *wĕlth′ĭ lĭ*, ad. richement.
wealthiness, *wĕlth′ĭ nĕs*, s. opulence, f.
wealthy, *wĕlth′ĭ*, a. riche, opulent.
wean, *wēn*, v. a. sevrer || priver de.
weanling, *wēn′ling*, s. enfant (animal) sevré, m.
weapon, *wĕp′n*, s. arme, f.
wear, *wār*, s. usage, m. || usure, f. || under-~, dessous, m.
wear, *wār*, v. a. & n. ir. user, consumer, employer, porter, montrer || s'user, vieillir || to ~ well, badly, être d'un bon user, n'être pas d'un bon user.
wearable, *wār′ă bl*, a. en état d'être porté.
weariness, *wēr′ĭ nĕs*, s. lassitude, fatigue, f. || ennui, m.
wearing-apparel, *wār′ing ăp′pār′ĕl*, s. habits, m. pl.
wearisome, *wēr′ĭ sŭm*, a. ennuyeux || -ly, ad. avec ennui.
weary, *wēr′ĭ*, v. a. fatiguer || ennuyer.
weary, *wēr′ĭ*, a. las, fatigué, ennuyé.
weasel, *wē′zĕl*, s. belette, f.
weather, *wĕth′ẽr*, s. température de l'air, f. || tempête, f. || ~ permitting, si le

temps le permet || ~-glass, s. baromètre, thermomètre, m.
weather, *wĕth′ẽr*, v. a. résister à || (mar.) doubler.
weave, *wēv*, v. a. ir. tisser || entrelacer || mêler, entremêler.
weaver, *wēv′ẽr*, s. tisserand, m.
weaving, *wēv′ing*, s. tissure, f.
web, *wĕb*, s. tissu, m. || toile d'araignée, f. || membrane, f.
webbed, *wĕbd*, a. palmé.
wed, *wĕd*, v. a. & n. épouser || se marier.
wedding, *wĕd′ding*, s. mariage, m., noces, f. pl. || ~-cake, s. gâteau de noces, m. || ~-day, s. jour de la noce, m.
wedge, *wĕj*, s. coin, m. || lingot, m.
wedge, *wĕj*, v. a. fendre || serrer, forcer.
wedgewood ware, *wĕj′wŏŏd wār*, s. wedgwood (faïence), m.
wedlock, *wĕd′lŏk*, s. mariage, m.
Wednesday, *wĕnz′dā*, s. mercredi, m. || Ash-~, mercredi des cendres, m.
weed, *wēd*, s. mauvaise herbe, f. || habits de deuil, m. pl.
weed, *wēd*, v. a. sarcler.
weeder, *wēd′ẽr*, s. sarcleur, m. || sarcloir. [m.
weeding-hook, *wēd′ing hŏŏk*, s. sarcloir, sarclet, m., serfouette, f.
weedy, *wēd′ĭ*, a. plein de mauvaises herbes.
week, *wēk*, s. semaine, f. || a ~ ago, il y a huit jours || this day ~, d'aujourd'hui en huit || ~-day, s. jour ouvrier, m.
weekly, *wēk′lĭ*, a. & ad. chaque semaine, par semaine || hebdomadaire.
weekly, hebdomadairement.
weep, *wēp*, v. a. & n. pleurer, déplorer.
weeper, *wēp′ẽr*, s. pleureur, m., pleureuse, f.
weeping-willow, *wēp′ing wĭl′lō*, s. saule pleureur, m.
weevil, *wē′vl*, s. charançon, m.
weft, *wĕft*, s. trame du drap, f. || tissu, m.
weigh, *wā*, v. a. & n. peser || examiner, considérer || to ~ down, s'affaisser || ~-bridge, s. bascule pour peser les voitures chargées, f.
weighing-machine, *wā′ing mă shēn*, s. bascule, f.
weight, *wāt*, s. poids, m., pesanteur, f.
weighted, *wā′ĕd*, a. chargé.
weightily, *wāt′ĭ lĭ*, ad. pesamment || avec importance.
weightiness, *wāt′ĭ nĕs*, s. pesanteur, f. || importance, f.
weighty, *wāt′ĭ*, a. pesant || important.
welcome, *wĕl′kŭm*, s. bon accueil, m.
welcome, *wĕl′kŭm*, v. a. faire bon accueil à.
welcome, *wĕl′kŭm*, a. bienvenu || agréable || ~! soyez le bienvenu!
weld, *wĕld*, v. a. souder.
welfare, *wĕl′fār*, s. bien-être, m.
well, *wĕl*, s. puits, m., source, fontaine, f. || ~s, pl. eaux minérales, f. pl. || ~-spring, s. source, f.
well, *wĕl*, a. & ad. bon, heureux || bien, comme il faut || as ~ as, aussi bien que || all's ~ that ends ~, tout est bien qui finit bien || ~ off, bien dans ses affaires ||

let ~ alone, le mieux est l'ennemi du bien ‖ ~-being, s. bien-être, m. ‖ ~-bred, a. bien élevé ‖ ~-meant, a. fait à bonne intention ‖ ~-met! heureuse rencontre! ‖ ~-to-do, a. à son aise ‖ calé ‖ ~-wisher, s. ami, m.

welt, *wĕlt*, s. bordure, f., bord, m.

welt, *wĕlt*, v. a. border.

welter, *wĕl'tẽr*, v. n. se rouler, se vautrer.

wen, *wĕn*, s. loupe, f., goître, m.

wench, *wĕnsh*, s. fille, f. ‖ donzelle, f.

wend, *wĕnd*, v. n. aller, poursuivre.

Wesleyan, *wĕs'li ăn*, s. méthodiste de la secte de Wesley, m.

west, *wĕst*, s. ouest, occident, m.

west, *wĕst*, westerly, *wĕst'ẽr li*, western, *wĕst'ẽrn*, a. d'ouest, occidental ‖ de l'ouest.

westward, *wĕst'wẽrd*, ad. vers l'occident.

wet, *wĕt*, s. humidité, f.

wet, *wĕt*, v. a. mouiller, humecter, arroser.

wet, *wĕt*, a. mouillé, humide ‖ ~-nurse, s. nourrice, f.

wether, *wĕth'ẽr*, s. mouton, m.

wetness, *wĕt'nĕs*, s. humidité, f.

whack, *hwăk*, s. roulée, f.

whack, *hwăk*, v. a. battre, rosser.

whale, *hwāl*, s. baleine, f. ‖ ~-boat, s. baleinière, f. ‖ ~-bone, s. barbe de baleine, f.

whaler, *hwāl'ẽr*, s. baleinier, m.

wharf, *hwŏrf*, s. quai, m.

wharfage, *hwŏrf'āj*, s. quaiage, m.

wharfinger, *hwŏrf'injẽr*, s. garde d'un quai, m.

what, *hwŏt*, pn. & ad. ce que, ce qui, que ‖ quoi ‖ quel, quelle ‖ ~? comment? ‖ he knows ~'s ~, il ne se mouche pas du pied.

what(so)ever, *hwŏt (sō) ĕv'ẽr*, pn. quel que, quoi que, tout ce que, tout ce qui ‖ quelconque.

wheal, *hwēl*, s. pustule, f.

wheat, *hwēt*, s. froment, blé, m.

wheaten, *hwēt'n*, a. de froment, de blé.

wheedle, *hwē'dl*, v. a. enjôler, flatter.

wheedler, *hwē'dlẽr*, s. enjôleur, m.

wheel, *hwēl*, s. roue, f. ‖ to break upon the ~, rouer un malfaiteur ‖ to put a spoke in one's ~, jeter des bâtons dans les roues de qn. ‖ ~-barrow, s. brouette, f. ‖ ~-wright, s. charron, m. ‖ ~-works, s. rouages, m. pl.

wheel, *hwēl*, v. a. & n. faire tourner ‖ rouler ‖ voiturer ‖ tourner.

wheeler, *hwēl'ẽr*, s. cheval de brancard, m.

wheeze, *hwēz*, v. n. respirer avec bruit ‖ siffler.

wheezing, *hwēz'ing*, s. sifflement de la respiration, m.

whelk, *hwĕlk*, s. pustule, f.

whelm, *hwĕlm*, v. a. accabler, submerger.

whelp, *hwĕlp*, s. petit chien, m.

whelp, *hwĕlp*, v. n. mettre bas.

when, *hwĕn*, ad. quand, lorsque, tandis que ‖ since ~? depuis combien de temps? ‖ since ~, depuis lors.

whence, *hwĕns*, ad. d'où.

whencesoever, *hwĕns sō ĕv'ẽr*, ad. de quelque endroit que ce soit.

when(so)ever, *hwĕn sō ĕv'ẽr*, ad. quand, toutes les fois que.

where, *hwār*, ad. où.

whereabout, *hwār'ă bŏwt*, ad. où, auprès de quel endroit.

whereas, *hwār'ăz'*, ad. au lieu que, attendu que, d'autant que, vu que.

whereat, *hwār'ăt'*, ad. de quoi, dont, sur quoi ‖ là-dessus.

whereby, *hwār'bī'*, ad. par lequel (laquelle, lesquels) ‖ par quoi.

wherever, *hwār'ĕv'ẽr*, ad. partout où.

wherefore, *hwār'fōr*, ad. pourquoi, pour quelle raison.

wherein, *hwār in'*, ad. en quoi, où, dans lequel (laquelle, lesquels, lesquelles).

whereinto, *hwār in'tō*, ad. où, dans quoi.

whereof, *hwār ŏf'*, ad. dont, duquel, de laquelle.

whereon, *hwār ŏn'*, ad. sur lequel, sur laquelle, sur quoi.

whereso, *hwār'sō*, wheresoever, *hwār sō ĕv'ẽr*, ad. dans quelque lieu que, n'importe où.

whereto, *hwār tō'*, whereunto, *hwār ŭn'tō*, ad. à quoi, où, auquel, à laquelle.

whereupon, *hwār ŭp ŏn'*, ad. sur quoi ‖ sur ces entrefaites.

wherewith(al), *hwār with' (ăwl')*, ad. avec quoi, avec lequel (laquelle), de quoi.

wherry, *hwĕr'ri*, s. bac, m. ‖ passe-cheval.

whet, *hwĕt*, v. a. aiguiser ‖ exciter. [m.

whether, *hwĕth'ẽr*, c. & pn. soit que ‖ que ‖ si ‖ lequel des deux. [f.

whetstone, *hwĕt'stōn*, s. pierre à aiguiser, f.

whey, *hwā*, s. petit-lait, m.

which, *hwich*, pn. qui, que, lequel, laquelle ‖ quel? quelle?

which(so)ever, *hwich(sō)ĕv'ẽr*, pn. quel que soit.

whiff, *hwif*, s. souffle, m., bouffée, f.

whig, *hwig*, s. libéral (en Angleterre), m.

while, *hwil*, s. temps, espace de temps, m. ‖ worth ~, cela vaut la peine.

while, *hwil*, v. a.; to ~ away, tuer le temps.

whilst, *hwilst*, ad. pendant que, tandis que.

whim, *hwim*, s. caprice, m., fantaisie, boutade, lubie, f. ‖ treuil, m.

whimper, *hwim'pẽr*, v. n. pleurnicher.

whimsical, *hwim'zi kăl*, a. (-ly, ad.) capricieux ‖ bizarre ‖ capricieusement.

whine, *hwin*, s. plainte, f. ‖ gémissement, m.

whine, *hwin*, v. n. se plaindre, geindre, gémir, se lamenter.

whining, *hwin'ing*, a. plaintif, dolent.

whip, *hwip*, s. fouet, m. ‖ riding-cravache, f. ‖ ~ and spur, au grand galop ‖ to be a good ~, être bon cocher ‖ ~-hand, s. avantage, dessus, m.

whip, *hwip*, v. a. & n. fouetter ‖ se précipiter.

whipper-in, *hwip pẽr in'*, s. chef de file, m. (au parlement).

whipping-top, *hwĭp'pĭng tŏp,* s. touple, f., sabot, tonton, m. [m.

whipple-tree, *hwĭp'pl trē,* s. palonnier, m.

whirl, *hwĕrl,* s. tourbillon, m. || tournoiement, m. [vitesse || tournoyer, pirouetter.

whirl, *hwĕrl,* v. a. & n. faire tourner avec

whirligig, *hwĕr'lĭ gĭg,* s. pirouette, f.

whirlpool, *hwĕrl'pōl,* s. tourbillon, m.

whirlwind, *hwĕrl wĭnd,* s. tourbillon, m.

whisk, *hwĭsk,* s. vergette, f. || petit balai, m.

whisk, *hwĭsk,* v. n. passer rapidement || voler. [favori, m.

whisker, *hwĭsk'ĕr,* s. moustache, f. ||

whisper, *hwĭs'pĕr,* v. a. & n. chuchoter in a ~, tout bas. [ment, m.

whispering, *hwĭs'pĕrĭng,* s. chuchotement, m.

whist, *hwĭst,* s. whist, m. || long, short ~, whist à dix, à cinq points || ~! chut!

whistle, *hwĭs'sl,* s. sifflet, m. || sifflement, m.

whistle, *hwĭs'sl,* v. a. & n. siffler.

whit, *hwĭt,* s. point, iota, m. || not a ~, pas le moins du monde.

white, *hwĭt,* s. blanc, m., blancheur, f.

white, *hwĭt,* a. blanc, pâle || pur || ~-heat, s. incandescence, f. || ~-hot, a. incandescent || ~-lead, s. céruse, f. || ~-lime, s. blanc de chaux, m. || ~-smith, s. ferblantier, m.

whitebait, *hwĭt'bāt,* s. ablette (de mer), clupée blanche, f.

whiten, *hwĭt'n,* v. a. & n. blanchir || devenir blanc. [ureté, f.

whiteness, *hwĭt'nĕs,* s. blancheur, f. ||

whitewash, *hwĭt'wŏsh,* s. blanc de chaux, m. [badigeonner.

whitewash, *hwĭt'wŏsh,* v. a. blanchir,

whither, *hwĭth'ĕr,* ad. où.

withersoever, *hwĭth'ĕr sō ĕv'ĕr,* ad. partout, n'importe où.

whiting, *hwĭt'ĭng,* s. merlan, m. || blanc d'Espagne, m. || ~-pout, s. molle, f., aigrefin frais, m.

whitish, *hwĭt'ĭsh,* a. blanchâtre.

whitlow, *hwĭt'lō,* s. panaris, m.

Whit-Sunday, *hwĭt'sŭn dā,* s. jour de la Pentecôte, m.

Whitsuntide, *hwĭt'sŭn tĭd,* s. Pentecôte, f.

whittle, *hwĭt'tl,* v. a. couper.

whiz, *hwĭz,* s. sifflement, m.

whiz, *hwĭz,* v. a. siffler.

who, *hō,* pn. qui, que.

whoever, *hō ĕv'ĕr,* pn. quiconque.

whole, *hōl,* s. le total || on the ~, à tout prendre, en somme.

whole, *hōl,* a. tout, entier, complet || sain.

wholesale, *hōl'sāl,* s. vente en gros, f.

wholesome, *hōl'sŭm,* a. (-ly, ad.) sain (ement) || salutaire, salubre. [f.

wholesomeness, *hōl'sŭm nĕs,* s. salubrité,

wholly, *hōl'lĭ,* ad. entièrement.

whom, *hōm,* pn. que || lequel.

whomsoever, *hōm so ĕv'ĕr,* pn. quiconque.

whoop, *hŏp,* s. huée, f.

whoop, *hŏp,* v. n. huer, crier || ~ing-cough, s. coqueluche, f.

whore, *hōr,* s. prostituée, f.

whortleberry, *hwŏrt'l bĕr rĭ,* s. myrtille, f.

whose, *hōz,* pn. dont, de qui, à qui.

whoso(ever), *hō sō(ĕv'ĕr),* pn. quiconque.

why, *hwī,* ad. pourquoi || mais.

wick, *wĭk,* s. mèche, f.

wicked, *wĭk'ĕd,* a. méchant, scélérat || -ly, ad. méchamment.

wickedness, *wĭk'ĕd nĕs,* s. méchanceté, f.

wicker, *wĭk'ĕr,* s. osier, m.

wicker, *wĭk'ĕr,* a. fait d'osier.

wicket, *wĭk'ĕt,* s. guichet, m.

wide, *wĭd,* a. & ad. (-ly, ad.) large(ment) || vaste, ample || loin || tout à fait || au loin.

wideawake, *wĭd'ă wāk,* s. castor, m.

widen, *wī'dn,* v. a. (& n.) (s')élargir || étendre || allonger.

widgeon, *wĭj'ŭn,* s. sarcelle, f.

widow, *wĭd'ō,* s. veuve, f.

widow, *wĭd'ō,* v. a. rendre veuve || priver.

widowed, *wĭd'ōd,* a. veuf, veuve.

widower, *wĭd'ō ĕr,* s. veuf, m.

widowhood, *wĭd'ō hŏŏd,* s. veuvage, m.

width, *wĭdth,* s. largeur, f.

wield, *wēld,* v. a. manier, tenir, porter.

wife, *wīf,* s. femme, épouse, f.

wig, *wĭg,* s. perruque, f. || ~-block, s. tête à perruque, f. || ~-maker, s. perruquier, m.

wight, *wĭt,* s. individu, m.

wigwam, *wĭg'wăm,* s. cabane indienne, f.

wild, *wĭld,* a. sauvage, farouche, agreste, inculte || irrégulier, dissolu || -ly, ad. à l'état sauvage || d'une manière sauvage || follement || étourdiment || ~-fowl, s. oiseaux sauvages, m. pl.

wilds, *wĭlds,* s. pl. désert, m.

wilderness, *wĭl'dĕr nĕs,* s. désert, m.

wildfire, *wĭld'fīr,* s. feu grégeois, m. || (méd.) dartre, f.

wilding, *wĭld'ĭng,* s. pomme sauvage, f.

wildness, *wĭld'nĕs,* s. férocité, brutalité, f. || irrégularité, f. || désordre, m.

wile, *wĭl,* s. fraude, fourberie, ruse, f.

wilful, *wĭl'fŏŏl,* a. entêté || prémédité || -ly, ad. opiniâtrement || à dessein.

wilfulness, *wĭl'fŏŏl nĕs,* s. entêtement, m.

wilily, *wī'lĭ lĭ,* ad. par ruse.

wiliness, *wī'lĭ nĕs,* s. ruse, finesse, f.

will, *wĭl,* s. volonté, f. || disposition, f. || testament, m. || of one's own free ~, de son gré, spontanément || with a ~, de tout son cœur. [or no, bon gré, mal gré.

will, *wĭl,* v. n. vouloir || whether one ~

willing, *wĭl'ĭng,* a. disposé || spontané || -ly, ad. volontiers. [lonté, f.

willingness, *wĭl'ĭng nĕs,* s. bonne vo-

willow, *wĭl'lō,* s. (bot.) saule, m. || weeping-~, saule pleureur, m. [gré.

willy-nilly, *wĭl'lĭ nĭl'lĭ,* ad. bon gré, mal

wily, *wī'lĭ,* a. rusé, fin.

wimble, *wĭm'bl,* s. vilebrequin, m.

win, *wĭn,* v. a. & n. ir. gagner || acquérir.

wince, *wĭns,* v. n. ruer || se reculer.

winch, *wĭnsh,* s. manivelle, f.

wind, *wĭnd,* s. vent, m. || haleine, f. || vanité, f. || flatuosité, f. || trade ~s, vents alizés, m. pl. || to break ~, (vulg.) péter || roter.

wind, *wind,* v. a. & n. ir. sonner du cor ‖
tourner, tordre ‖ conduire ‖ suivre à la
piste ‖ changer ‖ envelopper, entourer ‖
tourner ‖ s'entortiller ‖ serpenter ‖ to ~ up,
(a watch &c.) monter ‖ (com.) liquider ‖
(fig.) préparer, conclure ‖ ~-up, s. conclusion, f.

winded, *wind'ĕd,* a. essoufflé.

winder, *wind'ĕr,* s. dévidoir, m.

windiness, *win'dĭnĕs,* s. ventosité, flatuosité, f.

winding, *wind'ĭng,* s. détour, m., sinuosité, f. ‖ ~-sheet, s. linceul, m.

windlass, *wind'lăs,* s. cabestan, treuil, m.

window, *win'dō,* s. fenêtre, croisée, f. ‖
bow-~, fenêtre cintrée, f. ‖ ~-blind, s.
jalousie, persienne, f., store, m. ‖ ~-cur-
tain, s. rideau de fenêtre, m. ‖ ~-dresser,
s. étalagiste, m.

windpipe, *wind'pīp,* s. trachée-artère, f.

windward, *wind'wĕrd,* ad. vers le vent,
contre le vent ‖ (mar.) au vent.

windy, *wind'ĭ,* a. venteux.

wine, *win,* s. vin, m. ‖ ~-bibber, s.
biberon, m. ‖ ~-cooper, s. tonnelier, m. ‖
~-glass, s. verre à vin, m. ‖ ~-grower,
s. vigneron, m. ‖ ~-producing, a. vinicole ‖ ~-shop, s. cabaret, m. ‖ ~-stone,
s. tartre, m. ‖ ~-strainer, s. passe-vin,
m. ‖ ~-taster, s. dégustateur, m. ‖ tâte-
vin, m. ‖ ~-vaults (~-shades), s. pl.
caveaux à vin, m. pl.

wing, *wing,* s. aile, f. ‖ coulisse, f.

wing, *wing,* v. a. & n. donner des ailes ‖
s'envoler.

winged, *wingd,* a. ailé ‖ rapide.

wink, *wingk,* s. clin d'œil, m.

wink, *wingk,* v. n. clignoter ‖ fermer les
yeux sur.

winking, *wingk'ĭng,* s. clignement, m.

winner, *win'nĕr,* s. gagnant, m.

winning, *win'nĭng,* s. racquit, gain, m. ‖
~-post, s. poteau d'arrivée, m.

winning, *win'nĭng,* a. gagnant ‖ attrayant.

winnow, *win'nō,* v. a. vanner ‖ éplucher.

winter, *win'tĕr,* s. hiver, m.

winter, *win'tĕr,* v. a. & n. hiverner ‖
passer l'hiver.

wintery, *win'tĕr ĭ,* winterly, *win'tĕr lĭ,*
wintry, *win'trĭ,* a. d'hiver.

wipe, *wip,* s. nettoiement, m. ‖ coup de
patte, m. ‖ taloche, f.

wipe, *wip,* v. a. essuyer.

wire, *wir,* s. fil de métal, m. ‖ ~-puller,
s. joueur de marionnettes, m. ‖ intrigant,
m. ‖ ~-pulling, s. détours, subterfuges,
m. pl. ‖ ~-rope, s. cordage en fil de fer, m.

wiredraw, *wir'drāw,* v. a. tréfiler.

wireless, *wir'lĕs,* a. sans fil.

wiry, *wī'rĭ,* a. de fil de métal ‖ nerveux.

wisdom, *wiz'dŏm,* s. sagesse, f.

wise, *wiz,* s. manière, façon, f. ‖ in no ~,
d'aucune façon.   [grave.

wise, *wiz,* a. (-ly, ad.) sage(ment) ‖ savant,

wiseacre, *wiz'ā kĕr,* s. sot, imbécile, m.

wish, *wish,* s. souhait, m. ‖ désir, m. ‖
vœu, m.

wish, *wish,* v. a. souhaiter, désirer, vouloir.

wishful, *wish'fŏŏl,* a. désireux.

wisp, *wisp,* s. bouchon, m. ‖ touffe, f.

wistful, *wist'fŏŏl,* a. attentif ‖ pensif ‖
-ly, ad. attentivement.

wit, *wit,* s. esprit, m. ‖ bel esprit, m. ‖ to
live by one's ~s, faire le parasite ‖ to
~, ad. savoir, c'est-à-dire.

witch, *wich,* s. sorcière, f.

witchcraft, *wich'krăft,* s. sorcellerie, f. ‖
sortilège, m.

witchery, *wich'ĕr ĭ,* s. sorcellerie, f.

with, *with,* pr. avec, de, par, parmi.

withal, *with ăwl',* ad. & pr. aussi, de même.

withdraw, *with drăw',* v. a. & n. ir. retirer ‖
rappeler ‖ se retirer, s'éloigner.

withe, *with,* s. brin d'osier, m.

wither, *with'ĕr,* v. a. (& n.) (se) flétrir ‖
dépérir ‖ se faner.

withers, *with'ĕrz,* s. pl. garrot, m.

withhold, *with hōld',* v. a. ir. retenir,
détenir ‖ empêcher.

withholder, *with hōld'ĕr,* s. détenteur, m.

within, *with in',* pr. & ad. dans, dedans.

without, *with ŏwt',* pr. & ad. hors de ‖ dehors ‖ au dehors, en dehors.

without, *with ŏwt',* c. à moins que, si ce
n'est que, sans que.   [s'opposer à.

withstand, *with stănd',* v. a. ir. résister,

withy, *with'ĭ,* s. (bot.) osier, franc osier, m.

witless, *wit'lĕs,* a. sans esprit, insipide.

witness, *wit'nĕs,* s. témoin, témoignage,
m. ‖ to bear ~ to, témoigner de ‖ ~-box,
s. (jur.) banc des témoins, m.

witness, *wit'nĕs,* v. a. rendre témoignage,
attester.

witted, *wit'tĕd,* a. raisonnable, prudent,
sensé ‖ quick-~, qui a de la vivacité
d'esprit.

wittily, *wit'ti lĭ,* ad. spirituellement.

wittiness, *wit'ti nĕs,* s. esprit, m.

wittingly, *wit'ting lĭ,* ad. à dessein.

witty, *wit'tĭ,* a. spirituel, ingénieux, sarcastique.   [prestidigitateur, m.

wizard, *wiz'ĕrd,* s. magicien, sorcier, m. ‖

woad, *wōd,* s. guède, f.

woe, *wō,* s. douleur, f. ‖ malheur, m.

woeful, *wō'fŏŏl,* a. (-ly, ad.) triste(ment).

wold, *wōld,* s. plaine, f. ‖ désert, m.

wolf, *wŏŏlf,* s. loup, m. ‖ she-~, louve, f.

wolfish, *wŏŏlf'ish,* a. de loup.

woman, *wŏŏm'ăn,* s. femme, f. ‖ ~ of the
town, fille de joie, f. ‖ ~-hater, s. misogyne, ennemi du sexe, m. ‖ ~-hunter,
s. coureur de femmes, m.   [femme, m.

womanhood, *wŏŏm'ăn hŏŏd,* s. état de

womanish, *wŏŏm'ăn ish,* a. de femme ‖
efféminé.   [m.

womankind, *wŏŏm'ăn kind,* s. beau sexe,

womanly, *wŏŏm'ăn lĭ,* a. en femme.

womb, *wŏŏm,* s. matrice, f., sein, ventre, m.

wonder, *wŭn'dĕr,* s. étonnement, m., admiration, f. ‖ miracle, m.

wonder, *wŭn'dĕr,* v. n. s'étonner, admirer.

wonderful, *wŭn'dĕr fŏŏl,* a. merveilleux,
étonnant ‖ -ly, ad. merveilleusement,
étonnamment.

wondrous, *wŭn' drŭs,* a. merveilleux.

wont, *wŏnt,* s. coutume, habitude, f.

wonted, *wŏnt'ĕd,* a. accoutumé, habituel.

woo, *wō,* v. a. faire l'amour, courtiser ‖ supplier.

wood, *wŏŏd,* s. bois, m. ‖ forêt, f. ‖ ~-cutter, s. bûcheron, m. ‖ xylographe, m. ‖ ~-house, s. bûcher, m. ‖ ~-land, s. pays boisé, m. ‖ ~-louse, s. cloporte, m. ‖ ~-man, s. garde forestier, m. ‖ bûcheron, m.   [feuille, m.

woodbine, *wŏŏd'bĭn,* s. (bot.) chèvre-

woodcock, *wŏŏd'kŏk,* s. bécasse, f.

woodcut, *wŏŏd'kŭt,* s. gravure sur bois, f.

wooded, *wŏŏd'ĕd,* a. boisé.

wooden, *wŏŏd'n,* a. de bois, en bois.

woodpecker, *wŏŏd'pĕk ẽr,* s. pivert, m.

woodruff, *wŏŏd'rŭf,* s. (bot.) aspérule, f.

woody, *wŏŏd'ĭ,* a. ligneux, boiseux.

wooer, *wō'ẽr,* s. amoureux, m.

woof, *wōf,* s. trame, f.

wool, *wŏŏl,* s. laine, f. ‖ ~-comber, s. cardeur, m. ‖ ~-gathering, s. (of one's wits) distraction, f. ‖ ~-growing, s. industrie lainière, f. ‖ ~-pack, s. ballot de laine, m.

woollen, *wŏŏl'ĭn,* a. de laine ‖ ~-s, s. pl. étoffes de laine, f. pl.

woolly, *wŏŏl'ĭ,* a. laineux ‖ frisé.

word, *wẽrd,* s. mot, m. ‖ parole, f. ‖ terme, m. ‖ ~ of honour, parole d'honneur ‖ upon my ~! sur ma parole, parole d'honneur! ‖ to be as good as one's ~, tenir parole ‖ to put in a good ~ for one, to give one a good ~, louer, recommander qn. (à un autre) ‖ to take one at his ~, prendre qn. au mot ‖ to send ~ to, faire dire à ‖ to take one's ~ for it, croire qn. sur mot ‖ ~-book, s. vocabulaire, m.

word, *wẽrd,* v. a. exprimer, énoncer.

wordiness, *wẽrd'ĭnĕs,* s. verbosité, f.

wording, *wẽrd'ĭng,* s. construction, f.

wordy, *wẽrd'ĭ,* a. verbeux, diffus.

work, *wẽrk,* s. travail, m., occupation, f., ouvrage, m., opération, œuvre, f. ‖ broderie, f. ‖ open-~, ouvrage à jour, m. ‖ to have one's ~ cut out for one, avoir du fil à retordre.

work, *wẽrk,* v. a. & n. travailler, opérer, fabriquer, produire ‖ gouverner ‖ exercer ‖ broder ‖ être en action, s'occuper, agir ‖ to ~ one's passage, (mar.) acquitter son prix de passage en travaillant à bord ‖ to go the right, wrong way to ~, s'y prendre bien, mal.

worker, *wẽrk'ẽr,* s. travailleur, auteur, m.

workhouse, *wẽrk'hŏŭs,* s. dépôt de mendicité, f.   [ouvrable, s.

working-day, *wẽrk'ĭng dā,* s. jour

workman, *wẽrk'măn,* s. ouvrier, m.

workmanship, *wẽrk'măn shĭp,* s. manufacture, f. ‖ ouvrage, m.

workshop, *wẽrk'shŏp,* s. atelier, m.   [f.

workwoman, *wẽrk'wŏŏm ăn,* s. ouvrière, m.

world, *wẽrld,* s. monde, univers, m., terre, f. ‖ les hommes ‖ grand nombre, m.,

quantité, f. ‖ for all the ~, pour tout au monde ‖ ~-wide, a. universel, immense.

worldliness, *wẽrld'lĭnĕs,* s. mondanité, f. ‖ convoitise, f.

worldling, *wẽrld'lĭng,* s. mondain, m.

worldly, *wẽrld'lĭ,* a. du monde ‖ mondain ‖ intéressé.

worm, *wẽrm,* s. ver, m. ‖ tire-bourre, serpentin, m. ‖ ~-eaten, a. vermoulu ‖ ~-hole, s. vermoulure, f. ‖ ~-screw, s. tire-bourre, m. ‖ ~-seed, s. poudre vermifuge, f.

worm, *wẽrm,* v. a. & n. miner ‖ tarauder ‖ to ~ oneself into one's good graces, s'insinuer dans les bonnes grâces de qn.

wormwood, *wẽrm'wŏŏd,* s. absinthe, f.

wormy, *wẽrm'ĭ,* a. plein de vers ‖ rampant.

worry, *wŭr'rĭ,* s. chagrin, dépit, m., contrariété, f.   [tracasser.

worry, *wŭr'rĭ,* v. a. harasser, tourmenter,

worse, *wẽrs,* a. & ad. pire, plus mauvais ‖ plus mal, pis.

worship, *wẽr'shĭp,* s. adoration, f., culte, m. ‖ (title) Excellence, f.

worship, *wẽr'shĭp,* v. a. adorer.

worshipful, *wẽr'shĭp fŏŏl,* a. vénérable.

worshipper, *wẽr'shĭp pẽr,* s. adorateur, m.

worst, *wẽrst,* s. pire, pis, pis aller, m. ‖ dernière extrémité, f. ‖ at the ~, au pis ‖ let the ~ come to the ~, coûte que coûte.   [porter sur.

worst, *wẽrst,* v. a. vaincre, défaire, ‖ l'emporter sur.

worst, *wẽrst,* a. & ad. le pire, le plus méchant, le plus mauvais.

worsted, *wŏŏr'stĕd* ou *wŏŏs'tĕd,* s. laine filée, estame, f.

wort, *wẽrt,* s. racine, herbe, f. ‖ moût, m.

worth, *wẽrth,* s. valeur, f., prix, m. ‖ mérite, m.

worth, *wẽrth,* a. qui vaut ‖ digne de.

worthily, *wẽr'thĭlĭ,* ad. dignement, justement.

worthiness, *wẽr'thĭnĕs,* s. mérite, m.

worthless, *wẽrth'lĕs,* a. sans valeur ‖ indigne, vil.

worthlessness, *wẽrth'lĕsnĕs,* s. manque de valeur, m. ‖ indignité, f.

worthy, *wẽr'thĭ,* s. personnage illustre, m.

worthy, *wẽr'thĭ,* a. digne, de mérite, honorable.

would, *wŏŏd;* ~-be, a. soi-disant ‖ ~ to Heaven! plût à Dieu!

wound, *wŏŏnd,* s. blessure, f. ‖ plaie, f.

wound, *wŏŏnd,* v. a. blesser.

wove, *wōv,* a. vélin.

wrangle, *răng'gl,* s. querelle, f.

wrangle, *răng'gl,* v. n. se quereller.

wrangler, *răng'glẽr,* s. querelleur, chicaneur, m. ‖ senior ~, le premier entre les étudiants.   [cane, f.

wrangling, *răng'glĭng,* s. dispute, chi-

wrap, *răp,* s. vide wrapper.

wrap, *răp,* v. a. envelopper, entortiller.

wrapper, *răp'pẽr,* s. enveloppe, couverture, f. ‖ cache-nez, m. ‖ déshabillé, m. ‖ peignoir, m.

wrath, *rāwth,* s. colère, f., courroux, m.

wrathful, *rāwth'fŏŏl,* a. en colère, courroucé, furieux.

wreak, *rēk,* v. a. exécuter || infliger.

wreath, *rēth,* s. guirlande, couronne de fleurs, f.

wreathe, *rēth,* v. a. entortiller, entrelacer, tresser || couronner, ceindre.

wreck, *rĕk,* s. naufrage, m. || navire naufragé, m. || ruine, f.

wreck, *rĕk,* v. a. & n. ruiner || faire naufrage.

wreckage, *rĕk'ĕj,* s. naufrage, m.

wrecked, *rĕkt,* a. naufragé.

wren, *rĕn,* s. roitelet, m.

wrench, *rĕnsh,* s. torsion, f. || dé anglais, [m.

wrench, *rĕnsh,* v. a. tirer de force, arracher en tordant || se fouler.

wrest, *rĕst,* v. a. arracher || torturer || forcer.

wrestle, *rĕs'l,* v. a. lutter, contester, combattre.

wrestler, *rĕs'lĕr,* s. athlète, m.

wrestling, *rĕs'lĭng,* s. lutte, f.

wretch, *rĕch,* s. misérable, m. || malheureux, m.

wretched, *rĕch'ĕd,* a. (-ly, ad.) misérable (ment) || malheureux, méprisable || pitoyablement.

wretchedness, *rĕch'ĕdnĕs,* s. misère, f. || nature méprisable, f.

wriggle, *rĭg'gl,* v. n. se tortiller || frétiller.

wright, *rĭt,* s. ouvrier, artisan, m.

wring, *rĭng,* v. a. ir. tordre, tortiller, presser, torturer || arracher.

wrinkle, *rĭng'kl,* s. ride, f. || faux pli, m. || (fig.) nouveau tour, m.

wrinkle, *rĭng'kl,* v. a. (& n.) (se) rider || froncer.

wrinkled, *rĭng'kld,* a. ridé, froncé.

wrist, *rĭst,* s. poignet, m. || ~-band, s. manchette, f. || poignet, m.

writ, *rĭt,* s. écriture, f. || (jur.) assignation.

write, *rĭt,* v. a. & n. ir. écrire. [f.

writer, *rĭt'ĕr,* s. écrivain, m. || auteur, m. || commis aux écritures, m.

writhe, *rĭth,* v. a. (& n.) ir. (se) tordre.

writing, *rĭt'ĭng,* s. écrit, ouvrage, m. || écriture, f. || in ~, par écrit || ~-book, s. cahier d'écriture, m. || ~-desk, s. pupitre, m. || ~-master, s. maître d'écriture, m. || ~-paper, s. papier à écrire, m. || ~-table, s. bureau, m., table à écrire, f.

wrong, *rŏng,* s. tort, dommage, détriment, m., injustice, f. || to do ~, faire mal.

wrong, *rŏng,* v. a. faire tort à, léser.

wrong, *rŏng,* a. & ad. faux || injuste, impropre, mauvais || mal, mal à propos || -ly, ad. à tort || to go ~, s'égarer.

wrongful, *rŏng'fŏŏl,* a. (-ly, ad.) injuste (ment) || to accuse -ly, accuser à tort.

wrought, *rāwt,* p. & a. travaillé, ouvragé.

wry, *rĭ,* a. tors, tordu, difforme || ~-face, s. grimace, f. || ~-neck, s. torticolis, m. || ~-necked, a. qui a le cou de travers.

wryness, *rī'nĕs,* s. torsion, f.

X.

xebec, *zē'bĕk,* s. chebec, m.

Xmas = Christmas.

xylography, *zī'lŏg'răfĭ,* s. xylographie, f.

Y.

yacht, *yŏt,* s. yacht, m.

yachting, *yŏt'ĭng,* s. promenade en yacht, f. || ~-jacket, s. saute-en-barque, m.

yak, *yăk,* s. yac, m., vache grognante de Tartarie, f.

yam, *yăm,* s. igname, f.

Yankee, *yăng'kĭ,* s. (fam.) citoyen des États-Unis, m.

yap, *yăp,* v. n. aboyer.

yard, *yărd,* s. cour, f. || aune anglaise, f. || (mar.) vergue, f. || ~-arm, s. (mar.) bout de vergue, m. [m.

yarn, *yărn,* s. laine filée, f. || fil de caret,

yarrow, *yăr'rō,* s. mille-feuilles, f.

yawl, *yăwl,* s. yole, f.

yawn, *yăwn,* v. n. bâiller.

ye, *yē,* pn. vous.

yea, *yā,* a. oui || vraiment.

yean, *yēn,* v. n. agneler, mettre bas.

year, *yēr,* s. an, m., année, f. || leap-~, année bissextile, f. || last ~, l'année passée || a happy new ~! compliment de bonne année! || ~-book, s. annuaire, m.

yearling, *yēr'lĭng,* s. animal d'un an, m.

yearly, *yēr'lĭ,* a. (& ad.) annuel(lement) || par an.

yearn, *yĕrn,* v. n. soupirer après.

yearning, *yĕrn'ĭng,* s. élan, m. || aspiration, f.

yeast, *yēst,* s. levure, f., levain, m.

yell, *yĕl,* s. hurlement, m.

yell, *yĕl,* v. n. hurler. [jaunisse, f.

yellow, *yĕl'lō,* s. jaune, m. || ~-s, s. pl.

yellow, *yĕl'lō,* a. jaune || ~-boy, s. jaunet, m. || ~-fever, s. (méd.) fièvre jaune, f.

yellowish, *yĕl'lōĭsh,* a. jaunâtre.

yellowness, *yĕl'lōnĕs,* s. couleur jaune, f. || jalousie, f.

yelp, *yĕlp,* v. n. glapir, japper.

yelping, *yĕlp'ĭng,* s. glapissement, m.

yeoman, *yō'măn,* s. franc-tenancier, m. || garde national à cheval, m.

yeomanry, *yō'mănrĭ,* s. corps des gardes nationaux à cheval, m.

yes, *yĕs,* ad. oui, oui-da.

yesterday, *yĕs'tĕrdā,* ad. hier.

yet, *yĕt,* ad. & c. encore, cependant, toutefois || déjà || as ~, jusqu'ici || not ~, non pas encore.

yew, *yō,* s. if, m.

yield, *yēld,* s. produit, rendement, m.

yield, *yēld,* v. a. & n. produire, rendre, donner, accorder, procurer || céder, abandonner || succomber || consentir.

yielding, *yēld'ĭng,* s. soumission, f.

yielding, *yēld'ing*, a. complaisant.
yoke, *yōk*, s. joug, attelage, m.|| couple, m. || ~-elm, s. charme, m.   [accoupler.
yoke, *yōk*, v.a. mettre au joug || subjuguer ||
yolk, *yōk*, s. jaune d'œuf, m.
yon, *yŏn*, yonder, *yŏn'dèr*, a. & ad. qui est là || là-bas.
yore, *yōr*, ad. jadis, autrefois.
you, *yō*, pn. vous.
young, *yŭng*, a. jeune || nouveau || tendre.
younger, *yŭng'gèr*, a. cadet.
youngish, *yŭng'ish*, a. un peu jeune.
youngster, *yŭng'stèr*, s. jeune homme, m. || blanc-bec, m.
your, *yōr*, pn. votre, vos.   [vôtres.
yours, *yōrz*, pn. le vôtre, la vôtre, les
yourself, *yōr'sĕlf*, pn. vous-même || yourselves, vous-mêmes.
youth, *yōth*, s. jeunesse, f.   [jeune homme.
youthful, *yōth'fōōl*, a. jeune || -ly, ad. en
yule-log, *yūl'lŏg*, s. bûche de Noël, f.

Z.

zany, *zā'nĭ*, s. bouffon, m.
zeal, *zēl*, s. zèle, m.

zealot, *zĕl'ŭt*, s. zélateur, m.
zealotry, *zĕl'ŭt rĭ*, s. fanatisme, m.
zealous, *zĕl'ŭs*, a. zélé || -ly, ad. avec zèle, ardemment.
zebec, *zē'bĕk*, s. *vide* xebec.
zebra, *zē'brā*, s. zèbre, m.
zenith, *zĕn'ĭth*, s. zénith, m. || comble, m.
zephyr, *zĕf'èr*, s. zéphyr, m.
zero, *zē'rō*, s. zéro, m. || 10 degrees below ~, dix degrés au-dessous de zéro.
zest, *zĕst*, s. zeste, m. || goût, m.
zigzag, *zig'zăg*, s. zigzag, m.
zigzag, *zig'zăg*, a. en zigzag.
zinc, *zingk*, s. zinc, m. || ~-plating, s. zingage, zincage, m.
zodiak, *zō'dĭ ăk*, s. zodiaque, m.
zone, *zōn*, s. zone, f. || ceinture, f. || circonférence, f.
zoological, *zō'ō lŏj'ĭ kăl*, a. zoologique || ~-gardens, s. pl. jardin zoologique, m.
zoologist, *zō ŏl'ō jĭst*, s. zoologue, m.
zoology, *zō ŏl'ō jĭ*, s. zoologie, f.
zoophyte, *zō'ō fῑt*, s. animal-plante, m.
Zouave, *zwäv* ou *zō'äv*, s. zouave, m.
zounds ! *zōwndz*, morbleu !
zymotic(al), *zi mŏt'ĭk (ăl)*, a. de pourriture || épidémique.

bŏy ; — *fōōt, tūbe, tŭb.* || *chair, joy* ; — *game, yes* ; — *soul, seal* ; — *thing, there.*

List of such more important modern geographical names, as differ in the two languages.

Abruzzi, *ä brŏt'sĭ,* les Abruzzes, f. pl.
Abyssinia, *ä bĭs sĭn'yä,* l'Abyssinie, f.
Adriatic Sea, *ä drĭ ăt'ĭk sē,* la mer Adriatique.
Ægean Sea, *ē jē'än sē,* la mer Égée.
Africa, *ăf'rĭ kä,* l'Afrique, f.
Albania, *ăl bā'nĭ ä,* l'Albanie, f.
Aleppo, *ä lĕp'pō,* Alep, m.
Aleutian Islands, *ä lō'shĭ än ī'lănds,* les Aléoutes, f. pl.
Alexandria, *ăl ĕks än'drĭ ä,* Alexandrie, f.
Algeria, *ăl jē'rĭ ä,* l'Algérie, f.
Algiers, *ăl jērz',* Alger, m.
Alps, *ălps,* les Alpes, f. pl.
Alsatia, *ăl sā'shĭ ä,* l'Alsace, f.
America, *ăm ĕr'ĭ kä,* l'Amérique, f.
American, *ăm ĕr'ĭ kăn,* s. Américain, m.
American, *ăm ĕr'ĭ kăn,* a. américain.
Ancona, *ăn kō'nä,* Ancône, f.
Andalusia, *ăn dä lō'zhä,* l'Andalousie, f.
Antilles, *ăn tĭlz',* les Antilles, f. pl.
Antwerp, *ănt'wĕrp,* Anvers, m.
Apennines, *äp'ĕn nĭnz,* les Apennins, m. pl.
Apulia, *ä pū'lĭ ä,* la Pouille.
Arab, *ăr'ăb,* s. Arabe, m.
Arab, *ăr'ăb,* a. arabe.
Arabia, *ä rā'bĭ ä,* l'Arabie, f.
Aragonese, *ăr ä gō nēz',* s. Aragonais, m.
Aragonese, *ăr ä gō nēz',* a. aragonais.
Arcadia, *ăr kā'dĭ ä,* l'Arcadie, f.
Archipelago, *ärk ĭ pĕl'ä gō,* l'Archipel, m.
Armenia, *ăr mē'nĭ ä,* l'Arménie, f.
Armenian, *ăr mē'nĭ ăn,* s. Arménien, m.
Armenian, *ăr mē'nĭ ăn,* a. arménien.
Asia, *ā'shä,* l'Asie, f.
Asiatic, *ā'shĭ ătĭk,* a. asiatique.
Assyria, *ăs sĭr'ĭ ä,* l'Assyrie, f.
Athenian, *ä thē'nĭ än,* s. Athénien, m.
Athenian, *ä thē'nĭ än,* a. athénien.
Athens, *ăth'ĕnz,* Athènes, f.
Atlantic, *ăt lăn'tĭk,* l'Atlantique, m.
Attica, *ăt'ĭ kä,* l'Attique, f.
Augsburg, *ăwgs'bŭrg,* Augsbourg, m.
Australasia, *ăws trăl ā'shĭ ä,* l'Australasie, f.
Australia, *ăw strā'lĭ ä,* l'Australie, f.
Austria, *ăw'strĭ ä,* l'Autriche, f.
Austrian, *ăw'strĭ än,* s. Autrichien, m.

Austrian, *ăw'strĭ än,* a. autrichien.
Azores, *ä zōrz',* les Açores, f. pl.

Baden, *bä'dn,* Bade, m.
Baffin's bay, *băf'fĭns bā',* baie de Baffin, f.
Baltic Sea, *băwl'tĭk sē,* la Baltique.
Barbadoes, *bär bā'dōz,* pl. la Barbade.
Barbary, *bär'bä rĭ,* la Barbarie.
Basle, *băl,* Bâle, f.
Batavia, *bä tā'vĭ ä,* la Batavie.
Bavaria, *bä vā'rĭ ä,* la Bavière.
Bavarian, *bä vā'rĭ än,* s. Bavarois, m.
Bavarian, *bä vā'rĭ än,* a. bavarois.
Beirout, *bī'rōōt,* Beirouth, f.
Belgian, *bĕl'jăn,* s. Belge, m.
Belgian, *bĕl'jăn,* a. belge.
Belgium, *bĕl'jŭm,* la Belgique.
Beloochistan, *bĕ lōō kĭs tăn',* le Béloutchistan.
Benares, *bĕ nä'rēz,* Bénarès, m.
Bengal, *bĕn găwl',* la Bengale.
Bengalese, *bĕn gäl ēz',* s. Bengalais, m.
Bengalese, *bĕn gäl ēz',* a. bengalais.
Bermudas, *bĕr mū'däz,* les Bermudes, f. pl.
Bessarabia, *bĕs sä rä'bĭ ä,* la Bessarabie.
Bethlehem, *bĕth'lĕ hĕm,* Bethléem, f.
Biscay, *bĭs'kā,* la Biscaie.
Bœotia, *bē ō'shĭ ä,* la Béotie.
Bohemia, *bō hē'mĭ ä,* la Bohême.
Bohemian, *bō hē'mĭ än,* s. Bohémien, m.
Bohemian, *bō hē'mĭ än,* a. bohémien.
Bolivia, *bō lĭv'ĭ ä,* la Bolivie.
Bologna, *bō lōg'nä,* Bologne, f.
Bosnia, *bŏs'nĭ ä,* la Bosnie.
Bosphorus, *bŏs'fō rŭs,* le Bosphore.
Bothnia, *bŏth'nĭ ä,* la Bothnie.
Braganza, *brä găn'zä,* Bragance, f.
Brandenburg, *brăn'dn bŭrg,* le Brandebourg.
Brandenburger, *brăn'dn bŭrg ĕr,* s. Brandebourgeois, m.
Brazil, *brä zĭl',* le Brésil.
Brasilian, *brä zĭl'ĭ än,* s. Brésilien, m.
Bremen, *brē'mĕn,* Brême, f.
Britain (Great), *brĭt'n,* la Grande-Bretagne.
Britany, *brĭt'ä nĭ,* la Bretagne.
British, *brĭt'ĭsh,* a. britannique.

lāte, hăt, fär, läw; — hēre, gĕt, hĕr; — mĭne, ĭnn; — nō, hŏt, prōve; — hŏw; —

British (English) Channel, *brit′ish (ing′lish) chăn′l,* la Manche.
British Isles, *brit′ish ilz′,* les îles britanniques, f. pl.
Briton, *brit′un,* s. Breton, m.
Brittany, *brit′ă ni,* la Bretagne.
Brussels, *brŭs′sĕlz,* Bruxelles, f. pl.
Bucharest, *bŭ′kăr ĕst,* Boucarest, m.
Buda, *bŭ′dă,* Bude, f.
Bulgaria, *bŭl gā′ri ă,* la Bulgarie.
Bulgarian, *bŭl gā′ri ăn,* s. Bulgare, m.
Bulgarian, *bŭl gā′ri ăn,* a. bulgare.
Burgundian, *bĕr gŭn′di ăn,* s. Bourguignon, m.
Burgundy, *bĕr′gŭn di,* la Bourgogne.
Burmah, *bĕr′mă,* la Birmanie.
Byzantium, *bi zăn′shi um,* Byzance, f.

Cadiz, *kā′diz* ou *kă diz′,* Cadix, m.
Caffraria, *kăf frā′ri ă,* la Cafrerie.
Cairo, *ki′rō,* le Caire.
Calabria, *kă lā′bri ă,* la Calabre.
California, *kăl i fōr′ni ă,* la Californie.
Calmuck, *kăl′mŭk,* Calmouck, m.
Calvary, *kăl′vă ri,* le Calvaire.
Campania, *kăm păn′i ă,* la Campanie.
Campeachy, *kăm pē′chi,* Campêche, m.
Canary Islands, *kā nā′ri i′lăndz,* les Canaries, f. pl.
Candia, *kăn′di ă,* la Candie.
Candian, *kăn′di ăn,* s. Candiote, m.
Capetown, *kăp′town,* ville du Cap, f.
Cape Verd, *kăp vĕrd′,* le Cap Vert.
Capernaum, *kă pĕr′nă um,* Capharnaüm, m.
Capadocia, *kăp pă dō′shi ă,* la Cappadoce.
Capri, *kăp′rē,* l'île de Capri.
Capua, *kă′pū ă,* Capoue, f.
Carinthia, *kăr in′thi ă,* la Carinthie.
Carniola, *kăr ni o′lă,* la Carniole.
Carpathians, *kăr pā′thi ănz,* les Carpathes, m. pl. [f. pl.
Carribees, *kăr′ri bēz,* les îles Carraïbes,
Carthagena, *kăr thā jē′nă,* Carthagène, f.
Cashmere, *kăsh′mēr,* le Cachemire.
Caspian Sea, *kăs′pi ăn sē,* s. la mer Caspienne.
Castile, *kăs tēl′,* la Castille.
Catalonia, *kăt ă lo′ni ă,* la Catalogne.
Caucasus, *kaw′kă sus,* le Caucase.
Cephalonia, *sĕf ă lo′ni ă,* Céphalonie, f.
Cesarea, *sēz ă rē′ă,* Césarée, f.
Ceylon, *sĕ lŏn′,* Ceylan, m.
Chaldea, *kăl dē′ă,* la Chaldée.
Channel Isles, *chăn′l ilz,* les îles de la Manche.
Chile, *chil′i,* le Chili. [Manche.
China, *chi′nă,* la Chine.
Chinese, *chi nēz′,* s. Chinois, m.
Chinese, *chi nēz′,* a. chinois.
Circassia, *sĕr kăs′shi ă,* la Circassie.
Circassian, *sĕr kăs′shi ăn,* s. Circassien, m.
Circassian, *sĕr kăs′shi ăn,* a. circassien.
Cochin China, *kŏch in chi′nă,* la Cochinchine.
Columbia, *kŏ lŭm′bi ă,* la Colombie.
Como, *kō′mō,* Come, m. [f. pl.
Cordilleras, *kŏr dil′lē răz,* les Cordillères,

Corland, *kŏr′lănd,* la Courlande.
Copenhagen, *kō pĕn hā′gĕn,* Copenhague [f.
Cordova, *kŏr dō′vă,* Cordoue, f.
Corea, *kō rē′ă,* la Corée.
Corfu, *kŏr fū′,* Corfou, m.
Corinth, *kŏr′inth,* Corinthe, f.
Cornwall, *kawrn′wŏl,* le Cornouailles.
Corsica, *kŏr′si kă,* la Corse.
Corsican, *kŏr′si kăn,* s. Corse, m.
Corsican, *kŏr′si kăn,* a. corse.
Corunna, *kō rŭn′nă,* la Corogne.
Cossack, *kŏs′săk,* Cosaque, m.
Cracow, *krā′kō,* Cracovie, f.
Cremona, *krē mō′nă,* Crémone, f.
Cretan, *krē′tăn,* s. Crétois, m.
Cretan, *krē′tăn,* a. crétois.
Crete, *krēt,* la Crète, la Candie.
Crimea, *kri mē′ă,* la Crimée.
Croatia, *krō ā′shi ă,* la Croatie.
Croatian, *krō ā′shin,* s. Croate, m.
Croatian, *krō ā′shin,* a. croate.
Cyprus, *si′prus,* Chypre, f.

Dalmatia, *dăl mā′shi ă,* la Dalmatie.
Dalmatian, *dăl mā′shi ăn,* s. Dalmate, m.]
Dalmatian, *dăl mā′shi ăn,* a. dalmate.
Damascus, *dă măs′kus,* Damas, m.
Dane, *dān,* s. Danois, m.
Danish, *dān′ish,* a. danois.
Dan(t)zig, *dăn(t)′zig,* Dantzig, Dantzick.
Dauphinate, *daw′fi năt,* **Dauphiny,** *daw′fi ni,* le Dauphiné.
Deccan, *dĕk′kăn,* le Dekkan.
Delos, *dē′lŏs,* Délos, m. [f.
Delphis, *dĕl′fis,* Delphos, *dĕl′fŏs,* Delphes,
Denmark, *dĕn′mărk,* le Danemark.
S. Domingo, *sănt dō ming′gō,* St.-Domingue, m.
Dominica, *dō min′i kă,* Dominique, f.
Dover, *dō′vĕr,* Douvres, m.
Straits of Dover, *străts ŏv dō′vĕr,* le détroit de Douvres.
Dresden, *drĕs′dn,* Dresde, f.
Dunkirk, *dŭn′kĕrk′,* Dunkerque, f.
Dutch, *dŭch,* a. hollandais.
Dutchman, *dŭch′măn,* s. Hollandais, m.

East-Indies, *ēst in′diz,* les Ind s Orientales, f. pl.
Ebro, *ē′brō,* Èbre, m. [tales, f. pl.
Edinburgh, *ĕd′in bŭr rō,* Édimbourg, m.
Egina, *ē ji′nă,* Égine, f.
Egypt, *ē′jipt,* l'Égypte, f.
Egyptian, *ē jip′shun,* s. Égyptien, m.
Egyptian, *ē jip′shun,* a. égyptien.
Elba, *ĕl′bă,* Elbe, f.
England, *ing′glănd,* l'Angleterre, f.
New England, *nū ing′glănd,* la Nouvelle-Angleterre.
English, *ing′glish,* a. anglais.
English Channel, *ing′glish chăn′nĕl,* la Manche.
Epiros, *i pi′rus,* l'Épire, m. [Manche.
Equador, *ĕk wă dōr′,* l'Équateur, m.
Eretria, *ē ri trē′ă,* l'Éréthrie, f.
Ethiopia, *ē thi ō′pi ă,* l'Éthiopie, f.
Etruria, *ē trō′ri ă,* l'Étrurie, f.
Euphrates, *ū frā′tēz,* l'Euphrate, m.
European, *ū rō pē′ăn,* s. Européen, m.

European, *ū rŏ pē' ăn,* a. européen.
Euxine, *ū' ksĭn,* le Pont-Euxin.

Faroe Iles, *fā' rō ūlz,* l'archipel de Féroé, m.
Ferrara, *fer rä' rä,* Ferrare, f.
Ferro, *fer' rō,* l'île de Fer, f.
Fiji, *fē' jē,* les îles de Fidji, f. pl.
Finland, *fin' lănd,* la Finlande.
Finland, *fin' lănd,* a. finlandais.
Finlander, *fin' lăn der,* s. Finlandais, m.
Flanders, *flän' derz,* la Flandre, les Flandres, f. pl.
Fleming, *flĕm' ing,* s. Flamand, m.
Flemish, *flĕm' ish,* a. flamand.
Florida, *flŏr' ĭ dä,* la Floride.
Flushing, *flŭsh' ing,* Flessingue, m.
Formosa, *fŏr mō' zä,* Formose, f.
France, *frăns,* la France.
Franconia, *frăn kō' nĭ ä,* la Franconie.
Frankfort, *frănk' fŏrt,* Francfort, m.
French, *frĕnsh,* a. français.
Frenchman, *frĕnsh' măn,* s. Français, m.
Friburg, *frē' bŭrg,* Fribourg, m.
Friendly Iles, *frĕnd' lĭ ūlz,* les îles des Amis, les îles Tonga, f. pl.
Friesland, *frēz' lănd,* la Frise.
Frieslander, *frēz' lăn der,* s. Frison, m.

Gaelic, *gā' (ĕ)lĭk,* a. gaélique.
Gaeta, *gā ē' tä,* Gaète, f.
Galatia, *gā lā' shĭ ä,* la Galatie.
Gallicia, *găl lish' ĭ ä,* la Galicie (d'Autriche).
Gallicia, *găl lish' ĭ ä,* la Galice (d'Espagne).
Gallilee, *găl' lĭ lē,* la Galilée.
Ganges, *găn' jēz,* le Gange.
Gascony, *găs' kŏ nĭ,* la Gascogne.
Gaul, *gawl,* les Gaules.
Geneva, *jĕ nē' vä,* Genève, f.   [Léman.
Lake of Geneva, *lāk ŏv jĕ nē' vä,* le lac
Genevese, *jĕ nē vēz',* s. Génevois, m.
Genevese, *jĕ nē vēz',* a. génevois.
Genoa, *jĕn' ō ä,* Gênes, f.
Georgia, *jawr' jĭ ä,* la Géorgie.
German, *jer' măn,* s. Germain, Allemand, m.
German, *jer' măn,* a. germanique, allemand.
German Ocean, *jer' măn ō' shăn,* la mer du Nord.
Germany, *jer' mă nĭ,* l'Allemagne.
Ghent, *gĕnt,* Gand, m.
Giant's Causeway, *jī' ănts kăwz' wā,* la Chaussée des Géants en Irlande.
Golconda, *gŏl kŏn' dä,* Golconde, f.
Gold Coast, *gōld' kōst,* la Côte d'Or, la Côte de Guinée.
Gomorrah, *gō mŏr' rä,* Gomorrhe, f.
Göttingen, *gĕt' ing ĕn,* Gœttingue, f.
Granada, *grä nä' dä,* Grenade, f.
Great Britain, *grāt brit' in,* la Grande-Grecian, *grē' shŭn,* s. Grec, m.   [Bretagne.
Grecian, *grē' shŭn,* a. grec.
Greece, *grēs,* la Grèce.
Greek, *grēk,* s. Grec, m.
Greek, *grēk,* a. grec.
Greenland, *grēn' lănd,* Groënland, m.
Greenland, *grēn' lănd,* a. groënlandais.
Greenlander, *grēn' lăn der,* s. Groënlandais, m.

Grenada, *grĕn' ä dä* ou *grĕn' ädä,* Grenade, f. m. pl.
The Grisons, *thē grē' sŏnz,* les Grisons, m. pl.
Groningen, *grōn' ing ĕn,* Groningue, m.
Guelderland, *gĕl' der lănd,* la Gueldre.
Guiana, *gĭ än' ä,* la Guyane.
Guinea, *gin' nĭ,* la Guinée.

The Hague, *thē hāg,* la Haye.
Hamburg, *hăm' bŭrg,* Hambourg, m.
Hanover, *hăn' ō ver,* le Hanovre.
Havannah, *hä văn' nä,* la Havane.
Hebrides, *hĕb' rĭ dēz,* les Hébrides, f. pl.
Heligoland, *hĕl' ĭ gō lănd,* Héligoland, m.
Helvetia, *hĕl vē' shĭ ä,* l'Helvétie, f.
Herculaneum, *her kū lä' nē ŭm,* Herculanum, m.   [vine, f.
Herzegovina, *her zē gō vē' nä,* l'Herzégo-
Hesse, *hĕs' sĭ,* la Hesse.
Hessian, *hĕsh' ĭ ăn,* s. Hessois, m.
Hessian, *hĕsh' ĭ ăn,* a. hessois.
Holland, *hŏl' lănd,* la Hollande.
Hollander, *hŏl' lăn der,* s. Hollandais, m.
Holy Land, *hō lĭ lănd',* la Terre Sainte.
Homburg, *hŏm' bŭrg,* Hombourg, m.
The Horn, *thē hŏrn,* le Cap Horn.
Hudson's Bay, *hŭd sŭnz bā',* la baie de Hudson.
Hungarian, *hŭng gā' rĭ ăn,* s. Hongrois, m.
Hungarian, *hŭng gā' rĭ ăn,* a. hongrois.
Hungary, *hŭng' gā rĭ,* la Hongrie.

Iceland, *īs' lănd,* l'Islande.
Icelander, *īs' lăn der,* s. Islandais, m.
Illyricum, *ŭ lĭr' ĭ kŭm,* Illyrie, Illyrie, f.
India, *in' dĭ ä,* l'Inde, m.
Indian, *in' dĭ ăn,* s. Indien, m.
Indian, *in' dĭ ăn,* a. indien.
Indies, *in' dĭz,* pl. les Indes, f. pl.
Indus, *in' dŭs,* l'Inde, m.
Ionian Isles, *ī ō' nĭ ăn ūlz,* pl. les îles Ioniennes, f. pl.
Ireland, *īr' lănd,* l'Irlande, f.
Irish, *ī' rish,* a. irlandais.
Irishman, *ī' rish măn,* s. Irlandais, m.
Irish Sea, *ī' rish sē',* la mer d'Irlande.
Istria, *is' trĭ ä,* l'Istrie, f.
Italian, *ĭ tăl' ĭ ăn,* s. Italien, m.
Italian, *ĭ tăl' ĭ ăn,* a. italien.
Italy, *it' ä lĭ,* l'Italie, f.
Ithaca, *ith' ăk ä,* Ithaque, f.
Ivory Coast, *ī' ver ĭ kōst,* la Côte d'Ivoire, la Côte des Dents.

Jamaica, *jă mā' kä,* la Jamaïque, f.
Japan, *jă păn',* le Japon.
Japanese, *jă pă nēz',* s. Japonais, m.
Japanese, *jă pă nēz',* a. japonais.
Jena, *yā' nä,* Jéna, m.
Jerico, *jēr' ĭ kō,* Jéricho, f.
Jerusalem, *jēr ō' să lĕm,* Jérusalem, f.
Jordan, *jŏr' dăn,* le Jourdain.
Judea, *jō dē' ä,* la Judée.

Kalmuck, *kăl' mŭk,* s. Calmouk, m.
Kief, *kēf,* Kiev, f.
Kuriles, *kū' rŭz,* les Kouriles, f. pl.

Laccadive Islands, *lăk' kă dīv ī'lăndz*, pl. les îles Laquedives, f. pl.

Lacedæmonian, *lă sē dē mō' nĭ ăn*, s. Lacédémonien, m. [démonien.

Lacedæmonian, *lă sē dē mō' nĭ ăn*, a. Lacé-

Ladrone Isles, *lă drōn' ŭlz*, les îles des Larrons, f. pl.

Lancaster, *lăng' kă ster*, Lancastre, m.

Lapland, *lăp' lănd*, la Laponie.

Laplander, *lăp' lăn dẽr*, Lapon, m.

Lebanon, *lĕb' ă nŏn*, le Libanon.

Leeward Isles, *lē' wẽrd* ou *lō' ẽrd ŭlz*, les îles sous le vent, f. pl.

Leghorn, *lĕg' hŏrn*, Livourne, f.

Libia, *lĭb' ĭ ă*, la Lybie.

Lisbon, *lĭz' bŏn*, Lisbonne, f.

Lisle, *lēl*, Lille, m.

Lithuania, *lĭ thū ā' nĭ ă*, la Lithuanie.

Livonia, *lĭ vō' nĭ ă*, la Livonie.

The Lizard, *thē lĭz' ẽrd*, le Cap Lésard.

Lombardy, *lŏm' bẽr dĭ*, la Lombardie.

London, *lŭn' dn*, Londres, m.

Louisiana, *lō ĭz ĭ ăn' ă*, la Louisiane.

Low-Countries, *lō kŭn' trĭz*, les Pays-Bas, m. pl.

Lowlands, *lō' lăndz*, la Basse-Écosse.

Lucca, *lŭk' kă*, Lucques, f.

Lusatia, *lō sā' shĭ ă*, Lusace, f. [m.

Luxemburg, *lŭks' ẽm bũrg*, Luxembourg,

Macedonia, *măs sē dō' nĭ ă*, la Macédoine.

Madeira, *mă dē' ră*, Madère, f.

Majorca, *mă jawr' kă*, l'île de Majorque, f.

Malay Peninsula, *mă lā' pĕn ĭn' sū lă*, la Malaisie.

Malta, *mawl' tă*, Malte, f.

Maltese, *mawl tēz'*, a. maltais.

Manilla, *mă ĭl' lă*, la Manille.

Mantua, *măn' tū ă*, Mantoue, f. [f. pl.

Marquesas, *măr kē' zăs*, les îles Marquises,

Marseilles, *măr sālz'*, Marseille, f.

Mauritius, *mawr ĭsh' ŭs*, l'Île Maurice, f.

Mecca, *mĕk' kă*, la Mecque.

Medina, *mē dē' nă*, Médine, f.

Mediterranean, *mĕd ĭ tẽr rā' nĭ ăn*, la Méditerranée.

Mentz, *mĕnts*, Mayence, f.

Mesopotamia, *mĕ sō pō tā' mĭ ă*, la Mésopotamie.

Messina, *mĕs sē' nă*, Messine, f.

Mexico, *mĕk' sĭ kō*, le Mexique.

Minorca, *mĭn awr' kă*, l'île de Minorque, f.

Modena, *mō dē' nă*, Modène, f.

Moldavia, *mōl dā' vĭ ă*, la Moldavie.

Molucca, *mō lŭk' kă*, les Moluques, f. pl.

Mongol, *mŏn' gŏl*, s. Mongole, m.

Mongol, *mŏn' gŏl*, a. mongole.

Mongolia, *mŏn gō' lĭ ă*, la Mongolie.

Montreal, *mŏnt rē awl'*, Montréal, m.

Moor, *mŏr*, s. Maure, m.

Moorish, *mŏr' ĭsh*, a. maure.

Moravia, *mō rā' vĭ ă*, la Moravie.

Moravian, *mō rā' vĭ ăn*, s. Morave, m.

Moravian, *mō rā' vĭ ăn*, a. morave.

Morea, *mō rē' ă*, la Morée.

Morocco, *mō rŏk' kō*, le Maroc.

Moscovy, *mŏs' cō vĭ*, la Moscovie.

Moscow, *mŏs' kō*, Moscou, m.

Mount Salvage, *mŏwnt săl' văj*, Mont-salvage, m.

Mulatto, *mū lăt' tō*, Mulattress, *mū lăt' trĕs*, s. Mulâtre, m., Mulâtresse, f.

Neapolitan, *nēă pŏl' ĭ tăn*, a. napolitain.

Nemea, *nē mē' ă*, Némée, f.

Netherlands, *nĕ' thẽr lăndz*, pl. les Pays-Bas, m. pl.

Neuchatel, *nŭ shā tĕl'*, Neufchâtel, m.

Newfoundland, *nū fŭnd' lănd*, Terre-Neuve, f.

New Orleans, *nū awr' lē ănz*, la Nouvelle-Orléans.

New Zealand, *nū zē' lănd*, la Nouvelle-Zélande.

Nile, *nīl*, le Nil.

Nimeguen, *nĭ' mă gĕn*, Nimègue, f.

Nineveh, *nĭn' ĕ vē*, Ninive, f.

Norman, *nawr' măn*, s. Normand, m.

Norman, *nawr' măn*, a. normand.

Normandy, *nawr' măn dĭ*, la Normandie.

North Sea, *nŏrth' sē*, la mer du Nord.

Norway, *nawr' wā*, la Norwège.

Norwegian, *nawr wē' jăn*, s. Norwégien, m.

Norwegian, *nawr wē' jăn*, a. norwégien.

Nova Scotia, *nō vă skō' shĭ ă*, la Nouvelle-Écosse.

Nova Zembla, *nō vă zĕm' blă*, la Nouvelle-Zemble.

Nubia, *nū' bĭ ă*, la Nubie.

Numidia, *nū mĭd' ĭ ă*, la Numidie.

Oceania, *ō shĭ ăn' ĭ ă*, l'Océanie, f.

Olympus, *ō lĭm' pŭs*, Olympe, m.

Oregon, *ŏr' ĕ gŏn*, l'Orégon, m.

Orkney Islands, *awrk' nē ī' lăndz*, pl. les îles Orcades, f. pl.

Orleans, *awr' lē ănz*, Orléans, m.

Ostend, *ŏs tĕnd'*, Ostende, m.

Ostia, *ŏst' chĭ ă*, Ostie, f.

Otranto, *ō trăn' tō*, Otrante, m.

Oude, *ŏwd*, l'Aoude, l'Oude, m.

Pacific, *pă sĭf' ĭk*, le Pacifique, l'Océan Pacifique, m.

Padua, *pă' dū ă*, Padoue, f.

Palatinate, *păl ăt' ĭ năt*, le Palatinat.

Palermo, *pă lẽr' mō*, Palerme, m.

Parma, *păr' mă*, Parme, f.

Parnassus, *păr năs' sŭs*, le Parnasse.

Patagonia, *păt ă gō' nĭ ă*, la Patagonie.

Pavia, *pă' vĭ ă*, Pavie, f.

Pekin, *pē kĭn'*, Pékin, m.

Peloponnesus, *pĕ lō pŏn nē' sŭs*, le Péloponnèse.

Pennsylvania, *pĕn sĭl vā' nĭ ă*, la Pensylvanie.

Pernambuco, *pẽr năm bū' kō*, Fernambouc, m.

Persia, *pẽr' shă*, la Perse.

Persian, *pẽr' shŭn*, s. Persan, m., Perse, f.

Persian, *pẽr' shŭn*, a. perse, persan.

Persian Gulf, *pẽr' shŭn gŭlf'*, le golfe Persique.

---

bŏy ; — fŏŏt, tūbe, tŭb. || *chair, joy ; — game, yes ; — soul, zeal ; — thing, there.*

Peru, *pĕrŏ′*, le Pérou.
Perugia, *pĕrŏ′ji ā*, Pérouse, f.
Petersburg, *pē′ tèrz bŭrg*, Pétersbourg, m.
Philadelphia, *fĭl ă dĕl′ fĭ ă*, Philadelphie, f.
Phoenicia, *fēnĭsh′ĭ ā*, la Phénicie.
Phrygia, *frĭj′ĭ ă*, la Phrygie.
Piacenza, *pĭ ă chĕn′ să*, Plaisance, f.
Picardy, *pĭk′ ărd ĭ*, la Picardie.
Piedmont, *pēd′ mŏnt*, le Piémont.   [m.
Piedmontese, *pēd mŏn tēz′*, s. Piémontais,
Piedmontese, *pēd mŏn tēz′*, a. piémontais.
Piraeus, *pī rē′ ŭs*, le Pirée.
Pisa, *pē′ să*, Pise, f.
Poland, *pō′ lănd*, la Pologne.
Pole, *pōl*, s. Polonais, m.
Polish, *pō′lish*, a. polonais.
Polynesia, *pŏl ĭ nē′ zĭ ă*, la Polynésie.
Pomerania, *pŏm ĕ rā′ nĭ ă*, la Poméranie.
Pontus, *pŏn′ tŭs*, Pont, m.
Portugal, *pōr′ tŭ găl*, le Portugal.
Portuguese, *pōrt ū gēz′*, s. Portugais, m.
Portuguese, *pōrt ū gēz′*, a. portugais.
Prince Edward's Isle, *prĭns ĕd′ wărdz īl*, Ile du Prince Edouard, f.
Prussia, *prŭs′ shă*, la Prusse.
Prussian, *prŭs′ shŭn*, s. Prussien, m.
Prussian, *prŭs′ shŭn*, a. prussien.
Pyrenean Mountains, *pĭr ĕ nē′ ăn mŏwn′ tăns*, les Pyrénées, f. pl.

Quebec, *kwĕ bĕk′*, Québec, m.

Ravenna, *ră vĕn′ nă*, Ravenne, f.
Red Sea, *rĕd sē′*, la mer Rouge.
Rhine, *rīn*, le Rhin.
Rocky Mountains, *rŏk′ ĭ mŏwn′ tăns*, les Monts Rocheux, m. pl.
Roman, *rō′ măn*, s. Romain, m.
Roman, *rō′ măn*, a. romain.
Roumania, *rō mā′ nĭ ă*, la Roumanie.
Roumanian, *rō mā′ nĭ ăn*, s. Roumain, m., Roumaine, f.
Roumanian, *rō mā′ nĭ ăn*, a. roumain.
Russia, *rŭs′ shă*, la Russie.
Russian, *rŭs′ shŭn*, s. Russe, m. & f.
Russian, *rŭs′ shŭn*, a. russe.

Salonica, *să lŏn′ ĭ kă*, Salonique, f.
Samoid, *să mŏ′ ĭd*, a. Samoïède.
Saracen, *săr′ ă sĕn*, a. Sarrasin.
Sardinia, *săr dĭn′ ĭ ă*, la Sardaigne.
Sardinian, *săr dĭn′ ĭ ăn*, s. Sarde, m.
Sardinian, *săr dĭn′ ĭ ăn*, a. sarde.
Savoy, *sd vŏy′*, la Savoie.
Saxony, *săks′ ŏ nĭ*, la Saxe.   [navie.
Scandinavia, *skăn dĭ nā′ vĭ ă*, la Scandi-
Scheld, *skĕlt*, l'Escaut.   [îles Scilly, f. pl.
Scilly Isles, *sĭl′ lĭ īlz*, les Sorlingues,
Sclavonia, *sklă vō′ nĭ ă*, l'Esclavonie.
Sclavonian, *sklă vō′ nĭ ăn*, s. Esclavonien, m.
Sclavonian, *sklă vō′ nĭ ăn*, a. esclavonien.
Sootch, *skŏch*, a. écossais.
Scotchman, *skŏch′ mn*, s. Écossais, m.
Scotland, *skŏt′ lănd*, l'Écosse.
Scottish, *skŏt′ tĭsh*, a. écossais.   [gambie.
Senegambia, *sĕ nĕ găm′ bĭ ă*, la Séné-

Servia, *sér′ vĭ ă*, la Servie.
Siberia, *sī bē′ rĭ ă*, la Sibérie.
Sicily, *sĭs′ ĭ lĭ*, la Sicile.
Sicilian, *sĭ sĭl′ ĭ ăn*, s. Sicilien, m.
Sicilian, *sĭ sĭl′ ĭ ăn*, a. sicilien.
Silesia, *sĭ lē′ zhĭ ă*, la Silésie.
Silesian, *sĭ lē′ zhĭ ăn*, a. silésien.
Sinde, *sĭnd*, le Scinde.
Slave Coast, *slāv′ kŏst*, la Côte des Esclaves.
Slavonia, *slă vō′ nĭ ă*, la Slavonie.
Smyrna, *smèr′ nă*, Smyrne, f.
Society Islands, *sō sī′ ĕ tĭ ī′ lăndz*, les îles de la Société, f. pl.
Sodom, *sŏd′ ŭm*, Sodome, f.
Sorrento, *sŏr rĕn′ tō*, Sorrente, f.
The Sound, *thĕ sŏwnd*, le Sund.
Spain, *spăn*, l'Espagne.
Spaniard, *spăn′ yĕrd*, s. Espagnol, m.
Spanish, *spăn′ ĭsh*, a. espagnol.
Sparta, *spăr′ tă*, Sparte, f.
Spartan, *spăr′ tăn*, s. Spartiate, m. & f.
Spartan, *spăr′ tăn*, a. spartiate.
Staten Island, *stāt′ n ī lănd*, Ile de la Terre de Feu, f.
St. Helena, *sănt hĕ lā′ nă*, Ste-.Hélène, f.
St. Lucia, *sănt lŏŏ sĭ′ ă*, Ste.-Lucie, f.
St. Petersburg, *sănt pē′ tèrz bŭrg*, St.-Pé-tersbourg, m.
Stiria, *stĭr′ ĭ ă*, la Stirie.
Suabia, *swă′ bĭ ă*, la Souabe.
Swede, *swēd*, s. Suédois, m.
Sweden, *swē′ dn*, la Suède.
Swedish, *swē′ dĭsh*, a. suédois.
Swiss, *swĭs*, s. Suisse, m.
Swiss, *swĭs*, a. suisse.
Switzerland, *swĭt′ zér lănd*, la Suisse.
Syria, *sĭ′ rĭ ă*, la Syrie.

Table Bay, *tă bl bă′*, la baie de la Table.
Table Mountain, *tă bl mŏwn′ tăn*, la mon-tagne de la Table.
Tagus, *tă′ gŭs*, le Tage.
Tangiers, *tăn jērz′*, Tanger, m.
Tarentum, *tă rĕn′ tŭm*, Tarente, f.
Tarpeian rock, *tăr pē′ i ăn rŏk*, la roche Tarpéienne.
Tarragona, *tăr ră gō′ nă*, Tarragone, f.
Tartar, *tăr′ tĕr*, s. Tartare, m.
Tartar, *tăr′ tĕr*, a. tartare.
Tartary, *tăr′ tĕrĭ*, la Tartarie.
Tasmania, *tăz mă′ nĭ ă*, la Tasmanie.
Terra del Fuego, *tĕr′ ră dĕl fū ā′ gō*, la Terre de Feu.
Thames, *tĕmz*, la Tamise.
Thermopylæ, *thĕr mŏp′ ĭ lē*, pl. les Ther-mopyles, f. pl.
Thessalonica, *thĕs să lŏn′ ĭ kă*, Thessa-lonique, f.
Thessalonian, *thĕs să lōn′ ĭ ăn*, s. Thessa-lonicien, m.   [lonicien.
Thessalonian, *thĕs să lō′ nĭ ăn*, a. thessa-
Thessaly, *thĕs′ să lĭ*, la Thessalie.
Thracia, *thrā′ shĭ ă*, la Thrace.
Thuringia, *thŭrĭn′ jĭ ă*, la Thuringe.
Tiber, *tī′ bĕr*, le Tibre.
Tigris, *tī′ grĭs*, le Tigre.
Timbuctoo, *tĭm bŭk tŏŏ′*, Timbouctu, m.

Tirol, *tĭ rŏl'*, le Tirol.
Tirolese, *tĭr ō léz'*, s. Tirolien, m.
Tirolese, *tĭr ō léz'*, a. tirolien.
Toledo, *tō lē' dō*, Tolède, f.
Transylvania, *trăn sĭl vă' nĭ ă*, la Transilvanie.
Trinidad, *trĭn ĭ dăd'*, île de la Trinité, f.
Trent, *trént*, Trente, f.
Triers, *trērz*, Trèves, f.
Troy, *trŏy*, la Troie.
Turk, *tĕrk*, s. Turc, m.
Turkish, *tĕrk' ĭsh*, a. turc.
Turkey, *tĕr' kĭ*, la Turquie.
Tuscany, *tŭs' kă nĭ*, la Toscane.
Tyrol,Tyrolese,s.&a. *vide* Tirol, Tirolese.

Umbria, *ŭm' brĭ ă*, l'Ombrie, f.
United Kingdom, *ū nī' tĕd kĭng' dŭm*, le Royaume Uni.
United States, *ū nī' tĕd stăts*, pl. les États-Unis, m. pl.
Ural, *ū' răl*, l'Oural, m.
Ushant, *ŭsh' ănt*, Ouessant, m.

Valachia, *vă lā' kĭ ă*, la Valachie.
Valencia, *vă lén' shĭ ă*, Valence, f.
Venetian, *vé nē' shăn*, Vénétien, m.
Venezuela, *vé néz wē' lă*, le Vénézuéla.
Venice, *vén' ĭs*, Venise, f.
Verona, *vé rō' nă*, Vérone, f.
Vesuvius, *vé sū' vĭ ŭs*, le Vésuve.
Vienna, *vĭ én' nă*, Vienne, f.
Virginia, *vér jĭn' ĭ ă*, la Virginie.
Virgin Isles, *vér' jĭn ĭlz*, les îles Vierges, f. pl.
Vistula, *vĭs' tū lă*, la Vistule.

Wales, *wālz*, le pays des Galles.
Wallachia, *wŏl lă' kĭ ă*, la Valachie, f.
Warsaw, *wawr' saw'*, la Varsovie.
Welsh, *wélsh*, a. gallois.
West-Indies, *wést in' dĭz*, pl. les Indes Occidentales, f. pl.
Westphalia, *wést fā' lĭ ă*, la Westphalie.
Windward Isles, *wind' wérd ĭlz*, les îles au Vent, f. pl.

Zealand, *zē' lănd*, la Zélande.

bōy; — fōōt, tūbe, sŭb. || chair, joy; — game, yes; — soul, zeal; — thing, there.

List of the more usual christian names, not alike in both languages.

Adela, *ăd'ĕ lă*, Adèle, f.
Adolphus, *ă dŏl'fŭs*, Adolphe, m.
Adrian, *a'drĭ ăn*, Adrien, m.
Alexander, *ăl ĕkz ăn'dĕr*, Alexandre.
Ambrose, *ăm'brōz*, Ambroise, m.
Amelia, *ă mē'lĭ ă*, Amélie, f.
Anastasius, *ă năstā'zĭ ŭs*, Anastase, m.
Andrew, *ăn'drō*, André, m.
Angelica, *ăn jĕl'ĭ kă*, Angélique, f.
Ann, *ăn*, Anna, *ăn'nă*, Anne, f.
Anthony, *ăn'thŏ nĭ*, Antoine, m.
Arnold, *ar'nŏld*, Arnaud, m.
Arthur, *ar'thĕr*, Arthur, Artus, m.
Augusta, *aw gŭs'tă*, Auguste, f.
Augustus, *aw gŭs'tŭs*, Auguste, m.
Austin, *aw'stin*, Augustin, m.

Barbara, *bar'bă ră*, Barbe, f.
Bartholomew, *bar thŏl'ŏ mū*, Barthélemi, m.
Basil, *băz'il*, Basile, m.
Beatrice, *bē'ă trēs*, Béatrix, f.
Ben, *bĕn*, pour : Benjamin.
Benedict, *bĕn'ĕ dikt*, Benoît, m.
Bertha, *bĕr'thă*, Berthe, f.
Bertram, *bĕr'trŭm*, Bertrand, m.
Bess, *bĕs*, Bessy, *bĕs'sĭ*, Bet, *bĕt*, Betsey, *bĕt'sĭ*, pour : Elizabeth.
Biddy, *bĭd'dĭ*, pour : Bridget.
Bill, *bĭl*, Billy, *bĭl'lĭ*, pour : William.
Bob, *bŏb*, Bobby, *bŏb'bĭ*, pour : Robert.
Bridget, *brĭ'jĕt*, Brigitte, f.

Cary, *kă'rĭ*, pour : Caroline.
Catharine, *kă'thă rĭn*, Catherine, f.
Cecilia, *sēs ĭl'lĭ ă*, Cecily, *sēs'sĭ lĭ*, Cécile, f.
Christopher, *kris'tŏ fĕr*, Christophe, m.
Clara, *klă'ră*, Claire, f.
Claudius, *klaw'di ŭs*, Claude, m.
Clementina, *klĕm ĕn tē'nă*, Clémentine, f.
Constance, *kŏn'stăns*, Constantia, *kŏn stăn'shĭ ă*, Constance, f.
Constantine, *kŏn'stăn tĭn*, Constantin, m.
Cornelia, *kŏr nē'lĭ ă*, Cornélie, f.
Crispin, *kris'pĭn*, Crépin, m.

Dan, *dăn*, pour : Daniel.
Dick, *dĭk*, pour : Richard.
Doll, *dŏl*, pour : Dorothy.

Dominic, *dŏm'min ĭk*, Dominique, m.
Dorothy, *dŏr'ŏ thĭ*, Dorothée, f.

Edmund, *ĕd'mŭnd*, Edmond, m.
Edward, *ĕd'wĕrd*, Édouard, m.
Eleanor, *ĕl'lĭ nŏr*, Éléonore, f.
Elias, *ē lī'ăs*, Elie, m.
Elisa, *ē lī'ză*, Élise, f.
Emily, *ĕm'ĭ lĭ*, Emilie, f.
Eva, *ē'vă*, Eve, f.

Fabian, *fā'bĭ ăn*, Fabien, m.
Fanny, *făn'nĭ*, Fanny, f.
Felix, *fē'liks*, Félix, m.
Flora, *flō'ră*, Flore, f.
Frances, *frăn'sĕs*, Françoise, f.
Francis, *frăn'sĭs*, François, m.
Geoffry, *jĕf'frĭ*, Geoffroi, m.
George, *jawrj*, Georges, m.
Giles, *jīlz*, Gilles, m.
Godfrey, *gŏd'frĭ*, Godefroi, m.
Gregory, *grĕg'ŏ rĭ*, Grégoire, m.
Gustavus, *gŭs tā'vŭs*, Gustave, m.

Hal, *hăl*, pour : Henry.
Hannah, *hăn'nă*, Jeanne, Jeanneton, f.
Harriet, *hăr'ĭ ĕt*, Henriette, f.
Harry, *hăr'rĭ*, pour : Henry.
Helen, *hĕl'ĕn*, Helena, *hĕl'ĕn ă*, Hélène, f.
Henrietta, *hĕn rĭ ĕt'tă*, Henriette, f.
Henry, *hĕn'rĭ*, Henri, m.
Hilary, *hĭl'ă rĭ*, Hilaire, m.
Hodge, *hŏj*, pour : Roger.
Hugh, *hū*, Hugues, m.
Humfrey. Humphrey, *hŭm'frĭ*, Homfroi, m.

Ignatius, *ig nā'shĭ ŭs*, Ignace, m.

Jack, *jăk*, pour : John.
Jacob, *jā'kŏb*, Jacob, m.
James, *jāmz*, Jacques, m.
Jane, *jăn*, Jeanne, f.
Jasper, *jăs'pĕr*, Gaspard, m.
Jefferey, *jĕf'fĕr ĭ*, Jeffry, *jĕf'frĭ*, Geoffroi, m.
Jemmy, *jĕm'mĭ*, Jim, *jĭm*, pour : James.
Jenny, *jĕn'nĭ*, Jeannette, f.
Jeremy, *jĕr'ĕ mĭ*, Jérémie, m.

läte, hăt, far, law ; — hēre, gĕt, hĕr ; — mīne, ĭnn ; — nō, hŏt, prŏve ; — hŏw ; —

Jerry, *jĕr'rĭ*, pour: Jeremy.
Joan, *jōn*, Joanna, *jō ăn'nă*, Jeanne, f.
Joe, *jō*, pour: Joseph.
John, *jŏn*, Jean, m.
Johnny, *jŏn'nĭ*, pour: John.
Julia, *jū'lĭ ă*, Julie, f.
Julian, *jū'lĭ ăn*, Julien, m.
Julius, *jū'lĭ ŭs*, Jules, m.

Kate, *kāt*, Kit, *kĭt*, Kitty, *kĭt'tĭ*, pour: Catherine.

Laura, *law'ră*, Laure, f.
Laurence, *law'rĕns*, Laurent, m.
Lewis, *lō'ĭs*, Louis, m.
Lizzey, *lĭz'zĭ*, pour: Elisa.
Loo, *lō*, pour: Louisa.
Louisa, *lō ē'ză*, Louise, f.
Lucian, *lō'sĭ ăn*, Lucien, m.
Lucretia, *lō krē'shĭ ă*, Lucrèce, f.
Lucy, *lō'sĭ*, Lucie, f.

Magdalen, *măg'dă lĕn*, Madeleine, f.
Madge, *măj*, Margery, *măr'jĕr ĭ*, Meg, *mĕg*, pour: Margaret.
Margaret, *măr'gă rĕt*, Marguerite, f.
Mark, *mărk*, Marc, m.
Martha, *măr'thă*, Marthe, f.
Mary, *mā'rĭ*, Marie, f.
Mat, *măt*, pour: Matthew.
Matilda, *mă tĭl'dă*, Mathilde, f.
Matthew, *mă'thū*, Matthieu, m.
Maud, *mawd*, pour: Matilda.
Michael, *mī'kĕl*, Michel, m.
Moll, *mŏl*, Molly, *mŏl'lĭ*, pour: Mary.

Nan, *năn*, pour: Anne.
Nancy, *năn'sĭ*, Nannette, f.
Ned, *nĕd*, pour: Edward.
Nell, *nĕl*, Nelly, *nĕl'lĭ*, pour: Eleanor.
Nick, *nĭk*, pour: Nicholas.
Noah, *nō'ă*, Noé, m.

Otho, *ō'thō*, Othon, m.

Patty, *păt'tĭ*, pour: Martha.
Peg, *pĕg*, Peggy, *pĕg'gĭ*, pour: Margaret.
Peter, *pē'tĕr*, Pierre, m.
Phil, *fĭl*, pour: Philip.
Philip, *fĭl'ĭp*, Philippe, m.
Poll, *pŏl*, Polly, *pŏl'lĭ*, pour: Mary.

Ralph, *rălf*, Rodolphe, m.
Randal, *răn'dăl*, Randolphe, m.
Raymund, *rā'mŭnd*, Raymond, m.
Robin, *rŏb'ĭn*, pour: Robert.
Rowland, *rō'lănd*, Roland, m.

Sabina, *să bē'nă*, Sabine, f.
Sal, *săl*, Sally, *săl'lĭ*, pour: Sarah.
Sam, *săm*, pour: Samuel.
Sandy, *săn'dĭ*, pour: Alexander.
Sarah, *sā'ră*, Sara, f.
Sebastian, *sē băs'tĭ ăn*, Sébastien, m.
Sigismund, *sĭj'ĭs mŭnd*, Sigismond, m.
Solomon, *sŏl'ō mŏn*, Salomon, m.
Sophia, *sō fī'ă*, Sophy, *sō'fĭ*, Sophie, f.
Stephen, *stē'vn*, Étienne, m.
Susan, *sū'zăn*, Susannah, *sū zăn'năh*, Suzanne, f.

Ted, *tĕd*, Teddy, *tĕd'dĭ*, pour: Edward.
Theobald, *thē'ō bawld*, Thibaud, m.
Theresa, *tē rā'ză*, Thérèse, f.
Tim, *tĭm*, pour: Timothy.
Timothy, *tĭm'ō thĭ*, Timothée, m.
Tobias, *tō bī'ăs*, Toby, *tō'bĭ*, Tobie, m.
Tom, *tŏm*, Tommy, *tŏm'mĭ*, pour: Thomas.
Tony, *tō'nĭ*, pour: Anthony.

Ursula, *ŭr'sū lă*, Ursule, f.

Valentine, *văl'ĕn tĭn*, Valentin, m.

Walter, *wawl'tĕr*, Gautier, m.
Will, *wĭl*, pour: William.
William, *wĭl'yŭm*, Guillaume, m.

Zachary, *zăk'ă rĭ*, Zacharie, m.

bŏÿ; — fŏŏt, tūbe, tŭb. ‖ chair, joy; — game, yes; — soul, zeal; — thing, there.

Table of Irregular Verbs *).

Present.	Imperfect.	Participle.	Present.	Imperfect.	Participle.
abide	abode	abode	dwell	dwelt	dwelt
am	was	been	eat	ate	eaten
arise	arose	arisen	fall	fell	fallen
awake	awoke *	awaked	feed	fed	fed
backbite	backbit	backbitten	feel	felt	felt
bear	bore, bare	borne	fight	fought	fought
beat	beat	beaten	find	found	found
become	became	become	flee	fled	fled
befall	befell	befallen	fling	flung	flung
beget	begot	begotten	fly	flew	flown
begin	began	begun	forbear	forbore	forborne
begird	begirt	begirt	forbid	forbad, for-	forbidden
beheld	beheld	beheld		bade	
bend	bent	bent	forecast	forecast	forecast
bereave	bereft *	bereft *	forego	forewent	foregone
beseech	besought	besought	foresee	foresaw	foreseen
beset	beset	beset	foretell	foretold	foretold
bestride	bestrode	bestridden	forget	forgot	forgotten
betake	betook	betaken	forgive	forgave	forgiven
bid	bid, bad, bade	bid, bidden	forsake	forsook	forsaken
bind	bound	bound	forswear	forswore	forsworn
bite	bit	bitten	freeze	froze	frozen
bleed	bled	bled	freight	fraught *	fraught *
blow	blew	blown	geld	gelt *	gelt *
break	broke	broken	get	got	got
breed	bred	bred	gild	gilt *	gilt *
bring	brought	brought	gird	girt *	girt *
build	built	built	give	gave	given
burn	burnt *	burnt *	go	went	gone
burst	burst	burst	grave	graved	graven *
buy	bought	bought	grind	ground	ground
can	could	—	grow	grew	grown
cast	cast	cast	hang	hung *	hung *
catch	caught	caught	have	had	had
chide	chid	chid, chidden	hear	heard	heard
choose	chose	chosen	heave	hove *	hove *
cleave	cleft, clove	cleft, cloven	hew	hewed	hewn
cling	clung	clung	hide	hid	hid, hidden
clothe	clad *	clad *	hit	hit	hit
come	came	come	hold	held	held
cost	cost	cost	hurt	hurt	hurt
creep	crept	crept	inlay	inlaid	inlaid
crow	crew *	crown *	interweave	interwove	interwoven
cut	cut	cut	keep	kept	kept
dare	durst *	dared	kneel	knelt *	knelt *
deal	dealt	dealt	knit	knit *	knit *
die	died	died	know	knew	known
dig	dug *	dug *	lade	laded	laden
dip	dipt *	dipt *	lay	laid	laid
do	did	done	lead	led	led
draw	drew	drawn	lean	leant *	leant *
dream	dreamt *	dreamt *	leap	leapt	leapt
drink	drank	drunk	learn	learnt *	learnt *
drive	drove, drave	driven	leave	left	left

*) L'astérisque dénote que ce temps se conjugue aussi régulièrement.

Present.	Imperfect.	Participle.	Present.	Imperfect.	Participle.
lend	lent	lent	respeak	respoke	respoken
let	let	let	retake	retook	retaken
lie (être couché)	lay	lain	retell	retold	retold
			rid	rid	rid
lose	lost	lost	ride	rode	ridden
make	made	made	ring	rang	rung
may	might	—	rise	rose	risen
mean	meant	meant	rive	rove *	riven
meet	met	met	rot	rotted	rotted
melt	melted	molten *	run	ran	run
methinks	methought	—	saw	sawed	sawn *
misgive	misgave	misgiven	say	said	said
mishear	misheard	misheard	see	saw	seen
mislay	mislaid	mislaid	seek	sought	sought
mislead	misled	misled	sell	sold	sold
misshape	misshaped	misshapen *	send	sent	sent
misspeak	misspoke	misspoken	set	set	set
misspell	misspelt	misspelt	shake	shook	shaken
mistake	mistook	mistaken	shall	should	—
miswrite	miswrote	miswritten	shape	shaped	shapen *
mow	mowed	mown	shave	shaved	shaven *
must	must	—	shear	shore *	shorn
ought	ought	—	shed	shed	shed
outbid	outbid	—	shew	shewed	shewn *
outdo	outdid	outdone	shine	shone	shone
outgo	outwent	outgone	shoe	shod	shod
outgrow	outgrew	outgrown	shoot	shot	shot
outride	outrode	outridden	show	showed	shown *
outrun	outran	outrun	shred	shred *	shred *
outshine	outshone	outshone	shrink	shrank	shrunk
outshoot	outshot	outshot	shrive	shrove	shriven
outspread	outspread	outspread	shut	shut	shut
outwork	outwrought *	outwrought *	sing	sang	sung
overbear	overbore	overborne	sink	sank	sunk
overbid	overbid	overbid, over-bidden	sit	sat	sat, sate
			slay	slew	slain
overbuy	overbought	overbought	sleep	slept	slept
overcast	overcast	overcast	slide	slid	slid, slidden
overcome	overcame	overcome	sling	slung	slung
overdo	overdid	overdone	slink	slunk	slunk
overdrive	overdrove	overdriven	slit	slit	slit
overeat	overate	overeaten	smell	smelt *	smelt *
overhang	overhung	overhung	smite	smote	smitten
overhear	overheard	overheard	sow	sowed	sown *
overlade	overladed	overladen	speak	spoke	spoken
overlay	overlaid	overlaid	speed	sped	sped
override	overrode	overridden	spell	spelt *	spelt *
overrun	overran	overrun	spend	spent	spent
oversee	oversaw	overseen	spill	spilt *	spilt *
overset	overset	overset	spin	spun	spun
overshoot	overshot	overshot	spit (cracher)	spat	spat
oversleep	overslept	overslept	spit (embro-cher)	spitted	spitted
over-spread	overspread	overspread			
			split	split	split
overtake	overtook	overtaken	spread	spread	spread
overthrow	overthrew	overthrown	spring	sprang	sprung
overwork	overwrought *	overwrought *	stand	stood	stood
owe	ought *	owed	stave	stove *	stove *
partake	partook	partaken	steal	stole	stolen
pay	paid	paid	stick	stuck	stuck
pen (parquer)	pent *	pent *	sting	stung	stung
put	put	put	stink	stank, stunk	stunk
quit	quitted	quit, quitted	strew	strewed	strewn *
read	read	read	stride	strode	stridden
rebuild	rebuilt	rebuilt	strike	struck	struck
rend	rent	rent	string	strung	strung
repay	repaid	repaid	strive	strove	striven

Present.	Imperfect.	Participle.	Present.	Imperfect.	Participle.
swear	swore	sworn	undraw	undrew	undrawn
sweep	swept	swept	ungird	ungirt ✿	ungirt ✿
swell	swelled	swollen, swoln ✿	unlade	unladed	unladen ✿ unsaid
			unsay	unsaid	
swim	swam	swum	unstring	unstrung	unstrung
swing	swung	swung	answear	unswore	unsworn
take	took	taken	unwind	unwound	unwound
teach	taught	taught	unwring	unwrung	unwrung
tear	tore	torn	upbear	upbore	upborne
tell	told	told	updraw	updrew	updrawn
think	thought	thought	upgrow	upgrew	upgrown
thrive	throve	thriven	uphold	upheld	upheld
throw	threw	thrown	uplead	upled	upled
thrust	thrust	thrust	uprise	uprose	uprisen
toss	tost ✿	tost ✿	upset	upset	upset
tread	trod	trodden	upwind	upwound	upwound
unbend	unbent	unbent	wake	woke	waked
unbind	unbound	unbound	wash	washed	washen ✿
unbuild	unbuilt	unbuilt	waylay	waylaid	waylaid
underbid	underbid	underbidden	wear	wore	worn
underdo	underdid	underdone	weave	wove	woven
undergird	undergirt	undergirt	weep	wept	wept
undergo	underwent	undergone	will	would	
underlay	underlaid	underlaid	win	won	won
underlet	underlet	underlet	wind	wound	wound
underrun	underran	underrun	wiredraw	wiredrew	wiredrawn
undersell	undersold	undersold	wis	wist	wist
underset	underset	underset	withdraw	withdrew	withdrawn
understand	understood	understood	withhold	withheld	withheld
undertake	undertook	undertaken	withstand	withstood	withstood
under- write	underwrote	underwritten	work	wrought ✿	wrought ✿
			wring	wrung	wrung
undo	undid	undone	write	wrote	written

Les formes du participle drunken, holden, shrunken, stricken, upholden, withholden, ne sont employées qu'adjectivement et quelquefois en poésie.